HOW BELFAST SAW THE LIGHT

A CINEMATIC HISTORY

The Beginning

Published 2014 by Tom Hughes
All rights reserved
First Edition
First Impression

©2014 Tom Hughes except where otherwise noted

ISBN 978-0-9930767-0-1

Designed by April Sky Design, Newtownards
www.aprilsky.co.uk

Printed by W&G Baird Limited

Front Cover: Colour interior of Omniplex, Kennedy Centre.
Taken by author.

Frontispiece: Crowd outside the PICTURE HOUSE, Royal Avenue waiting to see Belfast's first feature length talkie April 1929.
Source, the Belfast Telegraph, with thanks

CONTENTS

Preface 7
Chapter 1: The Kinetoscope 11
Chapter 2: Animated Pictures 17
Chapter 3: The Excitement of the Cinematograph 33
Chapter 4: Queen Victoria, Ships and the Boer War 49
Chapter 5: Audiences Liked What They Saw 78
Chapter 6: Dancers and Clowns 91
Chapter 7: The Ire of Mrs Grundy 97
Chapter 8: Paddling in Holy Waters 103
Chapter 9: A Relic of Barbarism 124
Chapter 10: A Good Melodrama Town 134
Chapter 11: Goodbye to St George's Hall 155
Chapter 12: The Craze for Excitement 169
Chapter 13: From The Manger to the Cross 190
Chapter 14: The Perils of Pauline 198
Chapter 15: Birth of a Nation 225
Chapter 16: Censorship Again 257
Chapter 17: "Bright Goods For Drab Days" 275
Chapter 18: Horsemen, Sheiks and Valentino 307
Chapter 19: Worship and Weeping 348
Colour photographs 353
Chapter 20: The Arrival of Sound 394
Chapter 21: The Sound of Music 421
Chapter 22: American Twang, Slang, and the Ulster Accent 442
Chapter 23: Talkie Devil Development 461
Chapter 24: The Belfast Film Society 488
Chapter 25: Monstrous Events 515
Chapter 26: Good Feet and an Ability to Hold One's Tongue 538
Chapter 27: Why Worry? 566
Chapter 28: Is This Belfast? 589
Chapter 29: Big Men, Big Horses and Fine Big Girls 627
Chapter 30: Teddy Boys, Rock 'n' Roll and The Sash 659
Chapter 31: Revival 692
Map of Cinemas in Belfast 716

PREFACE

Idreamt I went to the Broadway again last night. It seemed to me that at the wide entrance I stopped and admired the smooth cream faience tiles of the facade always cool to the touch, the folding glass doors and the spotless shining green and cream marble of the foyer floor. My way was barred by a queue but in time the usher in his smart dark green uniform and peaked cap beckoned me to pass with a brief smile of recognition. I paused momentarily at the glass topped paybox ("back stalls, please") before walking to the left up the few steps and along the quiet red rubberised flooring past the uniformed usherette who tore my ticket in half. I could already faintly hear an alluring mix of music and voices as I pushed against one of the two black doors leading into the darkened auditorium. The film was "Rebecca" (1940, directed by Alfred Hitchcock), and the screen was glowing. Then I awoke. Memories...

But the Broadway is gone, destroyed by fire, a victim of the political Troubles. Its site is now occupied by houses and many of the new generation growing up there are probably unaware of its very existence, much less its importance as a local social and cultural centre for over thirty five years from 1936 to 1972. Sad, because there is so much happiness to remember, so many youthful memories to recall. Snow White, Dumbo, and Pinocchio; Mickey Mouse, Pluto and the irascible Donald Duck; Laurel and Hardy; Sabu uncorking the bottle and releasing the Genie in "The Thief of Bagdad" (1940, d.Michael Powell) and watching wide-eyed as he soared aloft shouting "free, free, free"; Bill Boyd as Hopalong Cassidy always with impeccable manners (except when dealing with villains) raising his stetson while addressing women as "ma'am"; Charles Starrett disappearing behind a large rock and reappearing like a medieval knight atop his charger, dressed all in black with a black mask as the Durango Kid; Randolph Scott restoring law and order with a "leetle" help from grizzled Gabby Hayes; mystery and thrills with Basil Rathbone as Sherlock Holmes or Sidney Toler as Charlie Chan; Claude Raines chilling all and sundry as the Phantom of the Opera; Charles Laughton as the Hunchback clambering about Notre Dame cathedral and sighing over the beautiful Maureen O'Hara; the same Miss O'Hara, dazzling in glorious technicolour, showing that she could handle a sword as well as any male pirate; Maria Montez and Yvonne de Carlo looking seductive - we didn't know the meaning of the word! - behind their veils; Johnnie Weissmuller as Tarzan giving his jungle yodel which we all tried to imitate; laughter, song and flashing feet from Gene Kelly, Bing Crosby, Danny Kaye and the ever elegant Fred Astaire, aided and abetted by Ginger Rogers, Debbie Reynolds, Jane Powell, Ann Miller and Rita Hayworth; Bing joining Bob Hope and Dorothy Lamour on the hilarious roads to Morocco and elsewhere; young Bobby Driscoll telling tall tales and suffering the consequences in "The Window" (1949, d.Ted Tetzlaff); Broderick Crawford with the assistance of the splendid Mercedes Mc Cambridge emoting and pointing up political corruption in "All the King's Men" (1949, d.Robert Rossen); Jennifer Jones being ethereal and mysterious in "The Portrait of Jennie" (1946, d.William Dieterle) and devout and suffering in "The Song of Bernadette" (1943, d. Henry King); Clarke Gable plaintively wondering why "they" must always change things in "The Misfits" (1961, d. John Houston) and Julie Andrews singing and dancing among the Alpine peaks in "The Sound of Music" (1965, d. Robert Wise).

Some things never changed and one of those was the recurring pleasure of recognising the familiar faces of supporting players in the background adding a touch of quality to the most mediocre offerings. It is easy to recall strong-jawed Charles Mc Graw or Joe Sawyer, Edgar Buchanan squinting sidewards through narrowed eyes, bluff Ray Teal usually in Western garb, Thomas Mitchell always bewildered, the wily Walter Slezak finally being caught out, polished villains Victor Jory and Lyle Bettger, Douglas Dumbrille with narrowed eyes and a moustache to match always up to no good, the delicious Gloria Grahame with marbles in her mouth, scatter-brained Spring Byington, motherly Jane Darwell and Sara Allgood, the menacing beauty of Gale Sondergaard and lots of others. They appear now when old films are shown on television and more mature filmgoers play the game: "Now who is that? I know the face but cannot remember the name..."

During the Thirties and the Forties the Broadway was crowded every evening - excepting Sundays, of course - and it was necessary to be there before 6:30 pm to avoid having to queue. After that normally three queues formed. The longest one, for the front stalls, stretched along a path on the uptown side of the building, while that for the back stalls curled down the front and around the downtown side, past the carpark which rarely held more than three or four cars because most of the patrons arrived on foot. The balcony queue occupied the middle ground and was always the shortest because the seats were the dearest. Performances were continuous from 2:00 pm and patrons arrived and left at all times in a pattern quite different from today's separate performances. And, of course, the big black front doors remained closed all day Sunday, every Sunday. When not being used the screen was always kept covered and there was usually a low but discernible buzz of excitement and anticipation when the draped curtain began to lift slowly as the front lights darkened through green to red to merge with the white projector beam which magically conjured up the images.

A typical show consisted of a main feature known as the "big" picture, a B-movie referred to affectionately as the "wee" picture, usually with a cartoon (always greeted with a loud cheer), a newsreel, a brief review of the coming attractions and the advertisements. The last main feature usually began about 9:00 pm and those still in the queues outside were brought in and allowed to stand along the walls and back of the auditorium. The usherettes and ushers moved quietly along the aisles and when they spotted empty seats they directed a beam from their torch across the hall to the two persons at the head of the waiting line who dutifully followed it around to be seated. The torch was a vital means of communication in the darkened auditorium and the waving torch beam was an integral and accepted part of the cinema environment. It was normally benign and helpful but it could semaphore anger or threats especially when it picked out unacceptable behaviour like excessive talking. Usually everyone was comfortably seated by 9:15 pm, but sometimes at very popular films or on crowded wet evenings people could be standing until 10:00 pm. By 11:00pm the screen was covered, the projectors were silent, the lights were out and the cinema was closed and locked.

That pattern was repeated daily in the many cinemas dotted across the urban landscape; but while the pattern was essentially the same each cinema was different. Each one had its own special atmosphere-ambience would be the term used today - and its own body of dedicated patrons who went regularly once or twice a week. While Hollywood was often accused - unfairly - by critics of making films for twelve year olds, in fact the cinema was the recreation of all age groups and the typical audience was always a mixture of young, middle-aged and old. Some of the more senior members even had their favourite seats and to find them empty and available increased their enjoyment of the occasion. To most people the cinema was a form of relaxation, a "night out," and they expected two and a half or three hours of entertainment. But it was more than mere entertainment. It was an integral part of their social environment functioning parallel to or competing with the other components of everyday life - namely, family, church, school and work.

Not everyone approved of the influence of the cinemas - darkened temples of sin one local street preacher called them - but despite an elaborate system of local and national censorship, plus warnings from pulpits and elsewhere the cinema did have a major impact on local society. The films, their stories and themes, the life styles of the stars, the fashions, all were major topics of conversation at home and at work. But the reaction of most people to what they saw and heard on the screens wasn't just a sponge - like absorption, but rather a form of mental challenge and response in relation to the values and standards they already held and adhered to. Also, in a city so tragically split by divisions, regular film going had a positive social value in that it was a unifying factor because the cinemas, especially the downtown ones, brought people of differing political and religious opinions together for entertainment and enjoyment.

On a personal level the cinema has given me much entertainment over the years plus artistic and intellectual stimulation. This account is by way of a recognition and a thank you. It is also a response to a natural curiosity as to how and why a seemingly simple mechanical Victorian invention became such a powerful and popular part of everyday life. I grew up in a quiet family that respected books and learning but also had a lively interest in theatrical entertainments. Youthful imagination was enriched by Christmas pantomimes in the Grand Opera House, the Empire, the Royal Hippodrome and local parish halls like St. Mary's in Bank Street and St. Paul's in Hawthorn Street. An early Christmas present from Santa was a toy projector along with a 35mm film of Charlie Chaplin. From there it was a short step to Walt Disney's "Snow White" in the Broadway cinema. My parents enjoyed their weekly visits to the cinema and they introduced me to a variety of carefully chosen films. My father was a Western fan who regarded William S. Hart as the ultimate cowboy, and with him I was introduced in the Forties to Joel McCrae, Randolph Scott, Johnny Mack Brown and John Wayne. My uncle, Joseph Hughes, a teacher, told me many tales of his early visits to silent films in halls with splendid names like the Panopticon in High Street, and the Alhambra in North Street. There were other stories of people fleeing from Lumière's approaching train in the Empire, or gaining entrance to some halls by paying with a jamjar. The cold realities of the business - and it was a business - have been submerged in an exotic mix of fact and fiction. This narrative is an attempt to separate fact from fable while still preserving the wonder.

In my research I have received support and help from many sources and I owe them all a debt of thanks. Firstly there are the family members and friends who shared their experiences with me; a special mention of my brother Stephen, my sister Kathleen who helped with the collection and arrangement of data; my brother-in-law Jack and my nephews Brian, John and Martin who advised on technical matters involving the computer; the managers and cinema workers who discussed the practical side of the business including most recently the staff of the Movie House on the Dublin Road especially Jim Simpson the chief digital technician who was a fund of information about recent developments in digital projection. The staff at Building Control Services in the City Hall were extremely helpful, especially Mr Mc Ferran and, above all, Robert Watton who was always courteous and knowledgeable. Special thanks are due to the many editors and reporters, past and present, of the Northern Whig, the Belfast News Letter, the Irish News, the Ireland's Saturday Night and the Belfast Telegraph who over the years recorded the relevant historical facts plus the views, attitudes and exploits of themselves and their fellow citizens. They described and discussed the local "amusements," the general term under which the theatre, music hall, cinema and similar divertissements were grouped. Access to that mine of information was happily facilitated by the staffs of the Belfast Central Newspaper Library (a special thank you to Brian), the Linenhall Library and the National Library in Dublin. Thanks are due to Patrick Close, my former student and later, colleague, who has tendered much practical and helpful advice, as have Dr Wesley Johnston and his staff at Colourpoint Creative Limited. Mention must also be made of Jack Cardiff, the British award winning cinematographer, who once described filming as "painting with light," a comment which inspired the title of this book.

One problem in going back in time is that the meaning and use of words have changed, but where possible for accuracy and atmosphere I have kept to the older denotation, and the same applies to values and distance. A few words of clarification may be useful for younger readers. Money may make the world go round but in those days it did so in the form of pounds, shillings and pence. The pound consisted of twenty shillings and each shilling consisted of twelve pence (written as 12d). There was also an up-market coin called a guinea which was worth twenty one shillings. At conversion in 1971 the decimal equivalent of a shilling was 5p. Similarly in those pre - decimal days lengths were measured in yards, feet, and inches. A yard consisted of three feet, and each foot contained twelve inches. Today the metric equivalent is one metre which equals about thirty nine inches. By now maybe it is easier to sympathise with Clark Gable's heart felt query in "The Misfits'" about change.

One regret is that my parents didn't live to see the completed work; or my sister Maureen; also my friend Manus Campbell OFM and my former student and colleague Liam Agnew all of whom would have, I'm sure, enjoyed it thoroughly. To them and to all filmgoers, especially those who encouraged me, this work is dedicated, with thanks.

Familiar sight during the Thirties and Forties. Source: Irish News

CHAPTER ONE

The Kinetoscope

Going to the pictures was an integral part of the social life of the majority of Belfast citizens during the 20th century. People visited the cinema once or twice a week on a regular basis, and while most headed for their favourite, usually local, venue they had during the peak period between the mid-Thirties and the Sixties, over thirty cinemas to choose from, distributed across the built-up area. Full houses and queues were the norm every evening. To gain an understanding of how that situation arose is the aim of this discourse. It is not a history of the cinema as such, nor is it a history of Belfast, though of necessity it touches upon aspects of both. It is, above all, the story of the growth of the cinema industry in the Belfast region, of the various personalities who influenced its success and of the reactions of the critics and, more especially, of the audiences who flocked to a new and exciting form of communication and entertainment. At the same time it is a study of the cinema's impact on the physical fabric of the city by way of its buildings and more importantly on the intellectual, social, political and economic life of the citizens. The cinema brought much more than entertainment to the local scene. It became a source of employment, a topic of conversation, a window on the world and a stimulating challenge to complacency. It was welcomed by the many, but treated with suspicion by those who were concerned about its impact on local society.

The spread of the cinema going habit was one of the most notable social characteristics of the early twentieth century, and regardless of their personal feelings or attitudes no one at that time could really have been unaware of the impact of the new Electric Theatres and Picture Palaces which became part of the urban landscape in the years before the first World War. Certainly the locals were quick to accept them and to incorporate them into their locational geography of the town. The Shaftesbury Pictoria, one of the first buildings in the city actually planned and constructed solely for the purpose of showing films, opened in late December 1910 and shortly afterwards on the 10th January an advertisement in the News Letter was offering a shop and house for sale at 8, Shaftesbury Square located "next door to the new Electric Theatre." A letter writer to the Irish News in April 1911 commented on how the new cinemas had "sprung up like magic," and went on to note that "they call themselves by the most catchy of titles, and at night time are emblazoned with electric light, the display of which never fails to arrest the eye."

From the beginning many of the films they showed, short, simple, primitive and innocent as they may seem today, challenged not only how people saw themselves and their world but also, directly and indirectly, long accepted social and moral attitudes. Thus in Belfast, like elsewhere, as the new entertainment medium spread it often found itself involved in disputes with individuals, groups and the authorities over attitudes to religion, Sunday observance, church attendance, education, crime, the behaviour of children and young people, and moral attitudes especially to sex, women, violence and race not to mention more pragmatic topics like safety and fire prevention in large darkened buildings. While theologians were contemplating how many angels could be assembled on the head of a pin the more down to earth town councillors of Belfast were trying to decide just how many yards should decently separate a cinema from a church.

The story of films and the cinema, as far as Belfast is concerned, began in February 1895 when a stranger arrived bearing a new technology in the shape of a free standing wooden cabinet called a Kinetoscope. Its exterior seemed familiar enough but the interior was revolutionary because it contained the world's earliest films. The man responsible for presenting them to the Belfast public and thereby planting the seeds of the local cinema industry was a Mr Quinn who arrived on a steamship from Liverpool. Mr Quinn was the latest in a long line of visiting showmen - cum - businessmen who came to sell a new "amusement." He was optimistic that it would be well received in Belfast.

A Kinetoscope

It is easy to imagine him leaning on the ship's rail enjoying the passing rural scenery of Antrim and Down and straining for a view of his destination. He probably heard it before he saw it as the sounds of industry and activity from the shipyards, factories and many mills, the clanking of the trams, the clacking of horses' hooves and cart wheels over the cobblestones and even the chiming of the many public clocks combined in a distant cacophony which reached his ears across the waters of Belfast Lough. Then the city came into view with its skyline of mills and factories under a cloud of gloomy industrial smoke. Some time before, the Northern Whig newspaper had commented on those murky conditions and suggested that the introduction of the recently developed electric street lighting would help to combat them. Mr Quinn would have understood and probably agreed with that suggestion because he was a member of that relatively new and growing body of skilled men, the electricians. But he was more, because he was also a salesman representing the noted American inventor, Thomas Edison, and held the position of manager of the Edison Kinetoscope Exhibition Company which had offices in London and Liverpool. As he arrived at the dock, no one, least of all himself, realised that his disembarkation represented the beginning of a new chapter in the local history of entertainment for he brought with him the first films to be viewed publicly not only in Belfast but anywhere in Ireland. The Irish cinema industry began when he put those little films on public display at ten o'clock on the morning of the 21st February 1895 in a small kinetoscope parlour rented at 22, Royal Avenue, next door to what was then the city's foremost hotel, the Grand Central. The site is now part of the Castle Court Shopping centre.

The lack of amusement often attributed to Queen Victoria gives a rather distorted view of the character of the lady herself, and of the society that takes her name. The Victorians had a great propensity for amusement and eagerly supported any new development in the field of entertainment. Belfast was no exception. In 1838, one year after Victoria's accession to the throne, the theatre critic of the Northern Whig wrote: "the great progress the sciences are making has among other agreeable and valuable advantages that of extending continually the variety of rational entertainments and recreations." The best known professional venue which catered for visiting showmen and their wares was the New Theatre, better known later as the Theatre Royal, which had been built in Arthur Street by Michael Atkins in 1793.

The theatre presented mainly live productions of well known dramas, melodramas and comedies, including plays involving some of the top actors of the day, like Sarah Bernhardt and Lillie Langtry, who was married to a local man. Also available was the rather exclusive Assembly Rooms in the Exchange Building in Waring Street, plus a few smaller rooms located in the Castle Street - High Street area. Those couldn't cope with the increased availability of new forms of popular entertainments, so, as the town expanded during the 19th century, besides the mills and factories, a group of assembly halls and other suitable structures were built to accommodate the needs of those new entertainments, and the audiences who wanted to see them.

In 1820 an Assembly Room opened in the new Commercial Building opposite the older Exchange Building, known today as the Whig Building. It was followed in 1851 by the Victoria Hall in Victoria Street, which quickly became a major centre for a wide range of popular attractions. The following year the new Corn Exchange, designed by Thomas Jackson, opened its hall, also in Victoria Street. In February 1881 St George's Hall opened in a new multi-functional building in High Street opposite Bridge Street. It was soon followed by the YMCA Hall in Wellington Place. At the same time a number of specially designed detached buildings were constructed for entertainment purposes, beginning with the Belfast Music Hall in May Street (March 1840). The Ulster Hall was built in 1862, while Dan Lowery's Royal Alhambra Music Hall brought smiles to many faces in 1871. St Mary's Hall opened in Chapel Lane during 1876 mainly to serve the needs of the growing Catholic population. The last decade of the century saw the addition of the New Star Music Hall (1892) in Church Street, the better known Empire Theatre of Varieties in Victoria Square (1894) and the Grand Opera House and Cirque (December 1895) in Victoria Square. Many of those would become involved later in showing films.

All those halls presented a wide range of amusements which included singers, dancers, musicians, magicians; lecturers like Oscar Wilde and Charles Dickens; exhibitions including wax work figures. The latter were regarded as educational, and educational material was treated with respect by critics and parents. New mechanical and scientific devices were especially popular and audiences flocked to see demonstrations of electricity and X-rays, or elaborate painted panoramas and dioramas. They thrilled to the mysteries of Phantasmagoria and Pepper's Ghost. But the greatest draw was the magic lantern which had the ability to project large scenes on a screen. The earliest scenes were painted on glass but after the discovery of photography and celluloid, audiences could watch slides of actual places and people from around the world. Magic lantern shows were usually accompanied by a lecturer who explained what was being illustrated, while increasingly background music was added using another new invention, the phonograph or gramophone. The lantern slides showed static scenes but ingenious methods were used to give the illusion of movement. Slides were often linked in the form of a story.

By the nineties audiences in Belfast were familiar with projected images in black and white or colour, with mechanical sound, and were aware of "instantaneous photography" which could show motion. They also knew about the photographer Edweard Muybridge and his experiments in photographing movement. In February 1890, at the invitation of the local Natural History and Philosophical Society, Muybridge gave two lectures in the

YMCA Hall in Wellington Place. He explained how he used a succession of closely spaced cameras to produce a sequence of photographs which, when viewed in order, illustrated the movement of the photographed subject. He then demonstrated his results on a Zoopraxiscope which used glass discs to project photographs of animal movement on a large screen, to the amazement of the audiences. Ingenious as it was, Muybridges's system of projected images on glass didn't constitute a film. The next practical steps towards that were taken at Thomas Edison's establishment in West Orange, New Jersey mainly through the efforts of William Kennedy Laurie Dickson. While few in Belfast had heard of Laurie Dickson the majority of the population were familiar with the work of Thomas Edison, famous for inventing the electric bulb and the phonograph. Edison had become interested in recording movement visually but passed the problem of how to achieve it over to his assistant Laurie Dickson who by 1891 had produced a working model of a contraption that met his employer's requirements, and more. It was called a kinetoscope.

The kinetoscope was given its first public exhibition in New York at 1155, Broadway on 14th April 1894 when a group of ten of them was assembled in a room called a kinetoscope parlour. It was an immediate success with the public and Edison realised that he was on to a commercial winner. By September the kinetoscope had reached Paris and on 30th October 1894 it went on show in London at 70, Oxford Street, drawing large crowds and causing much comment. At the end of the year the Irish News, under the heading "Science in 1894", summed up what it regarded as the major advances that had been made during the year in many branches of science including telegraphy, the telephone, and electric transport and then added with a flash of perception "nor should mention be omitted of the Edison kinetoscope which has been lately brought to the knowledge of the English public and consists in the production of what may be briefly called a living picture in photography."

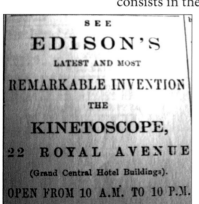

Advert for Kinetoscope with thanks to the Irish News.

Readers may have wondered what exactly a "living picture" was but they were soon to find out when, on Thursday 21st February 1895, with a time lag of ten months after their appearance in New York, advertisements appeared in the local papers inviting all to see "Edison's latest and most Remarkable Invention, the Kinetoscope" at 22, Royal Avenue beside the Grand Central Hotel. That was Ireland's first kinetoscope parlour and - stretching the imagination a little - proto cinema, with an admission charge of one shilling to view the contents of five machines. They were, of course, the machines that had been brought over from Liverpool and set up by Mr. Quinn. His aim was to demonstrate and, hopefully, sell some of them. He took one of the machines apart and explained its workings to the representatives of the local press, all of whom were highly impressed. The Irish News thought it was "a most ingenious contrivance." Each machine stood over four feet high, was made of hard wood in the form of what the newspaper called "an elegant cabinet," and was worked by electricity. At the top there was a small viewing aperture covered with glass with a magnifying lens below it. But it was the interior which held the real surprise. Inside there was a continuous narrow strip of transparent celluloid film 35mm wide and about fifty feet (16 metres) long stretched over a series of rollers, which ran for about one minute. It may have been short, and the content covered only one item, but it was a true film. The scenes involved had been photographed by a new type of camera called a Kinetograph which took a sequence of photographs on the celluloid at a speed of forty six frames per second. Muybridge's sequence of separate cameras taking images a split second apart on separate glass plates had been replaced by one camera which recorded the images in succession on a strip of flexible celluloid.

Today that may seem unexciting but in 1895 it represented a major technical advance. The celluloid strips were 35 mm wide with perforations in them to facilitate their movement past the viewing aperture, which became the basic technique used in most professional film making and projecting equipment throughout the 20th century, though that is now changing with the advance of digital technology. As the photographs, each lit separately and momentarily by a flash of electric light controlled by a shutter, passed rapidly before the viewer's eyes they gave the illusion of motion. The Irish News reporter was amazed by the accuracy and realism of the scenes and commented that the only difference between them and reality was the absence of colour. The assembled writers took turns peering into the darkened boxes where they experienced a series of short films, each running a minute or less, some of which had been photographed outdoors, but most of which had been completed indoors in the world's first film studio, the so called Black Maria (completed in 1892), which had been specially built at West Orange by Laurie Dickson for that purpose. He had experienced no real difficulties in persuading music hall acts, circus performers and celebrities like Jim Corbett or Loie Fuller to display their skills for the new invention.

The viewers saw an outdoor sequence from Buffalo Bill's Wild West Show in which the performers, dressed in their Western costumes, raced on horseback past the camera. There was a shot of Niagara Falls, one of lightning flashes and another of a horse race. Indoor shots included a comedy prize fight, two ladies fencing, a ballet dancer, an acrobat, and a bullet fired from a gun. The future of popular cinema was there in embryo - thrills and excitement, comedy, scenic beauty, a touch of violence, lovely ladies and something unusual. The newspaper representatives were enthusiastic in their comments. The News Letter thought the effect was "marvellous" and felt the invention had great possibilities. The Telegraph correspondent saw it as a complement to other recent inventions. As he put it "the telephone transmits the voice, the phonograph photographs sound and the kinetograph photographs motion." He looked forward to the time when the phonograph would be wedded to the kinetoscope to give natural sound and motion, and when scenes from around the world could be brought to the viewer's doorstep. The kinetoscope was perceived in terms of a machine akin to a telephone or phonograph which would be in peoples' homes in the future, in a situation more analogous to TV viewing. Some of what they wrote was obviously Edison sales talk though it must have struck them as having little immediate application in a city where most homes were still lit by gas or candles.

Mr Quinn emphasised that the Belfast kinetoscope parlour was the first occasion the Kinetoscope had been exhibited anywhere in Ireland so it is reasonable to conclude that the first films to be viewed publicly in Ireland were seen in that room on Royal Avenue. February 1895 is therefore a significant date in the social and economic history of the city, the cultural implications of which are still being experienced today. The Kinetoscope didn't arrive in Dublin until a month later when a parlour was opened at 63, Dame street where the films included a barber's shop, a skirt dance, a cock fight, a wrestling dog, a race horse exercising, and a serpentine dance. The Irish Times thought it was "one of the most remarkable of Mr. Edison's inventions" and commented on how vivid and detailed the films were. The writer was especially taken by the serpentine dance and noted that "the graceful movements of the girl were reproduced with amazing fidelity."

Of course the experience of using a kinetoscope was not the same as going to a cinema. Those little films were viewed only in miniature by single individuals. No actual projection was involved at that stage, though showmen were later to adapt them for showing on a screen. Also they were filmed from a fixed position by a large heavy camera which just recorded what happened in front of it. Despite their familiarity with the magic lantern, and the recent visit by Muybridge, few people seemed to realise that the resulting experience represented a step towards the projection of images on a screen that could be viewed by an audience, though that startling development lay only a short time in the future for Belfast audiences. In the meantime inquisitive crowds flocked to Royal Avenue, so large on occasion that they blocked the traffic in that thoroughfare, much to the displeasure of the local constabulary.

Mr Quinn returned to England after he had appointed a local agent, Thomas Tate of Rosemary Street, to sell or rent the kinetoscopes. Before leaving he announced that he intended to display the new marvel at the forthcoming Art and Industrial Exhibition in the White Linen Hall Building. Sure enough the normally drab interior of the White Linen Hall was transformed for the exhibition which opened in April. Its main aim was to illustrate and celebrate the industrial progress of Belfast with a display of products from local and overseas companies. By implication it also extolled the benefits of Victorian capitalism. The official opening ceremony was performed by Lady Londonderry in the presence of the Lord Mayor of Dublin, and other notables, including Sir Edward Harland. As Mr Quinn had promised, Edison had a stand at the Exhibition, located in a prominent position near the entrance, decorated with the American Flag and photographs of the inventor himself. The five kinetoscopes had been transferred from Royal Avenue, joining a range of electric lamps also on display. Mr S.T. Bitmead, an Edison representative from New York, was there to greet the local population which from all accounts was suitably impressed even if the new invention was well beyond the pockets of most of them. In fact very few of the machines became domestic fixtures anywhere, and most of the thousand units or so that were sold ended up in kinetoscope parlours, or displayed by travelling showmen. The Kinetoscope was dismissed by the more seriously minded as a trivial diversion, but it caught the public imagination wherever it was exhibited. There are references to it being displayed in a shop in Royal Avenue and at various fêtes and such. In later years it could be found in seaside funfairs where it was known as a "what the butler saw" novelty. Its lasting importance wasn't just in what it achieved itself but rather in what it led to. It was the gateway to the cinema.

Technology feeds off technology but Edison initially failed to see the wider possibilities of his invention. That leap of imagination was taken by others who dissected and adapted its technology, and the consequence was the projection of the first films on a screen to a paying audience by the Lumière brothers, Louis and Auguste, in Paris in late December 1895. What a Christmas present to the world!

CHAPTER TWO
Animated Pictures

Before the building of the Victoria Square shopping complex a plaque on the wall in William Street South at the entrance to the square stated that on that spot the first moving pictures were shown in Belfast on 26th November 1896. It referred to the well documented historic presentation in Dan Lowrey's nearby Empire Theatre at the corner of Telfair Street, which is traditionally regarded as the starting point for Belfast's cinematic history. That isn't entirely accurate. There was a very important showing in the Empire beginning on that date but it certainly was not the first in Belfast The first opportunity for local audiences to see the new phenomenon was actually made possible not by Dan Lowrey but by his friend and owner of the Alhambra in North Street, W. J. Ashcroft who pipped him by three months.

Sketch of W.J.Ashcroft owner of the Alhambra and the man responsible for the first film presentation in Belfast. Source, the Ireland's Saturday Night.

ALHAMBRA THEATRE OF VARIETIES, North Street.
OPEN ALL THE YEAR ROUND.
Proprietor and Manager...Mr. W.J. ASHCROFT.
General Manager............Mr. CON SALMON.
Extraordinary Engagement, at Enormous Expense, and positively for Six Nights only, the Most Marvellous Invention of the present century,
THE CINEMATOGRAPHE,
The Greatest Wonder of the age! Pictures endowed apparently with Real Life! Marvellous beyond the power of words to describe.
Return of the Belfast Favourites,
THE NORTHERN TROUPE,
Champion Male and Female International Dancers of the world.
Mr. DAN LEESON,
Negro Comedian and Pedestal Dancer.
Miss TESSIE VANDEAN,
Burlesque Actress and Song and Dance

Alhambra advert for Belfast's first film show with thanks to Irish News.

During 1896 there were many stories circulating in the city about a new form of music hall entertainment. There was normally much to-ing and fro-ing between Belfast and London for business and other reasons so word of mouth must have spread stories about an amazing new invention on display there that showed Animated Pictures. Readers of the

Graphic and the Illustrated London News would have been aware of what was happening as would those who perused the professional photographic magazines. The local papers, despite their admiration for the kinetoscope, showed little interest until a Belfast Telegraph commentator writing in his monthly Photographic Jottings in April, brought the matter up. He explained that a number of "ingenious contrivances" could be seen in a number of music hall venues in London. It is interesting that he perceived them as consisting of elements already available and familiar in Belfast, and his description of them as machines that projected kinetoscope films on a lantern screen would have made some kind of sense to his readers. His main emphasis was on the machine, not the films, though he did mention that the subjects were filmed at 15 frames a second and projected at the same speed, adding that all the "well known" kinetoscope subjects could now be seen on the big screen, while new scenes were also being photographed for future presentations. He introduced his readers to the names that they were to become very familiar with over the next months - the Lumière 'brothers' Cinematographe, R.W. Paul's Theatrograph, and "another by Birt Acres". Birt Acre's short lived machine was actually called a Kineopticon. In fact the public were soon to be deluged by a plethora of - graphs, scopes etc. as craftsmen and showmen vied with each other to take advantage of a growing demand.

The following month the Telegraph writer returned to the topic, which he referred to as "photography in motion." He seemed to be having problems understanding their growing popularity because, as he noted casually, they were just a development of the old "Wheel of Life," which was an earlier system in which a magic lantern was used to project figures from a slowly revolving disc to suggest movement. He had obviously gone over to London but had not been overly impressed by what he had seen with the exception of "The Derby" which he thought was so realistic that he expressed surprise that there weren't a few bookies in the audience. He found the shows "as far from being perfect as might be desired" and felt that they would have to improve technically if they were to become widely acceptable. Their present popularity, he suggested, was due more to the business acumen and persuasive powers of those involved rather than the novelty of the process. Without realising it he had put his finger on one of the enigmas of early cinema. Was its success due to the profit enthusiasms of the entrepreneurs who convinced audiences that they had to see the new marvel, or was it the result of some inherent qualities in the new medium itself?

The Belfast public had to wait another four months to make up their own minds and the man who gave them that first opportunity was W.J. Ashcroft who, with his neat beard and pince-nez, was a well known figure around the city. W.J. or Willie John, or the Solid Man as

Advert for the first Lumière film show in the Empire Theatre. Source: Belfast News Letter, with thanks.

Early Admission on all occasions.
BELFAST EMPIRE THEATRE
OF VARIETIES, VICTORIA SQUARE.
MR. DAN LOWREY............Managing Director.
Crowning Production of All !
London's Rage !..................Dublin's Rage !
Europe's Latest Sensation !
TO-NIGHT.........................TO-NIGHT.
Tremendously Expensive Engagement !
For This Week Only.
The Marvellous, Perplexing, and Original
LUMIERE CINEMATOGRAPHE
(From the Empire Theatre, London),
Where it has been the Sensation of the Metropolis for 6 Months past.
See It !.....................Simply Astonishing !
Living People brought from all parts of the World and placed in
REAL LIFE ACTION ON THE STAGE.
London's Streets and People Reproduced.
Czar's Coronation !......Royal Wedding Procession
Railway Station !—Train Arrival !—Bustle !
TO-NIGHT.......................TO-NIGHT
7..................Tiller's Troubadours ....
Charming Lady Duettists and Dancers.
3.....................The Sisters Lee.............
Most Amazing Contortionists Ever Seen.
Mr. Chas. Seel. | O'Brien and Collins.
Miss Amy Knott. | Miss Stella Starr.
Enormous Success of America's Genius,
MR. WILL. H. FOX.
Seats Booked Daily....................Telephone 83

he was affectionately known from his most successful song "Muldoon the Solid Man", had been born in Pawtucket in New England from Irish parents who had emigrated there, his mother being originally from Belfast. From an early age he showed an interest in the stage and often put on shows in the cellar of the family home including panoramas and dioramas. One of those was a panorama of "The Burning of Moscow" which he designed and painted himself. He also drew and put up the posters advertising it, collected the money at the door, played the music and gave the explanatory lecture. He started his professional career in 1861 when he joined a touring troupe of minstrels and over the next ten years he honed his talents as he experienced all aspects of music hall life in the United States and Canada. His success in America was followed by acclaim in England and Ireland, and he first came to the attention of Belfast audiences when he appeared in the Alhambra in 1879, and later that year when he bought the hall from Dan Lowrey. For some time he continued his singing and dancing career and left the running of the hall mainly to his managers, but in 1894 he decided the time had come to do the job himself. At the end of August his music hall, the Alhambra, announced "an Extraordinary engagement at Enormous Expense... of the most marvellous invention of the century, the Cinematograph, the greatest wonder of the age," and on Monday 31st August 1896 Belfast had its first public film show.

It was advertised as top of the bill in association with typical music hall fare which included dancers, singers, and comedians. The Belfast Telegraph, which had already commented occasionally on the new invention, ignored the event, leaving it to its sister paper the more chatty and laid back Ireland's Saturday Night not only to register its approval but also to celebrate the event with a charming cartoon showing the recently awakened Rip Van Winkle staring in amazement at a moving image of a girl dancing. The sketch has some historical significance because it includes the earliest known representation, rather crude admittedly, of a film projector in Belfast and perhaps even in Ireland. Rip Van Winkle was chosen because the play of that name was being presented during the same week in the Theatre Royal with Louis Calvert in the title role. The cartoon is interesting in other ways too. It brings together the popular stage and the screen face to face in close confrontation, the one old and set in its ways, the other young and full of vitality; the one encumbered with the weight of tradition and limited by the physical dimensions of the stage, the other presenting life in a vivid, attractive and startling new way. The Irish News critic congratulated the management of the Alhambra on allowing the local public to see the Cinematograph which he described as a "startling invention." He was very impressed by the pictures which showed street scenes with people and vehicles moving with amazing accuracy in what he described as a "mirror of motion." In all, he felt, it was "a novelty well worth seeing." The News Letter gave more details about the films noting that they included a fire, a coronation, dancing and bathing scenes and concluded that it was "a surprising invention that should be seen by everyone." The Whig thought the machine was wonderful but gave no details about the films except to mention that the images were very accurate and true to life. All the papers noted the fact that the audiences obviously enjoyed what they saw and they all agreed that the Cinematograph was an amazing invention.

The First Picture Show. Rip Van Winkle Meets the Serpentine Dancer. Source: Ireland's Saturday Night.

The show was presented by a Mr. B. Doyle who, despite his Irish sounding name, was an Australian. He was an entrepreneur who had trained as an engineer but had decided that there were commercial possibilities in the sale of projectors which, he claimed, he constructed at his workshop on the Loughborough Road in Brixton. He was travelling around the British Isles putting on shows mainly in the hope of attracting buyers. His "improved" model which could be worked with limelight or electricity cost forty pounds. The cinematograph and the screen were set up on the stage and the show consisted of about ten films with a total running time of around thirty minutes. The Ireland's Saturday Night's critic, who wrote under the pseudonym of Nomad, had already seen the Cinematographe at work in Dublin and London and thought that Mr. Doyle had largely overcome the problem of jerkiness which had marred other presentations and that his focussing was first class so that the pictures were clear and steady. The titles shown included "Haymaking," "A Card Party," "The Royal Wedding," "The Moscow Disaster," "Loie Fuller Dancing," and "The Fire Alarm." He was very taken by the latter film which ran for three minutes and he gave a detailed description of it.

The film opened with a view of the interior of a fire station which reminded him of the local station in Belfast. In one corner the horses were in their stalls while a big cat was stretched out contentedly in the foreground. Three firemen were chatting and joking while a dog frisked around their feet. "Suddenly," he wrote, "the picture of harmony and repose becomes one of briskness. Something has happened." Obviously the fire alarm had gone. The dog ceased its play and ran to the nearest fire engine. The firemen were galvanised into action. They quickly and efficiently attached the horses to the smoking fire engines, adjusted their brass helmets, jumped aboard and moved out, with the horses gathering speed. As they swept out of the picture and seemingly into the auditorium an "Oh" of surprise and delight came from all parts of the theatre and he noted that "the people in the front rows of the pit shifted uneasily in their seats." No - one was reported as leaving their seat or running out into North Street in panic, but obviously they were quite impressed by the reality of what they saw. There was a special reaction also to the dancer Loie Fuller, an artiste well enough known to get a mention in a poem by W.B. Yeats. Her movements were slow and graceful while every detail of her person including even the individual hairs on her head could be clearly seen, while "no tint of the vary-coloured limes which were thrown in all their gorgeous brilliancy upon her robes were absent." So, during that first historic show, the Belfast audience were treated to an early hand coloured film. When it ended they rose and clapped, and continued to clap and call until Mr. Doyle rewound the film and showed it again. After that the curtains closed but the clapping continued until the operator himself appeared and took a bow.

Mr. Doyle had a catalogue of fifty films which he claimed he had acquired from Paris. He had bought the films outright as was the normal procedure in those early days. Films were bought by length, so much per foot or metre and in time it became the practice to advertise them locally by length. Other films in the catalogue included "A Spanish Bull Fight," "Bathing at Trouville", "Holy Mass in Rome" and one that certainly would not be shown very widely in public in Ireland called "Going to bed of a Newly Married Wife - two hundred metres long." That sounds very much like a film whose French title was "Coucher

de la Mariée" made by Eugene Pirou. Nomad, who had a good sense of humour thought
that it "lent a spice of domesticity" to the proceedings. The clues given in the names of the
films, their origin in Paris, and the length of one in metres support Mr Doyle's claims that
the films were French, but from a number of different sources. Some were probably filmed
by George Méliès, a name that was to become very familiar to local filmgoers in the years
to follow. Méliès had begun filming earlier that year in Paris and in Trouville. Some may
have been Edison films that had been made originally for the Kinetoscope, and there is also
evidence indicating that a few of them were actually Lumière products. Méliès had filmed a
card game but the better known "The Card Game" (Partie d'Ecarte in the original French)
was filmed in Lyon the year before by Louis Lumière and showed three men around a table
outdoors playing a game of cards. The players meant nothing to the audience who were
more fascinated by the natural movements of the palm leaves in the background, but they
included Antoine Lumière the father of the Lumière brothers, and Felicien Trewey the
operator who was to present the first official Lumière picture show in the Empire a few
weeks later.

The coronation mentioned above almost certainly referred to some of the seven historic
films taken by the Lumière operatives Charles Moisson and Francis Doublier during the
ceremonies surrounding the coronation of the last Russian Tsar, Nicholas the Second, in
May; while "The Moscow Disaster" referred to the events which occurred two days later
when the new ruler was presented to his people. It was estimated that half a million people
were present on that occasion. In the crush a barrier collapsed and the crowd surged
forward. The police charged to protect the person of the Tsar and in the ensuing panic many
of the onlookers were killed. The Lumière cameramen continued to film until stopped by
the police who then confiscated their camera and film, probably the earliest example of
film censorship on record. What the audiences in the Alhambra saw were scenes of people
running away after the tragedy. Many must have been impressed by the fact that they
were watching incidents that had happened so recently, in terms of months rather than
the two years usually associated with panoramas and dioramas. Distance was becoming
less of a buffer between themselves and events overseas; the world was shrinking. If some
of the films were from Lumière the projector certainly wasn't because Lumière projectors
weren't put on general sale until 1897. Maybe it was a Paul model though Mr Doyle gave
the impression that it was of his own construction. That is not surprising because many
technically minded people were building and experimenting with simple projectors based
on the kinetoscope. Colin Johnston Robb, the historian, refers to a Frenchman, Louis
Fournel, in Belfast during the 1890's to study the linen industry, who claimed to have built
one such machine and used it to show films to a group of friends in his lodgings off the
Crumlin Road. There is no record of whether Mr Doyle sold any of his machines during
that momentous week.

Three weeks later Belfast had a second opportunity to appreciate the new Animated
Photographs when the Moore and Burgess Minstrels arrived from Dublin with their
show and fifty performers into the Ulster Hall, beginning on Saturday 19th September. It
was a superior minstrel show, full of singing, dancing, and humour. It had played Belfast
successfully before, but this time it promised some extras in the form of a series of tableaux

vivants based on "Uncle Tom's Cabin," plus what was billed as "the latest sensation of the London season" namely animated photographs projected by the Vitagraphe. The Vitagraphe was a French projector made in Paris. The News Letter critic gave a most comprehensive and enthusiastic account of the film exhibition which included street scenes, railway and other scenes "not the least interesting of which was a policeman making love to his sweetheart." That was the first story film shown in the city. Another reporter from the Ireland's Saturday Night who saw the same show in Dublin called it "The Soldier and his Girl" and was equally impressed, describing it as clever and refined. It was most probably actually called "The Soldier's Courtship," and had been filmed by R.W. Paul on the roof of the Alhambra theatre in London. It was a simple music hall sketch which involved a soldier (not a policeman as the reporter thought) sitting on a park bench with his sweetheart. A stern looking elderly lady arrived, sat down, and slowly inched along the bench pushing the lovers off. Suddenly they stood up and the bench tilted, toppling the aggressive old lady to the ground. The little film was photographed from a fixed camera position in one take and ran for less than a minute, but it was so popular that Paul remade it a few years later. The fact that the reporter choose that story film for special reference rather than the other documentary type offerings was an unconscious indication of the future direction that popular cinema was to take. The other films shown seem to have been a mixture of old kinetoscope films and some more recent ones. It was noted that large crowds arrived in the unreserved seats and many people had to be turned away. Obviously word of mouth from the Alhambra showings had spread the news in the factories, mills and other work places. Those two shows, historic and important as they are, were only the appetisers for the arrival of the original and better known Lumière Cinematographe. The man responsible for that was Dan Lowrey jr.

To understand what was happening, and the people involved, it is necessary to go back a year to Paris to the Boulevard des Capucines, not far from the Paris Opera where in December 1895 the Lumière Brothers rented a room called the Indian Salon. There they set up a screen, their new invention called a Cinematographe and installed one hundred chairs. The Lumières were a wealthy family who had a successful photographic business in Lyons where a work force of about 300 men and women turned out photographic plates in their factory there. The business had been founded by the father, Antoine, and was at that time being run by his sons Louis and Auguste. They had been intrigued by Edison's Kinetoscope and its strips of celluloid and realised that it contained the possibilities of projecting large moving images for an audience. After studying its mechanisms they produced their own apparatus which they called a Cinematographe. Unlike Edison's Kinetograph, it was portable and could be used as camera, printer, and projector. After successful private demonstrations in Lyons and La Ciotat near Marseilles where they filmed their historic Train Entering a Station they decided to go national and so the father headed for Paris and the Indian Salon. On 28th December they opened for business but were disappointed when they attracted only thirty curious customers who paid one franc each. Luckily, before their sceptical father Antoine could say "I told you so", their fortunes changed. The first day was the quiet before the storm. Word of mouth spread the news of their amazing invention and the crowds began to arrive and formed the world's first cinema queues. The crowds became so large and unruly that the police were needed to control them. Henri Brispot's first poster illustrates the occasion and, under the heading Cinematographe Lumière in large distinctive letters, shows a well dressed crowd pushing into the salon under the watchful eyes of the police. There are ladies in large hats guaranteed to cut off the view of anyone unlucky enough to be seated behind them, men in tall hats and a variety of other headgear, children and even a priest. Near the door one elderly gentleman raises his walking cane and shakes his bald head in anger as his elegant hat is dislodged in the crush.

One of the patrons who had been specially invited was George Méliès, a magician and proprietor of the Theatre Robert-Houdin on the nearby Boulevard des Italiens. The first scene which appeared on the screen was a frozen image of a street in Lyons and Méliès was wondering why he had been brought just to see another magic lantern show, when, to his amazement, everything began to move. As a showman and magician Méliès was enchanted by the "magic" qualities of what he saw and like everyone else he thrilled to the various scenes, especially the train from Marseilles rushing into the station and towards the audience. The show consisted of ten or twelve films which lasted approximately twenty minutes. There were minor problems of jerkiness and blurring plus the distracting noise of the projector, though that latter was quickly solved by the addition of piano music. The audiences were overwhelmed and many returned again and again. Some were obviously mystified because curious gentlemen were seen to approach and examine the screen carefully. Méliès knew he could make good use of a projector in his own magic shows so he asked Antoine to sell him one but the latter refused probably because he didn't want competition in what was clearly an eager market. The Lumière family obviously had a business plan and were well prepared to meet any demand. They had by the end of 1895 a catalogue of over fifty films - some of those would form part of Belfast's first film show the following year - and twenty projectors, while operators were being trained in readiness to take the Cinematographe around the world. Antoine asked his friend Felicien Trewey, a noted magician and shadowgraphist or ombromane, to go to London and arrange showings in Britain and Ireland. It was either with him or his assistant Matt Raymond that Dan Lowrey negotiated his film presentations in Dublin and in the Empire in Belfast. Meanwhile Méliès's lady love, the actress Jehanne D'Alcy, had been touring in England and had heard that Robert W. Paul in London was selling his own model of projector. When she told Méliès he immediately headed for London, a city he was familiar with, purchased one and was using it in his magic show by the following April.

Paul was an electrical engineer and manufacturer of precision instruments and his interest in films had been aroused when he noticed how large the crowds were waiting to view Edison's Kinetoscopes. He discovered to his surprise that Edison had not taken out a patent for them in Britain so he began making and marketing his own model, selling them with Edison films. Among his customers was Charles Pathé who took one back to Paris with the intention of doing what Paul had done, namely study its construction and then make and sell his own version in France to travelling showmen and such. Edison, who was obsessed with protecting his designs, was not pleased, so he cut off the supply of films surmising that the machines without the films would be useless. Paul then decided that he would have to make his own films but he didn't know enough about photography so he teamed up with a well known photographer, Birt Acres, and with his help produced a movie camera in early 1895. Acres used it that year to film the Oxford Boat race in March and the Derby in May for Paul's Kinetoscopes. Unfortunately, like Edison and Laurie Dickson, Paul and Acres quarrelled and went their different ways. Paul was attracted more and more by the idea of projecting films on to a screen for an audience and when he heard about the successful Lumière show in Paris he redoubled his efforts and by April 1896 had unveiled his own model of projector which he called the Theatrograph. It was one of those that he sold to George Méliès. But the Theatrograph was technically inferior to the Lumière model and Paul had to modify it, renaming the improved model the Animatograph and it was one of those he brought over to Belfast's Opera House later that year.

Paul also turned to making films early examples being "The Soldier's Courtship" which turned up in Belfast's second film show in the Ulster Hall, and the Derby of 1896 the atmosphere and immediacy of which greatly impressed the Telegraph's photographic reporter when he saw it in London. Paul also made an agreement with a man whose name was well known in Belfast, a conjuror called David Devant whose act was a big attraction at the Egyptian Hall in London's Piccadilly. A magician like Méliès, Devant saw the advantages of the cinematographe for his act so he approached Paul and bought one from him for one hundred pounds. Paul promised him a commission on any others he could sell to fellow magicians. Devant soon joined Paul not only in selling the equipment but also in making films for projection. Many of those were filmed on the roof of the Egyptian Hall. Devant put together a number of travelling shows combining conjurers with films and sent them touring outside London. It was one of those that played in Belfast in April 1897.

The situation in the new film business had similarities with the dot. com. revolution of 2000. Things were developing rapidly and there was a great feeling of excitement in the air allied with a certainty that there was money to be made so, as Jimmy Durante would have said, everybody wanted to get in the act. As the demand for films and projectors increased new "improved" machines popped up to meet that demand, each with a different name. A quick skim through the adverts in the technical magazines of the day turns up at least thirty different projector names. Nomad in the Ireland's Saturday Night found it quite confusing and suggested that the machine be called a cinemato - animato - theatro - graph but abandoned that in favour of a what - d'y - call - o - graph, and finally a somesortograph. Despite the humour he still insisted that it was "one of the most startling developments of science." The local audiences agreed and didn't seem to mind what the machine was called as long as they could see more films.

Dan Lowrey was aware of what was happening in London and of the success of the new animated photographs so he set about arranging Ireland's first film show in the Star Theatre of Varieties in Dublin beginning on the 20th April 1896. It was advertised as "The Cinematographe, The Greatest, most Sensational and Grandest Novelty ever Produced in Ireland'" which was being brought at the "enormous" cost of two hundred pounds for the week (it actually cost sixty pounds). Patrons were promised "Living people brought in animation from all parts of the Globe." It was quite a build-up but unfortunately, due to a fault in the projector or to an inexperienced projectionist the result was just a partial success. An expectant audience saw only flashes of light and a few faint figures on the screen representing acrobats, a serpentine dancer, Scottish dancers, a band and two boxing cats. The Irish Times was not very impressed, wondering if the Cinematogtraphe was any real advance on the kinetoscope. Lowrey's own growing disillusionment with it can be traced in the daily newspaper advertisements. The hyperbole of Monday's claims became "the world's most scientific invention" on Tuesday, "the latest scientific invention" on Wednesday, and finally just "the great invention" on Friday. Lowrey was relieved when the week was over and decided to set matters right himself. He went to London to see the agents of the Lumière Bros. and arranged for their Cinematographe with projectionist Felicien Trewey to come over to Dublin for a week at the beginning of November 1896. The result was a major success both artistically and financially. The Freeman's Journal described the event as "startling" and was very impressed by the overall presentation. The Irish Times was equally pleased with the quality of the pictures projected "with the aid of the magic lantern." But, above all, the audiences showed by their reactions that they loved it so it was only natural that Dan made arrangements to bring the show to his other variety theatre, the Empire in Belfast.

Although Belfast had already experienced two separate film shows Dan knew he had a number of important cards to play. The Lumière Cinematographe was not only the original but also had acquired the highest reputation for entertainment value and technical ability. Additionally members of the middle class, and especially ladies, who would never dream of entering the Alhambra would have had no hesitation in going to the newer, more comfortable Empire. Lumière opened on Monday, 16th November 1896 and, as Dan expected, the house was packed, and it continued that way all week. Observers commented that the response was overwhelming with audiences, as at the earlier Alhambra showings, standing, clapping and cheering. The Whig summed them up as "demonstrations of enthusiasm seldom witnessed from a Belfast audience." Technically it was agreed the presentation was the best yet with very little shake or blurring and there was much praise for the skill of the projectionist, Mr. Trewey. There was a catalogue of fifty films available and those actually shown varied from night to night but by comparing the commentaries of the main papers it is possible at least to reconstruct what was shown on the first night.

Lumière, the light arrives.

Pride of place went to Lumière's most famous film of a train entering the station which the Irish News gave special praise to. People were amazed at the passengers, some alighting from the carriages, others entering but all going about their own business, moving in different directions at different speeds. The Whig was impressed by the manner in which the animate and the inanimate were combined in the one picture. In an article in a local paper later, an unnamed cameraman commented that cameramen vied with each other over the years in making that type of shot more exciting by placing the camera as close to the train as was safely possible. It was finally realised by trial and error that a distance of five feet (less than two metres) from the edge of the platform was ideal for the most impressive picture. However few would criticise the positioning and framing used by Louis Lumière in the original film. That film was followed by the hustle and bustle of street scenes in Piccadilly Circus and on Westminster Bridge. The Fire Brigade Call (already shown at the Alhambra) was a great favourite and during it someone in the gallery caused a roar of laughter when he shouted, "Go it Parker," referring to the local fire brigade superintendent who had been appointed in 1892 and who had energetically set about modernising and expanding the local service. Royalty was represented by views of the wedding procession of Princess Maud. Then came a shot of sheep being led to the slaughter followed by an exciting charge of curvassiers which was very well received and much commented upon. A number of the reporters remarked on the realism of the clouds of dust which rose from under the horses' hooves. The show ended with two scenes of bathers enjoying the waters of the Mississippi and the Mediterranean. They seemed to fascinate the viewers, and the News Letter noted how the water rippled in the sunshine while the waves touched the beach with a quiet splash which "was all but heard" in the packed theatre. That was the only reference to sound, or lack of it and no - one said anything about the accompanying music, whether it was played on a piano or by the orchestra. Of some interest is what was not shown. There is no mention of either The Gardener Teased (L'Arroseur arrosé) about a gardener on whom a little boy plays a joke, or The Workers emerging from a Factory, two well known Lumière favourites. That doesn't mean they weren't shown sometime during the week and certainly they did appear in later presentations elsewhere in the city.

The week was a massive success and to put it simply: après Lumière, le déluge. By Christmas there were four separate film shows to choose from, and more followed in the New Year. That was in marked contrast to Dublin where no film presentations took place over that period. Dan Lowrey had intended to have the Lumière show back in the Star Theatre of Varieties over the Christmas period and had actually started taking seat bookings before announcing that the show was unavoidably postponed until January 14th. Meanwhile back in Belfast, where a greater enthusiasm for the new medium could be detected, Nomad in the Ireland's Saturday Night was amused not by the volume of offerings but by the tone of some of the advertisements. The exhibition at the Opera House was worthy of seeing because it had, he observed, "suffered the sacred gaze of her Majesty" at Windsor, while the presentation at the Ulster Hall had been "viewed by H.R.H. Teddy of Wales" at Marlborough House. Royal performances were always a good selling point because they implied quality and good taste and raised the show above common criticisms. But, above all, he hoped that people had noted that "the great, the marvellous, the original" Lumière at the Empire had been scrutinised by none other than Dan Lowrey the "Napoleon of Irish Theatres." Despite the sarcasm he knew that there was a feast of films available. The showmen offered other inducements to attract the public. In their advertisements, carried in the local papers, the emphasis was always on the machine which was presented as unique in some way and at the same time it was clearly coupled with the inventor's name. Thus the Lumière Cinematographe (always with an "e") was "the original" or "the premier," while Paul's Animatographe was described as "world famed" and "first time in Ireland." Audiences were promised pictures that were life size or full length to differentiate them from ordinary photographs and, at the same time, to imply greater value for money.

In December 1896 the Opera House presented its annual Christmas Pantomime, Bo-Peep, and had arranged as an extra treat for Robert W. Paul himself, often called the

Father of English Cinema, to come over and show some films on his Animatographe. Paul arrived with a catalogue of fifty films, presenting about ten each evening, with daily variations as was the general practice then. At the beginning he had some minor problems with his equipment but once those were solved the shows proved to be very attractive. "First class," the Irish News decided. The films included the familiar street scenes and the Derby, and there were also beach scenes at Brighton and at a cave on the Atlantic shore. An unusual addition was a bullfight. Those latter two were part of a popular series photographed by Henry Short for Paul during a tour of the Iberian peninsula earlier in the year. Music hall acts included the ever popular serpentine dancer, a conjurer (unnamed, but probably David Devant), and a beautifully coloured film of the White Eyed Kaffir, who was well known from local music hall appearances. One of the most interesting items historically however was a view of men working in a forge on Queen's Island. That must have been taken by Paul himself to add some local interest and is the first mention of a locally filmed view shown in the city. Strangely, only one of the papers, the Irish News, mentioned it.

The Lumière show at the Empire proved a major draw again and the Whig commented that the Cinematographe was certainly "a wonderful example of the application of science to recreative purposes," reflecting a very similar statement the same paper had made nearly sixty years earlier. The Ulster Hall also presented a film show though only for two days using, it was claimed, the same projector that was demonstrated before the Prince and Princess of Wales at Marlborough House. If the claim was valid then the instrument was probably one of Birt Acre's so - called Royal Cinematographs. Certainly the films presented were mainly older ones filmed by Acres for Paul. They included the Derby of 1895 (filmed for the Paul Kinetoscope), the Czar in Paris, Boxing Kangaroos, and the Arrest of a Pickpocket, with shots of the Prince and Princess at the exhibition in Cardiff. All the shows were crowded night after night.

In the New Year (1897) the Empire followed the departed Lumière with another French production, the happily named Prof. Jolly. It was actually named after Henri Joly a French engineer who had become well known in Paris by modifying kinetoscopes for Charles Pathé. Later he joined with Ernest Normandin and together they produced a projector - camera, which they called the Joly - Normandin Cinematographe, with which they took and showed films successfully in competition with Lumière, for example in the Cafe de la Paix and at many other Parisien venues. Prof. Jolly promised 48,000 living photographs and the Whig reviewer thought that his was one of the finest shows so far, with interesting films most of which hadn't been seen before. He was especially impressed by the fact that his version of the Czar's Entry into Paris ran for nearly five minutes. Other films included a charge of Lancers, some street scenes from Paris and a village smithy. Local scenes were promised but because of bad weather the filming was postponed. Finally, however, they were presented on January 18th. Dan Lowrey himself introduced them and began by apologising for the numerous delays, the latest of which he attributed to the fact that London had sent the wrong prints. The films, which included views of Donegal Place and the Queen's Bridge were received with enthusiasm and the latter scene had to be repeated to satisfy the calls of the audience.

Just over a week later the Belfast Natural History and Philosophical Society, always mindful of its aim to keep the city abreast of new developments, announced that there would be a lecture, repeated on the following night, on the subject of the Electric Cinematographe, to be presented in the Ulster Minor Hall. Those who attended were promised a history of the apparatus followed by a demonstration of its capabilities. The society lectures were usually one - off affairs so the fact that it was to be repeated reflected the high level of interest in the city. It also allowed professional people and those who would not normally frequent a music hall where alcohol was available, to acquaint themselves, in a suitably serious academic atmosphere, with the new scientific wonder. The power was supplied from Ewart's and a local electrical engineer J. H. Greenhill laid a cable across Bedford Street from their building into the Minor Hall. Despite travel difficulties due to heavy snow and frost that week, the lectures were crowded. The lecturer, William Nicholl, was well known to the society members as a lanternist and received a very warm welcome. He traced the origins of projection in some detail and showed how the modern cinematographe had evolved through the efforts of many investigators including Muybridge and Edison. He explained how the various projection machines worked and how the films themselves were photographed, giving in the process a detailed description of Edison's film studio, the Black Maria, which was built so that it could be turned to catch the sun's rays for photography.

The second part of the proceedings was the film show projected by Mr. Drennan. A great variety of films was shown most of which were from Lumière and included that old favourite, the Czar's Entry into Paris, plus the Card Party (which had appeared in the original Alhambra show), a Serpentine dancer, a Cavalry charge, Waves Breaking on a Coast, a scene of Nurses at Work, a Knife Grinder, an Obstinate Donkey, and the Exit of Workers from a Factory (La Sortie des Usines Lumière). The Whig singled out the latter as one of the finest. It is also one of the earliest and most famous of Lumière's films, in fact the first film shot by Louis Lumière. It was filmed in 1895 in Lyon and showed the workers emerging from their photographic factory to enjoy their lunch break. They formed an entirely natural group, talking and laughing, while a little dog ran between their feet. Through a door on the left of the picture a pram could be seen. They were not great artists, writers, clerics, leaders, society beauties or politicians. They were just ordinary working people who walked into entertainment and media history.

Reactions to those little snippets of film varied across the world. Almost everywhere there was enthusiasm mixed with varying levels of amazement and understanding. A journalist in Paris saw them in a more serious light as putting an end to death itself because people were preserved forever in movement on film. One can readily understand what he meant because watching La Sortie today and seeing those animated figures moving, talking, laughing and exhibiting all the characteristics of the living while at the same time knowing that they no longer exist, can stir an uneasy feeling regarding the true nature of reality. In Moscow a viewer, on seeing the train entering the station at La Ciotat, said it reminded him of Tolstoy's "Anna Karenina." In contrast Maxim Gorky was repelled by what he described as the silent grey world of the cinematographe, while in a rural area in deepest Russia peasants became convinced that the Cinematographe was the work of the Devil and burned the machine, the films, and the tent they were being shown in. The Lumière operatives who were presenting the show were lucky to escape with their lives and only reached their hotel with police protection. Elsewhere in Russia a Lumière cameraman photographed a Russian officer watching a Turkish dancing girl, but when he showed it publicly later, the police confiscated the film and expelled him from the country for bringing the Russian army into disrepute. The first films shown publicly in Australia were presented in Melbourne by the American magician, Carl Hertz, who had bought a projector from Robert Paul for one hundred pounds. That show took place nine days before Belfast's historic presentation in the Alhambra and consisted of a mixture of films supplied by Paul and some old Edison kinetoscope films. The Australians were impressed but took the matter less seriously than their European counterparts. In one of the films of a crowd crossing Westminster Bridge a man turned to look towards the camera. That became the point of an ongoing joke because every evening at the appropriate time someone, who had obviously been there before, whistled and the man dutifully turned around and looked at the audience, causing much laughter.

So, how did the reaction of our local audiences compare with what was happening elsewhere? In the five months following the initial Alhambra showing Belfast audiences had the opportunity to see a wide variety of films from the cameras of Lumière, Robert Paul, Birt Acres and Henri Joly, plus examples of older Edison - Dickson kinetoscope films. On every occasion curiosity ensured that there were packed houses and enthusiastic receptions. The general opinion was one of approval. The venues involved were the Alhambra, the Empire, the Opera House, the Ulster Hall and the Y.M.C.A. Hall in Wellington Place, which meant that they were accessible to all classes and sections of the populace, including children (at the Opera pantomime). Only those who wouldn't frequent the halls from religious or other reasons were unaware of the new novelty and even they had the opportunity to attend the Natural History and Philosophical society's lecture in the Ulster Minor Hall. The audiences that clapped and cheered with delight were not entirely unsophisticated or uninformed. They included music hall regulars who had seen panoramas and dioramas, special effects like the Ghost, and illusions involving skeletons, disappearing ladies, headless bodies and all types of wonders. They had grown up in an age of new inventions each with its own surprises. They had accepted the telegraph and the telephone and had experienced local demonstrations of Edison's phonograph and kinetoscope and most recently the amazing Rontgen rays (actually x-rays, discovered by Prof. Rontgen in Vienna) that could look through solid matter or humans, and photograph their interiors. In similar vein, the cinematographe was another such marvel to be experienced. There were also the skilled craftsmen with a technical turn of mind anxious to see how the machine worked, and the photographers both professional and amateur interested in a novel form of instantaneous photography. The new Cinematographe became a major topic of conversation in the workshops, in the homes and on the streets.

Interest increased when local scenes became available. Paul seems to have shown the first local views taken at Queen's Island but during January 1897 movie cameras actually appeared on the streets. On Friday, 1st January Lumière cameramen began taking local scenes. Excited crowds watched as two films were photographed of the Belfast fire brigade in action under the direction of Superintendent Parker. Cameras were then set up to record activity in Castle Place and on the Queen's Bridge. According to the Lumière catalogue those were part of a series of twenty five films taken in Ireland. The operatives arrived by boat from Liverpool and took nine films in Dublin and six around Belfast. The others were "panoramas" or shots taken from the moving train between Dublin and Belfast, one of them, for example, when passing Dammuray (Dunmurry!). Later in the month Prof. Jolly's cameramen also took local views. All that activity attracted curious crowds and must also have intrigued local lanternists and professional photographers like Alexander Hogg. Lizars and Erskine Mayne must have wondered if the latest novelty was just a nine day's wonder, or if it was going to last, and if it might even undermine their lucrative business of selling and renting magic lanterns and slides. The News Letter had no doubt that it was going to last and saw a great future for it especially in documentary material. The writer speculated that it would compete with and eventually supersede the many illustrated magazines then available. Others thought it would become an important tool of education especially for geography and history, while the Ireland's Saturday Night foresaw it in tandem with the phonograph becoming a medium for recording plays.

In December 1897 a special show was presented in the Great Hall of the Y.M.C.A. in Wellington Place. It was in aid of the Braille Library in the Workshops of the Blind located in Royal Avenue. The show was a mixture of music, song, Tableaux Vivants and the Lumière Cinematograph. A report of the affair was written up for the News Letter and in it the writer commented that it was a wonderful evening and the most wonderful part of it was the Cinematographe which to him was "a decided triumph of human ingenuity" involving an apparatus which didn't disappoint as one became more familiar with it. Through it one was able to "look at life represented in all its various forms and situations, to contemplate the sky sea and scenery all of which are things well calculated to strike admiration into the minds of the most oblivious and to make them pause and ask - what next?"

As part of its splendid programmes to celebrate the centenary of the cinema the Queen's Film Theatre presented on the 16th November 1996 a re-creation of that first Lumière show in the Empire. About twenty of the original films were shown, some from the first show with some which were filmed later in 1896 and 1897, but they did help to catch something of the early atmosphere. Of course there was a big difference between the perceptions of the audiences. The moderately sized audience in the Q.F.T. were film buffs, historians, students, and a sprinkling of senior citizens some of whom probably remembered seeing silent films. Many had a good idea of the outline history of the cinema so the overall reaction was a combination of the academic, the nostalgic and the curious. Their sense of wonder at seeing moving pictures may have passed but their quiet intensity and private smiles reflected deep satisfaction and pleasure. The original audience by contrast was numerous, noisy and in a state of high anticipation. What they were about to see was a complete revelation, a new type of photography. Old, worn and scratched prints often projected at the wrong speed have given a distorted view of early films so the first thing that probably struck the modern audience was the clarity and high quality of the photography. The original audience would have taken that for granted as they were well used to the high standards of Victorian photography. Each item began with a frozen image, a practice which had misled Méliès into thinking he was about to see another magic lantern show. One moment the viewer is looking at a large photograph say of a street with people on the pavements and horse vehicles on the road. Suddenly without warning the people are walking and the horses and vehicles are moving at differing speeds and in differing directions. It is still quite effective today but seeing it for the first time must have been astounding, all the more so because it was life size and looked quite natural.

The first film shown at the Q.F.T. was the delightful and popular one of the workers coming out of the Lumière photographic factory followed by some of the Lumière family "snapshots"; notably "Feeding the Baby" in which everyone, especially the baby, looks very relaxed. Fishing for Goldfish, On and Off the Horse and Jumping the Blanket were followed by the Gardener being teased by a young boy. The latter was a simple story such as might have appeared in a newspaper cartoon of the period, or on the music hall stage. A young boy puts his foot on a gardener's hose causing the water to stop flowing. The bewildered gardener peers into the hose whereupon the lad lifts his foot and the gardener is drenched. The hose is dropped and the miscreant is pursued and cuffed. In all it lasted less than a minute and was shot in one take without any cuts or camera movements. But that little comedy was the cinema's first fiction story, the progenitor of Chaplin, Buster Keaton, Harry Langdon, Laurel and Hardy and all the rest of the great comics and clowns.

The second half of the programme consisted of Irish scenes beginning in Dublin. Sackville Street (now O'Connell Street) had its horse trams, the women with their skirts to the ground and every man wearing some kind of headgear. The Dublin fire brigade went through its paces while the R.I.C. held back curious crowds on the pavements. The crowds watched the firemen and then switched their gaze to the camera, not quite sure which was the more fascinating. That was the shot that had inspired someone in the gods in the Empire to shout "Go it Parker" - but the modern audience remained quiet and pensive probably contemplating how fire fighting technology has changed. Scenes along the railway came next photographed from a moving train passing through Dublin, Drogheda, Lurgan, Lisburn and Belfast. The moving shot or panorama was discovered by Lumière's chief cameraman A. Promio when filming from a gondola in Venice, and there are strong indications that he was involved in the Irish scenes. Normally the camera didn't move. It was set up and photographed briefly whatever was happening in front of it. The earliest movements of the camera were the panorama shots which later developed into the so-called phantom rides causing great excitement when the camera was fixed to the front of a speeding train. Then came the scenes of the Belfast fire brigade which were filmed on 1st January 1897. That date is certain because the event is recorded in the Irish News which, like the rest of Belfast, was very proud of its brigade and its new equipment. The men put on a fine display which must have pleased Superintendent Parker who had been responsible for reorganizing the service over the period from 1892 to 1894. The horse drawn brigade looked very efficient as it swept past the camera, belching black smoke. That was followed by a demonstration of the new ladders with firemen in their new uniforms climbing upwards and out of the top of the frame. Little did they suspect that in a hundred years time they would be repeating their exercises before a curious Belfast audience again. Maybe there was an element of truth in that French journalist's comment about the end of death...

But what of the stories of people falling off their seats or even fleeing from the halls as vehicles raced towards them? The only story of that type recorded at the time involved an incident that happened at Strabane, not in Belfast. A travelling showman was presenting his films to an intent audience. Everything went well until he put on a serpentine dancer called Lucille Murray. The casual introduction of that detail suggests that the story is true because Miss Murray was a dancer who was persuaded in 1895 by Edison himself to perform for the camera at the Black Maria for the kinetoscope. Many showmen at the time used cheap old kinetoscope films as part of their presentation. Suddenly during her dance an irate man jumped up and shouted that the whole thing was obviously a fraud. The machine was only a magic lantern throwing a beam of white light while the girl was dancing behind the screen. Others joined in and things began to turn nasty. The showman tried to restore order and finally he appealed for a chance to prove that the films were genuine. He quickly took out the film of the train entering the station and put it on. The audience settled down and when it was over the showman pointed out that he couldn't have a train, a station and all those people behind the screen. They were convinced, so the film that had a reputation for frightening people out of their seats was the means of keeping them in their seats in Strabane. There's something very Irish about that.

Despite that it must be admitted that in the Thirties a different story appeared in Random Jottings in the Irish News. The reporter interviewed a former doorman of the Empire, by then retired and living in Cavendish Square. He recalled the first Lumière show in the Empire and related how a box had been set aside specially for the press but before the show they were entertained in the bar. According to his story some of them imbibed a little too much and were rather unsteady on their approach to the press box. When the show began and the train raced towards them at least one member fell off his seat while another departed the box erratically at maximum velocity. Allowing for the local penchant towards exaggeration and the frailty of memory, and if the reader is willing to accept the outrageous suggestion that some newsmen might actually overindulge, one might suggest that the report is a case of when the myth becomes history, print the myth, as suggested at the end of "The Man Who Shot Liberty Valence" (d. John Ford, 1962.)

CHAPTER THREE
The Excitement of the Cinematograph

During 1897 the cinematograph continued to infiltrate the local entertainment scene and made its presence felt in other commercial and social circles. In early February J. Lizar's, one of the city's best known photographic outlets, announced their annual sale of slides and equipment with a generous 20% reduction. But more important was a notice which accompanied it, namely that in future they would offer for hire Cinematograph shows using the finest apparatus and latest films. Lizar's had obviously decided that film shows were a natural and worthwhile extension to their magic lantern and slide hire business. They had purchased a number of cinematographs but there is no information about the type of machines involved or where they came from as all their early records have disappeared. Being opticians and camera makers Lizar's would have had the necessary know-how and business connections to get what they needed. In May the Lumière Cinematographe came on to the market and Lizar's obtained a number of them, and offered to put on exhibitions which included local views projected by "the most perfect machine made" showing pictures "free from flicker, noise or jumping." That decision represented the beginning of the local film hire business in the city and Lizar's was soon followed by a group called the Cinematographe Syndicate with offices in Donegall Street, and by another local retailer, Erskine Mayne.

The Cinematographe Syndicate was a London based company and was responsible for the film show which accompanied the Saturday Night Concert on 10th April in the Ulster Hall. Prior to then bookings had been made with similar companies or travelling showmen from England. One of those companies was H. Spencer Clarke of London with whom Cecil Hepworth, a noted English filmmaker, worked for a time. The Ulster Hall arranged a show through them in mid April, which is interesting for a number of reasons. It consisted of an illusionist Frank Kennard and a picture show described as "the largest collection of views yet shown in Belfast." It was put together by the magician David Devant, an associate of Robt. Paul. Kennard's act, especially his shadowgraphy, was highly appreciated by the audiences but their main interest was in the films. The projector was most probably a Lumière machine (Hepworth mentions H. S. Clarke having Lumières at that time) and the films were a mixture of British items photographed mainly by Paul, with a number of French scenes. Many were familiar Lumière favourites like the dancer Loie Fuller in colour, the Entry of the Tsar into Paris, the arrival of a train in a station, workers leaving a factory, Paris street scenes, and such. But there were many new ones notably David Devant conjuring, a gardener watering his garden and a gardener burning weeds all by Paul. Then there was a third group which included the Vanishing Lady Trick and the Haunted Castle. In the first a lady is turned into a skeleton before disappearing, while in the second a visitor to a castle is chased by ghosts in medieval costume.

They were the work of George Méliès the magician who had been invited to the first Lumière shows in Paris and had been so impressed that he decided to go into film making himself. He found the problems of filming in the streets, especially the unpredictable weather, so frustrating that he decided to build his own studio where he would have complete control over the whole process of film production and where he could bring his vast practical knowledge of stage craft and magic shows to bear on this new art form. He always insisted that from the beginning he saw film making not just as an entertainment but as an art form. Well, he was French. In 1897 he designed a studio and had it constructed in the garden of his property at Montreuil, a suburb of Paris. It was a more elaborate and substantial building than the Black Maria of Laurie Dickson, with a glass roof to catch the sunlight, blinds to control the amount of light, a specially built set for filming, and facilities for a workshop and the storage of props. It was the genesis of and model for the large studios that were to appear in Europe and America in the following century. Like the studio his films were elaborate and carefully constructed, and were always a delight to watch. They still are. They became great favourites with local audiences because, while no-one knew his name, they came to recognise his logo, a star, and Star films always drew a crowd. It is interesting that the Whig critic at the Ulster Hall show choose three films as the best of the bunch, and one of them was Méliès' The Vanishing Lady Trick.

Contemporaneously religious groups who had used magic lantern shows to attract crowds began examining the possibilities of using the cinematograph in a similar way. As it happened, a dispute was raging locally about the rights and wrongs of such attitudes. The directors of the Ulster Hall had decided to hold a number of concerts of Sacred Music on the Sundays of January and February. The aim was charitable; the proceeds were to go to the Lord Mayor's Coal Fund to relieve the distress of the poor who couldn't afford the price of fuel during the cold winter weather. Despite that, the decision outraged many people, especially the Lord's Day Observance Society who promised to do everything possible to put an end to the idea. Their secretary wrote to the papers objecting to the attempt to "turn the Lord's Day into a season of entertainment" and pointed out that they had prevented a similar decision being carried out two years before. Another letter from a concerned individual warned that "singing will never take the place of salvation." Despite the protests the concerts went ahead and were well supported. Letters continued to appear in support and one of those praised those clergy who were willing to use modern methods to attract an audience because once they had the audience they could, as the writer put it, "elevate and edify them."

It was estimated that about 75,000 local Protestants, mainly among the less well off, had no connection with any place of worship, and a number of religious groups had set out to try and gain their attention. One such group, the Belfast Central Mission under the leadership of their energetic superintendent, the Rev. Dr. Crawford Johnston, had for many years been putting on Happy Evenings - though never on Sundays - as an alternative to the public house for the poor. A typical evening's entertainment included music, singing, instrumentals, hymns and something special like a magic lantern show. The price of entry was nominal, only a few pence, and over the years the Happy Evenings had proved successful and were well supported. In the same spirit it was decided to hire a cinematograph as the attraction, and the first Happy Evening using films took place at the end of January 1897 in the Grosvenor Hall, the price of the seats being 1d and 2d. Those prices were the lowest yet for a local film show and brought the cinematograph within the reach of the very poor.

The wisdom of the decision was justified by the response, which was so great that hundreds of people were turned away - though with the promise that there would be a repeat show on the following Wednesday. The Saturday film show presented familiar scenes including the train entering a station, the turnout of a fire brigade, a march past of cavalry and children playing on the sand while the Wednesday show promised all those again plus some extras including an intriguing item described as "a carpenter's shop in Donegall Street." The pulling power of the Cinematographe didn't go unnoticed by other groups with religious aims and in the following weeks the Central Presbyterian Mission presented a repeat of William Nicholl's lecture on the Cinematographe in their Assembly Hall in May Street. The cost of admission was slightly higher than the Grosvenor Hall at 6d (3d for members) but Mr Nicholl addressed a large and attentive crowd "after devotional exercises." The new Queen Victoria Hall (the former Christ Church) in Durham Street also added the Cinematograph to its entertainment with a charge of 2d. In mid April the Y.M.C.A. announced the opening of their imposing new multi purpose building in Wellington Place and after the official ceremonies, which were photographed by A.R. Hogg among others, they issued a general invitation to the citizens of Belfast to come and inspect it the following evening. The facilities on show were very impressive because the building included every facility that was then perceived as necessary for the physical, moral and intellectual welfare of young Christian men. On show was the great hall which could hold 1,700 people, a minor hall for meetings of smaller groups, a gymnasium, a reading room, classrooms, a large cafe, and a special photographic unit with a dark room. The whole structure was lit in the modern fashion by electric light supplied by the corporation. To entertain the visitors on their tour the Royal Fusilier Band played selected pieces, while to ensure a good turnout a Cinematographe show was included in the proceedings.

The ease and indeed rapidity with which religious groups absorbed the Cinematographe into their systems might seem surprising especially in light of their general disapproval of the music hall and theatre. As recently as October 1890 the Y.M.C.A. Literary Society had had a lively debate on the motion that "theatre going is inconsistent with Christianity." By a large majority the answer had been "yes," a decision that had been greeted with loud cheers. But there were no such problems with the Cinematographe because it was seen essentially as a new form of photography and the Y.M.C.A. was already very proud of the achievements of its Amateur Photographic Society. In fact during the following month the Photographic Society held a "conversazione" in the new Minor Hall to celebrate the founding of the club eight years before. The evening was a great success. It started with tea followed by a short speech welcoming the members to their new surroundings and then a musical interlude. John Woodside then demonstrated a gramophone and a cinematograph. He explained how the latter worked and showed "some fine views." Woodside sold electrical goods for a living, and his name crops up on a number of occasions in connection with the cinematograph, which suggests very strongly that, like Lizar's, he had obtained a machine and had become proficient in its use, making him one of the earliest local projectionists. Another man who was to become well known in the same field was there that night. He was Alfred George, a lanternist, and future cinema owner, who gave a magic lantern show of slides made by A.R.

L. WALKER, Mus.?., (Hon.
J. MALCOLM.   / Secs.

27189

CITY Y.M.C.A.
IMPORTANT ENGAGEMENT.
ANIMATED PHOTOGRAPHY.

THE BELFAST Y.M.C.A. HAVE GREAT pleasure in announcing a most important Engagement with BIRT ACRES, Esq., the famous pioneer of Animated Photography, who will give an Exhibition of this most startling of all scientific discoveries in the NEW Y.M.C.A. HALL, on THURSDAY NIGHT, 28th October. By ROYAL PERMISSION, Mr. Acres has secured a number of magnificent Animated Photographs of her Majesty, H.R.H. the Prince of Wales, and other members of the Royal Family. These distinguished personages will be seen, LIFE-SIZE, moving to and fro in the scenes. The most complete Animated Photograph of the great ROYAL PROCESSION which took place in London last June will also be exhibited; Wedding of Princess Maud (taken by special command of H.R.H. the Prince of Wales), German Emperor Reviewing his Troops, Henley Regatta, Arrival of T.R.H. the Prince and Princess of Wales, accompanied by the Princesses Victoria and Maud, in State at Cardiff Exhibition, 1896 (life-size), &c., &c., &c. SPECIAL NOTICE.—This Exhibition is not to be confounded with the imperfect efforts with which the public are more familiar, but is the most Perfect and Complete in the United Kingdom, and is a great scientific success. During the Evening there will be Grand Organ Recitals, and a first-class Programme of Vocal Music by Miss McGreavi and Mr. Jack Spence, Amateurs. Prices

Mr Black introduces films to the YMCA (see page 44).

Hogg, which included shots of Fermanagh and slides of the recent opening of the new Y.M.C.A building. By the end of the year John Woodside had come to an agreement with the Y.M.C.A. secretary, D. Black, and was presenting highly popular film shows on a regular basis using a new Lumière machine worked by electricity.

Over Christmas 1897 that machine attracted large crowds and commentators noted how superior the pictures were, especially in steadiness and clarity, to those projected by limelight. He showed a total of forty pictures with scenes from all over the world. Local scenes caused great excitement like shots from the recent City Cup clash between Cliftonville and Distillery. Musical effects, described by one paper as "startling," were supplied by Fred Moffatt on the organ, while the commentary was given by an enthusiastic Mr Black himself. The capacity audience applauded some items so long and loudly that they had to be repeated. Over the same period the Grosvenor Hall shows were put on by Lizar's, their projectionists being A. R. Hogg and William Taylor. Hogg had a busy Yuletide because on Christmas Day when a group of voluntary workers from the Belfast Central Mission visited the poorest parts of the city to distribute food to the very needy he accompanied them and took a series of telling photographs. He then rushed back to the laboratory, developed them and mounted them as slides. He was able to show them with a magic lantern in the hall that evening. The following evening the Mission had its annual party for deprived children - the City Arabs, as they were called - and a film show was the most popular part of it. The following evening saw him back in the Grosvenor Hall again working the cinematographe.

On Tuesday 13th April 1897 Belfast was introduced face to face with another much talked about recent invention, the motor car. Two months before a motor car had appeared on the stage of the Theatre Royal in a melodrama called "Guilty Mother" and many in the audience had found it more interesting than the play. The excitement it had generated reappeared again as large crowds assembled to watch a parade of new vehicles through the city centre. Unfortunately a young schoolboy George Sibbons of York Street was knocked down and suffered cuts, bruises and shock. He is the first recorded case of of the victim of a car accident in the city. Commenting on the event the News Letter expressed regret but added that accidents could be expected when dealing with a new and popular invention. The writer was referring to road safety but his words were to prove tragically prophetic with regard to another much loved new invention, the Cinematograph, and the events surrounding it one month later at an annual Charity Bazaar in Paris.

Bazaars were an important and popular part of Victorian social life and the inhabitants of Belfast were very familiar with them. Their attraction lay in the fact that they combined entertainment with good works, usually the raising of money for worthy causes - a kind of early local Live Aid. Each bazaar was usually built around a theme. The themes were drawn from religion, history, geography, literature, or fantasy and many bazaars had become quite elaborate in their presentation. Specialised companies had grown up to supply the necessary raw materials and skills needed in their planning and building. The more elaborate were widely reported in the papers and became the talk of the town. There was no doubt about their popularity and crowds flocked to wander about and enjoy the exotic surroundings and the entertainments. Maybe the fun and fantasy tended to obliterate the true aims, as is hinted in a letter to the local press which complained that they would be splendid entertainment if it wasn't for being badgered at every turn by well meaning people selling ballots for this or that.

Some examples illustrate the appeal of bazaars. In December 1886 St. George's Hall was transformed into a Gypsy Encampment for a successful bazaar in aid of the Ulster Hospital for Children and Women, complete with gypsy music and all the trimmings. In October 1889 the Ulster Hall was impressively decorated with scenes representing places associated with the life of Our Lord, while the interior of the Church of the Nativity was recreated in the Minor Hall. The following year saw the Ulster Hall again transformed in a more elaborate manner for a bazaar put on in aid of St. Jude's church. A company from Leeds, J.T. Reach, was brought in to oversee the decorations and the result was an ingenious "submarine" bazaar which one paper described as "a fanciful picture" in which imagination and fantasy combined with scientific knowledge. Visitors found themselves walking in a marine wonderland. Green gauze was stretched across the hall to represent the surface of the sea while the balconies were covered with canvas on which were painted all types of sea creatures, real and imagined. The stalls were located underneath the balconies in a series of artificial "caves" made from wood and canvas, all of them painted in bright colours to show the great variety of creatures inhabiting the deep and given names like Mermaid's Retreat, Nymph's Bower, and Seaweed Shelter while the cafe suitably became the Sharkeries. The following year the same company returned and the Ulster Hall became a replica of Pharaoh's Palace in pursuit of an Egyptian theme. So Belfast became used to a succession of increasingly elaborate and fanciful affairs honeyed with all the traditional lures normally associated with collecting money for charity. The organizers were always on the alert for new and popular attractions so over the years it is not surprising that Edison's phonograph, the kinetoscope, Ronten rays and the Cinematographe were added to bring in the crowds.

In Paris there was an annual Charity Bazaar of that thematic type which raised money for the deserving poor of the city. It had been organized annually since 1885 by a Catholic charity group which included the crème de la crème of Parisian society, and had come to be regarded as one of the main social events of the year. In 1897 the committee under the usual presidency of Baron Mackam chose the theme of a medieval town and one was built of wood and canvas on the Rue Jean Gougon which today runs down to the Seine at the Pont de l'Alma, just across the river from the Quai d'Orsay. A Cinematographe was included as one of the attractions and the organizers turned to Dr. Joly who supplied a Joly - Normandin projector and a projectionist called M.Bellac. The projector was set up and partly screened from the audience within a canvas enclosure. Because electricity was not available, an ether vapour machine was used. It used an old and tried technique inherited from the magic lantern, that had often been used in the halls in Belfast, in which a mixture of oxygen and ether supplied a flame which heated lime to produce a bright projection beam. Because of the volatile nature of the gases involved great care had to be taken and a skilled projectionist was needed to ensure safety.

During the afternoon show the projecting light failed and the projectionist said it needed a fresh supply of ether. Someone suggested that he fix it outside, but he replied that wasn't necessary, and entered the canvas box which shielded the projector to attend to the problem. On that day a friend, Gregoire Bagrachow, was acting as his assistant and before Bellac could stop him he lit a match to see the equipment more clearly. In a split second the ether fumes ignited with an ominous roar and the flames almost immediately took hold on the nearby painted canvas and hanging draperies. The flames spread with lightning rapidity and panic broke out in the crowded enclosure. The whole area was covered by tarred canvas and drops of burning tar began raining down on the agitated audience. People rushed towards the one exit, many fell and were trampled upon. One man who had stepped out for a smoke before the tragedy struck told how he was almost bowled over by a sudden charge of screaming women, one of whom tripped but luckily he was able to catch her and pull her to safety. Inside, the women's long dresses with lace trimmings and the veils on their hats caught fire and helped to spread the flames. There were stories of gentlemen forgetting their code of manners and knocking women out of their way as they fought towards the exit, though that was later denounced as false during the inquest. Bagrachow managed to smash open a wooden wall and so saved many lives. One young woman reeled out with half her face burned off while others rolled over on the ground in an attempt to put out their burning garments. A man with his beard on fire plunged into a horse trough.

Because of the suddenness and intensity of the conflagration, those outside were beaten back and stood helpless as the air was rent with the hiss and roar of the flames and the screams of those trapped within. Workers from a nearby building site and from a nearby hotel rushed to the scene and after breaking their way in, did manage to save some people. Among those who managed to escape was an Irish girl, a Miss O'Meara who lived in Paris and whose father was a doctor who had attended Napoleon on St. Helena for a time. As the news of the tragedy spread all Paris, then France, was numbed. One hundred and twenty one people died of whom one hundred and ten were women, many of the bodies so badly burnt that it was impossible to identify them. It was announced that a special mass for the dead would be celebrated on the following Saturday in Notre Dame cathedral at which Cardinal Richard would officiate, to allow the nation to express its sorrow.

All the horrors were soberly reported and commented upon in the Belfast papers. There was great sympathy expressed on all sides throughout the city and the local Chamber of Commerce reflected that feeling in a telegram of sympathy to its counterpart in Paris. The papers dismissed an early conspiracy theory that the blaze had been caused by a bomb and agreed that it had been traced to the cinematographe. But they attached no blame to the machine itself nor was there any suggestion that it was a dangerous contraption or that it should be banned or its use otherwise curtailed as was being called for elsewhere. The Irish News sadly noted how the horrors of the disaster stood in stark contrast to "the innocent gaiety and frolicsome enjoyment which belonged to the nature of the entertainment," while the Whig had no doubts about where the real blame lay, in the "criminal carelessness" of those who had organized the affair. It pointed to the paucity of exits, the extreme flammability of the materials used and the lack of access to fire fighting facilities. There was a feeling that because of the elevated social rank of the organizers the police hadn't been as rigorous as they should have been in applying the law.

As the hurt and horror subsided, people began to put varying interpretations on what had happened. A minority saw it as a terrible warning to those who talked of the God - like ability of the cinematographe to replicate reality. Others perceived it in the light of the class struggle, contrasting the actions of the high born with those whom they regarded as the real heroes of the hour, the workers, who had rushed to their aid. Whatever was said or discussed in private, none of that appeared in public debate in Belfast, though those responsible for the licensing of halls for entertainment or involved in the growing cinematographe business must have paid attention to the more temperate and unemotional debate about safety which soon got under way. It was pointed out that the nitrate based film then in general use was highly inflammable and steps should be taken to develop and introduce non-flammable film. A sensible idea, and probably backed by good intentions, but it took nearly fifty years before that was widely achieved.

Another problem was that many projectors didn't use pick-up reels. The film was allowed to spool into a box or open basket and to lie there uncovered, an obvious source of fire danger. Many makers of projectors had already noted that risk and added pick-up spools. By September Robert Paul had a fireproof Animatographe on the market at a price of fifteen pounds, with two spools entirely enclosed in metal so that very little of the film was exposed during projection. The new Lumière machine which came on the market just after the fire incorporated a glass container of water to act as a safety condenser. Many halls already enclosed the projector in a box - like screen, partly because it looked more professional,but mainly because it inhibited curious members of the audience from approaching or interfering with the equipment, and it helped to reduce the noise from the machine. A demand arose that such screens should be compulsory and should be made of fire proof material like iron. Those safety boxes soon made their appearance locally and were the first step towards the separate fire proof projection booths which became standard in the future cinemas. Equally important was the realization that the projectionist should be properly trained. But human memory is short and all the lessons about safety that should have been learned from the terrible occurrence in Paris didn't prevail, as the population of Ireland came to realise when it experienced the shock and horror of a similar disaster nearly thirty years later in Co. Limerick.

The Charity Bazaar fire didn't reduce the popularity of the cinematographe in Belfast though the enormity of the disaster did concentrate official minds in the city as elsewhere across Britain and Europe. Admittedly the music halls eschewed it until August but that could very well have been because of the summer weather. On the other hand within three weeks of the tragedy the Y.M.C.A. Camera Club held a special meeting in their Minor Hall at which one of the items was a successful display of the Cinematographe put on by John Woodside. Newspaper reports indicate that one of the most popular items on any film show was the Fire Brigade Callout which can be partly explained by the fact that fire was never really far from public consciousness. On the one hand there was the threat of hell -fire from the local pulpits and street preachers. On the other, in a city lit mainly by gas and candles, actual fire was a recurring hazard and hardly a day went past without the daily papers carrying accounts of house fires, fires in factories, mills, warehouses and at the docks. During the early nineties there was an average of 120 major fires reported per year, but the citizens believed that their fire service could cope with any outbreak.

Recently the dangers of fire had been much discussed in the city because thoughtful and knowledgeable citizens knew that the city had been spared a major disaster not because of precautions and pre-planning, but mainly by good luck or chance. The fires that had destroyed Dan Lowrey's Alhambra Music Hall in March 1873 and the old Theatre Royal in June 1881 could have been serious tragedies if they had happened during performances, but. luckily they had occurred when the buildings were empty. More recently people had been shocked by events which had taken place in Raglan Street National School in December 1894. About 400 children were watching a stage production of "Uncle Tom's Cabin" when someone turned out the gas lights. In the darkness and ensuing panic five children were killed and many others injured. During the inquiry into the disaster the Belfast coroner warned that another disaster was just waiting to happen unless regulations were tightened up and adequately applied in places of entertainment.

Fire had long been recognised as a major recurring threat in the theatre. Before the use of gas became widespread (after 1830) the main means of lighting the stage was by large candles and their special light, smell and heat were part of the theatrical atmosphere. But such naked lights had to be carefully watched because theatre folk were well aware of tragic incidents when scenery or even the costumes of the players had caught fire. Most actors couldn't afford to emulate Sarah Bernhardt who had all her dresses made from fire - proof materials. The Theatre Royal kept a large container of water stored over the stage to cope with such a contingency.

Those in the Corporation directly responsible for fire safety were members of a body known as the Police Committee, a group who were to become better known later for their attempts at local film censorship. The fire service had been reorganised in the 1860's when new equipment had been ordered from Harland and Wolff's but nothing had been done since then. By the 1890's it was felt that the time had come to update and modernise the service. The Police Committee looked around for a suitably experienced man to undertake the task and finally appointed a new superintendent in July 1892, a Liverpool man G.W. Parker who had a fine reputation and a practical working knowledge of the fire service. When Superintendent Parker arrived in Belfast he realized that what his friends had told him about local conditions was true and that things were, as he put it, "antiquated." The equipment was old, inadequate and out of date, the service was undermanned and morale was low. The challenge was immense but he sat down and drew up a detailed plan of development. The Police Committee and the Corporation were both taken aback at its estimated cost of £5,000.

The Corporation had the reputation of postponing decisions that would cost the ratepayers more money but enough of them realised the urgent need for improvement, so the plan went ahead. Parker, a man of action, immediately began the necessary changes. He ordered five new steam appliances (called steamers) from England to replace the old out of date manual machines in use, also new hoses, ladders and other equipment. All the vehicles were horse drawn so he saw to it that extra horses were bought bringing the total available to ten and that they were then well trained and, above all, well cared for. New recruits were brought into the service on a permanent basis and the working conditions of all the firemen were greatly improved. Wages were increased and all were insured so that in case of accidents their families would have some recompense. They were also supplied with new uniforms and equipment. All men were expected to undergo rigorous training which included gymnastics and daily exercises to keep them fit. He saw to it that their working and living conditions were also improved and that suitable recreation facilities were supplied. In other words he laid the foundations of the modern fire service in the city. Speedy communications were essential for fire control and he encouraged as many establishments as possible to have their premises connected by telephone to his new modern headquarters in Chichester Street, so that warning of a fire could be sent quickly to the brigade. A network of secondary stations was established across the city with a fireman on duty in each one, day and night, to deal with local outbreaks until the main body of the brigade arrived. He also established a fire ambulance service which was badly needed, and insisted that his men became proficient in first aid. In 1894 the Telegraph praised him for his work and assured their readers that with regard to fires and the fire brigade "there is a new order of things." Besides undertaking and organizing all those developments Mr Parker also attended and directed his crews at major fires.

The News Letter described one of those fires which had engulfed two linen warehouses in Devonshire Street in May 1897. The paper was very impressed by the efficiency and competence of the whole operation and commented that "Belfast has just cause to be proud of its fire brigade which is one of the best in these islands." Like the voice from the Empire gallery it was echoing "Go it Parker." It was those new machines and those newly trained men that the Lumière cameramen filmed in January 1897 showing their skills in front of their admiring fellow citizens. When the films were shown on Lumière's new Triographe in the Empire during October 1897 - more details later - those same citizens raised the roof with their cheers. They were obviously proud of their firemen and their superintendent, who could be regarded as Belfast's first film celebrities.

In all the verbal heat there was no mention of places of entertainment, which might suggest that the Raglan Street coroner's fears were not unfounded. However there is evidence that the Police Committee was well aware of the need for fire precautions but had delegated that responsibility to the Superintendent of the Fire Service. On the plans for the renovations to the Alhambra in 1891, submitted to the Corporation for approval, a comment in pencil had been added which stipulated that all inner doors must be made to open outwards while all outer doors should be locked back, i.e. in an open position during performances or when the building was occupied. It added that water hydrants and fire appliances should be provided to the satisfaction of the Superintendent of the fire brigade. In the same year the question of fire precautions at the Olympia Palace in Glengall Street was discussed because, besides the availability of fire fighting equipment the manager, Mr Bernard, wanted a fully equipped fireman to be present at every performance. The Superintendent put the matter to the Police Committee who were sympathetic but wondered about the cost to the ratepayers. Again, in the same year E.W. Partick submitted plans for the conversion of a public house and two adjoining houses in Church Street into the New Star Music Hall to seat about 800 persons. With regard to the matter of fire prevention someone added a note in red ink to the plans that water hydrants would be required on each floor (it was a two storey building with the music hall on the first floor) and that the Fire Brigade Superintendent would determine the location of them. The proprietor also agreed to install a fire proof curtain across the stage.

The Star, which opened in October 1892, was located on the site which is now occupied by the R.O.A.B., about five minutes walk from the Alhambra. It was in direct competition with the older hall, catering for the same working class audiences who frequented it. Mr Partick had practical experience of what his patrons wanted because he had been proprietor of the old Buffalo Music Hall (seats 9d and 6d) in Victoria Sq. It had recently been bought by the Empire Music Hall Co., a group of local business men, who had it renovated and reopened as the Bijou Empire in December 1891. After a short period they sold it and it become the Empire Theatre of Varieties in December 1894, managed by Dan Lowery. Public reaction to the new theatre was less than enthusiastic and by June 1895 Dan Lowrey had submitted new plans for modifying and extending the Empire. At that time Superintendent Parker was in charge of matters of fire prevention and hand written notes added to the plans discuss details of the fireproof curtains and the availability of water hydrants. There is also a detailed report from Mr Parker, again handwritten, emphasising the need for proper fire precautions. He required a direct telephone line to fire headquarters. He noted that the doors leading to the orchestra were made of wood and advised that they would have to be replaced with iron doors. Also the stage would have to be completely closed off in case of fire. As the plans stood it was open and connected to the main auditorium and he felt that it would be very difficult to prevent a fire originating there from spreading rapidly to all parts of the building. All the suggestions were quickly incorporated into the plans which were approved by July 1895, so that the new theatre was able to open by October. It was as well that they were because the Empire did experience a fire the following year but it was confined to the dressing rooms and quickly dealt with.

Nowhere are there any safety comments with regard to the use of the cinematographe, which is hardly surprising as all the cases mentioned happened prior to the Charity Bazaar Fire. Being the man he was Superintendent Parker must have paid close attention to what had happened in Paris and its aftermath. The disaster involved many elements familiar in Belfast - the building of temporary structures for public entertainment, the use of cheap but highly inflammable convenience materials like wood and painted or tar covered canvas - and Parker must have pointed all that out to the Police Committee

Images from the terrible Charity Bazaar Fire in Paris. Source: Le Petit Parisien

The lucky ones rescued.

along with the need to control and regulate such types of buildings. It is of interest that in early December the Town Clerk, Samuel Black, published an official notice stating that in future no building could be put up until plans were submitted and approved by the city surveyor. That approval was contingent upon many factors one of which was usually fire prevention. As often happens the public memory seems to have dulled quite quickly and by the time the legal case resulting from the disaster ended in Paris and was reported locally in late August 1897, there was little or no reaction in Belfast to the news that Baron Mackan, the president of the Charity Bazaar Committee and the man ultimately responsible for matters of safety was fined only 500 francs, while the two men working the projector were sent to jail. M. Bellac was sentenced to one year while his assistant got eight months.

In 1895 Belfast was for the most part a gas-lit settlement but there was increasing pressure and enthusiasm from the business community for the introduction of the latest scientific wonder, an electric power system. In January 1895 Alderman Pirrie officially opened the town's first Power Station in Bank Street. It supplied only the town centre area, and the power was too expensive for normal domestic lighting so it's main customers were business and commercial establishments, and places of entertainment. The Theatre Royal and the Alhambra were immediately connected to the system. The owners of theatres and music halls recognised electricity as a more powerful and safer form of light and heat than gas. As early as 1889 Ginnett's Circus in Glengall Street had used a gas - fired generator to light its building inside and outside, while the redesigned Empire was lit entirely by electricity supplied from two large gas - fired generators. Projectionists quickly realised that electricity gave a brighter and more powerful light source than the widely used limelight and was safer to use than many of the other projection systems in vogue, so when possible they availed of it. There is no information about what light source was used in the earliest Cinematographs seen in the Alhambra, the Ulster Hall and the Empire but one can assume that it was limelight. The first documented case of a projector which used electricity was in the Ulster Minor Hall in January 1897 at the lecture arranged by the Natural History and Philosophical Society on the "Electric Cinema," when a special cable was laid from Ewart's across Bedford Street to the hall to supply the necessary power. More and more cinematographic shows incorporated the word electric in their advertisements and it became associated with good quality projection. The demand for the new power source increased, mainly from business and industry, so during the following year the East Bridge Street Power Station was opened, greatly increasing the availability of electricity. Without it the era of the Picture Palaces would not have been possible... though that still lay in the future.

Meanwhile in Paris the clergy had decided to purchase the site of the disaster and build a church on it dedicated to the memory of those who had died. Today that church, Notre Dame de Consolation, overlooks the Rue Jean Gougon, its light coloured stone darkened by a century of interaction with the Parisian atmosphere. It is approached up a series of curved steps and, within, the tragedy is commemorated by a simple but moving white marble sculpture of two draped female figures in mourning.

The Cinematographe was little seen in Belfast during the summer but it was much in the news elsewhere and in a more positive light. In June 1897 London experienced the

Queen's Diamond Jubilee celebrations and the great procession on the 22nd along its streets became the most photographed event of the year. Besides all the major British film makers photographers flocked in from Europe and America and set up their cameras, of which there were at least twenty, along the published route. There was much competition for the best sites and quite a lot of money changed hands. Among those present were names familiar to Belfast audiences: Robert Paul who had three cameras in action, Birt Acres, Prof. Jolly, Lumière, and a new group that they were soon to become acquainted with, the American Biograph. Thousands of feet of film were exposed that day which would soon be released to an expectant public. Belfast had to wait for its first glimpses until the August Bank Holiday when the Empire presented the "world famous" Cinematographe which showed scenes of the Jubilee Procession. There is no clear information about which company was involved, but the results were disappointing according to the News Letter and the Telegraph. The former found the introductory pictures "inferior" while the Jubilee scenes which had been looked forward to with such great anticipation received "but scant admiration." The scenes of the Queen in her carriage were rather blurred - spoiled, the reporter thought by too strong sunlight - but the audience cheered and when the orchestra struck up "Rule Brittania" they joined in while a lady dressed as the Queen - "in counterfeit presentment" as the Telegraph put it - bowed to them from the stage. The bogus queen just seems to have been tacked on to the end of the Jubilee film as a piece of showmanship to appeal to and augment popular patriotism. In such an emotive atmosphere it is doubtful if anyone was thinking about the dangers of fire.

When the evenings began to darken during Autumn and people turned more to indoor recreation, entertainments like the Cinematographe came to the fore again. In mid-October the Ulster Hall was transformed for a Centuries Bazaar the theme of which was the different centuries of the Christian era. The decorations were in the hands of a local firm, Morrow and son of Clifton street, and there is no mention of the use of canvas, painted or otherwise. There were lots of colourful tapestries illustrating scenes as varied as St. Patrick preaching, the battle of Hastings, the Magna Carta, Caxton and his printing press, the Spanish Armada, the submission of the Irish chiefs, the Boyne, the Pilgrim Fathers and Nelson's victory at the Nile. Almost certainly Superintendent Parker looked in to check the fire precautions especially in the Minor hall where John Woodside had set up his Cinematographe to present film shows, each thirty minute long, and including scenes from the Jubilee Procession.

About a week later the Y.M.C.A. announced a programme of views to be shown by Birt Acres, on his second visit here. The building of the new centre in Wellington Place had left the Y.M.C.A. with substantial debts and their energetic and enthusiastic secretary, D.A.Black, realised that the Cinematographe could attract the crowds and the money. He arranged a series of shows not only in the Central Hall but also in Bangor and Holywood where the unheard of (for the Y.M.C.A.) charge of one shilling was asked. To assuage any lingering fears of fire or such, audiences were assured that the instruments used had been thoroughly tested and were of the highest quality. The presentation included many Birt Acres favourites like the Derby of 1897, the Henley regatta and the fire brigade, but its great success was due largely to his shots of the Jubilee procession which were described as being very clear. One of the scenes showing members of the R.I.C. marching past the camera was always greeted with cheers. After the out-of-town shows the films were presented in the new Y.M.C.A. hall still at the high prices of one and two shillings. On the second night those were reduced to one shilling and sixpence respectively while on the third night, Saturday, all seats cost only three pence. So, the films were accessible to a wide range of people and pockets and reports indicate that all the shows were crowded. As already noted above, the Y.M.C.A. under Mr. Black's direction, continued with its successful film shows throughout the winter.

In the meantime the professional halls were preparing for the winter season. It is doubtful if they were unduly worried by the competition posed by the Y.M.C.A. and similar groups because most of their patrons wouldn't have attended such meetings, while those that did would have regarded the music halls with a jaundiced eye. Dan Lowrey had noted the unfavourable comments about his last film show in August and he decided to erase that memory by turning once more to Lumière. When he had advertised the return of the Cinematographe the previous December he had described it as "THE" Lumière, the Premier attraction and despite the varied and growing competition from other film makers the Lumière cinematographe had since its introduction kept its popularity and lived up to its reputation as one of the most dependable and high quality machines available. Part of that reputation was due to the control that Lumière kept over its products and the fact that the Cinematographe was not available on the open market. In May 1897 in a change of policy the machine, with an added safety condenser of water, was put on the market for sale. It was replaced for professional performances by a new machine, the Triograph or Lumière Cinematograph Model B, which had certain advantages. It was designed solely as a projector whereas the former was a combined camera, printer and projector. It was more versatile in that it used films perforated in the modern and more widespread Edison style in contrast to the older machine which used films perforated in the Lumière method with two circular holes to each frame. The Triograph made its first appearance in London in late July and was an immediate success with critics and public. The papers and magazines drew attention to the steadiness of the pictures, the large size (27 feet by 24 feet - about 8 metres by 7 metres) of the image, and the reduced flicker. Another change was in the personnel because M. Trewey had left the company and had been replaced by George Francis.

Mr Francis was already known in Belfast not only because of his association with Lumière, but also as a performer. He was a magician and in January of that year had presented his latest illusion called "Monsieur Trewey's Last Dream" on the stage of the Alhambra. The title seems to have been an injoke (maybe with an unintended jag) about Trewey's connection with Lumière, while the illusion itself was a stage version of George Méliès's little film "The Vanishing Lady." Mr Francis led his assistant, an attractive young lady, to a cabinet on the stage. She stepped delicately in, smiled at the audience and then to their amazement turned into a skeleton before their eyes. Then the bones themselves disappeared but after a dramatic pause the complete lady reappeared again. This time, at the behest of Dan Lowrey, Mr Francis reappeared in the Empire with the new Triographe and a batch of twenty new films including local scenes which were taken, according to the Whig, by M. Promio, Lumière's chief cameraman, himself. They were almost certainly the scenes referred to by the Irish News in early January. The local scenes were warmly received and were accompanied by a commentary by Dan Lowrey. The shots were of Castle Place, the Queen's Bridge, Belfast Lough and Albert Quay and also scenes from a Glentoran v. Cliftonville match. The latter caused much excitement with loud calls of "play up" from the audience. But the longest and loudest cheers were reserved for the scenes showing the new fire brigade and firemen going through their paces. Dan thanked Superintendent Parker from the stage for his co-operation during the filming. So popular was the show that it was held over for another week during which an extra shot was added to the football scenes showing Cliftonville attacking. Also included were scenes from Dublin and some "very lifelike" panoramas taken from the moving train between Dublin and Belfast. People were impressed by the fact that the pictures were clear and the episodes were longer than usual. Dan's reputation was restored!

The immediate catalyst that led to projected films had been Edison's Kinetoscope, but the Edison company had little impact on the early development of projectors and Belfast audiences had come to accept the dominance of French and English models, notably those of Lumière, Paul, and Acres. That situation was set to change as American competition increased. In mid-December the Alhambra advertised the arrival of Edison's Autograph while, at Christmas, the Opera House presented the new American Biograph for the first time in Ireland along with their annual pantomime, Dick Whittington. The Alhambra show was so well received that it was held over for a second week but despite that there are few details about the films shown and even less about the machine. A projector of Edison's own design wasn't available here until mid 1897. It was called a Projecting Kinetoscope, so one must assume that that was the instrument involved, renamed for its music hall appearances. Nomad, writing in the Ireland's Saturday Night, thought it stood up well in comparison with others he had seen and he mentioned some of the films shown. There was a snowfight, a Christmas scene and a piece called "His Last Chance". He had special praise for the accompanying music, a timely reminder that all films were backed not only with live music but often with special effects.

The Grand Opera House introduces the American Biograph to Belfast, December 1897.

There are no such problems of identification with the Biograph the origins of which go back to a machine, the Mutoscope, which was developed by a man called Herman Casler, to compete with Edison's Kinetoscope. It worked on the principle of a flip book. A sequence of photographs was attached to a cylinder which could be turned by a handle. When they were viewed through a peep-hole or aperture the subjects seemed to move. The Whig welcomed the Mutoscope in an editorial in February 1897 as "one more in the family of scopes and graphes reported from America," an entertaining device with educational possibilities showing how photography was being used for "the vivid portrayal of objects in motion." In October 1898 the machine itself arrived when the Irish Mutoscope Company rented premises at 2, Donegall Place and 117, North Street, installed a number of mutoscopes and set about persuading the populace to view them. They assured everyone that it was "an innocent amusement" and would be especially enjoyed by children. It was easy to use - "just choose your subject, drop a penny in the slot and turn the handle." Like the kinetoscope it successfully entered into popular culture and later generations visiting the seaside, where it remained an attraction until the 1950's, got to know it in a less innocent guise as another "What the Butler Saw" attraction.

The Mutoscope didn't use a strip of film but required a series of separate photographs, so Casler turned to the problem of making a camera to supply them. In that venture he was joined by W.K. Laurie Dickson who had parted company from Edison, and his skills probably contributed largely to producing the new Mutoscope camera. In the process both he and Casler realized that the same sequences of photographs employed in the Mutoscopes could also be used to make films so they went on to develop the Biograph projector. Both camera and projector used film nearly twice the width of the Lumière camera (nearly 70 mm) so they produced a much bigger and clearer image on the screen. They also worked at forty frames per second and were therefore well suited to photographing fast movement. Like the original Lumière, the Biograph wasn't sold on the open market. It could only be leased and was supplied complete with a skilled projectionist because, as it used film unperforated in the normal way, the film had a tendency to slip sideways and adjustments by knowledgeable hands were needed to prevent that. Laurie Dickson, building on his experience with Edison's Black Maria, constructed a roof top studio in New York on a turntable which could be rotated to catch the sun, in which indoor items and short stories were filmed.

The Biograph films made an impressive impact wherever they were shown with their large clear pictures, their increased length as many of them ran up to fifteen minutes, and their ability to catch detail at speed without blurring. Their films of American express trains became very popular and when they placed a camera on the front of the engine the results were really spectacular and audiences were bowled over. Such sequences became known as phantom rides. The Biograph made its appearance in London in March 1897 and was an immediate success. Besides its technical advances it introduced another innovation of displaying scenes from the films in front of the theatre with some suitable information. Belfast audiences were accustomed to colourful posters in front of the theatres with sketches of exciting incidents from the presentations within. Biograph, however, used large photographs and one presumes that they were displayed in front of the Grand Opera House in December giving information about the company and scenes from the films. If so, they were the first examples in the city of the front-of -house stills which became a popular feature of cinemas in later years.

While their main comments were reserved for the seasonal pleasures of "Dick Whittington" all the papers agreed that the Biograph show was very impressive and mentioned that most of the items were American, a mixture of outdoor scenery and events interspersed with a number of indoor situations and simple stories. The News Letter gave the most comprehensive coverage but said little about the picture size beyond the fact that it was "life size." The films shown included Hiram Maxim firing his Gun, Galtee More winning the Derby, the Diamond Jubilee Procession showing the march past of the

Highland Regiment, Jumbo the Horseless Fire Engine, Niagara Falls, a series of American trains at express speed and a sketch called "Love's Young Dream" which the writer thought was "comic and sentimental." Nomad, writing again in the Ireland's Saturday Night, praised the quality of the projection and mentioned two items he especially enjoyed. One was a pillow fight between young children and the other was a phantom ride which he enthusiastically responded to and commented upon in some detail for his readers. He recognised that the camera had been secured to the front of the locomotive and described the rapid approach to a tunnel. He was especially thrilled as the train rushed into the darkness. After a time a small bright light appeared away in the distance, getting larger and larger. Suddenly the train emerged into sunlight again passing through pleasant woodland country every detail of which stood out clearly. His obvious pleasure and delight give a hint of the impact that those early films had despite their simplicity and lack of sophistication.

Those fast trains may have made for spectacular viewing but they denoted something else, the fact that the Americans were coming. It may have been the end of the year (1897) but Edison and Biograph represented the beginning of the American invasion.

CHAPTER FOUR
Queen Victoria, Ships and the Boer War

The accepted wisdom is that the Cinematograph, with or without the "-e," became familiar to the populace as just another music hall act. Certainly it arrived in Belfast as part of music hall bills, heading the programmes in the Alhambra and the Empire but it soon developed legs of its own and became a special attraction at local bazaars or fairs and with religious and charity groups like the Belfast Central Mission in the Grosvenor Hall and the Y.M.C.A. in Wellington Place. While business men recognised its commercial possibilities the charitable and religious groups realised that it acted as a powerful magnet drawing in crowds of all classes - men, women and children. As a result cinematograph shows became widely available throughout the winter of 1898 at venues which had no connection with the music halls, presented by groups which in many cases would have regarded the music hall as a place to be avoided.

Near the end of January a Cinematograph show was advertised for the Carlisle Memorial Hall which set the general pattern for such happenings. The aim was strictly charitable, namely to collect funds for local orphans. The occasion was organized by the local vicar who opened the proceedings with prayers. The films were arranged and projected by local men, John Woodside and Mr Greenhill, and included familiar scenes of Sackville Street, a cavalry charge, the Scots Guards, a panorama of Venice, a hunt, the Fire Brigade, the Jubilee procession and shots of the Queen. During the lulls when reels were being changed five local ladies and two gentlemen continued the entertainment by singing songs and playing various instruments. In mid - February St. Enoch's Sabbath Schools presented a Grand Cinematograph Exhibition in their new hall in aid of the Orphan Society. Again in the intervals occasioned by reel changes there were songs and instrumentals. The films themselves included local scenes though there are no details of what was actually shown. Prices of admission were reasonably costly at one shilling, and sixpence. Despite that the hall was packed and the show had to be repeated the following week with new pictures and an Edison's phonograph added, while a wider audience was targeted by making seats available at three pence.

In Durham street the Queen Victoria Hall presented the Lumière Cinematographe with the promise of local views and seats at sixpence plus "eighty seats at three pence." The Crumlin Road Methodist Church had a show of live music and song, with a phonograph and new Cinematographic scenes in their lecture hall in Tennent Street in aid of the Poor Fund, with all seats three pence. In all those cases the entertainments were presented in nearby church halls but in at least one case the Cinematograph was actually in the church itself, which is interesting in light of the future relations between church and film industry. In late March the Macrory Memorial Presbyterian Church Band of Hope in Duncairn Gardens presented a Lumière Cinematographe Exhibition in the church presided over by the minister who gave suitable religious readings during intervals. The audience was promised the latest pictures with the best effects. Entrance was three pence but the doors were opened at 7:15 when there was an early charge of one penny extra. The practice of early opening with an extra charge, which in reality ensured a seat, was spreading and when the Ulster Hall introduced it for some music concerts an irate music lover wrote to the Whig to condemn the habit as unnecessary, exploitative, and liable to put people off. In early April Bloomfield School in Bread Street put on a Grand Cinematograph Exhibition with new films, limelights, songs, and an added attraction of the local school children performing on the trapeze. Children were normally welcome to such shows as long as they were with an adult but in mid February the Ulster Hall introduced a series of Saturday afternoon entertainments especially for children. At first they were built around an old favourite, Punch and Judy, but soon a Cinematograph Exhibition was added to attract a larger crowd.

The organizers of such shows had at least five professional enterprises to choose from in the city, all of them anxious for their business. John Woodside has been mentioned before but there is little information about him beyond the fact that he often worked in association with J.B. Greenhill. James A. Doyle - who might have been the man who presented the first film show in the Alhambra - had premises in Divis Street and Great Edward Street, and claimed to have the most recent machines and latest films. All his operators were very experienced men and the shows, he claimed, would not be marred by flickering or fuzziness. He also advertised for hire a bi-unial magic lantern which was a rather expensive two-in-one lantern for projecting complex dissolving views, indicating that slide shows were still holding their own. In October the Ulster Hall was transformed for a Masonic Bazaar by local firm George Morrow and Son to represent a street in Jerusalem. Besides the decorated stalls, there was a wide range of attractions including flash-light photography, the mutoscope and, in the Minor Hall, a Cinematograph supplied by James Doyle. The Minor Hall was used so often in those early years for showing films that it could reasonably put in a claim to be recognised as one of the city's first cinemas.

The Cinematograph Syndicate, an English based organization with premises in Donegall Street, tried one up-man-ship over the locals by playing the Royal card. They announced that the machine they hired out was the same as that used to show the Queen scenes from the Jubilee Procession at Balmoral on 25th October 1897. The show in question had been presented before the Queen by one William Walker of Aberdeen using a Wrench projector which was a very dependable machine, widely used, made by a firm of that name in London. But the oldest and best known names in the growing local business were J. Lizars at 73, Victoria Street and W. Erskine Mayne at 2, Chichester Street, both of whom at that time favoured the Lumière machines. Lizars was, of course, a firm of opticians and its founder hailed originally from Aberdeen. From there he had moved to Glasgow where he established the firm in Buchanan Street. With the growth of photography the firm expanded and established outlets elsewhere including Belfast. It also moved, like many other opticians, into the making of cameras which became well known to local photographers and were sold in its Belfast premises. Over Christmas 1898 they were selling not only their own make of Challenge cameras but also other makes of cameras, optical equipment, photographic materials of all kinds, magnifying glasses, Lumière cinematographs and phonographs. For the children there were toy magic lanterns and toy cinematographs, the latter another indication of how the influence of films was spreading. By the late 1890's the Glasgow workshop of the company employed over 200 workers.

When the Cinematograph appeared Lizars took a professional interest in its progress and in 1898 purchased a Lumière camera and began filming local Scottish scenes including the gathering at Braemar. When Queen Victoria heard of the films she expressed a Royal interest and so on 26th October, the day after Walker's exhibition, J. Lizar arrived at Balmoral Castle and presented his films in the ballroom. Besides the Queen and the Royal household, special guests included Empress Frederick of Germany and Princess Henry of Battenberg all of whom, it was reported, expressed delight at what they saw. Of course, in the light of that, Lizars weren't going to let the Syndicate have it all their own way and began advertising their machines as "under Royal patronage" and "exhibited by command of the Queen before the court at Balmoral." Certainly the standing and popularity of the company grew rapidly and they claimed to have presented 300 showings all over Ireland during their first season (1897) including twenty shows in the Y.M.C.A. In the following year the number of bookings went up to over 400. Their association with the Y.M.C.A. in Wellington Place is noted in many reports, along with references to their projectionist, the photographer A.R. Hogg. In an advertisement at the beginning of 1898 a mention is made of "my well known local views," and the "my" is significant. Contemporary reports make passing references to Lizars' exhibitions which included local street scenes (Donegall Place is particularly mentioned) and local events like Lifeboat Saturday (October 8th). Those comments, plus the fact that films were being shot by Lizars' cameramen in Scotland, plus the added fact that they had local photographers of the calibre of A.R. Hogg on their payroll suggests that not only were they successfully renting and exhibiting films (they had at least 150 films listed in their catalogues) but they were making them also. All of that only three years after the historic film show by Lumière in Paris.

D.A.Black was the general secretary of the Y.M.C.A. and, as already mentioned, he regarded photography as a very worthwhile hobby for the members of the association. He not only encouraged it but actively involved himself in its latest manifestation, the animated pictures, which he saw as not only a major aid to education but as a popular entertainment which could attract people to the Y.M.C.A. His weekly Cinematograph exhibitions soon became a popular fixture during the dark evenings of the autumn-winter seasons. In that work he was enthusiastically supported by other members of the association, especially from the Camera Club, in the organization required and in the showing of the films themselves. Names like John Woodside, J.B. Greenhill, Alfred George, James McCleery crop up with regularity. The shows took place on Saturday evenings at 8 o'clock with prices fixed at three pence and sixpence, and were well advertised. "The place to spend a Happy Two Hours," was one of his slogans. The words were carefully chosen because they weren't just an invitation or a statement, but were also a challenge to the Belfast Central Mission which held "Happy Evenings" in the Grosvenor Hall every Saturday at the same time.

While Saturday evening shows were the norm Mr Black never hesitated to try something new or different. At set times like Christmas or Easter he organized week - long film shows, Monday to Saturday, the first person locally to do so. Admittedly on occasion the Alhambra and the Empire showed films every day but always as part of a music hall bill, never as an item on their own. At first Mr Black got some of his film shows from London but he soon realised the advantages of having a local supplier and made an arrangement with Lizars who supplied the films, the projector and the projectionist. Lizars obviously valued the connection from a business point of view because they made special mentions of it in their adverts and offered their services when, during the last week in October, the Y.M.C.A. Camera Club decided to organize a Photographic Exhibition and Competition in the Great Hall in Wellington Place. The event was opened by the Lord Mayor himself (Alderman Henderson) and it proved to be the largest occasion of its kind so far presented in the city, attracting entries from all over Ireland, Britain and even the U.S.A.

The club's last public exhibition had been in 1894 but much had happened in the intervening four years. The growing popularity of photography was reflected in the increased membership which by then had reached over one hundred while in the new Y.M.C.A. building they had a splendid up-to-date studio and dark room in which to practise their skills. Special arrangements had also been made so that ladies could join and certain days were set aside for them to use the facilities. In his introduction the President of the Club, Frank Megarry, commented on the wide appeal of the photographic hobby and welcomed the fact that it involved not only men but also ladies. But he pointed out that it was much more than a hobby, being widely used in scientific studies, commerce and other activities. In the past, he noted, people had been content to sit and watch hand - painted Dioramas or, later, to enjoy limelights. But he felt they always hankered after more, "they wanted life as it really existed, to see it in active motion," and that was why they had taken to the cinematograph. At that point there was loud applause. The Lord Mayor expressed complete agreement with those comments and felt that photography could not be praised enough because "the limits of that wonderful art had not yet been reached." He praised Lizars who had shown their interest by putting up £200 in prizes and by running an exhibition of Lumière films in the Minor Hall, including some of their own local views. Lizars claimed that they used the latest Lumière projectors and that they were the only machines that produced steady clear pictures.

But Lizars weren't having it all their own way. The whiff of friendly competition noted between the Y.M.C.A. and the Grosvenor Hall became more obvious in the commercial field. W. Erskine Mayne, who still described himself as a bookseller, took up the challenge and announced that in response to increased bookings he had purchased another cinematograph and added more Lumière and English films to his stock. He offered a one hour or two hour programme including a projector and projectionist for a charge of two guineas (£2-20 p today) plus expenses. Lizars replied immediately with an advert under the heading "Don't be Misled," insisting that Lumière films could only be shown to their best advantage on a Lumière machine. Later they went further by claiming that they had the only Lumière machines in Ireland, and the best films. The machines in question were the older "one perforation to the picture" machines. Erskine Mayne replied by announcing that "I do not claim to be the only one to exhibit with a Lumière machine in Ireland but I do claim to have the very latest pattern Lumière Cinematographe yet produced." Then, in an appeal for local loyalty, he called upon people to "support an old established Belfast house" implying, quite rightly of course, that Lizars were not really local. Such was the general demand that the two rivals were kept busy with bookings for films, limelights (magic lanterns) and the phonograph for low profile events like small parties, meetings and such, and high profile events like bazaars, religious groups, the Y.M.C.A. and the Grosvenor Hall.

As part of their Happy Evenings on Saturdays the Belfast Central Mission introduced an item called "the latest news by limelight" which consisted of a commentator on stage describing slides based on pictures taken from the popular magazines Punch, the Illustrated London News, the Graphic, and Black and White. All of those were on sale in local booksellers like Shone's and Olley's but it was unlikely that the audiences who frequented the Grosvenor Hall could afford them. The programmes, which were put together and presented by Lizars, became a popular feature over the next few years. They indicated that the magic lantern could still attract an audience, while historically they represented a step towards future newsreels. Such was the increase in business that both firms announced by Christmas they would be moving to larger premises some time in the new year. Lizars intended moving to 8, Wellington Place where they still do business though now in partnership with Black's, while Erskine Mayne would transfer to 3, Donegall Square West. The promised moves took place in early May, 1899.

In January of the new year the main topic of news in Belfast was the impending launch of the "Oceanic" at Harland and Wolff's, a company at the apex of its reputation. It was the largest ship ever built and it incorporated all the latest shipbuilding technology, so interest in it was world wide. No one was rash enough to suggest that the vessel was unsinkable because, as the News Letter cautioned, it is unwise to ignore "the unforeseen which must always be reckoned with in the perilous work of navigating the sea." Prophetic words which could equally have been applied to another historic launch thirteen years in the future. There was a not unexpected local upsurge of pride in the shipyard and its workers and the launch was looked forward to with great excitement. Despite the time of the year the morning of the event, 14th January 1899, dawned bright and sunny. From an early hour crowds began to collect on both sides of the lough, including many photographers, both amateur and professional. At Victoria Wharf stands had been erected to hold about 5,000 visitors who included leading figures from local society, important personages involved in the shipbuilding industry from England, Scotland and North America, and those who had paid for the privilege of a close-up view. Money earned from the latter was given to the Royal Hospital.

A sign of the times was the platform specially constructed for the "cinematographic artists," as the News Letter referred to them. At least six well known firms had cameras there and among them were local cameramen from Lizars. That wasn't the only consideration shown the photographers. The ship wasn't painted in the usual colours of the White Star Line for whom it was built but overall in white so that it would photograph more easily and clearly. Some would see that as an early example of the growing tyranny of the camera. The films were rushed to London by boat and train and some of them were shown there that evening. During the following week Lizars developed and printed their own films, while Erskine Mayne and James Doyle obtained copies from England. Eager Belfast audiences were soon offered the opportunity to see them. D.A. Black announced that Saturday evening in the Y.M.C.A. would be "Oceanic Night" with full coverage of the launch. The films were almost certainly supplied by Lizars and the show was presented by the regular quartet of J. Woodside and B.J. Greenhill on the projection, commentary by W.J. Shields, and F.J. Moffatt at the organ. The Great Hall, which could hold about 1,700 persons, was filled to capacity and a large crowd of a few hundred had to be turned away. The show was a great success, the images greeted with bursts of applause and cheering and, as the ship finally slid into the water, "Rule Brittania" thundered from the organ. At the end it was announced that in response to public demand the films would be repeated on Monday evening, which they were to another capacity crowd.

On that Saturday evening Erskine Mayne presented a rival show on the same topic in the Ulster Hall. He promised views of the vessel from the laying of the keel to the launch, followed by 200 feet of film of the actual launching ceremony. Not only did he give the length of the films to be shown but the fact that they included 25,000 distinct pictures. It is well to recall that the majority of films were still very short, running for the most about a minute or less and costing in the region of £2-10-0 (two pounds fifty pence today) each to buy. Some distributors sold them by length, in feet, like cloth or floor covering, so it became normal for exhibitors to advertise the length of their total show, the implication being, the longer the film the better the value. As films were perceived as an extension of still photography the number of frames or pictures was also often mentioned to impress audiences. Again, the more frames involved the better the film. Erskine Mayne also laid on a cable so that the films could be shown by electricity. Seats could be reserved for one shilling, and for sixpence, but to ensure competition with the Y.M.C.A. the unreserved seats were only threepence. On the evening the hall was full including representatives of Harland and Wolff, and large numbers were turned away. The entertainment began with a magic lantern show of fifty coloured and black and white slides most of them taken by A.M. Carlisle, the manager of the shipyard, which illustrated the stages in the construction beginning with the laying of the keel. While the lantern was being worked by Mr Hogan, background music was supplied by a piano and an explanation added by a lecturer H.S. Morton, a photographer who had a studio in Lombard Street next door to the Lombard cafe. An interval followed while the cinematograph was being readied and during it the audience was amused with music and song from a phonograph. Then came the highlight as Mr. Taylor started the cinematograph. The pictures were large, clear and steady. After scenes around the dock the actual launch was shown to wild acclaim and there were loud calls for it to be repeated. Mr Mayne asked them to wait because it would now be shown again but from a different position. When that was done the excited audience kept calling to see them once more until Mr Taylor rewound them both and projected them again. How anyone heard the lecturer or the pianist through all the noise is not mentioned. At the end it was announced that the show would be repeated and so it was the following Friday when it was extravagantly advertised as "Britain's Triumph, Ireland's Boast, Belfast's Pride." Again the hall was crowded to the doors. It was obviously a popular and financial success, but beyond that it demonstrated to prospective customers that Erskine Mayne was determined to be a major player and could put on a show the equal of his rival, Lizars.

While all that activity was going on one could ask what the professional halls were doing. In simple terms they were presenting less cinematograph shows. The reasons are not clear. It certainly wasn't because of a decline in local audience interest or any difficulties with getting materials. The cinematograph industry was expanding on all fronts. More and more films were becoming available, as were new distributors and exhibitors. It is possible that the managers were worried about the implications of safety. Following upon the Charity Bazaar tragedy music halls and other venues became more aware of the dangers from fire. In January of 1898 the London County Council issued a series of safety regulations for cinematographic shows which, while they didn't apply in Belfast, must have given local managers food for thought and may even have brought Superintendent Parker to their doors. Whatever the reasons, the Alhambra and the Empire ignored celluloid for a time and returned to their normal music hall fare of singers, dancers, comedians, acrobats and such.

Among those presentations were a number of strong man acts. There was a cult of the body beauiful in Victorian society, especially acceptable if it was associated with strength and physical activity, which partly explains the popularity of boxers like John L.Sullivan and James Corbett despite the low repute of boxing itself. Such men took financial advantage of that interest by appearing in music halls and theatres - Johm L. Sullivan appeared in the Theatre Royal - usually in sketches or plays in which they demonstrated their fighting skills. But there were other strong men who made a living essentially in the circus and the music hall and they were always welcome in Belfast. Samson strode the stage impressively and then left for England where he appeared in court accused of assaulting a music hall manager, which must have brought a smile to many a performer's lips. The Alhambra presented a strong man and woman, Atlas and Miss Volcana, a brother and sister whose act the News Letter found "original and extraordinary." But the best known name in the business was Eugene Sandow, who had been filmed by Edison in the Black Maria for the Kinetoscope and who appeared at the Empire in May. His arrival, proclaimed as the Modern Hercules, the Anatomical Wonder, and the Monarch of Muscles, was the signal for packed and expectant houses. The Whig noted that he was not only very strong but displayed a striking "symmetry of form" and went on to comment that "the worship of muscle is not extinct in this intellectual and scientific age." His performance, which included feats like lifting a piano and carrying it around the stage took place in a gladiatorial setting with his assistants, male and female, dressed in classical apparel, all of which greatly impressed audiences. He was also into the keep - fit business and just before Christmas Blakely's Athletic Stores in Bedford street put on a special demonstration of Sandow's system of physical culture with a display of equipment which he endorsed.

The admiration of physical performance may actually have been whetted by a film. Earlier in the year, in April, the Ulster Hall presented the Veriscope film of the Corbett - Fitzsimmons fight which had taken place on St. Patrick's Day 1897 for a purse of 50,000 dollars. The fight had been at the centre of legal wrangles in the U.S.A. and various states, including Texas and Florida, had banned it. The promoter had finally succeeded in putting it on in Carson City in Nevada. The film is interesting for a number of reasons. Local audiences had seen brief shots of boxers in action since 1896, but this was the first fight to be actually staged for the camera and it was filmed by a camera specially designed to photograph the fast action in the ring. Furthermore it ran for an unheard of ninety minutes which made it the longest film shown in the city so far dealing with one subject, though it would still have been interrupted for reel changes. The film covered the full fourteen rounds and local reviewers were amazed at the clarity of the detail shown. The writer from the News Letter saw it as a contest between science (Corbett), and endurance and hard hitting (Fitzsimmons) with the outcome hard to forecast until Fitzsimmons landed a blow which felled Corbett. Fitzsimmons, who hailed from Cornwall, was declared the winner amidst wild scenes while Corbett staggered to his feet and rushed at him only to be restrained by his seconds who finally had to carry him bodily from the ring.

All of that was faithfully shown to the excited audiences who left the building well satisfied, and one can be sure that over the following weeks details of the clash were discussed and re-enacted at street corners for those who hadn't experienced it themselves. Despite its length the film wasn't shown on its own. It was accompanied by a concert which took place, as the Irish News put it, "before the combatants were put in motion." While there are no records of public censure, there certainly were those who disapproved of boxing on ethical grounds and would have regarded the film as quite unsuitable for popular entertainment; but despite that there obviously was an increasing interest in the sport. In September the Alhambra had a full house for a display "of the art of self defence" by J.J. Jeffreys, the World Champion who had in turn defeated Fitzsimmons. He was touring Ireland giving one night shows with an American heavyweight called John Dunkhurst. The prices for those events were high, being set for the film in the Ulster Hall at three shillings, two shillings and one shilling, while the Alhambra charged five shillings, three shillings and two shillings so they certainly were not targeted at workers, most of whom couldn't afford such sums. Despite the fact that the boxers were mainly of working class origin the sport itself, that noble art, was obviously regarded by the showmen as a pastime for the wealthier classes.

A specially interesting event of a different type took place in September when the redoubtable D.A.Black arranged for the Modern Marvel Company to occupy the Great Hall in the Y.M.C.A. for a two week period of films and slides. Marvels were promised that had already impressed the Prince of Wales (the Royal card again!) at a showing in the Crystal Palace. That it was something different was indicated by the prices which were two shillings (reserved), one shilling, and sixpence obviously aimed at the middle class and skilled workers, but from all accounts good value for money. The main attraction was a recent "beautiful artistic invention" called the Analyticon which today would be called a 3-D projector. Stereoscopes had been available from the 1840's but really came into their own after the Great Exhibition of 1851 and many middle class homes in Belfast would have had one. Like the Kinetoscope they were for individual viewing and were seen as a great aid to education, an attribute which many thought could be enhanced if they could be shown to an audience. Experiments in 3-D projection were carried out in the 1850's but in 1891 Louis Ducos du Hauron took the process a step forward when he projected two still images of the same scene, one coloured red the other green, on top of each other. When viewed through special glasses with red and green lenses the scene appeared to be three dimensional. It was that system that the Analyticon used.

The audience were each given a "lorgnette" as the News Letter called the special glasses, and the results were very impressive as the flat pictures appeared "solid." The Irish News thought the views were "remarkably good," while the Telegraph found them "marvellous," and noted the delighted reactions of the audience. That is the first recorded public showing of projected three dimensional views in the city. Granted they were only still pictures but contemporary experiments were going on to project 3-D animated pictures though for Belfast audiences that experience lay well in the future. Anyone who went to the cinema in the 1950's will remember the 3-D films that arrived then to compete with television, led by Bwana Devil (1952, d. Arch Oboler) which promised the audience "a lion in your lap."

But the marvels at the Y.M.C.A. didn't end there. There was also a display of photographic slides with dioramic effects coloured by a new system developed by Frederick Ives, followed by a film show. There is no indication of the type of projector used but there was general agreement that for clarity and steadiness the films were among the best ever shown in the city. The photography of the night scenes was particularly commented upon. Also included were five views of the funeral of W.E. Gladstone who had died in May and a dramatic tale taken from a popular novel called "Alec McLeod" The commentators were quite impressed by the latter especially by the way it told the story in a series of films. That "striking novelty," said the News Letter, "must be seen as well as heard." That suggests that there were actors involved, probably reading the lines from behind the screen. So Mr Black had certainly served up a rich dish full of tantalising titbits with a foretaste of menus of the future. Taken in conjunction with the boxing film they indicated, with the benefit of hindsight, the ways that films would develop - much longer, telling dramatic stories, making use of colour and, in time, sound.

What the managers of the professional halls felt about all that is not known. They certainly didn't rush to compete. In May the Grand Opera House presented those perennial favourites Sam Hague's Minstrels whose show included a Jubileeograph with some fine pictures and it wasn't until October that the Empire announced a presentation of a cinematogragh show. It was billed as the Edison - Thomas cinematograph and the show included scenes from the Spanish-American War and Gladstone's funeral. The name Edison led many people to assume that the great Thomas Edison himself was involved but actually he had no connection at all with it. The showman concerned was A.D. Thomas, a well known and well liked character from Manchester whom Cecil Hepworth once described as "an utter scamp". He changed his name to Edison - Thomas for publicity purposes and pursued a very successful career in film exhibition. He was noted for the good quality of his shows and had a reputation for care and safety. He was certainly well received and appreciated in Belfast, returning the following year twice to the Alhambra.

The Empire presented another film show that year over Christmas when it brought back the American Biograph with a series of new views that included shots of The Sirdar's Return, showing Sir Herbert Kitchener returning from his successful campaign in the Sudan. Those scenes were well received because Belfast had followed the military details of that campaign against the Dervishes - which was later to become the basis of a spectular film starring Laurence Olivier as the Madhi and Charlton Heston as General Gordon called "Khartoum" (1966, d. Basil Deardon) - not only from the newspapers but from lecturers giving first hand accounts. In late November Rene Bull, the war correspondent and artist of the magazine "Black and White," described the battle of Omdurman to a packed Grosvenor Hall, illustrated with slides based on his own photographs. He introduced a little local humour when he described how the night before the battle was very tense, the soldiers sleeping on the ground with their rifles at their sides, as a night attack was half expected. He had walked through the camp and as he passed one place he heard a soldier say to his companion, "Reminds me of Sandy Row before the Twelfth." He explained, amid laughter, that he didn't know then what that meant but since arriving in Belfast it had all been made clear to him.

A week later at the beginning of December another eminent reporter, Frederic Villiers, appeared in the Great Hall of the Y.M.C.A. and gave a talk called "Khartoum at Last" which covered Kitchener's entry into Omdurman. A real showman, he arrived on stage wearing his campaigning costume and explained to the audience that evening wear wasn't really of much use to a war correspondent. He illustrated his words with photographic slides taken by himself and projected by electric light. He began with a slide showing a map of the region and went on to describe his journey up the historic Nile from Cairo to Khartoum. He also showed the place of Gordon's death and a service that was held in his honour. While those slides were being shown F.J.Moffett played the Dead March on the organ and the audience stood quietly in remembrance. In later years he claimed that he had tried to film the actual battle but there is no mention of animated pictures in any of the reports in Belfast. Over the Christmas period however film of the battle was shown not only at the Empire but in the Y.M.C.A. The fascination with the war continued into the new year with another lecture in the Y.M.C.A. at the end of January by an ex Grenadier, A. Wellesley Chapman, who not only spoke about and showed slides of the campaign but also added some dubious "colour" by appearing in the gear of one of the Emirs who had been killed in one of the battles. He also displayed slave whips and a Dervish spear. Finally a month later Rene Bull returned, this time to the Alhambra, to repeat his lecture on the Soudan with new slides. His talk was followed by a concert and comedy turns.

The pattern of film shows presented during 1898 continued into 1899. The cinematograph appeared in only three showings in the professional music halls, covering a total of four weeks. Two of the occasions involved the Alhambra in late January and at the end of September and it was the popular showman Edison - Thomas who returned on both occasions. The September show included some quite interesting items. By then he was calling his machine the Royal Vitascope and he projected some local scenes which included the proprietor of the Alhambra W.J.Ashcroft and his assistant manager Albert Brooke which the Whig said were "well received." There is no clear indication of who took the pictures but the implication is that it was one of his own cameraman. Local views often "specially taken" for the occasion became increasingly fashionable during the year. But the "crowning item" according to the Whig was the series of views of the topical Dreyfus affair. During the showing Dreyfus himself was loudly cheered while the judges were roundly booed showing where working class sympathies lay. The films were accepted by the commentators and audience as actual scenes from the events, but most likely they were very realistic reconstructions filmed by George Méliès in his glass studio at Montreuil. He had filmed eleven small scenes there, and even appeared playing the part of M. Laborie the lawyer who defended Dreyfus. The films caused great excitement wherever they were shown in France with pro and anti Dreyfus factions sometimes coming to blows after watching them. In Belfast however the reactions and exchanges didn't go beyond the verbal stage.

There were also the usual comedies and among them was "The Astronomer's Dream" also made by George Méliès in Paris. It appeared in a number of other local venues throughout the year, indicating its wide popularity. When it was included in a show at Mountpottinger Y.M.C.A. a month later it was singled out and described as "the finest film ever exhibited." It was actually based on a sketch which Méliès had presented on the stage of his own theatre in Paris and consisted of three scenes. In the first an astronomer wearing a tall pointed conical hat looks through a giant cartoon like telescope at the moon before falling asleep. In the second the Moon with great big eyes descends to the room and swallows him. In the third he is on the moon where he meets the moon Goddess. He chases her and is just about to catch her when she disappears in a flash and he wakens. The film was just less than 200 feet long and ran for about three minutes.

The other show took place in the Empire in July and was described rather grandly as Gibbon's Bio-Tableaux. Few details are available of what was actually shown but among the films was the 1899 Derby from start to finish and scenes from a recent football final. Walter Gibbons was one of the more successful of the many showmen touring the British Isles at the time and according to reports he used a reliable Bioscope projector which he had adapted and improved himself. The fact that there were so few cinematograph shows in the music halls didn't mean that the opportunities to see films were restricted because the Ulster Hall, the Y.M.C.A., the Grosvenor Hall and other smaller establishments filled the void, using materials supplied on most occasions by the local firms of Lizars, Erskine Mayne and James A.Doyle. They all attracted large crowds and the reports often mentioned packed halls and disappointed people being turned away. There was one exception to the general tone of success and that was an interesting and intriguing show in the Ulster Hall at Easter.

Over the Easter holiday period there were a number of attractions to choose from. Mr Black announced a Grand New Cinematograph show in the Y.M.C.A. with suitable musical effects presented by Lizars, while the Grosvenor Hall had its familiar Happy Evening built around a film show. But the Ulster Hall promised something special appearing for the first time in Ireland, namely the New Model Bioscope, supported by music on the organ and a phonograph concert. One of the papers, quoting from a handout no doubt, mentioned that the new American projector from Mr Mayne was noted for the clarity and steadiness of its pictures. Up to forty films were to be shown including old favourites like a serpentine dancer and the turnout of the local fire brigade, military scenes, football, the launch of the Oceanic and new comedies called "The Billsticker's Dispute" and "Weary Willie in the Park." The latter was made by the Riley Bros in Bradford and is typical of the short one shot films of the period. Four elegantly dressed ladies and gentlemen are sitting on a park bench. An unkempt tramp arrives and pushes on to the end of the seat. The lady beside him moves away. He pushes up and in time the others depart one by one in disgust. When the bench is empty the tramp stretches out on it and goes to sleep. It was simple in construction, needed no dialogue and showed an affinity with R.W. Paul's earlier "The Soldier's Courtship." One difference was that it seemed to have been filmed in an actual park whereas Paul had used a backdrop. The other film had recently been completed by Paul and concerned the antics of two bill stickers. A billsticker is posting bills when another arrives and attempts to muscle in on his space. They quarrel and fight, firstly using their paste brushes, then the paste pots. Finally one empties the contents of his pot over the other's head. It was simple slapstick, the type of thing popular on the music hall stages. On the night the hall was packed with an expectant crowd but the results were, according to the Whig, disappointing and many of the audience left. The details of what happened were however more colourful.

When the projector began the spectators were taken aback because the pictures were very blurred and unsteady but that could happen on occasion so they waited expectantly for them to clear up. During the first reel change slides were shown which were impressively clear but when the second reel began it was as poor as the first. The audience began to show their disapproval, at first with groans and boohs then with loud whistling and stamping of their feet. The show was stopped and the lecturer, H. S. Morton, apologised and asked the audience to be patient, explaining that the machine hadn't arrived until 6.00 p.m. and the operator was having some trouble adjusting it. He tried again but things were as bad as ever. There were shouts of "fraud" and calls for money back, followed by demands for the manager to appear. There didn't seem to be anyone in charge and there was no indication of who was responsible, so the calls remained unanswered. By that time the projector had been stopped and in desperation Mr. Morton announced he had nothing to do with the matter as he had only been hired by Erskine Mayne to give the commentary. The phonograph was then turned on but the noise in the hall was so great that no one could hear it. As a last resort the organist struck up some Irish airs but after a while he accepted defeat and gave up also. By that time many people had left but it was some time before the younger members finally went. The evening had been a fiasco. But there was no firm information as to who had organized the affair. The only name mentioned, almost in panic, was Erskine Mayne who was the new local agent for the Bioscope.

That event took place on Easter Monday and on Wednesday all the local papers carried a statement from Erskine Mayne disowning the whole affair and emphasising that it had not been promoted by him and he had received no receipts from it. He promised that he would soon be presenting an exhibition of his own and, as a gesture of good will, offered free seats to anyone who had been at the Easter Monday show and felt disappointed. In early May he rented the Ulster Hall and presented another Bioscope Exhibition by electric light. William Hogan was the projectionist and that time the pictures were clear and steady and the show was a success, though the hall wasn't crowded.

Erskine Mayne presented another successful show in the Ulster Hall in mid September. The films shown included local shots of Donegall Place, Castle Place, a turnout of the Fire Brigade, and three different views of the Orange Procession, all of them taken during the month of July by his own operatives. There were also some comedies, various military subjects and a record of the launching of the battleship H.M.S. "Albion" at Blackwall on the 21st June, a film which had attracted some notoriety. During the ceremony a crowded gangway had collapsed throwing over one hundred people into the water. The event was being filmed by R.W.Paul from a small steamer he had hired, and when the viewing area collapsed he immediately steamed towards the people struggling in the water, with the camera still running, and managed to save twenty five of them. When the film was shown in London it caused a sensation. Today audiences are used to seeing death and destruction on screens in their own living rooms, but in the 1890's people were really shocked by such scenes. Paul was attacked in the papers by many, including Birt Acres, for filming under such tragic conditions while the ethics of showing such scenes as entertainment or for profit were questioned. Paul defended himself by pointing out that the camera worked off an electric motor and continued to photograph without attention while the efforts of those on the launch were directed towards saving the unfortunate people struggling in the water. Also, the film was being shown to collect funds for the relief of the relatives of the deceased before being sent to local distributors. If that was the one shown in the Ulster Hall, and the Telegraph report indicates that it was, there is no sign that it upset the audience who were more impressed by the fact that a series of films had been joined together to give nine minutes of screen time without a break.

The trend towards longer films with fewer reel changes was increasingly noticeable and appreciated at the time. Some of the films of Gladstone's funeral shown the year before by Edison - Thomas in the Empire had lasted three or four minutes. By Christmas 1900 D.A.Black at the Y.M.C.A. was able to dazzle patrons with the promise of "a magnificent film... the most remarkable ever witnessed in this country." It was suitable festive fare being a version of "Aladdin or His Wonderful Lamp" but it ran for nearly twenty minutes. The News Letter reported the excited reaction of the audience, and mused that the extended length indicated not only how films had progressed lately but how they could develop in the future.

During 1899 the big news items were the Dreyfus affair and later in the year the Boer War. Films made the news more immediate as the time lapse between actual events and their presentation locally was being continually reduced. In August 1899 the implications of Dreyfus were still being discussed in the papers but, as already noted, by mid September local exhibitors and visiting showmen were presenting films of the affair in the Ulster Hall, the Grosvenor Hall and the Alhambra. In October J.A. Doyle put on a show in the Ulster Hall which included scenes about Dreyfus but also for the first time the spectators saw references to happenings in the Transvaal with shots of President Kruger and those involved in the Jameson Raid. The city was beginning to be gripped by war fever again but this time the main topic of every day conversation was not the Sudan, Gordon, or the Madhi, but South Africa and the Boers. References to the war appeared at every turn. The papers were full of it, usually supporting the official line, except the Irish News which deplored what it regarded as the rampant jingoism involved. Anderson and McAuley read the public mood and erected a large colourful Panorama of the Transvaal War in their shop for which they charged an entrance fee of two pence, the proceeds going to the local War Fund. A series of Patriotic concerts, dances, and bazaars were arranged in the Ulster Hall and elsewhere to collect money for the support of the families of soldiers serving in South Africa, especially for widows and orphans. The Royal Studio - almost opposite the General Post Office in Royal Avenue, where visiting actors usually went to be photographed and where their admirers could purchase copies later - produced a series of small photographic war buttons which became all the rage. John Hanna in High Street announced the arrival of the latest styles in ladies' hats with special reference to "new sailor hats... including the new khaki colour." An Easter sports meeting at Ballynafeigh included a special attraction in the form of a tethered war balloon offering controlled ascents at 2/6 per person to show how they were used in South Africa to pinpoint enemy positions. Even the evangelical groups were not immune. During November the Y.M.C.A. put on a Great Patriotic Night which included the usual Saturday films, while on the same evening the weekly Happy Evening in the Grosvenor Hall became a Great Imperial Night with "Patriotic songs, Patriotic views and a Patriotic Lecture."

There was no shortage of films about the army and the navy showing marching, drilling and other aspects of military life. The authorities encouraged such shows and gave the photographers whatever facilities they needed because experience showed that they boosted recruitment. As the expected early victory didn't materialise and the war continued with the commander Lord Roberts asking for more and more troops such considerations became increasingly important. The Imperial Yeomanry was established to attract volunteers to fight alongside the regular soldiers and at least 260 young men from the city went along to Victoria Barracks and signed up. In early February 1900 the girls working in Arnott's department store in Bridge street organized a party in Ye Olde Castle restaurant in Castle Place - the finest restaurant outside London, it called itself - to say goodbye to three of their male colleagues Jack Whittle, Eddie Doak, and Tom Stephens, who had volunteered for service in South Africa. On the same evening the Empire put on a special Grand Yeomanry Night for the volunteers, which they and their officers were invited to attend. The original plan was for the volunteers to march from Victoria Barracks to the theatre but that was dropped, to the disappointment of the waiting crowds, when it was realised that many of them hadn't yet been issued with their khaki uniforms. So they arrived in twos and threes cheered by a crowd assembled in Victoria Square and took the seats reserved for them in the circle. The officers occupied the boxes. The rest of the theatre was packed and fire precaution regulations were forgotten as people pushed in and stood at the back and even in the aisles. The atmosphere was febrile with, as the Whig put it, "frequent outbursts of enthusiasm and patriotism."

All the acts managed to include some reference to South Africa and there were military songs, recitals and patriotic music. The events were further coloured by a youth in the gods who at every opportunity played airs on a tin whistle while another waved a large union jack. Then Mr Hogg set up his magic lantern and showed a sample of slides from Lizars illustrating the Transvaal and major figures connected with the war. The entertainment ended with the orchestra playing The Queen while the curtain was raised to reveal an easel supporting a portrait of Victoria with a member of the Yeomanry standing on either side of it. The audience rose waving their handkerchiefs and cheering. When silence fell the senior officer, Capt. Maude, came to the stage to thank the management of the Empire and the audience for their support and ended with the words that "every single man who goes there will be a credit to Belfast and to Ireland, and not only Ireland but to Great Britain."

The following evening the Opera House had a similar Yeomanry Night when 200 volunteers arrived in their uniforms to an equally enthusiastic and emotional welcome. There is evidence that both Lizars and Erskine Mayne filmed the volunteers, and shots of them were shown that week in the Y.M.C.A. Saturday night entertainment which for that occasion was labelled a Grand Military Night. A few days later the Lord Mayor entertained the volunteers to dinner in the Exhibition Hall at the Botanic Gardens and gave them an official send off from the citizens of Belfast before they left by rail for the Curragh for training. After a whole two weeks of training they sailed from London on the 28th February to face the hardened and experienced Boer fighters.

The showmen realised that war attracted the crowds and acted accordingly. In August 1899 Lloyd's Mexican Circus pitched a huge tent capable of holding 20,000 spectators on waste ground behind the Central Library (then called the Free Library) where the old streets had been swept away for redevelopment. One of their attractions was Professor Bosco's Cinematograph. Obviously some circuses had decided that with regard to animated pictures, if you can't beat them, join them. The professor promised over forty war subjects. It turned out that many of them were of past conflicts like the recent Spanish - American War and included shots of the blowing up of the battleship Maine, which was probably a reconstruction by Méliès. Carter's Waxworks in Castle Place which usually presented oddities, with an entrance charge of only two pence, also decided to try films and in the second week of October presented the Edis Bainton Cinematograph with a series that included some Dreyfus items. Running in conjunction with a palmistry act and a tank full of female swimmers it must have brought in the crowds because it stayed for four weeks. It seems to have been only a one-off because the new proprietor (the original owner died in July and was succeeded by his son - in - law, Charles Belbert) didn't repeat the experiment. During the exhibitions at Carter's the Boer War officially began (on October 11th) and the city screens were soon full of war subjects. At the end of the month the Mountpottinger Y.M.C.A. presented a series of "Red Hot War scenes," while a few weeks later the Y.M.C.A. in Wellington Place showed scenes of troops departing for South Africa. That show also included more films of the Dreyfus affair with the claim that that was their first showing in the city. They were probably the scenes shot by the Pathé company to compete with Méliès films. Certainly the problems of Dreyfus were well documented locally on film but by the end of the year they were superseded by the news from South Africa. Over the Christmas period none of the music halls showed films but the Y.M.C.A. and the Grosvenor Hall had their usual full houses.

Into the new century, and the Boer War dominated the screens. Both the Alhambra and the Empire included film shows in their presentations during the early part of the new year. The popular, and by then well - known, Edison-Thomas appeared in the Alhambra in February for a three week run with new war films and so popular were they that night after night he had to repeat them to satisfy the audiences. By late March he was still there and remained for another few weeks. During that period he mysteriously underwent several name changes. For a time he used his real name and became A.D.Thomas' Vitascope war pictures before changing to the Edisonograph, and then back to the familiar Edison-Thomas. Whatever the name he drew large and appreciative crowds. The Empire brought back the equally popular Gibbons' Bio Tableaux with a very impressive array of titles worth looking at because they give a good impression of the type of material that was typical of the time. They included Lord Roberts leaving for the front, the fifth Northumberland Fusiliers digging trenches near Estcourt, an armoured train passing (that became a great favourite with the crowds), the Scots Guards and Black Watch at Capetown docks, the

Gordon Highlanders marching through Capetown, Lancers fording the Modder river, a temporary bridge over the Modder replacing one destroyed by the Boers, and a troop train passing guarded by an armoured car and engine at both ends. As those little snippets were shown the orchestra played suitable military music while a lecturer explained what each picture meant or represented. One shot of a naval gun an the Modder was rather short and he apologised and explained in dramatic tones that the cameraman J.Bennett Stanford had been wounded by a shell exploding nearby after exposing only twenty feet of film. That must have brought home to the audience the dangers that the cameramen faced. The action at the Modder took place on the 28th November just about three months before so that gives some idea of the time taken to get the films back to the market in the British Isles.

In early March Erskine Mayne again booked the Ulster Hall to show off the American Bioscope projector with a sample chosen from the new films that kept arriving. He promised an evening which would combine war films, patriotic songs and music with "a thrilling illustrated lecture" called "From Boer Ultimatum to British Victory under Lord Roberts." Seat prices ranged from one shilling to two shillings, outside the budget of most workers. Despite that, the hall was crowded on the evening and the show, according to the Whig, was "excellent." There was one slight problem in that the lecture by J.F.Scott went on too long and the audience became restless. Some of them showed their feelings by whistling and stamping their feet which didn't stop until the projector was brought into operation. The films, accompanied by suitable music and sound effects, were as usual very well received. Lord Roberts was cheered, the Boers were hissed but there was complete silence during scenes showing Red Cross nurses attending to the wounded. To round off a successful evening the pain of war was lifted by a number of comedy films and local views.

Over Easter another combination show arrived in the Ulster Hall in the shape of Charles W. Poole's Boer War Myriorama. The Poole family were well known showmen who had been involved in the business of showing panoramas and dioramas for nearly sixty years during which they had often visited Belfast. They had six shows, each designated by a number, touring the British Isles and the one that arrived in Belfast was number two. It combined a panorama, magic lanterns, dissolving views, special effects, a Cinematograph show on the Eventograph and various music hall acts. Mr Poole insisted that he used the most up to date equipment and special effects and that his show would reflect the skill that came from decades of practical experience. The views were painted on canvas and silk by a group of artists working in his warehouse. The scenes of the fighting were kept up to date by artists in the war zone who made outline sketches and sent them back to England where they were completed. Older canvases, he explained, were stored in the warehouse in the hope that they would be of some interest to future generations.

Two years before, in October 98, the President of the Y.M.C.A. Camera Club had made the point that people would no longer watch painted panoramas or dioramas, no matter how beautiful they were, now that they had animated pictures, but the Myriorama ran successfully for four weeks. There were a number of reasons for that. The show had something for everyone. There were live acts, the nostalgia of a panorama which at the same time gave a different slant on the war, and a selection of films. All the reports agreed that the paintings, slides, dissolving views and special effects were excellent and that the variety acts were very entertaining. But the News Letter pointed out that "much as they deserve praise... they are a long way cast in the shade by the cinematograph views." The Edison-Poole Eventograph, as it was billed, showed a number of comedies and films from the war including the Lancers skirmishing, crossing the river Modder and the armoured train, but a study of the newspaper adverts over the period reveals an interesting development. At the beginning the Eventograph was nearly buried in small print at the bottom of the advertisement but as the days passed it moved upwards into a more dominant position with more impressive type. Obviously Mr Poole realised, like the newspaper reporter, that the films were the major factor in drawing the crowds. It is interesting that his response reflected the future of the Poole Company which slowly abandoned the panoramas and moved into the cinema business.

During the last two weeks of the engagement an extra film show was added to the programme. That was the Lubin Cinematograph of the Fitzsimmons-Jeffrey fight which had just arrived from America and hadn't been shown anywhere else in Ireland as yet. Understanding that many people disapproved of boxing, Mr Poole diplomatically announced that the complete Myriorama and Eventograph would be shown first and then there would be an interval so that those "who do not care for this class of entertainment can leave." There are no reports of how many left. The Irish News was very impressed by the immediacy and actuality of the boxing film and felt that the observer was really present on Coney Island rather than "within the sedate walls of the Ulster Hall" watching Jeffreys defeat "Lanky Bob" over nine rounds. In September the Theatre Royal, the original home of the Muse, also surrendered to celluloid and presented the Cinematograph with top billing combined with a drama set in Russia called "Under the Czar." The projector was an Edison model and the show was the usual mix of war scenes and comedies, but one gets the distinct feeling that the local critics disapproved of its appearance in the venerable theatre. In December Mr Poole returned to the Ulster Hall with his number one War Myriorama, complete with the Eventograph and live acts, a combination which proved successful again.

The chief cinematic event of the year was the appearance of Professor Kineto's Anglo-Parisian Biorama at the Empire beginning on the 5th March. He became so popular with critics and audiences that he remained until the end of April, a run of eight weeks, the longest of any cinematographer in the city up to that time. The name of his act was carefully chosen and suggests a man with a mind that was informed, organised and with a sense of history. The title "professor" was of course a widely accepted show business accolade implying knowledge and professional competence, with maybe a hint that theatre and academia had something in common. The many "professors" who graced the Belfast stages over the years didn't always display those qualities but in this case they were clearly manifest. The choice of Kineto reflected his recognition of the vital part played by Edison's Kinetoscope in the development of films and one can be reasonably certain that he was among the crowds that had flocked to Royal Avenue five years before to see the first machines and their contents. The words "Anglo- Parisian" referred to the sources of his films in England and France, while Biorama resonated with memories of the beautiful dioramas and panoramas which were so popular in the local halls before Lumière. Technically his shows were of a very high standard with clear and steady pictures. They were also topical dealing with the war and local events, leavened by good comedies.

But audiences really took to him when it emerged that he was a local man. His real name was J. Walker Hicks, born in 1863, and he had arrived in Belfast as part of the rural-urban migration which had so increased the population of the city during the second half of the nineteenth century. His family travelled in from Fermanagh in the 1870's probably because his father, a civil servant, had been transferred there and they settled on the Lisburn Road (as far as can be ascertained) where the lad grew up. Young John was fascinated from an early age by the magic lantern and took great pleasure and pride in putting on slide shows for friends and acquaintances. From there he became interested in photography and it was that interest which must have guided his footsteps to Royal Avenue to see the kinetoscope. By that time he had married and settled into the hotel business, having opened the Shaftesbury Hotel in College Square North. There he also practised photography and had a dark room specially set aside for visitors. That wasn't a unique idea as other hotels advertised similar facilities, for example the Glenmore Select Family hotel in Rostrevor had a dark room for guests interested in photography. There was a growing tendency to associate photography with relaxation and tourism. Lizars, for example, cleverly offered cameras which they described as being small and light enough to carry on a bicycle trip, thereby combining two hobbies, one to exercise the body and the other to test the mind and eye.

Mr Hicks was astute enough to combine business and pleasure. His interest deepened when he saw the first animated pictures in Belfast and he soon acquired a projector. But he also saw the business opportunities that were opening up so he set up a company, the Hibernian Vitograph Company, which he ran from his hotel, selling improved models of projectors. Part of his business duties involved him in putting on film shows to demonstrate his machines and he began to build up his technical skills and a concomitant reputation. At first he toured Ireland giving demonstrations and lectures in schools and colleges, probably realising that the cinematograph had the capacity to become a useful teaching tool. In February 1897, in response to a request, he put on a show for the St. Vincent de Paul in the Rotunda in Dublin which was highly praised and its success persuaded him to think in terms of more professional exhibitions, which led in time to his highly successful appearance at the Empire. His main strengths seem to have been his technical know-how and his organizational abilities. He demonstrated both those with flair and showmanship during his stint at the Empire.

The city, indeed the whole country, was agog with the news that Queen Victoria would visit Dublin on the 4th April 1900. The local papers showed an appropriate loyal appreciation. The News Letter, in an editorial, welcomed her while expressing the belief that she came because of her warm feelings for Ireland. The paper quoted approvingly her words to the Lord Mayor of Dublin how she wanted "to revisit the Motherland of those brave sons who have recently borne themselves in defence of my Crown and Empire with that cheerful valour as conspicuous now as in the glorious past." The hope was also expressed that she might come north to Belfast. The Whig had earlier described the preparations in Dublin, with the floodlighting of major buildings, the decorations, and the erection of viewing stands along the proposed route of her procession into the city.

The paper expressed approval, but added that such were the mistakes made in the past with regard to Ireland that it would not be surprising if many people had forgotten that they had a queen. The situation, the Whig felt, wasn't helped by certain English "jingo newspapers" who wrote as if the queen was visiting a foreign country. The country could also do without the "journalistic homilies and instruction" offered by those papers on how the Irish should behave. Ireland, the paper announced, would greet the sovereign in its own way and if she decided to come to the "cold North" she would get a warm welcome. Not everyone was entirely happy about the visit. The Irish News, also in an editorial, pointed out that she had arrived with a flotilla of warships which it felt was quite inappropriate for a private visit. Those ships embodied the armed might upon which British power rested in Ireland. However, the paper continued, reflecting the Whig's comments, the Irish were noted for their hospitality and would know how to treat the elderly Queen with respect. And so it was. Crowds flocked from all over the country into Dublin to see her and enjoy the pageantry.

A number of crowded trains left Belfast that first morning and on one of them was Prof. Kinetto with his camera. Special adverts in the morning papers promised that he would show "several snapshots" of the queen's procession into Dublin that same night in the Empire. He was aiming to reduce the time lag between an actual event and its presentation on a screen to a matter of hours. It was a brave thing to attempt publicly. He was putting his professional reputation to the test and it caused great excitement in the city. Of course he was well used to travelling to Dublin by train and he had worked out the times carefully, but things could still go wrong. But, he kept his word. He filmed the procession at a number of places, then caught the train back to Belfast where the film was speedily developed and printed. A crowded and expectant Empire watched scenes that had taken place earlier that day in Dublin, actually four days before those scenes appeared on screens in Dublin itself. The scenes showed the royal procession passing through Ballsbridge, then crossing the Leeson street bridge and finally in O'Connell street which was a riot of decorations. Praise was heaped on Prof. Kineto for his achievement but one wonders if the whole story was being told because a few days later an advertisement appeared from Erskine Mayne offering films of the Queen's visit to Ireland for rent. The advert emphasised that the films were taken on Wednesday, 4th April "by my own operator" who had rushed them to Belfast where they were developed and printed in Erskine Mayne's own workrooms, and one of

Prof. Kineto.
Source: Ireland's
Saturday Night.

them was shown in the city on that same evening. Does that mean there were two separate camera groups from Belfast in Dublin that day and that they both rushed back to screen their films? Prof. Kinetto was there and so was one of Erskine Mayne's cameramen, but whether they were working separately or in conjunction is unclear.

There is no record of any showing other than at the Empire that evening so was the Erskine Mayne film included in the show? It may have been that Kinetto and Erskine Mayne had a business agreement by which the expedition was organized by Kineto, but he hired the services of Erskine Mayne's cameraman and darkroom facilities. It is interesting that the Empire advertisement for the next day, Thursday 5th April, promised animated pictures of the Queen's procession entering Dublin with "several snapshots taken specially for the Empire Directorate by Prof. Kineto," clearly indicating that there were other films of the event involved. That takes nothing away from the professor's achievement but it indicates that Erskine Mayne was equally adventurous and willing to take business risks. Certainly his cameramen were busy around the streets of Belfast during the rest of that week. They filmed 'C' Company of the Imperial Yeomanry leaving the city on Thursday, shipyard workers on their lunch break on Friday and linen workers from a Crumlin Road mill on the following Monday, some of which were shown that weekend in the Y.M.C.A. As it happened the Queen didn't travel to the north, her spokesman explaining that the journey might prove too fatiguing, but Prof. Kinetto and Erskine Mayne between them softened the disappointment and presented the next best thing by way of her appearance in animated pictures.

The deluge of war pictures shown at the time were all of the newsreel type, but the local stage sometimes helped to add flesh and blood to them. In January the Alhambra presented a sketch called "Briton or Boer" which was so popular that it was held over for a second week. It was advertised as an Immense Attraction with the heading of War, War, War in large print. The outline of the short sketch could be the plot of one of the one reelers that were to appear on screens in a few years' time. It was a simple piece of propaganda which concerned a British farmer and his wife who were confronted by a Boer commander and his villainous hunchback adviser (not exactly subtle) and accused of being spies. They were arrested and imprisoned but a loyal Black servant, Old Joe, followed them to the Boer camp and managed to release them. He then led a group of British soldiers to the camp. It ended with a clash between the British and the Boers which the Belfast Telegraph found "very realistic" and which the audience responded to with loud cheers. The Telegraph, noting the popularity of the piece, went on to congratulate Mr Ashcroft on his excellent judgement of public taste. Sadly those were Ashcroft's last months at the Alhambra, and in October he put it up for sale by auction. The bidding started at £3,000, but it was finally sold for £4,500 to Hugh Smylie, an accountant acting for a local syndicate, who promised to give the building a make over and reopen it before Christmas. On Monday 17th December a special benefit was arranged by his professional colleagues at the Grand Opera House to say goodbye and thank you to the Solid Man. It was one of a number of similar events held in Dublin (at the Lyric), Liverpool and Glasgow organised by fellow professionals in recognition of his services to the music hall. It was a splendid and emotional evening of comedy, song, music and speeches and one of the highlights was Prof. Kineto's Biorama which must have been especially appreciated by the man who was instrumental in screening the first films in Belfast.

The film show included the inevitable war scenes but also a couple of interesting comedies called "What we saw through the Telescope" and "Let me dream Again." They were the work of an English film maker, G.A.Smith of Brighton. At that time Brighton was an important centre for animated pictures with a number of significant innovators working there. Smith was in the photographic business but he also had a deep interest in Astronomy and often gave lectures on the subject which he illustrated using a magic lantern. His familiarity with the latter led to his interest in animated pictures. The trick films of Georges Méliès intrigued him and he made a number of them himself, experimenting with what came to be known as close-ups. "Let me Dream Again" was a simple little film of only three shots, an example of minimalist story telling. In the first shot a man is in bed with his wife, he complete with nightcap, she with a bonnet. From the look on his face it is obvious that they are having a row and he is getting the worst of it. Suddenly in the second shot he is dreaming of their past life, celebrating and enjoying themselves, she wearing a party hat. Then just as quickly in the third shot without any camera movement they are shown again in bed reconciled, asleep, he with his arm around her. The New Alhambra opened at Christmas, repainted, with increased seating accommodation in the form of new pit stalls added at the front while the more expensive rear balcony had new seats which the Whig found "very comfortable."

Even more personal experiences of the Boer conflict were described by a number of speakers who gave illustrated lectures on the subject. At the beginning of May the well known war correspondent Rene Bull returned to the City Y.M.C.A. fresh from the front to describe what he had seen and to show two hundred slides that he had taken himself. The hall was packed for his reports but one obvious absentee was D.A.Black who had himself gone to S. Africa to do a six month's stint as a chaplain to the troops. He was there with them when Lord Roberts entered Pretoria. News of the fall of Pretoria and the flight of President Kruger reached Belfast at the end of May and resulted in a couple of days of celebrations. Flags appeared on major buildings, crowds thronged the centre of the city. At night bonfires blazed in loyalist areas of the Shankill, Sandy Row, Old Lodge and Mountpottinger. Bands marched the streets playing patriotic tunes to late in the night. There was of course the inevitable coat - trailing which led here and there to the exchange of verbal insults, leavened with intermittent stones and bottles, with Nationalist groups. The police used their batons on a number of occasions at Millfield and Divis Street to restore order. The incidents of disorder weren't all political. There was widespread condemnation when a group of youths harassed a lady trying to enter a tram in Royal Avenue and she had to be rescued by police. Whatever else one may think, its hard to deny that Belfast was always an exciting place to be in! At the same time there were reports of sadder news though it didn't seem to interfere with the general revelry. Companies of the Irish Yeomanry had been caught by the Boers in exposed positions at Lindley and in fierce fighting twenty eight of the Irish had been killed including five from the Belfast area, before the rest were forced to surrender.

The city had settled down again by the time D.A.Black returned in October. Soon afterwards a lecture about his experiences was announced for the great hall in the Y.M.C.A. for the 17th in the presence of the Lord Mayor, called "At the front with Lord Roberts", to be illustrated with 100 war scenes. Reserved seats were two shillings and long before the event every available seat was booked. There were also 500 seats at one shilling plus 1000 at sixpence. On the night itself the hall was crowded from an early hour and there was considerable confusion when some who had booked tickets arrived to find the doors already closed and a large crowd outside. In the pushing and shoving some managed to get in without paying. On the stage was a large twenty foot screen decorated with union jacks and the magic lantern was operated by the reliable Mr Hogg though nearly all the slides had been taken by Mr Black himself. Because of the public demand the lecture was repeated the following Tuesday with a warning that the scrum like conditions which had preceded the first lecture would not be acceptable. Over the following weeks he repeated the lecture in the Grosvenor Hall and at a number of out-of-town venues in Lisburn, Dromore and Lurgan, changing the name slightly to "with Lord Roberts to Pretoria." Everywhere Mr Black's reputation and his topic attracted maximum audiences. During all that time, no matter how busy he was he didn't forget his interest in films and quickly renewed his arrangement with Lizars to present the Saturday shows beginning with a promise of twenty films that had never been seen in Belfast before.

There was more to come. In late November citizens walking along Wellington Place were intrigued to see the letters WSC lit up by electricity on the front of the Y.M.C.A. building. It was the first example of public electric lettering in the city and it was erected by the local firm of William Coates. The letters stood for Winston Spencer Churchill M.P. and he had come over at Mr Black's request to give a lecture entitled "The War as I Saw it." It was an all ticket affair and the tickets were snapped up as soon as they came on sale, like the prelude to a modern pop concert. As with Mr Black's lecture there was a large screen on the stage decorated with union flags and Alex. Hogg was in charge of the magic lantern. Churchill, who was twenty six years old at the time, seemed rather nervous at the beginning and his voice revealed a distinct lisp. The talk began when a map of South Africa appeared on the screen and he set the tone of the evening by gesturing towards it and addressing the audience directly with the words, "Take a good look at it. It belongs to us." He then commenced, describing his many adventures in the area as the war correspondent for the Morning Post, his capture by the Boers, his imprisonment at Pretoria and his eventual escape. As time passed he became more confident, peppering his comments with flashes of humour and what the News Letter called "happy little phrases." He described the people he had encountered and speculated on their motives along with those of the chief players in the whole drama. He had special praise for the Dublin Fusiliers, comments which were greeted with applause. A slide of Mr Kruger was shown which roused the listeners to boohs, hisses and some cheers, and it was followed by one of Mr and Mrs Kruger which he described as "a family party for the Zoological Gardens," provoking much laughter.

The majority of Nationalists tended to keep the war hysteria and propaganda at some distance. Belfast had originated and grown with an essentially Protestant English and Scottish population, but during the nineteenth century the Nationalist - Catholic section of the population had greatly increased as rural dwellers migrated to seek employment in the growing industries of the town. By the 1870's it was realised that a large hall was needed as a focus for specifically Catholic social and other functions and therefore St. Mary's Hall was built and opened in Bank Street off Chapel Lane in February 1876. Over the years it was used mainly for meetings, concerts and similar social events but, despite their obvious and growing popularity, the new animated films were ignored. Those Catholics who were able to afford them could enjoy the Empire, the Alhambra, the Opera House and the Ulster Hall but the majority would have avoided the Grosvenor Hall and the City Y.M.C.A. which they would have perceived as centres of Protestant and Unionist entertainment. On the face of it the Nationalist population, especially the poorer sections of the working class, had less local access to early films than the rest of the population and they certainly had no venue which presented films with the regularity and economic accessibility (cheap seats) of the Y.M.C.A.

or the Grosvenor Hall.

That situation began to alter in the last month of 1900 when St Mary's Hall, in a change of policy, presented the first of a series of film shows. The programme was advertised as a Biograph Exhibition which would include filmed scenes of the then Pope, Leo X111. It would be supported by a Grand Concert, and the Bishop of Down and Connor, Dr. Henry, would attend. Seats at two shillings and one shilling were not cheap but it was mentioned in mitigation that the cost of hiring the Biograph was £80. That was a large figure in comparison to the few pounds that Lizars and Erskine Mayne charged and suggests that it was one of Biograph's roadshows complete with a projectionist, special 75mm negative, large clear images and a very large screen. There were those in the Vatican and elsewhere who argued that the Pope should not appear in a popular entertainment medium associated with music halls, but for local Catholics the positive attitude of their bishop implied that the event had Church approval. Also the Irish News carried a statement from the Apostolic Delegate which stated that it was "the expressed wish of His Holiness that those who see his Benediction in the moving figures of the biograph... and receive it in the proper spirit should participate in the happiness, in the glory and in the advantages of it as if it had been bestowed on them personally." There had been many reports about the pope's uncertain health recently and he felt that his appearance in the animated pictures would reassure Catholics everywhere and also bring joy and spiritual peace to the many Catholics who would like to see him and get his Blessing but couldn't afford the trip to Rome.

On the evening in question the hall was packed. As promised, the Bishop was present and there was a liberal sprinkling of clergy throughout the audience. The concert came first and was a most enjoyable success. Then an expectant hush fell over the audience as the lights were dimmed, the hum of the projector was heard and the first pictures appeared on the screen. They were clear and steady with "no painful tax on the eyes" as the Irish News explained. For some in the audience, especially the older members, and most of the clergy it was probably their first experience of the medium and from all accounts it was a memorable encounter. The whole show was carefully chosen so as not to give any offence. There was a series of Irish scenes including Jumping at the Dublin Horse Show, spinning in an Irish peasant home, feeding the pigs on a farm in the North of Ireland, feeding seagulls on the Irish coast described in the report as "a scene of great beauty" which produced an appreciative reaction from the audience.

In contrast there were some comedies which included the "Letter of Fate" and "Pussy's Bath." The latter is interesting because it can be dated. The Biograph was introduced to English audiences in March 1897 and caused a sensation. That first show included "Pussy's Bath" which showed a young child enjoying the process of washing her kitten. As would be expected the animal resented her well meant attentions and suddenly scratched her, putting an end to her pleasure. It was a simple incident but one that audiences everywhere recognised and responded to with sympathetic laughter. Then there was a number of documentary type scenes of the launch of the Oceanic, panoramic views of Venice, a Neapolitan dance among the ruins of Pompeii, religious processions, and one of Biograph's trademarks, a phantom ride, as an American express took on water at speed. Also among the latter was a recent picture of ex - President Kruger in France. He was shown leaving the Hotel de Ville in Paris and passing through a group of serious looking Frenchmen who raised their hats as a sign of respect. On reaching his carriage Kruger returned the salute by doffing his own headgear. At that a ripple of applause went around the hall. Most of the audience would have had very little in common with the dour Bible - reading Boer leader but they recognised him as representing a small country standing up for its rights against the might of the British Empire, and that was what they admired.

But the evening wasn't about politics, and when the film show reached its climax as the screen filled with the first view of the Pope the hall became charged with "an electrical spirit of reverence and intensity." In all, five views of the frail Pontiff were shown with his advisers and Papal Guard, travelling in his carriage, and walking in the Vatican gardens using a walking stick. They had been filmed on the 28th June 1898 by Laurie Dickson the man who had built the Black Maria and had made the first little films for Edison's kinetoscope. The series ended with a solemn moment when the Pope raised his arm and gave his Apostolic Blessing towards the camera and via it to those watching. It was an amazing and historic moment representing the beginning of a new and more open relationship between the Vatican and the outside world; today no-one is surprised when the present Pontiff appears on TV or even releases a CD. During the papal scenes the orchestra under the direction of Mr Boyle played Laudate, God Bless the Pope, Faith of Our Fathers and, seeing how it was Christmas, Adeste Fidelis. The evening ended with a spirited rendition of "God Save Ireland" by the orchestra. The crowds who streamed out into Bank street were well pleased. The reporter from the Irish News fully concurred and expressed the hope that the Biograph company would stay in Belfast and produce more shows of a similar high quality that contrasted so obviously with what he termed the trivial and jingoistic material so often shown in the city. However after a second packed and successful show Biograph packed up and hit the road again.

A few days later St Mary's Hall announced another concert and cinematograph show but this time it was built around scenes from the 1900 Oberammergau Passion Play. Seats cost two shillings, one shilling, and sixpence, opening the experience up to a wider audience. It was promoted by the branch of the Apostleship of Prayer in St Peter's parish who arranged for the show to be put on by Lizars. The religious theme attracted the bishop and many clergy again who, with a packed hall, enjoyed the concert which almost by tradition preceded the films. Recent adverts of Lizars had repeated the claim that they used Lumière machines so one can be reasonably sure it was a Lumière projector, but the films were from various sources. There were some war scenes but from the Spanish American war - Lizars probably thought it more diplomatic to ignore the Boer conflict - a march past of Spanish marines, scenes in Italy including Milan, Venice and Rome with a splendid interior in St Peter's. The inevitable comedies included a group of children having a pillow fight. There were also some views of the pope before three scenes were shown from the Passion Play: the birth of Our Lord, the Betrayal by Judas, and the Carrying of the Cross. The source of those films is not clear and whether they were genuine or reconstructions, but they had a dramatic impact on the audience which showed every sign of being moved. Indeed when Judas gave Christ the kiss of betrayal there were murmurs of indignation from the body of the hall. The success of the evening proved that a local representative could put on a dignified and moving entertainment and must have persuaded the management of the hall that film shows were not only good entertainment and educational but also financially worthwhile.

At the end of December citizens may have been taken aback by a newspaper claim that Kruger was in Belfast. They needn't have worried because it turned out to be an advert for a film. The Chapel Fields were the scene of a Christmas and New Year carnival promising "harmless amusement for all classes" and one of the diversions was a sideshow called Norman's Electograph, presumedly a travelling showman in a tent, who was presenting "the first and only film in Ireland" of the landing of Kruger at Marseilles. While Kruger may not have been physically in Belfast it is possible that some Belfast citizens may have actually seen him in the flesh when they went to visit the 1900 World Fair in Paris.

The main aim of the Paris Exposition was to celebrate the achievements of the nineteenth century so it is not surprising that the new animated pictures were represented in a big way. The site of the exhibition covered an area of about 550 acres and all the major industrial nations were represented there. It was opened by President Loubet on April 14th in time for Easter, and the local papers carried various reports on the affair describing the displays and the many attractions. One of the more popular displays was of a complete Boer farm and the writer detected a distinct anti - British feeling there among many of the French visitors. There was a more favourable comment on the latest development from America, a moving sidewalk which seemed to delight both locals and visitors. Scenes of people enjoying that experience were shown in Belfast early the following year in the Ulster Hall, the Y.M.C.A. and other halls. Another popular attraction was a giant telescope which was trained on the moon, reflecting the growing interest at the time in astronomy and surely among those who peered through it was George Méliès, soon to astound and delight audiences with his own "Journey to the Moon." There were at least seventeen different attractions which involved projected images as part of panoramas, dioramas and cinematographs which masqueraded under a variety of impressive sounding names like Mareorama, Cinoerama (an ambitious multi-camera system described by one reporter as a disaster), Stereorama, Phonorama, Theatroscope, and Phono-Cinema-Theatre. Reports suggested that some of the panoramas did very well, especially the Mareorama during which visitors experienced a trip around the Mediterranean on a liner which pitched and rolled and passed through a thunder and lightning storm. The passing scenery was painted on two canvas rolls moving on either side of the "ship."

While the panoramas and dioramas looked back at the entertainments of the nineteenth century the Phono-Cinema-Theatre pointed forward to the new century. From the earliest days of film there were attempts at perfecting a system that married sound to the images, and the Phono-Cinema-Theatre was an interesting experiment in that direction. It claimed to present "visions animées des artistes celebres." It was an early attempt at sound film in that it combined visuals and sound. It consisted of nineteen well known actors, actresses including Sarah Bernhardt, and music hall stars performing before a static camera while the sound of their voices was heard from a phonograph. The idea certainly impressed many people including visiting showmen looking for new novelties, and by the following March 1901 audiences in the Empire, who were probably still drowning their shamrock, were able by way of Gibbon's phono-bio-tableaux, advertised as his latest invention being presented for the first time in Ireland, to see and hear Vesta Tilley singing and dancing on film. Comments in the papers suggest it was a popular success. The News Letter thought that the visuals were very clear while the sound was quite distinct. There was no mention of the level of synchronization between the sounds and the images so it must have been reasonably accurate or it surely would have been noticed and commented upon. So on the evidence of that show the Empire could claim to have presented the first musical sound film in the country. Those historic little films, some in black and white, others hand tinted in colour, have been restored by the Cinematheque Francaise and were shown at the Flatpack Film Festival in Birmingham at the end of March 2014.

Without doubt the hit of the Exposition was the Lumière Brothers who presented a twenty five minute film show on a gigantic screen. Between shows the screen was lowered into a container of water and when it was raised again the wet white canvas was sufficiently transparent for the images to be seen from both sides. Over one million people visited that show for which the pioneering film makers won a top prize. So when Lizars claimed in their adverts that their Lumière shows were the best, maybe it wasn't an idle boast.

The early part of 1901 was dominated by the death of Queen Victoria who passed away on Tuesday 22nd January at 6:30 in the evening. Besides the public sadness and official mourning there was a general feeling, reflected also in Belfast, that an era had ended. The New Alhambra was presenting a comedy sketch "The Haunted House" at the time and at the end of the entertainment the whole cast assembled on the stage and sang the National Anthem while free photographs of the queen were distributed to the audience. On Saturday February 2nd, the day of the funeral, the shops closed and any afternoon matinees were cancelled though the theatres and halls opened as usual in the evening. On the following Monday the papers were full of detailed and impressive descriptions of the funeral procession and the associated ceremonials in London but in the midst of appropriate comments the Irish News astutely noted how it had all been carefully stage managed with "elaborate pomp and ceremony and a keener eye to spectacular effect." There is no doubt that the funeral was organized not only to pay tribute to the dead monarch but also to impress the world with the influence and power of her Empire. The one thing that could immediately capture and show that spectacle of course was the film camera and projector, and it is interesting that the new king Edward V11 famously stopped the funeral procession at one point so that the film maker Cecil Hepworth could get a good shot of the proceedings. The local audiences waited in anticipation for the record of an event that Ken Russell, the film director, has described as outdoing Elizabeth Taylor's famous entry into Rome as Cleopatra (Cleopatra, 1963, d.Joseph Mankiewich).

By the following day the Cinematograph Syndicate in Donegall Street had films of the event and showed them in St Enoch's School, while, at the weekend, D.A.Black and the City Y.M.C.A. had the first large scale showing as part of their usual Saturday night entertainment. It was another week before the Empire presented Gibbons Bio - Tableaux with a full coverage of the funeral, which the News Letter found to be "very vivid," and the Irish News described as "well received." As the month proceeded films of the funeral appeared in many halls across the city.

Around that time a new competitor appeared on the scene in late February to compete with Lizars and Erskine Mayne. A. R. Hogg had left Lizars and set up independently as a photographer at 13, Trinity Street from where he advertised a supply of recent films including the Queen's Funeral and the procession of the new king Edward V11 to open Parliament. Although essentially a professional photographer, A.R. Hogg also gave demonstrations and illustrated slide shows and was a very popular guest at meetings of local photographic societies. He retained his association with the Grosvenor Hall, continuing to present the cinematographic part of the Happy Evenings on Saturdays. After setting up independently he joined with his brother, D.J.Hogg, well known in the city as an amateur photographer, to form a lecturing duo. The first item presented by the Brothers Hogg, as they were advertised, was a description of the river Lagan from source to mouth illustrated by 150 slides. D.J. actually gave the lecture while the slides were projected by A.R. using a large and very impressive double lantern. When the slides were finished he added a special attachment to his lantern and then showed a number of animated pictures which he had filmed himself along the river. The lecture was given at a number of venues and was a great success. Hogg is rightly admired as a still photographer - most of his output still exists - but unfortunately little is known about the films he made to illustrate his lectures and, one suspects, to rent or show at his film nights. Occasionally mention was made of local films shown in the Grosvenor Hall which were almost certainly photographed by him. They included an outing of deprived children to Glenavy organized by the Central City Mission, Coronation Day at the Belfast Workhouse, and local street scenes of a funeral and Queen's Island workers (it was emphasised that the latter was "new" to differentiate it from other similar scenes that were already available).

The coronation of the new king was a major talking point even more so when it was postponed from the 26th June to the 9th August because of Edward's poor health, though, at his request, all celebrations already arranged were to go ahead. The film makers who were prepared for a momentous occasion had to pack up their cameras and change their plans, except George Méliès who had already filmed the coronation! Because of lighting difficulties and the excessive noise from the cameras no filming was allowed in Westminster Abbey so when Méliès was approached by Charles Urban the owner of the Warwick Trading Company in London on the matter he decided to replicate the event in his studio. The studio was cleverly decorated to represent the interior of the Abbey, actors and actresses were hired from the shows in Paris, a lookalike (reports say that he was a laundry worker) was found for Edward while a dancer played the part of Alexandra, and the filming went ahead. Urban held it over to August, added some actual outdoor footage filmed on the day and released it to popular acclaim. Some of those who saw it knew it was a "reconstruction" while others accepted it as the real thing. Any complaints were ignored because, at the time, such fake actualities were quite common and widely accepted. The first coronation films showing scenes of the outdoor processions were shown in Belfast on the Saturday following the event when Lizars projected them for Mr Black in the City Y.M.C.A. A.R.Hogg also showed 800 feet of film of the procession in the Grosvenor Hall some weeks later but when in September the New Alhambra included among its music hall acts the American Biomotograph it showed the King's Coronation. That must have been

Méliès's film and it proved popular enough to be held over for two weeks.

Throughout the year audiences also had the choice of three large and impressive touring cinematic shows which were presented in the Theatre Royal (Edison's Electric Animated Photographic Company), the City Y.M.C.A. (West's Our Navy), and the Ulster Hall (Our Army and Navy Animated Photographic Company). Edison's Pictures came to the Theatre Royal in February after a six week run in the Rotunda in Dublin and stayed for five successful weeks. There were no music hall acts involved, just films with appropriate music and songs. The latter were supplied by Lester King who also acted as lecturer, explaining and commenting on the pictures. The papers noted the quality of the projection which was clear, steady and, as the Irish News said, "much superior to what the public is used to." Over the period the mix of films was cleverly varied from week to week with the emphasis on quality combined with an appeal to the widest possible audience. The subjects involved varied from what would be called newsreel today (like President McKinley's funeral and shots of the yacht Shamrock 2 preparing for the America's Cup races) to historical drama (the Georges Méliès's film of Joan of Arc) to the serious and religious (scenes from the Passion Play) to melodrama (five scenes of Scrooge and Marley's Ghost from Dickens) to comedy and pantomime (Red Riding Hood, again from Méliès, and the Topsy Turvy Hotel) and a lengthy documentary called "The Toilers of the Deep" dealing with the lives of the cod fishermen of Newfoundland. The latter consisted of a series of short scenes joined together to give a comprehensive picture of conditions on the Grand Banks. Each scene was labelled and they were listed by a local critic as going aboard, hoisting sail, outward bound, cleaning fish on board, a boat run down, saving the victims, homeward bound, landing the catch, and returning to sea.

It is easy to understand why commentators stressed the educational qualities of the early cinematograph. But the exhibitors were interested mainly in entertainment so they included a group of "Singing Pictures" in which the images were accompanied by Phonograph recordings. The performers were the ever popular Vesta Tilly singing "The Midnight Sun", Vesta Victoria who would appear in person in the Empire later in the year with "Our Lodger", Lil Hawthorn with "Kitty Mahone," Alec. Hurley doing the Lambeth Cakewalk and a group called the American Comedy Four singing "Sally in our Alley". The News Letter found them all "very acceptable," the Whig was very impressed, while the Irish News commented on the wonder of hearing the actual voices. One of the most popular parts of the programme was called "Belfast, Day by Day" which consisted of scenes and events photographed locally by two cameramen who were members of the company. Each weekend the results of their efforts were taken to London by boat and train, processed, and brought back for projection on Monday. People were then invited to visit the Theatre Royal and see themselves on the screen. Quite a few local scenes were taken including the markets, workers leaving York Street mill and the Ropeworks, skating in Ormeau Park during the recent frosts plus local football matches, all of which reflected the perceived importance of the working class audience. In late February Ireland met Scotland at Balmoral for the twenty fifth time in a Rugby International and Edison promised scenes from the match if the weather permitted. Despite dull conditions the cameramen were there to record a victory by Ireland, all well received the following week, especially when Fred Warden was spotted in the crowd and got a good natured cheer from the audience. As a business man Warden must have been impressed by the success of Edison Pictures and the ability of the cinematograph to attract an audience and he surely noted the positive responses of the papers to the show. As the Whig summed it up, it was impressive on a number of fronts especially in the wide range of subjects it covered and in its ability to combine instruction, edification and amusement.

About a month later West's Electric Animatograph arrived in the City Y.M.C.A. for an eleven day run, arranged by D.A.Black. The West family hailed from Southsea near Portsmouth and were noted for their interest in recording seafaring scenes, an interest appreciated not only by the navy but also by Royalty. Their show, called West's "Our Navy," was given over to events involving ships and sailors. The first section dealt with the training of a young man who joins the navy, with scenes covering what happened to him from the moment he entered the recruiting office. The second section was a look at the navy of a rising power in the Far East, Japan. The final part concerned the races for the America Cup and the journey of the Prince and Princess of Wales around the world on the yacht Ophir. The images were accompanied by a commentary, plus rousing music. The News Letter thought it was "well presented" but added that the audience was rather sparse.

That wasn't the case however over Christmas when the Army and Navy Animated Photo Co. came to the Ulster Hall and was greeted by full houses. Audiences were promised that they would see "200,000 sensational pictures" reflecting "life at home and abroad" accompanied by music, song (Roy Ralston, baritone, singing songs of the sea) and bicycle tricks on a miniature track. Many of the films were in fact a repeat of those shown earlier by the Edison Pictures in the Theatre Royal, with some extras like "Ali Baba and the Forty Thieves," comedies, and local views. Even with the incomplete information available it is obvious that many of the best and most popular films showing in the city were from the imagination of Georges Méliès. It is doubtful if anyone in the audiences knew his name but they surely came to recognise his style and his trademark, a star symbol on the print. That mark was there to prevent the films being copied illegally, a ploy that failed especially in America where his films were duplicated to his financial loss, even by reputable companies like Edison and Lubin. Film piracy is nothing new.

One of his films to suffer that fate was "A Trip to the Moon" which was advertised to be shown in the Alhambra beginning on December 29th 1902. It was described as a unique coloured picture. That advertisement represented a significant development in the history of the cinema in Belfast because it was the first fictional film advertised by name, and represented a move from the machine to the film as the main attraction. The News Letter commented that the film was "very much admired."

George Méliès: screen magic.

CHAPTER FIVE
Audiences Liked What They Saw

By 1903 the film business in general was well organized making and supplying equipment and films to those who showed them. Inventors and technicians were still working away in France, England, the U.S.A. and elsewhere, developing more efficient and reliable machines which they then sold on to the manufacturing section of the industry. Some of the advances or changes caught on with the exhibitors and the public while others didn't. Typical of the former were the attempts to wed pictures to sound and after 1900 local audiences experienced numerous examples of those. While today those "singing pictures" seem very primitive, to the contemporary audiences they were quite amazing and must have been popular too because by 1903 Erskine Mayne had added Animatophone Entertainments, with new films and new records, to his other attractions. He promised to present shows involving a cinematograph, a magic Lantern and a concert phonograph anywhere in Ireland. His advertisements claimed that "distance is no obstacle."

On the other hand those trying to produce three dimensional films didn't make much headway though the topic kept turning up in the news. The News Letter reported in October 1903 that an English inventor Theodore Brown had produced a three dimensional film of a farmyard scene in which the figures were "not flat and bodyless but (had) a depth and fullness that invested them with a wonderful realism." The interesting thing, the writer claimed, was that the effect could be experienced without special glasses. The inventor used a new - secret - technique and he promised that colour sequences would soon be possible. Unfortunately nothing more was heard in public of his experiments which seem to have come to naught. Stereoscopic moving pictures without the need for glasses still remains an unrealised goal in the field of optics. There are no references at the time to any local technical developments associated with animated pictures. Lizars made and sold their own brand of still cameras (the Challenge Range made in Glasgow) but there is no evidence that they were involved in manufacturing movie cameras. Some local craftsmen and technicians of course, notably Prof. Kinetto, certainly modified and improved machines they had purchased in England, which was the main source of any equipment owned or used in the city.

Then there were the film makers who used the technology. During the early years many of them like the Lumières, Robert Paul, Birt Acres or Thomas Edison were fully involved in the development and making of the equipment but with the passing of time and the expansion of the industry most of the new film makers just used equipment made and supplied by others. The films shown in Belfast originated mainly in France, England and the U.S.A. but there was also a very popular minority made by local cameramen. Those intrepid Irish pioneers included Prof. Kinetto, A.R.Hogg, and one or two others, still anonymous, who worked for Erskine Mayne or Lizars. Sadly their records of city life which would be of immense historical and general interest to present generations have largely disappeared. In those days the usual procedure was to use films until they were worn out, and then scrap them. They weren't regarded as important enough to preserve.

The film makers usually passed their products on to the distributors who were concentrated mainly in London. One of the best known of those was the Warwick Trading Company whose managing director was Charles Urban, an American who began his career by managing a kinetoscope parlour in Detroit. From there he later moved to England and joined the Warwick Company which had introduced the kinetoscope into the British Isles. Under his guidance the company expanded and became agents for the distribution of films made by Lumière, Méliès, Robert Paul, G.A.Smith, and the Riley Bros. In 1903 he decided to set up his own business, called the Charles Urban Trading Company, successfully bringing his clients with him and remaining a major influence in the business. He was, like the early pioneers, interested in the technical side of the business and claimed to have invented the Bioscope projector, but he also arranged to have films made, like the Coronation of Edward V11, and he sent his cameramen across the globe to record interesting material. Many of the films he handled were shown in Belfast. All the films involved were for sale to showmen, magicians, fair ground operatives, and local traders like Erskine Mayne and Lizars. The Belfast traders had to buy their films outright from Urban and others like him because renting wasn't yet an option.

Erskine Mayne had accumulated a library of 10,000 magic lantern slides which could be bought or rented. The slides were often arranged in groups complete with descriptive and explanatory notes and were rented out at 6d for twelve slides. But films were treated quite differently. They were hired out as part of a package which included a cinematograph and an experienced projectionist. The equipment for showing them was portable and the railway network allowed the operators to travel widely, so the influence of Erskine Mayne and Lizars wasn't confined to Belfast. They put on shows in schools, colleges, clubs, parish halls and such locations all over the country. Both companies were kept busy because the demand was high, but so also was the appetite for new material. At the turn of the century Lizars claimed that it had the largest stock of films available in Ireland.

Strong competition came from the travelling shows, the majority of which came from across the Irish Sea. At the lower end of the scale were the one - man shows living literally from hand to mouth who pitched a tent or rented a room for a few weeks and charged a penny or two for admission to a show of mostly old, scratched pictures. They often occupied sites on the Chapel Fields and were popular with children and the poorer adults. Then there were the more up - market and better organized groups who arranged their presentations in the professional halls. Some of those were quite small, consisting of two or three people travelling with their equipment, usually as part of a general music hall bill which included singers, dancers, comedians, acrobats and such. Typical examples were some of those who appeared in the Alhambra: the Edisonograph (Dec. 1901), the American Biomotograph (Sept. 1902), the Royal Electric Animated Tableaux (Feb. 1903, "should be seen by all," advised the News Letter), and Andy Wright's Stereograph (Aug. 1903). None of those could compete with the larger outfits which usually arrived surrounded with or preceded by publicity in the way of informative adverts in the papers, handbills and posters. Among those that visited Belfast were Poole's Myriorama, Maskelyne and Cook, Gibbons, the North American Animated Photographic Company, West's Our Navy, and Edison's Electric Animated Pictures. Competition among them was intense.

A court case in Dublin in March 1902 involving the latter company throws some interesting light on the activities of such film exhibitors at the time. The Edison Company took the owners of the Antient Concert Rooms in Dublin to court on the grounds of having broken a booking arrangement. They sought an injunction preventing the proprietors of the Antient Concert Rooms from allowing the presentation of a rival film show, West's Our Navy, over the approaching Easter period. Edison's Irish manager, Mr Rosberry, explained to the court that in February his company had booked the hall in question from 28th July to 13th September for a fee of £100 and that part of the arrangement was that the hall would not be let before that date to any other film exhibitor. He explained that such restrictive arrangements were necessary because of the high level of competition with other exhibitors. Ireland, he explained, was regarded as a lucrative market and about six major companies were in keen competition to supply it. The Edison company was actually in the process of setting up a central office in Dublin to work that market and had already presented shows in Cork, Limerick and Belfast. It cost about £250 per week to put on those shows so it was necessary to attract as many people as possible to make the enterprise financially viable. Experience had shown that audiences became "exhausted" if too many shows were presented in succession or at the same time. Competition was actually greatest during the summer because the bright weather meant that their own photographers could produce a reliable supply of "day to day" local films, which were very popular and a major attraction. In winter the poor natural light meant they couldn't be guaranteed and that affected audience enthusiasm and numbers. For all those

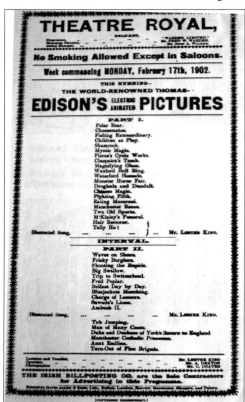

Edison in the Theatre Royal, 1902.

reasons they usually included a booking clause restricting their competitors, and believed that they had done so in that case. But when their show was at the Theatre Royal in Belfast Mr Rosberry discovered that the hall had been let to West's Our Navy over Easter for three weeks for £75, in breach of the agreement, so he returned immediately to Dublin to clear the matter up. He emphasised that his quarrel wasn't with the Wests but with the management of the Antient Rooms. To show his good will he had even offered to arrange a booking for Wests in Belfast in lieu of the disputed Easter booking. After hearing arguments from both sides the court concluded that technically the agreement had been breached, but allowed West's show to go ahead. During the same week however Edison, not to be outdone, rented the Round Room of the Rotunda and risked the "exhaustion" of the audience. When the Edison show was presented in the Theatre Royal in Belfast, there had been no competition but a month after the company's departure, West's filmed ships, following in its wake, dropped anchor in the Y.M.C.A. hall in Wellington Place.

So the general picture was one of nomadic individuals and groups travelling with their projectors and films and presenting their shows in a variety of venues. Wherever they appeared they were referred to by the name of the showman, the company or the projector used, usually in large print. If on rare occasions any films were mentioned by name they were always secondary to the above and were alluded to in much smaller print. But in 1903 three important developments occurred in the local entertainment scene which pointed to the future when the films would become the main attraction and only the films would travel. In fact the first of them overlapped the end of 1902 when the Alhambra - as already indicated - announced, in large print, the presentation of "A Fantastical Trip to the Moon", as its main attraction. That was the first time in Belfast that a film headlined an entertainment bill. There were no details of who made it or who was in it, just the name of the film. It ran for the first two weeks of the new year, attracting large crowds. The papers mentioned that the audiences greatly enjoyed it and the News Letter added that it was a work "of great merit." It had already been showing since mid - December at the Tivoli in Dublin to delighted crowds where it was described as "absolutely the most amazing, amusing, interesting and weird living picture ever put before the public." The Irish Times enjoyed it and thought it was "wonderful" while the Freeman's Journal not only agreed that it was sensational but also that it was "an astonishing instant" of the way in which such productions were being developed and improved. Film historians in the main today would agree with that conclusion.

Méliès Trip To The Moon.

In March 2002 the 20th International Festival of Fantasy Film took place in Brussels and the highlight was the screening of Méliès's historic film to celebrate its one hundredth birthday and to underline its position as the cinema's first important science fiction film. Martin Scorsese added his own special homage in his Oscar winning film "Hugo" (2011). Méliès may have sent his characters to the moon but equally the film sent his reputation as a film maker around the globe. There were no names on the film to indicate who made it or who acted in it and there were no intertitles to move the story forward though as was the custom a lecturer at the side of the stage would have supplied comments to clarify the action. However it must have been obvious to the more observant viewers that much had changed over the last seven years since they had watched the first simple "story" films of a soldier and his girlfriend tipping an old lady off a park bench, or of a gardener being drenched from his own hosepipe. Quite a lot of those changes were due to the efforts of George Méliès. His latest film was much longer, running for fourteen minutes in contrast to the one minute of the early efforts. It consisted of eighteen separate tableaux which told a detailed story which Méliès insisted could be understood without any verbal explanation.

There was more to its appeal than that because it was clearly linked to another form of popular expression - the novel - which tended to widen and deepen its meaning and enjoyment for audiences. The film was actually a gentle skit on the work of Jules Verne and H.G.Wells. The story tells how Prof. Barbenfouillis (Méliès himself) and his five companions, complete with umbrellas, build a space craft - whose shape has an uncanny resemblance to the Apollo craft - which is fired from a great cannon to the moon. There they have a number of adventures and meet the inhabitants of the Moon called Selenites who were played by acrobats from the Follies Bergere. The latter take them prisoner but, led by the resourceful professor, they escape, launch their spacecraft back to earth and land in the sea. In the final scene they are feted for their achievement. The film, which was coloured by hand, is still charming and beautiful to watch today despite the quaintness of the characters and the disregard for scientific facts. The screen, cluttered with Méliès's unique designs, which were recently paid tribute to in Moulin Rouge (d. Baz Lurmann, 2000), is always a delight to watch and positively vibrates with the energy of that essential element of cinema, movement.

Yet for all its qualities a modern audience would feel that it is not very cinematic. It was photographed entirely by natural light in Méliès's glass studio but more obvious is the fact that the camera remains in a fixed position and doesn't move at all. A tracking shot approaching the moon was achieved by moving a model of the moon towards the camera. The camera represents an observer sitting in the stalls in a theatre and what the spectator sees happens within the confines of the stage in front of him. Each scene is presented and photographed as a separate tableau. The camera does not become involved in the action; it merely observes and records. But that is not the whole truth because Méliès used a wide range of camera tricks to make the story more interesting. He was fully acquainted with slow and fast motions, insets, dissolves, double and multiple exposures and reverse action but all those were used within the overall conventions of the theatre. The popularity of the film is reflected in the fact that the Edison Company showed it at a number of venues around Dublin throughout the year, while it was shown in Belfast later in the year in the City Y.M.C.A. to delighted audiences, when the News Letter described it as "undoubtedly the funniest of the humorous pictures" on show.

The second development was contained in an announcement from the Warden company which owned the Opera House and the Theatre Royal. Since J.F.Warden arrived in Belfast in 1864 as joint manager of the Theatre Royal the family had become a major force in the local entertainment business. J.F. was an actor by profession and brought many of the top actors and actresses of the day to the Theatre Royal appearing in serious drama. He also presented not so serious melodrama because he knew that the latter attracted the crowds and the financial returns from them were vital in keeping the theatre operating. He was responsible for the building of a new modern theatre, the Grand Opera House, in 1895 but sadly died three years later, when he was succeeded by his son Fred Warden. Fred was a business man, not an actor and he set about solving the problem of how to fill two theatres. During 1901 - 2 he experimented by presenting high class music hall acts in the Opera House, while he introduced a scale of reduced prices in the Theatre Royal and announced that he wanted to "provide the masses of our city the best possible dramatic fare at cheap prices." In February 1902 he went further and introduced, in the Theatre Royal, a successful five week season of films presented by the Edison Electric Animated Pictures Company. Audience reaction was positive and Warden Ltd. were able to announce an increase in income for 1902 with an overall profit of £4671.

Fred Warden was aware of two trends in local entertainment, namely a decline in serious theatre going and a shift in popular taste towards light entertainment. He felt that economic success was more likely if the two theatres complemented rather than competed with each other. Therefore, he announced that beginning the following February (1904) one theatre, the Theatre Royal, would present serious plays while the other catered for less demanding entertainments. For that purpose the Opera House would be renamed the Palace Theatre of Varieties and would in fact become a superior music hall. It would operate the modern two - house system, similar to that introduced by the Alhambra in August 1902, to facilitate those patrons who had to travel some distance, and those who lived nearby. Also, he added, it would incorporate a permanent film show on a daily basis, the first hall in the city to do so. The promise of a regular film show clearly wasn't just an afterthought. It was a decision influenced by many factors. He knew that the Empire Theatre in Dublin already had such a show presented daily by "Louis, our cinnomatist" as the adverts put it. Maybe he had information from the U.S.A., where one of his directors had toured recently in search of suitable acts, about the growing popularity of films there and how in April 1902 Thomas Tally had actually opened the world's first cinema, the Electric Theatre, in Los Angeles given over entirely to the showing of films. Closer to home he must have noted the success of the recent Edison season in the Theatre Royal. Yet there is no evidence that he had a particularly high opinion of films because at Christmas 1903 he accompanied the pantomime "Dick Whittington" with Animated Pictures and a Monarch Gramophone but just as a "filler" for the forty five minutes between early doors and ordinary doors, which must have been a time of much noise, chattering and movement as people found their seats.

His attitude matches that of one of Belfast's well loved actors, Albert Sharpe (born in William Street South, April 1885), who began his career in the Empire and graduated from ministrel shows to Broadway and Hollywood. He described how in the English music halls which he toured around the outbreak of the Great War the film show was often relegated to the end of the bill when people were already moving out. The writer J. B.Priestley also complained about the quality of the film shows at that time in the music halls and wrote that he avoided them until the arrival of Charlie Chaplin. Despite such criticisms film shows became a fixture in the Belfast music halls and the newspaper reports suggest that in the main audiences welcomed them. Before the Palace could claim the honour of actually introducing permanent shows they were beaten to it by a new circus which established itself on the local entertainment scene. Since the departure of Ginnett's from Great Victoria Street there had been no permanent circus in the city until late 1903 when an English company, Carter and Bosco, took a site at the corner of Chichester Street and Cromac Street and arranged for a building to be erected there. The structure, made from corrugated iron and wood, was completed in five weeks with a length of one hundred feet and a width of seventy five feet and was called the New Imperial Hippodrome and Circus. From the outside the building wasn't as impressive looking as its name indicated but it met the Corporation's standards for safety and from the public's point of view it was in the tradition of "temporary" structures associated with circus performances. Inside it had seating for nearly 2,000 people, was well lit by electricity, well ventilated and was pleasantly decorated in crimson and gold with painted scenes on the walls. When it opened in November it was warmly welcomed by all the papers and attracted large crowds who paid prices ranging from three pence up to two shillings and sixpence for a reserved seat in the stalls. The acts were the normal circus fare but according to the Irish News one act that proved very popular with the crowd was a young man called John Fossett who did "clever juggling on horseback."

The advertisements had promised a Biograph as one of the attractions with a weekly change of pictures. It was the last item on the programme and showed a number of films of local interest like the recent visit of the king and queen to the city and the launch of Shamrock III with which Sir Thomas Lipton intended to contest the America Cup again. The Irish News commentator, who seemed to have a genuine interest in matters cinematic, thought the projector was a superior one and was particularly impressed by the steadiness and clarity of the pictures. Over the following months however the film fare presented was obviously unexceptional and the biograph was usually mentioned only briefly if at all, referred to as finishing the programme or, being up to date, or interesting. One could imagine, as Albert Sharpe recalled, the audience organizing their offspring, getting their coats and hats on, and preparing to leave with one eye on the flickering images.

During January of 1904 the two Warden theatres were closed for redecoration in preparation for their February reopening. The main interest was focused on the Palace Variety Theatre with its two evening shows, each two hours long presenting "quick, bright, refined varieties." There were no delays between the acts and the whole process was fast and furious. Too fast for the gallery who were denied encores from their favourites and who showed their frustration and disappointment. The first house was well filled but the enjoyment of those present was marred by the actions of the gallery which became so noisy that Mr Warden was forced to appear on stage and warn them. The News Letter commented that that type of behaviour would "have to be checked with a firm hand." The second house was packed and was a great success. The main attraction was the noted and skilled illusionist Carl Hertz who delighted and mystified the crowds but his appearance is quite interesting for another reason.

Hertz occupies a small but important niche in early cinematic history. He was an American on tour and happened to be in London in 1896 when the first Lumière film show was put on. As a magician he recognised the usefulness of the new attraction for his own show so he approached M. Trewey with the intention of buying one of the new cinematographs to take with him on his impending tour of the Southern Continents. Like Méliès in Paris he was refused and was about to leave by ship when he heard that Robert Paul had similar machines for sale. He literally forced Paul to sell him one for £100 and rushed with it to the ship, the S.S.Norman. As they sailed south he made history by presenting the first film show at sea and wherever he went in the Southern Hemisphere with his act he introduced his new attraction, to the delighted and amazed inhabitants of places like Johannesburg (May, 1896), Melbourne in Australia (Aug. 1896) and the cities of New Zealand.

There is no report of his opinion of the Palace Pictures which appeared at the end of the show in Belfast but as with the Imperial Hippodrome Biograph there were few details of what was actually shown beyond a brief reference that it was "interesting." The main topic of conversation in the city wasn't the pictures but the attitude of the Empire Theatre. The management of the Empire regarded the development of the Palace as direct competition and mocked the two house system as making proper performances impossible. They even offered a prize of two guineas to whoever would write a winning essay explaining the advantages of the one house system over the two house system in Belfast. In an unusual move they joined battle with a published piece of unmemorable doggerel in which they offered their patrons ease, comfort, courtesy, luxurious seating and "really first class entertainment." The opposition may imitate but it can never equal, they claimed, and ended with the battle cry, "Defeat we defy." Within a short time they had to introduce the two house system themselves, so it must have gained the approval of the audiences.

The big event of the summer of 1903 was the Royal visit of the new king and queen to Ireland, which included a day in Belfast. The royal couple arrived in Dublin soon after the announcement from Rome of the death of Pope Leo X111 but, despite the sadness felt throughout the country at the Pope's passing, the visit proved a great success. They reached Belfast on Monday the 27th July and the city was well prepared. Along the route of the royal procession stands had been erected and seats could be rented in them. Large buildings also offered view points at their windows. Prices ranged from four shillings to fifteen shillings and all spaces were filled with excited watchers. Among them were assorted photographers, amateur and professional, still and animated. The latter included the local photographer A.R.Hogg who took a number of shots including the street procession, the unveiling of Queen Victoria's statue outside the new but unfinished City Hall, and the Old Soldier's stand. To celebrate the occasion Mr Black had arranged for the North American Photographic Company to put on a show of Animated Pictures in the City Y.M.C.A. and in their advertisements they promised that scenes of the day's events would be shown that very evening in the Wellington Hall.

Belfast audiences were rather blasé about such claims since Prof. Kineto's coup but noted that the company's photographers were out on the streets as promised and sure enough that evening the show included the results of their efforts. The audience strained to catch a glimpse of themselves or their friends in the shots of cheering crowds in Donegall Place or on the Queen's Bridge. There were numerous views of the procession moving along the main thoroughfares, arriving at the City Hall, showing the unveiling of the statue there, and the Lord Mayor Sir Daniel Dixon presenting an address. Other shots showed the Royal couple at the Horse Show and finally their departure from the city. The speed with which the films were processed indicates that the work was done locally, almost certainly in the photographic laboratory in the Y.M.C.A. building. The News Letter praised the alacrity of the whole process, the skill of the photographers and the quality of the films themselves, noting that there was very little flicker or blurring when they were shown in the Wellington Hall. The same paper also mentioned reports of the success of A.R.Hogg's filming but that his films wouldn't be shown until later in the year. The pictures were actually shown during the autumn in the Grosvenor Hall and other venues, by which time Mr Hogg had added a few more of his local views notably shots of the Gordon - Bennett motor race, a hill climbing competition at Castlewellan and the Belfast to Ballymena walk. Obviously he was moving into animated films in a big way.

It is easy to forget that those films were very short, usually a minute or less but increasingly they were familiarising their audiences with a life - like visual dimension to the news that they read in the newspapers. In an age in which many people couldn't afford to travel much or too far the film camera increasingly became their extended eye stimulating their curiosity by allowing them to see and appreciate events near and far. Overseas incidents which were shown on local screens included the Delhi Durbar and the Russo - Japanese war. Despite the City Y.M.C.A. putting on a Great Russo -Japanese Night by Cinematographe (the 'e' came back for impact) in March 1904 the war never engendered the same enthusiasm or interest as the Sudan campaign or the Boer War. But the films did introduce audiences to aspects of life in the Far East and such educational qualities of the cinematograph were often noted and praised, especially when a film show like "The Unseen World" arrived.

When the Corporation bought the Ulster Hall in 1902 they found that it was rather run - down, so the building was refurbished and redecorated while its safety precautions were reviewed and brought up-to-date before presenting a programme of music, song and films over the Christmas period of 1903. The films got special attention and praise because they were largely of a scientific nature. They included studies of a boa constrictor, various small animals and the circulation of blood in a frog's foot. Of special interest was "The Unseen World" a series of films released by Charles Urban which his catalogue promised would "reveal Nature's closest secrets." In fact they explored new and unexpected environments by using a microscope to detail the minute life forms that inhabited every day foodstuffs, like cheese. Some food manufacturers objected to the showing of those films because of the effect they might have on potential customers and the sales of certain foods. When those same films were shown in the Pavilion Gardens in Kingstown the Irish Times critic commented on how instructive they were but added, with some surprise, that the audience seemed to find them funny. The attitude in Belfast was quite different and the News Letter warned its readers that the films had "an affect far from agreeable to those of tender appetite." The writer could also have added that while the topics were highly educational and visually fascinating, they were hardly Christmas fare!

While such subject matter was getting smaller the films themselves were becoming longer. Influenced mainly by the example of George Méliès, other European film makers, and, later, some Americans began to increase the length of their narrative films. That was the third development which became increasingly apparent during 1903 and into 1904. With longer films plot lines became more complicated and in time more sophisticated. The exhibitors realised that audiences responded well to the longer films so they began to emphasise length by giving not only the measured length in feet but also the viewing time in minutes. During the period 1903 - 1904 a number of interesting films were presented in Belfast, including Terrors of the Deep (City Y.M.C.A., Mar. 1903), The Rise and Fall of Napoleon (Alhambra, Nov, 1903), Daring Daylight Robbery (Alhambra, Dec.,1903), Wonders of the Deep (Alhambra, Dec.1903), How Capt. Kettle Discovered the North Pole (Alhambra, Dec.,1904), Pickpocket (Alhambra, Feb.1904), Don Quixote (City Y.M.C.A., Feb.1904), Uncle Tom's Cabin (City Y.M.C.A., April 1904), The Strike (Alhambra, Oct.1904), A Christmas Dream (Ulster Hall, Dec.1904), A Trip to the Sun (City Y.M.C.A., Dec.1904) and Whirling the World (Alhambra, Jan.1905). A closer study of those twelve films reveals the trends that were emerging as the industry moved from the days when a camera was set up and an incident, either factual or fictitious, was photographed in front of it in one shot covering a minute or less, to more organised, more carefully thought out, longer, multi - shot films.

The small films didn't disappear and some film makers continued to make and experiment with them. "Daring Daylight Robbery" and "Pickpocket" were two such examples. The former was made by Frank Mottershaw for the Sheffield Photographic

Company and shows a convict breaking into a house when he is seen by a young lad who runs for the police, who then pursue the villain and in time catch him. It is an early chase film and makes use of outdoor locations, including a chase across an actual roof. The News Letter critic recommended it as a comedy. "Pickpocket" made by Alfred Collins, which was described by the Irish News as "excellent" and by the Telegraph as "interesting," was in a similar vein, another early example of a chase film. It was actually subtitled as a chase through London. It begins with a thief stealing a man's watch and chain. He is seen and is pursued by increasing numbers of policemen who become involved in humorous situations like falling into a horse trough before he is apprehended. Those were early examples of a genre, the chase film, which was to become a staple of silent comedy and a major element in adventure films up to the present day. The chase sequence in the Attack of the Clones (d. George Lucas, 2002) may be visually more sophisticated, may make use of spectacular special effects and be filmed in digital format, but it still traces its roots back to those humble little films that delighted audiences in the Alhambra in the early years of the twentieth century.

Those two examples were English, but the dominant influence was French. Seven of the films were of French origin and four of those were by George Méliès. "The Wonders of the Deep" or the Chase after the Stolen Princess (1903), was a beautiful hand coloured film from Méliès which in French was called "Le Royaume des Feés." It was one of a series of feéries that he filmed, and it ran for fifteen minutes. The feéries, which were very popular at the time in the theatre, were part pantomime, part fairy tale, part comic opera, part ballet and one hundred per cent theatrical. In outline the story involves a Prince whose lady love, a Princess, is abducted by a wicked witch on the eve of their wedding. The valiant Prince sets out in pursuit, searching widely for her and having many adventures. Finally he is shipwrecked and ends up (down!) in Neptune's Kingdom where he meets and kills the witch. His beloved is released and returns home with him to live happily ever after.

As in all his other films Méliès was responsible for every aspect of the production from the scenario to the decor and the direction. He had the reputation of being a perfectionist and, like many later famous directors, was a hard taskmaster. Arguably he was the first film auteur. "The Wonders of the Deep" delighted the Belfast audiences who obviously appreciated his distinctive blend of wit, imagination, decor, eccentric characters and beautiful girls. "A Christmas Dream," made earlier in 1900, and running for nine minutes, was another typical Méliès creation. The fact that the Méliès style was not lost on contemporary observers is reflected in the comments of the News Letter which found it very entertaining with its "dissolving effects, tricks, spectacular tableaux, ballets and other effects being cleverly introduced." The same combination, only more so, characterised "A Trip to the Sun," (1904) also called "Whirling the World" or in French "Voyage a travers L'impossible." It was advertised as 1,200 feet long, running for an impressive twenty five minutes. It was shown originally in the Shankill Road mission - for the first time, it was claimed, in Ireland - before transferring to the City Y.M.C.A. for Christmas, venues that suggest that the local distributor was Lizars. Then it appeared in the Alhambra for a week's run. It was inspired by the success of "A Trip to the Moon" which it resembled in plot line as Méliès decided to travel further into space.

The Telegraph thought it was "most entertaining" but the Whig critic saw it as an example of "the ingenuity of the modern photographer" and was so impressed and enthusiastic that he felt that he had to describe the plot in some detail beginning with the building of the space machine which carried "a party of gaily dressed tourists" out through space to the sun and back again. The story was typically far fetched. It involved Prof. Mabouloff (Méliès himself) from the superbly designated Institute of Incoherent Geography who leads an expedition to the sun. Firstly he builds an Automabouloff which the Whig described as racing up a mountain slope at an amazing speed only to crash and send the party to hospital where they are ministered to by charming young nurses. Undaunted, the good professor has a special steam engine and carriages constructed which does take off and steams away into space, past the planets to the sun where the adventurers survive by living in a refrigerator. After some time they return to earth in a submarine - like craft where they are greeted by cheering crowds.

The success of Méliès influenced others including his fellow Frenchman Ferdinand Zecca. Zecca had met Charles Pathe during the World Fair and had later joined the expanding Pathe organization to make films. He revealed a natural talent for the process but was never slow to take his ideas from other successful film makers like Méliès, Paul, Williamson and such, though he usually reworked their themes and added to them. In that way he made "Terrors of the Deep" and "Don Quixote." There were two versions of the latter, a short version for fairground showmen and a longer version for showing in halls. It was the latter, running for approximately thirty minutes, which was shown in Belfast. Zecca also had a more serious side and his film "La Greve" (The Strike) illustrated it. Based on a story by Zola it was a very realistic view of the results of a strike and would have had a strong appeal to working class audiences. The News Letter described it as "intelligent."

The other film in the group worthy of comment is "Uncle Tom's Cabin" which was made for Edison by Edwin S. Porter. Porter was well aware of Méliès' films, which were shown in America and, looking for a "long" subject, he turned to the stage, to a well known and well established play namely the popular "Uncle Tom's Cabin." He filmed it in fourteen theatrical tableaux with a running time of nearly fifteen minutes. Using the stage as a source was merely following a tradition whereby the theatre had often turned to prose for its subjects. As Belfast audiences knew Dion Boucicault was very skilled and successful at it, but they were well used to seeing stage presentations of novels by eminent authors like Charles Dickens, Sir Walter Scott, Alexander Dumas, Victor Hugo and other less literary writers.

The most popular play in terms of the number of times it was performed in Belfast was without doubt "Uncle Tom's Cabin." The original material was published in book form in 1852 and in January of the following year it made its first appearance on the stage of the Theatre Royal. It attracted large crowds which by itself was quite an achievement, as the Whig pointed out, in those "unhappily, unthreatrical day" when the theatre was in the doldrums. That ability to draw audiences was recognised by managers and between then and the end of 1907 the play returned at least eight times to entertain local audiences. Most of the appearances were in the Theatre Royal but it also graced the stage of St. George's Hall (October 1893) and even the Alhambra. There were variations over the years in the quality of the presentations and on one occasion the News Letter warned that it was wise to approach all slave dramas "with suspicion." But "Uncle Tom's Cabin" never lost its popularity whether it came in musical form, or with a cast which included "real" negroes and even freed slaves. The singing and dancing by the negroes were always major attractions but its main strength was perceived to be its educational and uplifting themes. During its run in December 1905 the News Letter was able to comment that it had "lost none of its charm and attractiveness" while the Whig speculated that it would "probably remain a classic even after the colour problem is forgotten." In February 1907 it was back in the Theatre Royal billed as that "world famous musical drama" and the News Letter reiterated the observation that its hold on audiences was as great as ever and added that it "has taught imperishable lessons and truths to thousands of people." So Porter knew what he was doing when he filmed it and the Edison catalogue emphasised to exhibitors the selling point that "the popularity of the book and the play of the same title is a positive guarantee of its success."

Porter didn't tamper with the story but filmed it straightforwardly in a series of theatrical tableaux. He didn't dissolve from one scene to the next but separated them with simple explanatory inter-titles, one of the earliest films to use that technique. That development wasn't mentioned locally but it must have presented a problem to those who couldn't read properly. In later reminiscences early film goers in Belfast recalled that it wasn't unusual to see a group of non - readers sitting beside someone who read out the titles for them as the film progressed, often to the annoyance of other patrons. It also meant that the days of the lecturer standing beside the screen were numbered.

An historian of the cinema examining the above list of films and taking account of the date would almost certainly be struck by the absence of "The Great Train Robbery" which was made in 1903 by Porter. It is regarded as a key film and much has been written about its impact on audiences at the time. It was slightly shorter than "Uncle Tom's Cabin" but very different in content and style. In its telling it was much more cinematic. Porter took his camera and actors to outdoor locations and even included the use of an actual train. He abandoned the reverential theatrical approach and instead used parallel and overlapping action to tell an exciting story of a hold - up by bandits, their escape, and the pursuit by a posse which catches up and kills them after a shoot out. A startling - for the time - shot of the leader of the robbers, played by George Barnes, firing his revolver directly into the audience was included and exhibitors were advised that they could show it at the beginning or the end of the film. Who said that interactive cinema was a new concept! It has often been called the first true Western though it was actually made in the East, in New Jersey. There had been a few short Western scenes filmed before, but it can certainly claim to be the first plotted Western. The Edison catalogue claimed that the details of the plot were based on actual robberies in the West and modestly described it as "the superior of any moving picture ever made." Despite its fame there is no mention of it in the local papers though that doesn't mean that it wasn't shown locally. In fact there is no direct mention of it in the Dublin papers either.

In June 1904 John Lawson appeared in the Queen's Royal Theatre in Dublin in a play called "Humanity," and one of the supporting acts was Ruffell's Bioscope which presented a series of films among which the Irish Times noted a wrestling match, the recent Royal visit and a Train Robbery. Almost certainly the latter was "The Great Train Robbery." It is interesting that in April John Lawson had presented the same play in the Palace and, if the same supporting show accompanied him, it is just possible that the film was shown as one of the Palace pictures. At least one filmgoer is on record as having a vague memory of seeing it locally in some hall or other, while a mature friend recalled for the author how, as a young lad, he had seen the shot of Georges Barnes but he couldn't remember where, though he thought it was in the Alhambra. But certainly wherever it was shown no one thought it striking or memorable enough to mention. That is quite curious when one recalls that at the time Western stories were very popular in book form and on the stage, and indeed one of the actors in the film, the then unknown G.M. Anderson, was soon to become a great cowboy favourite with Belfast audiences in the guise of Broncho Billy, though they referred to him affectionately as Andy.

Audiences were not unfamiliar with Western stories at the beginning of the century having experienced them on the local stage. The presentation of a Western melodrama like "On the Frontier" in the Theatre Royal may have offended some theatrical purists but from the point of view of the management it was good business. In fact that particular play became a great favourite with local audiences and returned to the Theatre Royal in February 1896, May 1902 and again in May 1903. At that latter showing the News Letter enthused how it combined the ingredients of "the heroic scout, the despicable renegade, the untamed Redskin, a stage Irishman, a funny Dutchman, an Indian princess, and the U.S. army, with a sprinkling of songs and dances" to produce an entertaining tale from "that golden age when bowie knives, tomahawks, and revolvers" were the norm. In March 1903 the Grand Opera House presented another Western called "Arizona" which dealt with life in a U.S. cavalry unit, while in March 1906 the Theatre Royal had "At Cripple Creek" with a hero described by the News Letter as "one of Nature's noblemen" whose role was to "protect the orphan, to shield the weak, and to aid the defenceless." Many of the Western clichés were obviously already in place before Hollywood was even heard of.

Belfast audiences were soon to succumb to the lure and excitement of the cinematic Western, the first locally recorded presentation of which was "The Life of a Cowboy" made in 1902 by Edwin S.Porter for Edison and shown on the Alhambra Bioscope in September 1906. Like the later "The Great Train Robbery" it was actually made in the New York area but audiences, unaware of that, enjoyed it as the real thing. What they had read about, and heard about, and seen on the confines of the theatrical stage was happening in a "real" sense before their very eyes. They liked what they saw. Fred Warden and others in the business were correct in suggesting that there was a large audience out there looking for inexpensive popular entertainment, but no one yet realised that the main source of that entertainment would be the cuckoo that was already in the nest in the form of the cinematograph. In the long run it would prove most effective in fulfilling Warden's aims.

CHAPTER SIX
Dancers and Clowns

In 1904 the music halls still dominated local popular entertainment. Films were becoming longer with some running for up to ten minutes or more. Méliès's "Trip to the Moon," sometimes referred to as a Voyage or Journey to the Moon, had a duration of thirteen minutes while "The Great Train Robbery" unreeled in ten minutes. Films were a daily part of the Palace programmes and a weekly event in the YMCA and the Grosvenor Hall, but overall they were still widely regarded as just another music hall act or novelty, not to be taken too seriously. They tended to be overshadowed by the main music hall personalities and acts. That was especially the case when strong competition between the Empire and the Palace manifested itself following the opening of the latter in 1904. That competition continued and became more intense over the succeeding months and years, especially when the Royal Hippodrome opened in 1907. The Palace, as its management had promised, set about luring audiences with quality acts or acts of an unusual nature, and typical of those was one of the most talked about and exciting dancers of the day, Loie Fuller, who appeared in January 1906. She was credited with the development of the Serpentine Dance in which she combined a swirling costume with coloured electric lights. She had been filmed in France (by Lumière) and the USA (by Edison) and her Butterfly Dance had been recorded in colour and slow motion to bring out its full effect. Belfast audiences were familiar with her from those celluloid appearances which, at their insistence, often had to be rewound and repeated. Other notable personalities followed including the dancers Helen Roberts (in the Hippodrome,1908), Maud Allan (in the Theatre Royal, 1909), and a well formed young lady called La Milo (in the Empire, 1906 and 1908) who specialised in Living Statuary, and stirring up controversy. The Empire provocatively advertised her as "Mrs Grundy's pet aversion," while the News Letter critic noted that she "always calls forth criticism both laudatory and otherwise, but always draws the crowds." That was, of course, the main aim.

Another major audience puller was humour and one of the most successful magnets in that vein was Fred Karno's troupes of "speechless comedians" who appeared regularly in the Empire, and sometimes in the Palace, during the first decade of the century. The arrival of the troupes with up to sixty members usually caused great excitement in the city. Karno, who was born in Exeter in 1866, became a major force in the British music hall and has since gained a reputation as an important contributor to the art of slapstick humour. He was a self made man who had come up the hard way, working in a lace factory and trying his hand at plumbing and glazing before ending up in a circus where he learned the skills of the high wire, the trapeze, clowning and mime. Having little success as a performer he moved into management and organised groups of comedians to perform on the music hall circuits. He favoured clowning and mime rather than verbal humour and wrote a series of sketches that allowed his performers room to develop and perfect their gags and other funny business. He took part in many of the sketches so it is quite possible that he visited Belfast himself. He insisted on lots of rehearsals and careful preparation to produce the maximum number of laughs. "If in doubt," he would tell his players, "fall on your backside." He became very popular with local audiences who responded enthusiastically to the anarchic, knockabout, visual humour of sketches like "Jail Birds," "Early Birds," (described as a "screaming pantomimic absurdity"), His Majesty's Guests, "(a variation on Jail Birds), "Hilarity," "Saturday to Monday," "Mumming Birds" and others. The critics praised the shows, for example the News Letter noted how well written "Saturday to Monday" was while "Early Birds," which seems to have been a skit on Dickens, was "a cleverly conceived study of some aspects of London life."

But Karno's influence went further than local music hall stages, in fact right to the Keystone and Hal Roach studios in Hollywood where a number of his comedians found acceptance and success. Most famous was Charlie Chaplin who used many of Karno's ideas in his own films, and someone called Stanley Jefferson. There is no evidence that Stanley Jefferson ever appeared in Belfast at that period (he didn't join Karno until 1909) though he did come many years later as Stan Laurel, accompanied by a large man called Oliver Hardy. Chaplin came more than once, lodging in Joy Street. He himself recalled appearing in the city in a sketch called "The Football Match" and he also trod the Empire stage in "Mumming Birds" in January 1906 playing an inebriated toff in a dress suit and a red nose. In 1910 he was one of the Karno group which went to New York for an American tour during which "The Mumming Birds" was presented as "An Evening at an English Music Hall" and his performance attracted the attention of Mack Sennett which led to a contract with Keystone Studios. Both Chaplin and Stan Laurel later acknowledged their early debt to Karno and his music hall sketches which were the launching pad that rocketed them to international fame in the cinema. But who, watching "Mumming Birds" in the Empire in early 1906 could have foreseen any of that....?

While the Palace kept one eye on the Empire it also, in late 1906, had to look sideways - like an architectural Ben Turpin - at the site between itself and the Grosvenor Road where from September a new music hall began to take shape, to be called the Royal Hippodrome. It opened on Easter Monday 4th April 1907 and it was clear that it was intended to rival the Palace in size, grandeur and style and would, like its next door neighbour, take advantage of its location with access to public transport and proximity to the Great Northern Railway. It also incorporated the latest developments in building techniques. It was built on the cantilever system which did away with the need for too many pillars so that the view of the stage was improved. In the same way the seating (for 2,700) was laid out in a diagonal pattern which improved individual viewing. Spacing between rows was slightly wider to improve movement to and from seats. The dominant colours used in the overall decoration were crimson and gold relieved with flecks of white. Above the audience the impressive dome was in gilt and around it on the ceiling were painted figures of cupids and nymphs representing music and song. The emphasis was not only on comfort but also on safety and the plans had been scrutinised and the safety measures passed by the superintendent of the fire brigade, Mr G. Smith, as "suitable and satisfactory." A special safety fireproofed curtain was installed which could be dropped to cut the stage area off from the auditorium in the case of fire, while each section of the building had two exits and it was calculated that in an emergency the whole theatre could be cleared in less than three minutes.

Of special interest was the fact that for the first time in Belfast a projection room was built into the structure at the back of the circle. The accepted procedure was to enclose the cinematograph in a metal or wooden box so that it couldn't be seen by the audience. The projection room was different in that it was part of the building (though almost outside it, as one observer noted) but was designed as a separate fireproof unit with added asbestos shutters that could close it off in case of fire. The projection equipment, called the Hipposcope, was of the latest type with a throw of over eighty feet of what the News Letter described as a "strong and steady light." The inclusion of the projection room reflected the growing importance of films in the entertainment scene in the city because as the News Letter commented, "no entertainment today is considered complete without a display of moving pictures." The animated pictures were not yet perceived as standing on their own, but only as part of a bigger show. The new music hall was welcomed by all the papers as a "splendid palace of pleasure" as the Telegraph put it. One wonders if the choice of the word "palace" was a deliberate allusion for the Warden management to contemplate. The Irish News didn't doubt that a city the size of Belfast could support another music hall, especially one whose management promised high quality acts without any hint of vulgarity, and a theatre that would be run on strictly temperance lines so that women and children would be welcome. The building may have been new but it already included some familiar elements because the resident orchestra was under the baton of a well known local musician, Edgar Haines, while the manager was H.T.Downes, again well known in the city from his recent sojourn directing the fortunes of the Alhambra.

But what of the Alhambra when all that was going on? Like the other music halls it also felt the need for change and suddenly, to everyone's surprise, in June 1906 it abandoned variety and turned to live drama. It was a risky thing to do because its traditional patrons were not widely regarded as the playgoing type. The experiment seemed to work and was applauded by the critics. The two house system was retained and the newly formed Alhambra Dramatic Company presented a series of plays which included some serious though popular works (Uncle Tom's Cabin), mixed in with comedies, Irish subjects (especially by Boucicault and Whitbread) and, above all, melodramas with names like "Mysteries of London," "Her One Great Sin," "A Woman's Honour," "The Slave of Sin" and such. But that wasn't all because the plays were accompanied in double bills by the Alhambra Bioscope which presented films every night after the live show. The films were well advertised and the names of the main films were often given. Reference has already been made to one of them "The Life of a Cowboy" (Sept. 1906), made by Porter for Edison and described by the News Letter as "excellent" and by the Irish News as "depicted in an appreciable style." Although it was regarded as a Western it was filmed, like the later "The Great Train Robbery," (d. Edwin S. Porter, 1903) in the east near New York. It proved to be the beginning of what was to become a veritable flood or, more accurately, a stampede of Westerns which local audiences were to take to their hearts. An increasing number of the Alhambra films were of American origin with names like How the Office Boy saw the Baseball Game, or, And the Villain still Pursued Her (from Vitagraph, described by the Irish News as "interesting and entertaining") and Why Jones Signed the Pledge. The latter was one of a series of popular Jones pictures made by Porter and was recommended as "well worth seeing" by the News Letter.

Also shown was "The Poacher" made by a man called Walter Haggar and released by the Gaumont company. Haggar was a travelling showman of the type familiar in Ireland at the time. He traversed South Wales with a group of actors, putting on popular plays in the villages and small towns. After buying a projector he decided in 1898 to show animated pictures instead and that in turn led him to start making his own films. He succeeded in making an arrangement with Gaumont to develop, print and distribute the completed films. The Gaumont company would become well known in Belfast and represented another example of French influence in the early film industry. Leon Gaumont, its founder, had been involved in the making and selling of electrical and optical equipment in Paris when the Lumière Bros. demonstrated their projector. Like Charles Pathe, Robert Paul and many others he saw the commercial possibilities of the new invention and soon produced his own projecting machine which gained a reputation for being both dependable and fire-proof. He also built a studio to make films and to many people's surprise appointed a young woman, Alice Guy, to run it. By 1898 he had opened an office in London where his agents were Col. Bromhead and T.A.Welsh. In 1899 they built an outdoor studio at Loughborough Junction where Arthur Collins, in charge of stage direction, made a number of films including "The Pickpocket" and "The Curfew Shall not Ring Tonight," both of which were well received in Belfast. A.R.Hogg showed a tinted version of the latter in the Assembly Hall in early April 1907 which was advertised as having a length of 740 feet, which meant it ran for over ten minutes.

The Alhambra also showed "The Haunted Hotel" which was much shorter but is of greater historical interest because it was an early example of animated film, made by J.Stuart Blackton. Watching it audiences were amazed to see the furniture and other items in the hotel move about of their own accord. Blackton had been a mover himself, having emigrated from England to America at an early age and ended up as a cartoonist and caricaturist working on a newspaper in New York. But after an interview with Edison, and a session in the Black Maria where he demonstrated his sketching skills for the camera, he became fascinated with animated pictures. In 1897 with a friend Albert E. Smith, a professional magician, he established the Vitagraph company which was to play a major role in the growth of the American film industry. Pursuing his interest in illustration he developed a single frame technique that allowed him to photograph his drawings in movement. That technique, used in "The Haunted Hotel," remained the chief tool of animators until the more recent development of computer graphics. The Alhambra also included a number of titles that may have appealed to its female patrons like "When Women Rule the World" and "A Female Spy."

By the end of 1907 films were available to Belfast audiences on a daily basis (Sundays excepted) at five venues. One of the factors that facilitated that development was the changes that were taking place in the methods of film distribution, especially the fact that films could be hired for a period rather than having to be bought outright. So, the Palace had its Palace pictures, the Hippodrome boasted the Hipposcope housed in its state of the art projection room, the Alhambra led the field in quality films with its Bioscope, the

Imperial Hippodrome in Chichester Street had its Bioscope, as did the Empire. With the exception of the Alhambra there is little information about the films shown. Most of them were short comedies, or newsreel type records of sporting, tragic or spectacular events. The Grand National and other major horse races were popular and there is mention of pictures of Vesuvius in eruption and scenes from the terrible San Francisco earthquake (Empire Bioscope, June 1906).

Now and again there were some special events, as for example in June 1907 when the Empire presented a show of sound pictures which promised "the illusion of life with wonderful realism." It was in fact Gaumont's Chronomegaphone, one of the early and better attempts to produce sound pictures by combining a projector with a gramophone record. Gaumont used an electric motor to synchronise the two machines so that the sound could be recorded at the same time as the picture was being filmed. He first unveiled the system, called a Chronophone, in 1902 but while the synchronisation was satisfactory the sound was rather weak for a large hall. He overcame that drawback by using a more powerful gramophone and it was that improved system, the Chronomegaphone, that successfully made recordings around the world and which appeared in the Empire. He also made many recordings at the studio in Loughborough Junction of music hall favourites like George Robey, Victoria Monks, Dr Walford Bodie (whose electrical experiments had amazed some but repelled others in Belfast some years before), and Harry Lauder who sang well known songs like "I Love a Lassie" and "Stop Your Tickling Jock." Those latter pictures of Harry Lauder were the ones which the Empire showed to enthusiastic audiences. While some music halls had their own projectionists the usual procedure was for the stage electrician to work the machine but as systems like the Chronomegaphone became more complex and as worries about safety continued to be voiced, the need for specially trained personnel became obvious. By the following year Erskine Mayne's chief operator, W. Hogan, could claim to hold the only certificate in Ireland for high proficiency in operating gained after studies at Northampton Polytechnic Institute. On occasion local happenings were highlighted. In June 1907 the Empire showed scenes from a "go as you please" bicycle race to Lurgan. Those same scenes were shown some time later in the Grosvenor Hall, during a happy evening, by A.R. Hogg so it is almost a certainty that he filmed them himself.

Besides those there were the autumn-winter seasons of Saturday evening shows in the religious halls. They had become a tradition led by the City Y.M.C.A. and the Grosvenor Hall, but in recent years those halls had been added to. In June 1905 the new Presbyterian Assembly Building, which included a hall that could seat 3,000 persons, was opened in Fisherwick Place. One of its declared aims was to host meetings of the young men of the Central Presbyterian Association (the C.P.A.) but there was probably some surprise in the city when, in early December, a Cinematograph Entertainment was advertised for two weeks in the main hall to be presented by the London Bioscope Company. Audiences were promised "a mile of latest films every night" which included Méliès's "A Trip to the Sun." One suspects that the waters were being tested to see how the enterprise would fare with the faithful but as it turned out the "wholesome and bright entertainment," to quote the Telegraph, proved such a success that it was retained for another week over Christmas. A decision was then taken to present weekly Saturday evening Cinematograph and Musical

Entertainments and an arrangement was made with A.R.Hogg to supply the films and a projectionist. The latter was usually Alfred George, a name that would become well known in the city during the later cinema building boom. A.R.Hogg was also responsible for the film shows in the Grosvenor Hall while Lizars continued to attend to the needs of the City Y.M.C.A. St Mary's Hall also decided to start the Saturday evening shows and to that end made an agreement with Erskine Mayne to supply the films, an arrangement that lasted for many years.

It is no exaggeration to say that by the middle of the first decade everyone in Belfast regardless of religion, age, economic status or sex, had ample opportunities to attend animated picture shows in the social environment of their choice, and all the evidence suggests that a majority of the population did just that. Regular patrons must have noticed that not only was there a greater choice of films available, but that many of those films were longer, with running times of between ten and fifteen minutes, that an increased number were narrative films, and that their plots were becoming more intricate.

A composite of shows in religious halls.

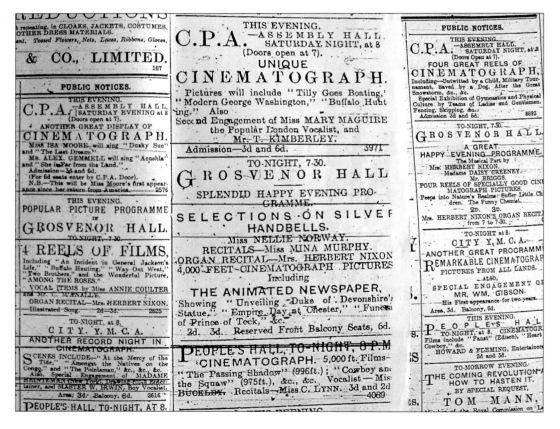

CHAPTER SEVEN
The Ire of Mrs Grundy

One of the fascinating aspects of the history of the early cinema in Belfast is the part played by the Protestant churches especially the evangelical groups. Knowing the city's reputation for religious extremism and conservatism one would suspect that their attitudes and influence would have been inimical to something as new and innovative as films but that wasn't the case. Influenced by the examples of the enthusiastic D.A. Black in the City Y.M.C.A. and the Rev. Dr. Crawford Johnson with his "happy evenings" in the Grosvenor Hall, religious groups all over the city, notably the Peoples hall in York street, the Shankill Road Mission and the east Belfast Y.M.C.A. at Mountpottinger, put on autumn/ winter shows of Animated Pictures for their parishioners and supporters which certainly played an important role in introducing the poorer elements of the population and children to the new medium. Films were seen as an acceptable extension of still photography and their projection a development from the magic lantern which those groups had been using successfully for many years in their missionary endeavours. While their entertainment value was recognised they were also seen to have an important educational aspect, not to mention a propaganda element.

The film fare presented often included scenes extolling Royalty and the class system, the army and the navy, and wars defending the Empire. In that sense they supported the status quo. The many humorous films often got their laughs at the expense of pride and vanity, feminism, the New Woman, or such targets that the churchmen readily approved of. The filmmakers for their part were usually careful in their treatment of religion which was not regarded then as a suitable topic for frivolity. During a well attended lecture on the subject of "Humour and Morals" in St. Georges Hall in May 1891 the Rev. Professor Davidson discussed the various aspects and appropriateness of humour and expressed the then contemporary politically correct view when he warned his audience that while it was unacceptable to poke fun at "sorrow or affliction" one must never use humour to "ridicule religious matters."

The short films of the day had no pretensions other than to entertain but they sometimes included unsettling undertones. Typical was "Wearie Willie in the Park." That film,which still exists, was very popular and widely shown in Belfast. The film begins with a bench in a park fully occupied by four well dressed and obviously affluent citizens. One of the men is wearing a silk hat while one of the ladies sports a large matinee hat. The mainly working class audience would have recognised them as members of the middle class who lived in the bigger and better houses of the suburbs with their bathrooms, indoor toilets, gardens, and servants.

Temperance films were very popular.

They saw them as typical of the people they worked for, or the "do-gooders" who lectured them about the need for temperance, and came to their doors with charity, welcome but at the same time resented. Willie the tramp arrived on the scene, obviously, from the others' reactions, as malodorous as the local Pound Burn. He pushed his way on to the bench so that the occupants were forced to leave one by one. The audience's sympathies were without doubt entirely on his side. When Willie finally stretched out and occupied the whole bench his victory was greeted by laughter, but its social and class implications may not have been lost on a perceptive few. Of course there is no evidence that that was the aim of the film makers and it certainly wasn't the intention of the well meaning people who presented it in local halls across the city, or in the Y.M.C.A. and Grosvenor Hall. Some of those early films about waifs, orphans, tramps and other deprived persons can now be interpreted as being quite socially subversive, but the Cinematograph itself certainly wasn't widely perceived in that light. It was continually praised in the papers as a marvellous invention which produced material which not only had the characteristics of Art – Art being defined as a true reflection of nature – but it was also a fine tool for education and science.

Not everyone approved of using such a worldly medium for religious purposes, especially one that was so closely associated with the music halls. As early as December 1897 a letter in the Whig condemned the use of animated photography by religious groups as degrading the Christian message. The "variety religious entertainments," as the writer called them with some validity, were shallow and only served "a morbid craving for excitement." Further, they tended "to drag sacred matters in the gutter." That letter reflected an exchange of views that had taken place the month before in the Telegraph, sparked off by rumours that Mr Black was about to persuade his committee to open a billiard room in the Y.M.C.A. building in Wellington Place. Mr Black was a much admired figure in the city but he discovered that the skin of tolerance in Belfast could be quite thin, as thin in fact as celluloid. An avalanche of critical letters descended upon him. One reminded him that the motto of the Y.M.C.A. was "Christ for young men and young men for Christ" not amusements for young men and young men for amusements, while another pointed out that billiards was "a contaminating Godless amusement" found on the "broad road that leads to destruction." Such people were not impressed by the argument that a billiard room would take young men off the streets. In that case, they asked, why not sell alcoholic drink also to take them out off the public houses? In defence of the Y.M.C.A. others contended that that type of link was without foundation and reversed the argument by asserting that there was no evidence, for example, that their (i.e. the Y.M.C.A.) concerts and cinematograph shows sent the young men to the Alhambra or the Empire. Back came the reply that there was no comparison because there was a very great difference between those concerts and cinematograph exhibitions and "many of the unsightly performances at the music hall." So even to some of those rather extreme critics the film shows were an acceptable form of entertainment though one suspects they perceived them as the lesser of a number of evils.

In contrast to the "unsightly performances" found in the music halls the contents of cinematograph shows must have seemed very innocent and harmless, so the religious halls not only continued to put them on but showed an increasing professionalism in their presentation. Advertisements emphasised the length of the films, four reels or 4,000 feet being the usual, about an hour of actual pictures. Competition between the downtown halls was keen so it wasn't unusual for them to publish the names of some of the films and the fact that they were "new" or "direct from London." The City Y.M.C.A. gained a reputation for the large size of its screen which according to commentators made the pictures "almost life-size." But all the shows had a similar format. They usually began with a hymn, a prayer or a few uplifting words about temperance or some similar topic. The films were shown in single reels and during reel changes the audience was entertained by a singer, a band or sometimes by exhibitions of athletics, or the whole assembly engaged in a sing-song usually illustrated by slides. On occasion singers and entertainers of the standing and quality of John McCormick and Cathal O'Byrne appeared.

As the entertainments became more organised, films were often grouped around a theme. In early December 1909 the Grosvenor Hall presented a special military night with the band of the First Battalion, the Cheshire regiment, and films that included "Invasion and its Possibilities," "Two Sergeants," and "Raised from the Ranks," with the promise of "stirring military exploits." Not to be outdone the City Y.M.C.A. had a special navy night the same evening which they called "Round the World under the Union Jack" with films including "Warships in Action" and "A Man Without a Country" but with an added extra attraction in the person of Cathal O'Byrne. The following week (18th December 1909) the C.P.A. in the Assembly Hall presented four reels of "Grand Cinematograph" which included a 700 feet version of incidents from the life of Charlotte Corday and what the Whig called "a fine American film called Shanghaied." Between the reels the audience was entertained by a recently formed group from Armagh called the O'Neill Pipers. They played the Uilean pipes, dressed in full Gaelic costumes and gave a selection of Irish music which consisted of old airs, marches and laments. Such was the enthusiasm of the listeners that they had to play many encores. At the end of the evening Francis Joseph Bigger thanked the audience for their warm welcome and presented the chairman with a Gaelic brooch similar to those worn by the musicians. It is interesting how an essentially Protestant audience responded so positively and warmly to Gaelic culture, reflecting conditions before the divisive bitterness of the Home Rule controversy.

Another typical evening on the last Saturday of the same year in the Assembly Hall is described in the Whig. Again, the hall was crowded. The proceedings were presided over by the Rev. Alexander Gallagher the minister of Fountainville Church, who introduced the evening with a short speech. A selection of light airs was then played on the Cuthbert organ by F.J.Moffett, who appeared regularly at the shows and often played suitable music to accompany the films. Alfred George had the projector ready and began the first of four reels. During reel changes there were sing-songs including a rendering of "The Old Folks at Home," illustrated by slides sent back from Philadelphia by a former member of the C.P.A.

A wide range of films was shown over those years but they can be grouped into comedies, Westerns which were very popular, detective stories, "pathetic" tales of orphans, widows or girls in jeopardy, documentaries and news items or "topicals" as they were often called. Most of them are now lost and indeed most were eminently forgettable as they were quickly made, often crude in technique, with acting (closer to mime) and make-up that would be regarded today as laughable. But the audiences loved them not only as entertainment but also as a source of information and even education. On February 5 1910, for example, the Y.M.C.A. announced that "the committee have succeeded in securing Cinematograph pictures of the AWFUL PARIS FLOODS." During the week the newspapers had been reporting the damage caused in the French capital as a result of the rise and flooding by the river Seine. To an audience, very few of whom had any experience of travel, such pictures thrown "life size" on the Y.M.C.A.'s special large screen, must have been real eye openers. A few weeks later the Grosvenor Hall showed "a vivid picture of King Edward opening Parliament" and as it filled the screen a James Dann set the mood by singing the National Anthem.

The documentaries were also well received and were often mentioned in positive terms in the newspaper reports. On the same evening that the king was on view in the Grosvenor Hall the C.P.A. presented "Wild Birds in their Haunts" which the Whig described as "beautiful and instructive." Accompanying it was "Naval Gun Drill" and a colour film from Yokohama celebrating a local jubilee. Other evenings included colour films of Denmark, and of the Pyrenees, while the crowd responded to "startling" pictures of Italian artillery crossing the Alps. Some of the films had a morally uplifting message. During a special American night in the City Y.M.C.A. in Dec. 1909 a typical message film was included called "What Drink Did" with its obvious warnings about the dangers of drinking. Such temperance films were widely shown and were gently satirised much later in a charming Doris Day musical called "On Moonlight Bay" (1951, d. Roy Del Ruth) while the subject was treated much more seriously in the Oscar winning "The Lost Weekend" (1945, d. Billy Wilder) and "Days of Wine and Roses" (1962, d. Blake Edwards).

Much has been rightly written about the qualities of the latter films but relatively few people have paid much attention to "What Drink Did." Yet it has a certain significance in that it was directed by a new talent, D.W.Griffith, who would go on to have a major impact on film making not only in the U.S.A. but across the world. Griffith, from Kentucky, a stage actor who hoped to become a playwright, joined the Biograph company in New York in 1908 attracted mainly by the five dollars a day paid to the actors. Within a short time he was directing one reelers. His first film was "The Adventures of Dollie," 700 feet long, the twelve scenes of which were filmed in two days which gives an idea of the speed with which films were turned out then. In 1908 alone he made sixty two such films and during the following year one hundred and forty three, including "What Drink Did," which was 913 feet long and described in the studio catalogue as a "temperance drama."

Temperance films were generally welcomed in Belfast and taken seriously. The need for temperance was a burning topic much discussed during the late nineteenth and early twentieth centuries. At a temperance mission in the Grosvenor Hall in April 1902 a speaker claimed that "it was impossible to draw an exaggerated picture of the ruin brought by strong drink, the great curse that lay like a foul blot upon 19th century civilisation." There were many in Belfast who agreed with those sentiments though they might have expressed themselves differently. During a lecture on "Temperance and Educated Women" Mrs Byers, the noted local educationalist and the founder of Victoria College, who had direct experience of the problem in her charitable work among the poor, expressed the belief that drunkenness was the main cause of "desolation, distress, impurity and impiety" among the working classes. A writer in the Telegraph, discussing the matter, pointed out that Christians of all denominations in Ireland were united in recognising the curse of intemperance in the country and were all working together for its eradication. There was widespread admiration in the city for the Catholic Pioneer Association and the Protestant Abstinence Union or Catch my Pal movement as it was called, and some observers felt that films like "What Drink Did" underpinned the work they were doing.

Of some historical interest is the fact that when Griffith was making the film (one of many temperance pictures he made) Mary Pickford, a young stage actress, arrived at the Biograph building at 11, East Fourteenth Street in New York to inquire about acting in films. She met Griffith who immediately gave her a trial walk - on part in the film. Unfortunately the scene was cut from the final released print, but it was her first contact with the film camera. Lest one think that such warnings were directed only at the poorer workers it is interesting to note that during the following week the Theatre Royal presented a play with the stark title "Drink" based on Emile Zola's "L'Assomoir" which dealt with the same problem though on a higher plane. The artistic gulf between Griffith's work and the play is reflected in the level of attention given to both. The film was just mentioned briefly in dispatches but the play was treated to a detailed critical analysis. The Whig was very impressed with how the audience was introduced to "the eminent French realist's picture of the misery and degradation caused by alcoholic excess." On the stage, he remarked, the "drunkard's gradual descent into a state of wretched demoralisation, and moral and physical ruin" is depicted with grim realism. He probably, however, would have found the realism of "The Lost Weekend" too much to accept.

The Saturday evening shows were a great success in attracting audiences. The reports often mention the fact that the halls were packed and when artistes of high calibre like John McCormack appeared large numbers were turned away. Actual figures are difficult to come by but the C.P.A. in January 1908 announced that over 40,000 people had bought tickets to see their shows that season over a period of about twelve weeks, which is very impressive and indicates the high level of popular support. The shows became important sources of income which usually went towards helping the poor, other charitable works, or helping to pay off the building debts on the halls. The City Hall officials were so impressed by their level of success that they decided that the halls should pay rates like any other entertainment centre, so in January 1911 they sent the Grosvenor Hall a rating demand for £18. 15d to cover the year 1909 to 1910. The trustees were taken aback because buildings "erected and used for public worship" were, according to the Borough Act of 1845, exempt from normal rate charges. The other religious halls watched closely as the Corporation took the matter to law and argued that the hall was often let for other purposes like cinematograph entertainments and organ recitals. The defence argued that the hall was still used primarily for religious purposes and, while admitting that it was also fully licensed for entertainments and cinematograph shows, pointed out that the act did not say that the use should be "exclusively" religious. The Corporation lawyer commented with some sarcasm that General Booth, the founder of the Salvation Army, had recently hired the Royal Hippodrome for a service but no one suggested that that establishment should now be exempted from rates. After a few weeks of deliberation the judge decided in favour of the Grosvenor Hall. The Corporation then appealed the case to the King's Bench in Dublin where the decision again went in favour of the Grosvenor Hall, so the Saturday evenings could be really "happy" again.

The halls had overcome that financial hurdle – the Grosvenor Hall management would probably have disapproved of this racing analogy – but in the professional entertainment scene developments were already taking place which would in time make their film shows redundant. The Picture Palaces were about to make an appearance in Belfast.

CHAPTER EIGHT
Paddling in Holy Waters

1908 was in many ways a seminal year for the infant cinema industry in Belfast because during it decisions were taken which had significant implications for it and for the future general entertainment scene in the city. The Warden management was faced with a decline in audience numbers and in income. The decision to reinvent the Opera House as a music hall and to concentrate serious plays in the historic Theatre Royal in 1904 had seemed a good idea at the time and for a period paid positive financial dividends. Indeed 1906 proved to be one of the best years financially ever in the company's history but by 1908 income had plummeted by nearly half to below the three thousand pound mark. The company publicly put the decrease down to the effects of local strikes and other economic factors that had temporarily reduced their audiences' spending power, plus competition from a new craze, American roller skating, that had swept the city. But they knew that those were only part of the problem and that the main cause was the successful competition from their next door neighbour, the Royal Hippodrome which had opened its doors in April 1907.

Both theatres had much in common. They were modern buildings with up-to-date stage technology specially designed to cope with the needs of the best of visiting groups and companies. They both demonstrated comparable high levels of comfort and audience safety and tended to draw their patrons from the same social and economic groups. Being side by side they were also equally well situated to take advantage of transport systems, either local trams which passed their doors, or the nearby Great Northern Railway which gave access to an out of town hinterland. Their close proximity also meant that audiences were able to engage in comparative shopping before choosing and it would seem that the Hippodrome was coming off better in that field. The Warden management came to the conclusion that Belfast could not realistically support two first class music halls, while at the same time they recognised that the stage of the Theatre Royal was too small to cope with the improved scenic and other requirements of large touring companies and as a result Belfast was missing out on many of the biggest shows from London.

An indication of the direction of their thinking was revealed in June 1908 when Madame Sarah Bernhardt made her fourth flying visit to the city and appeared with her company from the S.B. Theatre in Paris, not in her familiar venue the Theatre Royal, but in the Palace. The play was, again, "La Dame aux Camelias" but the turnout was large and the welcome was warm - hearted. The News Letter found her "as ever Sarah, the divine, the incomparable" whose marvellous voice thrilled the audience and who overpowered them with her moving death scene. It can be added in passing that that performance was the nearest she ever came to appearing in the Opera House. The Warden management bowed gracefully towards the Royal Hippodrome, referring to it as "no longer a rival or competitor," and in February 1909 reinstated the Grand Opera House with the promise that it would be run as a "first class theatre" and that, in association with the Theatre Royal in Dublin, the best of the London touring companies would be presented.

The demise of the Palace, of course, meant that the Palace Pictures disappeared though the fact that the projector was dimmed didn't mean that the Opera House was finished entirely with films. Over the next few years it was to present some exciting and even quite controversial celluloid. It is difficult to fathom the attitude of the Warden management to the animated pictures of the day. One suspects that they held the general theatrical view that they were artistically less worthy, less interesting and less important than legitimate theatre, though by way of compensation they were cheaper to put on and could attract large audiences and income. Thus there was a reluctance to abandon films completely, a reluctance that also extended to high quality music hall acts. That could explain how, a few months after the changeover, Warden announced the appearance of the internationally famed dancer Maud Allan, "the sensation of London," for three nights in the Theatre Royal at special prices, performing her "Vision of Salome." The turn of the century had coincided with a spectacular interest in the Biblical character Salome in artistic circles. She became the subject of plays (notably Oscar Wilde's one act "Salome"), paintings, operas and stage shows. In 1906 Maud Allan staged her own exotic and erotic dance interpretation which did much to popularise and spread Salomania across Europe. Helen Roberts had already brought a hint of its excitement to Belfast but that visit was only a taster of the real thing.

Miss Allan arrived in Belfast from Leeds with her parents and settled into the Avenue Hotel where, despite the fatigue of her journey, she granted an interview to a reporter from the Telegraph. She seems to have had a golden tongue and completely charmed the gentleman in question. She was a Canadian but she claimed that her mother was Irish, her maiden name being McKee, and that after performing in Dublin and Cork she and her parents were going to do the sights starting in Killarney. With regard to her act, she discussed the classical influences on her dancing but indicated her fundamental modernity by emphasising that she didn't follow any set pattern of steps because her movements sprang from "the feeling of the moment" and were "essentially inspirational and emotional." She explained that she responded instinctively to the music which she described as "soul expression" adding that the deepest human feelings were best expressed by actions rather than being "clothed in words." The question of her recent problems with local censors in England came up but she strongly refuted the suggestions that her dancing was scandalous in any way. She refused, she emphasised, to cut any part of her performance.

Her performance consisted of a number of dances based on Greig's Peer Gynt Suite, Chopin's Valse in A Major and the Mazurka in G Sharp all of which were "delightful" (News Letter), but, as the Telegraph pointed out, the Salome Dance was the main attraction. The curtain opened to great anticipation, revealing the stage decorated in an Oriental setting with dominant green tints and lit by torches attached to a series of pillars. Miss Allan appeared in her costume of veils and pearls, swaying, according to the Telegraph, in a sinuous and graceful dance which reflected the thoughts passing through Salome's mind. Those slow movements gave way to "impassioned frenzy" which in turn became "sensuous reflection" until the dancer seemed to "swoon under her own thoughts." The Whig described how she yielded to the exciting music "spinning, jumping, arms waving then collapsing." The News Letter found the whole presentation very dramatic, the dancing full of "passion and fire," all enhanced by the "charm and poetry of her movements." The critics all agreed that there was nothing offensive in her presentation though the Whig did mention that within the dance she "relived the murder with a dreadful vision of John the Baptist" which suggests that the severed and bloodied papier mache head did make an appearance. The critics certainly were suitably impressed and described her and her act in glowing terms ranging from "a great creative artiste" whose performance "stirred the imagination" (Telegraph), "a genuine triumph," (Whig), to "a dainty and captivating lady...... far superior to any who have imitated her" (News Letter). Audiences agreed and showed their appreciation by filling the theatre on the three evenings she appeared and giving her a "cordial and hearty reception" (News Letter) before she departed for Dublin, leaving behind memories and arguments.

Like other cultural fashions of its type Salomania faded as quickly as it had arisen and was finally overwhelmed by the outbreak of war in 1914. As people lost interest, so Miss Allan's career declined. She moved to California and, described as "the international danseuse," appeared in a film called "The Rugmaker's Daughter" (1915), described as a romance of two continents in which she played an Eastern dancer who falls in love with a visiting American. There is no record of it showing in Belfast and like many silent films it has disappeared which is a pity as it would have given modern students an idea of the true quality of her dancing. Later, ruined by scandal, she retired from public life and finally died in 1956 in poverty, forgotten. However, echoes of and variations on her Salome dance can be found down the years in silent and sound films. In 1918 Theda Bara played Salome as a Wildean temptress and performed a dance which prompted the News Letter critic, when discussing the film, to recall Miss Allan's local stage presentation. In 1922 Alla Nazimova produced, acted and danced in a version closely based on Oscar Wilde's play, with visuals influenced by Aubrey Beardsley's drawings. Rita Hayworth, a dancer of some ability, played the part in Salome (1953, d. William Dieterle) with a storyline that suggested rather unconvincingly that she was duped by her mother and that she really wanted to save the Baptist. Her dance was elaborate but essentially decorous because of censorship pressures. Ken Russell also had his say with his 1988 version called "Salome's Last Dance," a typically outrageous take supposedly on Wilde's writing of his play.

Miss Allan's comments on her art are interesting and while not wanting to read too much into her words, because she was speaking only of the dance, the implications of a performance revealing emotions essentially by movement, reinforced by music, could be applied in some measure to the emerging silent film, and implies at least the existence of a cultural and intellectual environment that could accommodate such a concept. The other basic elements of film, namely acting and plot development were, of course, already familiar through the theatre. It was hardly such theoretical concerns which drew the large audiences to popular performers like Maud Allan, Helen Roberts, La Milo and others, but while the managers delighted in putting up the House Full signs others complained that serious theatre was ill supported in the city. Typical was a letter writer in the Irish News who noted that any performance depending upon "the gyrations of semi - dressed females on the stage" attracted large crowds of those "ladies and gentlemen who can afford to patronise the higher paid parts of the house," armed with their "most powerful opera glasses." At such times he "trembled" for the safety of the dress circle. His plea to them was to show similar support for more substantial fare like the Ulster Literary Theatre (founded in 1902 to encourage local drama) which he observed always got its main support from the cheaper seats.

All the local critics had given a warm and positive welcome to the Ulster Literary Theatre and commented how pleasant it was to hear local speech on the stage, its naturalness contrasting with the often stilted delivery of some visiting actors. The Whig, however, pointed out that because a piece was good literature it wasn't necessarily good drama or, as the editor put it "when literature comes in the door, drama goes out the window." He felt that in a play - read "film" today - the literary and dramatic elements are as hard to blend as "oil and water." He suggested that the Ulster Literary Theatre drop the term "literary" because "to those who care for real drama it has an affected ring; to those who merely ask for something they can enjoy it acts as a positive deterrent; and in any case it is quite superfluous." Whatever the merits of that argument it is interesting that some individuals involved in the making of films, especially in France, were thinking along the opposite lines: namely that films needed to appear more serious and indeed literary in their subject - matter so as to appeal to a wider and more educated audience, a process that led to the production of the so called Films d'Art which were to become so popular in the city later. The key to success in both cases, both on stage or screen, was seen to be the ability to attract larger audiences.

In the midst of the arguments and doubts there was a group of businessmen who still had faith in the Belfast public and who believed there was a large enough audience there to support another theatre in the city. They got together in 1908 and raised £5,500 with the aim of building one in East Belfast, a populous working class area where none existed. They were interested in a site in Ballymacarrett at the corner of Station Street and Scrabo Street but it proved to be unsuitable so they turned their attention to the west of the Lagan and secured a large site at the corner of the Grosvenor Road and Durham Street on the Sandy Row side, relatively close to the Grand Opera House and the Royal Hippodrome. The plans for the Alexandra Theatre Co., as their group was called, were presented to the City Hall for approval and, after a delay until a Bioscope Box, as it was referred to, was included in the drawing, they were accepted and passed in January 1910. Thus during the last months of 1910 a new building began to take shape on the site, to be called the Alexandra Theatre, which in time would evolve into the Coliseum Cinema.

The decision in 1908 to build a new legitimate theatre was seen by many as a brave one because what seemed more obvious by then was that it was animated pictures that could attract larger audiences. As evidence of that, by October of that year there were three halls specialising in presenting them, the Alhambra, St. George's Hall and the Star Theatre of Varieties. The question naturally arises as to which of those can be described as the first local picture palace. Well, it depends on what is meant by a picture palace. If it means a distinctive building, specially designed and constructed for projecting films in surroundings of comfort, then neither the Alhambra, or St. George's Hall would qualify because neither had been built specially for the purpose of showing films, and even nostalgia cannot obscure the fact that the levels of comfort in both, while part of their charm, were rather basic and couldn't compare for example with other contemporary music halls like the Empire or the Royal Hippodrome. But at the same time it cannot be denied that the Alhambra and St. George's Hall were the first venues to present film shows on a regular weekly basis and that they were referred to by the local papers as picture palaces and accepted as such by the general population. In the contest however the Alhambra, described affectionately by the Irish News as "Ireland's Premier Picture Palace," must be given pride of place. Both halls were Victorian in origin and were in existence many years before the arrival of animated pictures, though the Alhambra (1872) predated its rival by about ten years.

The Alhambra had been built as a music hall and had the distinction - already noted - of being the first venue (in August 1896) to show films to a paying audience in the city. Since then it had under various managements maintained a connection, sometimes tenuous, with the new medium. Over the years the hall was periodically redecorated, repainted, and altered with the addition of new exits, and new seating to keep up with changing demands and safety requirements, but like some ageing celebrity it retained its magnetism and the affections of its mainly working class audiences. Even when it abandoned its traditional music hall format in June 1906 and introduced a period of popular plays and melodramas it kept its connection with animated pictures. During that time the Bioscope was given equal prominence with the plays and the main films were usually named. The Alhambra actually initiated the practice of advertising its weekly films by name in the local papers. That experiment lasted until February 1908 and then after a short closure it reopened on 9th March under a new manager, Will White, as a picture palace/ music hall. Audiences were promised a novel form of entertainment entirely new to Belfast and were reminded that the Alhambra was "copied by many, (but) excelled by none."

Will White, manager of the Alhambra and founder of the White Cinema Club. Source: Ireland's Saturday Night.

The new entertainment was a combination of films and live acts, which may seem old hat except that the traditional music hall order was reversed. The live acts were much reduced in number and the main emphasis was on the Famous Filmograph (with "miles and miles of new creations") which occupied not only the top of the bill but most of the fare also. The films, usually nine or ten in number, were supplied by a new distribution group called Films Ltd., a firm of "practical electricians and cinematograph specialists" (News Letter) with offices in Liverpool, which had recently opened an office in High Street managed by John Y. Moore a man who was to become an important player in the local growing cinema industry. The two house system, introduced to Belfast by the same theatre was retained along with popular prices of 2d, 4d and 6d. Music for the films was supplied by the resident orchestra under the baton of P.H.Boyle. A typical programme presented a few weeks after the changeover, which drew packed houses, consisted of a local film showing the final of the Charity Cup played the week before between Cliftonville and Linfield. The News Letter critic congratulated the cameraman, who despite poor light conditions, had managed to get pictures that were clear enough to easily make out the play and the players. It was an exciting interactive occasion with the audience applauding and shouting comments like "foul" and "offside," and probably other comments that couldn't be printed. Accompanying it was a group of narrative films which included "Christmas Eve" a film about a faithless lover which contained a "sensational scene" of a horse and cart falling over a precipice; Will He Overtake Them (no programme was complete without a comedy); Father's Lesson (another comedy - comedies usually arrived on split reels, that is two short comedies to

Film's Ltd an early major film distributor, managed by John Yeats Moore.

a reel); What a Razor can Do; A Corsican's Revenge; The Bond; and the Pneumatic Policeman. In all a relaxing mixture of thrills and laughs without any pretensions.

Mention was made above of the manager of Films Ltd. John Yeats Moore was a cousin of the poet W.B.Yeats but his importance lies not in literature but in being one of the pioneers of the cinema industry in Belfast. He was born in 1881 and became an apprentice in the firm of George Combe and Co. in Castle Lane where he studied electrical engineering. His work, installing lighting systems, took him to Britain where he worked on several theatres, including the London Coliseum. Like other electricians - notably Michael Curran - his knowledge of lighting led him to become interested in the new expanding cinema business. He even worked for a few years as a projectionist in Liverpool. From there he joined Films Ltd. and returned to Belfast to manage their new office. He soon became a well known figure driving around supplying films to the increasing number of venues requiring them. His ambition grew to own the Alhambra which he achieved later, and with Ferris Pounds went on to put together the group of cinemas known as Irish Theatres Ltd. But that lay in the future.

On August 17th, only five months after the launch of its new programme format the Alhambra faced real competition with the opening (strictly speaking, the re-opening) of St. George's Hall in High Street. St. George's, which had been opened in 1881, was a typical Victorian hall, 70 feet (22m) by 50 feet (16m)with a wrap around balcony located on the first floor of a multi - functional building just opposite Bridge Street, though a building that had the distinction of having been designed by Thomas Jackson who was also responsible for many fine buildings around Belfast including St. Malachy's Church in Alfred Street, the old Museum in College Sq. North and the Music Hall in May Street. During the last quarter of the nineteenth century the hall had been used for religious meetings, or lectures and had also presented magic lantern shows, panoramas, dioramas, the new phonograph and even popular plays. But it suffered from inadequate heating, uncertain acoustics, and the fact that it was difficult to see the stage from the back seats. In April 1894 the Whig had commented that "it had never been a complete success as a public assembly room" and added that it was closing and would be converted to a restaurant. A few months later it opened as a temperance eating house with a French chef, and so it remained until 1908 when a local company called Entertainments Ltd. took it over, remodelled it and presented it to the populace as "the family resort for first class entertainment" with a promise of music hall acts and Electric animated pictures. The early aims were definitely up market as reflected in the seat prices of 1/6, 1/-, and 6 pence (sixpence was the dearest seat in the Alhambra at that time), and the presence of a full orchestra under the baton of Fred Bathurst. The immediate response was one of immense excitement and anticipation: on the opening night the hall was packed long before the show was timed to begin.

The proceedings opened with the National Anthem followed by a few words from the manager, George Wilson, who in terms echoing the former Victorian showmen, promised that he would provide the public of Belfast with "high class, sound moral entertainments."

The star of the evening, Vernon Harcourt, was then called upon. He began a serious poetry reading which did not go down well with the gallery which remained quite noisy until the hall was darkened for the film show. There were about a dozen pictures, a mixture of documentaries, topicals but mainly fiction stories, including titles like the Dieppe Motor Race 1908, Tyrolean Customs and Manners, The Sleeping Beauty and, the hit of the evening, Blue Beard. Méliès had made a version of Bluebeard in 1901 but it is more likely that the one shown was a more recent production made by Gaumont in 1907, a film that had gained some little notoriety when earlier audiences complained of its "cruelty" so that it was withdrawn and modified. The projector used was the latest type and all the commentators admired the clarity of the pictures and the lack of quiver which may have been due to the fact that it was driven by an electric motor which eliminated the variations caused by manual cranking. Safety was a major concern and the apparatus was enclosed in a fire proof casing of iron and had a built-in automatic cut-off in the case of fire. The electrics were installed by a local firm that was to become a major player in the cinema business in Belfast, the Curran Brothers, and reflected their competence and professional skills. A special feature was that the lights were all controlled from the projection box, which meant that when the films ended the projectionist was able to bring the house lights on immediately so that, as the News Letter put it, "there was no period of darkness to doubt the audience." The remodelled hall had a seating capacity of 1,500 and new exits had been constructed to cope with the crowds in an emergency. The floor was still flat but commentators said that viewing was good from all parts, while the Telegraph made special mention of the clarity of the acoustics.

But despite the improvements and the promises, the undertaking was not an immediate success and after an early rush numbers fell off. Within two weeks the Alhambra model of two houses and low prices was adopted with charges being reduced to 3d, 6d and one shilling. Over the next few months other steps were taken to reduce costs notably the replacement of the orchestra with a pianist, Miss Renee Baker, and the appointment of a new experienced manager, Herbert Rogers. Mr Rogers accepted the Alhambra model but added two important extras, a gimmick and a determined effort to present films of quality. The gimmick was the Filmophone which was advertised as "talking and singing pictures." It first appeared at the end of March 1909 and became a regular and very popular attraction with the patrons. It was the latest system to use a recording by a well known singer or personality linked to an animated picture which illustrated the words of the song. The singer didn't appear on screen so the problem of precise synchronisation was reduced. On the first evening John Harrison and Robt. Radford sang "Excelsior" while the film showed scenes of wild Alpine scenery. It was followed by "the Galloping Major" and then, in complete contrast, a taste of Christmas with "While Shepherds Watch their Sheep by Night."

A great variety of contrasting music and song was presented in that form over the following months and a sample of the titles, which included an Apache Dance, "Oh oh Antonio," "Put me among the Girls," "I'm off to Philadelphia in the Morning," and "When Father was taken Away," gives a flavour of what audiences enjoyed and often sang along with. The singing pictures were used as a replacement for the music hall acts, which were temporarily dropped, though Mr Rogers cast all types of other lures to attract more people in the form of amateur singing contests, a competition for the best essay praising St George's Hall and he even went as far as putting an illuminated frame around the screen to "enhance the picture" as the Whig put it. He also introduced special matinee performances in the afternoon for the convenience of parents who wished to bring their children, and the Whig encouraged them to avail of the opportunity because of the "valuable instruction" in history and geography that many of the films contained. It is not clear which company Mr Rogers dealt with. Films Ltd, the new company which supplied the Alhambra, had their office on the ground floor of the same building within which St George's Hall was located and it is difficult to believe that such an aggressive new group would not have made approaches to him. The local suppliers were certainly feeling the impact of their competition, for example by the beginning of 1912 Films Ltd. had replaced A.R.Hogg as the film supplier to both the Grosvenor Hall and the Assembly Hall so that he was able to advertise that he was "free for other engagements in city or country using his own complete electrical or oxy-hydrogen apparatus." Also there is the fact that in the early weeks the Hall often showed films that had already appeared in the Alhambra suggesting a common distribution source. On the other hand there are also indications that Mr Rogers got some of his films directly from Dublin.

Whatever the source St. George's Hall began to show "quality" films based on plays or eminent novels associated with names like Shakespeare, Dumas, Hugo and others, acted by trained theatre personnel, often coloured and advertised as being shown here for the first time. The idea had flowered in France, where the Film d'Art Company was established in February 1908, and quickly spread to other European countries and then to America. Seen today the films are serious in intent, beautifully mounted and carefully made, but they are also just photographed stage plays with exaggerated stage acting which overall did nothing for the art or craft of cinema. At the time they caused a sensation and achieved their chief aims which were to raise the cultural stature of films and to make them attractive to a more educated and sophisticated audience. Mr Rogers obviously had a knowledge of Film d'Art and knew what was going on, and he also had sympathy with their aims. Above all he realised that the middle class represented a large and potential source of income if that market could be tapped.

The French films were generally welcomed by the local commentators who seemed quite impressed by the quality of what they saw. Among the earliest shown was "The Lady of Monsoreau," based on a story taken from Dumas. On seeing it the Whig critic commented that "those who still prefer to look down on cinematograph shows would speedily change their opinions if they could be persuaded" to see this film. "The Persecution of the Huguenots" was appreciated as "outstanding" and "seldom been equalled locally" while the "Lady with the Camelias" long associated with Sarah Bernhardt (though she wasn't in that version) was described as "superb" and the Whig made special mention of its glowing colours. It was shown just after Christmas 1909 when it drew extra large crowds with many people turned away from full houses. During comments on "The Fear" in July 1909 an important development took place in local reporting when for the first time ever in Belfast the main actor was named, representing a break with the normal cloak of anonymity surrounding the cast and makers of films. It was the Telegraph which praised the acting of the main player, M. Henri Desfontaines, a member of the Odeon Theatre in Paris. It is doubtful if that information meant much to the majority of the people who turned off High Street and climbed the wide staircase to the Hall, but it may have impressed some more serious - minded readers and encouraged them to sample the new medium. M. Desfontaines made a number of art films for a company called Eclipse and later became an important director for the same company.

Information about the films shown was given to the critics by the management. It consisted mainly of brief comments and summaries of the films taken from the official catalogues of the companies which released them. The comments that appeared in the papers were hardly detailed criticisms and more often consisted merely of plots summaries from the hand - outs with a few general words of praise or otherwise added. But increasingly the writers drew attention to certain aspects of the productions. In early January 1910 St. George's Hall presented another Art film "The Red Domino" dealing with European court life. It impressed the Whig critic with its fine acting and its visually beautiful tinted sequences, but above all with the complexity and detail of its plot. He praised the versatility of the film makers and the ingenuity of their plots before adding that some writers of fiction "must be gnashing their teeth when they see how the cinematograph is beating them at their own game." The following month the film highlighted was "The White Slave" which he described as "a charming Greek idyll of singular poetic and artistic charm." On the same programme he also drew special attention to a film showing the athlete Annette Kellerman demonstrating her skills. That was an American production made by the Vitagraph company and his comments represent only the second time an actual performer was mentioned by name. "The White Slave" was a major production from Nordisk, a company located in Copenhagen, and represented the vanguard of a series of distinctive Danish films which were to reach local screens over the following years. The logo of the company which consisted of a polar bear sitting astride the earth became a familiar and welcome indicator of quality entertainment.

Another source which Mr Rogers turned to was the increasing number of Italian films which were becoming available, films that proved to be very popular with his audiences. "The Last Days of Pompeii" which had been made by Luigi Maggi in Turin was presented in April '09 and its spectacular scenes gave some idea of the epics that would follow from Italian studios in the coming years. In direct contrast more serious fare also appeared like "Horrors of a Strike" six months later. As the name suggested it dealt with the effects of a clash between labour and capital. The Whig critic recommended it for its realism, and recalled that Belfast still had vivid memories of past strikes.

Films were also tending to become longer at the time. Instead of a brief few minutes an increasing number were one reelers and nearly every programme had one of those, running up to fifteen minutes on screen. Some were even longer. In May 1909 "The Three Musketeers" was described by the Telegraph as "one of the longest films exhibited, full of exciting incidents," while the Whig was impressed by its "vivid glimpses of French life in those days." It was an Italian production directed by Mario Caserini "in thirty tableaux" which indicated that it was a two reeler. The usual procedure was to show the reels on consecutive weeks or sometimes consecutive days, but Mr Rogers decided to present the two reels together, a thirty minute showing which must have really excited and impressed the audiences. The only other "long" films presented before then had been a few boxing contests. The following month he showed another two reeler "Napoleon, Man of Destiny" but divided it over two weeks with one reel each week. Made in 1906 it had William Humphreys as Napoleon and Julia Swayne Gordon as Josephine and stills from it reveal superior decor and costumes. It was actually made in New York by J.Stuart Blackton at Vitagraph, a company which was building a reputation for quality films, not least a series of one reel films based on Shakespeare, which it released during 1908 - 9. Many of those turned up in St. George's Hall. The first was "Romeo and Juliet" presented in Feb. 1909, the exteriors of which were filmed in Central Park, standing in for Italy. The film is interesting in that Juliet was played by Florence Lawrence who was to become well known later to Belfast filmgoers as "The Biograph Girl," while Romeo was played by an actor called Paul Panzer who would became equally familiar as a villain to be hissed at in "The Perils of Pauline." It was followed three months later by "Antony and Cleopatra" which the Whig found "full of vitality and artistic beauty" while the Telegraph noted it was "somewhat above the average and certainly worth seeing." It was so successful that it returned a few months later for another week long presentation. Then, at the end of the year, "Julius Caesar" was presented in colour with, in the words of the Whig, "elaborate stage settings and fine costumes."

Of course Mr Rogers didn't spend all his screen time educating and introducing his audiences to serious works. They would soon have baulked at that. He also showed a supporting mix of comedies, thrillers, Westerns and topicals which included football matches, local and national, and major horse races like the Grand National and the Derby. Among them were some films of special interest like "Fireside Reminiscences" (Edison, 1908) which the Whig commended for "its fine colouring and great beauty" the effect of which was greatly increased by the use of the illuminated frame around the screen mentioned above. It was actually one of the earliest films to use brief intertitles to explain the plot - which concerned an overbearing husband who quarrelled with his wife and in his anger put her out of the house. He then sat down at the fire where he began to regret his action as the flames dissolved into flashbacks of incidents from their earlier and more pleasant life. The outcome was that they were brought back together again to the general approval, it must be said, of the audience. It obviously played well for both critics and audiences but no one mentioned the use of the intertitles suggesting maybe that film historians have a different perception of what was important from that of the audiences of the period.

Another film of note was "1776 or the Hessian Renegades" which related an incident from the American War of Independence. It was made by D.W.Griffith at Biograph and reflected his interest in American history. The heroine, still anonymous of course to the audiences, was Mary Pickford who was soon to become a great favourite of those same audiences. While regular filmgoers couldn't yet put names on the actors and actresses they were becoming familiar with certain faces which reappeared frequently and were naturally curious about them. It wouldn't be long until audiences began to demand to know who exactly they were.

Will White, the manager of the Alhambra, always resplendent in his shiny black top hat and fiercely waxed moustache, was equally experienced, and had his own game plan. He saw to it that the building was continually improved by way of new exits and other fire safety additions until it was given a full cinema licence on the 17th November 1910. He also knew his audience and what they wanted so he gave them an entertaining mixture of comedies, Westerns, dramas, melodramas, thrillers and of course boxing matches. He was not averse to slipping in the occasional film of serious literary origin. In June 08 he presented an Italian production called "Beatrice Cenci" which Mario Caserini had filmed on the actual locations where her tragic story had unfolded. The News Letter recommended it it as "full of dramatic incidents". Unlike the Danes, the Italian film makers had the advantages of bright sunshine and Mediterranean light the clarity of which greatly impressed Belfast audiences. They also responded to "Joan of Arc" (August '09) which the Telegraph especially recommended with the added wry comment that the suffragettes could learn some lessons from it though exactly what wasn't clarified.

Such offerings were the exception and the normal fare was lighter and less intellectually demanding. Each show consisted of between ten and twelve films, mainly one - reelers though some were shorter. Many serious minded people looked down on such offerings but in fact they were often more cinematic in style than the slower, rather ponderous Art films. They celebrated cinematic movement with chases either on foot, on horseback, by carriage, car or train and they enlivened their stories with camera tricks involving sudden disappearances, quick motion and slow motion that defied gravity and logic. The comedies, short and quick paced, particularly used those techniques in presenting the adventures of characters like Foolshead and Tontolini. Foolshead was a French music hall actor called Andre Deed who had taken part in some of Méliès's entertainments but who only came to popular notice when he joined Pathé in 1906 before moving to Italy two years later where he developed a comedy character called Crettinetti in Italy, but known as Foolshead in the British Isles. Such multiple names for a character were not unusual at the time.

The Alhambra audiences loved him, greeting his films with clapping and cheering and literally falling about at his adventures and antics. He used all the camera tricks mentioned above, and more. In one film he escaped from his pursuers by disappearing through a crack in a wall, long before Terminator was thought of. Such was his popularity that his films were usually advertised by giving just his name, but sometimes their full titles appeared like "Foolshead Wrestling," "Foolshead Betrothed," "Foolshead Out For a Day" or "How Foolshead Paid His Debts," giving an idea of what he got up to. Another great favourite was Tontolini, also Italian, who was equally involved in all types of slapstick situations and who had, as the Irish News put it, "a strong tendency to tickle one's risible faculties." They were to be superseded later by the more sophisticated clowns like the French Max Linder, leading on to Chaplin and the great American silent comedians. As it happened one of those future funny men, the irascible W.C. Fields, appeared in person for the first time in Belfast at the Empire during August 1909 with his comedy juggling act, and endeared himself to audiences and critics. The former encored him enthusiastically while the latter praised his juggling skills, his "quaint humour" and his professionalism. To the News Letter he was "an artist of the highest ability" while the Whig pronounced him a "most accomplished artist." He returned the following year to similar accolades, appearing on the stage of the

Royal Hippodrome.

While many comedies were developed around a particular character, others poked fun at topics of contemporary concern or interest like the suffragettes (a great favourite) or fashion, especially female hats and harem skirts. A typical example was "The Butcher Boy and the Penny Dreadful" made by a small English company called Cricks and Sharp, located in Croydon, which specialised in local comedies. The Alhambra showed it as part of its programme in August 1909. The plot involved a boy who is sent on his bicycle to deliver meat to a customer. On the way he purchases the latest penny dreadful and becomes so wrapped up in its pages that he becomes oblivious to his surroundings and is the cause of humorous mishaps involving a lorry, a milk cart, a cart full of chickens and a group of road workers among others until he arrives at his destination and delivers the meat, completely unaware of the mayhem he has caused. To anyone familiar with the comedies of the day ("screamers," the Irish News called them) the theme wasn't very original and audiences would have been very familiar with plots where mayhem was caused among the population without anyone being really hurt. Such films were regarded by most people as harmless fun.

Others - and there were many in Belfast - were disapproving. They complained that penny dreadfuls with their lurid tales of crime and criminals were undermining the youth of the day. Not only the youth, because the cheap dime novels from America read by many adults were regarded as equally guilty, and not only here but across the continent. The American dime novel arrived in Europe in 1907, originally describing the adventures of Buffalo Bill, and soon there were French, German, Spanish and other editions available on a regular basis. In France Buffalo Bill was followed by detective stories, especially those involving Nick Carter ("le grand detective American") published in a weekly series, with each magazine containing about thirty two pages. They were exciting stories of crime and mystery, full of action and incorporating master criminals, secret organizations, ladies in distress, sliding panels, underground passages, murders, robberies, torture chambers, last minute escapes and dramatic unmasking of villains. They became immensely popular across the continent despite the protests and criticisms of clergy, teachers and others. Their writers realised the popular attraction of the cinematograph for their readers and were

Note the frame around the screen.

ready and willing to exploit it. Thus one of the stories carried the heading "Dans la cinematograph" over an episode called "The Man in the Biograph." It had an illustration on the cover, in colour, of Nick Carter at a film show, the screen bordered by a wooden frame as on a painting, the audience consisting of a mixture of ladies (one wearing a large matinee hat) and gentlemen. Another was "une affaire obscure" called "The Moving Picture Mystery." They not only entertained the ordinary people but had a seminal influence on many young film makers, notably Fritz Lang in Berlin and Louis Feuillade in France.

But the first to realise their importance as the raw material for film plots was the Eclipse company in Paris (mentioned earlier) and in 1908 they began releasing the first of a series of Nick Carter adventures. They were one - reelers with the main part played by Pierre Brussol. The Alhambra showed four of them in early 1909: - Nick Carter in A Kidnapping Case, the Great

Jewel Robbery, the Mystery of the False Coiners, and the Ruffian's Footprints. Two others, the Suicide's Club and the Sleeping Pills were shown later in the year in St. George's Hall. The success of Nick Carter was followed by the filming of the adventures of other fictional detectives like Nat Pinkerton (April '09) and Sexton Blake (November '09). The latter was an early English effort made by Douglas Carlile which according to the Telegraph "made a great impression" on the viewers in the Alhambra.

If one detective could draw the crowds, then two should prove an even bigger magnet so "Sherlock Holmes v. Raffles" had Holmes leading the hunt for and the recapture of Raffles, shown in the Alhambra during February 1909. That seems to be the first mention of Holmes on a local screen. One might have expected Holmes, who was referred to on the continent as the "king of detectives," to be the subject of earlier films, especially by English companies, but that wasn't the case. In June 1908 the Alhambra presented "A Case for Sherlock Holmes" but when it was reshown later in St George's Hall the Whig noted that it was "exceptionally funny" which suggests that it was actually an English comedy about the adventures of a dog called Sherlock chasing a gang of crooks, and had nothing to do with the detective. During the following year (in September '09) the famous detective did make his first solo screen appearance in Belfast when the Alhambra showed "The Grey Lady" which was described as an incident from the career of Sherlock Holmes. The date of the film suggests that it was probably one of a Danish series of thirteen one - reelers about the great detective made by the Nordisk company in Copenhagen between 1908 and 1911 starring Viggo Larsen in the main role. Later that year the City Y.M.C.A. showed "a thousand feet of Sherlock Holmes" but exasperatingly there are no details of the contents. Unfortunately the Nordisk series has suffered the fate of so many silent films and completely disappeared, so there is no firm information to confirm that either film was from the Danish series. Besides recommending the films, the local critics made no other comments about them - which is surprising because they were already very familiar with similar stories on the stage.

Sherlock Holmes was one of the most popular fictional detectives of the period He had first appeared in print in 1887, though it wasn't until the publication of the stories in the Strand magazine in 1891 that he began to catch on with the public. Conan Doyle however was never over enthusiastic about his "little creation," as he called him, and washed him out of his life down the Reichenbach Falls in 1893, much to the dismay of his readers. In fact public pressure forced him to bring Holmes back and one of the ways he did that, before the official return in "The Empty House" in 1903, was in the form of a play. He hoped that Beerbohm Tree would take the main part but after reading it Tree wanted so many changes that the idea was dropped and the play languished until it fell into the hands of an American actor and playwright, William Gillette. He rewrote it and, despite introducing a romantic interest for Holmes, got Doyles' permission to go ahead with the production. The play, called simply "Sherlock Holmes," opened in New York in November 1899 and was an immediate hit with the public. Gillette is credited with being a major influence on the popularly accepted appearance of Holmes. In the stories Doyle suggested that he was tall, over six feet, rather thin with piercing eyes and a narrow beak - like nose. Gillette's physique matched that description well enough. Sydney Paget the illustrator in the Strand magazine had produced a series of classic drawings of Holmes in action; or standing with his back to the fire before a high mantelpiece in his rooms in Baker street talking to Dr. Watson; or seated across from Watson in a railway carriage as they raced across England to solve another case, Watson in his bowler hat but Holmes wearing his distinctive deerstalker. The latter was actually Paget's idea, not Doyle's. Gillette had studied the illustrations and he adopted the deerstalker on stage but also added a long dressing gown and a pipe with a curved stem. That was how audiences saw him when he brought the play to the Lyceum in London in 1901 where it was equally successful.

The following year local theatre goers and Holmes enthusiasts were excited when the News Letter carried a report that two touring companies had been formed to bring the play to the provinces and so, in February 1903, the Opera House presented "Sherlock Holmes" on its stage to full houses. The detailed response of the local critics was very different from the few words they usually wrote about the films they saw, and reflected the low position that films still occupied in the artistic, cultural and entertainment hierarchy, despite recent progress in presentation and plot development. Gillete himself did not come to Belfast but the part was played by another popular actor Julian Royce, equally tall, complete with deerstalker, pipe and long dressing gown. The News Letter thought that his was "a lifelike picture" of Holmes while the Irish News, after expressing disappointment that Gillette himself did not appear, found him "a very acceptable substitute." The Whig critic thought he gave "a very able rendering of the part" but didn't approve completely of a "nasal twang" which marred his delivery on occasion. He felt that the play in general caught the essence of the character "altered of course to suit stage requirements." The Whig critic was always conscious of the need for changes or modifications when a work was transferred from one medium to another. Obviously he had the romantic interest in mind but probably agreed with the Irish News critic who noted that purists could complain about the inclusion of a romance but added that "seeing Christine McGill's portrayal (of the lady) makes one sympathise with Holmes." The News Letter was especially impressed by Royce's ability to project a persona that was cool, collected and calculated, a man who was daring, never lost his nerve and "who takes his hypodermic injections with the same amount of sang-froid as he meets the greatest and most terrible danger".

The Telegraph critic was in general agreement with his colleagues and felt that Royce accorded "pretty closely with the personality that most readers.... will have conceived." He did however have criticisms about the tendency of Royce to "overdress" and found his accent wrong for the part. Aside from those points he had nothing but praise for the production. Special tribute was paid to the impressive lighting effects and the Telegraph mentioned one scene which was especially effective and which gives a flavour of the production. Holmes is seemingly trapped in a gas chamber by Moriarty and his henchmen. Suddenly he grabs a chair and smashes the only lamp, plunging the stage into complete darkness except for the red glow from the tip of his cigar. "Track him by the cigar," shouts Moriarty but when a light is procured Holmes has disappeared and his glowing cigar is found attached to the window sash where the quick thinking detective had left it. The arrival of the play coincided locally with a period of severe weather of strong winds accompanied by widespread snow and sleet showers. As a result the first night saw a lot of empty seats but as the week progressed the crowds came in large numbers.

Exactly one year later the play was back again but in the Theatre Royal. Another ten years passed before Sherlock Holmes appeared on a local stage when Julian Royce returned again in the main part in Conan Doyle's adaptation of "The Speckled Band." There was general agreement that even though the plays were melodramatic and sensational they were superior melodramas and as the Ireland's Saturday Night pointed out they succeeded without "the three essentials of melodrama" - no killing, no shots fired and no kiss. The Irish News commended Sherlock Holmes as "the best and most readable series of detective stories that have ever been put on paper" but added that they "had cost (the author) his rapidly developing claim to be considered among the best of our latter-day writers." That didn't take away from the excellence of the stage productions which all the critics praised. The Whig and the Irish News were especially impressed by Royce's skill in fooling his audience when he adapted a disguise. No one suspected - in "The Speckled Band" - that it was he masquerading as Perkins the butler until they noticed in the programme that the butler was played by Mr C. Later.

Gillette's play has been revived on a number of occasions always with great success and not only on the stage. In 1916 it was filmed, silently of course, with Gillette himself in the main part, and was shown in the Picture House in Royal Avenue during March 1918. It's seven reels ran for one and a half hours and the Whig found it "most ingeniously adapted" while the News Letter was impressed by the "surprising and startling incidents" the plot contained. When 20th Century Fox made "The Adventures of Sherlock Holmes" in 1939 with Basil Rathbone and Nigel Bruce they claimed in the credits that the screenplay was "based on the play Sherlock Holmes by William Gillette with the permission of the executors of the late Sir Arthur Conan Doyle." Excellent as that film was, one would have to search very diligently to discover the actual connections between the play and the film beyond the performance by Rathbone, complete with deerstalker, pipe and dressing gown. The influence of the early stage Holmes, so appreciated and enjoyed by those audiences in the Opera House and the Theatre Royal during the first few years of the 20th century, has lived on to fascinate and entertain later theatre goers, cinemagoers and, today, T.V. watchers.

Certainly during the early years of the century the new films, including the early Holmes adventures, couldn't compete with the professionalism and sophistication of the stage. The plays presented in the Opera House and the Theatre Royal were well produced and widely advertised with colourful and even lurid posters aimed at attracting audiences with promises of exciting plots and eye - catching special effects which the films couldn't yet hope to match. Coincidentally during the same period a feature of the film programmes was the increasing number of one - reel versions of well known plays that were shown. As films became longer and plots more complex, film makers faced the problem of making them understandable to audiences. One way was by an increased use of inter - titles, and another was to film popular plays that audiences were already familiar with. Of course reducing a play to one reel or just over ten minutes screen time required much elimination of detail and an abridgement or even a distortion of the plot. An advantage was that, unlike the theatre, some scenes could be filmed out of doors in "real" surroundings though despite that the plays weren't really opened up or developed for the camera. In most cases the camera was just set up and the action filmed from a fixed position, as on a stage. Yet the results seem to have worked for and satisfied contemporary audiences.

Strangely enough the critics rarely referred to the original stage productions on which the films were based, or made any kind of professional comparisons between them. The only such reference, oblique at that, occurred when "The Silver King" was shown (June 08) and the Whig welcomed it and commented that "the absence of the spoken word passed almost unheeded." A similar welcome was given to other examples like "Jane Shore" (Oct.08) which had been presented many times on the stage of the Theatre Royal and the Opera House; also to "Mary, Queen of Scots" (in colour,Nov. 08), Kathleen Mavoureen (an Edison production directed by Edwin S.Porter in 1906 but not shown here until Nov. 08), The Shaughran (Jan. 09), and "The Sign of the Cross" (Nov. 09). The latter was described by the Telegraph as "a beautiful picture creation," but no mention was made of its impressive theatrical pedigree or of the exciting impact it had made locally. Written by the actor Wilson Barrett, it was one of the great blockbusters of the period. After major successes in America, New York and London it had arrived, heralded as "the greatest play of the century," in the Theatre Royal in October 1897, complete with a full chorus of male and female voices, specially composed music, new scenery, new costumes and in Act three a dance by Florence Fowler. A point often forgotten today is that most plays at that time were accompanied by a live "soundtrack" of music, song and sometimes dance.

When George Bernard Shaw first saw the production at the Lyceum in London he dubbed it an example of "scripturization" by which he meant that it sounded like something out of the Bible though it actually wasn't. The Whig in turn cautioned its readers that its plot shouldn't be confused with history because it was essentially an imaginative work. It was the first of many such epics to grace stage and, later, screen, which claimed to deal with the beginnings of Christianity, in which fictional characters were interwoven with authentic personages and events from that eventful historical period. "The Sign of the Cross" was set in A.D.64 during the reign of Nero, and the play contrasted the corruption and cruelty of the Roman system with the beauty and love of the new Christian faith. On a more personal level it told how Marcus Superbus, a prefect of Rome, fell in love with a pure Christian girl, Mercia, and finally sacrificed all by joining her in martyrdom in the arena. The local critics were in agreement about the high quality of the production and its aims. The Whig recognised its "high central motive" and thought that it was "one of the most interesting and instructive of modern stage creations," while the News Letter was impressed by its dignity. The Irish News saw it as a powerful piece, "a most impressive sermon," the aim of which was as much to instruct as to entertain and which stood in welcome contrast to "the coarseness of the dramatic tendencies of our time." Belfast with its well documented reputation for religious fervour embraced its coming warmly and many who wouldn't normally cross the threshold of a theatre were seen in attendance, including eminent professional men, clergymen, and "dear sweet Sunday school teachers" as Nomad put it. The result was "the melodious jingle of money" (Nomad again) at the box office. Panoramas, dioramas and exhibitions with religious themes had always been popular in the city but the play was different in that it didn't depend for its impact on the manipulation of inanimate painted pictures, photographs or wax models. Like the early

Medieval morality plays it used living breathing actors but added all the special effects of the modern stage to bring its message, the period, the characters and the incidents alive and immediate. Indeed the Irish News, following Shaw, complained that the scenes in the torture chamber were too vivid and that more scope should have been left in that scene to the imagination. On the other hand there was widespread praise for the costumes and the scenery, the latter being described by Nomad as "wonderfully realistic."

There had been criticisms too. The Irish News critic regretted that Wilson Barrett himself hadn't come because he had obviously tailored the main part to his special talents, and he further wondered if a play of such quality was best served by "an ordinary touring company." The Whig felt that the dialogue was "rather commonplace" while the Ireland's Saturday Night (referred to in future as I.S.N.) complained that it was aimed at the emotions rather than at the intellect, and agreed that its overall appeal would be mainly to the middle class, a comment that many film makers would have preferred to hear about their products. Nomad suggested that the audiences were too easily satisfied because the play was nothing but a "good old melodrama clothed in sham sancity" during which the audience could wonder sometimes if they were seated in a church rather than a theatre. He also found himself quite unable to accept or understand the final sacrifice of Marcus Superbus. In that conclusion he was in a decided minority in the city and the play was to return on a number of occasions, reflecting its popular appeal. Besides being much admired and discussed the production also generated many spin-offs. On one visit it was accompanied by an elaborate exhibition of its costumes, and on another occasion Rodmans put on show a large painting called "The Sign of the Cross" depicting a scene from the play of Nero's Palace with seventy figures, which attracted large crowds who paid sixpence a head to see it. But most important was the fact that, like Sherlock Holmes, it had a major impact on popular entertainment and aspects of it were to turn up in future cinematic "scripturizations" like Quo Vadis, Ben Hur, The Robe and indeed The Sign of the Cross itself. In fact the cinema was already paddling in those holy waters and, at the end of 1909, both the Alhambra and the City Y.M.C.A. were able to present an Italian one - reeler called "Nero and the Burning of Rome" which enthralled its audiences with its large cast, its fine scenery and its climax of the fire itself which one commentator described as "a triumph of scientific cinematography." (Whig)

Earlier in the year, in June, a film of a less elevating nature was shown which a local reviewer referred to as "Carried Off by an Eagle," and described it as an exciting story of a baby carried off by an eagle but saved by a man who happened to observe the event. Almost surely that was Edwin S. Porter's film, actually called "Rescued From an Eagle's Nest" made for Edison in 1907, which is remembered mainly because it introduced D.W. Griffith to the world of film. Griffith, a hard-up stage actor, was trying to sell Porter some story outlines at the time when the latter offered him the part of the woodman who climbs to the nest carrying his axe, does battle with what is obviously a stuffed bird and rescues the baby. When Griffith hesitated, reluctant to compromise his professional standing by acting in a "mere" film, Porter is reputed to have told him that no one would recognise him, so he acquiesced and took the five dollars a day that was the going rate. Griffith became fascinated with the new medium, but his skills didn't really lie in the field of acting and it wasn't long before he had moved to the Biograph company where he began to make films. If the film shown in the Alhambra wasn't that particular one it was a close copy because the copying or pirating of successful films was a widespread practice. George Méliès blamed the practice for his financial failure in America.

The well known, and widely accepted, practice of reconstructing or faking actual events on film had declined but hadn't completely disappeared. In September '09 the Alhambra presented "Hunting Big Game in Africa" (Selig) which purported to show ex-President Roosevelt doing just that. In fact the whole thing had been filmed in Chicago with a vaudeville lookalike playing Roosevelt, some very old lions from a local circus and a group of black extras pretending to be native Africans. Those minor drawbacks didn't prevent the film becoming a great success and there is no clear indication that the locals recognised it as a fake. When it was shown later in the year in the City Y.M.C.A. it was advertised as a "marvellous and costly picture" and after seeing it the commentator in the Whig wrote that it could only have been photographed "under circumstances of considerable danger" and that "the representation of the capture of a live lion, the excitement of the natives, together with the presence of ex-President Roosevelt created a scene seldom witnessed in this city."

Another film which made a great impression on the Alhambra audience was one of Griffith's anti drink stories, the well named "A Drunkard's Reformation," in which he cleverly used a play about a violent husband within the film to bring about the reformation of the real drunkard in the audience. Seen today the film shows Griffith's increasing understanding of editing as he cuts between the father in a drinking den and the wife and daughter waiting patiently at home, and later between the temperance play on the stage and the father in the audience. He had also continued to experiment with the lighting, adding to the impact of the final scene of the family reunited at home by placing the light source in the fireplace behind the fire around which they are grouped. Those watching may not have been aware of what he was doing but they certainly responded to the improved look and quality of the films. Commentators mentioned in their columns that during such stories an amazing silence often fell over the audiences. Among the faces in that film was one belonging to an anonymous actor, actually an Irish -Canadian called Mack Sennett, whose work would have the opposite effect on future audiences, provoking them to roars of laughter. In a similar vein another film called "The Salvation Army Lass" told how a young girl in the Salvation Army saved her fiancé from the evils of drink. One reviewer was intrigued and mystified by the final scene which showed the Army marching, led by the happy girl waving the Stars and Stripes.

Equally popular were what were called "pathetic" stories, which, like the temperance tales, were strongly Victorian in spirit. A characteristic example was "A Son's Atonement" screened in August 1909. It told the story of a boy who was expelled from school and as a consequence was put out of the family home by his angry father. Shocked and neglected, he wandered the unfriendly streets until finally in dire straits he decided to shoot himself. An officer in the Salvation Army saw him and wrested the gun from his hand. He then took the lad under his wing and arranged for him to emigrate to Australia. There he became a miner and struck it rich. Some years later he returned home, a wealthy man, just in time to rescue his parents who had been ruined by a bank failure. That plot of the stern or angry father casting a member of the family adrift in a generally uncaring society was recycled in many different forms over the years of the silent film and always retained its popularity. The stories were simple with stock characters and sentimental situations but usually with a positive moral, emphasising the mutual support of the family unit, the consequences of parental severity, and the importance of filial duty all rounded off with happy endings and everything forgiven. Audiences responded to them like modern day soaps.

One night in May 1909 mysterious lights were observed by quite sober citizens moving across the sky over south Belfast, leading to a lively discussion in the city as people wondered what they were. It was believed that some kind of airship had flown over but despite widespread inquiries it couldn't be identified and the mystery was never solved. That incident added a certain interest to "The Airship Destroyer" (distributed by Charles Urban) which the Alhambra presented later in the year. The Irish News described it - rather ominously - as dealing "with the aerial terror which is sure to figure largely in the next European war" and warned that in such a war victory will go to "the most scientific and highly trained nation." The film told the story of a young inventor whose warnings about aerial warfare were ignored but who was finally vindicated when his invention, which had been rejected by the authorities, saved their city from destruction during an attack by airships. So impressive were the special effects that the film was reshown many times over the following months. Not to be outdone St George's Hall also took up the theme of war with "Invasion: its Possibilities," and audiences were not only impressed but set to pondering the question that the film posed: was the country prepared for such an eventuality? The film began in peacetime and showed various aspects of army and navy life. Then an alarm was raised and both services went into action, showing how they would repel an invasion, a process suitably illustrated with scenes of land and sea action involving submarines, mines exploding and mighty battleships firing their guns. The Whig recommended it as a study of modern war and praised the way in which the excitement was built up by "incident upon incident, crisis upon crisis," while the Telegraph commented upon its length and the lucid way in which it was presented. Leaving aside the propaganda aspect for military recruitment, those films reflected the growing war fever that was already spreading across Europe. Some would argue also that the populace was being prepared psychologically for what was to come.

For a time the Alhambra and St. George's Hall were joined by a third hall showing films, called the Star Picture Palace. The origins of the Star go back to 1892 when Edward Partick, the former owner of the Buffalo Music Hall in Victoria Square, bought a public house and two adjoining houses in Church Street and had a local builder, Matthew Hearst, transform them into the New Star Music Hall which he opened in October of that year. It was located where the R.O.A.B. headquarters now stands and the site seems to have been chosen to take advantage of the crowds that thronged nearby North Street, the audiences attracted to the Alhambra located just around the corner and maybe the workers from local establishments like the Belfast Public Bakery. The building had a sixty feet frontage and consisted of two floors, with a bar and billiard room on the ground floor and the music hall on the first floor. The papers noted that it could hold 800 persons and that it was well lit, had good acoustics and satisfactory sanitary arrangements. Remarks added in red ink to the plans, stored in the City Hall, indicate that the building was inspected by the superintendent of the Fire Brigade who had discussed the positioning of fire hydrants and the provision of a fire proof curtain in the music hall. Within two years the business was sold by auction and a theatrical entrepreneur from Norwich named Dr. Redmondi reopened it as "a very comfortable bijou theatre" (Telegraph), charging 4d, 6d and 9d entrance. The Star functioned on the fringe of the entertainment scene and could never really compete with the Alhambra, the Empire, the Palace or the Royal Hippodrome in the quality of its acts. By 1908 it had a new manager, James Gyle, who decided that the cinematograph was worth trying as an attraction. He acquired an American Bioscope projector, putting on two shows at seven and nine every evening with an entry charge of 3d. The shows were a mixture of films with some vaudeville acts modelled on the Alhambra programmes. The films were "very clear and well thrown on the screen" (Telegraph). A typical show consisted of The Last Cartridge, The Cracksman and the Black Diamond, Poor Man's Romance, Two Orphans, Motor Ride in the Alps, Harmless Lunatics Escape, Lightning Postcard Artist, School Friends, and The Seaside Girl. They were accompanied by Cissy Baker and a Mr Harkness who sang sentimental songs like "Eileen Alannah" and "The Irish Emigrant," illustrated by magic lantern scenes. After a few weeks the price of admission was reduced to 2d which, according to the Telegraph, resulted in an increase in audiences.

Mr Gyle was responsible for one interesting coup when, during December 1908 he presented Hale's Tours of the World. Hale's Tours were a highly successful American gimmick in which the audience sat in a replica of a moving railway carriage and watched travel films projected on a screen which formed the end of the carriage. By 1908 the novelty and attraction had worn off and the Tours had become a pale reflection of the original. The Star programme was rather basic, consisting only of the films. Undeterred, the manager advertised in the local papers using railway terms. Pullman trains would run every 15 minutes from the depot, giving special trips to North America, France, Germany, Switzerland and elsewhere. Prices were 6d before 5:00 pm, 3d after that. According to one report audiences were large and "hundreds were turned away" in Christmas week. Despite such successes, the hall struggled to survive and, by the end of 1909, the twinkling Star had become a white dwarf. The projector was done away with, the hall was redecorated and the music hall format was fully restored. But the owner had other ideas and the hall later became better known for its boxing exhibitions. It played no further part in local cinema history.

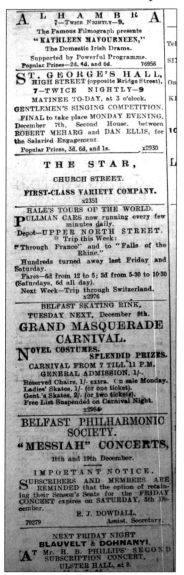

Hale's Tours in the Star.

So at the end of 1909 a theatrical and entertainment hierarchy of the professional and other halls available in the city could be detected. At the top the Grand Opera House occupied the position of the city's prestige theatre for the presentation of mainly serious and worthy subjects while the Theatre Royal was the comfortable home of more popular fare especially melodrama. Music hall was well represented by the Empire and the Royal Hippodrome both of which also offered short film shows, though mainly as an afterthought;

the Alhambra and St. George's Hall had made a break with the past and, designating themselves as Picture Palaces, had essentially come to depend on their film shows though still with a residue of music hall. Forming the base of the pyramid was a large group which included public halls like the Ulster Hall and the many religious and other local halls which presented lectures, concerts, local social functions and such entertainments. The latter often included film shows, especially at holiday times like Christmas and the New Year, usually organized and presented by Erskine Mayne, Lizars or Alex Hogg. Those shows were dominated by the weekend winter film seasons put on by the Y.M.C.A. in Wellington Place and elsewhere, the Grosvenor Hall, the C.P.A. in the Assembly Hall, and St. Mary's Hall.

Details of that pattern were continually being modified with new additions especially in response to public tastes and demands, and those tended to change quite often. Films weren't the only "new" attraction and the picture palaces had to face much more athletic competition. By 1908 the ping pong craze had been superseded by a roller skating craze and there were those, local and otherwise, always ready to satisfy the public appetite. The Exhibition Hall at the Botanic Gardens introduced skating but more importantly the American Roller Rink Company which had built rinks in London, Dublin, Liverpool, Glasgow, Bristol,Leicester and Edinburgh arrived and arranged to build a rink at Cliftonville, which opened its doors in November. It was a timber construction with a zinc roof supported by a steel frame which covered a spacious skating floor made from maple wood imported from the U.S.A. The well lit interior was described by the Whig as "a veritable fairyland of beauty and colour." Skates could be hired for one shilling and there were instructors on hand to give free tuition. Admission was sixpence, with a concession for ladies, who were admitted free in the afternoons. The new venue was widely welcomed and most people ignored the letters of complaint that building work on it had continued over two consecutive Sundays, which constituted a desecration of the Sabbath.

The local papers reflected the popular mood by giving considerable and favourable coverage to what was happening on the skating rinks over the following months. It is not surprising therefore that six months later, in May 1909, the Corporation received an application from a local businessman, W.J. Anderson, to convert an existing premises (a furniture store) at 308, Newtownards Road to a skating rink for the Princess Skating Rink and Amusement Company. The building was inspected by the Fire Service and declared safe for such a development, as long as all the doors were modified to open outwards. But Mr Anderson must have decided that, after all, skating didn't really represent the future, for within a few months of opening the rink he had applied for permission to convert the building to a Picture Palace. Whatever his reasons, whether practical (maybe the building was unsuitable) or economic (a good skating floor is expensive to lay and maintain) or what, his decision to open a picture palace may have been a lucky guess but, more likely, it indicated a canny recognition by a local entrepreneur of what road the popular entertainment business would take in the coming years.

CHAPTER NINE
A Relic of Barbarism

In its first issue of 1910 the News Letter, as was its wont, reminded its readers of the new laws which came into effect with the New Year. Well down the list it mentioned an "unostentatious act" called the Cinematograph Act (1909) which prohibited cinematographic exhibitions on premises that were not properly licensed for the purpose. Local councils now had the responsibility to inspect halls being used for film shows and issue licences costing £1 per year to those which met the necessary safety standards. The paper commented that "the Act should do not a little to prevent disasters which have become associated with exhibitions in which inflammable films are used." The main aim, in the words of the Act itself, was "to make better provision for securing safety at cinematographic and other exhibitions." Its provisions related to the use of inflammable film only, and did not apply to private houses or "structures of a moveable character." A constable or any person appointed by the Council for the purpose had the right "at all reasonable times" to enter premises, licensed or not, to see that the provisions of the act were being carried out. Unlike the arrangements for stage censorship it was clearly stated that the Act also applied to Ireland.

Few if any of the readers would have objected to the new law because they recognised that fire was a major hazard in all halls where people gathered for entertainment but especially so where highly inflammable nitrate film was used in conditions of low lighting. Many could recall the Raglan Street disaster where lack of lighting had precipitated a panic, or the horrific Charity Bazaar fire in Paris. The latter had concentrated professional and public attention on the problem and as a result some producers began to use non - flammable film, while in towns and cities, including Belfast, the music halls and exhibitors like Erskine Mayne and Lizars began to surround the projectors (and the projectionists) with box like structures made of wood, iron, or asbestos. The new boxes could be rather claustrophobic and daunting - which could well be one reason why women were rarely mentioned as projectionists as in such an enclosed space the voluminous clothing of the time could quickly become a fire trap. In Belfast all the early projectionists who are named in reports are men with one exception, a Mrs. Noyce, a member of the Salvation Army who is mentioned only once when helping her husband at a charity film show.

The nearest that Belfast actually came to a cinematograph disaster was in the Ulster Hall at Christmas 1904. The hall had been bought by the City Council for the use of the citizens the year before and it had been redecorated and its fire precautions checked and updated. On Boxing Day the hall was crowded for a cinematograph show presented by Our Navy and Army Animated Photographic Company which had hired the hall for the week. The company was well known in the city and had presented entertainments in the Ulster Hall before. The audience, which numbered about 2,000, was in holiday mood and included many women with children. Following the established procedure, a wooden projection box had been built at the front of the balcony for the projectionist and his equipment. The early part of the entertainment, which began at eight o'clock, consisting of films dealing with life in the army and the navy, accompanied by a commentary by a lecturer, Capt. Wilson, went very well, and held the attention of the audience. Then, in contrast, there followed "A Christmas Dream" made by George Méliès and described by the News Letter as "most entertaining (with) dissolving effects, tricks, spectacular tableaux, ballets and other effects being cleverly introduced."

But later, about 9:30 pm, during "A Stormy Sea," a film describing the crossing of the Atlantic, the film suddenly burst into flames. The projectionist, Mr Hogan, desperately tried to put them out, badly burning his hands and arms in the process. Someone in the balcony noted the red glow of the flames in the box and jumped up, shouting "Fire." The result was immediate panic and "wild scenes" as the Telegraph reported. On the ground floor seats were overturned and smashed to pieces in the rush to the exits. The air was filled with shrieks, shouts and the crying of children. Some people headed for the windows and broke them in an attempt to escape. The stairs from the balcony became jammed with a pushing mass of people. As they spilled out into Bedford Street and Linenhall Street the caretaker, after having telephoned for the fire brigade, joined the projectionist and some men in the balcony who were using the hall's fire fighting equipment to contain the blaze. When the brigades (three of them) arrived it was well under control and was quickly put out. Very little real damage was done, mainly some blackening of the ceiling and blistering of the paintwork, though the projector was ruined beyond use. The projectionist, a local man from Rochester Street, was the only casualty and was taken to the Royal Victoria Hospital to have his burns attended to. The papers the following day expressed "alarm" at the event but were thankful that there had been no loss of life. All were agreed that the fire was never out of control and that the main problem was panic caused by the person who had shouted "fire." There was also general agreement that a very significant safety detail was the availability of a sufficient number of exits all of which functioned properly, and they congratulated the Council on that fact.

The following evening the show went on again with a replacement projector and, in the words of the News Letter, "the crowds continued to come." But not everyone was so complacent as a spate of letters to the press about fire protection in local theatres indicated. There were worries expressed about the condition of the Theatre Royal, but the management was able to assure patrons that the theatre had been recently inspected by the fire authority as a precaution following the terrible Iroquois Theatre fire of December 1903 in Chicago during which over 600 people had perished. A fireman was always on duty during performances while hosepipes were available behind the stage and elsewhere in the auditorium. But there were criticisms that managers were too slow in introducing the latest technology like automatic sprinklers. They were being installed in theatres in England and had even been made compulsory in Birmingham, yet only one theatre in Ireland, the New Pavilion in Kingstown, near Dublin, had installed them. It was widely agreed that panic and the crush that usually accompanied it was as dangerous as the fire itself and that more attention should be given to coping with it. One writer insisted that audiences must be educated to remain cool - which seemed an inappropriate choice of term for coping with a fire. The local authorities emphasised the need for many exits with doors which opened outwards while corridors and passageways should be wide enough, with a minimum span of four feet six inches (about 1.4 metres).

As a result of the inspection of the Theatre Royal mentioned above certain exits were widened and all exits were clearly marked with black letters three inches high on a white background. Lamps were provided on stairs and corridors leading to the exits and those lamps had to be placed out of reach of inquisitive fingers. They had to have a protective covering and be kept lit whenever the public were present at performances. But the spectre of fire refused to go away. In 1909 the theatre added a new fire escape and in November of the same year the Alhambra drew attention to its recent improvements which included interior fireproofing and upgraded exits that enabled the building to be cleared, the management claimed, within thirty seconds. At the same time, as befitted its role as a popular picture palace, the outside was adorned with a display of coloured electric lights, giving it, the Telegraph reported, "a comfortable and animated appearance."

When fire struck again it was in quite a different zone of comfort. The following July (1910) the Kelvin Hotel located at 17-18, College Square East, went up in flames. The terrace of elegant four- storey houses which formed College Square East had been built just over a century before, but by the early twentieth century was undergoing rapid functional change from residential to mainly service functions. Edward Stringer, who lived on the Glen Road but who had a very successful tailoring establishment in Wellington Place not far from where Parson and Parsons are today, had bought two of the houses and combined them into the Kelvin Hotel. That name was chosen because Lord Kelvin, one of the most outstanding figures in science in the 19th century, had been born in one of the houses in 1824 as William Thompson, and had lived there for eight years as a child while his father taught mathematics across the road in the Royal Academical Institute. The fire broke out on the ground floor during the night and smoke from it was noticed about 5 a.m. by a policeman on patrol, who immediately summoned the brigade. Despite its best efforts, such was the speed that the flames spread and the ferocity of the fire that the building was gutted and six people of the twenty one who were in the hotel that night lost their lives. Some of the lucky ones escaped by climbing down knotted sheets, others by jumping and still others were rescued by the firemen. Contemporary photographs taken the next day show the remains with the front wall still standing, the only apparent damage being the letter "H" which was knocked off when one of the guests jumped from an upper storey and his foot caught the letter on the way down carrying it with him to the pavement. Sadly he was one of the victims and died later in the Royal Victoria Hospital. So intense were the flames that the Irish News reported how the mirrors didn't crack as in most fires but "literally boiled and the glass ran down to the ground like syrup."

The city was saddened and shocked - the Whig said that the citizens showed "consternation and genuine sorrow" - and again the same questions were asked about safety features and especially if the authorities were doing enough to enforce them. During the inquest it emerged that there had been no fire buckets or other fire fighting equipment available and that the City Hall actually had no power to ensure the presence of such safety devices in a converted building of its age. Most people agreed with the editor of the Irish News when he wrote that it revealed "a startling laxity in our building laws." The jury were unable to decide exactly how the fire began, but in their summing up they suggested that the Corporation seek whatever powers were needed to inspect all properties with regard to fire safety. They also stressed the need for exits to be clearly marked. The News Letter noted that the tragedy highlighted the fact that fire safety regulations should apply to all "places of public resort" and not only cinematographic halls, adding that the regulations were already there but that the Council wasn't applying them rigorously enough.

During that same month one of the attractions offered by the Royal Hippodrome was a return visit of Layfayette, "the man of mystery," an American entertainer of many talents whose skills, according to the I.S.N., included those of actor, sculptor, conjuror, mimic and illusionist. He promised a superior act of conjuring and illusions. His performance lived up to his reputation and his audiences were entertained, intrigued and thrilled. But those who saw him were shocked ten months later when news arrived that during his performance in the Empire Palace Theatre in Edinburgh fire had broken out on stage and spread with great rapidity. The safety curtain had been dropped immediately, protecting the audience and the main body of the theatre, but behind it the flames continued to rage. Layfayette and seven others died in the conflagration before it was brought under control. Another contemporary report described how a hall used for showing films in Tilbury was completely destroyed by fire, the cause of which was finally traced to a pet monkey "who had a habit of striking matches" (Whig). Because of such incidents the citizens of Belfast accepted the new Cinematograph Act on face value as a genuine and necessary attempt to deal with a serious problem. Few, if any, paid attention to those, especially in England, who pointed out that the new powers given to the local authorities could be used to control more than the danger of fire. They could be used to stop or curtail the showing of certain films themselves. There were those who warned that the act was actually the thin edge of censorship, and time would show they were correct in that judgement. But the local feeling was more attuned to the notion of who would want to censor a harmless piece of entertainment like a film. There were, after all, many other issues which the pulpits and newspapers drew attention to as causing serious moral concern.

The Rev. Prof. Todd Martin, addressing a public meeting in the Assembly College in 1911 summed up the problem as he saw it from a Presbyterian point of view, namely that all was not well with the world, a view shared by most of the local churches. In a lecture which today in certain quarters would still have a contemporary relevance, he put the blame for that situation on a number of reasons, most especially the many attacks on the stage and in print on marriage, "the lowered tone in regard to the family," the fact that there was too much emphasis in society on rights and not enough on duty, the unending pursuit of pleasure, excessive drinking, tainted literature and the trend in the "imitative arts" by which he meant the theatre and music hall, to stimulate the baser instincts. To those, newspaper letters and editorials added cheap trashy books, English Sunday newspapers and those magazines which published sensational serials in which dashing villains were often treated as heroes. It was felt that all those factors were undermining the moral fibre of the population, especially of youth both male and female. There was special condemnation of objectionable postcards which were on sale widely in the city. Some of those were probably cards of the seaside variety with vulgar jokes, other were revealing (for the time) pictures of stage actresses which prompted the Whig to regret how some actresses were willing to sacrifice "their self respect for the sake of advancement," and others again were imports with exotic names like "Paris at Midnight."

One letter in the Telegraph described how the writer had great difficulty getting along the pavement one morning near the city centre because of a crowd of men and boys staring at the latest "foul scenes" in a shop window. The editor of the Telegraph couldn't accept that such images would undermine "the national morality" but agreed that something should be done to control them because of their vulgarity. Complaints of that kind forced the police to act on occasion, confiscating the offending materials which were usually destroyed on the orders of a magistrate. But there was no mention of the youthful cinematograph in any of the local complaints concerning morals or behaviour. The problems of the cinematograph were not about the films themselves but about the conditions under which they were shown, conditions that the Cinematograph Act was intended to control.

Meanwhile the authorities and the film exhibitors had to come to terms with the new restrictions covered by that act. The Police Committee of the City Corporation had responsibility for overseeing matters of fire safety and the inspections of buildings but reports about their suitability were traditionally undertaken by the Superintendent of the fire brigade. Since the introduction of the legal requirement on presenting plans for all new buildings to the Council, the City Surveyor's office had also become involved. Added to that were the requirements of the Public Health Acts. At the monthly meeting of the City Council in February 1911 the Town Clerk, in the minutes of the Police Committee, highlighted the problems involved in getting a report on the suitability or otherwise of premises that applied for cinematographic licences. He pointed out that three different departments and the police all had to carry out inspections of the building and the apparatus. Recently the Committee had hired a man to make any necessary inspections at a fee of 10/6 for each visit. He suggested the matter could be greatly simplified and the procedures improved by the permanent appointment of one person, an overall inspector, to do the job. He believed that the person appointed should be "a properly qualified engineer" and he should be empowered to make regular and irregular inspections of centres of amusement and entertainment. The salary to be offered was two guineas per week. He added that Belfast was probably the only large city in the British Isles that didn't have such an inspector. The debate that followed showed that few members were impressed by that fact and that little seemed to have been learned from the Kelvin hotel disaster. Many members believed that such an appointment was unnecessary and that someone in the electrical department could well "make the inspections necessary in the few halls in Belfast." A minority thought that it was a good idea but that the salary was quite inadequate to attract a person of sufficient qualification. The Council, manifesting no sense of urgency, decided to postpone a decision on the topic. Meanwhile the office of the City Surveyor was still dealing with problems arising from the Kelvin tragedy.

Edward Stringer was typical of the small entrepreneurs who looked for opportunities to establish local profitable business ventures. The tragedy in the Kelvin convinced him that the hotel business wasn't really for him. His tailoring interests often took him to London on business and there he heard much about the expanding picture palace business. What he heard or noticed must have impressed him because after one such trip he decided that he would rebuild the Kelvin as a picture palace. He moved quickly and by the 28th October, only three months after the fire, he had presented his plans to the Surveyor's Office in the City Hall. That office hadn't forgotten the public criticisms regarding the hotel and the officials weren't going to make any mistakes this time. The plans were scrutinised but rejected on 12th November In the meantime the site had been completely cleared except for the front wall and part of the rear wall. A series of meetings then took place between Mr. Stringer and Mr. Forbes, the building inspector, during which the problems were discussed and a number of decisions taken which were added in hand writing to the plans, e.g., the building would be lit by electricity, all existing drains under the building would be removed and "all exits, doors, stairs, seating accommodation, etc. will be carried out in accordance with the Council's regulations."

Mr. Stringer then went ahead with the construction, laying a new foundation and reroofing the structure - until he received a summons to appear in court to answer the accusation that "he did within the past two months ..... proceed with the erection of a building, notwithstanding that the surveyor of Belfast had in due course disapproved of the plan thereof." The building was already completed and operating as a cinema when the matter came to court in January. The case involved the interpretation of the Cinematograph Act as to whether the building was a new one or an old one. The City Surveyor admitted that the projecting apparatus met the necessary requirements but under the definition of a new building, which he held it was, it did not comply with the stipulations regarding exits. The defence argued that the building was not a new one as defined by the act and after some deliberation the magistrate agreed and dismissed the case on its merits. Those fine points of difference may have made sense to the legal mind but to the public the structure was obviously a new building and regardless of its age it either met safety standards or it didn't. It seemed to many that Dickens may have been right in his assessment of the law as an ass, a conclusion that was reinforced by another case which didn't happen in Belfast but was widely reported there causing quite a lot of amusement.

It involved an incident that took place in Castlederg in Co. Tyrone earlier in the year, when a travelling showman, Allen D.Coon, put on a film show in St. Patrick's Hall. On the first evening the local sergeant of police and a constable entered the building at 7:30 p.m. to inspect the equipment. Mr Coon greeted them with "Good evening, I suppose you are coming to see whether we are going to blow up the hall or not?" The sergeant replied that they had, but after checking the projector and looking around, the two officers seemed satisfied but showed no sign of leaving. They stayed for the beginning of the show at 8:0 p.m. Mr Coon demanded two shillings payment if they intended to watch the whole show. They refused to pay, but stayed anyway. Some time later Mr. Coon received a summons charging that he and his assistant, John Joseph Richardson, had breached the Cinematographic Act (1909) because they had given a cinematograph show without placing the projector in a proper fire proofed enclosure, and without giving warning of their intentions to the County Council.

When the case was heard in June, Richardson's defence lawyer argued that the act had been introduced to protect audiences in large urban halls and that "it was simply disgraceful" that a policeman should try to apply it in a small rural hall where there were no more than forty people present. Mr. Coon, who had studied law and practised as an attorney for a period in America, organized his own defence. In his statement he said that the decision of the court was important for all the travelling showmen in the country as they were anxious to know where they stood with regard to this new law. When it emerged that he was using non - flammable film at the time, the case was dismissed. But that wasn't the end of it. Mr Coon was quite angry at what had happened so he sued the sergeant for the sum of two shillings, the cost of admission for two persons which he - the sergeant - had refused to pay. He - Mr Coon - claimed that it wasn't a matter of the money but of principle. He argued that the sergeant had not presented an official pass and therefore had no right to enter the hall. Above all he certainly had no right to remain and watch the show without paying. He had demanded payment but had been refused. Was he supposed to let in "this whole army of unemployed just because they wore a uniform?" He couldn't see that happening in Belfast or Derry.

The magistrate decided that under the conditions of the act the sergeant had the right to enter the hall to make an inspection, but whether he had the right to stay was another matter that he refused to comment on. He dismissed the case. Mr Coon's reaction was not recorded but it was probably quite colourful as he seemed to have been a rather flamboyant character. He was an American who had come to Ireland where he indulged and exploited his interest in still and animated photography. From his base in Derry and later in Letterkenny he distributed his own brand of postcards and travelled around the country putting on film shows. He later established cinemas in Letterkenny, Killybegs and Buncrana but was essentially a nomad whose travelling show became popular and well known across the north of the country.

While those matters were holding the public attention other events were conspiring to involve the cinematograph in fighting its first serious round against censorship over - a film of a boxing match. During the 19th century boxing had a very unsavoury reputation and certainly many of the early bare - fisted fights were long, brutal and bloody. Attempts were made to regulate and control the sport by the introduction of the Queensbury rules but when, in September 1910, the Bishop of Ossory described it as "a debasing and degrading form of amusement" there were still many in Belfast who would have agreed with him. On the other hand support for the sport had greatly increased, so much so that boxing exhibitions and matches became a regular attraction in the Star, the Empire and even the Theatre Royal. Local fans were especially pleased when the touring champions themselves arrived in the local halls and demonstrated their abilities. Household names like James Corbett, whom many held represented the change from old bruiser to modern boxer, visited Belfast in 1894 and was followed by Jim Jeffries (1899) and Bob Fitzsimmons (April,1909). They were all warmly received and praised, in the papers, for their achievements in the ring, their manly proportions, manifest skills and gentlemanly bearing.

From the early days of Edison's Black Maria and the Kinetoscope, exhibitions of the "noble art" had been filmed and had proved very popular. It wasn't long before complete fights were being filmed which the public appreciated and showed an appetite for more. The first films of early championship fights were shown in the Ulster Hall where crowds in

April 1898 saw the full fourteen rounds on the Veriscope when Bob Fitzsimmons defeated Corbett, while two years later Poole's Myriorama brought the Lubin Cinematoscope and showed the eleven rounds ending with Fitzsimmons being knocked out by Jeffries. In December 1907 the Palace (Opera House!) showed one of the few British boxing films of the period made by the Urban Company, in which Tommy Burns defeated Gunner Moir for the heavyweight championship of the world. After that it was the Alhambra which emerged as the mecca for the boxing films, presenting them on a regular basis. In mid 1909 the Telegraph in a comment on the latest example in the Alhambra was able to state simply but accurately that "fight films are very popular" in Belfast. Until then objections to boxing revolved mainly around its brutality and its doubtful moral suitability to be regarded as a sport but in that year another volatile element, racism, entered the argument.

From Texas there emerged a fighter called Jack Johnson who had his eyes set firmly on the World Championship. What was different about Johnson was that he was black. In June 1909 the Theatre Royal presented the film of his fight in Sydney with Tommy Burns which he won when the police stopped it in the fourteenth round with Burns in difficulties. In March 1910 the Alhambra presented the first contest between Johnson and Ketchell and, such was the interest, repeated it the following month. The audience watched in awe as Ketchell floored Johnson, who got up in a fury and in a flurry of punches knocked out twelve of Ketchell's teeth (Irish News), two of which were later found embedded in his glove. Critics could shake their heads at such incidents but the delighted crowds kept coming. The only fighter left capable of meeting Johnson was Jim Jeffries, and Johnson knew if he could beat him no one could deny him the title of World Heavyweight Champion. Burns had been much criticised for fighting Johnson at all and giving him the chance at the title and, when the latter won, there were those who pointed out that Jeffries had retired undefeated and was therefore still the true World Champion. Pressure was put on Jeffries to come back, regain the title and restore the honour and standing of the white race. Jeffries had retired to his farm in California and after seven years away from the ring was reluctant, but finally agreed and went into training.

When news of the contest was announced there was worldwide interest and excitement. Locally there were doubts expressed about the wisdom of Jeffries's decision because when he had visited the city there were those who thought he was already past his best then, and that had been over ten years before. The newspapers, especially in America, hyped the matter up and some began to talk in terms of the clash of the races. There were reports regarding negotiations about the prize money with the winner promised £3,500 while the loser would get £2,500, followed by details of a meeting with representatives of the film companies regarding moving picture rights. The main companies, Edison, Vitagraph, Essanay, Selig and the American Moving Picture Company had combined and agreed to pay £10,000 to each of the combatants, plus another £10,000 divided between their managers. They asked that the fight start early enough in the day when the light would be best for filming. The Irish News felt that there was too much money involved and deplored the "squalid commercialism" surrounding the whole affair. Then the Governor of California stepped in and banned the fight in the state so that the promoters had to look around for another venue.

After more bannings elsewhere permission was finally given to hold it in Reno, Nevada.

On the day itself the crowds, estimated at over 30,000, began arriving from midday to see what the Newsletter called "the greatest prize fight in history." Their report described how everyone was searched by the police looking for anything that could be used as an offensive weapon, so onlookers enjoyed the sight of cowboys and miners handing over their Colts, Smith and Wessons and even Derringers. Mrs Jeffries didn't appear, preferring to stay in her hotel, but Johnson's white wife sat there "under the shadow of one of the moving picture machines." That shadow was to spread much farther afield in the days and months to come. Around noon the betting was 10 to 7 on Jeffries but it wasn't until 2:46 pm that the bout got under way in a temperature of 85F, moderated by a slight breeze. Maybe a little warm for the exertions of boxing but perfect weather for filming. From the early rounds there was little doubt as to who would win, especially when an old wound over Jeffries's eye opened in the sixth, but he struggled on before finally going down in the fifteenth. But more than a gallant fighter went down because with him he carried white pride and supremacy. At the end he was heard to say sadly to his seconds, "I couldn't come back boys. Ask Johnson if he will give me his gloves." The Whig which reported that quote didn't add whether Johnson met his request or not.

Local fans wondered when, and if, they would see the fight especially when they read the final sentence in the Newsletter report which said that "a widespread movement to stop the moving picture reproduction of the contest is likely." The reason was the explosion of racial riots across the United States when the result became known. In an evening and night of clashes soldiers had to be called out to restore order, but not before thirteen people, mainly blacks, were killed and hundreds injured. Beginning with Washington D.C., city after city then banned the film and one of the major vaudeville groups said they wouldn't show it. Canada, Australia, New Zealand and South Africa followed suit. On this side of the Atlantic the news was not welcomed in the capitals of the colonial powers, in London, Paris, Brussels and Berlin where more widespread prohibitions were proclaimed. The Irish News commented that the film was turning into "a white elephant" (with no pun intended) for its makers, and went on to point out that the colonial rulers feared the political repercussions if their subjects were to see "an American negro with an African countenance thrashing a white man."

Suddenly it was realised that animated pictures could be much more than just a harmless entertainment. In India a magazine suggested that the negative be burned by the authorities who would then recompense the film makers for the loss. A letter to the London Times pointed out that if the film was shown, many children would see it, and called on the paper to "use your great influence to urge that no person with any proper sense of decency should be seen attending such exhibitions." There were even questions in the House of Commons and the Home Secretary was asked to use his powers to influence local authorities to prevent the exhibition of the film. Winston Churchill, who held that position, answered that he had no powers in the matter. The Cinematograph Defence League remarked that it was not good business to make and show films like that, and a report from America indicated that the owners of the film were considering the possibility of having to shelve it. Vitagraph, according to reports, had paid £52,000 for the exclusive rights to show the film in Ireland and the arrangements were in the hands of Films Ltd.

In late August it was announced that the first showing of the controversial film in Europe would take place in the Rotunda in Dublin during Horse Show week.

Immediately there were protests that such a development would offend American visitors, and eminent citizens including the Lord Mayor, the Commissioner of Police and His Grace the Archbishop Dr. Walsh tried to have the showing stopped. It was suggested that the Cinematograph Act be used to prevent the issuing of a licence. Dublin Council sent their inspector, Mr Butler, but pointed out that they could not refuse a licence if the conditions of the act were met. In fact the inspector discovered that the film was of the non - inflammable type and therefore the act didn't apply to it, so, everything else being in order, the necessary licence had to be issued. Only the Lord Lieutenant had the power to ban it, and he showed no inclination to act. The film went ahead much to the delight of the ordinary Dublin citizens who couldn't understand what all the fuss was about. The proprietor of the Rotunda, James T. Jameson, claimed that during the week he received no complaints. The large audiences included professional men, members of the clergy both Catholic and Protestant, many Americans and even "ladies of title," he insisted.

Will White in Belfast then made arrangements to hire the film and announced that it would be shown in the Alhambra during the first week in October. He paid the "enormous cost" (Irish News) of £550 for the week. That amount, if the figure is true, was certainly enormous when compared to the average cost of a show for a week which was usually about £10 or £12. It was presented as a roadshow event with six separate showings daily beginning at 12:30, with prices slightly higher than normal at 3d, 6d and one shilling. Surprisingly, that acted more like a magnet than a deterrent and on the first morning large crowds collected and formed queues in North Street well before opening time. So great were the numbers that the police had to be called to keep the busy thoroughfare open to traffic.

The film, which was 6,000 feet long and ran for seventy five minutes, was an overwhelming success with the crowds who obviously were not impressed by the argument that the contest was "a relic of barbarism," as the London Times had described it. It began with scenes in the two training camps giving views of the many visitors including John L. Sullivan and Jim Corbett, both of whom were greeted with loud cheers from the floor of the Alhambra. In Reno all the seats were taken by an obviously excited crowd and the Irish News was especially struck by the large numbers of women who were present, many wearing "gaudy" hats. The whole fifteen rounds were shown in detail until the "outclassed" Jeffries went down and was counted out. There were wild scenes then and when the fighters finally left the ring it was invaded by onlookers and "practically taken away by souvenir hunters." The Irish News critic praised the film for its clarity and its general interest and suggested that even those who had no real interest in boxing would find a visit to it worthwhile. There were no words of condemnation or criticism and no mention of the racial problem. The writer realised that those who went to see it were interested only in enjoying a good fight regardless of matters of taste, morality or public order. Reports suggest that Will White's gamble paid off and that he had full houses all week, ensuring a good return on his money. In fact it would seem that the only losers in the whole affair, besides race relations, were the film companies who were left with very few outlets for their expensive product. There is no reference to it being shown anywhere else in Belfast.

CHAPTER TEN
A Good Melodrama Town

Cinematograph halls were the dot. coms. of the second decade of the century and many entrepreneurs concluded that if one wanted to make money quickly the way was to get into cinemas. In Britain companies involved in the exhibition side of the cinema business mushroomed from under five in 1908 to nearly 300 in 1910 and then to 544 in 1913, according to the Board of Trade. The situation in Belfast reflected that general picture. At the beginning of 1910 those who wanted to see animated pictures in a professional hall had a choice of two main venues, the Alhambra or St George's Hall, but by the end of the year that number had increased to five and by the end of 1913 it had reached thirteen and that figure didn't include the Empire, the Royal Hippodrome, the Grand Opera House, the Theatre Royal and the new Alexandra Theatre, all of which had projection facilities.

The process of expansion began with a businessman W.T. Anderson, who is described as a pawnbroker in the local Directory and as a greengrocer by other sources. As already noted, his first venture was a roller skating rink (in 1909) but he soon abandoned that and switched to animated pictures. In March 1910 the I.S.N. was able to announce that Ballymacarrett was soon to have its own picture house and sure enough at three o'clock on Easter Monday 28th March the Princess Picture Palace officially opened its doors. It was situated in a working class area at 308, Newtownards Road, the first cinema in East Belfast and the first to locate away from the city centre area. It caused great excitement locally and large crowds attended the first shows. Anderson knew his potential audience and had pitched his prices and facilities accordingly. The prices of admission were 2d, 4d, and 6d and the patrons were promised "animated pictures and select vaudeville." There were two separate shows each evening at seven and nine plus afternoon matinees on Monday and Wednesday at four (for "scholars") with a Saturday show at three. The facilities, as indicated on the plans and as remembered by those who frequented it, seem to have been rather basic, though the Telegraph described the hall as "commodious and well equipped." According to the plans there were at least 800 seats though other estimates suggest over 1,000. The first show was the typical mix of drama, melodrama, Westerns and comedy with the audiences responding to "Gambling with Death," "The Devil Woman" and "Poorluck gets Married," among others. But there must have been some dissatisfaction expressed either from members of the audience or the management because the hall was closed during the last week in July for alterations. Exactly what work was done is unclear but when it reopened one observer commented on how much clearer and steadier the pictures were. Later, in September, the management were also given permission to build a large gallery to seat 800 at the back which was probably an attempt to overcome the fact that the floor wasn't raked. The policy of "fix it as we go along" indicated a shortage of capital or a lack of experience or, more likely, both. It was utilitarian picturegoing, films without frills, but the locals seemed to enjoy it

To be fair Mr Anderson served up an entertaining programme which included some interesting films. Many of them had already been shown elsewhere in the city, but not always. Among the early dramas shown was a one reeler by D.W.Griffith called "A Corner on Wheat" about a grasping trader who corners the wheat market, ruining many farmers in the process and causing distress among the workers by driving up the price of bread. It must have stirred the memories of the older members in the audience who could still recall how in 1867 bakeries across the town were attacked when workers from Ballymacarrett had joined fellow workers to protest at recent increases in the price of bread. At the end of the film the villain falls into one of his own grain silos and the final scene of his hand sinking slowly into the wheat, opening and closing as he desperately grasps at thin air, must have reduced the large hall to complete silence.

Another above average film was an Italian production called "The Sack of Rome" which was praised by all the local critics. George Méliès's "A Trip to the Moon," described by the Telegraph as "a splendid trick film" was shown and despite its age proved a great success. To celebrate the first anniversary of its opening in April 1911 a recently released one reeler from Crick's and Martin called "Pirates of 1920" was presented. It was a thriller set in the future with exciting special effects involving, for example, a battle between an airship and a liner. Every programme of course included comedies with Tontolini or Foolshead to the fore but at Christmas 1910 patrons were promised something special in the person of Max Linder (named) "the great French comedian" in "A Champion Boxer." While they could laugh at Linder's antics in the ring, films of actual boxing matches were always welcome also while topicals were popular especially when they included local events like the launch of the Olympic and the Titanic, major sporting events like football matches, the Grand National, the Derby or the boat race, and items about the Royal family.

Bronco Bill, Belfast's first Western hero.

But above all the crowds enjoyed Westerns and the Princess became associated with one cowboy in particular, Bronco Billy, the first Western star. He was played by G.M.Anderson and one wonders if the similarity in the surname to that of the owner had anything to do with his many appearances in the hall. Anderson, whose real name was Aronson, began his career on the vaudeville stage before joining the Edison company where he acted in a number of early films including "The Great Train Robbery" in which he played three separate parts. Later he moved from New York to Chicago and joined the Selig company with which he made numerous Westerns. In early 1907 he formed an association with George Spoor and they set up their own company called Essanay (using the first letters of their names, "s" and "a"). Their logo consisted of an Indian head with full headdress, a symbol that Belfast audiences soon became familiar with, and looked forward to. Anderson wanted to make "quickey" Westerns and he thought that could best be done in the actual West so he moved first to Colorado and then on to California. It was there he made the first Bronco Billy adventure in 1910 called "Bronco Billy's Redemption" and Bronco Billy first rode into town in December 1910 when that film was shown in the Alhambra. The Telegraph summarised it as a story telling how "an outlaw does a good deed." The Broncho Billy character was a loner who often lived on the edge of the law like a Western Raffles though he lacked the latter's social polish. He has been described as a "good badman" but audiences responded to his down-to-earth attitudes and his willingness to help those in trouble. Between then and 1916 he turned out about 400 of the films, mostly one reelers, each quickly but professionally put together in a week. Besides playing the main part he often directed and produced them. He became very popular in Belfast where he was affectionately known as Andy, nowhere more so than at the Princess. An indication of his standing is reflected in an announcement from the Princess in mid January 1912 that there would be a special cowboy programme the following week starring Andy "the hero of the Essanay company and the special favourite at the Princess." Also there in person would be a real cowboy, Frank Reilly, a man with Irish roots who would tell about his actual adventures and travels. Finally, every person who visited the cinema would get a free souvenir photograph of Andy.

Besides such attractions the Princess also had music hall acts from time to time. Typical was Harry Hollanda who appeared in Nov. 1910 billed as "a juggler and strong man." Mr Anderson liked to involve the audience in the proceedings so as part of the act a bag of flour was placed in the centre of the stage and men from the audience were invited to try and lift it and carry it from the stage. The man who did that in the shortest time would win the flour. Mr Anderson announced that if no one carried it off by the weekend he would divide it into smaller bags which would be distributed among the most deserving families in the area, which says something about local social and economic conditions. Singers both professional and amateur were popular and in 1911 the cinema even had a singing manager, Leslie Clare, who often entertained the audience with popular songs, sometimes accompanied by slides on the screen. The Princess quickly became an accepted and popular part of the physical and social environment and often advertised itself as the "East End Picture House," a position it could claim undisputed for nearly two years until local competition appeared on the scene.

Five months after the Princess changed its skates for films the Electric Picture Palace quietly opened its doors across the city at 19-21, York Street on the 22nd August 1910. Unlike the former it was rather small with only a few hundred seats but resembled it in that it was rather unprepossessing and catered mainly to a working class population that was down-to-earth, largely unsophisticated and poorly educated. The management promised 10,000 feet of film weekly including recent films from London, Manchester and Glasgow, which might suggest that the local distributors were being bypassed. The films would be presented in three shows daily at 3 pm, 7 pm and 9 pm with a complete change of programme every Thursday, all at the low admission prices of only 2d and 4d. The early shows were the usual combination of dramas, comedies, melodramas and pathetic stories and over the first few weeks the audiences enjoyed Her Terrible Ordeal, The Betraying Mirror, Old Kentucky, Across the Divide and Nick Carter, among others. They were supplemented with music hall acts like Pat White, an Irish comedian and dancer, and the Belfast Flower Girl who sang songs ("sweetly," said the Telegraph) accompanied by John McGrogan on the piano, and illustrated with slides on the screen. There was still a reluctance to make a complete break with the music hall. The manager was a Mr Cooke and he and Jack Baird attended to the projection.

There is little information about those early days but, as in the case of the Princess, there were obviously problems of such a nature that the owner, Fred Stewart, a Scotsman who had settled in the city, decided that the best thing to do was to close down (probably in October) and start again from scratch. So the Electric Picture Palace had one of the shortest histories of any cinema in Belfast and was never heard of again because when it reopened the following April during Easter week 1911 it not only had a new name but according to the Telegraph it was "under new management, repainted and redecorated, with every modern convenience introduced, additional exits provided and the auditorium completely rearranged." The reopening coincided with the official opening across the street of the Belfast Co-operative Society so it must have been an exciting week in York Street. The new manager was George Murphy, Jack Baird was joined by Mr Delaney as projectionists but the pianist had been replaced by Charles Hunter. The times of the shows were unchanged but admission now included an additional third section of sixpenny seats. One welcome technical change was a new, more powerful generator which resulted in very clear pictures "without the slightest flicker" (Telegraph). Mr Stewart had obviously decided that the road to success was to give his patrons quality and comfort and he wanted to distance himself from the former Electric. Thus the hall was advertised as the B.B. (Bright and Beautiful) Picture Palace and the P.P. (Perfect and Pleasant) Palace. Both the B.B. and the Palace were used for a time until the Palace became the sole name though even that was changed later to the Silver Cinema. Mr Stewart and his manager also tried to improve the quality of the films shown. For example in late May a programme consisted of a two reeler, "Drink" based on Zola's "L'Assomeir" a serious study of the decline of an alcoholic, supported by a coloured version of "Julius Caesar." Heady stuff for local textile workers. A few months later "Capt. Midnight" was presented, with the claim that it was the first Australian film shown in Belfast.

But local entrepreneurs were not left to have things all their own way. An indication of future trends emerged in mid-June when the I.S.N. told its readers that the London based Provincial Cinematograph Theatre Co. Ltd. (PCT) had acquired a prestigious site at the corner of Royal Avenue and Garfield Street on a 28 year lease and intended to build a new cinematograph theatre there. The company, which had been founded two years before with the aim of giving the public access to a better quality cinema going experience, promised continuous programming from 2 p.m. to 10.30 p.m. daily and a new establishment that would be managed "on thoroughly up to date and novel lines." Every effort would be made to make the theatre "one of the brightest and cosiest of its kind in the kingdom." The big guns of the cinema business were arriving armed with the type of capital resources and experience that the locals hadn't yet accumulated. That news only added to the speculation about what was happening. The keener eyed citizens had already noted the amount of building going on in many districts and were aware of the rumours that the sites in question were to be new picture palaces. They knew that work was progressing at the location of the former Kelvin Hotel in College Square East, at Joseph McKibben's property at the top of Northumberland Street and in a former butcher's shop in Shaftesbury Square.

What they didn't know was that the surveyor's office in the City Hall was also examining another two plans of prospective picture palaces that had been submitted for official approval. The Alhambra and St George's Hall contemplated the coming changes and knew their days of near monopoly were coming to an end. The Alhambra was granted a full cinematograph licence on 17th November and felt confident that it could depend on its traditional audiences for support no matter what the competition, but St George's Hall decided it had to act to improve its attractions. At the end of August it introduced a new element into the entertainment scene when it announced that free tea would be given to those in the sixpenny seats during the weekday afternoon performances. The idea of free tea can be traced back to New York theatres which had used it to attract female patrons to afternoon shows during the 1890's. The more recent development in association with films originated in Paris from where it spread to London. It became a popular attraction especially for women and children and some patrons must have commented on its suitability, recalling how the present hall was remodelled from a former restaurant.

The Christmas period saw the inauguration of the new halls led by the impressively named Shankill Picturedrome which opened its doors at 2.30 pm on the 19th December 1910. It occupied a site owned by Joe McKibben, a well known figure in the grocery trade in the Shankill area, and was located in the heart of a working class area on a very accessible site at the corner of Northumberland street and the Shankill Road. McKibben leased the site to Fred Willmot of Liverpool who had the grocery shop and club which stood there replaced by a small cinema which had an auditorium of the "shooting gallery" design-long and narrow-measuring about 80 feet long (nearly 25 metres) and 26 feet wide (8 metres), capable of seating 480 patrons. The plans were drawn by Campbell and Fairhurst of Southport who specialised in the design of picture palaces. Wilmot's company managed the cinema until 1919, when it reverted to the McKibben family. At the opening in 1910 the Telegraph reporter was very impressed by the design of the building which he thought reflected the work of someone who had good experience of the business. He found the interior comfortable, well lighted and spacious and commented on the quality of the projectors which produced pictures that were steady, without flicker or vibration so that they could be enjoyed "without eyestrain". The management must have been pleased to read that comment which challenged the criticism heard in some quarters that watching flickering images in a darkened atmosphere was bad for the eyes especially those of children. The managements of the early cinemas realised the importance of attracting children not only because they formed the core of a future audience but also because children were often accompanied by their parents especially their mothers. Whenever possible parents were assured that the cinema environment was safe, morally and physically, while being entertaining and educational at the same time.

The Picturedrome presented three separate performances daily at 3, 7 and 9 pm with a complete change of programme every Monday and Thursday. The prices of admission were the same as the Princess Cinema at 2d, 4d and 6d and, as in the Princess, the lively audiences enjoyed good value though in rather basic surroundings. But the raison d'etre of any cinema is to present films, and the manager, Edwin Sinton, announced that the programmes would reflect the motto of the new venture, which was "The World in Motion." The Picturedrome programmes were popular and entertaining combinations of

Westerns, comedies, melodramas with a sprinkling of documentaries (an early example was The Man to beat Jack Johnson), topicals and local items. Shows ran between sixty and ninety minutes.

From the beginning a special attraction, always popular, was Singing Pictures which were a combination of pictures with sound supplied by gramophone records. Some of the first films shown were "Pony Express Rider," "Modern Cinderella," and "Looking for Lodgings" followed later by "The Adventures of Lieut. Rose," and the more upmarket "The Slave of Carthage." The latter with its classical theme was also regarded as educational so a special children's matinee was put on at eleven on Saturday morning setting a pattern that was to become widespread in the city. Easter of 1911 saw the Oberammergau Passion Play on screen. It was the Pathé version which had been specially coloured and it brought "admiring murmurs" from the audience. So popular was it, with crowds being turned away, that it was held over and a few weeks later another version of the Life of Christ was presented, again to widespread acclaim. The Ireland's Saturday Night described the Picturedrome as "a boon" to the Shankill area and it quickly became an accepted part of the local social life for adults and children who supported it over the next forty eight years and there must have been some still around with fond memories of its opening day who expressed regret when it finally closed at the end of October 1958.

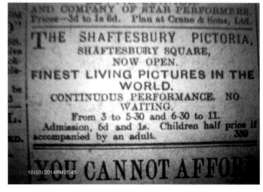

Advert for Belfast's first specially designed cinema

On the same day that the Shankill welcomed the first cinema in West Belfast, south Belfast also saw the opening of its first picture palace, the Shaftesbury Pictoria which modestly described itself as "the most luxurious and comfortable picture palace in Ireland." It was built for the Belfast Electric Theatres Ltd whose president was Isidore Clifford with an address in London. The first Electric Theatre Company in Britain was established in London in 1907 with the aim of building cinemas that would offer "cheap, elevating and popular entertainment for the masses" according to its Prospectus, a document that Mr Clifford seems to have been familiar with. The specifications for the new Electric Theatres were clearly set out. They were to be buildings of the bijou type, small, comfortable and tastefully decorated with an appeal to family groups. Admittance prices were to be low, at three pence and four pence, to attract patrons. The programming should be continuous and the business would function like a transport system which profited from a steady stream of users during the day. To ensure profitability costs had to be kept low so only the minimum of advertisement should be used, and patronage would be built up mainly by word of mouth from satisfied customers. Shows should run from one hour to seventy five minutes, while films, chosen with an eye to quality and variety, should be changed every Monday and Thursday. The Pictoria was to incorporate most of those suggestions in its design and management.

Mr Clifford leased two sites in Belfast, both of them former shops, one in High Street which would emerge later as the Panoptican cinema and the other at 6, Shaftesbury Square on the Dublin Road side near the corner with Fulton Street which he took on a twenty one year lease at an annual rent of £110. He chose Moore and Flanagan of Royal Avenue as the architects and they presented their beautifully drawn plans to the Surveyor's Office in early September. There are no indications of any major problems and the plans were quickly approved by mid September so that building could get under way. There were handbooks and guides available at the time for cinema proprietors and managers which gave advice on the general decor and running of a successful venture. They suggested that the frontage should be light coloured, tasteful and eye-catching, the foyer warm, bright and welcoming while the interior should have a dominance of dark or even sombre colours as those helped to make the screen shine brighter. Mr Clifford went along with many of those recommendations. The front of the Pictoria was painted in white and cream set off at night by rows of coloured electric bulbs resulting in "a handsome and ornate appearance." (Whig) but the interior had white walls, though covered with painted scenes, while crimson Kidderminister carpet covered the floor.

One problem discussed in some of the handbooks was the position of the screen and a minority opinion favoured putting it on the entrance wall with the projection room at the far end of the hall. Two reasons were given for that. One was that the cheaper seats would be near the entrance doors from where there would be less opportunity to slip into the dearer seats and at the same time it would necessitate only the higher paying, and by implication better behaved, patrons having to walk the length of the auditorium to reach their seats. The other reason was to do with safety. If a fire broke out in the projection booth it would be easier to evacuate the theatre away from the danger while it was hopefully contained at the far end of the auditorium. Mr Clifford favoured that suggestion so the screen was placed on the wall closest to Shaftesbury Square and the audience sat facing the entrance doors. That made the hall unique at the time in Belfast, yet none of the commentators mentioned the fact. It would also seem, in the system of continuous performances which the Pictoria introduced to Belfast, to have the drawback of causing an annoying distraction every time the doors opened during the show.

The cost of all the work was £813 and the results became available for inspection on Monday 19th December 1910 when the Pictoria opened its doors for business, and was warmly welcomed by the local papers. There was praise for the decor, the standards of comfort, the skill of the pianist and especially for the new system of continuous performances extending from 3 p.m. to 11 p.m. The projection was of a high standard, using two of the latest motor driven projectors, the Telegraph explaining that two machines were necessary for continuous performances. The reporter was very impressed by the steadiness of the pictures and the lack of accompanying eye strain. The prices weren't cheap at 3d, 6d, and one shilling but the manager, Mr Patton, implied that patrons would get good value when he declared that only the latest films from London would be shown and that they would be changed every Monday and Thursday. Yet from the beginning one can detect signs of uncertainty in management. Advertisements were irregular in appearing and those that did often didn't name the films showing. Also by February the continuous showing had been modified to an afternoon matinee between 3.30 and 5.0 p.m, with seats costing 6 pence and one shilling plus the added attraction of a free cup of tea; followed by continuous evening performances from 7.30 to 10.30 when seats cost 3 pence, 6 pence and one shilling. For the showing of the drama "The Sacking of Rome" - alone worth a visit, said the Telegraph -

three separate performances were put on. Most of the films however were run of the mill Westerns, melodramas, comedies and documentaries.

A letter to the Irish News a few months after the opening describes at first hand and in some detail a visit to a local suburban cinema, which could very well have been the Pictoria. The total programme lasted about an hour and the writer seemed surprised to discover that the audience consisted "mostly of grownups and respectable people." A variety of films was shown, many of which were "potted plays of a crude type some of them showing a domestic drama or a scene from a wild, 'woolly' West. All of them might have been culled out of the penny novelette or the 'Deadwood Dick' style of literature." What impressed him most of all was "the evident and unadulterated appreciation of the audience." His letter went on to say that the managers of these new picture houses (his words) had the opportunity to "educationally improve their clientele" by showing better quality material. There were actually occasional high spots at the Pictoria like the Italian film mentioned above or the travel pictures in colour and documentaries by Cherry Kearton, while the comedies included sophisticated capers by Max Linder.

One of the more interesting films shown was a Western called "Ranch Life in the Great Southwest," a Selig production directed by Francis Boggs. Selig had noted the growing popularity of the Broncho Billy films which were shot against splendid natural scenery in Montana and later in California. Boggs was anxious to do likewise so he took his crew to Oklahoma to take advantage of the outdoor attractions. The film impressed the local critics who admired its "daring feats of horsemanship" but their opinions only reflected similar reactions to the film wherever it was shown. It included an exciting rodeo sequence reputed to be the first ever included in a Western story and a local cowboy called Tom Mix had been asked by the director to take part in it. That was the beginning of his film career because the film had such a tremendous impact on audiences and was such a great financial success that Selig signed him up for more films. So, it was the Pictoria which introduced Belfast to Tom Mix, probably the most famous of the B-movie cowboys. In the credits he is listed as a former deputy U.S. Marshall but Mix was a classic example of the movie star with a manufactured private life. By his own account he had fought in the Spanish-American War, in the Boxer Rebellion in China and had been in South Africa delivering horses to the English army during the Boer War. After those adventures he had returned to the U.S. where among other things he acted as a Texas Ranger and a local lawman during which he was involved in a shootout with outlaws. In fact none of it was true. The stories were all exaggerations or pure tall tales which he told with such persuasion that many people, including Boggs, were willing to swallow them. In fact he wasn't even a real cowboy, having been born in Pennsylvania. His enthusiasm for the West had been kindled like so many others when, as a boy, he saw Buffalo Bill's Wild West Show. Over the years he had perfected the skills of riding, roping and shooting which he exhibited at Wild West Shows and circuses and it was those skills plus a willingness to undertake risky stunts that were to distinguish his films.

Many a fair maiden he rescued during his career but apparently even Tom Mix couldn't save the Pictoria. The cinema seemed to have everything going for it. It was located in an area that had no local cinema. It was near expanding residential areas, and trams passed its doors connecting to those areas. It overlooked the bustling Shaftesbury Square, a meeting place of six main routeways with their busy pedestrian flows. Yet within five months the cinema was closed and the company wound up. During those months the total takings were only £454, which implies that the cinema was operating half empty most of the time. According to the liquidator the main reasons for its failure were a lack of sufficient capital, the decision to pitch the prices for entry too high and an unreliable system of film supply. To those one could add the suspicion that Mr Clifford lacked real knowledge and experience of the cinema business. Also the high seat prices suggests that he had hoped to attract a more middle class audience but obviously the middle class didn't respond. While recognising its occasional worth they weren't yet prepared to accept the cinema as an equal with other forms of entertainment. As far as they were concerned most films couldn't yet match the effects of the best theatre productions like "Ben Hur" and even the finest Shakespearean adaptations lacked the beauty of the bard's poetry, while the cinemas themselves couldn't compare in comfort and architectural sophistication with the Grand Opera House, the Royal Hippodrome or the Empire.

It is not clear what the liquidator was able to salvage but it must have been enough to attract other interested parties because the cinema reopened under new ownership and with a new experienced manager (E.P.Baskeyfield) on Sat. 30th December 1911. Admission prices were more realistically set at 6 pence for all seats with children half price and with performances continuous from 6.30 to 10.30. The building had been completely renovated and repainted inside and outside so that, according to the Telegraph, it could withstand comparison with any in the city. The advertisement about the reopening confidently assured the public that "everyone is coming" and the hopes of the management were probably much boosted by the news that the Council had just announced the extension of the tramway system from Shaftesbury Square along the Donegal Road to the junction with the Falls, also up Botanic Avenue and along University Avenue to the Ormeau Road, and along South Parade to join with the Ravenhill all of which would increase the cinema's accessible hinterland. The opening programme wasn't distinguished in any way: the usual mixture which included a Western (The Sheriff's Decision), comedies (Double Deception and Betty Becomes a Maid), and drama (A Strike at the Mine and Faithful unto Death). There was sparse mention of the little cinema in the years that followed but it continued to occupy an unspectacular corner of the entertainment scene until it quietly closed and faded away in early 1917. The site was later occupied by a branch of the Ulster Bank and after that by Carlton House while the Pictoria itself settled into the archaeology of folk memory. Today (2014) a luxury hotel is being built on the site.

On the day following the double opening of the Picturedrome and the Pictoria, Belfast had another official addition to its growing group of cinemas when nearly 500 citizens responded to a special invitation to attend the opening of the Kelvin, located in College Square East near the City Centre. As the better informed citizens already knew, it occupied the site of the former Kelvin Hotel. The new building was carefully planned and designed as a bijou theatre right down to the potted ferns in the foyer and auditorium, and to the music supplied by the locally well known Wright's Bijou Orchestra. It was larger than the Pictoria, with seating for 495 persons, more than double the aforementioned, with luxurious tip-up seats fixed to a properly raked floor which facilitated good vision from all parts of the auditorium. Clarity and comfort were further enhanced by a superior ventilation system which removed smoke from the atmosphere yet kept the hall warm in winter and cool in summer. Visitors were assured that the building was completely fire proofed. There was no balcony and the cinema was to use that fact in their advertising by emphasising that there were no steps to climb. Decoration was tasteful and the manager, Henry Pulling, assured the visitors that the entertainment would be of a similar standard so that parents could bring their children "in perfect safety." Programming was based on separate shows at 7: 0 and 9: 0 p.m. though, a few months later, a 3: 0 p.m. matinee was added. Films were changed every Tuesday and Friday. Prices were 3 pence, 6 pence and 9 pence which could be described as moderate. Belfast seems to have taken to the Kelvin from the beginning and it survived many changes of ownership and name for over sixty years until it closed in 1972, and even then it took a bomb to achieve that.

There is a famous photograph of the Kelvin taken by A.R.Hogg showing its frontage painted in light colours, bedecked with small coloured flags and advertising the film "Rory O'More," which showed there in early December 1911. A rather impressive uniformed doorman sporting a moustache stands at attention while a group of eight very respectable looking men and women (two wearing large matinee hats) are waiting, presumably to see the matinee at three o'clock. Clearly visible near the door is a large poster with the name of the film and an action scene of a man reaching for a rearing horse entitled "Rory's Escape from the Gallows" while in the foyer it is possible to see what looks like a lobby frame containing photographs of individual actors. By that time the larger film companies were offering managers not only posters and frames but also front-of-house sets of stills for advertising purposes. Also patrons, or more correctly fans, could usually buy postcards of the more important players at one penny each in many of the new cinemas though there is no evidence that they were available there. A.R.Hogg must have known the manager of the Kelvin quite well because earlier in the year, in July, the cinema presented a film of the Orange demonstrations of the Twelfth taken by Hogg himself, the clarity of which, the I.S.N. thought, reflected "much credit upon him."

Besides news items the Kelvin presented the usual variety of Westerns, melodramas, and comedies but with an emphasis on quality; for example, the comedies included a number of Max Linder films which proved very popular. There were many historical films, often coloured and many of continental origin, with names like "The Bride of the Nile," the "Virgin of Babylon," "A Roman Campaign," "The Queen of Babylon," "Slave of Carthage" plus serious literary subjects like "King Lear," "Julius Caesar" or "Enoch Arden." The latter was actually a Biograph production directed by D.W.Griffiths and was one of the first American two reelers released with the reels to be shown together. But the manager let it be known in May that his patrons preferred Edison or Vitagraph films above all and the reporter from the I.S.N. commented that the filmgoers could by then recognise stars like Maurice Costello (known as the Dimpled Darling), Charles Kent and Florence Turner like people they met every day. That was an early indication of the growing awareness among the public about things cinematic and of the increasing influence and popularity of the American film industry.

Two important Vitagraph films shown in 1911 were that perennial favourite "Uncle Tom's Cabin" (in September) and "A Tale of two Cities" (in June). The former had already been shown in St George's Hall as three separate reels over Christmas and the New Year when it had attracted large crowds, but the Kelvin went one better by screening them together with a running time of over an hour, accompanied by specially arranged music played by a Miss Goodwin. The Vitagraph publicity emphasised the realism of the film due largely to the use of "real ice, real bloodhounds,(and) real negroes" but what mainly impressed the Whig critic was the beauty of the colour and the sense of movement as exemplified in the exciting scenes as Eliza made her escape over the frozen Ohio river in a blinding snow storm. The sequence had induced cheers from the more junior members of the audience in the High Street hall. One suspects that the response in the Kelvin was no less appreciative but probably more subdued. Of course a large part of the film's appeal was the association with its literary original and that type of link was to prove very important in the growing acceptance of animated pictures among the better educated section of the population, especially in a city like Belfast with its extremely conservative and traditional perception of art and "serious" amusements. If Harriot Beecher Stowe implied quality for a certain section of the population so also did the equally eminent and popular Charles Dickens. A look at the details of the connection between the Kelvin and Dickens helps to illuminate the process whereby the middle classes were finally lured into the cinemas.

Charles Dickens had been born in February 1812, so preparations were in hand throughout the country to celebrate his approaching centenary. The Telegraph, in an editorial in June, derided the "ocean of trivialities" that passed for contemporary writing and welcomed the "Dickens boom" as evidence of a "reawakening of interest in real literature." It warmly commended the evidence of that revival of interest, especially the lectures and the many stage plays based on his works that were being performed or prepared, and then added that "almost every one of the innumerable cinematograph theatres has a Dickens film on the bill." Special reference was made to the film "A Tale of Two Cities" and to the fact that it had become a special Coronation attraction. That was the first time that the cinema was mentioned in a local editorial on equal terms with literature and the theatre and it indicated a cultural step upwards for the new medium.

The following week the Kelvin, possibly in response, screened the film in question, giving the Whig critic, who impresses as the most observant and appreciative of those writing about films then, the opportunity to pursue his analysis of cinematic techniques and film theory. His main theme was that many early films suffered because the film makers kept too closely to the "the scenes and situations of spoken drama." He was probably thinking of the many Shakespeare adaptations and the Film d'Art works which, regardless of any qualities they may have possessed, were often little more than filmed plays. There should be a greater willingness, he suggested, to make use of those opportunities in the story which the camera is best suited to exploit. He believed that the contemporary experiments and attempts to produce film drama represented "one of the most interesting developments of the day" but admitted it was still "largely tentative and experimental." He felt that the novel "A Tale of two Cities" was well suited to cinematic adaptation and the way it had been done showed a decided advance in story telling techniques so that he didn't hesitate to recommend it as "perhaps the most remarkable" film yet shown in the city. The narrative was clear and the various episodes combined into a harmonious whole. He liked the way the main characters took on "form and shape" though he didn't mention, what the audience almost certainly knew, that it was Maurice Costello who played Sydney Carton and Florence Turner, the Vitagraph Girl, who played Lucy, while other players included Charles Kent who was also in "Uncle Tom's Cabin," and William Humphrey. He was particularly impressed by the way the "whirl and fury of the days of the Terror" were captured and even more so by the trial sequence with its "roaring crowds." It is clear from his comments on both films that he didn't want filmed plays but a narrative that was comprehensible despite the lack of dialogue, had a sense of movement and used the camera to best advantage to add visually to the overall effect. His comments indicate that local criticism was moving beyond the usual simple plot description followed by a recommendation.

If on the one hand the cinema courted respectability by referring to the literary precedents of its more important products, on the other it played the education card. During the nineteenth century panoramas and the magic lantern were often praised for their instructional potential. The Ulster Hall presented the last major panorama seen in Belfast when Poole's Myriorama visited the city in December 1907 and even in its dying days the News Letter could still recommend it as "an entertainment as well as an education." From its beginning commentators also realised and extolled the educational possibilities of the new Cinematograph and living pictures. Parents were often exhorted to bring their children to certain films because of their educational value, and the halls co-operated by putting on special matinees. Of course the more cynical pointed out that getting and holding the attention of children was also good business while most cinema owners continued to emphasise the positive moral as well as educational value of what they were presenting. The debate over children and the cinema was to become more acrimonious as the years passed. Fears were already being expressed about the dangers to children's eyes from watching "flickers" and the moral dangers of improperly supervised darkened halls.

But any actual or perceived harmful influences were as yet minority fears and the main thrust of the argument involved the educational value of the medium. Certainly there was a continuing supply of historical subjects which, despite their limitations, helped introduce children and, in many cases, their parents also to the characters, way of life, dress, architecture, and events of past eras while there were increasing numbers of films, often coloured, showing life in foreign and exotic lands. The still popular Saturday evening shows in the City Y.M.C.A., the Grosvenor Hall and the Assembly Hall often included films with names like The Wonders of Nature, Wild Birds in their Haunts, Elephant Hunt in India, Birds of Africa, Leopard Hunting in Abyssinia and Cherry Kearton's Lion Hunting (the real one this time, not the Selig copy). Most of those were filmed for their entertainment value and not primarily as tools for education. The three halls however regarded education as an important part of their programmes and took every opportunity to enlighten their audiences. When "A Tale of two Cities" was shown in the Assembly Hall in late November the Rev. J. Woods Gibson read aloud appropriate sections from the novel while the reels were being changed.

In February 1911 the Telegraph aired the topic in an editorial, noting that society had been "surprisingly slow to realise the educational possibilities of the cinematograph" and had allowed it to become merely a producer of "funny fake pictures for more or less harmless entertainment." But the editor felt it had the capacity for more than that and he drew attention to the many "wonderful films" being made about Nature, travel, foreign places and peoples showing everything from "weird primitive savage ceremonies (to) the most gorgeous pageantry of modern Europe." Such films, he suggested, went beyond textbooks and inspired the imaginations of students and added, in a burst of enthusiasm, that he hoped for the day when "the cinematograph and the pointer began to be more important to the school than the blackboard and the cane." Later he was to add that "the more the possibilities of the cinematograph in the school are looked into the more important they become."

A few months later, in April, the challenge was taken up by the Belfast Technical Institute, whether by chance or design is uncertain, and the Kelvin found itself involved in a unique demonstration about the educational value of films. The cinema was hired by the Tech. for a morning in early April and the Principal, Mr F.C.Forth, addressed an expectant audience of students, headmasters, teachers and representatives of film companies. The aim of the project, he declared, was to show how films could be used in the teaching of such subjects as science, geography, history and art. He felt it was an historic moment for two main reasons. Firstly because it was the first time to his knowledge in Belfast that the cinematograph had been used for purely scientific purposes and, secondly, it was very appropriate that it should happen in a building that stood where one of our most distinguished educationalists, Lord Kelvin, was born. Normally, he pointed out, this annual lecture would be accompanied by slides but "after all, a lantern view is a dead and lifeless thing and if we can impart life, reality, vividness and movement to a picture then by all means let us employ cinematography."

To illustrate his theme, about fifteen films from Britain, America and the Continent were shown, supplied by Lizars, Films Ltd. and Jameson and Sons of Dublin, all accompanied by an explanatory lecture from the curator of the local museum, Mr Deane. The films included The Birth of a Flower, Cheese Mites, studies of plants, insects and other animals (some by Cherry Kearton). The Birth of a Flower had been made the year before by an English photographer Percy Smith who had developed a form of stop-go photography which allowed him to take a series of spaced photographs over a long period of time which were then linked and shown as a speeded up version of nature. He had tried to interest the Board of Education, where he worked as a clerk, in the educational aspects of films but they weren't interested so he left and took a job with Charles Urban. The News Letter expressed special admiration for his film and also drew attention to the films of the flight of Wilbur Wright's aeroplane, the views of Niagara Falls, and a visit to the Le Creusot iron and steel works in France. It praised the entire venture, finding it "not only thoroughly original but also highly successful" and hoped it "would have an important bearing upon the future of education in the country." The paper admitted that everyone in education wasn't yet convinced but dismissed their criticisms as "short sighted."

The manager's policy of associating the Kelvin with such worthy causes and 'literary' films wasn't short-sighted. It brought him into contact with the type of informed and well-off audience he was anxious to cultivate. In December, to celebrate the Kelvin's first year in business, he showed his partiality for quality by presenting the early Film d'Art production "The Assassination of the Duc de Guise" with the claim that it was its first showing anywhere in Ireland. During its first year he pointed out that the Kelvin had screened 920 films which, if they were all joined together, would form a ribbon of celluloid stretching from Belfast to Dublin. Over Christmas, with a flourish of showmanship and confidence, he put on a Colossal Attraction consisting of "over six miles of specially selected pictures." On Christmas Day and Boxing Day the cinema opened at ten in the morning and six separate shows were presented during the day between then and the last show at nine in the evening. Patrons were promised a complete change of programme at each performance and as an added treat Madame Emmanuel-Lane entertained them with songs. Belfast had

never experienced the like of it before but comments in the papers suggest that the city was ready for it. The Irish News remarked that by then the cinematograph held "a place among our amusements which it would be hard to equal" while the News Letter was so impressed by its recent growth that it saw it as "a formidable rival to the theatre" and the Whig observed, significantly, that for many people going to the pictures was becoming as important as life itself. Obviously increasing numbers of people were falling under the spell of what the Telegraph called "the cinema magicians" of the day.

Picturedromes, the World in Motion.

During 1911 while the Pictoria floundered and the Kelvin went from strength to strength three more halls opened to cater to the public demand. On Saturday 25th February east Belfast got its second picture palace when the Mountpottinger Picturedrome opened its doors with the claim that it was "the largest and most elaborately furnished Picture Hall in Ireland." It was located in a working class area on the Mountpottinger Road just below the junction of the Castlereagh and Albertbridge roads. In keeping with the accepted wisdom of the day its frontage was painted white to attract attention as did its rather exotic dome which gave it the "appearance of an Eastern temple." (News Letter). As the name suggests, it had certain affinities with the Shankill Picturedrome in that it was planned by Campbell and Fairhurst of Southport for Fred Willmot of Liverpool and was built by the same Belfast company J. and R. Thompson. The Southport company specialised in "picturedromes" and their competence is reflected in the fact that it took just over a week from making their application on 4th October 1910 for the plans to be approved. The interior had comfortable seating for 900 persons and the raked floor ensured clear viewing. Careful attention was paid to safety with the provision of five exits, and suitable fireproofing in the projection room, which had three of the latest projectors. That number of machines might suggest that the programming was to be continuous but the manager, Ferris Pounds, decided on separate shows at 3 p.m., 7 p.m., and 9 p.m. with seat prices ranging from 2d, through 4d and 6d up to one shilling. As a further enticement he announced that free tea would be served in the afternoons to those in the dearer (6d and shilling) seats, following the example of St George's Hall and the Pictoria.

One of the handbooks available at the time for managers pointed out that people didn't go to a picture palace to look at the paintings on the walls or the decorations, but to see the films. Ferris Pounds, the manager, was well aware of that and on that first evening he presented a well balanced programme of films. But firstly he wanted to make sure that all his customers could see the screen clearly so the show began with a lantern slide depicting three ladies wearing "immense picture hats" (News Letter) followed by a second slide with a written request to remove them. The third slide caused howls of amusement because it showed the hats removed to reveal a man behind the ladies, who had been trying unsuccessfully to see the screen. The films shown included Westerns (The Deputy's Duty), comedies (Stolen Boots, Wiffles Tries to Work, Bobby's First Smoke), and beautifully coloured travelogues from South America and S.E. Asia. The star film however was a coloured version of "David and Goliath" made in France with the players from the Comedie Francaise which went down very well and was warmly applauded at the end (Telegraph).

There was also a special attraction called the Vivaphone which had recently come on the market and which was actually another system where a gramophone was synchronised to the film. It differed from other models in that it had been perfected by the British film maker Cecil Hepworth who had produced an adaptor costing only five guineas that could be attached to any projector. A pointer on the gadget was connected electrically to the gramophone and when the two machines were properly synchronised the pointer covered a light below it. If the speed of one got out of sync the pointer moved and allowed a green or red light to show. The projectionist then adjusted the speed of his machine until the light disappeared. The Vivaphone was much praised at the time because it was simple and effective and could maintain a high level of accuracy, though its success at any time depended largely on the skill of the projectionist. It was used sometimes for speeches but mainly for song and dance items which were filmed while the artistes mimed to the records. In his later years Hepworth was rather dismissive of it and similar systems, describing them as feeble attempts to bestow "the gift of tongues" on the medium that couldn't be compared with the real talkies. Such criticism would have been lost on the audience that first evening as they watched "Ship Ahoy" a nautical song and dance sequence on the screen. Other music was supplied by the pianist Tom Whitehead.

Under Ferris Pounds' guidance the Picturedrome soon became an integral part of local working class life and crowds flocked to see the Westerns, thrillers, dramas, comedies and singing pictures that changed every Monday and Thursday. He must have noticed the large numbers of children in attendance because three weeks after opening he introduced a Saturday morning matinee for them at 11a.m. Being aware of the criticisms from some quarters he sent a message through the Telegraph newspaper that "parents need not have any fear of allowing their children to attend because the class of films for which the hall is noted, the excellent accommodation provided and the large staff of attendants ensures even the youngest child's safety both morally and bodily." The Picturedrome put down deep roots and for nearly sixty years weathered changes, modifications and rebuilding until it finally closed in May 1970.

On Monday 10th April the Alexandra Theatre at the corner of Grosvenor Road and Durham Street opened with a large audience which included the Lord Mayor and his wife. It was an impressive looking building designed by J. D. Swanston of Kirkcaldy, with a facade of red McGladdery bricks, styled after the Italian Renaissance, opening into a bright vestibule which contrasted with the oak panelled walls of the comfortable auditorium decorated tastefully in ivory and gold, with crimson curtains. Seating capacity was nearly 3,000. Admittedly it was not a Picture Palace but it did contain a projection room located for safety behind the stage and the intention was to back project the films from there on to a transparent screen, a technique that Belfast hadn't seen since the turn of the century. The director and chief mover behind the whole project, J.Leicester Jackson, told the audience that recent films would be shown as part of every programme but that the main emphasis would be on good quality live entertainment. There would be two shows each evening at 6.50 and 9.0 p.m which implied fast moving entertainment without any frills. He reminded them that he was a native of Belfast and he had every confidence that the city could support another theatre. He had always found Belfast to be "a good melodrama town" and he promised patrons that in the Alexandra they would always experience "cleanliness, order, courtesy and attention." Prices for seats ranged from 3d to one shilling though boxes cost five shillings and seven shillings and sixpence, a very wide range indeed. The season began with a good Victorian sounding melodrama, "Her Path of Sorrow," during the first week, followed by a musical comedy which starred Dolly King who, according to the Irish News, had recently performed at the Folies Bergeres where "her harem skirt dance created quite a sensation."

The harem skirt had been the cause of much controversy since its recent appearance in Europe. A few weeks before the opening of the Alexandra, examples of the latest dresses and skirts, including harem skirts, arrived in Belfast from Paris and were displayed in the windows of the Bank Buildings for all to see, though only the well-off could afford them. Large crowds of appreciative women gathered, mixed with what the News Letter called, "members of the sterner sex" and there was much humorous comment. The prevailing attitude in the city seems to have been light hearted. For those who felt so inclined the Electric Studio nearby in Royal Avenue offered while-u-wait photographs in a harem skirt, and a range of other comical poses including the Harem Scarem Girl. A sketch of one of the dresses appeared in the Whig and, as the paper commented, it was nothing like the caricatures which were presented to the public in the comic papers or, it could have added, in the comedy films. In fact the garment looked exceptionally elegant and modest, though that didn't prevent some adverse reaction. When similar dresses appeared in the windows of Robinson and Cleaver's someone showed their disapproval by breaking the windows. Needless to say the Alexandra gained from the publicity and then went on to present other popular fare like "My Irish Molly" a superior musical play (Irish News) which was "well received" (News Letter); "A Dark Secret" a thriller in which during one scene the stage was transformed into a river with real water for an exciting rescue sequence; "Hush Money" a Sexton Blake mystery; and "Secrets," an exciting melodrama set in a Turkish harem. Films were shown with every presentation as in the Empire and the Royal Hippodrome, and Mr Jackson must have believed that the two forms of expression could coexist peacefully. But the fact remained that the two latter halls were music halls and the early cinema had been nurtured to some extent within the music hall format, but no such relationship existed between the theatre and films. Films had often borrowed from theatre and basically were a competitor with it. In fact those two elements of borrowing and competition were to be illustrated at the opening of the city's next picture palace.

During June there was much excitement in the city surrounding the approaching Coronation of the new king, George the Fifth, on Thursday the 22nd. Many buildings were decorated and there were plans for outdoor parties in the parks for the children and bonfires in the streets. Such celebrations were generally regarded rather coolly by the Nationalists many of whom showed more enthusiasm for the event which preceded the Royal occasion by a few days. On Monday 19th June 1911 a specially invited group saw the High Sheriff, Councillor Crawford McCullogh, officially open the latest and most luxurious addition to the city's cinemas, the Picture House, located at the junction of Royal Avenue and Garfield Street where Castlecourt Shopping Centre now stands. It was an impressive looking building designed by Naylor and Sale of Derby and its superior facilities reflected how far things had progressed for filmgoers in the one year since the opening of the Princess.

The exterior was finished in polished granite and the main door, which faced in the direction of the City Hall, opened onto a foyer floored with marble. The walls of the interior were panelled with oak and in the auditorium the panels were carved with scenes illustrating the history of ships and their cargoes. The comfort levels in the auditorium itself, which contained 600 seats on ground level with another 120 in the balcony, were controlled by a powerful ventilation system which renewed the air every six minutes. The seating was of the latest tip-up type and the rows were designed to allow maximum space for movement while a clear view of the screen was facilitated by the sloping floor. The overall colour scheme was deep red with a touch of green, while the screen curtains were of luxurious red velvet. The screen itself was deeply recessed and surrounded by black velvet, a contrast aimed at ensuring bright clear pictures. The source of those pictures, the projection room, was, according to the News Letter, among "the finest in existence" with all the latest equipment. The plans indicate a little more, in that the "lantern room" was connected by a door to the winding room where the films were rewound after projection, while on the other side, though separated from it, there was a developing and printing room. That meant that films could be photographed locally and then developed and printed for showing in the cinema. Upstairs, behind the balcony, there was a tea room, the impressively named Oak Room Tea Lounge, where people could have something to eat, write letters or just peruse the latest newspapers and magazines. A cloakroom and even a telephone were available for patrons and every modern precaution was taken against fire and to ensure their safety.

The Picture House introduced a new dimension to "going to the pictures" in Belfast. The cinema was owned and built by the Provincial Cinematograph Theatre Ltd and its high levels of comfort and luxury reflect the capital resources and experience of the company which already owned and operated fifteen other cinemas throughout the Br.Isles, including the historic Volta Cinema in Mary street in Dublin which had been managed briefly by James Joyce. Joyce and his two Italian business partners had actually visited Belfast in the latter half of 1909 looking for a suitable site for a cinema but nothing came of it. Councillor McCullogh welcomed and praised the facilities of the new building and wished its owners every success. With the memory of the recent closure of the Pictoria still fresh in his mind he dismissed the pessimists who still thought that the cinematograph was just a passing fad and, injecting a note of reassurance, emphasised that a business that was well managed and treated the public "in a fair manner" was certain to succeed. In reply the managing director assured the public that only the most recent and best of films from all around the world would be shown and that there would be nothing of a sensational nature included. Besides the normal fare, he promised "special and exclusive productions of outstanding interest." The introductory programme of nature films, documentaries and such included one such production, a two reel version of Shakespeare's "Henry VIII" with Sir Beerbohm Tree and his entire company from His Majesty's theatre in London.

The presence of such an eminent theatre actor in a film was quite unusual, but the film had other claims to fame. Tree was well known in Belfast and had spoken kindly of the city and its theatregoers despite the fact that during a visit in 1903 to the Opera House the attendance was so sparse that complaints even reached the London Times. When he returned in 1907 to the then Palace it was to full houses with a production of "The Red Lamp" which the News Letter described as "pure melodrama, but the undisguised and sterling article" for all that. During 1910 Tree and his company put on a very successful production of Shakespeare's "Henry VIII" in His Majesty's Theatre in London in which he played Cardinal Wolsey, with Violet Vanbrugh as Queen Katherine, Henry Ainley as Buckinham and Arthur Bourchier as the king. During its run he was approached by Will Barker who asked him if he would be willing to have the play filmed.

Barker is a very important figure in the history of the British film. He had started his adult life as a commercial traveller but by the beginning of the century he was involved in film making, especially topicals and news items. In 1909 he set up his own film company and built a small studio of brick and glass at Ealing Green which marked the beginnings of Ealing Studios. Tree was not unreceptive partly because he already had some experience of the medium, having taken part in the filming of a short sequence from Shakespeare's "King John" in 1899. But what convinced him was the unique deal that Barker offered. Tree would receive £1,000 for his trouble and only twenty prints would be made and they would be available for renting at special rates for a limited season of six weeks. To make certain that the film wouldn't compete with the play or undermine its ticket sales, all copies would be recalled at the end of that period and destroyed. Tree's fee was very high for the time but Barker gambled-rightly-that the restricted release, fuelled by his careful publicity, would stimulate interest and rentals. In fact the six week period was soon fully booked. Tree and the whole cast with their props travelled to Ealing on 9th February 1911 and five scenes from the play were filmed by Barker himself. The players were already well prepared so all they had to rehearse was where to move in front of the fixed camera. The prints were ready for release on 27th February by which time a considerable excitement had built up which, as Barker had anticipated, translated itself into full houses

After six weeks the prints were recalled and the Kinematograph and Lantern Weekly described how they were burned to ashes in full view of an invited audience on April 13th. If they had been burned because of censorship problems there would most likely have been protests of one kind or another but because it was for economic reasons there was little comment. Some people weren't entirely convinced. Barker was known as an astute businessman and some argued that he was unlikely to have destroyed the original negative.

Also, despite reports to the contrary, Tree would almost surely have wanted to keep at least one copy for posterity. There was a suspicion in some quarters that the burning was partly a publicity stunt and that copies of the film were still available. The events surrounding the opening of the Picture House give some credence to that view because two months after the supposed destruction of all copies of the film it was definitely being screened in Belfast by a very reputable and eminent concern. Neither Tree or Barker ever threw any light on the matter. Strangely enough, beyond mentioning the film and the appearance of Tree and his company, none of the local critics made any comment about the qualities of the film. The combination of such an eminent actor and Shakespeare would normally have stimulated remarks at least about the educational virtues of the cinema.

Certainly the management of the new cinema regarded instruction or education as an important part of their function. Documentaries and travel films became a familiar part of the programmes and during the first few months audiences were able to see such contrasting subjects as "A Tour of Pisa," "Iron Making at Donetskiy," "The Making of an Aeroplane," and "Flight Over Pau" in which the Telegraph promised that "one can actually experience the sensations of flight." Another aspect of their devotion to knowledge was their use of newsreels, and they often advertised one item of news which they regarded as important as their main attraction. They were just a few weeks too late for the launch of the Titanic on May 31st but another equally newsworthy topic occurred in the opening week, the Coronation of the new king in London, which took place on Thursday 22nd. The London Times noted that the crowds in the streets during the Coronation procession were not as large as expected and put it down to the belief that many people were waiting to see the event in comfort in their local picture palace. The PCT let it be known that they had made an agreement with Will Barker (the same man) to supply film of the procession. Barker had the sequences filmed on Thursday morning and rushed to his laboratories for processing. By 2.0 pm the first prints were ready and messengers took them to the railway stations for distribution throughout the country to all the picture palaces owned by the company. Thus the Picture House was able to put the film on show from 11 am - "something unprecedented" commented the Irish News - on the Friday morning. They didn't have things all their own way because the Alhambra had a version from another source later that day, and by the following week it was showing all over the city. Dazzled by all the speed and efficiency there was probably much local talk of progress though younger citizens probably paid little attention when their elders recalled how Prof. Kineto and Erskine Mayne had equalled such feats many years before.

The association between entertainment and education was highlighted by the local critics often in the following months with regard to a number of major films presented in the Picture House. The management realised the importance of the critics in their attempts to get the support of the middle classes so they introduced the practice of morning previews or press shows for special presentations when the films could be viewed in comfort, without the distractions of an audience. The idea paid off in longer and more detailed comments in which the films were treated more like works in the theatre. The first of those, in early August, was "The Crusaders," a four reel Italian epic which told the story of the capture of Jerusalem from the Saracens. To the delight of audiences it ran unbroken for an hour. The introduction of a second projector, first experienced in the Pictoria, meant that the annoying breaks for reel changes every fifteen minutes were being eliminated. In Belfast there were no complaints about the length but there was widespread admiration for the clarity of the image and the detail of the story telling, for the research to ensure the historical accuracy of the dress and the weapons and for the organization of the battle scenes.

The Italian films which were arriving in increasing numbers on local screens often specialised in colourful historical subjects which were filmed with flair and confidence using actual locations where possible. In that the film makers were greatly aided by the long hours of sunshine and the peculiar quality of the Mediterranean light. But beyond that, Italian directors had discovered the concept of space within the scene and had begun to explore it with the camera. Where possible they did away with painted backdrops and moved out of the studio into the countryside. Some critics have seen that development as analogous in significance to the discovery of perspective in painting. The impact certainly wasn't lost on the local critics. The News Letter admired the beauty of the scenery and commended the way in which the action cast off the restrictions of the stage as, for example, when the fighting scenes took place "in open country...with marvellous realism," while the Irish News was impressed by the visual impact and noted that "the grouping of the characters was always excellently done." The Telegraph summed everything up by advising "all who admire the aesthetic, the intellectual and historic should not fail to see it."

A few months later another Italian epic arrived on the Picture House screen, based on a revered work of literature. It was "The Adventures of Ulysses," a Milano production directed by Guisippe de Liguoro, who also played the part of the wily Ulysses, with a running time of forty-five minutes. It was just what the critics wanted, the indisputable evidence of how the cinema could combine entertainment and education at the highest level. The glories of a Homeric epic, a knowledge of which was essential to anyone who regarded themselves as educated, presented in a visual form, readily accessible to all. All the local papers welcomed and praised it. The News Letter was especially impressed at how "the atmosphere of Ancient Greece (had) been recreated" with a realism, the writer felt, that rivalled the stage. The Telegraph felt that "the educational value of cinematography was never more strikingly exemplified" than in that film, and the Irish News critic praised "this wonderful film" for the clear way it presented the events from Homer's narrative with a vividness which would surely encourage students to go back to the original. The film gripped his attention from the beginning and he found the departure of Ulysses from his beloved wife Penelope in a galley "swan-like in shape, propelled by oars and wafted by the wind on a pair of sails" with the "brilliant sunshine falling on the dazzling whiteness of the garments" very impressive. For the audience it must have been a vivid experience and in the 1950's a relative of the author described seeing the film as a young teacher and, without any prompting, recalled that scene involving the rather quaint looking craft and above all the reflections of the sunlight, not from the clothing but from the water. The Whig thought the fall of Troy was effective and realistic as was the meeting with and the blinding of the Cyclops who according to the Telegraph responded "like an Eastern Finn McCool (hurling) massive rocks after the escaping boat." It was, said the Whig "a real feast of cinematograph." The News Letter regretted the absence of dialogue but added that "the artists who figure in the picture know their business and one can be intensely interested and even thrilled by their expressive gestures and the play of emotion suggested by their mobile features." An audience today would find the film too theatrical and would probably respond to the style of acting with a smile, but audiences of the period sat in respectful silence and even awe at what they were seeing.

The third film, shown in early December, was quite different in that it was a documentary shot by Herbert G. Ponting, the official photographer of Scott's expedition to the South Pole, covering the period from leaving New Zealand to the arrival in Antarctica. By sheer chance while it was showing news arrived from the Antarctic that Roald Amundsen had reached the Pole and that he had seen no sign of Scott or his party on the way. The resulting speculation about Scott's whereabouts naturally increased popular interest in the film. In the papers praise for its obvious educational aspects was equalled by critical enthusiasm for its visual impact. The Whig referred to its "scenes of rare novelty and beauty" and all the critics were impressed by the human detail depicted against the magnificent scenery.

At the beginning of the film, to the delight of all, Capt. Scott posed for the camera and smiled out at the audience. Today viewers, bombarded continuously by visual imagery, accept such images as normal but in 1911 they were rare and memorable. One could imagine the buzz of excitement and recognition that went round the hall as fathers and mothers drew the attention of their children to the screen, while others recalled having seen and heard Scott when he had given a lecture in the City Y.M.C.A. in December 1904. After the Terra Nova sailed snippets of life on board were shown, including scenes of the cinematographer himself preparing for work. The critics praised the clarity of the black and white pictures, and the Telegraph especially mentioned "a marvellous picture taken from a platform built over the starboard side of the Terra Nova (showing) the ship cutting through the ice," followed later by views of Mt Erebus, and of a massive iceberg looking like "the great cliffs of the Antrim Coast." Mention was also made of the "beautiful sky and water effects" and of some charming shots of gulls and penguins "of interest to natural history lovers." In all, the Telegraph told its readers, the film was "a tremendous revelation" while the Irish News added just one word, "magnificent." The film is an important historical document which, seen today, is still visually impressive. One must admire Ponting's achievement under difficult physical conditions, though of course his film has a more poignant significance for a modern audience in view of what subsequently happened to Capt. Scott and his party.

CHAPTER ELEVEN
Goodbye to St George's Hall

St George's Hall, which advertised itself as "the family resort for first class entertainment," catered for audiences belonging mainly to the same social and economic groups as those who frequented the Alhambra and did so with the same entertainment mix though with a touch of distinction now and again in the form of a Shakespeare film, a Continental drama or a spectacular. Typical of the hall's style was the management approach to the ubiquitous Western. Because of their obvious audience pulling power increasing numbers were being shown. Many of them were standard material, and no less popular for that, but some more interesting ones appeared - like Thomas Ince's "Across the Plains" (Sept. 1911) which was much praised. In August, in response to their patrons' requests, an All Western Week was announced, the first example of themed programming and an idea which was to be taken up by other managers later. The Whig approved of the concept and emphasised that the one - reelers shown were well chosen, not only for their variety but also for their high quality, so there was no question of boredom or repetition. The critic supported his judgement by noting the main films, the themes of which seem familiar enough: "The Man from the Foothills," about a cowboy saved from lynching; "A Romance of the West," in which a brave woman stands her ground; "The Justice of the Desert," dealing with the results of a bank failure; "His Side Pard," a dispute over a gold claim; and at least two comedies "The Hobo's Round-up" and "Calino as a Cowboy."

Advertisement for a Film D'Art, Ulysses.

But the Hall is noted above all for introducing the Kalem Irish films to Belfast. The Kalem company was formed in New York in 1907, its name representing the initials of the founders George Kleine, Samuel Long and Frank Marion. Their main director was Sydney Olcott, born in Canada of Irish parents, who recruited actress Gene Gautier for the new company. Miss Gautier not only became famous as the Kalem Girl but showed an aptitude for writing screen plays and outlines. She and Olcott became a very successful team, she writing, he directing. Kalem favoured outdoor location shooting (for one thing it was cheaper) over indoors studio work. In the winter of 1909 they sent Olcott and Gautier from snowy New York to sunny Jacksonville in Florida to make some films and the venture was so successful that they were dispatched again the following year. They had hardly settled in when they were instructed to go further afield, to Ireland in search of scenery and stories. So it was that Kalem arrived in the Killarney area and began filming a one - reeler, "The Lad from Old Ireland," in 1910. The film was finished off with scenes in New York and released later that year in November The story was a simple and straight - forward one about a young Irishman Terry, played by Olcott himself, who emigrates to America where he makes his fortune. He returns to Ireland just in time to save his mother and sweetheart (Gene Gautier) from the horrors of eviction. The film was a great success in the U.S. and Mr Rogers, the manager of St George's Hall, presented it to local audiences in April 1911, advertised as "a romance of one of Erin's Emigrant Sons." The Whig, responding to the location shooting, was much impressed by the realism of the Irish scenes and enthused that the film "was bound to appeal to anyone with a drop of Irish blood in his veins." The crowds agreed and long queues formed into High Street.

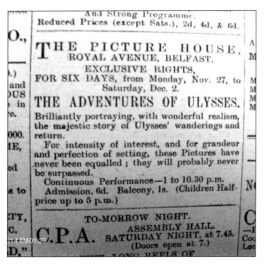

Advertisement for same film, Picture House.

The film is important in the history of cinema in this country because it was the first time a major company from overseas actually made a fiction film in Ireland. Irish inventors had played no major part in the development of the original projecting equipment though local entrepreneurs and photographic enthusiasts like Professor Kinetto soon learned how to use and even improve the machines. Most of the early films made in the country were non - fiction and were the work of outsiders like Robert Paul, the Lumière cameramen and others. The earlier fiction films dealing with Ireland were nearly all made in the U.S.A. In 1906 Edwin S. Porter made a one - reel version of "Kathleen Mavoureen" for Edison which was shown in the Alhambra in November 1908. During the same month "Shamus O'Brien" billed as "a great Irish drama" was also shown but despite the Irish characters and plot the scenery and backgrounds were American. In early 1910 the Alhambra also showed "The Irish Boy" describing it as the story of an Irish emigrant, though the action again took place entirely in the United States.

Sydney Olcott's photoplay was different. It had a greater ring of authenticity because he filmed in Ireland, bringing his own Irish temperament and sensitivity coupled with American technical experience to the subject, and the success of the film showed there was an audience for such material. The film was a blend of those elements and themes that have continued to appeal over the years: the magnificent scenery (around the Lakes

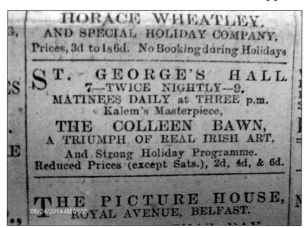

Advertisement for Colleen Bawn.

of Killarney), the oppressive social system, the lure of America, the returned affluent emigrant and his love for a beautiful colleen. It could be an embryonic outline for "The Quiet Man." "The Lad from Old Ireland" lacked a political dimension but Olcott supplied that in his next film, "Rory O'More," the story of an Irish patriot, played by Jack Clark who is captured by the British but who escapes and departs with his sweetheart in a ship bound for America and freedom. It reached Belfast on 30th October 1911 showing simultaneously in St George's Hall and the Alhambra. According to the Irish News it caused "a sensation," attracting large and enthusiastic crowds. The paper recommended it while the Whig was impressed by its "picturesque representation of striking scenes." Over the following months it was brought back "by special request" to both cinemas and also showed in the Kelvin and in the Princess on the Newtownards Road. It is interesting though that St George's Hall balanced its rebel content by including in the same show a much praised Edison film of "Trafalgar," complete with suitable sounds and other effects. The Irish slant was not abandoned and the entertaining "Kathleen Mavourneen," proved to be another success in both the Hall and the Alhambra during mid - November. The Whig described it as "a delight to the eye" while the Irish News found it "vivid."

Irish films.

A month later, at Christmas, St George's Hall announced a "triumph of Irish art," another film made by the Kalem company in Killarney. It was that old favourite "The Colleen Bawn" and the Whig congratulated the manager, Mr Rogers, on how he had managed to secure the film from the distributors in Dublin. It was a three - reeler which ran for over forty minutes. The cast again included Jack Clark, Olcott himself as Danny, and Gene Gautier as the colleen. Miss Gautier became strongly identified with the part and in studio advertisements over the next few years she was often referred to as the Colleen Bawn. The Whig encouraged those "who believe in Ireland and Irish work" to support it as it was "Irish every inch and the very best at that." The I.S.N. praised its lack of artificiality which it put down largely to the use of location shooting in Kerry, with scenes including "the world famous Colleen Bawn rock and cave." The crowds responded and Mr Rogers enjoyed the experience of queues and full houses, which persuaded him to bring the film back in February - to a similar reaction.

What no one local knew was that pressure had been put on Kalem about the subject matter of Olcott's Irish films. The company had suggested to their director to avoid political controversy so he had decided to turn, temporarily at least, to that perennial favourite Boucicoult. "The Colleen Bawn" was quickly followed by "Arrah na Pogue," 3,000 feet in length, running for an hour, which, when it was shown in February, the Telegraph thought was "the best of all the Irish series" so far. The Kelvin advertised it with the slogan that "Arrah na Pogue is still the vogue." The same could be said about Olcott who made about fifteen other films in the Killarney area which were so successful that he contemplated building a permanent studio at the village of Beaufort there, but his plans were thwarted by the outbreak of War. However his films continued to arrive in Belfast.

Two weeks after "Arrah na Pogue" St George's Hall showed an "all Irish romance from Kalem" called "The Fishermaid of Ballydavid" and then a month later had "The O'Neill," not about the great Northern chieftain but a story about an Irish highwayman which according to the Telegraph teemed with "interesting and exciting episodes" that kept one's attention "riveted to the end." At the end of January 1913 St George's Hall showed "Michael O'Dwyer, Irish Outlaw" which the Irish News praised for its beautiful mountain scenery and commended it as "a fine film rich in dramatic incident." A month later it was "The Kerry Gow" which was advertised as "a thrilling Irish Romantic Drama, produced at Killarney by the Famous Kalem Company of Irish players who have become so popular at St George's Hall." Referring to it, the I.S.N. commented that it was "safe to predict record attendances." It was a three - reeler, the plot of which involved a wronged father, his lovely daughter, a wily land agent and a gallant hero all photographed in magnificent surroundings. Typical of the critical comments were those of the Whig which warmly welcomed and endorsed it because of its many "exciting scenes including a race course where the farmer's son wins a race and clears the mortgage on his father's farm, arriving just in time to save the day." Sounds like a rerun of the lad from old Ireland with a few new twists! The following month it was "The Shaughraun" in the Alhambra, another three - reeler running for an hour. Many of the films were brought back by request and appeared all over the city, even turning up in the winter Saturday evening shows in St Mary's Hall, and as part of a Grand Irish Night in the Grosvenor Hall in November. For over two years the Kalem films were major topics of conversation and discussion in the city and, besides their obvious widespread popularity, one detects also in the many recorded comments distinct feelings of pride in their Irishness. Their memory remained fresh over the following years. In May 1915 the "Colleen Bawn" was showing in the Crumlin Picture House and in March 1916 the Kelvin presented "The Shaughran" again, brought back by the special request of its patrons.

Despite the success of the Kalem films and other productions the manager of St George's Hall knew that he would soon face competition nearly on his doorstep. Each time he walked along High Street he could see and hear how the former premises once occupied by furniture makers were being converted to a new Picture Palace to be called the Panopticon. The site, extending from numbers 42 to 46, was located just diagonally across the street, between Sugarhouse Entry and Skipper street. The Panop, as it came to be widely called, was originally planned by Isadore Clifford as a companion hall to the Shaftesbury Pictoria and the earliest plans, dated October 1910, (by Moore and Flanighan, Royal Ave.) show some affinities with the latter in its rather basic facilities, in its size, and especially in the projecting arrangements, with the screen on the High street wall near the entrance and the lantern room at the far end of the building. There were unspecified delays in the undertaking and a final amended plan was not approved by the Surveyor's Office until 18 March 1911. It was for a cinematograph hall to seat 500 persons, but the most obvious

Lad From Ould Ireland (Kalem).

change in the internal geography concerned the projection room which was now located at the High Street end of the building while the screen was transferred to the far wall. It is very possible that the disappointing performance of the Pictoria was a contributory factor influencing Mr Clifford in making that change. When, some time later, the Pictoria closed and the Belfast Electric Theatre Company was wound up Mr Clifford departed the scene leaving the Panopticon unfinished.

The situation was saved when Fred. Stewart took over the project. Mr Stewart was typical of one group of entrepreneurs who entered film exhibition from the fairground end of the entertainment spectrum. He was Scottish and had been born in Brechin in Forfarshire. As a lad of sixteen he had been apprenticed to the jewellery trade, but his real interest lay in entertainment and he was soon touring in south England with a small flea circus. From there he moved into waxworks. He took many jobs connected with fairgrounds and even did a stint as an assistant manager in the famous Coney Island in New York. On his return to England he became interested in the new animated pictures and for a time managed a cinematograph hall in London before returning to Scotland where, according to the Whig, he acquired interests in Picture Palaces in Edinburgh, Leith and Glasgow. He arrived in Belfast in 1910 to survey the opportunities in the entertainment scene and soon opened a Grand Waxworks in vacant premises at 78, Ann Street. His first cinema was the

Electric Picture Palace in York Street and its success persuaded him to look around for other suitable ventures, a search that led to the Panopticon. As an experienced showman he realised immediately that it occupied an excellent city centre site which offered attractive business possibilities.

The official opening was on Thursday 22nd February 1912 before an invited audience who were promised "a revelation in cinematography" and "the last word in living pictures" and who were, by all accounts, not disappointed by what they saw. The front of the building was "tastefully designed" (Whig) and, in keeping with accepted practice, was pure white in colour though with an Irish touch in the form of edgings of emerald green. It looked particularly impressive at night when it was illuminated by electric bulbs, and it certainly brought a splash of colour to the business premises along High Street. The green tints were continued in the interior decorations but blended tastefully with gold and red, while the ceilings were light cream within black mouldings. The seats for 340 persons were of the latest tip -up type, covered in green and gold and were placed for maximum viewing comfort on a sloped floor. The screen was surrounded with an impressive gold frame. The electrical system, significantly installed by a firm (Robertson and Hogg) brought over from Edinburgh, incorporated the latest technical developments while the projection used Gaumont machines which gave clear steady pictures that posed "no injury to eyesight." (Whig) The pianist was D. Walsh, who had tinkled the ivories in the Electric, but now he had at his disposal a special electronic piano, technically described as a synphonista - carona - xylophone which could reproduce the instrumental range of a full orchestra. The sound of that must have appealed greatly to the showman in Stewart and it was probably with difficulty that he restrained himself from joining in and shouting "roll-up, roll-up."

He was very pleased at the response of the public who rolled up in large numbers but he soon realised that there were problems. The hall was too small and as the plans indicate one wall in the auditorium was curved, which tended to distort its viewing harmony. Also, most importantly, the projected pictures weren't bright enough. That drawback was quickly remedied when a new metallic screen was installed three weeks after the opening, with a promise of fifty percent more light. Playing upon the theme of an electric theatre the showman in him invited the populace to come to his "High Street Electric Power Station (where) the Power was Switched on Daily at 2:30." They were promised "live wire" films with a "fun accumulator (which made) resistance to laughter impossible." Added to that were selections varying from Wagner to ragtime on the "electric orchestra." By that time he was already well advanced in the planning of the next stage of the development. Showing a reluctance to cast off his fairground associations, a month later he opened his Panoptican Grand Exhibition next door to the cinema.

It was an elaborate waxworks with some fairground attractions added, spread over three rooms. In the first hall there were figures of Royalty with politicians and military men while in the second hall there were six scenes from a gambler's life "with a suitable moral warning", plus figures from the realm of sports, religion and crime. Added to those were curios, distorting mirrors, penny - in - the slot machines (probably including mutoscopes) and such. Various attractions were promised for the future and one of those turned out to be a flea circus which was organised and presented by Mr Stewart himself.

Obviously he had a special affection for the novelty that had started his career. Another was a fasting man who set out to do without food for the Biblical forty days, existing only on a diet of soda water and cigarettes. After thirty nine days the doctor ordered food to be taken but it was announced that the exhibition would remain on show for another week with the subject "feeding up." With stunts like that one could, with good cause, have felt uneasy about the type of future fare to be presented in the cinema. At the opening of the waxworks he explained that his role as proprietor was "to make this exhibition always fresh and attractive by constant changes and additions.........and no effort or expense will be spared to keep this establishment in the forefront." He obviously applied those guidelines equally to his cinema.

He understood from his dealings with the public the fascination that people had with the cinematographic screen. Charles Laughton put it well when he said that in those early days people leaned forward in their seats, not like today when they tend to loll back. Mr Stewart decided to give them quality entertainment that would definitely encourage them to lean forward. He tried the tested favourites like Lt. Rose and P.C.Sharpe and even the trusty Westerns but decided that something extra special was needed. Thus, a few months after opening, he presented the prestigious Selig production "Christopher Columbus" which the Whig thought was "well done" and which the Irish News praised for its production values, its excitement, its realism and the way it evoked the past with "details that words fail to express" so that it held the audience's interest to the end. It was followed by the Vitagraph version of "Vanity Fair" and the "Charge of the Light Brigade" in which viewers were promised a meeting with Queen Victoria (the showmanship still tended to show through). Knowing that a touch of the exotic never did any harm from a commercial point of view, he delighted audiences and local critics with "Mysteries of Paris" based on Eugene Sue's novel, "Dante's Inferno," and "Paris, the Siren," a sensational vein that he was to continue to mine in the future.

"The Mysteries of Paris" was a Pathé production directed by Albert Capellani which had been released the year before and arrived in Belfast with the reputation of being the most sensational and financially successfully film ever made. The public were assured that it had taken more money at the box office than any other dozen films together, an advertising ploy that hasn't really changed over the years. Added to that was the fact that it ran for an hour and a half. All the critics welcomed it as a familiar work and pointed out how it had evolved from sensational novel to stage and then to screen. The original novel by Eugene Sue was a great popular success but it wasn't great literature, claimed the News Letter. Sue wrote "at white heat" and tended to sacrifice everything for the sake of effect, but when his work was adapted for the stage the resulting melodrama had been equally successful and many in Belfast still remembered it from performances in the Theatre Royal. The News Letter critic commented that that type of sensational story was very suited to the cinema or, as he put it, was "very effective in dumb show for the cinematograph." The plot involved the nefarious activities of a criminal gang consisting of a cruel Schoolmaster, his wife the Screech Owl and his retarded son Hoppy. He found the story "coherent," the action "vividly depicted," and the acting "vigorous." The Telegraph agreed about the high level of excitement while the Irish News noted that in its telling "thrill follows upon thrill." Scenes in a disreputable tavern were especially highlighted. The Telegraph described how when the hero is searching the tavern he is tricked and falls through a trapdoor into a secret cellar from which he is rescued just in the nick of time. The Whig was equally impressed by the scenes in the tavern which showed "the squalor of the buildings and the cruel and cunning expressions on the faces of the people." There is much about the film that sounds familiar and quite modern - an example of how a mediocre novel can make a highly successful film, advertised and promoted with an emphasis on action, sensation and commercial success.

Dante's "Inferno" had equally sensational connotations but had a much superior literary pedigree. It was an Italian production made by Milano Films in 1909 and directed with some flair by Giuseppe de Liguoro. De Liguoro knew his Dante and was also aware of the engravings illustrating the work completed by Dore which he used to shape his visuals, adding his own imaginative touches like periodically turning the screen red, a device that Hitchcock was to use later to great effect in "Marnie" (d. Alfred Hitchcock, 1964). The film was made in three parts which could be shown separately or as a unit. Mr Stewart opted for part one which ran for thirty minutes, but the response was so positive that he showed the remaining two parts spliced together two months later.

There were and still are those who would argue that a work like the Inferno is diminished when it is translated to the screen and that many who would go to see it would be unaware of its religious and allegorical content. The News Letter observed that the film had generated much discussion - Mr Stewart must have been pleased to read that - but added that "the poem itself is one of the most remarkable in the literature of the world and by reason of its wonderful complexity and deep seated knowledge of human frailty cannot readily be adapted for cinematographic purposes." De Liguoro was well aware of that and while he catered for the educated elite - the film was made according to the News Letter "with scrupulous regard for detail" - he depended on the demons, the torments and the other fantastical elements to attract the crowds needed for worthwhile commercial returns. He also persuaded many of his wealthy friends in Milan to play the parts of the damned, which they seem to have done with enthusiasm. The local critics were well pleased with what they saw and after explaining for those who hadn't read the original text that the film dealt with Dante's journey to the Underworld, to the circles of Hell itself guided by the poet Virgil, they heartily recommended it. The Whig was above all impressed by the "elaborate scale" of the production and commented that many scenes were so "remarkable" that they left a "deep impression on the mind." The Irish News agreed, praised the "fine dramatic effect" and felt it would appeal greatly to students of literature. The Telegraph found it "outstanding" and drew attention to the apt musical accompaniment which added to the overall impact. The News Letter responded to the serious nature of the subject and thought that overall the film could only be described as "excellent." When parts two and three were shown in April all agreed that it was even more impressive. The Whig critic thought it was probably the "strangest film that has yet been produced" and found the scenes of the damned souls with sinners being whipped by demons and Lucifer himself eating some of his victims, quite disturbing. The Irish News noted that the cinema itself was "overflowing" which, of course, was Mr Stewart's main aim.

With such a response it isn't surprising that also in April the Panopticon presented a kindred subject called "Satan" which had a screen time of one hour and forty five minutes. It was another Italian production made by the Ambrosio Company and illustrated the continuing evil influence of the Devil on human affairs by way of three stories set in Biblical times, the Middle Ages and the modern era. The local critics gave it very favourable reviews, using terms like "most remarkable" (Irish News), "a triumph" (Whig), "vivid and realistic" (News Letter) and "spectacular" (Telegraph). Only the Telegraph raised the problem of whether the Devil was a fit topic for the screen but set the question aside for others to answer. The News Letter thought that the subject was treated "with reserve and dignity" and while the Irish News agreed, it emphasised that the film was quite unusual. The Telegraph felt that the early impressive scenes of the expulsion of Satan from Heaven were influenced by Milton, while the Whig was intrigued to see how, when the Devil reached earth, he metamorphosed into a serpent to tempt Eve and Adam and later was responsible for showing Cain how to make a weapon to kill Abel. From then on he fomented wars and conflict and encouraged the building of the Tower of Babel in a series of scenes which The Telegraph thought were "very effective." In the New Testament sequence he tempts Christ but, as the Whig pointed out, it is the only time in the film when he is defeated. In the Middle Ages he is responsible for the spread of the knowledge of how to make alcohol and the misery that accompanies it. The modern sequence sees him maliciously causing the separation of two young lovers which leads the man to crime, until pursued by the police, in desperation he blows up the house where he is hiding. The Whig was very impressed by the final scene showing "his Satanic Majesty standing over the ruins of the house and calmly lighting a cigarette" and went on to praise the performance of the actor playing the difficult role of Satan, and also the high quality of the photography.

Empire Theatre knew what its patrons appreciated.

The film showed to full houses and must have made a deep impression on many of the viewers to whom the Devil was a real person but one whom most of them perceived as having horns and a tail. The idea of him being a modern sophisticated citizen surely caused much discussion and debate. Since then a number of actors have distinguished themselves playing him as "normal" looking, notably Walter Houston as "Mr Scratch" in "The Devil and Daniel Webster" (d. William Dieterle, 1941). The structure of the film with three stories linked by a common character and theme is also interesting and one wonders if D.W.Griffith saw it before developing his epic "Intolerance" which used a similar framework though worked out in a much more complex manner.

In contrast to such exotic content "Paris the Siren" had a more familiar theme, that of the provincial or rural dweller being seduced by the attractions of the big city. Indeed a number of plays on that theme with names like "How Girls are Brought to Ruin" and "The Lure of London" had been presented in the Theatre Royal in which the main character was usually an innocent young girl but in this case it was a male student who is "ruined by the seductiveness of Parisian life" (News Letter). The story enfolds against the well known scenic attractions of Paris and so is part travelogue, but also includes scenes of the "infamous" bohemian lifestyle. Mr Stewart carefully leavened such visual provocation with a careful sprinkling of quality products of literary origin from the Hepworth studio - like "Oliver Twist" and "Lorna Doone" - but he really struck gold dust when he made an agreement with the Walturdaw company to give him exclusive releases on the films of Asta Nielsen.

Asta Neilsen: European star of note

Miss Nielsen is often referred to as the first international film star and she certainly became very well known and popular in Belfast due mainly to the efforts of Fred. Stewart. The adverts for her films always carried her name and in the local papers she was often referred to as "the German Sarah Bernhardt," a label which was meant as a compliment but which was misleading on both counts. She was actually Danish, born in Copenhagen and made her first films there for the Nordisk Company before moving to Germany and while she was a fine actress her style was much less flamboyant and more naturalistic than the divine Sarah. Her first film, "The Abyss," (1910, d. by Urban Gad, who became her husband) tells of the moral decline and fall of a piano teacher who is enticed away from her boyfriend by a cowboy in a travelling circus. It was actually shown in the Q.F.T. as part of the Belfast Festival in September 2000 and gave modern audiences an insight into the quality of films that Belfast filmgoers watched in 1910. The results were surprising to many. From a technical viewpoint the photography was startlingly clear and the opening scene which showed Miss Nielsen walking across a city centre square is almost three dimensional in its impact. The camera follows her as she boards a tram and flirts with a man standing on the platform at the back. During the scene the long interior of the tram extending to the driver is in perfect focus (long before "Citizen Kane"!). Miss Nielsen is not only attractive looking but her acting is quite naturalistic and in the main lacks any exaggerated gestures, while she moves with grace and style. The plot develops clearly and is easily understood despite the almost complete absence of intertitles. Only at the climax when, during a violent quarrel, she stabs her lover to death is there a modicum of arm waving and dramatic posing. The final shot is of her, in shock, being led away by the police while her boyfriend covers his face in his hands.

Beginning in November 1912 the Panopticon showed a series of her films beginning with "The Dance of Death" which was the story of a dancer who suffered because of her husband's jealousy. It was followed in quick succession by "The Outcast" which the Irish News praised for its "natural manner" and realism, "Gypsy Blood," "The Great Moment," "Falsely Accused," (the News Letter noted the large crowds it attracted), "When the Mask Falls "("with the well known actress Asta Nielsen," wrote the Irish News), and "The Secret Code," (a strong plot concerning a female spy "well played by Asta Nielsen," said the Whig). By that time she was an accepted part of the entertainment scene and the Telegraph was able to comment how she continued to gain in popularity. Her films tended to be highly dramatic and the News Letter pointed out that each had some distinctive feature, noting that her latest, "A Girl Without a Country" had a "dramatic and unconventional finale." She often played an independent woman and tended to endure a lot in her films, many of which didn't have the customary happy ending. Her attraction for local cinemagoers seemed to be a combination of her personality and the fact that her films were well made with highly dramatic unconventional plot lines. Once that image had been established, Mr Stewart surprised everyone in April 1913 when he presented her in a lighter mood, in a comedy called "In a Fix," part of a programme which also included the inimitable

The Melbourne
Cinema opens

John Bunny in "Mike O'Shayne, Matchmaker" one of the films he had made on his visit to Ireland.

Watching the success of the Panopticon from across the street the management of St George's Hall knew that, like Asta Nielsen, they were in a fix, but there was nothing funny about it. The owners, Entertainments Ltd., decided that expansion was the answer. Their experience told them that the majority of filmgoers were workers so they decided to open a new Electric Theatre in a working class district. They acquired an old Methodist mission hall in Melbourne Street, just off Townsend Street, which they renovated and decorated before announcing that the Melbourne Electric Theatre would open on Monday, April 1st 1912 "as a picture house for the masses." They appealed to the local residents to regard it as "a branch of a popular and old-established Belfast house" which was unnamed but which everyone knew was St George's Hall. Significantly the advertisement added in heavy print that "we know your tastes and shall cater for them," - maybe a rash promise. There is little information about the new hall except that it had seating for about 400 and that it was "spacious, lofty and well ventilated" (Telegraph). The walls were painted in light colours decorated with the likenesses of well known music hall artistes. The Irish News reported that Mr Rogers would manage the business but, while he had overall responsibility, the man in direct charge of the hall was a Mr William Robinson. The hall charged "people's prices "of 2d and 4d (similar to St George's Hall and the Alhambra) which were, according to the Telegraph, "well within the reach of the purses of the working classes seeking enjoyable and instructive entertainment for themselves and their families." The new venture caused much excitement and anticipation in the area and a large crowd, mainly of young people, turned up for the opening programme. They joined heartily in singing along with the pianist, Mr Mc Henry, as he played a medley of popular songs.

The film programme which followed was a mixture of the "grave and gay, the farcical and tragic" (Telegraph) consisting of "The Roman Tyrant" (in colour), "Tested by the Flag," "A Woman Paul Revere," "A Miser's Christmas," "The Family Pet's Revenge," "His First Row," and "A Monkey's Bite." Despite the rather mediocre content the films were received enthusiastically and were often interrupted by clapping and cheers of appreciation. The following week saw equally large crowds to enjoy "Kit Carson's Wooing" and "Saved From the Torrents" among others and then the Melbourne disappeared from the public awareness. It's owners realised that its appeal was strictly local so it stopped advertising in the papers and depended on front - of - house posters and word of mouth. The emphasis on its working class appeal really meant that it was run on a shoestring and that its facilities were rather basic. That didn't diminish its local welcome or the pleasure it obviously gave, and it continued in business for a few years. It appears in the Directories for 1913 and 1914 but in 1915 the building had reverted back to a mission hall. That suggests that it closed sometime in 1914 and it is interesting that adverts for the "mother" hall St. George's also ceased in April of that year, the last known films shown there being ' The Mexican Spy "and a railway drama called "A Race With Time." Despite a valiant struggle neither hall could compete with the new picture palaces with their higher levels of comfort and improved projection facilities.

St George's Hall continued to operate though without showing films, and the name remained on the building into the Thirties. Its occupants included the Ulster Sports Club. St George's Building was bomb damaged in the Seventies but after a facelift which retained the original facade but greatly modified the interior it was bought and occupied by J.G.O'Hare, a firm of solicitors. Today the hall is for most people a forgotten location as is the part it played in the early history of the cinema. From August 1908 to April 1914 St George's Hall was a cinema to be reckoned with. Amazingly it is still in existence - at least in part - but access is forbidden because the Fire Service has sealed it off because the floor is deemed to be unsafe. The interior is in a dilapidated state but, according to one report, contains the remains of a boxing ring, a reminder of the Ulster Sports Club. One wonders what else may be hidden there.

Improvements were a necessary concomitant to attracting audiences because films were becoming longer and more complex in plotting so that going to the pictures was becoming more of an event. One man who realised the truth of that was W.J. Anderson, the owner of the Princess Picture Palace on the Upper Newtownards Road. In July 1912 he let it be known that the days of the Princess were numbered and that the week beginning 15th July would "positively be the last week of entertainment in this building." By way of clarification a writer in the I.S.N. added that the management felt that a larger, more comfortable hall was needed and that would be supplied by a new building, the New Princess, just across the road, to which the business would be transferred. Thus began the sequence of events leading to the presence of two Princesses on the Newtownards Road. It is not unusual for cinemas to cluster but what is unusual is for two cinemas to face each other in competition carrying essentially the same name.

The new cinema was being built for a new company Irish Electric Palaces Ltd and their architect, Thomas Houston of Wellington Place, set out to produce something out of the ordinary. The plans, approved in March 1912, were beautifully executed in colour on linen, and show a building designed to hold 900 and fronted with a dramatic windmill - like construction which would be lit by coloured lights at night. Unfortunately, the arms of the windmill were never completed; but despite that the building - "of unique design," to quote the I.S.N. - remained striking in appearance. The original Princess closed on Saturday 20th July and the new Princess opened with a fanfare on Monday 29th. On the surface it seemed an agreed transfer of business so the expectant public were not surprised when it was announced that the new cinema would continue to charge the same prices of admission and would carry on the traditions of the former. A clear indicator of that was that the main film on the first programme was "The Deputy's Love Affair" a new adventure of their favourite cowboy, Andy. The experienced manager, W.J.Bowering from London, exhorted the public to "give the splendid new building a bumping opening week." And they did just that, with an estimated 20,000 patrons attending in that period. They found a much improved facility with a spacious interior, the walls decorated with panels painted pale green and with a fine painting of Shaw's Bridge drawing the eyes to the back of the wide stage. The stage was an important addition because live entertainment was promised as well as the films, while music would be supplied by a special "fifty guinea Collard and Collard piano" played by the resident pianist Miss Cook. The total seating was greater than the plans indicate, with 100 comfortable seats at sixpence, 200 upholstered seats at fourpence and a noisy sea of 800 seats on wooden benches at twopence. The floor was sloped to allow clear views of the latest type of aluminium screen. Full attention was paid to safety with the use of fireproof materials while the projection room had fireproof self - closing doors and was separated from the auditorium by a brick wall 18 inches thick. The programming consisted of two separate shows at seven and nine each evening with children's matinees on Mondays and Saturdays.

It seemed to be business as usual but obviously behind the scenes the business arrangements went sour for suddenly Mr Anderson announced that the original hall would reopen after renovation. On August 10th the New Princess announced that "we have completely severed connections with the Old House opposite. Ours is the Windmill House." Once battle was joined the new hall set out on a vigorous advertising campaign claiming to be a People's Palace while the older hall, like the Melbourne, contented itself with front - of - house posters and word of mouth to draw its audiences. It rarely advertised, one unusual exception being in January 1915 when it described itself as Ye Olde Princess offering a last opportunity to see "la Belle Hedida" which wasn't a French film but referred to a visiting English dancer. The competition between the two halls was well known in the trade but in the end the more modern facilities and greater financial resources of the Windmill House won out though the original Princess carried on for over thirteen years before closing in the mid Twenties.

Another local entrepreneur who saw a lucrative future for the entertainment business was John Donnelly who was in the coal trade and owned property, including stables, on Albert Street located between the Cullintree Road and McDonnell Street, backing on to Lady Street. In 1909 he had part of that property renovated as an Entertainment Hall "complete with ladies and gents retirement rooms, WC's and cloakrooms" (according to the plans) for music hall turns and social functions. But he had noted the spread of the film going habit and the growing network of cinemas catering to it. As yet the densely populated Falls Road had no cinemas, the only local centre presenting films being St Mary's Hall in Bank Street, with its Saturday night winter shows. Donnelly decided to do something to rectify the situation. He formed the West Belfast Picture Company and in December 1912 applied for permission to alter and convert his hall to a picture theatre. The plans, by Robert Lynn of Ann Street, indicate an auditorium about sixty feet long (19m) and thirty five feet wide(10m), to accommodate 390 seats. Yet when the West Belfast Picture Theatre opened on Wednesday 18th December the Irish News remarked that it could hold up to 600 people. The opening was quite an occasion for the lower Falls and the hall was packed for the first film, a detective thriller called "The Adventures of Tom Butler." The Irish News described the hall as "splendidly equipped" and noted that the projection room, where Walker Browne worked the machines, had fireproof doors between it and the winding room, and between it and the outside corridor. The latter led to the balcony which was equipped with the latest tip up seats. In contrast, the pit had wooden benches which were regarded as normal in those days. Prices were pitched at a working class level at 2d and 4d, with 6d for the balcony. Shows were presented at 7 and 9 in the evening with the programmes being changed on Mondays and Thursdays. The manager, Jeremiah Mc Cavanagh, decided to present popular material, and thus, later weeks saw "Broncho Bill Outwitted," "The Ranchman's Trust" and "The Adventures of an Army Colonel" - all of which drew large crowds.

Not unexpectedly Irish films or, more correctly, films with Irish themes or settings also proved to be great favourites. A short time after the opening audiences enjoyed a week of Irish material including that old favourite "The Colleen Bawn," plus "The Death of Michael O'Grady," "One Round O'Brien," "Kathleen Mavoureen," "Shamus O'Brien," and "Life at Hogans." To add to the Irish atmosphere Belle O'Neill appeared and sang Irish songs, for despite the attraction of the films, live entertainment was always a part of the programmes from the opening night, when the noted Irish baritone Denis Glasgow sang. One advantage of having a cinema on the Falls was that films with particular Catholic interests could be shown and be certain of support. In October 1913 it was announced that a special film, 2,500 feet long, of the Irish National Pilgrimage to Lourdes which had taken place the month before had been secured from Dublin "at great expense" and would be shown at special prices of 4d for the pit, 6d for the balcony and one shilling for reserved seats. The result was packed houses for two weeks. The Irish News whetted appetites by commenting that the photography was crystal clear and that the Belfast pilgrims were well represented on screen - which was another way of telling its readers that they might catch a glimpse of themselves, their relations or their friends. The reporter described how the film began in London and then followed the party on the sea - crossing from Folkestone to Boulogne followed by the railway trip to Paris where Mass was heard in the magnificent church of the Madeleine at the top end of the Rue Royale. From there the pilgrims travelled across the city in large vehicles, each drawn by four horses, to the railway station for the journey south via Bordeaux and Tarbes. Finally the ceremonies in Lourdes were shown in great detail, along with splendid scenes of the town with the river Gave and the snow - capped Pyrenees in the background. Besides its financial success it became clear that a religious film could also reduce the noisiest of audiences to silence.

During the last week of the year another film with a religious theme was shown to great acclaim. It was "By the Cross" an Italian spectacular made by the Savoy Film Company of Turin which dealt with the events surrounding the decision of the Emperor Constantine in 312 AD to declare Christianity a "religio licita" or legally permitted religion. The publicity emphasised that, while the actual narrative was fictional, every effort had been made to keep to known historical facts. The News Letter critic was impressed by the fact that the script was original in that it wasn't based on an existing play or novel. He noted that the story dealt with the trials of the early Christians and contrasted their calmness with "the turmoil, passion, brutality and ignoble strife of the pagan world." He felt that the blend of fact and fiction meant that "it should appeal to the ordinary picturegoer, also the student, historian, archaeologist and churchman." The Telegraph equally felt that it "combined and blended world - moving and stirring incidents with educative, moral and love interests." The Irish News also indicated its approval and drew particular attention to the "very impressive" scenes of Constantine's army crossing the Alps from Gaul on their way to Rome, and the sequence before the battle of Milvian Bridge when the symbol of the cross appeared in the clouds and Constantine had his soldiers engrave it on their shields as a sign of their coming victory. No one thought it unusual that an average working class audience, including children, should understand and appreciate a foreign film, because it was accepted that the silent film was an international medium accessible to all. The West Belfast Picture Theatre became a much loved part of the local social scene and went on to be much better known later as the Arcadian; but no matter what its official name was many locals continued to refer to it simply as "Johnny Donnelly's." The coalman and the emperor, Johnny Donnelly and Constantine, seemed an unlikely combination for success, but such was the nature of the cinema industry that was beginning to dominate the local entertainment scene.

CHAPTER TWELVE
The Craze For Excitement

1913 was a special year in the history of Belfast because it was the tercentenary of the granting of the Charter to the settlement which gave it town status but, in view of the rising tensions over the Home Rule issue, it was decided that celebrations were not in order. The political uncertainties over Home Rule did not disrupt the optimism of the picture palace business. In the early years of the century there were those who had held the view that the cinematograph was just another fad and that in time public interest in it would fade but by 1913 it was widely accepted that that wasn't the case and that films had come to stay. "There is no end to new picture theatres," declared the Telegraph, not in a spirit of exasperation or criticism, but as a simple statement of fact about what was happening in the city. At the opening of the Clonard in December the Irish News agreed that "picture houses have come to stay" and forecast accurately that more would be built because the then total of thirteen halls was "not excessive" for a city the size of Belfast.

In March the annual stockholders meeting of the PCT which owned the Picture House in Royal Avenue took place and was widely reported locally. The managing director R.T.Jupp, a man highly regarded in the trade and well known in Belfast, addressed the meeting about the extremely healthy state of the film business. As an insider he had his finger on the pulse of that business and was well aware of what was happening. He pointed out that there were approximately 6,000 cinemas in the British Isles and that attendances continued to increase, with eight million people visiting the cinema each week. The opportunities for development were there and their own company had seen profits increase from £47,000 to £80,000 over the previous twelve months. He saw films as "the rational amusements of the masses" and felt that people would continue to support the industry as long as they got "clean, light, wholesome entertainment." Many in Belfast would have agreed with his general analysis while believing that the reasons for the local cinema's success were not difficult to find. It was a cheap form of entertainment and, as its critics pointed out, it required very little effort on the part of the viewers to appreciate it so that it tended to appeal to the unsophisticated, a view that was certainly held in certain circles in Belfast.

In a letter to the News Letter in December 1913 a rather severe critic of the cinema deplored the fact that "working people practically keep the picture halls up" and claimed that every night of the week one can see "poor ill clad people who can least afford it filing into these places and wasting money which might have been spent on better dress or beautifying their homes." He couldn't understand why people wanted "to be amused like babies with pictures." Such an unsympathetic vision overlooked the multi-layered response that films could trigger and especially their power to appeal to the imagination of the audience in a way that other entertainments didn't. The screen presented something for everyone from the young girls and boys in the front benches sucking brandy balls and smelling of Finlay's soap, to the young men who had recently "slid down the bannisters" into long trousers, the sign of manhood, with their bright eyed girlfriends beside them, and the quieter more mature mothers and fathers. They forgot their cares as they collectively roared with laughter at the antics of Pimple and John Bunny, or gazed from the cover of darkness upon the fabulous and the unattainable. Before their eyes the past was recreated and they saw the burning of Troy, watched the Roman legions march again, thrilled to Maciste as he saved his mistress Cabiria from the flames of sacrifice in ancient Carthage, admired the great figures of history like Columbus, George Washington, Napoleon, Nelson and Queen Elizabeth. They could accompany Lieut. Rose or Nick Carter on their perilous adventures or ride the Western plains with Bronco Billy or Tom Mix. Children emerging from the picture palaces mounted their invisible horses and raced off along the pavement slapping their hips for greater speed while their pointed fingers became sixshooters and the drab streets were transformed into ravines and valleys.

Some, of course, entered too seriously into the game, like the young seventeen year old lad from Hind Street who became fascinated with the West to the point that he wanted to become a cowboy. He dressed in Western garb and "attended a picture palace in a regular fashion" (Telegraph). Finally, in an act of desperation, he took his father's best boots and pawned them for ten shillings before setting off on his great adventure. He was caught by the police on a train at Newtownards with four shillings and two pence in his pocket and ended up in court accused of stealing a pair of boots. There were those who shook their heads at such evidence of how the picture palace could lead immature people astray, but despite some isolated incidents of that kind the cinema above all brought colour, excitement and "wonders" (Telegraph) into the drab lives of the poor.

It is difficult for modern citizens to visualise the extent of poverty among the workers of the period. A reporter from the Manchester Guardian visited the city at the time and wrote that he couldn't believe the poverty of the textile workers who lived with hardships of long working hours, low wages, inferior housing, inadequate diet and poor health. Over the years those conditions were highlighted and criticised by local newspaper editors, politicians like Joe Devlin, various visitors and many local men and women of conscience like the clergy and helpers associated with organizations like the Belfast Central Mission (Grosvenor Hall) and the St Vincent de Paul. In December Dr Traill, a Co. Antrim man who was Provost of Trinity College, Dublin, and a group of C. of I. clergymen added their voices to the critics. Dr Traill painted a depressing picture of the industrial poor in Belfast living without religion or hope "in narrow parallel streets of small houses without amusements." While the overall situation he described was accurate, at least the lack of amusements was being ameliorated by the new cinemas where people could go and, for a few pence, spend an hour or so being entertained in a warm social environment.

The cinemas, unlike theatres which tended to locate at city centres, were willing to go to their audiences. Thus across Belfast new cinemas had been constructed on York street, Shankill Road, Newtownards Road, and the Falls Road, all working class areas. Each one was building up a faithful audience of fans, mainly of locals who identified specially with it. The Irish News astutely pointed out that if a film was shown in a city centre hall it wouldn't exhaust its audience potential because it could still find an audience elsewhere in the city. Thus a film shown, for example, in the Picture House on Royal Avenue could later be shown successfully in the Princess, the Shankill Picturedrome or the West Belfast Picture Theatre where it could still attract an audience. Unlike plays and music hall, films went to the audiences and most people tended to wait until they arrived at their local where they could see them at their convenience and at prices they could afford. A system of first runs at the city centre followed by showings in the suburbs evolved to service that state of affairs.

At the beginning of the year (1913) a discernible pattern was emerging in the distribution of cinemas which was to persist in its essentials until the nineteen sixties. A cluster of halls located near the city centre where they availed of the heavy pedestrian flows in that area, while at the same time depending upon the up-to-date facilities of their halls plus the presentation of well advertised latest films to attract audiences from widely across the city. They included the historic and popular Alhambra in busy North street which, although built originally as a music hall and still inclined to include one or two live acts in its programmes, had been remodelled and modified to show films so that it regarded itself, and was regarded so by its audience, primarily as a Picture Palace; St. George's Hall in High Street which had a fine location but struggled to overcome the deficiencies of a hall which was never designed for the comfortable viewing of films; the Panopticon also in High Street successfully attracting large crowds with its modern facilities and first class films; the Kelvin in College Square East offering all the comforts of a bijou hall; and the Picture House at the heart of things in Royal Avenue, without doubt the premier picture hall in the city due largely to the fact that it benefited from having the resources of a large British circuit behind it. The Telegraph described it as being "the pioneer of comfort and high class entertainment" with programmes that appealed "to all classes of the community and to all shades of intellectuality." In the older working class residential areas outside the city centre area were the Melbourne Electric Theatre in Melbourne Street, a rather basic hall though no less popular for that; the renamed Silver Cinema in York Street; the more elaborate Picturedromes on the Shankill Road and at Mountpottinger; and the recent West Belfast Picture Theatre in Albert Street off the Falls Road. Outside that again in what was then approaching the suburbs were the two Princesses on the upper Newtownards Road and the Pictoria in Shaftesbury Square. A total of thirteen halls to which, as the Irish News had forecast, three more were added during the year: the West End, the Clonard and the Central.

As the number of cinemas increased the competition between them intensified. In his address Mr Jupp emphasised the need for what he called "attractive and exclusive films" in the successful running of a cinema. The same year he established a film unit called London Films at Twickenham and imported American technicians and talent to produce the quality films he needed for his cinema chain, It was an astute move that gave him control of production, distribution and exhibition in one business organisation. Belfast audiences were soon to benefit from the new arrangement and quickly became familiar with the logo of London Films whose first film "The House of Temperley" based on Conan Doyle's play "Rodney Stone" showed successfully in the Picture House in mid - November. The film, advertised as "the finest ever shown," starred Ben Webster and Lillian Logan a name that means little today but about whom the News Letter wrote that she was "already too well known to cinematograph audiences to call for further comment." The film was well received by both critics and audiences. The Picture House, under the direction of its manager Noel Hobart, applied Jupp's benchmark of quality during 1913, and presented a series of interesting and significant films during the year, including "Custer's Last Fight," "The Count of Monte Cristo," "Les Miserables," "Theodora," "Pickwick Papers," "Shylock, Merchant of Venice," "Ivanhoe," "Fantomas," "Hamlet," "The Speckled Band," and "Silver Blaze." Together those films of French, Italian, American or British origin give a comprehensive view of what direction cinema in general was taking.

The first named film, shown in early January, was a three - reeler that had been produced in California by Thomas Harper Ince. Ince was an Irish American born in Newport, Rhode Island in 1882, who became involved in the film business in New York before deciding in 1911 to move westward to California with his leading lady Ethel Grandin, to make Westerns. He established a studio with excellent outdoor and indoor facilities four miles north of Santa Monica whose personnel included a large company of real cowboys and native American Indians. His production methods proved very influential in the development of the early film industry in California. He always used a detailed script and believed in careful preparation at all levels before filming started. "Custer's Last Fight" was typical, a reconstruction of an encounter from 1876, which became better known later as Custer's Last Stand, in which George Armstrong Custer and his men of the Seventh Cavalry were overwhelmed and wiped out by a superior band of Sioux and Cheyenne Indians. The details of the Battle of the Little Bighorn were carefully researched and he even questioned Sioux Indians on the lot who had seen the battle as children. They added little information, insisting that the fighting was over so quickly that they could remember none of the details. The film was directed by Francis Ford who also played the part of Custer. Ford was the elder brother of John Ford and he is probably best remembered in Ireland as the old bearded man in "The Quiet Man," dying in bed until he hears about the fight between John Wayne and Victor McLaglen whereupon he jumps to the floor and races off in pursuit of the action, pulling on his trousers as he goes. The film, which ran about fifty minutes, went down very well in Belfast and was warmly greeted by the critics who recognised it as a Western of above average quality. They praised the effective way in which the story was told (News Letter), and how the action moved along with never a dull moment (Telegraph) especially in the vivid and striking battle scenes (Whig), all of which was presented in a fine style (Irish News). At the end the story was brought right up -to - date with a touching (Whig) unveiling of a special memorial to the fallen men. The name Custer meant nothing to the audiences of 1912 but was to become very familiar to filmgoers in the years to come as numerous films mythologised his life and deeds while many different actors interpreted the part, including Dustin Farnum, Frank McGlynn, Ronald Reagan (dealing with his early career), Errol Flynn, Phil Carey and Robert Shaw.

In his keynote address on the state of the cinema Mr Jupp commented - to widespread laughter - on how the Western had become one of the staples of the industry, but added that there were many other subjects waiting to be filmed as "the mine of the world's fiction had scarcely been touched yet." Beginning essentially with the Films d'Art a belief developed that longer films based on successful plays and novels of acknowledged quality would gain merit, and audiences, by association. By 1913 film makers on both sides of the Atlantic were convinced that the works of writers like Dickens, Hugo, Dumas, Scott and others were suitable sources for their films and thus the Custer film was followed by another three

- reeler, "The Count of Monte Cristo." It was a Selig production with the part of Edmond Dantes played by Hobart Bosworth. The Whig thought the plot was "well treated" and was particularly impressed by the costumes, the News Letter found it "dramatic," while the Irish News commented favourably on the settings and the characterisation. While that was still showing the Picture House announced its next attraction, a version of Victor Hugo's "Les Miserables" made in France by Pathé Brothers, in nine reels with a running time of two and a half hours. A ripple of excitement ran through the city at the prospect of a film that took two and a half hours to show. More mature people recalled that less than twenty years before individual films lasted only about a minute and sceptics speculated that people just wouldn't sit still for such a lengthy production. Others pointed out that cinemas were now warm and comfortable while the projection was clear and steady with no strain on the eyes, and suggested that if what was shown was interesting enough people would be willing to sit through it. The Picture House added to the general excitement by treating the film as a road house event. The film was scheduled for only one showing each day, in the evening at 8 o'clock, with all seats reserved at special prices of one shilling and two shillings. Normal programming, when the main attraction would be "The Woman in White" based on the novel by Wilkie Collins, would continue during the day at normal prices until 7:45.

A special preview was arranged for the critics and a few invited guests. The critics approached the film with the same sense of respect normally reserved for the theatre, essentially because of its source material. It wasn't dismissed in a few sentences but was discussed in detail. The Whig reflected the views of many literary persons by confessing a certain unease on hearing that the novel was to be filmed and wondered if such "a great and noble tale" could be brought "within the limits of a screen play." The writer feared that the result might be akin to presenting a "grisly skeleton to imitate with its rattling bones the graceful and sinuous movements of Pavlova." He had to admit though that the result was quite splendid and showed that a complex work could "be made intelligible in dramatic form by the aid of the cinematograph." All the critics agreed that it was not necessary to have read the book to understand the plot which, according to the I.S.N., was developed with a "wonderful completeness". The story, according to the News Letter, unfolded "with astonishing vigour and realism" and all the main characters and incidents were there except, as the Whig discreetly put it, those "entanglements which only speech could explain." There was praise for the acting and what today would be called the production values. It was a magnificent film (Whig) which held the attention of the audience riveted to the screen from start to finish (Irish News). The readers were encouraged to see it and they certainly responded because there were full houses over a fortnight with a return visit for another successful week in March. There was little doubt that Belfast audiences agreed with the writer in the I.S.N. who enthused that films of such a length were "one of the most extraordinary forms of entertainment of the time" and showed a willingness to sit through such quality productions regardless of their length.

The emphasis on quality was maintained with two contrasting Shakespearean presentations, "The Merchant of Venice" and "Hamlet." The former was a French Pathé production which the Irish News praised for its clever acting and effective settings without giving any details. "Hamlet" was treated as a major production, with a special preview and lots of publicity. The film had been commissioned by Gaumont but it was filmed by Cecil Hepworth at a cost of £ 10,000 mainly in his studio at Walton-on-Thames, with exteriors at Lulworth Cove in Dorset where a replica of the castle at Elsinore was built. Hepworth had a reputation for making quality films and his productions of "Oliver Twist" and "David Copperfield" had been very popular in Belfast, but the special importance of this film was that it represented the last appearance of the eminent English actor Sir J. Forbes Robertson who was retiring - with a sense of relief, as he put it - at the age of sixty. His stage Hamlet was regarded as the finest of the time and, as part of his farewell, his company presented his version of the play in the Theatre Royal, Drury Lane with Forbes Robertson as the Prince and his wife Gertrude Elliott as Ophelia. Hepworth and the actor agreed on a three week shoot and it was only a question of organising the transfer of the seventy strong cast to Walton-on-Thames. While much of the production was essentially filmed theatre, both men wanted it to be more cinematic so Forbes Robertson was persuaded to include visual action and other business to explain Shakespeare's dialogue. But more importantly, he understood the demands of the camera, especially the need for underplaying and adapted his performance accordingly. The film opened in London on 22nd September and a week later was showing in Belfast and Dublin. The Whig refers to "crowded houses" so that suggests a positive response from the population.

One can imagine the scene in the Picture House before the film began, the tea rooms crowded with many mainly middle class family groups, fathers and mothers chatting while watching their well - behaved children some of whom were examining the souvenir pictures of Forbes Robinson as Hamlet they had purchased for three pence in the foyer. For them it was not only a night out but also a part of their education. The film is still extant (the British Film Institute has a copy) and is, as the Telegraph wrote, a golden opportunity to study a great actor at work. Despite the absence of the poetry his performance still comes across as "fascinating in its force and power" (Telegraph) and "the absence of the spoken word is at times almost forgotten". The film ran for one hour forty minutes and the Whig, always alert to the educational aspects, warned its readers that "a high level of attention" was needed. The critic emphasised that the pictures were very clear and steady, thereby assuring parents indirectly that they needn't worry about any damage to their children's eyes. The film was presented in a series of scenes separated by intertitles of explanatory text taken from Shakespeare but overall he thought that the play had been "skilfully condensed." He also noted that certain scenes were especially impressive, a reference probably to the Ghost scenes which were widely praised elsewhere.

The Picture House never forgot that it was mainly a place of entertainment and that most patrons went to the cinema to relax and enjoy themselves so the management didn't hesitate to include a variety of adventure films and thrillers in their programmes. Typical in early September was a three - reel version of "Ivanhoe" starring the splendidly named King Baggot, and directed for Universal in the area around Chepstow by an Irishman called Herbert Brenon. The News Letter was impressed by the fact that the cast involved 500 actors, but added approvingly that the plot closely followed the book, while the Irish News praised its many "striking episodes." The following week, in complete contrast, Belfast was introduced to the sensational escapades of Fantomas, a French criminal known as the Master of Crime who continually outfoxed his pursuer, Inspector Juve. The first of a controversial series based on popular French detective novels, it was a one - reeler directed by Louis Feuillade for Gaumont. The main character was a master of disguise, a "mysterious villain" (Telegraph) with "an elusive and ever changing personality" (News Letter). Both the News Letter and the Irish News, which rarely agreed on anything, described the film as "astonishing," most likely because of the strong visuals that Feuillarde used to evoke a bizarre environment, resonant of later film noir, through which Fantomas and his associates moved, often hooded and dressed entirely in black. The Telegraph praised the competence with which the plot unfolded and the Whig emphasised how the film maker cleverly kept the interest "at fever pitch" to the very end. In the episode in question Fantomas was finally captured and condemned to the guillotine but managed to escape and substitute an innocent man in his place. It was only at the last moment that Juve realised what had happened and intervened to save his life. In the final scene a grim looking Juve sat at his desk vowing to catch the criminal when an image of a black garbed Fantomas suddenly appeared on the wall behind him, laughing in derision, before disappearing just as quickly. Their duel was obviously not over yet. Audiences were intrigued and looked forward eagerly to subsequent episodes.

With its murders, kidnappings and violence it was clearly adult material, while the depiction of a "hero" who was obviously a successful criminal offended and upset many people. It probably influenced the editorial which appeared in the Telegraph that same week expressing sympathy with the current campaign against sensationalism "in literature, in the theatre, and on the screen." But the writer also called for caution in condemnation and pointed out that not all adventure stories were objectionable and that they were a great source of harmless pleasure to many people. "We are not even afraid of a realistic burglary scene," the editor wrote, a comment directed at those who claimed that young people were learning to be lawbreakers by watching such material, and went on to suggest that critics must differentiate between "honest sensation" which was acceptable and the "piled - up horrors" of some films, plays and novels which were not. He named no names but left it up to individual readers to decide which was which.

A few weeks later in another contrast a very different thriller, an example of "honest sensation," without the dark undertones of Fantomas was screened. It was "The Speckled Band" the first of a new series of adventures of Sherlock Holmes, followed a month later by "Silver Blaze" and then at the end of December by "The Beryl Coronet." A few years before, audiences had enjoyed a Nordisk series with Viggo Larsen as Holmes. Holmes had been popular on the Continent for many years but British film makers were slow to adapt his stories for the screen. However Conan Doyle sold the rights to an Anglo-French group in 1912 and the result was a series of two - reelers made for the first time in England. What wasn't widely known was that they were directed by a Frenchman, Georges Treville, who also played the part of Holmes. Despite that the local critics welcomed them, applauded the skill with which they were made and noted that the adaptations had "lost none of the stories' force and mystery" (Whig). Sadly, like so many of the early silent films, the series hasn't survived the ravages of time so it is necessary to depend on contemporary comments and stills to determine their quality. The Irish News thought the acting was "very realistic" and the action was well staged. After their "exclusive" run in the Picture House they moved to the Alhambra where they proved very popular.

Although the trend was towards longer films the majority of films were still two reels or less in length, though that didn't affect their general popularity as the success of the Sherlock Holmes series showed. In fact a new studio called Keystone was to prove that not only did short films still have a future but that they could have a major influence on the whole industry. The Keystone Film Company was the brainchild of Mack Sennett, a Canadian of Irish extraction, born two years before Thomas Ince, who had migrated to New York hoping for a career on the stage. He ended up working in burlesque, but became intrigued with films especially the early French knockabout comedies which he enjoyed immensely. His interest took him to the Biograph studio in 1908 where he became friendly with a young actress called Mabel Normand and with director D.W.Griffith. From the latter he learned the basics of film making and especially the importance of editing. After raising the necessary capital he travelled to California and in August 1912 set up his organization in the old Bison studios which Ince had also used for a time at Edendale in Los Angeles. His original players, who joined him from Biograph, were Mabel Normand and Ford Sterling who were soon to become great favourites of the Belfast audiences. Keystone was unique in that it produced only one type of film, comedies, the first of which were released in late September 1912. They were all one reel or shorter, and in style they were fast and furious.

The Keystone world was a place of frenetic movement. People and events rarely stood still for long and the narrative, such as it was, usually culminated in a wild chase involving animate and inanimate objects. It was a world where authority was undermined, where the large were defeated by the small, where pomposity and haughtiness were deflated by a swift kick to the pants or a pie in the face. In all the mayhem the imposition of order was in the hands of the Keystone cops who usually ended up adding to the general madness. A calming influence of a sort were the Bathing Beauties, flitting delicately through the scene like ballet dancers through a rugby match. Keystone comedy was a blend of music hall and circus clowning given an extra dimension by the special power of film, and the world loved it. Belfast was no exception. The first mention of the word Keystone was in the Irish News in October 1913 with reference to a film showing in the Panopticon called "The Sleuth's Last Stand" a parody of the detective thriller which the critic described as "the most amusing item on the programme." Amusing proved to be an understatement because the laughter of Belfast audiences watching Keystone comedies could soon be heard on the moon. It is ironic that as the European continent tipped into the abyss that became the Great War, and as Ireland moved down the slippery slope towards civil war, cinema audiences in Belfast were probably laughing louder than ever before at the antics of the Keystone clowns.

The Picture House hadn't things all its own way because Fred Stewart in the Panopticon was also pursuing a successful policy of bringing quality and popular films and he was quick to recognise the drawing power of Keystone. He realised that his ambitions were being curtailed by the drawbacks in the design and size of his cinemas, so he decided to rectify the problems. Firstly he had his Electric Cinema in York Street modernised and it reopened on Monday 16 December 1912, renamed the Silver Cinema. Shows were continuous from 6:30 p.m. and there was a change of programme every Monday and Thursday. The films were decidedly popular as the first show indicated, consisting of "Broncho Billy for Sheriff," "Tontolini Among the Clouds," "The New Woman and the Lion," "The Tenant's Children," and "The Clay Industry." He then travelled over to Glasgow to study the picture palaces in Sauchiehall Street and to consult his contacts on the latest design developments in cinema construction. The task of updating and enlarging the Panopticon was given to the architect W.J. Moore of Royal Avenue. The latter presented his plans to the City Hall in late February 1913 and they were quickly approved by 14th March. The cinema closed on 19th May and the work began to rebuild it "on a luxurious scale," as the I.S.N. reported.

Around that time fears began to be expressed about the possible health risks in buildings that were in continual darkness in that the lack of light might lead to the breeding of certain unspecified "microbes." Fred Stewart, never the man to lose any opportunity for advertisement, announced that the new Panopticon would deal with the problem by incorporating special daylight ventilators in the roof which would allow the auditorium to be flooded with natural light in the mornings before opening time. "Daylight kills germs, darkness breeds them," he declared. The new findings didn't seem to deter anyone however and the reopening on Friday 13th September - Mr Stewart mustn't have been the superstitious type - was looked forward to impatiently. The "elaborate reconstruction" (Irish News) cost £5,000 and the results showed impressively from the new frontage with its four marble steps leading up to the entrance and into the brightly lit foyer. The box office was straight ahead in the centre with the swing doors leading to the auditorium on the right. The interior, the walls of which were decorated in dark oak and brown, had been completely altered. The roof had been raised to twice its original height, according to the Telegraph, and the ceiling with its discreet concealed lighting was painted green and cream to contrast with the darker walls. The seating for 400 was of the latest tip - up type, and was divided into three groups by two passageways running the length of the building. Seat prices were very affordable at 4d and 6d. The screen, made from aluminium surrounded by a golden frame, was 14 feet by 12 feet making it bigger than the original by nearly five square feet.

But the main changes were not only in size, though the increase of 190 seats was impressive. The wall along the left hand side (for someone facing the screen) had been straightened out and, most impressive of all, a new balcony for 130 seats (9d) now stretched across the back and along the left side. The emphasis there was on comfort and luxury, the seats being covered with green corded velvet while the lighting showed a touch of the exotic in the form of Egyptian style bowls. Behind the balcony was a lounge area and above it the new projection rooms which housed two of the latest Gaumont projectors controlled by the head projectionist, E. Mathieson. There were other touches that registered, especially the latest innovation, an electric clock with an old style opaque dial located to the right of the screen and the enlarged orchestra which now consisted of two violins, a cello and a piano. The orchestra pit had been deepened so that the players were in no way obtrusive. The general murmurs of appreciation were reflected in a comment in the Telegraph which held that the remodelled Panopticon equalled "any first class picture palace in the U.K."

Mr Stewart knew that it was the films that drew the audiences and he indicated the continuation of the policy he had been following before the makeover by reopening with another Asta Neilson film "Spanish Blood," followed the next week by her "Temptations of Drink" a three reel drama which the Telegraph praised for her acting and the "extraordinary vividness and realism" of the production. Lest the audience be too depressed by the theme it was supported by an unnamed Keystone comedy. Obviously the studio name was enough to let the audience know what to expect. Miss Neilson appeared again some time later in the topically named "Suffragette" which the Irish News described as combining aspects of the suffragette movement with a romance. She played Asta Panbourne, a young woman who meets and falls in love with a stranger whom she knows nothing about. Meanwhile under the influence of her mother she becomes a member of a band of militant suffragettes and is sent to place a bomb in the home of the Prime Minister, timed to explode at midnight. Some time later she discovers to her horror that he is actually the stranger that she loves. She races to him and tries to persuade him to support a bill for women's rights. Failing in that she rushes off to defuse the bomb, but before she can reach it there is an explosion. Luckily no one is hurt and obviously no blame is attached to her because in the final scenes the Prime Minister introduces her to his friends as his future wife.

Between Miss Neilson's appearances there were other major attractions which included the Vitagraph production of "Cleopatra," filmed in New York, starring Helen Gardner, an actress who is almost forgotten now. It was an impressive five - reeler running for one and a half hours and the publicity claimed that it had cost £9,000 - the Elizabeth Taylor version of 1963 cost forty million dollars - and was the longest film made in America until then (1912). Significantly none of the local critics commented on its length but the Irish News thought it had great dramatic power while the Whig found it "very impressive." A still from it shows a grieving Miss Gardner with long black hair down to her knee holding the lifeless body of Mark Anthony, the scene that presumably prompted the Whig critic to the original summation of how in the end "Anthony at fifty died for a queen of forty." Other exotic presentations were "The Wandering Jew" based on Eugene Sue's novel, an Italian five - reeler which the critics thought was "skilfully adapted," and the ever popular "Last Days of Pompeii." It was also an Italian film made by Ambrosio of Turin and directed by the talented Mario Caserini. Its seven reels gave it a running time of about one hour and forty minutes so Mr Stewart gave it roadshow publicity with five separate houses at two hour intervals beginning at one o'clock. Normal prices applied until 6:30 with special prices of 6d for the ground floor and one shilling for the balcony after that. All the critics drew attention to its educational worth but also found it entertaining, well made and exciting, especially the scenes involving the eruption of Vesuvius and the subsequent destruction of the city.

While the Panopticon was being modernised the residents of the Shankill road noticed that Joe McKibben had undertaken a new development at the corner of Carlow Street consisting of six shops and a hall. The hall occupied the corner site and turned out to be another cinema called the West End Picture House. The architect was the dependable W.J. Moore who deposited the plans with the Corporation on 4th January and received permission to proceed on 21st June. Four months later the hall opened at 3:30 p.m. on Monday 6th October 1913 under the watchful eye of the manager George Malcolm. The main entrance looked on to the Shankill and from it wide steps led to a circular foyer with the paybox on the left near the entrance to the stalls (seats, 4d). There was a separate entrance and paybox in Carlow street for the pit (seats, 2d). The prices indicate that the facilities were rather basic, but the local patrons didn't seem to mind. On the plans the auditorium looks to be long and narrow but the Telegraph described it as "a fine roomy building, well ventilated and heated." Again the plans indicate seating for about 620 persons but during the construction that number was obviously greatly increased, possibly without official permission, because the final total was kept rather vague with the papers giving seating figures varying from 1,100 to an unbelievable 2,000. Programmes were twice nightly at 7 and 9 with matinees on Monday, Wednesday, Friday and Saturday at 3:30 p.m. Films were changed every Monday and Thursday.

The opening was low key and the lack of reports means that there is no information about the first programme beyond that it consisted of "a mixture of little pictures," but a few weeks later a typical evening consisted of "Blue Grass Romance" (a two - reeler), "The Mirror" (drama), "A Woman's Heart" (drama), and four comedies including "Merry Pimple's Ladder," all of them entertaining but eminently forgettable. Westerns and comedies were frequent visitors especially Broncho Billy and Pimple, or epics like "A Wild Ride" which promised a story about "a plucky girl (who) escapes from a ranch under attack from savages, on an ostrich"! Regardless of quality, they were watched by what the Telegraph called "large and enthusiastic audiences." Occasionally more superior and interesting fare was presented like the three - reeler "The Curse of Drink," the very successful "The Battle of Waterloo," or "The Intruder" - advertised as a Vitagraph two - reeler featuring Maurice Costello. Then, in early December, the West End secured a minor place in the history of local cinema by presenting Edison's "What Happened to Mary" featuring Mary Fuller. It was a series of twelve episodes or chapters following the adventures of Mary. Each film was complete in itself but the series was shown in sequence over a number of weeks, the link being the main character. It wasn't an action cliff - hanging serial of the type that was to appear during the next few years in which the plot developed from week to week, but it is regarded as a first important step in that direction. Mary Fuller was the model who led on to Kathlyn Williams, Pearl White and the other serial queens yet very few remembered her when she died in a mental hospital in 1973, thirteen years after the West End itself had closed its doors.

Monday 22nd December saw the simultaneous opening of two more cinemas, the Clonard at 4:00 pm and the Central two hours earlier, both of them designed, built and decorated by local talent and labour. The cinema industry was no longer just a frivolity for entertainment; it was also contributing substantially to the local economy as a growing source of employment. John Donnelly had built the West Belfast Picture Theatre to entertain the workers of the lower Falls, and the Clonard (named after the district where it was located) aimed to do the same for what was then the upper Falls. A company for that purpose had been formed of local men with W.J. Moore the architect as chairman and Joseph Maguire, Hugh McAlinden, D. McCann, John Duffy and Maurice Sullivan as directors. They acquired a site opposite the Falls Library where John Horner's foundry had stood and Mr Moore undertook the task of designing a picture palace to replace it.

What he produced was arguably one of the most distinctive and delightful looking buildings to be erected on the Falls Road (see page 354). The frontage could be described as delicate Renaissance, with a tasteful and well proportioned upper building supported by four elegant pillars, the two central ones having been retained from Mr Horner's original house in a gesture of continuity with the past, despite the major functional change. The dimensions were so perfect that the building seemed to float above its three entrances, an effect increased by its pure white colouring which contrasted vividly with the browns and greys of the other buildings nearby. At night a revolving coloured light shone invitingly from a lantern which topped the roof. From the pavement, which had been specially widened and raised at a cost of £27.15. 6, one entered a foyer floored with marble and terrazzo, the walls covered with oak panels. To the left, an entrance led to the lounge with its red carpet and luxurious tip up seats (6d) while to the right swinging doors opened on to a corridor, also panelled in oak, which ran the length of the building and gave access to the pit with its wooden benches (2d), and the stalls (4d).

At the end of the auditorium there was an orchestra pit occupied by six musicians under the direction of J.Boyle, though there was room for twice that number. Above the orchestra the screen was an impressive twenty feet by fifteen feet (approx. 6m by 5m) with the unique feature that it was on wheels and could be pushed back to reveal a large stage to accommodate the music and live shows that the owners announced would be an important part of the entertainment. The roomy auditorium, which could hold over 1,000 patrons, was lit by hanging lamps with an Oriental design. It was well heated and ventilated and Mr Moore had added another unique feature. Since his work on the Panopticon he had experimented with methods of introducing daylight into cinema buildings and he incorporated into the Clonard an ingenious system of louvred wooden shutters over the windows that could easily be moved aside to allow the hall to be flooded with natural light, an innovation which caused much favourable comment. Many years later senior citizens recalled those early days for the author and their comments inevitably included references to the ingenious shutters. The electric power was supplied by a new model Crossley gas engine which ran quietly at the rear of the building. The projection room was fire proofed and contained two of the latest Gaumont projectors which produced pictures that were sharp and clear with "no eye strain" (Irish News). The owners claimed it was the most luxurious hall in the city and the Whig emphasised that it was "splendidly equipped." In keeping with the high standards of comfort and the quality facilities a manager experienced in the business was appointed. He was W.J.Hogan, one of the earliest local projectionists to have proper professional training, a man who had worked for many years as a projectionist with Erskine Mayne, in which position he had become well known in St Mary's Hall and other venues both inside and outside Belfast. His qualities were widely recognised and he had risen to the position of manager with that firm before accepting the situation at the Clonard. Under the scrutiny of his practised eye one would expect clear steady pictures.

His introductory show also reflected his past training. It began with pictures of local public figures including the chairman and members of the board of the Clonard Picture Hall Co. which were greeted with cheers. A similar reaction also took place when a newsreel shown later included shots of the Pope. The main films were "Snatched from Death," a two reel thriller which was described as exclusive to the Clonard, followed by a Keystone comedy "Mabel's Strategem," which involved Mabel Normand dressing up as a man to get a job but then finding herself pursued by the amorous wife of the boss. Then there was a Western "Unwritten Law of the West" and a series of comedies including one of Pimple's adventures. The second half of the week saw an Irish - American three - reeler called "Kelly from the Emerald Isle," with in later shows, "Brennan of the Moor" and John Bunny comedies. That set the general pattern for the immediate future with a combination of thrillers, Westerns, comedies, and material of Irish or Catholic interest all of which assured that the "Klondyke," as it affectionately became known, occupied a prominent position in local affections. Like most suburban cinemas there were two separate shows at 7 and 9 o'clock in the evening while the films were changed every Monday and Thursday.

The Central represented a contrast in many ways. As its name suggested it was located in the city centre area, in Smithfield near the junction with Garfield Street and not too far from the Royal Avenue Picture House. In fact the security light at the back of the Central could clearly be seen from the latter. It was owned by a local group called the Belfast Picture Co. and the architect was H.E.Barron of Garfield Street. The design he produced had a frontage with an Oriental flavour in traditional white, lit by rows of electric bulbs. The foyer was small with the paybox on the right near the doors which led to the auditorium which had a seating capacity of 520 persons, of whom 120 were accommodated in a balcony with tip - up seats. Overall it was less luxurious than the Clonard though its prices were in the same range at 3d and 6d, with children charged only 2d and 3d before six o'clock. The interior, with its colour scheme of green and red, was well ventilated by electric fans and graced by an electric clock near the screen. Projection was from two Gaumont machines, and accompanying music was supplied by a piano and violin. Like most other city centre halls its programming was continuous from 2 o'clock to 10:30. with changes of films on Mondays and Thursdays.

The notion of a film running for a full week was exceptional and its implementation was reserved for the longer and more outstanding productions that it was felt could attract larger audiences across the social divides. The manager, Edward MacKavanagh, had promised that only the best quality films would be shown, "the greatest masterpieces of filmdom," and to back up that claim he decided to build his programmes around the longer films - the earliest feature films - that were becoming increasingly available. The first presentation was "By the Cross" the spectacular four reel Italian production from Savoy Films of Turin which had already been shown in the West Belfast Picture House, and which had the distinction of having been shown to Pope Pius X before a copy had been deposited in the Vatican library, where it probably still resides. The sweep of the film was impressive, moving from Milan across the Alps to Gaul and then back to Rome. The local critics had already praised it and had encouraged their readers to see it because of its strong plot, its depiction of early Christianity, its positive morality and its educational content. Mr McKavanagh must have been happy with the large crowds that packed the new cinema, but he knew that not everyone went to the cinema to be educated so he followed it with a Barker production "Younita," another four - reeler, but on a very different theme. It detailed the career of an Italian dancer in London "from the gutter to the footlights." On her way upwards she selfishly made use of and destroyed the careers of many men but finally met her end when one of them shot her. The News Letter found it "gripping" while the Irish News praised the realism of its acting comparing it favourably to that found on the stage.

Such a comparison was meant as a compliment because the older theatrical traditions were still regarded as culturally superior. Films were seen mainly as vehicles for superficial action plots rather than for more thoughtful themes that needed the elucidation of the spoken word. But that didn't prevent some theatre managers from eyeing the new and developing upstart as a competitor and envying its power to attract audiences. Neither the Grand Opera House, the Theatre Royal or the Alexandra could ignore the new cinemas that were springing up across the city and they had to formulate policies to compete successfully with them. During 1913 the Theatre Royal fought for audience attention by presenting tried and tested stage favourites like "East Lynne" or more sensational melodramas like "The Devil's Mistress," a thriller in which Winifred Maude played "a fascinating but wicked woman who incites a man to commit murder" (Whig). A few weeks earlier she had played a female detective in "The Woman from Scotland Yard" about which the Whig commented that it was "quite an original idea to throw the burden of the plot into female hands" adding that she carried the part off "with grace and charm." The News Letter described how her performance so thrilled the audience that when she finally unmasked the spy there were "shouts of applause" in the theatre.

Miss Maude's heroines with their intelligence, their more aggressive physical presence, their feminine allure and their ability to survive in a man's world were far removed from the retiring and swooning Victorian maidens who had been the norm on the stage in the recent past. Though they didn't know it, the audiences were being conditioned to accept the action heroines like Kathlyn Williams and Pearl White who were soon to appear, not on the stage, but on the screen in the popular serials. Miss Maude obviously understood how to attract attention and during that summer season she also presented a number of plays which "dealt with the more sensational questions of the day" (Whig). They included "Sins of the City" about the attractions and perils of the seamier side of urban life; "The Mormon's Wife," about the perceived dangers to young women from Mormonism; "Poor White Slaves," about the evils of the traffic in young women as prostitutes; and "Black Passion," about miscegenation. The critics, while recognising that such topics needed "careful treatment" (Whig), praised the plays as serious attempts to highlight contemporary problems while Miss Maude and the theatre management must have been encouraged because their efforts were also "well supported and appreciated" (Whig).

The Opera House decided that films could no longer be completely ignored but that only the most outstanding should be shown as roadshows with special prices. Thus on May 12th Paul J. Rainey's "African Hunt" was presented with prices ranging from 6d (gallery) to 3 shillings (dress circle). The film, which was accompanied on stage by an explanatory lecture by Henry Latimer, was a record of an expedition by Paul Rainey, a wealthy sportsman from Ohio, to British East Africa as it was then called. According to the publicity his outlay was £50,000, a lot of money in those days, but from all accounts it showed on the screen. In all, the group he organised consisted of 350 individuals including a scientist from the Smithsonian Institute, a doctor, animal handlers, expert cameramen and 300 local tribesmen. His main aims - a mixture of sporting, commercial and scientific - were to study the habits of the wild animals, to catch specimens for zoos in Britain and the U.S.A. and to film the whole process. The educational aspects of the film were highlighted in the hope that those parents who could afford it would feel that it was imperative that their children should see it. But at a time when foreign travel was experienced only by the few it was not just the children who watched wide - eyed. The News Letter found the pictures "deeply instructive and entertaining" and technically of a very high standard. The Irish News agreed, describing the scenes as "remarkable" or "unique" and commended the lecturer whose comments greatly added to their interest.

The film began with the preparations in Nairobi followed by impressive scenes as the column moved off with 135 camels, 40 horses, 60 dogs, 54 oxen and 150 sheep. Certain scenes delighted the critics and the audiences, especially those at a waterhole where animals of all kinds collected to wash and drink. There were exciting incidents involving the dogs pursuing a cheetah which tried to escape by climbing a tree, and a lion "at bay in a thicket snapping at its tormentors," scenes according to the Whig which were "worth a thousand of the faked dramas that are at present the standby of the picture houses." There was also humour notably a "dance" by a group of ostriches the description of which reminds one of the later True Life Adventures produced by Disney in the Forties and Fifties. A great favourite was the "shy" giraffe looking down imperiously at passing rhinos.

Such images are almost commonplace today on television but in 1913 they were a revelation to many, making the film a great talking point. Added to that was its length, an impressive nine reels with a running time of over two hours. The success of the film encouraged the Royal Hippodrome next door to present a similar type documentary in July, "Nature's Zoo," a record of popular Yorkshireman Cherry Kearton's adventures in East Africa. The wild animals were again filmed in their natural surroundings and there were thrilling scenes showing attempts to lasso the likes of zebras, rhinos, cheetahs and giraffes. There was also a lion hunt, with Masai warriors confronting the beast armed only with spears. The film was shown each day at three o'clock while the normal music hall programme was presented in the evenings. It proved so popular that, despite the early showing time, it was held over for another week.

The success of those films strengthened the views of those who believed that the true vocation of cinema lay in the educational field, but the management of the Opera House knew better and announced their next major attraction, the controversial life of Christ called "From the Manger to the Cross" which will be discussed in some detail later. A few months after that the billboards proclaimed the imminent arrival of the Italian spectacular "Quo Vadis?" - causing a ripple of excitement across the city. Those with an interest in films were obviously delighted, those of a religious mind recognised that it dealt with themes similar to "The Sign of the Cross" and those of a political mind might have noted that the question posed seemed germane to the political future of Ireland but no one, least of all the Unionists, said so especially when they realised that the plot line led to Rome.

If a film buff was asked what is the connection between Cushendall and the silent version of "Quo Vadis," he or she would be hard put to find an answer. But there is a connection and it is the Grand Opera House. The Warden Co., with its commitment to drama, had organised a competition to encourage the talents of local amateur dramatists and the first prize went to the young Miss Margaret Dobbs of Cushendall for her play (or playlet as the Telegraph called it) "The Doctor and Mrs Macauley". In a bizarre double bill this little rural story, an "amusing if farcical piece" (Irish News), set in Cushendall in 1813 which told the story of how a man falls in love with a maid and finally marries her, was presented with "Quo Vadis" during the week beginning 18th Aug. 1913. The contrast between the domestic events in Cushendall and the more lurid happenings in Ancient Rome must have caused many in the audience to smile. "Quo Vadis?," advertised as "the picture that has stirred the world," was the latest of the Italian spectaculars filmed by Enrico Guazzini in Rome for the Cines company. The film arrived in a blaze of publicity from a very successful showing in the Albert Hall in London. The News Letter assured its readers that they would see the original six - reel version, eight thousand feet long and running for over one and a half hours. The film boasted having the largest cast and the most elaborate sets of any film yet made and an article in the Graphic, which many in Belfast would have read, described it as "the finest and most expensive film yet exhibited." The writer went on to praise the settings and costumes which showed a "scrupulous fidelity to the period." The article was accompanied by a spread of seven excellent stills to illustrate these points, though nowhere was there any mention of the names of those involved in the production.

The Belfast critics were similarly impressed by what they saw. The Telegraph writer noted how the audience was swept up in the action and found themselves transported back "to that period of carnival and crime, of license and laughter, cruelty and luxury which preceded the fall of the great Roman Empire." He was especially impressed by the burning of Rome which "for sheer strength and terrifying realism nothing could surpass." The scenes in the amphitheatre involving Christians, gladiators and wild animals were "wonderful in conception and magnificent in stage management." The acting, especially of the "mad and licentious Nero" was very impressive. All in all he felt it was a "screen drama to be seen and considered." The Whig critic summed it up as "a triumph" and praised the skill of the production and the direction, especially with reference to the burning of the city and the bloody confrontations in the arena. But he was also much intrigued by lesser background scenes and detail, especially those showing everyday life - like the slaves grinding corn - and he contrasted the quiet nobility of the Christians worshipping "in a gloomy crypt" with the "rabble of Nero's courtiers reeling about in orgies." In conclusion he expressed a criticism that has been echoed down through the years about spectaculars, that "as always in cinemaplays emotion has to be sacrificed to action" and he felt that the film would have been greatly improved if the love interest and "pathetic incidents" had been cut, comments that didn't deter the crowds. Overall the film was a great success and its compelling combination of professional expertise, sensational historical spectacle, religion and long running time was to be much copied in the years to follow.

Around the corner on the Grosvenor Road at its intersection with Sandy Row the Alexandra Theatre was facing the same problems of competition for audiences but its response indicated an element of uncertainty about how to cope. At the beginning of the year the hall was advertised as the Pretty Alexandra when it presented Chalmers Mackay and his company, well known throughout the country, in a series of favourite Irish plays including "The Wearing of the Green," "The Shaugraun," "Eileen Oge," "The

Colleen Bawn," and "Arrah-na-Pogue." Some time later local favourite Cathal O'Byrne and his Celtic Company of forty members took the stage with "The Rising of the Moon" and scenes of domestic comedy, poetry, music and Irish dancing. By March it was the Beautiful Alexandra when "Uncle Tom's Cabin" was being presented with "real negroes and a full chorus." That was followed by George A. Street, a "real American cowboy actor" in a Western drama, "The Cattle Thief." But the manager, Leicester Jackson, mustn't have been fully satisfied with the response to those and he decided to make better use of the projection facilities which the hall had had since its inception. At the beginning of June he combined a sensational play "A White Slave" with a showing of the film "Dante's Inferno." The following week he continued the theme of prostitution but went over entirely to films with a three reeler, "The White Slave Traffic, or In the Hands of the White Slave Merchant." The Irish News thought the film was "of undoubted human interest." The plot, which fuelled the popular imagination regarding the white slave trade, revolved around a young girl in England who became infatuated with a Count and, disobeying her father, ran away with him to Hamburg from where he took her to S. America. There he revealed his true nature and sold her into prostitution. She experienced a series of "soul harrowing" ordeals until, fortunately, she was rescued by the Mate of an English ship who arranged to get her back home to her father. Today it would be regarded as an exploitation film but at the time the News Letter thought that it was "intensely dramatic" and "a striking illustration of the necessity for the Bill recently passed through Parliament with the object of dealing with that nefarious traffic."

By the end of June the adverts were describing the Alexandra as Belfast's Perfect Picture Palace and the uncertainty over its programming seemed to have ended. John Bunny, Broncho Billy and Pimple were regular visitors and the Whig commented on the technical quality of the pictures shown, describing them as "exceptionally clear and steady," and further noted the enthusiasm of the audiences who cheered loudly, for example, when "The Indian Outcast," a Western, appeared on the screen. The second week in July saw "East Lynne" on screen, actually during the same week that Miss Maude was presenting her version on the stage of the Theatre Royal. Familiar stage plays often arrived in film form but never together, and the critics rarely made any comparisons. However, "East Lynne" proved an exception. The Whig critic admitted that the film showed certain advantages in that some of the incidents gained greatly in naturalness by being acted in outdoor surroundings while many scenes were enriched by the beauty of the scenic backgrounds. He also found that the special effects of a train crash were very impressive and noted how "the sides of the compartment are seen to collapse over the heads of the occupants who are buried in the debris and then extracted from the ruins of the wrecked train." Miss Maude and her company had the reputation and the spoken words but he wondered, with cause, if they could compete with that kind of realism. The News Letter took up the same theme with regard to a Western play presented in the Theatre Royal but came to different conclusions. The play, seen in October, was "The Prairie Outlaw" by Mr and Mrs Kimberley's company. The critic noted that stage plays set in the West were very popular and put that down to the influence of the cinema, but added that "superb as many of the films are, people prefer to see actors in the flesh with the advantage of the spoken word, the timely and restrained gesture and proper scenery." One could go along with his comments regarding the flamboyant acting of the silent films and the lack of speech but hardly about the scenery. Painted deserts and mountains could only rarely compete with moving images of the real thing. Also his arguments don't stand up, especially in view of what finally happened to the Theatre Royal.

The Alexandra seemed to be transforming itself into a picture palace and that suspicion was strengthened by the announcement in July that it was closing for redecoration and would open in September. Then in mid - August it was announced that the hall would be sold by public auction "with fixtures, fittings, utensils, stage scenery, properties, gas engine, dynamo and fittings, four cash registers, piano and all internal furnishings." About a month later, on 29th September., it had a "very successful opening" (Irish News) under the direction of a new owner, John Lawson who was well known locally, and who modestly described himself as the foremost Hebrew actor in the country. As an indication of its new beginning the theatre was renamed the Palladium and it was announced that it would be run as a first class music hall and picture palace. Much work had been done to it during the summer to lure back audiences. The auditorium had been completely repainted and redecorated, the seats had been re-upholstered and the ventilation and lighting improved. Besides comfort the safety aspect had been addressed and the exits had been widened to allow quicker and easier movements in and out. There were to be two shows every evening at 6:50 and 9 and prices were pitched at a popular level at 3d, 6d, and one shilling.

The reopening involved John Lawson and his company in a play, "The Looms of Mayfair," supported on screen by a Keystone comedy, "How Fatty Made Good," starring Fatty Arbuckle. Over the next few weeks the new Palladium attempted to make good with a mixture of stage plays, music hall acts and films often together on the same show. An outline of a typical programme indicates that there certainly was value given for money. It opened with the orchestra playing the overture followed almost immediately by John Bunny in "The Stenographer's Troubles." The curtain then went up on music hall acts consisting of Florrie and Wee Lena (a singing and dancing act), and Jack Chambers, described as a ragtime coon, who sang and danced. Then there was a comedy playlet "Squaring the Missus" followed by Miss Jenny Costello, a singer. The show ended with another film "The Clue of the Broken Finger" an exciting action thriller, the highlight of which was a chase on top of an express train speeding at over forty miles an hour. It was popular material with no attempt at sophistication or pretentiousness, aimed mainly at pulling in the crowds.

Mr Lawson was a seasoned showman who also understood the value of gimmicks and similar attractions. He announced that postal orders would be distributed to patrons, enclosed randomly in the printed programmes, and he was not averse to a little glamour. At the beginning of December he presented Henriette de Serris from the Palace Theatre in London along with 15 models "from the Academy of Sculpture in Paris" who staged tableaux vivants of well known art productions in the evenings, with a fashion show of gowns and corsets in the afternoons. The reports of those events describe "packed houses." Besides his acting ability Mr Lawson had a reputation for being controversial. During his first visit to Belfast sixteen years before he had presented, in the Alhambra, a short play - it lasted about twenty five minutes - written by himself called "Humanity." The story involved the attempts of a villain, an Englishman (a Christian) to destroy the hero Silvani (a Jew) and ended with a mighty fight which the Jew wins.

The play was praised at the time but its unusual subject matter stirred up some anti - Semitism locally and the actor became involved in heated exchanges on the subject. The implication that a Jew couldn't be a hero was, he wrote, "a gross libel on the Jewish people." Soon the old chestnuts were being dredged up in a number of letters which accused the majority of Jews in Belfast of being "tickmen" or moneylenders, "foisting their shoddy goods on the Belfast public at three times their value." In reply another letter signed "Only a Jew," - which was the title of a song Lawson sang in his play, - refuted those allegations and, while admitting that many local Jews were in the money lending business, emphasised that they were as honest, and often more so, that their Christian equivalents who in recent years had been involved in "ballot frauds, insurance frauds, putrid meat dealing," and other scandals.

Lawson continued to present "Humanity" without further incident on his many visits to the city and by 1913 he was generally welcomed as a popular entertainer. His play was expanded by the Magnet Film Company into a three reel film acted by Lawson and his company which showed very successfully at the Alhambra in early November, giving him welcome publicity, and critics and audiences another opportunity to compare the techniques of stage and screen. The I.S.N. approved of how the action had been opened up beyond "the narrow confines of the stage" to include an exciting car chase, while the Irish News thought that the plot had the essential ingredients for a good film as the material allowed "the film manager (= director?) full scope to his imagination."

In December Lawson, despite his knowledge of the conservative nature of Belfast society, decided either as a publicity ploy or just to stir the pot to write a letter to the papers suggesting that it was time for Sunday picture shows of the type recently allowed by the L.C.C. He presented himself as a public benefactor in the matter. He explained that he would be willing to put on such shows of carefully chosen inoffensive material which would have the advantage of taking young people off the streets on Sunday nights where they often caused a nuisance, especially in the city centre. He would take his expenses from the proceeds and hand the surplus over to the Lord Mayor's Coal Fund. The latter was a very worthwhile and necessary charity set up annually at Christmas to supply coal to poor families during the cold days of winter, a charity declared the Irish News, that should not be ignored. The chairman of the Coal Fund committee had recently pointed out that the fund had "the warm approval of the various denominations" and that it was "a practical illustration of the sympathy which the citizens feel for those in circumstances of urgent need." Mr Lawson's offer would alleviate both public order by reducing rowdyism, and poverty by assisting the fund.

Satisfied that he was playing with a good hand he sat back and waited. There were a few isolated voices raised in his support. One letter writer felt that "Sabbath performances of moving pictures - provided of course the pictures are not marred by extravagant flippancy - are in many ways desirable." Another welcomed the aim to take noisy crowds off the streets as a positive suggestion, especially as "the entertainment presented by Mr Lawson is of no harm and the pictures usually have a moral attached." Also, he added, it was time that the citizens of Belfast were treated like adults and "not as a lot of babies." But such sentiments were decidedly in the minority and Mr Lawson soon felt the full ire and outrage of the Sunday Observance supporters. He was accused of "putting picture performances before religious devotions" and, even worse, of trying to introduce the Continental Sunday into Belfast. One writer felt that young people suffered more harm in a music hall than on the streets and that the Coal Fund didn't need money from events that desecrated the Sabbath. Another indicated that the judgement of someone who staged "corset parades" could not be entirely trusted and that this "most mischievous proposal" should "receive the emphatic and immediate condemnation of every right thinking citizen." To Mr Lawson's disappointment Sunday cinema didn't materialise, and citizens were encouraged to continue to desist "from work and worldly amusements for one day out of the seven." So the year (1913) ended on a note of controversy surrounding a topic that was to recur with increased vigour in future years.

Parallel with the verbal clashes over Sunday performances there were moral fears expressed about a new craze that was sweeping the city, the Tango dance. While some admired its style and grace others condemned it for what one female letter writer called its "manifold iniquities." Despite such criticisms Belfast seems to have gone tango mad. Tango slang was soon heard on the streets and tango dresses adorned the shop windows. Even the Great Northern Mineral Water Company in Boundary street brought out a new non - alcoholic drink named after the dance. Ask for Tango, said the adverts. Dancing schools presented Tango Teas and one of those in late October in the Carlton Restaurant in Donegall Place organised by the pupils of a Mrs Gardiner was filmed and shown in the Panopticon the following week, supporting "The Last Days of Pompeii." Usually local material was filmed outdoors where sufficient light was available but the fact that the dancing was indoors indicates the use of improved equipment and film stock. Unfortunately the name of the cameraman is not recorded though photographers from Charles and Russell of Royal Avenue were present. The manager of the Panopticon must have had an arrangement with some local cameraman because he often presented local events. A month before, in September, he showed film of Carson's review of the Ulster Volunteers at Balmoral only a few hours after the actual event. Meantime the News Letter observed that the Tango fad had "swept aside bridge, roller skating and even ragtime." But films were not included in its list.

Obviously the cinema was no longer regarded as just a craze, but as a permanent fixture on the entertainment scene. That new eminence didn't prevent film makers from making use of popular fads, and on 10th November the Panopticon presented "Her Supreme Sacrifice" with the comment that it introduced "the famous Tango dance." The film got high praise, the Telegraph critic describing it as "excellent." The story doesn't sound all that original, being about a young woman from the American West who gave up wealth and position to be with the man she loved. One scene introduced the Tango "splendidly presented by cabaret dancers from the U.S.A." Soon other films followed with tango sequences, or given over entirely to the dance. In mid - December the elegant Picture House included "The Tango" in its programme, shown daily at three o'clock, a film which illustrated the correct steps for the dance, while the less elegant West End Cinema had its own version called

"Tango Dancing." The newly opened Palladium presented afternoon Tango Teas, charging one shilling (with tea) and six pence (without tea) with demonstrations by Henrietta de Serris and her models, to full houses. Later Mr Lawson went one step further, attracting crowds with a Tango competition open to all, combined with a ragtime competition. There were those who saw all that as examples of what the Telegraph had called "the craze for excitement" that was gripping society, a trend they believed that didn't augur well for the future. Puritan mistrust of the entertainment business was never far from the surface in Belfast.

CHAPTER THIRTEEN
From The Manger To The Cross

The 1st January 1913 saw the inauguration of the workings of the British Board of Film Censors, established in October of the year before to oversee the content and suitability of films, indicating that the years of cinematic innocence - if they ever really existed - were over. It was not a statuary body and the government was not involved directly in its operations. It was a voluntary self - regulatory body established by the film makers themselves under the guidance of men like Will Barker and Cecil Hepworth who feared the effects of government or local authority interference in their industry. G.A.Redford, who had twenty years experience of censoring plays in the Lord Chamberlain's office, was appointed its first President and he had four examiners to assist him. There was no written code for film makers to follow beyond two guidelines: no nudity and no impersonation of Christ. Mr Redford's remit was that he and his team examine all films presented for exhibition in the country, inform producers of objectionable scenes which could then be removed and grade the films either "U" which were suitable for children, or "A" which were deemed unsuitable for children. The grading was merely advisory and there was no legal backing to enforce it.

The system depended mainly for its success on the co-operation of film makers, distributors and local authorities, co-operation that was not always forth coming, especially in the early years. Film makers resented the interference and maybe the fact that they had to pay thirty shillings a reel for the vetting process while many local authorities including Belfast felt that the final decision with regard to objectionable material should lie with them. Surprisingly Belfast, despite its reputation for sternness and religious extremism, showed little reaction to the new development because films did not really rank high locally on the list of anti - social activities. Criticism of them was usually rather general and concerned practical matters like the danger of eyestrain and the spread of germs in the darkened environment, though there were worries expressed on occasion about the possible connection between crime films and juvenile delinquency. But even there the association was not yet widely accepted in professional circles where undesirable reading material was often seen as more "dangerous." In July 1912 a case was reported concerning a young Belfast lad, Denis Hanna, who ran away from home and was apprehended some time later in Armagh after breaking into a house and stealing some articles from it. In court his mother pleaded for him and put the blame for his behaviour on the "penny dreadfuls" that he was addicted to. The judge tended to agree with her because, he explained, in his experience those cheap papers with their emphasis on crime and criminals were responsible for leading many young people astray. It was the lad's first offence so the judge was lenient and let him off with a warning.

In contrast films were more often praised for their educational value and the fact that they offered an alternative attraction to the public houses and so were helping to reduce excessive drinking in the population. In August 1913 the Belfast Harbour Commissioners issued one of their quarterly reviews of the trade of the port, mentioning among other things that there had been a reduction recently in the amount of alcoholic beverages being shipped. Commenting on the report the Telegraph felt that the news would cause temperance workers to rejoice, and claimed that while some felt there were economic reasons for the decline it had also been "confidently asserted" that it was partly due to the increasing popularity of cinema going. The severest criticism was still reserved for the stage and while attitudes had mellowed somewhat from the attacks of the mid nineteenth century they hadn't disappeared entirely.

When the Grand Opera House brought back the stage play "The Sign of the Cross" in August 1912 a local cleric, the Rev. Dr. Murphy the Rector of St George's Church, advised people to go and see it. In reply a letter appeared in the Whig which described his advice as "incredible" and dismissed the theatre in Biblical terms as "a corrupt tree (which) cannot bring forth good fruit." The writer went on to say that he had never heard of any conversions resulting from a visit to a theatre and that anyone going there had - in his words - to leave Christ at the door. Local pundits however felt that society faced more immediate and serious problems like the excessive sensationalism of certain books, newspapers, stage plays and films and the increasing tendency in the media towards what would be called "dumbing down" today, or as a letter writer to the Irish News put it, the "flood of triviality in art, literature and drama." The same writer deplored the fact that people no longer supported thought - provoking matter but preferred lighter plots which, in his opinion, explained the popularity of stage melodramas and, the "output of the cinematograph." There was also widespread concern about the continued sale of objectionable postcards in the city and calls for the police to take more effective action against the shops which engaged in the trade. An editorial in the Telegraph called for a sense of balance in the matter pointing out that it was most unlikely that the "national morality" would be undermined by "stupid and ugly picture postcards" and, if it ever was, it was hardly likely that censorship of the theatre, picture palace or the bookstall would save it. What was needed was proper education to raise people's horizons, a process which takes time. In the meantime the editor suggested that a voluntary system of control of the type "recently initiated by cinematograph film makers and exhibitors" was advisable.

Unease was also expressed about recent trends in modern fiction, and trashy literature was attacked, especially cheap novels, serials in magazines including "penny dreadfuls" and certain Sunday newspapers. The serials, which were very popular, were widely criticised because, it was claimed, they usually dealt with crime and criminals in an uncritical manner which gave them a certain appeal and implied that "rascality is all right so long as it is daring and clever enough to escape punishment." Such lax attitudes were seen as a danger to society in general and to immature and impressionable youths in particular, but while a small minority still felt that all forms of censorship should be abolished the general response in Belfast was in agreement with the editor of the Telegraph who felt that "some form of supervision was advisable." What form that should take wasn't always clear because, he cautioned, while the aim of censorship was often of the highest "its results in practical working are seldom satisfactory." In early 1911 the anxiety about the state of the national morals led to the formation in England of the National Council of Public Morals to study the subject. It examined a wide range of matters concerning sex and population, including evidence for the White Slave traffic which was regarded as a growing and serious evil. It did not immediately concern itself with the cinema though it was later, in 1917, to publish an important report on its influence on society. In April 1913 after a meeting in the City YMCA an Irish Council of Public Morals was set up with the same aims, one of which was to monitor white slavery, or prostitution, in the city.

Despite such concerns when controversy about a film did arise during the following month the objections raised were not about sex but about that other equally sensitive topic, religion. The Grand Opera House announced that during the last week in May (1913) it would present the recently completed "From the Manger to the Cross" based on the life of Christ and billed as "the most remarkable religious film ever produced." The question of how suitable the stage or the cinema was to deal with sacred topics was a very touchy one. Yet Belfast already had some experience of cinematic attempts to deal with the life of Christ. During the Christmas season of 1900 Lizar's had presented a show in St Mary's Hall before large and appreciative audiences including clerics which contained three scenes from the life of Christ, the birth, the betrayal by Judas and the carrying of the cross. Later in August 1908, also in St Mary's Hall, Erskine Mayne showed the "Life, Miracles, and Passion of Our Lord" which the Irish News described as a beautiful hand - coloured film based on paintings of the events. It was most likely a French film made by Alice Guy. At Easter 1911 the Shankill Picturedrome presented another coloured "Life of Christ" based on the Passion Play. All those were received warmly and welcomed by critics and audiences alike but this new film was different in that it arrived surrounded by contention. The six reel film was presented as a road house performance with prices ranging from two shillings for the circle and stalls to sixpence for the gallery. As readers of "The Graphic" would have been aware it was a Kalem production made by the same people who were responsible for the series of Irish stories which were so popular when shown at St George's Hall, the Alhambra and elsewhere in the city.

While travelling across the Mediterranean in 1911 in search of topics to film, Gene Gauntier and Sidney Olcott developed the idea of filming the life of Christ in the actual locations where the events had occurred. Following their usual arrangement Miss Gauntier wrote the script while Olcott attended to the direction and production. The first scenes filmed were the Flight into Egypt with dramatic views of the pyramids in the background. Miss Gauntier played the part of Our Lady, James Clarke was St Joseph but Olcott chose an Englishman, Henderson Bland, for the important and challenging role of Christ. Despite the difficulties of communications the company travelled over poor roads with their equipment around the Holy Land in search of the correct locations, and Bland described how Miss Gauntier spent long hours in the saddle without complaining. Scenes were filmed at Nazareth, Tiberias and around the Sea of Galilee. In Jerusalem a replica of part of Solomon's Temple had been built causing Bland to marvel at the skill of Kalem's craftsmen. As word spread crowds gathered to watch the filming and the police often had to called to control them. During scenes along the Via Dolorosa people pressed in on Bland and to his embarrassment some local women reverently kissed his robes. Nearly the whole European population of Jerusalem turned out and mixed with the locals to see the scenes of the Crucifixion and the actor heard moans and sobs from the crowd as they watched the reconstruction.

Gauntier were convinced they had a good film in the can and they returned to America to edit and prepare it for release. To their disappointment they found that the owners of Kalem were not too pleased. There were complaints about the high cost of the production though in fact in time it made a substantial profit for them. They were unsure of how the public would receive the film and felt that there would be controversy, especially if word got around that Miss Gauntier, who played Our Lady, was actually divorced. Because of those worries the company decided to release the film without credits, with no mention of the actors or the director. That explains why the film is completely anonymous and there is no mention of anyone connected with the project in any of the reports in the local papers. Angry at the way they were treated, Gauntier and Olcott severed their connections with Kalem and set up their own independent company, the Gene Gauntier Film Players, before returning to Ireland (where they became known as the Gee Gee's) to make more films. Meanwhile the released film faced the expected controversy. In England it wasn't submitted to the Censorship Board for a certificate and wherever it was shown it raised a storm of both protest and support.

Scene from "The Manger to The Cross": reverential but controversial.

Early in the year (1913) its imminent arrival in Dublin was announced with plans to show it in the Antient Concert Rooms. Immediately there were complaints and articles of condemnation appeared in The Irish Catholic, the Irish Times, the Irish Independent, Freeman's Journal and the Daily Express while many clerics used their pulpits to attack the film. In February an action was brought in the courts to stop the showing by having the license of the Antient Rooms suspended or revoked. The main objections centred around the fact that an actor personated God and that he was paid for doing so. The Recorder contended that that alone represented an outrage, a comment that provoked an outburst of applause in the court. James O'Connor K.C. for the defence argued that the person of Christ often appeared in paintings of sacred subjects and even the Oberammergau Passion Play had been performed in Dublin without giving offence. The response was that the film was different because it had been made solely for profit and that anyway the stage was not the proper place to treat Biblical subjects. One witness, the assistant secretary of the Y.M.C.A., said he found the scenes of the Crucifixion very objectionable and that certain other scenes, he felt, bordered on the blasphemous. Mr O'Connor marshalled a number of eminent clerical witnesses who defended the film and declared it would do no harm "if approached in the proper frame of mind." The Recorder asked why the Dublin corporation hadn't refused a licence for the film and was told that it didn't need one because it was "non flammable." At that Mr O'Connor injected some much needed humour into the proceedings by commenting that it seemed to him that it was a very inflammable film indeed. The Recorder was not particularly amused but admitted that despite the objections there was nothing legally he could do to prevent the showing. The film ran for five weeks and an estimated 85,000 people saw it.

The hostile sentiments expressed in the Dublin court found wide support in Belfast among both Protestants and Catholics yet the film faced no organised opposition. The matter of its showing was raised in the City Hall by Councillor M.J. Burke who suggested that after the controversy surrounding it in England and Dublin its exhibition in Belfast was "a scandal and disgrace." In reply Alderman J.S.Finnegan admitted that he also had criticised some films shown recently but he noted that this film had actually been a success in Dublin and that prominent ecclesiastics including the Archbishop of Canterbury had praised it. He went on to say that when picture palaces "were conducted with decorum and the films were educational in the highest degree there could be no possible objections to them," a sentiment which was greeted with a chorus of "hear, hear." The management of the Opera House probably felt that the controversy represented good publicity and that, regardless of what was said or written, the film would attract audiences with a similar disposition to those that had supported plays with religious themes like "The Sign of the Cross" and "Ben Hur." Their publicity emphasised the special nature of the production and the care and detail that had gone into it, all of which, it was pointed out, had increased its costs so that the Opera House had only obtained it "at enormous expense." Despite that the management offered everyone who paid one shilling or more on the opening night a free special souvenir containing eleven stills illustrating the main scenes. It would be interesting to know if any copies have survived to form a tangible connection to that Monday evening of 26th May 1913, though a hint of what was included can be found in a series of scenes shown in "The Graphic" about ten months before.

The local critics treated the film with all due seriousness. From their comments it is obvious that the complete film was shown, including the Crucifixion scenes which had upset some viewers elsewhere. Beginning with the infant Jesus in the manger the film covered the visit of the Magi, the flight into Egypt, the boyhood years, teaching in the Temple in Jerusalem, the meeting with John the Baptist, preaching by the Sea of Galilee with Christ calling the apostles Peter, Andrew, James and John, the marriage feast at Cana, the events of Holy Week, the Last Supper, the arrest and trial, the crowning with thorns, the carrying of the cross to Calvary and the Crucifixion. The Telegraph critic commented that "judged solely from the point of view of a moving picture - and that is all we are here concerned with - it is a beautiful piece of work." He was much impressed by the freshness, clarity and beauty of the outdoor scenes (George Hollister's photography was widely praised at the time), and the obvious care taken to be accurate in the presentation. Overall one got a "vivid impression of the Master's life with all its pathos, dignity and tragedy." The News Letter took a similar approach, pointing out that the vexed question of whether the subject was a suitable one for the cinematograph was not the critic's concern. The film itself was "exceedingly beautiful and largely....... characterised by the simplicity and impressiveness" of the Biblical story. The critic was especially struck by the scenes of the Crucifixion but added that he wished "one could have been spared the pain of some of the scenes." He also praised the scenes of the Last Supper with the apostles reclining around the table and particularly appreciated "the most effective departure of Judas." On the negative side, he thought the miracles were over emphasised and were rather clumsily done. But his main complaint concerned the acting which he found too flamboyant and he wished that the actors had used more restraint and economy. The Irish News indicated its disapproval by completely ignoring the event though when what was described as a "revised edition," presumably cut, appeared the following year and was shown during Easter Week in the Clonard on the Falls

Road, their critic was very impressed and described the film as "wonderfully graphic." He added a number of interesting comments, noting how the audience watched the scenes in reverential silence and also praised the quality of the accompanying music.

The most detailed critical analysis came from the Whig critic. Dipping his pen in some slightly cynical ink he acknowledged the controversy surrounding the film with "clergymen laying down the law on aesthetics, artists at grip with subtle problems in theology and commentators in general devoid of expert knowledge delivering judgements on points of good taste." All of that had produced discussions which he had found "exciting rather than instructive." The core of the problem as far as he was concerned was whether or not it was irreverent to deal with Biblical subjects in the cinema, and he argued that if a painted picture could be accepted as reverent then why should a moving picture be irreverent. If a picture is reverent, he mused, that doesn't necessarily mean that it is artistically successful. He found the film "hopelessly inadequate from a purely aesthetic point of view" and felt that it never got to grips with "the loftiest theme in history." It was a superficial rendering of the Gospel story which reflected "religiosity rather than religion," a criticism that has been made of many religious films since. The acting was stilted and mannered and many of the scenes were directed in a way too reminiscent of the stage. What he did like were the incidental details of local life, the "glimpses of the unchanging life of the East" as he put it, referring especially to the camel caravans, the water carriers with their "squelching skins," the fishermen with their nets at the Sea of Galilee, and the natural way the crowd on the Mount of Olives moved and shifted as they listened to Christ. All of that seemed to him "vivid and real" and gave texture to the film.

The film proved a success with the Belfast public who came out in large numbers and watched it "with great respect and interest" (News Letter). The film has never been accused of inaccuracy or of distorting the Gospel story. Audiences of the day would never have tolerated that. Olcott told Henderson Bland that the story would be filmed with suitable reverence and indeed he seems to have been inhibited somewhat by the seriousness of the topic, and his desire to be traditional may explain the staginess of some of the scenes. He and Gene Gauntier deserve credit for what was a pioneering step. In cinema history the film is important in that it was the first full length Life of Christ actually filmed in the Holy Land, but its real significance is that it broke the taboo of presenting a sacred subject in a popular medium, like a modern Miracle Play, and, equally important, of a professional actor playing the part of Jesus. It opened the door for different and often contentious and, many would contend, even dubious interpretations of Christ by actors such as George Fisher (Civilization, 1916), Howard Gaye (Intolerance, 1916), H.B.Warner (King of Kings, 1927), Jeffrey Hunter (King of Kings, 1961), Max Von Sydow (The Greatest Story Ever Told, 1965), Enrique Irazoqui (The Gospel According to St. Matthew, 1965), Willem Dafoe (The Last Temptation of Christ, 1988) and Jim Caviezel (The Passion of the Christ, 2004) not to mention the censorship rows surrounding religious subjects like the innovative "Green Pastures" (1936, d.William Keighley), the funny but decidedly tasteless "Life of Brian" (1979, d. Terry Jones) and the disappointing "The Last Temptation of Christ" (1988, d. Martin Scorsese) all of which were to engage, and enrage, Belfast audiences - and their moral defenders - in varying degrees in the future.

While the arguments over the film were still raging Sir Beerbaum Tree asked permission of the Lord Chamberlain to stage a Biblical story, "Joseph and his Brethren" at His Majesty's Theatre in London and much to many people's surprise the necessary consent was given. Whether the decision was related in any way to the success of "From the Manger to the Cross" cannot be known, but it is significant that it paralleled it and suggests that a change in attitudes was under way. The Telegraph thought the matter important enough to give an editorial over to it. Without mentioning Olcott's film the editor emphasised that traditionally most people had objected to attempts to present sacred dramas based on Scripture on the stage and that "such convictions deserve to be treated with respect." It was difficult to preserve the dignity and moral message of Holy Writ in what was essentially a medium for entertainment. The editor felt that the decision by the Lord Chamberlain's office was premature because "public opinion on the whole is not in favour of such performances on the stage." However valid such considerations were, they were soon to be overwhelmed by the calamitous developments in Europe which were to change public attitudes in many different spheres of human behaviour.

While some serious - minded persons were involved in ascertaining that the content of films was "safe," other more practical groups were more concerned about the safety surrounding the showing of the films. The Fire Service and the City Surveyor's office were, as the law required, particularly worried about the fire risks but felt that their vigilance and periodic inspections allowed little opportunity for such an event. Their minds were concentrated somewhat in early 1914 when a report from the Select Committee on the precautions necessary in the production, handling and storage of celluloid materials, including film, was published as a White Paper. The report was wide ranging and thorough in its treatment of the problem. It emphasised that celluloid was a particularly flammable material and that every precaution was needed in dealing with it. But it also felt that a sense of balance should be maintained in approaching the problem and pointed out that the number of fires caused by celluloid was not as great as might be expected, which was a cause for optimism. With regard to the cinema it welcomed the introduction of non - flammable film and felt that the authorities should do more to encourage that trend. Finally it reminded the authorities of their obligations to make certain that all the regulations surrounding public exhibitions were rigorously applied so as to cope not only with a possible fire but with the panic that often accompanied it.

While the City Hall was still mulling over the contents of the report any trace of complacency on their part was erased by the events in the early hours of 2nd May, 1914. A local citizen, James Donnelly, was walking past the Royal Hippodrome about 12:50 a.m. when he heard a crash and suddenly to his amazement a mass of flames and sparks shot out of the back of the building. He immediately took off in the direction of the City Hall in search of a policeman and to inform the fire service. Another man, a worker in the building, also called the brigade and soon a number of appliances reached the scene. They discovered that the fire was raging in the stage area so they set about trying to douse it and at the same time prevent it from spreading to the nearby Opera House, or into the auditorium of the theatre itself. In the latter their efforts were greatly helped by the fire curtain which stayed in place and held the flames in check as they devoured the scenery and other stage props. The early indications were that the fire had started in a room near the stage and that the cause was a careless smoker. Seemingly it had nothing to do with the cinematograph which was located at the other end of the building.

An observer who managed to get into the back of the theatre described the scene as eerie, being lighted only by the glow from the stage. Suddenly someone switched on the Hipposcope and directed its strong white beam towards the stage where one could clearly see the extensive damage not only to the stage area, but to the ceiling and roof above, to the front rows of seats which were badly scorched and even to the front of the gallery scorched by sparks. By three a.m. the fire was out and the firemen left, widely praised by all for the professional way in which they had brought the flames under control, thereby saving a fine theatre not to mention the nearby Opera House. Despite the destruction there was a general feeling of relief that the fire had occurred when the theatre was empty and there was no loss of life. Those who knew their local history recalled the fire which had destroyed the old Theatre Royal (in 1870) which had also started when the theatre was empty, though on that occasion the building couldn't be saved. By the next morning the manager, H.T. Downs, had already taken steps to undertake the necessary repairs. He also consulted with the management of the Opera House and arranged that in the meantime the "Hippodrome Season" would be transferred there. As far as the public was concerned everything was under control and it was only a matter of waiting until the Hippodrome was up and running again.

In official circles the matter was in no way closed, nor was it regarded as just a local incident. A few days after the fire a letter arrived at the City Hall from the Superintending Architect's Dept. of the London County Council referring to newspaper reports of the fire and asking for detailed information about the building, the number and position of the exits, the cause of the fire and the extent of the damage done. "Special interest attaches to the behaviour of the fire resisting curtain which is said to have protected the auditorium to some extent." The City Surveyor replied and gave all the data requested about the age of the building, when it was built, its layout and such. He also included details of the curtain, pointing out that it was made of iron, was quite rigid and was covered on both sides by asbestos. He noted that it did protect the auditorium until the fire men arrived but added that "the origin of the fire remains a mystery." The exchange continued with questions about how the regulations of the 1909 Act were applied in Belfast (the Hippodrome had opened in 1906 before the Act became applicable) and a copy of the L.C.C. regulations were forwarded for consideration. On the surface the letters were polite and well mannered and seem to have been a data collection exercise by the L.C.C., reflecting the seriousness of how the fire hazard in places of entertainment was perceived. If the City Surveyor felt there was any innate criticism of how Belfast applied the safety regulations, he made no official comment on the matter though what he felt and said in private may have been less charitable.

CHAPTER FOURTEEN
The Perils of Pauline

1914 was a year of rising national and international tensions. On the home front the Home Rule Bill made its way through parliament towards what the Irish News called the "sunrise of Irish freedom" while Unionists flocked in large numbers to the U.V.F. and threatened civil war over the matter. For one penny supporters could buy from the Telegraph a portrait of Sir Edward Carson in characteristic speaking mode with the legend "we will not have Home Rule" printed on it. Every public move of Sir Edward Carson and his supporters was watched by cameramen and duly appeared on the local screens. There was so much coverage that T.P O'Connor, the future film censor, commented that the events unfolding were beginning to resemble the script of a film, though he also admired the way the Unionists were using the newsreels as a tool of propaganda. The Picture House often screened local events, and those increasingly included scenes of the many U.V.F. demonstrations and parades taking place in Belfast and elsewhere, which were presented week after week almost like a serial.

Typical, in April, were scenes of a visit by Carson when he reviewed a parade of marching men and cavalry who greatly impressed the News Letter critic with their "fine physique and splendid marching qualities." The Panopticon also showed many scenes involving the U.V.F., often giving them top billing. March was a particularly tense month of rising confrontation between the Unionists and the Government and the cinema asked (via its adverts) a question that was on many peoples' minds: Are the Ulster Volunteers Prepared to Fight?, and as evidence showed scenes of the S.Antrim regiment at Langford Lodge taking part in a series of exercises including marching, drilling, shooting, and changing guard. The Irish News didn't directly answer the Panopticon's question but commented that real conspirators didn't conspire before the cinematograph and called on the British government to call their "bluff." On the Shankill Road Joe Mc Kibben presented a film called "The British Army" in the West End and, in a reference to the Curragh Mutiny, encouraged his patrons to "come and see the making of the officers and soldiers who refused to fight against Ulster."

The local tensions were relieved, at least temporarily, by more momentous events on the Continent, precipitated when Gavrilo Princip opened fire with his Browning pistol and killed the Archduke Ferdinand and his wife Sophie in Sarajevo in June. By August Britain had declared war on Germany and calls were soon being made across Ireland for volunteers to fight, while the newsreels were reporting the latest war news. By September local problems had been swept aside and the Panopticon newsreel headline was "Belgium at Bay" followed over the following weeks with "The Defence of Alost," and "The Siege of Antwerp." In early December the Panopticon invited audiences to "come and see the boys" referring to the new recruits of the Ulster Division of Kitchener's army training at Ballykinlar camp. The same newsreel was also shown in another of Fred Stewart's cinemas, the recently opened Crumlin, with the claim that the scenes had been specially taken "by our own photographer." According to the I.S.N. the film showed men from north Belfast settling into their new surroundings and training, "preparing to take part in upholding the might of Britain and vindicating her honour on the war - scarred field of Belgium."

In November the Clonard showed film of Irish National Volunteers - "Ireland's other army" as the Telegraph called them - leaving Belfast by rail for Fermoy to join the Irish Brigade. A few weeks later, in December, special film was screened of those same volunteers undergoing their training. The Irish News commented on the clarity of the pictures and was very impressed by shots of the soldiers "in their neat uniforms" marching to church behind their officers and bands. Like Fred Stewart the Clonard insisted that they had sent their own photographer to Fermoy to take the film and added that shooting had been delayed by bad weather. It is difficult to discover if local cameramen were actually involved or if those were official films (more likely) flavoured with a little showmanship. Whatever the truth, the films themselves were greatly appreciated and there were reports of members of the audience recognising and responding to the sight of friends and relations on the screen. Unusually the Clonard held the film over for a second full week and followed it up a few weeks later with an "exclusive" film of Joseph Devlin visiting Fermoy to meet the Irish Brigade. For many people the newsreels were major connecting points with the war.

During the same period the cinemas were deluged with such a mass of fiction films about the war or with war themes that the News Letter critic complained that "the cinematograph operator seems to be seeing a good deal more of the campaign than the Press correspondent." Some of those films were heroic action stories involving well known characters like Lieut. Rose or Lieut. Daring; others were comedies with Pimple showing how the war could be won, but most were just basic propaganda showing the Hun as a murderer of children and a despoiler of women. Among them were some serious films that were felt to be appropriate at the time, notably a three - reeler which the Alhambra presented called "Florence Nightingale" which traced her life from her early youth to her work among the wounded in the Crimea. The main part was played by the "famous cinema artist" (I.S.N.) Elizabeth Ridson who, from contemporary accounts, gave a very dignified performance. Miss Risdon is forgotten today but in 1915 she was voted the most popular film actress in Britain.

Despite the problems posed by the war the local cinema business continued to flourish and three new cinemas opened during the year: the Crumlin in March, the Great Northern Kinema in April and the Imperial in December. The Crumlin was an addition to Fred Stewart's holdings making him, with three cinemas, an early local mogul. Although the Crumlin described itself as "the most luxurious suburban cinema in Ireland" allowance must be made for the exaggerations of showmanship. It was in fact a modest, moderately sized hall measuring about 100 feet (30m) by 50 feet (15m), designed by the experienced architect W.J. Moore who had already designed the Shaftesbury Pictoria, the Panopticon, the Clonard and the West End Picture House. The balcony, with 176 seats at 6 pence and the back stalls (4d) were certainly comfortable with tip - up seats and carpeted floors, but the cheaper seats (at 2d) were only upholstered benches fixed to a cork floor. Some reports gave the seating as 1000 but in fact it was nearer 850. Some care had been taken in the layout of the seating to ensure a clear view of the screen and to improve comfort by giving more legroom between the rows. The latter was especially welcomed by many commentators. The front elevation had a romanesque design with a main entrance surmounted with a rounded top above which there was the faint impression of two medieval towers, with a small balcony worthy of Juliet between them. Inside, Mr Moore had gone to some trouble to produce a relaxed atmosphere with subdued colours (dark greens and reds), the clever use of concealed lighting and efficient ventilation. To ensure good hygiene and protect the patrons from germs the auditorium could be flooded with natural light every morning. Projection was by the latest Gaumont machines and the screen surface was a mixture of aluminium and mica which was guaranteed to give a bright picture. All the work was carried out by local firms and Mr Stewart was congratulated on availing of local skills and giving much local employment. The main contractor was Alex Murdock of the Cullingtree Road, the decorations were added by Oswald Jameson of Middlepath Street, the electrics by Maynes of Divis Street, the seating by Maguire and Edwards of Arthur Street, the plumbing by Hildersley and Co. of Oldpark Road and the ventilation system by Musgrave and Co. The Irish News found the building "up-to-date and luxurious," the News Letter commented on its modernity while the Whig thought it "handsome and commodious."

Fred. Stewart, with his showman's understanding of urban geography, had chosen the site carefully. It was located at 189, Crumlin Road near the junction with the Oldpark Road and not far from the top of Agnes Street serving a working class area that had no cinema. Mr Stewart himself welcomed and addressed the first audience. He explained that the cinema would be run on a policy of continuous programming from 6:30 to 10:30 p.m. between Monday and Saturday, with matinees at 3:30 on Mons., Weds., and Saturdays, with an added special matinee at midday on Saturdays for children. The films would be supplied by the well known firms of Jury in London and Weisker in Liverpool and the programme would be changed every Monday and Thursday except for some outstanding films which might be kept for the whole week. An essential of any silent cinema was music and that would be supplied by an all female orchestra, which turned out to consist of two ladies, a Miss Donovan on violin and a Miss Bruce on the redoubtable piano. He then introduced the manager George Stewart, his son, who had helped him put the Panopticon successfully on the city entertainment map. The first films shown were "Secret Service Sam" (a detective mystery thriller), "When the Clock Stopped" (another thriller), "The Line Rider's Statement" (a Western), a selection of comedies and the news. That programme set the general tone and pattern of Westerns, comedies, and thrillers interrupted with an occasional "special" - for example in November the Famous Players production of "The Sign of the Cross" starring William Farnum ran for a week while, in December, audiences were treated to Edison's "Wonderful Talking Pictures."

A few weeks later, on April 7th, the Crumlin's medieval frontage was joined by the mock Tudor design of the new bijou style Great Northern Kinema opened at 19A, Great Victoria Street just next door to the Great Northern Railway. The owner-manager was Alfred George a well known figure in the local film business. He had been a member of the Y.M.C.A. camera club and as early as 1896 was a member of the club's committee when he was described as a "lanternist." Another member of that committee was A.R.Hogg whom he must have known well because for a time both of them worked as projectionists for

Lizars, and lived a few doors from each other in Thorndale Avenue. When A.R.Hogg set up his own business George went to work with him. They became well known through their cinematograph shows in the City Y.M.C.A. but more especially in the Assembly Hall and the Grosvenor Hall. Later, George joined Films Ltd. located in High Street where he became familiar with the distribution side of the business and probably built up many useful contacts. In 1913 he decided to move into the exhibition side of the business and was able to acquire a site beside the busy Great Northern Railway station that was also near the city centre and readily accessible to both city transport and trains. He engaged William J. Roome of Kingscourt as his architect and what he produced was described in the advertisements of the day as a "most picturesque and artistic home of the Moving Picture Art."

Roome's building was certainly very distinctive, exhibiting a mixture of styles with black and white mock Tudor design on the outside and classical features inside. The entrance hall was spacious and impressive with tasteful wooden panelling, multi - coloured floor tiling and a small fountain complete with goldfish. The overall structure was, like the Crumlin, up -to - date with a modern ventilation system installed by the Musgrave Company, while the louvred windows could be opened to allow "the germ-destroying rays of the sun (to) daily penetrate to every part of the house, purifying and sweetening the atmosphere."

A unique little cinema.

Knowing that some of the audience would probably be travellers with trains to catch, he installed a Sharman D.Neill electric clock in a prominent position above the screen. The Whig was later to comment on the quality of the screen and the brightness and clarity of the pictures projected on it, completely free of flicker. Like the Kelvin, which it resembled in size, there was no balcony but the floor was sloped to give clear views of the screen. There were 550 seats, of which 500 cost 6d while the remainder could be booked for one shilling. The seating was comfortable and one critic commented favourably on the elbow and leg room available. Music was supplied by a small orchestra. Mr George offered his patrons comfort in tasteful surroundings ("a quiet and subdued decor" as the News Letter referred to it) and the cinema soon came to be known as Belfast's "drawing room" kinema, with a "k." The side walls of the auditorium were covered with tapestries or engravings of well known paintings while the back was decorated with a restful Irish landscape complete with a castle, painted by a local man, Joseph Carey.

Mindful of the admonition that people don't go to the cinema to look at the decorations, Mr George promised to show "strictly high grade films by all the most eminent producers" though the first week's offerings of "Silent Heroes" (a war drama), "House of Discord" and some forgettable comedies doesn't exactly sound too exciting. Programmes were continuous from 3:30 to 10:30 with a change of films every Monday and Thursday. His adverts tended to be quite detailed and often mentioned the actors involved and the companies which made the films. Many of the films were routine two - reel comedies, Westerns (like Broncho Billy), thrillers, melodramas and such, but he also included longer quality subjects like "David Garrick," "David Copperfield" (a Cecil Hepworth production with a running time of one hour forty minutes, presented in separate shows at 3, 5, 7, and

9 o'clock), another Hepworth production of Dicken's the "Old Curiosity Shop," and the Vitagraph production of that old favourite "Uncle Tom's Cabin."

The majority of the cinema managers showed strong Unionist sympathies but in his early months George's advertising was almost aggressively loyalist. In late May he celebrated Empire Day by bringing back Will Barker's "60 Years a Queen," the life of Queen Victoria and put on special shows for students and their teachers. Later, "For the King," a patriotic film about the army and the navy, was accompanied by the suggestion that it should be seen by all Volunteers. A few weeks later he lightened the atmosphere with a "Laughter Week" showing films involving Pimple, Maurice Costello, and Florence Turner, the proceeds from which went to the Young Citizen's Volunteer Force. However, he never forgot the comfort of his patrons and nearly a year after opening he introduced glow lamp teas which could be enjoyed in comfort while watching the films. Patrons were promised that they could sit at "dainty tables" and enjoy the film while drinking their tea.

The idea of having tea in the cinema was not an original one. The Shaftesbury Pictoria, St. George's Hall and the Panopticon had all used it as an attraction. The latter's "picture teas" which were served free in the balcony in the afternoons were well known and much appreciated. Many cinemas, like the Picture House in Royal Avenue, had separate tea rooms included in their buildings where patrons could dine either before or after seeing the film but the idea of enjoying a cup of tea while actually watching the film was a more recent innovation. In the early 1970's the Classic, on the site of the Kelvin, revived the idea and sometimes presented senior citizens at the afternoon show with a cup of tea "in their hand" without any frills. The Kinema however seemed to have used a tray which probably could be attached to the back of a seat as in an aeroplane. The idea caught the imagination of some observers at the time and a contemporary article gives a flavour of their thinking. The writer, with a hint of Jerome K. Jerome in his style, felt that the new cinemas fulfilled "many of the purposes of a good club." He dismissed those "superior persons" who criticised the average programme as "melodramatic fare (which pandered) to a morbid public taste" and pointed out that the cinemas were dry, warm and comfortable places where travellers could wait in luxury for their connections, sipping their tea, while listening to "a not intolerable orchestra while the plot of some thrilling drama of cowboy life unfolds itself." He even suggested that they were suitable places to meet a business colleague for a discussion over tea and toast with the surprising (to a modern audience) rider that privacy was insured because there was "just enough noise to prevent one's conversation being overheard." How noisy the silent cinemas were is difficult to ascertain but one cannot imagine managers like Alfred George or Fred Stewart allowing too much disturbance. It mustn't have been a major problem in the downtown cinemas because none of the local critics ever mentioned it.

The Great Northern Kinema was the last of the pre - war cinemas to be built but the War didn't dampen the cinema - going habit or curtail the cinema business. Quite the opposite. Cinema going increased during the next four years, a period which also saw the opening of twelve new cinemas which added nearly 10,000 extra seats to those already available in the city. Despite that increase, long queues could be found at most cinemas every night of the week. A letter writer complained that unless one was downtown before seven o'clock it was impossible to get into any cinema. He suggested that one answer was for cinemas to set aside a number of seats that could be booked, but the only manager to consider the idea was Alfred George. The other cinemas retained the policy of first there got the seats. Another writer described being faced with a long wait in a queue followed by having to stand through most of the last show before getting a seat. Some managers filled the auditorium for the last show allowing patrons to stand around the walls or even to sit on the steps in the aisles. News of that reached the authorities and the City Hall issued a statement reminding managers to keep the aisles and passageways clear at all times in case of fire and panic.

Charlie and Mabel. Top favourites with local audiences.

The News Letter put the increased attendance at films down to people seeking relief from the shortages, pressures and realities of wartime. That was certainly one of the reasons but there were others. The Whig critic believed that what he called "the resurgence of cinema going" was due largely to the emergence of one man, Charlie Chaplin, ably supported by the other Keystone clowns and comedians like Ford Sterling, Mabel Normand and Fatty Arbuckle. Nor can one overlook the impact that the sensational new Serials had, with the emergence of the Serial Queens like Kathlyn Williams, Pearl White and Ella Hall. The film makers and producers also realised the drawing power of the star system that was developing and they released more and more information, both factual and fictional, about their actors and actresses. Advertisements in the press increasingly included the main players' names besides the title of the film and the company which made it. Film goers became more and more familiar with names like Annette Kellerman, Mary Pickford, Francis X. Bushman, Elizabeth Risdon, Gene Gautier, and Suzanne Grandais. At the same time films were becoming longer and more artistically satisfactory and a number of them like Cabiria, Quo Vadis

Pearl White in peril

and Birth of a Nation added stature to cinema as an art form and proved attractive to the middle classes. Finally the new cinemas which were spreading in a close network across the city were architecturally seductive, increasingly luxurious, technically superior in their equipment and efficiently managed.

Typical was the Imperial, the first of the wartime cinemas to be completed, though it had been planned long before hostilities broke out. The original plans had been deposited with the Council in September 1913 for the Ulster Picture House Company formed by a group of local entrepreneurs led by two businessmen, James Barron and Councillor Turner, a well known fruiterer with twelve retail outlets across the city. The belief at the time was that the cinema was designed by a third member of the group, R.E.Forbes, but the official plans were actually the work of the architects Naylor and Sale from Derby. Those plans indicate a moderate sized cinema seating just over 500 which was part of a complex extending from High Street to Corn Market. The cinema had its entrance and foyer in Corn Market where the Box Office for the Titanic Experience operated (2013), allowing access not only to the auditorium but also to two elegant and well appointed tearooms called the old English Tearoom, situated to the right of the entrance where citizens could dine in the comfortable surroundings of a Tudor decor, with an open log fire and carved oak furniture, and the Empire Tearooms with its furnishings finished in mahogany, located on the first floor. From High Street one entered an equally elegant cafe, passing a fountain into a marble Palm Court which also gave access to the cinema foyer. There obviously were major modifications to that original plan (maybe by Mr Forbes) because none of the commentators at the time mention the High Street connection, which seems to have been abandoned, while the auditorium which the Whig described as "elegant and commodious," was expanded from its original conception, with a balcony added to give a total seating of nearly 1000 people.

The Imperial overlooks the busy Arthur Square. Source: Irish News.

The building's frontage abandoned the traditional white decoration associated with cinemas and there is no mention of coloured lights. Its grey Carrara stonework extended about fifty feet (16 metres) across 18 - 24, Corn Market, a site that had formerly been occupied by two shops, a fishmonger and a drysalter, forming a dramatic contrast to what had preceded it. Structurally it incorporated the latest building developments being constructed with a reinforced concrete raft foundation and cavity walls which together, the builders claimed, would keep it entirely damp free. The final result was a splendid cinema capable of competing with the luxuries of the Picture House in Royal Avenue. The newspapers described it as one of the finest and most up-to-date cinemas in the country and the public were given the opportunity of appraising it when it opened on 7th December 1914. The official opening was an elaborate occasion and it certainly didn't manifest any obvious wartime austerities. Attendance was by invitation only and there was a cameraman on hand at three o'clock to film the arrival of the Lord Mayor, Councillor Crawford Mc Cullagh, and other prominent citizens. That film - well advertised - was shown in the new cinema later in the week, causing much comment. It was a further reflection of the importance that managers attached to showing local events. Besides the obvious political happenings all types of occurrences of local life were filmed and proved popular with audiences. Sadly they also proved to be transient and most of them, which would have formed a fascinating film archive, are now lost.

The Lord Mayor was an enthusiastic supporter of local business enterprise and congratulated the local men on their initiative. He pointed out that it required quite substantial capital to build a cinema of that quality but he felt the venture would be a success because "picture entertainments possessed a wonderful popularity with all classes and so far from waning, as had been predicted, that popularity was increasing year by year." He noted that most of the work had been carried out by local firms which pleased him very much not only because of the high quality of the results but also because it gave local employment. The building had been completed by C. and W. Mc Quoid of Roden Street, the heating and lighting had been installed by John Robinson of Library Street, the furnishings which were much praised were by Robert Watson of Donegall Street and the electrical installations, which included two gas National engines to supply the power, were completed by Wm. Garmany of Donegal Street. The fibrous plaster work on the ceiling of the auditorium, which impressed all, was carried out by a London firm, John Tanner and Sons, who specialised in the process. There were a number of complementary references to the elegance of the ceiling with its refined Greek character. If well done, fibrous plaster work could be very beautiful but it also had the added property of improving the general acoustics and was therefore used in many cinemas. One might ask why acoustics should be so important in a hall for silent films but every major cinema had a large orchestra. Music was an important and integral part of the entertainment and details of the orchestral pieces to be performed were often published with the name of the film. The Imperial was no exception and advertised the excellence of their large orchestra directed by Herbert Mortimer from Nottingham, a much respected and experienced musician who played both violin and piano.

After the speeches the guests were entertained to tea in the Empire Tearoom where the catering was in the hands of the Bloomfield Bakery and afterwards they retired to the cinema to enjoy the films where, according to the Whig, the music was "attractive" and the pictures were "remarkably clear and steady." The show consisted of "Little Lord Fauntelroy," a John Bunny comedy "The Vases of Hymen," another comedy "Who Got the Trousers?" "George Robey as an Anarchist," war news and the Pathe Gazette. The main thrust of the newspaper reports was the magnificence of the cinema itself and there was little comment about the films shown. The Whig however did mention that the main feature was a popular story that "lent itself appropriately" to the film format and added that it was "splendidly filmed." It was most likely a Kineto production released just a few months earlier and reports elsewhere suggest that it had an extra attraction in that it was photographed in Charles Urban's Kinemacolor system. The cinema was opened to the public at 6 o'clock and was "thronged" (Whig) until 10 o'clock. The management opted for continuous performances from 1 o'clock until 10. 30 p.m. with seat prices of 6d for the stalls and one shilling for the balcony. Children, always an important consideration, were half price until 5.30. Films of the highest quality were promised and the programme would be changed every Monday and Thursday. The Imperial opened in style, it maintained high standards throughout its working life, and from all accounts it departed the entertainment scene in style when it closed in November 1959 aged 45 years.

Of course the main concern of most people was the War which was reported in great detail in the press and presented visually in the cinemas. All the cinemas had newsreels with the "latest war pictures" as had the Empire, the Royal Hippodrome (on its Hipposcope), and at weekends during the winter the Y.M.C.A. and Grosvenor Hall. Mr George in the Kinema House went one better and introduced "war talks," a series of short addresses given before the main film by professors from Queen's University, the aim of which was to promote enlistment. Despite the fact that it was a daily topic of conversation and that it permeated all aspects of life, the actual war seemed far away until suddenly in February 1915 a German submarine, the U21, appeared in the Irish Sea and sank three ships. Another vessel, the Graphic, belonging to the Belfast Steamship Company only escaped because its speed enabled it to outrun the raider and reach the safety of the Mersey Estuary. There was a mixture of excitement and consternation in Belfast as cross channel services were suspended and the port was closed as a precaution. There was also some irritation that the Navy had allowed such a thing to happen. Rumours were rife about sightings of the submarine and how it had even stopped a ship at sea to refuel. The Panopticon announced that the expected print of "The Spoilers" hadn't arrived from London for the Monday showing because of the scare but by Wednesday Mr Stewart was able to screen it "with grand orchestral music." With uncanny - or lucky - timing during that week the Picture House presented "Defenders of our Empire" which dealt with the problem of how invaders to these shores would be dealt with.

The Picture House continued to emphasise quality combined with instruction in its programmes along with a liberal sprinkling of local affairs, presented in attractive and comfortable surroundings. The Imperial did likewise even to the showing of local material but the emphasis was on quality or unusual films. Early in January a drama called "Three Faces" was presented in which Gene Gauntier played three different characters. The News Letter critic wrote that it was the first time that had been attempted and that the actress appeared on screen playing the three parts in the same scene "to the general wonder of the audience." Many years later Joanne Woodward was much praised for attempting the same feat in "The Three Faces of Eve" (1957, d. Nunnally Johnson). After the appointment of a new manager, B.N.McDowell in June, there was a further promise of quality films which turned out to be the products of a new American company called Paramount Pictures. Paramount was founded in 1914 by William Hodkinson as a financing and distribution company and he persuaded a number of film making companies to join him, notably those of Adolf Zukor and Jesse Lasky. Zukor, a Hungarian who had immigrated to the U.S.A., had made his name when he imported and successfully exhibited the French film "Queen Elizabeth" (shown in Belfast as "Queen Bess") starring Sarah Bernhardt. Zukor believed that audiences would respond if they were given good quality material presented in attractive surroundings. Thus he presented the film (a four - reeler) as a road show in theatres giving it the extra prestige of theatrical quality, a policy that was also favoured by the Grand Opera House. To that end he set up a company called Famous Players in Famous Plays and began filming a series of well known plays, the first of which was "The Count of Monte Cristo" starring James O'Neill, a well respected stage actor and father of Eugene O'Neill. The film was directed by Edwin S. Porter, without much imagination, using painted backgrounds as on the stage. Seemingly O'Neill was drunk most of the time but he knew the play so well that it didn't show in the final product, which might say something about the acting style of the period.

The film appeared in the Picture House in early 1913 and was well received. Others followed, notably "Tess of the D'Urbervilles" with five reels, and the popular "The Sign of the Cross," a four - reeler with William Farnum, both of which were screened in the Panopticon. The latter with its special music was very well received in Belfast, the I.S.N. finding it "most beautiful" while the News Letter felt that it had improved on the stage version by using natural outdoor scenery instead of "a faded back cloth." The critic had actually put his finger on one of the problems of the early Famous Players productions, namely that they were, like the Films d'Art before them, merely filmed plays. Critics pointed that limitation out to Zukor and added that the exaggerated histrionics of some of the stage actors were quite unsuited to films. There was also the fact that many of them were middle

- aged or older and that they photographed badly in the harsh lighting of the period.

At the same time Jesse Lasky, Samuel Goldfish (later changed to Goldwyn) and Cecil B. De Mille had founded the Jesse Lasky Feature Play Company (1913) with the aim of making longer films. De Mille and his crew left New York by train to make their first film, a Western called "The Squaw Man" with stage actor Dustin Farnum, a brother of William, in the main part. They ended up in a small place called Hollywood and rented a barn to be used as a studio. On completion the film proved a major success though there seems to be no record of it having been shown locally. Later productions from the same company, like "The Virginian," were shown very successfully.

It is doubtful if anyone in Belfast was aware of those developments but they soon became familiar with the names of the companies and with the Paramount logo of a snow capped mountain surmounted by stars, especially after the Imperial made an agreement to show Paramount films. That early association with Paramount remained strong all through the cinema's life time and the major Paramount releases over the years premiered in Belfast in the Imperial. The perceptive Fred Stewart in the Panopticon had also noted the arrival of the quality productions from Zukor and Lasky and tried one or two to test their drawing power, after which he decided to leave them to his competitors in the Picture House and the Imperial. He felt more at ease with a touch of the exotic and drew the crowds with a series of films "exposing" the evils of White Slavery in "Dealers in Human Lives," "Souls in Bondage," and "Society and its Sins." In contrast to those actual or imagined scenes of female degradation he also lightened his screen with the froth and frivolity of "Neptune's Daughter" starring one of the city's favourite actresses, the glamorous Annette Kellerman, who could be described as the silent era's Ester Williams. In 1952 Miss Williams actually played her in the M-G-M tribute "Million Dollar Mermaid" (d. Mervyn LeRoy).

Miss Kellerman had suffered from polio as a child in her native Australia but had overcome her physical disability by taking water based exercise. She then turned the swimming skills acquired in that way to her advantage in sport (by the age of fifteen she was an Australian champion) and on the stage, becoming the world's first aquatic star. Her father brought her to Europe where she demonstrated her ability by swimming in the rivers Seine, Rhine, Danube and Thames. She began her stage career in London, diving into a large glass tank and performing a water ballet. She had also attained some notoriety by her campaign to promote the single piece bathing suit, the wearing of which complemented her billing as "the perfect woman." The I.S.N. illustrated that claim with an impressive array of vital statistics for its readers: height 5 feet 4 ins, head 21. 3 ins, neck 12.3 ins, chest 33.1 ins, waist 26.2 ins, hips 37.8 ins, thigh 21.2 ins, calf 13.0 ins, ankle 7.7 ins, upper arm 12.0 ins, forearm 9.6 ins, and wrist 5.9 ins which was probably as close as one could get to virtual reality in those days.

"Neptune's Daughter" was directed by an Irishman, Herbert Brenon, for Carl Laemmle at Imp (later, Universal Studios). Brenon had a fondness for what the American writer Terry Ramsaye called "moist stories" about the sea and its mythical inhabitants. He portrayed a fantasy world in which Annette Kellerman was a mermaid, the daughter of King Neptune, who wanted to avenge her younger sister who had died trapped in a fishing net. The story gave her ample opportunities to display her swimming and diving skills, not to mention her impressive physical charms. She discovered that the offending net had been set by a king but when she met him, instead of exacting vengeance, she fell in love, abandoned the sea, her immortality and her existence as a mermaid to marry him. The I.S.N. described it as a "wonderful picture play." The film, a five - reeler, was retained for a whole week in late August, rather than the usual three days, drawing large crowds. Later in the year Mr Stewart presented a more serious piece of work, Barker's epic about the English Civil War, "Jane Shore," which had been staged many times in the city over the years, and then capped it with one of the most famous of silent films, "Cabiria," billed then as "the World's Greatest Picture," which for once wasn't an understatement. As he watched the passers by stopping to read the posters in front of the cinema he had every right to feel that he had a hit on his hands, a film that arrived with a hefty reputation. Belfast filmgoers were about to be amazed and awed by what they would see. In fact this epic of Ancient Rome proved to be an eye - opener, a lesson in film technique which showed up the visual inadequacies of the filmed stage plays. An American critic claimed, maybe over enthusiastically, that it was the film that finally freed the camera from the proscenium.

The film made an impact wherever it was shown. It impressed audiences, critics and film makers like D.W.Griffith and Cecil B. de Mille, and film historians today still regard "Cabiria" as an important and seminal event in film development. It was essentially the work of one man, the Italian Giovanni Pastrone, who wrote the script and directed and produced the film. A story at the time claimed that the noted Italian poet Gabriele D'Annunzio was responsible for the story and the script but that was an advertising ploy used by Pastrone to solicit serious literary attention and to appeal to middle class educated audiences. He paid the poet 50,000 lire in gold for the use of his name and in return D'Annunzio wrote the intertitles and gave the characters their distinctive names. The intertitles were certainly very literary, even flowery, and full of classical allusions. Just before the eruption of Mt Etna the titles read: "The mighty chest of Typhon upon which rests the celestial column gives a sudden start and shatters the peace of the evening." What the down - to - earth linen workers and shipyard workers made of that is anyone's guess, though they were probably too absorbed watching the drama of the erupting mountain and the fleeing inhabitants to think about it..

While D'Annunzio was playing with words, it was Pastrone who planned the practical details from the beginning. He thoroughly researched the period, the third century B.C., thoroughly, visiting the Louvre Museum in Paris to study costumes, buildings and details of everyday life. The story was set during the Second Punic Wars as Rome and Carthage struggled for control of the east Mediterranean so it contained many of those elements that had already made Italian epics like "The Last Days of Pompeii," and "Quo Vadis" widely known and enjoyed. Taking his basic historical facts from Livy, Pastrone wove around them a fictional tale of the adventures of a young Sicilian girl called Cabiria. The story begins in Sicily where the family villa is destroyed when Mt. Etna erupts. The child Cabiria is saved by a servant Croessa and they flee the scene only to be captured by Phoenician pirates and taken to Carthage where they are sold in the slave market. The High Priest Karthalo buys them as he intends to sacrifice the child to Moloch the fire god. Also in Carthage is Fulvius Axilla, a Roman spy, accompanied by his servant, the strong man Maciste (a name which means "breaker of chains"). In response to Croessa's pleas Maciste saves Cabiria from the flames but during the ensuing chase is forced to leave her in safety with the princess of Carthage, Sophonisba. Maciste is captured and chained to a mill wheel (Victor Mature suffered the same fate as Samson in Cecil B. deMille's "Samson and Delilah" made in 1949) where he spends ten years during which Cabiria grows up as one of the princess's servants. Intercut with all this are striking scenes from the war, of Hannibal crossing the Alps, the destruction of the Roman fleet at Syracuse by fire, and the siege of Cerba. As Scipio and his Roman army finally approach Carthage Fulvius returns to the city secretly and helps Maciste to escape. Incident piles upon incident culminating with the death of Sophonisba by poison. Cabiria is rescued once again and reunited with Fulvius who brings her back to her parents in Sicily.

Critics of the day were impressed by the complexity of the story line, the variety of major characters, the skill and visual flair with which Pastrone drew the many threads of the plot together. A video version is available today and it still stands up to critical viewing allowing one to appreciate in some degree what awed the contemporary audiences. The sets are solid looking and have depth. Pastrone filled them with people and he often tracked smoothly in among them to the amazement of audiences. The critic of the New York Dramatic Mirror described how scenes were "brought slowly to the foreground [tracking] or moved from side to side [panning]." Some of the sets were massive, like the temple of Moloch where struggling children were tossed into the furnace roaring in the god's belly. The audiences in the Panopticon must have been reduced to silence by the scenes in the temple, its vast size dominated by the ugly statue of Moloch whose hinged stomach opened periodically to reveal the flames therein, the strange decor, the exotic rituals, the striking and effective lighting, the atmosphere heightened by the strains of the specially composed music "Symphony of Fire." Whether the latter was played or not in the Panopticon is uncertain because none of the critics mention the accompanying music, though such an omission was not unusual.

In scenes such as those Pastrone showed his mastery of using space, and especially lighting, for dramatic effect. His outdoor sequences were equally impressive, and audiences enthused over scenes of snow - covered mountain slopes with long lines of Hannibal's trudging troops stretching away into the background, or the arid desert landscape with slow moving lines of camels silhouetted against the sky in images worthy of John Ford. The scenes at the siege of Cerba where he used dolly shots to show soldiers attacking and scaling the city walls amazed audiences, as did a sequence when Roman soldiers built a human pyramid with their shields to allow Fulvius to climb the walls of Carthage. The acting was naturalistic and in the main lacked the exaggerations of the stage, with the exception of Italia Manzani as Princess Sophinista. Pastrone commented later that her performance was a tribute to Sarah Bernhardt and she certainly strikes some Bernhardt - style poses. How Bernhardt would have relished her death scene! After seeing the film the critic of the New York Dramatic Mirror concluded that "high art and the motion picture are not incompatible."

The filming took place in Italy, the Alps, and Morocco over seven months during which 20,000 metres of celluloid were exposed. Pastrone edited his raw footage down to ten reels which were presented in Turin in April 1914 complete with special music played by a large symphony orchestra. A month later it was shown in New York where the New York Times thought it was "well done." In London a critic described the audience sitting in silence hardly able to believe what they were seeing. It was, he wrote, "a triumph of triumphs." It reached Dublin in October 1915 where it showed at the Theatre Royal every afternoon for over a fortnight. The Irish Times critic thought it was "one of the most interesting cinema films ever exhibited in Dublin." It was, he explained, full of "remarkable scenes" among which he included the eruption of Mt Etna, the destruction of Cabiria's house, the army crossing the Alps, and the destruction of the Roman fleet. It is interesting that two of those - the eruption and the burning of the fleet - involved special effects and the use of models. He was impressed by the scale of the spectacle and the "remarkable realism" of many scenes. The acting was "dignified and convincing." He concluded that it was a remarkable production which "should be seen by all."

Belfast had to wait another month until mid -November when Mr Stewart presented it at the Panopticon for a week in separate shows at I,3,5,7, and 9 o'clock, ten days before the official opening in Paris. The version that had been premiered in Turin ran for three hours as did those in New York and London but the print shown in the Panopticon was obviously just less than two hours. The video version today runs for 123 minutes so it is probably similar to what audiences watched in 1915 in High Street. The critic of the Whig commented that the extra length of the film meant that most of the usual supporting programme was not screened but felt that was more than compensated for by seeing the film "unabridged." There must have been two versions available, a longer one (the director's cut?) for road house showings and a shorter version for normal cinema viewing. From the local critics' comments the version shown included all the spectacular elements with "gorgeous, weird and striking pictures" (Whig). It was, continued the Whig, "one of the finest films ever shown at the Panopticon, which is saying a good deal." The critic praised the complexity of the plot which he described as full of murder, treason and suicide "that are dear to the Italian heart." The Irish News drew attention to the involvement of D'Annunzio, "one of Europe's leading literary figures" in the project and recommended it for its "scope and immense detail." Equally the News Letter was impressed by the succession of spectacular scenes and closely echoing the Irish Times found it a "triumph of film production" with acting that was "dignified and convincing."

Maciste (right) in "Cabiria".

One of the actors in particular made an impression on audiences: Bartolomeo Pagano, who played the part of the strong man, Maciste. In fact he wasn't an actor at all but a docker whom Pastrone found working in the docks in Genoa. Impressed by his muscular frame he signed him up though he had no previous acting experience. Under Pastrone's guidance he produced a fine performance and came across with a natural dignity and humour. So popular was he that a series of very successful Maciste films followed, built around the character. Mr Stewart must have been impressed because when he opened his new cinema, the New York, in York street a year later the first film shown was "Maciste" starring the same Bartolomeo Pagano. Maciste introduced the strongman into Italian cinema and the tradition has continued with stories involving Samson, Hercules and similar heroes. He also influenced American cinema which was soon to start producing the first Tarzan films starring Elmo Lincoln. The more recent success of Arnold Swartzenegger still owes something to Cabiria and Maciste.

There was nothing unusual in audiences in Belfast enjoying and appreciating an Italian film. European films were an important and accepted part of normal cinema fare prior to the Great War, including Italian, Danish, Swedish, German and especially French films. During the war European and British production declined due to disruption, lack of raw materials like film stock and, above all, a shortage of technicians as more and more men were called up to be sacrificed to a war god every bit as voracious as Moloch. The deficit on local screens was made up by increased numbers of American films. Of course there had been films of American origin from the beginnings of the cinema and local audiences had always enjoyed them, especially the Westerns, but they had never dominated the screens. One of the first indications of the coming change was the steady flow of Paramount productions which arrived at the Imperial; but even more prominent were the waves of Keystone two - reelers which released Ford Sterling, Mabel Normand, Fatty Arbuckle and, above all, Charlie Chaplin on to local screens.

The first Keystone comedies began appearing as supporting fare during 1913 and the first recorded reference to the studio is in the Irish News at the end of September of that year. Referring to the programme in the Panopticon the critic commented on the main film, a Vitagraph production called "One Good Turn" starring Miss Florence Turner and then added that "The Sleuth's Last Stand," a parody of detective dramas by the Keystone Company was "the most amusing item on the programme." During the same week the Palladium screened another Keystone, "How Fatty Made Good," as support for its stage show though there was no reference to who was in it (Fatty Arbuckle) or who made it. Included in the opening show of the Clonard was "Mabel's Strategem," another Keystone with Mabel Normand, which was mentioned without comment. In early January 1914 the Picture House presented "Our Wives" and again the Irish News drew attention to a supporting film, "Mabel's Dramatic Career," though with no details. It is an interesting film in that it starred Mack Sennett himself with Mabel Normand who was to become a great favourite of the local crowds, and it gives a good idea of the type of subject Sennett liked to present. Sennett plays a rustic in a tight jacket and a bowler too small for him. He visits a nickelodeon to watch a film starring his girlfriend who is played by Mabel Normand. He becomes very involved with what is happening on the screen and when she is menaced by the villain, Ford Sterling, who ties her up and threatens her with his pistol Sennett loses control, whips out his own gun and begins shooting in all directions. The result is mayhem.

Despite its basic appeal the Keystone style was obviously making an impression on the cinematic consciousness and during 1914 even the fastidious Picture House showed a number of Keystone films starring Fatty Arbuckle, Ford Sterling and Mabel Normand. There was no mention of Keystone's latest recruit, one Charles Chaplin, though at least one of his early films, "Mabel's Strange Predicament," only the second in which he wore the tramp costume, was shown in the Empire in October. One wonders did anyone make the connection between the character on the screen and the real person who had clowned on the very same stage a few years before. By the end of the year local patrons were familiar with Ford Sterling (a particular favourite, according to reports), Fatty Arbuckle and Mabel

Normand who was often referred to as Keystone Mabel or just Mabel. However they were all soon to be outshone by the new arrival.

Charles Chaplin, as he was referred to in the early advertisements, was a member of the Fred Karno Company which had often performed in Belfast where he was just regarded as part of a very funny music hall act. In 1913 he was touring in the U.S.A. with one of Karno's groups when Mack Sennett and Mabel Normand saw his performance. The result was that Chaplin arrived, somewhat reluctantly, at the Keystone studios later that year and was soon involved in his first film, "Making a Living." By the end of 1914 he had made thirty five films at Keystone and had clowned with Mabel, Ford Sterling, Mack Sennett, Fatty, Chester Conklin, Mack Swain, Edgar Kennedy, Slim Summerville, Minta Durfee, Gloria Swanson and many others whose names are revered by film buffs. The earliest local mention of Charles Chaplin is in an advert for the Alhambra which presented "Caught in a Cabaret" during the second week in January 1915, calling it the "absolute limit in Keystones" and promising the audience "a smile, a scream, a yell!" That same week the Central offered "two hours of continuous laughter" in what it called Keystone Nights, consisting of a series of films with Keystone Mabel and Charles Chaplin. The West Belfast Cinema also called upon its patrons to "come and see Charles Chaplin" with his name in heavy black print, but, significantly, felt that it wasn't necessary to indicate what the name of the film was. In February the Alhambra showed "Mabel's Busy Day" with "The Masquerader" in which Chaplin demonstrated his versatility by playing a woman and was joined by the Panopticon which also showed the latter. By April Charles Chaplin was being billed as "the world's greatest comedian" and the mere mention of his name attracted the crowds.

Another manager who became aware of Chaplin's potential during early 1915 was Alfred George in the Kinema House. Like many others he had come to realise that the War wasn't going to be over as quickly as had been predicted and that the country was probably in for a long difficult slog. He now agreed with those who felt that people needed something to lift their spirits and such thoughts moved him to announce that "laughter is treasure for the people.... the antidote to intolerable hours of gloom. Wars are not won by brooding, nor victories achieved by gloom." In January he presented one of his Laughter Weeks with Ford Sterling, John Bunny, Flora Finch, Pimple and Mabel as the named attractions, but a few weeks later he was advertising "Mabel's Busy Day" starring Mabel and Charles Chaplin, following it with "A Busy Day" featuring Charles Chaplin. The next month he presented a week of Special Keystone Comedies featuring Chaplin, Ford Sterling, Mabel Normand and others named in that order. It was clear who the main attraction was. The Imperial also began to include Chaplin films regularly in its programmes as did the Panopticon and the Central. In every case Chaplin got top billing.

The cinemas vied with each other in presenting Charlie's latest, or Charlie's funniest, until the Panopticon topped them all by presenting "Tillie's Punctured Romance" in early May, which could have been described as Charlie's longest. It was a completely new departure for Keystone in that it was a six - reeler which ran for one and a half hours. It was the first feature length comedy and it was directed by the boss himself, Mack Sennett. The film, which was based on a successful musical stage play, "Tillie's Nightmare," was designed as a showcase for the star of that play, a comedienne called Marie Dressler who was paid much more than the other feature players, Chaplin and Mabel. The three main players were supported by all the old Keystone favourites. The result was a major success in America where one critic called it "the Cabiria of comedies." Charlie plays a city slicker who has a girlfriend, Mabel, in the city but who, while hiding in the countryside, meets Dressler and persuades her to steal her father's savings and accompany him to the city for a good time. When the money runs out, so does Charlie. Later when he hears that she has inherited money from an uncle, he returns and persuades her to marry him. Dressler finds out about Mabel, and the rich uncle who had "died" in a climbing accident suddenly reappears alive and well. Dressler is poor again, Charlie is frustrated and at the end Dressler and Mabel become friends and go off leaving him alone in the hands of the police. All of this is enlivened by the usual Keystone slapstick and above all by Charlie's superb clowning which was widely commented upon and praised.

Despite its historic importance and the fact that it made him a major star, in later years Chaplin showed little interest in or respect for the picture. That could be due to a number of reasons. He always found taking direction difficult and restrictive, was unhappy at playing the villain again, and at the time was anxious to develop his own directorial skills. None of that seemed relevant in May 1915 when the film arrived in Belfast and there was no doubt that the main attraction for the crowds that flocked to High Street was Chaplin. Mr Stewart had promised them "a real banquet of FUN....NUF SED." The News Letter critic noted the unusual length of the film and mused that a prolonged dose of unadulterated farce could become "tiresome" but assured his readers that that certainly wasn't the case. It was a very funny film dominated by Chaplin who was "supported" by Marie Dressler and Mabel Normand. His conclusion was that Chaplin had few equals. The Whig critic found the film "quite Keystonian" with the fun coming fast and furious. It proved that Chaplin was without doubt "the greatest comedian in the cinema world at the present time." His drawing power was "magnetic," as the packed houses in the Panopticon indicated.

Over the next weeks the film showed in nearly every cinema in the city, a feat unequalled by anything that had gone before it. When the Alhambra showed it only one name was mentioned, Chaplin, along with the information that the film consisted of six parts which were described as a progression through the stages of smile, laugh, scream, roar, hysterics to convulsions. No film comedy today could live up to that level of promotion. Suddenly Chaplin was everywhere and screens all over the city were showing Charlie's Elopement, Champagne Charlie, Charlie in the Park, Charlie's Night Out, Charlie's New Job, Getting Acquainted, Charlie the Perfect Lady, Charlie at the Bank, Charlie Shanghaied, Charlie at the Show, His Prehistoric Past, and by July 1916 the Kinema House could claim to include the "Charliest Chaplin ever shown" in its programme, without giving any name.

The Chaplin phenomenon, which would probably be jargonised into Chaplinmania today, spread well beyond the cinema screens and invaded all levels of society. Children in the streets copied his walk and sang songs about him, one could buy a Chaplin walking cane in the city centre, soldiers marched to war singing "the sun shines bright on Charlie Chaplin," intellectuals admired him and Chaplin lookalikes were ten - a - penny. The Opera House caught the mood of the time when it presented "Charlie Chaplin Mad" in September

1915, a musical review that promised beautiful girls, a riot of fun and frolic, with a stage full of Charlie Chaplins including the only female Chaplin impersonator in the country. What a sight the Opera stage must have presented crowded from one end to the other with dancing Charlie Chaplin lookalikes. The Whig critic reckoned that there were sixty Chaplins on stage, dancing, or copying his walk, or trying to perfect "his wonderful kick." Chaplin, he suggested, had an individual style and that was what endeared him to cinema audiences. It wasn't so much what he did but the way in which he did it. It was all good fun, said the News Letter, but at the same time it reflected many aspects of the contemporary Charlie Chaplin craze. The writer felt that Chaplin's new and distinctive style of "pantomimic art" had allowed him to succeed John Bunny as the main comedy draw in the cinema. There was no doubt that he now reigned supreme in "broad comedy" which contrasted with Bunny's more subdued and subtle style, a style which had depended more on facial expressions. The stage impersonations were very enjoyable and the audiences in the Opera certainly responded to them but the critic added that "No-one can really do Chaplin," though that didn't stop many trying. During the Easter holidays of 1917 the Clonard, in addition to its films, put on a special stage presentation by Bob Robinson, described as an eccentric character comedian, doing his impersonation of Chaplin which according to the Irish News proved to be "a great success." As part of the show there was an amateur Charlie Chaplin contest which was won by a local man, Charles McDonnell. Two weeks later the Clonard presented another live Charlie Chaplin sketch called "The Waiter," with Mr Mc Donnell playing Chaplin and Bob Robinson playing Chester Conklin. The crowds loved it though the Telegraph found it no more than "acceptable."

There was however one man who could "do" Chaplin quite well and he was Billy West. West had been born in Russia but was taken to the U.S.A. as a child. He worked in vaudeville and during those years perfected his Chaplin routine. In 1917-18 he made a number of comedies for King Bee pictures in which he played the Little Tramp, copying every movement of Chaplin. His playing was so authentic that many people thought they were actually watching Chaplin himself and some experts have even been fooled into accepting his films as the real thing. It was Fred Stewart at the Panopticon who introduced West to Belfast in October 1917 but he clearly advertised him as "Charlie Chaplin's double" in "Back Stage," "Bombs and Boarders," "Doughnuts," "Cupid's Rival," "The Villain." and "The Millionaire." The fact that he showed so many of his films suggested that West was popular with local audiences though the critics made no comment beyond the fact that he was "funny." When the Clonard showed "Back Stage" some time later it was advertised as "two reels of machine gun laughter featuring the New Chaplin," which must have confused a lot of people. The Clonard doesn't seem to have shown the other West films though he did turn up in the newly opened Popular and the Crumlin. During those same weeks Fred Stewart showed a number of comedies involving a character called Lonesome Luke and went so far as to describe one of them, "Luke's Busy Day," as "très drole." Sadly they were very sub - Chaplin and made no real impact on audiences or the local critics, despite the fact that Luke was played by an as yet little known actor called Harold Lloyd.

On one occasion the Whig critic commented that the appearance of Chaplin's name on the screen always caused "an anticipatory chuckle" among the audience. Another attraction, the serial, also caused a noticeable reaction, but it was more a gasp of suppressed excitement. During the war years the Serial or Chapter play as it was often called became an integral part of most cinema programmes. The Chapter Play originated in 1913 in America when the Chicago Tribune, in an effort to increase its circulation, joined with the Selig company to produce a film serial, The Adventures of Kathyln. The aim was to release thirteen episodes or "chapters" in sequence, each one accompanied by a written description in the newspaper. The arrangement proved to be a big success with audiences and the newspaper buying public, and that persuaded other newspapers to do likewise. The Chicago Herald combined with Universal while the Hearst group approached Pathé and a new film genre was under way. Audiences in Belfast were already familiar with series of films (like James Bond or Harry Potter today), each one complete in itself, built around the adventures of a distinctive character like Broncho Billy, Lieut. Rose, Nick Carter, Detective Daring, P.C.Sharpe, the Girl Detective, Fantomas and even Sherlock Holmes. The serial was different in concept. The episodes, each between 1600 and 2000 feet, i.e. up to two reels long, were linked in one thrilling and exciting story well spiced with sensational events, but each episode ended with the hero or heroine in a perilous situation from which there seemed to be no escape. Such cliff hanger endings sent the audience away in a state of suspense wondering what would happen next. It was a simple but direct device to lure people back to see the next episode and, in most cases, it worked.

The serials didn't originate mystery plots or thrills, and a look at some of the films showing in the city at the time makes it clear that audiences were well used to sensational material. In early 1915 the Alhambra presented "London's Underground with Detective Daring." Daring was a popular hero of the day, a man of action designed to compete with Lieut. Rose. The advertisement for the film breathlessly encouraged people to come along and see "the dash through a plate glass window on a motorcycle, Daring suspended head downwards 60 feet (18 metres) above the ground, the escape along telephone wires, the dive from a tramcar over Kingston Bridge into the river 70 feet (21 metres) below." A little later the Imperial screened "The Ghost Breaker," a Lasky production which ran for over an hour and involved the hero, W.B.Warner, in a succession of adventures while exploring a mysterious old castle. It was, wrote the Whig critic approvingly, crammed with thrills involving "every up-to-date stage device - portraits with peepholes, chambers whose walls move together to crush an occupant, dungeons with skeletons in armour, rats galore - very clever and startling."

Today the serials are often derided and dismissed as dross. Many histories of the cinema ignore them yet they had an important impact on audiences at the time. They were splendid entertainment and played a major role in attracting people to the cinema on a regular basis. Their format, somewhat camouflaged, is still very much alive today. Films like "Star Wars," "Indiana Jones" or "Speed" are really serials without the breaks and they present an interesting exercise to incipient film editors as to where they could be cut and presented as separate episodes. Television soaps like "Coronation Street" and "Eastenders" use the serial format and there are even hints of it in some news broadcasts. Modern audiences are not all that different from those of 1915 in what they respond to. The serials helped take peoples' minds off the war and at the same time presented them with new heroes and heroines of the time who seemingly could cope with any situation no matter how dangerous or hopeless. Above all, audiences took to the serial queens who have become epitomised today in folk memory by one name, Pearl White. They weren't superwomen or the toned and muscled automatons who grace today's screens spinning on their toes or swinging about on invisible wires like circus performers. They were everyday down - to - earth girls who displayed intelligence, pluck, tenacity and ingenuity in the face of all kinds of danger. Some of the dangers were quite real and involved hazardous stunts which many of the girls performed themselves, or coping with unpredictable wild animals that could - and did on occasion - bite or claw.

The serial arrived quietly in Belfast in December 1913 courtesy of Joe McKibben. "What Happened to Mary" (Edison) is regarded as a link between the film series and the serial and, as already mentioned, its twelve episodes were shown in the West End Cinema just a month after it opened on the Shankill Road. The first true serial however appeared in the Kinema House in November 1914 and its fifteen episodes continued until May 1915. It was Selig's "The Adventures of Kathlyn" starring Kathlyn Williams who was already well known in the city. The plot involved Miss Williams in a perilous search to mysterious India, though it was actually filmed in Florida. Sadly, like so many of the early silents, it has completely disappeared and all that remains are stills of Miss Williams being menaced by the villain Charles Clary, or by fierce looking wild animals (a Selig favourite), or being rescued by hero Thomas Santschi. Those names mean nothing to most people today but they were much talked about personalities in 1915. So much for fame! There was little comment by the local critics on the content of the serial though the News Letter did note that "it was more and more looked forward to" as the weeks passed, while the Whig commented that it "illustrated" the written serial running concurrently in a paper called "Ideas". Alfred George however must have been pleased at the response to it because when it ended he followed it with another serial, "Dolly's Adventures." The idea was obviously catching on because at the same time the Central presented the "Trey o' Hearts" another mystery thriller in fifteen chapters starring George Larkin and Cleo Madison who played two parts, twin sisters, one good, the other evil. That was followed in September by the fifteen episodes of "The Black Box" which caused much comment among the cinema goers. What is the secret of the Black Box... come and find out! Pearl White called that kind of lure a "weenie" while Alfred Hitchcock much later referred to it as a Mc Guffin. Meanwhile "Dolly's Adventures" had ended in the Kinema House and was followed immediately by "The Master Key" with Ella Hall searching for a lost gold mine supported by hero Robert Leonard and menaced by villain Harry Carter.

The Black Box serial in the Central

The success of the cliffhangers in attracting audiences was not lost on other managers and an important event occurred in October 1915 when the up - market Imperial announced that it would present its first serial, the "Exploits of Elaine" starring the most talked about of all the serial queens, Pearl White. Miss White had already made her name as the heroine of "The Perils of Pauline" and "Elaine" was a follow - on to it. There was great anticipation as the city awaited the arrival of a "quality" serial. Elaine was not regarded as a programme filler; it was given top billing in the advertisements and was treated seriously by the critics.

The titles of the episodes give a flavour of its contents - the Clutching Hand, the Twilight Sleep, the Vanishing Jewels, the Frozen Safe, the Poisoned Room, the Vampire, etc. The first episode introduced the sinister villain known only as the Clutching Hand and people who saw it recalled for the author many years later the startling impact it had on the audiences. An elderly aunt who had seen it as a young girl shivered with a combination of fear and pleasure as she reminisced to the author about it. The Clutching Hand became a topic of widespread conversation and in many homes children and others were "frightened" by clutching hands appearing unexpectedly around doors or from behind curtains. The News Letter found it to be "of compelling interest, (with) sensational scenes, excellent photographic work... brimfull of thrills.... splendid acting...(and) drawing large crowds." Over the next few years the Imperial programmes were built around a Paramount release, a serial and a Chaplin film, a shrewd combination that proved immensely popular with the patrons.

At the end of 1917 the I.S.N. observed that serials were "immensely popular" in the city and added that some of the best were shown in the Imperial. Among them was the eagerly awaited "The Perils of Pauline" (Pathé) which was screened starting in early August 1916. It was given top billing over Mary Pickford, being "supported by" that popular star in "Poor Little Peppina." It is probably the most famous of the silent serials, the one most often spoken off even by people who know little about the cinema. It introduced Pearl White, the action heroine. The details of her early life are rather vague and she never made any serious attempt to clarify them. There were stories that she had been a circus performer but what is certain is that by 1912 she was making films in New York, mainly comedy one - reelers and Westerns but she made no real impact on audiences until the release of the twenty episodes of "The Perils of Pauline." The story line was quite simple. Pearl plays a girl who wants to become a writer so she postpones her marriage for a year to pursue her ambition. Unfortunately her plans are disrupted when her foster father is cruelly murdered and it is revealed that he has left his estate to be divided equally between Pearl and his villainous secretary (Paul Panzer). The latter immediately sets out to eliminate her by any means so that he can take all the estate. Thus she finds herself in all kinds of dangerous situations. Audiences - and Belfast was no exception - responded to her plucky character who gave as much as she got, with her fists, guns or whatever she could lay her hands on. She fought her foes in balloons, aeroplanes, trains and fast moving cars, doing most of her own stunts. All of the Perils still exist but there is some confusion about the sequence and the names of some episodes. The version shown in the Imperial covered ten episodes which the Whig critic found "ingenious and sensational." The titles certainly suggest action and thrills, and the order of presentation was: Twixt Earth and Sky, Held Up, Race with Death, The Gypsy's Revenge, A Double Catastrophe, A Dash for Life, The Poisoned Chocolates, Vortex of Adventure, The Counterfeiters, and The Target of Death. The serial actually ran to twenty chapters but the discrepancy can be explained by the fact that each showing - good value from the Imperial - included two episodes.

Soon the Imperial was showing two different serials each week, one over Monday, Tuesday and Wednesday and the other over Thursday, Friday, and Saturday. They included "Girl of the Lost Island" (Pathé) set in the South Seas and "Peg o' the Ring" which involved murder and mystery in a circus. The latter starred a notable serial team who not only acted the main roles but also wrote and directed the script. They were Grace Cunard and Francis Ford who had already made a name for himself directing Westerns for Thomas Ince. Pearl White returned in "The Laughing Mask" and "Pearl of the Army," both made by Pathé which was the most famous company associated with the silent serials. In episode one of the former called "The Vengeance of Legar," audiences were impressed by scenes where a sluice gate on a dam was opened and a great mass of water swept over the countryside pushing houses and other buildings aside. The makers claimed that it was the "greatest water scene ever filmed." It has often been said that the serials were made for children and that may have been true later, especially after the coming of sound, but the early silent serials were definitely made for adults and were treated as such by the critics. The first serials concerned mysterious goings on, sinister hooded characters and murder but other themes soon began to appear. In April 1916 the Coliseum presented a Western serial "Deadwood Dick," while the Kelvin screened an Irish serial comedy called "Patsy Bolivar," (Lubin). The Irish theme surfaced again when the Kinema House and the Clonard, and later the Willowfield, presented "The Adventures of Terence O'Rourke," which the Kinema House recommended for "its delightful Irish flavour," while the Clonard noted that the main part of "the fighting Irishman," was played by J.Warren Kerrigan. The title of the first episode, "His Heart, His hand, His Sword," suggests that it was an early form of swashbuckler.

The serials usually arrived in a flurry of advertising and publicity. Typical was a thriller, "Diamond from the Sky" which opened in the Central in June 1916. It starred Lottie Pickford, Mary's younger sister, with Irvine Cummings and ran to twenty - two episodes. The producers had hoped to persuade Mary Pickford herself to star but she refused so they approached her sister instead hoping that the name would be a magnet. Patrons were invited to pick up details of a competition in the cinema foyer where £500 was offered to the person who could write five winning episodes to follow episode 22. The I.S.N. was very impressed by the quality of the serial and noted that it had "taken Belfast by storm." Later when it moved to the Clonard the Irish News concurred and insisted that it set the standard against which other serials should be measured.

Some of those other serials deserve a few comments. In May 1917 the Imperial began screening the fifteen episodes of "The Shielding Shadow" (Pathé) with Grace Darmond and Ralph Kellard. The Irish News critic was intrigued by the story line which introduced a dimension of what the writer called "mysticism," with events being presented which seemed to have no logical explanation and which kept audiences "at fever heat." The attraction was increased by the acting qualities and charm of Grace Darmond, the new serial heroine. She had, the critic believed, the three qualifications necessary for a serial queen: she was "pretty, graceful and fearless." The I.S.N. critic agreed and thought she was a "worthy successor to Pearl White." Another lady who for a time drew much attention was Neva Gerber who appeared in the Panopticon in "The Voice on the Wire." She made eleven serials in all, many of them with Ben Wilson: both were very popular among local cinema goers. Equally well liked was spirited Marie Walcamp and one of her best known serials "Liberty, a Daughter of the U.S.A." (Universal) was screened in the Central starting April 1917. One scene in episode one where she dived from an aeroplane into the sea below was described by the Irish News critic as "breath taking." Another serial much admired at the time was presented by the Imperial in December 1917. It was "Patria" (Pathé) starring the dancer Mrs Vernon Castle who played a dual role. The villain was an actor who was to become very well known to local audiences in the Twenties and especially in the Thirties. He was Warner Oland who had been born in Sweden before emigrating to the U.S.A. In "Patria" he played an Oriental villain, Baron Huroki, and over the years came to specialise in such roles. He later became a household name as Charlie Chan in the detective series filmed in the Thirties. "Patria" was shown on Monday, Tuesday, and Wednesday, followed during the rest of the week by a superior serial called "Judex," starring Rene Creste in the title role. It was different in that it was French, was released by Gaumont and was directed by Louis Feuillade, the man who had already thrilled audiences with the adventures of Fantomas. Judex, impressive looking in his great black hat and his long cloak, was dedicated to fighting evil, like an early Batman.

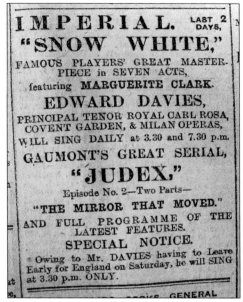

Snow White and the French serial, Judex in the Imperial.

While Chaplin, Keystone and the serials were drawing large crowds on a regular basis there were those who believed that the future of films lay in their ability to reproduce nature as accurately as possible, especially by the addition of colour and sound. Of course those ambitions had been apparent from the very early days of the cinematograph and Belfast audiences had experienced coloured films, many of them quite beautiful, in the late 1890's, tinted painstakingly by hand. By the turn of the century they had also seen and heard rather crude attempts at sound using synchronised discs. But in March 1914 it was announced that the Picture House, the only downtown cinema to ignore the serials, would soon present Edison's Talking Pictures. The magic of the Edison name conjured up visions of technical perfection and an air of excited expectation built up as the opening day, 23rd March, approached. The apparatus was called a Kinetophone and it had been first unveiled to the public in New York exactly one year before. It arrived in London in July 1913 and was shown to the King and Queen. Technically it incorporated the much tried system of a synchronised long playing record and a gramophone with its own amplifier placed behind the screen connected to the projector by a series of pulleys and belts. Many experts expressed disappointment and felt that it was inferior to other systems then available in Europe.

The public ignored such comments and flocked in large numbers to see it. It ran for four weeks without any reported snags in the Picture House during which time the Irish News pronounced it "an unprecedented success," while the News Letter felt that it could initiate a new period of "enterprise and conquest" for the cinematograph. The Irish News agreed that sound was the thing of the future but pointed out that if it became a fixture it would mean the end of the cinema orchestras because the films would supply their own music. The more perceptive members of those orchestras must have seen the "talking pictures" as more of a threat to their livelihood than a mere technical advance. The Irish News also pondered the fact that there were so many new inventions that the public had lost their sense of wonder but felt that the Kinetophone would help to restore it. The Whig critic obviously agreed because he thought it was "a most wonderful apparatus" which represented "a great advance in the cinematographic world." He described it, quite accurately, as sounding like a gramophone, only much louder and clearer. All the local critics agreed that the sound quality was of a high standard and, equally important, that the level of synchronisation was very good.

During the first week the programme was introduced by Thomas Edison himself who appeared on screen and explained the system and its significance to the audience. That was followed by an excerpt from the opera, "Faust" which the Irish News critic thought was very well done. He wrote that the Soldier's Chorus "was sung with a fullness of tone which made it difficult to realise that the chorus of a big opera company was not really somewhere behind the screen." The Edison Minstrels then entertained with a wide variety of popular songs. Over the next few weeks the programme was periodically changed and, in all, a wide range of music hall variety was presented which according to the Whig included demonstrations of singing, dancing, poems, jokes and many different musical instruments. Besides the Edison Minstrels the little films had names like "Songs of Old Ireland," "Old Songs are the Best," and the Ohio Minstrels.

After its successful run downtown the Kinetophone moved to the Clonard in June where the people of the Falls received it "with enthusiasm." (Irish News). Later appearances were in the Crumlin (in December) and the Central (in January 1915). Never a man to be outdone, when Fred Stewart heard that the Picture House was bringing the Kinetophone he immediately took steps to compete. He announced that the Panopticon would present the "wonderful" Electrophone which would show the "loudest and clearest of all singing pictures." It was actually a machine called an Auxetophone which had been developed as early as 1902 and had proved its worth for use outdoors and in large halls. He acquired it from T.Edens Osborne, an old family firm which claimed to have sold the first gramophones in the city, recognised specialists in talking machines, whose premises were located at 11,Wellington Place. People passing their shop often stopped on the pavement to experience what the latest developments in sound recording were, and to listen to the music emanating from the interior. Sadly, the Electrophone doesn't seem to have made much of an impression on either critics or audiences and quietly disappeared from the scene. Mr Stewart did however manage to get the original Edison Kinetophone in late February 1915 and presented it for a short "farewell visit" to the city.

1915 saw the opening of two new cinemas in the city, in February and December, like bookends to the year. The Alexandra Theatre on the Grosvenor Road had been struggling for some time to maintain audience levels and had developed a policy of live theatre interspersed with film weeks before finally closing. A group of businessmen including representatives from Films Ltd. formed the Belfast Coliseum Company to buy and run the hall essentially as a cinema. They felt they could build up an audience from Barrack Street, the lower Grosvenor Road and Sandy Row, an area which still lacked a local cinema. They informed the City Surveyor in January that they intended to modify the building for that purpose and the experienced and reliable W.J. Moore was asked to carry out the necessary alterations. The whole ground floor was cleared and new leather tip - up seats installed while the projection booth was modified and improved. It was announced that it would reopen on Monday 8th February under completely new management, with the aim of presenting high class variety and pictures. A new manager, James Burt, with many years experience was brought from Derry City to oversee the establishment and the programming. On that day the Irish News carried a large advertisement which declared "tonight's the night" and at six o'clock the doors of the new Coliseum were opened to large and enthusiastic crowds. Prices were aimed at a reasonably wide range of pockets with 2d for the ground floor, 4d for the balcony, 6d for the circle and one shilling for the box seats. Value for money was emphasised and patrons were assured that all refreshments would be charged "at outside prices." Like the Alhambra there were to be two houses each evening at 6:50 and 9:00 with a matinee on Saturdays at 3:00 p.m. and the films would be accompanied by music hall acts. During the opening week the live acts were Fits and Starts (comedy acrobats), and Royde and Villiers (songs and comedy) followed by "The Land of the Lost" a three - reel drama, a newsreel and the latest film from the war zone. The Irish News critic was impressed by the quality of the projection and especially by the new screen which he described as "massive." He also noted that the new company consisted of men experienced in the cinema trade, including one of the earliest pioneers of cinema in Belfast. Unfortunately he named no names, though he was probably alluding to J.Y. Moore. The following week the films shown were "When London Sleeps," and "The Stranglers of Paris," thrillers which set the pattern for the general quality of the future programmes.

The conversion of a theatre to a cinema disturbed serious playgoers, but for most people it was just a trend of the times. However when the Willowfield Picture House opened in December at 215, Woodstock Road (near the junction with Cherryville Street) it caused some surprise because it was owned by Willowfield Unionist Club. In August the City Surveyor received a letter from W.Taggert, an architect of Wellington Place, writing on behalf of the members of the Willowfield Unionist Club who had asked him to draw up plans to convert the Drill Hall in their premises to a cinema. The plans suggest a hall without frills consisting of a ground floor area divided into front and back stalls, and a gallery incorporating in all about 900 seats. R.Carothers, a former projectionist with Films Ltd., who was well known in the Grosvenor Hall and the Assembly Hall, was hired as manager and the building was opened on Monday 20th December. The official opening was at 3:00 p.m., by special invitation only, and to the public at 6:00 p.m. Shows were continuous from 6:00 to 10:30, with matinees on Monday, Wednesday and Saturday at 3:30 and admission prices were moderate at 2d to the front stalls (nearly 500 seats), 4d to the back stalls and 6d to the gallery (120 seats).

Mr Carothers had chosen his first programme carefully with an eye to his employers and to the local population. There was a four - reel quality film from Paramount, "The Commanding Officer," a newsreel, and a special film showing an inspection of the Ulster Division. All proceeds from the first day were donated to the Ulster Women's Gift Fund for the comforts of the men of the 8th Battalion, Royal Irish Rifles. On Thursday the programme changed to lighter material with "The Love Route" another Paramount release from Famous Players plus a comedy called "When Wifey Sleeps." Later films included popular hits like "Girl of the Golden West" and "The Four Feathers," plus some Charlie

Chaplin comedies. But the obvious local favourite was Mary Pickford. In the following months Mr Carothers presented many of her films including "Dawn of a Tomorrow," "Such a Little Queen," "Fanchon the Cricket," (a film which also introduced Fred Astaire and his sister Adele to the world of cinema), "Mistress Nell, "and "Rags." He also introduced serials beginning with "The Adventures of Terence O'Rourke" popular because of its strong Irish flavour, followed by "Judex" with its very different French mood.

The growing popularity of Mary Pickford was obvious across the city and during 1915 her films appeared with increasing frequency, especially in the Panopticon and the Central. The latter had no doubt at all about her artistic qualities and introduced her as "the world's greatest cinema actress." When, in early August, the Panopticon advertised her film "Eagle's Mate" the advert was accompanied, uniquely, by a photograph of Mary. Advertisements are one thing but for a manager the real proof lay in the box office and Mr Stewart showed his faith when in July he gave a whole week over to her films. His "Mary Pickford week" presented a different one of her films each day -- The Eagle's Mate (Mon), Hearts Adrift (Tues), Caprice (Wed), A Good Little Devil (Thurs), Tess of the Storm Country (Fri), Zena and the Geese and The New York Hat (Sat). There had been Comedy weeks and Western weeks before, but that was the first time that a star had been singled out in a special way and it reflected her popularity and high standing. When the Panopticon presented her in September in "Mistress Nell" the News Letter referred to her as "the world's Sweetheart" the tag that was to stay with her for the rest of her screen life.

But there was more to Mary Pickford than golden curls, smiles, innocence and charm. The local critics agreed that she was also a fine actress. The I.S.N. critic summed it up when commenting on the film "Behind the Scenes," which the Panopticon showed in October. He wrote: "We are always pleased to see Miss Mary Pickford in a picture whatever its" vein "as she never fails to distinguish the role she plays." That view was endorsed a few months later when, under the heading "A Popular Cinema Star," the paper published a tribute to Mary Pickford detailing her life and career, the first time any film actor or actress had been singled out locally in that way. It was only one indication of how the film industry was changing, Filmgoers could enjoy and choose from an impressive array of delights by the end of 1915: an evolving star system backed up by a highly organised publicity machine; longer films with credit titles; Charlie Chaplin, the Keystone comedies, and the excitements of the serials; all of which made for excellent if undemanding entertainment in cheap, accessible but comfortable surroundings.

Theda Bara, The Vamp

A key factor was the publicity which aimed to meet the increasing demands of filmgoers for information about the films and, above all, about the people who appeared in them. Much of the publicity was manipulative at a low level, especially in relation to serious actors and actresses like Mary Pickford and Lillian Gish, but sometimes it went over the top as with a new female personality who emerged with amazing suddenness in America in 1915, called Theda Bara. In contrast to the two ladies mentioned above, she was presented as a mysterious and exotic creature with a baleful attraction to men. She was, according to the publicists, the child of an Arabian princess and an Italian artist born in an oasis within sight of the Egyptian pyramids.

Even her name had sinister overtones, Theda being an anagram of death, while Bara is Arab in reverse. To the amazement of many, including the lady herself, the public seemed to swallow the whole story which newspapers (excluding our locals) continued to embellish. In reality she was Theodosia Goodman born in Cincinnati, Ohio of a respectable family. She had built up a minor reputation on the stage often playing femmes fatales which contemporary reports say she was quite good at.

It was in one such role that she was seen by Frank Powell, a director working for William Fox, who was looking for the lead in a film he was about to begin, called "A Fool There Was." The film was based on a Broadway play of the same name which in turn had been developed from Rudyard Kipling's poem "The Vampire." It was the latter which inspired the ludicrous publicity stories which added a certain soupcon of spice as Miss Bara played the vampire, using her wiles to lure a number of men to their destruction over six reels. Today her attempts at seduction would tend to raise smiles but that was not the case then. Men and women reacted strongly to her image; the men were fascinated but many women detested her. Miss Bara herself described how some women passing a cinema where her film was showing kicked her publicity stills. But maybe that was just part of the publicity! As film history has it, when she first appeared with her black make-up, come - hither looks and slinky walk the screen vamp was born.

Theda Bara in Redemption in the Picture House.

Actually the Belfast public was not entirely in the dark with regard to the deadly charms of the female vampire. The year before Fred Stewart, never slow to recognise a new trend or fad, screened "The Total Enchantress" at the Panopticon. The producers had thoughtfully accompanied the film with an explanation of its theme which the I.S.N. published without comment. "Throughout the ages history has furnished numerous examples of women possessed of beauty or some indefinable fascination for whom even kingdoms have been lost. Human vampires to whom men are simply puppets to amuse an idle hour, to be cast aside ruined and broken." The film was described as a compelling drama with "intense" scenes though the local critics seemed to be more interested in the backgrounds and scenes of local life which had been filmed in Brittany. As for the furore emanating from the U.S.A. surrounding Miss Bara, audiences would have to wait to make up their own minds because the British censor thought that "A Fool There Was" made quite unsuitable viewing and banned it completely.

1915 ended with another mystery more down-to-earth than the aura surrounding Miss Bara. It involved the opening of the Queen's Picture House, an event which seems to have been completely ignored by the local papers, even by the I.S.N. which usually commented on most matters of local entertainment. What is known for certain is that plans for a cinema at 248, York Street were submitted to the City Hall on the 4th June 1915 to be built for Joseph Russell of 20, Lewis street. The plans indicate a rather basic hall to seat about 500 persons The site was at the bottom of the Limestone Road, next door to the Salvation Army hall (where one can be sure the plan was not welcomed), just opposite the Midland Railway. It was also not too far away from where Joe McKibben would open his Midland cinema in Canning street in early 1916. The plans were approved by mid - September so an opening in December is not improbable. However, no details are available though it seems that Mr Russell wasn't completely satisfied with how things progressed because by October 1916 he had sold out to the Gaiety Theatre Company, an offshoot of the Imperial. The new owners presented plans drawn up by R. Lynn and signed by the manager of the Imperial which entailed modifications to the frontage, the seating and the exits. What attracted the company to the Queen's is uncertain unless it was the attraction of opposites. The Queen's was everything that the Imperial was not. It was decidedly downmarket and casual, but despite a poor reputation it was popular and must have been profitable because it continued in business until April 1941 when it closed as a result of German bombing during the blitz.

CHAPTER FIFTEEN
Birth of a Nation

Despite the horrors of a world at war 1916 was a good year for the cinema and for cinemagoers in Belfast. Like the weather, films had become one of those topics that one could hear being discussed openly in the home, in the workplace, on the trams, and in non professional and professional circles. Complaints continued about crowded halls in the evenings and the inconvenience of queueing, especially in the damp and cold of winter weather. The Coliseum turned those criticisms to its advantage by cannily pointing out that it had large waiting rooms where patrons could wait in comfort for the beginning of the show. The editor of the Whig noted with some astonishment the rapidity with which cinema attendance had swept across the globe. There were now, he commented, in excess of 60,000 cinemas in the world, over half of those in the U.S.A. Films had also reached places like Borneo and even isolated Pacific islands where people from pre - industrial societies and even "former cannibals" were watching and enjoying fare that had been made for the more sophisticated audiences of London, Paris and New York.

There actually was no need to quote such exotic evidence because industrial Belfast itself reflected that same growth. Despite the wartime shortages of materials and workers six new halls were opened during the year, adding an extra 4,500 seats to what was already available. Of the six, only one was located in the City Centre area, Warden's Royal Cinema which replaced the historic Theatre Royal in Arthur Street, a change that seemed to suggest checkmate for serious theatre in the city. The Midland, New York and the Gaiety were built on inner city sites in or near working class areas while the Duncairn and Lyceum were located farther out in what was then suburban surroundings.

Intolerance in the Lyceum.

The first to open its doors was the Midland built for Joe McKibben in Canning Street nearly opposite the Northern Counties Railway station (now York street station). The architect was the experienced W.J. Moore with offices at 35,Royal Avenue who produced what was requested, namely a basically plain but functional hall. According to the plans there was only one level with no balcony. The floor was sloped but with a steeper angle at the rear were there were six rows containing 150 seats (4d) in an area referred to as the Lounge. The rest of the hall consisted of 28 rows of cheap seats (sic), totalling 700 (2d). All seats were of the modern tip-up type. At the end of the hall there was a space for the musicians, a stage for live acts and a large screen. There were a few problems with the building notably the danger of flooding, which of course was a general hazard in the lower parts of the city. The management had to agree to accept full responsibility for controlling it, but that was quite usual for downtown and low - lying sites. The planning office also queried the position of the rear emergency doors and suggested that they be recessed. Mr McKibben however requested that they be left as they were because the presence of recessed spaces "would permit undesirable persons to harbour in same." Some things obviously

Intolerance in the Opera House.

haven't changed all that much over the years.

The cinema was built quite close to a school and to St Paul's Church, at a distance of about eight metres away, but that didn't seem to cause any problem as it certainly would have in later years when there was much discussion as to how much distance should separate a cinema from a church. The building was opened on the 6th March but the papers uncharacteristically ignored the event except for the Telegraph which greeted it rather optimistically as "the most up - to date and sanitary house in the kingdom." The latter comment meant that the building had windows that could be opened in the mornings to allow the natural healthy sunlight in. There were two separate programmes daily at 7 pm and 9 pm with a matinee on Saturday at 3:30. The cinema depended mainly for its audience on word of mouth and avoided the expense of newspaper advertisements, reflecting the fact that it was essentially a popular hall for local people. There are few details about what was shown but it was most likely the popular mix of Westerns, comedies and thrillers. Also from the start there were serials, beginning with Pearl White in the "Exploits of Elaine," also Charlie Chaplin comedies and nationalistic documentaries like "Our Navy." Despite the lack of luxuries the Midland flourished as a silent and later as a sound hall for twenty five years until it was destroyed by German bombs, forcing it to close on 15th April 1941. By the fifties the site had reverted back to its original function of a warehouse.

Four months later, on Monday 3rd July, and just a few days after the beginning of the historic Somme offensive the Duncairn opened its doors at 12, Duncairn Gardens. From the beginning it described itself loftily as "Belfast's Super Cinema" and it certainly seemed to have ambitions of grandeur. The original plans were presented to the City Surveyor on 2nd September 1914 by P.J. Waddington, an imaginative architect with offices in Blackpool. The beautifully drawn and coloured document was for a picture palace to be built for the Duncairn Picture Theatre Company by Henry Laverty and Sons of Cambridge Street. The comprehensive plans show an entrance between four shops through a foyer into a large hall aligned, T shaped, at right angles, with the screen to the left and a dress circle to the right plus, to top it off, an unusual addition in the shape of a roof garden. The pit and stalls seated 600 while the circle held another 100, giving a total of 700 which is a lot less than the 1000 seats that are widely mentioned. The owners were obviously not satisfied with the original design and an amended plan was presented on the 23rd December 1915 in which the roof garden had been abandoned (pity!) while a cafe and promenade were added at the rear of the circle. There is no indication that the seating capacity was modified but later comments by observers suggest that it had been increased. Interesting additions to the drawing were a ray line from the projection booth to the screen plus eye lines of a person seated and of a person standing, evidence of the care given to the problem of insuring clear uncluttered vision. The construction was completed by the local builders already named, Laverty and Sons, and the important electrical system was installed by another local firm, J.Dowling. The local people watched in excited anticipation as the building took shape. They were soon to have their own picture palace and from what they could see it was going to be worth waiting for.

When the doors opened they were not disappointed. The entrance from Duncairn Gardens was floored with marble tiles while the pay-box was adorned with glass Roman - style tiles. To the right a wide carpeted staircase led up to the circle with its buffet, cafe and promenade while to the left swing doors led directly into the large auditorium (26m by 15m). The overall decor was subdued with a hint of Italian Renaissance in the decorations. The walls were panelled in African mahogany which contrasted with the pure white ceiling. On one side of the screen was an electric clock, a familiar fixture in most of the new cinemas, while on the other was a device which must have been unique in the city, a counter which was worked from the projection booth to show the number of the scene being shown at the time. Careful attention had been given to the comfort of the patrons. All seats were tip - up. Six large fans in the roof area withdrew the foul smoke filled air while a system of recessed radiators dealt with the heating. The placing of the radiators in recesses was another innovation that caused much comment and it was pointed out how that simple innovation improved safety because they no longer interfered with the movement of patrons in the low - light conditions. It was claimed that the building could be cleared in seconds if there was a fire emergency. To protect against the latter the projection room was at the back of the auditorium but, as the law demanded, it was isolated from it by concrete and fire resistant materials. The professional critics summed the building up as spacious, impressive, imposing and comfortable. They also welcomed the experienced guiding hand of W.J.Hogan as manager. Programmes were continuous from 6:30 to 10: 30 with a complete change of fare every Monday and Thursday, while prices were moderate at 4d (front stalls), 6d (back stalls) and one shilling to the circle.

The opening programme consisted of "Jewel" starring Ella Hall, the Pathé Gazette news, a travel item on Srenagar plus comedies including "Foiling Father's Foes" and "Pansy's Papas." Despite competition that evening from the Crumlin which was screening Charlie Chaplin in "His Prehistoric Past", the Central with the thriller "Ultus, Man from the Dead," and the Alhambra with another thriller "In the Whirlpool," long queues formed well before opening time and packed houses became the norm. Mr Hogan's policy was to show material of quality which was also popular in appeal, with an emphasis on entertainment and education. Thus, supporting the main films, he favoured topical newsreels, documentaries and travelogues. The Duncairn, for example, was one of the first cinemas to show "The Battle of the Somme" in early September. In the following months Mr Hogan screened a number of quality productions including "Tom Brown's Schooldays," "Hazel Kirke" starring Pearl White, "Annie Laurie" with the very popular Alma Taylor, "Samson" starring William Farnum, and "Macbeth" a Triangle Drama with Sir Herbert Tree. Lighter material included thrillers like "Ultus and the Grey Lady," and "The Gilded Spider" featuring "the beautiful Louise Lovely," and comedies like "Dust of Egypt." The latter was a Vitagraph production, a comedy starring a lady called Edith Storey who played a 3,000 year old princess whose mummy comes back to life and she finds herself coping with modern life and its mysterious gadgets like telephones, safety matches, cigarettes and such. In the end it all turns out to be a dream and the heroine wakens up happily in her own century. While the new cinema was a success there were also stories of occasional rowdyism and high spirits. Within a year it was closed for redecoration and when it reopened it had a new manager, Will White, formerly

Battle of the Somme in the Duncairn.

Battle of the Somme in the Picture House (see page 244).

of the Alhambra, who presented the latest war record "The Battle of Messines" followed by the Italian epic "Salambo" set in old Carthage.

Despite the increase in American films shown on local screens the name of the next cinema to open had nothing to do with the U.S.A. The New York cinema, which unlocked its doors at 68,York street at 3:30 pm on 31st July 1916 was so named because of its location on busy York street, in the block between Great Georges street and Lancaster street. As the locals watched the structure taking shape word spread that it was being built for Fred Stewart - a name according to the Whig that meant quality - who was the owner of the nearby Silver Cinema which had recently closed. He probably intended the new building to be a more up-to-date replacement. The architect was Thomas Houston of Wellington Place and he produced an unfussy, compact looking building with a basic classical facade. Three doorways at ground level were separated by two large advertising spaces. The auditorium was spacious though smaller than the Duncairn (approx. 22m by 12m) with a high ceiling which concealed two large extractor fans installed by the Musgrave company, plus ventilators that could be opened to flood the hall with natural light in the mornings. Seating was for 750 patrons, reasonably priced at 2.5d and 4d for the ground floor with 5d and 7d for the balcony. Mr Stewart emphasised that those low prices included the new war tax which had been introduced in May. All the seats were tip - up except the cheapest which were the traditional wooden benches. The ground floor was sloped to give all a good view of the screen but the balcony floor was especially raked so that people could see over the ones in front even if they were wearing hats. At the screen end there was a large stage and a space for the musicians. All the electrical equipment was installed by the very experienced Curran Bros. The manager was Sam Stonehouse who had been the manager of the Empire during the previous six years, so Mr Stewart obviously believed that running a cinema was little different from organizing a music hall. Of course in contrast to the latter programming was continuous from 3:30 to 10:30 pm. with films being changed on Mondays and Thursdays.

The Irish News critic found it a "handsome and well arranged house" and commented specially on the fine music which accompanied the opening film. Remembering his success in the Panopticon with "Cabiria" Fred Stewart had chosen "Maciste" about the further adventures of that film's slave hero. The following week saw another typical Stewart choice, a Nordisk production "Flaming Sword," described as containing "scenes of flood, fire and destruction." Supporting the main films were the ubiquitous Westerns (Broncho Billy became a near permanent resident), comedies, newsreels and topicals. "The Battle of the Somme" showed to great acclaim in October. Obviously someone's expectations were not fully realised because by early 1917 Mr Stonehouse had moved on and a new manager in the form of J.B.Mc Candless had taken over. But, whatever the problems, Mr Stewart never sold his audiences short. He and his manager continued to present programmes that were entertaining with films made by some of the top stars of the day. A sample over the following twelve months included "A Welsh Singer" with Florence Turner, "Betty of Greystone" a Triangle production starring Lillian Gish, "The Lamb" another Triangle production starring Douglas Fairbanks, "Infidelity" with Theda Bara, "East Lynne" also with Theda Bara, and "Mothers of France" with Sarah Bernhardt. The New York soon became a popular venue and its future seemed secure. Yet after a relatively short duration of about five years it went out of business in the early twenties for reasons that are not too clear. In 1919 plans were submitted to the City Hall detailing changes to the ground floor seating and the exits. Approval was refused so whether the alterations were ever carried out is uncertain. What is certain is that in June 1924 an application was submitted to the City Surveyor to convert the building to two shops and a warehouse for a Joseph McManus of Great Patrick street. The New York had passed into history.

Meantime the commercial success of the Imperial had convinced its owners that films were definitely there to stay and that expansion was financially worthwhile. They set up a new company, the Gaiety Picture Theatre company, and purchased a site in North street consisting of a shop and showrooms extending from 155 to 163. They asked architect Robert Lynn to draw up plans to convert the space into a picture and variety theatre to be called the Gaiety. Events moved quickly. The plans were submitted on 13th May 1916 and were approved by the 23rd. The building itself was erected by W. McQuoid of Roden street and was ready for opening on 14th November 1916. All the main work was completed by local firms, a point that the critics noted with approval in their reports. The building itself was greeted with equal approval. The auditorium was described as "spacious" and the decor, according to the Irish News, reflected "a very satisfying sense of taste and judgement" with none of the garishness and overelaboration found in some recent picture palaces. The writer was very taken by the paintings on the walls and especially that of the Irish castle covering the rear wall with the beam from the projector shining from one of the turrets. There was no mention of the fact that a similar scene had decorated the rear wall of the Kinema House. The ceiling was of "a refined Greek character" (Telegraph). The building was well lit and had efficient heating and ventilation systems. At the front there was a stage and orchestra pit with the musicians under the baton of Frank Doherty. The programming was for separate shows at 6:40 and 9:00 with a matinee on Saturdays at 3:00 pm, films being changed on Mondays and Thursdays. Seat prices were very reasonable at 2.5d for the pit, 5d for the stalls and 7d for the balcony.

The manager, Ernest Forbes, promised quality presentations of films and music hall artistes and must have been pleased that such large crowds turned up for the opening that many had to be turned away. The introductory film was "The Eternal Grind," dealing with the contrasting lives of three sisters who worked in a sweat factory. That may seem a rather serious subject to begin with, especially for a working class audience who wanted to be entertained, until it is remembered that it was a Famous Players production starring Mary Pickford. A still from it shows Mary staring rather dreamily at her sewing machine which recalls a similar scene in the much later talkie "The Perils of Pauline (d. George Marshall, 1947) when Betty Hutton, in an analogous situation, sings a spirited but sardonic paean to her Sewing Machine, a Girl's Best Friend. Mary was supported by a serial "Peg o the Ring," comedies, newsreels and the music hall turns of Lil Cadbury ("the essence of refinement") described as a "chocolate coloured" singer, dancer and pianist, plus Pony Sam, the cowboy vocalist. On the following Thursday the film chosen was "Lydia Gilmore" starring that "unsurpassed emotional artiste" Pauline Frederick, a Broadway star who was proving very popular with filmgoers. It was another Paramount release and like "The Eternal Grind" indicated the influence of the Imperial owners. The manager went along at first with those

Mary Pickford, first star to appear in the Gaiety.

quality products but came to appreciate that his audiences wanted more light - weight material and gradually introduced more comedies, especially Charlie Chaplin, as well as Westerns and thrillers.

The News Letter commented almost with a sigh of resignation in December 1916 that there seemed to be no end to the building of picture theatres. The writer was referring to Belfast's latest addition, the Lyceum, which occupied a site at the corner of the New Lodge and Halliday's road. Cinema had finally arrived on the Antrim Road. The building with its distinctive dome and impressive Oriental appearance (Irish News) was designed by James Barron of Garfield street for Michael Curran who was already well known in cinematic circles because of his successful electrical business. The plans, signed by Michael Curran, were submitted on 29th July 1915 but final approval was not granted until May 1916 and the cinema itself opened on Monday 11th December at 6:30 in the evening. Curran and his fellow owners, who included Ferris Pounds, ensured that the building was completely up - to - date with a sloped floor to give maximum vision, good ventilation, concealed lighting and seating comfort, the work being carried out by local businesses and craftsmen. The electrical installations were carried out, not surprisingly, by Curran Bros. of Kent Street, the furnishings by R.Watson's and the heating by the Musgrave company. The newspaper accounts give the total seating as around 1000 but the plans give a lower figure, with 300 seats in the front stalls at 4d, 350 in the back stalls at 7d, and 200 in the circle at 11d. The entrance foyer was circular, gleaming with black and white tiles which covered the floor and walls. It gave access to a spacious auditorium, the walls of which were cream coloured though the overall brightness was subtly tempered with panels of dark brown tapestry, while the high ceiling was crossed with dark oak beams. The screen and stage were flanked by two Grecian columns reminiscent of a theatrical proscenium and there was space below for the six piece string orchestra led by E.J.Popplewel, and a small sound effects team.. The manager, Herbert Harrington, announced that programming would be continuous from 3:00 to 10:30 pm daily.

The opening proceedings began formally with Mrs Ferris Pounds singing the national anthem, after which the audience settled down to enjoy the show. The films shown were "Maritana" based on an opera, comedies including "Romance and a Rough Horse," and "She Was a Vampire," a documentary on the International Censorship of mails, a cartoon involving a tank, and a newsreel, the Topical Budget. Hardly popular fare, but soon the Lyceum was calling itself "Belfast's smartest picture house." A week later the presentation was Charlie Chaplin in "Carmen" described as a burlesque of two recent cinematic Carmens which had starred Geraldine Farrah and Theda Bara. Chaplin had made it as a two - reeler for Essanay but when he left that company to join Mutual, Essanay enlarged the film to four reels (the company's cut !) by including out - takes and other material shot by Chaplin but rejected at the time by him. They also added a sub - plot involving Ben Turpin and released it as a four - reeler. In America the film was criticised as repetitive and well below Chaplin's usual standards. Chaplin publicly disowned it and took Essanay to court to prevent its further distribution. He argued that the two reel version which he had written, directed and acted in was "his" definitive version and the studio had no right to modify it as they had done. His argument was an early defence of personal authorship having precedence over commercial ownership, of creativity having priority over money. His case, unfortunately, failed - auteur theory hadn't yet emerged - and it was the despised four reel version that showed in Belfast. Regardless of all the legal and artistic arguments local audiences flocked to the Lyceum, and later the Panopticon, to see "an hour of Chaplin" which one critic described as "fun, fast and furious." (News Letter). It seemed that in matters cinematic, entertainment outranked all other considerations.

Subsequently, a film pantomime called "Robinson Crusoe" drew large crowds to the Lyceum over the Christmas period but the general policy of presenting films of quality or special interest was adhered to. The films that followed the Christmas fun including "Typhoon," starring "the famous Japanese actor Sessue Hayakawa," "Ambition," with the "celebrated Russian actress Bertha Kalich," and Thomas Ince's "Civilisation." Ince was noted mainly for his Westerns and it was he who introduced W.S.Hart to world audiences, but he also produced a whole series of other types of films including "Japanese" films like the above - mentioned "Typhoon" which introduced the talented Sessue Hayakawa to local audiences. Hayakawa is probably best known to modern audiences as the wily Colonel Saito who faced Alec Guinness in the "Bridge on the River Kwai" (d. David Lean,1957). In 1915 the U.S.A. hadn't yet entered the war and there were many voices in the country raised against such a move. Ince was one of them and decided to make "Civilisation" to show the futility of war. The film was dedicated "to that vast army whose tears have girdled the universe - the Mothers of the Dead." The story is set in the fictional European country of Wredpryd whose leaders go to war inflicting death and destruction on their neighbours. The terrible details of that are depicted in part one. In part two Christ Himself (played by George Fisher) comes down on earth in the cause of peace, conducts the king of Wredpryd across the battlefields, like Vergil with Dante, showing him the real horrors of war and convincing him to sue for peace. The aims were worthy but critics found the latter part rather too sentimental and there was also criticisms of the standard of the acting. The British authorities, anxious to pursue the war, were not too happy about its pacifist ideals but allowed the film to be shown because the uniforms of the "baddies" looked quite Germanic and with a few changes in the titles it was made made to appear as an anti - German tract.

It was announced that "Civilisation" would be shown in the Lyceum on Monday 19th October 1917 and a special Press showing was arranged for the Friday before, in the Alhambra. The Whig critic was particularly impressed and congratulated the management of the Lyceum on their initiative in getting the film for its first public showing anywhere in Ireland. He recognised the film for what it was, a commentary on the war in Europe and a powerful condemnation of the futility of that war. He was overwhelmed by the "colossal scope and magnitude of the film" and by the realism of many scenes especially the battle scenes in part one. He described how villages were destroyed before one's eyes by shelling, including their civilian populations, the air "thick with aeroplanes" while the ground trembled under the movement of armoured cars and "every type of invention war has produced." The war at sea was equally well done and had involved the co - operation of the U.S. navy. Scenes showed the destruction and sinking of ships, one of which was blown 500 feet into the air "while all about the sea is tortured into a thousand seething spouts by bursting shells." The religious elements were not mentioned and he dismissed part two briefly, merely describing how the guilty king "forced by a realisation of his inevitable and complete defeat by the Allies" sued for peace. That was hardly Ince's original intention and suggests the type of official tinkering that had modified his vision. Chaplin obviously wasn't the only film maker having his work amended at the time.

In conclusion the critic praised "Civilisation's" appeal "to humanity" and emphasised that it should not be missed, promising that those who went to it would have "a rare and inspiring treat in store." The I.S.N. added that the film consisted of ten reels with a running time of two hours, and was accompanied by an enlarged orchestra playing specially composed music to add to the occasion. Because of its special status continuous programming was suspended and instead there were separate showings at 3:30, 6:30 and 9:00 pm. The Irish News noted that the hall was crowded and that the film was "greatly admired" by the enthusiastic crowds. With films of that stature and interest the Lyceum declared its objective to be a major player in the local entertainment scene, and so it proved until its closure in 1966. During its early years there is evidence of disagreements behind the scenes between the owners. An indication of the strained relations emerged in January 1921 when Curran sued Ferris Pounds in court over non payment of £221 which he claimed was due to him. When Michael Curran emerged as sole owner and manager, it represented the first step towards the creation of the Curran chain of cinemas which was to emerge in the Thirties.

Michael Curran is a major figure in the history of the cinema in Belfast. He was born in Larne in 1872 and during his career he embraced the Victorian attributes of self improvement, hard work and recognition of entrepreneurial opportunities. In pursuit of those aims he moved to Belfast where, with his brothers, he built up a successful electrical business, Curran Bros, located in Kent Street, and later at Long Lane. Part of his work involved wiring and lighting and he soon applied them to the new cinemas that were springing up in the city at the time of the Great War. He wired St George's Hall, the New York cinema, the Lyceum, and, in the Thirties, the main Curran theatres in Belfast. After his death in 1940 the company carried out similar electrical work in the Metro (1956) and the Scala in Keady (1956), where they also installed a panoramic seamless screen. In the Lyceum he added to his technical skills as he experienced the practical problems of running a cinema. He soon realised that besides comfort and good value audiences were attracted by quality entertainment of a positive type in a well organised welcoming environment. Thus he often vetted his films to ensure they were suitable for family audiences and fostered good relations with his workers and the Trade Unions. Unlike Fred Stewart he kept a low public profile though, like the latter, he was always open to try new technical advances in the business, as will be discussed later.

In the meantime competition continued to increase with the opening of yet another quality cinema. It could be argued that the writing was on the wall for the venerable Theatre Royal when the Imperial Cinema opened diagonally across Arthur Square, one minute's walk from it. The management of the Theatre must have noticed, and envied, the large audiences attracted to programmes of what then were regarded as quality films. Thus when it was announced that the show on the 10th March 1915 was to be the last on the boards of the historic theatre before it closed, very few in the entertainment business were really surprised. The final show was a benefit for the staff and consisted of an impressive line -up of local talents, with acts from the Hippodrome, the Empire, the Alhambra, and the Coliseum, while the staff themselves presented a comedy called "The Press Gang." On a more serious note the band of the Royal Irish Rangers played selections as soldiers demonstrated, on stage, how they were trained for war. Finally the curtain dropped on what the I.S.N. described as years of theatre history. It soon became clear that the historic home of the Muse in Belfast was not to be converted but was to be knocked down to its foundations and replaced with a modern picture palace. Theatregoers were outraged. They recalled the great names, from Tyrone Power to Sarah Bernhardt, who had performed there and protested that the traditional theatre was being undermined by the seductive new vamp, the cinema, with its pervasive electronic wiles. But the decision, drastic as it appeared, had been taken on essentially commercial considerations. The Warden Company had become convinced that they could no longer ignore the cinema, and that it would be more advantageous to concentrate live theatre at one venue, namely in its more modern theatre, the Grand Opera House. In August the I.S.N. reported sadly that the interior of the old building was already gone and that demolition work was beginning on the outer walls. The following week the same newspaper continued the theme by publishing a photographic sketch and description of what would replace it, a "handsome building" that was expected to be open "before Christmas."

But events seemed to conspire against the new building. The architect chosen was the well known and admired theatre architect Bertie Crewe, who had designed the Royal Hippodrome, and he duly submitted his plans to the City Surveyor on the 30th April. Unfortunately there were problems with staircases, the position of exit doors, fire proofing and the arrangements for flood control which were discussed and dealt with in an exchange of seventeen letters between the Surveyor's department and Mr Crewe's London office. As a result final approval was delayed until 16th October 1915 when a local firm, H. and J. Martin who had built the City Hall, were able to proceed with the actual construction. Scarcity of materials due to the war caused further delays so that it wasn't until Saturday 16th December 1916 at 3:00 pm that it finally was able to unlock its doors to the public. The opening was accompanied by suitable pomp and circumstance and the Lord Mayor Sir Crawford McCullough was present to add a dash of distinction by lending his official prestige to the occasion.

THE NEW ROYAL CINEMA

Theatre to cinema.

The ceremonies began rather properly when the audience stood as the orchestra struck up the National Anthem sung by Ouida Mac Dermott, the principal boy from the current Grand Opera pantomime, in a subtle piece of Warden advertising. The Lord Mayor then performed the opening ceremony with a flourish and expressed his admiration not only for the building but also for the man behind it, Fred Warden. He recalled the former Theatre Royal and commented on the high quality of the artistes who had appeared there. He felt sure that those same high standards would enhance the programmes soon to be presented in the new cinema. At that the manager, W.A.Salmond, visible evidence of continuity with the old theatre which he had also managed, must have nodded and smiled in sympathetic agreement. The Lord Mayor went on to note the many new cinemas that had been built recently in the city but added that "there was always room for something better and he felt that this was it."

Observers on the day agreed with his conclusions. They were greatly impressed by the exterior dominated as it was by a high tower which contained a welcoming light though that couldn't be turned on until the war was over. Directly below the tower at pavement level was the main entrance located at the corner of Castle Lane and Arthur Square leading to a spacious circular foyer floored with marble mosaic with contrasting mahogany covered walls. The foyer contained the pay box and another office where bookings could be made for its sister theatre, the Grand Opera House. That latter convenience was drawn to the attention of the crowds and they were encouraged to take the opportunity of booking seats for the current Christmas pantomime, Cinderella. The auditorium, accessed through swing doors, had all the most up - to - date projection equipment and facilities to ensure comfortable clear viewing. The sloped ground floor had 592 tip-up seats all at the same price (7d). At the screen end there was a stage with a space for a large orchestra, while overlooking the rear was the circle with 332 seats (1/2d), decorated in cream and gold, and a tea room - accessed by a staircase leading up directly from the foyer. While the main building was erected by a local firm most of the decorations and furnishings were the work of English companies. Like most downtown cinemas the programming was to be continuous from 1:30 to 10:30 pm.

The Royal Cinema called itself the Centre of Cinema Art, a worthy aim though the first show hardly lived up to that high ideal. It was a traditional programme with comedies (like Vitagraph's "Pa's Overalls"), a documentary ("In Old Brittany"), a newsreel (Gaumont Graphic) and a rather forgettable main feature, "Just a Girl," a romance starring Owen Nares. Mr Salmond knew that he had to compete for patrons with the neighbouring Imperial and the nearby Panopticon. Over the following months he did that mainly by bringing big name stars like Vesta Tilley ("The Girl who Loves a Soldier" with its echoes of the music hall!), Lionel Barrymore (in "Dorrian's Divorce"), Olga Petrova (in "The Scarlet Woman" and "Extravagance"), Norma Talmadge (in" Going Straight "), and that "alluring actress" (Telegraph) Theda Bara in "Romeo and Juliet" and as Cigarette in "Under Two Flags." He also brought back Griffith's "Birth of a Nation," at normal prices for those who hadn't seen it during its initial run in the Opera House, though it barely merited a comment in the critics' columns. The mention of the Opera House in connection with films is a reminder that Fred Warden's interest in cinema wasn't entirely recent.

The Warden Company played a major role in the entertainment scene in Belfast from the mid-nineteenth century or more accurately from when Joseph F.Warden arrived in 1863-4 to

Advertisement for Grand Opera House, the 'Gone With The Wind' of its Day.

manage the Theatre Royal. His personal influence remained strong until his death in 1898 when his son Fred Warden took control. Through their management of the Theatre Royal and the Grand Opera House the Wardens were responsible for bringing some of the most outstanding actors and personalities of the contemporary stage to the city. Those included actors of the quality of Sarah Bernhardt, Mrs Patrick Campbell, Lillie Langtry, Sir John Irvine, Ellen Terry, Sir Beerbaum Tree, Dion Boucicault, Tyrone Power, Sara Allgood and Barry Sullivan, and international artistes like Loie Fuller, Maud Allen and Anna Pavlova. Most of them performed in the Theatre

Royal, with many returning to make later appearances in the Opera House. Sara Allgood, for example, was introduced to local audiences in the Theatre Royal and returned with the Abbey players to comparable triumphs in the Opera House. Sarah Bernhardt swept into Belfast on six occasions between 1881 and 1908 on one day stands, appearing four times in the Theatre Royal, once in the Ulster Hall when the old theatre was unavailable because of a disastrous fire, and once in the Palace of Varieties (May 1908). So, strictly speaking, she never appeared in the Opera House as such, though she did trod its boards when it was masquerading under another name.

There is no doubt that the interest of the Wardens was mainly in live theatre though that was interpreted elastically to encompass the circus, the music hall (especially when the Opera House was the Palace), and it was not entirely unusual for the Theatre Royal to present evenings of boxing after the latter became more socially acceptable in the early years of the 20th century. Their attitude to the cinematograph (with or without an "e") was always ambiguous but they recognised a crowd pleaser when they saw it and regardless of their attitude to mechanical entertainments they didn't hesitate to include the new contraption in the shape of Robert Paul's Animatograph in their Christmas pantomime, Pretty Bo Peep, on the stage of the Opera House in December 1896. Thus they were indirectly responsible for one of the earliest films made here when Paul filmed and projected scenes from the Harland and Wolff shipyard at Queen's Island in early 1897, as reported in the Irish News. The following Christmas the pantomime, Dick Whittington, was again used for another first, with the introduction of the American Biograph into Ireland. There were also experiments with animated pictures in the Theatre Royal which from reports were very successful, but instead of pursuing that line the bizarre and commercially unsuccessful decision was made in 1904 to go into music hall. That involved renaming the Opera House the Palace of Varieties and initiated an experiment which lasted until 1909 when the Opera House was reinstated as the main centre for serious drama.

As part of the change in policy the Theatre Royal specialised in popular melodrama with stage productions like "The Corsican Brothers," "East Lynne," "The Woman from Scotland Yard," "How Girls are Brought to Ruin," which delved into the seamy side of London life, "A White Slave Victim," "Nick Carter" which the Whig described as being "full of thrills, hairbreadth escapes and blood curdling scenes," and even Westerns with names like "The Frontier Queen," "His Indian Wife," "The Indian Scout," "The Prairie Outlaw," and "The Kelly Gang," (an Australian Western). Such fare competed directly with the Alexandra on the Grosvenor Road which presented George A. Street, described as "Belfast's Favourite Cowboy," in a series of Westerns called "The Cattle Thief," "The Cowboy," and "The Yuma Valley." Stagebound as they were those outdoor sagas were were well received by both critics and audiences, and the Whig critic went so far as to suggest that the live cowboy was preferable to the celluloid one. The stage Western could not really compete in "authenticity" with the cinema which had the advantages of the actual outdoors with its fine scenery, exciting horse chases over long distances, gunfights and realistic battles with the Indians. It was for those reasons that audiences flocked to the Westerns of Griffith and Ince, to films like "The Battle of Elderbush Glutch" and" Custer's Last Fight." In presenting those stirring melodramas of town, country and the West with their clearcut heroes and villains and their emphasis on the sensational the Theatre Royal and the Alexandra were actually functioning like embryonic cinemas and it is interesting that that was the direction in which they eventually evolved.

In the meantime the management of the Opera House had decided that the cinematograph could no longer be ignored. The technology was continually improving, films of quality were being produced, films that were longer and more complex in construction. It was agreed that it would be worthwhile to introduce a number of special roadhouse shows of special films at special prices. Adolph Zukor in the U.S.A. had shown with Sarah Bernhardt in "Queen Elizabeth" that such presentations could be financially successful. That decision meant that the Opera House began to play a major, though often neglected role, in elevating the status of films in the city. As a character in a Thirties film might say, the Opera House environment gave them a touch of "class." Each item shown was distinguished in some way and was chosen with reference to either its level of technical innovation (a new colour system or a camera that could for the first time film under water); its educational content (documentaries set in exotic regions like East Africa); controversy (like a life of Christ that offended conservative Christian sensibilities or a story of the Civil War which offended black sensibilities); cinematic quality (D.W. Griffith's impressive and much discussed "Birth of a Nation" and "Intolerance"); effective war propaganda (documentaries of army and navy life) or just sheer entertainment (Annette Kellerman cavorting in a bathing suit).

The first major success in March 1912 was the presentation of Charles Urban's record of the visit by the King and Queen to India, in Kinemacolor. The film included superb colour shots of the Delhi Durbar which, according to one commentator allowed the audience to see more of the event than if they had actually been there. Also shown were scenes of the Calcutta races, the Niagara Falls, Winter in Sweden, and a scientific film of The Birth of a Flower. The viewers were fascinated by the clarity and the naturalness of the colours and it is no surprise that the programme ran for three weeks. It was followed in 1913 by the success of Paul Rainey's "African Hunts," the controversial "From the Manger to the Cross," and the stately "Quo Vadis." The following year saw "With Capt. Scott in the Antarctic "described as Herbert G.Ponting's "moving picture lecture." In 1915 and 1916 the trend was towards war subjects and the Opera House performed its patriotic duty by presenting "With Fighting Forces in Europe," "Britain Prepared," and "British Army in France."

"With the Fighting Forces in Europe," shown in May 1915, also had the advantage of being shot in Kinemacolor which brought out the distinctive colours of the uniforms, flags and other military paraphernalia. There was no actual fighting shown but the action covered scenes of armies marching or taking part in manoeuvres, and troops manning trenches, all of which were "very impressive visually" (News Letter). "Britain Prepared," shown in May 1916, was a more elaborate film which was made with the co-operation of necessary Government departments including the Admiralty, the War Office and the Ministry of Munitions - which meant, according to the Newsletter, that it "could be relied on." The First Lord of the Admiralty, Mr Balfour, praised the film at its premiere in London and suggested that it resonated with "lessons of the deepest import to us and to all the world." It was divided into two sections namely enlistment and the rigours of training, followed by a review of the Fleet which must have reminded older viewers of the popular series called "Our Navy."

Details of training had of course been shown in other films and it was really in the naval section that Kinemacolor came into its own. The cameras showed minesweepers at work, an armed liner being coaled at sea, a submarine submerging, a battle squadron at sea and destroyers on patrol. Audiences found the scenes exciting and, above all, reassuring because, as they were told, those ships were "the Sure Shield of the British Isles and Empire." It's easy to forget that those silent films were accompanied onstage by lecturers who not only explained what was being shown but who cleverly interwove propaganda, including the need for more young men to sign up, into their comments. The News Letter critic was also impressed by the quality of the photography and commented that "the cloud and sky effects were magnificent." Scenes were also screened of how the vital munitions were made for the guns etc. and the work of women was emphasised and praised in that process. Under the pressures of war the New Woman was morphing with official sanction into the Working Woman.

It's educational potential was always one of the foremost benefits lauded by early advocates of the cinema with its ability to bring strange places and peoples to its audiences. The Opera House went one better with its next film, a documentary called "Submarine" screened in July 1916 which, despite its name, had nothing to do with the war. It actually introduced its audiences to a completely new environment, the world beneath the waves. A Capt. Williamson had invented one of the earliest housings, a collapsible submarine tube, that allowed a camera to function underwater. His two sons took the contraption to the warm clear waters around the Bahamas and made a series of startling underwater films showing scenes that had never been filmed before. The Whig critic praised it as another step in the cinema's forward technical advance and described the results as "wonderful." He marvelled at the "coral formations, beautiful vegetable growths and various types of marine life." The camera also gave tantalising glimpses of sponge divers at work, of an old decaying shipwreck, and of the Atlantic cable, that vital communication link between Europe and America. All of those wonders were commented upon by a lecturer, Cyril Bradshaw, so that the whole was, according to the Whig, "extremely entertaining and instructive." The film ended with a note of excitement when a blue shark was encountered and one of the sons, Ernest, engaged it in battle and after a struggle killed it under the gaze of the camera. The David Attenboroughs of the day would most probably not have approved but contemporary audiences were amazed at such scenes.

The following month saw large advertisements in the papers for "The Birth of a Nation" which opened at the Opera House on Monday 7th August, with seat prices varying from 7d up to a substantial three shillings and three pence. "Birth of a Nation" is a problem picture in that, like the much later "Triumph of the Will" (d. Leni Riefenstahl, 1935), it combines cinematic brilliance with objectionable content, but there is no doubt that it caused a sensation with Belfast critics and audiences, who had never experienced anything quite like it before. Its length alone was intimidating, running as it did, for over three hours thus exceeding even "Cabiria," and "Les Miserables." There were still those who argued that it was too much to expect people to sit for that length of time to watch a mechanical entertainment. After all, only twenty years before the typical "film" lasted about one minute or less. However, much had changed in that time not only in the expectations of audiences but in the style, content and artistry of films. So audiences did sit willingly for the three hours, held by the power of

D.W.Griffith's direction.

The aim and scope of the film was expansive, to tell the story of the events leading up to the American Civil War, the terrible details of the war itself and its aftermath with the assassination of Lincoln, the depredations of the carpetbaggers, the reactions of the freed slaves and the emergence of the Ku Klux Klan. Griffith allowed the great events to pass like a panorama before his audience while he personalised the impact of those events on the members of two families, the Stonehouses from the North and the Camerons from the South. According to the I.S.N. the film was "a liberal education," but not everyone saw it in that light, pointing to showings in America that were accompanied by protests and riots as black people complained that the film was marred by racism in the way the negro population was presented. Griffith, a Southerner by birth and upbringing, vehemently rejected those arguments and insisted that he showed historical events as they had happened. There is no doubt that he omitted or changed incidents in the original source novel to reduce the level of racism, but there is also no doubt from evidence in the film that he believed that the South's political problems originated with the forced migration of Africans to work on the plantations. In early scenes he paints an idealistic view of the plantation workers as happy, easy - going, friendly and contented and later contrasts that with the violence and the desire for revenge among the freed slaves. Scenes in the newly elected State Legislature show the Blacks as little interested in the minutiae of government, and easily manipulated. One of them persists in taking surreptitious nips from a hidden bottle of alcohol, a scene which must have caused local laughter when the titles indicated that he was "the member for Ulster." It is difficult to find even one sympathetic character among the Blacks and modern audiences would certainly find it offensive. On the positive side however, seen today, the film is still an overwhelming experience, full of cinematic riches which the local critics recognised and praised with enthusiasm.

Griffith prefaced his film with two statements. In one he demanded that film be given the same rights as literature to show the darker side of human behaviour, and in the other he set out the main aim of the film which was to convince people that war was an "abhorrence" that should be ended for ever. Belfast audiences didn't seem to be much impressed by all the political furore surrounding the film. Instead they read in the papers how it consisted of 3,000 scenes involving 18,000 actors, actresses and ordinary citizens, with 5.000 horses and that the whole had taken eight months to complete at the unheard of cost of £100,000. The I.S.N. found the result of all that effort a thrilling and inspiring record of events "staged with consummate art and skill," and told its readers that it should on no account be missed. The Telegraph critic agreed. Nothing, he felt, in cinematic history equalled "the magnitude, the scope and the beauty of Mr D.W. Griffith's great spectacle .... it is hard to find language that even dimly indicates all that the film conception conveys." He went on to describe how the film covered the whole gamut of human feelings while at the same time showing the great events of history. "Here are burning cities red with flame and blood, fiercest conflicts of men and machines intermingled with gladsome scenes of domesticity and affectionate relationships." He evidently saw Griffith as an early example of an auteur and advised his readers to ignore all the much publicised details of size and cost because all of that became lost sight of in the stupendous spectacle of history unfolding itself in one man's vision. Words cannot give the slightest indication of the tremendous effectiveness of this conception. Those were sentiments of praise that could be directed at very few films today. He exhorted "every man, woman and child" in Belfast to see it because those who did not would miss the "experience of a lifetime."

The Whig critic was in full agreement with his colleagues that Griffith had produced an amazing film "a brilliant, vivid, thrilling masterpiece of historical fiction," which combined both grandeur of scale and a minuteness of detail. Griffith's strength, he felt, lay in the fact that "he thinks all the time in terms of his medium and uses it to get effects peculiar to itself instead of making it the humble and bond slave of literature and drama." Griffith, he suggested, understood that films move, and action is the primary factor that drives them, but the choice of action was important, in that it must suggest the emotions required. As an example he chose how truth is conveyed in two key scenes. In the first the Southerners march off to Bull Run, confident young men in Confederate grey, acknowledging the cheers of the spectators. Later another scene shows the same men before the fall of Richmond - "ragged, unshaven, hollowed eyed, greedily devouring their starvation rations as they wait in trenches for the final assault." He felt that those two scenes summed up the whole tragedy of all wars in a flash. He praised the fluidity of style of many scenes which he contrasted with the woodenness of the old fashioned tableaux that were once so popular. He had criticisms too. The sentiment was laid on too thickly but that, he felt, was a minor fault of most American films. More seriously he believed that Griffith had overstated his case. While no real defence could be made of the Carpetbaggers it was ridiculous to suggest that the Ku Klux Klan represented a new order of chivalry. They were anything but "angels of light." Despite that he praised the skill and power of those final scenes as the K.K.K. rode to the rescue of the Whites, cheered on by the Opera House audience. He also noted the relevance of the film to contemporary events in Europe. He mentioned especially the war scenes and the fierce fighting in trenches only yards apart and related them to the bloody Somme campaign and to what the soldiers involved in it were suffering. He could also equally have highlighted Griffith's scenes of the battlefield strewn with the dead - "war's peace," as the film title called it. No wonder the Telegraph critic described audiences emerging from the Opera House with "their feelings overcharged and drained" because what they had just experienced was "not a pageant but a revelation."

For three weeks the Opera House screened the film twice a day at 2:00 pm and 7:30 pm to packed houses. People sat transfixed at what they saw on the screen. During the K.K.K. sequences, especially during the ride of the Klan the audience often came to their feet with "frequent and hearty outbursts of applause" (News Letter). At other times they sat quietly, emotionally involved in scenes that were "moving in the extreme," like the death of Lincoln. Special music had been composed to increase the impact of the visuals but strangely enough none of the critics commented upon it though one can be sure that the Opera House Orchestra made a good hand of it. Like the racialist overtones it was just accepted, and merited no special mention. As the audience emerged into reality again many were consulting their souvenir booklets to discover who the actors and actresses were who had so convincingly conveyed Griffith's vision to them, names like Henry B. Walthall (who played the heroic colonel Ben Cameron, later leader of the K.K.K.), Mae Marsh and Miriam Cooper (his sisters Flora and Margaret), and Lilian Gish (the heroine, Elsie Stoneman) whom they could look out for in the future.

Even after the Royal Cinema opened, the Opera House continued to present roadhouse film shows, though with less frequency. Exactly one year later, during the first fortnight of August, the screen attraction was William Fox's production "A Daughter of the Gods" starring the statuesque swimmer Annette Kellerman in what was described as "a fairy film fantasy" dedicated to all "who love Beauty, Joy, the laughter of Children and the Love of Brave men and Fair women." It's theme was far removed from Griffith's serious view of history but it shared certain characteristics with his film. It was long running at nearly three hours, it was expensive with a reputed bill of £200,000 and it was surrounded with a whiff of controversy. The latter involved the skimpiness of Miss Kellerman's costumes. At its release the New York Times commented unapprovingly that there were long sequences where the heroine just wandered around aimlessly in a state of undress. In one scene she dived completely nude into the sea causing shock in certain quarters. The British censor, T.P.O'Connor, left that shot in because it was, he explained, very brief and involved the lady, a world famous swimmer, in her natural element, the sea. Other shots of her reclining in tight or brief clothing were regarded as suggestive and were removed.

The local critics recognised that the film wasn't to be taken too seriously but that it was just very good escapist entertainment, well filmed in beautiful surroundings on Jamaica by the Irish director Herbert Brenon. The Whig described it as a "treat" and praised it for its "many impressive scenes" which included an exotic marble harem ruled by a villainous sultan, the diversion of a river and a great battle between the forces of good and evil, during which a specially constructed city was spectacularly destroyed. There was high praise for Annette Kellerman and for the "delightful exhibitions of her prowess as an expert swimmer and diver." During the filming the producer, William Fox, and the director quarrelled, mainly over the rising costs, and as a result Brenon was banned from the première though it is reported that he slipped in disguised in a large pair of whiskers. Or maybe that was just another fairy story.

Annette Kellerman, swimmingly attractive. Source: US Library of Congress.

The question of Miss Kellerman's nudity or near nudity seemed rather low key in relation to what was to follow, namely the appearance of the so called sex hygiene films in the city. During February.- March of 1918, in the midst of increasing worries about the war, Belfast experienced a period of confronting certain contemporary social evils, a process in which the Opera House played its part. It began when the Ulster Temperance Council initiated a week long campaign calling for Prohibition. Rallies and meetings told the public that drink was the ally of the enemy, weakening and undermining society. It was "a greater enemy than War, Pestilence and Famine combined .... the enemy of Christianity, of Social Purity, Healthy Homes and the Emancipation of Women ....more destructive than the submarines." In the midst of all the hyperbole the use of the terms social purity and healthy homes was interesting in that they represented a veiled reference to the growing belief that drinking played a part in what was referred to as "race suicide," a term increasingly used by those who were worried by the decrease in the size of Anglo - Saxon middle class families brought about by birth control, abortion and the debilitating effects of venereal disease, or VD as it was popularly referred to. Those were not topics that could be discussed openly in polite social circles though they had been addressed in a much praised report by the National Council of Public Morals on the National Birthrate Commission published in June 1916, a report described by Sidney Webb as "the most candid, the most outspoken and the most impartial statement "yet published on the question of birth control within marriage. There were critics who felt such reports didn't go far enough and that what was needed was a system that insured the availability and spread of information on sexual matters to the public at large. In America attempts were being made to do that in print and more controversially on the stage.

Venereal disease (as it was called then) had been referred to obliquely in Ibsen's "Ghosts" but the play had been attacked and banned in Britain. One eminent critic at the time described it as an attempt to dramatise the Contagious Diseases Act. When the ban was lifted the Opera House decided to present it in October 1917 with the added warning that it was suitable "For Adults Only," causing the ISN to comment that the War had resulted in "a remarkable broadening of opinion on certain subjects which were previously tabooed." The first play to use the term syphilis publicly on stage had been Eugene Brieux's "Damaged Goods" in New York in 1913. It was of course a succès de scandale and, as a result, was quickly made into a film. It was the original play that the Opera House presented in February 1918 with the warning again, that it was "For Adults Only." It was billed as "the Great Play on the Social Evil." Tradition and good taste, one presumes, prevented the naming of the evil in question either in the adverts or newspaper criticisms and suggested that prospective audiences were already aware of the subject - matter. The play had no artistic pretensions, a fact that the Whig critic recognised. He admitted that it was well acted but otherwise found it "decidedly unpleasant." He felt that its didacticism undermined the drama and added his personal opinion that anyway "certain topics are not suited to portrayal on the stage." He didn't mention the film based on it though it was doing well at the box -office in America, where it was being presented as having an important educational content. Its financial success convinced others that there was a market for such films and soon the beginnings of a cycle of sex hygiene films could be detected.

Belfast had already experienced one such cycle of white slavery films which had been received and commented upon as serious attempts to warn people, especially young women, about the dangers and horrors of prostitution. The sex hygiene films purported to have similar positive aims and the Opera House presented two of them in early March at special prices and with the "For Adults Only" tag prominently displayed. The films were "Where Are My Children?" which had the blessing of the National Council of Public Morals, and "An Ancient Evil."The former film was made by an American married couple, Lois Weber and Philip Smalley, in 1916 and it had proved to be both controversial and financial successful. The story concerned a young man who during a party before his marriage has too much to drink and in a state of confusion consorts with a prostitute which results in him contracting V.D. In time he infects his new wife and first born child, and the former becomes barren. The film condemned abortion as a means of birth control but called for the legalization of information on contraception. The News Letter noted its American origin but thought that overall it was done "in an earnest dignified manner"; but the other critics, put off by its sensational plot line, either ignored it or made the minimum of comment. There was a reluctance about dealing with the content and one suspects that the film and its message were not widely approved of in the city.

The key problem was whether those types of film were "educational" or just "exploitative" and that argument was to run and run inside and outside the City Hall until the 1960's. In the process the label "For Adults only" with its hints of the sexually sensational was to become very familiar to filmgoers. Indeed within a few months the Royal Cinema and the Central were to screen "Shadows on my Life" based on the turn of the century sensational Stanford White murder trial in New York with a warning, or maybe a promise, to its audiences that it was "for Adults only." It starred Evelyn Thaw (neé Nesbit) a former chorus girl and artist's model and a main player in the actual events. She was described in the advertising as "the most talked about woman in the world," but the Whig critic referred to her as "a notorious personality" and deplored the fact that such happenings could draw the large audiences who flocked to the cinemas in question. He was probably aware that as early as 1907 Miss Nesbitt had appeared in "The Great Thaw Trial" based on the same case, a film which had caused uproar when shown in New York because of its drug and murder scenes. Little did he know that her exploits were to be savoured by future generations because the case was used many years later as the source of the plot of "The Girl in the Red Velvet Swing" (d. Richard Fleisher, 1955) in which Joan Collins played Miss Nesbit, while the same character also appeared in "Ragtime" (d. Milos Forman, 1981) impersonated by Elizabeth McGovern.

The following month, beginning in Easter Week, saw the Opera House present a film that really was aimed at adults. It was D.W.Griffith's massive and intelligent "Intolerance" which opened with showings twice a day at 2:00 p.m. and 7:30 p.m. and prices ranging from 8d to three shillings and sixpence. Its arrival was preceded by details of its making, surpassing Griffith's earlier epic - it cost £500,000, took two and a half years to complete, involved massive outdoor sets including the largest ever constructed for any film, and a cast of 125,000 performers. But, critics asked, with all those excesses was the final product worth it? When it had opened earlier in America it was received with mixed feelings. The New York Times referred to its "utter incoherence" and questioned the wisdom of an actor depicting Christ, something that was sure to offend many people. The film involved four separate stories of bigotry and intolerance from different historical periods which Griffith had cleverly intercut, moving from incidents in one story to another until the four climaxed together at the end. The conceptual sophistication and the skill of the editing technique were well ahead of the time and the complexity of the multi - layered plot left many viewers bewildered. Many didn't seem to understand the main link that Griffith used between the narratives, an image of Lillian Gish rocking a huge cradle, inspired by Walt Whitman's line, "Out of the cradle endlessly rocking," a reference to the cradle out of which mankind had emerged.

Some of that confusion is apparent in local reviews where no mention is made of the important fact that the film was Griffith's answer to those who had accused him of being racist in the "Birth of a Nation." The Whig critic, usually very perceptive in matters cinematic, thought the film was "remarkable" but didn't say why. He noted the four separate stories - the Babylonian episode, the Judean (Christ) episode, the St Bartholemew Day's Massacre, and a modern story of a man wrongfully accused of murder and only saved from execution at the last moment by the perseverance of his wife and some nifty editing from Griffith. He made no comment on how the stories were integrated though he did praise the way Griffith handled the "ancient stories" and was impressed by how he incorporated historical detail from the periods in question. The acting of Bobby Herron, Mae Marsh, Miriam Cooper and Constance Talmadge, many of whom had appeared in the "Birth of a Nation," also came in for special mention. The I.S.N. critic was impressed by the visual quality of the scenes, the massive sets especially for the Babylonian section which included defensive walls over 100 feet high, and wide enough to allow a chariot to move along them, the "realistic" war scenes and the fact that overall the film appealed "to the heart as well as the mind." It's a film that still resonates with modern film makers and, hopefully, filmgoers. Watching the siege of Jerusalem in the "Kingdom of Heaven" (d. Ridley Scott, 2005) one can clearly see the parallels with Griffith's magnificent staging of the siege of Babylon.

The film ran for two weeks which under the circumstances was quite commendable, but it didn't have the impact of the "Birth" maybe because tolerance wasn't exactly the flavour of the period. Tolerance was particularly lacking in many war films of the day where it was the Germans (the Huns) who were usually shown as abusers of women and children. Indeed Griffith himself was soon to depict them as such in "Hearts of the World" starring Lilian Gish which showed in the Royal Cinema in April of the following year. In September 1918 the Royal Cinema touched that popular mood and had a great success when it showed "The Kaiser, the Beast of Berlin" an American film "full of sensational incidents .... though a good deal of dramatic latitude is taken" (the Whig). Playing the part of Admiral von Tirpitz in it was an actor called Lon Chaney, as yet unknown to local audiences but who

Film; Beast of Berlin: film as propaganda.

would become very popular with them during the Twenties. The anti-German feelings were widespread locally and even led to a demand to remove all German street names from the city. Thankfully good sense prevailed and the motion was defeated in the Council in August but it indicated that public tolerance was in short supply.

The War, its implications and its consequences infiltrated the consciousness of all levels of society and people were hungry for news of what was happening. They sought out that information in the newspapers, magazines and the cinema newsreels. For many people, especially those with reading difficulties - and in the prevailing social conditions where many poor children worked as half - timers in the textile mills - there were many of those, the cinema newsreels were of vital importance. Every cinema in the city showed weekly newsreels and even the music halls like the Empire and the Royal Hippodrome included the "latest" war news on film among their live items as, periodically, did the Y.M.C.A., the C.P.A., the Grosvenor Hall and other local halls who could turn to Lizars, Films Ltd and Weiskars of Pottenger's Lane for their programmes. The newsreels were more complex entities than their name may suggest. The makers perceived them essentially as a form of entertainment and saw to it that besides serious news they included items of sport, with a sprinkling of frivolities like the latest fashions, fads and such. The government came to regard them as effective channels of propaganda while the public regarded them as sources of information.

During the first months of the war the Army did not welcome or allow cameramen near the front lines so the early newsreels were about soldiers preparing for war: training, marching, scenes of camp life, relaxing with a game of football. Many such scenes involving Irish and other troops were shown locally as already mentioned. Typical was a Pathe Gazette shown in the Kinema House in September 1915 which included Winston Churchill addressing munitions workers, the London Irish at play, the Cheshire Volunteers on parade, the Port Sunlight and Birkenhead Volunteers being inspected and, in colour, the latest fashions from Paris. One of the more impressive offerings at the time was "With the Fighting Forces of Europe" which had the added attraction of being shot in Kinemacolor. The cameramen kept asking, and when the Germans bombarded the east coast settlements of Scarborough, Whitby and Hartlepool killing 100 persons, mainly civilians, they were allowed to photograph the aftermath, which quickly appeared on local screens. That unsettling event was followed in mid January 1915 by a Zeppelin attack on Great Yarmouth and King's Lynn in which 20 more people were killed. As the scenes of destruction were shown, audiences in Belfast began to feel that no-one was really safe in this war. By June Zeppelin attacks had started on London and some anxious eyes here were raised skywards. Anti - German feelings rose accordingly.

By 1915 the Army had relented in their opposition to the newsreels, having realized their propaganda value, so they allowed certain cameramen including Geoffrey Malins and J.B.McDowell supervised access to the front where they filmed the trenches, explosions, machine guns firing and heavy guns being brought into action. Those scenes reached the screens as official War Office films. The Picture House usually showed them first before they appeared across the city. In late January 1916 those official films presented "With the British Army at the Front," in February it was "A Machine Gun at the Front," in April the official pictures of the Irish at the Front. When the latter was screened in the Clonard the Irish News gave some details of its content. The writer prefaced his words with the comment that "this official film gives an excellent idea of the unparalleled heroism of our (sic) soldiers at the front," and then went on to describe the main scenes which showed the Irish Brigade in action, the Munsters marching to Mass, the R.I.R. moving into trenches, Capt. William Redmond M.P. leading his company, the Connaughts capturing an enemy position, the bombing of German lines and such. The film was watched with rapt attention broken only by bursts of applause. But all those snippets were only a prelude to the most famous extended newsreel of the war, the Battle of the Somme, which used material shot by the two men mentioned above.

The official pictures of "The Battle of the Somme" opened simultaneously in the Picture House, the Duncairn (where it was supported by Pearl White in "The King's Game") and the Crumlin on Monday, 11th September six weeks after the beginning of the actual attacks in France. The Picture House modestly described it as "the greatest moving picture in the world" while the Duncairn advertised it as "the most wonderful picture of actual warfare ever produced," adding that "the King recommends all to see it." Seen today - it was screened in the Ulster Museum as part of the Belfast Festival in February 2001 - the film is an important historical artefact but artistically it hardly lives up to its commercial promotion. It was based on events which began at 7:30 am on Saturday 1st July when 120,000 men began to move forward along an 18 mile (29 km) front in N. France, a fact that was reported in the local papers. The Telegraph stated simply a few days later that the battle of the Somme was "in progress" while the Irish News commented that reports of the fighting were "fluctuating."

The advance had been preceded by an eight day bombardment which among other things had warned the Germans that something major was about to happen so they weren't entirely taken by surprise. By the end of the first day it is estimated there were 60,000 casualties of whom 20,000 had been killed, but the film gives no indication of that horror. Yet its impact at the time in Belfast was sensational and it attracted long queues to the three cinemas that waited patiently for admittance. Viewers felt that they had never been so close to the action before. Of course, as the Telegraph pointed out, it was not meant to be an overview of the battle, more a microcosm of events in a small area that reflected what was happening along the whole front but which nevertheless gave the public a "thoroughly realistic impression" of the conflict. The writer pointed out that there had been arguments about the wisdom of showing certain sequences which had resulted in the film being cut at some venues, but he assured the Belfast public that they would see the complete film as passed by the War Office. The I.S.N. warned its readers that some scenes were "too vivid" while others "may appal the faint hearted." Without exception the critics encouraged the public to see the film to get an understanding of the conditions the soldiers were actually experiencing. The Irish News commended its "wealth of details" and found some scenes very moving. The News Letter thought it "a masterpiece of its kind" and again mentioned the detail like how close the trenches of the opposing forces were, and the poignancy of certain scenes.

The incidents shown had been filmed between the end of June and mid July and had been edited into an hour - long film that was divided into five sections: the preparatory action, the bombardment of the German trenches, the attack, the toll of war, and cleaning up. At the beginning the soldiers are shown in relaxed mood, looking "cheery and devil may care" (Telegraph), before getting ready, checking their weapons and equipment like the vital wire cutters. The bombardment of the enemy trenches is very spectacular with "plum puddings" (mortars) causing massive explosions which send masses of soil and debris up into the air. The attack follows with soldiers waited tensely for their officers to lead them over the edge of the trench into no - man's - land. As they go a number fall and one man slides slowly backwards, inert. That scene impressed everyone, not only the critics but the audiences some of whom cheered the bravery of the men while others who had lost relatives or friends sat quietly feeling a terrible sadness. Even today it still has the capacity to move people. The Telegraph was especially saddened by the images of the dead but commented by way of justification that "they had done their duty, and their bit." Yet that famous scene was not filmed in France but was cleverly reconstructed, or faked, later on Salisbury Plain which says something about the power of art over reality. The scenes in the trenches and in no-mans-land showed the ubiquitous barbed wire fences but none of the mud and water usually associated with them because the attack took place after a dry period. The Whig felt that the features of the battlefield shown would "be historic for many centuries to come." All the critics expressed satisfaction with the scenes showing German prisoners being rounded up and moved behind the lines and praised the efforts of those who dealt with the rescue and treatment of the wounded. The Telegraph found the whole film "very moving without being depressing" which seemed to reflect the feelings of the people who saw it also.

Audiences today are more detached and recognise that the film was above all a propaganda exercise in the guise of an extended newsreel. They also find the lack of sound a disadvantage in that a whole dimension of the conflict, the thunder of explosions, the crackling of the rifles and machine guns, the shouts of the men is omitted. That lack was compensated for at the time by special effects in the halls, and above all by the musicians playing music that was specially written to heighten the impact, though only the Irish News critic mentioned it. The style of the film is rather static with camera movements that show no advance since the newsreels of the Boer War. Most shots are from a fixed position with the camera recording what is happening before it, and there is no sense of involvement with the action. Of course that doesn't detract from its historical and human value because as the generation that fought that war slowly disappear those faces staring from the trenches at the camera will remain as silent accusing witnesses to the folly and waste of war. The Telegraph thoughtfully struck the right note when it described the film as "a work of historical as well as immediate value."

A new weapon is introduced.

"The Battle of the Somme" was only one of a series of official pictures about the war. The actual battle continued with a terrible and increasing cost in young lives until November when more pictures of the conflict became available. The Clonard on the 6th of the month could announce the arrival of another special film on "The Advance on the Somme," while in the weeks that followed another official film of the King's visit to the war zone was screened in the Kinema House, the Duncairn and the Picture House. It was a two - reeler which showed the king's arrival at Boulogne, his inspection of the battlefield including fortified areas "that had been wrested from the enemy during the last four months"(Whig). In February 1917 the Imperial, Lyceum,Crumlin and Royal Cinema all showed the "Battle of the Ancre," also using scenes shot by the same photographers, with official pictures of the Irish Division in the front line and also for the first time a new weapon, the tank, in action.

There is a description of the film by a young boy at the time which is full of detail and highlights the impact of the propaganda elements. "Crash! Boom! the cinema band is imitating the battle. You see the tanks in action, also men slushing about in mud. Now you see a transport wagon being guided round a shell hole by an officer; he takes an unlucky step and has a bath in mud. Now the eighteen pounders in action, making frightful havoc over in the German trenches. Now the whistle shrills, and they leap over the parapet, rat, tap, tap, tap go the German machine guns, but nothing daunts our soldiers. Crack! and the gallant captain falls. This enrages the men to fury. At last they reach the German lines. Most of the Germans flee. Now the British and German wounded are brought in, some seriously, others slightly. Soon after follows the German prisoners, some vicious looking scoundrels that I should not like to meet on a dark night, others young boys about sixteen years of age." (The Cinema, its present position and future possibilities: Cinema Commission of Inquiry 1917, p.280.) Another lad of eleven years described the terror among the Germans as "snorting, creaking, waddling, the huge bogey started for the front line trenches," his imagination filling in the necessary sounds.

Later in the year the reopened and redecorated Duncairn presented the next "official," "The Capture of Messines." Again it was a two - reeler which opened with troops behind the lines relaxing before making preparations for another attack. A massive bombardment follows, including the explosions of mines. Scenes also showed the Irish Regiments who had taken part in the fighting and, sadly, the grave of Major William Redmond M.P., killed in action. By then a pattern can be detected in the films. Each contains scenes involving specific regiments, there are scenes of smiling men playing football or engaged in some other sport, some humour, a few safe war scenes like shots of the trenches, no -man's land, soldiers running forward to engage the enemy, or something special like trundling tanks, and maybe a reconstructed shot of fighting. That pattern continued until the end of the war with increasing emphasis on the soldiers involved, as the filmmakers realised that the human element appealed above all to audiences.

Even in late 1918 the Coliseum and Royal Cinema simultaneously screened an official film of the Irish fighting men. In the latter it was called rather formally "With the Irish Regiments in France" but the Coliseum advertised it as the more friendly even fraternal, "Our Boys in France," adding that it covered incidents from the base to going over the top. Patrons were assured the these were the finest pictures ever taken of the Irish troops in France and they were promised views of the Irish Guards, the Royal Irish Rifles, the Royal Irish Fusiliers, the Royal Munster Fusiliers and others. Also promised was an impressive array of tanks. "Come and see this picture," the advert advised, "you are sure to recognise some of your friends." As an added attraction it was supported by "Behind the Lines,"described as a thrilling war drama in six reels. In contrast to the war themes on the screen the accompanying live music hall acts put the emphasis on humour, with comedians and eccentric dancers Morris and Moore supported by Ronaldo, a boy juggler. All of that for only 3d, 5d, 9d or 1/3d depending on the state of one's finances.

Besides the official pictures there were the weekly newsreels like the Pathé Gazette and the Gaumont Graphic which continued to supply pictures of other events around the country. The Gazette boasted that it was "always right there with the latest" and the public expected it to live up to that claim. As a result cameramen crossed the country seeking interesting pictures not only of major events like the Grand National or major football matches but of the unusual and the unexpected - such as happened in Ireland at Easter 1916. In late April the managers of cinemas like the Picture House and the Panopticon apologised for the non - arrival of new films from Dublin because the railway schedules were disrupted by what was described as rioting in that city. On May 8th the Imperial and the Panopticon followed up those reports with a special newsreel called "The Dublin Revolt" which presented unbelieving audiences with scenes that were visually every bit as shocking as some coming out of France. The News Letter was struck by the realism of the scenes from central Dublin which showed "terrible damage," with devastated buildings in various stages of collapse. Other shots showed Sinn Féiners marching into Dublin, a group of wounded in hospital, a parade of the National Volunteers, and scenes around Liberty Hall. Beyond shock there was little comment on the matter and the disturbances didn't seem to have had much immediate impact locally. War news continued to dominate, not only the fighting in Europe but the increasing incidence of Zeppelin raids on S.E.England and London. The Zeppelin had caught the imagination of the populace as a flying machine that was both beautiful and sinister. Fiction films that included sequences involving them proved very popular and even Pimple tangled with them with hilarious results. The real things were not very funny and the civilian death rate continued to rise as a result of their raids.

Lillian Gish was in London at the time with her sister Dorothy and her mother to make a film for D.W.Griffith. He had been asked by the government, in the person of Lord Beaverbrook, the head of the Cinematograph Committee, to make an anti - German war film which it was hoped would help bring the U.S.A. into the conflict. He had been promised full co-operation by the authorities and so had come across to scout locales in N. France that he could use. He had also summoned his foremost star, Lillian Gish, who was to play the female lead in the film, to be called "Hearts of the World," in which she would suffer badly at the hands of the Hun. In fact she experienced much more than she had anticipated due to a series of Zeppelin raids on London while she was staying there. She described how they occurred without warning by day and night. Suddenly there were loud explosions followed by the sounds of breaking glass and the screams of women and children. She found the nights especially fearful as "those horrible big things in the sky" arrived without warning "dropping death wherever they go." At first the air force was impotent to stop them until the development of explosive bullets which could pierce the skin of the Zeppelin before exploding.

The Whig gave its readers an eye witness account of an engagement between aircraft and one of the Zeppelins, a huge monster about 700 feet (215 m) long, carrying 2,000 gallons of fuel. There were the sounds of aircraft, of gunfire and shells bursting around the intruder. Suddenly she (sic) was hit and a white arc of flame swept along her body, lighting up the sky "like a celestial torch." The metal framework glinted momentarily through the spreading flames "like the giant ribs of a mastodon ripped bare by the tusk of an invisible yet mighty enemy." Slowly the "doomed giant" dropped earthwards breaking into two parts, scattering its remains over two miles of the countryside. The newsreels weren't able to rise to those descriptive heights but the following week the Picture House had film from Essex of the burnt and twisted remains of the same craft with hundreds of sightseers rushing excitedly to see them, some waving and smiling in a carnival atmosphere - St George had killed the dragon! Most were walking, others were on bicycles and some on carts.

Griffith meanwhile filmed some scenes in N. France and on Salisbury Plain before returning to the U.S.A. He was dissatisfied with the dramatic content of the European scenes so he scrapped most of them and made the film in California where he had the artistic control he needed. The film had its première in Los Angeles on 12th March 1918 and was well received. It did very good business until peace was declared in November when the public seemed to lose its appetite for war themes. It reached Belfast in April 1919 and opened in the Royal Cinema, in the presence of the Lord and Lady Mayor, where it ran for a week to crowded houses at normal prices, but in separate shows, at 3:00 pm, 6:30 and 8:30. It was welcomed by the critics but with none of the enthusiasm that had greeted "Birth of a Nation" and "Intolerance." The Whig critic, always an admirer of Griffith, praised its "masterly perfection of detail" and "grimly realistic battle scenes." The scenario, which shows clear parallels with "The Birth of a Nation," opens with idyllic village scenes involving the hero and heroine who are to be married, including the first appearance of Noel Coward on film, but the war soon intervenes and the lovers are separated. The incidents that follow become more and more grim and Lillian Gish suffers like a true Griffith heroine, beaten and threatened sexually by beastly Huns, one of whom was Erich von Stroheim who later became known as "the man you love to hate." Her scenes of madness after the death of her mother, especially when she wanders across the battlefield carefully carrying her folded wedding gown in search of her lost love, reduced audiences to tears and confirmed her reputation as an outstanding actress. In true Griffith fashion there is a last minute rescue from the attacking Germans with the arrival of American troops. What influence, if any, the film had on American public opinion is difficult to gauge but certainly before it was released the U.S., despite its large German immigrant population, had entered the war in April 1917 in support of the Allies. By late June American troops were landing in France and the Imperial was able during that same week to show scenes of the arrival of American ships and soldiers "in British waters." As they watched that newsreel people must have felt and hoped that the nightmare would soon be over.

One of the characteristics of the contemporary films was the unflattering portrait of the German characters involved, a portrait that was widely accepted without question. One can easily see why. It was a time of war, relatives and friends were dying at the hands of the Germans and the population was being primed by propaganda to detest and resist the enemy. An image of the Hun as a barbarian was carefully, and often not too subtly, conceived and presented by non - Germans and there were no films of German origin allowed that might contradict that picture. Belfast audiences seem to have forgotten the German made films of Asta Nielson which had presented a quite different view of the German character. Thoughtful people - and Belfast, thankfully, had its share - must have queried that perception and may have pondered how accurate the cinematic image of any nation was, and they could have started by examining the screen image of their fellow Irishmen.

Such an evaluation might have been precipitated by a large advertisement which appeared on the front page of the Irish News on the 16th August 1916 announcing the arrival of a new completely Irish film company, the Film Company of Ireland. Ireland and its inhabitants had been much defamed during the 19th century and earlier by the cartoon activities of the stage Irishman, presented as an aggressive hard - drinking and basically stupid clown, though Dion Boucicault and writers like J.M.Synge and G.B.Shaw had taken steps to modify that image. Sydney Olcott continued that process in his Kalem films which proved so popular when they were shown in St. George's Hall. Despite his good intentions Olcott was still an outsider, albeit a sympathetic one, from America and his films were aimed mainly at the American market, though he used genuine Irish locations peopled by native Irish. His films also touched upon real Irish concerns: the poverty and depressing social conditions, emigration and, increasingly, the political resentment against the English. The Irish nationalism of his life of Robert Emmett, "Bold Emmett, Ireland's Martyr," made in 1914 so displeased the British authorities in Dublin that it was withdrawn. It wasn't shown at all in Belfast. Yet his films, while welcomed at the time, are not regarded today as genuinely Irish. All that seemed about to change with the Film Company of Ireland.

The company had been founded earlier in the year, in March, by two Irishmen, Henry Fitzgibben and James Mark Sullivan, with the aim of making films in Ireland which they promised would deal with Irish subjects and use only Irish talents. Their original offices in Dublin had been burned during the Easter Rising and they had lost some films but they now had a headquarters at 34, Dame Street and had just released their first production "O'Neil of the Glens," a three - reeler, which was doing good business in the Bohemian Picture House in Dublin. They had also completed four comedies to be released soon, two two - reelers "The Miser's Gift" and "Woman's Wit," and two one - reelers "Food of Love," filmed in the beautiful surroundings of Glendalough, and "An Unfair Love Affair." Over the next months they promised an ambitious programme which included The Upstart, Blarney, the Irish Girl, a series called the Shanachie's Tales, an Irish Jarvey Tale, Bye Ways of Fate, Treasure Trove, Willy Reilly and The Girl from the Golden Vale.

The first of those reached Belfast when the ever vigilant Fred Stewart presented "O'Neil of the Glen" in the Crumlin for three days followed by a downtown showing in the Panopticon. The following week it appeared in the Clonard accompanied by special music played by the cinema orchestra directed by W.L.Richards. The film was adapted by W.T.Lysaght from a novel by the Ulster writer Mrs M.T.Pender and boasted a cast which included Abbey Players. The main part was taken by one of those players, J.M.Kerrigan, appearing in his first film role. Kerrigan not only acted in many of the films but also directed them. He was supported by Nora Clancy, Fred O'Donovan and Brian Magowan. Unfortunately the film has completely disappeared but the Irish News praised it as a wholesome story of Irish life and history which appealed to local audiences because "it touched a chord in their Irish hearts that was inaccessible to the imported production." The film certainly proved popular wherever it was shown, including runs in the Kelvin and the Kinema House. In October the Clonard and the Kinema House presented the next film from the company, "The Widow Malone," which was advertised by Alfred George as "the first comedy produced in Ireland." The following month saw the same cinemas showing the "all Irish" comedy, the Film Company's "Puck Fair Romance," while before Christmas the Clonard presented "The Food of Love." Much more was to follow because over the next four years the Film Company of Ireland was to become the most important Irish film company of the period by making around twenty films including the highly successful and popular "Knocknagow" and "Willy Reilly and his Dear Colleen Bawn."

During the week that "O'Neil of the Glens" was screened in the Clonard it was accompanied by music specially composed by a Rev. A. Greven plus selections and solos chosen by the musical director W.L.Richards, the quality and suitability of which were greatly praised by the Irish News critic. Many films were accompanied by original scores written for them or put together by the orchestra leaders, and increasingly the critics referred to and commented upon the music. The presence of live musicians made visits to a silent cinema a very different type of experience from modern day cinema going. Music had been an integral part of the silent film since its inception, probably because the earliest examples were shown in music halls and music hall acts were usually accompanied by music. Silent films without music are akin to Laurel without Hardy. The traditional view of a silent movie is of screen visuals augmented by an expressive piano and it was that perception which is illustrated in "The Smallest Show on Earth" (d. Basil Deardon,1957) - a film that all film buffs should see - to maximum effect in a very moving tribute to the beauty of the silent film. The sequence begins when the owner of a noisy fleapit, played by Bill Travers, arrives unexpectedly and discovers the elderly attendants (Peter Sellars and Bernard Miles) watching a Cecil Hepworth production in admiring silence while a dignified Margaret Rutherford plays a suitable piano accompaniment. A product of the sound era himself, Travers withdraws quietly from what he respects as a personal and enriching moment for his elderly employees.

But the solo piano became confined to the smaller and poorer halls as the cinema business expanded and cinema orchestras became the norm. The medium sized halls like the Panopticon, Kinema House, Kelvin, Duncairn and the Clonard had small groups of six or seven musicians, but the more up - market downtown cinemas had much larger ensembles. The Picture House, the Imperial and the Royal Cinema were very proud of their orchestras and regarded them as major attractions often rivalling the very films themselves. They drew attention to them in their advertisements and clearly persuaded the critics to mention them in their columns also. There was quite a level of musical competition between the downtown cinemas and successful orchestra leaders could pick and choose their venues. In January 1914 the News Letter praised the Panopticon's grandly named Royal Bijou Orchestra and its leader Mr Wright but the following month noted that the the orchestra was being enlarged and a new conductor, Jack Read from the Royal Hippodrome, was being engaged, while Mr Wright was moving to take charge of music in the Central. When the Panopticon showed the much praised "The Last Days of Pompeii," directed by Mario Caserini, Mr Read's "splendid music" was duly commented upon. A few months later the same cinema showed the "Sign of the Cross" and again Mr Read was complimented on his "special music." The critic noted that the latter included fine violin solos and impressive organ solos by a Mr M. Burns. The Panopticon was the first commercial cinema to make extensive use of an organ (it had often been used from an early date of course during cine-musical evenings in the Y.M.C.A. which couldn't afford an orchestra and where there already was a resident organist) and sometimes the entire film was accompanied by the solo organ. In October 1916 the Irish News critic commented particularly on the expressive organ solos by Edwin Thomas that accompanied the Triangle thriller, "A Submarine Pirate," which starred Sydney Chaplin. Some notion of the atmosphere surrounding such an event was experienced by an audience of over 300 people in March 2013 when the Ulster Hall presented Carl Dreyer's silent masterpiece "Le Passion de Jeanne D'Arc" accompanied by a solo musical background on the Mulholland Organ. From its opening the Imperial put great emphasis on its resident orchestra which by 1916 included sixteen players under the direction of Herbert Mortimer. The critics often expressed admiration for his arrangements and, as the I.S.N. put it, his "use of orchestral music to compliment the films."

To what extent the musical accompaniment actually influenced the average filmgoer in his\her choice of film is uncertain but cinema managers certainly seem to have considered that it did have a bearing. In February 1916 the premier cinema the Picture House decided to up the musical stakes and emphasise its pre- eminence by announcing that it intended to increase the size of its orchestra to 40 members (surely the largest ever of any

Belfast cinema) by engaging members of the Scottish Symphony Orchestra under a new conductor, Enrico Cinganelli. The new symphony orchestra would accompany the films as usual but would also give separate recitals at 3:00 p.m. and 7:00 p.m. daily. Critics and audiences were suitably impressed. When "The Christian" starring Elizabeth Risdon was screened the following month the Telegraph critic described the experience as two hours of "throbs, hopes, heartaches and heartbreaks" all enriched by excellent music from the symphony orchestra, and added that Signor Cinganelli showed "great tact and dramatic fitness in the synchronisation of picture and music." The symphony orchestra remained a special attraction at the Picture House until May 1916 when it ended its run, an event which caused much regret locally, according to the News Letter. The Imperial Symphony orchestra continued to perform, however, with sessions of "exquisite music" (Whig) and mention was often made of how appropriate its renderings were to the films. In May it supported one of Lasky's impressive new rising actresses, Blanche Sweet, in "The Case of Becky," and in July it drew large crowds to hear the special music enhancing Mary Pickford's performance in "Madame Butterfly," directed by that Irish favourite, Sydney Olcott, before he left the U.S. again to return to Ireland with a new leading lady Valentine Grant. Mary herself disliked "Madame Butterfly" and thought it was so slow moving that she called it "Madame Snail."

The musical fallout from the symphonic competition between the large halls also enveloped the smaller halls where there is some evidence of a growing appreciation of the interaction between film and music. In July the Irish News critic referred to the musical director of the Clonard, W.L.Richards, as "the right man in the right place" and praised his choice of music for a war picture, "The Survivor," which had a lively plot full of intrigue and adventure marked by "graphic views" of a battlefield blasted by battery fire. One can be sure that the percussion section earned their keep that week. A month later the I.S.N. critic drew attention to the fine work of Mr J. Monaghan, leader of the Kelvin orchestra, whose music was "now more adapted to the mood of the film being shown." But competition even in musical circles could lead to difficulties as was revealed the following year when a dispute arose between Mr Mortimer and members of the Imperial orchestra who complained that he had become too strict and "harsh" in his treatment of certain players. Today the problem would be perceived as one of harassment, but then it was a question of discipline and of workers doing what they were told. The Imperial management supported the leader's drive for excellence and dismissed the complaints. In reply the orchestra downed instruments and walked out, the first recorded incident of a strike in a local cinema. The stoppage doesn't seem to have lasted long and there are no details of how the matter was resolved but one may wonder if the Imperial was reduced to having their films supported by the traditional piano again for a time.

The other cinema which promised from its opening that it would provide a "magnificent orchestra "was the Royal Cinema and it lived up to that promise. In reply to the Picture House and the Imperial, special orchestral recitals were put on daily at 3:00 p.m. and 7:00 p.m. and they often included well known Irish singers like Lilian Dalby and John West. The Royal orchestra enjoyed a high reputation in the city, a fact that the I.S.N. played upon when, in its amusing series "Chronicles of the Coort," it described a night out by Mrs Twigglety and her daughter Margit Bella to the cinema. The event was written up in broad Belfastese and the hall wasn't named but behind the humour it was obviously a visit to the Royal Cinema. Firstly they went to the cafe where "the tay was graun and ivirything was that nate an' clean an' brite." Their shillings were taken by a young lady wearing a spotless white apron and cap and they were escorted to their seats. The film was very enjoyable but Mrs Twigglety was completely bowled over by the music. "A dunno when A enjoyed anything so much before." In future, she promised, when Margit Bella had a headache she would cure her with "a dose of the picthirs." Everything that night was just "louvely." Margit Bella came away completely cured and "it was the gud musick dun it, A ses."

Important as the music may have been, the vast majority of people went to the cinema to see the films and, increasingly, the stars. During 1916 the star names which dominated the screens were Mary Pickford and Charles Chaplin whose films continued to attract large crowds. Following closely behind them were Pearl White, Pauline Frederick (the Mrs Patrick Campbell of the screen according to the I.S.N.), Elizabeth Risdon, Geraldine Farrar, Petrova (who was actually an English girl called Muriel Harding), and Blanche Sweet who appeared in a number of films one of which was "The Secret Sin" set in the opium dens of Chinatown, in which she played two contrasting parts. The Irish News critic was impressed by its "grim realism" and added that Miss Sweet displayed "histrionic powers of a high order." William S. Hart, who had played Shakespeare on the stage, was making an impact as a tough Western star and the Whig critic wasn't alone when he described his acting as "powerful and impressive" and praised his fighting abilities. The author's father, who claimed to have seen all his films, agreed with that evaluation and always referred back to W.S.Hart as the touchstone of what a screen cowboy should be. Another Triangle actor Douglas Fairbanks was also making a local impact as was Francis X. Bushman, Fannie Ward, Lotte Pickford (Mary's sister), Sydney Chaplin (Charlie's brother), Marguerite Clarke, and Gerald Ames, while a host of old favourites like the Keystone clowns, the serial heroes and heroines, Pimple and Broncho Billy could still bring in the crowds.

W.S. Hart, top western star.

Even a superficial perusal of the cinematic year indicates the increasing dominance of American films and personalities, while European faces like the once popular German star Henny Porten, had largely disappeared mainly due to the disruption of the War. The Telegraph critic cannily noted the change and regretted that British films especially were struggling to hold a place in the marketplace. The war wasn't the only reason for the changes. Audiences found the American films superior in many ways. They seemed bigger, more challenging, with higher production values and more exciting characters than the local products. Typical was "The Eternal City" which was actually filmed in Rome with Zukor's new find, Pauline Frederick. It opened in the Imperial during the first week of 1916 and the comments of the News Letter critic expresses much of why the local filmgoers found the American product so attractive and entertaining. The critic praised "its beauty of finish, its smoothness, its magnificent staging, its perfect photography, its fine acting (which) are all marvels in its way ...... (with) nothing jerky in the telling of its story." Zukor's Famous Players and Lasky merged in July making their new company the largest film producer, while Fox, Metro and Triangle were increasing production to supply their large home market but also with an eye to the European and British markets.

In Britain on the other hand production was shrinking. During 1916 three major

figures decided to leave the film scene: Charles Urban, Dr. Jupp and Will Barker. Urban's monopoly on Kinemacolor ended and he sold his interests and returned to America. An ailing Dr. Jupp who had done so much to improve the standards of comfort and cleanliness in his purpose - built cinemas (like the Picture House) and who had set up the London Film Co. to supply his cinema chain, and the American market, with quality films found himself in financial difficulties and after deciding to cease film production he then over the next few years sold his interest in Provincial Cinematograph Theatres and his studio at Twickenham. Will Barker is a major figure in British cinema, a showman who had been involved with films since the heady days of 1896 and was responsible for the first films made at Ealing Studios. He specialised in large scale but popular films like "Sixty Years a Queen," "East Lynne (1913)" and "Jane Shore." The latter was typical, a five reeler involving 250 scenes and over 5,000 players with a civil war plot based on events during the reign of Edward VI and starring his leading lady, Blanche Forsythe. It was strongly influenced in style and content by Griffith's "Birth of a Nation." It showed in the Panopticon (usually an indicator of a popular success) and the Crumlin during November 1915 and in the Kinema House in October 1916. After twenty years in the business and despite such successes, age persuaded him to retire. That left only one major film maker, Cecil Hepworth who continued large scale production at Walton - on - Thames with his leading stars, the dark - haired and beautiful Alma Taylor (who was much admired in Belfast), Chrissie White and Henry Ainley.

That wasn't the complete picture because British production had always included a clutch of small producers located mainly around London, whose names were as well known to local filmgoers as the large studios. They included the Clarendon Film Co at Croydon which made the Liet. Rose series, Cricks and Martin also near Croydon who produced the P.C.Sharpe and Paul Sleuth series, the Bamford Film Co. in Holmfirth with its comedy Winky (Reggie Switz) series, the Phoenix Film Co at Twickenham, run on a shoestring, but making the profitable Pimple series, and the British and Colonial, originally at Barnet before moving to Walthamstow in 1912, where the Liet. Daring series was completed. Their films were small scale with an emphasis on action and humour and had a decidedly local appeal but they were popular with ordinary filmgoers and turned a profit. The Pimple films, for example, were knockabout shorts often no more than ten minutes long and turned out on a weekly basis. But they were topical, usually based on recent events or characters, quick and cheap to make, and had no pretensions at all beyond making people laugh. Will Evans, a former music hall star, played Pimple and often made public appearances, music hall style, at local cinemas in England to the delight of the audiences. He never visited Belfast but his films were a welcome part of the local staple diet and were shown widely across the city, especially in the Panopticon (e.g. "Capture of the Kaiser by Lieut. Pimple" which delighted audiences in November 1914 when the war was still expected to be over by Christmas), the Kinema House (almost a weekly appearance), and even on occasion in the Imperial ("Pimple and the Stolen Plans," January 1915) and the Picture House ("Sexton Pimple," March 1915).

The small studios were joined in 1914 by G.B.Samuelson who had moved from renting and distribution into production. He had actually financed Will Barker's "Sixty Years a Queen" and its success persuaded him to enter enthusiastically into the more creative side of the business. He set up his studio at Worton Hall, Isleworth and signed up a former teacher, George Pearson, who had made a name for himself in educational films, as director. After a hectic year during which he filmed "A Study in Scarlet" with James Bragington as Sherlock Holmes, "The Great European War - Day by Day" which included fake newsreel material, "Christmas Day in the Workhouse," "The Life of Lord Roberts," "A Cinema Girl's Romance," and at least four other films, Pearson decided in 1915 to join Gaumont who had studios at Lime Grove, Shepherd's Bush where he hoped he would have a less onerous schedule. His new employer asked him to come up with a rival to the French success, the mysterious Fantomas, and the result was Ultus (a name he discovered in a Latin dictionary, meaning avenger) and a successful series of mystery thrillers starring Aurele Sydney that lasted until 1917. Four of the Ultus thrillers were shown in Belfast beginning with "Ultus, The Man From the Dead" a six - reeler which opened in the Alhambra during May 1916 before moving on to the Central. It caught the imagination of audiences and people, just like their modern counterparts, looked forward to the follow-up, "Ultus and the Grey Lady," which arrived at the Duncairn in October. It was followed by "Ultus and the Secret of the Night," a five - reeler, at the Alhambra in February 1917, described by the I.S.N. as "fascinating."

What is really fascinating about it is that during its showing the star, Aurele Sydney, made a public appearance on the stage of the Alhambra, talked about the making of the film and answered questions from the excited audience. The old theatre had done it again. Not only was it the first place in Belfast to show films but it was the first venue in the city to host a personal appearance by a real live popular film star. The event proved to be a great success and the I.S.N. arranged an interview with the visitor which it published under the heading "Ultus in Belfast." According to the star he had been born Aurele Labat de Lambert in Sydney, Australia; hence his simpler stage name which he insisted had been suggested by none other than Sarah Bernhardt herself. He presented himself as a confident and talented all - rounder with an interest in sport, travel, philosophy (he was writing a book on the subject) and music - besides acting. His acting career began in Sydney from where he moved to London and then to Paris where he acted in the Theatre Sarah Bernhardt, meeting the great lady and Jane Hading. In Paris he was persuaded to take part in a few films which whetted his appetite for the medium, before being asked to take the part of Ultus whom he described as "a man of high spirits and firm determination who takes the law into his own hands to administer justice." He insisted that he had an input into the preparation and making of the Ultus films but made no mention of George Pearson. He was enjoying his trip to Ireland, being received everywhere "with enthusiasm and appreciation."

As it happened there was to be only one more Ultus adventure, "Ultus and the Three Button Mystery" which showed in the Royal Cinema in November 1917 and was described by the I.S.N. as "a good clean exciting drama." The following month less affluent audiences welcomed it in the Alhambra. After the Ultus series - which the sophisticated Whig critic described as "remarkable" - Mr Sydney signed a remunerative contract to stay with Gaumont and continued to star in a number of films including Pearson's version of "Sally Bishop" with Peggy Hyland which appeared in the Panopticon in February 1918. Fred. Stewart advertised it as "a picture for grown ups only" while the Whig critic thought it was a well acted and well produced melodrama. In the following year he appeared in another thriller "The Green Terror," and followed that up with "Angle Esquire." He died soon after, in 1920. Despite being involved in about two dozen films made in Britain, France, Italy and Spain he never really became a major star and probably today only film buffs are aware of either Ultus or Aurele Sydney.

In contrast in early 2006 his French prototype, Feuillade's more stylish Fantômas, was reissued on D.V.D. for modern audiences to contemplate and enjoy.

CHAPTER SIXTEEN
Censorship Again

Cinematically the year 1916 ended with a distinct tendency towards escapism. The Panopticon presented "Undine" described as a water pantomime, a fantasy of the sea; the Imperial had Chaplin in "The Floorwalker"; Kinema House favoured "Cricket on the Hearth" based on Dickens, while the Lyceum presented another pantomime, a film version of "Robinson Crusoe." Some time previously the takings from the opening day at the new Royal Cinema had been presented to the group responsible for the support of Ulster Limbless Soldiers, a reminder that the harsh realities of the war were never far away. The situation in Europe had long since reached a stalemate, but the lists of dead and wounded from the front were not decreasing. It was not only on land that things didn't look promising but also at sea and in the air. During the early months of 1917 the U - boats were decimating shipping approaching the Br. Isles while the German airforce brought into service a new specially designed long range bomber, the twin - engined Gotha. The country had been relieved when the Zeppelin menace had been beaten off but from late May large scale bombing began again over S.E. England and London. During the early raids among the dead in London were eighteen children killed when a bomb made a direct hit on a school. The Germans apologised for that but the incident strengthened the popular image of the barbarian Huns who had to be defeated at any cost. Sir John Lavery caught the drama of one such incident in his painting of a daylight raid seen from his London studio window in July, and now displayed in the Ulster Museum.

The cinemas continued to show official newsreels, usually with an upbeat message which ignored the setbacks. In July the Picture House presented the battle of Arras with welcome pictures of the Germans in retreat while the following month the renovated Duncairn reopened with "The Capture of Messines" which the Irish News critic thought was "quite as good as the Somme picture," and he particularly praised its "magnificent cinematography (which gave) an excellent idea of modern warfare." There was praise also for the fighting abilities of the Irish Regiments, with scenes involving the Dublin Fusiliers, the Royal Irish Fusiliers, the Royal Irish Regiment (enjoying an issue of stout), and the men of the Ulster Division. The Royal Cinema had a weekly series called "Our Navy" which showed how the men and the ships were coping with the war situation, while the Imperial promoted Pathe's Animated History of the War, presented also in a weekly series. The Imperial later presented a selection of French official war newsreels which were used to illustrate an accompanying lecture by Major Treves, a surgeon in the French army. He was touring Ireland explaining the situation in France with particular reference to the treatment of wounded soldiers.

Both sides were watching the Americans and waiting to see what they would do. There was general relief and welcome when the Americans entered the war on the side of the Allies in April 1917, and their soldiers were soon be seen on local screens. It took a year however before the Picture House offered a special film "America's Answer to the Hun," specially made for and presented by the British Ministry of Information, detailing how the U.S. was gearing up for war. Obviously all the governments regarded the cinema as a vital weapon in the propaganda war. Despite the fact that the Yanks were coming there were continual calls for more men to enlist and for the women to do their bit also. In July the local museum put on exhibitions of photographs detailing how women were working successfully in the munitions industry and how citizens in general were adapting to the war time economy. In September it was announced that a new auxiliary corps of women was to be established to undertake clerical and other non combatant duties for the army, thereby releasing more men for active service. They would be stationed in the Grand Central Hotel which was being requisitioned for the purpose. Belfast was to lose not only its premier hotel with the hundred jobs it provided, but its plush furnishings and contents were to be sold off. According to the Irish News such a decision was "a remarkable departure as far as Ireland was concerned" and caused disquiet in the city. Progressive women may have felt that their economic importance was being recognised at last but, at the same time, when women working in the poorly paid handkerchief and embroidery sections of the linen industry asked for an increase in wages their request was refused, resulting in over 4,500 of them coming out on strike; while at much the same time a strike was narrowly averted in the gas industry, another sign of underlying social discontent.

Tensions were also rising again in the city over the vexed question of Home Rule and there was increasing anger towards the British Government in Nationalist circles at the treatment of the leaders of the Dublin Revolt who had been executed in Kilmainham Jail during May 1916. As the shootings continued there were calls for clemency from many quarters, including the President of the U.S.A., John Redmond and Sir Edward Carson. Those humanitarian appeals were ignored and when it was reported that the already wounded James Connolly had been carried into the prison yard and propped up on a chair before being shot there was profound shock, not only in Ireland. That was the last of the executions and the other Sinn Féin prisoners, including De Valera and Countess Markieviez, were imprisoned. Not surprisingly Irish affairs began to feature again in the newsreels. Sinn Féin prisoners in Wales were unexpectedly released in mid - June 1917 and on the 25th the Clonard announced the showing of a specially elongated newsreel of their arrival and reception in Dublin. They showed scenes of welcome for Countess Markievecz with a procession through the city and a reception at Liberty Hall.

It is thought that one reason for their release was to avoid the problems arising from possible hunger strikes. Another local S.F. leader Thomas Ashe was already on hunger strike in Mountjoy Prison and in September he died. On 1st October the Panopticon highlighted a special newsreel on "Thomas Ashe, the Sinn Féin Hunger Striker" giving it precedence over the main film "The Perils of Divorce," episode 3 "The Spider's Web" of the serial "The Voice on the Wire," and even Pimple in "Oliver Twisted" by Darles Chicken. The newsreel was watched in complete silence. The Clonard also gave it top billing and it was later shown in the Central and the West Belfast Picture Theatre. The film showed the lying - in - state in the City Hall, the funeral procession to Glasnevin, the scenes at the graveside including the firing of a volley over the grave, and the playing of the Last Post. All of the proceedings in Dublin were watched by "vast throngs." (Irish News). A few months later, in February 1918, the Panopticon and the Imperial highlighted another newsreel of the arrival of Sir Edward Carson in York Street station on a visit to Belfast and a month later the Picture House and the Imperial both showed film of the funeral of John Redmond in Wexford which the Whig described as "unusually clear and vivid" but when it was shown in the Clonard it was, according to the Irish News, "followed with melancholy interest." "Melancholy" was hardly the term that most people would have used about a visit to the cinema which was perceived mainly as a form of entertainment, an escape from the tensions of daily existence. The Central caught that mood over Easter 1917 when it presented Charlie Chaplin in "Behind the Screen," advising patrons not to miss "our all - smiling holiday programme," and adding a short piece of uplifting doggerel:

> Smile awhile
> For while you smile another smiles
> Soon there are miles and miles of smiles and life's worth while
> If you but smile.

In contrast to the political and economic gloom there was much to smile about on local screens during 1917. It was above all the year when Belfast audiences were introduced to the much hyped Fox star, the mysterious Theda Bara, mainly through the efforts of Fred Stewart. Mr Stewart's instincts as a showman told him she would be a major popular draw though he was probably slightly uneasy about the strength of the reaction from certain conservative sections of society. His fears evaporated when in January the Lyceum presented her in a modern version of the well tried and inoffensive "East Lynne," without any protests. That must have decided him and beginning in March she appeared in his New York cinema in "Infidelity" directed by Herbert Brenon, a story of an unfaithful wife who comes to a bad end, in which she was billed as "the queen of the silent stage." Throughout the rest of the year she reigned in the Panopticon in "The Two Orphans," "The Galley Slave," (full of incidents, very emotional, with moments of tension..... Miss Bara a competent actress.... according to the Irish News), "Secrets of Society" (as Lady Audley whose secret was that she was a murderess), "Gold and the Woman" (as a wronged woman who seeks revenge on the man responsible), and ended the year in December playing an artist's model in a modern version of Alphonse Daudet's Sapho called "Bohemia".

Over the Easter holidays the Royal Cinema also presented her in "Romeo and Juliet" which impressed the critic of the I.S.N. who described her as "that alluring actress" and praised her highly, especially for her acting in the balcony scene. The following month she returned to the Royal Cinema as Cigarette in "Under Two Flags," a role that was to be repeated many years later by Claudette Colbert. The Picture House waited and eventually found a suitably serious vehicle in "The Darling of Paris" based on Hugo's Hunchback of Notre Dame, in which she emoted in the part of the gypsy Esmeralda. Audiences weren't told that a few changes had been made to the plot, notably that Quasimodo who rescues her from torture was no longer a hunchback but a handsome French knight. Anything could happen on the silver screen!

One of the reasons for updating or modifying traditional plots was that there was often more than one version of a story going the rounds, so audiences had to be persuaded to choose. Theda Bara's "East Lynne" was competing with the recent Will Barker's production of the same story, while "Romeo and Juliet" vied with the Metro version starring Beverly

Bayne and Francis X. Bushman. Also available was Mary Pickford's "Esmeralda" while Pauline Frederick appeared in "Sapho," which the Whig critic thought "was handled in a masterly fashion" and he was especially impressed by the depictions of life in Paris which "were presented with a realism and effect that were positively startling." The I.S.N. also praised it but pointed out that the ending had been changed so that Miss Frededick becomes "a repentant woman conquered by the power of love who enters a convent to expiate her past offences." The Whig critic thought that despite the changes the moral of the original was retained while agreeing with his fellow critic that "much of the sordidness (had been) removed." So Miss Bara hadn't things all her own way and had to work hard to retain her popularity. The general reaction of the local critics was that she achieved that by a combination of a pleasant personality and average acting talents and none of them made any direct or detrimental references to her vamping reputation. Whether any of Belfast's young ladies adopted her dark eye make-up and slinky walk is not reported.

Another name which appeared regularly on the bill boards was Marguerite Clarke, whose personality and films were at the opposite end of the spectrum from Miss Bara's. She was one of Zukor's new faces whom he had seen on Broadway and signed to a three year contract. Being a Famous Players star, all her films reached local audiences via the Imperial. Photographs and stills indicate that she was an attractive and petite young lady with large beguiling dark eyes and a mass of chestnut hair. She had real talent and quickly realised that films needed a less flamboyant acting style than the stage. Her bubbly personality made her a strong competitor for a time to Mary Pickford and she was certainly very popular with Belfast audiences. Her films were usually light hearted romantic comedies and included a number of fairy tales like "The Goose Girl," "The Seven Swans," but most famously "Snow White" which was the main attraction in the Imperial just before Christmas 1917. When that film had been shown earlier in the year in Kansas City the audience included a young lad watching his first full length feature and the memory of that experience stayed with him into adult life. His name was Walt Disney (see page 219).

The showing in the Imperial didn't inspire any local animators but the appearance of the "adorable" (I.S.N.) leading lady was certainly widely welcomed. The News Letter critic praised her "daintyness" and mentioned the excitement the film caused, as many parents brought their children to see it. Her films had begun arriving in mid 1915 with "The Crucible," a story about a girl who runs away from a reform school and finds romance. There was no immediate response and indeed one of the papers referred to her erroneously as Margaret. But "The Goose Girl" proved a big success a month later and was followed by "Of Mice and Men," described as a romance of the Old South, "Out of the Drifts," a romance of the Alps, "Molly Make - Believe," about a country girl who finds romance in the town, "Silks and Satins" in which she played a dual role, "The Fortunes of Fifi," about a girl finding romance in the theatre in Paris during the Napoleonic era, and then a series about the romantic adventures of a flapper called Babs beginning with "Bab's Diary," which the Irish News described as "charming."

With all that romance in the air it is clear that her appeal was mainly to women but critics at the time noted that her beauty and natural charm also intrigued the men, so her fan base was quite wide. How wide can be gauged from the fact that one of her comedies

"Seven Sisters" was even shown in the C.P.A. The aura of innocent romance that surrounded her personality didn't prevent her tackling at least one serious story, "The Pretty Sister of Jose," which was described in the advertising as "a tragic romance of Old Spain." Knowing what her audiences expected exhibitors were offered an alternative happy ending. Which ending was projected in the Imperial is not recorded but seeing that the film was shown near Christmas 1916 one can guess that it was the happy one. The film is surprising also in that it was shot on location in Southern California to take advantage of the scenery around the historic Missions and because Miss Clarke, like many Broadway actresses of the period, was quite reluctant to travel westward. She insisted that most of her films were made in and around New York.

Around the same time there was a young actor called Douglas Fairbanks (real name Ulman) making a name for himself on Broadway. He had been approached by a representative of Triangle Films and persuaded to sign a three year film contract. His films began filtering into Belfast from late 1916 via the Imperial, before appearing across the city. The Clonard was quick to realise their appeal and began presenting them regularly, referring to Fairbanks himself as "America's Whirlwind Smiler." The earliest, such as "The Lamb," "His Picture in the Paper," "Facing the Music," "The Americano," were comedy action productions and Fairbanks came across as an athletic fighting hero of the old type, laughing at danger and defending imperilled heroines. Every young man or boy who went to the cinema to be thrilled saw himself as a Douglas Fairbanks. The success of the films was helped by the zesty subtitles written by Anita Loos, whom some regard as the originator of the wisecrack, and by the hero's competent acting skills. In April 1917 the Telegraph critic could refer to him as "that gifted film actor" while some time later the I.S.N. commented on his increasing popularity with the Belfast public. His public stature was to increase further when he joined with D.W.Griffith, Charlie Chaplin and Mary Pickford in February 1919 to set up United Artists to release their own films, and a year later when he married the queen of the screen herself, Mary Pickford. Audiences were spoiled for choice and that choice was informed mainly by the stars in the films because their names indicated what they might expect. The range was wide, extending through the exotics of Bara, the heavy emotions of Pauline Frederick and Olga Petrova, the outdoor exploits of W.S.Hart, the delightful charm and humour of Marguerite Clarke and Alma Taylor, the heroics of Fairbanks, the humour of Chaplin, the artistry of Lilian Gish (a delightful and accomplished actress according to the Whig critic), and the appeal of Mary Pickford.

But everything wasn't as perfect as it seemed in cinema paradise. In contrast to the building activity of the year just past, 1917 was a year of entrenchment for the cinema industry. There were those who argued that the city was approaching cinematic saturation level and now had sufficient halls and seating for its size. As evidence they pointed to the closure of the Shaftesbury Pictoria and the Kinema House which they put down to the result of increasing competition for an economic share of the audience. The entertainment tax introduced in May 1916 has been blamed for cinema closures at the time, but even though money was scarce it's difficult to see how increases in seat prices of one to three pennies could have been that crippling unless the cinema was already operating at the limit of profitability. The Pictoria just faded away like an old soldier early in the year, and maybe the tax did play a part in that but it is more difficult to explain the demise of the Kinema House. From all accounts it was a comfortable and well run hall with an excellent location near the main railway station and with easy access to the tramways. Yet there must have been worries expressed about a drop in audience numbers - maybe Mr George couldn't get the quality films he wanted - because the Irish News critic, most unusually, mentioned that he detected an increase in numbers during May.

There were other hints that audiences were shrinking. In early July the Royal Cinema announced that it was reducing prices and that in future all seats would cost only sixpence, including entertainment tax. It was pointed out to the public that queuing was no longer a problem because with such a large building there were always seats available and furthermore that patrons could be sure of seeing the best pictures, perfectly projected in a perfectly ventilated hall. The paramount claim was that no other cinema in Ireland gave such good value. The Picture House also faced a similar situation and some time later, in a change of policy, advertised their first serial, a detective thriller called "Jimmy Hope" to attract more patronage. The Imperial with its Paramount releases and its access to the quality products and top stars of Famous Players - Lasky, and the Panopticon guided by the canny Fred Stewart dominated the business. In contrast Alfred George obviously found no improvement in his situation, so he threw in the towel and moved sidewards to become the manager of the Crumlin picture house. The last adverts for the Kinema House appeared in the papers at the end of July but it is not quite clear exactly when the cinema closed its doors. What is certain is that by February 1919 plans had been passed to convert the building to a garage for the Stanley Motor Company. In 1954 it was converted again to shops, one of which was leased by the Gestetner Company, while from 1970 it was occupied by an amusement arcade. Today it is occupied by a car rental firm. The Royal Cinema wasn't happy with the results of its experiment and after only three months announced that in response to "many requests" from its patrons it was introducing a new pricing system as follows: the front parterre consisting of six rows, 5d; the middle parterre of twelve rows, 8d; the back parterre of four rows, one shilling and three pence; and the balcony, 8d. Prominently displayed in the foyer was a notice pointing out that those prices included the entertainment tax of one penny in the front and middle parterre, two pence in the balcony and three pence in the back parterre.

Despite those developments not everyone agreed that the city couldn't support more cinemas, especially a group of businessmen in East Belfast who formed a company with Thomas McAdam as director with the aim of building a new cinema, the Popular, on the lower Newtownards Road. Mr McAdam was well known in sporting circles especially as a director of Glentoran football club and was most enthusiastic about the project. He promised that the new cinema would be "the Pride of Ballymacarrett" and as a first step in that direction he acquired the services, as manager, of P.J.Hogan who had recently shown his abilities by getting the Clonard and the Duncairn off to good starts. Thomas Walker, former musical director at the Empire, was hired to direct the six piece orchestra, always an important element in the success of a cinema. The architect was F.M. Shaw, a new name in local cinema design. His plans were submitted to the Surveyor's office on 12th July 1916 but problems with the design and the materials involved delayed approval so that the building didn't open until Monday 29th October 1917. The site extended from 49 to 55 along the lower Newtownards Road near Bridge End, between Keenan Street and Young's Row. It was an inner city location and the cinema was meant to serve a populous working class district, which included Unionist and Nationalist neighbourhoods.

The owners wanted an efficient structure without any frills and Mr Shaw gave them a compact red brick building with a bright attractive faience frontage. The overall concept was traditional and uninspired, and the interior, while functional, held no real design or decorative surprises. The main entrance from the Newtownards Road led into a circular foyer with a terrazzo floor. To the left of the paybox one went up a few steps into the auditorium which held about 730 seats. The back stalls had comfortable tip - up seats unlike the pit at the front which had "polished seating of the latest kind" (I.S.N.) which was a polite way of indicating wooden benches. The pit had its own access from Keenan Street and the pit area was securely separated from the stalls. To the right of the paybox stairs led up to the balcony with its 175 seats. What luxury there was was concentrated in the balcony with its upholstered tip - up seats including some "cosy corner settees," protective plush curtains along the back to reduce draughts, carpet underfoot and an emergency exit leading down fireproofed stairs to Young's Row. The heating was installed by the Musgrave Company and indeed all the work was done by local firms. Mr Hogan, a former projectionist, applied his expertise to the projection, seeing that the best Gaumont projectors were installed and having the screen so aligned that flicker and eyestrain wouldn't be a problem. Below the screen was a stage with two dressing rooms for live acts, and of course an orchestra space. Essentially basic as it was, the Popular was heaven to the local population. There were two shows each evening at 6:50 and 9:00pm and charges were moderate at 2 and 1\2 pence for the pit, 5d for the stalls and 8d for the luxury of the balcony.

The first show consisted of "The Ploughshare" an Edison drama set in the Old South, plus Billy West, advertised as "Charlie Chaplin's double" in "Back Stage." Comedies and Westerns became the staple fare but in his three year stint as manager (he departed in November 1920 to emigrate to Australia and was replaced by John Greenwood) Mr Hogan also presented some above average films including, "The Eternal Question" with Olga Petrova, "The Iron Hand" with Hubert Bosworth, "The White Raven" starring Ethel Barrymore, Pauline Frederick in "Paid in Full," and not least in May 1920 the first Tarzan adventure, "Tarzan of the Apes" with Elmo Lincoln which the I.S.N. insisted was "a marvellous production which should not be missed." To them he added exciting serials like "The Secret Kingdom" with Arline Pretty, and "The Red Ace" with the popular Marie Walcamp. The audiences loved them and often expressed their enthusiasm noisily. On such occasions it was only the films that were silent!

But it would be unfair to dismiss the Popular merely as a place of noise and tumult because it also had a strong family atmosphere and it was not unusual, unlike today, to find whole families there together for a night out. People identified strongly with their local cinema which was not only part of the physical landscape but of their social landscape like their church hall, school, public houses and shops. In those days before cars most working people didn't travel too far for entertainment so a local cinema could prosper without showing first run films as long as it supplied good entertainment in a friendly atmosphere.

Many cinema managers still defined entertainment as involving live artistes, thus no one was surprised when the new Popular was seen to include a stage and dressing rooms in its structure, and for a time described itself as a house for film and variety.

Live entertainment was a vestige of the days of music hall where the cinema had its beginnings and across the city singers, dancers and novelty acts continued to appear on stage in conjunction with films, notably in the Alhambra, Central, Coliseum, Duncairn and Clonard. When a new manager was appointed to the Clonard in early 1917 he decided to give greater emphasis to live entertainment in his programmes, a move welcomed by the Irish News critic who suggested that it gave some relief from the "monotony" of an all film evening. Unfortunately Mr Irvine soon found himself in court accused of not having the requisite amusement licence. His lawyer explained that due to his youth and inexperience he had been unaware of that requirement but on being informed he had immediately applied for one. The judge, actually or metaphorically, looked over his glasses, accepted the explanation, and granted the licence, but reluctantly. He felt there were quite enough places for such entertainments already available in the city, and complained how every wall space was covered by posters advertising them. Mr Irvine, undeterred, decided that improvements were needed. He began by having the cinema completely redecorated using local craftsmen. The main work was undertaken by Maurice Sullivan of the Falls Road who produced what the Irish News described as "an imposing and chaste design" consisting of tapestry supplied by J.F.Magill of North Street on a black background. Plasterwork was completed by Charles Breen of the Kashmir Road while the electrics were brought up to date by the Curran Bros. of Kent Street. The cinema reopened on 30th July with packed audiences and the proceeds of the first day were given to the Mater Infirmorum Hospital. It was intended as a new beginning and Mr Irvine lived up to his promise.

The advertisements soon advised the public to come to the Clonard "where the best is screened and staged." He presented Dervaux a female impersonator from London, who amazed the Clonard audiences with his magnificent gowns. That was an improvement on an earlier act, a Dancing Bushman from Central Africa (?) who was reputed to be one hundred years old. Bob Robinson brought down the house with his Chaplin impersonations and there were appearances by Irish and local artistes like singers William Johnson and child star May King, when the cinema rang with the sounds of Irish dancing, music and songs. But his most unusual decision was to present a series of stage plays in conjunction with the films. Plays were performed before enthusiastic audiences by the Celtic Players, a group that included R.H.McCandless, the Ulster Players who presented "Thompson in Tir-na Og" and "Ireland First," and the Lamh Dherg Players in "The Matchmaker."

Celluloid was not neglected and the local plays were accompanied by films featuring the top names of the day, including Chaplin, W.S.Hart, Mary Miles Minter presented as a rival to Mary Pickford, Tyrone Power, Douglas Fairbanks in "The Good Bad Man" a Western in which he appeared as a Robin Hood type outlaw, and "Facing the Music," a comedy which also starred another up-and-coming actress, Bessie Love. Also prominent were Norma Talmadge, Elizabeth Risdon and "the Queen of Dramatic Art" herself, the indestructible Sarah Barnhardt in a superior war film called "Mothers of France." When it was released in America in March 1917 the critic of the New York Times commented that "it atones for most of the sins of the movies" and when it was shown in the Imperial two months later the local critics tended to agree with that assessment. The Irish News critic welcomed its arrival in the Clonard, praised its theme as "most inspiring," urged local audiences to see it and drew attention to the scenes of actual warfare it contained, including a glimpse of the damaged Rheims Cathedral.

The same critic was very supportive of what he saw as Mr Irvine's efforts to bring quality material to the local Falls Road area. He recognised that people didn't travel far for their entertainments and that films already screened downtown or elsewhere in the city could still draw crowds when shown in the local cinemas like the Clonard, or, he could have added, the Duncairn, the Popular, the Picturedrome and others. The Clonard had in its short existence not only become an integral part of social life on the Falls but an instrument of its Nationalist cultural identity in its choice of Irish (or, some would argue, pseudo-Irish) material, whether it be the films of Sydney Olcott, the output of the Film Company of Ireland, the Irish-American films from Edison, Vitagraph, Triangle, Famous Players-Lasky and others, the carefully chosen newsreel snippets, and the local stage presentations. It had become a Picture Palace with attitude.

An interesting aspect of 1917 was the relatively large number of Shakespeare related films that were shown. The year before had been the tercentenary of Shakespeare's death and that had concentrated some film makers' minds here and in California on his plays. Polls taken of managers at the time indicate that they were not too keen on Shakespeare films because they rarely did well at the box office. Some put that down to the lack of sound and asked what is the point of Shakespeare if one cannot hear his poetic dialogue. You didn't need the mellifluous tones of Olivier, Burton or Gielgud to make a silent Shakespeare. The emphasis was on the plot line though important speeches were usually interpolated as titles. The managers of the poorer cinemas complained that many of their patrons found that technique boring because they couldn't read the titles and as far as they were concerned they only held up the action. But such was the eminence of the Bard that his plays continued to be filmed and there were always managers willing to risk presenting them, if only to emphasis the cinema's educational virtues. Such men included Fred Stewart, Alfred George, W.J.Hogan and the management of the Royal Cinema with its august theatrical connections.

The most prestigious project of the period was the filming of "Macbeth" by D.W.Griffith for Triangle. He persuaded Sir Herbert Beerbaum Tree to come to America and take the main part. At the time Griffith was still involved with "Intolerance" so Macbeth was actually written and directed by John Emerson though under Griffith's general supervision. The approach was to be visual, opening up the plot with duels and battles but keeping to the spirit of the original. Production values were high and large expensive sets were built e.g. the electrical effects in the witches' cave cost over $10,000. Sir H.Tree was overwhelmed on arrival with his reception in California which included cowboy outriders firing their guns in the air. He got on well with his director and adapted quickly to "this strange new art" as he called it. The film ran to six reels and on release in the U.S. the critics praised it, but it was largely ignored by the public. Professionals shook their heads and pointed to the play's dire reputation in theatrical circles but others put its poor showing down to the lack of sophistication of the American audiences. To widespread surprise the same thing happened in London. Undeterred Mr Hogan brought it to the Duncairn in January 1917 and it must have performed well financially because it quickly reappeared in the Kinema House. From comments made at the time there was obviously much in it that appealed to the general public, like the eeriness of the witches' cave with its mysterious gloom and floating phantoms, the impressively frightening ghost of Banquo, the moving wood of Birnam, the battle scenes and of course the acting of Tree, with Constance Collier as a very convincing Lady Macbeth. Not to be outdone Fred Stewart engaged "The Merchant of Venice" for the Panopticon in February. As a film it contrasted in many ways with "Macbeth." It was an English production running to five reels and starring Matheson Lang as Shylock, a part he had made famous on the stage. When his company was presenting the play at the St James Theatre, arrangements had been made for them to travel with their scenery to the Broadwest film studio at Walthamstow where the play was photographed. The technique used was old - fashioned and static with no attempt made to open up or adapt the play for the camera, yet when it was released it proved a popular and financial success. It was probably that fact which drew it to Mr Stewart's attention.

In April another favourite, "Romeo and Juliet," was presented in the Royal Cinema. Actually, as already mentioned, two versions were available, a much praised one from Metro starring Francis X. Bushman, and a Fox version starring Theda Bara made at the same time as the above. The Royal Cinema went for the Fox version, probably because of the high profile of Miss Bara. Like so many silents, the film has disappeared so it is difficult to assess her performance though, as already mentioned, the I.S.N. critic was quite impressed. The film must have done well because only two months later Shakespeare returned to the same venue though in the very different guise of "A Modern Taming of the Shrew" produced by the Triangle Company and starring Enid Markey. She played a spoiled New York society beauty who travels to Alaska where she meets her nemesis, another New Yorker who is seeking the natural life. After some rough handling during which she is kidnapped and forcibly married she succumbs to his charms and they return to the Big Apple to raise a family. The Shakespeare cycle continued into the following year when the Crumlin showed "Macbeth" and the Willowfield presented "The Merchant of Venice." Obviously some of the Belfast managers agreed with a critic of the day who claimed that even those who go to the cinema "for amusement" appreciate Shakespeare if given a chance.

While managers worried about the extent of the audiences in their halls others outside the film business were more worried about the content of what was being shown therein. In September 1916 a report in the local papers quoted a naturalist called John Burroughs who suggested that moving pictures impaired people's brain power. Most critics of the medium didn't go that far but there was unease expressed about the effect of continued exposure to films, especially on the young. Research indicated that many young people were attending cinemas on a regular basis, often twice or more times per week. It was suggested that such behaviour involving long hours in a darkened environment could result in dangers to their physical and spiritual well being. Also, as one judge put it, they were being educated "in the wrong way," which was a reference to the so called "crook" films which many people thought glamorised wrong - doers, and showed young people details of how to commit burglary and other crimes. Parents worried about the impact of depictions of violence A writer in the Telegraph, who obviously enjoyed the cinema, described how he had taken his wife and three children to a suburban cinema (unnamed) and for one shilling they had a very enjoyable few hours with tea and biscuits plus a programme of films which contained lots of shooting, a murder, a hanging and a suicide. The final film was a comedy about a young lad who comes into possession of a box of tools and immediately sets out to commit all kinds of silly mischief with them. Finally he runs outdoors with a saw and cuts the head off a woman sleeping on a bench nearby. Now, argued the writer, adults would realise that the figure was a dummy but a young person may not. What, he supposed, if he went home and tried to do the same to his baby sister. Films themselves, he admitted, were perishable and after a time the scored and scratched negatives usually ended up "in smoke" but he could only wonder what impact they left on the minds of the younger generation. One may ponder in passing what he would have made of "The Texas Chain Saw Massacre" (d. Tobe Hooper, 1974), a film which gave new meaning to the term director's "cut."

The implication behind such remarks was that stricter censorship was needed. Not everyone agreed and, in an editorial, the Irish News pointed out that since the introduction of censorship there had been no real problems with the films shown in the city, though that fact didn't prevent criticisms bubbling up. Some argued that the voluntary system of censorship in operation wasn't strict enough and that many major films were released without being submitted for vetting, films like "From the Manger to the Cross," "Intolerance," and "Civilisation." Others argued that those films were not immoral in content or ignoble in concept but they breached one of the prohibitions of the censorship guidelines in that they presented actors playing a living, breathing Christ. That fact alone outraged many people, some of whom already, for religious reasons, didn't approve of the cinema in any form. Others criticised the places where the films were shown, especially those in working class districts, for being unhygienic and germ - filled, and expressed worries about what could happen to children sitting without proper supervision in darkened halls for hours on end. Some children, they suggested, were so desperate to go to the pictures that they stole pennies for that purpose. In July 1917 the St Vincent de Paul Society, a much respected and responsible charity that undertook good work among the poor, held a debate on "Cinema and the Young" in which those and similar objections were aired. The discussions so incensed one observer that he wrote a letter to the Irish News headed "In Defence of the Cinema." He described how one speaker at the conference boasted that he had never entered a cinema during his lifetime but that it annoyed him to see "the rising generation drifting to desolation after shadows and nonsense," while another condemned cinema going as "a waste of money and, what was worse, a waste of time." The letter writer pointed out that cinema going was a pastime that "the majority of respectable citizens approved of" so he found such ill - informed criticisms to be of little use, and asked if readers of the newspaper were actually expected to take such "vaporings" seriously. He admitted that the topic posed certain problems but insisted that they would never be solved by "the vehement denunciations of a few unbalanced enthusiasts." He implied that a detached and balanced investigation was needed to ascertain the facts and thereby highlight any problems that required remedies. And, strangely enough, that is exactly what happened.

The leaders of the film business felt that such criticisms voiced by a vocal and literate minority could result in government censorship, a situation they did not relish. Thus it was that in late November 1916 the National Council of Public Morals, which had a branch in Belfast, received a letter from the Cinematograph Trade Council representing the Cinematograph Exhibitors Association of Gt. Britain and Ireland, the Incorporated Association of Kinematograph Manufacturers Ltd. and the Kinematograph Renters of Gt. Britain and Ireland, that is, the main branches of the industry, asking them to undertake an inquiry into the physical, social, moral and educational influence of the cinema, with special reference to young people. The Council agreed on condition that there would be no interference from either the film trade or the government. A commission of twenty - five persons, male and female, was appointed consisting of eminent clergy, educationalists, professional teachers, child experts, the chief censor (T.P.O'Connor M.P.) and expert members of the film trade. They began taking evidence on 8th January 1917 and finished on 19th July. A very wide range of witnesses was interviewed including prominent ecclesiastics, the chief censor, chief constables, prominent film makers like Cecil Hepworth, teachers, eye doctors, representatives of organizations like the Y.M.C.A. with experience of film shows, schoolboys and girls who attended film shows regularly, and even spokesmen for the bill posters and the cinema musicians. The report regretted that some of those who were most vociferous in their criticisms of the medium refused to appear to back up their claims.

All aspects of the subject were examined: its history, its rapid growth and widespread acceptance, the films themselves, their content and their influence on young people, the strengths and weaknesses of the present system of censorship, the medical and health factors resulting from a darkened environment where viewers could be subjected to flickering, glare and such, the quality or otherwise of the projection, the layout of cinemas, the number of attendants needed for proper supervision and the influence of the music played at the shows. The result was a comprehensive and detailed description of the state of cinema going in the British Isles at the time. Every facet of the cinema going habit was investigated and suggestions made about changes or improvements where necessary. The report ran to nearly 400 pages and while the language is very formal and highly moral in places it is required reading for anyone interested in the silent cinema. Fred Stewart, Will White, P.J.Hogan and the other Belfast managers must have read it with some trepidation wondering what new regulations they might soon have to contend with. They probably would have agreed wholeheartedly with the statement of one of the witnesses that the cinema was already faced with more regulations and restraints that any other form of popular amusement.

The report recognised that the film industry formed a highly organised and sophisticated system in which producers, renters, and exhibitors were interconnected by a network of financial and technical communications involving mainly steamships at sea and steam trains on land. Belfast for example received its films by train from Dublin and by train and boat from London and Liverpool. In the Br. Isles the system serviced 4,500 cinemas which employed over 80,000 workers and projected about 70,000,000 feet of celluloid every week to millions of people of all ages and backgrounds. The report calculated that over half the population visited cinemas every week and drew special attention to the fact that its appeal was to all classes and all groups including children. In fact it was the only form of popular amusement that regularly produced material suitable for children. Added to that was its cheapness, with over 50% of patrons occupying seats costing 3d or less and as the prices of the seats decreased the number of children attending increased. The presence of such large numbers of children on a regular basis was seen as a matter of concern and was in itself advanced as sufficient cause for the present inquiry. Before the publication of the report there were rumours that the Government favoured banning children entirely from cinemas and the Cinematograph Exhibitors' Association had warned its members, including those in Belfast, that such a decision would result in many cinema closures and would have to be resisted. As it turned out such scare mongering was unnecessary.

To the surprise of many the report, published in mid 1917, did not condemn the cinema but had much to say in its favour. Typical were the comments of Bishop Welldon, the Dean of Manchester, who stated that "I cannot at all associate myself with the general condemnations of the cinemas." He praised the educational advantages of films and as an example recalled the scenes of the Delhi Durbar, noting that anyone who had been there wouldn't have seen as much of it as the cinema audiences did. Also, he continued, sitting in a cinema was much better for people than being in a public house. Other witnesses agreed that cinema going had reduced the incidence of drunkenness, while others showed how the opening of a local cinema reduced hooliganism because instead of roaming the streets in the evening young people went to the pictures. People who worked among the poor emphasised that the cinema was the main relaxation and recreation of the poor, especially poor children. One experienced social worker said that "to be able to make the poor, pinched - faced, half clad and half nourished boys and girls in crowded slums in the cities forget their pain and misery and their sad lot is a great thing and the pictures do it." A number of witnesses were at pains to put the cinema in a positive social context and emphasised its role in bringing relief from the pressures of poverty and in helping to reduce discord in the mean streets. One witness felt that part of the remedy was for the government to take steps to relieve poverty and to improve the standard of housing available to workers.

The Council never forgot that the main raison d'etre of the whole exercise was to confront the problem of censorship. There was no disagreement about the need for some kind of control, but there was a lively discission about what kind of censorship was appropriate. The Trade felt that the voluntary method already in operation was sufficient while others, including the then Home Secretary Herbert Samuel, felt that a compulsory official (i.e. government) system would be better. The President of the Board of Film Censors T.P.O'Connor and one of the assistant censors had been questioned at length about the present system. It was recalled that that the Board was established relatively recently, in 1912, and that Mr Redford was appointed the first President, taking up his duties on 1st January 1913. He was chosen and approached because it was felt that his experience with the Lord Chamberlain's office suited him for the job. Thus in a sense film censorship was an extension of theatre control despite the fact, emphasised by the report, that films were a very different medium. When Mr Redford undertook his duties there were two main guidelines - no nudity and no depictions of the living Christ. Over the following two years those prohibitions increased to forty three, covering details of sexual relations, female dress, the depiction of violence and crimes, the need to show proper respect for religions and religious beliefs, no criticisms of prominent citizens both here and abroad, and no criticisms of army personnel.

When Mr Redford died in November 1916 the position was offered to T.P.O'Connor M.P. who took up his duties on 1st January 1917. He described how he had four assistant censors none of whom had any connection with the film business, but all were men of experience and high character. One had left to join the army and he had replaced him with a person of equally high moral character whom he had known and respected for many years, a "good Irish Catholic." The censors worked in a small room in central London, which contained two projectors with two men assigned to each film. If the two couldn't agree about the merits of a scene or a film then the four examined it together. If they couldn't agree then the matter was passed to Mr O'Connor. He was guided by the principles mentioned above but his approach was flexible and he was willing to discuss any problems with the producers so that offensive material could be removed. When he was finally satisfied, the film was given a certificate, either a "U" suitable for all including children, or "A" suitable for adults only. He acknowledged that the system was voluntary but the Trade had proved to be very co - operative and about 97% of films released passed through the Board of Censors.

It was noted however that Mr Samuel, the Home Secretary, believed there was a connection between cinema attendance and juvenile crime and the Inquiry wanted to pursue that line. In his interview on the subject Roderick Ross, the Chief Constable of Edinburgh, described a situation that the citizens of many cities including Belfast were familiar with. The cinema, he declared, had proved very popular with all classes of society and there were now picture houses on the main roads and in every district, surrounded most evenings by long queues. He put its popularity down to the fact that it was "an educative, morally healthy and pleasure giving entertainment...given at a price within the reach of all." He recognised its part in reducing rowdyism and drunkenness, but admitted there were critics. On a few occasions he had had complaints of indecency in some films but on investigation his officers had found nothing that was illegal though he felt that such scenes should be eliminated. He accepted that some critics insisted that films caused juvenile crime by showing methods of burglary and such, or that children could be driven to theft to get money to go to the pictures. In his experience and in that of his officers they had never come across a case that indicated a direct link between a juvenile offence and the cinema. However, he felt that certain crimes and criminal types should not be presented on screen, but while supporting the principle of censorship he emphasised that the cinema "has had little or no effect on the crimes committed by children and young persons." The Commission sent copies of his statement by letter to all the Chief Constables in the Br. Isles and asked them for their comments. One hundred and eighteen replied and the majority of them agreed with Mr Ross that some form of censorship was needed but that the cinema was not a source of crime.

There were three replies from Ireland, from Dublin, Cork and Derry. The Chief Commissioner of Police writing from Dublin Castle felt that certain crime films could excite "the imitative propensities" of young people but noted that such films usually showed the evildoers being caught and punished which must have a "deterrent effect." Generally he believed that the cinema was "a source of much innocent amusement" which also had a great educative potential. D.I. Walsh of Cork had some reservations but in the main regarded the pictures as "a very harmless form of amusement for the working classes and others who have not the money...to go to the theatre." Added to that was his belief that "the benefit they confer outweighs any harm they may do." The message from D.I.Ryan in Derry was similar, though he also favoured a strict censorship. Unfortunately there is no record of a reply from Belfast. It is unlikely that the matter was ignored or overlooked so maybe the Chief Constable agreed with the letter or the police just didn't regard the cinema as a cradle of crime or a cause for concern.

Certainly the evidence collected suggested that many of the criticisms usually put forward were highly exaggerated. Despite that the Inquiry came down on the side of those who favoured an official government - backed compulsory form of censorship. They complemented that decision with comments that praised Mr O'Connor and his assistants for the work they were doing and they admitted that the Trade had good arguments when it suggested that Government censorship, probably by civil servants, could become too rigid, unimaginative, and out of touch with popular taste and artistic developments. They also pointed out that local authorities were often quite jealous of their rights to influence what was shown in their areas, a fact that Belfast managers were to be made very much aware of in the years to come. The favourable tone of the report certainly blunted the arguments of those who wanted to exercise excessive control over the new medium. Other factors conspired to insure the continuance of the status quo. Mr Samuel was replaced by Sir George Cave who was not keen to get the Home Office involved in the matter. The tact, good judgement and friendly personality of T.P.O'Connor played a major part in engendering public support for the Board of Censors and the work it was doing. The worst fears of the Exhibitors were not realised and the Belfast managers could continue to sleep easily - well, reasonably easily - in their beds.

As the clock ticked into 1918 the censorship debate faded and other more pressing problems arose, especially involving scarcities due to the war. Skilled technicians like projectionists were leaving to join the forces and the supply of new films began to decline because of transport problems. Some films arrived late for Monday showings and some older favourites were reissued to fill the gaps. The Panopticon presented a series of past successes which Fred Stewart called Old Masters, which included "The Last Days of Pompeii," "Quo Vadis" billed as "the greatest picture of all time," and "A Daughter of the Gods," with the glamorous swimmer Annette Kellerman. The problems and dangers of transport were brought home cruelly on 10th October 1918 when a U-boat attacked and sank the Irish mail boat, the Leinster, sailing from Kingstown (Dun Laoghaire) to Holyhead. Two torpedoes split the ship in two with a loss of 587 lives including many women and children. A sense of shock and anger swept the whole country at what the Irish News described as a "ghastly Hun crime." A few days later scenes of the aftermath of the disaster were showing in the Panopticon under the heading "Germany's Latest Crime."

Since August the Irish Recruiting Council had been arranging a series of recruiting demonstrations in Belfast, Bangor, Newry, Portadown and other centres including even small settlements like Cushendall, to encourage men and women to volunteer because "your fellow Irishmen at the front need you." The Belfast demonstration took place at the City Hall where three military bands paraded and the crowds were harangued with patriotic speeches often interrupted by loud cheering. The machines of war so familiar on the cinema screens were there to be seen. Armoured cars manoeuvred while aeroplanes flew overhead firing rockets and dropping leaflets. Overwhelmed by all the propaganda a group of potential recruits marched to the Grand Central Hotel to volunteer and there they were warmly welcomed by the Lord Mayor who was somewhat disappointed by the turnout, and complained about those men still "lurking behind counters doing the work of women they should be out defending." Unsurprisingly the Recruiting Council immediately took advantage of the surge of anti - German feeling following the Leinster disaster to increase the calls for volunteers.

At the same time the Irish News in an editorial rightly predicted that Peace was within Sight, though that didn't relieve the immediate situation. Flour was in short supply and people were asked to reduce their intake of bread, while meat, butter and margarine were rationed. There were calls also for the collection of waste paper which was needed for recycling but, above all, there were worries about the increasing shortage of domestic coal supplies. The Coal Controller called for economies in the use of heat and light with the aim of making savings of 25% in the use of coal. In September a special meeting of the Council took place in the City Hall to discuss Belfast's response to the problem. It patriotically called on all citizens to co-operate and suggested that the early closing of businesses would be a useful start in saving power. It was suggested that shops should close at 6:30p.m. on weekdays and 8:00p.m. on Saturdays; public houses at 9:00; and places of entertainment to open only between 6:30 and 10:00 p.m.

Jeremiah MacCavana, until recently the manager of the Central, but now the chairman of the Belfast and North of Ireland Cinematograph Exhibitioner's Association, complained in a letter to the newspapers that there had been no prior consultation about the matter, that the opening hours suggested for cinemas were not financially viable and, if applied rigorously, would result in widespread closures. He called for a meeting to discuss the matter. He received much public support from those who pointed out that picture houses were "communal parlours," as one letter writer put it, where thousands gathered rather than sitting at separate fires using separate lights. In that way cinemas surely represented a saving of power. Also it was argued that picture houses were "a boon to soldiers, sailors, tired and war - weary people." There was also the fact that they offered a source of entertainment and education for the young and that they were an important means of propaganda and information. That latter fact was verified on Tuesday 6th August when a special message from the Prime Minister to the population was read out in all cinemas, appealing to all citizens to stand firm and to do everything in their power to help win the war. Also, as already mentioned, the official newsreels continued to give a very upbeat and optimistic view of the war. Typical was "With the Irish Regiments in France" which caused a great stir in the city when it was widely shown during September and October. Made by David Frame, it ran for thirty minutes, showing Irish soldiers at the front or relaxing behind the lines. The Irish News emphasised that it had special local interest whether the scenes shown had been filmed at base camp, in billets, in the trenches or during a thrilling dash "over the top." The photography was so clear that some members of the audience recognised relatives and friends.

The special social position of cinemas was recognised by the authorities so they remained open to inform and, above all, to entertain the populace. Crowds flocked to the Imperial to see W.S.Hart in an exciting Western "Wolf Larsen" or Wallace Reid in "The Hostage" or Mary Pickford in "Romance of the Redwoods"; to the Lyceum to enjoy William Farnum in a Western "The End of the Trail," or Marguerite Clarke in a new version of the ever popular "Uncle Tom's Cabin" in which she played the two parts of Little Eva and Topsy: or to the Picture House to enjoy Lillian Gish in "Diane of the Follies." That film was much commented upon at the time because it revealed a completely different Lillian Gish playing an outgoing chorus girl who abandons her husband and child for the excitement of the musical theatre. She admitted later that she enjoyed the experience which was so different from the "gaga-babies" as she called the sweet innocent child - women she usually played. Unfortunately the film is lost but the Whig critic relished it, praising the actress's versatility and highlighting her "clever imitation of Sarah Bernhardt."

The Panopticon, always good for thrills, pulled in the crowds with a Pearl White serial, "The Fatal Ring" and later "Sherlock Holmes," billed as the world's greatest detective. The latter was a seven - reel version starring William Gillette, complete with deerstalker, and his original London company, filmed by the Essanay company. Like the Lillian Gish film, it also has disappeared with the exception of a few stills but the Whig critic found it "as enjoyable as the play itself," which was high praise indeed. Memories of Miss Bernhardt were also rekindled when, in October, the Panopticon presented "The Lady of the Camelias" starring Clara Kimball Young whose performance the Whig found to be "impressive." Meanwhile in America the Triangle company had collapsed when D.W.Griffith, Thomas Ince and Mack Sennett withdrew from it, but those producers then made agreements with Paramount to release their films. That greatly strengthened the position of Paramount as the main source of quality films in the United States and indirectly the importance of the Imperial as Paramount's main outlet into the Belfast market.

The downtown managers realised that the Imperial was the competition to beat. The Corn Market cinema very nearly fumbled the pass when during a Saturday evening show on 7th September a fire broke out in the room where the film reels were stored. Luckily the fire - proofing contained the flames while the fire brigade was summoned and the outbreak was swiftly brought under control. There was no panic reported, and the manager, Mr McDowell, insisted there was no real danger, the only inconvenience to the audience being smoke and smell. The films were destroyed but the manager obtained a replacement set of films within fifteen minutes so that the programme could continue. That reflects well on the efficiency of the local distribution system but the incident must have been a reminder of the need for continual vigilance in handling celluloid entertainment.

As the year progressed there was rising concern at the serious recurring outbreaks of the Spanish flu in the city. All sections of the community were prone to it. At one point in June up to 100 tram drivers and conductors were ill with the symptoms and the general manager told the Council that it was a struggle to keep the system going. It was agreed that there was a need to distribute information to the public on the best methods of coping with the threat. One problem was that the causes of the disease were not fully understood. One report in the

Whig blamed it on the amount of dust in the air and called for more water carts to clean the streets. Dr. Bailey, the Medical Superintendent of Health, took a more scientific approach and advised people to stay away from large gatherings and to take quinine a few times a day as a protection. On advice, the Council closed badly hit schools across the city for a time, and Queen's University suspended lectures for a week in early November. As the disease continued to spread large business premises and picture houses were regularly inspected and disinfected. Cinema managers realised how vulnerable their large darkened halls were to infection and were aware that cinemas were being closed in other countries, but, hoped for the best. The Alhambra, ever to the fore, faced up to the problem and announced in November that the hall was fully sprayed and disinfected between shows, so it exhorted the public: Why fear the flu? come and enjoy an All Star Picture and Variety programme in Camphor Comfort. The first cinema in Belfast to show "smellies"!

During the first half of the same month the newsreels and newspaper headlines that people had been hoping for and looking forward to began to appear. "Huns in Throes of Defeat and Revolt....The German Rout.... abandoning guns and materials... resistance failing... Allied troops advancing in driving rain..... Kaiser Abdicates." On Monday 11th November news began to filter through to Belfast of the signing of the Armistice. Work immediately stopped in the mills, factories and shipyards and crowds poured into the streets to celebrate. Bands appeared and there was widespread music and singing. Colourful American, Allied and gold and green Irish flags were waving everywhere and as evening approached rockets and fireworks added to the general scenes of merriment. One reporter described a large "ring of roses" in Castle Street and how uniformed soldiers and sailors were loudly cheered wherever they went. Such was the density of the crowds at the City centre that the trams could only crawl towards their destinations.

Most of the rejoicings were good natured and heart felt but a minority took advantage of the general relaxation to engage in rowdyism. Some shop windows were broken notably Woolworth's, and a crowd broke into the Imperial Cinema and began damaging the seats, but were quickly evicted. The most serious incident happened about 12:45 pm when a group of rowdies broke into the Panopticon in High Street and began attacking the fixtures. Pictures and gas lamps were smashed and some pipes pulled from the walls causing serious gas leaks. The seats were attacked and some of them were wrenched from their moorings and carried out into High Street. Seven of them were never recovered. Some of the crowd demanded a film show, but Fred Stewart refused saying that the gas had to be made safe as he feared an explosion. He calculated that damage had been done to the value of nearly £100 but with the help of his staff had the building ready for the evening performance.

That night the face of the Albert Clock was illuminated for the first time in four years and tired crowds went home with that image of normality in their minds. They left behind a city centre that was quiet but strewn with the litter of celebration. Some practically minded officials wondered when the debris would be cleared up because the city was in the grip of a strike by street cleaners but luckily two days later the strike was settled and the workers set about the task of cleaning up. "Thank God, it's all over" was a sentiment expressed in many households that night.

CHAPTER SEVENTEEN
"Bright Goods for Drab Coloured Days"

If there were people in Belfast naive enough to believe that life would return to normal when the war ended they were quickly disabused of the idea. The true horror of what had happened over the previous four years slowly became apparent as the soldiers who had survived returned from the battlefields, many of them scarred in body or mind. But besides the visible human cost the impact of the war had also sent invisible seismic shock waves of such intensity through the social, economic and political systems that things would never be the same again. The magma of discontent was stirring just below the surface. The signs were there for those with the perspicacity to see them. There was a general feeling that after the terrible sacrifices things should somehow be better; people's aspirations were high but were to be cruelly disappointed. Instead of peace and plenty the returning warriors found a city still blighted with widespread poverty. There followed strikes and threats of strikes over low wages, working conditions and working hours, coupled with rising vocal demands for social change, while, in the background, the growing political storm winds that would soon fan the glowing embers of Home Rule to destructive flames were blowing again. So the city entered a prolonged period of disruption and uncertainty that affected all levels of the community.

It began in February 1919 with strikes in the shipyards, the electricity and gas industries which resulted in what the I.S.N. called "a fortnight of darkness." The lack of power disrupted the tramway system and affected many businesses, big and small, including the entertainment sector, forcing cinemas and theatres to close their doors. When the workers showed no sign of relenting, the army was brought in and soldiers occupied the electricity stations and gasworks. The Lord Mayor called for civilian volunteers to help and soon the strike collapsed. In retrospect those two weeks of physical darkness can now be seen as an ominous augury of a terrible darkness of the mind that was descending on the city. The cinema managers had to get used to closed doors and to the army on the streets. By 1920 the situation had further deteriorated. A strike by coal handlers at the docks, over the question of Sunday working, caused severe shortages of fuel in the city. Many poorer families found themselves without coal to heat their homes against the winter cold. An irate citizen wrote to the Irish News describing one such family of shivering children. Their embittered father, unemployed, could do nothing for them, a situation the writer found intolerable because the man in question was a veteran of the trenches. Was that, the writer asked, the nation's thanks for his sacrifice? Finally, in scenes worthy of a Chaplin film, crowds of poor people invaded Queen's Quay one Saturday morning searching for coal, and whatever fragments they could find were quickly carried away in carts, prams, buckets and bags before the police arrived and cleared the area. One observer described bare footed boys and girls scuttling about searching through piles of slack and other debris looking for a few lumps of coal.

From today's perspective that post - war period of austerity doesn't seem conducive to the establishment of new entertainment centres, but despite the depressed conditions there were optimistic business men in the city then who still felt that new cinemas were financially viable, and made plans accordingly. Their emphasis was firmly on small local cinemas. Typical was the Ligoniel - known locally as the Henhouse - which opened in 1918. It was a small converted hall, on the lines of the Melbourne off Millfield, with a totally local appeal. It didn't advertise, but depended largely on word of mouth to attract an audience to its mixture of films and variety. Because of that there is regrettably very little hard information about it and the films it showed. It added nothing of distinction to the cinematic landscape and, like the Melbourne, its existence was short lived, probably only a few years. During the disturbed and dangerous times to come it formed a welcome and safe environment which the locals could enjoy without having to leave the relative safety their own neighbourhood.

The Tivoli Picture House in Christian Place, which lay between Albert Street and Irwin street, belonged to the same category, though it was better designed and was built from scratch as a cinema. At the behest of Patrick Kelly, a spirit grocer of Irwin Street, architect W.J Moore presented plans for a long narrow building to seat 537 persons, on 2nd June 1916, which were approved by August. Unspecified delays meant that the hall wasn't opened until July 1918 and didn't begin advertising until February 1920, by which time it was well established with the local population. There were two separate shows daily at 6:45 and 8:45 with admission prices of 3d, 5d, and 8d, and special children's matinees on Mon., Thurs. and Saturdays at 3:30pm, costing only one penny. Those rather noisy shows were the source of stories about children presenting a jam jar as payment for entry. In fact the glass and stone jars of the day were recycled by the manufacturers and could be returned to the shop for a penny refund. Mr Kelly was a grocer, so he was being practical when he accepted the jars as payment. To him they were worth the one penny admittance. The Tivoli showed a popular mix of comedies, Westerns and serials along with longer films like "The Great Game," a story set in the boxing world starring Bombadier Wells, "Bonds of Honour" with Sessue Hayakawa and "The Foolish Virgin" starring Clara Kimble Young.

A major attraction was the live variety which often accompanied the films. The acts were local, and included the likes of Pat Killen, the Singing Goalkeeper or Billy Ryan, a coon (sic) comedian and dancer, or Terry Lincoln who gave a demonstration of skill with ropes and whips which was followed by a lassoing competition for boys under sixteen, the winner of which was presented with a "special medal" by the management. Amateur competitions were very popular and caused much local excitement. One such talent competition judged by the audience offered a first prize of one pound plus a week's engagement in the Tivoli, a second prize of one pound and a third prize of ten shillings, substantial amounts of money for those days. The winner Edward Brown, had his week on stage while the runner - up, James McKelvey, was also engaged for another week. A singing competition for the Championship of Ireland, no less, was a great popular success and the winner received an "impressive" cup from the management. During another week a free ballot was held every night and eight bags of coal were given away, as much appreciated as money by poor families. It may all seem rather simple and naive now but to the local families struggling to keep their heads above subsistence level a night out at the Tivoli was like a tonic, a cheap, enjoyable and sociable occasion. During the "troubles," in late June 1922, they lost that opportunity when the cinema was bombed and burned, though by December Mr Kelly had applied for and received permission to rebuild, a sure sign that the Tivoli not only met a local need but had been economically viable.

The normally astute Joe McKibbin also felt there was room for more cinemas and to that end he acquired two corner sites, on the Falls Road, and the lower Ormeau Road. As befitted a successful business man he had bought a house and settled on the upper Ormeau, so he couldn't have but noticed that the area had no local cinema. He intended to rectify that omission by building one on his new site where Agincourt Avenue joined the Ormeau Road. On the 8th February 1919 Jackson G.Smyth, the architect, submitted plans for a cinema on that site. The building was to be about 80 feet by 64 feet (approx. 24 by 18 metres) with a ground floor space for 1200 people and a balcony holding another 357 people. The plans were approved in May 1919 but the building was never erected. Why, is not clear, and following Joe's death in February 1921 the site remained undeveloped until the early 1930's when his vision was fulfilled and the Apollo cinema was constructed there, though by another entrepreneur.

The site chosen on the Falls Road was at its junction with Cupar Street, not too far from the Clonard, and was obviously aimed to compete with the latter. As early as April 1917 another architect, Norman H. Grahame of Fountain Street, submitted plans for a cinema to be raised there. The plans were for a long narrow auditorium of the type known in the U.S.A. as a "shooting gallery," about 96 feet by 21 feet (approx. 30 metres by 7 metres), to accommodate 600 persons, but for some unknown reason the building was delayed. Amended plans were submitted in July 1919 and again in early 1920. By that time, in addition to other minor

A rare early advert for The Diamond (circa 1920).

changes, a balcony seating 100 had been added and the Diamond finally took shape and opened in early 1920, an event that was ignored by the press. The Diamond was not a showy place and its first manager, J. McCann, obviously had to watch the pennies. There were only rare press advertisements, and the films shown were generally just run - of - the mill, so the elegant Clonard felt no real competition. Yet the cinema was popular with those locals who could only afford a cheap night's entertainment, and it tends to be remembered today through a haze of nostalgia and myth. Its opening in 1920 meant that the Falls Road with its large working class population, had five cinemas to choose from (six if one included the occasionally cinematic St. Mary's Hall). In contrast the Shankill Road inhabitants had only two local halls, or three if the nearby Crumlin cinema was included. The York Street area fared better with four halls though, in addition, the inhabitants would probably have claimed a fifth, the Alhambra, as "theirs." East Belfast also had five halls to choose from.

In contrast to all those, one of the most distinctive working class areas, Sandy Row, had no cinemas at all, and according to a local minister "didn't need them." From a group of cottages located along the old road to Dublin, Sandy Row had grown, through rural immigration during the 19th century, into a densely populated area characterised by parallel streets of small houses interspersed with a liberal sprinkling of mission halls, on either side of Sandy Row itself. The locals worked in the nearby textile mills, the railway yards, the shipyards, the tobacco works and the myriad small industrial units, businesses and service industries scattered throughout the area. During 1867- 68 a brewery was built between Rowland Street and Boyne Square for the Belfast and Ulster Brewing Company, and though brewing operations ceased in the eighties the imposing structure remained and continued to be called the Brewery Building. It was divided into small units occupied by offices, warehousing, and small manufacturers grouped around a central yard, at the rear of which there were stables owned by David Allen. In December 1918 those stables were the subject of an official Notice from the City Hall "Requiring the Abatement of Nuisance." The nuisance in question was the accumulation of horse manure from the stables. In the pursuance of proper sanitation the owners were required to remove the manure and keep the area clean. Someone had complained to the surveyor's office about the smell.

There was soon to be cause for another complaint but of a very different kind. Over the years the original brewhouse had been converted into the strictly non - alcoholic Emmanuel Mission Hall, but in 1918 the lease had run out. In July 1918 an application was made to the Surveyor's Office by W.J.Bourke of Botanic Avenue to convert that hall at 69A Sandy Row into a picture house, a request that was accompanied by a plan drawn up by the architect Robert Lynn of Ann Street. The plan was simple and straight - forward indicating a narrow rectangular room with a pit to accommodate 600 persons, and a stalls for 164 persons. There were no frills or extras. Approval was delayed by protests from other occupants of the building who highlighted a number of perceived problems. The first of those was the question of proper exits from the hall. Besides the main door leading directly on to Sandy Row the only other exit was through the brewery yard. The other occupants objected to the use of that route as they felt it would jeopardize the security of their goods and properties. They also knew that without that emergency exit the City Surveyor would refuse planning permission on grounds of safety. Mr Bourke, in response, was able to demonstrate that the lease gave him the right to use the route through the yard, and the gate onto Sandy Row. It is interesting that the letter to the City Surveyor clarifying the situation was signed by W.K.Gibson, later to become the managing director of the company that built the Classic cinema in Castle Lane.

The objectors then changed tack. They called a protest meeting of the occupants, which was addressed by the local minister, the Rev. Mr Higgins, Mr Jameson and others. Their theme was that the area didn't need a picture house and that the opening of one would be "detrimental to the well - being of the community." They also deplored the fact that a former mission hall should be chosen as the site for a picture house. That was the first recorded salvo in the struggle over the location of cinemas in relation to places of worship, which was to become so dominant during the Thirties. The Sandro won that first round, and deserves recognition for the fact. The City Surveyor rejected the protests, and the plans were approved at the end of September allowing the work of conversion to proceed. As word spread throughout the area there was general delight that an obvious and sorely felt social omission was about to be rectified. A local cinema was regarded by many as an essential convenience, especially for the elderly and the young who would no longer have to walk across the Boyne Bridge to the Coliseum, or down to Great Victoria Street to the Kinema House, which had recently closed anyway.

The new Sandro opened quietly early in 1919. The exact date is uncertain because, like the Diamond, the press ignored the event but by the 1st March the crowds were flocking twice nightly to separate performances at 7:00 and 9:00pm, paying 3d to occupy the wooden benches in the pit, 5d to the back stalls or 8d to the gallery. When the author first came to know the Sandro in the early 1950's it was well past its best, rather rundown and dilapidated. In the mornings, about 9:30 am, when the front doors were opened for cleaning, passersby were assailed by a distinctive parfum de cinema ancien - a heady brew of strong disinfectant, stale tobacco smoke, foul air and other indeterminate elements. It shared that fragrance with other equally decaying establishments of the period, like the Diamond on the Falls Road and the Central in Smithfield. The folk stories about the Sandro tend to lean towards an evocation of that rundown environment. Certainly the building was rough and ready but it wasn't neglected. Notes on the plans indicate that the gallery was rebuilt in 1920, and in 1926 a new stage and dressing room were installed. In November 1919 the I.S.N.'s critic referred to it as "such a bright spot these dark nights" and the following winter it was still that "comfortable rendezvous" on the Row.

What was most impressive was the range, type and quality of the films shown during its early years, described again in 1922 by the I.S.N. as "bright goods for drab coloured days." That choice was the decision of the early managers who obviously respected their audiences and worked to see that they got the best films available. The first recorded manager was the energetic Harold Buckley who held the position for over a year and a half before being succeeded by Charles H. Rogers, who moved from the Palace in Bangor to take the position. The screen may have been a whitewashed wall, though one wonders if that was really true in those early years, but the shadows that graced it were among the most popular at the time. In the first months Charlie Chaplin had audiences roaring at his antics in "Tillie's Punctured Romance," "The Floorwalker," "Easy Street," and "The Cure." Mary Pickford, Norma Talmadge and Mae Murray also appeared but the locals obviously preferred men of action. Douglas Fairbanks did his stuff in films like "A Modern Musketeer" and "Mr Fixit" but the man who appeared most often in those early years was the stern visaged W.S.Hart, in stories with names like "Blue Blazes Ramden," "Selfish Yates," "Breed of Men," and "Square Deal Sanderson." Audiences responded to his exciting Westerns, in which he usually played a loner of uncertain morality. He inevitably succumbed to the innocent charms of the heroine and under her influence went forth to restore order and justice with guns and fists. Westerns were especially popular, and another great favourite was Harry Carey, the actor who later had such an influence on John Wayne. Carey Westerns shown included "A Marked Man," "Bare Fists," "Riders of Vengeance," and "Ace in the Saddle."

Comedies abounded, including the adventures of Harold Lloyd, Buster Keaton and Charlie Chaplin, while thrillers were always welcomed. An interesting example shown in early 1921 was "The Mystery of the S.S.Olympic" advertised as taking place on "the Belfast built liner." It was in fact one of a series of Sexton Blake mysteries going the rounds then. No show was complete without a serial and the Sandro presented some fine ones, beginning, during its opening weeks, with Pearl White herself in "House of Hate," which was followed some time later by the same lady in "The Black Secret. "Other popular early serials included "The Great Gold Swindle," "The Red Ace" with Marie Walchamp and the interesting and unusual "The Master Mystery" starring Harry Houdini.

The Sandro was one of only a few cinemas in the city that showed the Houdini serial, another being the Alhambra. The cinema industry especially in the U.S.A. was voracious in its search for new talent so it was almost inevitable that Harry Houdini, the famous escape artist, would be approached and persuaded in 1918 to make a film. The result was "The Master Mystery," a serial which he made in New York. He collaborated on the script and insisted that no camera tricks were to be used but that he would extricate himself from dangerous situations by his own skills. The story involved a secret agent, played by Houdini, trying to thwart the evil plans of a wily robot called the Automaton. The serial ran to fourteen episodes and Houdini found himself in all types of dangerous - but to him familiar - predicaments, typical of which was having to free himself after being left hanging in chains over a large container of boiling acid. Seen today the robot looks far from sinister, resembling something that might have appeared in the Dandy, or a man in an unwieldy metal suit, which is actually what it finally turned out to be. Like the Sandro audiences, Jesse Lasky was impressed by what he saw and signed Houdini to make two "proper" films. The first of those was "The Grim Game" which was filmed in California and as befitted the star was full of amazing escapes. Mr Rogers who had obviously noted the positive reaction of his audiences presented it in July 1921. Its most famous sequence involved a wing - to - wing transfer by the hero but, unusually, Houdini was unable to do the stunt because he had injured his wrist in an earlier incident, so a stunt man stood in for him. The stuntman completed the manoeuvre successfully but unfortunately the two wings touched and the planes plunged earthwards as everyone held their breath. Luckily the pilots managed to separate them before they struck the ground. The cameraman had kept the camera rolling so the whole episode was recorded, and appeared uncut in the final print, with shots of Houdini edited into it.

The Sandro audiences must have felt they had got their money's worth that week, but not only that week. More thrills followed with action man Charles Hutchinson in the serial "The Whirlwind," with William Duncan in "The Silent Avenger" and other assorted heroes in "Thunderbolt Jack" and "The Call of the Jungle." The Sandro, of course, couldn't afford the really top films like "Salome" with Theda Bara, but did present "Salome v. Shenandoah" Ben Turpin's wickedly funny burlesque of that epic. In it the cross - eyed one played both John the Baptist and a Confederate spy involved in typical Keystone mayhem. Other highlights were Charlie Chaplin in "Shoulder Arms," and "Pay Day." "Garryowen" with a horse racing theme went down well, especially as it starred local girl Moyna MacGill.

There was even a special D.W.Griffith production "A Romance of Happy Valley" starring Lillian Gish and Bobby Harron, one of a series of rural stories Griffith made for Jesse Lasky. The public were promised "a human and pathetic story of life in a peaceful village" but what they got was much more interesting. It is not one of Griffith's better known films but Miss Gish herself has described it as a "little poem." It was thought to be completely lost but in the 1960's a copy turned up in Moscow which can now be seen in the Museum of Modern Art in New York, allowing scholars and film buffs to see and study it. The story is set in a small settlement in Kentucky, the state where Griffiths was born and spent his youth, and is regarded as being partly autobiographical in that he used places, scenes and incidents remembered from those early days. The theme is about youthful ambition, about a young man who leaves his sweetheart (Lillian Gish) and his home to find success in the city. That success proves elusive but meanwhile the girlfriend waits patiently at home. Lillian Gish gives one of her most natural performances, both attractive and humorous, peeking under her bed each night before retiring to see if anyone is lurking there. The scenes of village life are artfully sketched in, as when the congregation at church pray that the young man won't be led astray by the wickedness of the big city. Needless to say he does meet an urban seductress but he rejects her and remains faithful to his village sweetheart. In true Victorian fashion, despite complications caused by robbery and murder, good is finally rewarded and the lovers are happily reunited. Rural - urban migration in search of work, a positive moral outlook and the rejection of wickedness were concepts that the audience would have been familiar with and could relate to, especially those who attended the local mission halls. Some in the audience may even have contemplated the possibility that the gap between film and religion was not all that wide on occasion. What is certain is that while the Sandro may have lacked the polish of certain other local cinemas it was no inconsequential fleapit in its silent days, as has been suggested. It really did give its audiences "bright goods," as the I.S.N. critic suggested.

As the Twenties progressed the economic and social deprivation of the working class areas was made worse by the deteriorating political situation. 1920 began with Sinn Fein proclaiming an Irish Republic in Dublin in January and ended with the Government of Ireland Act establishing Northern Ireland in December. The Nationalist minorities in the city began to see themselves surrounded by a rising, angry and vociferous sea of Loyalists intent on cutting them off from what they regarded as their rightful roots. Their response to that challenge was an increasing emphasis on their Irishness and that process revealed itself not only in political and religious matters but even in the local entertainment sector. In the largest Nationalist enclave, the Falls, the Clonard in particular became a conduit for Nationalist feelings, showing films with Irish themes and presenting stage plays and acts with a local appeal involving the likes of Cathal O'Byrne and his Celtic Company, or singer -comedian Albert Sharpe, both of whom always attracted large audiences. With its main films it showed the Pathe Gazette news, but emphasised that it was the Irish Edition, that is the version shown in Dublin. That version often included excerpts from Irish Events, a local and successful newsreel produced in Dublin by the General Film Supply Company, owned and run by Norman Whitten. Scenes of the funeral of Thomas Ashe and the release of Sinn Fein prisoners, which the Clonard had screened, were Whitton's. The Irish News expressed approval, adding that such material kept local audiences "versed in the most recent happenings of importance in the country."

But the Clonard had competition from an unexpected source, St. Mary's Hall in Chapel Lane, which normally restricted its cinematic presentations to Saturday evening shows during the winter months. During February the Panopticon held trade showings of two important new Irish films "Willy Reilly and his Colleen Bawn" made by the Film Company of Ireland, and "In The Days of St. Patrick" filmed by Whitten's General Film Supply

Company, which were attended by local managers and film agents. Normally such films, made in Ireland and starring Irish actors, would have attracted much attention and have been snapped up by Mr Stewart or other enterprising managers, but nothing of the kind happened on that occasion until St. Mary's Hall, seeing an opportunity, acted. Starting in April the management committee decided to go full -time into films with two shows daily at 7:00 and 9:00 p.m., and seats priced reasonably at 5d, 9d and one shilling for the balcony. Their projectionist was Harry Mc Mullan, the assistant manager of Weisker's, who normally supervised St. Mary's Saturday evening shows, which suggests also that Weisker's was handling the renting of the films.

The season began with "In The Days of St. Patrick" which attracted large crowds. The Irish News critic thought highly of the production which consisted fashionably of a prologue, followed by five reels of narrative, and an epilogue, the whole having taken nearly a year to complete. It dealt with the life of the saint as a boy on Slemish, as an ecclesiastic in Rome and as an adult (played by the well known Irish actor Ira Allen) on his return to Ireland. The production was as lavish as Whitten could afford to make it, with scenes involving chariots, pirate ships, burning buildings and conflict, causing many critics to praise its epic qualities. Liam O'Laoghaire, the noted Irish critic, recalled seeing it as a small boy and finding it "thrilling." The Irish News critic noted "its excellent spectacular effects" and the fact that where possible the scenes were enhanced by being filmed on the actual locales at Tara and Croagh Patrick. Of special interest was the use of both Gaelic and English intertitles which the critic felt would appeal especially to Gaelic scholars. The epilogue consisted of a quick tour of contemporary monuments to the saint's memory plus shots of Cardinal Logue giving his blessing to his flock, which some felt may have put off non - Catholic viewers. Finally much credit was given to the orchestra under the baton of John Curry for their special selection of appropriate Irish music. The popularity of the film can be judged by the fact that it made two return visits to St. Mary's, accompanied by newsreels of scenes outside Mountjoy prison during the hunger strike and emotional scenes at the funeral of the late Lord Mayor of Cork, Alderman Mc Curtain - "murdered by Crown forces,"- all most probably taken by Whitten's cameramen.

Another Irish film followed called "Rosaleen Dhu" or Dark Rosaleen, a four - reel story whose action and storyline were set in the days of the Land League "when land-lordism was the curse of a down - trodden people," and told of the adventures of a Fenian patriot who had to leave Ireland. He joined the French Foreign Legion and fought in North Africa where he married an Algerian girl who, rather improbably, ended up inheriting an Irish castle. Even more improbable was the fact that it was made in Bray by a local barber called William Power for his Celtic Cinema Company. He also acted in it. The film included an eviction scene in Ireland, and shots of fighting in Morocco which the Irish News critic described as "scenes of a particularly thrilling character." He also thought that the action scenes were "vividly portrayed." The film was well received though it didn't have the same impact as the life of St Patrick. The critic also mentioned that it was supported by "a splendid comedy of rural life" which almost certainly was another film made by Power just the year before called "Willie Scouts while Jessie Pouts." He also felt that the general reception given to the Irish films showed "ample evidence of a strong local demand for genuine native films."

St. Mary's Hall management obviously felt the same because they followed it up with a showing of "Willy Reilly and his Colleen Bawn," a famous film which is still remembered with affection today. Much has been written about its significance and there are those who regard it as the finest native silent film made in Ireland. The importance of its presentation in Belfast was underlined by the arrival from Dublin of M.F.Reynolds the manager of the Film Company of Ireland to supervise the arrangements for its showing, though the projectionist was still Weisker's Harry Mc Mullan. The film was modestly advertised as "Ireland's most famous love story" and "the greatest film ever produced in Ireland." It was based on an 1855 novel by William Carleton with a story set in the mid 18th century which dealt with conditions under the Penal laws. An Irish landowner, Willy Reilly,(played by Brian Magowan) saves a neighbouring Protestant squire from a band of outlaws and through that act meets his beautiful daughter Helen, (Frances Alexander) the Colleen Bawn of the title. They fall in love but are unable to marry because of the prohibitions of the penal laws. The squire tries to persuade the hero to change his religion so that the marriage can go ahead but he refuses, a decision that Helen supports, telling her father that if he did he would no longer be the same person that she loved. She has another suitor, Sir Robert Whitecraft, a bigoted Protestant landowner (Jim Plant), the villain of the story who sets out to destroy Willy by having him falsely accused of robbery and abduction. That proves to be too much for other Protestant landowners who join with the squire to reveal Whitecraft's treachery. After many setbacks the film ends with Willy and Helen happily married. Throughout the story the Protestants and Catholics show understanding and toleration of their respective positions and on one occasion the Protestant minister tells Willy that despite their differences they were "fellow Irishmen." The final mixed marriage of the happy lovers suggested that Protestant and Catholic could live together in peace and harmony (see page 357).

The film did not preach but presented a good story, well acted and finely directed by John MacDonagh, a man experienced in stage and film work who had actually taken part in the 1916 Rebellion. He filmed the story during the summer of 1919 mainly in and around St. Enda's in Rathfarnam, a locale associated with Patrick Pearse and Robert Emmett, so there were strong Republican undertones. The political message was implicit in the material but the Irish News critic was silent on that score. Instead he praised the production, the quality of the acting and the fact that the adaptation had kept so closely to the original novel, commenting in passing that the film was doing very well in the U.S.A.,which was true. Despite its success it proved to be the last film made by the Film Company of Ireland which sadly passed into history. Most of the company's output has disappeared but luckily a print of "Willy Reilly" is preserved in the Irish Film Institute in Dublin. The film drew large audiences to St Mary's Hall, and there were packed houses also later when it was shown in the Clonard, but how people responded to its message of toleration is not recorded. The political landscape looked a lot different from Belfast than it did from Dublin where the film was made and as nationalist unity broke down into civil war and partition loomed larger on the horizon the film's message was lost in recriminations and spilt blood. One suspects that those Irish made films recalled for some the earlier Kalem films made by Sidney Olcott near Killarney. In November St Mary's Hall became, temporarily, a Picture and Variety

Theatre managed by a local actor Terry Mc Govern and one of the films he presented was, according to the Irish News, a "real Irish picture showing the lakes of Killarney" which was very probably one of Olcott's productions. That suspicion is strengthened by the showing of another famous Olcott production "From the Manger to the Cross" in December. At its original showing in Belfast in 1912 it had been the centre of controversy and ignored by St. Mary's Hall, but in December 1920 it was hailed as "a masterpiece" and when it returned to the same hall in February 1921 it had become "a great sacred masterpiece."

As Northern Nationalists perceived their politicians to be failing them they fell back on their religion more and more to emphasise their identity. Films with religious themes or Catholic connotations were very popular during the early Twenties and, after St Mary's Hall was occupied by the police and Army in early 1922, the Clonard continued to present them. They included films like "The Rosary" (which Mr Stewart, to be fair, also presented in the New York), "Fabiola," "The Victim," produced by the Catholic Art Association of America which the Irish News commented was "recommendation enough," a two - reeler called "Daniel in the Lion's Den," which must have appeared to some locals as rather appropriate to their situation, and "The Life of Our Lord." in three reels. The crowds flocked to them, and a contemporary described the atmosphere during their projection as often being as reverent as in a church. The Clonard also continued to show newsreels of Irish events like the emotive funeral of Terence Mac Swiney, the Lord Mayor of Cork, which included scenes shot in London and Cork. The Irish News critic was impressed by the "great realism" of the camerawork and described how the audience was "visibly moved." Two years later audiences were still facing the fact of death as they "watched respectfully" newsreels of the funerals of Arthur Griffith and Michael Collins.

How the Unionist audiences would have perceived the Irish films is a matter for speculation because they weren't shown outside the Falls area and the Unionist newspapers, which had so often in the past praised Olcott's films, ignored them. But obviously there were those in the film community who didn't want the social hairline cracks that the differing reactions to Irish films indicated deepening into ravines. A group of aficionados of music hall and films, brought together by popular manager Will White, established a society, named after Mr White, and called the Belfast White Cinema Lodge. Its aim was to promote social welfare and good fellowship among its members, who included representatives from the music hall and cinema trades plus a small number of honorary members connected with the business. It was emphasised that the organization was completely non - sectarian and non - political and that it was there to allow people of like interests to meet periodically to discuss and debate topics associated with films and music hall. Several major social occasions were organized throughout the year including outings. In early 1922 a successful outing took place to the Downpatrick races and it was followed on the second Sunday in May by a motor excursion through the Glens of Antrim to Ballycastle for a meal. Then on to Bushmills and the Giant's Causeway for tea and back home through Ballymoney and Antrim, ending in front of the Panopticon in High Street where they parted, happy and tired. While in Ballycastle they held a formal meeting and it is interesting to note the names mentioned on that occasion. The President was Will White (manager of the Duncairn), Vice Presidents were George Dobler (manager, Royal Hippodrome) and T.

Connor (of Weisker Bros.), honorary secretaries were John Quinn (manager, West Belfast Picture House), Fred. Stewart (Panopticon), W.G.Bradley (manager, Alhambra), and A. Moore(of Messrs J.P.Moore). Others present included J McCann (manager, Diamond) and W.J.Hogan (returned from Australia and manager again of the Clonard), in all a very representative and wide ranging group.

They were right to worry about the direction local society was taking and some of them and their employees had already experienced its darker side. People in general were becoming edgy in their relations with each other, and with society. One R.M. complained that too many people were appearing in court over altercations in cinemas. In fact, he added, he had come to the conclusion that "cinemas were a curse on the city." One such case in 1920 involved a young man from Hillman street who used a penknife to switch off an electric light on a stairway in his local cinema. That was not only a piece of vandalism but also a breach of safety regulations and in court it was claimed that that type of incident had become quite prevalent lately. On being reprimanded by the manager the miscreant had assaulted him. The solicitor for the manager claimed in court, that Belfast at that time had gained an unenviable reputation for "vandalism, bad breeding, and bad manners." The editor of the Irish News replied that such criticisms of Belfast youth were excessive. The Germans, he argued in an editorial, who had recently burnt the library at Louvain and shelled the cathedral in Rheims were true "vandals" but local youths had never done anything so extreme. If manners and behaviour had deteriorated we should be looking into why and deciding what should be done instead of making wild accusations. Not long after that another case was heard which involved two men who had assaulted an attendant in the Gaiety, one of them threatening, gangster - style, to put "an ounce of lead" in the victim. The reason for the attack was not given but the R.M. deplored the fact that people in their daily work were not safe. Both those cases paled into insignificance when compared with the horrific event which occurred in the Crumlin cinema at the end of August 1922 when the assistant manager, Peter Mullan of Joy street, was shot and killed during an actual performance. Witnesses described how, the week before, Mr Mullan had had trouble from some men and how he had put some of them out of the cinema. A female attendant overheard one of the men say they would "get him" and a police spokesman admitted that the assistant manager had to have police protection on his way home on occasion. On Tuesday evening, the 29th August, while a film was being shown, a group of six or eight men suddenly appeared in the darkened auditorium, shots rang out and Mr Mullan fell dead. Confusion followed and even a special constable who was present at the show was unable to describe what had actually happened. It was unclear whether the killing was sectarian or a personal grudge. The coroner finally brought in a verdict of "willful murder by members of an unlawful assembly." Life in some cinemas seemed to be becoming as dangerous as that often depicted on the screen; but in fact it was just imitating what had been happening only too often on the streets of the city.

In the political calendar July was usually a troublesome month in Belfast and the situation wasn't helped in 1920 when Loyalist workers in Workman's shipyard called a lunchtime meeting on the 21st to condemn what they regarded as Sinn Fein atrocities taking place across Ireland. The News Letter explained that the protest was about "the long continued and extreme provocation to which the loyal people of our city have been subjected." The meeting was addressed by a number of speakers and as the verbiage became more extreme, the News Letter explained, feelings rose and "disturbances ensued." Sinn Feiners (a euphemism for Catholics) were told "that in their own interests it would be advisable for them to return to their own homes." According to the Irish News what actually happened was that inflammatory statements made at that meeting initiated "wantonly and suddenly" a "mad campaign of persecution, riot and bloodshed" which included the forcible expulsion of 10,000 workers, "mainly Catholics and Socialists" from the shipyards, engineering works, factories and mills across the city. Rioting and street battles followed, and the sound of gunfire filled the city streets, the whole sad activity driven by an intensity which shocked everyone. The editors of both the papers mentioned above called on all citizens to desist from any type of provocation. The Lord Mayor appealed for calm but no one seemed to be listening.

Finally on Tuesday 31st August the army imposed a curfew on the city. All citizens, without exception, had to be indoors between 10:30 pm and 5:00 am. The Corporation announced that the last trams to the suburbs would leave Castle Junction around 9:00 pm, which meant that all places of entertainment had to be closed at the latest by 9:30 pm to allow their workers and patrons to get home in time. Some local cinemas closed for a time but soon theatres and cinemas adapted by putting on just one performance in the evening. The Clonard announced that their last show would commence at 7:30 pm and most cinemas did likewise. The Alhambra scheduled one performance at 7:45, the Coliseum at 7:15 while the Hippodrome managed two at 5:45 and 7:45 with the stated proviso that the second show must end at 9:30. The Popular managed two shortened shows at 6:00 and 7:45 while the New York decided on continuous showing from 6:00 to 9:30. The Royal Cinema also became continuous from 3:00 to 9:00pm while the Panopticon was continuous to 9:00 pm. Managers had to adapt to the controls on movement and the reduced income that resulted, with the hope that the restrictions would not last too long. They weren't to know that with short breaks and some modifications the curfew was to last to 1924 and that before then worse, much worse, was to come.

In early September the situation was still very serious and the News Letter described how "the lust of destruction continued to run rampant on the Shankill, the Oldpark and the Falls," though with time the fierceness abated somewhat. But despite appeals to the authorities the restrictions remained. The period that followed, until late 1922, became a rollercoaster of sporadic violence broken by short periods of relative calm which were matched by equally short spells of relief from the restrictions of curfew. By 18th September the curfew had been lifted and cinemas quickly reverted to their former times; but by 27th October the curfew was back in place and the restricted openings applied again. Over Christmas and the New Year the I.S.N. reported that, despite the curfew, every cinema in town had "Q" signs clearly displayed, but it would be wrong to draw the conclusion that all was well again. The cinemas were struggling to survive and the first casualty was the Coliseum which at the end of April closed "until further notice." By high summer the I.S.N. critic reported that all houses were "suffering" (financially, one presumes), and he suggested that the beginning of curfew should be postponed another half hour to give some much needed relief, a suggestion that was ignored.

The cinema managers fought back with their most powerful weapon, a range of films that would tempt the public to risk the dangerous streets. Before that fateful outburst in July 1920 crowds had been flocking to see top performers like Mary Pickford ("one can never tire of Mary Pickford" the Whig declared), Chaplin, W.S.Hart, Douglas Fairbanks, Annette Kellerman, and Theda Bara. There were also lesser but increasingly popular players like Elmo Lincoln, Tom Mix, Harry Carey, and Sessue Hayakawa while coming over the horizon was Gloria Swanson and a new European star called Alla Nazimova. In May both the Popular and the Clonard showed "Tarzan of the Apes" starring Elmo Lincoln and it was so successful that the Clonard followed it two weeks later with the "Romance of Tarzan" a sequel which began with some scenes from the original. The Irish News critic had described the first Tarzan adventure as "terrific" and he found the sequel "a most absorbing film which holds the audience to the end." Elmo Lincoln has his place in cinema history as the first Tarzan but he also played other Maciste - like strong men, for example in a serial called "Elmo the Mighty" with Lucille Love, which was shown successfully in many local cinemas including the Lyceum. The character of Tarzan had been forged in the imagination of Edgar Rice Burroughs in 1912 but the book wasn't filmed until 1917, in Louisiana and around Los Angeles, not in Brazil as the film publicity claimed at the time. The person chosen to play the main role was a little known actor called Elmo Lincoln (born Otto Lincolnhelt) and the film shot him to fame immediately as the Lord of the Jungle. Tarzan entered into the vernacular and became part of everyday conversation and communication in Belfast as elsewhere in America and Europe. For example, an animal act involving Great Apes which appeared in the Royal Hippodrome in October 1921 was billed as "Tarzan's Playmates." Lincoln was familiar with the technicalities of film making because he had been around the studios for some time playing small parts in early D.W. Griffith films, notably "Intolerance" where he swung a mighty sword against the enemies of Belshazzar. He was rather bulky in build but was fast on his feet and entered into the fights with enthusiasm. He prospered for a few years but his acting skills were meagre and his range limited, so the parts gradually dried up. He ended up playing small parts in the Durango Kid Westerns with Charles Starrett, dying in 1952.

In contrast, Tom Mix began in Westerns and made his name in them. He was a flamboyant character and it is difficult to separate fact from fiction in what was written about his early life. He was a skilled horseman and fearless in carrying out dangerous stunts. The Western environment of his films was somewhat removed from the real thing, presenting a mixture of the traditional and the modern but always exciting with lots of stunts, fist fights and gunplay. Commenting on a typical example, "Ace High," a four - reeler which reached the city in January 1920, the critic of the Irish News wrote that it "was replete with all that goes to make an enjoyable and interesting Wild West picture - a fine love story, thrilling fights with Indians, wonderful horsemanship and great sweeps of prairie." His films were pure entertainment and a population struggling with economic depression, unemployment and other problems in their day - to - day lives welcomed them as preferable to the more serious and more historically accurate fare of W.S.Hart. The Tom Mix films, produced by Fox, were introduced to local audiences mainly by Fred. Stewart in the Panopticon, the star usually headlined as the King of the Cowboys, with titles like the afore mentioned "Ace High," "Fame and Fortune," "Mr Logan U.S.A.," "Treat 'Em Rough" and "Roaring Reform," all of which were shown during 1920. Both W.S.Hart and Tom Mix had competition from another rising Western star, Harry Carey, who, as already mentioned, was to have a major influence on John Wayne. He was closer to Hart in his interpretation of the Western hero, but with a greater sense of humour.

In contrast Sessue Hakawaya was a serious actor and as the Whig critic put it, he was "always artistic in whatever he played '" and gave "wonderful impersonations." He had built up a sound reputation working for Thomas Ince but really made an impact on the general public when he moved to Paramount where Cecil B. de Mille starred and directed him in "The Cheat '" in 1915 with Fannie Ward. It was a powerful but lurid story of a society woman (Fannie Ward) who gambles away money she was holding for a charity. In desperation she goes to a wealthy Japanese admirer (Sessue Hayakaya) and borrows the money from him, with a promise of favours to be granted in return. Later she reneges on her bargain whereupon the furious Hayakaya claims her as his property and in a shocking scene brands her as such on the shoulder. She in turn shoots him, a crime that her husband is accused of, but she wins the jury over when she exposes her branded shoulder in court. In spite of, or maybe because of, its sensational content "The Cheat" was a great success at the box office and praised critically especially for Hayakaya's fine understated acting. It didn't reach Belfast until February 1920 when it was shown in the Imperial, which introduced it with cinematic modesty claiming that it was "a masterpiece production which stands alone among pictures by reason of its tremendous story, exceptional dramatic situations, and brilliant acting." The Whig critic agreed that the plot held the interest and felt that overall it was "tastefully done.". Large crowds dutifully turned up and from all accounts were not disappointed. Hakawaya had meantime become a major star both on the screen and in his luxurious private life. It required seven servants to run his home, a converted castle, and they were kept busy with daily parties and looking after hundreds of guests. He and his wife made quite an impression as they travelled around Los Angeles in a Pierce-Arrow motor vehicle with its distinctive gold plating.

During 1920 in the Panopticon Mr Stewart presented as supporting films a series of two - reel comedies starring a seemingly new comedian called Winkle. The films had names like "Going, Going, Gone," "One Night Only," "Blue Blazes," "The Girl and the Game," and "Look Out Below""which included some hair raising escapades on a skyscraper, and all proved very popular with audiences. As the Irish News critic put it, Winkle and his antics were "well worth seeing" and were always greeted "with great success." People began asking who exactly Winkle was because they liked to know as much as possible about their favourites. Some of them probably recognised him as Lonesome Luke whose one - reel comedic adventures, often in the company of Snub Pollard and the delightful Bebe Daniels, had often been part of the Panopticon's supporting programmes until recently. But Lonesome Luke had only been a pale reflection of Chaplin, with little originality about him, in contrast to the new Winkle character. Mr Stewart knew that the public were intrigued and that a new personality was in the making, so he supplied the answers they wanted over the weeks. In September his adverts described him more fully as Harold Lloyd

Winkle in "His Prehistoric Way," which some time later became Harold Lloyd Winkle (Him with the Goggles) in "A Crooked Round-up."

Chaplin had his bowler, Max Linder had his shiny top hat, Buster Keaton had his flat hat and Harold Lloyd had his "goggles" or more accurately horn rimmed spectacles. The glasses - actually he only used the rims because the glass reflected the studio lights - set Lloyd apart, giving him a rather studious and serious look though he was far from being an academic. He was a man of comic action not averse to using his fists or a gun to get his way, which in most cases meant getting the girl. His pleasantly optimistic and capable personality, splendidly caught by James Fox in "Thoroughly Modern Millie" (d. George Roy Hill, 1967), combined with his comic inventions quickly made him a hit with local audiences. By Christmas even the Imperial was headlining him as plain Harold Lloyd in "High and Dizzy," a sure sign that he had arrived. "High and Dizzy" was still a two - reeler but it was different in that Lloyd had a new leading lady, a young blonde called Mildred Davis who had replaced the dark haired Bebe Daniels in 1919. Miss Daniels had accepted an invitation and a contract from Cecil B. deMille which involved a move to Paramount studios. She was soon appearing on local screens in major films like de Mille's "Why Change Your Wife?" with Thomas Meighan and Gloria Swanson. When it showed in the Panopticon the Irish News critic noted that it was "followed by keen interest by the audience," one reason probably being that in de Mille's "sex stew," as one American critic called it, they saw more, literally, of the lady than they had ever seen in all her adventures with Lonesome Luke. Bebe Daniels went on to a successful career, later married Ben Lyon and moved to England to make the popular "Life With the Lyons" series on BBC radio and TV in the Fifties.

In 1921 Lloyd and his new leading lady made "A Sailor Made Man" in which he played a rich and spoiled young man (the Boy) who joins the navy to impress Miss Davis (the Girl). The result, of course, is that he becomes a better person, even rescuing his ladylove from the harem of the Maharajah of Khaipura-Bhandanna where she had been imprisoned. It was a four - reeler, not quite a feature film, though it was released as such. Harold Lloyd explained that it had been planned as a two - reeler but when it was finished it included so many good sight gags that the decision was taken not to cut it down but release it as filmed. Audiences loved it when it was released in December 1921 and Lloyd never returned to making two - reelers though his old ones continued to turn up across Belfast in the following years. "A Sailor Made Man" arrived in the Picture House one year later in a flurry of anticipation. The usually staid Royal Avenue hall used a distinctive black - edged advert which warned the public that there had recently been a terrible outbreak of "laughing sickness" which had affected one million people already. So "get inoculated before visiting the Picture House to see Harold Lloyd in 'Sailor Made Man.'" Unfortunately the film was engaged for the second half of the week, that is, for Thursday, Friday and Saturday, so there are no critical comments in the papers, Tuesday being the normal day for reviews. Fred Stewart must have seen the queues because two months later the film appeared for a week in the Panopticon when the Whig critic noted its extra length with approval and commented on the large crowds who had turned out to see a film that "was very funny without being vulgar." As his popularity increased Lloyd moved to longer films and at the same time initiated a new fad for horn rimmed glasses which became one of the "in" things for trendy types during the Twenties (think "Harry Potter" glasses: do people really change?).

But the star who was still really riding high at the time was Theda Bara. In July 1919 Fred Stewart delighted the Panopticon regulars, and others, by presenting her expensive and much hyped epic "Cleopatra." an eight reel spectacular which pleased audiences and critics. The Whig critic found it "daring and dazzling" and praised its overall look and skilled execution, especially of its land and sea battles. The Irish News scribe noted its attention to detail and thought that Miss Bara was "magnificent" especially in her final scene which he described as "a triumph of emotional acting." During 1920-21 at least eight new films appeared from her all presented at the Panopticon before making the rounds, attracting crowds with their eye - catching and provocative titles. All of them, like most of her films, were competently directed by a man she greatly admired, J. Gordon Edwards the grandfather of Blake Edwards. They included in February 1920 "The Forbidden Path," a story of life among the artists of Greenwich village which the News Letter critic thought was "vividly realistic," while the Irish News commented on its "scenes of a startling nature." Both agreed with the Whig that in the proceedings Miss Bara showed "skilful acting and a fine stage presence." The use of the latter term indicates how strongly critical reaction to films was still influenced by the conventions of the theatre. In an attempt to imply quality some films were referred to as plays in their advertising, and the inclusion of stage actors in the cast was also seen as desirable despite their uncinematic posings and overacting. Some critics wickedly declared that the skills of some film actors were due more to chance than training, maintaining for example that Miss Bara's effectively sensual stares in close-up were the result of her being myopic rather than of good acting, a criticism that didn't worry her in the least as long as she could see the road to the bank.

During the period in question the cinematic highlight was the eight - reel spectacle, "Salome," which Mr Stewart presented in April 1920 at special prices of one shilling and two shillings, describing it as "the greatest thing that ever happened on the screen." It ran for a complete week with House Full notices, in contrast to the usual three days, and large numbers were turned away every evening. Belfast had in the past experienced the excitement of Salome mania and there were many who could recall the stage performances of Helen Roberts and Maud Allan, but Miss Bara's film was something quite different. It gave the producer William Fox a part that suited the talents of his leading star, a story which offered the opportunity for spectacle and exotic locations with the added benefit of known biblical associations. The scenario however was not based directly on the narrative in the Bible but was taken from the turn of the century Oscar Wilde play. It depicted Salome as yearning for John the Baptist, who firmly rejects her, so she plots her revenge and the Baptist's death by taking advantage of Herod's infatuation with her. The News Letter critic thought that overall the film was "a fine achievement on the technical side" but he also praised the artistic construction and noted how every episode advanced the dramatic development of the plot. The Whig critic thought it was "a thoroughly good film" with Miss Bara proving that she was "a cinema artist of the first order." Like his fellow critic he commended the production values, especially the technical quality of the photography which enhanced the "splendid scenery." He found the costumes "daring" which seemed, perhaps, at odds with the News Letter critic who commented that Miss Bara was robed in "rich apparel" and wore about twenty five different costumes throughout the proceedings. The general tone of the film is suggested by his description of Salome's dance, a "climax wherein the passion - swayed siren dances madly before a besotted monarch" though he adds that the effect of the introduction of the Baptist's severed head "is softened by lighting effects which eliminate the harsh blunders that brought such severe criticism on the stage presentation." The Irish News gave it a rather brief review, finding it elaborate and picturesque and "a triumph of the spectacular in film drama." There was no mention at all of Miss Bara or her dance and one feels that the critic didn't fully approve of what he saw.

Like most of Miss Bara's films "Salome" had censorship problems, especially in parts of the U.S.A., and there were references to cuts in the opening bathing scene, later in John the Baptist's prison cell where Salome made sensuous advances to him, and finally, in the dance sequence where a scene of her stretched on the floor with John's head on a platter was shortened. In those drab and depressing days an event like "Salome" must have brought some excitement and colour (not literally, the film was in black and white) to the city. While the general populace obviously enjoyed the experience, pastors condemned it from their pulpits, academic historians and biblical scholars threw up their hands in horror, followers of serious theatre blenched, but Mr Stewart and Mr Fox smiled and enjoyed the sound of the tinkle of coins at the box office. In December "Salome" was shown in the Crumlin and the I.S.N. critic had the last word when he urged all to see it because he felt it would "become a classic of the screen." How wrong can one be.

A month later Miss Bara was back in the modern world in "When a Woman Sins," using her myopic stares plus some suggestive wiggling to good effect in a story about a nurse who takes to the exotic life as a dancer called Poppaea, "the idol of libertines," appearing as the Irish News critic described her "in one of her most arresting moods." That was followed in mid December by "When Men Desire" a story of spying during the recent war in which she gave ' "a characteristic exhibition (which) kept interest alive to the finish. "At the beginning of January 1921 she was in the Panopticon again in "A Woman There Was," which transported her to the South Seas for a romantic interlude. The Irish News critic praised the well developed plot and her performance, adding that the enjoyment of the film had been greatly helped by the playing of the orchestra. In contrast in "The Siren's Song" she played a poor peasant girl in Brittany who becomes a great singer, causing the Whig critic to comment that he felt that her performance showed that she could act parts other than vamps, an evaluation that would have pleased her. Finally in November Mr Stewart presented the "Lure of Ambition" her last role as a serious vamp. Fred Stewart had been Theda Bara's most consistent supporter in Belfast, showing most of her films, though even he didn't attempt to present her disastrous Irish film "Kathleen Mavoureen," based on a play by Dion Boucicault which, though advertised as a gentle Irish love story, caused widespread resentment among the Irish in America, who objected to someone with her reputation playing an Irish heroine. In some areas cinemas showing the film were subjected to physical attacks, with stink bombs being let off in the auditoriums.

From 1919 to 1921 Miss Bara was a prominent part of the cinema scene in Belfast and then as suddenly as she had appeared she vanished from local screens. The abruptness and

Theda Bara as
Cleopatra

completeness of her departure at the end of 1921 is quite dramatic. But the signs were already there that audiences were tiring of her brand of playing. The Irish News critic mentioned that when he went to review "When Men Desire" in December 1920 in the Panopticon he was surprised by the paucity of the audience, and the following month he was to make the more telling statement that "Nazimova has become all the rage." Cartoonists and humorists were beginning to lampoon her darkened eyes and gait. She didn't walk, one commented, she prowled. Theda Bara herself was tired of the bad publicity and complained that many people actually believed that she was like the character she played on screen. Also, like the Whig critic, she felt she could play other more serious roles, especially on the stage. She had made nearly forty films for Fox Studios between 1915 and 1919 and she felt the time had come for a change. Despite the fact that the profits from her films had been the mainstay of his operations, William Fox didn't prevent her leaving because he felt that audience tastes were swinging towards a new type of heroine, the outgoing flapper, and anyway he had a new star called Betty Blythe who, he believed, could fill her shoes. So Miss Bara retired from the screen leaving mainly a legacy of only stills and memories because most of her films seem to have disappeared. She returned to the stage but didn't have the success she had hoped for and in 1925 was lured back to the cinema to make two more films.

By then her great days were over. Wisely she decided to retire to private life with her husband, the director Charles Brabin, away from the public gaze. Behind the hype and the manufactured persona one detects an intelligent woman with a well developed sense of humour, who would have been a pleasure to meet. The Belfast critics, to their credit, ignored the sensationalism and treated her with professional respect from the beginning. As the films continued to arrive they began to praise her acting and above all her ability to catch and hold the interest of an audience right to the end of the story, which was quite an achievement in view of the ludicrous nature of many of the plots. But even in private life she could, right to the end, still play the role she was famous for. The story is told how many years later she had arranged for her chauffeur to collect her from a party. Unfortunately he was delayed by traffic and was a few minutes late. At the appointed time when he hadn't arrived she rose, called a taxi and swept out saying "Theda Bara waits for no man." The queues outside the Panopticon in the early Twenties indicated that many men were only too willing to wait for her. She died of cancer in April 1955, ignored and forgotten by the cinema - going public.

Violent death had become so much a part of the local social landscape that it was easy to overlook the natural demises that continued to affect families and organizations. One of those occurred on 13th November 1921 when it was reported that W.J.Moore had passed away peacefully at his residence, the large and impressive looking villa called "Maureen" on the Andersonstown Road, at the early age of 47 years, leaving a widow, Minnie, and eight children. Mr Moore was a well known public and professional figure in the city, especially in Nationalist circles. The Whig described him as a "respectable, well liked and kindly" citizen and could have added that he was public spirited and an "eminent architect," as the

Irish News pointed out. He had represented the Falls Ward capably on the City Council between 1907 and 1919, had been an Alderman and vice - chairman of the Improvements Committee. He was also a Director of the Irish News, a Director of Belfast Celtic Football club, and the Managing Director of the Clonard Picture House. By profession he was an architect with offices in Royal Avenue, and his name was associated with many fine buildings including the Whitla Street Fire Brigade Station and the Catholic churches in Portstewart, Cushendall and Glenariff.

Reference to all those achievements appeared in the obituaries but there was only brief mention of the fact that he was also much involved in the design of local cinemas from the earliest days and that many cinemas across the city bore the imprint of his expertise. He had designed the Shaftesbury Pictoria and the early Panopticon for Isadore Clifford in 1910 and later completed the plans of the Panopticon for Fred Stewart, before planning the Crumlin for the same owner. He also worked with Joe Mc Kibben producing the plans for the West End Picture House (1913) and the Midland (1915), followed by the Tivoli for Patrick Kelly. When the Alhambra decided to become a cinema it was W.J. Moore who was called in to design a completely new frontage and make other necessary interior modifications during 1910-11. A few years later (1915) he made the necessary design modifications to convert the Alexandra Theatre to the Coliseum Picture House, and in 1917 carried out renovations to improve the New Princess for Ferris Pounds. But the Clonard, which he planned and built in 1912, was his cinematic masterwork, combining a dainty and elegant frontage with a comfortable, modern and well proportioned interior. He was very proud of the Clonard, as he had a right to be, and his early death meant that thankfully he didn't have to witness the damage that political vandals were soon to inflict on it.

During early 1922 the violence on the streets continued sporadically. Most cinemas struggled on but the Popular and the Gaiety decided it was wiser to close their doors temporarily. Fred Stewart obviously believed that music could sooth the savage breast so he reorganised his orchestra as the New Pan Orchestra, consisting of seven experienced musicians under the baton of W.B.Currie. The Whig critic expressed his approval and found their sound just sufficient for the size of the hall. The canny manager went further and had a specially built cinema organ installed. He had used an organ type instrument briefly before but the new instrument could claim to be Belfast's first true cinema organ. The Whig critic again commented favourably, mentioning that he had consulted with a number of music students and all had praised the quality of its tone. Music continued to be a vital element in the cinema programmes and the orchestras in the downtown halls gave musical interludes at announced times as well as accompanying the films. At one time or another all the local critics emphasised the importance to a film of a good musical accompaniment. They pointed out that all major films were accompanied by advice from the producer regarding the music to be played with the film and that the suggestions could be quite detailed. A recent "ordinary" five - reeler (unfortunately, unnamed) had arrived with fifty accompanying musical suggestions, which the local musicians reduced to six which proved "quite adequate for the occasion." Such a selective procedure had become normal and it was only with exceptional productions that the music score was rigidly adhered to.

On the streets a different type of "music" was being heard, accompanied by the lyrics of fear. "Your liberty is in danger" sang one song but the reference was not to the political changes taking place but to the recurrent theme of Prohibition. One local film critic noted that if prohibition was being rigorously applied in America it certainly didn't show in the movies where drinking continued "unabated." There were strong rumours going around Belfast that certain politicians, who believed that alcohol fuelled the present violence, wanted to introduce prohibition locally. In response members of the drink trade, especially owners of public houses and spirit grocers, had established the Ulster Anti-Prohibition Council. One of its main aims was to alert the general public to be careful whom they voted for in future elections if they wished to retain their freedom to have a drink. Their slogan, widely advertised, was moderation itself: "Wisely to eat...... wisely to drink....happily to live in peace with your neighbour." The sale of drink wasn't completely banned but the Special Powers Act was used to drastically restrict the opening hours of spirit grocers and public houses to between midday and 7:00 pm. At least, for once, the violence was not being blamed on the cinema.

A characteristic of the civil disturbances was the increasing bomb and incendiary attacks on economic targets which involved a wide variety of buildings including workplaces, shops, hotels and even noble structures like Shane's Castle and Garron Tower. The cinema managers suspected it would only be a matter of time before halls of entertainment would be attacked, so they braced themselves and hoped that if such attacks materialised they would not happen when audiences were present. Straight - faced contemporaries tell many humorous stories about that period and at least one is worth retelling. There were genuine worries about attacks on cinemas while a show was in progress and it was decided by concerned citizens to post a rota of guards at the door of the Clonard to prevent such an occurrence. One of them, well known in the district, was rumoured to be a member of the I.R.A. One quiet afternoon during a children's matinee he decided it was safe to move into the auditorium and quickly became very involved with the film that was being shown. Unfortunately there was a lot of noise from the pit but his calls for silence went unheeded. Finally in desperation he pulled out a gun and fired a shot into the air. The result was like the climax of a Mack Sennett comedy with bedlam breaking out and children racing to the exits. Within a few minutes the cinema was nearly empty. The manager was, to say the least, not impressed and the "guard" was barred from any future attendance. The mark of the bullet, the storyteller insisted, could be seen in the ceiling for quite some time after that.

In March the army occupied the Ulster Hall and all concerts arranged for there were cancelled. A week or so later the police moved into St. Mary's Hall and according to the Whig "raised the Union Jack over it, "a move that angered Nationalists, and ended its short spell as a cinema. Then it was the turn of the Falls Road library. As the violence spread the curfew was extended at the end of May to cover all of N.Ireland, so it was no longer possible for the better off to spend their weekends in Bangor or further afield where they could enjoy longer hours of evening entertainment. Things deteriorated dramatically through May and June into what the Irish News described as "one of the most terrifying campaigns of slaughter and incendiarism ever experienced in the blood stained history of this city," and many working class areas experienced what could only be called an "unabated reign of terror" for a time.

The cinemas didn't escape. The first hall to be targeted was the Imperial, on the 19th May. The caretaker, John Killen, opened the doors about 8:30 am and admitted the women who normally cleaned the cinema. As they were getting organised to begin their tasks a group of twenty to thirty men forced their way in, carrying cans of petrol and paraffin. Some had candles and at least one had a handgun. The women were ushered into seats at the side and the intruders began pouring the fuels over the seats in the stalls and the balcony. At that point Mr Killen appeared and there was an altercation during which he was struck with the gun. He managed to pull free and using his superior knowledge of the geography of the building escaped through the projection room down the back stairs and into the street, where he called for help. Within a short time the police arrived to find the building empty except for the frightened women. There was a strong smell of petrol but thankfully the men had fled without starting a fire. After a thorough cleaning the cinema opened for business as usual later in the day though the number of people admitted was probably small because rioting, which claimed 14 lives that weekend, kept most people in their own districts. Also, a land mine was discovered nearby, in Arthur Square, and had to be defused, so the Imperial and the Royal Cinema were almost certainly closed for a time. The same applied to the halls in York Street, where six people died, the Falls Road, Albert Street, Short Strand and the Crumlin Road. On Tuesday 23rd. at about 7:00 in the evening two bombs were thrown at the front of the Gaiety cinema starting a fire but the brigade arrived quickly and got it under control before much damage was done.

The situation in York street was especially serious and it became very dangerous for the inhabitants to venture out of their homes. The hardy Alhambra which drew a large part of its audience from that area announced that it was closing because of "the civil commotion in the city." The New York, in the middle of the trouble zone, struggled to stay open but on Saturday 27th it was attacked with incendiaries which started fires. When the brigade arrived the roof was well alight but the flames were quickly extinguished. As people milled around in the confusion a shout went up that there was a bomb at the main door. Luckily it hadn't gone off, either because the fuse was faulty or the water from the hoses had softened it to the point that it had malfunctioned. It was a sad sight that met the gaze of Fred Stewart when he arrived later. The building was still standing defiantly but the roof was severely damaged and there was smoke and water damage everywhere. One can understand why he decided later to abandon it. Conflict was also extremely fierce and prolonged on the lower Newtownards Road and Short Strand areas causing the Popular and Mountpottinger Picturedrome to close. The city centre emptied quickly after working hours as people rushed home to the safety of their homes. The Royal Hippodrome closed in early June blaming the disturbed state of the city, and the Central announced it was closing until further notice. The I.S.N. reported that by the 10th June nearly all the cinemas in the city were closed, though it is interesting that through the worst of the troubles the Panopticon, the Imperial and the Lyceum continued to advertise and one presumes struggled to stay open.

The Falls area, according to the Irish News, experienced nights of "unprecedented terror" when workers were unable to get home and had to spend the night with friends or relatives. Places of entertainment must have been severely restricted in their opening hours yet there are reports that the Conard was crowded on the evening of 12th June 1922 It was a different story on the following evening because at 5:30 pm bombs exploded at both the Clonard and the nearby Diamond, drawing large crowds on to the road. An attendant had arrived to open the Clonard and make preparations for the show at 6:30 when he noticed that someone had been there before him. He could smell petrol and paraffin which had been splashed over the seats, the cushions of which in many cases had been slashed open. Candles, waste material and empty cans were lying around. As he surveyed the scene a loud explosion occurred in the right hand corridor breaking windows and bringing down part of the roof. Almost immediately another device exploded on the stage starting fires by which time the man, lucky to be alive and unhurt, was racing for the front door. The brigade arrived and began to tackle the flames, soon bringing them under control.

The Diamond escaped with less damage and announced it would reopen in a few weeks. Actually five bombs had been left in it but only two had exploded, the one near the paybox doing most damage, blowing down part of a wall. A few days later three fires were discovered burning in the Central which was already closed. Three rows of seats in the gallery and some in the stalls were destroyed before the brigade managed to put the flames out. But the building was saved. A few days later the bombers returned to the Clonard and Moore's elegant structure suffered severe damage; but the directors decided the building would be restored as soon as possible. On the same evening, around 7:00 pm, before the doors were opened the Tivoli, off Albert Street, was targeted with fire bombs and damaged, and a few hours later the nearby West Belfast Picture House went up in flames and was completely gutted. The Tivoli was still standing but at 4:00 pm the following day another bomb went off in it, destroying the roof and most of the walls. About a week later another unexploded bomb was found in the ruins which was defused and removed by the police. In the space of just over a week the Falls Road area lost all its cinemas except of course St Mary's Hall which was still occupied by the police.

Into July things quietened down and a resident of the area recalled how people would usually close the wooden shutters on their windows about 9:30 pm and move indoors for the night. If footfalls were heard passing on the pavement outside one knew it was an army or police patrol. Regularly the low whine of a passing "cage" of Specials broke the silence, sometimes followed by the sound of shots or an exploding bomb, indicating an ambush. The man in question said that his family was lucky because his brother, who was training to be an engineer, had built one of the new fangled crystal radios using a cat's whisker and they each took turns putting on the earphones and listening to music heard faintly from London. Across the city people were fearful, and most halls remained closed with a few exceptions, one of which was the Willowfield.

Like most halls the staff of the Willowfield enjoyed an annual outing for a day but unlike most halls the outing usually took place mid - week and the management closed the cinema for the day so that the staff didn't have to rush back to work. 1922 proved to be no exception. In early July two large charabangs carried the staff to Bangor and the Ards peninsula for a most enjoyable day. Mr Carrothers, the manager, accompanied them and in a post - prandial speech thanked them for their dedicated service and rejoiced in the fact that despite the troubles "business was booming." In the light of the bombings it may not have been the most diplomatic of statements but it indicated that the appetite for films was still there and that given the opportunity people would come out to see them. That was an important factor in understanding how the local cinema industry survived the disruption of the early Twenties. When a similar situation developed fifty years later it proved terminal for many cinemas though it must be admitted that many were already in decline from the impact of television.

The fact that the disruptions of the Twenties had a different outcome didn't mean that the cinema industry was free from problems. Quite the opposite, in fact. In Britain and America owners and managers were complaining about declining audiences and income. In Britain the reason was put down mainly to the burden of the entertainment tax which was condemned as unfair and unnecessary. The trade argued that the tax was not only a factor in the numerical decline of patrons but that it weighed unfairly on the poorer classes who occupied the cheaper seats. The tax of one penny levied on a threepenny seat represented an increase of 33% while the tax of two pence on a seat costing one shilling and sixpence represented less than 10%. Finally, in 1922, the industry launched a major campaign which had already got the support of at least 80 M.P's and which included the use of all cinema screens to highlight the iniquity of the tax. Meetings, discussions and a petition to be signed by cinemagoers were all planned. Comments in the local papers indicated that it had widespread support. The government was unwilling to lose such a lucrative income even though it had been introduced as a "temporary" measure during the war, and showed its resolve by pursuing cinema owners who they believed were avoiding it, in the courts.

Local owners and managers watched the outcome of one such case in Banbridge in May 1922, a case that many felt had been brought as a warning. The Irish News noted that it had aroused a lot of interest especially among the "promoters of public entertainment." The case was brought by the Commissioners of Customs and Excise against a local cinema owner, accusing him of breaking the regulations of the Finance Acts. He was accused of selling tickets at 10d (that is 8d admission and 2d tax) and 6d (that is 5d admission and 1d tax) whereas the tickets should have been clearly stamped as including 3d and 2d tax respectively. That meant, the prosecution held, that he was keeping 1d per seat which should have been paid to the government. His hall had a maximum of 700 seats which implied that a substantial amount of money was involved each year. He was also accused of issuing tickets on which the amount of tax involved was illegible, of reusing tickets and of issuing tickets that had no stamps at all on them.

His solicitor, Mr G. Hanna, pointed out that his client had been running a well organised cinema since before the recent war, without any complaint of any kind. The present problems had arisen not through any intent to defraud but because he was ignorant of the complications of the law. He himself found some of the regulations "mystifying" and was surprised to discover for example that a patron who didn't retain his half of the admission ticket was liable to a fine of five pounds. In fact one of the summonses had been issued in respect of a man who was found to have no ticket, but who actually had free access to the cinema because he worked for the defendant. The Crown Solicitor argued that a large amount of revenue was involved and that the new state of N. Ireland needed all the revenue it could get, but Mr Hanna replied that the summons had come from London and that the revenue would go to London, not to the local Exchequer. The magistrate declared that ignorance of the law was no excuse and he fined the defendant accordingly. The message was clear, the tax had to be paid.

But the financial problem was more complex than the matter of tax, as the local film commentators intimated. They pointed out that in Britain the industry was suffering from a lack of investment which meant that there wasn't enough money to attract and pay top quality talent, especially writers. In its efforts to save money the British film industry was still turning out too many cheap one and two - reelers, while the trend elsewhere, especially in America, was towards the longer features that people were demanding.

Not that short films were unpopular in Belfast. The films of Pimple may have been short, snappy and cheap but were always welcomed, and when he appeared in person in March 1922 on the stage of the Royal Hippodrome, in a short comedy called "The Hidden Terror" he was received with great enthusiasm. He explained that he had long wanted to visit Ireland because his wife was of Irish extraction, and added that he was enjoying his visit immensely. He had his own film crew with him and hoped to film in Belfast, Dublin and the country's best known beauty spots. He couldn't resist a little advertising, and told audiences that he was just completing his own version of "The Three Musketeers" to compete with a recent production from France (which was showing at the time in the Lyceum in serial form), and another skit about Douglas Fairbanks. It's worth mentioning that a few weeks later another comedian who was to impact on films in the future arrived in the Royal Hippodrome in a burlesque called 'Find the Needle'. Described as the Scholastic Humorist, but better known as Will Hay, he played a dithering schoolmaster "assisted by schoolboys and other insects" in a performance which the Whig critic praised as "full of originality and farcical incidents."

In complete contrast to the comedies another series of popular shorts began to appear in local cinemas under the general title of Secrets of Nature. They were one - reelers which ran for only eight to ten minutes, and dealt with unlikely topics from Natural History. They were photographed by experts like Edgar Chance and Percy Smith, who had made similar pictures in colour for the Charles Urban Company in 1910 - 11 which more mature members of the audience probably remembered being shown locally. This time they were organised under the enlightened guidance of Harry Bruce Woolfe who had started a small company called British Instructional Films in 1919 with a capital of only £3,000. The films had names like "The Cuckoo's Secret," "The Lair of the Spider" and "The Evolution of the Caddis Fly" and to everyone's surprise they caught on with the public and became steady favourites right through the Twenties. They were usually shown firstly in the Picture House before going on release to the other cinemas. They were much enjoyed by the local audiences who were amazed to see the antics of small insects in gigantic close ups, and to watch plants rapidly growing into flowers before their eyes. At the same time they garnered praise from the critics who appreciated their use of stop-go photography and slow motion techniques to reveal those wonders of nature. Even critics of the cinema praised their educational value. They were the worthy forerunners of the nature documentaries that are so popular on television today. The critic from the I.S.N. also commented that they and similar topics were a "welcome change from Deadwood Dick" but above all else they showed that there was an audience for interesting and intelligent fare.

Equally popular were a number of series of two - reel thrillers and mysteries, notably "The Adventures of Sherlock Holmes" made by the Stoll Company which turned out fifteen of them during 1921, followed by fifteen more in 1922, and again in 1923. The great detective was played by a former stage actor called Eille Norwood and to cinemagoers in the Twenties he became the authentic Holmes. Another British series was The Mystery of Dr. Fu Manchu, based on stories by Sax Rohmer, of which fifteen were made in 1923, with eight more in the next year. The name part was played by H. Agar Lyons and when the first one was shown in the Alhambra in May 1924 the I.S.N. warned audiences that they would be seeing "the most sinister and terrifying being ever created in fiction." The Alhambra emphasised that that was the first showing in Belfast, and followed it with the rest of the series over the subsequent weeks. Another great favourite was a new series of detective tales involving that old favourite "Nick Carter." Nor had the weekly two reels of the serial lost their appeal. Nothing improved a cinema's programme like a good serial, one of the critics announced, and he certainly would have approved of the American produced "A Dangerous Adventure '" a new 15 part serial announced for the Crumlin in early January 1923 which concerned a search for treasure in the Jungle. Patrons were promised exciting events which would include the most realistic electric storm ever screened, the heroine captured and offered as a sacrifice to a sacred tiger, her rescue by an ape-man and her being shot 100 feet upwards into a cave while the hero fell into a lion's den. On top of all that there would be an earthquake, a volcanic eruption, and an underwater struggle with a crocodile before the treasure was recovered. Obviously taking advantage of the popularity of the Tarzan pictures it had everything but the kitchen sink included. Other serials going around were the more stylish French offerings "Fantômas" and the 18 part "The Three Musketeers" which the Irish News praised for its accurate detail, its use of actual locations and its adherence to the original novel.

Eille Norwood: The authentic Holmes during the Twenties.

But films like those didn't help the British industry and often only showed up the inadequacies of the latter. Britain had no one to compete with the likes of Mary Pickford, Charlie Chaplin, Theda Bara, Douglas Fairbanks, and W.S.Hart - to name but a few. The box office returns in Belfast and elsewhere told the story which, simply stated, was that audiences preferred the slicker, fast - moving American product. But that didn't mean that the American films weren't without their problems also. The I.S.N. complained that there were too many "duds" among the American films. Their critic insisted that the average five - reeler consisted of four reels of padding and only one of impressive plot and acting, which was one reason why he favoured the return of the two - reelers. William Fox, whose studio produced all of Theda Bara's films, was quoted as saying that the answer was fewer but better pictures and he promised a series of "super" productions which would bring the public back. Other producers agreed with him and Belfast was to experience "super" and "super - super" productions over the next few years.

But the Americans faced a more serious problem, one of image. The cinema had always had its critics and enemies, people who watched and waited for any evidence of what they regarded as immorality. They highlighted stories and rumours which periodically circulated of wild parties, orgies, and alcohol and drug use among the film colony in Los Angeles, though the population as a whole paid little attention until early September 1921 when matters came dramatically out into the open. After a period of intensive film making Fatty Arbuckle and a few friends had driven up to San Francisco to relax at a Labour Day party in the St. Francis Hotel, a party which from all accounts was wild, with lots of alcohol and pretty girls. During the proceedings one girl, a starlet with a shady past, became ill and had to be attended by a doctor. She was seen later by two other doctors before, a few days later, being transferred to hospital, where she died. It was then that her friend, for her own reasons, accused Fatty Arbuckle of her death, claiming that he had raped her with violence. Friends of Arbuckle like Charles Chaplin, Mack Sennett and Buster Keaton, who knew him well, sprang to his defence, saying that such an accusation was completely at odds with his nature. Their words got little publicity because the Hearst press had decided to run with the story, putting the emphasis on its scandalous aspects. Rumour, innuendo, and half truths were used to paint Arbuckle as a monster. At first Paramount defended and supported their star, seeing that he got a good legal team, but as the pressure increased the film industry turned its back on him. In mid - October the I.S.N. announced, without comment, that Roscoe Arbuckle was "apparently down and out in filmland" and would be replaced in some of his planned roles by Will Rogers. The essence of what followed was reported locally in a factual manner without comment of any kind.

Fatty Arbuckle underwent three trials, with two hung juries until a third jury, on April 22nd 1922, not only found him not guilty but added a rider that he had suffered a great injustice, and that he was entirely innocent and free from all blame. But it was too late for the comedian. There were stories of his films being boohed off the screen in places in the U.S. though it is difficult to ascertain how truthful or exaggerated such reports were. What is certain is that his career was destroyed, his good name had been dragged in the gutter and his films, despite being completely inoffensive in themselves, were withdrawn from public showings. A month after his acquittal the Irish News reported that the Cinematograph Exhibitors Association of Great. Britain and Ireland had recommended its members "not to exhibit Arbuckle pictures already banned in America." The last recorded showing of a Fatty Arbuckle film in Belfast was in the Imperial at the beginning of February 1921, called "Good Night Nurse" in which "Fatty is seen at his best" according to the Whig. After that he just disappeared. The critic of the I.S.N. later mentioned his absence from the screen and contemplated what seemed to be the fate of "fat funnymen," recalling wistfully the great days of John Bunny who had audiences rolling in the aisles around 1910-11 and who now was never even mentioned.

The matter didn't end there because the film makers were worried about the increased calls for censorship of their medium and decided that they would have to be seen to be doing something positive. They set up the Motion Pictures Producers and Distributors of America (the MPPDA) and invited William H. Hays, a practising Presbyterian, a Republican and former Postmaster General to take the reins. His remit was to take steps to clean up the image of the film colony and to ensure "the highest possible moral and artistic standards in motion picture production." On 11th Feb. 1922 the I.S.N. reported that he had been "appointed to control the American picture industry" but wondered just what he could achieve. The Irish

News also noted the fact that "the business of reforming the moving picture" was under way and suggested that something should be done to eliminate the insulting caricature of the Irish - always poor, ignorant and intemperate - that was often presented on the screen in the same way that the stage Irishman had been banished from the theatre. One of Hay's first acts was to banish Fatty Arbuckle from the screen and then he let it be known that he expected film actors to lead exemplary public lives, an aim that was undermined more than somewhat, as Damon Runyon would have said, by a number of new scandals.

In February 1922 the successful director, William Desmond Taylor, was found murdered in his home and the Whig reported the matter under the heading "A Cinema Sensation" adding that the movie colony at Hollywood had been shocked by the crime, and that Mabel Normand and Edna Purviance were being questioned by the police. The report is interesting for a number of reasons, especially in that it contained the first reference in a local paper to Hollywood; prior to that in local articles, film criticisms and other comments, film making was usually referred to as being located on the West Coast, in California or in Los Angeles. The name Hollywood had not yet attained the eminence it was to reach as the main centre of film production in later years. The use of the term "sensation" turned out to be an understatement in light of the details that appeared over the following days, details that were more "juicy" as far as the newspapers were concerned, than anything in the Arbuckle affair. There was not only a mysterious murder but stories of illicit love affairs involving well known names, plus hints of drugs and worse.

It seemed that Mr Taylor was not who or what he claimed to be. He was regarded as a polished and cultured Englishman who had arrived in Hollywood in 1914 and since then had directed over forty films, and as a respected President of the Motion Pictures Director's Association he had often spoken out in defence of films. In fact he wasn't English at all but, as the Whig correctly pointed out, was Irish and his real name was William Cunningham Deanne -Tanner. He was an adventurer and rogue and the details of his life before Hollywood have never been fully clarified. The Whig report also intimated that Mabel Normand and Edna Purviance were involved in the case. Miss Purviance lived nearby and was interviewed merely about what she had heard and seen in the vicinity of the victim's house, but Mabel Normand was more deeply implicated. It emerged that she had been the last person to see him alive, and after the shooting was observed searching his rooms for love letters she had written to him. There was no sign of forced entry at the crime scene and nothing had been stolen so there were suggestions that his killing had been a crime passionnel, and some went so far as to suggest that Mabel herself had shot him because of his involvement with another woman. That woman was Mary Miles Minter, a Paramount star, who was very popular in Belfast where she was advertised as a rival to Mary Pickford. The publicity, whether true or not, put an effective end to her career in America though her films continued to appear in Belfast; for example the Imperial showed "All Soul's Eve" in December 1922, and as late as February 1924 the Clonard presented her in "Drums of Destiny," described as an African romance, which prompted the Irish News critic to comment, without any hint of moral disapprobation, that "Miss Minter, who is considered a woman of rare beauty, gives a fine emotional performance." Three months later the Imperial again presented her in "The Cowboy and the Lady," suggesting that local audiences hadn't abandoned her completely.

The Taylor murder was never solved though it continues to be the cause of much speculation and there have been many theories about who really committed it including one, never proved, that Mary Miles Minter's outraged mother was the culprit, or another that he was the target of a hitman sent by drug distributors. Mabel Normand was luckier than Arbuckle or Miss Minter because despite severe attacks on her character, including hints of drug taking, audiences continued to support her strongly, though her survival proved to be only temporary. During the darkest hours of the scandal Mabel's latest film "Molly O" was in release and continued to play well. It arrived at the Royal Cinema during the first week in January 1924 and was warmly greeted by critics and audiences. The News Letter critic encouraged its readers to go and see the film which was the story of an Irish heroine Molly O'Dair, a plucky girl played by "that talented actress Mabel Normand" fighting for her place in the world. The I.S.N. was equally enthusiastic, describing the film as "exciting" with splendid stunts. The writer described one which gives a flavour of the action. The heroine is abducted in an airship which is pursued by the hero in an aeroplane. As the plane flies over the airship he drops on to its roof, reaches and rescues the girl before they both parachute safely to the ground. Who said that James Bond stunts were original? The incident must have reminded those viewers with good memories of an early flying film "A Dash Through the Clouds" (1911) which had caused quite a stir in Belfast, in which Mabel, armed with a pistol, carried out a daring rescue using an airplane. The critic thought the airship stunt, though dangerous, was real and hadn't been faked but he could have recalled that such feats could go wrong. Some time before the Irish News had published a report with the sad heading "Young Film Actress Dies" which described how a young girl, Madeline Davis, while trying to transfer from a moving car to an aeroplane lost her grip on the rope she was using and fell fifteen feet to her death, in New Jersey.

People had hardly digested the Taylor affair when in January 1923 another bombshell exploded, with the news that the popular young actor, Wallace Reid, had died from cocaine addiction. His family made no attempt to cover up the circumstances and blamed the pressures of cinematic fame and a heavy workload as the reasons. Like young Madeline Davis he had also been holding on in his own way, trying to break the habit until he literally lost his grip on life. His studio, Paramount, launched a major publicity campaign to convince the public that because of his struggle he had died a hero, not an addict. None of that, however, was published in the local papers. Meanwhile Mabel's latest film "Suzanna" reached Belfast and drew large crowds suggesting that she would survive her critics. Unfortunately it was not to be and she found herself involved in another scandal when in January 1924 her chauffeur, Joe Kelly, shot and wounded one Courtland S. Dines while she and Edna Purviance were in the next room clearing up after a party. The shooting was followed, as in the Taylor case, by other astonishing disclosures, notably that Mr Kelly was actually Horace Greer, a fugitive from a chain gang. He claimed that he shot Dines to protect Miss Normand, whom Dines was controlling with the use of drugs. The reporters had a field day and the public couldn't believe what they were reading. Their love affair with Mabel ended and her latest film "The Extra Girl" was withdrawn while demands for film censorship and for Hollywood to be cleaned up became louder. Mabel made a few films for Hal Roach during 1926 but her career was really over. Her health deteriorated and she contracted tuberculosis. Finally on the evening of 22nd February 1930 she asked for a priest, made her peace with God, and died quietly during the night, aged only 38 years.

There are those who insist that Mabel Normand was the finest comedienne of the silent screen. She had worked and held her own with John Bunny, Charlie Chaplin, Roscoe Arbuckle and of course her mentor, Mack Sennett, and had brought smiles to the faces of millions of people including thousands in Belfast who recognised her simply as "Mabel." Among the pallbearers at her funeral were Mack Sennett, Charlie Chaplin, Roscoe Arbuckle, Ford Sterling and D. W. Griffith, all of them fully appreciative of her outstanding talent, but who, as they contemplated the untimely passing of a sad unhappy clown, must have asked the questions that are still pertinent: was she socially naive, too trusting or just unfortunate in her choice of friends?

Such questions have not been asked about William Desmond Taylor whose career is being reassessed. In Ireland his birth town, Carlow, has, since September 2012, presented an annual Taylorfest honouring him in lectures and discussions as one of the country's major silent film directors. A number of his films have been shown with special musical accompaniment, including "Soul of Youth" (1920) and "Huckleberry Finn"(1920). The positive aspects of his life and achievements are now being presented to a modern young generation who for the most part had never heard of him.

Remembering Irish director William Desmond Taylor.

There is no indication in 1922 of how seriously Belfast audiences took the Taylor and Wallace Reid scandals, though they must have formed the basis of many a conversation in the cinema queues. Filmgoers were almost certainly fully aware of them - the Sunday papers and the fan magazines saw to that - but they were too involved with their own problems of trying to survive the bombs and bullets, to be seriously concerned. For their part the owners and managers who drove the entertainment business were certainly more worried about the troubles in Belfast than those in Hollywood. Closed doors meant no income, and they were determined to reopen their premises as soon as was possible. The only hall that became a permanent casualty of the violence was the New York cinema in York Street which Fred Stewart decided to sell rather than repair. Across the city other damaged halls were soon resounding to the sounds of repair and redecoration. The Big Four in the city centre, the Imperial, Panopticon, Royal Cinema and the Picture House had all managed to keep going with only temporary closures of a few days, and they were soon joined by the Grand Opera House and the Royal Hippodrome which reopened fully in early July, 1922. The annual Twelfth passed relatively quietly which was an encouraging sign though some sporadic violence continued. On 21st August the Clonard reopened, "beautifully restored" according to the Irish News, and large crowds thronged the Falls Road in welcome. The bombing of the Clonard had caused much anger on the Falls Road not just because it meant the loss of a popular centre of entertainment but also because people identified closely with their local cinema which they regarded as a symbol of modernity and progress. Thus their manifest delight when it reopened, decorated and restored to its former self.

Three weeks later the Coliseum was back in business after structural alterations, but instead of showing films it reverted back to its former theatrical function and presented an eight week season of plays by the Denville Stock Company. By early November it had reverted to films and variety again, with a series of Maciste films and a new serial, "The Great Reward." Just as people were rejoicing at the return of their favourite halls the Alhambra suddenly closed its doors again, in early November, and was put up for sale with the offer of a 71 year lease at £400 per year. However the hiatus was short and on 2nd December it reopened with a flourish under new management. The new manager was Henry Houston, a Belfast stage performer whose connection with the Alhambra went back to W.J. Ashcroft, the Solid Man himself. Houston was a successful magician who had travelled widely with his own show and had now returned to his native city. He had a wide experience of the entertainment business and was expected to get the old Alhambra back to popularity and profit. "You will get the best at the Alhambra," his advertisements promised, and he showed that he appreciated the tastes of the hall's traditional audiences by presenting the film of the controversial Carpientier v. Siki fight. He retained the customary separate performances (at 6:50 and 9:00 pm) and keen prices of 5d, 9d, and one shilling. On 11th December 1922 the Gaiety reopened, in direct competition, with separate performances at 6:40 and 9:00pm and similar prices, and set out to attract its patrons back with a series of Sherlock Holmes two - reelers starring Eille Norwood.

The city's main halls were by then back in operation with a few notable exceptions like the Popular, the badly burned Tivoli and West Belfast Cinema, but it would be wrong to assume that things were returning to normal. There was still anger and unease, especially among the Nationalist minority and they responded with cynicism to Sir James Craig's call to forget the past. "Let us wipe it out and think only and solely of tomorrow," and he added the hope that Catholics would return to the shipyards. In reply the Irish News pointed out that there were 51,000 unemployed in Belfast, that wages were generally depressed and it was almost impossible for Catholics to get work in the shipyards or elsewhere as long as there were Protestants unemployed. Some employment was promised from an unexpected source, when, in the midst of the recent closures, a group of local business men announced that they had formed a company to build a new luxury cinema to seat 2,000, be called the Classic, in the city centre at Castle Lane. The reaction was mixed. There were those who asked: are they mad? In the midst of bombs, bullets and fires they want to build what could become another target. Others were more optimistic and regarded the decision as a positive vote for the future.

Despite the difficulties and interruptions to normal cinematic service, the year 1922 had much to offer to filmgoers with films from Nazimova, Buster Keaton, Larry Semon, Harold Lloyd, not to mention the Gish sisters, Gloria Swanson, Chaplin (whose "Pay Day" had an amazing success in the city), and Mary Pickford, who still brought the crowds in with "Little Lord Fauntelroy" and "Madame Butterfly" though, as the I.S.N. reported, she had recently announced her intention to change her image, grow up, remove her "curls and pigtails", wear longer skirts and "do romance with Doug Fairbanks." British films continued to arrive and the Royal Cinema manager, Frank Pearse, presented a number of them, including versions of Dicken's works, notably "The Old Curiosity Shop" and "The Adventures of Mr Pickwick" with Bransby Williams, which were welcomed by the local critics because of their literary and educational values. A group of exciting adventure yarns showed widely across the city including "The Great Air Robbery" which dealt with the exploits of a gang of air pirates. The Irish News critic thought it was excellent entertainment with "spectacular effects" including a series of night battles in the sky filmed "with great realism." Another film which attracted a lot of attention was an early science fiction story "A Trip to Mars" in which an astronomer built an airship in which he and his son flew to the Red Planet. There they were warmly greeted by the peaceful and well organised Martians who showed them "the beauties of their planet."Later they returned safely to Earth with a very contemporary message of peace and international understanding. From the descriptions in the newspapers the production actually seems to have been a Danish film called "Heaven Ship" made a few years before. The relationship between films and international peace was a popular topic at the time. In an article published in the Irish News Jesse Lasky described film as no less than "the common tongue of the League of Nations," while on a visit to London in November 1922 with her sister Constance, Norma Talmadge returned to that theme with the comment that the cinema had done much to foster better understanding between countries and suggested that what was needed was "a cinema League of Nations to put an end to war." The I.S.N. published her comments with obvious approval.

But the highlights of the year were the new much hyped Super Productions, notably "The Three Musketeers" which the Picture House presented in September, starring the energetic Douglas Fairbanks. The film was preceded by a prologue and accompanied by specially written music which impressed the local critics, who also praised the film's vitality and the performance of its star. The director Fred Niblo was commended for his staging of the action and his handling of the actors, who, besides the popular Fairbanks, included Marguerite de la Motte, Barbara LaMarr, Adolphe Menjou and Eugene Pallette. Long queues were the norm for the whole week. In November the Imperial presented another major production though of a completely different milieu. It was a modernised version of that old favourite "Camille," starring the "incomparable Nazimova." The Irish News critic was overwhelmed by Nazimova, whom he described as "beautiful, exotic and always sympathetic" and he pronounced her performance to be "marvellous." The Whig critic was equally impressed by the outstanding quality of her acting. Her co -star was one Rudolph Valentino but none of the critics even mentioned his name.

The movie of the year from the public point of view was the William Fox super production of "The Queen of Sheba" starring Betty Blythe, which arrived at the Royal Cinema in mid - November. Its appearance was preceded by a storm of publicity so that everyone could know that it was "the world's greatest motion picture, the love romance of the most beautiful woman the world has ever known." Potential viewers were bombarded with a wealth of statistics to back up those claims. The film had cost over £250,000 to make, and its cast involved 10,000 people, along with 500 horses and camels. The massive sets included the interior and exterior of King Solomon's palace, and an elaborate arena constructed for the chariot races covered over 150 acres. "Terrific" battle scenes were promised, added to such spectacles as the Queen of Sheba's caravan arriving in Jerusalem. The queen herself was played by a rising star, Betty Blythe, whom William Fox hoped would replace Theda Bara as the new femme fatale. Stills show Miss Blythe looking beautiful and exotic in a series of costumes of veils and strings of pearls. In the film she wore 28 different costumes, and she commented wryly that if she had worn them all at once she would still have had difficulty keeping warm. To show the story in all its detail required ten reels, so the film was presented as a road show, with three separate showings daily at 3:00, 5:30 and 8:15pm, with special prices of one shilling for the stalls, and one and sixpence for the balcony.

The city literally went Sheba mad and in the face of such publicity and the undoubted charms of Miss Blythe the critics probably felt - like many critics today - that serious comment was superfluous, but they did what they were paid to do. The News Letter writer emphasised the escapist qualities of the production and noted how audiences found "something intensely fascinating in the mystery and romance of past ages." The film didn't fail at that level and he found it "enthralling in its interest," pictorially spectacular and pulsing with scenes of great power. He expressed approval that in the midst of all the spectacle there were intimate scenes of moving human intensity especially when Solomon called on the God of Israel to grant him wisdom. The critic made no mention of Betty Blythe at all but took time to draw attention to the qualities of the special accompanying music by Weber (Euryanthe), Beethoven (Coriolan), Monti (Legende Arabe), and Lingini (Ballet Egyptienne) which also gives some idea of the atmosphere the makers were attempting to conjure up. The Whig critic agreed with his colleague but felt that the key to its success was the director J.Gordon Edwards who had directed many of Theda Bara's films. He praised Edward's control and how he was able to produce "scene after scene of extraordinary power," while he commended his striking use of pageantry.

Around the corner, in High Street, Fred Stewart in the Panopticon was impressed but not overwhelmed. He fought back with a seven - reel Goldwyn super production called "Theodora," described as a story of politics and violence set in 6th century Byzantium. With a typical flourish Mr Stewart informed the public that his film had taken three years to complete at a staggering cost of £700,000, with a cast of 25,000 persons, clearly putting the Queen of Sheba in her place. Belfast was quite familiar with the details of Theodora, which had often been performed as a melodrama on the boards of the old Theatre Royal, and indeed had also appeared in an earlier silent film version. The practice of remakes has a long history in the cinema. The story told of how Theodora, a dancer, had married the Emperor Justinian and became involved in a life of indulgence and corruption, which was ended by a popular rebellion. But the new film was presented as "bigger and better" than its predecessors, and the critics seemed to agree. The Irish News was impressed by its "awe inspiring realism, "and the Whig thought it was "a feast for the eyes" while at the same time - in a throwaway but telling comment on silent film making - admiring the ease with which the story could be followed. The News Letter noted its educational value in that the dress, customs and manners of the period seemed to be accurately portrayed. The film was given added importance by being presented in separate shows at 2:30, 4:30, 6:30 and 8:30 pm and the result, as the Irish News reported, was "crowded houses." On that optimistic note the cinemas faced into 1923.

Betty Blythe as The Queen of Sheba: the super epic.

CHAPTER EIGHTEEN
Horsemen, Sheiks and Valentino

After the dark days and the tribulations of 1920 - 22 the years that followed must have seemed a golden age which brought smiles to the faces of both managers and filmgoers. There is no doubting the popularity of the cinema during the Twenties not only with the working classes, but increasingly with the better educated middle classes and even groups of the more serious - minded. Every aspect of the medium was discussed, examined, and commented upon not only in the film fan magazines like "Picturegoer" and "Picture Show," which appeared weekly, priced at an affordable 2d, but in the daily newspapers where a sequence of reports, articles and readers' letters combine to build up a lively picture of a topic that ranked only second to politics as a source of local conversation. The public's craving for information about films and their stars was boundless. Such enthusiasm was a response to many factors, beginning with the obvious fact that films were still, above all, a cheap and satisfying form of entertainment, presented with highly organised but essentially seductive advertising campaigns. The studios and film makers were becoming more successful in the presentation and packaging of their products, while, at the same time, more talented personnel were being attracted to the industry, which in turn was having an improving effect on the content and quality of many films. In the hands of directors like Erich Von Stroheim, Maurice Tourneur, Fritz Lang, Rex Ingram and Cecil B. deMille the silent film was becoming more complex and sophisticated, a trend clearly recognised by the local critics.

In November 1920 the Irish News published a long article by Jesse Lasky on the cinema, taken from an impeccable source, the Manchester Guardian. One could be reasonably sure that the article was actually written by Mr Lasky himself or at least it reflected his thoughts on the matter. The article was concerned essentially with describing and explaining the growth of the American cinema since the War, a process which he naturally enough saw as worthwhile and beneficial. He argued that its world-wide success had earned the industry the capital to build large studios in Los Angeles (there was no reference to Hollywood) with all the most up to date facilities, in which up to seven films could be made at the same time. The studios also had the money to offer high salaries and in that way to attract the best talent among actors, directors and writers from around the world. The stars, he emphasised, were particularly well paid, with favourites like Alla Nazimova earning over 13,000 dollars per week, while successful personalities like Chaplin, Mary Pickford, Doug Fairbanks, W.S.Hart and Sessue Hayakawa were able to set up their own production companies. Increasing numbers of authors now reaped financial benefits by adapting their work for the screen and saw their efforts reach a much wider audience. Improved quality now meant that film was no longer "a cheap and vulgar business having no relation to the life of Art." He predicted, correctly, that the time would come when every settlement would have its own cinema, and that films would become part of the curriculum in schools, and part of the entertainment available in hotels, and on the machines of long distance travel. While the article was basically serious and informative it also for many young people confirmed their perception that a career in films was a road to money, glamour and success.

When the Royal Hippodrome presented a live entertainment called "Making Films" accompanied by the intriguing question: would you like to be a picture star? it played to packed houses. It was actually an exercise in film making, involving professional actors and members of the audience, all presented in an entertaining fashion. The stage was organised to represent a film set complete with lighting, props and camera. A simple story with four scenes was outlined and volunteers from the audience were invited on stage to play the characters. As they were costumed and made up, the processes were explained in a humorous manner to the audience. Then, when the preparations were completed, the story was filmed and projected later in the show. The event was a great success with people and critics, and actually returned the theatre the following year, to equal acclaim. The Whig reporter describing it as "novel and unique," while the Irish News commented that it attracted packed houses despite the curfew. The films made during the week were also shown later in the Alhambra and the Coliseum with the invitation to "come and see talent on the screen."

The fascination with the cinema affected all levels of society. Writing in the I.S.N. in November 1922, local man Sir Robert Baird described a visit to the Famous Players - Lasky Studios in Hollywood, one of the rare occasions on which the film centre was mentioned by name in the local papers. There he met and spoke with Cecil B.de Mille who invited him to watch an indoor scene set in a fashionable apartment, in a new film "Adam's Rib," which he was filming. Baird was intrigued by the whole process and highly impressed at the care taken to achieve certain effects. He described the rehearsals with the three actors involved, and noted that there were two cameramen and twenty five other individuals working behind the scene getting the effects, and especially the lighting, right. He counted twenty one large electric arc lights at work. He toured the studio, visiting the workshops where the props were made and admired the detailed models of planes, ships and cars that were on show. In the special effects department he was shown some of the tricks of the trade, for example how a small jump of a few feet could be made to look like ten times that distance. Some time later other tricks of the trade were discussed when, in February 1923, the Irish News published a review of Frederick Talbot's new book "Moving Pictures." The reviewer praised the volume though he felt that it tore away "the veil that hides the real working of the film." The tricks and special effects used to fool the public were fully described but, despite that, "the fascination of the movies is heightened rather than otherwise." He could have been writing about today's audiences.

The heightened public interest manifested itself locally in the form of crowded halls and "House Full" notices. At the popular level the average citizen's immediate concern, as a prelude to an evening's entertainment, was the ready availability of seats, rather than having to face a long wait in a queue. To wait or not to wait was often the question. In the evening the front exterior of the typical cinema was ablaze with white and coloured lights beckoning patrons into its warm interior. Large colourful posters and front - of - house stills gave hints of the delights that were in store within. But equally prominent usually was a large letter "Q" indicating that the hall was temporarily full. Queuing became a familiar feature of the

Belfast social landscape during the war and post - war years and the I.S.N. took to referring to the "queue fever" which gripped the city every evening, but especially on Saturdays when patrons would wait in line for up to an hour and a half to see a film of similar length. In early January 1924 the paper reported that D.W. Griffith's "Way Down East," starring Lilian Gish had attracted queues one quarter of a mile long outside the Royal Cinema.

As already indicated there were those who regarded queues as an inconvenience and complained loudly and often about them, and especially about those managers who seemed to do little to reduce them. The Coliseum, for example, pragmatically accepted them as a fact of life and in its advertising exhorted its patrons to "meet me in the queue at the Coliseum," while the Picture House just ignored them and called on their patrons to "meet me at the Picture House." But some owners did listen, among them Fred Stewart, who announced at the beginning of 1923, that the Crumlin was opening large waiting rooms so that patrons in future would be "saved the inconvenience of standing in queues and would be protected from inclement weather." Others had canopies attached to the outsides of their buildings with the same aims. But not everyone complained and some local writers in the papers took a more down - to - earth approach by suggesting that queues were to be welcomed as a clear visual indicator of the enthusiasm of the citizenry for "the pictures." Still others were more philosophical and held that queues fostered a sense of patience in the population. One writer admired the forbearance of his friends who were willing to wait patiently and quietly to see a particular film. Another commented how queuing encouraged conversation, most of which was usually about films and their stars. He added that he had discovered the most interesting and amazing information about the lives of film favourites like Nazimova by listening to the conversations around him.

Another writer saw the queue as the prelude to a great adventure which began when a fully caparisoned male attendant beckoned the waiting and expectant crowd from the dark night into the welcoming foyer, and up to the paybox. From there you entered the darkened auditorium, and were confronted by a uniformed girl selling sweets and cigarettes from a tray suspended around her neck. Then another uniformed young man or woman, he wrote, guided you by torch to your seat, but usually disappeared quickly, leaving you in the dark, to edge past the other seated patrons, trying not to step on their feet or to collapse on the lap of a large female. He suggested that a certain leeway was permissible and acceptable regarding those problems, during one's progress but that you still felt a sense of achievement when you reached your seat and settled between its comfortable arms. All negative feelings soon gave way to pleasure as you turned one's attention to the screen. There could still be minor irritants, like the tobacco smoke that hung in the air, though most people just accepted that as part of the cinema environment. More annoyingly one could end up seated near someone who insisted on reading the titles aloud, probably to others who couldn't read or who read too slowly. But even that was forgotten, he insisted, as you became involved in the film. That general scenario - minus the reading aloud of titles after 1930 - remained familiar to cinemagoers right up to the late 1950's when cinema going here went into decline. The author remembers many epic waits, including queuing for nearly ninety minutes with a friend one Saturday evening in 1957 to get into the Imperial to see Cecil B. de Mille's "The Ten Commandments".

Queuing wasn't the only aspect of cinema going that survived into the later sound era. The convention of continuous shows, with patrons entering or leaving during the films, may be difficult for a modern audience to understand but it was the norm in most cinemas. "Come when you like, go when you like" was typical of the advertising used by some cinemas in the city. It may sound illogical but it was not unusual for people to arrive in the middle of a film and then watch the programme until that point came round again, before exiting, so that in fact they saw the climax or ending before the beginning. Not everyone approved of the continuous programming, and Random Jottings in the Irish News in 1936 complained that some people abused the system, staying to watch the main film twice or more. Displeased managers had, by then, taken to projecting a slide on the screen asking patrons to think of others, and vacate their seats when they had seen the complete programme to make room for those waiting to get in. Despite complaints, the majority of filmgoers liked the system and it remained in operation well into the Sixties. Also, even in the downtown cinemas, films were usually booked for a run of three days, with programmes being changed on Mondays and Thursdays. Only the top films were kept for a full week, and on rare occasions some were held over for a second week. Unlike today there was a wide range of new and older films available and no two cinemas in the city normally showed the same film at the same time. New films began their runs in the city centre cinemas before moving outwards in the following weeks to the suburban halls. Most films were in black and white - but more about that later.

The idea of the queue as a social phenomenon where information was freely available and easily exchanged is an attractive one and certainly the people standing in line had much to talk about in the Twenties. Almost certainly local personalities were much discussed, because, despite political and religious differences, people were fiercely proud of their fellow citizens who had made a name for themselves. Chattie Mc Ildowie was one such success and, better known by her stage name, Moyna Magill, can claim to be Belfast's first film star. She was the daughter of Willie McIldowie, a well known local solicitor who had a keen interest in the amateur stage. He was a member of the Belfast Amateur Operatic Society and had been much praised for his performances in Gilbert and Sullivan. His daughter had honed her stage skills locally during the war years before moving to London where she soon attracted the attention of the critics. There she also met George Pearson who persuaded her to take parts in two of his films which were released in 1920. The first was a story with a horse racing background called "Garryowen," in which she starred with Fred Groves. When it was shown in the Duncairn during October 1921 the Irish News noted that it starred "that popular Belfast artiste Chattie McIldowie (Moyna Magill)," with the implication that that was sufficient recommendation to see it. Her second film "Nothing Else Matters" was a major critical success in London and here, when it was released in August 1920. Reports described how the critics at its preview had so enjoyed it that, at their insistence, it had to be shown immediately for a second time. The film, which also introduced Betty Balfour, dealt with the clashes and jealousies behind the scene in the theatre and George Pearson maintained that it was one of the best films he had ever directed. The Whig critic noted that it had "a strong story which made no concessions to sentimentality," and had special praise for Miss McIldowie. The film didn't reach Belfast

Moyna MacGill, the pride of Belfast.

until November of the following year when it was screened in the Royal Cinema, before being shown across the city. The I.S.N. drew special attention to the fact that it starred "Belfast's own screen actress, Moyna Magill" (or MacGill).

Miss Magill became an attractive supporting actress and later went to Hollywood where she appeared in films with her daughter, Angela Lansbury. Miss Lansbury, who has had a long and successful career in films and on stage, but is probably best known for her "Murder She Wrote" series on TV, may appear to be quintessentially English in many ways but on a visit to Belfast she expressed her admiration for her mother and declared that she was proud to be fifty percent Irish. Elsewhere she claimed that in her everyday activities she was English but once on screen or stage her Irish half took over, and she put that down to the influence of her mother. Another Belfast actress often mentioned in the local press was Cathleen Nesbitt, though her talents were as yet confined to the stage. Originally a member of the Irish Players, she had charmed audiences and critics here, in America, in Europe and in London where she was based for many years. She made a film in England in 1922 called "The Faithful Heart" but didn't really make much impact until the sound era.

Another local personality who must have been a source of comment was Albert Sharpe, the future Darby O'Gill. He hadn't yet appeared in films, but his music hall act was welcomed in cinemas throughout the city. He had grown up in the vicinity of the Empire Theatre and from his early youth had been fascinated by the stage and especially music hall. Beginning in the Empire, he built up a reputation as a black face singer, dancer and comedian. Experience was gained the hard way by touring in England with a friend enduring low wages, uncomfortable digs, and dingy and seedy halls. Audiences were difficult to please and he mentioned how hecklers would stand up and shout at the younger performers demanding to know why they weren't in the army fighting the Germans. He expressed no interest in the "flickers," as he called them, that were shown as part of the bill, maintaining they were usually old, scratched, jerky and difficult to watch. Managers, he insisted, regarded them merely as "fillers" and often put them on at intervals, or at the end of the show when the hall was being cleared before the next performance. J.B.Priestly has made similar comments and recalled that he avoided flickers until Charlie Chaplin appeared on the scene and he realised what film was really capable of.

Mr Sharpe never suggested that the local music halls in Belfast had such a low opinion of the early films, and all the evidence indicates the opposite. They occupied a prominent position on the bills in the Empire and the Alhambra, where they were greatly appreciated by local audiences. In the early Twenties minstrel shows made a comeback, welcomed by local critics who claimed that they livened up the entertainment scene, and Albert Sharpe became a well known member of Alfred E. Dodd's Dixie Minstrels. But it was mainly as a solo performer that he became familiar to picturegoers as a result of his frequent appearances on the stages of the Alhambra, the Clonard, the Duncairn and other venues. During one of those bookings the I.S.N. reviewer summed him up as "simply a comedian with something new." One can be sure that the retailing of the choicest of his jokes helped shorten the wait in many a queue.

Another topic that must have been discussed, especially among the waiting male members, was sport. Admiration was expressed for the fine silver cup, the Alhambra cup,

The main venue for filmed boxing matches.

presented by the directors of that hall to the Irish Football League in November 1920, a gesture that reflected the long standing enthusiasm of the Alhambra management and its audiences for sport. An earlier manager, the flamboyant Will White, had reared and raced greyhounds, one of which was called Alhambra's Beauty, much to the delight of the patrons, while the hall was always crowded when films of major boxing matches were shown. Over the years the Alhambra had built up a special reputation for showing films of "the noble art" even before it was regarded as especially noble. By the Twenties, the sport had a high profile throughout the whole city and no eyebrows were raised even when boxing films were shown in the city centre cinemas. Boxing had come to be perceived as a healthy pursuit which instilled discipline and self control in the young, and boxing lessons were available even in the conservative surroundings of the Y.M.C.A. and the C.P.A. A writer in the Whig commented that professional boxers were treated with the awe and respect once reserved for the gladiators of old and were even welcomed on stage and in films. Of course there was nothing really new in that because since the days of John L. Sullivan and Gentleman Jim Corbett boxers had toured the music halls and theatres, giving demonstrations of their prowess and enjoying the adulation of the crowds. Following in that tradition Bombadier Wells visited the Royal Hippodrome in March 1923 in a play called "A Question of Honour" wherein he was called upon to give a boxing display.

Many boxers had also over the years taken parts in silent films, and in the comments mentioned above the Whig critic was actually referring to Georges Carpentier who had followed in their footsteps by appearing in leading roles in films like "The Wonder Man" (shown in the Imperial in February 1921) and "A Gypsy Cavalier" (in the Royal Cinema in March 1923), in both of which he acquitted himself with credit. The latter was a British costume drama made in 1922 and set in 18th century Bath, in which he played a gentleman who was forced by circumstances to become a gypsy boxer. Later that year Carpentier returned to the ring to fight Battling Siki from Senegal, in Paris. It was a scrappy fight by all accounts during which Carpentier was accused of butting Siki, while, later, Siki was thought to have kicked Carpentier in the ankle, tripping him up. At that point the referee stopped the fight, disqualified Siki and awarded victory to Carpentier. There was immediate uproar in the hall, and the police had to be called to restore order. The referee and judges consulted together, decided to change the verdict, and awarded the victory to Siki. The event caused widespread arguments, but it was announced that the match had been filmed in actual motion and slow motion, and an examination of the film would settle the matter. Needless to say it didn't, and the boxing critics remained divided. One French critic went so far to say that Carpentier was defeated because he had entered the ring like a picture hero, and had acted like one, instead of a scientific boxer. The arguments were closely followed in Belfast and enthusiasts could scarcely restrain themselves until 9th October when the Royal Cinema presented the film of the affair. The public were promised "an impartial witness" in the form of the slow motion sequences from which they could form their own conclusions. The reaction of the local critics was summed up by the I.S.N. which stated that the slow motion "was used to great effect," but one can be sure that it led to heated exchanges among boxing fans The film then transferred to the Lyceum and later, in December to the reopened Alhambra, where it was watched by noisy and appreciative crowds.

Some time later excitement soared again when it was announced that Siki's next fight would be with the Irishman Michael McTigue from Clare, for the cruiser - weight championship of the world, in Dublin on St Patrick's Day 1923. The venue was to be the La Scala Theatre in O'Connell Street. The night of the fight saw great excitement both inside and outside the hall with large crowds milling around awaiting the result. Suddenly, at about 7:30 pm, there was a loud explosion and rumours spread that an attempt had been made to blow up the La Scala. It soon became clear that the bomb had gone off further up the street at the back of the Pillar Picture House, which occupied number 62. It damaged the exit doors and blew some of the musicians to the ground, though luckily no one was badly injured. The main building was only slightly effected and as far as the management was concerned it was business as usual. The damaged doors were wrenched off, the patrons were persuaded to resume their seats and the film was restarted. Meantime the crowds waited good humouredly in the street as the fight went the whole distance of twenty rounds. Suddenly the word spread: "McTigue has won," and there were thunderous shouts and cheers that would have drowned out the sound of any bomb. As in Paris, Siki protested again, claiming that he had won 17 of the rounds, but the verdict stood, and the disappointed African left by boat in a sulk, heading back to France. Two weeks later the film of the fight arrived in Belfast, showing in the Royal Cinema for a week. How many rounds did Siki win? the advertising posters asked. The News Letter critic didn't give an answer but thought the film was "sensational," as did the crowds on the Falls Road who cheered Mc Tigue when it was shown in the Clonard. Boxing films continued to attract large audiences, who much appreciated the slow motion sequences. In October the Irish News critic congratulated the Alhambra for living up to its slogan "you always see the best in the Alhambra" by allowing fans to see Carpentier, back on form, flooring Beckett in a "careful" slow motion sequence lasting 15 seconds.

While many young men were attracted by the excitement of the ring, it seemed that every young girl's ambition was to act in films, an attitude that the film studios encouraged for obvious reasons. In February 1924 the Picture House presented a Goldwyn film which dealt with that aspiration. It was called, rather enigmatically, "Souls for Sale" and according to the Irish News, was the story of how an unknown young girl with no acting experience worked her way upwards to become a star. It is a story not unfamiliar to modern audiences, though the success today would probably be in the popular music industry. Direction was in the hands of Rupert Hughes, the uncle of the better known Howard Hughes who twenty years later was actually to take an unknown and turn her into a major star called Jane Russell. "Souls For Sale" starred Eleanor Boardman and purported to parallel her own career. But the film was also a piece of subtle advertising for the industry. Thirty five stars took part, including top names like Charles Chaplin and Eric von Stroheim, both of whom were shown directing scenes from their latest films. Glimpses of the private lives of the stars were shown, an approach which the critic found to be "entirely new." There were also insights into the use of special effects, with spectacular desert scenes and a circus fire, while stuntmen performed and explained their impressive feats. It was a carefully constructed window on a world of glamour, excitement and talented friendly people, showing what the News Letter called "all the bustle of studio life." For that reason alone it would be academically interesting to see today, but in 1924 it was a "must" for any film fan, and the Picture House experienced long queues all that week.

One of the ways for an aspiring actress to gain entrance to that world was to win a talent competition. Many of those were organised by unscrupulous manipulators and led nowhere but one of the more reputable examples, which produced much queue gossip, was sponsored by the Daily Sketch. That paper, in conjunction with the newsreel company Topical Budget, organised a nationwide competition in 1922 to discover a new female film personality who would be chosen, in London, by the Talmadge sisters, Norma and Constance. The winner was promised a trip to America and a part in a film. Local heats were to be arranged across the country and the winners would go to London for the final. The popularity of films was reflected in the fact that 300 local girls, would be stars, came forward and by a process of elimination were whittled down to two, a Miss Tinsley (18) and Suzanne Stewart (17), the daughter of cinema owner Fred Stewart. They departed by steamer for London with the best wishes of their friends and the whole city. Joe Schenck, a producer from Metro had travelled over with the Talmadge sisters and the whole affair was filmed by Topical Budget. Neither of the local aspirants was successful but the winner, chosen by Norma Talmadge, was called Margaret Leahy, a name that suggested Irish connections. There was much excitement in the city when it was revealed that one or both of her parents actually came from Belfast. The newsreel of her success, her subsequent tour of England and her departure with her mother from Southampton on the Aquitania was shown throughout the city in December and ran for two weeks in the Lyceum.

Miss Leahy was feted in America where her bubbly personality won her many friends. As promised, she was given a part in a new film, and the one chosen was the Buster Keaton comedy "The Three Ages," produced by Schenck and directed by Keaton. Buster was reluctant to accept a complete amateur with no acting experience on the set but, under pressure, finally agreed. The film was a gentle parody of Griffith's "Intolerance" and consisted of the same story retold in three separate eras........the Stone Age, the Roman age and the modern Twenties. In each age Margaret was the heroine and Buster the hero. By the conclusion of each section the principals were married and the final scenes give some idea of the humour. At the end of the Stone Age Buster and Margaret appear surrounded by a large and lively family; at the end of the Roman episode they appear again with a large but slightly smaller family, but, at the end of the modern story, they emerge accompanied only by a small dog. The film arrived in Belfast at the Panopticon in August 1923 with a flourish of showmanship from Fred Stewart, who indicated that Miss Leahy herself would visit the city on Thursday. Unfortunately she was unable - or unwilling - to come and sent a telegram to Mr Stewart which he published. "Regret cannot accept invitation to visit during showing of "Three Ages" because, very busy making new British film, but hope to visit later. Best wishes to yourself and people of Belfast." The Whig summed the film up as "a delightful comedy" and thought that Miss Leahy had made a good impression "supporting that droll player, Buster Keaton." In the trade however the general opinion was that the lady was no actress and, unlike Eleanor Boardman, she doesn't seem to have made any more films but quietly and sensibly disappeared from public view. She had had her experience of fame, short as it was. Andy Warhol would have approved.

The dominant topics of discussion in the cinema queues were the films and their stars, and not just the top stars. There was a whole raft of lesser performers who were immensely popular, and whose films appeared regularly downtown and across the city, always drawing large crowds. Typical were the Western heroes like Hoot Gibson, Harry Carey, Buck Jones and the self styled "king of the cowboys" Tom Mix, with his trusty horse Tony. Their action - filled stories were replacing the more severe and historically accurate depictions of W.S.Hart, whom audiences were beginning to regard as out - of - date. On the comedy front Larry Semon, a white - faced clown wearing a black bowler and rather tight - fitting overalls, was a great favourite and the Irish News critic described how his "side splitting reels" always delighted audiences. The name is not a familiar one today but especially on this side of the Atlantic he was, in the early Twenties, regarded as a serious challenger to Chaplin. Another favourite whom one never hears mentioned today was the dark - haired Louise Glaum. She had been around in films since 1914 but only came to the fore in the vamp era. One critic referred to her, rather unkindly, as a second rate Theda Bara. She attracted notice as a seductress tempting W.S.Hart in westerns like "Hell's Hinges" and "Hell Hound of Alaska," and built up a large following in Belfast, where she kept her fans satisfied in films like "Sahara," which showed in the Royal Cinema in April 1920. The Whig thought it was a "delightful entertainment" which brought "the atmosphere of the Ancient Nile and the weird charm of the desert night before you." Other epics included "Sex" which the News Letter described as "lavish, arresting, startling," while "The Leopard Woman" and "I Am Guilty" were passed over in silence.

Her biggest success in Belfast was "Love," released there in 1923 which, besides Miss Glaum, had the added attraction of being coloured by hand. All the local critics praised the quality of its "natural" colours which seems to have been an important factor in its popularity. The story line sounds familiar and involved the often filmed eternal triangle with a wife's (Miss Glaum) jealousy leading to violence and murder. The I.S.N. critic dismissed it as "a stereotyped drama" in which "the heroine is turned into a murderess, her husband into a corpse and her car into a wreck," which is as succinct a summary as anyone would have wanted. That didn't prevent it becoming a major attraction wherever it was shown in the city. Crowds flocked to see it in the Duncairn, the Central and the newly reopened Mountpottinger Picturedrome, where special guests included the Minister of Home Affairs Sir Dawson Bates, Capt. and Mrs Dixon, Major and Mrs Hall Thompson.

Pearl White in action

Another magnetic name was the better known Pearl White, and one could find her serials like "The Black Secret," and "The Lightning Raider" both made in 1919, still showing in the suburban cinemas in the early Twenties, though by that time she herself had decided to move into feature length films like "Without Fear," "Know Your Men," and "Mountain

Woman." The local critics were circumspect in their comments but never overwhelmed by them with the exception of one called "The Thief" which showed in the Royal Cinema in April 1922. It had what the News Letter described as "an intriguing plot" which concerned a frustrated but ambitious woman (Miss White) who aspired to a position in society, but was constrained by the economic reality that her husband couldn't afford to buy her the quality of dresses required. She, however, managed to obtain a supply of them by other, rather dubious, means and for a time enjoyed the friendship of the women she envied, along with the attentions of their menfolk. Unfortunately the truth came out and she had in the end to face the consequences of her behaviour.

The News Letter critic found Miss White "very watchable," while the Whig noted the large crowds that the film attracted. In February 1923 the News Letter, in an unusual departure, published a photograph of her under the heading Popular Cinema Actress which probably had to do with the fact, announced a short time before in the I.S.N., that she had decided to retire from what she called "her hectic existence" and had gone to live in Paris. She was suffering from back trouble brought on by the exertions of her earlier stunts (she consistently refused to use doubles) and her eyesight was failing; but, despite the physical problems, she had made one last serial called "Plunder." Stills from it show her involved in near - death situations, fights and other lively escapades. She seemed her old self again, the original action girl, departing in a warm blaze of glory. The serial reached Belfast in the following month and was shown, not in the Imperial where her early adventures had premiered with such excitement, but in the Crumlin and the more down - market Midland. It is amazing how her memory has survived, and how many people, who have never seen a silent serial, react positively to the name Pearl White while the names of many other actresses popular at the time, like Pauline Frederick, Mae Marsh, Betty Balfour, Peggy Hyland, Evelyn Nesbitt, Alice Terry and Baby Peggy hardly register a flicker of recognition today.

The same applies to many of the male stars of the day. How many today recognise the name Thomas Meigham that "tall, handsome Irishman" as Gloria Swanson described him, an actor who was extremely popular with Belfast audiences, or William Farnum whom the Royal Cinema once referred to as "the idol of 10,000 picture palaces". One name that still does resonate is Gloria Swanson whom the local critics admired, praising her beauty, her poise and her dress sense. The News Letter on one occasion referred to her as "the fashion model of the screen" and described her gowns as "amazing." She actually began her career with more minimal covering as one of Mack Sennett's Bathing Beauties, before moving to Paramount where she was moulded by Cecil B.De Mille, who directed her in her early successes like "Why Change Your Husband?" with the aforementioned Tom Meighan, which showed in the Picture House in December 1921. When it reappeared in the Panopticon the following September the Irish News critic noted that it was "followed by keen interest by the audience." The same applied to "Something to Think About" which appeared in the Panopticon in November 1922, drawing packed houses. That was followed by "Don't Tell Everything," "The American Wife," "Her Husband's Trademark," "Her Gilded Cage," and "Prodical Knight," all directed or produced by deMille. They made her a household name and part of the attraction was her wardrobe of exotic and much admired dresses which de Mille had specially designed for her.

Discussion of Miss Swanson's professional and personal doings soon rivalled those of the really top stars Mary Pickford, Douglas Fairbanks, Charlie Chaplin and Harold Lloyd. It is noteworthy that nearly all the names mentioned were of American performers whose personae outdazzled the more local names. There were a few British players who were beginning to make an impact. George Arliss impressed in "Disraeli" and even more so in "The Devil" where, according to the I.S.N. his performance was a superb study in "subtle villainy." Basil Rathbone, a future Sherlock Holmes, was also favourably commented upon, but the new personality that drew the most attention was a young actor called Victor Mc Laglan. Born in England, his family had emigrated to South Africa where he had taken part in the Boer War as a boy soldier. Back in civilian life he had made his living for a time as a heavyweight boxer, going six rounds with Jack Johnson and three with Jess Willard. He also spent time as a strong man in a circus, and had many other adventures, including being shipwrecked, before returning to England and enlisting when the Great War broke out. He spent most of the war fighting in the desert campaign in Mesopotamia. After the war he decided to try his hand at acting in films and discovered he had found his true vocation. Local audiences took to him and enjoyed his appearances in films like "A Romance of Old Baghdad," and "Corinthian Jack" (1923) which had a boxing background and allowed him to display his skills in the ring.

By 1922 the local critics made it clear that the three stars who dominated the affectations of the Belfast crowds were Alia Nazimova, Rudolph Valentino and Jackie Cooper. Miss Nazimova was a serious Russian stage actress who, like Sarah Bernhardt, had a Jewish background and a Catholic education. After a successful appearance on Broadway in 1905 she decided to stay in America, and it wasn't long before she moved into films, firstly in New York and then in Los Angeles. Her introduction to Belfast was by way of the Picture House which in May 1920 presented "An Eye for Eye," described as a story of

Valentino dominates the page in Cobra.

love, treachery and revenge. Audiences were promised an actress with "an alluring and magnetic personality" worthy to be called "the Bernhardt of the screen". In the film she played an Arab girl who falls in love with a young French officer whom her tribe had captured. She releases him and he escapes, as a result of which she is abandoned by her tribe in the desert to die. She is found by another tribe and sold to a circus as a dancer. Meantime the officer has led his soldiers back to the camp where he had been imprisoned and kills many of her relations. When word reaches her she plans her revenge but cannot go through with it, and, in the end, love conquers all. Hardly world shaking material but the Whig critic found it "vivid and thrilling" in its execution, and directed great praise at its new star whose acting he found "superb," while he also had particular praise for the skill and grace of her dancing. It is interesting that he greeted her as a new star because the film in question was actually her fourth, though her first to be shown locally.

In July the Picture House again presented her as "the star of 1000 moods" in a drama of the sea called "Out of the Fog" in which she played a double role as a mother and daughter, a feat that once more impressed the Whig critic who described her as "talented." The following month saw the Picture House present "Revelation" allowing the Whig to praise her "wonderful versatility." One can understand the writer's enthusiasm because stills from the period reveal her as having a slightly built frame that belied her forty years, enhanced with a fine and delicate beauty, large luminous eyes, and luxurious dark hair, while her acting revealed a subtle combination of experience and skill reinforced with intelligence and beauty. By that time she must have been attracting the crowds because Fred Stewart, always with his finger on the popularity pulse of the city, began to show her films in the Crumlin and later in the Panopticon, while the Clonard gave the Falls Road audiences the opportunity to appraise her abilities in "Revelation." But it was with the arrival of her next film "The Red Lantern" at the Panopticon in mid January 1921 that she really impacted on the city. The "great" Nazimova, as the advertising referred to her, played the part of a Chinese

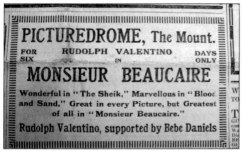

Valentino in M,Beaucaire: not his best known film.

girl in whom "ran the blood of a foreign devil," as a result of which she had to endure discrimination and rejection from both ethnic groups. The Irish News critic emphasised her wide popularity and implied that he wasn't surprised because of the "intensity of feeling and power in her acting." He was very impressed by the subtle way in which her character embodied "all the mysticism and fatalism that we associate with the people of the East." The result, he claimed, was a "fascinating" study and he strongly recommended the film. His colleague at the News Letter agreed with him, describing her acting as "thrilling in its poignancy and intensity." Intensity was a word often used with reference to Nazimova's performances, and one admirer described her as "emoting as only Nazimova could." Later in the year the Picture House presented "Stronger than Death" which gave the Whig critic an opportunity to join again in the general paean of praise. She was, he believed, an actress with few equals, and certainly no superiors. He was continually impressed by the power of her acting which he felt was "always effective, never exaggerated."

While her public reputation and acting skills kept the crowds coming, Nazimova herself was increasingly disappointed by the quality of the material she was asked to appear in and decided to turn to more theatrical and artistic fare. The first of those was the well tried stage success "Lady of the Camelias" which arrived in the Imperial in November 1922 under the title "Camille." As the Whig pointed out, it conjured up warm memories of past theatrical and operatic occasions, especially the visits to the city of Sarah Bernhardt, and indeed another film based on the play, starring Clara Kimball Young, had been screened as recently as October 1918. The new film proved to be a modern updated version of the story, which disappointed many people, though the Whig critic thought it "a fine and effective screen adaptation" while the Irish News described it as "marvellous." All the critics were, as usual, overwhelmed by the power of the main performance but only the Whig mentioned that her co-star was one Rudolph Valentina (sic). In Hollywood, in real life, Nazimova was regarded with a combination of awe and distaste. As a European artiste and intellectual she was admired and honoured by being known by her surname alone, but, in her private life, she was strong willed and often overbearing. She also made no secret of her lesbian tendencies and surrounded herself with a coterie of female acolytes anxious to do her bidding. One of them was Jean Acker, Valentino's first wife, who famously locked him out of her bedroom on their wedding night. Another was the wealthy, talented and impressively named Natasha Rambova, who had been educated in Europe, and who carried the aura of a European intellectual until it became known that she was actually Winifred Shaunnessy from Salt Lake City, Utah. She acted as Nazimova's designer and was responsible for the design and costumes for "Camille" and for the distinctive look of her next film, a version of Oscar Wilde's "Salome," which was presented in the Royal Cinema at the end of January 1924.

The locals were well prepared for an experience that was to be very different from the average film. The advertisements promised them "the screen's most amazing actress in a most amazing picture," a picture that would deliver "phantasy, history, beauty, allurement, tragedy, comedy, spirituality and passion." Whether anyone in Belfast actually believed such hype or not, what they saw was certainly out of the ordinary. It was, said the News Letter, "a splendid interpretation of Oscar Wilde's poetic drama." Rambova based her designs on the drawings that Aubrey Beardsley had completed for the original play, and her efforts gave the film a most distinctive art nouveau look which impresses even in the surviving stills. The acting was highly stylised and Nazimova's strangely boyish figure moved through the whole brooding affair, wearing a series of unusual and distinctive wigs, "a capricious but innocent figure" while the plot pointed up the "controversies and quarrels of the Jews, the flirtatious deportment of the effeminate Greeks, and the solid indifference of the Egyptians" according to the I.S.N. probably quoting from the producer's blurb. Salome was presented as a woman with many love affairs, who falls in love with John the Baptist, is firmly rejected and in revenge dances for Herod in return for the Baptist's head. On seeing that "grim relic" (I.S.N.) Herod is revolted at what he has done and orders his soldiers to kill her. As she expires the words on her lips appear as a final title: "The mystery of love is greater than the mystery of death."

Valentino in Blood and Sand

The popular response to "Salome" was rather cool, but the local critics were very impressed by what they saw, especially by Nazimova's acting which they agreed dominated the film. "Who" asked the News Letter writer, "can get away from the witchery, the grace and vivacity of this great artiste?" There was praise for the "barbaric splendour" of the settings and for the final dance which was presented "without offence." Nazimova, the critic claimed, slipped out of the last veil "without giving any basis for censorship." All of which meant that it was a film that should not be missed. While all the comments were positive, no attempts were made to compare the production with former Salomes despite the fact that Theda Bara had danced before Herod only a few years before in 1920, nor to emphasise that Nazimova's film was an Art film in every sense, with an appeal to a rather specialised audience. It is noticeable that it ran for just one week at a time when major successful films were usually being held over for a second week. In fact the Royal Cinema followed "Salome" with Douglas Fairbank's "Robin Hood," which did just that, its success reflected also in the "large crowds" that were recorded.

Significantly "Salome" was ignored by Fred Stewart, who had shown many of Nazimova's earlier films, and who often gave audiences a second chance to see local successes. Added to that is the fact that it appeared in only one other cinema in the city, when Ferris Pounds presented it two weeks later in the Mountpottinger Picturedrome. One suspects that word spread by grapevine that it was just too esoteric for popular entertainment. Also those with strong religious feelings were offended by what they regarded as as a distortion of the Biblical story, while its association with Wilde didn't help in some quarters. Nazimova's drawing power was declining at the time and it is known now that she suffered a serious financial loss on "Salome," which helped persuade her to return to the stage. The Royal Cinema, which always maintained that it was the home of Art, didn't desert her but presented one more of her films in April, her version of Ibsen's "A Doll's House" which the News Letter critic defiantly declared was "a treat, one of her best." She disappeared from the screen for many years but her memory has lingered on like a potent perfume. The public, fickle as ever, transferred their adulation elsewhere and the Irish News could note at the end of 1923 that the triumvirate of top favourites in Belfast had been reduced to two, Rudolph Valentino and Jackie Coogan.

From the point of view of cinema in Belfast, 1923 was the year of Rudolph Valentino. So much nonsense has been written about him that it is often difficult to separate reality from fiction. What is certain is that he was born in Southern Italy and at the age of 18 years, like so many other Italians, he emigrated first to Paris and then to New York, which he reached in 1913. He arrived as Rodolfo Alfonzo Raffaelo Pierre Filibert Guglielmi de Valentino d'Antonguollai, obviously a man with a proud family background, but short on funds. After a mix of employments it was his skill as a nightclub dancer that finally brought financial rewards and led him to the West Coast and Hollywood. There his dancing attracted attention from established figures like Mae Murray, who in 1919 arranged parts for him in some of her films like "The Delicious Little Devil" which showed in Belfast though without any mention of him. Other small parts followed, usually as a gangster or villain, all of them best forgotten. The only one recorded in Belfast was when he appeared in the Alhambra, named in the credits as Rodolpho de Valentino, in "The Wonderful Chance" in April 1923, described by the Whig as a Raffles type adventure. No one seemed to notice him, yet only a few weeks later the whole city was talking about him under his new name Rudolph Valentino when the Royal Cinema screened the much praised super production "The Four Horsemen of the Apocalypse" the film that made him a star.

"Horsemen" was released in America in 1921 but took two years to reach Belfast, a time lag that was not unusual then for major films. So great was its impact that Valentino was rushed into further pictures which were quickly given worldwide release. Thus his films did not arrive in chronological order. In January he made his first billed appearance quietly at the Imperial in "The Conquering Power" which, being based on a story by Balzac, was received seriously and favourably by the critics, who thought it was "powerful, and impressively told" (News Letter), with "splendid backgrounds" (Irish News). The film however ran for only three days and there was no special mention of Valentino though interest was to built up during the next two presentations of "The Sheik" and "Blood and Sand" in the Picture House, until, with the "Horsemen," Valentino arrived in style. The Four Horsemen galloped into Belfast in a cloud of advance publicity and stabled in the Royal Cinema on 19th May 1923. Its success was assured because everyone had heard of it, and the hysteria which surrounded its leading man. The critics praised its quality and the skilful use of a spoken prologue, while there were stories in the papers of even mature women fainting in the cinemas as Valentino danced the tango with Alice Terry. The Royal Cinema modestly announced that it was the world's greatest picture, the most sensational film ever shown in Belfast, and because of its length and the expense involved in its making, there would have to be separate shows (at 3:00pm and 7:30 pm) with special prices of 3/ 6 for the balcony where seats would be numbered and reserved, 2/ 4 for the parterre (back stalls) and 1/ 3 for the the front stalls.

The Four Horsemen had a new format, beginning with a spoken prologue, and it was accompanied by detailed instructions about the use of house lights, coloured footlights, music and special effects. To all that, the Royal Cinema added vocalist Madame May Reid who would sing appropriate songs during the screening. Every attempt was made to make the event memorable and value for money, beginning with the prologue. The I.S.N. thought the spoken prologue was "a worthwhile novelty" but the Whig and Irish News critics were so impressed that they described the opening of the film in some detail. As the house lights were dimmed an expectant hush fell over the packed auditorium, and out of the darkness the orchestra began to play solemn music "giving an uncanny effect as of souls in twilight regions" (Whig). Then above the music came the voice of local actor and author, Charles K.Ayre, intoning the relevant passage from the Revelation of St. John. "I watched as the Lamb broke the first of the seven seals and I heard one of the four living creatures say in a voice like thunder 'Come.' There before my eyes was a white horse and its rider held a bow. He was given a crown and he rode forth, conquering and to conquer." And so he continued describing the second horse, red in colour, riding to slaughter; the third was black and finally the fourth, sickly pale in colour, bearing a rider called Death. They were the Four Horsemen of the Apocalypse, traditionally representing Conquest, War, Famine and Death. As his voice tailed off the music picked up again, the footlights changed colour, the curtains opened and the film began.

The first sequence was set in a seedy nightclub in Buenos Aires where Valentino entered, took Alice Terry in his arms and swept her around the floor in an exciting tango. In the original script it was a short sequence but the director, Rex Ingram, recognised its potential and expanded it, giving Valentino his head. Women in the audience were overwhelmed by his grace and power and as he bent Miss Terry to his movements there had been stories of women in the audience swooning away. The ladies of Belfast proved more disciplined and there were no reports of untoward reactions, though one can be sure that a keen ear could have detected a scattering of quiet and well mannered sighs. Under Ingram's skilled direction Valentino showed that he could act also, and almost overnight the film made him a star. The Belfast critics ignored the hoopla surrounding him and concentrated on the film which they praised to the sky.

The News Letter thought it was a "remarkable production that lifted the silent drama to an artistic plane never touched before," and the critic went on to praise the acting, the direction and the "exquisite" photography. The Irish News drew attention to the "startling realism" especially of the war sequences and how the impact was increased by the clever use of lighting, the dramatic tap tap of the drum and the special effects with their recreations of the sounds of artillery and gunfire. The film was in black and white but in two scenes Ingram used colour with dramatic effect. In one the French flag was coloured and in another Alice Terry held a single red rose. It is interesting that Steven Spielberg used the same device in "Schindler's List" (1993) with a little girl wearing a red coat. The film was held over for a second week in the Royal Cinema, a sure sign of its success, and wherever it was shown later in the city it drew large crowds. It had much going for it: a respected source in the novel by the Spanish writer Vicente Blasco - Ibanez, a good script by June Servais who had also suggested Valentino for the lead part, the personality and fine acting of Valentino, a beautiful and talented heroine in the person of Alice Terry, a strong anti - war theme which struck a popular chord at the time, and an underlying touch of mysticism. The final scenes with the Horsemen crossing the sky, the camera panning across the graves of the fallen, and the mystic Tchernoff (Nigel de Brulier) saying "I knew them all," before disappearing, impressed people deeply. The success of the film was due largely to the skill of the man who gave shape, form and meaning to all those disparate parts, the director, a very talented Irishman call Rex Ingram (real name Hitchcock).

Rex Ingram was born in Dublin, the son of a Church of Ireland minister, and was raised and educated in Ireland, before emigrating to America in 1918, aged 18 years. There, he studied sculpture for a time at Yale, adding its skills to those of sketching. In New York he met the son of Thomas Edison and through that meeting went to work in the Edison film studios where he built up his knowledge of film making. Moving to the West coast he began directing for Universal, and later Metro, gaining a reputation as a stylist, until he was asked to direct the Four Horsemen, a Metro super production. The result not only made Valentino a star but propelled Ingram into the top bracket of Hollywood directors, making his name as familiar to Belfast audiences as Alfred Hitchcock was to later filmgoers. When his version of "The Prisoner of Zenda" arrived at the Imperial the following March the News Letter critic praised "the inspired direction of that young wizard of the screen, Rex Ingram" and the skilled performances of Lewis Stone, Ramon Navarro and Alice Terry whom he referred to as being "as beautiful as a lily." Similar approval was heaped on "Trifling Women" and the highly successful "Scaramouche" both of which were shown in the Royal Cinema. "Scaramouche" had the same leads as "Zenda," with Ramon Navarro, Lewis Stone and Alice Terry who had by then married Ingram. The I.S.N. critic described the film as "fashioned by the deft hands of a master" who had given it not only "heart and soul....but also a brain." The critics obviously didn't regard Ingram as a flash in the pan but as a gifted director with style and technical ability.

With regard to the Valentino phenomenon the impact of the Horsemen may have been reduced somewhat by the fact that the city had already experienced "The Sheik" which although it had been made after "Horsemen" arrived in the Picture House two months before it, in March, claiming to be "the finest production ever attempted." The papers were saturated with daily adverts calling it "the best film of the week" and a "wonderful production." But there was no need because Valentino's reputation as an exciting personality had preceded him, and expectant crowds literally besieged the cinema during the whole week. "The Sheik" was a lurid desert romance of a type that was very popular at the time. Audiences flocked to stories set in the Middle East, with scenes of dashing heroes, veiled women, swordplay, oases, warm sands, moonlit nights and a Western damsel in distress, especially if she was trapped in a harem. The year before had seen "A Romance of Old Baghdad," "The Virgin of Stamboul" which the Irish News thought was "daring" but which nevertheless gave a good picture of the "unchanging East," "The Lamp in the Desert" and "The Right to Love" which starred Mae Murray as a young American sold into slavery in a Turkish harem, where she had to cope with "one of Nature's degenerates." Like those "The Sheik" would have been forgotten by now if it wasn't for Valentino. As it was, it increased the public appetite for such films and they became an increasing feature of programmes during the next year or so.

"The Sheik" was based on a romantic novel by an English farmer's wife who wrote under the name E.M.Hull, and Metro tailored it to Valentino's new image of the strong and overpowering lover. The story involves a young English girl (played by Agnes Ayers) who travels to the desert in search of adventure, and finds more than she bargained for. She is kidnapped by a dashing but rather brutal sheik (Valentino) who carries her off and bends her to his will, at least as far as the Hays Office would permit. She wasn't the only one in the cinema to succumb to his hypnotic stare and flaring nostrils. The romantic sequences were interspersed with many scenes of galloping horses, and much sword play. In the final reel it turns out that the sheik is actually an English lord who had been abandoned as a child and brought up in the desert, so all ends happily. Natasha Rambova, whom Valentino had married, couldn't believe that he would have anything to do with what she regarded as trash, and she tried to steer him towards more artistic ventures. However, to women all over the world Valentino was and has remained "The Sheik." When recalling those early days of cinema the author's mother, with a smile, often referred to him as "the sheik without a shirt" which was probably how he was perceived in Belfast. The local critics ignored that aspect of the film. The News Letter described it as a romance of Araby with "beautiful settings and some daring horsemanship." There was no mention of Valentino or Agnes Ayers but much praise for David Curry's accompanying music, especially his foxtrot version of "The Sheik of Araby," which the audience really appreciated.

That song was being played and sung literally everywhere at the time, and was only one sign of the popularity of the film. Another was that Ben Turpin made a famous skit on it called "The Shriek of Araby" which was shown in the Royal Cinema, supporting Nazimova's "Salome," a strange combination to say the least. Over the next few years Valentino's films continued to arrive and were always well attended, mainly by the women who would drag reluctant boyfriends or husbands with them. The producers knew that and attempted to make his films more attractive to men by pairing him with attractive female stars. A good example was "Beyond the Rock" in which he co-starred with the most glamorous woman on the screen, Gloria Swanson. Off screen she found him good - mannered and gentlemanly, a charming companion, a fine horseman and well spoken. Besides English, which he spoke with an attractive accent, he was fluent in Italian, French and Spanish. It is intriguing that the women who adored him, never heard him speak because he died before the coming of sound. His appeal was down to the image alone.

Jesse Lasky set out to make "Beyond the Rock" opulent and visually impressive. It was based on a love story by Elinor Glyn, which gave both principals opportunity to emote

323

with passion. Miss Swanson later described the expensive furs and jewels she wore. One of the highlights was a tango danced, as she put it, with the master himself. For it she wore a specially designed lace gown embroidered in gold, which shimmered as she moved, causing great discussion among the female members of the audience. The film appeared in the Imperial in December 1923 showing to full houses, after which it quickly transferred to the working class Midland. What a poorly paid, semi -literate linen worker sitting on a wooden bench in the darkened hall clutching her shawl actually made of the luxurious goings -on on the screen is difficult to understand. It was happening only fifty feet (16 metres) away, yet it might as well have been a million miles. At the very least it represented a few hours escape from the cramped housing and the damp floors and continual noise of the spinning rooms.

There is no doubting Valentino's exceptional popularity in Belfast at the time. His films were major attractions in the downtown halls, and were also shown right across the city from the Clonard to the Willowfield, with the critics usually recording long queues and full houses. Between October 1923 and January of the following year the Clonard screened "Moran of the Lady Letty," "The Sheik," "Blood and Sand," and "The Four Horsemen," complete with spoken prologue, special effects and music under the baton of J.Finlay. The Irish News critic described the large crowds attending every showing and how the films were often interrupted by clapping and cheers, scenes one can be sure that were repeated in other venues. Fred. Stewart was quick to recognise what was happening, and beginning with "The Sheik" in November 1923, gave Valentino's films second runs, usually a few months after they had appeared in the Picture House. He would probably have approved when his premier cinema the Panopticon, which had closed after his sudden death, reopened as the Lyric in October 1924, and the first film shown was Valentino's "Cabaret Dancer."

While people were arguing or swooning over Valentino, his popularity in Belfast was equalled only by child star Jackie Coogan. Coogan came from a music hall family but became a major figure in films when, at the age of four years, he was chosen by Charlie Chaplin to appear in his new film "The Kid." The result was amazing, with young Coogan becoming a major star almost immediately. Certainly in Belfast he was taken to the hearts of both audiences and critics. "The Kid" arrived in the city in 1921 and was still being reissued and shown locally in 1924. Fred Stewart showed it on two separate occasions, a week each time, in the Panopticon and the Crumlin while the Clonard, the Willowfield, the Alhambra and the Lyceum gave it long runs. Other films like "My Boy," "Oliver Twist" and "Trouble" arrived in quick succession during 1923. Young Master Coogan could do no wrong and audiences asked for more. They could buy Coogan dolls and Coogan caps in the big shops downtown, while the papers and magazines kept them up - to - date on his latest activities. When he disembarked at Southampton in September 1924 with his parents on the beginning of a European tour there was great interest in the city, and rumours that he might come to Belfast to see his fans, though the I.S.N. thought it unlikely because Belfast was too small "even for the diminutive star." His fans could still follow the details of his travels in the papers, and on the newsreels including his attendance at mass in Westminster Cathedral, his visit to the League of Nations in Brussels and being honoured by an audience with the Pope in Rome.

Child stars had been around since the early days of the cinema but they usually played characters of the "Just William" type, causing minor mayhem and upsetting unsympathetic adults. Jackie Coogan was different in that he was mentioned in the same breath as Mary Pickford, Douglas Fairbanks and Valentino because he made feature films which required acting talent. But he soon had a rival, though few people remember her now. She was Baby Peggy (Montgomery) and her films were very popular for a time in the city, where she was advertised as "the million dollar little screen star." She appeared mainly in short comedy films but also in features like "The Darling of New York" and "The Law Forbids" both of which began their local runs in the Royal Cinema in May and August 1924. The I.S.N. often mentioned her and referred to her as a "wonderful child actress."

Defenders of the cinema welcomed successes like Coogan and Baby Peggy because they could then reasonably argue that films weren't all about sex, violence and crime. The effects of the cinema on children were still being hotly debated, especially the relationship between films, juveniles and crime. There was increasing support for the idea that no child under 16 years should be admitted to a cinema without an accompanying adult, while others argued that there was a need for an Adults Only category of selected films from which children would be debarred entirely. The I.S.N. critic found the concept of adult only films "suggestive of nastiness" and wondered where our society was heading. He asked: would the Royal Hippodrome soon have to announce that some of its live acts were suited only to certain classes of citizen? Meantime critical attention became focused on the local Children's Matinees which many cinemas organised, usually on Wednesdays and Saturdays. A group of concerned ladies led by the Lady Mayoress (Mrs Turner) expressed disquiet that such cheap matinees in overcrowded and unhygienic halls helped to spread disease, while the films shown were often unsuitable to young minds. They felt that such matinees should be better organised and supervised in more pleasant surroundings. They approached Mr Broughton, the manager of the Picture House, with the aim of introducing children's programmes on Saturday mornings, and he agreed to try them for a time.

The first was scheduled for 7th May 1923 from 11:00 am to 1:00pm, and parents were promised "clean, instructive, interesting films" which would assist children in their homework. The financial arrangements were straightforward. The cinema would take its running expenses and any surplus would be distributed among children's charities in the city. The scheme was widely praised for its worthy aims and the first day was a great success with the cinema packed. The audience including the Lord Mayor and other city worthies, along with representatives of the Ministry of Education, who declared the occasion to be "a unique gathering" and expressed the hope that the children would be encouraged to comment on what they had seen. The Lord Mayor declared that the films shown were "wholesome and proper," though only two are mentioned in reports, an Aesop fable and "The Last King of Scotland." Like other commentators the I.S.N. critic supported the idea, but showed some irritation at the suggestion that films were bad for children, adding that many things were bad for them not least cold, hunger and ignorance. He recalled how juvenile delinquency was once blamed on the "penny dreadfuls" and pointed out that though they were now gone the problem still remained. The other cinema managers made no comments, but continued as usual to present their penny matinees with their programmes of comedies, Westerns and serials. They knew that the children who attended the Picture House matinees were mainly from the middle classes but that after a week in school their patrons from the poor streets wanted entertainment on Saturdays. The halls may have been overcrowded and noisy, but the children enjoyed and looked forward to the experience. They roared with laughter at the antics of Ben Turpin and other clowns, cheered Tom Mix, Hoot Gibson, Buck Jones and the other Western heroes and thrilled at the hairbreadth escapes of Pearl White and her ilk. After ninety minutes or so they poured out of the cinema riding invisible horses, fighting Indians, swinging through jungles, all in the world of their imaginations. Only the management of the Coliseum reacted - tongue in cheek, one suspects - to the new educational Picture House matinees by announcing a competition for children who attended their Saturday matinees. Those who could spot the mistakes in an essay based on the serial being shown would be entered in a draw for a free pass covering the next eighteen weeks. The I.S.N. critic was amused by the offer and commented that it was educational in a way, a "sort of sugar coated school lesson."

Most of the cinema managers were married with families so they understood the value of education, but they would have argued that they were in the business of entertainment rather than education. The local critics would have agreed with them, but they still found educational aspects in many of the films presented for enjoyment. They drew attention to and praised the Secrets of Nature films, as well as travelogues and documentaries like those on Howard Carter's recent discoveries in the Tomb of Tutankhamun in the Valley of Kings in Egypt, but they left the decisions on what the children should see to their parents. They often detected educational worth in the most unlikely of places. When Douglas Fairbank's version of "Robin Hood" arrived in the Royal Cinema (February 1922) it was welcomed by both critics and audiences. It ran for two weeks and then returned to the same cinema in August for another week. The News Letter praised the overall impact of the film, its atmosphere of historical veracity, the fine camerawork and, above all, Fairbanks as "a joyous dare devil Robin." The I.S.N. critic agreed that his interpretation was "magnificent" making it the most entertaining film he had seen recently. Quoting probably from the producer's blurb, he emphasised the careful research that had gone into recreating the costumes and manners of the 12th century. That, he felt, gave it an educational value that added to its enjoyment. He didn't see why educational school outings of the type that accompanied Shakespeare plays in the Opera House couldn't be arranged to the cinema. Whatever truth was in that and whether any parents or schools gave it serious consideration, the fact remained that the large audiences who flocked to "Robin Hood" were more interested in a night's relaxation in warm comfortable surroundings, and they kept coming because they were hooked on films.

An interesting and somewhat bizarre indication of the strength of that addiction occurred in the Panopticon on Tuesday 7th November 1923. The cinema was crowded with a rapt audience watching a recent remake of "Secrets of Paris" based on Eugene Sue's sensational novel. It was a thrilling melodrama that had enthralled local readers as a novel, and later audiences as a stage play and an early silent film. About 6: 30 pm some patrons complained of smelling smoke and one of the ushers, John Castle, checked the heating equipment and turned on the extractor fans but the smell persisted. It was only then that he realised that the building next to the cinema, owned by Currie and Co., ironmongers and hardware merchants, was on fire. He rushed up to the manager's office but Fred Stewart had gone home and had locked the room so he wasn't able to get to the telephone. Rushing across High Street he reached a phone and called the fire brigade. On arriving the firemen discovered a large fire out of control at the back of the building just behind the Panopticon. Soon brigades from all over the city were summoned as there were fears that the flames could spread to the whole block. Because of the narrow width of the alleyways leading from High Street the firemen had great difficulty getting their equipment into position and some of them had to reach the fire through the cinema. Crowds collected in High Street as flames and showers of sparks rose in the air and the sound of heavy machinery crashing downwards through burning floors could be heard beyond the rear wall of the cinema. The firemen struggled for three hours before bringing the flames under control, and during that time they entered and exited the cinema, while water ran in along the floor and smoke filtered across the screen. Yet during all that commotion no one moved but kept their eyes glued on the screen. It seemed that the fictional drama was more enthralling than the real drama on the other side of the end wall. No attempt was made to evacuate the cinema and the Irish News correspondent expressed amazement at the "stoical" response of the audience which he saw as a reflection of "the power of the pictures."

With the demand for films so high and competition so keen, cinemas took steps to improve their facilities. Many, like the Imperial and the Clonard, closed for a few days for complete redecorations. Others added adornments to make their cinemas more attractive. The usually staid Picture House added coloured electric flaming torches to its frontage which lit up Royal Avenue, prompting one of the local critic to comment that Belfast was "getting past the big village stage." The Classic and Royal Cinema followed with bright new adornments, while the latter also kitted its staff out in new uniforms which had a flash of white on them, making them "easily seen in the gloom." (I.S.N.). Ferris Pounds decided on an upmarket overhaul of the The New Princess and began by renaming it the New Princess Picturedrome. Alterations to the auditorium resulted in the balcony being extended to hold 126 seats while the downstairs could accommodate about 810 patrons. Also in East Belfast, the Popular and the Mountpottinger Picturedrome both closed during the worst of the riots in 1922 and were slow to reopen. However by 1923 both had been redecorated and in the case of the Picturedrome, remodelled.

The Picturedrome changed hands, coming under the same ownership as the New Princess, (Irish Theatres Ltd.) with Ferris Pounds as the new managing director though day to day management was in the hands of James Fletcher. The cinema was completely overhauled with new extended seating including 160 extra seats, new entrances and exits, a new waiting room to cope with queueing, new carpeting and decor. The latter was in subdued gold, blue and cream and the News Letter found the whole effect "tasteful." On the technical side new projecting equipment and a more up to date heating system were installed, while an orchestra under the baton of Cyril Mortimer replaced the former lone piano. The emphasis in future was to be on quality and comfort and, as befitted those aims, the re - opening on August 27th 1923 was attended by the Lord Mayor (Alderman Turner) and his wife. Ferris Pounds promised quality and he backed that up in the months that followed with good films that attracted the crowds. There were reliable old favourites

The Pride of East Belfast.
Source: N. Whig.

like Mary Pickford in "Pollyanna," and "Little Lord Fauntleroy"; new favourites like Valentino in "The Four Horsemen," and "Blood and Sand"; comedy with Mabel Normand in "Molly O" and Max Linder in "The Three Must Get Them" a skit on the "Three Musketeers"; Westerns with Tom Mix; exotics like "Madonna in Chains" starring Natacha Rambova, though she was billed as Mrs Rudolph Valentino which wouldn't have done her ego any good at all; and even foreign fare like Fritz Lang's "Dr Mabuse." A mixed bag but with something for everyone because Mr Pounds wanted to widen his audience base and make the Picturedrome the premier cinema east of the river Lagan.

As part of that policy he emphasised the accessibility of the site and its proximity to the major tram routes. He had also paid attention to the discussions regarding children's matinees and at the end of May 1924 he introduced a Saturday matinee with a festive touch. Every child who attended was given a balloon and the programme of films was carefully chosen with a balanced mixture of entertainment and education. The films included a comedy, "Young and Dumb," a travelogue called "Across the Alps," an "Aesop's Fable" and "The Birthplace of William Tell" which was accompanied by an essay competition. The News Letter was quite impressed, describing the whole proceedings as "splendid" and "very educational." Local parents and the children must have agreed because the weekly event became a popular fixture in Ballymacarrett.

But the dominant event of the period was the opening of the Classic Cinema in Castle Lane, a building that not only claimed to be the largest in Ireland but which proved to be the last luxury silent Picture Palace built in Belfast. It was the brainchild of a group of local businessmen who set up a company for the purpose. The managing director and main driving force was W.K.Gibson, supported by directors H. Smylie M.P., S Donald Cheyne J.P. and Sir Crawford McCullagh. Their aim was to use local talent where possible so they engaged Sam Stevenson of Royal Avenue, the man who had planned the Kelvin Cinema, as architect. His plans were submitted to the Council in 1921 and quickly passed. The site chosen was the old Castle market at Castle Lane, a location now occupied by the British Home Stores. Extensive piling was needed to support the impressive building of steel, brick and concrete which was ready by late December 1923. Work continued right up to the time of opening, at 5:30 pm on Christmas Eve. Two days before, a celebration lunch was held in the nearby Carlton Restaurant in Donegal Place to which the press and local businessmen were invited. It was of course an opportunity for the exchange of good - mannered wishes of success, especially from the press in the persons of the editors of the Northern Whig (R.J. Lynn), the News Letter (W.G. Anderson) and the Irish News (W.H.Smith). Sir Crawford McCullagh welcomed the guests and emphasised and praised the role of a "clean Press" in encouraging the development of the city and its many institutions including the cinema. He referred to the impressive growth of the entertainment business over the previous twenty five years and what it had contributed to the life of the city. He praised the cinema, especially its educational role and its economic contribution. The new Classic, for example, gave employment to 300 persons most of whom were local. and the declared aim of the cinema was to present the public with worthwhile films of quality. After the exchange of toasts the guests were invited to inspect the new building and as they sauntered down

Castle Lane in an aura of cigar smoke they were advised that work was still continuing in preparation for the opening.

The main entrance was located where Castle Arcade meets Castle Lane and the visitors stepped into an impressive circular vestibule bordered with Doric columns of granite looking down on a floor of black and white marble. Beyond it were wide marble steps leading upwards to the spacious foyer, complete with a homely oak fireplace and decorated in bronze. There were two ticket offices with the latest automatic ticket machines, the first to be installed in Ireland, according to the manager, Noel Hobart. Bronze fittings and doors gave a feeling of luxury even before one entered the auditorium - which impressed by its size. It was fan shaped, extending 80 feet (25m) across and 140 feet (43m) in length, seating 1,250 persons in surroundings decorated in gold, orange and black, and had six safety exits. The balcony, the last word in luxury, was connected to the Tower Cafe with its distinctive green decor and to the Rotunda cafe with its blue and gold finish. An elaborate ventilation system allied to a new Lewbart Disinfector guaranteed clean air throughout the building without any "offensive odours."

A true picture palace, the Classic in Castle Lane.

Behind the balcony was the hub of the system in the form of the projection rooms, with the most scientifically up to date projectors available, made by the Ross Optical Co, of London, incorporating the latest safety devices which meant that "there was no possibility of fire," according to the manager. The souvenir programme which accompanied the opening also emphasised that safety point. The projectors had an automatic electrical switchover system which eliminated any problems as one reel followed another, while the screen was so constructed and installed that no discernible distortion of the image was noticeable from anywhere in the seating areas. The visuals would be complimented by an orchestra under the baton of T.S. Clarke - Brown, a former conductor with the Carl Rosa Opera Company who had wide experience also of cinema music. The emphasis was on modernity and quality, and the man responsible for delivering them to the public was the experienced manager Noel Hobart, who had guided the new Picture House in Royal Avenue on its way. The visitors were impressed with what they saw and the word went out across the city where the filmgoers waited impatiently. Programming was to be continuous with prices of stalls, 6d and balcony one shilling until 4:30pm, then increasing to one shilling for the stalls, and two shillings for the balcony. The seats weren't cheap but it was a luxury cinema and the opening days saw packed houses.

The inaugural film was a British production "Chu Chin Chow" based on a well known successful musical stage show. It was the first film directed by Irish born Herbert Wilcox who was to become well known later for his films with Anna Neagle. Despite being British, the film had an American star, the Queen of Sheba herself, Betty Blythe, and had actually been shot in the U.P.A. studios in Berlin. Musicals were hardly best suited to the silent format. They gave the orchestra an opportunity to shine, but problems arose with the songs. In this case the complete lyrics were included in the titles which must have been boring for some and certainly slowed down the action of the film. the Belfast audiences didn't seem to mind and the opening was a great success, a topic of lively conversation in the following weeks. That was followed by another film with a musical theme, "The Tales of Hoffmann," introduced on stage by a prologue played by the Mayfair Quartette in period dress which, according to the News Letter, helped to create an appropriate atmosphere for the film. Unfortunately the early promise doesn't seem to have been fulfilled and one suspects that things didn't go too well for the manager because in February, after only two months in the position, he declared that he was leaving for a new post in London, though, in fact, he actually became the manager of the Coliseum.

One film of interest to film historians and film buffs that he showed before leaving was "Woman to Woman." It was a superior romantic drama about a British officer played by Clive Brooks who during the war went to Paris on leave where he had an affair with a dancer (Betty Compson) from the Moulin Rouge. Later, during the fighting, he was shell shocked and lost his memory, forgetting about the woman and not knowing that she had borne a child from their liaison. After the war he returned to England where he met and married another woman. Some time later at a party arranged by his wife, as part of the entertainment a dancer was carried in on the shoulders of four Nubians (one of whom was Victor McLaglan in blackface). It was his former love and her dancing jolted his memory, forcing him to face his responsibilities. It is a plot that has been used often since then but at the time the film was regarded as adult and sophisticated. The interesting aspect is that the Art Director was a young man called Alfred Hitchcock, who also acted as assistant director and helped write the script. The editor was a young woman named Alma Reville, who was to become Hitchcock's wife and life long collaborator. The beginnings for the Hitchcocks, but the end, as manager, for Noel Hobart.

After a short delay W.K.Gibson announced the appointment of Harry Houston, the former manager of the Alhambra and the Coliseum, to the post. It was a shrewd move. As already noted, Harry Houston was a Belfastman with a long and wide experience of music hall and popular entertainment. He had once been hired by W.J. Ashcroft himself to appear on the Alhambra stage as a magician and maybe the directors of the Classic felt that his skills in that direction might help. He quickly took the reins and began making changes. Advertising became more emphatic, with larger adverts, often illustrated, in which the cinema was described as the Classic Supreme. New Ross type mirror arcs were installed in the projectors, a first for Belfast, which dramatically improved the brightness of the pictures on the screen. The orchestra was increased in size to 30 members, producing a sound more appropriate to the extent of the auditorium, and its contribution was increasingly emphasised in the adverts. He announced that the Rotunda cafe would soon be open for business and that the distractions and noise caused by the workmen still putting the finishing touches to the building would cease. Using his knowledge and understanding of music hall he began to introduce live musical supporting acts of quality, top name singers like Gordon Monro and Ella Mayne from the Cal Rosa Opera, and more popular items like the Famous Syncopating Quartette playing dance music. He added two neon flaming arrows to the front of the building pointing to the main entrance which an observer described as "pretty and effective." The interior also benefitted from improved ventilation which left the atmosphere free of smoke.

But his main attention was directed at the films, with an emphasis on those with proven popular appeal, like Jackie Coogan in "Daddy," or "Armageddon" about Allenby's campaign in Palestine, accompanied by special music arranged by the orchestra; "The Love Light" with Mary Pickford, still a major draw; "Samson and Delilah" starring Maria Corda, based on the opera of the same name and enhanced with live music by the "eminent harpist" Norman Feldman; "Unseeing Eyes" with Lionel Barrymore; "Blinky" a thrilling Western with Hoot Gibson; a reissue of Rudolph Valentino in "The Sheik;" Lon Chaney in the "While Paris Sleeps;" a new British version of "The Colleen Bawn" starring Stewart Rome; Maurice Tourneur's "The Isle of Lost Ships;" "The Death Ray;" Colleen Moore in the controversial "Flaming Youth;" and Hepworth's swansong "Comin Through the Rye." All of those were supported by live acts in the form of singers or musicians and by a wide selection of shorts including the popular Pathé News, Pathé Pictorial, comedies like Baby Jane, cartoons notably the adventures of "Felix the Cat," travelogues, documentaries on topics like the treasures of Luxor, and specialities like a series of colour films showing the latest fashions from Paris, which the Irish News described as "gorgeous."

Items of unusual interest were often included, as when in mid - June he announced that the Plastigrams were coming. They turned out to be a 3D film viewed through special glasses, and proved very popular and a great local talking point. Figures walked right out of the screen, a chimpanzee swung on a rope over the audience, a speeding car careered wildly towards them and a man with a hosepipe turned it directly on them. The audiences loved it and responded just as audiences do today. They gasped and shouted with astonishment, waved their hands before their eyes in an attempt to touch the images. The critic from the I.S.N. looked down from the balcony at what he described as an amazing sight of row behind row of people wearing coloured glasses. In the low light they seemed to him to be wearing masks and he felt he was looking at a Ku Klux Klan meeting. Mr Houston's response to that was not recorded but he was probably too happy at seeing full houses to bother. A few months later the Plastigrams showed in the Alhambra to wild enthusiasm. Some time later audiences were also able to appreciate the Vitasona, a new sound effects machine specially designed for large halls, one of only a few available in the Br. Isles.

The new manager also introduced serials beginning with "The Eagle's Talons," shown during the first half of the week followed by "In the Days of Daniel Boone" during the second half. That was an unexpected move because the downtown cinemas no longer showed serials. They had lost their shine and were regarded as somewhat down - market, though they were still immensely popular in the suburban cinemas, especially the Lyceum which continued to show some fine French examples like "Fantomas" and "The Three Musketeers", the Duncairn, and Crumlin plus the less salubrious halls like the Sandro and Midland. They had also become an integral part of most children's matinees where they were greeted with loud and prolonged cheers. If any eyebrows were raised they soon dropped again when it was realised that during Easter Week alone the cinema sold 27,122 tickets, and in the first year over one million patrons passed through its doors. On Christmas Eve 1924, its first birthday was celebrated with a special evening graced by the presence of the Lord mayor and Lady Mayoress. The Classic had arrived and the manager could announce that in the year just past they had sold a total of 1,002,332 tickets, or, as he put it, they had paid entertainment tax on that number of tickets. The Classic had obviously taken off and it never looked back until the sad bad days of declining audiences in the Fifties, thirty years later, which affected all cinemas in the city.

After the Classic Belfast added one more name to its list of cinemas, the Lyric, which opened on Monday 13th October 1924. A new name but not a new cinema because it was the old Panopticon disguised by renovation and re decoration. Sadly, in June, Fred. Stewart had died suddenly, and the Panopticon closed in mourning. Mr Stewart, an immigrant from Scotland, was a pioneer in the establishment and growth of the early cinema industry in Belfast. From his first establishment, the Electric, opened in August 1910 in York Street, he went on to build the Panopticon, the New York and the Crumlin. He also became a prominent and much respected figure in the social side of the business, and his bearded visage was a popular sight around the Panopticon, which he personally managed and, in the process, made into a leading attraction in the city. He was above all a showman, always ready to use any gimmick or new technical development like sound on disc or coloured or tinted films to attract patrons. His adverts were usually more personal than his competitors and he was not averse to a dash of humour. He couldn't compete with the Imperial, the Royal Cinema or the Picture House in the size of his orchestra but often referred to his orchestra leader as the chef d'orchestre, and to his group of about seven players as the famous Seem - Phonny orchestra. He was quick to install the latest in cinema instruments for special effects and was the first manager to use a cinema organ in the city. When some cinemas began boasting about the length of their films he parodied their adverts by announced a showing of an improbable 14 reels - which actually turned out to be two films of seven reels each. On one occasion a comedy called "Mary's Ankle" was accompanied by a short poem describing the plot:

"Mary had a little ankle
Injured it one day
Now the doctor who repaired it
Just can't stay away."

Pola Negri

When he showed the re - release of Griffith's complex "Intolerance" just a month before his death there was no mention of its serious dimension, but it was described as starring Constance Talmadge, Lillian Gish, Mae Marsh "supported by 4,000 dancing girls." He knew what attracted the crowds and didn't hesitate to show the films of the "notorious" Evelyn Thaw, Annette Kellerman or Theda Bara, but equally prominent in his programmes were Mary Pickford, Asta Neilson, Tom Mix, Sessue Hayakaya, Bebe Daniels, Nazimova and Pola Negri. He was very well informed about films and played a major role in introducing quality films to the city. He was among the first managers to show the comedies of Mack Sennett and especially the films of Chaplin, Ford Sterling, Mabel Normand and Roscoe Arbuckle, not to mention Lonesome Luke (Harold Lloyd). It was he who first showed "Cabiria" and introduced local fans to Maciste. He also presented the first examples of post - war German cinema in the form of Ernst Lubitsch's spectacular "The Loves of Pharaoh" which starred Emil Jannings, "Passion" starring Pola Negri, and

"The Golem." While the comment by the I.S.N. that the local industry had suffered "a sad loss" with his passing was true, it was also an understatement.

The Panopticon was sold to a group of enthusiastic local businessmen who had it made over. They installed the latest technically up -to - date projectors which produced a brighter picture and eliminated flicker, and had the screen slightly realigned to reduce distortion. Extra musicians were appointed along with a new manager, T.G.Harris, formerly of the Lyceum, who promised that only the best films available would be shown, regardless of expense. The newly named Lyric opened on 13th October 1924 with a presentation of "The Cabaret Singer," starring Rudolph Valentino and Mae Murray. Programming was continuous and prices were fixed at 6d and one shilling until 4:30 pm, after which they rose to 9d and one shilling and three pence, making them overall more competitive than the nearby Imperial, Royal Cinema and the Classic.

With the opening of the Lyric the pattern of silent cinemas was completed that was to last into the sound era, and audiences found themselves catered for by twenty three halls varying from the most luxurious at the city centre to the barely basic in the poorer working class areas. As the I.S.N. pointed out, competition between them was high for the best films, because while audiences were willing they were also becoming more selective in their choices. At the same time there was literally a new prospective form of competition in the air called radio, by which people could be entertained in the comfort of their own homes. In September 1922 the Irish News felt there was enough local interest in the topic to print an article on How Radio Worked, while the I.S.N. often poked gentle fun at the new addicts of crystal sets. In many homes, the writer insisted, a new tyranny had arisen in the shape of the crystal set. When Father set up the equipment in the evening the family came to attention, and watched quietly while he carefully put on the headphones to hear the latest news and music from London. During that daily ritual wife and children sat motionless. A shadow of silence was spreading through our homes putting an end to "fireside debate," a criticism that was to be repeated many years later with regard to the spread of television.

The new form of communication was quick to get organised and by early 1923 the News Letter had a regular column on radio matters, plus the broadcasting details of three stations in London, Manchester and Glasgow. In March 1924 the papers carried the news that Pope Pius XI had had a radio installed in the Vatican, and it was claimed that over ten million people listened regularly to the radio in Britain. Soon there was talk of a radio station in Belfast and on 25th October 1924 the BBC opened a broadcasting station in the Ulster Hall. Between 7:15pm and 9:00pm on that evening music was broadcast locally before the station joined the national network in Britain. The Lord Mayor praised the new venture, adding that over 1,400 licenses had been issued in Belfast since January, suggesting that radio had a great future locally. Marconi wireless sets could already be purchased in certain city shops for £22: 8d, while the Co-Op in York Street was selling crystal sets costing between 7/ 6 and 90/ - along with more complex valve sets at £11:10 to £45:00. Those prices were still too high for most working people, but well within the means of the middle classes, an audience that cinema had already targeted and didn't want to lose. Some local managers perceived the danger. In the same week in October as that first local broadcast Ferris Pounds' advert for the Mountpottinger Picturedrome read: You cannot LISTEN to the screen's greatest drama - you must SEE Pola Negri in "Bella Donna."

In Europe and America inventors were already working towards the time when audiences could both hear and see such dramas at the same time. The solution to that problem lay in the future and didn't unduly worry managers, who increasingly recognised the need for good films, and looked to the production companies to supply them. The response of the film makers was, as usual, many sided and as the Twenties progressed Belfast audiences were spoiled for choice as they experienced a heady mix of super productions, remakes and reissues of films with a reputation, plus some new and original material. The super productions with their popular stars and high production values led the attack. Douglas Fairbanks could do no wrong with the likes of "The Three Musketeers" and "Robin Hood" while Rudolph Valentino continued to attract the women with "Beyond the Rock" (with Gloria Swanson) and "The Young Rajah" which brought long queues to the Picture House. Rex Ingram's "Trifling Women," "The Prisoner of Zenda" and "Scaramouche" were the talk of the town as was their star, Ramon Navarro, the Latin rival to Valentino. D.W.Griffith's "Orphans of the Storm" and "Way Down East" were amazing successes and had all the local critics praising the talents of the "magnificent" Lillian Gish. Chaplin, Buster Keaton, and Harold Lloyd all had their fans and their exploits were discussed animatedly in factories, mills, shops and offices, as were the extraordinary roles of Lon Chaney, known as "the man of 1000 faces." Mary Pickford still drew the crowds but it was also the era of Gloria Swanson, Bebe Daniels, the Talmadge sisters and Pola Negri, who had replaced Nazimova as the foremost "emotional" actress.

A few British films made their way into the top attractions. "Paddy, the Next Best Thing" a charming story starring Mae Marsh and set in Ireland, where it was largely filmed, was shown in the Royal Cinema and then across the city. Besides the fine scenery of mountain and bog, its attractions included scenes of hunting and yacht racing. Its success was enhanced by the fact that it was based on a popular play which had had a successful run recently in the Grand Opera House. Another British film which drew the crowds to the Classic in December 1924 was Cecil Hepworth's "Comin Through the Rye" though by that time his studio, where he had made so many enjoyable films, had been sold and he was out of business, a victim of changing tastes and fashions. Audiences preferred the fast - moving American style of story - telling such as characterised the Goldwyn production called "Moriarty" which the Picture House presented earlier in May accompanied by "special music."

The film, which was photographed mainly in London, caused quite a stir because it starred John Barrymore as the ever popular Sherlock Holmes. According to the director, Barrymore spent most of his free time during the making of the film in an alcoholic haze, but that didn't seem to affect "the Profile's" acting, which was widely praised. The Irish News critic found Barrymore's performance realistic, detailed and resonant with "vivid truth and power." The film wasn't based directly on Conan Doyle but on William Gillette's play, "Sherlock Holmes" which local audiences had enjoyed on stage and as an earlier silent film. Purists were not pleased because, like the play, the film involved Holmes in a romance, so that, as the Irish News critic put it, Holmes "at a stroke captures his man and loses his heart." The villain Moriarty was played very effectively by an experienced and well known Austrian actor, Gustav von Seyffertitz who was then resident in Hollywood.

Another Austrian also living in Hollywood at the time was Erich Von Stroheim who had emigrated to the U.S. around 1906 and joined D.W. Griffith's company. He was a man of many parts, quick to learn, and by 1919 his talents had brought him to Universal Studios where he wrote, directed, designed and acted in "Blind Husbands." But it was his next picture "Foolish Wives" that really brought him to local notice. Advance publicity had emphasised that the film had cost nearly £300,000, involved 15,000 of a cast, and had taken a year to complete. Von Stroheim was a stickler for detail and tended to work slowly, characteristics that were to cause clashes with his producers and studios in the future. Picture Show magazine, read by many local fans, carried an article about the making of the film, illustrated with shots of him acting, and behind the camera, so expectations were high when it opened in the Royal Cinema during August 1923. Large queues were the order of the day though the I.S.N. critic commented that though it did not please everyone "it caught everyone's attention." Von Stroheim was a cultured man who brought a sophisticated European outlook to the problems of human behaviour, including sex. His film dealt with the seduction of an innocent American wife by a cynical Russian army officer, played out against the opulent and decadent background of Monte Carlo. Von Stroheim, who was advertised tantalisingly as "the man you will love to hate" played the callous officer with "great force and vitality" (News Letter). The Irish News critic thought his acting was superb with "every expression, every gesture" illuminating the character, while his direction mercilessly revealed the "sins, snares and follies" of society. The Whig critic agreed that the acting was splendid and was equally impressed by Von Stroheim's evocation of the atmosphere of Monte Carlo, "the whole spirit of the place" as he put it. He relished the carefully chosen detail, the scenes at the gaming tables, the hectic crowds, the smart set mixing easily with soldiers of fortune. He found the film visually striking and especially commended a water carnival imaginatively photographed at night. It was a film, he concluded, that "should be seen by every movie lover." Despite its sordid theme the local critics recognised its original style and intelligence, and felt that overall it had a positive moral message. They encouraged their readers to see it.

Hollywood was always ready to avail of European skills and another fine director working there was the Frenchman Maurice Tourneur. Tourneur was the father of Jacques Tourneur who later impressed Belfast audiences with a number of atmospheric thrillers like "Cat People" (1942), "I Walked With a Zombie" (1943), and "The Night of the Demon" (1957). He obviously inherited his approach from his father, who was strongly attracted to stories of mystery and imagination, stories that greatly appealed to local audiences. But Tourneur was above all a stylist and his films had a distinctive pictorial look which combined beauty with imaginative presentation, traits that were not lost on the local critics. His versions of "Treasure Island" and "While Paris Sleeps" both with Lon Chaney, his remake of "The Christian," "The Last of the Mohicans" and "Women," all drew eager crowds. The latter film dealt with the impact of women throughout history from the time of Adam and Eve, and consisted of separate stories in the form of a Prologue, four episodes and an Epilogue. The Whig critic found it "enchanting and fascinating" while the Irish News praised its originality, finding it "inspiring, appealing and fascinating."

But the Tourneur film that caused the most stir was "The Isle of Lost Souls" which showed in the Classic in early April, 1924. It was advertised as "a tale that staggers the imagination with thrills to make your teeth chatter." It had a plot that was original at the time but which has been much copied since. A ship is wrecked in a storm in the Sargasso Sea with only three survivors, a convicted murderer, a detective who has him in charge and a young society girl. They discover a strange floating island which is ruled by a cruel dictator who doesn't make them welcome. After a series of incredible adventures they come across an old submarine in which they eventually make their escape. The Irish News critic praised Tourneur's direction which he thought was "very imaginative." The News Letter gave a more complete though concise commentary describing it as "a fascinating tale which stimulates the imagination..... weird and romantic.....wonderfully pictured....the audience enraptured."

The Hollywood studios were also looking to Germany again for talent. Before the war Belfast had been familiar with German films but when hostilities broke out it became illegal to import or show "enemy" films and the only Germans to appear on screen for a number of years were of the despicable Hun variety. In December 1921 the I.S.N. announced that the ban on enemy films would soon be lifted. During the war film making in most European countries had suffered from lack of materials and personnel but in Germany the authorities had recognised the entertainment and propaganda values of the cinema and film production was encouraged, to supply the cinemas of German - speaking regions. In 1917 the authorities helped in the establishment of the U.F.A. production company by merging a number of smaller film units. The U.F.A. studios were to nurture a group of film makers and actors including Ernst Lubitsch, Fritz Lang, F.W.Murnau, Paul Wegener and others whose combined talents produced a golden age of silent classics which are still watched, enjoyed and studied today.

The films dealt with themes of crime, master criminals, myth, monsters, legend, murder and madness, photographed in a distinctive style called German Expressionism which took its inspiration from painting and the theatre. They presented a strange world shaded in dramatic light and shadow, a world of distorted images and realities wherein slow moving figures wrestled with good and evil. The first of the German films, Fritz Lang's "Dr Mabuse," advertised as "the wonder film of the world," arrived in the Picture House in September 1923. While "Moriarty" was being shot in London a few years earlier Fritz Lang, an Austrian by birth, was directing "Dr Mabuse" the story of another master criminal in Berlin, but the result was very different from the Sherlock Holmes story. The film finally emerged in two parts... "The Great Gambler," (120 minutes) and "Inferno" (93 mins) and was previewed on two consecutive evenings, 27th and 28th April 1922 in Berlin. At that time Germany was politically unstable, lurching from one crisis to another and the capital, Berlin, reeked of corruption and moral turpitude. Extreme poverty and want existed side by side with wealth and all kinds of carnal and indecorous behaviour. Unabashed sex, drugs, gambling and alcohol were all freely available in the city's nightclubs, cabarets, gambling and other dens. Writers of the time compared that behaviour to the excesses of Biblical Babylon, Sodom and Gomorrah. It was that environment of moral decay that Lang brilliantly recreated and interwove into the story of the rise of a sinister master criminal who manipulated and destroyed men and women in his insatiable search for wealth and power. Many have since seen Mabuse as a grim foreshadow of the rise of Hitler, though

Lang himself actually compared him to Al Capone.

The film caused a sensation and was an immediate success with both audiences and critics. The acting, and above all, the direction were greatly praised and many scenes were picked out and commented on. Typical was a gambling sequence during which Mabuse's face initially appears as a small white dot on the completely black screen before the camera zooms in rapidly until it fills the whole screen, its evil eyes glaring at the audience. The climax where Mabuse and his gang are besieged by police in an exiting shoot out, was also praised for its execution. At the end an obviously mad Mabuse was captured and taken away to a mental asylum. Belfast had its problems of politics and violence but Mabuse was something else and the Picture House was literally besieged by people seeking admission. The management drew attention to the excessive length (over three and a half hours) of the film and that it was usually shown in two separate parts. For the first time, they claimed, the film would be shown as one unit, which meant there would be only three shows a day. Those shows were all packed, and there were reports of many disappointed patrons being turned away. It was the same story when the film was shown later in the Mountpottinger Picturedrome, the Clonard, the Coliseum and the Duncairn even though in those more suburban cinemas the film was shown in two separate parts during Mon., Tues, Wed. followed by part two on Thur., Fri., and Saturday. The local critics were all quite impressed. The News Letter critic found it an exiting experience, especially the climax, and he noted the quality of the sets, the acting and the production. The Irish News critic described how it held the audience "in an unbelievable grip" and how the events on screen were watched "with breathless interest." He also went out of his way to commend Rudolf Klein - Rogge, who played Mabuse, in a "powerful and convincing manner."

After such an experience many cinemagoers must have asked for more German films and Fred Stewart at the Panopticon responded quickly. He turned to a director whom many regarded as the equal of Lang, another German called Ernst Lubitsch and, in January 1924 during the same week that the Royal Cinema showed Nazimova's "Salome," presented his "Passion." It was known in Germany as "Madame du Barry," because it was the story of her rise and eventual fall, a victim of the Terror. It starred Lubitsch's favourite actress Pola Negri, a new face to Belfast audiences, but one that was soon to replace the afore - mentioned Nazimova in their affections. It was accompanied by an impressive advert with a sketch of Miss Negri who was described as "the famous continental actress," starring in the "Romance of the world's most daring adventuress." The News Letter praised the "scenes of great splendour" in the film while the I.S.N. commented on the careful research that had gone into its preparation, so that besides its dramatic interest it had a definite educational value. The Irish News critic was the only one to mention the star, finding her acting "impressive," though it was the direction that really caught his attention. He found many scenes not only sensational but presented with spectacular effects. The incidents depicted around Madame Guillotine were so realistic that "one could hear the sound of the trumbrills and the fall of the knife." The idea of "hearing" a silent picture gives some indication of the impact that quality film making had on the imaginations of contemporary audiences.

Fred Stewart followed its success with another Lubitsch production, "The Loves of

Pharaoh" Germany's first spectacle film. It came at an appropriate time when everyone was talking about Howard Carter's amazing finds in the Valley of the Kings in late 1922, and people couldn't get enough of things Egyptian. Typical was an advert from W.H.Alexander of May Street, the local agent for Morris cars, which referred to the finds at Luxor and added that even the chariot of the greatest Pharaoh who ever lived was "a Poor Thing compared with the Modern Motor Car." The film had everything a spectacle film needed... a fine cast including Emil Jannings who played the tragic Pharaoh who falls in love with a lowly slave girl, impressive sets, scenes of luxury and debauchery within the palace, court intrigue and murder, and battles fought in vast desert vistas. The critics praised its "splendid atmosphere" but noted also that the director never let the spectacle overwhelm the human dimension. The undoubted popularity of Lubitsch's films must have tempted Fred Stewart to try an example of Germany's more esoteric films, but even he wasn't brave enough to present Anthony Weine's "The Cabinet of Dr Caligari," a fascinating study of murder and madness as seen through distorting lenses, to his audiences. In March 1924 he did present "The Golem" at the Panopticon, promising his patrons "something entirely new in pictures... drama like nothing you have ever seen before." The story, described as "a fantasy of faith and fury," was set in the 16th century and concerned the Golem, a precursor of the cinematic Frankenstein monster, a large and massive clay figure made and brought to life by a Rabbi to protect the Jews in the ghetto of Prague. After fulfilling its main task, however, the monster became destructive, abducted the Rabbi's beautiful daughter and was finally only subdued by a playful young child. Innocence overcoming evil. The I.S.N. thought it was a "remarkable" film. It was shown a few years ago in the Q.F.T. and still looks very eloquent and impressive, though probably too slow moving for a modern audience. Overall its impact tends to be more beautiful than horrific; visually it is a rare treat.

During 1923-4 Germany was staggering from one political crisis to another; there were protests and riots in the streets, unemployment and poverty were widespread and inflation was rampant as the mark steadily lost its value. Lang, an Austrian, took out German citizenship in 1923 and partly to celebrate that and partly to counteract the contemporary political pessimism he decided to film the 13th century epic poem, the Nibelungs, which described the adventures of the noble Siegfried and Kriemhild. The final film was released in two parts: part one called Siegfried, and part two called Kriemhild's Revenge.. It was part one which arrived two years later in the Picture House in late January 1926 and amazed both critics and audiences. The Northern Whig critic admitted that he had seen nothing quite like it before and the audience around him sat "astonished" at what they were watching. He felt that words alone couldn't convey its impact and that it had to be seen to be really appreciated. The Irish News critic noted its German origin but added that with its many spectacular scenes "it could hold its own against most American films." The latter were obviously the template for cinematic entertainment. All the critics were impressed by the power of the story telling with its combination of myth, fantasy and special effects. They described Siegfried beginning his journey to woo Brunhilde, the beautiful princess of Burgundy, carrying his newly forged invincible sword, a journey that took him through a magic forest which the Whig described as a cinematic "miracle." In the forest he had to overcome a tribe of dwarfs and do battle with a fierce dragon. The dragon, described by the News Letter as "a marvellous mechanical achievement," was 70 feet long and was worked by a crew of 32 men hidden in a pit beneath it. The Whig was quite impressed at how natural its movements were, whether eating, drinking or fighting. After overcoming it Siegfried bathed in its blood which made him impervious to weapons except for one place on his shoulder where a falling lime leaf rested leaving a point of vulnerability which, as is often the fate of mythical heroes, was later to prove his undoing. The News Letter praised the beautiful settings and "the great attention to detail" which would have pleased Lang who was a stickler for accuracy.

The Siegfried saga was very popular in Germany and had been the inspiration for novels, plays and opera, notably by Wagner. Lang wanted to present a popular alternative to Wagner but, despite that, the Picture House orchestra poured on the Wagner - which must have added substantially to the general atmosphere. That association with Wagner and the fact that the film later became a favourite of Hitler has caused the film to be criticised as preparing the way for the Nazis, a charge that Lang has dismissed. He knew nothing, he claimed, of the Nazis when he was making the film and his intention was to look back to the past and not to the future. When Hitler came to power in 1933 he fled the country and finally settled in Los Angeles.

Some time before that he had travelled to America on a visit and was greeted in Hollywood as a special guest. On a tour of the studios he watched the making of scenes for Conan Doyle's "The Lost World" which caused quite a stir when it came to Belfast in 1926. The plot involved the discovery of a plateau area in S. America which time had by -passed, leaving an environment inhabited by prehistoric animals. Bessie Love, the star, recalled that the exotic locales were actually all filmed around Hollywood and that the prehistoric animals were small models animated by Willis O'Brien, who went on to do the same for the first and best "King Kong." The models were made of rubber and manipulated by internal bellows, wires and stop-go photography. As in Kong, the explorers brought back two animals who break loose and go on a rampage in London, before disappearing down the river Thames. Lang showed deep interest in O'Brien's work and suggested that Hollywood was well ahead of UPA in such special effects.

Another German film shown in the Lyceum was F.W.Murnau's "The Last Laugh" a complete contrast to the fantasy, violence and spectacle of "Siegfried." Unlike the former film whose players were generally unknown here "The Last Laugh" had Emil Jannings, whose face was very familiar to Belfast audiences, as its star. Also, in contrast to Lang's film with its complex structure and many narrative strands it had a simple linear plot without any trimmings. The story concerns a hotel porter (brilliantly played by Jannings) a man of importance in the high class hotel where he worked, in his family circle and in his neighbourhood. That social importance was reflected in the impressive uniform which he wore with pride. Because of his advancing years the unpleasant manager demotes him to lavatory cleaner, depriving him of his signature uniform and replacing it with a simple white coat. With that he loses his dignity and his ability to cope with life. A subjective camera records the insults and snubs directed at him by those he thought his friends and the images spin, tilt and go out of focus, reflecting his reactions and state of mind. When things are at their worst he unexpectedly comes into a legacy and so regains his dignity and humanity. The story is so skilfully told that it required no titles with the exception of one near the end. The first showing in the Lyceum began with Mr Fowler, the leader, calling the orchestra to order before they played "The Last Laugh" foxtrot, complete with vocals, which was well received. During the film there was complete silence as the audience sat fully absorbed. When it ended it became clear that the story had certainly struck a chord with the watchers because they spontaneously broke into applause. The Irish News critic approved, but also expressed some amazement because, as he wrote, "Belfast audiences are not too easy to please." But obviously many in the cinema felt a certain empathy with the old man, and understood only too well the effect of losing one's job or position. Former soldiers recognised the significance and symbolism of the uniform. During the war they had worn one with pride and the public had respected them for it. After the war when their uniforms were discarded they became just one of the crowd again, struggling to survive in an era of rising unemployment.

The new German films may have been slow moving, with touches of Teutonic ponderousness, but the best of them had style, stimulating content, technical quality and a wealth of talented and creative personnel. Hollywood, with its money and studio facilities, beckoned and over the following years many of the latter took the journey to the U.S.A., especially after the rise of the Nazis. One of the first to go was Lubitsch, and Belfast audiences soon became familiar with Lubitsch productions from America which the local critics praised for his light and elegant directorial style and his understanding of human nature. He was followed by Pola Negri who signed for Paramount and went on to become, in the words of a local critic, a household name. She was Polish but according to Jesse Lasky the language difference didn't prevent her swearing like a trooper if she didn't get her way off screen. Paramount rushed her into two remakes, the first of which was "Bella Donna" based on an earlier Pauline Frederick vehicle. The story concerned an unscrupulous woman who goes to Egypt where she becomes romantically involved with a sheik. Infatuated, she decides to murder her husband but he foils her plans and evicts her from the family home. She returns to Egypt and, she hopes, the arms of her lover, but finds him dallying with another woman. Stunned and rejected, she wanders off into the desert and disappears into a raging sandstorm. The desert often appeared in contemporary films as an image either of a moonlit vista for exotic romantic adventures or equally as a sunblasted landscape of moral barrenness.

Today the plot line would probably raise a few laughs but in the Twenties those themes of the fallen wife, the exotic lover, the betrayed husband and moral retribution were all the rage, so when the film arrived in the Imperial near the end of May it caused quite a stir. The News Letter critic thought it was a "magnificent production" and he praised the Egyptian sets. Above all it was Miss Negri's performance that really impressed him. He expressed admiration for the way she dominated the film, "expressing both the passionate and lovable sides" of her character yet retaining the sympathy of the audience to the end. The Irish News critic went even farther. The film was "a crushing rejoinder to those high - brow critics who are wont to sneer at the film as a medium of art." That was a pointed reference to the debate on the value of the cinema which was occupying the minds of many writers and artists at the time. He also praised the leading lady's acting which he felt "put her among the greatest tragediennes." He added that the film was visually beautiful and that the accompanying music was "delightful." The Irish News critic never forgot that no silent film was complete without its music.

"Bella Donna" was followed six months later by "The Cheat," another remake of the Cecil B.de Mille melodrama starring Fanny Ward which had shown in Belfast only four years before. Miss Negri suffered nobly in the old Fanny Ward part and the I.S.N. critic's response was to find her acting "full of fire, verve, power and magnetism." The Northern Whig was more restrained, describing her efforts as "clever." Her third American film, "The Spanish Dancer," arrived in the Imperial, early in the following year, described as a romantic story of Old Spain. The advertising promised a "fiery dynamic personality flashing like a comet through reel upon reel of nerve tingling action." The Irish News critic thought it was a "delightful" film though the audiences who flocked wherever her films were shown across the city probably agreed more with the billboards. To the critics Miss Negri was the latest "emotional actress supreme," following in the footsteps of Pauline Frederick, Theda Bara and Nazimova.

In complete contrast to the seductive images, dark eyes and dramatic posturings of the great screen goddesses, Robert Flaherty's simple "Nanook of the North," which came to the Royal Cinema in July 1923, proved to be a revelation. It claimed to be "the most remarkable film ever shown" and for once the publicity was near the truth. The local critics were overwhelmed by its simplicity and the fact that it had no plot, no trained actors, no stars or studio sets. It was revolutionary in that it was the antithesis of the studio product, its style, content and presentation being a long way from the technically polished productions of Doug. Fairbanks and Gloria Swanson. It was real life presented visually by a poet, and some critics greeted it as a new form of film making. It was in fact an early example of a documentary film though no one used that term because John Grierson, the critic and film maker, didn't coin it until a few years later. Grierson, whose cinematic writings and work were widely admired at the time and who became more widely known when he launched his programme on documentary films called "This Wonderful World" in October 1957 on Scottish Television, believed that the cinema had benefited from the work of five great innovators: Georges Méliès, D.W.Griffith, Mack Sennett, Eisenstein and Robert Flaherty.

Flaherty was an American with Irish roots, an explorer and geographer who had turned to film making. He brought a poetic eye to the problem of showing pre - industrial cultures and was able, according to Grierson, to turn the ordinary into the remarkable with his camera. There had of course been actuality films from the earliest days of the Lumière Brothers but whenever native peoples were shown the camera was looking at them and their culture from the outside. Flaherty's approach was quite different. He lived with his subjects and illustrated their way of life and culture from within. As a film title explained, Nanook was a member of the Itivimuit branch of the Eskimo people and Flaherty stayed with him and his family for a year filming his struggle for survival in a harsh environment, the cold desert of the Barren Lands of N. Canada. At the beginning Nanook may have seemed rather backward, with his lack of sophistication and his simple tools, but as the film progressed he emerged as a complete human being, humorous, intelligent and above all self - reliant. The audience could identify and sympathise with him and understand what he was doing as he ventured into the frozen wastes in search of food in his continual struggle to stave off hunger and starvation. The latter was always a real threat and sadly, according to reports, Nanook himself succumbed to it two years after the film was completed. The News Letter critic described the film as "a unique experience" and noted how it "held the audience from start to finish," a detail that the writer in the Whig agreed with while also describing it as "a splendid achievement." It was, he felt, a plain "unvarnished" story which showed that truth can be stranger than fiction. He also pointed out that the success of Nanook locally reflected a growing interest in actuality films like the Secrets of Nature series. There was some truth in that.

The memory and shadow of the recent war of course lay darkly across the Twenties, but as the decade progressed, books began to appear describing and highlighting the true horrors of what the soldiers had gone through. It is not surprising that the details of the conflict also became a suitable subject for film makers, especially when the success of "The Four Horsemen" indicated that people were willing to accept war themes again after a period of revulsion following the peace in 1918. The War was fought again on the cinema screens in both fictional and documentary form. A series of war films passed before receptive audiences with titles like "Reveille" with Betty Balfour, described as a story of how the war had affected a group of ordinary people; or "Havoc" with Madge Bellamy, accompanied by an advert reminiscent of the Four Horsemen, and praised by the I.S.N. for the authenticity of its war scenes. The critic was especially impressed by the terrible realism of scenes of soldiers going over the top into a maelstrom of liquid fire attacks, bursting shrapnel and machine gun fire, all lit by blinding rockets and star shells, scenes which he felt would convince people of the need to ensure that there would be no more wars. That was followed by "Roses of Picardy" and "Mademoiselle from Armentieres" starring the popular Estelle Brody, and described as "a soldier's story of the war" which, when shown in the Alhambra, was accompanied by "full effects as only the Alhambra can." The I.S.N. thought it was "the most appealing of all war films." Also shown were "Victory," "The Big Parade," "Wings," and "What Price Glory? Those last three were American, and are the best remembered films of the period." The Big Parade "starred John Gilbert, that "useful and talented artist" as the Irish News reviewer called him, who had a large following in the city; while William Wellman's "Wings" dealt heroically with the war in the air.

Entertaining and exciting as the fiction films were, it was the documentaries that had the most immediate local impact. In March 1922 the Wellington Hall (Y.M.C.A.) presented a Lowell Thomas travelogue dealing with the campaigns of Allenby and Lawrence of Arabia in the Middle East. It took the form of a combination of a lecture by a Mr Courtenay who had been involved in the actual fighting, accompanied by slides and film clips. The Whig described it as "one of the most thrilling and fascinating entertainments ever given in Belfast… an artistic combination of the motion picture, the coloured slide and the speaking voice (which) depicts the campaign against the Turks with vivid realism." The crowds came in large numbers and such was their enthusiasm that the display returned a few months later to the Ulster Hall. On that second occasion Lowell Thomas himself arrived to give the lecture. The prices of admission ranged from one shilling and threepence to three shillings and sixpence, too expensive for most ordinary workers, but their needs were soon met by the British Instructional Company, the same company responsible for the Secrets of Nature, which decided to make a documentary of the same campaign using maps, photographs and actual wartime newsreels interspersed with short sequences involving actors. The film, called "Armageddon," was relatively inexpensive to make but proved a great success with the public. It arrived in the Classic in April 1924 where it was presented to packed houses, enhanced with special music. The I.S.N. recommended it highly for its accuracy.

It was the first of a series of similar documentaries dealing with Zeebrugge, Ypres, Mons, and The Battles of the Coronel and Falkland Islands, all by the same film makers which appeared in Belfast during the following years bringing back memories, good and bad, to those who had fought through the campaigns. They were welcomed by large crowds and praised in the local press for their quality and their educational value, though some critics elsewhere felt that they tended to romanticise war. "Ypres (Wipers)" arrived in early 1926 described as "a pageant of heroism" and "an imperishable story," followed by "Mons" which showed in the Classic during Armistice Week later that year. The management invited 200 soldiers from Victoria Barracks to the opening evening performance. The group included 150 "Old Contemptibles" who marched in full uniform displaying their medals through the city preceded by a band. On Armistice Day itself the Classic Symphony Orchestra played special music, including songs that were popular during the war. The Whig described the film as "a lesson in patriotism" and that it was a suitable reminder of the debt owed to the old soldiers for the hardships and sacrifices they had endured.

There was even more emotion the following year, 1927, when a new version of "The Somme" appeared in the Royal Cinema during Armistice Week causing interest even in circles that normally ignored the cinema. "All Belfast must see this pageant of heroism where Ulstermen won Undying Fame" ran the advertisement, and such was the enthusiasm that the film was retained for a second week before being shown widely across the city. The I.S.N. found its realism so "startling" that the viewer became fully involved in what was happening on the screen, and the reviewer picked out particular scenes for praise: the troops waiting in "eerie light" to go over the top when the creeping barrage of heavy gunfire stopped, scenes of fierce fighting, individual deeds of bravery, and the problems of getting ammunition and food up to the front lines. During that particular November week, besides "The Somme," the downtown cinemas also presented "The Battles of the Coronel and the Falkland Islands" in the making of which the navy had cooperated fully, and "The Unknown Soldier." The latter was a fictional American film about the experiences of a young soldier during the War. Unsuccessful attempts had been made earlier in England by a group, who thought it "unsuitable," to prevent it being shown during Armistice Week. The local critics found it very moving and recommended it to their readers.

War, its futility and its horrors were much in the news during those years and there was widespread approval when in August 1927 fifteen countries including Britain, Germany and the U.S.A. signed a treaty in Paris outlawing it. The local papers mentioned that there was a greater spirit of compromise abroad in Europe and welcomed it. Against that background another war film, British this time, arrived in the city during the following year, surrounded by controversy. It was Herbert Wilcox's "The Dawn" in which Sybil Thorndyke played the part of Nurse Edith Cadell who was shot as a spy by the Germans in Belgium in 1915. Some argued that it was such a sensitive topic that the film would stir up resentment against Germany, and the German Ambassador had complained to the Foreign Secretary Austen Chamberlain who in turn had put pressure on the Film Censor, T.P.O'Connor. The result was that the film, in an early example of political censorship, was refused a certificate. Wilcox cleverly persuaded the LCC to view it and after an all night sitting the members narrowly passed it as fit for general exhibition. After that it was widely shown in the country and garnered much praise. The News Letter referred to its first public showing in the London Palladium as "crowded but normal" and wondered what all the fuss had been about. A few days later it reported that the film would be shown in the U.S.A. and two weeks later that the Police Committee here had viewed it and given permission for it to be shown in the Royal Cinema, where it opened on 28th May 1928, a month after its original release.

The response was immediate. All five showings on the first day were packed and the waiting crowds became so great that police had to be called to keep Arthur Square open to traffic. The critics were very impressed especially by "the ennobling and genuinely tragic quality of Sybil Thorndike's acting" (News Letter) and were agreed that the furore that had accompanied its making was completely unnecessary. The Telegraph described it as setting out "coldly and clearly to demonstrate the ghastliness of war" while the Whig thought its theme could best be summed up in Nurse Cavell's last words, "Patriotism is not enough - I must have no ill feeling or bitterness towards anyone." The News Letter pointed out that the film as presented was not exactly what Wilcox had intended. Scenes at the end where Rammler, one of the German soldiers in the firing squad, refused to raise his rifle and was shot for disobeying an order, and where Nurse Cavell fainted and was shot dead while lying on the ground by the German officer in charge, were cut out. Instead the film ended with Nurse Cavell facing the firing squad followed by a quick cut to her grave. The actual execution was not shown. The paper attacked "the wholly indefensible attitude" of Sir Austen Chamberlain who refused even to see the film, yet used his considerable influence against it. As such, the paper felt, there was no blame on the censor and no suggestion of political censorship.

The Irish News and many others saw it differently, criticising T.P.O'Connor for giving way before Chamberlain's pressure in what could only be perceived as a clear case of political censorship. In an editorial headed "A Film Fiasco" the editor wrote that if "Dawn" had not had censorship problems it would have been shown, have excited a passing interest and by now would have been forgotten. The editor felt that the whole affair reflected badly on the film censor and called for a "more decisive attitude" in the censorship of films and plays, similar to that favoured by the Government in Dublin. The trade made it clear that it still objected to official government censorship, and favoured the voluntary system in operation. The arguments about the nature of censorship were to resurface with increasing intensity often during the Thirties and succeeding decades.

A documentary of a different kind was the "Epic of Everest" the official record of the 1924 attempt on the great mountain which was shown in the Royal Cinema in Sept. 1925.

People would already have been aware of its tragic consequences with the deaths of the two climbers, George Leigh Mallory and Andrew Irvine. The cameraman on the expedition, Capt. J. B. Noel, arrived with the film to give the explanatory lecture. He explained how special permission had been obtained from the Dalai Lama to approach the mountain from Tibet and the film included unique scenes of the people and scenery of that secretive country. Noel used the traditional panning shots to show the landscape but on the climb he had used a powerful telescopic lens which must have impressed the audience. The final scenes were filmed from over one mile away and showed the two climbers within 1000 feet (approx 300m) of the top before they disappeared into cloud and bad weather. They were never seen again. Noel described whistling and making other noises, hoping that they would hear the sounds and follow them down through the cloud but to no avail.

The lecture was accompanied on stage by an exotic item consisting of seven lamas from Tibet who played their native instruments and performed local dances. They had been recruited from the successful British Empire Exhibition which had opened the year before at Wembley. The aim of that exhibition was to make the people of Britain more aware of the extent and variety of the Empire, and there were displays by representatives from the main countries of Africa under British rule along with those of India, Canada, Australia and New Zealand. There were also other attractions including an Amusement Park with dodgems organized by a certain Billy Butlin, a stadium for sports and a rodeo. A special attraction was a replica of the Tomb of Tutankhamun which had already appeared in so many newsreels and documentaries. The exhibition gained favourable comments in the local papers and many of those who could afford it went to London to see for themselves, while the rest of the citizenry had to make do with what the newsreels showed. The Exhibition's aim was to bring the realities of the varied countries of the far flung Empire to the people of Britain, but there were those who felt that the future involved the opposite, namely that people should be able to travel abroad and see for themselves. Foremost among them were the airmen, those popular heroes of the sky, whose exploits increasingly dominated the news reels during the Twenties.

It was the era of Alcott and Browne, of Lindberg and Alan Cobham. Cobham believed in the commercial future of air transport and had flown from London to Capetown and back to show that it could be done. A film of the venture, "With Cobham to the Cape," appeared in the Classic in August 1926. The Irish News critic praised its lack of sensationalism, noting that there were no cannibals, no man - eating lions, just vivid depictions of African life. The journey did have its excitements as when crossing the Victoria Falls the plane was caught in spray causing the engine to cut out, but luckily Cobham was able to get it restarted and continue in safety. The Whig thought the documentary was a fine example of its kind combining as it did "travel, entertainment and education." Cobham later used the same seaplane, a double - winged de Havilland 50J, to fly from London to Australia and back. Newsreel shots of him approaching London and landing on the Thames were shown locally in October. The following Easter week, April 1927, he appeared in person in the Royal Cinema to a warm reception and gave an illustrated lecture on both flights. His popularity and drawing power were verified a year later when he appeared in a British film, "Flight Commander," about a group of Europeans under siege in a town in N. China who are saved by some fancy precision bombing by Cobham. Thus fact and fiction merged as it often does in the cinema, but if boxers could act in films why not airmen?

Aviation was a much debated topic during the Twenties in Belfast as elsewhere, and Alan Cobham was a familiar figure in the city, having flown there on many occasions. In June 1921 he landed in a field at Balmoral to deliver copies of the London Times, and during 1924 he was fully involved as chief pilot of the De Havilland company when a local company, Northern Airlines, with commendable initiative organized Ireland's first air service using rented De Havilland aircraft. The City Council purchased land for an airfield at Taughmonagh on the Malone Road contiguous to Balmoral Golf Club and Alan Cobham piloted the first flight to it from Aintree in Liverpool on 30th April. He carried airmail for the post office, and London newspapers which were collected and distributed by Eason and Sons. Flights carrying mail, newspapers and passengers were tried later to Carlisle, Glasgow and Derry but the worthy venture collapsed after a year, with the last flight in June 1925. The Malone Road field continued to be used spasmodically for local events. During August 1928 a Col Henderson from England offered flights from it over the city and local countryside for ten shillings a time.

Near the end of the decade an Irish News editorial deplored the fact that the Malone Aerodrome still lay "useless" while new air routes were being successfully opened elsewhere. A new airmail service had been recently inaugurated between London and India "with less publicity than that foreshadowing the exhibition of a new picture." There was a need for local action, the writer claimed, pointing out that an Irish aviator, Col. Russell, who was flying a new mail service from Galway to London had recently landed in the Harbour Estate showing its feasibility for aircraft, while an English company had shown an interest in locating an airfield there. Nothing was done and Belfast's familiarity with the air remained mainly on the silver screen. Films with flying sequences or involving pilots were common and some suggested, rather rashly as it proved, that the aviator was displacing the cowboy as the great cinematic mythic hero. Even Tom Mix exchanged his saddle for a cockpit.

The outstanding flying film of the period was "Wings," a Paramount production starring Richard Arlen, Buddy Rogers, Clara Bow and, in a small part, a new actor called Gary Cooper, which appeared in the Royal Cinema in January 1929 and made such an impact that it returned again in the following June. It had been filmed for maximum effect in Magnascope, which meant that it could be shown on a screen four times the normal size, but there is no indication that that format was used in the Royal Cinema. It also had special effects supplied, including recorded machine gun fire, which were played on gramophones located behind the screen during the air combat scenes. The Whig commented that the film was worth seeing for the aerial combats alone, scenes that were so realistic that the critic wondered how they were filmed at all. "Wings" wasn't a documentary but, like many fiction films, it contained sequences of heightened reality often commented upon by the local critics.

A totally authentic depiction of reality has long been the Holy Grail of film makers and photographers, but it still remains tantalisingly out of reach - unreachable, some would argue - though that hasn't deterred artists from trying. Flaherty's poetic visions were only one attempt, albeit a noble one, which has since been followed by neorealism in the Forties, cinema - verite and "direct cinema" in the Sixties. The Seventies reality of four letter words and explicit sex just seems in most cases crude and vulgar now, while today's computerised reality is still too bland and too technically "clean" to suggest real life. During the Twenties audiences seemed quite happy with what they were seeing and intrigued by the special effects produced by the cinema orchestras, the organs, the gramophones or new equipment like the Vitasona, all of which aimed to make the films more real. It seemed that the silent film was acquiring every type of sound except the human voice.

The Vitasona was the latest special effects machine and in late 1924 the Classic, in pursuance of its policy of keeping up to date, installed one. The Irish News critic described how it was set up in the orchestra pit from where it was worked "electrically and pneumatically" by a specially trained operator, probably one of the cinema's electricians. The machine had a switchboard covered with switches and buttons which when manipulated could produce over fifty different sounds including smacks, bumps, gunshots, machine gun fire, cannon fire, bells, galloping horses, running water and a steam train which could be used with any film. It was operated in conjunction with the orchestra and its first demonstration delighted the audience as they experienced a specially made film "A Motor Ride," "accompanied by full Vitasona effects." It was soon overshadowed by the arrival of the Panatrope which made its first appearance in Belfast in the Picture House on the 4th July 1927, described as "a novel musical installation" which would complement the orchestra with vocal and instrumental numbers including organ recitals. It was in fact an early form of record player, but more information about it became available a few weeks later when the Imperial announced the installation of another Panatrope as part of a major overhaul and redecoration process. The News Letter critic was impressed by the fact that it combined "modern electrical recording with electrical reproduction" and thought that it added greatly to the musical side of the programme. The Whig, quoting most likely from the manufacturer's blurb described it as "the musical marvel of the century" - without further comment. Made by the American company, Brunswick, it certainly represented a major technical advance and was in fact the first all electric machine capable of recording and reproducing sound. Electrical recording would soon completely replace the older system of using horns. It had the advantage that it produced much superior sound, with increased volume. It was the beginning of modern style sound recording, and was welcomed by the local critics as adding to the quality and variety of the music available in the Picture House, the Imperial and the Mountpottinger Picturedrome when it was installed there in October.

A new reality was manifesting itself as the cinemas adopted that latest electronic gadget. Some producers were already beginning to distribute special effects and background music on records with their films, and the new Panatrope could play those records (or discs, as they were called). Whatever else those developments meant for films and audiences, they were certainly ominous for the players in the cinema orchestras. Whether anyone in Belfast realised it at the time, the foundations were being laid for the introduction of sound films.

CHAPTER NINETEEN
Worship and Weeping

During the early Twenties Belfast experienced at first hand the difference between screen violence and the real thing as an incendiary cocktail of culture, politics and religion led to riots, shootings, murders, bombings, and other horrors which shocked right - thinking people. Thankfully after a few years the initial intensity and savagery of the incidents decreased and at the end of 1927 the News Letter announced that the events of the year just past indicated clear signs of "peace and progress." By Easter 1929 the Irish News felt that there was a good feeling in the air and that "happiness was general." There was much to support that attitude, with indications that political and religious differences had been relegated to the back benches. The entertainment industry, especially the cinemas, which had endured loss of audiences due to bombs, fires, closures and the curfew experienced full houses again. In May 1929 the Abbey Players returned to the Grand Opera House after an absence of ten years and were greeted with real warmth and appreciation. In the newspapers the arguments and discussions were about problems like the urban transport system, the cleanliness or otherwise of the streets, youthful behaviour, the granting of the vote to women over 21 years and the new fad of flapperism. The General Election of 1929 was referred to as the flapper election and the media, including the newsreels, poked fun at politicians courting the new flapper vote. The flappers had their critics who dismissed them as silly and irresponsible, interested only in fashion. The flappers for their part regarded themselves as being modern.

Going regularly to the cinema was also regarded as modern. The weekly newsreels were still the city's main eyes on the world, and they brought images of everything from Paris fashions to the latest journey of the giant Graf Zeppelin airship. Sporting events featured often, like the 1928 Olympic Games which took place in Amsterdam. Among the gold medal winners was an American swimmer, Johnny Weissmuller, who was to become even better known in the early Thirties as the latest cinematic Tarzan. The Grand National always drew the crowds and in the same year when it was shown in the Classic, the Irish News critic drew special attention to it, pointing out that forty cameras had been used to cover every jump, some in slow motion, showing the thrills and spills that had allowed Tipperary Tim to win at one hundred to one.

Despite the long queues and packed houses the cinemas had their own problems. There was keen competition between them to book the top films and managers complained that major films, especially American, were slow to reach the city, usually after a time lag of up to two years. There were rental agents in the city whom the cinemas could and did access. Films Ltd. was still operating successfully in High Street, managed by the energetic John Y. Moore who was also the proprietor of the Alhambra. Gaumont had offices in Donegall Street, Irish Picture Productions were located in Skipper Street, European Picture Productions were in upper Church Lane, Weisker Bros. had premises in Pottinger's Entry and Wardour Films Ltd were in the Garfield Chambers in Royal Avenue. Most of the downtown cinemas got their films directly from England, many after their initial run was completed in London. Adverts for major films often emphasised "direct from London" as part of their attraction. The Classic had the many benefits of a large organization behind it in filling its programmes, the Imperial had the advantage of its long standing arrangements with Paramount and the Royal Cinema availed of the many connections that the Warden family had in the entertainment business.

The Picture House had originally been part of the PCT chain but had changed hands probably when PCT was absorbed by Gaumont in the Twenties. J. Boughton was then appointed manager, a position he held all through the Twenties. The new owners were an imaginative and innovative local company called Northern Theatres one of whose directors was James Barron, an auctioneer and estate agent whose premises were located in Garfield Chambers near the cinema. It competed for audiences by introducing new

Good value for money.

technology, being for example the first cinema in Belfast to install a Panatrope in July 1927. Also as part of its declared aim to give value for money, it combined that with impressive double bills, giving its patrons two full length films in one show. The success of that policy - unheard of today - is reflected in the fact that all the big downtown cinemas were soon doing likewise. One of those double bills in January 1926 consisted of a popular British film "Decameron Nights," directed by Herbert Wilcox and starring Lionel Barrymore, in a story set in Damascus at the time of the Crusades which was praised by the News Letter for its "gorgeous Oriental settings" and by the Irish News for its "scenes of splendour" with sultans, princes, princesses and dancing slave girls. It was coupled with an early version of "The Wizard of Oz" directed by and starring Larry Semon, one of the top clowns of the day, though rarely mentioned today. The film also starred Oliver Hardy as the Tin Woodsman, racing around in perpetual motion, waving his arms madly and falling all over the place. The News Letter thought the result was "intriguing" and "quite a change from the usual slapstick," while the Irish News noted that it caused continuous merriment in the audience. Also included in the programme was a special musical interlude by the orchestra, the newsreel, and another short comedy starring Stan Laurel. It is therefore the first recorded appearance of Laurel and Hardy on the same programme in Belfast, though in separate pictures.

The Picture House, or Avenue as it was increasingly called, also developed a distinctive advertising policy. During the General Strike in England in May 1926 the film "The Blackguard" was accompanied by what could be described as a topical advertisement which read: "the title may STRIKE you as being TERRIBLE but the film is CERTAIN to more than please." Later, when the furore over "Dawn" was raging, it published a cleverly worded advert which seemed to suggest that its next presentation was that film. A closer reading revealed that the actual film to be shown was "Nurse and Martyr," described as the story of an heroic nurse in Belgium. The advert was actually in the form of a question which asked: why was "Dawn" (in large capitals) refused a certificate when "Nurse and Martyr" (in smaller print) wasn't? "Nurse and Martyr" was actually a British three - reeler based on a script by Edgar Wallace, which was rushed into cinemas to take advantage of the publicity over "Dawn". It was described as the story of Nurse X, but everyone knew that it was about Nurse Cavell. It showed in the Picture House for only three days due, according to the advert, "to heavy bookings," and then moved on to the Mountpottinger Picturedrome and the Lyceum with little comment from the local critics, only the News Letter critic taking time to describe it as "an exciting drama."

When "Dawn" did arrive at the Royal Cinema some weeks later it was advertised as the "authentic" film about Nurse Cavell. The Picture House also looked for unusual fare and in October 1928 presented a double bill consisting of "The Wrath of the Gods" and "A Blonde for the Night," starring Marie Prevost, with the added rider, "what a blonde and what a night!" Despite the implications, the Irish News critic thought the Marie Prevost comedy was "delightful," but found the other film much more interesting. It was in fact a German production, and like most German films of the day, he was impressed by its superb setting, its fine photography especially the night scenes involving skiers, and its subtle use of light and shadow. It was an example of what is known as a "mountain," film and dealt with events in a ski centre "set amid giant glaciers, majestic mountains and roaring avalanches." He noted - and this is the film's main claim to attention - that it introduced a new actress called Leni Riefenstal to the screen. He praised her dancing (she was actually trained as a dancer, not an actress) and "her well trained athletic body" which stood to her in the exciting mountain climbing sequences. Time was to show that there was more to Miss Reifenstal than dancing and mountain climbing, because, with her striking blonde Nordic looks, she later became a favourite of Hitler and directed a number of films for the Nazis including the amazing but distasteful and much criticised "Triumph of the Will" (1935) and the two part "Olympia" (1938).

By the time "The Wrath of the Gods" was showing the astute management of the Picture House had become aware of what was happening in America since the public presentation in 1927 of "The Jazz Singer," and was probably already contemplating the possible future impact of sound on the cinema. In the meantime it continued to attract its audiences with major stars like Pola Negri, challenging films like "The Nibelungs," and top American productions like "Covered Wagon," "The Ten Commandments" and "King of Kings" along with the drawing power of its musicians who were presented as "Ireland's Finest Orchestra."

Like the other cinema owners in the city the management of the Picture House had to cope with the demands of the Films Act which came into effect at the end of September 1928. The act introduced compulsory quotas, making it a legal obligation to ensure that 5% of films shown in a year were British, a figure that would rise to 7% in 1929 and 10% by 1931. All managers had to take out a special licence, and keep a record of every British film shown. The aim of the act was to encourage the production of British films and to protect the industry from foreign, especially American, competition. The result was a flood of poor quality British films which neither exhibitors or audiences favoured. The Irish News quoted Sir Oswald Stoll's criticisms of the Act, probably reflecting the feelings of local managers on the matter. He complained that money was now being invested in British films that were not performing well, and he argued that it was wrong to force unwanted films on exhibitors. Instead, he suggested that foreign films should be taxed at 1d per reel per day of projection and that the income from that policy should be invested to make better pictures. Whatever local managers thought they tholed the situation quietly but were more outspoken about another problem which they regarded as more serious, namely the impact of entertainment tax on their industry. They saw the tax as unfair and more oppressive than the situation over the water in Britain. They argued that the tax burden made survival economically very difficult for the smaller and poorer halls, and it is probably no coincidence that the Old Princess hall closed in the mid - Twenties, while other cinemas like the Coliseum, obviously struggling, reduced their admission charges.

Even the Pottinger Picturedrome, the premier cinema in East Belfast, reduced its admission charges during the summer months, and tried to improve the level of comfort by having the seating reupholstered. The manager also decided to prepare for the rigours of winter queueing by opening a new waiting room in early December 1928 built, decorated and heated by local firms. It was a spacious hall capable of holding 200 people, designed in the form of an Italian piazza with a tiled floor bordered by pillars, and illustrated by panels between them showing sea scapes. The Irish News reporter commended the overall decor, especially the blending of gold and blue which produced a "magnificent effect." The room was not only well heated with equipment supplied by Messrs Musgrave and Co., but the waiting patrons were entertained by the novelty of piped music, probably from a Panatrope, while sweets, cigarettes and the latest evening newspaper were available from a kiosk.

A letter to the Irish News from a local cinema manager (unnamed) clearly set out the problem. He pointed out that after representations from the industry the Imperial Parliament in the budget of 1924 had abolished all tax on seats up to 6d, while, above that, the tax on one shilling seats was reduced from 3d to 2d and on dearer seats from 4d to 3d. Those changes came into effect in England, Scotland and Wales but the local Minister of Finance ignored them and the full tax remained in force here until June 1927, when, reluctantly, the tax on the cheaper seats up to sixpence, was abolished, though the higher taxes on the dearer seats remained. The letter writer claimed that the tax was "unique" in that it was a charge, not on profits, but on receipts. In view of Lord Craigavon's claims of equal treatment with the rest of the U.K. he couldn't see why the tax shouldn't be equalised. In April 1928 a deputation representing 59 local cinemas, employing 1398 persons, met Mr Pollack, the local Minister of Finance, to ask for relief. They explained that the modification of last year had been very welcome and had actually saved a number of smaller establishments from closure, but that the cinemas still faced serious competition from dance halls (a fast growing craze) and from greyhound meetings and other outdoor sports during the summer. The Minister listened, as politicians do, with apparent sympathy but when the budget was announced in June the tax remained unchanged. The seats above 6d would still pay 3d and 4d tax. A meeting of the White Cinema Club, the umbrella group consisting of representatives of cinemas, variety halls and dance halls, expressed "disappointment." They pointed out that they paid more for their films and had greater difficulty getting them than their colleagues in England. They agreed that a political campaign should be undertaken to bring about equality with England, and felt that they would have the support of their audiences, regardless of their political colour, in that.

Despite its popularity and its mixed audiences, the cinema wasn't completely divorced from the prevailing political and social divisions. It was unlikely for example that many filmgoers from the Shankill district visited the Clonard on the Falls Road, or vice versa, though both groups did frequent the same downtown cinemas. The latter were generally not overtly political though there were rare exceptions. During the showing of John Ford's "The Iron Horse "in May 1926 the Classic decided to celebrate Empire Day in a special way. The cinema was decorated with Union Jacks and a speaker addressed the audience on the meaning of Empire. That was followed by a colourful pageant, put on by the Haines School of Dancing, which illustrated "the growth of the power of the Empire." One can be sure there were few Nationalists in the audience that evening. Local managers knew what their audiences would or would not accept and choose their material accordingly. In Nationalist areas newsreel items about Royalty or events like the Twelfth parades were usually omitted while in Unionist areas references to the Pope, the Catholic church or Republicans were likewise left unseen. Slip-ups in that local censorship could result at least in booing and catcalls or something more extreme. During the early Sixties a patch appeared on the screen of the Clonard for a time which the operator explained, with a rueful grin, was caused by a bottle, when by an oversight the Queen appeared in a newsreel. Yet all such "touchy" items were shown in the downtown halls, usually without incident. One topic of dissention however was the playing of the National Anthem at the end of the day's performance which often led to an undignified rush to the exits around 10:30 pm. It was not unknown for staunch Loyalists to occupy the end seats on a row and try to prevent those who wanted to leave before the anthem, from doing so. In the main relations in the downtown cinema were sociable and both groups relaxed in comfort, enjoyed the same films, admired the same stars, laughed at the same comics and paradoxically mourned together.

One of the top favourites of the period, especially with the female audiences, was Rudolph Valentino. His films had been arriving regularly over recent years in the local cinemas and always attracted large crowds. 1926 had seemed no different. In late January the Royal Cinema presented his latest release "The Eagle" directed by Clarence Brown, which promised "romance, love and mystery" as he enthusiastically pursued Vilma Banky. In it he played a Russian gentleman who is forced to become a bandit, which gave him the opportunity to rival Douglas Fairbanks with a deft combination of humour and impressive athleticism that delighted critics as well as his fans. One commentator was impressed by the skill, as he put it, with which he turned animal magnetism into at least the semblance of talent. He was physically and artistically in top form, a standard which he maintained in his next film "Cobra" which arrived in the Classic two months later. The I.S.N. informed its readers that the title referred to "the lure of a fascinating, sensuous woman, resembling the hypnotic charm which the cobra wields over its victims." A cobra was, in fact, a female sheik, and the story was a case of a femme fatale meeting the Great Lover. The film is interesting in that it is the only one of his major films in which he actually played an Italian though the plot is set in modern New York. Valentino's character was a young man who is very susceptible to female charms but, as he struggles to reform, he falls under the spell of "the cobra woman" in the person of Nita Naldi, "more alluring than ever." She also happens to be his best friend's wife but, regardless, he goes with her to a hotel. However his conscience gets the better of him and he leaves before anything happens. Unfortunately

THE BUILDINGS

The Oldest.
St George's Building. Opened in 1881, included St George's Hall which was one of Belfast's oldest Silent Cinemas functioning between 1908 and 1914. The hall still exists in a very dilipated state.

The Survivor. The Strand, front view.

The Strand, side view. The only surviving Picture Palace from the Thirties, still functioning as a cinema, part of the Strand Arts Centre.

The Hints of Past Grandeur. The former Majestic, Lisburn Road. Now (2014) unoccupied.

The former Ambassador, Cregagh Road. Now a supermarket.

The former Curran cinema, the Apollo, on the lower Ormeau Road. Now an Asian supermarket.

The Castle. *Photos by the author.*

The Lost Legends. The Cannon Cinema, formerly the ABC, and Ritz before its demolition in 1993.Now Jury's Hotel. In the background the New Vic, formerly the Odeon and Royal Hippodrome is also gone.

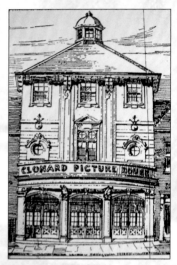

Unique and elegant design added distinction to Falls Road. *Thanks to Irish News.*

Entrance to Cannon cinema.

ENTREPRENEURS

Michael Curran, the Founder of Curran Theatres.

P. Murray Bass, J. Y. Moore and Ferris Pounds at the opening of the Forum. (Nov.1937) The men behind Irish Theatres Ltd.

James Curran, managing director of Curran Theatres (second from right).

Sir Crawford McCullagh, Belfast's longest serving Lord Mayor, strongly supported the local cinema industry. Studing a projector in the newly opened Savoy (Nov. 1934) with Mr W.J. Hogan (centre).

Michael MacAdam, owner of the Movie House chain following in the footsteps of J.Y.Moore and Michael Curran. With thanks to Movie House.

Gaston Brothers, owners of the Curzon.

George Lodge. Involved with down town cinemas.

THE PERSONALITIES

Moyna MacGill. Belfast's first film star.

Her daughter Angela Lansbury who visited Belfast in search of her family roots.

Liam Neeson who began his career in Belfast. *With thanks to Irish News.*

Deanna Durbin, even more popular in Belfast than Shirley Temple.

Stephen Boyd, Belfast's first international star.

Albert Sharpe alias Darby O'Gill with his wife.

George Shanahan who gave the author his first tour of a projection room.

Errol Flynn being formal with Greer Garson...

Loie Fuller, early hand tinted film.

...and informal with Maureen O'Hara.

NOSTALGIA

The Broadway, a
Curran cinema,
where the author
saw his first films.

The former QFT
entrance. Up an entry.

See the epic
struggle for freedom filmed as it
actually happened!

"MISE
ÉIRE"

Royal Cinema

BELFAST

14-19 NOVEMBER, 1960

Arna léiriú ag

gael-linn

Mise Eire, a fine
documentary
with an Irish
sound track.

D.W.
GRIFFITH'S
- AMERICAN INSTITUTION -
THE BIRTH OF A NATION
"THE SUPREME PICTURE OF ALL TIME"
NEW YORK MAIL

Advert for Griffith's
controversial epic.

"Le Film d'Art"
LE RETOUR D'ULYSSE
Pièce Cinématographique de Mr JULES LEMAITRE de l'Académie Française

A silent epic
shown in St
George's Hall.

WILLY REILLY
AND HIS COLLEEN BAWN

PRESENTED BY

THE OFFICE OF PUBLIC WORKS
AND
THE IRISH FILM INSTITUTE

The Coleen Bawn
always very popular
in Belfast.

In from the Rain'

The Quiet Man in the Linenhall Library.

Jimmy Durante, a unique personality.

The screen discreetly covered in the Forum.

THE CURZON

The Curzon shortly before closing.

Notice of closure on the paybox.

The modern entrance hall.

Curzon Children's Club with Roy Rogers on Trigger.

Projection room with projector and reels loaded with celluloid.

The last reels to be shown. The last film: Shakespeare In Love.

The original projectors from 1936.

The original RCA sound power unit. All Curzon photos by author.

TODAY

Modern attractive foyer. Plastic has replaced marble and wood, The Omniplex, Kennedy Way. With thanks.

New Multiplex in Victoria Square.

The Modern Cinema, part of the Victoria Square complex.

Back to the future: the new Ritz.

Projection room, Movie House, Dublin Road. It's all done by computers - well, nearly all.

The author with Jim Simpson, the chief digital technician.

Despite the warning the cinema carries on.

during the night the hotel burns down and the lady dies, leading to what the I.S.N. described as "a strong ending." The Classic promised its patrons a special treat in the form of a live prologue in which a noted European exotic dancer called Nada would perform a snake dance with a nine foot reptile. Her performance was described as "unusual, daring and fascinating" and quite unlike anything ever seen in the city before. The News Letter thought that "Cobra" was a fine film, and noted that the cinema was packed, despite the fine weather (see page 317).

In June Valentino's fans were watching him with less enthusiasm in "Monsieur Beaucaire" but in August crowds were flocking to the Clonard to enjoy "A Sainted Devil," which co-starred the popular Bebe Daniels. It was only a few days later that a small item appeared in the local papers saying that Rudolph Valentino had been taken ill and had been admitted to hospital in New York. People, even his greatest fans, paid little attention because after all he was a young man of only 31 years, at the height of his physical powers, famous and wealthy ensuring that he would receive the best medical attention available. Thus it was a major shock to all when the papers of 24th August carried the news that he had died the day before. Belfast took the news quietly, with people at first expressing surprise and even incomprehension but as the news sank in the situation began to take on the physical and psychological attributes of the Princess Diana tragedy. Some young women became distraught, others just refused to believe it, others said prayers for the repose of his soul, preachers used the event to point up the superficiality and transience of earthly things especially fame, while classical scholars probably contemplated past heroes whom the gods had given the choice of a short life full of fame or a long uneventful one. Here was a modern Alexander the Great who had achieved world fame, conquering and causing havoc (mainly in female hearts and imaginations) only to be struck down at the height of his powers. The papers published detailed accounts of his career, while the local critics mourned his untimely passing. The Irish News editor summed up their general attitude when he described him succinctly as "a notable artist in his particular field." The Whig carried a piece which acknowledged his "virile simplicity" and described the private person as "a man entirely without pretence, quiet spoken, unassuming (but) mysteriously magnetic." The writer suggested that in his films the cinema actor "has an immortality which does not belong to his elder brother of the stage" and forecast that in death Valentino would enjoy a new popularity.

But while Belfast absorbed the shock with dignity, the news from New York was quite different. Whipped up by sensational newspaper reporting and radio commentary a large crowd, mainly of women, converged on Campbell's Funeral Parlour where the body was displayed. Pushing and shoving turned quickly into a mini riot. The crush caused a large picture window to shatter, women fainted, while others were knocked over, trampled upon and injured. The police finally had to be called to restore order though it required 120 men, including 20 on horseback to do so. The News Letter described the scenes of hysteria as "extraordinary" but the editor of the Irish News was appalled and under a heading "Degeneracy" he condemned the crowd for their lack of respect towards the dead, and described them as "de - Christianised and decadent people" whose behaviour recalled that which used to accompany public executions in the past. It is believed today that those scenes were probably stage-managed for publicity purposes by Valentino's manager and the funeral undertaker, but if they were, they quickly got out of hand and in view of the unfavourable reaction elsewhere in America and overseas stern steps were taken to see they didn't recur.

The Whig described the scenes the next day in the funeral parlour, where the body lay in full evening wear, in an open coffin that was almost filled with with flowers. Large candles burned at its four edges where four Fascist guards dressed in black shirts "gleaming with medals" stood to attention. Private detectives and ushers kept the crowds, which included many sobbing women, moving as thousands filed past the catafalque. The local critics drew their reader's attention to the fact that the newsreels in the Classic, Imperial and other cinemas carried "impressive" scenes of that event. So great were the numbers that it was decided to extend the lying in state for another three days until the following Monday when the funeral took place. From early morning crowds lined the pavements until at eleven o'clock the cortege of over a hundred cars left to travel the two miles from the funeral parlour to the Church of St Malachi where the Requiem mass was celebrated by a long standing clerical friend. The local papers carried full reports describing how boys climbed poles and workers leaned out of upstairs windows to get a glimpse of the passing cars carrying friends, actors and others connected with cinema and theatre. Prominent among them were his first wife Jean Acker and Pola Negri, whom the media claimed had been recently engaged to the dead actor. She was attended, dramatically, by a doctor and nurse and during the ceremonies in the church "her sobs were plainly audible above the dirge - like notes of the organ." The Whig regretted "the flagrant publicity" that attended the sad event, but felt that in contrast to the "disorderly scenes" of the week before the funeral service was carried out "with adequate solemnity, and the crowds behaved with respect and orderliness." Locals had to wait until the following Monday to decide for themselves when the Imperial presented a film of the complete funeral ceremonies giving people, the Irish News claimed, the opportunity to see the passing of "one whose death affected the whole world."

Cinema is a business and the film companies were anxious to cash in on the widespread sympathy for the late actor, so they quickly organised the reissue of some of his films. Before the end of September the Imperial was able to present "The Sheik" again to full houses, followed a few weeks later by "Blood and Sand" while the Classic, in response, the manager claimed, to hundreds of letters from fans, showed "The Four Horsemen of the Apocalypse," proclaiming it as "the film you will remember him by." The Irish News described it as "the picture of the age" which like a good book rewarded a second viewing. The News Letter confirmed that the crowds which arrived to see it, were "enormous." Then on the 1st November the Royal Cinema climaxed the season by screening his last and as yet locally unseen film, "Son of the Sheik," declaring it to be "his last and greatest picture. "The critics agreed that it was worth seeing and to no one's surprise it soon broke all records at the Royal so that it had to be held over for a second week. In the film, which was a sequel to the original, Valentino played a double part of father and son while Agnes Ayres reprised the part of the Sheik's wife. The main body of the story involved the adventures of the Son and his involvement with a dancer played by Vilma Banky. On their first meeting she says (by intertitle of course) "Who are you my lord? I do not know your name," to which he replies, "I am he who loves you. Is not that enough?" For most of the audience it obviously was. The I.S.N. critic described the film as "full of thrills and sensations" and remarked that the nightly queues were "a remarkable tribute to the popularity of the dead star." The film continued to be shown across the city during 1927 and as late as October of that year the Royal Cinema presented it a second time, "by special request." In June of the following year the Classic brought it back for another short appearance and it was warmly received again by critics and public. The Irish News praised Valentino's "dare devil horsemanship and athletic stunts," an aspect of his screen character that is often overlooked, while the Whig enjoyed the film's clever combination of romance, spectacular action and humour. In early August 1929 the Imperial, responding, - it claimed, - to further requests from fans, brought back one of his early (released in 1921) and lesser known films "The Conquering Power" directed by Rex Ingram in which he starred with Alice Terry. After that Valentino disappeared for the most part from local screens, though his memory endured.

No history of the silent cinema is complete without reference to the Valentino phenomenon and his name has joined those of Mary Pickford, Chaplin, and Pearl White which people who have no knowledge of the cinema are familiar with. Much later he was personated by Anthony Dexter in "Valentino" (d. Lewis Allen, 1951) and more sensationally by Rudolf Nureyev in another film of the same name (d. Ken Russell, 1977). But the magic was lost and while both films illustrated the excitement surrounding his character neither explained it satisfactorily. Modern audiences have the opportunity to judge for themselves because DVDs of some of his better known films are now available, including the one with which he is most associated, "The Sheik." He was a better actor than he is usually given credit for but, while one may appreciate his performances in a detached academic fashion, it is impossible today to experience the special excitement that surrounded his screen appearances in the Twenties. Sheiks and Cobras may seem rather old fashioned and even somewhat risible to our modern sophisticated and politically correct audiences. Or maybe our society is just losing its sense of humour.

An important part of the cinema going experience was the comfort of the surroundings. The I.S.N. critic, who was much given (thankfully) to recording his personal feelings, mentioned a visit to the Classic on a cold winter's night in the mid - Twenties. He was struck initially by the comfortable environment of the cinema which was greatly augmented by "a big crowd, jolly music, good pictures and a genial sense of warmth." Those sentiments would have applied more or less to most of the cinemas in the city, especially the downtown ones. But an event occurred in 1926 which gave many people pause for thought that maybe they were taking a lot for granted in their evening's entertainment. As crowds were converging on the Classic and other cinemas to watch the funeral of Valentino in rapt silence, others were reading the shocking news about what became known as Ireland's worst cinema disaster. Fire prevention was a high priority in the cinema business and indeed the owners of the Classic had emphasised its importance when that cinema opened a few years before. What the citizens read highlighted the consequences of ignoring or neglecting it. The News Letter described it as "one of the most ghastly catastrophes to be recorded in the history of Ireland," the Belfast Telegraph equally found it "awful," while the Irish News reported it as "a ghastly and horrible tragedy." They were referring to the terrible events that took place

The scene of Ireland's worst cinema disaster.

in the little village of Drumcollogher in Co. Limerick on the evening of Sunday 5th September 1926 when 48 children, women and men died in a fierce fire which broke out in a hall being used as a temporary cinema.

Local shock and horror were followed by world wide expressions of sympathy and support. One of the first came from the entertainer Will Rogers who was in London, enclosing £100 for a relief fund, and promising to come immediately to Dublin to present a concert for the same fund. He kept his word and two days later the concert raised £400. Messages were also sent from the King and Queen, the Governor of N.Ireland, a representative of the Six Counties Government, the Salvation Army in Belfast, the Belfast Rotary Club, which also donated £10 to the Relief Fund, and many Protestant churches. The Telegraph felt there was something especially terrible in the thought that a group of people innocently enjoying "the pictures" were suddenly faced with an agonising death by asphyxiation and fire. Differences of politics, religion and culture were forgotten. "The sympathy of North and South alike will go out to those who have been so cruelly bereaved, especially those denied the consolation of being able to identify the remains of their loved ones," one editor wrote.

The papers printed photographs of the smoke blackened walls of the stricken building alongside harrowing descriptions by survivors of what they had experienced. There were also details of the continuing search for remains, the decision to bury all of the victims in a communal grave and the moving funeral service in the small overcrowded church "with its bare distempered walls and six tall candles burning on the altar" (Irish News). One observer, writing in the Irish Independent, described the scene in the graveyard after the Requiem Mass with the large open grave which had been dug by twelve men, and the coffins laid out in rows beside it. There were also 13 other boxes of mud and fine debris which might contain human remains, which were also being interred with the coffins. "The awful grave is made. Silence, utter silence safe for the stifled sobs of some afflicted one. It began to rain. A woman cried." Another reporter poignantly noticed the bicycles lying around the village which had never been reclaimed. There was none of the theatricality of Valentino's passing, just simplicity, sadness and numbness which began to turn to anger when details emerged at the inquest which indicated clearly that the disaster had been completely avoidable. The night after the funeral the first indication of that feeling manifested itself when windows in a shop owned by one of the organizers of the film show were broken.

It was the News Letter which pointed out that there was a big difference between the level of precautions taken in the "palatial cinemas" of a centre like Belfast and the conditions that prevailed in small villages throughout the length of Ireland. Yet, in those villages and parishes there were many people who wanted to enjoy an evening of films, and their needs were supplied by travelling showmen, and local businessmen. Drumcollogher was typical of those centres, "an out of the way village in a remote part of Ireland" as the Telegraph described it. Located about 30 miles from Limerick City, it had a population of about 400 and was the centre of a parish which had a total population of around 900. A local businessman, Mr Forde, noticed that a man from Cork had put on a few filmshows in a local hall and that they were well supported. He decided to organise the shows on a more regular basis so he approached another businessman, Mr Brennan, and arranged to show the films in a hall he owned on Church Street in the village. The hall in question was located above a store and was approached by a wooden ladder which led to a narrow doorway just over a metre wide, which opened inwards into a hall about fifty feet long and fifteen feet wide containing wooden benches. The hall itself had a wooden floor and walls, and the single door was the only means of exit. There were two windows at the far end of the hall but both were barred. There were no buckets of water or sand available, or blankets to fight a fire.

Mr Forde knew nothing about the mechanics of the film business so he contacted a Mr Downey from Cork, a projectionist with twelve years experience in the business and on the Sunday he drove from the city bringing the projector and films with him. Because they were rather bulky he didn't carry the reels in their metal containers but in an asbestos lined portmanteau, which he insisted was quite safe. He later admitted that when he first saw the hall he was reluctant to proceed with the show, but was persuaded to continue. Thus, on Sunday evening people began to arrive for the performance and by nine o'clock there were 150 men, women and children seated on the wooden benches. Also present were two representatives of the law, the local sergeant and a guard. On ascending the ladder the eager customers entered through the single door and paid their nine pence to Mr Brennan, who was seated at a table on which a number of candles were lit to give him sufficient light to sort the money. The only other light was from a single electric bulb hanging in the centre of the room. The power for that and for the projector was supplied from a lorry parked just outside the building. On the same table lay uncovered reels of film. The sergeant said later that he quenched one of the candles which he thought was too near the film. The projector sat on another table behind the audience, and, like the film reels, was open and unenclosed. The possible source of any fire in the projector, or among the reels of inflammable film, was therefore located between the audience and the one door.

Nearly every regulation or recommendation in the Cinematograph Act 1909 which covered film safety in cinemas was ignored, or broken. It was a situation, wrote the editor of the Irish News, which reflected "carelessness and inconceivable ignorance." Why, he asked, didn't someone foresee what could happen and act accordingly? What did happen became clear later. The first film, a Western called "The Decoy" went well and the main feature, Cecil B. de Mille's "The Ten Commandments" was running about ten minutes when someone shouted "fire." A dropped cigarette or, more likely, a candle had ignited one of the reels of film on the table. A number of men, including the sergeant, rushed to put it out, but the fire spread with a frightening rapidity. There was an immediate stampede past the flames towards the one door, and people spilled out and fell down the ladder to the ground floor. As women and children clutched each other screaming, some men ran in the opposite direction, wrestled with the bars on the windows, and managed to push a number of women through them to safety. Within a few minutes the wooden floor and walls were blazing, the heat became intense and soon the floor collapsed, sending burning bodies ten feet to the ground below. Outside, men collected buckets but the local pump was broken, and they had to rush to the nearby river for water. The nearest fire brigade was in Limerick over 30 miles away, and by the time it arrived it was all over. No one slept in the village that night. First thing in the morning the grim task of recovering the remains began. Arguments also raged as to what exactly had happened to cause such a tragedy.

The jury at the inquest decided that the calamity was caused by a lighted candle falling on an uncovered film reel. They found the projectionist, Mr Downey, guilty of negligence for having exposed film on the table, and the lessee, Mr Forde, guilty of carelessness. Both men were placed under arrest and charged with manslaughter, and, a few days later, the owner of the building, Mr Brennan, was likewise arrested and charged. The trial took place in Dublin in February and, there, the jury acquitted Brennan but couldn't make up its mind about the culpability of Forde and Downings. As a result all further criminal charges were dropped and a verdict of nolle prosequi was entered. Calls for an inquiry were also rejected by the authorities, as it was felt that the trial and the publicity had already achieved its aim of warning people of the dangers.. All through the sad affair the local papers assured their readers in Belfast that such an event was impossible here though the Irish News pointed that there was a continued need for vigilance "We trust," wrote the editor, "the frightful lesson..... furnished by these shocking events will not be ignored by governments, local authorities and the general public." All the papers emphasised the need for rules and restrictions and chided those who complained about them. The Irish News noted that personal liberty was "a precious heritage" but not to the detriment of the community at large. There was, the editorial warned, often a need for "the restraining hand of authority."

The spectre of fire in a crowded cinema was always in the background ever since the dreadful Charity Bazaar fire in Paris in May 1897, and the Drumcollogher fire was a wake-up call to local authorities both North and South of the border to check the status of safety measures not only in cinema halls but also in the new popular dance halls that were springing up across the land. It must have had some positive impact because Ireland remained free of similar disasters for 55 years until the Stardust Ballroom fire of February 1981 in Dublin, in which 48 people lost their lives in equally horrible conditions. Drumcollogher also drew attention again to the dangers of using inflammable film stock and added urgency to the need for film producers to introduce non - inflammable materials as soon as possible.

A minor but interesting sidelight is the fact that "The Ten Commandments" was the film showing when the fire broke out, a fact that was widely reported by the papers. Paramount was so worried by that association with the fire that they issued a statement that its presence in Drumcollogher was impossible because there were only four prints of the film in Ireland and three of those were in their vaults in Dublin, while the fourth was showing in Newtownards. However, survivors insisted that the film on that fateful night was "The Ten Commandments." When Cecil B. de Mille remade the film in sound, it premiered in the Ambassador in Dublin in 1956. The star, Charlton Heston, was there, and a reporter from the Limerick Leader interviewed him in the Gresham Hotel. He was pleasantly surprised to discover that Heston was fully aware of the details of the 1926 disaster. Today Drumcollogher, or Drumcolliher as it is now spelt, is a neat village noted mainly for its Irish Dresden factory which turns out beautiful porcelain figurines. The site of the fire on Church Street is occupied by a circular shaped Memorial Library which carries an explanatory plaque on its wall, while in the modern church, one of its fine windows is engraved with the simple inscription The Fire, 5th September 1926. Pray For

Them. Through the glass one can see the mass grave surmounted by a tall stone copy of a traditional Celtic Cross with the names of the dead cut into its base. The memory of that fateful night still lingers on.

The Memorial Library plaque.

Drumcollogher naturally enough focused official and public attention on the dangers inherent in badly organised or poorly supervised film shows, and the papers pursued that theme by printing accounts of other contemporary disasters from around the world. In January 1927 a cinema in Manchester was partly destroyed by fire but luckily no-one was hurt. A week later during a show in a cinema in S. Italy flames suddenly burst from the projection booth causing panic, with some members of the audience jumping from the balcony to escape. In the melée three people were killed and fifteen injured. But the worst disaster was in Montreal when fire broke out during a children's matinee causing panic, and a stampede for the exits. Children fell and were trampled upon and in all 77 died. Investigations concluded that the hall was overcrowded, with children even standing at the back, and there was inadequate adult supervision. There was even an incident - a false alarm as it proved - closer to home, on 7th February during a children's matinee in the Market Street cinema in Lisburn. Smoke was smelt in a ventilator and though there were no flames, a boy shouted "Fire," causing a wild rush to the exits. Some children were knocked over and one young boy was hurt. Those and similar incidents were duly noted by the authorities concerned with safety, but they had no noticeable impact on local cinema attendances, with reports continuing to mention full houses and long queues.

They did contribute in certain quarters to an increasing unease about a perceived wider social malaise which was summed up by a writer in the Irish News as "the inordinate craze for amusement and pleasure" which was sweeping through society, and which revealed itself in excessive drinking, gambling, the increasing popularity of evil literature and a general disregard for modesty. Those problems were often highlighted and commented upon by all the local papers. The Irish News tended to report criticisms made by the Catholic clergy, the News Letter those by Protestant ministers, while all the papers reported those of lay professionals including judges, magistrates, teachers and their representatives. The latter were mainly concerned with the behaviour of young people and the factors influencing it. The old chestnuts of films being a major cause of juvenile crime and delinquency were often repeated, arguments that the film critic in the I.S.N. had no time for. He felt that much delinquent behaviour was more likely caused by what he called "native cussedness." But many professional people who dealt with children and their problems were worried by their regular attendance at film shows, and by what they watched even during special children's matinees.

The comments of the National Union of Women Teachers were widely reported in the local papers. "No one," the Union claimed, "can defend the presence of children of school age at cinemas where dramas of love, passion, crime and sordid misdoings are shown" and went on to assert that even at children's matinees murders, burglaries and other "terrible things" were shown. One speaker had attended some matinees and was alarmed by the level of involvement shown by the children as they hissed the villains and cheered the hero. She felt that such an amazing medium could be a factor for positive education and good if only it could make films without villains. In an address to the Association of Headmasters in London a speaker, sounding quite modern, complained that education shouldn't be a political shuttlecock and highlighted the practical problems that schools faced coping with large classes, inadequate buildings and poor academic standards. Then he went on to single out the cinema for special attack, claiming that it was "typical of all that deserves our most vigilant hostility as protectors of the young." Such views were not only read in Belfast but were prevalent in certain sections of society. A typical reaction came from the Girl's Friendly Society in April 1928 when, at one of its meetings, the president, Mrs Kinahan, called for stricter censorship of films and agreed to the setting up of a committee of women from the organization to attend cinemas as often as possible, and complete monthly reports on the contents and suitability of the films viewed. If one is to go by the lack of reaction in the editorial and letter columns the majority of parents in Belfast seemed quite happy with what their children were watching during the Saturday matinees across the city and, certainly in working class areas, middle class women like Mrs Kinahan were liable to be dismissed as "old busy bodies."

But events were to show that there was a need for vigilance, and to realise that the dangers weren't confined to the content of the films, as parents and Alfred George, the manager of the Crumlin Cinema, discovered on Saturday the 3rd August 1929. The usual Saturday afternoon matinee was nearing its end and a packed house of children was enjoying the film when a boy suddenly stood up, flashed a torch and shouted "Fire." There was an immediate rush of children towards the exits and in the crush some children were bowled over, trampled and injured. Two girls, one aged 10 years from the Oldpark Road area and the other, only three, from the Shankill had to be detained in the nearby Mater Hospital over the weekend suffering "from bruises and internal injuries." Mr George the manager described how the programme was progressing normally and he was in his office when he heard the commotion. He rushed into the auditorium and joined the attendants who were trying to restore order. They soon calmed the children but, by then, four had collapsed in one of the doorways. While the hall was being cleared he and the attendants carried them out into the fresh air. Mr George then went to the projection box where the operator told him that nothing was amiss technically. "The whole thing was a boyish prank," he explained, "and the boy in question obviously didn't have the slightest idea of the serious nature of his conduct." There was no suggestion that the manager or his staff had been negligent in their duties, but questions were asked about what level of supervision was needed on such occasions and why such a young child, aged only three years, was present at all. Many parents and Mr George, a manager of many years experience in the business, must have breathed a sigh of relief because the results could have been much more tragic, as the Whig pointed out in an editorial comment headed "Cause for Thankfulness." The safety regulations in place may seem irksome on occasion but without them, the editor wrote, there might have been another Drumcolligher or even a repeat of the Charity Bazaar disaster that had sent all Paris into mourning many years before. Also, he added sternly, the incident is a reminder that the only "cure" for certain practical jokes is the birch, a sentiment that a fair proportion of his readers would probably have agreed with.

Many commentators felt that the problem went well beyond what children were watching, and where they were watching it. The Bishop of Raphoe, Dr Mc Neely, quoted in the Irish News just after the Drumcolligher tragedy, had summed up the situation, as he perceived it, by saying that halls supplying entertainment should be organised so that audiences were faced neither by physical danger or moral degradation. He deplored the spirit of "indifference and laxity" that was widespread among young and old, which he maintained emanated from the impact of the recent European War and "our two domestic wars." Organizers of popular entertainments, he continued, should have a keener sense of their responsibilities and audiences should be on their guard not only against physical dangers but must be ready to protest when they found themselves presented with "objectionable and scandalous pictures or other forms of amusement that should be regarded by decent Christians with disgust and reprobation." Near the end of the year a row erupted in Limerick City over a request for the Council to allow the Sunday opening of cinemas. The Irish News, aware that a similar suggestion had been mooted locally, gave it much prominence and quoted an address by Fr Cleary - who was well known in Belfast, having spent a few years there ministering in Clonard Monastery - to the Limerick Confraternity. In his speech he condemned the request and added that if he had his way the cinemas would be closed not only on Sundays but on weekdays too. He felt that many films projected pagan standards of behaviour and that many of the actors and actresses involved in them led far from moral lives. Being published in the Irish News those comments were read mainly by Nationalists, but the sentiments contained in them had a sympathetic acceptance in sections of the Unionist population whose preachers often condemned filmgoing and cinemas which they perceived as despoiling their city.

Worries expressed over safety, dark unhealthy environments and objectionable content weren't ignored by cinema owners and managers but they faced more immediate challenges from the increased popularity of radio and, especially, the spreading craze for dancing, a topic that caused much reaction in the letter columns. One writer in the Irish News condemned the new dances like the Charleston and Black Bottom - "borrowed from West Africa via the U.S.A. and London" - and suggested that greater efforts should be put into encouraging Irish dancing, which he felt was much more beneficial physically. The Charleston reached London in mid -1925 and soon spread across Britain into Ireland where it joined the more formal waltz, quickstep, and foxtrot in the local dance halls. The Tango, much favoured during the Valentino era, was soon replaced in popularity with the less elegant and more frenetic Charleston and Black Bottom. They were soon being demonstrated on the stage of the Royal Hippodrome, and in November the Picture House presented as part of its supporting programme a short called "How to Dance the Charleston," which was warmly received. The following year the same cinema showed another short "The History of the Black Bottom" which the News Letter thought was "a novel feature,"while the Whig recommended it as enjoyable light entertainment, "cleverly conceived," and enlivened by lots of pretty girls and humorous sketches. The Black Bottom was technically difficult to perform properly, and was never as popular as the Charleston in the Plaza, the Carlton and the other local city dance halls.

Daytime tea dances and evening dances were so well attended that one local cleric felt called upon to suggest that excessive attendance at dance halls created "an indisposition for work" while another pointed out that people should realise that "work, not play, was the appointed occupation of man." Disquiet about excessive dancing also extended into secular circles as was reflected in the way that the Whig critic drew attention to the film "Dancing Mad" starring Maria Corda. It was a cautionary tale of a woman so addicted to the new dances - jazz mania the critic called it - that she nearly loses her home and husband. Part of the general disapproval was aimed at what was regarded as the poor quality of the syncopated music and jazz from America which accompanied the new dances. A letter in the Irish News from the conductor of the Savoy Orpheans informed its readers that the "weirdest effects" of jazz were achieved by breaking all the rules of music, while a writer in the Whig described the new syncopated sounds as consisting of instruments making "funny noises in the name of music." He complained that "the saxophone has been reduced to a clown, the strong stirring trumpet has been demoralised, the clarinet clowned out of its legitimate functions and even the staid romantic violin is called upon to play the fool." The only way, he argued, they could regain their "lawful and legitimate character" was to play "real music." The same paper also published the comments of Frederic Austin, the artistic director of the British National Opera Company, who criticised the prevalent "jazz culture" and complained that he felt that the musical taste of the general public was "at a very debased level."

For many people one of the main sources of music was in their local cinema, and the critics often praised the local cinema orchestras for the quality of their "real music" and drew attention on occasion to specific items. One such was the Masters of Music series which showed in the Picture House, in which the life of a particular composer was shown on the screen while David Curry's Orchestra played selections of their music on cue. Composers covered included Schubert, Liszt, Brahms and Bizet. The Irish News critic called on music lovers not to miss them. The critics also mentioned the many occasions when the orchestras played popular music, and how it was welcomed and appreciated by the crowds. They drew particular attention to the Ko - Ko Song Cartoons, or "cartunes" as they were usually spelt, which were made in the Max Fleischer studio in Florida, and were actually filmed versions of the song slides which had been used in theatres and music halls since the days of the magic lantern. They obviously still retained their popularity as the critics described the enthusiasm of the audiences laughing at the antics of Koko the clown while singing along with the orchestra as the lyrics of Ta Ra Ra Boom De Ay, Dixie, Kentucky and other favourites appeared on the screen.

The cinema managers were in touch with the mood of the public and were quite willing to satisfy their appetite for the new sounds. In March 1925 the Lyric in High Street announced that their musical accompaniments in future would be supplied by the Lyric Orpheus Band which was described as the latest type of American syncopated band, under the baton of J.W.Esplin. A few months later the Classic announced the introduction of the Classic Syncopating Five which played 30 minutes of the latest foxtrots and jazz each evening. The Irish News praised it as "a very popular innovation" but pointed out that the music for the main films would still be played by the thirty strong Concert Orchestra. In July 1926 the Classic was bought by the Provincial Cinematograph Theatres Company (P.C.T.), the company that had opened the Picture House in Royal Avenue in 1911 and which now owned 75 cinemas around the Br. Isles. The following month the new manager,

Frank Sparkes, announced, as part of a modernising process, the reopening of the cinema's two cafes, the Tower and the Rotunda, which had been redecorated and put under the direction of a new chef, Signor Ostenelli, supported by a staff of 75 workers. The new catering manager promised good food at reasonable prices and added that one cafe would contain a "real" American soda fountain and that diners in both would be entertained by jazz orchestras, or "combinations" as the Irish News called them, suggesting that they were small groups of musicians. The cinema itself retained its large traditional orchestra. The extra employment resulting from those changes was welcomed and the Irish News noted, with approval, that the addition of cinema restaurants over the years had greatly enhanced Belfast's reputation as a centre for catering.

The soda fountain and jazz music, symbols of creeping Americanisation, were accepted by audiences without comment. The Classic continued to cater to the musical tastes of its patrons and on 14th March 1927 it introduced Belfast to its first Wurlitzer organ inaugurated by Fitzroy Page who demonstrated its capabilities to an admiring audience. The instrument, which cost £8,000 and involved the installation of 150 miles of electric cable, according to the I.S.N., not only produced marvellous music but could "bark like a dog, roar like the the Atlantic, sound like the wind and sing like a bird." It became an integral part of the musical side of the Classic's programmes, enriching singalongs and delighting audiences with a wide range of classical, popular and jazz music. By August 1927 the Imperial Orchestra, directed by Victor Norman, was also supporting the films in that cinema with musical interludes which according to the Irish News included Irish melodies "and the latest jazz." The Alhambra, not unexpectedly for a hall with its entertainment tradition, went one better and in the following month complemented its films with a week long Grand Charleston Contest with prizes of £7 for the winner, £3 for the runner-up and £1 for third place.

The trans - Atlantic music with its catchy rhythms was soon all pervasive and because of the increasing availability of gramophones and radio was heard not only in the cinemas, dance halls like the Plaza, and music halls like the Royal Hippodrome and Empire but also at parties, in cafes and other social meeting places, in shops and in the streets. The Irish News was moved to report an interview with Sir Thomas Beecham who felt that such music had become "a public nuisance." He complained that there was nowhere left for people to rest and talk quietly in public anymore. What would he think today when canned music pursues people even into the toilets! But in 1928 it was already too late and such opinions were increasingly voiced by a minority as the majority of citizens seemed to have been seduced by what Noel Coward was to call "the potency of cheap music."

Locally the loudest voices of disapproval were directed against the behaviour and dress code of the flappers. One typical letter condemned the scantiness of dresses worn by young women at formal dances, a clear indication, the writer felt, that parental control was no longer having its effect. There were expressions of shock, outrage and amazement at the behaviour of young girls and women, many of whom were publicly smoking, drinking, using lipstick, cutting their hair short and wearing dresses that revealed bare arms and legs. One of the most "fateful" issues facing local young girls at the time, the I.S.N. noted with mock horror, was "to bob or not to bob." Mature citizens, familiar with the notion of long tresses as a mark of feminine beauty, couldn't understand why girls would want to cut them off. At the same time they accepted the wearing of long elegant skirts down to the ankle as the norm and were shocked as hems began to rise towards the knee. As hair and skirts shortened the faces of the censorious lengthened, and the warnings of social catastrophe from those in authority, including politicians, increased in intensity. The letter columns of the papers were full of dire predictions but equally of spirited defence. A young flapper added her personal view saying that she had bobbed her hair, wore a short skirt, silk stockings and lipstick but otherwise, she insisted, her behaviour was above reproach. Another, pre-empting Betty Boop (who was actually a caricature of the flapper girl) by a few years, asked what was wrong anyway with the occasional glimpse of a garter. A mother argued that fashions changed and it was "silly" to equate that with modesty, while a young man claimed that men liked their girlfriends to look smart and modern. Modernity was seen as the key and those who praised or defended the skirts signed themselves "modern," as in modern man, modern parent etc.

Films were seen as an integral part of the problem by both reflecting and encouraging a view of life and behaviour that undermined well tried and tested traditional values. The Whig critic, usually well balanced in his comments, noted cautiously that the cinema was being widely accused of "neglecting substance for shadow" but he didn't say if he agreed or not. But his paper did publish details of an address to an Educational Conference under the heading "The Cinema and Life" by a Dr Ballard in which he defended certain aspects of films. He claimed that he had never seen anything really demoralising in the cinema and thought that the majority of films could hardly be described as offensive. Indeed he felt that many were educational and even instructive, while some were really worthwhile culturally and dramatically. Having said that, he added there was a debit side in that many of the more popular films presented false aspects of life, often leading the spectators through "the crudest and sensational melodramas in which virtues and vices were distorted into grotesques."

In early 1927 the News Letter pursued that theme when it published comments from the Glasgow Educational Authority attacking the inappropriate standards of behaviour presented in Hollywood films, and calling for stricter censorship to protect young people. The paper itself expressed unease at the moral models often illustrated on the screen and suggested that a tightening of censorship might be the answer. Such criticisms were not confined to the local papers. An even more severe attitude was taken in early 1927 by the Irish Times in Dublin which deplored "the license of these latter years" with sordid plays on the stage and "vile" books in the shops but, the editor continued, "the worst that the stage and the meaner press have done for the debasement of civilised manhood is as nothing to the ravages of the cinematograph." The main problem, the editor argued, was the dominance of the "degraded" American film. He pointed out that European producers made films of quality like the recent "Les Miserables" and "Mademoiselle from Armentières" - both of which had been shown in Belfast with great success - but that the industry in general couldn't compete with "the cheap popular American films that fill the cheap houses." There was some truth in that argument, but he could also have pointed out that audiences both in Belfast and Dublin seemed to prefer the fast moving, lively Hollywood products regardless of their quality or cost. Also, while the local girls may have copied Clara Bow's dress, walk and make up with her round eyes and bee-sting lips, the imitation tended to stop there. There was little opportunity for the much publicised excesses of the Bright Young Things in Belfast with its strict licensing laws, strong traditional morality, village mentality and firm policing. Also a 6:00 am start in the nearby spinning mill didn't exactly encourage late night partying. Pleasure was strictly controlled in a city where even the children's playgrounds were closed on Sundays. The News Letter noted that the Chief Censor T.P.O'Connor was aware of the widespread criticisms of the contents of films, and of his office. The paper published his response in which he defended the level of censorship and suggested that, in the case of children, the answer was stricter supervision, while in other matters "local authorities should exercise their discretion." Future filmgoers in Belfast were to experience the implications of that last piece of advice.... but that's another story to be saved until later.

Despite the criticisms, the local critics maintained a sense of balance, avoided any tones of high morality or preaching, and continued to discuss the films shown in the city on their own merits. They made it clear that they expected good on the screen to be rewarded, and evil to be punished. They all accepted, like most responsible people of the day, the need for censorship and, in general, they seemed to believe that T.P.O'Connor and his team were doing a good job. They were also probably aware that in intellectual and cultural circles attitudes towards the cinema were changing and that it was increasingly seen as an art form capable of intelligent and perceptive comment on life and human behaviour. The Royal Cinema and the Classic often referred to themselves as centres of cinematic Art and the critics weren't slow to praise certain films like the recently shown "The Last Laugh" as having artistic value.

In London some cinemas began to show specialist films to select audiences who wanted something more than just entertainment, and it is interesting that some of the films involved like Gosta Berling, the Nibelungs, The Last Laugh and The Student of Prague were screened with appreciation and success in Belfast. The local press also reported recent exhibitions, in London, of actuality films from the beginnings of cinema in the 1890's, which amazed audiences with their clarity and lack of flicker, not to mention their historical content. A minority of critics began to discuss the need to preserve such films for the nation and in 1924 the first step in that direction was taken when the war films preserved in the Imperial War Museum, snippets from which had been incorporated into "The Battle of the Somme" and other war documentaries, were transferred to the keeping of the H.M.S.O. and put into the charge of a Government Cinematograph Adviser. Those films were to form the nucleus later of the National Film Library founded in 1935, and today run by the British Film Institute. Local editors expressed approval of that move though there was no suggestion that commercial entertainment films should be treated likewise. In 1925 a Film Society was founded in London for the showing of quality films that weren't available in the commercial cinema. It was supported by a cross section of British intelligentsia and among its many members were Julian Huxley, George Bernard Shaw, H.G.Wells, Augustus John, Ivor Montague and Adrian Brunel. The London Film Society was to become the model for later film societies established across the country including Belfast, though the Belfast Film Society as such wasn't formed until 1935-6.

Running parallel to the theoretical enthusiasm was an increasing amateur interest in actual film making. Indeed by late 1928 a group of local enthusiasts had got together to establish a film society called the Provincial Film Society of N. Ireland which, according to the Irish News, intended to make amateur films of local interest. It was the brainchild of a professional photographer, Louis Morrison, located at 83, Royal Avenue who announced in January 1929 that preparations were well under way, including the acquisition of a studio, equipment, professional cameras and projectors. He called upon all those with an interest or knowledge of amateur acting, scenario writing, dancing, stage management, costumes, scene painting, make - up, and filming to join the Society and "show the film world what can be done in Ulster by Ulster people." There were plans for a series of "Ulster comedy plays" (which, sadly, never materialised) but, before that, their first production was to be a newsreel coverage of the Ulster Motor Race later in the year. Obviously plans were changed for within a few months they had actually completed their first short film called "Easter Holidays," which turned out to be a travelogue of local scenery. It included scenes filmed at Bellevue, Bangor and in the Glens of Antrim and was shown to the public in the Picture House during the week beginning 15th April 1929, which was, interestingly enough, the last week that the Picture House projected silent films. It was welcomed by the Telegraph while the Irish News critic commended its photography as "good" and hoped that its local interest would attract "many spectators."

That growing enthusiasm for the medium carried over into print and in 1927 a magazine of serious criticism appeared called "Close - Up" describing itself as the only magazine devoted to the study of films as an art. With its esoteric discussions of filmic theory, its promise of "no gossip," and its decided bias against popular Hollywood and British films it was very different from the fan magazines available in the bookshops in Belfast. There is no direct evidence to indicate whether the local critics read it or not - there are hints in their columns that they did - but because of their professional interests they were surely aware of it, and of the developments in London and elsewhere. Even in Hollywood there was a growing desire to recognise quality in film making and in January 1927 a group of eminent film makers met to discuss the issue. The result was the setting up of the Academy of Motion Picture Arts the following month and the beginning of the presentation of annual Oscars for excellence shown by film makers. The first Oscars were presented in May 1929 in the Rooseveldt Hotel in Hollywood, without much ballyhoo, and with only a brief mention in the local papers. Yet the ceremony had a connection with Belfast. The first ever award for Best Writing was won by Ben Glazer for his adaptation of the silent film "Seventh Heaven" (d. Frank Borzage, 1927). Glazer was a Hungarian Jew whose family had migrated westwards across Europe, heading for America. They settled for a time in Belfast were young Benjamin was born in May 1887, and where he spent his early years. The family moved onwards to America where he studied law, before becoming a journalist. He translated European plays for American theatre and ended up in Hollywood as a script writer, and later a producer and director. He died there in March 1956. But the fact remains that a Belfastman won one of the first Oscars awarded.

The influence of films for good or otherwise, and their impact on society at large was rarely out of the news at the time, but, still, on the morning of the 21st October 1923, readers of the Irish News must have been surprised to find a letter from the eminent stage actress Fay Compton, about a problem she perceived for the theatre in what she called, "this cinema-ridden era." She highlighted the increasingly "direct competition between the footlights and the film." She argued that certain sophisticated plays would never be "relegated to the dead silence of the picture palace" but wondered what would happen in the case of action plays like "The Prisoner of Zenda." Could the stage, she asked, survive the competition from such productions? That competition certainly existed. The local critics mentioned it on occasions, while film publicists made effective use of it. When the Classic showed "Ghost Train" based on a well known play by Arthur Ridley, who was later to gain nation - wide fame on television as Godfrey in "Dad's Army," it boasted that the film was accompanied by "full effects that were not possible on stage." Miss Compton wondered if Belfast audiences had any thoughts on the matter. The answer came a few days later, not from a citizen of Belfast, but in another letter from London. The writer, who worked in the cinema industry, understood her "apprehension" but he believed that "the art of the cinema" only appeared to threaten the stage. He argued that the cinema was already developing new techniques and scenarios that were no longer bound by the conventions of the traditional stage. To his optimistic eye the cinema had at last cut the apron strings to the theatre and was "stepping out on its own." He predicted that it was entering a sphere "where the stage cannot follow... and it will not be long before it calls forth a Shakespeare of its own." The lack of a local response to Miss Compton probably didn't surprise the critics because they knew that the majority of their readers were little interested in such matters, and went to the cinema mainly for relaxation and entertainment, and, above all, to see their favourite stars, both male and female.

The death of Valentino had caused widespread and genuine sorrow among his fans and many of them probably bought the sheet music of the popular song "There's a New Star in Heaven Tonight" which his passing inspired. But, as is the way of the world, there were new stars waiting on earth. Valentino's departure didn't end the reign of the so called Latin Lover because the studios had been building up competitors, the most successful of whom was Ramon Novarro who was already well known and liked in the city. He made his greatest impact with "Ben Hur" which arrived in the Classic in January 1928, where it was shown "with full effects." The populace had been well primed with stories in the fan magazines and the press, and anticipation levels were high. Many would already have read the original novel "Ben Hur: A Tale of the Christ" by Lew Wallace, and some more mature citizens may even have recalled the stage presentation which had caused a sensation in London earlier in the century. The religious aspects of the story also give it a special interest even to those who didn't normally go to the cinema. The filming had begun in Italy but accidents and other calamities had resulted in spiralling costs until the newly formed M.G.M. company took drastic action. The cast and crew were dismissed and the whole production was recalled to Hollywood. A new director, Fred Niblo, was appointed and the main part of Ben Hur was given to Ramon Novarro, though Francis X. Bushman was retained as his adversary Messala, the part that was to be taken in the remake thirty four years later by Belfast's Stephen Boyd. Bushman was very popular in Belfast, especially with the ladies, and his romantic films with Beverly Bayne always drew large crowds.

As expected, the film was warmly received by critics and public and its popularity can be gauged from the fact that later in the year it returned to the city centre and showed in the Royal Cinema, something that happened only rarely. The religious sequences involving the Nativity, the Three Wise Men, the Procession of the Palms, the Pool at Siloam and the Last Supper were filmed in colour, with suitable respect and reverence. There was always a problem with depicting the person of Christ because many people, including the British Censor, still objected to an actor playing the part and some went so far as to call it blasphemy. The film makers were anxious not to offend religious sensibilities so, in "Ben Hur," the presence of Christ was indicated by shots of his arm, a hand or a footprint combined with reaction shots. Some people, including Cecil B. deMille, suggested that the hand shown was too effete but that minor criticism was generally ignored. When the film was remade in the sound era the director William Wyler used the same approach but the hand and arm shown were strong and muscular belonging to a Man who made his living as a carpenter.

While religious feelings were respected, years later it was the deadly duel between Ben Hur and his former friend Messala in the chariot race which remained in the memories of those who had seen it. The chariot race was the most exciting piece of film - making people had ever seen. It was organized by the second unit director Reeves Eason a name remembered today only by film buffs and historians. In a massive crowded set he used 42 cameras to expose nearly 200,000 feet of film which was edited down to 750 feet in the completed film. The audience was swept along by the excitement of what they were seeing on the screen, enhanced by the orchestra at full throttle, plus the special effects of pounding horse hooves and crashing chariots. One elderly filmgoer who recalled watching it in the Classic added ruefully: "And they call them silent films!" The I.S.N. critic summed the experience up in one word - "amazing," adding that the film was "the talk of the city." The News Letter on the other hand was inclined to draw attention to the "fine acting" of Ramon Navarro.

Audiences were already familiar with stories about the early days of Christianity, complete with pagan revels, cruel Romans and a chariot race, because the Classic had earlier also shown a version of "Quo Vadis" advertised as "the immortal story of the dawn of Christianity." It was an Italian production, not to be confused with an earlier version in 1912 which had made quite an impact on the city then. The Italians had decided to show that the memory of "Cabiria" and other prewar epics was still alive in their studios and had undertaken to remake "Quo Vadis" on a grander scale. Thus the Whig critic was able to tell his readers that the film had taken two years to complete, and had a cast of over 20,000 including Emil Jannings who played Nero, plus 150 lions specially imported for the bloody arena sequences. The management played the religious card very cleverly with an open invitation to the local clergy to attend the initial showing, which many accepted, some of them entering a cinema for the first time in their lives. Another invite went out to the Lord and Lady Mayoress to honour a showing with their presence, which they did. Special music was played during the film and the Classic Quartette sang hymns and other vocal items in keeping with "the sacred atmosphere of the picture." The result was, as the

News Letter commented, "full houses," and the critic went on to praise the realism of the crowd scenes and the chariot race. However, as so often in the past, he preferred the human dimension, and reserved his greatest praise for the acting of Jannings which he described as "splendid." The Irish News critic thought that the film gave "a wonderfully vivid picture of the persecution of the early Christians." He agreed with his News Letter colleague that it was a feast for the eyes filling the screen with impressive spectacle especially during the "very realistic" burning of Rome and during many other scenes of "great splendour and terrible cruelties."

In complete contrast, other less spectacular films of a religious nature were shown and, from accounts, their simple veracity had a wide appeal. Typical was the French made "The Miracle of Lourdes" which the Royal Cinema presented, while the Clonard showed another French film called "The Vow" which dealt with the life of St Thérèse of Liseux. That film ran for a full week to packed houses, with a special matinee on Saturday for children only. The Irish News commended the management of the Falls Road Clonard for its enterprise and "its desire to cater in a most dignified way for the people of that most populous district." Praise was heaped on the film's direction, the acting and the orchestra whose rendition of sacred music produced a result that was both "impressive and devotional." How many films could be described in those terms today! East Belfast was not neglected either because during Holy Week 1928 the Mountpottinger Picturedrome "respectfully" announced the screening of "INRI," a simple straight forward life of Christ which attracted full houses. The News Letter felt that the story was "reverently portrayed" with suitable sacred music from the Panatrope and the orchestra, while the I.S.N. praised the fact that it eschewed "the stuff that emanates from Hollywood."

Meanwhile, in Hollywood, the director Cecil B. de Mille, a name well known to Belfast cinemagoers, had already noted the continuing popularity of stories with a religious theme and, in the early Twenties, he decided to try his hand at one. He was a skilled director and showman who excelled, as the I.S.N. critic pointed out, in ultra modern society dramas characterised by "gorgeous settings, luxurious backgrounds, beautiful women, flashing gowns and an all star cast." He could also have added that de Mille liked to show his leading ladies, including Gloria Swanson and Bebe Daniels, in various stages of undress, and that he had often caused raised eyebrows with his bathing and orgy scenes. Much has been written about de Mille since then, a lot of it negative and highly critical but, whatever their drawbacks, his films were always entertaining and popular with audiences including those in Belfast. Arthur Miller and others dismissed him as a super egotist, but he knew what he wanted and dominated his sets like a petty tyrant to ensure that he got it. Adolph Zukor, who knew him well, held that his success was due to the fact that he made films mainly for the public not for the critics, while Graham Green, who wasn't easily fooled, described him as a sentimental salvationist.

When de Mille announced in 1922 that he intended to make a film called "The Ten Commandments" there was widespread surprise, but that decision was to prove to be the beginning of a new phase in his career. His brother William put it well when he commented that having applied himself to the underclothes, bathrooms and matrimonial problems of his fellow citizens he decided it was time to turn to the question of their salvation. De

Mille knew that audiences wouldn't sit still for a dry visual lecture and he believed there was nothing wrong in presenting religious beliefs enhanced with some sex and spectacle. In February 1925 his "Ten Commandments" arrived in the Picture House two years after its New York premiere, which was the normal time lapse for major films to reach local screens. It was applauded by the critics and audiences, who came in such numbers that it was retained for a second week, before moving to other cinemas across the city, notably the Clonard, the Picturedrome and the Coliseum. It arrived in the city at the beginning of Lent in the midst of Lenten Pastorals and other calls for spiritual renewal, though whether that was by chance or design it is impossible to say. De Mille the showman would certainly have approved of the timing.

The film was in two sections with a relatively short Biblical prologue, photographed in colour, depicting how Moses led the Israelites out of bondage in Egypt and received the Commandments from God amid scenes of "powerful dramatic appeal..... and novelty" (News Letter). That was followed by a modern story set in San Francisco and filmed in black and white illustrating the need for their application today. The critics concentrated mainly on the Biblical section with its massive and exotic sets, ignoring the Golden Calf orgy but expressing particular admiration for the crossing of the Red Sea which the News Letter found "impressive," the Irish News described as "a marvellously ingenious piece of photography, wonderfully realistic," while the I.S.N. thought it was so "startling as to be unbelievable." The moral of the film was emphasised, namely that the keeping of the commandments was vital for the survival of society. The modern section illustrated that theme by showing the struggle of good against evil as taking place between two brothers, and how one of them destroyed himself by breaking those fundamental laws. The Irish News noted, with approval, that the story was characterised by "dramatic scenes and a thrilling climax."

The reported success of the film was achieved against strong competition, because another film, "The Moon of Israel," which also dealt with the subject of Moses and the Exodus from Egypt, was screened in the Classic during the same week as de Mille's epic. It was an Anglo-Austrian production based on a popular novel by Rider Haggart. Austria specialised in spectacular films at that time and stills indicate that the sets used in "The Moon Over Israel" were indeed large and impressive. The film was expertly directed by a Hungarian Mihaly Kertesz who changed his name to Michael Curtiz and went on to make many successful films in Hollywood. It starred another Hungarian, the glamorous Maria Corda, who had begun her career in Budapest where she met and married Alexander Korda, who took her to Austria and Germany before moving on to Hollywood and later England. Some English critics thought that "The Moon of Israel" was superior to de Mille's effort, and while the local critics didn't go that far they were quite impressed, especially by the special effects. They encouraged their readers to see the film and described the depiction of the Pillar of Fire that protected the Israelites, and the opening of the Red Sea as "really marvellous." Today the film is generally unknown while de Mille's epic marches on in DVD format. As if that wasn't enough, during the same month the Coliseum presented another Biblical epic, "Sodom and Gomorrah" from the same Austrian studios, starring Maria Corda and directed by Michael Curtiz. The Irish News described it as "sensational" and not unexpectedly noted that it was attracting full houses. Like the "Ten Commandments" it combined elements of the present and the past. The story compared the depravity of modern Vienna with the evils of the Biblical cities and, as the critic pointed out, showed that "evil does not go unpunished."

Twenties Glamour.

Not all the spectacle films had religious or moral themes. The popularity of Rider Haggart persuaded a British producer G.B. Samuelson to make a film of his novel "She." To ensure as wide an interest as possible he brought over American actress Betty Blythe to play the main part of Ayesha, the mysterious white queen, and had the production filmed in one of the best equipped studios in Germany. Modern critics who have seen the film have dismissed it as badly made, badly acted and slow moving though modern audiences used to the almost frenetic pace of many present day films would probably find most silent films leisurely. In the mid - Twenties tastes were different and the film proved a popular success when it showed in the Classic in early April 1926. The News Letter critic, reflecting the theme put forward by Fay Compton, praised the novel but suggested that the excitement conjured up by the written word was trebly enhanced "by the camera's magic aid." He praised the film as a "faithful portrayal" of the novel and added that Betty Blythe combined the required beauty with "high histrionic ability" in the main part. The I.S.N. critic was equally complimentary but saw that Miss Blythe was the main attraction of the piece. Quoting probably from the producer's blurb, he described the well known scene at the end where "she casts aside her gossamer garments and enters the flames....... wonder changes to horror as she begins to fade...... the flames roar as she writhes within their bondage.......... (until) she is no more." What red blooded young man could resist seeing that! The success of the film probably encouraged the Royal Cinema to bring back Miss Blythe's version of the "Queen of Sheba" for another outing a few months later. Of course it wasn't the end of Ayesha as later filmgoers discovered. She was reborn in the person of Helen Gahagan in 1935 when the story was inexplicably relocated to the Arctic (d.Irving Pichel, and starring Randolph Scott) and again in the Sixties by Hammer with Ursula Andress (d. Robert Day, 1965, with Peter Cushing). There was even a modern day sequel, the "Vengeance of She" by the same studio a few years later starring a Czech actress, the rather wooden Olinka Berova (d.Cliff Owen 1968).

During the Twenties British and American film makers, including for example Alfred Hitchcock, often made use of the excellent facilities available in Austrian and German studios. There they came into contact with the Expressionist visual style of filming. It was the period usually described as the Golden Age of German cinema, and German films with that distinctive visual style continued to appear on local screens, notably Fritz Lang's "Metropolis." It opened in the Royal Cinema during the last week of 1927, billed as "the screen sensation of the age," accompanied by "special music and effects by the Premier Cinema Orchestra," and continued through the first week of the New Year. Filmgoers had read about it in the papers and magazines but were still intrigued by the posters outside the cinema showing part of a city of skyscrapers with the image of a gold coloured female metal robot in the foreground. The film had an amazing impact in the city and attracted, according to the I.S.N., "enormous crowds." The News Letter critic described it as a "stupendous spectacle" while the Whig critic found it "bewildering in its intensity" and added that it was "impossible to describe" in words but "must be seen."

The critics, and the audiences, expressed wonder at Lang's vision of a future city with an upper zone of skyscrapers - influenced by Lang's experience of New York - occupied by a ruling elite of managers who lived in luxury, and a lower underground region where the workers lived in appalling conditions. The skyscraper section with its massive buildings, its moving crowds of people, its vehicles, connecting railway tracks and flying machines was, in fact a large detailed model built by the German craftsmen to Lang's requirements, a technical marvel in its own right which still impresses. To the citizens of Belfast in 1927 it represented the city of the future, the city of the year 2000AD. Viewers also marvelled at the scenes showing the making of the robot Maria, played by a new German actress Brigitte Helm, complete with flashing electrical discharges of the type which were to accompany the making of another famous monster many years later (1933, Frankenstein, d. James Whale). Miss Helm described the filming of those scenes as "torture" and claimed she passed some of the worst moments of her life on the film submitting to Lang's "tyrannical" direction. The result, many critics believe, was one of the finest pieces of silent film acting still on view. Robots or automans had long been part of the entertainment scene in Belfast and just over a year before audiences in the Lyceum and the Coliseum had marvelled at the antics of Sparks, the Wireless Man, brought over from the London Palladium. He, or it, was a life sized male figure who came on stage dressed in an Admiral's uniform. According to the Irish News he did everything but talk. He answered questions from the audience using signs and even conducted the orchestra. At the end of his performance he was taken apart on stage to show that he was completely mechanical. The I.S.N. found the performance "puzzling,"as most of the audience probably did, but Sparks was nothing in comparison with the exotic Maria. Other impressive sequences in the film, specially mentioned by the local critics, were the Tower of Babel scenes, the rebellion of the workers, the smashing of the machines and the flooding of the underground city.

One of the earliest serious science fiction films, "Metropolis" included many elements which have reappeared in or influenced later films including, "Star Wars" and "Blade Runner." It is of interest to a modern audience not only because the story is set at the beginning of the twenty first century but because it is still worth seeing for its own sake, having an intrinsic quality that has survived severe cutting and re-editing over the years, and even attempts in the Eighties to "improve" it with the addition of a rock soundtrack. The film that had premiered in Berlin on 10th January 1927 ran for two and a half hours but the version that reached Belfast a year later was only two hours long which suggests that it was the official edited version from Germany, released by the UFA studio. The editing was an attempt to meet some of the criticisms directed against it at the time, above all that it was too long and too violent. Critics had highlighted its sources tracing them especially to H.G.Wells, Karl Marx and the Bible, and Lang was particularly annoyed when Wells, whom he admired, described it as one of the silliest films he had ever seen. A complex work, it dealt essentially with the conflict between Capital and Labour, though the final romantic scene of the hero and heroine holding hands, capital and labour united by love, does seem rather naive and strangely at odds with Lang's left wing politics.

That optimistic ending caused no problems for the local critics at the time. The I.S.N.

pointed out that the film was full of contrasts - light and darkness, wealth and poverty, the differing life styles above and below ground, the two Marias - the one good the other evil - but he thought the solution, based on love, was "splendid." Since then others have suggested that Lang believed that in a society dominated by technology there must always be a place for the heart. What made the film riveting, then as now, are the visuals, and Belfast audiences certainly responded positively to them. After running for two weeks in the Royal Cinema the film was quickly transferred to the Crumlin, the Alhambra, the Picturedrome and the Midland in turn, allowing a wide cross section of the population to see it. Over the years the film has been the cause of much heated debate, and cineastes have searched fruitlessly for the missing thirty minutes that would hopefully clarify some obscure points in the narrative, and give a more complete picture of Lang's vision. The QFT bravely screened a version in May 2002 which ran for only 79 minutes but even in that truncated state, as the accompanying notes pointed out "it still has resonance today." There was, therefore, widespread surprise and delight in critical circles when it was announced in mid - 2008 that a complete copy of the film had turned up in an old film museum in Buenos Aires. The discovery was authenticated by German experts on the silent cinema and they promised that the complete version would be made available to the public as soon as possible. In September 2010 the QFT screened "a fully reconstructed and restored" version of Lang's film complete with its original score. Local modern students of film history, and other film aficionados, were able to see a more complete, and satisfying, "Metropolis" than had been available to local audiences in 1927, or in 2002. The complete version is now available to all on DVD.

In the meantime Cecil B. deMille had decided to continue with the religious theme and to make a life of Christ. Friends cautioned against it because devout people regarded the depiction of Christ on a screen for profit as a form of blasphemy while many others thought that it just wasn't right or respectful. DeMille went ahead with the project, saying that he wanted to rectify the overly pious Sunday School images that many were familiar with. The film was to be called "King of Kings" and he choose H.B.Warner to play the lead. The first day of shooting began with prayers from an ecumenical group representing Protestant, Catholic, Jewish, Moslem and Buddhist faiths and every effort was made, according to the publicists, to maintain a reverent atmosphere on the set to the point of having a short period of meditation after the scenes of the crucifixion. During the filming a clerical advisor was present on the set to give advice, though that didn't mean that the director listened. The completed film premiered in April 1927 in New York amid large crowds, and lively controversy, which preceded and accompanied it wherever it was shown, including Belfast. The main criticisms were very similar to those that had accompanied the showing of "From Manger to Cross" many years before. The film had its severest critics among the clergy, scholars of the Sacred and in America some Jewish groups, though, in general, it was well received by the paying public. The British censor refused a certificate to any film showing a living moving Christ so it was released in Britain without being submitted to the censor's office. When the LCC passed it as suitable for screening the main hurdle was crossed and it went on view around the country.

The News Letter reported that it was seen by the local Police Committee in December

1928 and that no objections were raised to it being shown in Belfast. In early January the Picture House announced that "King of Kings, Unquestionably the Greatest film of all time" would be opening on 7th January for a two week run, presented in separate shows at 6:00 and 8:15 pm daily. The Friday before, a special morning showing was arranged for the critics and above all for the local clergy, large numbers of whom attended. The News Letter found their reactions mixed, but generally negative. One elderly cleric dismissed it out of hand as "blasphemous and absurd," but younger men were less extreme and were willing to accept that the atmosphere was reverent though, as one commented, he felt that "the Gospels had been played about with." The introduction of scenes that had no Biblical basis offended many of the religious though the film never descended to the fictional levels of daftness depicted in "The Last Temptation of Christ" (1988, d. Martin Scorsese) or "The Da Vinci Code" (2006, d.Ron Howard).

The critics, on the other hand, were more positive. The Irish News critic found the whole experience quite acceptable. He thought that the film itself was elaborately produced with splendid settings and costuming, that the plot kept close to the Bible and that the whole was enhanced by the use of appropriate sacred music. He did admit that de Mille had added extra details "based on early Christian legend or tradition." He didn't say if he approved or not, but praised the acting and the "wonderful" colour photography which was used in the introductory and final scenes. De Mille based many of his scene compositions on traditional paintings, a fact noted and commented favourably upon by the Whig, but the result is that while the film is often beautiful to look at it tends to be rather static. The Belfast Telegraph writer thought that the approach was "most reverend" and he drew attention especially to the scenes in which Our Lady appeared, describing them as "full of grace and beauty." Unfortunately many people were put off by the opening sequence which showed De Mille at his most ridiculous, introducing Mary Magdalene (Jacqueline Logan), in colour, living in decadent luxurious surroundings and complaining about her absent lover Judas, who was played by the excellent German actor, Joseph Schildcraut. The Irish News critic felt the sequence was overdone but accepted that her later "contrition and atonement" adequately restored the balance. It has one particularly hilarious moment when the lady, preparing to leave her sumptuous home, orders her servant to "harness my zebras." Luckily the mood changes after that and becomes more serious.

People who saw it at the time recalled that the audience was soon reduced to complete silence when the figure of Christ Himself appeared. De Mille used a young blind girl for that key moment and the camera takes her place as she is cured. As her sight returns the completely dark screen lightens slowly until she, and the audience, see Our Lord's features for the first time. It is a moment which, once seen, remains long in the memory. The main incidents in the life of Christ are shown ending with the mystery of the Resurrection, and the Ascension into heaven. After its downtown run it quickly moved to packed houses in the Clonard, the Midland and the Lyceum proving once again that films with a religious theme usually did well in the city. Despite its faults the film became a favourite with audiences and was shown regularly in the Silent Movie Theatre in Los Angeles every Christmas up until the Fifties. Who would have forecast that over eighty years later it would actually be shown in Clonard Monastery on the Falls Road as part of the Belfast Festival, when it was described as "a masterpiece......visually stunning and deeply moving."

For a time the Western had been eclipsed by the religious and other spectaculars, though Tom Mix, Buck Jones and Hoot Gibson continued to entertain their many fans. W.S.Hart's last major Western "Tumbleweeds" arrived in 1926 and though it drew sizeable crowds to the Clonard and the Crumlin the popularity of Hart himself was obviously declining. The public gaze had turned to a new type of Western which didn't deal with gunmen, stage and bank robberies or such. The epic Western had arrived and it concerned itself mainly with great historic themes like the opening up of the West and the unification of the nation. The seeds of that approach could be traced back to Griffiths, Thomas Ince and even W.S.Hart, but the new trend was initiated by James Cruze's "The Covered Wagon." which arrived in the Picture House in February 1925 preceded by rave reviews, and Royal approval as the Prince of Wales had actually called in unofficially to see it in London. As befitted a major production from Lasky, it was presented in separate shows though there were no increases in prices. The Picture House often pointed out that London prices varied from 2/ 6 to 10/ 6 but "ours are 8 pence and 1/ 3," while the Imperial insisted that its policy was always to give the best value available for money. The patrons certainly got good value whatever they paid, and "The Covered Wagon" was no exception. Each show was preceded by a Prologue given by a Major Kelly who set the historical scene, along with Chief Laacnig who performed native American dances and songs, while suitable music, including the new Covered Wagon theme, was supplied by David Curry and his orchestra.

The film dealt with the trek of 1849 when 500 wagons left Kansas City for a 2,000 mile journey, some going to Oregon and others to California. There was the prerequisite love triangle story between two wagonmasters (J.Warren Kerrigan and Alan Hale) and the female lead (Lois Wilson) that tended to get in the way of the main story, which concerned the pioneer families in the wagons and how, as the Whig put it, they overcame the problems of the trail. Cruze took his crew to the Snake Valley region of Nevada to film authentic outdoor locations of plains, valleys and mountains. According to the critics the local audiences were amazed and entranced by the wide landscape vistas, with the line of wagons nearly three miles long moving slowly on, and thrilled especially to the crossing of the River Platte, a prairie fire, a buffalo hunt and an exciting attack by Indians in full war paint. Wherever it was shown in the city it drew large crowds. Critics have since argued about the artistic qualities of the film and have complained that the versions available to modern audiences are incomplete, being much shorter than the original 108 minutes. The Queen's Film Society showed a copy in the mid - sixties describing it in the accompanying notes as "splendid" but unfortunately included no details of its running length. Regardless of today's opinions the film was a great popular and financial success in the Twenties, and it turned a new page in the history of the Western.

The Western grows up.

Registering that success,William Fox decided to go one better and choose an up and coming director, John Ford, who was making a name for himself, to do it. The result was "The Iron Horse" which reached Belfast in early May 1926. One day citizens going about their business in the city centre were amazed to be confronted by an American Indian in full war paint and bonnet riding a splendid bay horse. It turned out that he was

only advertising the arrival of the "Iron Horse" in the Classic. The film was conceived and directed in the epic mould and Ford, like Cruze, took his crew to Nevada to film actual locations, despite a lack of facilities and bitterly cold weather. He insisted that every detail be authentic down to the interior of the log cabins. The result, said the News Letter, was "a vivid and striking narrative." The story revolved around a vital step in the growth of the U.S.A: the building of the first continental railway across America, a milestone involving what the News Letter described as "a struggle against Nature and unfriendly Indians," which welded the East to the West. The I.S.N. emphasised the historic and epic qualities of that achievement, comparing its significance to the voyage of Columbus or the opening of the Suez Canal. All the critics and the audiences, one suspects, appreciated the feeling of authenticity of the temporary townships, the saloons with their gamblers, dance hall girls and tough workers, which permeated the film.

Charles Chaplin in Gold Rush. Box office gold.

Ford filmed the rivalry between competing gangs of track layers, - the one Irish and Italian the other Chinese, - who between them actually laid about a mile and a half of track. As the track lengthened Ford interwove the arduous work in a masterly way with the struggle against the elements, attacks from Indians and renegades, a buffalo stampede with the animals actually thundering towards the camera (and audience), and the adventures of the hero played by the athletic George O'Brien, all intercut with small but moving personal details involving individuals. He also introduced real characters into the plot, notably Abraham Lincoln, Buffalo Bill and Wild Bill Hickok, and recreated the moment when the tracks of the Union Pacific and the Central Pacific railways met on 10th May 1869 and the Golden Spike was driven in to celebrate the event. To the audiences it was history in the making. The final shot was of Lincoln accompanied by the title "His truth is marching on." The Western was certainly marching on and had travelled a long way from "The Great Train Robbery" and the simple adventures of Bronco Billy Anderson.

Vying with the spectacle and the West were the many comedies from Harold Lloyd, Buster Keaton, Larry Semon and a host of others especially, a young man called Stan Laurel, whose two - reelers the Irish News drew attention to with increased regularity. But the master was still Chaplin and he proved it when he released his latest full length film, "The Gold Rush," in America in early August 1925 to high praise from the critics, the New York Times describing it as "an outstanding gem." Major films could take up to two years to reach Belfast but "The Gold Rush" was in the Royal Cinema in less than five months, to the obvious delight of both critics and public. Without hesitation the Whig hailed it as "Chaplin at his best," the News Letter referred to "packed houses," while the Irish News noted succinctly that "Chaplin proves that he has many rivals but no equals." The public obviously agreed because beginning on the 9th January it settled in for a four week run, but such was the demand that it quickly returned to the same cinema for another fortnight. Even that wasn't enough and during Christmas week it was back in the city centre, "by popular request," showing in the Picture House. No other film had ever performed in the city to that level of popularity. During that same year it also showed in the Clonard, the Picturedrome, the Duncairn and the Alhambra. It ran for a full week in the Clonard with two shows every evening (except Sunday, of course) at 6:50 and 9:00 pm, and a special matinee on Wednesday. At times the cinema seemed to be under siege and the Irish News critic described the scenes at the box office as "another gold rush."

The film dealt with Charlie's adventures as a prospector searching for gold in Alaska, with hilarious set pieces played out against a grim background of intense cold and the threat of starvation. The scenes of the frozen wastes of the tundra were worthy of "Nanook of the North." One outstanding sequence involved Charlie cooking his boot and eating it with refined delicacy. Another had his hungry companion, Big Jim McKay (Mark Swain), imagining Charlie as a huge fowl ready to be cooked, and pursuing him around their cabin for that purpose. Outside the cabin a blizzard raged and murder was committed. The News Letter commented that "besides farce the film depicts grim realism, giving it a rare distinction" while the Irish News referred to it as a "dramatic comedy." The Irish News also commended Chaplin's personal input into the film and praised his working methods as superior artistically to the widespread "factory system" of film making which tended to produce mediocrity.

The critics were well aware of Chaplin's serious side because the year before they had praised and enjoyed his "A Woman of Paris" which he had written and directed. The plot concerned a young country girl (Edna Purviance) who after a misunderstanding with her boyfriend ran off to Paris where she ended up as the mistress of a wealthy man (Adolphe Menjou). Later the boyfriend met her again and tried to win her back but, when he discovered her situation, he committed suicide. In revenge his mother acquired a gun and set out to kill her, but was reconciled when she realised that the girl did truly love her son. The Irish News critic admitted that it wasn't typical Chaplin and that it dealt with life "far outside the beaten track" but nevertheless found it a "work of surpassing interest." He also thought that Edna Purviance in the main role was "splendid," which would have pleased Chaplin because one of the reasons he made the film was to show off her talents, which he greatly admired. The film did reasonable business in Belfast but created none of the excitement that normally surrounded a Chaplin production. While the critics were pleased, the public wanted to see the skilled clown and were disappointed that he appeared only very briefly as a bungling porter early in the story.

Besides laughs, the public enjoyed thrills and there was no shortage of them available. Lon Chaney was a great favourite and his amazing but bizarre make - up and unusual characters never failed to draw the crowds. When his "Hunchback of Notre Dame" came to the Royal Cinema in January 1925 it broke all records with 23,528 patrons paying to see it during the first week, which ensured that it was retained for a second week. The critics praised the acting and the vast sets especially of the cathedral. The Irish News critic was impressed by the skill with which Chaney portrayed emotion despite a grotesque makeup and was still able to play effectively upon the feelings of the audience "moving them to the extreme." When the film was shown in the Clonard, queues formed one and a half hours before the opening time. Equal enthusiasm was shown for another quite different film, "Beau Geste" which boasted a marvellous cast of Ronald Colman, Victor McLaglan, Noah Beery and William Powell with the added promise of "battles, mutiny, mad Arab raiders, sudden death in the hot Sahara......... spine tingling mystery, murder, fire, heroism, self -

sacrifice, escape, and finally the astonishing solution of a jewel theft." In other words it had, as local fans would have put it, everything but the kitchen sink. No wonder it ran for two weeks in the Royal Cinema and then returned later for another week, not to mention successful runs in the Mountpottinger Picturedrome, the Alhambra and elsewhere.

Besides the manly heroes, romantic leads and menacing villains there was also a wide variety of female stars and players on show. Between them they presented every aspect of feminine personality, and local fans had their favourites whom they followed loyally. There was Gloria Swanson, the epitome of Twenties glamour, though her appearances became rarer as the decade progressed. Bebe Daniels, known equally for her humour and glamour, remained a great favourite while the talented Pauline Frederick continued to attract crowds with her more serious roles. The Whig critic was of the opinion that Miss Frederick was "probably the cleverest tragedienne to appear on the screen." Pola Negri had displaced Alla Nazimova as the latest European exotic and her films, which arrived regularly in the Picture House and the Classic, were greeted with acclaim by critics and audiences. The I.S.N. commented at the beginning of 1925 that "her name was a household word" locally, while the Irish News quoted with apparent approval the official studio blurb that in "The Spanish Dancer" (Imperial, February 1925) she displayed a "fiery dynamic personality flashing like a comet through reel upon reel of nerve -tingling action." Later in the alluringly titled "Forbidden Paradise" (Imperial, February 1926) he thought that she "excelled herself..... her facial expressions convey volumes." Her popularity can be gauged from the fact that during one week in December 1926 two of her films, "A Woman of the World" and "Flower of the Night" were showing at the same time in two downtown cinemas, the Classic and the Picture House, something that happened very rarely indeed, and only to stars of the calibre of Charles Chaplin or Mary Pickford. Her intense acting style impressed all, though modern critics feel that her American films were never as good as her German productions, a criticism that would have fallen on deaf ears at the time in Belfast. But over - exposure has its inbuilt risks and, as the decade progressed, she in turn was superseded by Greta Garbo, who dramatically increased the romantic temperatures in her films with John Gilbert.

It wasn't just female fire and glamour that attracted the crowds. The perennial favourite Mary Pickford still ranked high in local affections and when her "Little Annie Rooney" arrived in the Royal Cinema the Whig critic could still write that she "was at her best, still the World's Sweetheart." Lilian Gish, probably the greatest of the silent actresses, was also widely admired as a woman of talent and principles. Her films were never as popular as those of Miss Pickford but they still drew large audiences. When D.W. Griffith's "Orphans of the Storm," in which she appeared with her sister Dorothy, showed in the Royal Cinema in January 1923 there were long queues for a week, according to the I.S.N., which also praised her acting as "wonderful," while the Whig critic, always an admirer, thought her performance was "most clever." No one in the audiences that week suspected that over seventy years later (in 1994) the film, beautifully restored, would return to Belfast for a packed presentation in the Q.F.T. Neil Brand from Dublin sat in for the Royal Cinema Orchestra and supplied the solo piano accompaniment for what proved to be an evening to remember.

During the Twenties Lilian Gish left her mentor Griffiths, moving away from impersonating retiring and much-put-upon Victorian child - women, to reveal an engaging versatility. In "The White Sister" (Royal Cinema, 1925) she played a nun who sacrifices herself to save others. The I.S.N. thought it was one of her most difficult roles and that she handled it "with great depth." That was followed by "Romola" again with Dorothy, then "La Boheme" (Classic, Oct.1927) with John Gilbert in which she gave "a remarkably vivid and satisfying character study" according to the News Letter. Her death scene was much talked about for its realism. She always prepared with great care for her performances and for Mimi's demise she visited the wards of tuberculosis hospitals and during the filming refused to allow any liquid to touch her lips. In "The Scarlet Letter" (again in the Classic a month later) she played an unwed mother, which was regarded by some as quite shocking and unsuitable for a film, but religious and other groups in America only agreed to the project because of her high personal reputation. There is no mention of the film causing any waves in Belfast and, in it, the Whig found her "a most sympathetic heroine." Her next film, "Annie Laurie," also in the Classic, was lighter in theme, described enthusiastically by the Irish News as "a mixture of fable and song," in a story of love and war. Set in Scotland at the time of the massacre of Glencoe it proved very popular across the city where its presentation was often accompanied by a Scottish piper or, as in the Midland, by a pipe band.

The great Lillian Gish battles The Wind.

Then, in complete contrast, in late 1928 the Imperial presented "The Wind," described as "the story of a woman's conflict with man and the elements." The film was a serious work directed by the eminent Swedish director Victor Sjostrom, and told the story of Letty, played by Lillian, a refined but penniless lady from Virginia who is worn down and driven to murder by the continuous terrible winds and harsh personal manners she encounters in the bleak mid - West. It was photographed in the Mohave Desert and besides the intense heat the actress, who often suffered for her art, had a gruelling time struggling in a howling man - made wind produced by aeroplane propellers, and filled with stinging sand particles. She described the experience as one of the worst of her long career. The Telegraph's reference to her "spirited acting" was from all accounts an understatement. It arrived in the Imperial during the early years of the talkies when audiences were responding to the new light - hearted musicals and wise cracking comedies, and didn't receive the attention it deserved though it was well supported in the Picturedrome and the Clonard. Many found the story too depressing and the sight of Miss Gish with her crowning glory tumbling abundantly to her waist seemed rather incongruous in those days of flappers and bobbed hair. Attitudes change and when the film was restored and reshown in London in 1983 it caused a sensation. It is now regarded as a superb piece of work which, despite a "happy" ending imposed by the studio M-G-M, is cinematically superior to most of what is being produced today. In it the unique Miss Gish gives a demonstration of silent acting at its best. No-one who appreciates quality cinema should miss it.

Colleen Moore in Flaming Youth. The flappers arrive.

It was inevitable that the flapper or jazz baby would reach the screen, complete with all the cultural paraphernalia of her group: the bobbed hair, lipstick, cigarettes, knee length skirts, a penchant for jazz music, dancing and parties. F.Scott

Fitzgerald dated the flapper's arrival in films from the making of "Flaming Youth" with Colleen Moore in 1923. Regardless of the fact that the Jazz Age had already been around for some time, it is a good starting point for Belfast. The film in question, banned in Canada, and the subject of much criticism in the U.S.A., arrived in the Classic on 6th October 1924. It was, stated the I.S.N. solemnly, "a startling exposure of modern society" though the large advert that accompanied it described it more colourfully as "a picture aglow with the wine of life, aflame with the spirit of youth." There was no doubt about the age group it was aimed at and it emphasised that by adding; "Dance to the mad merry tune of flaming youth, youth that demands love, youth that craves kisses and new thrills, youth with its jazz, its flapperism, its petting parties, its reckless disregard of Conventions." Even for a film poster it went as far as it dared, but said enough to alarm parents, clergy, teachers and others involved with youth from the Falls and Shankill roads to the Malone, who quickly made their feelings known.

In response the Classic issued an invitation; "Come, join the dance" and to further attract the younger set promised a prologue of a special band playing jazz. That was probably the first time a jazz band of black players appeared in the city. The film played to packed houses and the critics were soon referring to Colleen Moore as "a local favourite" or "the tomboy of the screen" while praising her "charm and vivacity." They had plenty of opportunity to comment because her films, introduced usually by the Classic or the Imperial, flooded the screens, one after another, with names like "Her First Love" "The Huntress" "We Moderns" "It Must Be Love" and "Orchids and Ermine. "She had her imitators and competitors, notably the beautiful Corinne Griffiths who, according to the papers, was a great favourite locally. She is rarely remembered or mentioned today but in films like "Modern Madness," (Classic Sept. 1926), "Mlle Modiste" (Classic, July 1927), and "Syncopated Sue" (Classic, Dec.1927) she charmed and delighted critics and audiences. A flavour of the content of those films was given by the I.S.N. when it described the latter film as "a vivacious comedy of a modern girl -- her pluck, her charm and her little failings."

The 'It' Girl: Ciara Bow.

Another who illustrated those "little failings" on screen, and who came to represent the ideal flapper even to the present day was a red - haired bundle of energy from New York, the It Girl herself, Clara Bow. She entered the world of films by winning a talent contest in late 1921 and slowly made a reputation as a vivacious, out -going type in supporting roles in a number of forgettable films. She is first mentioned in Belfast in June 1925 when she appeared in the Classic with Baby Peggy in a romantic comedy called "Helen's Babies" which the I.S.N. described as "charming." The film was part of a double bill with another comedy which would have been more appropriate for Miss Bow, called "Flapper Fever" starring Bobby Dunn, a former Keystone Cop and Charlie Chaplin lookalike. That was quickly followed by "Wine" the story of a family of bootleggers who lived high on their ill gotten money. Clara Bow played the flapper daughter who, according to the I.S.N. "went pleasure mad" giving a portrayal that showed decided improvement as an actress due to "proper direction." He added, significantly, that Colleen Moore would have to look to her laurels. The Irish News critic found the film "vivid" and described with approval how it showed that a price had to be paid for the character's illegal and immoral living, with the father ending up in prison and the daughter mired in scandal, but added that the actors did excellent work. In "The Adventurous Sex" (Imperial, Feb. 1926) she again played a flapper heroine but on the side of the law, who becomes involved in a series of adventure around Niagara Falls. The Irish News praised her depiction of a "girl of high spirits and up -to -date notions" and thought the film was worth seeing also for the splendid views of the Falls.

Her signature film "It" arrived in the Royal Cinema (Mar. 1928) without any fanfare. In fact it formed the lower half of a double bill, the main attraction being "Chang" a natural drama in the style of Robert Flaherty which had caused quite a lot of positive comment since its release in New York. "Chang," made by Merian C. Cooper and Ernest Schoedsack, and financed by Jesse Lasky, was filmed under very difficult conditions in the isolated jungle of N. Thailand, or Siam as it was called then, and illustrated the struggle of a local native family to survive in a challenging environment which included snakes, man - eating tigers and rampaging elephants. It is mainly forgotten now, but has some historical importance in that it contains the seeds of "King Kong," which its makers went on to produce some years later. Most people today have at least heard of "It" which has come to represent Twenties sex appeal. The film was the idea of Elinor Glyn who wrote the script especially for Clara Bow. In it Miss Bow plays a shop girl who uses her considerable charms to attract and finally marry the head of the department store where she works. The film became closely associated with the actress who became known as the It girl, the epitome of the Twenties flapper and Jazz Baby.

Its association with "Chang" may be more appropriate than first appears as "IT" can also be perceived as the struggle for survival of a working girl in challenging surroundings. There were those who saw Clara Bow as a sexual predator in a predominantly male environment, while others regarded her as a hunter using her wiles as bait to trap her quarry. If there were any anthropologists in the audiences in the Royal Cinema - and there could have been considering the reputation of "Chang" - they could possibly have reflected upon such coincidences. Her fans and the local critics, however, took a softer view of her antics on screen, enjoying her outrageous joie de vivre, her ability to manipulate stars like Antonio Morena, Gilbert Roland and Gary Cooper, and her developing skills as an actress. The fact that the film makers often manoeuvred her into situations where she lost her outer garments outraged many of those responsible for youth, but did nothing to dent her popularity. In "My Lady of Whims" she again played a flapper enthusiastically pursuing the men with "her usual good style" (Irish News) and the critic noted how warmly the audience responded to her. The formula was repeated in "Red Hair", again scripted by Elinor Glyn, where she was a manicurist called Bubbles who carried on a triple flirtation. The Telegraph thought it showed her "at her best." Unfortunately in her private life Miss Bow seems to have been a very insecure person and she began emulating the fictional life she played on screen. Stories of wild parties, gambling, alcohol, drugs and excessive sexual gymnastics began to circulate. The pressure of that life style allied to press intrusion and studio disapproval took its toll on her health and by 1933 she had retired from the screen. She died in a sanitorium in Los Angeles in 1965 but her image has lingered on as a window into the Twenties.

By the mid - decade the flapper styles were being adapted widely throughout the medium and when a major star like Norma Talmadge filmed a version of "Camille" (Classic, Dec. 1927) it turned out to be a modern update in which she appeared complete with bobbed hair, though "strikingly gowned" according to the I.S.N.. Nearly two years later the "world's sweetheart," Mary Pickford, arrived in the Classic in "Coquette," her first talkie, playing a flapper with bobbed hair and all. To some older filmgoers it must have seemed that their world was ending, and of course in a sense it was. Not all the popular actresses were flappers, jazz babies or vamps as the appeal of Janet Gaynor showed. The petite red haired star became a great favourite in the late Twenties, "the screen's most adored actress" according to the Irish News. Her films, especially those with co -star Charles Farrell, drew large crowds, and were highly praised by the local critics. Their film "Seventh Heaven" was described by the Irish News as one of the outstanding films of 1928, while equal praise was showered on "The Street Angel" and Murneau's very beautiful "Sunrise" in which she acted with George O'Brien. For her acting in those three films she was awarded the first Oscar (1927-8) given for an outstanding female performance. Other personalities from the period, who delighted local managers by attracting full houses, included Mae Murray, Dolores del Rio, Barbara La Marr, Laura LaPlante, Bessie Love, Marion Davies, the beautiful and exotic Anna May Wong and, of course, in a different category, the Wonder dog himself, Rin Tin Tin, or Rinty as he was known in Belfast. Praised by local critics as "the dog with human intelligence" and referred to on one occasion as "that sagacious canine," his films were amazingly popular and were shown with equal success in the downtown cinemas as well as in the suburbs and poorer halls.

Seeing their favourites on the screen was one thing, but many local filmgoers nurtured the hope, often expressed, of seeing them in the flesh. They read about the stars who crossed the Atlantic to London, often on their way to Paris and elsewhere in Europe. Mary Pickford and Douglas Fairbanks, Jackie Coogan, the Talmadge sisters, Norma Shearer with her new husband, Irving Thalberg, all received amazing receptions in London. Dolores del Rio arrived wanting to see where the poor people lived because, as she explained, she usually played poor people on screen. Charles Chaplin made a pilgrimage back to his poverty -stricken roots in East London before going on to an ecstatic welcome in Paris. Only Thomas Meighan seems to have come to Ireland and that was to make a film called "Irish Luck" about the adventures of a New York policeman. When it was shown in Belfast in 1927 it was advertised as "the one they came to Ireland to make". Meighan, an Irish American from Pittsburg, was a great favourite with Belfast audiences. The girls enjoyed his rugged good looks and romantic attitude while the men responded to him as a man of action. In November 1925 the Irish News quoted him as criticising the cinemas in Dublin because of their excessive smoke haze, which he claimed took away from the clarity of the photography but he praised one cinema in Belfast (apparently the Classic) as being the equal of any on Broadway. The mystery is that there is no reference to him ever having visited the city.

However a number of screen personalities did visit the city, mainly through the efforts of the management of the Grand Opera House. In July 1926 the theatre management announced that Miss Betty Ross Clarke would appear on stage in "The House of Glass." Hardly a name to conjure with. Photographs show her as a pretty, rather unassuming young lady, but she had made a few films in Hollywood and was willing to talk about the experience to local reporters. What she had to say wasn't exactly what the fans wanted to hear. She found filming really hard work - what with early starts, long hours, continual retakes and wearing location photography often in harsh physical conditions. Most actors, she emphasised, had to work hard. They lived normal lives and most of the stories about Hollywood's high life, she insisted, were untrue or greatly exaggerated. Not everyone was willing to believe that.

In October of the following year the British actor Matheson Lang made his first visit to Belfast, to the Opera House. Lang is remembered as an eminent stage actor - manager and matinee idol but he had also been making films in England since before the Great War, so he was known to both theatre goers and filmgoers. In a newspaper poll of favourite British stars in 1924 he had been voted into the top five in the company of such as Betty Balfour and Ivor Novello. He had appeared on local screens as the Wandering Jew and the highwayman Dick Turpin, though his most famous role was as the Scarlet Pimpernell. He had a reputation for using disguises and elaborate make-up on stage and one critic had gone so far as to compare him with Lon Chaney, though the comparison doesn't stand up to any serious scrutiny. He did have an opportunity to display those skills in the melodrama at the Opera House, a play called "The Chinese Bungalow" in which he played a Chinese gentleman who is deceived by his English wife. The production was well received, the Whig describing it as a mixture of Othello and Sherlock Holmes, distinguished by fine acting and a sombre atmosphere. The story dealt with the question of miscegenation and involved a young English girl who marries a Chinese merchant and then is unfaithful to him. When the merchant discovers what has happened, events take a tragic turn, which results in his death by poisoning. Three weeks later his film version of the same play arrived in the Picture House and the News Letter critic compared the two productions. He seemed to prefer the stage acting but felt that the Chinese - Malay atmosphere had been caught more successfully in the film. The film, he suggested, with its ability to move outdoors had an advantage in that particular field. The Whig critic thought the film was "excellent" and felt that in many ways, notably the magnificence of its settings, it was more satisfying than the stage play. While the critics praised Lang's stage performance and audiences gave him a friendly reception, the city didn't become overly excited about his visit.

A month earlier the atmosphere surrounding another celluloid visitor had been quite different. The only major Hollywood star to come to Belfast during the Silent Era was Pauline Frederick, and when it became known that she would be appearing in the Opera House at the end of August 1927 a sense of anticipation built up in the city. The papers pointed out that she had been born in Boston to parents who had hailed from Glasgow and that she had made a name for herself on Broadway before moving to Hollywood in 1915 under contract to Adolph Zukor. As an actress Miss Frederick was regarded as top class and her films, which had been appearing locally since 1916, were immensely popular in the city with both critics and audiences. She was classed as an "emotional" actress, which meant that her style was serious and intense. In 1927 she was in her forties but still a beautiful woman who photographed well, though no reference was made publicly to such personal facts in those well mannered days. She arrived in Belfast quietly but every seat in the Opera House was occupied on the Monday night, many by fans anxious to see her up

Pauline Frederick: Top ranking star.

close. The play was the melodramatic "Madame X" in which she had her most famous role as Jacqueline Floriot, the wife who abandons her husband and young son to go off with a lover, a path that leads to drugs and shame. The husband becomes a man of importance while the son completes his studies for the law and becomes a barrister. Meanwhile the wife sinks lower in the mire and in a weak moment reveals the details of her early married life to her new lover, who decides to use the information to blackmail the husband. A row ensues as the despairing woman tries to stop him and in the struggle she shoots him dead. She is brought to trial and as fate (and the dramatist) would have it, she is defended by the son she hasn't seen since a child, a son who doesn't know her. She had already filmed the story with great success and it had shown across Belfast in 1924, so many in the audience would have known what to expect,

As it happened they got more than they anticipated because according to all the critics what followed was one of the most extraordinary evenings the Opera House had ever experienced. The curtain rose and the audience was plunged into over two hours of "unrelieved tragedy" according to the Whig. Transported "on the wings of emotion," the time passed like so many seconds wrote the Telegraph critic, with the audience held "spellbound" (Whig). The News Letter writer commented that Miss Frederick was well known and admired from her films but her impact in the flesh was "remarkable." He sat back and watched "a great actress" play on the audience's emotions like a musician playing a delicate instrument, and in the process moving a Belfast audience in a way that it rarely allowed itself to be. After a short time one forgot who she was and thought only of the character she was playing. He agreed with his Whig colleague who felt that such acting was "a rarity in Belfast." One of the attractions for the audience must have been the thrill of hearing her speak for the first time and the Telegraph critic praised the clarity of her diction, with a voice that was "soft and appealing," without any strong accent, and capable of reaching all parts of the auditorium.

But it was the sheer intensity of the acting that gripped the audience. When the verdict of "not guilty" was finally brought in they watched in complete silence as she collapsed in her chair "a pathetic but beautiful figure" (Telegraph) moaning "I must die, I must die." The scene of reconciliation with her son was "utterly pathetic" (Whig) but when the happy ending that all expected didn't take place, the audience were distraught. Women were openly weeping and even some of the men were seen to raise their hands furtively to their eyes. When the curtain descended there was complete silence and then it rose again to reveal the whole company who were "saluted with applause."(Telegraph). Then Miss Frederick was led forward on the arm of the young man who had played her son (Ian Fleming) and the audience went wild "giving expression to the ardour of their affection." Clapping and cheers rang out, with calls for a speech. One observer hadn't seen anything like it since the Abbey Players had come to Belfast on their first visit twenty years before, while another said it recalled a visit by Sarah Bernhardt herself. The audience just wouldn't let her leave and the actress took ten curtain calls. Finally she came to the front of the stage and said she couldn't make a speech but thanked everyone from the bottom of her heart for their welcome. One critic observed sympathetically that she seemed worn out by the efforts of her acting, while another added that she may not have been a great speechmaker but "she was a great actress." The crowds leaving the Opera House that evening would all have agreed, overwhelmed as they were by the combined impact of superb stage craft and Hollywood glamour. The Telegraph heading of "Worship and Weeping for Pauline Frederick" caught the tenor of the evening perfectly, and though the paper's critic felt that the play raised themes worthy of discussion, the event represented essentially a victory of emotion over intellect, and was long the talk of the city.

The excitement over Miss Frederick's week long visit was only one indication of the power and influence of the silent cinema. Every week thousands of Belfast people, young and old, went to the cinemas in pursuit of relaxation and entertainment. They were able to choose from a variety of approximately twenty major films with supporting programmes of shorts which included Westerns, thrillers, comedies, travelogues, cartoons like Felix the Cat and Koko the Clown, singalongs, information films like the latest fashions from Paris, usually in colour, and newsreels which kept them up to date with regional and world events. The serials had passed the peak of their popularity but a few halls including the Alhambra, the Crumlin and the Midland continued to show them. The downtown cinemas no longer looked upon them with favour but as often happens were willing to screen them under a new format. In mid 1928 the Imperial presented a five week series of connected shorts called "The Masked Players" in which well known actors appeared heavily disguised. The audience had to decide who the players were and at the conclusion of the series enter their names in a competition for prizes. The Royal Cinema showed a weekly series called "Haunted Houses and Castles," each with its own story of mystery. The overall aim was to lure the fans back week after week and the various baits seemed to work only too well. The silent film industry had given every appearance during the early Twenties of being completely secure, yet by the end of the decade it had almost disappeared, and at the popular level silent films were regarded as old - fashioned and out of date. At a professional level the industry was in turmoil and disarray.

The first indication in Belfast of the cause of all that change was an innocent advertisement for the Lyceum Cinema, which appeared in the papers at the end of October 1926, stating simply: the motion picture talks.

Pauline Frederick,
a sensation in the
Grand Opera House.

Scene from the film "Madamex" with
Pauline Frederick in the part she
played on the Grand Opera stage.

CHAPTER TWENTY
The Arrival of Sound

Mention has already been made of Jesse Lasky's informative article on the growth of the American cinema industry which the Irish News published at the beginning of the decade in November 1920. In his discussion he had suggested that films could still be improved technically to make them more attractive to audiences. The clarity of the images, he felt, would benefit from the introduction of stereo photography. Many people were aware that 3D could certainly do that through their familiarity with stereoscopic viewers. Because of their cost they had been a popular pastime mainly among the better off citizens but recently as prices had dropped they had become more widely available and accessible. In tobacconist shops in the city during the Twenties each packet Army Club cigarettes, which sold at ten for sixpence, included two cigarette cards showing views from around the world. When they were viewed through a simple Camerascope they gave clear three dimensional pictures. Static images of that type were one thing but, when it came to projecting 3D moving images, the system was encumbered by the need for viewers to wear special glasses, a fact that has always restricted its development and popularity. Until recently cinema managers have regarded 3D as essentially a gimmick with a limited appeal despite attempts to develop it for full length films. Belfast experienced one such gimmick when the Plastigrams swept the city cinemas in 1924.

Lasky also thought that the use of natural colour would be worthwhile and he was on firmer ground there. The first picture show in Belfast presented in the Alhambra at the end of August 1896 included a hand tinted snippet of a Serpentine Dancer which so fascinated the audience that the showman had to rewind it and show it again. So colour was an "added attraction" from the earliest days of cinema and in the years that followed colour films, usually tinted or coloured by hand, were enthusiastically welcomed. The success of the Arabian adventure "A Thousand and One Nights" in 1922 with local audiences was in part due to its hand - coloured scenes which according to the Irish News were "the last word in colour" while in the following year "Love" starring Louise Glaum owed its success and popularity largely to it being coloured. In all those cases the colour was added after filming but what Lasky meant by "natural colour" was a process by which colour was captured in the camera. The first company which successfully achieved that was the Technicolor Motion Picture Corporation which was founded in 1915 by Herbert Kalmus, Daniel Comstock and W.B.Westcottand. The first commercial film using the rather cumbersome two strip Technicolor was completed in America in 1921 but didn't reach Belfast until three years later. Based loosely on "Madame Butterfly" it was called "The Toll of the Sea" and starred the young Chinese actress Anna May Wong. While receiving honourable mention it caused no great waves locally. It was followed by the more popular "The Black Pirate" starring Douglas Fairbanks which the I.S.N. described as being "exquisitely photographed." Technicolor had its competitors and one of them was Prizmacolour which was used in the British production "The Glorious Adventure" which showed at the Picture House in January 1923. According to the local critics it was an historical romantic drama set in the period after the Restoration. The elaborate costumes looked well in colour and the film also had the benefit of starring the well known society beauty (the equivalent of today's celebrity) Lady Diana Manners, later Cooper. The Picture House management was impressed with the audience reaction and announced that in future it would introduce its films with a special system of colour projection - which probably involved no more than the use of colour filters. The Irish News seemed quite impressed by the results.

By the middle of the decade colour was increasingly accepted as a part of the cinema - going experience. Typical was a series of short colour films from Paris showing the latest fashions while with increasing regularity full length films included sequences which looked impressive or benefited from colour, such as fashion parades, dance routines or raging fires. In October 1928 the Imperial presented "Fire" a two hour epic about heroic firefighters, parts of which were filmed in natural colours. Colour was also used to highlight special religious events and was so used in "Ben Hur". "The Ten Commandments," and "King of Kings." Some filmgoers and particularly critics complained that the colours were often garish, and many regarded colour as unnecessary, preferring the beauty and greater subtlety of the black and white photography which was still used in the majority of films. Modern picture goers raised on a diet of colour would certainly have been amazed at the high quality of the monochrome photography which characterised many silent films. Such considerations didn't prevent the quest for perfect colour continuing and even the critics were impressed when Paramount's first full length feature in Technicolor, called "Wanderer of the Wasteland" arrived in the Picture House in July 1926. It was a Western based on a Zane Grey novel and its marvellous outdoor locations looked magnificent in colour. The response of the Irish News critic was typical. He found the outdoor scenes shot in the Painted Desert of Arizona and Death Valley "very beautiful," while the News Letter critic noted that the colour system was a decided improvement over those used in the past, and was "very impressive," especially in the desert scenes. It was the first time that Belfast audiences had seen the West "in glorious Technicolor" and it added an extra dimension to the already considerable attractions of the Western.

Lasky made no mention of sound in his article though he must have been aware of the technical experiments and advances taking place in that field. Certainly anyone in Belfast who was interested was reasonably well primed in what was going on because the local editors often published comments and reports on the matter. Recent developments in electrical recording and reproduction - highlighted by local shops that sold records and gramophones - had allowed far greater clarity and amplification of sounds and had turned the attention of some inventors in the U.S.A once more to the system of pictures accompanied by recorded disks known as the sound on disc system. Examples of that had played in Belfast on a number of occasions in the past but no matter how interesting the experiments were they had all suffered from tinny sound, poor amplification and uncertain synchronization. As early as July 1922 the Irish News commented on contemporary attempts to marry sound and visuals or what the writer called "the unification of the phonograph and the kinematograph." He noted that one of the major problems was correct synchronization or as he put it, "the problem of keeping the two in step." He assured his readers that steps were being taken to deal with that problem but that the results were still secret.

The following year the paper returned to the topic and under the heading "A Speaking Picture" discussed details of a technical breakthrough whereby sound waves were translated into electrical impulses which in turn produced light fluctuations that could be photographed and printed alongside the visuals to give perfect synchronization. The following month the Whig supplied more information and explained that an American, Dr.Lee De Forest, had done just that and had produced what he called a Photofilm with the sound occupying a narrow strip along the side of the film. Though no one knew it at the time that system, known as the optical system, was eventually to be the one that the major studios would adopt before the end of the decade. By the time that the Whig had printed its comments De Forest, building on his success in the U.S.A., had established a company in London (in 1923) and purchased a studio at Clapham where he began making short Photofilms involving singers, comedians, musicians and actors for the local market. It was those plus a mix of American products that were shown in the Lyceum when Michael and James Curran, respectively father and son, the owner and manager of the cinema, signed an exclusive year - long contract to show Photofilms at that venue. The Currans recognised the technical superiority of De Forest's system and decided to give it a try.

The first showing at three o'clock on Monday 22nd November 1926 represents the beginning of the sound revolution in Belfast and indeed in Ireland because the Lyceum was the first cinema in the country to publicly screen sound - on - film pictures. Photofilms didn't reach Dublin until nearly twelve months later. At last, a Telegraph reporter exulted, talking pictures have come to Belfast. The De Forest company, as agreed, sent over a number of engineers under the direction of Mr L. Bland Flagg to modify the projectors by adding special equipment which produced the sound - including a mysterious potion, a small glass tube filled with gases which according to the Whig glowed with a bright violet light when it was operating - and a photo - electric cell. They also installed extra wiring and two large speakers on either side of the screen. For its part the cinema paid a weekly fee for the hire of the equipment and about 3,000 feet of film which would be changed every week. According to one of the trade papers a figure of about £16 was mentioned as the weekly hire rate. Large audiences were obviously needed to ensure its financial success and that entailed a careful advertising campaign. The appeal was pitched without verbal excess on an historical level. The advertising began at the end of October with the simple but dramatic statement already mentioned: The Motion Picture Talks. Although the Telegraph was later to carry an advert claiming that the Photofilm was "the most amazing invention of the century" the overall approach was more subdued. At the beginning of November the Irish News

The Motion Picture Talks in The Lyceum, a Curran cinema

advert claimed that "a long cherished dream had been realised. You will shortly be able to see and hear De Forest Phonofilms at the Lyceum." That was the first local use of the term "see and hear" which was to become the advertising catchphrase for the new sound films in the following years.

During the week before their introduction the Lyceum showed a film called "The Talker" starring Anna Q.Nillson which was described in one of the papers as the story of a woman "who forgot that silence is golden" and as a result suffered for it. It seems an ironic coincidence in that film makers were soon to adopt the same approach to their medium though with a different outcome. At the end of that week the Irish News carried an article under the heading "The Talking Films," preparing its readers for the coming premiere and telling them to ignore the rumours going around that the special equipment hadn't arrived yet. All was in readiness for Monday's programme, with the equipment already installed and tested. There was also talk in the city, the writer noted, that the new technology was nothing more than a large gramophone, but to show that it was actually a new departure the management had arranged for anyone who was interested to inspect the equipment any morning during the following week except Monday. All they had to do was to make an appointment with Mr Curran and they would be shown the technical details by Photofilm engineers. There is no information about who actually took up the invitation but one can guess that other interested managers and their projectionists including those from the Picture House in Royal Avenue must have availed of the opportunity. Special prices of two shillings and one shilling were charged for the first show and James Curran announced that all proceeds from the presentation would be donated to the rebuilding Fund for the Samaritan Hospital on the Antrim Road. The doors opened at 2:30 pm and the cinema was soon crowded. Uniformed nurses sold special souvenir programmes and one wonders if some of those are still lying in a drawer or a loft somewhere in the city waiting to be rediscovered. Distinguished guests included Lady Craig and the Lady Mayoress, and when Lady Craig and her party arrived they were met in the foyer and greeted by Mrs Curran and Mrs McKenzie, the Hon Sec. of the hospital, before being led to their seats to the strains of "God Save the King" played by the Lyceum orchestra under the baton of Mr Finlay. In the enthusiasm of the moment it is unlikely that anyone in the orchestra realised that the "novelty" or "wonder" that they were about to see would in time prove to be the death knell for cinema orchestras and would result in unemployment for many of the musicians.

De Forest Phonofilms' November 1926.

The audience was addressed by Mr Levy, the Irish representative of the company, who explained how the system operated and then added with surprising candour that it wasn't perfect yet but that it soon would be. The Photofilms followed. They consisted of four shorts lasting in all thirty minutes. The first was of a well known singer and comedian, Dick Henderson, the father of Dickie Henderson who became so popular on television in the Sixties, who sang a popular song "I Love Her All the More." The sound was a little distorted at the beginning but the projectionist quickly fine tuned the equipment so that it registered clear and distinct. The Telegraph reporter thought that the performance was "very realistic" and expressed satisfaction that the words were quite audible even at the back of the cinema, while the Irish News scribe found it difficult to believe that the words were emanating from the loudspeakers at the sides of the screen and not directly from the singer's lips. When the film finished there was a spontaneous outburst of applause with people looking at each other and nodding their heads with approval. Mr Levy's comments about the lack of perfection were forgotten. Dick Henderson was followed by an American group, The Radio Franks, who sang two songs "in perfect harmony," then by an "eccentric" musician who demonstrated his skills on the guitar, banjo and violin. The programme ended with an orchestra playing "The March of the Toys" and as it did a buzz of appreciation went around the auditorium. The Whig critic made no comments on the content of the films, which were really music hall acts, but agreed that the device was "an interesting innovation" and admitted that technically it was much superior to the "talking machines" that had reached the city in the past.

The Irish News felt that once news of the quality of the sound was spread by word of mouth large crowds would soon be flocking to the Lyceum. He also drew attention to the rest of the programme, the normal silent material, which consisted of a short comedy called "Fresh Faces", a film with dancers giving a demonstration of the Charlston, the Pathé Gazette news, and the main feature which starred Norma Talmadge in a delightful romantic comedy called "Graustark." Miss Talmadge played Princess Yetive in the mythical European kingdom of Graustark who is caught between marrying a Prince whom she doesn't like and a handsome commoner whom she met on a trip to America. At the end of the show the cinema was cleared and after a brief interlude it reverted to its normal prices of 6d, 1| - and 1|6 with continuous programming and the Phonofilms timed for screening at 4:00 pm, 6:30 pm and 8:45 pm daily. The Irish News prediction turned out to be accurate and in the following months there were reports of large crowds and packed houses, especially over Christmas when people had to be turned away. Patrons came from all over the city and the cinema was able to take advantage of its well advertised location at the end of the penny stage on the tramway from the city centre. In early December, as public enthusiasm continued James Curran arranged for the programme to be changed twice a week (on Monday and Thursday) and the Irish News commented that the pictures continued to improve. In January the same paper noted that "the talking pictures continue to hold the public enthralled by their sheer marvellousness and distinct novelty."

The programme pattern remained unchanged with short films of singers like Dick Henderson, who was a particular favourite, though more serious items from opera and classical composers were also introduced. The I.S.N. described one week's offering as being a case of opera versus jazz, singing and dancing. The system also revealed its versatility by having some items in Technicolor while others boasted large casts; for example one cabaret sequence involved a cast of about fifty. Comedy situations were introduced and excerpts from plays like the Quarrel Scene from "Julius Caesar" with Geoffrey Keen which had been filmed at Clapham. The Helen Lewis All - Girl Band was a great success, as was Lillian Russell in a Temple Dance, and not expectedly there was a warm welcome for a compilation of Irish Airs. In one film a comedian, Phil Baker, spoke directly out to the audience from the screen which according to the Telegraph "added interest" to the proceedings. But one of the most interesting aspects of the films was the use of outdoor sequences. One of the problems of early talking films was the need to make them in special studios but De Forest equipment worked well even outdoors. One such film presented over Christmas was "A Trip to Long Island" which showed people at work in or enjoying the resort. It began with the arrival of a train - memories of Lumière ! - complete with the hissing of steam etc. and went on to show humorous scenes at a funfair, at an aerodrome and in a farmyard complete with various animal noises which caused great laughter in the audience. An elderly relative of the author recalled the excitement that the Phonofilms caused. He remembered the sound as being quite loud, natural and distinct though he admitted that some of his friends had difficulty at first understanding the "strange" accents of the American players.

As the months passed familiarity bred acceptance and the advertisements reflected that by just referring to "a De Forest Phonofilm" or sometimes "a Phonofilm number," alluding to its musical content without giving any details. Sometimes the critics didn't even mention them in their weekly film comments. Mr Curran must have noticed the change and when the early enthusiasm cooled he restricted the Phonofilms to the second half of the week to take advantage of the larger crowds at the weekends, but they continued to be shown until the end of October. One of the last to be screened was an outdoor short of the historical attractions of London which the Whig critic found fascinating, especially scenes of the Changing of the Guard where the combination of visuals and sound proved most impressive. It was, he informed his readers, not to be missed. But such commendation was by then rare. The Irish News critic may have put his finger on the reason when he described the Phonofilms as a novelty because people notoriously tend to lose interest in novelties. It is noticeable also that no other cinema in Belfast decided to show Phonofilms. Maybe the financial arrangements were not suitable or the managers felt that their contents hadn't yet developed a sufficiently wide appeal. People became rather blasé about what in many cases were just superior music hall acts. If De Forest had moved more quickly into feature films the history of the sound film would have been very different, and not only in Belfast.

The main reason the managers delayed was probably that they were aware of events taking place in America and were waiting to see the consequences of them. Warner Brothers, in agreement with the Western Electric company, had decided to test the waters of sound using the Vitaphone sound on disc system. The sound was recorded on discs 17 inches in diameter each one running the equivalent of 1000 feet of film. Film and disc were synchronised by a motor attached to the projector. On 6th August 1926, only a few months before Phonofilms opened in Belfast, Warners had presented their first sound programme in New York consisting of eight shorts of mainly classical music and song followed by the film "Don Juan" starring John Barrymore and Mary Astor. In the film Barrymore lived up to his reputation as "the Great Lover," (he bestowed 191 kisses on his lady loves according to the publicity) and still had enough time and energy to outdo Douglas Fairbanks with his athletic prowess. It was actually a silent film complete with subtitles but Warners had added a detailed soundtrack of music on disc which greatly impressed the audience. When "Don Juan" came to Belfast in December 1927 and showed in the Classic, no mention was made of its musical soundtrack, or of the part it had played in Warner's historic presentation. It was screened as a normal silent film because the cinema was not wired for Vitaphone sound, as indeed no cinema in the city was. The Whig critic was, as usual, impressed by Barrymore's performance, describing (without detailing the number of kisses) how he "lavished his love" on a large group of ladies who included Mary Astor, Estelle Taylor, Myrna Loy, Helene Costello, Phyllis Haver, June Marlowe and Hedda Hopper (later to become an acid - tongued journalist), and praising his skill with the sword, especially during a splendid duel with a master swordsman at the end of the film. The News Letter commented that Barrymore was "brilliant" and that he had"excellent support from the orchestra." The reports of large crowds indicated that Barrymore was still popular in the city even without sound.

In the USA Warners had presented their second sound show two months after the first, consisting again of a silent film, "The Better 'Ole," a comedy with Sydney Chaplin, which had added music and sound effects, preceded by a selection of shorts. That latter programme had a broader audience appeal and included more popular music, notably a sequence of Al Jolson singing "Red, Red Robin," "April Showers," and "Rockabye Baby." The Sydney Chaplin film reached Belfast during the same week as "Don Juan" was drawing crowds in to the Classic, and showed in the Royal Cinema where it was welcomed as a "rollicating" silent comedy with music supplied by the cinema orchestra. Another similar programme had followed in early February 1927 but by then there were indications that audiences were tiring of what some American critics were already calling a "gimmick." In fact, as events had shown locally with the Phonofilms, what the public was bored with was the repetitive sequence of shorts shot in a way which, in contrast to the flowing camera style of the silents, seemed unimaginative and static. While those events, momentous in the history of cinema, were unfolding in the U.S.A. the only audiences in this country able to experience the future of the medium in a comparable way were those visiting the Lyceum. The management sensed that and proudly, and rightly, announced that the Lyceum was the only talking picture house in Ireland.

Al Jolson in The Singing Fool in the Picture House, Royal Avenue. Feature film sound arrives 29 April 1929.

Meantime back in America the astute producer William Fox, whose epics like the "Queen of Sheba" were always welcomed in Belfast, and never one to ignore competition, had purchased a sound on film system derived from De Forest's, which he renamed Movietone. By May 1927 he had presented his own sound programme which included a sound recording of Lindberg taking off in his Spirit of St Louis on his historic trans-Atlantic flight, plus the film "Seventh Heaven" which had an added musical soundtrack. Warners replied with "The Jazz Singer" which is regarded as the first feature film with synchronised voice and music, and which was premiered in New York on 6th October 1927. Despite a silent style including subtitles, and a maudlin storyline audiences responded warmly to Jolson's personality, his singing (which included "Toot, Toot Tootsie" and the lachrymose "Mammy") and above all his natural sounding ad-libs, especially the famous "You ain't heard nuttin' yet" a catchphrase that he had often used in his stage shows. "The Jazz Singer" reached London a year later on 27 September 1928 and shortly afterwards the Irish News carried a commentary on the proceedings there under the heading "The Talking Films: First Impressions."

The article began with the statement that "the Vitaphone has evidently come to stay" and the writer noted the positive reaction of the audience which included "outbeaks of spontaneous applause" from the moment that the curtains opened and a Fanfare of Vitaphone Trumpeters lit up the screen. Despite being impressed by some of what he saw and heard he also expressed some doubts. He thought the sound was uneven, and on occasion the level became almost deafening. Voices varied in clarity and he found the "lisps" (probably caused by surface hiss on the disc) and what he called the "bronchitic resonance" of the sound rather annoying on occasion. He admitted that those drawbacks involved technical matters that would be overcome in time. He also had problems with the content of the programme and concluded that what was needed was for "men of taste and talent" to recognise and use the possibilities of the system. At the moment he felt that the restricted and repetitive camera movements were boring, and didn't endear the films to those who really appreciated cinema. That was only one comment from the many that the local papers published about the impact and future of sound. Theorists deplored its introduction and argued that the challenge of the lack of sound was what had raised the silent film to an art form while, in contrast, others pointed out that improved sound effect machines and developments like the Panatrope were indications of a long - standing desire to add sound to films. Others felt that sound was only a novelty that would soon pass.

In Hollywood there was no desire or pressure for sound from top film makers like Chaplin and a major producer like Jesse Lasky could ask: what can sound do that subtitles cannot convey? Samuel Goldwyn, among others, claimed - for a time - that there was still a great future for silents. Of course that approach may have been influenced by economic considerations because both producers had large numbers of silents on the shelf, waiting for release. On the other hand the Telegraph quoted the actors Seymour Hicks, who had recently appeared at the Opera House, and who described the arrival of sound as "a marvellous thing," and Gerald du Maurier who was less enthusiastic and expressed worries about its impact on the live theatre. The Irish News reported comments from John Mc Cormack who visited the city for a concert in April in which he welcomed the development and even expressed an interest in making a sound film, though he added that sound would never take the place of live opera. Some time later the Whig reported that the tenor had signed with Fox to make a talkie film - "Song of my Heart" - with scenes to be shot in Ireland, that would be "good propaganda" for the country. The News Letter gave other details of the project, especially that location shots would be filmed in Ireland during August by the director Frank Borzage, who also had discovered a new young Irish actress to join John Mc Cormack. She was 19 year old Maureen O'Sullivan, and after filming, she sailed with her mother and fifteen other members of the Fox film crew on the White Star liner "Baltic" for New York to complete indoor shooting in Hollywood.

Many people were uneasy about the impact of sound upon traditional theatre culture, and Queen's University may have been trying to ease their fears when it put on a special series of lectures dealing with the Theatre as the Temple of Art. Those who attended must have taken heart from reports that the actor Richard Hayward had approached the Empire Theatre, and the manager Gerard Morrison had agreed to the setting up of the Empire Players (who became better known as the Belfast Repertory Theatre) a group of local actors who would present plays of local interest. Their first production, an Irish - American subject called "The Land of the Stranger," staged at the beginning of March, attracted good reviews and substantial crowds. The News Letter reflected the feelings of most theatre goers when it wished the new venture well but added pragmatically that its success lay - as in the case of the new talkies - in the hands of the paying public. A month later the same paper reported that the BBC in Belfast had recently been impressed by a demonstration of a system of "home talkies" which used a home projector connected to a gramophone by an adaptor, which cost about five pounds. Was that, some asked, the entertainment of the future? Could live shows survive such developments?

Those matters were the subject of discussion among interested people in Belfast as elsewhere, and some of them probably recalled Fay Compton's worries of a few years past, but ordinary cinema goers who just enjoyed a good film tended to ask when, if ever, the "talkies" would come to Belfast. They must have taken heart from an article carried by the Irish News in early January written by "an authority on the film industry" which claimed that 1929 would be a transitional year for the cinema which would see a decided move in favour of sound. The writer commented that the "talkies" may have been "unwanted" a few years before, but that attitudes had altered since then. The matter had been settled largely by the impact on producers and studio heads of audience reaction to, and financial returns from the "The Jazz Singer" which was well on its way towards earning $ 3,000,000 while Jolson's second film "The Singing Fool" released in September 1928 was also a resounding success. The article highlighted one factor that might restrict the move to sound, namely a shortage of necessary equipment but it could also have mentioned the problem of the cost of that equipment which many of the smaller independent cinemas might find prohibitive. In fact the Irish News, probably reflecting conversations with local owners, showed awareness of that problem and wondered if such cinemas could survive the change to sound. Another problem was the lack of a decision on which system the big studios would adopt, either sound on disc or optical sound on film. The struggle for technical dominance was akin to the later competition between Betamax and VHS or more recently between HDVD and Blue - ray, but in early 1929 there was no clear indication which system would triumph. Films were being released in both formats and cinemas had the choice of installing one or both of the systems.

The first cinema in Belfast to face up to the problem, and do something about it, was the Picture House. The cinema already had a reputation for its innovative approach to film going and few were surprised when it announced in late March that "the two most perfect talkie systems in the world" were coming. Two weeks later the film on show was "Red Hair" with Clara Bow and a second teaser was added that Al Jolson was coming "soon" in the Vitaphone production "The Singing Fool." Anticipation continued to rise in the city, and was finally rewarded with the announcement that the cinema would close on 20th April to allow for the installation of the Vitaphone and Movietone sound systems "the only two perfect sound systems in the world," and would reopen on 29th April 1929 when people could see and hear Al Jolson in "The Singing Fool." Meantime the last silent film shown in the Picture House was "The Fifty-Fifty Girl" starring Bebe Daniels. The simple and direct advertisements took it for granted that the people of Belfast were already familiar with the technical changes taking place in the industry, and also with the entertainer Al Jolson, whose records were available in the city.

But Belfast wasn't to have the honour of presenting Ireland's first talking feature because on Monday 22nd April, a week before the premiere in the Picture House, the Capitol in Dublin premiered the same film amid scenes of great excitement. The Capitol was well known to Northerners over many years as the La Scala Theatre but it had been purchased by Paramount in 1927 and renamed. During that first week it was literally besieged by people wanting to experience the latest novelty and the cinema, with a seating capacity of just less than 2,000, reported selling 50,000 tickets. Clery's opened a stall in the foyer where patrons could buy the book of the film and recordings of the songs by Al Jolson. The people were obviously overwhelmed by the experience and the Irish Times critic commented that it was almost impossible to criticise a film that pulled so blatantly at the heart strings so that most viewers left the cinema "in a state of prostration." The story line, he felt, was trite but the presentation was so superb that it became irresistible. The film was dominated by the personality of Jolson whose voice, whether talking or singing, came over clearly and with maximum effect. He found the star's personality "amazing," and his singing "masterly," so that his presence was sufficient alone to carry the picture. He was also impressed by the clever way in which sound had been integrated into the story and the many touches which indicated its future dramatic possibilities. He noted the overall impact of the music, the chattering of diners in a restaurant, the sound of doors closing, and the ringing of telephone bells which added realism to the scenes. He implied, without saying so, that what was needed was directors with intelligence who would use the new medium with suitable imagination. He also mentioned in passing the advantage to the actors of having a pleasant speaking voice, a factor that was to become a serious talking point in the near future.

While Dublin audiences were experiencing at first hand the pleasures of the new medium the Picture House was being prepared to initiate local patrons. Wisely, both sound systems, disc and optical, were installed at a cost of thousands of pounds (Whig) thereby giving the cinema a wide choice of films. At the same time the hall was redecorated and extra seats were installed. No mention was made of the orchestra pit which of course became redundant because "Ireland's finest cinema orchestra," as it was referred to only two weeks before, was the first casualty of the new technology, and the Picture House musicians found themselves in the queue heading for unemployment. In the excitement of the moment no one mentioned their fate. The first show was on Monday morning at 11:00 am and Mr Barron addressed a packed hall to whom he introduced the Lord Mayor, Alderman Sir William Coates, who, in turn, congratulated the management on their initiative, wished them every success and thanked them for donating the proceeds of the first show to the Belfast Hospital for Sick Children. Then the curtains parted and Belfast entered the sound era. Thus, in Belfast, the Silent Era, the period during which silent films alone were available, lasted just 33 years less four months (1896 to 1929), and that relatively short timespan in turn suggests that there were those present in the audience who clearly remembered the earliest film show in the Alhambra

The film was shown in four separate programmes beginning at 1:00 pm, 3:30 pm, 6:00 pm, and 8:30 pm with the doors opening thirty minutes before and potential patrons, used to continuous programming, were warned that the theatre would be cleared after each performance. As expected, prices were increased to 9d (stalls) and 1| 8d (balcony) during the afternoon, rising to one shilling and two shillings after five o'clock, increases that did nothing to reduce attendance numbers. The results that first day were long queues, packed houses and many disappointed people turned away, a situation which continued unbroken for the next four weeks. The excitement that "The Singing Fool" engendered equalled that of Dublin. Special trains were even put on to allow people from outside the city to join in the spectacle. The Star Music Stores which had outlets in Church Lane and Royal Avenue, had a stall in the cinema cafe where records of Al Jolson singing songs from the film could be bought. They included "There's a Rainbow Round My Shoulder," "I'm Sitting on Top of the World," and of course "Sonny Boy," all of which were soon to be heard whistled or sung along the city streets.

The Irish News recognised the importance of the event with an editorial in which the writer summed up the situation aptly and concisely with his opening statement that "Belfast has caught the craze." He described watching long queues of "eager people braving yesterday's weather nastiness to see and hear their first talking picture." He felt that the "talkies" were here to stay despite any arguments put forward by critics of sound, because the people had taken wholeheartedly to them. He admitted that the system wasn't technically perfect yet, and audiences at the first shows had noticed a "blurring" of the sound in places and had experienced difficulty in understanding some of the American accents, but those were minor problems that would be eliminated in time. The significant fact was that the "silent stage" had found its tongue. The local critics were enthusiastic in their praise also. They all congratulated the management of the Picture House on being responsible for what the Whig called "a notable step forward in the history of the cinema in Belfast," while the Irish News wrote that in future years when the talkies were fully accepted "the Picture House will be able to look back and feel a just pride in having been pioneers in their introduction to Belfast." With regard to the film itself the Whig critic described it as "an instant success" and he praised the clarity of the sound. The Telegraph thought it was "a remarkable piece of work" and the writer was particularly impressed by the accuracy of its "tonal reproduction," though he admitted that "the awful American twang" of the speaking voices was a shock that had to be got over. The Irish News critic agreed that one may "dislike" aspects of the American accent, but couldn't deny that technically the voice reproduction was clear and audible. He thought that the film was "well staged and dressed" and overall it was well worth seeing. The News Letter critic suggested that sound was "a mechanical wonder" which instilled life into the film and was certainly very effective "at least in that style of picture." He was impressed by the way the film began in silence, even using subtitles, thereby heightening the viewers' expectations until they experienced the "thrill" of the first spoken words which came "mysteriously" from the screen. He praised Jolson's speaking and singing voice which "could be heard clearly in all parts of the theatre." During close-ups the effect was so real that he had to remind himself that Jolson wasn't really there in person.

All were agreed that the success of the picture was due mainly to the acting and singing of Al Jolson. The story concerned a singing waiter who marries and has a son but his wife runs off with another man taking the child (played by David Lee) with her. As the waiter struggles to become a successful entertainer he watches as his son's health deteriorates and the boy finally dies in his arms in hospital. It was the type of emotional role that suited Jolson and he played it for all it was worth. The scene where he sang "Sonny Boy" to his dying child reduced most of the audience to tears. The Irish News found those scenes "heart rending" and admitted that they wouldn't easily fade from the memory. The critic, however, refused to discuss the details of the plot, instead urging his readers to go and see the film "where it is told more vividly than any words could make it." He hoped that when the novelty aspect had worn off people would realise that "the talking film will be found more expressive and possessed of a greater power and range than even the best silent film ever could be." The News Letter agreed that the talking picture was "the film of the future."

After four weeks there was no sign of a decline in the enthusiasm of the public and queues continued to form every night. Those who argued that as the novelty aspect wore off the talkies would lose their appeal were quickly proved wrong as large and enthusiastic crowds continued to collect to see the next presentation called "In Old Arizona." It was a complete contrast to the Jolson film, being a Western, most of which had been filmed outdoors using the more flexible Fox Movietone optical system. "The Singing Fool" was an indoor film because the Vitaphone system worked best in controlled studio conditions but the Movietone system, which Fox used for recording their newsreels, could function well out of doors, especially under the control of imaginative directors like Raoal Walsh, the man who set out to make "In Old Arizona." The story about the adventures of the Cisco Kid (Warner Baxer) was shot in the Mojave Desert, the San Fernando Valley and Utah amid scenery that impressed all the local critics. The film was advertised as "100% talkie" but the Whig summarised it also as a film with "action, thrills, a love theme, gorgeous settings and scenery." The Irish News thought that as a talkie it was "quite successful" and while some of the diction was not as clear as in "The Singing Fool" there was on the other hand none of the strong American accents of the former.

Obviously much depended on the individual listener because, in contrast, the Telegraph noted that "all the dialogue could be clearly heard" and there was clever use of natural sounds. Walsh had integrated the sound dramatically into the story using, for example, the ticking of a clock to increase the tension before a gunfight or emphasising the sizzle of ham and eggs cooking over a camp fire. The sound of footfalls receding or approaching, the opening and closing of doors and such may seem trivial matters today but in 1929 local audiences found such details fascinating and responded accordingly. Their reactions recall the very early days of films in the last decade of the nineteenth century when viewers had been captivated by simple natural phenomena like waves breaking on a shore or leaves fluttering in a breeze. A few weeks later they enjoyed natural sound again used expertly by another master director, John Ford, - who like Walsh was of Irish extraction, - in "Napoleon's Barber," a short story about Napoleon on his way to Waterloo who stops for a shave by a country barber who doesn't recognise him. The barber describes what he would like to do to the former Emperor if he had him in his barber's chair, all the while expertly wielding his razor at Napoleon's throat. People were thrilled when they heard sounds such as the rumble of the Emperor's coach wheels crossing a wooden bridge.

When "Lights of New York, "described as "the first all-talking picture," followed, the Telegraph praised it for its "clear and natural voices." It was a gangster film set on Broadway and in one scene the Boss tells one of his henchmen to get rid of a certain character. "Take him for a ride," he orders. It was the first time filmgoers had heard the phrase and for some unknown reason it quickly entered into the vernacular. Whether local audiences noticed it and began using it is not recorded. "The Ghost Talks" starring Helen Twelvetrees, and "The Terror" were old dark house types of mystery, the latter based on an Edgar Wallace story, full of thrills and comedy which went down well with local audiences, some of whom probably compared it with the stage version that they had seen in the Grand Opera House in November 1927. Courtroom dramas became quite popular not only because of their plots but also because they were indoor productions suited to the Vitaphone system. The first of those to arrive in July was "On Trial" starring Pauline Frederick, still remembered vividly for her appearance in the Opera House. The film had been much criticised in America because of its poor sound quality but the local critics certainly didn't agree with that. The Irish News found the courtroom sequences "realistic" and the whole presentation "very dramatic." The Telegraph wrote that Miss Frederick "registered well," while the Whig praised her "beautiful voice." Mention was also made of the vocal clarity of another character in the story, a well known stage - trained Dublin actor called Holmes Herbert who turned up as a murder victim. When the Picture House installed sound equipment the management decided to make a complete change from the past, and every programme thereafter consisted entirely of sound films. Thus "On Trial" was supported by the first boxing match filmed in sound, a fifteen round bout between the Spaniard Paolino and the German Max Schmeling, which the latter won. The Irish News was impressed by the extra dimension that sound brought to the proceedings, especially the noise and the cheers of the crowd. The critic was amazed to clearly hear the instructions given by the referee to the fighters.

While the Picture House was going from strength to strength the Classic announced that it would introduce sound, and on 15th July it presented a version of "Showboat" starring Laura La Plante and Joseph Schildkraut, with the admonition to the public:"You have seen the play, heard the music, now see and hear the picture." The opening day was blessed with splendid weather but, despite that, the cinema was packed. The film, produced by Universal, was a part talkie which had begun life as a silent, with songs and dialogue added later. It also had a special prologue introduced by no other than Carl Laemmle, the founder and President of Universal studios, aided by Florenz Ziegfeld the Broadway producer who had brought Jerome Kern and Oscar Hammerstein 11 together in 1927 to write "Show Boat". They began the proceedings by presenting songs and extracts from that original stage show, including "Ole Man River" sung by Jules Bledsoe. The local audiences were quite impressed, and the film ran for two weeks. The Irish News thought it was a "superb presentation" while the Telegraph critic found the voices "clear and distinct though a bit nasal" but added that the dialogue could be followed with ease. He further commented, rather ruefully, that everywhere one went in the city someone could be heard singing "Ole Man River." The latter is associated mainly with Paul Robeson who had recently had a major success with it in the stage production in London, but his fans had to wait another nine months to hear his version when he made a personal appearance in the Ulster Hall.

Unlike the Picture House the Classic didn't switch entirely to talkies, but usually programmed a new talkie or synchronised talkie with a silent feature. The orchestra was dispensed with and music for the silents was supplied by George Newell on the Wurlitzer organ. Mr Newell was also responsible for much appreciated interludes of popular music played during the intervals between the feature films. The combination of talkie and silent wasn't always appreciated by the audience and during one such programme the Telegraph detected a "cool reception" for the silent. In December the cinema invited filmgoers to "see and hear" Vilma Banky talk in "This Is Heaven." Audiences were always anxious to hear the voices of their favourites from the silents and responded in large numbers. Miss Banky, who had acted with Valentino in his last two films "The Eagle" and "The Son of the Sheik", was Hungarian with an accent to match, but Sam Goldwyn cleverly got around that by having her play a Hungarian immigrant. Unfortunately she only spoke in one short sequence at the end of the film, which didn't please the locals at all. The Telegraph insinuated that the second feature, the silent "Woman in White" in which Blanche Sweet played a double part, with atmospheric organ music supplied by George Newell, was much superior in every way. Many of the films shown in the Classic were in fact only sound - synchronised which meant that they were filmed as silents and a mainly musical soundtrack was added later. That procedure meant that the studios could show their backlog of silent films and satisfy audience demands for more sound at the same time. The resulting films were too often unsatisfactory.

But interspersed between them over the weeks the Classic did present some talkies of quality notably "Blackmail", "Bulldog Drummond" and "Coquette." The latter was Mary Pickford's first talkie in which she appeared as a flapper complete with a short hair style, the famous curls having been sheared. The Whig thought that the dialogue was "extremely arresting" and audiences declared themselves well pleased with the new Mary. "Bulldog Drummond" was a thriller starring Ronald Colman, and proved a great success with audiences. The critics noted the crowded houses and the Irish News praised, in particular, Colman's voice. The Telegraph critic was also much taken by his "clear talking" and commented on his lively personality which, he felt, added much to the entertainment. "Blackmail" is regarded as the first British talkie and was directed by Alfred Hitchcock who, like Walsh, Ford and other talented directors, wasn't just interested in talk for its own sake, but faced the challenge of integrating sound dramatically into the plot, which he did with great skill. One major problem was that his leading lady, Anny Ondra, was Czechoslovakian and, like Vilma Banky, had a very pronounced accent which didn't record well. Hitchcock had her dubbed on the set by an English actress who spoke the words while Miss Ondra mouthed them. Technically primitive, but effective. The Irish News critic thought the result was "a fine picture" and noted with approval that it was "well attended." He did admit to one criticism regarding Sara Allgood who had a small part in the film. He was disappointed that despite having "a beautiful speaking voice" she didn't get to say a single word, though she "laughs once and screams once."

Some critics argued that dubbing was a form of cheating but one could ask what else in a film is really what it seems. Voices, accents and delivery were much discussed in both professional and popular circles. While audiences were becoming more familiar with American vocals, they weren't always completely accepted. The Telegraph critic described being at a talkie in the Classic called "Nothing But the Truth" starring Richard Dix, during which the audience roared with laughter, not at the jokes, but at "the atrocious nasal accents" of the minor players. It would be wrong to suggest that all American voices evoked mirth or were difficult to understand. Local audiences had no problems when listening to the first words of the likes of Mary Pickford, Doug. Fairbanks, Pauline Frederick, Norma Shearer, Marion Davies and even John Gilbert, despite reports that American audiences had actually laughed at his vocal efforts. The film in question was "His Glorious Night" but when it showed in Belfast there was no criticism of Gilbert 's diction and the Irish News critic praised his performance, and the fact that "he made love charmingly."

When the eminent actress Ruth Chatterton was brought from Broadway to film in Hollywood American audiences in their turn laughed at her stage - trained accent which they regarded as superior and upper class. However when her film "Madame X" was shown here in the Picture House her diction was praised and welcomed. Similarly when "The Last of Mrs Cheyney" arrived in Belfast the critics welcomed the fact that the dialogue was taken directly from Wilde's play and emphasised that it was a pleasure to hear it spoken by the "cultivated voices" of Norma Shearer and Basil Rathbone. When Richard Barthelmess spoke in his first talkie "Weary River" his voice came across strong and clear, but audiences in the Picture House were really amazed by his singing, though it emerged much later that the singing voice had been dubbed. Ramon Navarro also spoke for the first time in "The Pagan" and bowled his listeners over in the Classic with his singing of "The Pagan Love Song ' which he did actually perform in a clear tenor voice. It became a great favourite on record and radio.

Criticism continued not only here but across the British Isles and parts of Europe about what the Irish Times called "Californian English." The I.S.N., which had complained about the "stranglehold" that American films had on British and European cinemas, carried an interview with the director Raoul Walsh on the topic in which he argued that American and English were actually two different languages. He accepted that "some impressionable people" could be influenced by the American idiom and he understood that that was a source of worry to some educationalists and others, but he emphasised that Hollywood had no plans to change the American vernacular in their films. His message was that our society would have to learn to live with it. The Irish Times, which often criticised what it regarded as the poor quality of many American films, worried that sound would speed up the Americanisation of our society.

While the talkies were getting most attention, the majority of films showing in the city during 1929 were still silents, often films of quality that, according to the Mountpottinger Picturedrome, "spoke for themselves." There were still twenty - one silent cinemas in operation showing a wide range of films which according to reports were well supported. Each evening queues of eager fans pushed into the foyers past the colourful posters, the front - of - house stills and other advertising items, under the welcoming but quizzical gaze of the uniformed attendants. People continued to flock to see their favourites who included Chaplin, Buster Keaton, Harold Lloyd, Tom Mix, Hoot Gibson, Lon Chaney, Victor MacLaglan, William Boyd, Ivor Novello, Bebe Daniels, Dolores Del Rio, Colleen Moore, Clara Bow, Pola Negri and many others. A new elaborate silent version of the old favourite "Uncle Tom's Cabin," the eighth to be filmed, arrived and received good reviews. It was accompanied by a colourful and elaborate prologue of "plantation songs, dances and spirituals" according to the Irish News, which also recommended it as "well worth seeing." The Telegraph described how when it reached the Alhambra the stage was decorated as a log cabin in which the songs and dancing by members of the staff took place under the direction of the hall's musical director, John White. The critic wrote that the story's appeal was still powerful and agreed with his Irish News colleague that the film was "worth seeing."

Also recommended was something completely different, "Gentlemen Prefer Blondes," Anita Loos's lively comedy of the adventures of two gold diggers Lorelei(Ruth Taylor) and Dorothy (Alice White), ably supported by oldtimers Ford Sterling and Mack Swain. The Telegraph was of the opinion that it had "one of the funniest plots" around and the acting of the two principles was widely praised. Some who saw it at the time preferred it to the later version starring Marilyn Monroe and Jane Russell. The Irish News told its readers to ignore the trivially sounding title of another film, "The Private Life of Helen of Troy," with Maria Corda and Lewis Stone, but to go and see it because it was actually a fine satirical comedy, "a novel trans - Atlantic view of Homer", beautifully directed and presented with "good satire in both the acting and sub titles." The latter comment is an interesting sidelight on how silent comedy could be appreciated. The much more serious "Flesh and the Devil" with John Gilbert and Greta Garbo also drew the crowds.

In October the Lyceum announced the showing of "The Jazz Singer," regarded as the first talking picture, but local excitement subsided somewhat when it was realised that it was the silent version. It wasn't unusual for silent and sound versions of the same film to be available because so many cinemas weren't yet wired for sound. Before the film was projected there was a special prologue of the music and songs it contained presented by Mr Finlay and his orchestra. The Irish News commented that it was "well received" though the sound version had been shown only two months before in the Picture House where it had run for a week. The Duncairn presented the silent version of Hitchcock's "Blackmail" while the Imperial showed the silent version of Clara Bow's first talkie "The Wild Party," and crowds rushed to enjoy another "throbbing, pulsing, thrilling story of youth." Audiences and fans of Miss Bow had to wait another month to actually hear her a speak in "Dangerous Curves" a circus drama in which the Picture House claimed her voice "glowed with new charm'." During the latter half of the year "Wings" had a successful rerun, "The Wind" featuring a much put - upon Lilian Gish impressed the serious minded, while "Our Dancing Daughters" in which Joan Crawford played a flapper, complete with a tabletop dance, attracted large crowds to the Imperial. Although there was a sound - synchronised version available it was the silent version that was shown and appreciated. It seemed that in Belfast at least there was still audience support for both sound films and silents.

There were actually four types of film going the rounds that they could choose from. There were the genuine silents which had been planned, scripted and filmed in silent form, though they were becoming fewer and fewer. Then there were synchronised silents which were silent films that the studios had adapted by adding music, some natural sounds and a few lines of dialogue to make them more saleable to halls already wired for sound. There were also silent versions of successful sound films which a writer in the Irish News referred to as "dumb talkies," and finally there were the new talkies, all talking, or all talking, singing and dancing as the case may be. The aforementioned writer in the Irish News, seeing the funny side of that confusion, described being at one such "dumb talkie" in which there was a scene where two characters were in conversation (by subtitles, of course) when both suddenly, without apparent reason, turned their heads and looked up. The next shot was of a door which opened. Obviously, the writer commented, someone had knocked or a doorbell had sounded in the sound version, causing their reaction. People near him were in their turn reacting to that and similar situations where they would guess what sound was missing. The commentator felt that it added a new dimension to the enjoyment of the film - guess the missing sound !

While suburban Belfast was still cinematically silent more and more of those who could afford it were making their way downtown to SEE and HEAR the new novelty of the talkies or "talkers" for themselves. Most emerged into the light impressed and not only by the feature films but also with the supporting featurettes. From the beginning the Picture House gave its audiences full sound programmes and the main film was always supported by Vitagraph shorts, usually of singers or musicians performing, similar to the Phonofilms that the Lyceum had presented earlier. The critics made no comment about them but their reactions to the accompanying cartoons were a different matter. The often seen conventional symbol of the inauguration of the sound era is the famous image of Al Jolson in blackface but it could just as easily have been a little black and white mouse because Mickey Mouse arrived in Belfast, as elsewhere, with sound. Mickey was essentially the creation of a new talent, Walt Disney, whom the critics began to mention and praise in their weekly columns. Mickey's first sound film, "Steamboat Willie" - an oblique reference to Buster Keaton's recent "Steamboat Bill Jr" - got its first public viewing in the USA in November 1928 and exactly one year later was showing in the Picture House much to the delight of critics and audiences. Mickey became a star almost immediately in Belfast, as elsewhere across the globe. His antics, according to one local reporter always provoked "roars of laughter.'

He was so popular that he often received equal billing with the main feature. The Telegraph compared his antics to Felix the Cat which was a great compliment then, while the Irish News declared that the only problem with his cartoons was that they were too short. When the Picture House showed Mickey in "The Jazz Fool," a skit on Jolson's film, the Irish News critic thought that it showed "exceptional originality." Besides Mickey's personality the main appeal of the films was the masterly synchronisation of sound, especially music, and action. Disney wouldn't tolerate any sloppiness in the process and he and his fellow artists and technicians developed more subtle techniques to achieve his aims. Those improvements led to Mickey introducing the Silly Symphony cartoons in which music and motion combined to further the stories. The first of those under the title of "The Skeleton Dance" was, according to the Irish News, "amusing." It was the beginning of the great love affair between Walt Disney and the public, especially the children and parents. In the years that followed many parents, seeking wholesome fare for their young offspring, expressed their thanks for the output of Walt Disney and his Studio.

Another popular item in every programme was the newsreel and audiences were amazed at the Movietone News in Natural Sound which allowed them to experience not only what the world looked like but what it sounded like. It was advertised as "the newsreel that speaks for itself" which was no idle boast because many critics at the time held that technically the newsreels were much more advanced in their use of sound than many fiction films. Sporting events took on an extra dimension and audiences reacted excitedly when they heard the thunder of horses' hooves and the cheers of the crowd when Trigo, the Belfast horse, won the Derby in May 1929, or when they experienced the roar of engines from the Motor Grand Prix in Phoenix Park. It was the same with football matches and special events like the Boat Race and the Grand National which the Picture House not only showed but advertised as major items.

For the ladies the latest fashions from Paris came not only in colour but with a commentary which sometimes fuelled argument and discussion. Local arguments about female fashions still continued but the sting had gone out of them though the news from Paris occasioned differing reactions from women and men. Suggestions that skirts would be lengthened again were seen by some local women as an attack on hard - won female freedoms. They argued that the short skirt went along with the right to vote and greater independence, and that the reimposition of the longer garment was part of a plan by "them" to restore male control. The men in the audience had other, not so serious, ideas. They thought that some of the latest fashions looked rather ridiculous, and one writer in the I.S.N. called on the girls of Belfast to form a Society for the Prevention of Freak Fashions, the slogan of which should be: Comfort and Common sense, Flappers and Freedom. "

That sounded like something that George Bernard Shaw would have approved of, and he was one of a number of well known personalities who appeared in the newsreels to speak directly to the audience which he did "most entertainingly," according to the Telegraph. Politics were not neglected, and when Ramsey Mac Donald formed the second Labour Government in July he presented the members of his cabinet one by one to the audience from his garden at 10, Downing Street. His voice, wrote the Telegraph critic, came over "clear as a bell." The following week he introduced the female members of Parliament in the same way and sometime later another member of the government, the noted Socialist Sir George Lansbury, the grandfather of Angela Lansbury, spoke from the screen about his plans for improving the quality of life in London. On another occasion former Prime Minister Lloyd George was interviewed. People were amazed and impressed that politicians could now be seen speaking to the whole country, but others, more cynical perhaps, suggested that maybe it was a mixed blessing.

Significant world events also appeared on screen and became the subject of daily conversation as, for example, when the great airship the Graf Zeppelin circled the globe in 21 days, 7 hours and 26 minutes with stops in Germany, Tokyo and Los Angeles before landing at Lakehurst, New Jersey. There were shots also of its British competitor, the R101, scenes that turned to reality when during one of its trials it appeared over Ireland in mid November. It circled over Dublin early in the morning and later passed over Holywood so low that locals could read the lettering clearly on its side. There were reports of buildings reverberating from the sound of its engines. It was also seen over Belfast and citizens stood in awe as they watched it silhouetted against the moonlit sky like "a great silver fish" (Telegraph). In the papers it was described as the largest airship in the world with a length of 777 feet (about 240 metres). Unfortunately the lucky sevens didn't protect it and it crashed in flames in France the following October, killing 44 of its passengers. The newsreels showed dramatic shots of its burnt out metal frame. The tragedy was keenly felt in the city and in the following week the Irish News critic drew his readers' attention specially to the fact that the Pathé Super Sound Gazette was entirely given over to the funeral of the victims. The newsreels had to entertain as well as inform but that didn't prevent them from illustrating a selection of sad events. Patrons were reminded of the passing of Lily Langtry, the Jersey Lily, with her Belfast connections, who died that year, as well as the Father of the House of Commons the popular T.P.O'Connor who had been President of the Film Censorship Board for many years.

One event which became a talking point among cinemagoers was the report in a local paper that Alma Rubens, the popular star who had been appearing on local screens since Griffith's "Intolerance," had suffered a seizure in public in Los Angeles and had to be taken off to an asylum. The shock was increased by the fact that many of those reading the report had only recently enjoyed her much praised performance in the talkie "Showboat" in the Classic. What the report didn't reveal was that she was struggling with a serious problem of drug addiction, which was ruining her health and career. That became clearer two years later, in January 1931, when the Telegraph announced her death from pneumonia at the early age of 33 years. The report made quite clear that the main cause was drugs, and added that a recent search of her rooms had uncovered drugs to the value of five thousand dollars (£1000). Barbara La Marr, another popular young star had also died recently at the age of 30 years, her career ruined by drug problems. To the more observant it was just another hint that life in Hollywood as described in the movie fan magazines and presented on the screen wasn't as happy and glamorous as suggested.

In Belfast, those who kept their fingers on the moral pulse of the city were worried about other more immediate issues. Gambling was seen as an increasingly serious problem and the authorities were asked to look into reports that it had invaded the schools where young children were actually making penny bets. Another worry was the perceived immorality of much of contemporary literature, which was widely condemned by local churchmen. At a meeting of the Church of Ireland Young Men's Literary and Debating Society in November the modern novel was described as "decadent" and condemned for its obsession with sex, and its attacks on the sanctity of marriage. Speakers felt that such novels were undermining the morals of the younger generation and called for some kind of local censorship. The cinema didn't escape entirely but the criticisms were of a different nature, emanating from a political source. As early as April when the first talkies were showing in Belfast the Irish News carried comments from Mr Baldwin, the then Prime Minister, about the many films showing across the world which he felt were "a travesty of our Western civilisation." Echoing the fears which had been expressed following the victory of black boxer Jack Johnson back in 1908 - 9, he claimed that such films undermined the respect for white rulers in the Tropical dependencies, and could actually put their positions at risk. He felt so seriously about it that he intended to bring the matter up for discussion at the next Imperial Conference. There certainly were many films set in the tropics in which the heat, the humidity, the insects and the exotic locales seemed to sap the moral strengths of the white heroes. A typical example was the talkie "A Dangerous Woman," which appeared in the Picture House a few months later, described sensationally as "a tale of the Tropics, of love maddened men and a beautiful woman who is as dangerous as she is beautiful." The story, which the Telegraph critic praised for "its scenes of intense realism," involved upright Clive Brook falling for the charms of Olga Baclanova, Hollywood's latest import from Russia, a lady probably better remembered today as Cleopatra, the haughty trapeze artiste of the controversial cult horror film "Freaks" (d. Tod Browning, 1932) who ended up as a freak herself in the form of a human chicken. In August the I.S.N. carried a follow - up in the form of an article under the heading "Cinema and Natives. Damages White Prestige," which dealt with reaction to a report on the matter drawn up after the Imperial Conference.

A former Colonial Governor Sir Heskett Bell, giving evidence in the House of Commons, insisted that such films had done immeasurable harm to the standing of white rulers in the Tropics and he described how he had seen at first hand the adverse reactions of natives to scenes showing the worst side of behaviour among white people. He condemned above all long drawn out kissing scenes and added that "the worst thing was the showing of white women in cabaret scenes." The chief culprits in the matter, he held, were the Americans but regardless of who was responsible he felt that a stricter censorship was needed. He rather overstated his case when he traced the beginnings of political unrest in the colonies to the arrival of the cinema, an intriguing idea but one which would hardly stand up to serious academic investigation. The reports caused little reaction in the city at the time but it was obvious that with the arrival of sound the calls for more control and censorship were increasing again, and certainly the principle of film censorship for political reasons was not to go away either in London or here where it fell on fertile ground as the activities of the City Hall's Police Committee were to show in the years that followed.

The newsreels claimed that they showed the most important news happenings but, of necessity, they had to pick and choose, so it was inevitable that events, attitudes and talking points especially of a local nature which Belfast audiences regarded as "news" weren't reported. At ground level the world seemed a different place from that projected on the screen, even if sound did add a new reality. There was a dark side to life in the city, with insidious politico - religious tensions infiltrating nearly every aspect of society. There seemed little to celebrate, though there were exceptions as when Sir John Lavery, one of Belfast's most famous sons, made a gift of thirty of his paintings to the Museum and Art Gallery. In gratitude the Council decided to confer the Freedom of the City on him and on the 22nd April 1930 of the following year Sir John and his wife Hazel arrived off the Liverpool boat to receive the honour. The decision was welcomed by the newspapers and by people across the city but the Irish News, while praising the Council for their action, felt it had to point out the he was only the first Catholic ever to have been honoured in that way.

Most citizens' concerns revolved around day to day matters far removed from the rarified atmosphere of the Arts. The working class could relate to the newsreel scenes of the Depression from America, following the Wall Street Crash of October 1929 because they reflected a reality that they were familiar with, a reality in the form of serious unemployment, strikes and threats of strikes, long working hours and low wages combined with widespread poverty and poor housing. A report on housing was debated in the Northern Senate in December and during it Senator T.J. Campbell strongly criticised the local Government saying that its housing policy was "a thing of shreds and patches" incapable of coping with the problem. As evidence he claimed that within half a mile of the city centre there were belts of inner city slums that were "a disgrace to civilisation." In that area, he claimed, there was unhealthy overcrowding with 2,700 families each sharing one room, 8,000 families each two rooms, and 10,000 three rooms. It was against that background of deprivation and economic struggle that the cinema business had to operate, offering an escape from the everyday hardships. Interviews with people recalling the Twenties and the Thirties often emphasised that no matter how difficult things became there was always a penny or two, sometimes in the form of a jam jar, for the children to visit the local cinema matinee, while those lucky enough to work in the mills or factories put aside a few shillings most weeks for a visit to a local or downtown cinema.

In August John Y. Moore announced that the Alhambra would celebrate the Silver Jubilee of W.J.Ashcroft's purchase of the old hall with a programme of old style variety, an event that stirred up much nostalgia and reminiscences about the past. But Mr Moore and the other cinema owners had to live in the present and couldn't ignore what was happening around them, if only because it influenced the number of people who could afford to visit their halls. Suitable pricing was a key part of their business strategy and in 1929 three distinct pricing levels or strata can be detected. The cheapest halls, that is, those that served their immediate working class neighbourhoods were priced from 3d to 9d with special children's matinees at 1d on Wednesdays and Saturdays. The 3d was for the pit, an area usually of wooden benches located near the screen; 5d for the stalls, an area of tip - up seats at the back of the ground floor behind the pit; and 9d for the balcony, which had the most comfortable seats and even pile carpet on the floor. The halls in that group are remembered with great affection and have entered into local cinema mythology, in the process becoming encrusted with highly colourful stories of noisy patrons, stalwart attendants and other employees, often of a distinctive eccentricity, overseen by patient or harassed managers. Their programmes consisted mainly of second or third run films, B films, Westerns, comedies, cartoons and such with music supplied by a few musicians or a single piano.

Some were better run than others but all shared one characteristic in that their programmes were advertised and perceived by their patrons as excellent value for money. The Queen's Theatre in York Street for example proudly described itself as "the wee house with the big attractions." It would be wrong to suggest that they showed only the cheaper rejects of the trade, as an examination of programmes presented at the nearby Midland just before the arrival of sound indicates. Audiences there were able to see John Gilbert in a fine war film "The Big Parade," Ivor Novello in Hitchcock's thriller "The Lodger," advertised as "a story of the London fog," Fritz Lang's "Metropolis," de Mille's "King of Kings" (only two months after its first run in the Picture House), and the Anita Loos comedy "Gentlemen Prefer Blondes." Many of those cinemas didn't need to advertise because their customers came back uncritically every week sometimes more than once. Most of them, though not all, operated on a system of separate shows with a complete change of programme every Monday and Thursday. Outwardly they may not have been very distinguished architecturally and inwardly they proudly carried the scars of rough wear and tear, but to the people that frequented them they were palaces of exotic pleasures. They included the Midland and Queen's Theatre in York Street, the Central at Smithfield, the Gaiety in North Street, the Kelvin in College Sq. East, the Coliseum and Sandro in the Sandy Row area, the Arcadian, Diamond and Tivoli in the Falls Road area, the West End Picture House (better known locally as "Joe's") and Picturedrome on the Shankill, the Crumlin, called after the road it stood on, the Popular and Willowfield (the Winkie) in East Belfast.

The second group was more up - market, with better and more comfortable facilities aimed at both better paid workers and middle class patrons. They were well run by capable and respected managers like P.J.Hogan, Ferris Pounds, J.Y.Moore and H Mac Dermott. Their price range was from 5d to one shilling and financially they were differentiated from the former group by their higher balcony prices They included the historic Alhambra which in 1929 was charging 5d, 9d and one shilling; the Mountpottinger Picturedrome, the pride of East Belfast, and the New Princess Palace on the Newtownards Road, both with seats at 4d, 6d, and one shilling; the Lyceum on the Antrim Road, which had introduced "real" sound films to the city, charging 6d, one shilling and one and six (balcony); the Duncairn Super Cinema with 4d, 6d and one shilling; and last but by no means least the Clonard on the Falls Road charging 3d (pit), 5d (stalls),9d (lounge), and one shilling (balcony). Those halls had high standards, and showed the top films often only a few weeks after their first run downtown. They were quick to introduce improvements whether technical, like the Panatrope, practical like under cover queueing, or topical like speedily acquiring material of local interest. In June 1929 the critic of the Telegraph went out of his way to congratulate P.J. Hogan who was able to screen scenes from Dublin of the Centenary Celebrations of the introduction of Catholic Emancipation (1829) in the Clonard the day after they took place. The film, which the critic described as "wonderful," showed the special Mass in Phoenix Park attended by one million persons and the procession which followed through the centre of Dublin. The cinemas had medium sized orchestras and often supplemented their films with quality music hall and concert personalities including local favourites like Albert Sharpe. Some cinemas hovered on the invisible divide between the two groups. For example the Coliseum could charge one shilling for circle seats and even one shilling and sixpence for boxed seats, while the Gaiety for a time charged one shilling for its best seats.

There were no problems recognising the city's top cinemas, all located downtown in what was the original walled town. They were Belfast's luxurious picture palaces and they included the Picture House in Royal Avenue, the Classic in Castle Lane, the Royal Cinema in Arthur Street, the Imperial in Corn Market and the Lyric in High Street. They showed first run films, the best that were available and they presented them in very comfortable, clean, well organized surroundings. Their prices were high, pitched at the better paid workers and the middle class, and normally were one shilling for the stalls and two shillings for the balcony, though the Classic sometimes made balcony seats bookable for three shillings. Lower prices applied before 4:30 weekdays, but even then the balconies cost one shilling. Leaving aside special attractions the dearest seats cost two shillings, which in today's money is only ten pence but the obvious comparison isn't really valid. A seat for 10p today is unbelievable with top prices in the city cinemas now normally between £5 and £ 6 (2013) but two shilling in 1929 was substantial when one realises that most workers earned only about 35 shillings (£1- 75 today) per week while 50 shillings (£2-50 today) was regarded as well paid. Also in those days, when a man invited a lady out for the evening convention dictated that he paid for everything so a visit to a downtown cinema with a girlfriend who had to be impressed with the best seats and a box of chocolates could add up to about nearly 20% of a weekly wage. Adding to his expenses the young man also had to take into account that twenty cigarettes (and nearly everyone smoked) cost one shilling, a pint of stout was six pence, while a complete suit (and one had to wear one's best on such occasions) at the likes of Hyams in North Street cost ninety shillings (£ 4 - 50). In all the evening could be quite expensive. But, on the other hand, an evening spent in comfortable surroundings with a pleasant companion watching the latest from Hollywood was regarded as something special, the height of luxury that couldn't be measured in mere financial terms. The downtown cinemas for their part had to compete for audiences with the theatres and music halls and therefore had to keep their prices competitive.

The premier theatre, the Grand Opera House, was the most expensive venue in town with a price range from one shilling to five shillings and ninepence. The Royal Hippodrome, the premier music hall, was cheaper with prices from sixpence to three shillings, while the older Empire charged from sixpence to two shillings and fourpence. Differences in social standing within audiences in a particular cinema or between audiences in different cinemas was widely recognised in the Twenties and Thirties. The I.S.N. carried a series of chatty articles written by an unnamed reporter who described, accurately he claimed, life in different sections of the city on Saturday nights. In one article he described passing the Picture House in Royal Avenue with its queue waiting quietly and patently for admission to the last show of the day. It consisted of well dressed young and mature people talking quietly to each other while moving forward in an orderly fashion when the doorman indicated. He walked to North Street which at the time (about 8:00pm) was all bustle, with people everywhere, but dominated by the Alhambra queue which was "doing its best to fill the street."

"Can you imagine North Street without the Alhambra?" he mused as he studied the crowd waiting for admittance, which in contrast to the Picture House patrons, was noisy and lively. It was in two sections, and he was impressed by the "distinct social differences" they exhibited. One section for the dearer seats stretched down the street past Hyams and "had a touch of quality about it." It was orderly and characterised by "soft hats and hard hats, and no hats; top coats and burburrys; fair damsels that seemed all silken legs and sleek heads." The other section heading for the cheaper seats stretched unevenly up towards Church Street. It was much livelier and consisted mainly of males who instead of impressive headgear and outer coats sported "the duncher and the white knotted muffler (and) the baggy concertina grey flannels." Scattered among them was a small number of women wearing shawls and looking "far from prosperous." The reporter crossed Royal Avenue "through the perpetual swirl of traffic" into Upper North Street where the shop windows were full of sale goods (it was January) passing a group of men admiring a display of tweed caps offered at only 18 d (7 1/2p) before reaching the Gaiety. There the inevitable queue was moving in for the last show, a queue that in composition looked much like the Alhambra one. The attendants had divided it into sections for easier control, letting one section at a time up the steps to the box office. The movement up the steps was more of a rush than an orderly approach. A few policemen stood on the pavement watching that all went to plan.

On another Saturday evening he walked along Castle Lane which he described as "bright with lights and congested with cars," past the long queue which was moving slowly up the steps leading into the Classic, past a "depressed looking man" who was entertaining them with his fiddle on which he was playing, rather badly, "Dancing With Tears in my Eyes." Similar well organized queues decorated the outsides of the Royal Cinema and the Imperial, who were being harangued by "a lone preacher" standing in the middle of Arthur Square. It was a scene which would be repeated weekly there until the Fifties. Another reporter wrote that there was no avoiding a cinema queue on a Saturday night and it was not unusual for people to have to wait up to an hour and a half before admittance. He joined one (cinema unnamed) to discover what it would be like because he admitted that he was not a regular filmgoer, and found the experience required "endurance and patience." He passed the time observing the other members of the queue, most of them in animated conversation with their friends because there were very few individuals standing, like himself, alone, and what he heard he did find quite interesting and informative. The younger members discussed the films they had seen recently and it became obvious that many of them had been to the pictures two or three times already that week. They knew all the stars and personalities, the latest film news and gossip, and spent a lot of time discussing the likes of Marlene Dietrich. So it was across the city, with lines of eager people, poor or of moderate means or well off, animated or otherwise, with or without hats or overcoats, heading for the seats that they could afford to enjoy an evening's entertainment.

A study of cinema prices during the Twenties suggests a tension between the cinema owners' desire to hold prices steady and thereby keep their traditional audiences, and the need to adapt to local political and economic troubles which were hostile to business, with the added burdens of entertainment tax and increases in the costs of film hire. Many regarded price stability as vital to retain their patrons. In 1922 the Alhambra for example pegged its prices of admission at 5d, 9d and one shilling and so they remained throughout the decade. The Clonard charged 3d, 5d, 9d and one shilling in 1923, prices which remained unchanged until 1930. During the same period the Imperial kept its prices steady at one shilling and one and sixpence. The Picture House was charging one shilling for the stalls and two shillings for the balcony in 1920 and held those prices until April 1929 when sound was introduced. The Royal Cinema tinkered quite a lot with its price structure before settling on one shilling for the stalls and two shillings for the balcony which remained the norm during the decade, except for special "roadshow" presentations like "The Four Horsemen of the Apocalypse" when balcony seats were made available as bookable for three shillings and sixpence. The Crumlin on the other hand held its prices at 3d, 5d and 8d throughout the Twenties until 1930 when they were reduced to 2 1/2 d, 4d and 6d, as the hall remained silent and obviously struggled to hold its audience in the face of the spread of sound. In the main the policies followed by the cinema owners worked in that audience numbers remained high during the decade though a writer in the Irish News suggested their success was also due to clever advertising and he called on other ailing industries to learn from that and remember that it paid to advertise. Some firms did actually think along those lines. During British Empire Week the match - making firm of Maguire and Patterson located on the Donegal Road took a large advertisement in that paper calling upon people to "buy Ulster made goods" because by buying local made goods they would help to reduce unemployment. Be loyal to your own people the advert advised, don't buy inferior foreign matches when you can buy Swift, Bo-Peep and Yacht matches made in Belfast.

Prices weren't a consideration for a small group of enthusiasts who were interested in the technical and creative side of film making. They were the members of the city's first film society, The Provincial Film Society of N.Ireland. They had already made and shown one short film, a local scenic documentary, in early 1929 and they had plans for more subjects. In early October the society held a meeting in the Ashleigh Studio in Royal Avenue when a little film called "Trying Conditions" was projected by their technical director, Louis Morrison, on a screen "half the size of a cinema screen "(Irish News). It showed a simple situation where a number of the society's members, male and female, all amateurs, displayed their acting abilities by expressing various emotions while using a telephone. The film was silent and the Irish News reporter seemed more amused than impressed by what he saw. The society was earnest in its aims, and announced optimistically that they would soon be undertaking a new film to be called "Kitty of Coleraine" based on the well known song. The script was to be written by Clifford Carter and the action would include scenes shot in the shipyard, Bangor, Bellevue and the Glens of Antrim. When completed it would be the first story film actually made in the area and as such was something to look forward to.

What most people were looking forward to was Christmas and the New Year, which would signal not only the passing of 1929 but the end of the Twenties. As expected that fact stimulated some soul searching. All the papers welcomed Christmas as the greatest festival of the year with its emphasis on peace, charity and the family. The welcome was tempered with some reservations. The editor of the Whig was quite pessimistic about what he saw as the waning influence of the Spirit of Christmas. He felt that at that time of the year eyes should be raised to the Star at Bethlehem and what it represented but from evidence around the world people seemed to be acting more like the oxen in the stable, uncomprehending and unaware of what Christmas really stood for. He went on to ask could we still be described as a Christian nation because as a community we seemed to have become "blind to moral evils." He complained that locally the Prince of Peace was "overshadowed by crime and poverty" and for many "there would be no glad tidings" but for the generosity of individuals and charitable groups. The News Letter also emphasised the need for charity and praised those who gave so much at Christmas, because in the poorer parts of our city there were "disheartened men, poorly clad women and insufficiently nourished children" who needed help. The elements seemed to concur because the holiday period turned out to be one of the wettest and windiest that people could recall, though it didn't dampen the spirit of enjoyment in the city. All over Christmas there were reports of crowds relaxing and enjoying themselves and especially on the evening of the 31st December the halls of entertainment were packed. A large audience was in attendance in the Grand Opera House at the annual pantomime, "Dick Whittington" a colourful, elaborate and spectacular affair praised by all the critics as marvellous Christmas fare. The Whig critic even lectured the citizens that "they were lucky to have such a fine production." The Empire was less opulent maybe but equally crowded, for "Bo Peep" which the Irish News praised especially for its beautiful settings. The dance halls from the Plaza to the smaller Victoria Hall pulsated with the rhythms and sounds of special New Year parties, and the cinemas offered a wide variety of attractions which drew the usual long queues.

The Picture House had a Fox all - singing musical called "Hearts in Dixie" which, as the name suggested, was set in the the Deep South. It had been much criticised in America for its depiction of the blacks and especially for the obsequious performance of Stepin Fetchit, a black actor with a particularly annoying style, who was to become very familiar to Belfast audiences during the Thirties. Local audiences were agreed that its main attraction was its music and songs like "Swing Low, Sweet Chariot," "Deep River," and "Nobody Knows the Trouble I See." The Classic also presented a talkie called "Pleasure Crazed" described by the News Letter as "a crook picture" which was accompanied by supporting shorts including cartoons and a newsreel, along with J.F.Newell playing "seasonal selections" on the organ which went down very well with the audience. The Imperial announced the last few days of "Our Dancing Daughters" starring Joan Crawford. Also in the cast was Kathlyn Williams whom many older filmgoers would have recognised from the days when she had thrilled them in her popular serials. It was supported by straight faced Buster Keaton as "The Cameraman."

Across Corn Market the Royal Cinema presented two old favourites, Tom Mix in "Son of the Golden West" and Charlie Chaplin in "The Ice Rink," accompanied by "Belfast's Premier Orchestra" under the baton of F.M.Doherty. When visiting the Royal one could also, and indeed was encouraged, to book for the pantomime in the Opera House. Outside the city centre the Alhambra presented an adventure story with Victor McLaglan in "Captain Lash," the Clonard on the Falls was screening "Revenge" with the beautiful Dolores Del Rio, the Pottinger Picturedrome had a reissue of "Wings" accompanied with appropriate music by David Curry and his orchestra, the Duncairn had a comedy "Adam's Apple," while the Crumlin and the Lyceum were showing "Submarine" starring grim - jawed Jack Holt, and Ralph Graves, described as "a drama of a crew trapped in deep water." It was directed by Frank Capra and had proved a critical and financial success for Columbia Pictures. The film was inspired by two underwater tragedies that the US navy had suffered recently but Capra got full cooperation from the navy with the use of an actual submarine, the aircraft carrier Saratoga and other ships and men which helped to add reality to the proceedings. The film contains many scenes that are now submarine clichés - the panic of the trapped crew, the frantic attempts to conserve air, the attempts at rescue, the brave divers working against time under dangerous conditions and the final realization that crew members were still alive from faint tappings on the hull. It is usually described as Columbia's first sound film but it was actually filmed as a silent with the sounds added later. The version shown in Belfast was silent but no less gripping for that.

When the halls began to close their doors after 10:30 pm crowds poured on to the streets and converged on the Albert Clock. A reporter from the Irish News estimated that over 20,000 people mainly between the ages of 17 and 26 years filled the nearby streets. A carnival atmosphere prevailed and young people wearing coloured paper hats linked arms and danced up and down High Street singing popular songs from the new talkies, records and radio. As the clock began to chime midnight the crowd became quiet before breaking into Auld Lang Sang. On all sides there were happy faces, happy voices and wishes for a Happy New Year. The editor of the Irish News, echoing the earlier comments of his colleague on the Whig, wished that those feelings could be extended throughout the whole year but knowing the city and its people he suspected that that was a forlorn hope.

As the crowd dispersed some of those walking up High Street past the Lyric Cinema and shops like Goorwiches and Robb's, with their Winter Sales notices, must have contemplated the decade just past and it is unlikely that many regretted its passing. To Belfast those years were the Terrible Twenties when the city had suffered under the dark shadows of political bitterness and change, street violence and sectarian bigotry though thankfully as the Whig put it "the volcano (was) now at rest." However, the concomitant social ills of unemployment and poverty still presented major problems to be solved, and many must have wondered what the new decade would bring. The cinemas had offered temporary but welcome relief from the everyday pressures of life, but even that industry was changing under the impact of sound. Cinematically the Twenties had seen an increasing technical and artistic sophistication in silent film making and there was a greater willingness among intellectuals to treat the medium more seriously, though many of them did not take kindly to the arrival of talkies. Audiences, for their part, were more excited about the impact of sound and how it would add to the entertainment value of a night at the pictures. Despite the good humour and the high hopes expressed around the Albert Clock and across the city the year ended on a sad note which seemed to suggest that things were not about to change suddenly for the better. The day before, news came of a fire in Cashel which had completely destroyed a local cinema but thankfully it had occurred when the hall was closed so there were no casualties, though the newspapers made much of the fact that the film showing that week was called "Doomsday."

But the news on New Year's Eve was more serious. That afternoon, across the sea in Paisley, the Glen Cinema had been packed for a children's Hogmanay matinee. A reel of film caught fire in the projection room but the projectionist managed to manhandle it down the stairs and kick it out on to the pavement where it burned harmlessly. Unfortunately smoke from the flames drifted into the cinema auditorium and someone shouted that dread word "FIRE." The result was immediate pandemonium as frightened children rushed wildly towards the exits. They climbed over seats, some falling in the process. Others were caught on the stairs from the balcony, tripping and falling in a heap that others tried to climb over. In all seventy children died in the terrible crush as a result of panic, not fire. Everywhere the public were appalled, including Belfast, where memories of the Raglan Street Disaster and the terrible events in Drumcolliger were recalled, and what might have been a few months before in the Crumlin cinema. Over the following weeks the memories remained vivid as local cinemas showed newsreels of the sad aftermaths of the event and collected for the Disaster Fund set up for the relief of those families and individuals who had suffered in the disaster. In the cinemas 1929 had begun with the hope for mankind implicit in the "King of Kings" but ended with the sad realities of "Doomsday."

Little did anyone realise that that scenario would prove to be equally appropriate for the "low dishonest decade" (Auden) that was just beginning.

CHAPTER TWENTY ONE
The Sound of Music

At the beginning of 1930 there were only two cinemas in Belfast with the facilities to show sound films, the Picture House in Royal Avenue and the Classic in Castle Lane. Those cinemas shared a tenuous link in that one (the Picture House) had been built originally by the PTC company and then later sold to a local group, while the other (the Classic) had been built by local entrepreneurs and then sold to the PTC company. In contrast, at the same time, Dublin could boast five sound cinemas, including the recently completed Savoy. The Savoy, which is still operating successfully, was opened on 29th November 1929 and occupied, according to the Irish Times, "a magnificent building which added to the architecture of O'Connell Street." The official ceremony was carried out by the Taoiseach, Mr Cosgrove, before an expectant audience of about 3,000 persons including "business men, and government officials" (Irish Times) which reflected the

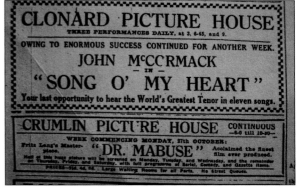

Song of my Heart, an Irish musical.

importance that the Government attached to the cinema industry. It must be emphasised that the official interest was primarily practical because the Dail, like its Northern equivalent, regarded cinemas mainly as a source of employment, and revenue for the Exchequer. The film content was highly censored to a level which provoked the I.S.N. to comment that if films were sausages then Dublin audiences were being offered only the skins. In reply Dublin filmgoers could argue that at least they could see (or eat) them on Sundays, a contentious luxury that Belfast filmgoers didn't yet have. Unlike all the other talkie adapted halls north and south, the Savoy had the advantage that it was planned and constructed as a sound cinema, the first in Ireland to be so designed. It was a pointer to the future.

The Belfast Telegraph reported in May 1929 that across the British Isles 300 new cinemas were being planned or built, but could have added that there were no plans for similar developments in Belfast. The local cinema owners knew that the costs of installing sound equipment were high and hesitated until they felt that they would get a worthwhile return on their investment. As the decade ended it became increasingly clear that sound represented the future, and that they would have to adapt to survive. It was obvious from the queues outside the Picture House and the Classic that the people had taken to sound and wanted more of it, while reports in the specialist magazines emphasised the large profits that sound productions were making. The news from London, and especially from Hollywood, was of the major companies converting their studios or building new expensive sound studios. Even the local press reported on such changes. In May 1929 the Irish News noted that Fox were soundproofing their stages and would soon abandon making silent films entirely. It was also becoming clear that the preferred technology would be sound - on - film. Modern researchers have discovered that the quality of the sound recordings on records at that time was high, but no matter how technically good records were they presented a number of problems for the projectionists. They were brittle and easily chipped, cracked or broken. Also, when being played they were prey to hissing and clicking. But most of all they were bulky and difficult to transport. Each recording ran for about ten minutes so an average film required ten or more discs, while longer and more prestigious productions needed even more. Sound-on-film, while not entirely problem free, was more compact and straight forward to use. An added incentive was that the prices of sound - on - film systems were dropping as more and more manufacturers produced new equipment, though lower prices didn't necessarily mean better reproduction, as some of the local cinema owners discovered.

The first Belfast cinema in 1930 to announce the technical changeover was the Lyric in High Street, a decision which would have pleased the building's former owner, Fred Stewart, who always favoured innovation. It installed a wholly British made system and on the 13th January presented its first talkie, a Universal production, "The Mississippi Gambler" starring Joseph Schildkraut. The advertisements described the film as "100% talking and singing." It was accompanied by a second feature, the silent "Woman From Moscow" starring Pola Negri. Though the Lyric began calling itself the "home of talkies on High Street" and invited all to come "and see and hear our talkies without effort," it actually showed a mixture of sound (all talkie), synchronised sound (part talkie) and silent films. That became the policy in many of the cheaper cinemas, indicating that the break with the silent era wasn't sudden and clean but tended to be gradual and uneven. Another characteristic of the changeover, which was widely introduced, was a rise in prices to meet the cost of the new equipment and the increased rentals for sound films. The Lyric increased its evening prices to one shilling for the stalls and one and sixpence for the balcony. On visiting the hall the Telegraph critic found the auditorium "well filled" and thought that the sound was "of good quality," which was hardly an overwhelming endorsement. In fact the system proved unsatisfactory and in November the management abandoned it and installed the new and superior American system called RCA Photophone. The initial change to sound was accompanied by modifications to the hall which allowed an increase in revenue by the addition of 26 extra seats. Those plans came under the scrutiny of the City Surveyor who insisted on certain structural changes to bring the establishment up to the latest safety standards, especially, the insertion of new steel supports to strengthen the gallery.

Five weeks later the Lyric was followed into sound by the Coliseum which presented Al Jolson again in "The Singing Fool." Like the Lyric the Coliseum installed one of the cheaper British systems and, like the High Street hall, found it ultimately unsatisfactory so that in mid - October, after sampling the superior sound being used by then in the Alhambra, it closed to install "the latest and world famous British Thompson Houston talking picture apparatus." It reopened with the very popular "Gold Diggers of Broadway" but went against the prevailing trends by keeping to separate shows, and more importantly for its patrons, by reducing its prices to 4d, 6d and one shilling. The I.S.N. welcomed that decision and expressed amazement that a film of the quality of "Gold Diggers" could be seen in the city for as little as four pence. The price reduction only reflected the increasingly harsh economic realities facing people in a city with over 70,000 unemployed, and it is significant that around the same time the main bakeries of Barney Hughes, Inglis and

Windsor reduced the price of their bread twice, bringing the cost of a 2lb loaf down to three and a half pence. The Irish News welcomed that move, which, it claimed, made the cost of the staff of life "probably the lowest in the British Isles," but wondered how long the bakeries could afford to maintain a price that was obviously "uneconomic."

The wiring for sound of the Coliseum was important socially because it brought the new technology within reach of the pockets of ordinary working people, and many who had until then just heard or read about "The Singing Fool" could at last afford to see it. During the week that the Coliseum installed sound the Lyceum on the Antrim Road announced the imminent arrival of talkies. The Curran management went for quality and decided to install Western Electric Sound. That company's representative, F.W. Gallon, duly arrived and announced that the Lyceum would be the 5,000th installation worldwide of the system. From then the cinema described itself as "a Western Electric Talkie Theatre" and encouraged the populace to come and "hear every word distinctly at the Pioneer Talkie Theatre." Obviously the sound wasn't as clear in some other cinemas as it ought to be. The Irish News critic pointed out that the staff of the Lyceum already had experience with talkies from the phonofilms they had shown, and when he attended the first presentation on the 3rd. March 1930 he admitted that he was not disappointed at the clarity of both the sound and the visuals.

The film chosen by Mr Curran was, surprisingly, the Vitaphone production "Noah's Ark" which had already been shown in the Picture House and which was only a part - talkie, the first thirty five minutes being silent. The I.S.N. mentioned that fact without comment but added that the film had other compensations, beginning with a cast of 10,000 and a running time of over two hours. It was directed by Michael Curtiz who had much experience in the making of epics and its construction followed that of other recent epics by having a Biblical section and a modern story set during the Great War. The sets and set pieces were much praised at the time, especially the building of the Tower of Babel, the orgies of a decadent lifestyle, the building of the great Ark and the Flood itself. The latter was magnificently staged in actuality without special effects, but sadly during its filming a number of extras had been injured and at least one was drowned, causing some outrage in America, though the local papers omitted those details. Adding to the visual excitement was a fine cast which included George O'Brien, Dolores Costello, Noah Beery and Myrna Loy. It is of some interest that "Noah's Ark" was reissued in late 1960 with a soundtrack added and was seen again in Belfast cinemas, though, by then, regarded more as a curio. The main film was supported by sound versions of Pathé Pictorial, Pathé News and a Mickey Mouse cartoon which caused "roars of laughter." Programmes were continuous from 2:00 pm but prices were adjusted upwards. Before 4:30 entry cost 3d to the pit, with the stalls 6d and the balcony 9d increasing in the evening to 6d, one shilling and one and sixpence. A short time later the Central in Smithfield introduced sound, with no increase in prices, though its subsequent programmes tended to alternate between silents and sound for a time.

In mid - June the people of the Falls area rejoiced when they heard that the Clonard was closing for two weeks for redecoration, and the installation of the much praised Western Electric sound system. It reopened amid great excitement on 30th June with a Fox "all talking, all singing" musical called "Sunny Side Up" starring two great favourites from the silent era, Janet Gaynor and Charles Farrell. The Irish News critic declared that the Clonard was then the most up-to-date cinema in the city and that the film was "sparkling." Despite an increase in prices so that the pit cost 4d, the stalls 6d and the balcony one shilling and three pence, long queues were the norm all week. The sound proved to be clear and the crowds came away delighted, many singing one of the film's hit songs, "If I Had a Talking Picture of You."

As 1930 progressed everybody seemed to be discussing talking pictures as they became more available, and financially accessible, to wider sections of the population. That process continued rapidly with the conversion of the Alhambra a week later, the Queen's Theatre in August, and the Mountpottinger Picturedrome and the Midland in September. Sound venues had by then spread along York Street and across the river Lagan into East Belfast. Because of its reputation and its place in the entertainment history of the city the Alhambra became the focus of much attention as to when it would change over, and its owner John Y. Moore made the most of that interest. The hall closed in early June for an overhaul that would initiate what he called "a new era" and when it reopened on Monday the 30th June 1930 at three o'clock the manager R.J. Mac Dermott welcomed elated audiences that expressed great satisfaction with the changes. The frontage had been completely remodelled into what most people associated with the Alhambra up to and after the second World War. The interior had also undergone what the I.S.N. called a "transformation" though the emphasis was still on "comfort and homeliness of atmosphere." In the lounge area the latest tip - up seats had been installed in a staggered plan so that everyone would have an uninterrupted view of the screen. The auditorium had been redecorated in cream and green and the familiar coat of arms above the proscenium with its motto Cead Mile Failte shone with a new covering of gold. The proscenium itself was decorated with painted flowers and shrubs with - indicating that Mr Moore knew his audience - a scene showing Donegall Quay and the cross channel steamers with Cave Hill in the background on the left, and Queen's Quay and the shipyard on the right, all the work of a local artist, Robert Shaw.

Mr Moore had chosen the best British sound system available, the British Thompson Houston or B.T.H. as it was known, and three engineers had travelled over from England to install it, the Alhambra being the first cinema in the city to use it. The film chosen to show it off was a comedy, "The Cock Eyed World" with Victor Mc Laglan. Prices of admission remained unchanged at 5d, 9d and one shilling, and programming also kept to the traditional two separate performances. The following week recalled the heady days of the old Alhambra with the advertisements screaming "A Big Scoop," when the cinema presented "the official and first Talking Film of a World Heavyweight championship Contest" between Sharkey and Schmelling, supported by "Speakeasy" - described as an "exciting all talking drama." A few weeks later Al Jolson's "The Singing Fool" was presented and the Irish News critic expressed some trepidation because, as he put it, Alhambra audiences could be quite "critical," and the film had already done the local rounds. The film attracted packed houses and the crowds even joined in with the songs indicating that the film "still held the public fancy." It also reflected the amazing drawing power of Al Jolson. Not all the films shown were second runs. In November the Alhambra was the first cinema in Belfast to show "The Virginian," starring Gary Cooper in his first talking role. Audiences were invited to come and "see the gripping action of those glamorous cattle ranch days...... cowboys with their red - blooded dialogue (and) stirring songs." The I.S.N. thought it was a film "that no patron could afford to miss." Cooper's dictum, directed grimly at the villain, "When you say that - smile," was to enter into the local vernacular.

In January of the following year the Alhambra presented a film with great local interest, described as "the Leviathan of Talkies," based on the sinking of the "Titanic," though that ship wasn't mentioned in the film. The advertisement solemnly advised its regular patrons "not to miss this tragic episode of the sea." The critics praised the production, describing the early scenes on a great ship, with elegant couples dancing in the ballroom while others sat on the deck or strolled in the cool evening air. Suddenly those scenes of enjoyment and contentment were disrupted by a rending crash as the ship hit an iceberg. The scenes that followed, wrote the Telegraph critic, were "inspiring" and shot "with wonderful realism." They showed women and children being transferred to the safety of lifeboats while others waited patiently. Then panic breaks out as passengers struggle to get the few remaining seats. The I.S.N. was impressed by the way the film highlighted "in a remarkable way how the certainty of death affected various people."There was special praise for one courageous clergyman who explained "how men ought to die," and for the radio operator who continued sending signals for help as the ship foundered. Those scenes evoked themes that were to reappear in later filmed versions of the sad event. The film, which had been shot at Tilbury Docks and Elstree studios, made a deep impression wherever it was shown in the city. The makers of "Atlantic,"as it was called, were among the first to face up to the divisive impact of sound on their international marketplace, and compensated by releasing the film with French, German and English soundtracks. That was an expensive and slow process, because dubbing wasn't yet available and scenes had to be filmed over again with a French or German cast.

There was by then no doubt about the warmth of the public welcome for sound, and more cinemas moved to take advantage of it. By August the Queen's Theatre in York Street had installed the equipment but also continued to include live music hall acts in its programmes. J.Y.Moore's business partner Ferris Pounds, with whom he had set up Irish Theatres Ltd., then converted the Mountpottinger Picturedrome, using the same British system that had been installed in the Alhambra. He opened on the 1st September with "The Desert Song" which, when it had been shown in the Picture House, the Irish News critic had described as "a powerful argument in favour of the talkies." He followed that with the conversion of the New Princess Palace and the presentation of "The Singing Fool" there on 3rd November. The I.S.N. critic noted how, almost immediately, sound produced an increase in audience numbers attending the Princess. Moore and Ferris showed their enthusiasm for sound by announcing at the end of October that they had purchased the Picture House in Larne and the Picture Palace in Bangor, both of which would be renovated

and wired for sound with the BHS system. They had begun to expand their cinema circuit outside the city and by the Forties would control a circuit of thirteen cinemas.

Circuits consisting of groups of cinemas had been a feature of the business since before the Great War and were organized on a national, regional or local basis. Their size gave them certain advantages over the single independent owners especially in striking more favourable rental terms for their films. The earliest examples in Belfast were those owned by Fred Stewart, and local businessman Joe Mc Kibben. By 1930 Stewart's group had been broken up and the individual cinemas either closed or sold, but the Mc Kibben family members continued to manage the original cinemas owned or built by Joe in working class areas: the Shankill Picturedrome and West End Picture House on the Shankill Road, the Midland in Canning Street and the Diamond on the Falls Road. They quickly realised that their audiences wanted sound and began the process of change with the Midland in early September, using the BTH British sound system.

When the Alhambra changed to sound it meant that there were only three downtown cinemas still using the silent format, namely the Kelvin, the Imperial and the Royal Cinema. The Imperial competed by putting on impressive double bills and emphasising the quality of its orchestra. A typical show from January 1930 consisted of King Vidor's "The Crowd," a moving and beautifully directed film about ordinary people, coupled with "The Fleet's In" starring Clara Bow. A few months later patrons could enjoy the silent version of "The Wild Party," once again with Clara Bow pursuing Fredric March, directed by Dorothy Arzner, one of the few female directors working in Hollywood, along with "The Yacht of Seven Seas" starring the striking Brigitte Helm, plus of course the Imperial Orchestra. "The Wild Party" was also filmed with sound and was Miss Bow's first talkie but, as already mentioned, silent and sound versions of major films were not unusual at the time. Greta Garbo films also appeared regularly and always attracted the crowds, but finally the Imperial owners accepted the inevitable and decided that the time had come to change. So, on the 27th October 1930 the cinema converted to sound with Ramon Navarro in "Devil May Care," parts of which were also in colour. Sadly, no more was heard of the Imperial Orchestra.

The Royal Cinema continued to fight a strong rearguard action, putting the emphasis on quality. During 1930 films of the silent greats were presented in what constituted a roll - call of the silent era and must have brought back fond memories to many of the more mature patrons. Tom Mix, Lillian Gish, Chaplin, Buster Keaton, Harold Lloyd, Rudolf Valentino, John Gilbert, Lon Chaney and D.W.Griffiths all graced the screen along with more recent personalities like Garbo, Colleen Moore, Bebe Daniels, Joan Crawford, Janet Gaynor and Charles Farrell, Clara Bow, Anna May Wong (in "Piccadilly" which also introduced Charles Laughton), and Corinne Griffiths in "The Divine Lady" based on the life of Emma Hamilton in which, according to the I.S.N., Miss Griffith's "beauty outshone her performance." With the nearby Imperial and Classic both drawing large crowds who wanted "to see and hear" the films, the Royal Cinema began to feel the cold wind of empty seats and finally gave up the struggle at the end of January 1931 when it closed, to reopen on

9th February with the Western Electric Sound System installed. The News Letter reporter expressed his sadness at seeing "the departure of the last of the large silent cinemas in Belfast" but admitted that the modified Royal Cinema was "now the equal of any" in the country. The Telegraph critic commented that until two weeks before the Royal Cinema was "the stronghold of the cream of the silent pictures" but had now successfully entered the sound era "with marked success." No mention was made of the fate of its fine orchestra that had entertained its patrons over the years.

For its first talkie the management chose a comedy, a British film, "The Middle Watch," described rather optimistically as "a sparkling story of feminine complications on board a warship," and as an "all talking, laughing success." Programming was continuous from 1: 30 pm and afternoon prices were popular at 6d and one shilling increasing after 4:00pm to one shilling and two shillings. The introductory film may not have been world shaking, and is remembered today mainly for the appearance of two actors in minor roles, who were to become very well known later as Stewart Granger and Michael Wilding. It was followed by films that are still remembered and discussed today, like "King of Jazz" with John Boles accompanied by one of the top entertainers of the period, Paul Whiteman and his Orchestra. It boasted eight hit tunes and a first brief appearance by an up - and - coming crooner called Bing Crosby. Not only was the technology changing but to the audiences' delight and excitement, the personalities also. Later that year the Royal Cinema showed an early Hitchcock, "The Skin Game," with the director's name mentioned prominently for the first time in local advertisements. In August it presented an old favourite with Charlie Chaplin's latest production, "City Lights" which ran for three weeks, followed by the Marx Bros. in "Animal Crackers" and a few months later "Morocco" starring Marlene Dietrich (with top billing), Gary Cooper and the ever polished Adolph Menjou. The Royal Cinema was to continue that policy of quality films right through the Thirties.

To those in the business, and to the weekly picturegoers, the conversion of the Royal Cinema was no real surprise but an event that occurred soon after did cause widespread surprise and debate. In June the Royal Hippodrome, the city's premier Music Hall, announced that it had been purchased by the London based circuit Associated British Cinemas which already owned about 200 cinemas across the country, and that it would close for renovation and conversion to sound, before reopening on 20th July as a Picture Palace. Prior to the final closing of its doors two special benefit nights were put on for the staff, and for the orchestra, most of whom would soon be out of work. Like other music halls the Royal Hippodrome had felt severe competition from the talkies especially from the new all singing, all dancing musicals. Throughout 1930 and ' 31 the Hippodrome l had fought back with a colourful combination of shows starring the likes of George Formby and Dick Henderson "fresh from his American vaudeville and film successes." Also prominent were well known local favourites like Cathal O'Byrne, and Jimmy O'Dea with his company from Dublin. On the occasion of the latter's Christmas Pantomime, "Babes in the Wood," in January 1931 Jimmy was accompanied by Miss Marie Mc Crystal who conducted the orchestra. The News Letter critic commented that it was a new departure to have a lady conductor and "most unusual," before adding that she performed "most efficiently."

Patrons also enjoyed a series of fast moving London revues like "Tune In," described by the I.S.N. as "new and novel," and advertised as having "a galaxy of stars, gorgeously mounted and beautifully dressed." Another London revue "Un Vent de Folle" promised all the above plus "20 dancing beauties," while "Clowns in Clover" included the Tiller Girls. "Painted Dolls" again emphasised its full London company, including "lovely and alluring girls, girls, girls (in) original costumes and whirlwind dances." It is easy to detect the spectre of the attractions that Hollywood was offering, lurking in the background and finally in November 1930 it came out into the open when a Revue arrived which included two dancers called Al and Val Reno, and much was made, by way of recommendation, of the fact that they had danced in "The Gold Diggers of Broadway," a film which the I.S.N. commented "had taken exceptionally well in Belfast." Again, in the following March, when it was announced that Sophie Tucker was coming, she was described in the same paper as being "known only from the talkies until now." That was a reference to the film "Honky Tonk" which had shown in the Classic and other cinemas the year before, but the News Letter pointed out that she was also a household word from her gramophone records, which, of course, were easily and readily available in the city shops.

Miss Tucker arrived quietly from Dublin where she had had a "rapturous welcome" (News Letter) the week before. When the curtains parted on Monday evening in the Royal Hippodrome the audience was "devastatingly enthusiastic" (Telegraph) and welcomed her with three minutes of clapping, to which she responded with a performance that was "full of verve and vitality." She sang the songs associated with her from her gramophone records and films, including "The Last of the Red Hot Mamas," and "I'm Doin' What I'm Doin' for Love" (from "Honky Tonk") while the audience shouted and clapped their appreciation. The Irish News writer was impressed by the rapport she built up with the audience, who responded to many of her songs with "unmeasured enthusiasm." He was particularly taken by the way that she could be funny at her own expense. At the end of the evening she thanked the audience and explained that before coming on stage she had been worried about how her special brand of American song and humour would go down in Belfast, but the response had made her "very happy indeed." She then asked what she should sing for an encore and the audience replied with "one vast shout" (Telegraph) "Tall, Dark and Handsome." According to reports everyone, including the singer, the audience and the critics were happy at the results.

Films had flourished originally within the embrace of music hall but by 1930 the talkies were beginning to silence the latter, and the Royal Hippodrome only followed the path other music halls had already taken. The Empire noted what was happening but, as the only true music hall left in the city, was determined to hold on and survive with live entertainment. Typical Empire fare included appearances by Richard Hayward, Cathal O'Byrne or Jimmy O'Dea. The latter presented a revue called, "Irish Smiles," (March 1930) which promised, among other delights, to solve the Border Question. The Irish News praised it as "a splendid skit on a thorny subject" and drew special attention to a hilarious sequence where Jimmy showed how to deal with a Custom's Officer on the border. The I.S.N. praised Jimmy's skill as a comedian and described the show as "glorious entertainment ...... without a dull or discordant note from start to finish," which "kept the audience in roars of laughter." The Empire retained a certain flexibility in its programming, and didn't entirely ignore or disdain the use of technical attractions. It followed Jimmy O'Dea with an attraction called "Recordia" (April 1930) which it described as "the greatest novelty of the century." It was however more of a gimmick which recognised the growing popularity of the gramophone. It actually involved members of the audience performing and making their own records on stage to take home, while at the same time competing for free gramophones.

Films weren't entirely ignored either and a few months later, in November, the hall had a successful showing of a silent documentary "Cape to Cairo" presented in person by its maker, the explorer F.N. Redhead. The Empire management were neither out - of - date or old - fashioned with that decision because they had detected that there was still an audience for silent documentaries in the city, especially if they had an educational aspect. In January 1931 the Grosvenor Hall showed "In the Land of the Lion" a silent documentary made by Cherry Kearton about wild animal life in Central Africa. Tickets, available at Erskine Mayne's, were quite expensive at 1/3d, 2/6d (res.) and 6d for children, but the hall was crowded nevertheless. Mr Kearton, an experienced explorer and film maker, already well known in the city from his earlier films, appeared personally on stage describing and explaining the filmed sequences and, according to the News Letter reporter, he transported his audience via an excellent commentary from "the rain and fog of Belfast to the sun and heat of Africa." He clarified the ecology of the region and illustrated the part that each animal played in it, while also discussing the problems and dangers faced by a film maker like himself who, he emphasised, never carried a rifle. He would have been quite at home on television today.

The papers of the day were already carrying reports about the feasibility of television, and one in the I.S.N. went so far as to suggest that it would be the entertainment of the future in the form of a set "sitting on the living room table," - an idea received locally with some scepticism. A few weeks later the YMCA Hall in Wellington Place presented another, but contrasting, silent documentary on "Palestine" which dealt with the people of that area and their problems, illustrated by showing sequences filmed in the main centres like Jerusalem, Bethlehem, and Nazareth, along with traditional scenes of rural life. The commentary, on stage, was by T.H.Baxter FRGS. The News Letter critic praised its educational value, especially "for all students of the Bible" and, as expected, it drew packed houses. But despite those successes the thrust towards sound continued, with the Hippodrome just the latest to take the step in that direction.

The new owners, Associated British Cinemas Ltd., took nearly a month over the conversion. The architect W.R.Glen thankfully retained as much of the old theatre as he reasonably could, but had to make some changes. A new entrance was opened on Great Victoria Street leading directly into the ground floor with access to the stalls, which were modified to improve the viewing quality of the 1000 seats it contained. Above it the circle, the most expensive area, had 520 seats while above that again the steeply raked gallery, where one had to move carefully in the darkness, had 550 seats. The prices were attractive for a luxurious downtown cinema at one shilling, 6d and 3d in the afternoon rising after 4:30 pm to 1/6d, one shilling and 6d. A reporter from the Whig visited the hall during the week preceding the official opening to see how the work was proceeding. He described groups of workers installing new plush tip - up seats even in the pit where the old wooden forms had been removed. Women were at work with needles and thread on the carpets and a painter was varnishing a wooden trellis that had been placed over the former orchestra pit. That trellis, as was the norm in most converted halls, would soon be covered with containers of flowers and plants. The stage was bare and empty except for a large, "gaunt" white screen. His emotions were very mixed as he viewed the scene. He recalled the many occasions when he had witnessed the hall packed with audiences laughing and reacting to the music and the antics of "singers, dancers, comedians, conjurers and jugglers." He had always admired the acoustics where the lowest whisper on stage could be heard quite clearly in "the gods." Now, he added, there was only "a bare white screen, stretched taut on its framework, lifeless before a silent house."

That silence ended on the following Monday (July 20th.) when the doors opened to admit a large and expectant crowd who admired the luxurious surroundings and expressed "delight" (Whig) at the clarity and distinctness of the dialogue. The new owners promised that they would show the best of British films and that they would be presented in comfort and with technical excellence. The best equipment available had been installed with a combination of Western Electric Sound using a single Roxy speaker, Ross projectors, high intensity arcs, and a special rubberised gauze screen for extra brightness. Where possible local craftsmen, materials and labour were used in the conversion, and George Dobler was reappointed as manager, a popular and very visual connection with the former theatre. The prefix Royal was dropped, and the opening of the Hippodrome Picture Palace brought the addition of a first class hall to the downtown entertainment scene. It was widely praised and the Newsletter reporter encapsulated the general opinion when he declared that it was "the last word in cinema comfort," though he regretted that the inaugural films weren't British. The films chosen for the occasion were American, a version of Tolstoy's "Resurrection" with John Boles and Lupe Velez, plus Universal's "Bad Sisters" which is remembered today as the film which introduced another new personality, Bette Davis, to local audiences.

The public continued to make it clear that they wanted sound and as more owners and managers reacted to that pressure by converting their cinemas the number and variety of sound films available to audiences increased. Silent films were still being shown in the city and there was a steady flow of synchronised productions. Even old silent successes were "updated" in the hope of milking extra profits from them. In July 1932 the Clonard and the Lyceum showed the reissue of "Ben Hur" with the added attraction of the chariot race enhanced by "the thunder of hooves, the rattling of wheels, the crack of whips and the cheers of frenzied spectators" (I.S.N.). In the studios development in sound recording went ahead quite rapidly and the local critics often commented on the improved clarity of speech and technical efficiency of the new films. The sound cameras were beginning to recover their former fluidity and mobility so that films were beginning to "move" again and as directors became more confident some films of distinction began to appear. Shakespeare was seen as suitable material for sound and Mary Pickford and Douglas Fairbanks made a version of "The Taming of the Shrew" which showed in the Lyceum and Clonard in March 1931, advertised as "the screen's most famous lovers in their first talking picture together." The Irish News critic recommended it for retaining Shakespeare's dialogue, but added the proviso that the producers had filmed it solely as a comedy and that it succeeded mainly on that level. Purists probably preferred to wait for the Bard until the following January, when Sir Frank Benson came to the Opera House on a farewell tour as part of a special Shakespearean Festival.

Of more significance cinematically was the arrival of the Oscar winning "All Quiet on the Western Front" (d. Lewis Milestone, 1930) in the Picture House on 19th January, two months before Miss Pickford, when it played for two weeks to packed houses. To highlight the theme of the film the cinema directors invited patients, former soldiers, from Craigavon Hospital to attend the first performance. Over thirty accepted and were greeted by the manager C.F. O'Dowda, who saw that they were comfortably seated and attended to. Others who were unable to leave the hospital were given cigarettes by the "Not Forgotten" Association. Based on a novel by Erich Maria Remarque the film gave a view of the Great War from the German point of view. It is still widely accepted today as one of the strongest anti-war statements to appear on screen, though it was, as the Irish News pointed out, banned at the time in Germany. The critics, describing it as "eagerly awaited," welcomed it enthusiastically with the I.S.N. commenting that it was "worth studying and thinking about." They recognised it as a serious attempt to translate an important novel to the screen and on that account advised their readers not to miss it. Audience reaction was suitably serious but the film's unrelenting depiction of trench warfare must have brought back painful memories to former soldiers, who would surely have approved of the fact that it was "dedicated to those who were destroyed in the war" (News Letter). The acting was widely praised but, above all, the film impressed audiences with its "remarkable impression of life during war years" (News Letter) and with its scenes of battle. The Irish News critic noted it had moments of romance but that in the main it dealt with "the remorseless side of life and death." He found it "an unforgettable experience" which left "deep memories." The Telegraph critic was impressed by the acting and the "stupendous scale" of the production and concluded that overall it presented "an accurate picture of Remarque's sensational work." The realism of the scenes in the trenches and on the battlefield proved too much for some viewers, and a writer in the Irish News described how he had felt his skin "creep" at the horrors which were shown on the screen "almost too graphically." That didn't stop it being shown to large audiences across the city in the Lyceum, the Clonard and the Alhambra, among others.

But the war was already receding into history and for some, especially the young, its impact was less immediate. While "All Quiet...." was drawing in the more serious filmgoers others were enjoying, at the same time, in the Classic, a comedy with Leslie Fuller called "Not so Quiet on the Western Front," while the Royal Hippodrome (not yet converted to films) was staging "All Right on the Western Front," proclaiming it as the "funniest" war burlesque ever. A writer in the I.S.N. continued in that lighter vein, using the title as an excuse to comment on the many advertisements around the city, selling films and everything from sunlight soap to Guinness. Referring to them as "the poor man's picture gallery," he praised their pictorial merits but found their juxtaposition often unintentionally amusing. He mentioned strolling along Royal Avenue past the Picture House with its impressive frontage which included a neon sign proclaiming it as "the House of Perfect Sound, "while just below it that there was another advert which read "All Quiet...."

While "All Quiet On The Western Front" was, as the Irish News put it, "arousing widespread interest," the Imperial presented another serious film, the M-G-M version of Eugene O'Neill's "Anna Christie," starring Greta Garbo. It arrived preceded by widespread praise and was described modestly in the cinema foyer as "the most eagerly awaited event in Screendom." There was no mention of the famous advert "Garbo Talks" though the main popular attraction of the film was that it was indeed her first talkie. The News Letter critic thought the production lived up to its reputation in every way. He praised both the "realistic settings" of old New York's dockland and Garbo's acting which he found "very clever." The Irish News critic went further, praising Clarence Brown's direction, Eugene O'Neill's dialogue and, above all, Miss Garbo's performance. He thought that "this intensely emotional actress" was excellent in the role and that "even her voice with the slight Swedish accent" was perfectly suited to the part. Only when the film transferred to the Mountpottinger Picturedrome was it advertised as Garbo's first talking picture. In the film Garbo played a former prostitute who returns home but has to reveal her past life to her new Irish boyfriend. When it reached the Coliseum some time later it carried the warning "For Adults Only," which suggests that there had been some local criticism of its content.

While such films were stimulating serious discussion in intellectual and academic circles the vast majority of people took a more relaxed approach to the cinema. As numerous writers in the local press pointed out, the conversations in the queues were usually about more mundane or trivial matters like the wardrobes and personal lives of the stars. Audiences, out for an evening's entertainment, enjoyed the many comedies available with the added attraction that they could now hear as well as see old favourites like Harold Lloyd, Buster Keaton, Will Rogers, Laurel and Hardy. New faces and voices had appeared too, including Joe E. Brown, Andy Clyde, Jimmy "Schnozzle" Durante, Jack Hulbert and the Marx Brothers. When the latter's first two films, "Cocoanuts"(Picture House, April 1930) and "Animal Crackers" (Royal Cinema, Oct. 1931) arrived here, critics and audiences were introduced to a new zany humour that depended for its effect on both visuals and verbals. Fans were soon reeling off the names of the four brothers, Groucho, Chico, Harpo and Zeppo, described by the Irish News critic as the funniest men in the world. Westerns also drew large crowds to see stars like Gary Cooper and Richard Dix, Tom Mix, Ken Maynard and Buck Jones who were now talking (drawling !) as well as shooting. For the first time the posters outside the Classic for "The Big Trail" (June 1931) proclaimed a new star, a tall lean man in a wide brimmed Stetson and fringed buckskins, called John Wayne. The Western heroes attracted widespread approval because they stood for positive values like good and fair-mindedness which they struggled to apply in a healthy outdoor environment, in contrast to the much criticised cinematic gangsters who projected evil, greed and violence in enclosed and often depressing urban surroundings.

Audiences were soon appreciating fast - moving crime stories dominated by the edgy acting and terse snarling speech of James Cagney, Edward G. Robinson, Paul Muni, George Raft and Chester Morris among others. When Warner's "Little Caesar" (d. Mervyn Leroy, 1930) showed in the Hippodrome, before moving on to the Lyceum and Alhambra, the I.S.N. praised Robinson's "splendid performance," while the Irish News commented that "it showed the gangster as he really was." The film detailed the bloody rise and fall of Rico

Bandello, to the final scene when Edward G. Robinson expiring from gunshot wounds, rejected and forgotten by all, asks in disbelief: Mother of Mercy, is this the end of Rico? It certainly wasn't the end of the gangster film, with classics like "Public Enemy" (d. William Wellman, 1931) and "Scarface" (d. Howard Hawks,1932) quickly following. The not so well known "Up the River" went over well in the city, introducing two new personalities, Spencer Tracy and Humphrey Bogart, to audiences. The picture was originally intended as a tough story about convicts but the director, John Ford, saw it more as a comedy and that was how it was received locally. The critics welcomed Spencer Tracy for his skill as "a comedian" but made no mention at all of Bogart. "Dance, Fools, Dance" described as "a stirring drama of the underworld" starred Joan Crawford and Cliff Edwards with a relatively new actor called Clarke Gable who greatly impressed the local critics. There were also fresh female faces to admire, but behind their good looks they were a new breed of tough, sharp tongued ladies or "broads" as the gangster slang would have it. They included Barbara Stanwyck, Ann Dvorak, Ida Lupino, Joan Blondell, Jean Harlow (a woman of "unusual beauty" according to the Irish News) and Mae Clarke, the latter famously on the receiving end of a breakfast grapefruit from James Cagney in "Public Enemy." Belfast audiences didn't see that particular scene until many years later, because the censor at the time decided it made unsuitable viewing, and removed it.

In the years that followed, the well reported exploits of Al Capone, Dillinger, Legs Diamond and others provided a fertile soil for stories involving the struggles between gangsters and the forces of law and order represented by crusading district attorneys, the police, and the F.B.I. There were those in society who shuddered at the depiction of violence, the drinking in speakeasies, the gambling, the sexual immorality, and the political corruption shown in those films, which they felt had a deleterious effect on the youth, especially by way of what they saw as the glorification of the gangster. Others saw them as a type of morality tale in urban surroundings offering a warning to youth that crime did not pay. Both those contrasting views were to come together much later in the enigmatic ending to "Angels With Dirty Faces" (d. Michael Curtiz, 1938), as tough guy James Cagney is dragged off, screaming and protesting, to face execution. The local critics accepted the films as serious attempts to deal with a modern American phenomenon, but many in Belfast would have agreed with the Rev. H. Atchinson, the pastor of Donegall Pass Presbyterian Church who, in a lecture on the cinema in January 1933, complained that gangster films were "'" leading young men to crime."

Of all the genres available on screen it was the new "all talking, all singing, all dancing" musicals, many of them partly or completely in colour, that audiences rushed to see. The earliest Jolson films were musicals of a kind and they were followed by filmed stage musicals and musical comedies like "Showboat," "The Desert Song" and "Rio Rita." When "The Desert Song" came to the Picture House in January 1930 it caused great excitement among critics and audiences. It ran for four weeks, showing to packed houses, and made John Boles, who played the Red Shadow, the talk of the city. The later "Rio Rita" was another success for him and audiences were delighted to discover that the female lead, Bebe Daniels, also had a fine and pleasant singing voice. Throughout 1931 audiences who wouldn't normally go to the theatre had their cultural horizons widened with the opportunities to enjoy good quality music and superior singing in "New Moon" with Laurence Tibbett and Grace Moore (Imperial) wherein they sang that "entrancing duet" (Irish News) called "Wanting You," or Romberg's "Viennese Nights" (Picture House), or "No No Nanette" (Lyceum), or "The Vagabond King" with Jeannette MacDonald. Seen today many of those films seem static and stagey but audiences of the day flocked to them, obviously enjoying the music and the singing, and demanded more.

Equally popular were the revue films in which the main studios competed with each other to show off the talent on their books. The first film of that type to reach Belfast opened in the Classic in March 1930 and was called the "Hollywood Revue of 1929," produced by M-G-M. It boasted 25 stars who took part in a series of singing and dancing acts, comedy sketches and other novelties. The various acts were introduced by the comedian Jack Benny, who also played his violin. A typical sequence involved a miniaturised Bessie Love who appeared out of Benny's waistcoat pocket before becoming full sized to sing and dance. Laurel and Hardy raised laughs as fumbling jugglers, Marion Davies sang along with marching soldiers, Buster Keaton clowned as only he could, Joan Crawford sang "Low Down Rhythm" and, in colour, Norma Shearer and John Gilbert played the balcony scene from "Romeo and Juliet." The scene was played twice, once using Shakespeare's dialogue, followed by a modern version using flapper slang. The climax of the film was in colour, an elaborate dance number involving chorus girls and the stars built around the song "Singing in the Rain," which the Telegraph described as "a notable event." The song itself was also sung elsewhere in the film by Cliff Edwards, better known as Ukelele Ike. Edwards was a major performer on Broadway but was known locally to collectors of gramophone records. He sang with a decided American "twang" but that only increased his appeal locally. Over the next twenty years he appeared in over 100 films and became a familiar face and voice on local cinema screens. "Singing in the Rain" was to go on to greater things with Gene Kelly, but in 1930 it still caused quite a stir in Belfast and anyone with 1 / 6 d to spare - and a gramophone - could buy a recording of it. The Classic management added to the fun by having their front - of - house staff wear colourful rainwear while the film was showing, which provoked much mirth and comment among the patrons.

About six months later the Picture House screened Warner Bros response, called "Show of Shows." Filmed in colour, and compered by the so called "profile," John Barrymore, it claimed to include 77 stars and was advertised as "a hundred shows in one." The I.S.N. was impressed and described it as "fine entertainment." The Irish News critic found it enjoyable but a little too much for one sitting. It was "a bewildering sequence of acts by scores of famous cinema stars '' with everything from the serious (Shakespeare) to jazz. He picked out two items for special praise, the musical number "A Bicycle Built for Two," and "A Chinese Fantasy." The latter was an elaborately staged number, introduced by no less than Rin Tin Tin, which involved Myrna Loy as a dancing Chinese princess, and Nick Lucas a popular crooner of the day, backed by a chorus of "one hundred Oriental beauties." That sequence can still be seen and admired today because it turned up recently in WB's vaults and is now available on DVD. Other examples arrived from Paramount - "Paramount on Parade" introduced by Jack Oakie, in the Classic, April 1931 - and other studios but they all followed the same general format. The best remembered is "King of Jazz" with John Boles again, and

Paul Whiteman and his Band. The Irish News critic thought it was "tuneful .... delightful."

The third type of musical was the backstage story which intercut a story about the lives of the performers with singing and dancing numbers. They presented a stratum of society very different from anything experienced in Belfast, teeming with fast - talking, wise - cracking chorus girls, ambitious singers and dancers, distraught producers and directors, monied ladies and gentlemen and a whole range of gangsters, gamblers and other unattractive individuals. It was a world that disturbed many local mature people, and they criticised the films as loud, noisy and vulgar, the music as cheap, the dancing as indecorous, and the whole atmosphere of obvious sex and pursuit of money as morally dubious. However, like the gangster films, the general audiences didn't take them so seriously, seeing them essentially as good undemanding entertainment, and, as a consequence, queued up in large numbers to see them. The early Jolson films were of that type and they were quickly followed by "Broadway Melody" from MGM which ran for three weeks at the Picture House (Sept. 1929). It was the story of two sisters from out of town played by Bessie Love and Anita Page, who arrive in New York and quickly lose their illusions about show business. The story line has been much copied in later musicals but "Broadway Melody" is significant in that it was the first film to have had music and songs especially written for it. It arrived in Belfast after winning the Academy Award for best picture and was advertised as having "the song hits you will want to hear again." It broke all records at the Picture House with reports of long queues and packed houses. The Irish News critic praised its song and dance numbers especially "You Were Meant for Me" and "The Wedding of the Painted Doll," which, he wrote, were put across "in a real American way."

That was what audiences appreciated and they responded wholeheartedly again when Warner's "Gold Diggers of Broadway" - the epitome of back stage musicals according to the I.S.N,. - appeared in the Picture House in August 1930. It ran for four weeks and the management apologised "to the thousands who had to be turned away." As a result of its popularity it was brought back to the same cinema in December, "by special request," for another crowded week. Filmed completely in colour it was greeted as "the brightest, most tuneful and most entertaining of all recent musicals." The I.S.N. summed it up as "magnificent" while the Irish News found it "hilarious and fast moving," which together reflected the general local critical reaction. The I.S.N., always ready to be of assistance to its readers, explained "for the unsophisticated" that "a gold digger was a girl who seeks to deprive gilded youth of as much money as possible." The story concerned the adventures of three such ladies in show business played by Ann Pennington, Winnie Lightner and Nancy Welford, names that would ring no bells today. The story was told," with many flashes of humour and some shades of satire," (I.S.N.) the whole enhanced by tuneful music and songs. The Irish News critic enjoyed the latter, picking out "Painting the Clouds with Sunshine," and "Tiptoe Through the Tulips with Me" for special praise.

Backstage musicals became regular visitors to the city. Universal's "Broadway" introduced a new twist with its story of a dancer who innocently becomes involved in a murder. The film was for the main part in black and white, but, by contrast, the local critics were impressed by the imaginative use of colour used in the nightclub scenes. "Queen of the Nightclubs" which starred former Western star Texas Guinan was described as "rich in incidents," while the Picture House once again experienced packed houses with Warner's " On With the Show," a backstage story with "wisecracking dialogue." The film starred Betty Compson, in her first major talkie, ably supported by comedian Joe E. Brown and a chorus of "100 Beautiful Girls." Miss Compson had always been popular with Belfast audiences but her career had been in decline recently and she hadn't graced local screens for some time. That had changed in the Thirties, and her career had been revitalised, because she was one of the silent actresses who took naturally to the new technology and actually benefited from sound. The critics welcomed the film with its by now familiar story of an understudy who goes on to success when she replaces the overbearing leading lady. It was Warner's first all colour musical and the Irish News critic was suitably impressed, describing it as "a riot of colour." Miss Compson was soon welcomed back in another musical, "The Street Girl."

The craze for musicals ended in America at the beginning of the Thirties, but the films continued to arrive regularly in Belfast because the time lag between their release in the U.S. and their appearance in the city was about twelve months. But no matter how beautiful the girls, how talented the performers, how tuneful the music and how glowing the colours, there came a time when people began looking for something different. When "The Rainbow Man," starring Marion Nixon, arrived in the Classic it was warmly welcomed by the critics as a different type of musical. The Telegraph critic expressed relief that it wasn't just another series of "illustrated gramophone records." He and the other critics were relieved and delighted to enjoy "a refreshingly human romance" in which there was "no vamp, no other man and no questionable scenes." Another musical that was greeted in a similar manner was Paramount's "Innocents of Paris" (Picture House, Feb. 1930) which introduced Maurice Chevalier, that gift to local imitators. The gentle story of Parisian life delighted audiences, though the main attraction of the film was Chevalier himself. The Irish News critic thought that he had a charming personality superbly suited to talking pictures and, above all, a fine singing voice. Many patrons who had found Jolson's aggressive personality a bit overwhelming agreed, and there was much praise for his singing of "Louise," recordings of which were soon selling like hot cakes in the local record shops. The Telegraph critic noted that he sang effortlessly in both French and English which he thought was "quite a feature" while adding that his acting was "very clever." The I.S.N. reviewer had the last word, describing the film as "a refreshing entertainment."

The musical that really broke the mould, as far as Belfast was concerned, was "Song o' My Heart," the first talkie to be made in Ireland, which arrived in the Picture House in September 1930. The citizens were well prepared because the local newspapers had carried details about its making, mainly because it starred John McCormack whom the papers didn't hesitate to call "the world's greatest tenor." John McCormack, born in Athlone, had become one of the world's best known singers whose name was mentioned in the same company as Gigli and Caruso. He had a wide following in Belfast and his concerts were always "full house" affairs. He had, over the years, visited the city many times, most recently in 1929 when he came twice (in January and May) and received the usual warm welcome. The papers had written then about his interest in performing in one of the new talkies. He later signed a contract with William Fox to make a film in Ireland which he promised would not include any stage Irish characters. The director Frank Borzage, whose wife came from Dublin, supported him in that aim. The announcement was welcomed throughout Ireland where there had been growing, and sometimes aggressive, criticism of how the Irish were depicted on screen. Hitchcock's recent "Juno and the Paycock," despite featuring Abbey actors, had been much criticised in the Free State and a copy had actually been seized by a group of men in Limerick and burned.

Frank Borgaze didn't intend to enter any delicate political territory and supporters of the film pointed out that the location shooting, mainly around Bray, would encourage the tourist trade by highlighting the beautiful natural scenery. The filming began in August giving employment to Abbey actors like J.M.Kerrigan and a new discovery, Maureen O'Sullivan, but the main attraction was John McCormack, or to be more accurate, his voice, and his admirers were not disappointed. He sang eleven songs including the title song, plus A Pair of Blue Eyes, Kitty My Love, Paddy Me Lad and Little Boy Blue. The critics agreed that the film was excellent entertainment and the public obviously supported their opinions because it ran for four weeks to packed houses before transferring to the Clonard, where it was eagerly awaited, and where it ran for another three weeks. At the end of that run the Irish News reported that the cinema was "still packed." In January 1931 it reached the Coliseum for another successful week and the I.S.N. critic recommended it as "a rare treat for those who love good singing." When the Duncairn changed to sound two months later it chose "Song o' My Heart" as its inaugural talkie presentation, describing it warmly as "the soul of Ireland revealed in song and scena." The story was rather sentimental and concerned a singer, played by McCormack, who gives up his career when the girl he loves is forced to marry another man, who proves to be a bad husband who later abandons her with their children. The hero secretly saves them from ruin with the proceeds from a song recital he gives. There were reports of tear - filled eyes in the audience as the plot progressed. The Irish News critic described the story as "a delightful lyrical romance" and praised its "clean humour." He extolled McCormack's singing but said nothing about the other actors with the exception of newcomer Maureen O'Sullivan whom he described as "a pretty young Dublin girl who played the heroine with charming effect." The refreshing naturalness of the proceedings was noted, and the I.S.N. compared the Irish accents favourably with the "American twang" usually heard in the cinemas.

Today "Song o' My Heart" is not regarded as a great film, but its combination of a simple story with strong Christian virtues, John McCormack's superb voice, Irish characters who acted in a normal everyday manner, and a background of fine scenery made it irresistible to audiences of the day. Over the years its memory faded but not that of its young heroine. Some critics felt, probably correctly, that Maureen O'Sullivan's lack of experience showed in her performance, but most agreed that it was due to the fact that it was only her first film. She had been born in Boyle, Co. Roscommon but educated in England before being spotted in Dublin by the director Frank Borgaze. Under contract to William Fox she made a number of undistinguished films like "The Princess and the Plumber" which showed in the Clonard in April 1932. After moving to M-G-M, she burst upon the cinema scene as Jane in "Tarzan the Apeman" (d. Woody Van Dyke, 1932) which arrived in the Classic in

October 1932. Described on the poster outside the cinema as "Ireland's Own Star" she was teamed with "the Swimming Adonis" and five times Olympic gold medal winner Johnny Weissmuller in what was to be the first of five Tarzan films. Later of course she was to marry the director John Farrow and become famous again as the mother of Mia Farrow.

The nearest that Maureen O'Sullivan came to music in the Tarzan film was the incessant chattering of Cheetah (a nasty and spiteful animal, according to the lady), and the famous melodious call of the hero as he swung through the trees, a sound that soon became part of the local scene as youngsters vied with each other trying to replicate it. The author remembers, as a boy in the Forties, often hearing the Tarzan call echoing through the trees in the Falls Park or along the streets off the Springfield Road. That desire to copy or replicate what had been seen and heard in the cinema was widespread and much commented upon at the time, and for the most part was regarded as innocuous. It represented an attempt to relive the enjoyment of what had been seen on the screen. There were, however, criticisms that young persons in particular sometimes admired and copied things that were not so innocuous. With regard to the new musicals and the gangster stories complaints were often aired about the pollution of local speech with the American slang that was so prevalent in those films.

Critics pointed out, with disapproval, that girls and ladies were referred to as dames, and addressed as honey, baby or sugar. A gangster's ladyfriend was a moll and the gangsters themselves used a gat or rod to rub out opponents. Typical was an article in the News Letter in June 1931 under the heading "Ulster and the Cinema," with a sub heading "Cuties and Kiddos." After reiterating the statement, almost a cliché by then, that the talkies had become a dominant part of the entertainment scene, the writer pointed out that large numbers of people were in the habit of visiting the cinema at least once per week, and that what they watched were mainly films of American origin. Continued exposure to American culture in that way was, he felt, having a deleterious effect on their language. He deplored the use in everyday speech of yeah for yes, and the habit of addressing individuals as kid, cutie or sweetie. One can detect an approach to apoplexy as he recalled hearing a local young man's farewell to his lady love, with the words "goodbye, good - looking." The newspapers approached the matter with differing levels of seriousness. The I.S.N., which had such fun guying the lifestyle of flappers, tended to take a rather frivolous attitude towards the new idiom. A typical cartoon in January 1931 showed an "old - fashioned young man" addressing his ladyfriend rather seriously: Darling, may I kiss your hand? To that request a casual "modern Jane" replies: Sure, kid. Hop to it. But mind you don't burn your nose on my cigarette. Some time later a commentator in the same paper admitted, more seriously, that continued exposure to the new slang was undermining traditional speech. He described his surprise at hearing a mature citizen address his wife as "baby" and noted that the man in question got an Arctic stare in return. But the young people took to the new means of expression with enthusiasm. An irate letter writer complained that he had recently been in the Great Northern Railway where a group of young people, their conversation peppered with the new slang, were seeing some friends off on holiday. If he had closed his eyes, he wrote, he could have been listening to a scene from a Hollywood film.

The musicals had an immediate and more positive impact on the local music scene.

Everyone seemed keen to hear and even to sing the popular tunes from the films and one result of that was an impressive increase in business in the record shops. Patrons who flocked during 1931 to the Classic, Lyric, Clonard and other venues across the city to see "Sunny Side Up" greatly enjoyed its hit song "If I Had a Talking Picture of You," an ambition that was out of the financial reach of most of them. Today it is possible to enjoy a favourite film again by obtaining such a "talking picture" on DVD, but in the Thirties fans remembered their films by collecting photographs of the stars, cuttings from newspapers and film magazines, or sometimes by buying front-of-house stills. Most stills were in black and white but a number of beautiful hand - tinted examples have survived and to get one of those must have been quite a prize. Very few people collected posters and the manager of the Curzon on the Ormeau Road recalled for the author how during the late Thirties and into the Forties old posters were sometimes disposed of by being spread out on the floor like carpet and walked over before being dumped.

The most immediate way to recall a musical film in the Thirties was to buy gramophone records of the songs and music from it. A symbiotic relationship based on a mutual desire to sell their products grew up at an early stage between the new talkies and the established gramophone companies. It was the record industry which had first introduced the benefits of electrical recording to the public. As early as October 1927 Smyth's. "the Gramophone Specialists," located in Queen's Arcade advertised Columbia records, produced by a new process of electrical recording which gave clear reproduction "without scratches." The double sided shellac records sold at three shillings each. The other gramophone and record shops, like the newly opened Premier Records in Smithfield, the Anglo-American Gramophone Company in Rosemary Street, Johnsons in Gresham Street and York Street, the Grosvenor Gramophone Salon at 16, Grosvenor Road, the Star Music Stores in Royal Avenue and Church Lane, and Crymbles in Wellington Place were soon stocking and selling electrically recorded products. The records were grouped for sale into classical, sacred and religious, Irish (John McCormack was the great favourite) and popular, and free publicity exhibitions of new records were put on for the public in halls like the Y.M.C.A. in Wellington Place. The companies also took advantage of the periodic Wireless and Gramophone Exhibitions that were held in the Ulster Hall to advertise the latest technical developments in the industry.

The local newspapers were quick to introduce weekly Gramophone columns, described variously as Chats, Notes or such, which kept their readers up-to-date on the equipment and the recent releases. Those who could afford them, mainly the middle classes, bought the latest records and gramophones. At the upper end of the range expensive elaborate cabinet type gramophones began to replace the traditional pianos in middle class parlours. Those who couldn't afford such equipment could still hear the latest records played on the Panotropes in those cinemas that had them while the Empire Theatre, recognising a popular trend, played popular records between the live acts. Outside the record shops groups of citizens could be seen loitering, without criminal intent, listening to the music wafting out from the interior. Inside the shops, which by 1930 were describing themselves grandly as "salons," there were listening booths where the latest music could be experienced in comfort and silence.

People were therefore quite familiar with recorded sounds before the talkies arrived in the Picture House. Those who saw "The Singing Fool" there were not surprised that they could also buy recordings, supplied by the Star Music Stores, of Jolson singing the songs from the film, in the cinema itself as well as in the city shops. The cultural and economic links between the record industry and the cinema were highlighted from the first days of the sound film in Belfast. The talkies, especially the musicals, had a dramatic impact on the sale of popular records. As each new film arrived songs from it went on sale in the gramophone shops and adverts in the papers reminded the population of the fact, though, from reports, people didn't need any encouragement to buy. As the market expanded the competition increased and new venues opened. Typical was Polland's which opened at 18, High Street in February 1930, described as a bright cheerful salon with private audition rooms. They stocked "all the latest" records.

The event which probably had the most impact on the local trade was the opening in November 1929 of the Cliftophone Salons at 110, Upper North Street, "next to the gas office," which supplied both cash customers and the trade. Cliftophone sold a bargain label called Piccadilly, double sided 10 inch (26 cms) discs, at only one shilling and sixpence, which was half the price of a recording from Decca, HMV, Brunswick, Parlophone or Columbia. Such was the initial rush for their products that their shelves were cleared within a few hours, but they promised that they would be restocked with "shiploads" of recordings within a few days. Cliftophone had a comprehensive and aggressive advertising policy, and always had the hits from the latest musicals showing in the city, on sale. By the end of January 1931 they were selling new Warner Brunswick recordings "by original cinema stars," using the slogan "follow the stars on Brunswick." Other salons quickly followed in their footsteps. The Central Music Stores in Gresham Street claimed that it stocked "all the latest talkie hits" though it also highlighted recordings by Irish artistes like Jimmy O'Dea, who appeared personally to autograph his records, and by locals like Cathal O'Byrne (whose Belfast dialect was emphasised), Richard Hayward and gospel singer Carson Andrews.

The Gresham Street store also offered gramophones to play them on, costing only one pound, while the Grosvenor Gramophone Salon had models at an equally reasonable price of fifty shillings (two pounds fifty). What the quality of reproduction was like was not mentioned but cheaper equipment meant that popular music was heard increasingly both indoors and outdoors at parties, in parks, on beaches and at picnics, something that not everyone appreciated. That trend was further facilitated when prices of the records also fell with Shearer's of Smithfield offering Decca records for 1|6 each while Hart and Churchill of Wellington Place sold quality Columbia recordings for 2|6 each. The local critics often noted the link between records and films and one (Telegraph) sometimes referred to some musicals disparagingly as "illustrated gramophone records." Even the rather staid Belfast Museum wasn't unaware of what was happening. On Saturday mornings the museum usually presented free programmes of educational films, which always attracted large crowds. Included in one selection, in January 1931, was a sound film which was much appreciated by the audience. It detailed the steps by which a gramophone record was produced from the factory floor to the recording studio. Sound was becoming ubiquitous.

Cowboys, gangsters, singers and dancers weren't the only characters to inhabit the cinema screens. The talking detective was a great favourite and William Powell was greeted warmly as the suave Philo Vance; Ronald Colman impressed as Bulldog Drummond and

Raffles; while straight backed Clive Brook and Raymond Massey starred in the first Sherlock Holmes talkies. Purists of the Holmes stories were not over - impressed by the results though the films were welcomed by the local critics and well supported by audiences. The Irish News expressed the opinion that Raymond Massey in "The Speckled Band," which showed in the Classic in November 1931, filled the main part adequately, and that the film was "thrilling.....and at times quite eerie." An aunt of the author recalled seeing it in the Clonard and being suitably thrilled. The following year (in February 1932) the Hippodrome introduced audiences to Sam Spade when it showed the first filmed version of "The Maltese Falcon," with Ricordo Cortez as the famed detective. Dashiell Hammett had written the novel in 1929 and the rights to it had been bought by Warner Bros., who called on Roy del Ruth to direct a script based quite closely on it. Del Ruth's film has been overshadowed by the later (1941) version starring Humphrey Bogart, but it deserves better recognition. The film, described at the time by the Irish News as "a clever drama," is taut and fast moving with Cortez and the splendid Bebe Daniels giving excellent performances. Ricardo Cortez had been groomed at one time to replace Valentino but was unhappy as "a great lover." He never made much impact in Belfast, and one suspects that the film's main attraction for locals was Miss Daniels, who had been very popular in the city for many years. The Irish News critic was intrigued and surprised by her appearance in an unfamiliar blonde wig, but praised the excellence of her performance, deeming it a major asset to the film.

Without doubt the most popular detective of the day was Charlie Chan, as interpreted by Warmer Oland. Today Charlie Chan films are seen as 'B' movies but in the early Thirties they were main features which played as such in downtown cinemas like the Royal Cinema. Audiences responded to the skilfully presented mysteries, and especially to Warner Oland's believable characterisation of the Hawaiian - Chinese detective, despite being of Swedish origin himself. Soon "number one son" and other amusing Chanisms had entered into the local vernacular. Warner Oland showed another side of Oriental characterisation by appearing also as the sinister and mysterious "Dr Fu Manchu" in the Picture House, with Jean Arthur, a film which drew "crowded houses" (Irish News).

As an alternative to war, mystery and murder there was, thankfully, an abundance of comedies, both two - reelers and full length features. Most programmes included short comedies with the likes of Andy Clyde, or cartoons with the wildly popular Mickey Mouse. New comedians Joe E. Brown, Jack Oakie, Jack Hulbert and Jimmy "Schnozzle" Durante were appearing regularly on screens across the city. It was also the heyday of Laurel and Hardy who always brought the house down in a way that one rarely experiences in the cinema today, while other well loved figures like Buster Keaton and Harold Lloyd continued to surface though, sadly, less regularly than in the silent days. Charlie Chaplin seemed to have disappeared as the physical comedy of the great clowns gave way to the humour of the spoken word. Elsewhere the silent heroines with their great haloes of long hair, and their large luminous, expressive eyes ringed with dark make - up were being replaced by equally beautiful but slinky, fast talking "dames" with short hair and cloche hats, their features often wreathed in tobacco smoke.

The silent film with its distinctive visual style was dead or dying, regarded as passé, and it seemed in the early Thirties that there were few among the cinema audiences in Belfast who mourned its passing.

CHAPTER TWENTY TWO
American Twang, Slang and the Ulster Accent

If the cinema owners and managers had any regrets about the passing of the silents they are not publicly recorded. After all they were businessmen and their personal feelings wouldn't have prevented them from seizing the financial opportunities of the day. Those opportunities clearly lay in sound films and by the end of 1930 thirteen cinemas had made the necessary technical changes, usually accompanied by some degree of redecoration. During 1931 the process continued and at least another ten cinemas converted to sound. On the Falls Road the Clonard had been the first to install the new equipment (June 1930), with obvious success, and it had things all its own way until February 1931 when competition arrived from the Arcadian in Albert Street. Little had been heard of the Arcadian since it was burned during the political troubles of the early Twenties. Within two years of that tragedy the Arc, or "Johnny Donnelly's" as it was known locally, 'had been rebuilt and was back in business, serving its faithful though noisy patrons, who crowded its wooden benches every night. On the evening of Monday 2nd February 1931, after installing the British Thompson Houston sound system, it presented its first talkie, called "Song of the West" starring John Boles. The poster informed passers - by in Albert Street to expect an "all colour, all talking, all singing" musical set in the exciting Gold Rush days of 1849. According to the Irish News the cinema had been extensively renovated and redecorated "in a modern style" for the occasion. That evening the atmosphere was highly charged, and the critic commented on the "enthusiasm" of the audience, who thoroughly enjoyed the good quality reproduction. That popular programme was succeeded on Thursday by another musical, "Broadway Scandals," supported by the antics of Mickey Mouse whose appearance elicited loud cheers from the younger members present. The Arcadian retained its pattern of separate evening performances at 6:45 and 9:00pm, and locals recalled how queues for the first house sometimes began to form as early as 5:30pm, especially at the weekends. The nearby Tivoli had also suffered during the Troubles of the early Twenties but had been quickly repaired, re - roofed and returned to business. Probably for financial reasons it

Cinemas in 1938.
37 available.

was never wired for sound and by 1935 had abandoned films and reverted to its former function as a store.

One week later the Diamond, following the Arcadian's example, opened its talkie period after installing the BTH system, with another musical, the already widely shown "On With the Show," starring Betty Compson. Like the Clonard and the Arcadian the film was presented in separate shows at 6:50 and 9:00pm. In the published advertisements attention was drawn to its "outstanding natural colour," and the fact that it was all talking, singing and dancing. After three days it was followed by another musical, the less known "Dark Red Roses" starring Stewart Rome. It has a certain historical interest in that it was one of the earliest completely talking films made in England, and was filmed using De Forest's Phonofilm system. The film also has a local significance - unnoticed, it would seem, at the time - because among the cast was Una O'Connor, making her film debut. Una O'Connor had been born in Belfast in 1880, where she had been baptised as Agnes Mc Glade. She had attended St Dominic's High School on the Falls Road before studying to fulfil her ambition of becoming a teacher. Some time later her family migrated to Dublin and there she changed careers and joined the Abbey Theatre, before moving on to critical acclaim in London and on Broadway.

Una O'Connor, a fine Belfast actress.

Artistically, "Dark Red Roses" was an interesting film in that, unusually, it included a ballet sequence by George Balanchin, danced by Lydia Lopokova and Anton Dolin. Audience reaction in the Diamond is not recorded. The following week saw more down - to - earth material with Pauline Frederick and Myrna Loy in a thriller called "Evidence." The Diamond was, of course, owned by the Mc Kibben Estate who had already adapted the Midland in Canning Street to sound in September 1930. The changeover of the Diamond suggests that their other cinemas, the Shankill Picturedrome and the West End Cinema on the Shankill Road, had been converted during the intervening five months, if not earlier. The problem with precise dating is that neither cinema advertised in the local papers. The same difficulty arises with the Sandro on Sandy Row, and the Popular in East Belfast.

During the following month, March 1931, two more cinemas made the change, the Duncairn Super Cinema (with "Song o' My Heart") and the Gaiety in Upper North Street (with "Rio Rita") both on the same day, the 16th March. The Willowfield made the change on 9th May with a showing of "High Society Blues." Most managers obviously felt that musicals were the best way to show off the the qualities of their new new systems, as well as to attract large crowds. An exception was Alfred George, the manager of the Crumlin, who stayed with silents as long as he dared, before closing for a week to install the RCA sound system, which he described as "the most perfect and up-to-date talkie equipment available." He also reminded prospective patrons that because of its large waiting rooms the Crumlin had no street queues, a decided advantage on wet or cold evenings. He finally presented his first talkie on June 8th 1931. It was a new film, which had shown in the Royal Cinema only the week before. It was a comedy called "The Cohens and Kellys in Africa," the latest in an ethnic series involving the friendly rivalry between an Irish and a Jewish family. The series, which starred Charlie Murray and George Sydney, had begun in 1926 as silent comedies, and over the years involved the families in visits to New York, Paris, London, Scotland

and, of course, Hollywood. The films were well received in Belfast and the Telegraph critic commented that they were always "a pleasant experience", not readily forgotten. Their latest, in Africa, he summed up as "a jungle of laughs," a phrase probably lifted from the publicity literature that the critics were supplied with. The Crumlin programme was continuous from 6:00 to 10:30 pm, and an added incentive was the reasonable pricing at 3d, 5d and 6d. After three days Mr George changed his programme from a comedy to another staple, a Western, "Sons of the Saddle" starring Ken Maynard. He obviously believed in popular entertainment without frills, for among the supporting films was a sound serial about circus life called "Tinsel and Tears."

At the beginning of 1932 there was at least one cinema that was still showing silent fare, the Kelvin in College Square East. There had been little mention of it during the former decade because it had ceased to advertise its programmes. Comfortably situated near the Falls and Grosvenor Road working class neighbourhoods it had, over the years, built up a faithful and substantial following. In April 1925 the owners applied to the City Surveyor for permission to make renovations aimed at increasing the seating to 485 units, which suggests that financially the cinema was doing well. The application was signed by Violet Crothers, a director, and one of the few women involved in the cinema business at the time Like Alfred George, the directors and manager couldn't completely ignore the competition from sound if they wished to stay in business, so in early 1932 the decision was taken to install the new technology. On 30th May 1932 they presented their first sound programme with a film called "The Big Party," followed three days later with a double bill, "In Line of Duty" and "Annabelle's Affairs." Pricing was competitive at 6d, and one shilling for front and back stalls, while substantial double bills gave added good value. Continuous programming from 2:00 to 10:30pm was introduced, and by Christmas they were advertising the cinema as "all talkie with perfect sound." In the following months it was decided to make more changes and the hall was closed for what was called "an extensive overhaul," which included the purchase of the latest RCA sound system. Newly painted and decorated, with "perfect sound," the Kelvin reopened on 26th June 1933, optimistic that it could hold its own against the other downtown halls. Prices were adapted to the harsh economic conditions of the time at 3d and 6d before 5:00 pm, rising to 6d and 9d in the evening.

The period from 1929 to 1932 was one of change and adaptation for the local cinema business. It saw not only technical updates but also improvements in the physical conditions of the buildings, many of which were showing their age. The Currans decided to give the Lyceum a complete overhaul to meet the needs and demands of the sound era, and, in the process, to make the experience of going to the pictures even more attractive and luxurious. The hall was redecorated in a colour scheme of amber, cream and gold and the seating was improved. The theatre was completely re-carpeted and, as might be expected from the Curran Bros, new electrical fittings were installed which produced a lighting system which was "splendid" (Irish News). An added incentive, when the cinema reopened on 14th July 1931, was the film shown, a gentle romantic comedy called "One Romantic Night." It was Lilian Gish's first talkie, which she had made with some reluctance, but her fans and admirers were delighted to discover that she had a clear and attractive speaking voice. In support, with the standard newsreel and cartoon, was a sound serial called "Fingerprints."

The serial, once so popular, was beginning to creep back into programmes.

While Michael Curran and his sons were planning their changes to the Lyceum, Ferris Pounds did the same to the Mountpottinger Picturedrome, but for different reasons. On Friday the 1st May 1931, just following the afternoon matinee, attendants smelt smoke in the auditorium and to their horror flames suddenly appeared near the stage. The fire brigade was called and arrived quickly. By that time the fire was spreading across the front of the auditorium and for a time it was feared that the whole building would be lost. However, quick work by the firemen brought it under control though by that time the screen had been completely destroyed along with the loud speakers behind it. Rows of seats at the front were also badly burned, and there was damage to walls and fittings. Mr Pounds, ever the showman, publicly dismissed the effects as "minor," and announced that the cinema would be closed for a short period for necessary repairs. On closer examination, it became clear that the damage was much more widespread and severe than expected, leading to heartfelt expressions of thanks and great relief that the hall, which just a short time before had been well filled, had been empty at the time. After discussions it was decided to use the opportunity to completely overhaul the building, a process that took nearly five months. A Mr Shaw, a painter and decorator of Ardenlee Avenue, was dispatched to London to familarise himself with the latest developments in cinema design and decoration in the West End, and elements of what he saw were incorporated into the reconstructed building.

The cinema finally reopened on Monday the 12th October with the popular comedy team of Wheeler and Wolsey in "Hook, Line and Sinker," and the curious patrons were able to experience the changes. A new impressive verandah had been added above the main entrance, through which the public entered into a much enlarged vestibule where they could purchase their tickets, the prices of which remained unchanged. The auditorium, discreetly lit by new concealed lighting, glowed in tangerine, blue and gold, and was much quieter because of a new marbled rubber floor covering. Ferris Pounds, representing what the Irish News called a "progressive management," welcomed the first audiences and promised them a season of top films. On Thursday the first of those was presented in the form of the talented and sophisticated Norma Shearer in "Let Us Be Gay."

Audiences and newspaper commentators showed continued interest in and expressed continued approval of the architectural changes taking place in cinemas across the city as a result of the sound revolution, as it was called. Sadly there was little or no reference to the less attractive effects. Few mentioned the disappearance of the orchestra pits whose empty spaces usually displayed potted palms for a time before being removed where possible and replaced with rows of seats. The great orchestras and smaller ensembles that had accompanied the silent films, and entertained the audiences for so many years, were disbanded and their musicians found themselves unemployed. The Irish News drew attention to that development in an editorial on 6th January 1930, when the editor quite rightly recognised the talkies as part of a wider revolution in sound technology, which included the gramophone and the loudspeaker, as he put it. The rapid spread of "mechanical music" he argued, was causing widespread unemployment and hardship among musicians. He deplored the loss of musicians and their live music in the face of what he termed as, not

Norma Shearer: the author's mother's favourite star.

music, "but mere din."

The paper returned to the subject the following year when Samuel P. Swanton, the conductor of the Opera House Orchestra, announced his imminent retirement after 46 years as a professional musician. In an article in the Irish News describing his career, he recalled that he had been born in Cork but had studied music in Liverpool, before coming to Belfast. His parents had been members of John Warden's stock company and through that connection he had gained a position playing violin in the old Theatre Royal orchestra. From there he had, over the years, graduated to the Opera House and his present position. He obviously relished the great days of live performances, and recalled the songs of the music hall which he felt were superior to most of what was being published, sung and played in 1931. He seemed less enthusiastic about playing musical accompaniment to silent films and had a low regard for some players in cinema orchestras. He admitted that the arrival of the talkies had proved to be a serious "menace" to professional musicians, and expressed great sympathy with those musicians who were now "on the street." He also suggested that the present unhappy situation was inevitable because the silent cinema had created a "false market" which had encouraged too many to enter the musical profession. Many of them were now paying the price of that situation. Despite the present downturn he was optimistic - rightly as it turned out - about the future, because he felt there would always be a demand and need for "good musicians." Some players had already joined dance bands and had migrated from cinema to dance hall music.

Another group that suffered from the arrival of sound were the deaf. Deaf people had no difficulty in following the "dumb show" of silent films but, as a letter in the I.S.N. in July 1932 pointed out, they could not make head nor tail of most sound films. The letter, from local man Edward Collins, went on to explain how in response to a recent proposal made at the annual meeting of the Mission Hall for the Deaf in College Square North, the British Deaf and Dumb Association had undertaken the task of furnishing local missions with projectors and a regular supply of silent safety films which would "restore to the deaf their chief pleasure." It was hoped that the venture could even become a commercial success if other members of the public who still "sigh for the old time silent film" decided to attend the showings. It was a worthy and interesting idea, and he appealed to all cinema-goers to support the project by subscribing towards the cost of the home projectors which would be used in the small mission halls. Despite its high ideals there is no indication that the enterprise became more than a local experiment, though the desire to keep films accessible to the deaf was not entirely abandoned by the commercial cinema.

Despite such negative effects it was clear by 1931 that the talkies were not a passing craze but were there to stay, and as such their impact would have to be faced up to. For many, a major concern was the dominance of American films being shown in the cinemas, and how they were influencing the behaviour of young people especially with regard to behaviour and slang. That led one commentator to ask where all the "well spoken" films from England, France, Germany and elsewhere had gone. Why, he asked, weren't there films with Ulster scenes and, one presumes, Ulster dialects on the local screens? His comments were welcomed in certain quarters because others were thinking along similar lines.

The Film Society of Northern Ireland was still operating despite the serious handicap of a shortage of funds. A few months before, in January, its President, Charles Haig, explained that it hadn't the resources to compete with Hollywood - nor did it wish to - but that it had completed a number of short films on local subjects which were shown successfully at small functions like house parties or whist drives. The response to them convinced him that there was an audience for local films. The society was a small amateur group and he appealed to anyone with an interest in filmmaking or acting to join the Society, or at least to support it financially.

While "Ulster films" weren't yet available, the influence of Belfast wasn't entirely absent from the screen, with the appearances of Una O'Connor, Moyna Magill, and Cathleen Nesbitt, who made her first film, "The Case of the Frightened Lady" in 1932. When, in September 1933, the Classic showed "Cavalcade" with Clive Brook and Diana Wynyard, it attracted large crowds mainly on account of its author, Noel Coward. The critic in the Telegraph went out of his way to draw attention to Una O'Connor, "the Belfast actress," who played the role of Ellen Bridges. He recalled that she had first appeared on stage in London in 1913, and had recently had a major critical success playing Ellen Bridges in the Drury Lane Theatre. As a result she had been invited to Hollywood to play the film role, and put under contract to Fox Studios. Audiences, he predicted, would be seeing more of her in the near future. Earlier in the year the Picture House presented "The First Mrs Frazer," based on a play by St John Irvine. The local critics praised the film for its fine acting, and drew attention to its "splendid" cabaret sequence enhanced by music from Billy Cotton and his Band, and Geraldo's Tango Band. The author's local connections were noted and the Irish News congratulated the management of the Picture House for bringing a film "from a playwright who still has an affection for Belfast, the place of his birth."

Despite such honourable mentions, the idea of Ulster competing with Hollywood for the affections of local audiences still sounded somewhat optimistic, and the I.S.N., for one, found it a bit of a joke. The paper printed a cartoon showing two ladies in conversation. One claimed that her fiancé was now in the movies. "I know," replied her companion, "I saw him driving a furniture lorry the other day." But the suggestion that Ireland could produce its own films was being seriously discussed by some and they got support from a visiting actor later in the year. In October, Percy Marmount came to the Opera House in a play called "Lucky in Love." It was described as a "farcical comedy" which was being tried out before being presented in London. It was, according to the Irish News, "well received" by the audience though the critic felt that part of its success was due to the appearance on stage of "a film star in the flesh." Percy Marmount was a well known English stage actor who had also made a name for himself on the silver screen. In an interview he recalled that he had appeared once on stage in Belfast "about twenty years ago" but since then had travelled and acted worldwide. In America he had made a number of successful silent films (including "The Shooting of Dan McGrew"), and had become friendly with the likes of Ronald Colman, Clive Brooks and William Powell.

The Irish News, which showed a continuing interest in the cinema, persuaded Marmount to write an article headed: Why Not an Irish Hollywood? In it he discussed his considerable experience of working in films in England and California, and claimed that Hollywood's success was due to a combination of facts. It had the necessary finance, it attracted talented people from all over the world and, above all, it took its "art" seriously. Anyone wanting to compete with the American cinema would have to do likewise, and he concluded that this country had the talent and the scenery to succeed. He felt that Ireland and the Irish had been badly treated by English and American film makers who had presented a distorted view of the country and its people. That could be changed, but only if the industry was organized by what he called "an Irish - thinking brain." He praised Irish audiences - and whiskey - as wonderful, and expressed delight that a number of local people had stopped him in the street to talk about his films. A few days later he held what would today be called a workshop, in the Opera House, for aspiring film actors. The Irish News sent one of their reporters along and he was quite impressed by what he saw and heard. It was a mixed group that had turned up, with a few girls including "a couple of bewitching blondes," a larger number of men and a scattering of children. On that showing he decided that Belfast obviously had "more budding John Gilberts and Clive Brooks than Greta Garbos and Clara Bows. "An interesting choice of established names, with no mention of James Cagney, Edward G Robinson, Paul Muni, Barbara Stanwyck or other up - and - coming stars. The discussion proved worthwhile and the reporter felt the group was genuine in its interest, and asked sensible questions. Mr Marmount replied in great detail. He emphasised to the group that acting was not an easy life, that it demanded hard work and personal sacrifice, and that in the end, the chances of success were small. The chief deciding factor, he felt, was the possession of a definite personality "that could be projected on the screen."

That problem of what actually made a successful film star intrigued many writers in the business at the time. When "Christopher Strong" showed in the Picture House (September 1933) the News Letter critic had high praise for the acting abilities of Katherine Hepburn but at the same time was intrigued by her success. He wrote that "this young woman hasn't a film face, she is scarcely even pretty.... her raw voice lacks any trace of trained enunciation.....yet she compels concentration with every word and movement." Some time later the Lyceum presented a film called "What Price Hollywood" which dealt, in its own way, with the points Mr Marmount had raised. It starred Constance Bennett, and, according to the Belfast Telegraph, it "gave a faithful impression of everyday life in the studios and streets of Hollywood," with scenes of many well known stars at work. The story, which developed against that background, concerned a young waitress - like a typical Belfast girl - who, driven by ambition, and hard work becomes a screen star "with the world at her feet." Sadly, fame proves to be empty and the critic commented that "beneath the glitter, gaiety and applause she is unhappy for her home and children." One wonders if any of those who attended Mr Marmount's discussion saw it or were influenced by its underlying message. During the Thirties the ambition or hope to be a film star occupied the minds of many of the young in the same way that the desire to be a pop singer motivates many teenagers today. People recalled the excitement of the Daily Sketch Girl competition in which two local girls had reached the finals in London. There was also the example of the Belfast actresses mentioned above, and the newspapers continued to encourage such hopes. In November 1934 the Irish News (in its Random Jottings) drew attention to a play on the radio called "Our Miss Gibbs" in which an actress from the city, Helen Gilliland, was playing a major role. The writer mentioned approvingly that, after success on the London stage, she had travelled to Hollywood and was now back in England with plans for another film. He finished his column with the comment that "no doubt (the play) will be listened to critically by many of our Belfast girls with ambitions in that direction."

The achievement of eminence in Hollywood was often mentioned in the local newspaper columns and was reinforced, for example, in the I.S.N. by an article on the success in the film industry of Belfast born Brian Desmond Hurst, which was given prominence in February 1934. His life, according to the reporter, read like a film story, leading from Belfast to Hollywood. He maintained that, over the years, many Belfastmen who had emigrated overseas had "made good" in literature, painting, drama and music but were noticeable by their absence from film making, "until now" with the emergence of Mr Hurst. Hurst was born in the Castlereagh district of Belfast in 1900 into a large family. His father was a blacksmith in the shipyard, but Brian Desmond's interests didn't lie in that direction. He was educated in London, where he studied Art. After service in the Far East during the Great War he travelled, went to America and ended up in Hollywood where he made a living painting murals in the homes of the rich. He had the good luck to meet and become friends with John Ford, a friendship which lasted until Ford's death in August 1973. Ford got him employment as an assistant art director in one of the studios, and then appointed him as his own personal assistant. In that way Hurst not only broke into films but learned the skills from one of the great masters. Later when he returned to London, he entered the business there and directed his first film, a version of Edgar Allen Poe's "The Tell Tale Heart," (1934) which was well received by the critics. Encouraged by that success, the writer claimed, he now had plans for more films and was poised for great things. In fact Hurst, though based mainly in London, went on to direct a number of films with Irish themes, beginning with "Irish Hearts" (1934) which is often described as the first Irish all sound fiction film; J.M. Synge's "Riders To The Sea" (1935) which Gracie Fields funded to the tune of £6,000, and which starred Sara Allgood; and "Ourselves Alone," (1936), a quota quickie and the first British film to deal with the Irish War of Independence. There is no record of the Synge film showing locally, but when "Ourselves Alone" reached Belfast it was banned. Hurst was interested in the establishment of an Irish film industry, but based in the South. In the early Fifties he was a member of the Irish Film Industry Committee along with Lord Killanin and John Ford which looked into the possibilities of setting up such an indigenous film industry.

A surprising omission from the article on Percy Marmount was any mention of standard English diction, which was surely of vital importance to anyone wishing to act in the talkies. Despite all the fuss about the impact of American twang and slang, regular cinemagoers were familiar with the clearly enunciated tones of Clive Brooks, Basil Rathbone, Claude Raines, Boris Karloff, and no one could fault the diction of American actors like William Powell, Richard Dix, Adolph Menjou, Frederick Marsh or Norma Shearer. Despite that many commentators continued to criticise the American accent. When "The Sky Hawk" came to the Classic in April 1930 it was greeted as "the first talking epic of the air war" and praised by the local critics for its magnificently staged Zeppelin raids on London. When it showed later in the year, in the Alhambra, the I.S.N.. also commented how attractive it was to hear actors speak "English rather than American."

But, some observers asked: what of the Irish and Ulster accents; were they suitable for international productions? Certainly the Abbey actors and actresses had no difficulty being understood in Belfast, London or New York. An English director, Alfred Hitchcock, so admired them that he filmed what was essentially their 1925 production of Sean O'Casey's "Juno and the Paycock," even persuading O'Casey to write a new short introductory scene for the film. He got little thanks in Ireland. Cyril Cusack, for example, described the result as "awful." Reference has already been made to the fact that when the film was screened in Limerick a number of men hijacked the reels and burned them on the pavement outside the cinema. During its showing in Dublin in the Savoy in November 1930, hissing and booing broke out and the manager, after trying to reason with the audience, withdrew it and replaced it with a silent film. The Irish News reported that many patrons then left and had their money refunded. Some time later it was announced that it would be shown in Derry, but not unexpectedly in light of its theme, that promise was not realised and it was withdrawn before the opening date. It never reached Belfast, until the Q.F.T. showed it in February 2000 as part of their Hitchcock Centenary series. It is not the type of film that one associates with Hitchcock but one can be grateful that he made it because, despite its faults, it is a fascinating historical document. It illustrates the simple, direct style adopted by the Abbey Players and the quality of their acting, especially the skills of the magnificent Sara Allgood as Juno Boyle. The evening that the author saw it there was a large school party present and despite the film's age Miss Allgood easily and quickly reduced them to attentive silence. For Belfast viewers it was also amusing to see a large bottle of Dunville Whiskey prominently displayed on a table in one scene. Despite the primitive state of sound recording - for example dubbing was not yet possible - the dialogue was clear and easily understood, giving some inkling of auricular conditions in the cinemas of the time.

"Song o My Heart" had done well internationally, and the diction of John McCormack and Maureen O'Sullivan had been favourably commented upon. But, as the News Letter writer had intimated, the Ulster dialect hadn't appeared on screen in any form. Locally there were many who argued that it was unsuited to serious drama, and had no attraction for audiences outside Ulster. They felt that geographically its appeal was distinctly limited, while artistically it should be restricted to humorous situations and comedy. Certainly it was in such circumstances that it was often heard on contemporary Belfast stages, especially in the Empire, where performers like Cathal O'Byrne and Richard Hayward used it mainly to humorous effect, a tradition that was to be carried on by James Young, Albert Sharpe, and today by May Mac Fettridge. Not everyone accepted those narrow views and since the early days of the century the plays put on by the Ulster Literary Theatre had shown that local dialect could be used effectively in serious drama. Richard Hayward, described on one occasion in the I.S.N. as being "involved in the furtherance of Ulster Dramatic Art and the preservation of local character studies on stage and in song," supported that supposition. In 1929, as already noted, he had founded the Belfast Repertory Theatre Company (also known as the Empire Players) in conjunction with J.R.Mageean, and with the enthusiastic support of the manager of the Empire Theatre, Gerald Morrison. He then set about presenting local plays about ordinary people using everyday speech, especially the works of Thomas Carnduff.

Carnduff, a Socialist, often described in the local papers as "an unemployed shipyard worker," was a man ahead of his times in many ways. He had a firm belief in the importance of local culture and revealed an artistic ability to illustrate it in dramatic form. During a lecture called "A Shipyard Worker and Drama," delivered in the YMCA hall in Wellington Place in February 1933, he told his audience that "it was about time that the stage Ulsterman followed the stage Irishmen into oblivion." He reminded them that it was vital "to keep our historical customs and dialect from dying out," and to remember that "our literature and poetry are Irish and should remain Irish." He believed that if local literature and drama were lost then Ulster would become just "a second rate English county." Drama was a vital means of keeping that local culture alive, and he congratulated the many lively drama societies across the land that were doing just that. His own plays, which incorporated everyday speech and idiom, were part of that objective also, and he told a receptive audience in the Empire on one occasion that his aim was to write about "commonplace people........ my people.......ordinary people who live in mean streets" and to show that they have as much "tragedy, comedy and sentiment in their lives" as kings, queens and lords. (Belfast Telegraph, 21st March 1933).

Carnduff's first two plays were "Workers" and "Machinery" and the mainly working class audiences in the Empire took to them with enthusiasm. For his next play, also set in Belfast, Carnduff turned to the Ninety - Eight Rebellion, and produced "Castlereagh," which was presented on the stage of the Empire in January 1935 by Richard Hayward and his Players. It then transferred to Dublin for a week in the Abbey Theatre and while there an excerpt was broadcast on radio. The Irish News critic was an admirer of Mr Carnduff's work but his response to "Castlereagh" was mixed. He admitted that the play dealt with a "difficult theme" but he felt that the author hadn't really "cleared all the obstacles that history raises." On the positive side he felt the play did catch "the atmosphere of intrigue, of exciting danger in which the United Irishmen plotted their rebellion (and) the atmosphere of ruthlessness with which it was put down." Audiences were thrilled to see figures like Henry Joy McCracken whom they knew about from their local history, walk the stage in the garb of the day. The critic felt that the actors not only filled their costumes impressively but also caught the manners of the day. He praised the quality of the acting. Richard Hayward, he felt, had the most difficult role to fill as Lord Castlereagh and he interpreted it well, but Harold Goldblatt as his sinister secretary was outstanding. He relished the "rich creamy malevolence" of his playing which reminded him of the villains of a bygone age. R.H.McCandless was splendid as the weaver James Hope. His diction and delivery were so natural that the sense of unreality which marked the speech of some of the other actors was banished.

The critic also perceived "an ingenious borrowing" from the cinema. He pointed out that a problem facing the playwright was to introduce and explain to the audience the pertinent political issues of the period, and the many characters involved in the plot. That was done by adapting the technique of rapid cutting used in films. The main characters were introduced, briefly, between quickly raised and lowered curtains while a voice offstage explained who they were and what they represented. It is interesting to speculate on the origin of that introductory sequence. It may have been Mr Carnduff's idea but it is more likely to have been suggested by Richard Hayward who, in recent years, had become involved in film making and was therefore more familiar with cinematic techniques. "Castlereagh" was more than just a night out at the Empire. It represented an interesting amalgam of a local writer, local actors, local history, local speech and hints of a convergence of traditional theatre and cinema. Though no one suspected it at the time, the dramatic groundwork was being laid which would in time propel a group of local actors, complete with local accents, on to the international screen where they would prove their worth. World audiences were to have no difficulty understanding and appreciating the accents of Stephen Boyd, Joe Tumelty, Albert Sharpe and Liam Neeson to name a few. Richard Hayward and his Belfast Repertory Theatre Company led the way in that development, and took the first steps towards putting the Ulster accent on the cinema screen. In his book, "In Praise of Ulster" (William Mullan & Sons Ltd., 1938) Richard Hayward claimed, with justification, that he was "the first person in the world to use the Ulster dialect on radio, on gramophone records, and in talking pictures." How he achieved that in films will become clear soon, or as Hayward himself would have said, "in a wee while."

The nature of cinema and how it differed from the theatre was one topic that was often discussed. It was widely held that the theatre attracted a more sophisticated and highly educated audience than the cinema. The latter, in contrast, was supported by an intellectually less demanding audience, one moreover that included a high proportion of young people and children. The Censorship Board held that view and used it as one reason (or excuse) for censoring many films. At the same time many argued that films were less subtle than plays, and therefore of less importance culturally. Elements of those arguments surfaced following the local banning of the film "Frankenstein" in April 1932, a matter to be discussed later, along with the thorny question of censorship. The Irish News, which tended to defend the cinema, and treat it with the level of seriousness it warranted, stated in February 1932 that "the cinema is a feature of social life which cannot be ignored." It had become a "constant theme of discussion in the newspapers, on the platform and in serious reviews." It then illustrated the truth of those comments by quoting, without comment, from an article on the nature of the cinema which had appeared recently in the pages of the serious "Quarterly Review."

In the article the writer, a Mr Rowland, expressed disappointment at the achievements of the cinema and complained that it was "suffering from a plague of restlessness and sensation (resulting in) a quite unnecessary corruption of taste." He put the blame for that situation squarely on the film producers who "repeated the same hackneyed hotch-potch" because they believed that was what the public wanted. There was too much emphasis in films on the sensational which appealed mainly to those with a shallow "jazz type of mind." That attitude, he felt, underestimated the public appetite for knowledge as reflected, for example, in the success of recent Workers Educational Schemes. The cinema could, he argued, meet audience needs better with documentary films which would record contemporary life not only for present audiences but also for posterity. There was also great scope to be found in filming the lives of important persons from the past though, he warned, care must be taken to avoid "embroidering" their actions with fiction. Greater care should also be taken in the choice of fictional subjects for filming and he thought that the works of Charles Dickens were especially suited to the cinema.

George Coulter, writing in the I.S.N. took a more frivolous approach to the topic. He ignored the calls for an educational, documentary type cinema. He recognised that for most people films were essentially an entertainment, a relaxation, and that, in the main, they described a world of make - believe inhabited by handsome heroes and beautiful heroines. It was a world, he wrote, of "charming fictions.... in which beauty never loses her lustrous eyes and love is the first occupation." Its characters, exquisitely gowned and suited, moved in elegant social circles, visiting night clubs and drinking sparkling wine. No matter what perils befell the heroines they never showed a hair out of place but continued to gaze out agreeably at their audiences from under "glistening eyelashes," and from behind perfect makeup. When, after an evening at the pictures, one stepped out from the warm and glowing cinema into a "dark and dingy street" one could reasonably say to oneself that if that was the real world I have just been watching then "this one I'm standing up in must be a blasted swindle and I've been had." The writer's final ironic comment was that in real life they do things so much more unhandsomely than in the pictures.

Belfast audiences, realists all, understood those sentiments only too well. They knew that behind the bright lights of the cinemas, theatres and city centre shops a recurring and widespread characteristic of social life in the city was what the newspapers referred to as "distress." Today it is called deprivation, but the underlying causes were the same, namely poverty and its associated blights of unemployment, low wages, poor housing and lack of education. The newspapers highlighted those problems and called on the authorities to do something to relieve the misery of the destitute and the poor. The entertainment industry was one group which responded. Throughout the year the White Cinema Club gave financial support to schemes aimed at helping the less well off, and, at Christmas, collections were taken up in cinemas to give parties for poor children. Many cinemas organized free festive matinees for poor children, a tradition which recalled the annual Christmas celebrations organised at the turn of the century in the Grosvenor Hall for poor and neglected children, the highlight of which had always been the silent comedies.

The children's parties which became a feature of the Classic during the Thirties were equally entertaining, with the added benefit that the surroundings were more palatial. Typical was the one organised for Monday 2nd January 1933. The arrangements were made by a committee consisting of the Lord Mayor (Sir Crawford McCullogh), the editor of the Irish News (S.Redwood), the editor of the Telegraph (T.Moles), and the manager of the Classic, T.H.Mac Dermott. The Lord Mayor attended in person, and the cinema staff gave their services free for the two hour "treat," which began at 10:00 am with thirty minutes of community singing. To ensure a fair representation from both communities, the audience of boys and girls, Catholic and Protestant, was chosen by organizations that had first hand experience of child poverty in the city. The St Vincent de Paul Society (600 children), the Grosvenor Hall (300), the Salvation Army(200), the North Belfast Mission (200), the Shankill Road Mission (200) and the Industrial School (50). Each child was given a parcel which contained a meat pie, fruit, sweets, a toy and a new penny. The morning was crowned with a film show which included a Charlie Chaplin comedy, a Mickey Mouse cartoon and an Andy Clyde comedy. According to reports the morning was enjoyed by all, children and adults. The Hippodrome, not to be outdone, also organised a party which catered for a smaller number of children, but was no less enjoyable, culminating as it did with a feature film starring Shirley Temple.

The long queues outside Belfast's cinemas most nights of the week were visible evidence of what filmgoers enjoyed, but what they were watching was increasingly criticised by a minority who believed that films could and should be of better quality. In January 1932 a literary reviewer in the Irish News complained that the filmgoers of Belfast tended to accept "bovinely" whatever was presented for them. He would like to see them demand films with more intelligence and taste. The occasion for his comments was his recommendation of a new book on the history of the cinema by the eminent film critic, C.A.Lejeune. Miss Lejeune had been the film critic on the Manchester Guardian for many years and had then moved to the Sunday Observer. She was, he acknowledged, known by name and reputation to anyone who had "a lively interest in the cinema." He admired her knowledge of the cinema and the fact that she treated it seriously. The book, he wrote, was a well informed bird's eye view of the development of the cinema and, thankfully, not a sermon on its iniquities. It showed the potential that the cinema had as an art form, but also raised the question of why so many of the films shown in commercial cinemas were trivial and undemanding. He complained that of the ten best films of last year, as chosen by London critics, only three had been shown in Belfast, hinting that part of the problem lay with local management.

Another film critic and historian who was often quoted in the local papers was Paul Rotha. The Irish News referred to a lecture he gave in Liverpool at the beginning of October 1934 in which he claimed that the future of the cinema lay in documentary and instructional films. The editor disagreed and expressed the view that if people wanted to go to the cinema for relaxation, and if they found that relaxation mainly in fiction films, there was nothing wrong with that. "There is no reason," he wrote, "why this type of picture should not be good art, or why film fans should not be instructed in some degree as well as entertained." There was no direct mention of censorship but he did emphasise that one important criterion of such films was that they "should not be degrading in their influence." A few weeks later the eminent English author and dramatist John Drinkwater visited Belfast and during a lecture on "The English Theatre" to the Alpha Club in the Grand Central Hotel, attacked the arrival of the cinema as "an unmitigated curse to mankind." He claimed that it had lowered artistic standards and, above all, had undermined the viability and popularity of the legitimate theatre. No genuinely creative person, he claimed, would want to write a film scenario and went on to predict - rather rashly - that within a decade there would be no cinemas. Again the Irish News came to the rescue and in an editorial called "A Word for the Cinema" the editor defended the junior medium, emphasising its potential for good and for education. Despite its success he doubted that the cinema had taken patrons away from the theatre. There would, he argued, always be people who enjoyed theatre, others who preferred the cinema and even those who enjoyed both. The competition from the cinema had actually revitalised and improved the theatre, and he hoped to see more co-operation between them in the future. Both could survive because both were of benefit to the public, if run on the right lines. The public, he claimed, would always pay for good entertainment whatever the medium.

John Drinkwater's attack also provoked a letter to the papers from Sydney P. White, of Balmoral Avenue, the Hon. Sec. of the recently formed N.Ireland branch of the British Film

Institute, which will be discussed in more detail later. He found Mr Drinkwater's comments to be without real substance, and argued that what was needed was not wild, negative and intemperate accusations about the qualities of films, but the creation of "an educated public opinion.... equipped with the knowledge necessary to criticise constructively." He admitted that film makers had in general underestimated the level of taste of the cinema audiences but was confident that situation could be changed with education. The British Film Institute had been established in London in October 1933 for that purpose, and, within a year a branch had been formed locally, which was already attracting enthusiastic support.

In December a local dramatist, Richard Rowley, addressed the Fisherwick Presbyterian Literary Society on the subject of "The Drama and Life." During comments on the cinema he claimed, with some justification, that over 90% of films were "pathetically bad" because they were made by people who had no real idea of art and were mainly interested in box-office returns. Like Mr White he felt that many film producers had a low opinion of the public taste, but, if attitudes changed, he believed the cinema could produce "a more beautiful and newer form of dramatic art." Despite that optimistic forecast the general consensus from those discussions was that the theatre was artistically and culturally superior to the cinema, was intellectually more challenging, and was less concerned with financial returns. Most local filmgoers paid little attention to such discussions and continued with their weekly visits to their favourite cinemas.

But the debate continued across the city. Could Ireland or Ulster improve cinematic quality by producing their own films, and was there a market for them; was the Ulster accent suited to the cinema screen; was the cinema a threat to the future of the traditional theatre; could the cinema and theatre co-exist side by side in a spirit of positive co-operation; were films worthy of serious artistic consideration? One man at least thought he had the answer to most of those questions, and he was Richard Hayward who, though essentially a man of the stage, decided to become involved with films. In 1932 he agreed to take part in a film to be made in Ireland, to be directed by Col. Victor Haddick. Victor Haddick was a novelist and poet, and one of Ireland's pioneer film makers. He was described in some reports as an Ulsterman, though the consensus was that he came from Limerick. He wrote the script, directed the film and spoke a commentary on the soundtrack, while Richard Hayward did the acting and singing in his own inimitable style. The film was called "The Voice of Ireland" and it ran for only 49 minutes, but it was greeted like an epic in Belfast. The I.S.N. described it as "a remarkable film of Irish life." The official handout that accompanied it described it as "a film of types.... which involved a concert singer, a farmer, a huntsman, a fisherman, a country girl, a Tyrone poteen maker, an Irish dancer and a wandering musician... in a simple story related in a setting of exquisite beauty, sporting thrills and sweet melody."

"The Voice of Ireland" can claim to be the first sound film made in Northern Ireland for commercial release. It was released in early August 1933 as the supporting feature in the Picture House, where it attracted much attention, and curious crowds. It was an uncomplicated comedy, essentially a travelogue with music and song, about a returned emigrant who, as he travels around the country of his birth, finds himself out of step with changed social conditions. The theme wasn't original and, indeed, a few years before, Cathal O'Byrne had entertained Empire audiences on stage with something similar called

"The Returned Swank," while there were echoes of Jimmy O'Dea sketches in some of the situations. The Whig critic thought it was "out of the ordinary, admirably produced, and well worth seeing", while the Irish News welcomed it as "all Irish" (which it was) and commented favourably on the "haunting" melodies on the sound track. The I.S.N. was especially impressed by Richard Hayward's performance and described his antics in one particular scene, where he played a poteen maker, as "uproariously funny." In October it arrived in the Alhambra, with the added attraction of Richard Hayward himself appearing on stage, where he sang Irish songs and entertained the audience with local anecdotes and stories told in the local vernacular. The crowds loved it and many of the more mature patrons were heard to express delight in "the glad sight of flesh and blood" on the Alhambra stage again. The Ulster accent was welcomed uncritically in Belfast on both screen and stage in what was a piece of pure popular entertainment.

The theoretical debate on the nature and quality of films may have passed over the heads of most local filmgoers but it strengthened a minority in their belief that there was a need for a more intelligent approach to the cinema. The establishment of the Film Society for N.Ireland had shown that there were locals with a serious interest in the medium, though the society was essentially of a practical nature, with the aim of making films on an amateur basis. The few small films they had produced were however complimented by other amateur efforts completed outside the society. The number of people involved in making their own films was necessarily restricted by the high cost of movie cameras and other equipment, but films of interest often came from unexpected quarters. On an evening in early January 1936 an audience gathered to enjoy a programme of films in Thompson's restaurant in Donegal Place. It was a charity event held in aid of the Benn Ulster Eye, Ear and Throat hospital. Of special interest is the fact that all the films shown were shot, as a hobby, by Mrs W.A.Anderson, who was a member of the ladies' committee of the hospital. Mrs Anderson was obviously a dedicated and skilled photographer, and she presented a comprehensive series of films shot overseas on her travels, as well as local material. She began with scenes taken on a holiday in N. America, showing town and countryside in Quebec, and along the St Lawrence river, followed by Niagara Falls, before moving to New York. Another film showed life in the rural areas of the Wye valley. The main body of her work was local, and the audience was entertained with scenes taken in and around Belfast, including a visit to Bellevue to see the recently opened Zoo, followed by general views of the Province taken from an aeroplane. Sporting events were included, especially the 1932 T.T. race, and a special colour film of the Co. Down Staghounds which used a new American colour system not yet available in Ireland. Finally she presented a short subject called "Summer time" with Ulster scenes filmed in "mist and sunshine." The News Letter reporter was very impressed by the films, describing them as being "of a remarkable quality," while the Whig reporter found them "artistically and realistically satisfying."

The artistic value of films was being increasingly recognised locally. During October 1935 the Ulster Museum put on an exhibition of original drawings from Walt Disney's animated films, which caused much excitement and comment. The Irish News celebrated the event by claiming that Mickey Mouse had now rightfully become "art." At the death of George the Fifth a few months later, in January 1936, the News Letter emphasised that the king had been a patron of the cinema, had supported it, and had often spoken of its "wonderful possibilities." The paper even published a list of the many films which he had viewed privately with his family during the year before, an eclectic list that included Eleanor Powell in "Broadway Melody of 1936," "Top Hat" with Fred Astaire and Ginger Rogers, "Anna Karenina," starring Greta Garbo, "Mutiny on the Bounty," with Charles Laughton, and Alfred Hitchcock's "39 Steps." The arrival of Charlie Chaplin's "Modern Times" in the Classic during the following August stimulated much discussion about quality film making, and the long queues it attracted suggested that people were interested in seeing intelligent films. In October 1936 Fred Storey, the vice chairman of the N. Antrim Regional Education Committee put forward the idea that a Film Fund be established "to produce an Ulster film worthy of the province." The following month Alderman Tommy Henderson suggested to the Library, Museum and Art Committee in the City Hall that important events in the city should be filmed and preserved in the museum for future generations. That worthwhile idea was unfortunately not acted upon at the time.

It was against such a background that, in mid 1934, a small local group of concerned persons including cinema managers, clergy and teachers established a local branch of the British Film Institute, called the N.Ireland Film Institute Society, with Lord Dufferin as President. The British Film Institute had been established the previous year with government financial support, to educate public opinion about the cinema and thereby "to raise the standard of films and get a wider public to realise its artistic, educational, cultural and entertainment possibilities." During the following months they held a series of lectures on the art of the film in the Grosvenor Hall, and the Whig commended them for the efforts they were making "to encourage serious cinema going." Lord Dufferin addressed the society at one such meeting. He argued that Art could follow two paths in dealing with the realities of life. One way was to escape from those realities into a dream world, and the other was to face up to those realities and treat them in serious and memorable ways. The latter path was the one followed by serious artists. The cinema on the other hand, he felt, had tended to follow the first path, with important artists like Chaplin and Disney producing works, that were essentially just entertainment. The worthwhile aim of the Institute was to inform and educate people so that they would demand and support more serious films. Like Paul Rotha he recommended the realities of documentary films. During the debate that followed, his suggestions were criticised and a number of speakers rejected documentaries as "propaganda" and spoke in favour of entertainment films. They went to the cinema, they insisted, to be entertained.

On the 19th November 1936 the Institute opened their second season, again in the Grosvenor Hall, with a full programme of films, an event which was welcomed warmly by the local critics The main attraction was a German speaking film, with English subtitles, called "Masquerade in Vienna," supported by a puppet film called "On Parade," and a travelogue called "Journey to Flanders." The films were on 16 mm stock, and the level of comfort in the hall couldn't compare with that of the downtown cinemas, but, from all accounts, the evening was a great success. The main film was directed by Willy Forst, a Viennese actor who had turned to directing, and it starred another Viennese personality, Paula Wessely. Miss Wessely was new to local filmgoers, but many would have remembered

Willy Forst from a number of silent German films, including "Atlantic" based on the tragedy of the Titanic, which had been shown in the city. The explanatory notes that accompanied the film pointed out that an American version of "Masquerade in Vienna" had been screened recently in the city, titled "Escapade," and starring William Powell.

The policy of making Hollywood versions of continental films is not a recent idea. The opportunity was taken to compare both films. The continental film was praised for the beauty of its visuals, the subtle use of light and shade, and the effective way the camera movements were used for dramatic impact. Adding to the overall impact was a fine musical score, and the "impish naturalness" of Miss Wessely. In contrast the American version was essentially a star vehicle that shifted the emphasis to William Powell, who admittedly gave an attractively humorous and light hearted performance. It was felt that, in the transition, the Hollywood film had lost the special atmosphere and gaiety of Vienna, which was one of the main attractions of the original. The Irish News critic praised the "superior direction" of the original, and added that English and American directors could learn much from German film makers.

For a variety of reasons, not every cineaste in the city was willing to support the Film Institute Society. Some argued that the BFI was too academic and too formal in its approach, and that its use of lectures and debates tended to alienate some people. Others were suspicious of the fact that the institute had government support, and that representatives of the cinema industry were included in its Board of Governors. They felt that their influence compromised its independence, and would mean that the society wouldn't be adventurous enough in its choice of films. What was needed, they argued, was a truly independent organization modelled on the London Film Society, with the essential aim of showing quality films. It was that group of enthusiasts who met on Friday 22nd January 1937 in the CIYMS Hall and founded the separate Belfast Film Society. According to the Whig, the idea had been discussed for some time but its implementation had been delayed by the reluctance of the local cinema managers to agree to let the society use their cinemas for Sunday showings. The inaugural meeting was presided over by Prof. Montrose of Queen's University who complained that Continental films were rarely shown in the city, and that even some good quality English and American films were denied screening for one reason or another. The aim of the society, he declared, was to raise the level of appreciation of films partly by showing such quality films not normally available on the commercial circuits, and by encouraging debate and discussion about matters pertaining to film making.

The original prospectus declared that the Society's aim was "to bring to Belfast for exhibition to its members films of special interest and value which are either not shown in local cinemas or are unlikely to secure the revival they deserve." The approach would be concerned with the theoretical aspects of the subject and there would be no attempt to make films. As a beginning it was planned to show three films during the first season, before the summer. Prof. Montrose emphasised that there was "no conflict" intended with any other association already in existence in the city, and he hoped for future co-operation in arranging lectures and debates, especially with the Belfast branch of the British Film Institute. A number of important issues were then discussed including the need to attract at least 200 members if the society was to become financially viable, and the problem of obtaining suitable premises where the films could be shown. With regard to the latter problem they hoped, at some future date, to persuade a sympathetic cinema manager to co-operate, but in the meantime they would have to be nomadic. Officials were then elected to undertake the necessary organisation, including a chairman (Mr Woodside), a treasurer (J.S.Dodd), secretaries (Ian Mc Clelland and Edward Selwyn), and a committee which included Hazel Armstrong, Dr Price Clarke, and Prof Harrison. Frazer Mayne and Richard Hayward were to be technical advisers. It was a formidable team, and they soon got things up and running.

The first official meeting took place six weeks later on 6th March 1937 in the Kerr Memorial Hall in Glengall Street, and attracted an audience of about 300 persons, who enjoyed a stimulating programme. The main film was quite a surprise, and proved a lively talking point. It was "Hey-Rup!" made in Czechoslovakia. It seems strange that a film was chosen from a country that hadn't a great reputation for film making. The inspiration for the decision was probably the Venice Film Festival which had been established in 1932, with the aim of showing the best films available, without the restraint of censorship. The first festival had been a great success and had won the approval and attention of those who, like the members of the Belfast Film Society, regarded films as more than just entertainment. The second festival took place in 1934 and gained much publicity in Ireland when the Grand Prix was awarded to Robert Flaherty's "Man of Aran." That festival also raised the profile of Czech cinema because of the notoriety which surrounded the Czech entry. The film in question was "Extase" in which the leading actress, Hedy Kiessler, appeared in an extended nude sequence. Miss Kiessler was to become familiar to Belfast audiences many years later as the very beautiful but emotionally placid Hedy Lamarr.

The society members were well aware of the furore surrounding the film but they also knew that any attempt to screen it in Belfast would cause, not ecstasy but outrage, in certain quarters. They managed to secure another Czech film to give their members a taste of east European fare, but if anyone went to the Kerr Memorial Hall in the hope of being shocked they were pleasantly disappointed. "Hey-Rup!" turned out to be a comedy with "a general air of frolic "(Whig). It dealt with the relationships among a group of industrial workers, and while its style was often that of slapstick it also exhibited, according to the Whig critic, original flashes and, above all, a serious social undertone. He put its appeal down especially to the skill of the director, Jindrich Honzl, with his clever use of the camera, and novel editing. The main feature was supported by Paul Rotha's" Shipyard, "which was a twenty minute documentary about the construction of a ship at Barrow-in-Furness, a topic that had a special appeal in Belfast. It was a film that showed "real artistry," and the Whig critic was impressed at the way Rotha linked the progress in the building of the vessel to events in the lives of the workers. To finish the evening there were two rather specialised Nature documentaries, Julian Huxley's "The Tortoiseshell Butterfly" and Mary Field's "Thistledown." It was a rich and varied programme that reflected the taste and enthusiasm of the organising committee, and augured well for the future.

That was followed three weeks later by the third meeting (on 25th March) in St Mary's Hall in Bank Street, by which time the membership had reached 420. The organizers were delighted at the response but appealed for even more people to join the society, because if they could reach a membership of 600 they would no longer be legally restricted to 16mm non- inflammable films. Their choice of films would therefore be greatly increased. As it was, the main feature that evening was another East European production, "Road To Life" (1931), directed by Nickolai Ekk, which interestingly enough had been shown at the first Venice Festival in 1932. Historically it has some significance in that it was the first talkie made in the Soviet Union. It was also the first time that a work of "socialist realism" was shown in Belfast. There were those in the city who would have regarded it with suspicion, and some probably muttered about Communist influence in the Society. The film dealt with the problem of the anti - social behaviour among homeless juveniles in Russia, and showed how the delinquents changed their ways when they discovered a purpose to life, in their work on a collective. What the members of the Society made of it is not quite clear. The critic Paul Rotha had found it rather theatrical, and another critic had dismissed it as "Louisa May Alcott on a collective farm." Our own critics remained non-committal, except the News Letter reporter who commented that it all seemed "rather naive."

The Soviet film was followed by John Grierson's superb documentary, "Night Mail," in which visuals, spoken commentary (by the poet Auden), music and content all came together in an unforgettable and poetic vision of a speeding mail train. With such challenging and tasteful programmes the Belfast Film Society was well and truly on the right track, and was to remain so for the next decade. It rapidly increased its membership, and extended its influence. Prof. Montrose's suggestion of co-operation was acted upon and the society went on to publish a monthly Belfast Film Review in conjunction with the British Film Institute, which carried serious reviews of new films including those showing locally in Belfast, new publications of interest and other cinematic matters.

The Dublin Film Society was established at much the same time - the Irish Times first mentions it in mid September 1936 - with aims similar to their colleagues in Belfast. Belfast members in time made contact with it and trips were made to Dublin for discussions and debates. Members of the Dublin society are on record praising those meetings, and, above all, the unbounded enthusiasm of the Belfast members especially Ian McClelland and Hazel Armstrong. But the society remained a minority group within the filmgoing public. Membership figures suggests that at most they numbered under 1000 persons. The owners and managers of the commercial cinemas did not see that as serious competition to their business and, despite early concerns, some of them, notably the managers of the Imperial and the Apollo, exhibited a willingness to co-operate in its success by allowing the Society to use their premises and facilities.

All of that lay in the future as the audience left St Mary's Hall that March evening, many already looking forward to the next meeting that had been arranged for April 26th, in the Imperial cinema. Some of them probably crossed Bank Street and headed for the nearby Kelly's Cellars to discuss what they had just seen over a glass of the black stuff. Even for serious cineastes film going included a dimension of entertainment.

CHAPTER TWENTY THREE
Talkie Devil Development

During the early Twenties there was no hint that anyone in Belfast, either in the cinema business or among the viewing patrons, realised that a decade on the experience of going to the pictures would be so radically different. The change to sound, when it came, was surprising in its rapidity, as some of the local critics noted, taking place over three short years following April 1929. In an article in the Irish News (January 1933) recalling the delights of Belfast's old theatres, a writer recognised the overall impact of the cinema on stage shows and public taste. It involved, he admitted, a "marvellous machine" which had made shadows move, then talk and sing, thereby adding a new dimension to entertainment. But he also saw it as part of a wider "rush along the road of progress" to a mechanical age before which the "more pleasant" old order was giving way. It is an argument that is still heard today.

Audiences, especially the young, quickly accepted the new sound films as a natural technical development, but the silent experience, which had spanned thirty three years from the Alhambra's historic introduction, had left a residue of pleasant memories which continued to reveal themselves in various ways. Among the older generation there was an upwelling of nostalgia for the old days, with reminiscences that must have brought smiles to the faces of the young trendy film fans. Typical were the comments of a writer in the I.S.N. who recalled his experiences with the magic lantern shows and the first films. He conjured up the excitement and atmosphere of an early silent cinema beginning with the novelty of an usher guiding him safely through "the Stygian darkness" to his seat. The entertainment that followed was, he claimed, much superior to the "talkie devil development" of the modern sound cinemas. Another scribe, writing in the

All singing dancing pictures.

Whig under the pseudonym "An Old Fogey," went back even further in time and memory. He recalled, as a child, playing with a Zoethrope, spinning its wheel and watching, fascinated, as the little figures moved. But that was nothing, he wrote, compared to the excitement in Belfast years later when Edweard Muybridge demonstrated his Zoopraxiscope to the members and friends of the Natural History and Philosophical Society, taking their breath away with its projection of "really lifelike motion." He had seen the cinema change dramatically in its short history, and he regretted the passing of what he called "the shadow theatre," because the best silent films, he claimed, were the equal of anything being produced in sound. They were beautiful to look at, and satisfying on an intellectual level, especially those from France, Italy, Germany and Sweden, whose productions regrettably no longer appeared on local screens. Those films were made by people who regarded the cinema as "more than a vehicle for cheap melodrama."

Such comments are no longer regarded as the opinions of a backward - looking minority. Martin Scorsese has referred to the "sheer beauty and sophistication of silent cinema," and has added the weight of his professional standing to support those who are working to restore and preserve the old silent films that have survived. Local elderly people who remembered going to the silent cinemas were interviewed by the author. Many of them retained vivid recollections of the experience and while they sometimes forgot the names of some of the productions, they could recall major stars and certain scenes or episodes in great detail. Charlie Chaplin, Buster Keaton, Harold Lloyd, Pearl White, W.S.Hart, Valentino, Clara Bow, Laurel and Hardy were names that often turned up in their conversations. While accepting and enjoying sound films, they agreed that there was something special about silent films, and silent cinemas.

Attempts have been made in the last quarter century to recreate that special atmosphere at events in London, Dublin and locally at the Q.F.T. and the Ulster Hall. which, while fascinating to specialist audiences, were never completely successful. But they do ensure that silent films continue to be shown, and have contributed to a continuing and increasing interest in silent films today. In December 2008 the Ulster Orchestra accompanied a programme of six silent Chaplin films in the Waterfront Hall, while the ninth Belfast Film Festival presented a well attended showing of the 1923 version of "The Hunchback of Notre Dame" starring Lon Chaney, in St Anne's Cathedral in late March 2009. During that showing a young Queen's student sitting behind the author whispered to his girlfriend: "This is fantastic!" It was. In March 2013, during Lent, the Ulster Hall presented a special screening of Carl Dreyer's silent masterpiece "La Passion de Jeanne D'Arc" made in 1928 and starring Maria Falconetti. The organist of Westminster Cathedral, Martin Baker, supported the visuals with a rich and superbly timed score played on the Mulholland Organ. An audience of about 300 persons, including many young people, sat in silent awe and appreciation of film making of the highest order.

In the early Thirties those in Belfast who read the serious newspapers, or film magazines like Film Weekly or Sight and Sound, knew that some of the top stars in Hollywood had their reservations about sound. Lillian Gish pointed out that in silent acting the whole body was used to express feelings and emotions, but in the talkies the voice became dominant and as a result, she believed, much was lost. That was one reason that she decided to turn her back on the cinema for a time and return to her first love, the theatre, much to the disappointment of her local fans. Her theory would have found some support in Belfast. Edward Collins in his letter - already referred to - to the I.S.N. on behalf of the deaf, wrote that a deaf friend had complained to him that "since speech was added, the quality of acting had deteriorated." Of course defenders of the talkies argued that a new style of acting was required for sound productions, with new skills adapted to the requirements of the microphone. Lillian Gish's friend Mary Pickford seemed to agree because it was reported that she had bought up all her old silent films and withdrawn them from exhibition because she felt they now looked "ridiculous." Not everyone would agree with that.

Charlie Chaplin was another who resisted the change to sound, and he had both the influence and finance to do so. His many admirers in Belfast waited with patience and anticipation to see what he would do, and he didn't disappoint them. His latest film was "City Lights,"a nine reeler which he completed in 1930. It was artistically a silent film with a sentimental and essentially Victorian plot, with no spoken dialogue, though he did use natural sounds and music on the soundtrack. The Royal Cinema, loyal as always to silent Art, presented it on 24th August 1931. Filmgoers responded enthusiastically and it ran for three weeks to packed houses. There is no way of knowing what the composition of the audiences was, but one could suspect that they were made up mainly of the more mature elements of the population, with a sprinkling of those who felt they were seeing an important part of movie history. With regard to the film, the critics were overwhelmed. The Irish News praised the artistry of Chaplin, and described the film as having a story that was simple, but brilliantly told, with not one word spoken, though music and sound effects were included. The Whig critic welcomed the film as "long awaited" and added nostalgically that "a silent film in a house converted to talkies drew packed crowds." The film itself, he claimed, had "all Charlie's qualities that made him famous, crammed into it (so that) it vibrated with fun and emotion." Another critic referred to "the heroic and hilarious Charlie" who, in the story, gives up so much so that the heroine (Virginia Cherrill) can have an expensive operation to restore her sight. In return for his sacrifice, which included a period in gaol, he received only her thanks and a final title "Yes, I can see now," which the Little Tramp accepted, without resentment, as his reward. As "The End" appeared on the screen many in the audience must have felt that those familiar words represented the closure of the Silent Era, but they were to be pleasantly surprised later, because Charlie had another silent ace up his sleeve.

The film in question was "Modern Times," which reached Belfast on 24th August 1936. The traditional venue for a major Chaplin film was the Royal Cinema, but it was the Classic that claimed the distinction of showing Chaplin's last silent masterpiece. On that day Mr Mac Dermott, the manager of the cinema, hosted a special Lunch a La Chaplin in the Classic restaurant, to which the Press were invited, to celebrate the premiere of the film. The meal, which included courses like Classic Hors d'Oeuvres, Hungary Kid Soup, Lame Duck and Pompadour Pauline (the leading lady was Pauline Goddard) was a great success. The head waiter, known familiarily to all as Bobby, joined in the general gaiety by serving in a Chaplin bowler and moustache. The Irish News reporter approved and commented that the result showed that Mr Mac Dermott could chose not only a good film but a good meal. The Press were introduced to the special guest, C.H. Hurst (known as Hush Hush) who was the publicity man for Gaumont British Films. He had been involved in the cinema business almost from its inception,and he had many stories to relate about those early days. He recalled that 25 years before he had been one of a group of bioscope operators who could be hired for twelve guineas (£12: 60) to present a film show of "living pictures" in a local hall. He usually travelled by train, carrying the bioscope machine, with about 6,000 feet of film in a tin box. He would set up his projector and show the short films, often accompanying them with a running commentary. The projector was hand cranked which, he claimed, required special skills, and a sympathy with the medium. Romantic scenes, for example, were cranked slowly with feeling, while chase sequences needed liveliness and fast turning. Advances in technology had brought about many improvements and the modern projectionist, he noted, needed quite different skills. He intimated (humorously, of course) that the modern projectionist had a much easier time, a conclusion that local projectionists would not have agreed with. They felt that the new technical developments, and working conditions, brought increased working pressures. In July of the previous year projectionists from across the city had met in Gaumont British's private cinema in Donegall Street and took the first steps to set up a Belfast Projectionist's Guild. It was to be a social club with premises where members could enjoy "a quiet hour" away from their work. It also aimed to organise outings, dances and other recreations for the members.

After the meal the guests moved into the auditorium to see the film, which dealt with the impact of changes in industrial technology on workers. Without exception the critics welcomed it as an outstanding achievement, which showed that Chaplin was still a major figure in cinema. Only Charlie Chaplin, wrote the Whig critic, would have dared to make a silent film today, and to make it so brilliantly. There was only one act working in the talkies that might have pulled it off, and that was the Marx Brothers, some of whose "larger lunacies" might be compared with Chaplin in that they were in the true tradition of the great clowns. The Irish News critic described the film as more than just a comedy. It was, he felt, "a rich and often bitter satire" on the machine age, presented with all the inventive genius that one expects from Chaplin. Artistically it was a silent film but he admired the way that Chaplin incorporated natural sounds like the roar of machinery, or traffic or even a radio, to complement the plot. Chaplin himself was superb, "full of his old funny tricks." The Whig critic agreed. In appearance Charlie hadn't changed, with his small moustache, his bowler, baggy pants and cane, while in his art he was still the symbolic figure "expressing the inarticulate longings of the little man." Many in the audience would have had sympathy with the film's message that the workers hadn't benefited from the wealth that machines produced, but were like sheep at the mercy of the machines and those who made money from them. The Irish News critic had the last word. Overall, he wrote, the film was a reminder of how "completely satisfactory the old silent films were." It was, he concluded, a film that should be seen by all and he took heart from the fact that queues began forming along Castle Lane from as early as 11:00 am. The Whig critic reflected those sentiments as he noted, approvingly, that the six showings on the first day were packed, while management responded to the public interest by retaining the film for a second week. It went on to further successful showings in the Clonard and the Picturedrome.

When Charlie and Paulette Godard walked off towards the horizon their demeanour indicated a hint of optimism about their future, but for all intents and purposes that scene represented the end of the silent film era in Belfast. Soon after that, a report in the Irish News referred to silent films as curios from the past. Even the "Old Fogey" admitted that the younger generation wanted to see talkies, and regarded silent films as an out of date novelty. A film going the rounds at the same time treated them in a similar light. Called "Cavalcade of the Movies" it represented a final chapter in their history. The film was a documentary which the News Letter described as the first attempt to show the development of the cinema, in a cinematic manner. It consisted of "a hundred oddments of screen history," and it vividly recalled the great names of the past - Valentino, John Bunny, Lon Chaney among others - illustrated by clips from their films. It was, said the News Letter critic, "a novel attraction." Today it wouldn't be out of place on television.

References to silent films and silent stars continued to surface in local reports. One of those referred to John Gilbert the man who had romanced Greta Garbo both on screen and off, and whose career illuminates the human tragedy that lay behind the change to sound. During the silent Twenties his handsome good looks and intense love - making had caused many a local female heart to flutter. He didn't disappear completely from the screen with the advent of sound as is sometimes suggested. He continued to make films but, in general, he had become a pale shadow of his former self. During the early Thirties his sound films arrived at regular intervals, usually showing in the Imperial or the Royal Cinema before moving on to the Picturedrome, the Clonard, the Duncairn and elsewhere. When the lively "Way For a Sailor" showed in early 1932, Gilbert was co-starred with Wallace Beery, and the Irish News critic wrote that it was "a splendid film, with good scenic effects and superb acting." A few months later the Imperial showed "Gentleman's Fate," in which, according to the same critic, Gilbert combined "the romanticism of his silent films with a more dashing personality." The following year he appeared in "West of Broadway" playing a rich young man who returns from the Great War broken in health. He takes to the bottle to help face up to changed conditions, which causes his fiancée to leave him. The Irish News critic thought that he gave "a fine performance in a difficult role." Ironically the part reflected the problems facing Gilbert in his private life where, frustrated at the parts he was offered, he had begun drinking heavily. His next film, "Downstairs," really surprised his admirers. The script was written by the actor himself and, as the Whig critic pointed out, it represented "a new approach," with Gilbert playing "a sinister villain." The following year the Royal Cinema presented "Fast Workers," which the critics and fans found more entertaining, welcoming it for its "thrills, romance and laughter." That was followed by "Queen Christina" in which he was reunited with Greta Garbo.

His career seemed to be looking up again, but behind the scenes, he was an ill man, an alcoholic, a far cry from the dashing hero of the Twenties. In early January 1936 his admirers were saddened when the local papers announced, in brief reports, that he had died suddenly of a heart attack. The Telegraph referred to him as a "famous star of the silent picture days" whose fame had declined with the coming of talkies, while the Whig described him as the "screen's perfect lover." He was only 41 years old, approximately the same age as the cinema itself. A cynic once suggested - after the death of Valentino - that, for an actor, an early death was "a good career move," but for a star who, only a decade before, had dominated the screen and attracted long queues at Belfast cinemas, the local reaction was muted, to say the least. The death of John Gilbert was another indication that the silent era had passed well and truly into history.

The audiences of the Thirties preferred talkies and in Belfast, as elsewhere, the film industry responded accordingly. The result was the most intensive period of cinema construction that the city has ever experienced. At the beginning of 1933 there were 26 cinemas available, with a total capacity of around 23, 900 seats. They were all former silent cinemas that had been modified and partly redesigned to meet the technical needs of the new medium. Such changes and improvements were deemed vital to maintaining the attractiveness of what the Irish News called "the retail end of the business," where the films were presented and sold to the public. In April 1935 even the prestigious Picture House closed its doors for a week "for renovations," before reopening with "Disraeli" (d.Alfred Green,1929) starring George Arliss, one of the most acclaimed actors of the day. It was the type of film that was much admired in responsible quarters - serious, theatrical in style, educational in tone and accompanied by an aura of quality and respectability. That combination paid off when Arliss won the Oscar for best actor that year. A short time later the less prestigious but equally popular Crumlin also closed for an overhaul which involved new furnishing and decoration.

After only four years of sound businessmen like Michael Curran, Ferris Pounds, John Gaston, Harry Wilton and others had come to realise that what was really required were new modern buildings specially designed for sound reproduction, incorporating the latest technology and offering the maximum in cinema comfort. Through a combination of their initiative and business efforts, plus the professional skills and imaginative plans of architects like Thomas Mc Lean of Howard Street, and J. McBride Neill of Ann Street, a total of 17 new cinemas was built, beginning with the Apollo on the Ormeau Road (which opened on 20th March, 1933) and ending with the Forum on the Shankill Road (which opened on 20th Nov. 1937). It is difficult to be completely precise about seat numbers as totals vary slightly between those recorded on the the architects' plans, in the newspaper reports and in the official figures from the cinema owners. Despite that, it is clear that in all, the new cinemas added approximately another 22,000 seats, thereby nearly doubling the number of seats available in a period of only four years.

The Whig described 1937 as "a record year for cinemas" but, with a total of 43 halls, others protested that there were already too many cinemas in the city. A writer in the Irish News commented wryly that the persons who made such remarks should try to find a seat in a cinema on a Saturday evening, and pointed out that over the Christmas holidays that year all the downtown halls displayed "House Full" notices. The Northern Ireland Caterer's Association, or White Cinema Club as it was better known, held their annual meeting in the Imperial Hotel in late November and were addressed by the President, James Curran. In his survey of the twelve months just past he noted the increased number of new cinemas, but added that, despite the increased capacity, overall business had remained "regular and satisfactory." He could have put the situation into perspective by suggesting that the number of cinemas was not exorbitant for a city that, according to the Whig, also supported 56 pawnbrokers, 40 official moneylenders, 504 public houses and spirit grocers, 169 Protestant churches, 19 Catholic churches and a multitude of mission halls.

The roads in Belfast converge towards the centre like the fingers and thumb on a hand. The earlier cinemas were built mainly in the palm of the hand but, after 1933, the new sound cinemas moved out and located along the fingers where they had ready access to extensive new housing areas and spreading suburbs. The owners preferred sites fronting on the main roads, often at major intersections where they could tap extra pedestrian flows (the majority of people still walked to their local cinema), bus and tram routes and, with an eye to the future, even cars. Many boasted car parks for that purpose, and there were rumours of roof top parking though that never materialised. Accessibility to residential areas was a key consideration. With reference to the buildings themselves the emphasis was firmly on modernity, comfort and quality.

After the sites were chosen and secured the next step was up to the architects. The architects were faced with a number of challenges. On the outside the buildings had to have a style that distinguished them and indicated their function. They had to look modern and inviting as became a modern entertainment form. That was achieved by using a variation of the new Art Deco style with its emphasis on clean smooth perpendicular or horizontal lines. Domes such as adorned the Lyceum, the Mount Pottinger Picturedrome, the Royal Cinema and the New Princess were rejected as were other fussy adornments. There was also a clear break with the traditional architecture associated with theatres, music halls and silent cinemas.

The contrast and change in style was brought home dramatically to the people of East Belfast, especially those who lived on or near the Mountpottinger Road. The Picturedrome had been a familiar sight there since its erection in 1911, and the light from its tower had become a friendly beacon after dark. However, the fire damage it had suffered in 1932 was more severe than first suspected and, despite renovations, Ferris Pounds and his fellow directors concluded that the building had been overtaken by recent developments in cinema construction and "had become obsolete." It was decided to knock it down and replace it with a brand new building. The architect given the task was J. Mc Bride Neill and he produced a cinema which impressed all on its opening night, Monday 12th November 1934. The building was designed in the new international style that had originated on the continent, especially in Germany, and Mr Mc Bride Neill involved himself in every detail of the project even down to the comfort of the seating. Four experimental models of seats were made for testing before one was chosen.

The work was completed in four months, mainly during the summer, using local firms and workers. On the outside the clean, almost severe, horizontal lines contrasted with what they had replaced. The frontage was white, lit at night with green and red neon strips and bulbs. A canopy protected the four black entrance doors which led into a spacious tiled foyer. From it there was access to a long waiting room where queues could wait away from the wet and cold without. Carpeted stairs led up to comfortable lounges, with access to the balcony, which seated 250 patrons. The main auditorium, which seated another 800, had a decor dominated by shades of gold. It was characterised again by spaciousness, the smooth walls leading up to a wide stepped ceiling subtly lit by concealed lighting. Mr Mc Neill felt that the lack of superficial decoration resulted in improved acoustics, a view that would be shared by modern designers. The prices were announced as front stalls 5d, back stalls 6d and the circle one shilling. Circle seats could be booked for an extra 3d.

The opening ceremonies went well and after the speeches the staff presented Mr Pounds with a large decorated horse shoe which was then hung in the foyer, to bring good luck. The well known soprano, Chrissie Manning, travelled from Dublin and entertained the enthusiastic assembly with Irish songs including "The Rose of Tralee," as a prelude to the main attraction. The initial film was "The Lily of Killarney," described as "a musical romance of the Emerald Isle" but actually based on the story of the Colleen Bawn. The Irish News praised its music, and its "picturesque settings with unrivalled views of Killarney." The News Letter critic agreed that the scenery was magnificent, but felt that overall the film was "disappointing." He partly blamed the main players, John Garrick and Gina Malo, and suggested that if Sara Allgood and Stanley Holloway, who had supporting roles, had taken the main parts it would have been a much better film. The Belfast Telegraph again praised the photography and added that the plot "was skilfully worked out." The I.S.N. critic added that the film had "a real Irish atmosphere."

The other owners weren't encumbered by the problems that Ferris Pounds had faced in that they were building from scratch. Like the Picturedrome their buildings, in the main, exist now only in plans, photographs, newspaper descriptions and memory. Fortunately some details of their style can still be discerned in those buildings that have survived, though with changed functions, like the Majestic on the Lisburn Road (until 2013 a furniture store), the Ambassador on the Cregagh Road (a supermarket), the Castle on the Castlereagh Road and, until recently, the Curzon on the Ormeau Road (now an apartment block). The true impact of those fine structures as entertainment centres can still be experienced to some degree in the lone survivor, the Strand at Gelson's corner on the Holywood Road. Professional attitudes to cinemas in the Thirties and Forties were mixed but in general they were not held in high architectural esteem and many architects regarded them as unworthy of their skills. By the time that their true social value was recognised it was nearly too late, many already having been modified out of all recognition, vandalised for other commercial purposes, abandoned or demolished. For Belfast it is certainly too late because of the 43 halls that enriched the cityscape at the end of 1937 only one remains as a functioning cinema, the Strand.

In 1937 it was a very different picture. Along whatever road people travelled into the city, with the exception of the high quality residential Malone Road, their eyes were drawn to those highly visible centres of popular Thirties culture. On the Shore Road stood the Troxy near the intersection with Fortwilliam Crescent; on the Antrim Road the Capitol, a Curran Theatre at the corner with Alexandra Park; on the Crumlin Road the Savoy dominated the corner with Tennant Street while the Forum stood opposite the recently opened Twaddell Avenue; on the Oldpark Road the Park occupied the corner with Torrens Avenue; on the

Opening of the Astoria: Curran Theatres expand, Dec. 1934. Source: Northern Whig.

Shankill Road the Stadium stood at Tennant Street; on the Falls Road the much loved Broadway at Willowbank just across from the populous Beechmount district; on the Lisburn Road another Curran Theatre, the Regal, while further down at the corner of Derryvolgie Avenue, the stately Majestic. Across the Lagan the picture was similar with the the Apollo, and John Gaston's Curzon at the corner of Raby Street on the Ormeau Road; the Ambassador on the Cregagh Road; the Castle on the Castlereagh Road; the Astoria on the Upper Newtownards Road and the Strand on the Holywood Road. No one resided too far from a cinema.

The original plans for the Strand cinema were drawn by Thomas Guthrie, an architect from North Parade, at the request of Harry Wilton of 707 Antrim Road. Mr Wilton had acquired a triangular shaped site at Gelson's corner on the Hollywood Road with the aim of erecting a cinema there. The plans were submitted to the City Surveyor on 26th March 1935. Before any actual building work began Mr Wilton sold the site to the English based Union Circuit which then asked J. McBride Neill to draw up plans for the new building. Mr McBride designed his building in the Art Deco style and when it opened on 7th December 1935 it impressed all who saw it. The official opening was performed by the Lord Mayor, Sir Crawford McCullogh, and the proceedings were specially filmed for Movietone Newsreel, and were screened in the cinema the following week. The Lord Mayor and the local reporters were seduced by the sleek appearance, the smooth curves, the horizontal lines and the clever lighting which characterised the building. They praised the skill with which the architect had overcome the drawbacks of the less than adequate site and had produced a fine structure which from a certain angle reminded some observers of a great liner. Despite TV, the Troubles and other problems the Strand managed to stay afloat and in 1999 its owners asked the architectural firm of Robinson Patterson to refurbish the building. In an attempt to recreate McNeill Bride's original concept the architects went back to the original 1935 plans as their starting point. The work was completed in just over four months at a cost of around £212,000. The interior atmosphere has been lost by the division into four modern cinemas, but the impressive exterior now gives a worthy window into the past and some idea of the impact the original had on the local landscape. It is Belfast's only surviving Thirties Picture Palace.

Opening of the Broadway with Richard Hayward in person.

While the main aim of the cinema owners was to tap the residential areas of the suburbs a number of the new buildings were also located within the city's "palm." The first of the new cinemas, the Apollo, was hardly suburban in location. It was situated on the front of the Ormeau road on the city side of the Ormeau Bridge, at the corner of Agincourt Avenue. Modest in size (it seated fewer than 1000 and had no balcony), it was designed by J.McNeill Bride for the Mc Vea family. Its target audience was the areas now known as the Holy Land and the Lower Ormeau but the inclusion of a car park suggested that it was hoped to throw its net further afield. Its programming was continuous from 6:00pm, with reasonable charges of 5d, 6d and one shilling. The opening film was "If I Had A Million," the impressive cast of which included Charles Laughton, Gary Cooper, George Raft and W.C.Fields. It opened rather quietly on 31st October 1933 and inspired few comments from the newspapers. It soon became a great favourite of the locals, who came to refer to it as the Polo, where they could catch up with and enjoy the likes of the Marx Brothers in "Horse Feathers," and "Monkey Business," Brigitte Helm in "Atlantide," and Clara Bow in "Call Her Savage." From the end of 1937 it also went up-market artificially when it became the main venue for the programmes of the Belfast Film Society. It remained in the ownership of the McVeas until 1939 when it was bought by the Curran Brothers.

Another non - suburban cinema was the Windsor which was built on the Donegal Road in a densely populated residential area that still lacked a local cinema. The opportunity to rectify that omission was recognised by a J.D.Finney of Banbridge who acquired a large site on the front of the road between Empire Street and Richview Street. The cinema was built in conjunction with a number of shops, as many of the new cinemas were. The architect was Thomas McLean and he designed a building that was rather basic though "commodious and comfortable," according to the News Letter. One didn't really go to the Windsor because of its level of comfort, though the sight lines and the acoustics were excellent. At 62 feet across (about 19 metres), the auditorium impressed as one of the widest in the city, and its straight walls and high ceiling were simply decorated in cream and crimson. The large screen was made of perforated rubber to give maximum brightness and when not in use was hidden decorously behind a draped curtain of crimson silk. The sound system was British Thompson Houston and while it and the projectors had to be brought from England all other fittings and work on the building was carried out by local labour. The cinema had its own electrical supply which was an advantage because during the Thirties there were often annoying breaks in the electricity service. At the side of the building near the generator there was a "free car park."

For the official opening on Saturday 23rd March 1935 all seats had a special price of only 6d, though normal pricing was stalls 6d and balcony one shilling. All proceeds from that first evening went to the RVH and Mater hospitals. The special film for the occasion was "Yes, Mr Brown," starring Jack Buchanan. Normal working conditions began on the following Monday with two separate evening shows at 6:45 and 9:00pm, when the introductory film was a British production called "Danny Boy" with Frank Forbes Rorinson. It was described by one critic as "a sentimental musical." The Windsor was located in a well established working class area, where it was welcomed and strongly supported. During the Forties and Fifties it was always packed and early attendance, before 7:00pm, was necessary to ensure a seat. By the late Sixties it was in decline. The fabric was allowed to deteriorate and an essentially young audience (their elders were at home watching television) tended to be rather boisterous. It never showed first run features, but it compensated with long double bills of quality films which represented good value for money. That was the secret of its success, which continued for over forty years.

After the successful launch of the Strand the Union circuit turned its attention to the more affluent Lisburn Road. The Upper Lisburn Road was already served by the Regal which the Curran Brothers had opened in October 1935, while John Gaston had acquired an excellent site at the corner of Derryvolgie Avenue and had arranged for J.McBride Neill to design a luxurious cinema to be called the Majestic. The plans were submitted in April 1935 and were approved three months later for a three layered building consisting of ground floor stalls, a lower and an upper circle to seat 1400 in all. Union Cinemas bought the cinema and it was opened on 25th May 1936 by the Lord Mayor, Sir Crawford Mc Cullagh.

There had been complaints from local residents and from members of the nearby Windsor Presbyterian Church about the unsuitability of the location, and at least one of those residents wrote to the Whig calling for stricter planning laws to protect the cityscape. He complained that the new building "ruined irremediably the contour of the road," and interrupted what had been "a pleasing prospect." He much preferred the graceful church spires and trees which added to the beauty of the area. But that was a minority opinion and on the evening of the opening, the cinema was crowded, while a large number of people collected outside to see the Lord Mayor arrive. Those inside heard him congratulate the architect on his splendid vision, and warmly welcome the Union Circuit into the city. The company, he explained, already controlled over 200 cinemas across the Br. Isles, and had optimistic plans for N. Ireland, including the new Ritz which was already taking shape near the city centre. In November a representative of the circuit, Mr J. Kean, held a press conference in the Grand Central Hotel to clarify their plans for further expansion in N. Ireland. The company was very satisfied with the public response to the Strand and the Majestic, and aimed to build a further 21 new cinemas across the area, some of which were already under way. The most impressive one would be located in downtown Belfast.

The site chosen for the new Ritz was acquired from a local businessman, James McCartney of Shaftesbury Square. It was a large, flat accessible area, where Jury's Hotel now stands, located at the bottom of the Grosvenor Road at the intersection with Fisherwick Place. Across the Grosvenor road was the Hippodrome cinema, while opposite, in dramatic contrast, was Church House the headquarters of the Presbyterian Church, with its grave and sobering frontage. It was situated within five minutes walking distance of three other cinemas (the Hippodrome, the Coliseum and the Kelvin in College Sq. East), and the city's premier theatre, the Grand Opera House. By 1936 the citizens were well used to seeing sites being fenced off with signs announcing the construction of another cinema, but the Grosvenor Road site was different. It was bigger than normal with over 500 workers, mainly local labour, involved in the construction. No recent building in the city aroused such a high level of public interest and comment, much more indeed than that other "union" building recently opened at Stormont, an event largely ignored by the Nationalist community.

During the weeks prior to the opening, Union Cinemas added to the general excitement by releasing titbits of information to the Press aimed at whetting the public's curiosity. It would be the largest and most luxurious place of entertainment in the city with an auditorium that would seat over 2,000 patrons; its facilities would include the most up to date projection equipment allied to first class sound from Western Electric; included would be a large stage with every modern device capable of handling 30 complete changes of scenery and producing a wide range of impressive lighting effects; beneath the stage, housed in two rooms, would be a specially built Compton organ costing £10,000 with nearly 1000 pipes varying in diameter from a few millimetres to two feet, and up to 16 feet long. It all sounded too good to be true. According to the Belfast Telegraph curious eyes watched and noted every move daily (including Sundays) as the building "took on grace and form."

Building the Ritz.
Source: News Letter.

The architect was Leslie Kemp from London. He was an experienced professional who had entered the profession in 1922 and had designed cinemas in London, and across southern and northern England. His work had included a number of much praised Gaumont super cinemas, elaborate and luxurious buildings that included the latest projection and sound equipment, with complete stage facilities and, in many cases, an organ. He understood that many provincial centres desired such super cinemas in downtown locations, regarding them as symbols of modernity and success. He therefore designed the Ritz as Belfast's super cinema, a sign to the world that Belfast was a modern thinking, up-to-date metropolis. When the scaffolding and the protective fencing were finally removed the building appeared in all its glory. On -lookers were suitably impressed.

It was certainly large, extending from the Grosvenor Road to Murray Street, and it gleamed under its covering of cream faience tiles. The main entrance with its large double glass doors, approached from the pavement up wide marble steps, was at the corner where one turned from the Grosvenor Road into Fisherwick Place. A canopy extended the whole length of the building so that queues for all parts could wait under cover, while the walls above the canopy glowed with the light of coloured neon strips and concealed bulbs. The foyer was spacious with walnut panelling and deep pile carpet. On the right side of the foyer a wide marble staircase led up to the spacious cafe, its walls covered with paper in a tapestry design, with gold leaf decoration and tastefully located mirrors, all lit by an elaborate chandelier. A small dance floor added to the relaxed elegance. To the left a wide carpeted staircase gave access to the circle, while straight on a short corridor led to the auditorium.

A few days before the opening it was announced that preparations well nearly completed, that only about fifty seats were still available to the public, all in the most expensive (10/6 each), evening dress, upper circle area. An elaborate stage show would precede the inaugural film, introduced and compered by Harold Ramsey, the popular BBC organist, who would also play the new organ. The show would star Gracie Fields who planned to come over from England via Dublin, from where she would be driven north. She would be supported by the well known band of Sonny Farrar and his Sunny Boys plus other variety acts. Jack Hylton, the band leader, would also fly over to be present, though without his musicians. For the first time ever the BBC would broadcast the opening of a new cinema on radio, while Paramount newsreel cameramen would be present to record the event on film. There was no doubt that Union Cinemas had pulled out all the stops in their desire to impress. The event was the talk of the town and the evening of Monday, 9th November 1936 was looked forward to with unconcealed excitement. Equally, from today's viewpoint, it can be seen now as a highlight in the history of the cinema in Belfast, an acceptance of the cinema as an integral and proper aspect of social living..

The doors were officially opened at 7:00 pm but long before that crowds began to converge on Fisherwick Place to enjoy the experience and above all, to see Gracie Fields. The front of the building was a blaze of light which formed a brilliant backdrop as fifty policemen struggled to control over 2,000 excited people, while keeping access to the cinema open. The ticket holders, who included Belfast's "famous, near famous, and not-at-all famous citizens" (Irish News) had to push through the large crowd to reach the steps which they mounted, with some relief, into the foyer. There they were met by bright Klieg lights set up to allow the Paramount news cameramen to film the scene. By 8:00 pm every seat in the auditorium was filled by nearly 2500 eager patrons. They sat holding their souvenir programmes, quietly listening to music played by the band of the First Battalion, the Border Regiment, overawed by the size of the space, admiring the high ceiling and its supporting walls decorated with horizontal bands of mottled reds and blues. The Irish News reporter summed up the occasion, describing it as "the largest, best dressed, and most expensive audience which ever saw a theatrical

Notice of opening.

show in Belfast, the largest crowd of spectators which ever gathered outside a Belfast theatre,(and) the largest traffic block ever caused by a theatrical show in Belfast. "Outside, the crowd was waiting for Gracie Fields. Her car, which was late in arriving, had some difficulty reaching the pavement but with the assistance of the police she reached and mounted the entrance steps. At the top she stopped and waved at the cheering crowd before disappearing into the foyer through a door held open by a young pageboy called Billy Hall.

At 8:00 pm the stage curtain was raised to reveal the official party of special guests including the Lord Mayor, Sir Crawford McCullagh, representatives of Union Cinemas, the architect, members of the many firms involved notably the builders H. and J. Martin, and representatives of the charities, the Newspaper Press Fund and the Lord Mayor's Coal Fund, which the gala opening would benefit. After the traditional self - congratulatory speeches in which thanks were showered like confetti on all involved, the Lord Mayor performed the official opening. The hour long stage show began immediately with a special item dedicated to Belfast's major industries which was introduced by the hull of the SS Prosperity moving slowly across the stage. The message was not lost on the watchers that the success and popularity of the cinema industry in Belfast was an indication that the recession was ending. People had more money in their pockets and could spend it on entertainment. A parade reflecting aspects of local interest followed, during which Harold Ramsey introduced Jim Salmon, the oldest riveter in the city, along with, by contrast, one of the youngest apprentices from the shipyard, also Jenny King the well known flower seller, and John Geddis the oldest jaunting-car driver. At the end came a group of ushers and other workers from the Ritz accompanied by the manager, Mr Russell. Harold Ramsey then gave a demonstration of the musical capabilities of the organ with a selection ranging from Tiger Rag to Danny Boy. But the performer whom everyone wanted to see and hear was Gracie Fields.

When Miss Fields appeared there was warm and prolonged applause. Her popularity, which emanated from her stage appearances (she had appeared in the Opera House a few years before, in September 1933), her records and her films, couldn't be doubted. Seeing her on stage, the Irish News reporter wrote, she combined "good looks, a voice that seems super human and acting ability with an overflowing joy of life." Her working class background in Rochdale, where, for a time, she worked as a part - timer in a cotton mill, and her down to earth personality added to her local appeal. She showed that facet when she put a finger from each hand in her mouth and gave her famous loud whistle to quieten the audience so that she could begin singing. At the end of her act the audience were reluctant to let her leave the stage.

After the live show the main film was shown. It was "Queen of Hearts" starring Gracie Fields herself. The plot, which reflected scenes from her own life, told the

The new Ritz shows its domination.

Gracie Fields at official opening. Source: News Letter.

story of a working class girl with the ambition to become a star of musical comedy......
which, of course, she does. The Irish News reporter found the film "fast moving, with
hilarious scenes that kept the audience in uncontrollable laughter." So, what the Belfast
Telegraph called "a sensational night," ended but many in the audience were reluctant
to leave their seats. They sat there chatting and gazing about. Some commented on the
comfort of the seating with its salmon pink colouring, or how clear and fresh the air in the
auditorium was, while others were impressed by the effectiveness of the lighting, though
not a single bulb could be seen anywhere. Meanwhile 300 specially invited guests ascended
the marble steps to the cafe for a meal, and danced to the music of Sonny Farrer's Band.
Gracie Fields wasn't one of them because she was already on the boat sailing out of Belfast
heading for Heysham, and another engagement.

Estimates put the combined crowd (indoors and outdoors) which assembled at the
opening around four thousand men, women and young people. The main attractions were
the novelty of the occasion, and the promise of seeing Gracie Fields in person, factors
which tended to temporarily obscure the fact that the other downtown picture houses were
offering fine entertainment also, though as a young man who was there told the author,
business elsewhere was rather "quiet" that evening. The Classic had a musical with Jesse
Matthews in "It's Love Again," the Picture House was showing "The Early Bird" with local
actor Richard Hayward, the Hippodrome had Spencer Tracy in Fritz Lang's thoughtful
"Fury," while the Royal Cinema presented a comedy called "The Rainmakers," with
Wheeler and Woolsey. The Grand Opera House was staging musical comedy in the form
of "The Merry Widow." The suburban houses were also showing crowd pullers. Typical was
the Clonard delighting the Falls Road audience with "Top Hat," while across the city the
Duncairn had the talented Shirley Temple in "The Little Colonel."

The Ritz had arrived in style and its owner's plan was to make it Belfast's premier
cinema - the adverts referred to it as Ireland's Wonder Theatre - and in that they were more
than successful. During the following three decades long queues stretched back along the
pavements on the Grosvenor Road and Fisherwick Place. For those, including the author,
who stood in those queues and frequented the Ritz words alone don't evoke the special
feeling of walking up the steps, past the uniformed ushers and through the glass doors
into the spacious foyer with its deep pile carpet. The change from traffic noise to luxurious
quiet was sudden and dramatic. One had entered a different world. The building was, as the
Telegraph commented, truly a "cinema of cinemas," and anyone who spent an evening in
the Ritz never really forgot the experience.

The cafe opened at 10:00 am to cater to the public while the cinema opened its doors
at 11:30 am with continuous performances from midday to 11:00 pm. The aim was to give
value for money with first class films combined with live stage shows. Films and live acts
on the same bill were quite familiar to older filmgoers, especially those who had frequented
the Alhambra, but in 1936 it was presented as something new called Cine Variety. It proved
to be an instant success and indicated that despite the amazing popularity of "canned"
entertainment people would still respond to quality live acts. Cine variety became especially
associated with the new Ritz, or the Union Cinema Ritz, to give it its full title. The highly
praised opening show was typical cine variety and it was retained for a second week, to be

followed by Myrna Loy, Clarke Gable and Jean Harlow in "Wife v. Secretary," with Nina Mae Mc Kinney on stage supported by Snakehips Johnson and His Emperors of Jazz, plus Sidney Torch on the Compton Organ. Miss Mc Kinney was a black singer who had appeared in a number of films including "Sanders of the River" with Paul Robeson. Unfortunately after her Monday appearance she went down with a bout of influenza and was unable to appear. The complete show was held over for a second week and, fully recovered, she was able to fulfil her engagement. The following week saw another Myrna Loy film, "Petticoat Fever "with Ambrose and his Orchestra on stage. Ambrose was one of the top dance bands of the period.

The Thirties were the era of the big swing bands which attracted large crowds wherever they appeared. Highly organized and well drilled, they consisted of neatly dressed, well turned - out musicians, plus singers and a leader, who usually gave his name to the orchestra. Their main venues were the dance halls like the Plaza and the new Floral Hall where crowds enjoyed the music while dancing waltzes, quicksteps, and foxtrots. The most successful bands often appeared in films so their appearance on the Ritz cinema stage caused no real surprise, only delight. Over Christmas a new organist called Alex Taylor took up residence in the Ritz and he introduced and demonstrated an extra attraction called the Phantom Piano, described as "the only one of its kind in Ireland." The instrument in question was a full Grand Piano, supplied by Crane's of Belfast, which was connected by remote control to the Compton organ. It could therefore be played from the organ without anyone sitting at its keyboard. A piece of technical magic that the audiences obviously enjoyed.

Cine variety became progressively more elaborate, and in 1937 the local critics were marvelling at programmes of three and a half to four hours of top class entertainment. Typical, at the end of January, was a double film bill of "Dracula's Daughter" with the polished and soft spoken Otto Kruger, plus "Nobody's Fool" a comedy. On stage was Nat Gonella and his Georgians playing swing music, including superb versions (according to the Whig) of "Its A Sin to Tell a Lie" and "Tiger Rag" in both of which Gonella dazzled the audience with his trumpet solos. The band was supported by the "lunatic humour" of Three Loose Screws, the Five Canadian Wonders ("aerialists"), Harry Moore, a paper tearer and Cecil Chadwick on the Compton organ. In early March, another show consisted of two films, Wheeler and Woolsey in a comedy, "Mummy's Boys," set in Egypt, along with Chester Morris in a thriller, "Counterfeit," accompanied on stage by comedian Tommy Handley, along with The Fayre Four, a group of female accordionists, the BBC Mystery singer, tap dancers Freddie, Phyllis and Anne, and the Chevalier Bros. a team of knockabout comedians. Added to that was Frank Matthews, one of the earliest organists to broadcast on radio, on the Compton, plus a newsreel and the coming attractions. Amazing evenings for as little as one shilling.

The Ritz, of course, had the advantage of a prominent downtown location plus the financial and booking resources of a large circuit behind it. Not everyone could afford the Ritz prices and the company realized the value of its more suburban and less expensive venues, the Strand and the Majestic. They announced their intention to build another suburban cinema on the Crumlin Road at the corner of Cliftonpark Avenue on a site acquired from the former owner of the original Ritz site. The plan never materialised and most suburban cinemas remained in the hands of local entrepreneurs, either as individuals or groups. One of the most successful local groups was the Curran Circuit owned and organised by Michael Curran and his family. From their commercial base in the electrical industry (in Long Lane) they had moved into the cinema business with the Lyceum Cinema on the Antrim Road. One of their achievements there, which earns them a prominent place in the history of the cinema in Belfast, was the introduction of the first modern sound films (the Phonofilms) to local audiences. It is not surprising that when a similar sound - on - film system became established, they decided to move into sound films in a big way. Once the decision was taken they proceeded quickly. Over a period of two years (December 1934 to December 1936) they built and opened four major suburban cinemas, the Astoria, Regal, Capital and Broadway, and also acquired the Tonic in Bangor in November 1936, followed by the Apollo on the Ormeau Road in September 1939. Although neither was built by the Currans the Tonic and Apollo met the standards they demanded.

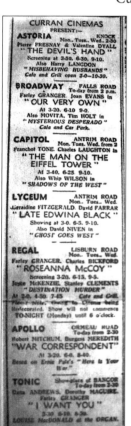

Quality and comfort at reasonable prices.

The Tonic was built by a local businessman, John H.O'Neill, at a cost of £76,000, on the Hamilton Road, and opened on 6th July 1936. It was an impressive and well appointed building which boasted a Compton organ which had cost £10,000 to build and install. Despite a warm welcome by the residents of Bangor Mr O'Neill experienced problems of cash flow and found himself in court in Belfast sued over non - payment of a bill for cinema furnishings. It was no surprise in some quarters when it was announced that the Tonic had been acquired by the Curran circuit. Thus their suburban chain was completed just before the outbreak of the Second World War, and they were able to take advantage of the surge in cinema going which took place in the war-torn city during the dark years that followed.

The Curran policy was simple and direct. It was to bring quality cinemas to suburban areas of upper working and middle class residents, not yet served by a local cinema. Sites were carefully chosen that were spacious, uncluttered and fronting a main road. The Astoria was the first to be completed, located on the Upper Newtownards Road, to serve the Knock and Ballyhackamore districts. It opened on 22nd December 1934 under the management of James Curran and his assistant manager Stendal Todd, whose accomplishments included the ability to play the organ, though that particular skill wasn't required in the Astoria. After the official proceedings and speeches the film billed for showing was Frank Capra's "It Happened One Evening" starring Clarke Gable and Claudette Colbert. The excitement of the evening was dampened somewhat by a technical problem when it was discovered that one of the projectors had been damaged in transit from England, and the films had to be abandoned. It fell to Mr Todd to apologise, which he did with style and humour, adding coyly that any money paid was going to charity and wouldn't be returned. By way of recompense, as the audience left, each member was presented with a box of chocolates which they carried off in addition to their souvenir programmes. Two days later the cinema was fully operational and audiences could enjoy Capra's fine film comedy (see page 468).

There were no such snags when the Regal and Capitol opened. The Regal site was on the front of the upper Lisburn Road, at number 366, between Bawnmore Road and Lancefield Road. By coincidence the site had formerly been owned by Edward Stringer who had built

476

one of Belfast's earliest silent cinemas, the Kelvin. The Regal opened on 23 October 1935. In colour and design it was a rather severe looking building, and, in keeping, the introductory film was Katherine Hepburn in "The Little Minister," though it was accompanied by a fine Disney cartoon, "La Cucaracha" in technicolor. Less than a month later the Capitol opened its doors. It was located at 407, Antrim Road on the corner with Alexander Park Avenue about equidistant from the Duncairn and the Lyceum. The site and the building were both impressive. The cinema design was dominated by horizontal lines and dramatic colours. The exterior gleamed with cream tiling while the canopy over the double glass entrance doors was finished in horizontal gold and red bars. The interior had a pink and silver decor. The upper floor incorporated a director's boardroom and the Curran organization made it their headquarters.

The Regal. Source: Belfast Telegraph.

The core Curran cinemas, the Astoria, Regal, Capitol and Broadway, were designed and built under the supervision of local architect Thomas Mc Lean of Howard Street, all to the same high standards. They were characterised by what the Belfast Telegraph called "new standards of style and luxury" which audiences could enjoy at reasonable prices of 6d for front stalls,1/ - for back stalls and 1/ 6d for the balcony. The News Letter commended them for being among "the best appointed and most comfortable" in the city. The Irish News concurred, listing for example, the attractions of the Regal as including its "perfection of equipment, clarity of sound, smoothness of vision, comfort of patrons and general hygiene." Stylistically they were characterised by the clean geometric and "bold" (Irish News) lines of Art Deco on the outside, clad overall in bright cream coloured faience tiles which glowed with coloured neon lighting after dark. The buildings were large but not too large, with seating varying from 1,100 in the Capitol to nearly 1,500 in the Broadway. The interiors were tastefully decorated with subtly shaded plastic paints, but without unnecessary frills. Mr McLean believed that uncluttered walls improved the acoustics, and the critics seemed to agree. The cinemas offered what for suburban cinemas were many innovations. Those included concealed lighting, high quality heating and ventilation systems, cloakrooms, cafes and free car parks. The Curran cinemas had all the facilities associated with downtown cinemas like the Ritz, but packaged in a smaller, less flamboyant way. They also had the advantage of adjacent car parks, something the downtown venues lacked. They were well organized, quiet and clean, with well turned - out staff wearing distinctive uniforms. But, above all, they showed good quality, non - controversial, entertaining films that all the family could enjoy.

The Capitol.

The Broadway was a paradigmatic Curran theatre. It was the pride of the Falls Road, and the building with its distinctive ambiance reflected clearly the standards and aims of the Curran Circuit. The plans by Thomas Mc Lean were submitted to the City Surveyor on the 18th February 1936, were approved by April, and the building was ready for opening in December. It was located at Willowbank, sited prominently on the front of the Falls road, where it rose gradually towards the Whiterock and the City Cemetery. It was set back some distance from the road, which made the building look more impressive, but also gave it the advantage of easy uncluttered access for pedestrians and cars. The frontal space also meant that queues did not interfere with the normal pedestrian traffic. Cars were catered for in a good sized carpark along the side of the building. The latter had a clean perpendicular style emphasised by cream coloured faience tiles which gave it a bright look and artfully reflected the coloured neon lights which adorned it after dark. The tiles also had the practical value that they were easy to clean so the Broadway always looked bright, pristine and inviting. The Irish News commentator thought that the building presented "a well balanced facade, modern in concept, carried out in lines of classical simplicity." Particularly impressive were the four projecting piers which adorned the frontage, rising fifty feet to the top. The main entrance, which was protected from the elements by a fine canopy, consisted of double swing doors which gave access into a hall floored in green and cream terrazzo. Beyond that another line of swing doors led into a spacious foyer whose walls were decorated with plastic paint, its overall beige colour relieved with flecks of gold, scarlet and black. Unlike the hall its floor was covered with red and green rubber tiles, quiet to the feet. The paybox was straight ahead in the centre, with a cloakroom located to its left, where a corridor led to the stalls, while stairs on the right led to the cafe and the balcony, which seated 270 patrons. The cafe had modern Thirties style tubular tables with polished plate glass tops and matching tubular chairs.

Past the paybox, black doors opened quietly on to the auditorium, 120 feet long and 62 feet wide, floored with Wilton carpet on top of which were slightly curved rows of tip - up seats, 1,020 in all, covered in rich red material, and separated by three aisles, one in the centre with two along the walls. The walls repeated the gold and scarlet colours of the entrance and reached up to a high curved ceiling which shimmered with old gold. The atmosphere was one of spaciousness and roominess. At the far end there was an extensive stage with two dressing rooms, and above it a large screen hidden behind draped curtains, which slowly changed colour from green to red before opening upwards at the beginning of the film. The seating was divided into front stalls (330 seats) and back stalls (690 seats), the division marked only by a tasselled cloth chain across the aisles, though there was a completely separate entrance and exits for the front stalls. Access to the latter was through a double black door to the right of the main entrance, into a long wide corridor which ran parallel to the auditorium (though completely separate from it) the full length of the cinema. It had its own paybox, and proved very welcome to queues on cold wet nights. A similar door on the other side of the main entrance added balance to the front of the building, but it was used only for emergencies.

Much attention was given to safety with the availability of sufficient exits, while the projection room, located behind the balcony, was constructed of fire proof materials, and could be isolated from the auditorium in an emergency by a system of steel shutters which automatically closed off all the portholes. In such an event it had an alternative exit for the staff to escape to a flat roof. The sound system was high quality Western Electric, and the acoustics were generally agreed to be excellent. The whole combined comfort and luxury with practicality. The Belfast Telegraph summed it up as being of "modernistic design, pleasing to the eye, where comfort hadn't been sacrificed to ultra modernism." It was also in many ways a family cinema drawing its clientele from the middle and upper Falls, Beechmount and the lower Springfield Road. It was well run, always clean and airy, with audiences that were well behaved.

By the Thirties the Falls Road had three cinemas which contrasted in design and atmosphere. Down the road nestling among the spinning and weaving mills, the Diamond, a typical Mc Kibben cinema, was basic in price and facilities, and looked it. Nearby, directly across from the Falls Library, the elegantly designed Clonard was socially more upmarket though it was beginning to display a rather decayed elegance. By contrast the Broadway wasn't hemmed in by houses or industrial establishments, but looked across at the open grass meadows and trees of the Beechmount estate, conscious of the new standards it offered.

The Broadway opened its doors on Saturday 12th December 1936 at 7:30 pm with a ceremony that was, according to the Belfast Telegraph, "delightfully informal." Michael Curran, the founder and chief director of Curran Theatres, was present in the foyer with his sons James and Paul, to greet the patrons. Inside the auditorium the audience assembled and waited, listening to the music of the Frank Mohan orchestra. The official party arrived on stage to warm applause and the official opening was then carried out by Owen Kelly, the President of the St Vincent de Paul Society, who thanked the Curran family for donating the first night's takings to the charity. James Curran replied and assured those present that "nothing would be left undone to provide the best possible entertainment for our patrons." The speeches were followed by a cine variety show which was compered by an up and coming actor, Billy Milton. The Ritz had presented Gracie Fields followed by her latest film; the Broadway emphasised local interest and talent by introducing local actor Richard Hayward as the star of the evening, followed by his latest film. Hayward - who told the Irish News reporter that he couldn't bear to leave Ireland for more than a month at a time - charmed the audience with his humorous banter before singing, "The Bright Silver Light of the Moon," and "The Old Man of Killyburn." Then for the first time the draped curtains rose and the name of the main film was flashed on the screen. It was "The Early Bird," an Irish or, more accurately, Ulster comedy, the exteriors for which had been filmed around Glenarm, and the details of which will be discussed later. The author's mother was in the audience that December day and while she recalled it as "a great evening" she admitted that the cinema wasn't completely crowded. She put that down partly to the distractions of the approach of Christmas, but mainly to the belief that people were becoming blasé about such events. New cinemas seemed to be opening every other day!

In fact, the Broadway opened on the same day as two other cinemas, the Park on the Oldpark Road and the Curzon on the Ormeau Road, followed two days later by the Ambassador, which unlocked its doors for business on the Cregagh Road at the corner of Willowholme Parade. The Curzon was designed by J.McBride Neill for John Gaston and was located in Ballynafeigh on the front of the Ormeau Road at its junction with Raby Street. The plans also included five shops. It was a spacious (1424 seats) and impressive structure faced with cream faience tiling Its opening recalled that of the Ritz because the first film shown was "Queen of Hearts" starring Gracie Fields. The manager, H.Sheppard, promised similar top quality programmes, a policy that the cinema maintained to its last days. The Ambassador (known locally as the Ambo) was designed by John Mac Geagh, who had offices in Donegal Square East, for D.D.Young of High Street who was also an owner of the Lyric. It was a well proportioned building with a balcony, with

Three cinemas open on the same day.

total seating for about 980 patrons. Beginning with "Charlie Chan in Egypt" it showed family fare for many years but, in its twilight days, it turned to sex films though even then it could spring a surprise by presenting a quality film like Bunuel's "Belle de Jour" starring Catherine Deneuve.

No matter where the cinema was located the procedure in every case was similar. After the purchase of the site an architect was consulted and given the task of planning an appropriate building. When the plans were completed to the satisfaction of the owner they were submitted for official approval to the City Surveyor. They were examined and scrutinised by his department to ascertain that they met the legal requirements of the Cinematograph Acts, and local by-laws. If not, changes and modifications were advised which the architect had to incorporate into the drawings. Only when the plans were approved by the City Surveyor was the application placed before the Council for its approval. Most of the plans were passed without debate but others led to heated exchanges with approval being withheld.

The original plans for the Savoy, to be built for Mr M.Logan of Oldpark Road, on a site at the corner of Tennant Street and the Crumlin Road, were submitted by the architect T.R.Eagar at the beginning of July 1933. They were for a cinema with 850 seats. They were rejected a week later and the project became stalled. A new group emerged under the directorship of Joseph Maguire, from the company that owned the Clonard Picture House, who engaged a different architect, the experienced and dependable Thomas McLean. His amended plans for a cinema of 1150 seats were approved in May 1934. The cinema was quickly built and opened on 5th November 1934 with W.J.Hogan, also from the Clonard, as manager.

Meantime, Mr Logan had decided to build another cinema, to be called the Park, on the Oldpark Road at the corner of Torrens Avenue, adjacent to a site where the Oldpark Baptist church had already been given permission by the Improvements Committee to erect another church. Mr Eagar produced the required plans which were submitted to the City Surveyor in September 1935, and quickly approved. Unfortunately there were objections by local residents, especially by religious groups, and Mr Logan found himself involved in an unwanted planning ménage-a-trôis involving the Improvements Committee and the objectors, especially the Churches. The situation became further complicated when Irish Theatres Ltd. submitted plans for another cinema, to be called the Stadium, to be located on the corner site where the Shankill Road was joined by Tennant Street. If completed, the Stadium would be only 22 yards from the already existing Shankill Baptist Tabernacle Church. From the point of view of the cinema proprietors their new buildings would be well placed to serve the large residential areas nearby. Not everyone had the same geographical perceptions of the situation, especially members of existing churches nearby, who felt that the cinemas were invading their space.

One of the objections put forward by church groups was that the proposed cinemas were too close to existing churches and other places of worship. The earliest recorded incident of such a church - cinema conflict was in May 1918 when the Rev. Mr Higgins led a protest about the site of the proposed Sandro cinema. He contended that it was inappropriate to build a cinema on what was originally a mission hall. His arguments were overruled by the Corporation at the time. The problem resurfaced again in the Thirties when members of the Windsor Presbyterian Church on the Lisburn Road objected to the siting of the new Majestic nearby. Cllr. Clark Scott brought the matter up in the Council in July 1935, claiming that if the cinema was built at nearby Derryvolgie Avenue the crowds that would be attracted to it would clash with and disrupt church services. There were no seconders for his complaint, which was not proceeded with. But some architects paid attention and when the plans for the new Forum cinema on the Crumlin Road were submitted in November that year they included a note addressed "to the Improvements Committee" making clear that the "nearest wall of the theatre will be 147 yards from the nearest wall of Holy Cross Roman Catholic church." Disquiet remained among local residents and even those who had no connection with the church complained that a quiet, middle class residential area was no place for a centre of popular entertainment. The first organised protests involved the Park cinema.

At the monthly meeting of the Corporation on 1st October 1935 a deputation consisting of representatives from the Protestant churches and the Rate and Taxpayer's Association of Cliftonville and Oldpark lodged an official objection to the proposed site of the Park cinema. The main objection was that the site was too close to several places of worship. They further argued that the area was a quiet residential district and that a cinema would attract large crowds which would put an end to their peace and tranquillity. One result would be a decline in the value of their property. No one locally had requested the cinema and they felt that the city's attractions should not be imposed on them on their doorsteps. The churchmen argued that the crowds would interfere with church services. Also they felt that a cinema would undermine good behaviour. The Rev. Mr Warren held that schools were inculcating high ideals into the local children but the cinema would be "an instrument in lowering the tone" of the area. He insisted that much juvenile crime in the city could be attributed to "the pictures." In reply Alderman Pierce dismissed the attacks on the cinema as misleading. He had always found the films he saw "enjoyable and artistic." Councillor Cole argued that it was the duty of the Police Committee to make certain that no improper films were shown. The City Surveyor, in turn, indicated that he would give permission for the building to go ahead. Alderman Byrne strongly disagreed. He felt that picture houses shouldn't be forced on any community that didn't want them, and the majority of the councillors were inclined to agree, so the matter was referred back for further consideration. The Improvements Committee discussed the matter a few days later and decided that there was merit in the suggestion of an actual geographical separation between cinemas and churches. They decided on an arbitrary distance of 300 feet. (approx 93 metres). They suggested that, in future, no new cinema should be built less than 300 feet from an existing church. Under that guideline the Park could be built but the Stadium could not.

The question was raised again at the November monthly meeting when two deputations, again from the Protestant churches and from the Oldpark Ratepayer's Association, challenged the figure of 300 feet and asked the Council to double it to 600 feet. Councillor Hill compared those who introduced the proposal to the Bolsheviks while Councillor Agnew declared that the objections to cinemas had gone too far. Tommy Henderson, who always spoke up for the workers, saw the complaints as an attempt to "deny the poor of the Oldpark the opportunity of going to a picturehouse in their own district." He suggested that if certain members of the council went to the cinema more often, "it might broaden their minds." That was a sentiment that was widely accepted outside the council chamber and not only by those of the same political persuasion as Mr Henderson. A contemporary letter in the Irish News decried the attempts to restrict the building of cinemas in certain areas, by "old fashioned people whose sense of sound judgement was still controlled by conventionalism." They ignored, the letter writer continued, the many benefits of the cinema, which had brought "enchantment, inspiration and moral vision" to the populace. Like all good art, he believed that the best films elevated the mind and gave expression to the soul. Mr Henderson would certainly have agreed in principle because he is on record as stating that "picture houses are the educational centres of the workers." Despite such comments the majority of councillors felt that 300 feet was still too close, but, after discussion, a compromise of 360 feet (110 m) was agreed, and a resolution to that end was passed by 22 votes to 11. It became official then that, in Belfast, thou shalt not construct a cinema less than 360 feet (120 yards) from a church. In such a situation the Park cinema could still go ahead, but not the Stadium, and a few weeks later the plans for the latter were rejected on the grounds that the cinema would be too near the Baptist Tabernacle church in Tennant Street.

The matter didn't end there because the owners of the proposed Stadium decided to appeal the Corporation's decision to a higher authority, the Minister of Home Affairs. Almost in tandem, those objecting to the Park also decided to appeal upwards to the Prime Minister, with whom they requested a meeting. The Prime Minister declined to meet them, but in a letter he pointed out that the Corporation had the authority to close cinemas on Sundays, thereby averting any interference with worship. As everyone was aware the Corporation used that power and no cinemas in Belfast opened on Sundays. The objectors claimed that noise and queues would still disrupt mid - week services. They approached the Corporation again, in February 1936, asking that the plans for the Park be disapproved. In reply the Improvements Committee said that nothing could be done until the matter of the Stadium appeal had been settled. By April the Ministry made its decision and informed the Corporation that it had no authority to restrict the building of cinemas by distance. The proposed distance of 120 yards could, after all, be unreasonable to the cinema proprietors. Each case had to be decided on its own merits. The Corporation bowed to that decision and rescinded the resolution of November 1935.

In response, representatives of the Protestant churches met in the Shankill Baptist Tabernacle on Tennant Street in mid - April to discuss that development and to plan their strategy. They agreed to send another deputation to the Corporation with the aim of having a by-law introduced whereby no cinema could be legally built near a church. To show the extent of their opposition a Mass Meeting of Protest involving churchmen and concerned lay people, under the chairmanship of W.J.Stewart MP, was called for the evening of 27th April in the Assembly Hall - opposite the imposing Ritz Cinema. The topic for debate was the Building of Cinemas near Places of Worship, and the rallying call was "Unity is Strength." To anyone who lived through the political turmoil of the Seventies the pattern of events seems familiar. The hall was filled with an enthusiastic crowd. At the beginning Mr Stewart made it clear that they "did not condemn cinemas as such," though deep down many of those present regarded films as morally suspect or worse. The MP went on to assert that the Protestant churches had the support of the Roman Catholic authorities in the matter, though there is no evidence that any Catholics were present in the hall, and, significantly, the Irish News, which reported the proceedings, made no comment. The speaker insisted that the problem was really a question of town planning. The Corporation should have some kind of say in where cinemas were located; it should be able to legislate on something that was of concern to Christian people generally. Pastor Ravey of the Baptist Tabernacle added that people should be able to worship "without interference and annoyance.": He thought that a distance of 120 yards was reasonable and was "in harmony with the views of the mass of the people." A resolution was agreed that "no cinema could legally be built within 120 yards of a place of public worship."

As the debate continued across the city, a letter of clarification from representatives of all the churches present at the meeting appeared in the Whig in mid - June. It referred to the decision of the Minister but insisted that disturbance was possible in some cases. In such cases they still felt that 120 yards was a reasonable guide. With reference to the Shankill Baptist Tabernacle, the new cinema would occupy the corner site and would completely box the church in. There would inevitably be interference with worship "regardless of arrangements of doors and entrances, or police supervision." In cases like that of the Stadium cinema, owners should look for sites further away from churches. There was widespread sympathy and support in the Corporation for the position taken by the churchmen but under the circumstances they legally had no choice but to give permission for the construction of both cinemas. The Park was opened on the same day as the Broadway by none other than the Lord Mayor, Sir C. McCullagh. He praised the building, which seated 1,200 persons, and congratulated the architect, T.R.Eagar, who had designed an impressive structure which blended admirably with its surroundings. The local area was a relatively recently developed one of modern shops and streets of red brick houses. The cinema had a distinctive exterior decoration which reflected that, consisting of horizontal bands of rustic brick alternating with more characteristic cinematic plain white. The Lord Mayor noted that the building had been finished in four months, and he praised the local workers for their skills. He also appreciated the fact that the first night's takings would be donated to the Coal Fund which, he emphasised, supported the poor without reference to their religion or politics.

The Stadium opened ten months later on 16th October 1937, with a showing of Fred Astaire and Ginger Rogers in "Follow the Fleet." The official ceremony was performed by the man who had always defended it in the Corporation, Alderman Thomas Henderson. He warmly welcomed the occasion because, he claimed, "after schools there is no better means of education available to working men and women than the cinema." He was proud of the fact that from start to finish the whole venture was local in concept. The building had cost £30,000, all of which had been raised in Belfast, while the design and work had been carried out by local firms and workers. Others praised the impressive design by R.Sharp Hill who had been designing cinemas for over 26 years. It had a white frontage which according to the News Letter gave it the appearance of "a great and shining palace." The interior was designed like a sports stadium and had no balcony. Its comfortable seats cost only 4d and 6d, prices which local workers could afford, a point made by Henderson. The proceeds of the first performance went to the Royal Victoria Hospital for the purchase of extra beds. The Stadium became a popular venue on the Shankill Road with three shows daily at 3:00pm, 6:45pm and 9:00pm. The conflicts over its site were soon forgotten.

It is interesting to speculate why, after so many years of cinema expansion the churches suddenly began to question their locations. Many early silent cinemas had been built near places of worship without serious opposition. The position taken by the churches has to be seen in the context of what was happening in society both locally and in Europe. The victory of atheistic Communism in Russia, combined with the rise of heavily armed dictatorships in Germany and Italy were perceived as dire portents of the future. The local papers carried almost daily reports of comments by eminent politicians, churchmen and others about the dangers of the time. Many held that democracy itself was in peril and Mr Baldwin, in a controversial speech in May 1936, even claimed that the next war would result in the end of civilisation. Unease and uncertainty permeated local thinking, and in such an atmosphere conservative churchmen concluded that they had to defend traditional values, which they felt had stood them well over the years. They decried the creeping secularisation around them which they saw as undermining those values, and many of them regarded the cinema as a major contributor to that secularisation. Protestant traditionalists pinpointed, above all, the changing attitudes to Sunday Observance as indicators of society's declining standards, and there were complaints on that score from pulpits, in letters to the press and from the General Assembly of the Presbyterian Church. One letter in the Whig called for action and complained that the City Fathers seemed "powerless and inert" in the face of these changes.

At the General Assembly of June 1936 speakers expressed alarm at the rate at which Sunday was being changed into a holiday. One speaker complained that "even in Protestant districts" boxing, games (especially golf), flying exhibitions and band performances were taking place on Sundays, and there was actually talk of opening cinemas also. Another was disturbed by the number of ice cream and confectionery shops that were opening for business, while another noted that among those who could afford it, the habit of Sunday motoring for pleasure was increasing. Yet another drew attention to the increase in football matches being played on the Sabbath. By football he meant the G.A.A., because he went out of his way to congratulate the Irish Football League on their ban on Sunday matches. He emphasised that he was no dictator (a dirty word in the Thirties) to tell others how to behave, but people (meaning mainly Nationalists) should understand that they couldn't play such games in predominantly Protestant areas. He thought that the Church should co-operate with the Orange Order to deal with that problem. There were complaints that in many rural areas licences were being issued for Sunday dances and the next step surely would be Sunday opening of cinemas. Cinemas were tolerated on week days but never on a Sunday, though even that toleration became progressively strained as the cinema was increasingly perceived as a vehicle for exclusively secular behaviour, and an opponent of traditional values.

During the Thirties, Church spokesmen in Belfast were involved in fierce verbal exchanges with filmgoers and exponents of free expression on the problem of film censorship, relating to a number of films which included "Frankenstein" and "Green Pastures," which will be discussed in detail later. It was in that general atmosphere of suspicion and discord that some Protestant clerics decided to take a stand on the continuing spread of the cinema and its propaganda at, as they saw it, the expense of the churches.

Of course there was never any possibility of Sunday opening of cinemas in Belfast. The Corporation members, mainly Unionist, and many with a strong Sabbatarian bent, were almost completely unified in their opposition to such a move, in which they had the support of all the churches, the Orange Order and others. In the Nationalist - Catholic community attitudes to Sunday observance were more relaxed and the Irish News reflected those views by often calling for a less strict attitude to Sunday, and condemning the closure of public amenities. While the church - cinema problem was under discussion the Corporation, after a debate, refused a request to open the Municipal Art Gallery and Museum on Sundays. The Editor of the Irish News, who admitted that he often found the Belfast mind "a source of constant bewilderment," deplored the decision and pointed out that after a long struggle the Zoo had recently been allowed to open on Sunday afternoons, and that the large crowds who flocked there every week indicated that the citizens favoured such moves. The majority of Catholics attended Sunday mass, and in Belfast masses were on the hour, every hour, from 7:00 am to midday, with most of them packed to the doors. Cinemas as such were not condemned, but mass goers were often warned from the pulpit about "unsuitable" films. After attending mass, relaxation could include outdoor games, and evening dances or a visit to one of the few rural cinemas that were open. A minority of non-Catholics respected those views and attitudes, as long as they were confined to areas where the local people wanted them.

A case in question concerned the mainly Catholic village of Cushendall in the Glens of Antrim. The local cinema there, the Moyle, had a seven day licence and showed films on Sunday evenings. In May 1936 Unionist members of Antrim County Council who supported strict Sunday Observance, attempted to reduce that to a six day licence. Speakers in the council attacked the Sunday opening of the cinema, and a lively debate followed. But some members revealed a more tolerant approach. One speaker admitted that he was no supporter of cinemas at all. "If I had my way, I know what I would do with them," he declared ominously, but added that he knew that the local people wanted the cinema open on Sundays and "it savoured of dictatorship" - that dirty word again! - to vote against their wishes. The aptly named Mr Kirk said that, as a Presbyterian, he did not approve of Sunday entertainments, but he would not force his views on others. Another member argued that films, on Sunday or any day, were "more elevating" than dances. The Chairman, Lt Col. J.Patrick, did not personally approve of Sunday entertainments, but he agreed with the last two speakers, and when the vote was taken his casting vote supported the continuance of the seven day licence. There were those in the Protestant community in Belfast who agreed with that decision, and, while recognising the secular changes that were taking place in society, felt that maybe their more enthusiastic colleagues, in their opposition to films and the cinema, were tilting at the wrong windmills.

It was against that background that each application was processed on its merits and, when all the problems had been ironed out to the satisfaction of the Improvements Committee, the City Surveyor gave permission for the project to proceed. The building was carried out by local firms so the new cinemas gave employment to construction companies, workers and a wide range of suppliers during a period when the economic depression was "unrelenting," according to one local paper. As each was completed an opening date was announced and arrangements were made to make the occasion a memorable one. The first day's takings were usually donated to local hospitals, especially the RVH and the Mater, or to deserving charities like the Lord Mayors Coal Fund, the Newsboys Club, the St Vincent de Paul, the Lifeboat Association and others. The official opening was performed by an entertainer like Gracie Fields (the Ritz) or Richard Hayward (Broadway), or more often by a prominent local representative or politician. The Lord Mayor during the cinema boom of the Thirties was the Unionist Sir Crawford McCullagh who was elected to the position in 1931, and remained in the office for 16 years. He was a film fan and a strong advocate of the cinema. He personally attended the opening of six of the new cinemas - the Castle, Savoy, Strand, Troxy, Ritz and Park. He showed particular enthusiasm for those halls which were financed, designed, built and run by local people. He supported the cinema as an industry which gave employment, but equally so as a cheap form of relaxation for working people of all social levels.

At the opening of the Castle in October 1934, on the Castlereagh Road, Sir Crawford told his capacity audience, "The cinema has come to stay........ which is not surprising for no other form of amusement gives pleasure to so many people for such a small outlay. "He felt that cinemas brought real benefits to their local communities, and the Castle, he predicted, would be no exception. The Castle, which seated just over 1000 patrons, was owned by James Crawford and managed by W.V.Winters, and was built in four months using a workforce of 40 men. Its staff consisted mainly of local women and men and its audiences were mainly from the Castlereagh and Cregagh districts, who welcomed its opening with enthusiasm. Because of the dominance of old gold in the colour decoration of its almost square shaped auditorium - even the seats were covered in gold coloured moquette - it was described in the papers as the Old Gold cinema. The latest RCA high fidelity sound system was installed and the management claimed that the Castle was the first cinema in Ireland to do so. Value for money was promised with double features the norm, beginning with "Identity Parade" with Marion Nixon, plus "The Lady is Willing" starring Leslie Howard. Its prices were very reasonable with seats costing 6d for front stalls and one shilling for back stalls; there was no balcony.

Besides the Lord Mayor a number of members of the City Council were present, including the influential Lt. Commander Harcourt, who was in charge of the Police Committee which oversaw matters of film censorship. When, the following month, he opened the Savoy on the Crumlin Road, whose audiences were mainly Nationalist, the Lord Mayor returned to his favourite theme of a hall built by local enterprise, and added that he always liked going to the pictures. However he expected to see "clean pictures" and thankfully he found that was what Belfast cinemas usually presented. Two years later he officiated at the inauguration of the Troxy, and took the opportunity again to emphasise his support for the cinema, pointing out that films were not only an amusement, but a source of education and news. He was impressed by the clean geometric lines of the architecture, and congratulated the architect J.McBride Neill; also the builders who had completed the work in five and a half months. The cinema, which boasted a screen 25 feet by 18 feet, seated around 850 persons. It was owned by Harry Wilton who emphasised that a special long waiting foyer had been included which would eliminate the problem of outside queueing in the cold and wet.

The Thirties cinema boom ended in November 1937 with the opening of the Forum by Irish Theatres Ltd., on the Crumlin Road near Ardoyne. The News Letter praised its simplicity of design, while the Whig was impressed by the "good taste" of the interior decorations, with the use of textured plastic paint to produce a subtle mix of gold, rose, pink and russet shades. Prices were very reasonable at 4d (pit), 6d (stalls) and one shilling for the rear stalls. By then the city had 43 cinemas serving a population of 438,000, and as already noted, attitudes to them varied among the citizens. Some criticised them, others welcomed them, but the majority of the population embraced them with enthusiasm, and returned week after week to experience the talent and entertainment that brightened the screens. The cinema rode on a wave of popular support which continued throughout the Thirties, the Forties and well into the Fifties, before a rapid decline set in. People who didn't "go to the pictures" were the exception rather than the rule.

Within its political framework, local society functioned around five main supports -- the family, the church, the school, the workplace and the cinema. One might be tempted to suggest that the latter was the most trivial and least significant of those, but that doubtful premise would have to be tempered by the medium's obvious appeal, influence and popularity. As stated above even the city's first citizen, the Lord Mayor, freely admitted to enjoying films, and often going to the cinema. The writer of the Random Jottings column in the Irish News, who often detailed the more mundane aspects of Belfast life, mentioned in April 1938 that when walking past an evangelical meeting house his eye was drawn to an uplifting message which stated that "every day should end with a look at the stars." He interpreted that, rather impishly, as a call to the faithful to daily attendance at a cinema. He could have added that if one was so inclined, one certainly had plenty to choose from and plenty to see in the city venues.

CHAPTER TWENTY FOUR
The Belfast Film Society

By 1937 the basic geographical pattern of cinema distribution in the built-up area was fixed, and the habit of weekly cinema going firmly established in the population. It was a situation that was to prevail for the next thirty years. Every day, excepting Sundays, filmgoers across the city were faced with a range of about forty feature films to choose from. Programming was of two types, with cinemas that opened their doors around 2:00pm or earlier and screened their wares continuously until approximately 10:30pm, and those that had two separate evening shows after 6:00pm. The downtown cinemas belonged to the former group. During the afternoon they admitted a steady stream of patrons who benefitted from lower prices, but in the evenings they came into their full glory, bathed in coloured neon lights, their foyers invitingly decorated with coloured posters, pictures of stars and front-of-house stills. Each evening after 6:30 pm a view from above the city would have revealed streams of people, young and old, moving from working class streets and converging on their local cinema. Others waited for buses (including trolley buses after 1938) and trams to carry them to downtown venues, while a more affluent minority travelled independently in the same direction in their cars. They didn't go to admire the buildings, their architectural styles or decors. What they wanted was a few hours of good entertainment in comfortable to luxurious surroundings. And normally that was what they got.

Most cinemas offered a double bill of two films, consisting of a feature or main film with top actors, supported by a shorter B - movie with lower production values and less famous - though not necessarily less popular - stars. Those films were supported by added extras which could include a cartoon (Disney, Popeye, Betty Boop or such), a travel documentary from the likes of James A. Fitzpatrick, (he always concluded his travelogues with the oft mimicked "...and so we say farewell to beautiful..."), the coming attractions which consisted of a rapidly edited series of scenes from next week's film, and a newsreel. Added to that, in the top cinemas there was an organ recital, or cine variety. The Ritz had its Compton with, by 1937, the resident organist, Joseph Seal. The Classic competed with Leslie Simpson on the Wurlitzer, while the Tonic in Bangor had Stendal Todd. An evening spent in one of those cinemas, with up to three hours of entertainment was, despite the smoke from hundreds of cigarettes and pipes, a very pleasant experience.

The main attraction of course was the films. What is impressive is the variety of films available, with a wide range which included thrillers, Westerns, musicals, adventure stories, tales of horror (or, "weird" subjects as the local critics termed them), comedies, historical epics, biographies, literary standards, and by the end of the decade full length cartoons following upon the completion of Walt Disney's wonderful "Snow White and the Seven Dwarfs." The film makers had no pretensions and made no secret of the fact that their main aim was to make financially successful films for entertainment. The source material, whether fiction, historical fact, literature, or popular novels was reorganised and modified to meet that aim. What reached the screen reflected the efforts of skilled and often dedicated craftsmen and women. The best, and there were many, of what they produced were never less than interesting, and included many worthwhile films that have stood the test of time. The local newspaper critics often recycled the comments in the production handouts they were given, but they also recognised quality of content or form and directed their readers towards it, whether it was the visual artistry of Walt Disney, the professional skills of Fred Astaire and Busby Berkeley, the acting abilities of Charles Laughton, Spencer Tracy, Greta Garbo and others, or the directorial expertise of John Ford, Alfred Hitchcock, Fritz Lang, or De Mille. The picturegoers in their turn were well informed not only by the critics' comments but also from serious newspaper articles and, above all, from the fan magazines which were published on a weekly or monthly basis, and were prominently displayed in local newsagents. Some were actually sold in the cinemas, notably Film Review which could be purchased for six pence at the paybox in the Ritz. A growing minority had progressed beyond the fan mentality and were becoming quite sophisticated in their appreciation and understanding of film art.

Advertisement for colour production of film Becky Sharpe in Curran theatres.

The release system was very different from today when, with saturation release, all cinemas show the same films contemporaneously. In the Thirties it was very rare indeed for a film to be showing at more than one cinema at the same time, and film titles changed every week, or, in the suburbs, every three days. The basic run was normally for one week at the town centre or three days in the suburbs. A batch of new feature films arrived each Monday and were presented in the Picture House, the Classic, the Imperial, the Royal Cinema, the Ritz and the Lyric. They usually ran for a week though if a film proved to be especially popular it could be retained for a second week, or, on rare occasions, longer. The best musicals, top quality productions and films of special local interest were often held over to meet local demand, or, some cynics claimed, to engender it. "The Charge of the Light Brigade," starring Errol Flynn, ran for an amazing four weeks in the Picture House during October 1937 though the News Letter dismissed it as having "a rambling story .... with no historical pretensions." Audiences ignored such comments, because they regarded Errol Flynn as a local man. After the initial run the new films were withdrawn, until they reappeared in the suburban cinemas a few weeks later. After that they moved, at lower rental rates, to the less salubrious venues before disappearing from local screens entirely. There were some exceptions which were reissued for extra showings but, in the main, filmgoers had only a few months at the most to catch up with the films they wanted to see. For anyone interested in films, and wanted to keep abreast of developments, a weekly visit to the cinema was not only a pleasant habit, but a necessity. There were no VHS tapes or DVD's for home viewing, and only a minority could afford a 16 mm or 8 mm projector for personal viewing.

The monopoly that the six downtown cinemas had on new releases was accepted as normal, but no-one was surprised when the odd exception occurred. In February 1933 the Alhambra showed its artistic mettle by announcing the showing of Fritz Lang's "M" for a week instead of its usual three days. Not only was it a first for the city but it was also that increasingly rare event on local screens, a film from the continent, from Germany. A large advertisement described the film as "the sensation of the year," and the I.S.N. increased local anticipation by advising its readers that it would be "the most unusual film you have ever seen." Based on fact, it dealt with a child murderer, played with a combination of chilling menace and sympathy by Peter Lorre. Lang caught the atmosphere of a large city gripped by fear, with the police seemingly helpless, and protective parents wondering where the murderer would strike next. Finally the "monster" (I.S.N.) was hunted down by the police with the help of the local underworld. The film was warmly welcomed by the local critics and those interested in serious cinema. It attracted large crowds, though there were criticisms that such an abhorrent subject was not a suitable theme for popular entertainment. The Whig critic described it as "a masterly example of the macabre film, brilliantly directed and acted," while the News Letter was impressed by its artistry and the fact that "a horrific theme was saved from sensationalism by Lang's direction and Lorre's ability to infuse his character with humanity." Among those who saw it were members of the Belfast Film Society and they opened their 1937 - 38 film season with a special late night showing of "M" in the Imperial cinema at 11:00pm on 17th November 1937. It was its last showing in the city before being withdrawn from general circulation.

There were other above average pictures shown notably Fritz Lang's first American film "Fury," starring Spencer Tracy, which arrived in the Hippodrome in November 1936. The Irish News critic approved of its "hard hitting indictment of mob rule" and declared it a personal triumph for Lang. Tracy also appeared with Jeannette MacDonald and Clark Gable in "San Francisco" which drew crowds to see the impressive earthquake scenes. In contrast the Classic presented Frank Capra's comedy "It Happened One Night," which the Telegraph greeted as a "sparkling entertainment with a romantic quality nicely spiced with amusing situations." There was special praise for the two leading players, Clarke Gable and the very feminine and sophisticated Claudette Colbert. Alfred Hitchcock continued to add to his reputation with "Secret Agent," and "The Thirty Nine Steps," which showed in the Classic during January 1936. The News Letter critic thought that the latter was a "truly brilliant film" which exhibited a "combination of gripping excitement and dramatic suspense." He praised Hitchcock's direction, and the acting, especially the "delightful nonchalance of Robert Donat." Such was the film's popularity that the Classic arranged a special showing for an invited audience of blind people. The manager, Mr T. MacDermott, welcomed them and gave a running commentary on the plot so that they could understand and enjoy the film. According to the newspapers the event was a resounding success.

The laughter in the cinemas contrasted with the increasingly somber atmosphere outside, in the seats of government and elsewhere, as political observers contemplated the activities of Adolf Hitler on the continent. The buildup of German armaments, the pogroms by the Nazis against their political opposition, their treatment of the Jews, their attacks on artists, writers and others who disagreed with them caused increasing concern. As Hitler's expansionist ambitions became clear, local editors, fearing for the future, began to write ominously about a drift towards war. Thus, to some, it seemed entirely apt and timely when, in January 1937, the Ritz announced the imminent presentation of Alexander Korda's latest British film, "Things To Come" (d. William Cameron Menzies, 1936), starring Raymond Massey and Ralph Richardson. The film was scripted by H.G.Wells and dealt with the perennial problem of war. The theme was summed up by a character near the beginning of the film who announced that "if we don't end war, war will end us." The topic wasn't original in concept - it had been put forward eloquently and effectively a few years before in, "All Quiet on the Western Front," - but in its futuristic exposition it was novel and, in ways, frighteningly accurate. The bombing of Guernica was only four months away, and the beginning of the Second World War less than three years. The film story prophetically begins on Christmas 1940 with waves of bombers coming across the Channel and attacking Everytown, actually London, resulting in scenes of civilian deaths, devastation and widespread destruction. The more sensitive in the audiences in the Ritz must have felt uneasy because they were aware of recent public meetings in Belfast, and newspaper articles explaining what to do in the event of such an air raid.

As early as the end of October the following year they were to be startled when the local papers carried the disturbing heading: War Planes Roar Over Belfast. It was thankfully only a series of mock raids arranged by the ARP (Air Raid Precautions) to forewarn the population. The fourteen planes involved came from Aldergrove and consisted of five Hawker "Hinds' bombers accompanied by eight of the latest Hurricane fighters. At midday the bombers swept low over Harland and Wolff's, to the delight of the workforce. They dropped smoke bombs which crackled and gave off flames, before the Hurricanes began to repel them. In the afternoon a second "raid" took place over May's Market. Incendiary bombs were ignited on the ground which, according to the Irish News, added "a touch of grim reality" to the proceedings. The local ARP officer, who had arranged the demonstrations, emphasised that in the event of war, Belfast, with its docks and industries, would certainly be a target. He called for volunteers to join the ARP where they would be trained to protect the civilian population. His predictions proved to be deadly accurate. Little did those sitting in the comfort of the Ritz realise that in four years time Belfast itself would suffer a devastating attack similar to what was being enacted on the screen and, sadly, some of those watching might well become victims of it.

In Korda's film the initial attack is followed by scenes of warfare which according to the Irish News were alone well worth a visit. The period of war is followed by "a state bordering on barbarism" (Irish News) which, in turn, is ended by the emergence of a powerful and enlightened scientific elite. Their efforts produce a new scientific world which has no disease, a population that lives longer, factories that function without the need for labourers and a social environment which is ordered, clean and tidy. The Irish News critic found that aspect soulless and "almost painful to look at." He criticised its "glaring efficiency" as depressing, but nervelessly concluded that it was an integral part of a serious film that should be seen. The Whig critic agreed that the film was aimed at "thinking people," but he added that it included enough action scenes to entertain those who just wanted thrills. The News Letter critic was equally impressed. He appreciated its cinematic attributes and suggested that "not since Metropolis has the scope of the screen as an imaginative medium been as fully realised." He recognised the artistic and technical continuum with Lang's silent film though H.G. Wells, who had famously dismissed Lang's vision, insisted that "Things To Come" represented an entirely opposite vision of the future. What those patrons in the Ritz who had already seen Lang's film thought is not recorded but certainly "Things To Come" didn't cause anything like the excitement that accompanied "Metropolis" when it had arrived in the city. Seen from today's viewpoint, "Metropolis" comes over as a superior work. The News Letter critic was right to praise the visuals because the director, the American William Cameron Menzies, was essentially an art director, and he produced sets and images that still impress today. Despite the positive comments the critic wasn't completely happy with the film and complained, rightly, that despite its "technical marvels" it lacked "intimacy and warmth." It suffered, he claimed, from a philosophical "aloofness" that lessened its impact from the point of view of entertainment, though overall it remained "a spectacle of unequalled dignity and vision." He joined his colleagues in saying that it should be seen. The average Belfast cinemagoer disagreed with the critics however, and looked elsewhere. "Things To Come" was not a commercial success, and quickly disappeared from local screens.

Later in the year another film surfaced which also dealt with the search for peace but, from a very different, more personal, viewpoint. It was Frank Capra's "The Lost Horizon" which arrived in the Classic in November 1937, accompanied by a full page advert in the News Letter, and a special exhibition of photographs and sketches of the costumes used in the film, in Goorwiches in Castle Junction. The script was based on James Hilton's novel of the same name and Capra intended the film to be a definitive statement of his attitudes to society and human behaviour. The story was contemporary, beginning on March 1935, and involves a British colonial administrator (Ronald Colman) who becomes disenchanted with his life style in particular and Western values in general. He turns his back on the pressures and bustle of civilisation, and finds his own Utopia in Shangli-La in the inaccessible Himalayas, a place where war and conflict have been eliminated. There, the High Lama, who is actually a European, tells him that his hope is that when the strong men of politics have destroyed themselves by wars the Christian ethic will prevail and the meek will inherit the earth. Peace and contentment will become the norm. Filming took place in Hollywood between March and July 1936 and Capra's first enthusiastic cut - the Director's cut? - was over six hours long. Further cutting and retakes followed until January 1937 when the film premiered in San Francisco with a running time of 132 minutes. Mainly because of an unenthusiastic response that was further cut to 118 minutes for the general release, and an examination of the times of exhibition in the Classic indicate that it was that version which showed there.

To Capra's disappointment the general public's response remained lukewarm, while critics were mixed in their comments. Grahame Green, for example, described it as a very long picture, and a very dull one. Ten months after the premier it was showing in Belfast, where the comments of the local critics would certainly have pleased Capra. The News Letter described it as "weird,(by which he meant unusual), fantastic, but very beautiful, full of glorious concepts." The Whig critic thought it was "an engrossing picture which falls just short of brilliance." He praised Capra's direction as "imaginative" and was especially impressed by the Shanglia-La sequences with their "fine example of quiet, isolation and happy contentment." He admitted that the film had a specialist appeal, which he suggested would be "little appreciated" by ordinary cinema patrons who wanted continuous action. Such people would probably "fret uneasily" at the slow pace. It was a criticism that is equally valid today. The idea that one had to travel to the Himalayas to find contentment seemed rather silly to an audience who found it weekly in their local cinema. The film was not a financial success but its worth was realised much later when the American Film Institute spent over ten years restoring it - and in the process, its reputation - to its original length in 1986. Seen today the film stands up to scrutiny better than "Things To Come," and has much to say to modern audiences. It is a thoughtful treatise on human behaviour, especially on the politics of war and violence. The opening scenes in China showing frightened Europeans struggling to board the last planes to safety presages the departure of the last American helicopters from Saigon at the end of the Vietnam War. The discussions that follow between the characters, but especially between the hero and the High Lama about power, wars, and the meaning of life for the individual, suggest that very little has basically changed since the turmoil of the Thirties. It must have sent the more serious minded out of the Classic in a thoughtful frame of mind.

There were many films going the rounds that would not cause the least evidence of "fretting" in an audience and among those were the spectaculars. As the News Letter commented, when one thinks of spectacle one thinks of Cecil B. DeMille. Most films depended on their stars to attract audiences but DeMille was an exception. Although a producer and director he was as well known to filmgoers as any star. He had made his reputation with over fifty silent films in association with the likes of Gloria Swanson and Bebe Daniels, and had enhanced it later with the films "The Ten Commandments," and "King of Kings." His reputation carried over into the sound era and a "Cecil B.DeMille production" usually attracted large audiences. He often appeared, like a pedagogue, in the trailers to his films explaining their significance and discussing the research that had gone into the script to ensure that all artifacts shown were accurate in detail. Audiences were suitably impressed and tended to overlook the historical inaccuracies that often occurred in the plots. They were probably unaware of them anyhow, and didn't really care as long as they got colourful characters, and lots of spectacle. They got that, with the added extras of sex, violence, religion and more in "The Sign of the Cross" which he made in 1932.

The script was based on Wilson Barrett's 1894 play of the same name which had caused great excitement when it was presented on the stage of the Theatre Royal in early October 1897. The theatre had been packed every evening of its run and when a silent film, based on the same play came to Belfast a few years later it repeated that success. With his greater financial and technical resources DeMille was able to open up the plot, which dealt with the persecution of the Christians by Nero. He retained the main message - lauded by the local critics - which showed how a cruel pagan society was defeated by the beliefs of a new religion, in the person of a young Christian girl, played by Elissa Landi. Her spiritual values and her fearless rejection of the decadence around her sent her to her death in the arena. Her behaviour so impressed a Roman prefect played by Fredric March that he joined her on that last journey. Their sacrifice was watched with satisfaction by Nero (Charles Laughton in great form, "superb" according to the Whig) and his wife, the notorious Poppaea.

One of the great surprises of "The Sign of the Cross" was the choice of Claudette Colbert, a sophisticated light commedienne, to play the part, a task which she seemed to relish. DeMille introduced his trade mark bathing scene when Poppaea, surrounded by

OBER 14, 1933.

THE PICTURE HOUSE - Royal Avenue
ALL NEXT WEEK

A PICTURE WHICH PROUDLY LEADS ALL THE
ENTERTAINMENTS THE WORLD HAS EVER SEEN!

CECIL B. DeMILLE'S
Greatest Dramatic Spectacle
Of Our Generation

THE SIGN
OF THE
CROSS
WITH
FREDRIC MARCH
ELISSA LANDI
CLAUDETTE COLBERT
CHARLES LAUGHTON
WITH 7500 OTHERS

FROM THE PLAY BY WILSON BARRETT

It's a Paramount Picture
A

THE BIGGEST THING THAT HAS HAPPENED IN PICTURES!
You'll Never Forget It!

De Mille at full
throttle.

handmaidens, stepped into a pool of asse's milk. According to reports real asses milk was used and it curdled and smelt under the heat of the studio lights. If so, it didn't show on the screen, as Miss Colbert appeared to luxuriate in her lacteal ablutions. What local audiences, most of whom lived in houses without bathrooms, and who washed daily in a sink or in the scullery, thought, is not recorded. DeMille didn't hold back on his depiction of the pagan lifestyle he was criticising, so there were orgies with lots of dancing girls, while the scenes in the arena involving gladiators, lions and Christian martyrs were quite violent and bloodthirsty.

The film was released in America in November 1932 and reached Belfast eleven months later, where it showed in the Picture House. The posters outside the cinema claimed that it was "the greatest dramatic spectacle of our generation," and guaranteed audiences that they would "never forget it." As expected, it drew large crowds and - a sure sign of success - was retained for a second week. The reaction from the critics was mixed. They recognised the worth of its underlying message, the skill of the direction but seemed uneasy about the general presentation. None of them mentioned the source of the film, or the fact that it had been seen before in Belfast on stage and screen, though some of the more mature members in the audience must have known that. The Belfast Telegraph praised its wonderful screen work, its elaborate settings, its spectacle and the fine acting of the principals. The Irish News found its plot "gripping" and the general presentation "luxurious," but the brevity of the comments suggest that the critic, who usually approved of deMille's work, was less than impressed by the production. The News Letter critic made no secret of his disappointment. He summarised it as being dominated visually by orgies, gladiators and persecutions. He admitted that it was a magnificent screen spectacle but felt that that aspect was so overdone that "the underlying story was swamped .... its emotional appeal and human interest sacrificed." He was impressed by the performance of Elissa Landi which he found to be "very touching." Frederik March struggled manfully but was hampered in his interpretation by a poor script. Claudette Colbert, he complained, in no way suggested the "vicious and ruthless Poppaea." The dialogue of the principals was acceptable but, he felt that some of the lesser parts "smacked of gangster films." Needless to say most of the general public ignored such critical broadsides and packed those cinemas across the city where it was shown.

Many years later the author, as a young boy, was regaled by some adults with descriptions of scenes which they could still vividly recall, and was advised to see the film if it was ever re-released. DeMille would certainly have been pleased at that because he always claimed that he made his films for the public and not for the critics. Did you see .....or, do you remember ....? It was by such word of mouth that information about films was spread, though in the process it was not unknown for details to become exaggerated and distorted.

The success of "The Sign of the Cross" encouraged DeMille to make another spectacular and he decided on a new version of "Cleopatra," which he filmed between March and May, 1934. The main part went again to Claudette Colbert, with an English actor, Henry

Wilcoxon as Mark Anthony, Warren Williams as Julius Caesar and Joseph Schildkraut as Herod. While the latter character suggested a Biblical connection, neither the Old or New Testament texts were involved. It was a non - Biblical tale of political ambitions destroyed by love. The film was released on 24th July 1934 and was showing in the Hippodrome only four months later. Advertised as "history's most seductive woman," it was greeted warmly by critics and public. Belfast audiences had experienced the sultry queen as early as 1913, in the Panopticon, in the form of a French silent version starring a stately Helen Gardiner. It had cost £9,000 to produce, a mere trifle to DeMille who spent $ 900,000 on his epic. Later, Theda Bara had played her as a vamp, but Miss Colbert's Cleopatra contrasted conspicuously with Miss Bara's femme fatale approach, and with the later grandeur of Elizabeth Taylor. The beautiful Miss Colbert was suitably seductive but used her skills as a comedienne to infuse the character with touches of sardonic humour. Her performance, wrote the Whig critic, was imbued with intelligence and physical charm. DeMille's control of the medium revealed itself in the spectacular staging, outdoing himself especially in the scenes aboard Cleopatra's barge - a remarkably roomy vessel, according to one of our local critics - where Mark Anthony was greeted with exotic Egyptian hospitality. Groups of dancing girls are everywhere, some of them, dressed only in seaweed, being swept in from the sea in giant nets.

A story in circulation at the time described how the censor watched the filming of those scenes with DeMille to ensure that female modesty was preserved. While unlikely, the director never denied it because he knew what would draw the crowds in. In that atmosphere of sensuous Eastern music and dance Mark Anthony finally succumbed to Cleopatra's charms. As they embrace, veils are drawn around the lovers but not before Miss Colbert raises one arched and pencilled eyebrow as a signal to her minions to get the barge under sail. At that moment the camera begins to move backwards and upwards in an impressive crane shot. It glides past the dancers and the ranks of muscled rowers, moving in unison to the thunder of a mighty drum that would put any Lambeg in its place. It may be ludicrous and over the top but in its own way it is magnificent; one of those scenes which once seen stay in the memory. In contrast the ending of the film is subdued with the queen dying from the bite of the asp, and the camera again moving backwards from her. There are no revellers, no music, only the silence of an empty dark throne room. The Irish News critic summed up the critical reaction, praising DeMille's spectacular direction and Claudette Colbert's "fine performance." Paramount Pictures mounted a concerted advertising campaign, and for a time the film was the talk of the city, with Egyptian motifs appearing in shop windows and elsewhere. Despite the enthusiasm the film ran for only a week, though with reports of full houses. When it reached the suburbs the following year, and the cheaper halls, the public needed no convincing and wherever it showed it attracted large crowds.

There were other films that contained spectacular sequences which people continued to recall and talk about in later years. There was "She" (1935, d.Irving Pichel) in which Helen Gahagan stepped into the youth - restoring cold flames before spectacularly crumbling physically as age caught up with her, watched by Randolph Scott in his pre - Western days. Another was "San Francisco" (1936, d.Woody Van Dyke) in which Clarke Gable, Spencer

Tracy and Jeanette Mac Donald contemplated the realities of life against the backdrop of the superbly staged 1906 earthquake, a sequence that still impresses even in these days of CGI. "In Old Chicago" (1938, d. Henry King) starred Tyrone Power, who had to compete with an impressively realistic recreation of the great fire of 1871, while "The Last Days of Pompeii (1935, d. Ernest Schoedsack) filled the screen with a dramatic eruption of Vesuvius. After the disasters of earthquake, fire, lava and ash, audiences were then almost literally blown away with Jon Hall and the exotic Dorothy Lamour (known as the Sarong Girl) by the howling and realistic storm winds of" Hurricane "(1937, d. John Ford). But, unlike many of today's empty spectacles, those films had worthy subtexts about the need for strong moral and spiritual values.

Cecil B. De Mille also turned his eyes westwards and produced "The Plainsman" (1936). It was a part historical, part fictional story about the exploits and death of Wild Bill Hickok, reputedly the fastest draw in the West. The main role was taken by Gary Cooper who gave his usual laconic performance, while Jean Arthur played Calamity Jane. The film had fine scenery, gunfights, attacking Indians, and lots of action. Belfast audiences took to it immediately and it played across the city to crowded houses. It is interesting that the city experienced a fascinating taste of the real West when Grey Owl, a 42 year old member of the Obijway Indian tribe from Canada, visited in January 1936. His reputation as an early conservationist had preceded him, mainly from his writings, and he was greeted as "a modern Hiawatha." It was, wrote the Whig reporter, "difficult to write with restraint about Grey Owl." His brief stop over was part of a British tour he was making, and had been arranged by W.Erskine Mayne, who presided at the two lectures he gave in the Grosvenor Hall, in the afternoon and evening. There was some mystery about his antecedents but he claimed to be the son of a Scotsman and a native Indian woman, and that he had been reared by the Obijway tribe, from whom he had learned to live simply in communion with Nature.

Grey Owl's appearance on the stage of the Grosvenor Hall was dramatic, dressed in full hunting apparel of buckskin trousers and a beaded and frilled jacket, set off with a large feather in his black hair. He looked, according to the Belfast Telegraph, "a true son of the wilderness." He explained, with telling sincerity, that for many years he had lived as a trapper in the wilderness of N. Canada until he realised that humans were needlessly destroying the natural wildlife. He made the decision to do something to protect the wild animals before they were eliminated and lost. He illustrated his talk with a series of official Canadian government films shot in the forests of that country. The only civilised way to shoot wild animals, he claimed, was with a camera and he expressed his pleasure that the rifle was being slowly replaced with the camera for that purpose. His audiences were very impressed by his message and, above all, by the bearing of the man himself. Thus it was with shock that they read in the local papers of his death from pneumonia only two years later. More shocks followed when it was subsequently revealed that he had no native American Indian blood but was actually an Englishman, born in Brighton. His fascination with the wilderness and the West had led him to emigrate to Canada, and to live the life of a hunter and trapper. From that experience he had developed his ideas about conservation and the protection of wildlife. The details of his life continue to attract attention and were recently the basis of a film by Richard Attenborough in which Grey Owl was played with dignity by Pierce Brosnan.

Grey Owl's fascination with the West was shared by many in Belfast, but whereas he had integrated into the "real" Western wilderness even to the point of "becoming" a native American, cinema audiences in general preferred the imagined West, the myth, as presented on their cinema screens. The Thirties were not noted for many really great Westerns. The genre was still popular, and children played cowboys and Indians in the streets, but the films themselves were mainly B movies or fillers which occupied the lower half of popular double bills, whether in the Royal Cinema or the Midland. Tom Mix, Hoot Gibson, Tim McCoy and Ken Maynard were still regular favourites, but had been joined by new faces like William Boyd as Hop-a-Long Cassidy of the Bar Twenty, and an - up - and coming action man called John Wayne who appeared often in the Royal Cinema. By the mid - decade audiences enjoyed a new phenomenon, the singing cowboy. For a time even John Wayne entertained local audiences as Singing Sandy but thankfully quickly abandoned his guitar. Wayne's films were fast moving with lots of hard riding, fights and gunplay and included actors like Gabby Hayes and Yakima Canutt, who were to make cinematic names for themselves in later years. The leading singing cowboy, with a wide following in Belfast, was Gene Autry who appeared regularly in the Royal Cinema, before moving on to less opulent screens, accompanied by his faithful sidekick, Smiley Burnett. Gene Autry's recordings were also in great demand in the record shops and the author's earliest memory of a gramophone was listening to him singing, at 78 rpm, "Old Faithful," a sentimental ode to his "four footed friend." Screen cowboys were expected to treat their horses well and many of the popular heroes appeared with the same animals in film after film. Many of them became equine stars in their own right, and were recognised with affection by the public. Most famous was Tom Mix's "Tony," Ken Maynard's "Tarzan," the Lone Ranger's "Silver" and, later, Roy Roger's "Trigger." The tradition continued into the Forties and Fifties when major stars like James Stewart and Randolph Scott regularly rode their own favourite steeds.

Running parallel to the B movies were the Western serials, the most famous of which was "The Lone Ranger," which ran with great success in the Imperial during 1937. The serials had made a comeback with sound in the early Thirties though they never had the breath taking impact of the silent serials. The new heroes were mainly men, and there was no one to equal the early silent serial queens. In mid - 1938 one of the best known of them, Pearl White, died in Paris and that news moved a writer in the Irish News to recall her screen adventures, and her immense popularity in Belfast. The sound serials became a staple ingredient of the programmes in the cheaper cinemas like the Crumlin and the Midland but, on occasion, showed in some of the downtown cinemas. As already mentioned the Imperial screened "The Lone Ranger," and followed it with "Flash Gordon's Trip To Mars" starring Buster Crabbe, while the Royal Cinema showed the John Wayne Mascot serial "The Hurricane Express" in which he attempted to foil the dastardly plans of The Wrecker, whose aim was to destroy the local railway.

For the most part the sound serials were quite unsubtle, being just an excuse for fights, chases on horseback or in cars, trains or aircraft. There were thrills galore as the intrepid heroes clashed with mysterious hooded or otherwise disguised villains. They were regarded as suitable for children because, like the B Westerns, they had brave, upstanding, honest heroes. They showed clearly that crime did not pay, and that good prevailed in the end. The Westerns in particular had an unwritten code of behaviour which their heroes adhered to. The Western hero was strong but used his strength to protect the weak and dispense justice. He was good mannered, especially in his treatment of women, whom he addressed as "ma'am" accompanied by a slight raising of his Stetson. He never used violence towards a woman. There was no escape for anyone found to be a "woman killer." In his dealings with villains he was ready to use his fists or guns but even then there were conventions. Fights were fair and gunplay was used to disable rather than kill an opponent. Backshooting was forbidden and a villain was always given the opportunity to draw first. In some cases, notably the Lone Ranger, the rules extended to the verbal exchanges. The Lone Ranger always spoke correct English, without slang, and certainly without profanity of any kind. In modern parlance the Western hero was presented as a role model for young people, and the boys especially responded enthusiastically.

While the positive attributes of the Western hero could be admired, the same couldn't be said for the urban villains. Fears were often expressed that young people, especially young males, could be impressed by the spurious glamour surrounding crime figures. Film makers were under pressure to show the evils of a life of crime, and to make sure that the villains paid the penalty for their misdeeds. Thus gangsters played by the likes of Edward G. Robinson and James Cagney usually ended their days under a hail of police bullets. A popular series shown in most cinemas was the thirty minute long Crime Does Not Pay stories based, it was claimed, on actual cases. In each a serious crime was shown taking place, followed by details of the investigations by the F.B.I., Scotland Yard or other police forces which led to the apprehension of the criminals involved. The style adopted was part documentary with the action being commented upon by a sonorous but commanding voice whose final words were always "crime does not pay." The stories, "taken from actual police files," were tautly directed and the documentary style convinced audiences that what they were seeing was "real." Similar type series remained popular throughout the forties into the fifties, the latter being fronted by serious faced personalities like Edgar Lustgarten (the Scotland Yard series) or Valentine Dyall of the sepulchral voice. Both the latter made the connecting link to television in the Fifties, as did other series, notably the Lone Ranger and Hopalong Cassidy. When the B-movies disappeared from the cinema screens in the sixties they didn't die, they just migrated to television.

Fred and Ginger: poetry in motion.

The musical continued to dominate local screens during the Thirties, to the delight of critics and audiences. The Hippodrome in particular got the reputation of bringing the latest and brightest musicals, while the Picture House was often congratulated by the critics on its policy of reviving older and much loved musicals. Always welcomed were the romantic comedies starring Fred Astaire and Ginger Rogers. Fred especially was praised for his superb dancing skills, his witty persona and his elegance. The dancing couple first appeared together in "Flying Down to Rio" (d. Thornton Freeland, 1933) which showed in the Hippodrome in October 1934. The Irish News found the story "full of life and colour," and had special praise for the dancing skills of Astaire and his partner. The News Letter was impressed by the spectacular nature of the production and the dancing, making special mention of the Carioca, in which Fred displayed "a clever and amusing dancing turn." Overall the critic was much taken by his "dry wit" which, he felt, added greatly to the general enjoyment of the film. No mention was made of Ginger Rogers. Wherever the film was shown in the city it proved to be a great hit, attracting long queues and large crowds. Eddie Cantor was another popular performer who was much praised especially in "Whoopee," "The Kid from Spain," and the titillating "Roman Scandals."

The musicals, with their rapid cutting and fluid camera work were awash with energy, high spirits, good humour and, of course, - one of their main attractions - lots of beautiful girls. The routines of Busby Berkeley, with their lines of well drilled dancers, often photographed from above to show ever changing patterns, were a great favorite with audiences and often earned the praise of the local critics. The musicals were usually light hearted in tone but some, like "42nd Street" (d. Lloyd Bacon,1933), which showed in the Hippodrome in October 1933, could be grittier in their depiction of stage life. The News Letter critic described it as "a backstage story with splendid music and dancing .... one of the bigger and better musical spectaculars." The Irish News praised its plot and commented on the spectacular dance sequences originated and directed by Busby Berkeley. When the Q.F.T. showed the film 66 years later (April 1999) its attractions obviously hadn't faded with time. The accompanying notes not only reflected those early comments but further insisted that it was "without doubt one of the half dozen finest musicals of all time." There was special praise for "the unforgettable Ruby Keeler." Miss Keeler soon appeared again in "Gold Diggers of 1933," aided and abetted by Ginger Rogers (not yet teamed with Fred Astaire), Dick Powell (crooning soulfully in his pre - Philip Marlowe days), and the incomparable Busby Berkeley dance routines. Audiences in the hungry Thirties appreciated the irony of songs like "We're In The Money," but they rarely emerged from the cinemas in pensive moods. They were usually smiling the smiles of people warmed by first class entertainment.

The musicals reflected and buttressed the dance crazes of the period. Dance halls like the Plaza, the Orchid, the Orpheus, the Floral Hall and many smaller halls competed with the cinemas for audiences. Dance halls, cinemas and record shops all competed with each other, but also complemented each other in the musical field, as elements in popular culture tend to do. Many of the top bands of the day appeared in films and the fans who went to see them also visited the ballrooms and theatres where they made personal appearances, and bought their recordings. Despite its popularity dancing, like the cinema, had its critics. There were those who felt that it was somehow immoral, and it was condemned from many a pulpit and at many a local council meeting, especially when requests for licences for Sunday dances were being debated. Despite such negative comments young people flocked to the local dance halls to enjoy the music, the bands, the company and the general atmosphere. The dance halls were generally well supervised and there was a high level of formality with regard to personal dress and behaviour. Each dance, whether a waltz, quickstep, foxtrot or tango, had its own special steps, and most aspiring dancers attended dancing classes before braving the big dance floors. Many discovered that the moves weren't just as easy as Fred and Ginger made them look. The Haines School of Dancing which had instructed many generations of local dancers had been superseded by names like Joe Dosser, Betty Staff and

Albert White. When Mr White, who was married to Eve Dosser, opened his new dance hall, or ballroom as it was technically called, on 2nd October 1937, in the former Victoria Hall in Victoria Street, he commented on the amazing growth in the popularity of dancing among young people during the Thirties. He recalled how he had been teaching dancing locally for over 19 years. He had started with 4 pupils, while today he had about 800.

Besides its social attributes there was an increased realisation of the physical advantages of some forms of dancing, especially tap dancing. Dance routines were increasingly incorporated in the activities of keep - fit clubs, particularly those aimed at women. One such organization was the Women's League of Health and Beauty, based on a German concept, which in a few years had grown from small beginnings to over 130,000 members across the Br. Isles. It was organized into local branches of enthusiasts and in November 1937 the Ulster Branch hosted a major Midnight Charity Matinee in the Ritz Cinema. The cinema was crowded for the occasion, and those present enjoyed displays put on by branches throughout the Br. Isles, including one from the Free State. There were gymnastic exhibitions involving large hoops, with skipping, jumping and dance routines. One of the warmest welcomes was given to the branch from Dublin, wearing red and gold, who put on an energetic comedy dance routine. Prunella Stack, the daughter of the founder of the movement, was present, and gave a speech followed by a gymnastic display which greatly impressed the audience.

The musicals also introduced audiences to fine singing by the likes of Nelson Eddy and Jeannette McDonald, Paul Robeson, John McCormack, Bing Crosby, Richard Tauber, Jessie Matthews, Alice Faye and Grace Moore who was a particular favourite in Belfast. Such cinematic pleasures were available to all who had the money to pay for the seats though there were some notable exceptions like the blind, of whom there were 1161 registered in Belfast in 1937. A number of concerned citizens and organizations like the White Cinema Club, and the Corporation's Blind Persons' Committee felt that some effort should be made to accommodate groups like the blind, who despite their visual disability could still appreciate the soundtrack, and enjoy the special ambiance of a cinema. The local cinema industry had always been ready to help the socially deprived and other deserving minority groups with special charity shows and such, and responded sympathetically. As already indicated, in late January 1936, the Classic had presented a showing of Alfred Hitchcock's "39 Steps" to a specially invited group of blind people. While it was a welcome gesture, much appreciated by the audience, the film wasn't really suited to the situation.

A year later the experiment was tried again with a different type of production, a musical. It was felt that after a brief outline of the story the blind could then enjoy the music and songs. In January 1937 the Hippodrome put on a special morning showing of Grace Moore's latest musical "The King Steps Out." 800 blind persons were invited, and the importance of the occasion was reflected in the fact that the Lord Mayor, Sir Crawford Mc Cullagh, was present, as was W. J. Kennedy the clerk of the Blind Persons' Committee. The group were welcomed by the manager of the cinema, George Dobler, who in turn introduced Gerald Morrison, the manager of the Empire Theatre. He explained the setting of the film and gave an outline of the story. Then the film was projected and from all accounts was thoroughly enjoyed by all. Grace Moore's next film, "I'll Take Romance," arrived in the Ritz in June of the following year and the experiment was repeated with an invited audience of 600 blind patrons. The event was arranged by John Archer, the Town Clerk, in association with the manager of the cinema, John D. Russell. After being welcomed by Mr Russell the audience, which included members of the Corporation's Blind Persons' Committee, was entertained by Joseph Seal on the cinema organ before the curtains parted and the film was shown. In it Miss Moore played an opera singer who had to choose between her career and love. Hardly an original theme, but it was just an excuse which allowed her, in the process of deciding, to sing often, including a wide range of popular excerpts from Manon, La Traviata and Madame Butterfly. Again the occasion was a great success, and at the end the audience erupted with cheering and clapping.

In December 1936 the Classic showed the remake of the popular theatrical extravaganza "Showboat" (d. James Whale, 1935) with a star cast which included Irene Dunne, Charles Winniger, Paul Robeson, Allan Jones and Hattie McDaniel. One of the main attractions, and talking points, in Belfast was the performance and singing of Paul Robeson, which the local critics drew special attention to. He had visited the city in February 1934 for a concert in the Ulster Hall and had impressed audiences then with his vocal prowess and his personal character. The Irish News critic was enthusiastic in his praise of the film. He intimated the extent to which sound films had progressed technically since 1929, when, he recollected, he had seen the original talking film of "Showboat" in the Classic in the very early days of sound. It was that cinema's first talking picture, and he recalled the "tinny sound of both speaking and singing voices." Even natural sounds like the steamer horns were distorted and he particularly remembered "the walled in impression of the sounds in open air scenes." All that was much improved in the new production and Paul Robeson was heard "as perfectly as if he was singing in a concert hall," with the added advantage that close-ups clearly showed the emotions that accompanied his singing. He praised the purity of the deep bass notes in his voice, whether speaking or singing, especially in his rendition of "Ole Man River," which he described as "a thing of joy." In conclusion, he added that along with the technical and vocal improvements there was more comedy in the new version. Praise for Robeson was reflected in the comments of the other critics while the long queues outside the cinema spoke of the public's approval. Another observer noted how quiet the Belfast audiences were. They had the ability to sit through the most lively songs and enjoy them in silence. In contrast, audiences in Dublin cinemas were known to join in the better known songs on occasion.

Many local people were saddened when John McCormack announced at the beginning of April 1936 that he would retire after one last concert tour. The singer had been a frequent visitor to the city over the years and always spoke highly of Belfast audiences. He gave his farewell concert in the Ulster Hall on 10th October 1938 in an atmosphere that was highly emotional. A writer in the Irish News described him as "the greatest glory of Ireland in the world of music," and pointed out that while many associated him with popular and emotional songs like "The Rose of Tralee" and "The Star of County Down" he was equally at home in classical music and opera whether singing in English, German, Italian, or French. The writer regretted his going, adding that he would be greatly missed, not only in Ireland, but also from the international concert stage. He made no mention of the singer's films. His last screen appearance was in the Technicolored "Wings of the Morning" (d.Harold Schuster,1937) which starred Henry Fonda. It was Britain's first film in three - strip Technicolor and even today it looks magnificent. The plot was based on a story by Donn Byrne and involved gypsies, a curse, horses and, of course, true love. When it showed in the Curzon in October 1937 it was praised by the News Letter critic for its lovely Irish scenery, and the "superb" singing of John McCormack. As expected, it drew large crowds and when it reached the Clonard a few months later the cinema was packed every evening. Today, film historians recall it mainly for its pictorial beauty, and the singing of John McCormack.

Mystery and detective films vied with musicals for popularity. The decade had begun with Clive Brook and Raymond Massey giving their very different personations of Sherlock Holmes but by the mid - Thirties they had been superseded by an English stage actor called Arthur Wontner in the role. Wonter looked remarkably like the original Paget drawings of the great detective, and his films proved popular with audiences. The Whig described his "Triumph of Sherlock Holmes," in July 1935 as "a succession of thrills." On the American side William Powell continued to entertain as the Thin Man, and local critics agreed that each successive film was better than the one before. Charlie Chan always drew large crowds even after the original player, Warner Oland, died suddenly in 1937 and the part was taken over by Sydney Toler. Chan was a Hawaiian Chinese and he soon had another Oriental competitor in the person of the Japanese Mr Moto. Mr Moto, who was probably the first hero to use ju jitsu on screen, was played by the German actor Peter Lorre. The series had its first showing in Belfast with "Think Fast Mr Moto," in January 1938, followed by "Thank You Mr Moto," which appeared in the Imperial in August 1938 and "Mr Moto Takes A Chance" in the same cinema a few months later. Needless to say the Mr Moto series didn't survive Pearl Harbour. By then a third Oriental sleuth had surfaced, called Mr Wong, played with typical aplomb by Boris Karloff, though he never reached the level of popularity of Charlie Chan. The Wong films had intriguing plots but, like most Monogram products, suffered from low production values, and were quickly forgotten.

Another name that did live on, also appeared contemporaneously on local screens: Perry Mason. Perry Mason emerged in book form from the imagination of Erle Stanley Gardiner in 1933 and the following year appeared in his first film. From 1934 local audiences in the downtown cinemas enjoyed a sequence of typical titles like "The Case of the Howling Dog," "The Case of the Curious Bride," "The Case of the Velvet Claws," and "The Case of the Lucky Legs" in which the lawyer detective was played by Warren William, a tall sophisticated actor, complete with moustache. As a matter of interest the corpse in the "Curious Bride" was played by an unknown Australian actor called Errol Flynn, appearing in his first American film. Different leading ladies came and went as Della Street. After three more cases the series ended, until resurrected in the fifties on television with Raymond Burr in the name part. Warren William was well known to Belfast audiences. He had impressed as Julius Caesar in De Mille's "Cleopatra," and during the Forties appeared in various private eye mysteries as Philo Vance, and the Saint.

One of the many pleasures of such series for regular film fans was the recognition of the familiar faces of bit players who always turned in watchable, predictable but entertaining performances. Also, on occasion, former stars whose best days were over appeared in supporting roles. Such was the case in "Mr Moto Takes a Chance" when Pauline Frederick appeared in a minor role. Her visit to Belfast in the Twenties had caused great excitement and many of the more mature picturegoers would have remembered that, plus her many successes as a major star in silent films. The Irish News critic, probably with such memories in his mind, drew special attention to her presence in the film. He didn't know then that her health was in decline, and, soon after, the papers carried brief reports of her death, aged only 53 years. When those old films appear on television today, or are made available on DVD, film buffs still play the game -- spot the face!

There were also adventure films to supply outdoor thrills. Of those Tarzan was the great favourite and the local critics praised Johnny Weissmuller's swimming prowess, and emphasised that Jane was played by an Irish actress, Maureen O'Sullivan. Other actors, notably Buster Crabbe and Herman Brix, were appearing in Tarzan serials at the time but for audiences and critics Weissmuller was THE Tarzan. When "Tarzan and his Mate" reached Belfast in December 1934 the Belfast Telegraph critic praised its fast action, but suggested that "credulity was stretched" by the antics of some of the animals. The Irish News critic joined him in admiring the film, and the attributes of its hero. He praised Tarzan's bravery and ingenuity, and was impressed by his "sensational battle with a man - eating crocodile." Tarzan, he wrote, had become as well known as the most famous international figures. "He fills a great human need, inspiring grown-ups and children alike."

Apes featured largely in the Tarzan films but, appealing as they were, they couldn't compare with the biggest ape of all, King Kong, who arrived in the Picture House on 4th November 1933. Critics and audiences were both intrigued and amazed. The News Letter described the film as based on a really fine idea, and was impressed how the story exploited "the scope and technical ingenuity of the cinema." The Whig recommended it but refused to take it too seriously, commenting wryly that Kong, like most "gentlemen," seemed to prefer blondes, a reference to the much put upon heroine played by Fay Wray, whose screams entered into screen mythology. The Irish News saw it as "a weird drama of strange happenings." No one seemed to notice that it was a clever variation on Beauty and the Beast. People queued wherever it was shown in Belfast and it became the talk of the town, not only while it was in the cinemas, but for long after.

There were also films with more serious literary origins. The film companies regarded them as essentially prestige projects, and they were often undertaken without the expectation of making money. The film companies knew that such films pleased censors, parents, educators and even some critics. Certainly they were well received in Belfast and the critics usually overlooked their shortcomings and encouraged their readers to support them. One of the most unusual was Warner Brothers production of Shakespeare's "A Midsummer Night's Dream" starring James Cagney, Mickey Rooney, Dick Powell, Joe E. Brown, Frank McHugh and Olivia de Havilland, which opened in the Picture House on 25th May, 1936. What was even more surprising than the cast was the fact that it was directed by Max Reinhardt, the talented and greatly respected figure of German theatre. Reinhardt, a Jew, had fled from Nazi Germany to work in the United States. He had presented a successful stage version of A Midsummer Night at the Hollywood Bowl, with a cast that included Olivia de Havilland and Mickey Rooney. Warners were subsequently persuaded, reluctantly, to let Reinhardt direct a film of the play. While some traditionalists and critics, especially in Britain, were appalled at the result, the local scribes remained receptive and appreciative. They attended the trade show arranged for them and members of the local film trade on the Saturday morning before the official Monday opening, and what they saw, according to the Whig, was "a unique and challenging film" made with great imagination. A retired teacher who saw it at the time described it to the author as "fascinating," though, as he recalled, poorly supported.

James Cagney was very popular in the city and some cinemas, like the Strand, put on special Cagney weeks of his films, but even his most ardent supporters were uncertain of what to expect. The original plot was followed closely, but the longer speeches were judiciously shortened. It took some time getting used to James Cagney and others speaking the Shakespearean dialogue with an American twang, but the Whig critic thought that Cagney was a "revelation" as Bottom, while Mickey Rooney brought an "impish devilment" to his playing of Puck. Max Reinhardt had expressed satisfaction with Cagney's performance, and admiration for his acting style which, as he described it, was characterised by a mysterious and dangerous uncertainty that never allowed the audience to relax. Cagney's reactions, he noted, were always unexpected, fresh and never conventional. The main surprise and attraction of the piece for the local critics was the beauty of the photography, especially in the scenes involving the fairies in the enchanted forest. The dances were a "free and fantastical interpretation" (Whig) and the sequences were handled with intelligence and imagination. No one mentioned that the film had obviously been cut for local presentation. The original length is given as 132 minutes yet the special showing times advertised for the Picture House were 12:15, 2:20, 4:25, 6:30 and 8:35, which indicates that the running time was less than two hours. Nearly fifteen minutes must have been removed.

During the silent era films based on Shakespeare that used only an outline of the plots were always popular in Belfast, but by the Thirties that interest had declined. Reinhardt's film showed for only one week in the Picture House, and then disappeared. It doesn't seem to have been shown anywhere else in the city. Films based on Shakespeare continued to attract only a relatively small audience in Belfast. Even M-G-M's sumptuous "Romeo and Juliet," starring Norma Shearer and Leslie Howard, with Basil Rathbone and John Barrymore, which arrived soon after, suffered the same fate despite its fine cast. For many filmgoers Shakespeare was associated with school, not with entertainment. For others he represented literature and was therefore more suited to the stage rather than the cinema screen. The Whig critic disagreed with such views and argued that the cinema added an extra dimension, noting for example that "A Midsummer Night's Dream" had a visual impact superior to anything the stage could produce. Any casual filmgoer who consulted the cast list and then went to the Picture House that week expecting to see a gangster film must have been very disappointed, to say the least.

Disappointment wasn't always the popular response to the literary films. The works of Dickens were always well supported and large crowds were reported at M.G.M's "David Copperfield" (d. George Cukor, 1934) and "A Tale of Two Cities" (d. Victor Fleming,1935 with Ronald Colman). The Whig critic described David Copperfield as an "impeccable production," while his colleague on the News Letter thought it was one of the finest adaptations of a book for the screen that he had seen. There was special praise for W.C.Fields as Mr Micawber and a warm welcome for a young English actor called Freddie Bartholomew, who for the next ten years or so became the epitome of what a well mannered and properly brought up young boy should be. Similar praise greeted "Treasure Island" (d. Victor Fleming, 1934) a beautifully made, rousing pirate adventure with Wallace Beery as Long John Silver, and Jackie Coogan as Jim Hawkins. Another local success, "The Barretts of Wimpole Street" (d.Sydney Franklin,1934), wasn't based on a great novel but it dealt with the love story of Elizabeth Barrett (a "brilliant" Norma Shearer), and Robert Browning (Fredric March). Special mention was made of the presence of two Irish actresses in the cast in the persons of Maureen O'Sullivan and Una O'Connor. The local critics agreed that the most memorable performance in the film came from Charles Laughton as the stern father. He was to appear even sterner in "Mutiny on the Bounty" (1935), but the crowds and the critics, loved him for it. No one could project refined nastiness like Charles Laughton and his name on a cast list meant long queues either at the city centre or in the suburbs. The author can recall an aunt, a practical and well balanced woman, praising his performance in "The Barretts of Wimpole Street" but adding that there were times when she felt like climbing up into the screen and walloping him. Films and performances were not taken lightly by local audiences.

Some time later, in January 1936, the Classic announced the arrival of "Becky Sharpe" (d. Rouben Mamoulian, 1935) based on Thackeray's novel, "Vanity Fair." The film represents an important technical advance for the cinema because it was the first full length commercial film made in three - strip Technicolour. Colour had been a part of film going from the earliest silent days but the tints were usually added, often by hand, after the filming was completed. With Technicolour the colours were fixed within the camera and the results were certainly spectacular. Colour is taken for granted today but for audiences in the mid Thirties "glorious technicolour," as it became known, was an eye opener. The local critics were completely delighted with the clarity and richness of the colour and impressed with the way the director, Rouben Mamoulian, used it for dramatic purposes. They praised the visual beauty of the rural landscapes, the colours of the dresses and uniforms, the rich reds of the soldiers' cloaks swirling as they went to battle, contrasting them with the dark greys of the church where the waiting women prayed. There was praise also for the acting, especially of Miriam Hopkins as Becky. While praising and recommending the film the Whig critic, rather astutely, wondered if the colour represented a dramatic addition to the story telling, or a distraction from it. The public in general weren't interested in such distinctions but went in large numbers to see what they regarded as a new attraction. After a successful run in the Classic, the Curran family, who had demonstrated a long standing interest in new technical developments in the medium, booked it into their circuit, and It actually showed in three of their cinemas, the Capitol, Astoria and Regal, at the same time, most unusually for those days (see page 489).

One of the arguments put forward in favour of prestige productions was that they introduced people who normally didn't read, to good literature. Another was that many of the stories were more suited to young filmgoers than the sensational fare they normally watched. The release of increasing numbers of prestige films in the Thirties coincided with a renewed and widespread debate at all levels of society about the impact of films on children, and the need or otherwise for educational films. The local newspapers entered fully into the discussions with reports of conferences, debates and pieces on the topic, plus suitable editorial comment. The writer of Random Jottings in the Irish News was a regular filmgoer, someone who enjoyed and appreciated good films. He often commented on matters concerning the cinema which he felt held local interest as, for example, in January 1933 when he referred to a questionnaire on cinema attendance that had been carried out in England by a doctor. From a mixed group of 500 children the doctor had discovered that around 10% never visited a cinema, but 44% went at least once a week, including visits to the late showings. Boys went more often than girls. When asked what they learned from films, some said "slang" but most replied, "nothing." For the boys cowboys and comedies were their favourite films, while love themes and murder were the least liked. When asked for suggestions to improve cinemas a small number made quite sensible suggestions, such as that there should be no smoking allowed, nor should children in arms be admitted. While the research wasn't very scientific it suggested that the topic of children and the cinema wasn't as simple as some observers suggested.

Many "experts" insisted that films had a derogatory impact on the young minds of children and that their exposure to the medium should be restricted. Films, they argued, glamourised violence and anti - social behaviour, and made crime seem too attractive. Such opinions received substantial support in responsible circles in Belfast. Magistrates and others who dealt with children were often reported condemning films as a major cause of juvenile delinquency, despite statements by eminent legal personages in England to the contrary. The local chief justice, Lord Justice Andrews, stated clearly at the opening of the Belfast Commission in the Courthouse on the Crumlin Road in 1934 that films were a major cause of the recent increase in juvenile delinquency in the city. Shortly afterwards he chaired a meeting of the Belfast branch of the British Film Institute held in the Grosvenor Hall, and he repeated and elaborated on his comments. He admitted that he didn't go to the cinema often, and that he knew very little about film making, but insisted that he was well informed from discussions with responsible people who were familiar with and very knowledgeable about the subject. He recognised that films were a source of education and had introduced audiences to aspects of literature, art, history, science and geography, but at the same time they had done a lot of harm. He had seen some good films, but too many contained scenes that were "loathsome." He especially condemned gangster films, and those which undermined marriage, and family values. He believed that there was a need for some type of control on what was shown, especially to young people.

Around the same time the Women Citizens' Union held a debate on "The Influence of the Cinema on the Community," presided over by the Rev. Sydney Whitehouse, the hon. secretary of the local branch of the B.F.I. It proved to be a lively affair. During it a Mrs Belshaw, who seems to have been a valiant woman with strongly held views, bravely defended the cinema. Despite some problems, she felt that overall it offered positive social advantages. At one level it represented an escape from the grim realities of life into "a world of romance, excitement and laughter," and she felt that for the very poor and unfortunate their lives would be "intolerable" without it. At the very least it provided a place of warmth and comfort for a few hours, and on a practical level kept young people off the streets, and out of public houses. At a higher level she held it introduced them to beauty. In her experience most films contained some elements of beauty, and she believed that beauty was a most powerful influence for good. She admitted that her Puritan ancestors were probably "turning in their graves" at her words, but despite all the good they had done she had come to the conclusion that they had missed much about life. They had feared Beauty and thought it was dangerous, which wasn't the case.

Others disagreed vehemently with her and insisted loudly that films had a very adverse effect especially on the young. One speaker said that she couldn't see how "the orgies of squandering, idleness and loose living" depicted in many films could do other than corrupt a child's mind. She was also worried about the impact of such scenes on native peoples throughout the Empire and how they coloured the perceptions they held of their white rulers. Another debate along similar lines took place in the Belfast CPA, arranged by the Literary and Debating Society. The theme was "The Film in Modern Life," and the main speaker was local man Ruddick Millar. He traced the amazing growth of the medium from its small beginnings to its modern influential position, but expressed disappointment at its achievements. He reflected the views of Mrs Belshaw when he described the cinema as "a distraction from worry and work ......a kind of drug that transported people to a world of beauty and romance ....where dreams became reality." He felt that entertainment alone was not a sufficient objective but the cinema could reach much greater heights if it recognised itself as "a definite form of Art." He praised certain aspects, and was particularly impressed by its educational possibilities. At the same time he had reservations about the impact of films on young people, and advised strict control of what children watched.

While recognising that children's viewing needed to be supervised, the Belfast newspaper editors took a more liberal attitude to the problem of films and juvenile crime. In February 1936 the News Letter published research carried out by the LCC which rejected the link between films and crime. The work had been carried out with the co-operation of teachers in LCC schools and from the data collected the Chief Inspector of schools concluded that there was no need to be alarmed by the sight of children going to the cinema. What they saw, he explained, was no worse than the contents of the "penny dreadfuls" read frequently by children until recently, and there was no evidence that those stories had done any harm or influenced the reader's behaviour. Furthermore, the inspector stated, the cinema was an effective means of widening children's experience of the world, and was therefore a significant tool for educators. In November 1936 the News Letter returned to the theme and, in an editorial entitled Children and Films, pointed out that the Home Office rejected the theory that there was a direct connection between juvenile delinquency and the cinema. Research indicated that there was little concrete evidence to support the view that juvenile crime was due to films. Children may imitate or play at gangsters, but their motivation was not criminal. What attracted them was the action and speed of the films, and, importantly, the defeat of the bad men. In December of the same year the Belfast Telegraph reported the Lord Chief Justice in England as stating categorically that "criminals are not made by films."

The connection between films and juvenile delinquency continued to be accepted in ruling circles in Belfast, especially in the courts, despite the research that suggested otherwise. Typical was a case in November 1937 when seven boys appeared in Children's Court before a magistrate, Mr W.F.McCoy. One boy had stolen 4 shillings to go to the cinema, and the other six had broken into a shop to steal flashlights. They all pleaded guilty. The magistrate obviously regarded films as the source of their actions so, when they gave a promise that they would not go to a cinema for twelve months, he put them on probation. If they broke that undertaking, he warned them, they could be sent to an industrial school. The matter came in for local official examination when the government of N.Ireland set up a Committee of Inquiry to investigate the existing legal provisions for the protection and welfare of the young. The result was a wide ranging study of the law and youthful crime. The Committee's recommendations were published in March 1938, and among the conclusions, stated clearly that "there was insufficient evidence to show a connection between juvenile delinquency and the cinema." In conservative Belfast not everyone was convinced, and the accusation that the cinema undermined good behaviour continued to surface locally, though with decreasing effect. During the Fifties and later, horror comics and television became more convenient scapegoats to explain juvenile problems.

The fears expressed may have been genuine but now seem exaggerated. Hollywood films presented a wide range of youthful personalities and behaviour, with the balance tilted in favour of good behaviour. On the female side proper behaviour was personified by the likes of Shirley Temple, Judy Garland and Deanna Durban all of them talented, outgoing and without guile. Their films, strongly family oriented, were always welcomed and well attended in the city, as were those of Binkie Stuart. That name probably causes interrogatory raised eyebrows today, but in fact she was Britain's answer to Shirley Temple. The local critics usually referred to her as "charming," or "delightful" in films such as "The Rose of Tralee," but no one suggested that she posed any real competition to the talented Miss Temple. On the male side perfection was presented in the form of Freddie Bartholomew, Jackie Coogan, Bobby Breen and Mickey Rooney. Mickey Rooney's enthusiastic and wide eyed performances were enjoyed by both adults and young people. His immensely popular series of Andy Hardy films were aimed directly at family audiences. They were personally supervised by the chief of M-G-M, Adolf Zukor, who allowed no slur on the reputation of American mothers, nor unseemly behaviour that would offend them.

Mickey Rooney also made a series of teenage musical films with Judy Garland which were amusing, warm hearted and charged with a youthful energy which flooded out from the screen over the audiences. Crude language, violence and suggestive sex were nowhere to be seen or heard. The values highlighted were those of middle America, and the images were the screen equivalent of Norman Rockwell paintings. Mickey Rooney did also appear as a delinquent, notably in "Boy's Town" (d. Norman Taurog, 1938) with Spencer Tracy, which illustrated the story of Fr. Flanagan, and his attempts to establish a home for orphans in Nebraska. Spencer Tracy played the priest with fine conviction and was rewarded with an Oscar for best actor of 1938. Tracy presented the award to the real Fr. Flanagan in recognition of his work. Mickey Rooney played the uncooperative troublemaker who finally saw the error of his ways, proving, as Fr Flanagan claimed in the film, that "there is no such thing as a bad boy."

There were many in Belfast who disagreed with that conviction, and pointed to the Dead End Kids, among others, as evidence. They were a gang of fast - talking, street wise young toughs from the slums of New York, who represented the opposite end of the social spectrum from small town and rural values. They swaggered onto local screens in May 1938 with Joel McCrae and Humphrey Bogart, in the socially conscious "Dead End" (d. William Wyler, 1937), and had an immediate impact. When "Crime School" showed in the Classic in late 1938, the Dead End Kids were given top billing over Humphrey Bogart, which reflected their popularity. They moved in a noisy, overcrowded, multicultural environment, quite alien to local experience, which tended to reduce the impact of their behaviour. In time their toughness was further blunted by humour, and by the end of the Second World War they had evolved into the Bowery Boys, whose adventures were played mainly for laughs. The Bowery Boys, who seemed to have had a permanent residence in the Royal Cinema, were led by Leo Gorcey complete with a battered hat, the brim of which was incongruously pinned up at the front. He was ably supported by his second - in - command, Huntz Hall, who wore a baseball cap, sometimes backwards, a headgear and style then unknown in Belfast. Rather than encouraging local crime, the audiences in Belfast were more bemused than impressed by their speedily delivered slang and odd dress.

Meantime there was increasing support for the use of films in education. All the local papers praised the Ulster Museum's policy of showing free educational films on Saturday mornings and expressed satisfaction that demand for tickets resulted in packed showings. The Irish News, in an editorial in late 1936, praised recent government plans -- never fully realised -- to equip local schools with projectors to show educational films, but cautioned that "the film can only be an aid to the teacher and pupil. It can never be a substitute for personal instruction and study." Those opinions were highlighted again at a convention of the Federal Council of Teachers of N.Ireland, which claimed to represent all types of teachers, from elementary to university. The meeting took place in the Museum and Art Gallery where the main guest was Mr W. Farr from the BFI who addressed the teachers on "Films in School," illustrating his comments with examples of suitable films. He claimed, rightly, that there was some prejudice among teachers against the use of films but he felt that films could make a unique contribution to education. Mr A.N. Bonaparte Wyse, another member of the local BFI, also spoke about the practical considerations, like costs, of using films in the classroom, but hoped that in the future they would be accepted as a normal part of the teaching process.

Children were rarely consulted on such weighty matters but over Christmas 1936 Curran Theatres announced an essay competition for children on the topic "Should Educational Films be shown in School." The winners were announced at free matinees on Christmas Eve in the Broadway, Astoria, Capitol, Lyceum and the Regal. First prize was one guinea. The company expressed delight with the results, not only with the large and enthusiastic response but also with the quality of the ideas put forward. So much so that they released extracts. One scholar wrote: why shouldn't homework be a pleasure, if it was to describe some picture you have seen recently, like David Copperfield, or A Tale of Two Cities. Another took the view that "the chief objections to using educational films are raised by old - fashioned people." Yet another held that "the eye is the most important retentive and observant organ of the body and if educational films were shown in schools they would play an important part in the acquiring of knowledge." Finally, one budding young geographer commented that "to read and learn about different countries is most interesting, but to actually see them reproduced would be thrilling. It would be the next best thing to be travelling the world." Children in the Thirties obviously weren't just sponges soaking up crime and violence from what they viewed. They saw, and hoped for, more than some adults gave them credit for.

The debates and discussions indicated two positive approaches to the question of the educational worth of films. There were those who felt that specially made films could be used directly by teachers in schools, and there were those who held that even entertainment films had an intrinsic educational content which impacted on audiences. The BFI supported such views, and they were taken up by the Irish News and the Whig. In an editorial the Whig welcomed the increase in biographical films which introduced audiences to the important personages of history. The editor drew attention especially to such recent films as The Story of Louis Pasteur, Lloyds of London, Cardinal Richelieu, and Rembrant which had shown successfully in Belfast. But not everyone agreed that history was accurately represented on screen. The financially successful "The Private Life of Henry VIII" was strongly criticised for showing Henry as a "comic buffoon," as one writer put it. Another complained about John Ford's "Mary, Queen of Scots" for including a scene showing a meeting between Mary and Queen Elizabeth, a meeting which never took place in actuality. General criticisms were aired at many local meetings with complaints that the Hollywood domination of British and Irish screens meant that audiences, including children, absorbed an American perception of historical events.

One recurring worry was heard from certain quarters that the depiction of white persons in "unedifying situations" undermined the standing of colonial governments with native people. The Whig replied that it was all a matter of interpretation and one must remember that the film makers were producing dramatic works, where some poetic licence should be tolerated. The antidote to those criticisms was an educated public opinion. The editor found no fault with those who went to the cinema to enjoy the likes of Charlie Chaplin, the Marx Brothers, Will Hay and W.C.Fields, or to appreciate the "feminine allurement" of Greta Garbo and other lovely ladies. Such enjoyable outings were beneficial, and acted as a relief from "the dullness of everyday life." However he also welcomed the emergence in Belfast of a minority who showed increasing discrimination, and judged what they saw "by artistic standards" and not by "the shallow standards of entertainment."

Belfast had its fair share of societies, clubs and other groups whose members met periodically for lectures and discussions. Many had long been a feature of city society and they indicated the lively intellectual spirit that pervaded certain sections of the population. In the early Thirties a new society was added, called the Young Ulster Society, the aim of which was the promotion of the Arts in Ulster. It met in the Lombard Cafe to listen to lectures given by prominent figures on the local art scene. By July 1935 it had over 80 members. Its first president was the shipyard dramatist, Thomas Carnduff, who naturally gave a lecture on drama. Other speakers including Denis Ireland, Norman Hay and Richard Hayward who addressed the members respectively on literature, music, painting and the cinema. What is interesting is that the cinema was included, without protest, as an example of the arts. The cinema's profile had been raised by the type of debate mentioned earlier, and especially by the establishment of the local branch of the British Film Institute.

The BFI had an aura of academic formality about it, and its lectures were usually serious and technical in content, but it took its task of improving public taste seriously. In pursuit of that aim during 1938 it renewed its call for new members. Its Director, Oliver Bell, came over specially from London and gave a lecture in the Art Gallery on the "History of the Cinema," with the local BFI chairman, Bonaparte Wyse, in the chair. Mr Bell traced the development of the medium from 1896, which was only 42 years before. It was an exercise in living history because there must have been many in the audience who remembered seeing the first silent films, and responded to the early examples that the lecturer had brought with him. Those included "The Life of Charles Peace," and "The Great Train Robbery," both of which had been shown in Belfast at the turn of the century. After discussing the silent period he dealt with the talkies and the problems that the sound pioneers faced, problems that, he claimed, were only then being satisfactorily solved. But already, he insisted, the cinema had moved into its third chapter, that of colour. Unlike John Drinkwater, who had forecast the demise of the cinema, he saw a bright future ahead, but to get the most from that he encouraged people to take a more serious interest in films. One way to do that, of course, was to join the local branch of the BFI. Later, the Chairman, Bonaparte Wyse, in a letter to the local papers, continued that theme and took the opportunity to explain the practical advantages of membership. For one guinea a year each member received a copy of the Institute's quarterly magazine Sight and Sound, (which is still in production, though now on a monthly basis) plus a monthly Film Bulletin which detailed all films released in Britain, with critical notes on each. Added to those was the Belfast Film Review which discussed the "better films" being shown in the city cinemas, and any pamphlets published by the Institute on aspects of the cinema. The package also included entry to all BFI lectures in Belfast. Above all the Institute pointed its members towards the better films, those worth seeing. To those who argued that the press critics already did that, he replied that they only gave guidance "to a certain extent," inferring that newspaper critics were under pressure not to offend important advertisers like cinema owners, managers and film distributors.

Members of the Belfast Film Society would probably have agreed with that last comment, but they also had their reservations about the artistic independence of the Institute itself. Such matters were probably discussed in Methodist College, where the teaching staff included members of both organisations. In fact the two groups had much in common and in time came closer together, co-operating in producing the Belfast Film Review. In the meantime the Film Society went from strength to strength, and by 1938 had nearly 600 members. It also succeeded in overcoming a major problem by renting suitable venues for its shows. For its second, and later, seasons the Apollo cinema on the lower Ormeau Road became its main venue with shows arranged on designated Wednesday evenings at 8:00pm, beginning on 15th December 1937. A local resident and filmgoer recalled those special shows but could give no details. "We just ignored them," he commented casually. Those sentiments probably reflected the attitude of the majority of filmgoers in the city.

The members, however, enjoyed five foreign films during that second season, two

French, one Austrian (with the popular Paula Wesselly), one German and one Swiss with supporting documentaries and shorts. Each member could buy one guest ticket, but individual guests could attend only one film during the season. Outside those normal society meetings a number of special late night showings were arranged in the Imperial cinema. The first of those -already referred to - was Fritz Lang's "M," screened at 11:00 pm for members only, by ticket costing two shillings. The tickets had to be purchased beforehand from the Hon. Treasurer at 2, Upper Crescent. "M" had already had a restricted release in Belfast, having been shown in the Alhambra, but the Society announced that the Imperial screening would be the last before the film was withdrawn from general release. The showing was a great success, with the News Letter critic claiming that "the screening of 'M' fully vindicated the Society's policy of late night matinees." He admitted that it was not a film "for sensitive minds", but added that "its dramatic and technical brilliancy renders it invaluable to the student of the cinema." The supporting short, Lotte Reiniger's "Puss in Boots," also received great praise. The Whig critic described it as "artistic." Lotte Reiniger was a German who made silhouette films using paper cutouts, photographed one frame at a time. The results were quite exceptional in style, including sequences of not only great but mesmerising beauty. Like many artists working in films she fled from Nazi Germany in the Thirties, and settled in England where she made a number of films for the BBC in the Fifties.

A second late night showing followed in mid - April and was supported with equal enthusiasm. Unfortunately it had one unwelcome outcome. The Film Society was an idealistic cultural grouping, but when it entered the commercial side of film making it found itself scrutinised by the law. By law each entry ticket purchased had to carry a duty stamp attached to its back. On entering the cinema the ticket had to be torn in two by an attendant so that the stamp was rendered useless. One half of the ticket was retained by the cinema while the other half was returned to the patron. A government inspector had visited the Imperial and discovered that a number of tickets (97 in total) were untorn, while some had no duty stamp attached. As a result the Society was summoned, in the person of Ian Mc Clelland, the Hon Sec., for breaching the Entertainments Duty Regulations Act of 1916. The magistrate regarded the offence as a serious one, and fined the Society £50, which was a large sum in those days. On hearing that the organization was non - profit making and that no fraud was involved, he reconsidered and mitigated the fine to £12.10, with a warning that a similar situation mustn't happen again. Despite such setbacks the Film Society continued to flourish and gradually introduced an atmosphere of intelligence, continental allure and variety into the cinematic scene in the city.

Most of the regular filmgoers in the city ignored the activities of the Film Institute and the Film Society. To them films were an entertainment far removed from the realm of art. They gleaned their information about them mainly from the weekly and monthly fan magazines, notably Picturegoer and Picture Show. The latter, which appeared in newsagents every Tuesday, priced 2d (less than 1p of today's money), described itself as "the paper for people who go to the Pictures." Its readers were assured that if they perused the magazine every week they would enjoy the pictures more. Each issue promised "fresh news and pictures of the stars, the latest films, a pictorial souvenir of the week's releases, and a guide to the best films." From such sources the fans knew what the most popular films making the rounds were, and they were aware of what new films were being readied for release. Above all they could indulge their passionate admiration for their favourite stars, and readily absorbed the heady mix of fact and fiction that the magazines printed about them. Many younger fans wrote to their favourites via their studios and received copies of signed photographs by return. When, in "Broadway Melody of 1938," Judy Garland gazed wistfully at a photograph of Clark Gable and sang "Dear Mr Gable" it was not only one of the high points of the film but it struck a responsive chord with young girls from the Falls and Shankill, as it did in every city across the English speaking world. The cinema owners and managers encouraged such undemanding support, often with bizarre gimmicks. The Random Jottings scribe described how, on leaving a suburban cinema (unnamed), he and other puzzled patrons were given small boxes of dog biscuits. It transpired that a Bulldog Drummond film was showing the following week. There is quite a gulf between Lotte Reiniger and dog biscuits, but it was all accepted happily as part of the cinema scene. But not everyone in Belfast was satisfied with the situation.

Because of the widespread popularity and influence of the cinema there were many individuals and groups who felt that some type of local control of films was needed. Various Watch committees were set up by interested groups to monitor the films being shown in the city. One of the most influential of the pressure groups was the Joint Film Committee set up in the early Thirties by the Protestant Churches of N.Ireland. In early reports it was referred to as the Joint Committee, or the Protestant Film Committee, but was best known as the Belfast Film Committee. Dissatisfaction was often expressed about the decisions of the London based BBFC, and the local Corporation was called upon to take action. Within the Corporation responsibility for the scrutiny of films regarding their suitability for public exhibition was in the hands of the Police Committee, who had appointed a Film Committee to deal with any problems. The leader of that - mainly Unionist - Film Committee was Lt. - Commander Harcourt, and its fifteen members applied themselves vigorously to defending the moral fabric of their city. Their deliberations and decisions over the next forty or so years earned them praise, criticism and ridicule in equal measure. One irate letter writer to the Irish News in April 1932 during the Frankenstein controversy described them and their supporters as a collection of "kill - joys, spoilsports, disappointed spinsters, nosey Parkers, narrow minded cranks and grundies." Another, writing to the News Letter, noted that they represented a minority view, and, as such, he found their actions "gross interference" in his personal freedom, while yet another in the same paper thought that their activities were making Belfast "the laughing stock" of Britain.

Others defended the Police Committee as guardians of conservative Christian values, and upholders of the stern moral values that Belfast was noted for. Today they are seen by many as creaking relics unable to understand or cope with a changing society. In mitigation it must be said that the newly emerging values of that society were causing widespread unease in certain circles, both Protestant and Catholic. At the beginning of the decade the Whig, in an editorial, could ask its readers: Are we still a Christian people? Many people in Belfast were beginning to wonder. While films received high profile reporting there were also calls for the control of certain novels, objectionable English Sunday newspapers, magazines, and sexy postcards which were on sale in the city. The police were pressed especially to take action against shops that sold the latter and often did so, prosecuting the owners and confiscating their stocks. The moral disapprobation even extended to student activities and in May 1932 the rag magazine Pro Tanto Quid was banned by the Disciplinary Board of Queen's University.

The cinema and its films remained the main target of the watch committees. In February 1932 a group of 30 members representing the Joint Film Committee met the Police Committee officially to discuss film censorship. Their basic demand regarding the cinema was simple. A firm and decisive local Censorship was needed that could ban objectionable films. At the meeting it was agreed that if the Joint Committee became aware of a film being shown in the city which they regarded as objectionable they would inform the Police Committee, who would then examine the film and decide what action to take. The door was opened, and the ban - the - film supporters would soon enter.

CHAPTER TWENTY FIVE
Monstrous Events

The self regulatory system of censorship practised by the British Board of Film Censors (BBFC), had been established for silent films but continued to function, and to develop, when sound arrived in the Thirties. The Free State government introduced its own system and set up a Film Censor's office in Dublin in 1923. The office was part of the Dept. of Justice and the appointment of the censor was made by the Minister of Justice, though he had no power to change the censor's decisions. Unlike the British system which operated in N.Ireland, the film companies had no say in the running of the office, or in its decisions. The Irish censor was empowered by law to prevent the general exhibition of any film which he believed to be indecent, obscene, blasphemous or contrary to public morality, or subversive of it. It was a wide remit and the early censors interpreted it vigorously, so that the Free State acquired an unenviable reputation for cutting and banning films submitted to it. That oppressive, and to many people, negative approach remained until the Eighties, when the then censor Sheamus Smith began to liberalise the system.

During the Thirties the rigorous and forthright approach of the Dublin censor was admired and even praised by a minority on both sides of the religious and political divide in Belfast. In early January the minister of Donegall Pass Presbyterian Church compared the effectiveness of the system in Dublin with that in Belfast which he described as "nominal and a farce." The films which came to Belfast had already been examined and passed for exhibition by the BBFC, and the majority of people accepted that situation as adequate. Even the Irish News, never slow to criticise British policy, in an editorial in October 1935, conceded that the censorship system was working well, and that "Belfast has not a great deal to complain of as regards objectionable plays and films."

There was, nevertheless, one bone of contention which was often mentioned in letters to the local press, and in local discussions. The BBFC used only two categories of classification; "U" was for films suitable for all, while "A" indicated films suitable only for persons over 16 years. Children under 16 years could be admitted to such films but only if accompanied by a parent or guardian. The Home Office accepted that not all films given an 'A' certificate were harmful to all children, and felt that parents should be left to "exercise a discretion" in the matter regarding what their children saw. Critics argued that if a film was unsuited for a child alone, it was equally unsuited when that child was accompanied by an adult. Also, the system was open to abuse by children asking adults to let them accompany them into the cinema. The author recalls that situation even in the Forties. Young persons waited outside the cinema, money in hand, with the request: "Take me in with you, mister." Once in the darkness, the child abandoned his temporary "parent" and disappeared to find his own seat. Pressure was put on the Police Film Committee to take appropriate action to put an end that situation. That pressure increased when, in late 1931, the Secretary of State at the Home Office in London, announced the appointment of a sub-committe to study the current system of film censorship in England and Wales, and to make recommendations on any problems, including the vexed question of the "U" and "A" certificates. His declared aim was to promote better co-operation between the licensing authorities and the BBFC. The conclusions and suggestions of the sub-committee weren't published until March 1933 and the Police Committee duly received a copy. The contents consisted essentially of information updates, and guide-lines for the licensing authority, but in the light of happenings involving the Police Committee before 1933, the reaction of many in Belfast who read them was one of déja vù.

Although its deliberations didn't directly involve N.Ireland, the recommendations of the sub-committee were awaited with interest in Belfast where the decisions of the Police Film Committee, along with the effectiveness of their attempts at film censorship were often criticised. One highly critical group was the newly formed Belfast Film Committee - the joint committee mentioned above - and the minutes of the Police Committee include a letter from that Committee, dated 29th January 1932, which informed them that it had been formed "from practically all the Young People's Organizations in the city, and from members of all the churches including the Roman Catholic Church and the Jewish Synagogue," and that the sole aim of the members was to "promote the purity and the morality of our city, and the welfare of our young people." They didn't wish, they claimed, to usurp any of the powers of the Police Committee but wanted its members to consider three suggestions: the exclusion of all children under 16 years of age from "A" rated films; the need for large notices to be displayed at the entrances of cinemas stating clearly whether the film being shown was for adults or children; and the establishment of an effective local censorship in the city. Reference was also made to the advertising of films, especially to the objectionable posters which were "a blot on the hoardings of our city." Besides its comprehensive nature there are two significant points about the letter. It highlighted the film "Frankenstein" (which hadn't yet been shown in Belfast) as being among those films that should be censored, and secondly, one of the signatures to the letter was the Rev. W. Popham Hosford, who was to play a significant role in later attempts to censor locally booked films.

The matters mentioned in the letter were discussed a few weeks later, in February, by a sub-committee of the Police Committee at a meeting to which representatives of the Belfast Film Committee, and of the Amusement Caterer's Association (better known as the White Cinema Club) were invited. The Belfast Film Committee declined the invitation but the film trade was represented by W.J.Hogan, T McDermott, B.N.McDowell and F.A.Spiers, who found themselves on the defensive. They argued that the exclusion of children from "A" films was unreasonable as many films were given the "A" certificate because of their intellectual content rather than being morally objectionable. Such a decision would result in an unnecessary loss of revenue for the cinemas. They also maintained that a local censorship was unworkable because the time available from a film's arrival in Belfast, to its showing, was so short that every film couldn't possibly be examined. As a compromise, the sub-committee suggested that two members of the Belfast Film Committee should be given special passes which would admit them at no cost into any cinema in Belfast, except on Wednesdays (the shopping half day, and a busy one for the cinemas), and Saturdays. If they decided that the film they saw was unsuitable for children they would arrange for the Police Committee to see it, and take appropriate action.

The cinema representatives, who felt that one level of censorship was enough, were not too happy with the idea, and only agreed reluctantly. They also agreed, where necessary, to put a large notice in their foyers indicating that no one under 16 years would be admitted to the film being shown. The restriction didn't just apply to tawdry productions. In October 1932 the I.S.N. reported there was a large notice in the foyer of the Classic during the presentation of the prestigious and - prize winning "Dr Jeykll and Mr Hyde" (d. Rouben Mamoulian, 1931), starring Fredrik March, which stated that no-one under 16 years would be admitted. Most responsible filmgoers, except some disappointed 16 year olds, agreed with that injunction. The film dealt with a serious topic in an adult fashion, and was welcomed as such by the critics. It was, wrote the Irish News critic, "not just a sensational thriller; its theme has beauty as well as horror, and behind all there is moral and purpose without which the story could not have lived so long." He could have added that many of the scenes between Mr Hyde (F. March) and Miriam Hopkins were violent and sexually charged, and quite unsuited to children. Despite the absence of children - still perceived as a loss of revenue by some managers - the film was a major success across the city, showing in the Alhambra and the new Apollo. In November 1938 it was revived - by special request - and played to crowded houses for a further week in the Royal Cinema.

The deficiencies of the "A" certificate were further highlighted by the artistic and popular success of Universal's new series of horror films, beginning with "Dracula"(d.Tod Browning, 1931) and "Frankenstein" (d. James Whale, 1931). Those films, with their adult themes and strong visuals, prompted calls for a special category, other than "A", forbidding all children from seeing them, with or without an adult. The writer of Random Jottings in the Irish News highlighted a popular complaint, especially among parents, when he described cases of children having nightmares after watching frightening films, and called for action. Similar calls from professionals and others interested in the welfare of children led to the introduction of the special "H" for horror category in 1933. Before that happened, however, the matter had come to a head in Belfast with the sudden and unexpected banning of "Frankenstein." It was the first of a series of high profile censorship controversies which were to plague the city and its cinemas until the Seventies.

Frankenstein banned April 1932.

Mary Shelley's novel had been a popular success since its publication in 1832, so it wasn't surprising that it generated a number of equally successful stage productions. The latest of those was a much praised play by Peggy Webling. The Grand Opera House announced that the Webling play would be coming to Belfast direct from London, and promised that it was "more sensational than Dracula," and guaranteed "to make your flesh creep." A notice in the foyer of the theatre warned parents and others that the play was unsuited to children. It opened on Monday 30th March 1931 and, according to the Whig, it held the Belfast audience "enthralled" on that first evening. The Irish News critic was impressed by the quality of the production, but nevertheless concluded that it was "not a pleasant play." He praised David Basil Gill who played the part of the monster with great effect, even arousing pity in the audience for his unfortunate state. The Whig critic agreed, and gave more details. Here, he wrote, was a tragic, frustrated, man-made creation which had no soul, and no understanding of life or death. It desired human sympathy, but that was denied it. Mr Gill played the creature like a robot, speaking in the manner of a mechanical creation but "by gesture and inflection" investing his performance with humanity. All the local critics agreed that it was a serious play which dealt with adult themes - "strong meat" according to the Irish News - and quite unsuited to children. Its presentation wasn't marred by any protests about its content, and it proved a hit with local theatre goers. Mr Gill thanked the audiences from the stage for the way they had supported the play. In Hollywood Universal Studios had already seen the potential in it, bought the rights and had it rewritten and developed for filming. The studio had recently had a critical and financial success with "Dracula" (d. Tod Browning, 1931) starring the Hungarian actor Bela Lugosi, based also on a stage play, by Hamilton Deane. That same play had impressed local playgoers when it was presented on the stage of the Opera House in July 1926. Universal hoped to repeat its success with "Frankenstein."

The film of "Dracula" didn't reach Belfast until four months later (July 1931), when it was presented in the Classic. It was well received by the critics, though not as a horror film. The term "horror film" was not yet in general use, nor was horror perceived as a separate genre. The Irish News critic described it as a good thriller "with plenty of creeps," well made, and distinguished by the "good" acting of Bela Lugosi. The Whig critic thought that it was the best thriller he had seen for ages, a welcome change from "go - go girls and red-hot mammas." It was, he warned, completely unsuited to children, but for adults "with good nerves" it was utterly absorbing. He promised that grown men and women would be so absorbed that they would let their cigarettes go out while the normally garrulous would not even whisper, but would sit there tingling from head to toe. He marvelled how a completely unreal sequence of events became "real" through the skill of the camera. The story, he suggested, was "completely ridiculous," but, "you don't think so while watching the film, so marvellously is it produced in sound, scene and effect." The public agreed, and the Classic was besieged with long queues night after night. It drew equally large crowds across the city when it showed at the Clonard, the Alhambra and elsewhere.

Managers expressed satisfaction and looked forward to equally full houses with "Frankenstein." Audiences, for their part, eagerly followed reports on the progress and impact of that film in the fan magazines. Finally, in April 1932, the Classic announced its forth coming debut with the invitation "if you like an unusual thrill you will find it here - it will chill you and fascinate you." Audiences were advised that the film was booked only for a week, and they would see "the most gigantic thrill picture ever presented." But, mindful of the debate over the efficacy of the "A" certificate, a warning was added from the manager, Mr McDermott, that "the management earnestly recommend that children should not see this picture."

It is difficult for a modern audience to comprehend the impact that "Frankenstein" (d. James Whale, 1931) had in the early Thirties. The clutter of the Munsters, Young Frankenstein, Abbot and Costello and the Hammer films form a distorting mirror that partly obscures the original. The film caused a sensation in Belfast, some idea of which can be gleaned from the local reviews, and letters to the papers. The News Letter critic, in particular, disliked it and used the opportunity to criticise the modern craving for "thrills" in films, in stage plays or novels. "Frankenstein," the writer felt, was an example wherein "this mania" was carried too far. The film combined ingenious contrasts, devilish make-up and unnatural scenery to convey "a vivid and repulsive impression to the mind." Despite the censor's cuts, he forecast that many picturegoers were so inured to thrills that they would still have no hesitation in welcoming a film which, he insisted, was more gruesome than any they have ever seen. The Belfast Telegraph critic agreed that it was a film with its share of thrills, but he preferred to describe it as a "shocker" and warned his readers that those who went to see it would indeed be shocked by some scenes. Despite that he recommended it as a film that should not be missed because in many ways it was remarkable. The storyline was unusual, the acting was "excellent," and Boris Karloff with his "devilish make-up" was "an awe - inspiring spectacle as the Monster." The whole was embellished with ingenious stagecraft and impressive visuals. He emphasised that the film was completely unsuited to children and asked parents to note the manager's warning about its content.

Viewed today "Frankenstein" impresses with its imaginative direction, superb Gothic sets and, above all, with Boris Karloff's frightening but sensitive portrayal of the Monster. Jack Pierce, who was responsible for the special make-up, perceived the Monster as an electrical gadget whose life force was lightning. The film makers had a deeper meaning in mind for the creature. At the beginning of the picture a character addressed the audience directly with a message, and a warning, from Carl Laemmle the head of Universal Studios. What they were about to see was the story of a man of science "who sought to create a man after his own image, without reckoning upon God." The story had the capability to shock and even horrify, so... "we've warned you." The local critics ignored that serious subtext, but many thoughtful people see that warning as being every bit as pertinent today, when biochemists continue to manipulate the genetic code of DNA, and even, like Craig Venter in May 2010, claim to have mimicked the creation of life in a laboratory. Venter's new synthetic "creature" has been called - what else - a "Frankenbug."

When "Frankenstein" opened on Monday morning the 18th April the manager described it as a thrill picture. From the first programme it fulfilled the News Letter's predictions and did good business, with large crowds and long queues. Over the following two days a total of 10,000 patrons paid for admission. No one complained to the manager about the film or its content. However on Tuesday 19th a member of the Belfast Film Committee saw the film and after consulting with other members, wrote to the Town Clerk demanding that, as agreed in February, the Police Committee take action, as the film was in their opinion, unsuitable for public exhibition in Belfast. The Town Clerk in turn contacted Mr McDermott and requested a special showing for the Police Committee, a showing which was arranged for 10:00 am on Wednesday. Only five members of the Police Committee attended the viewing: Lt-Commander Harcourt the chairman, Councillors George Gray, Hopkins and McClelland, and Alderman Nixon. After watching the film the group retired to a room in the Classic and twenty minutes later emerged to announce that by a vote of 3 to 2 the film would be banned. Mr McDermott was informed officially of the decision a few hours later by the Town Clerk (Sir Robt. Meyer) and told that the film must be withdrawn after the 3:00 pm showing that day. An angry manager complied and quickly made arrangements to replace it with Lewis Stone in "Strictly Dishonourable." He personally went on stage before each showing of the replacement film, explained to the audience what had happened and apologised to them. The reactions and comments of those who arrived for the evening shows are not recorded, but can easily be imagined.

The development caused what the Irish News called "a mild sensation" in the city. It was the first occasion on which a film had been banned and withdrawn during its advertised run. Among those involved in the cinema industry there was disbelief and anger. A special meeting was called of the Cinema Managers Association of the White Cinema Club. It met in the Imperial Hotel in Donegall Place and was presided over by its founder Will White, who set the tone of the meeting by declaring that the Belfast Film Committee was out to give them all the trouble they could. He pointed out that the industry had always co-operated with the City Council and ensured that a Trade Show of any new film was arranged where members of the Police Committee were welcomed and could raise any problems before the film was presented to the public. No problems had been raised about "Frankenstein," though there were rumours going around the city that certain individuals were determined to stop its presentation. Mr McDermott was highly critical of how the ban was imposed. After the special showing the members of the Police Committee had refused to give him a reason for their decision beyond the fact that the film was "blasphemous and unedifying." They took special exception to the scene where the Monster caused the drowning of a little girl. That scene had caused problems in the U.S.A. but the version that reached Belfast had already been trimmed by the censor, with cuts that actually remained in place until 1986. They ignored his offer to have the sequence excised and were unmoved by his arguments that no-one had complained to him about any part of the film, that it had been passed by the BBFC in London with an "A" certificate, and had been shown widely in Britain. Also, the same version had been screened in Dublin, running for three weeks in the Corinthian cinema without protest. He added that some people seemed to think that the cinema was a branch of the educational system. They were now, he warned the meeting, facing a serious threat of local film censorship. Great exception was taken to the fact that only five members of the Police Committee had attended the special showing and that the decision to ban was reached on the basis of one vote.

The president of Universal Pictures Ireland, Robert Mc Kew, also addressed the meeting. The Police Committee had refused, he said, to give a reason for their action and he found their whole attitude "high - handed." His company took a very serious view of the affair and he had been authorised to take legal action, if necessary, to test the validity of the ban. It is doubtful if that would have achieved anything because in law the local Council still had the right to override the BBFC and stop the showing of any film locally. The cinema managers agreed that they couldn't run their business properly if films were to be banned with such suddenness, at the whim of a few people. The events of the past few days alone had cost Mr McDermott over £100 in lost revenues. The meeting finally decided to send an official protest to the Police Committee, and asked Mr Mc Kew to arrange another special showing of the film for Saturday morning in the Classic to which the entire Corporation should be invited. The members would then have the necessary information to discuss the matter at the next monthly meeting. Unfortunately when a group of councillors and others arrived at the cinema on Saturday morning they found that the Town Clerk hadn't yet given permission for the showing. If it went ahead the Classic would technically be in breach of the ban and the cinema could lose its licence. Mr McDermott felt he couldn't take that chance so he apologised to a very disgruntled group, who went off about their business. After discussions with the City Hall the Town Clerk gave the necessary permission and a showing was arranged for the following Saturday morning, 30th April. That showing did take place before a "small but critical group" (Irish News).

The matter was debated by the whole Council during the monthly meeting, on the following Monday. The debate lasted one and a half hours during which the qualities of the film, its content and its suitability for exhibition in Belfast were all discussed. It was a noisy debate, high in opinions but low in facts, enriched by typically Belfast humorous exchanges that verged on insults. Above all it revealed that many local representatives knew very little about films or the cinema, a fact that didn't stop them having clear opinions about what should be done. The film was robustly defended by Alderman Harry Midgley, the member for Dock ward, who reminded the council that they were dealing with an important industry which had invested over half a million pounds in the city, and was a major source of employment, and revenue in the form of rates. It deserved, he declared, to be treated in a serious manner. He found these "spiritual saviours of society" who had banned the film, inconsistent in their approach. They often allowed films to be shown that were dubious with regard to ethics and morality. By contrast, no matter what test one applied to "Frankenstein," it passed. The film might be controversial, but he found it neither blasphemous or unedifying, and it had an underlying theme which was intelligent and moral.

Some councillors objected to certain sequences, especially the one where a little girl, who had befriended the Monster, was drowned, while others considered the whole idea of collecting body parts for the monster distasteful and gruesome. They ignored Mr McDermott's offer to remove such scenes. Some of the criticisms were quite extreme. Councillor Agnew condemned most pictures that were allowed to be shown in Belfast, and averred that he had "no high opinion of the people who went to see them." He added however that, while he found "Frankenstein" sensational, it was neither blasphemous or unedifying. He objected strongly to the fact that only 5 members out of 15 could decide a matter which involved individual liberty. Councillor McMahon was of a similar frame of mind. To him the film had an important educational aspect and he suggested that the Police Committee would be better occupied censoring other films which reached the city, and which deserved to be banned. Some members attacked the BBFC as being too lax and argued that Belfast needed its own system of censorship, a suggestion that seemed to have wide support in the Chamber. In future years the local cinema industry was to feel the full impact of that attitude.

Alderman Dr Williamson expressed worries about the psychological impact of the film on the sub-conscious of certain unstable people and suggested that such films played a part in producing "mental defectives and otherwise abnormal children." Councillor Adgey supported the action of the Police Committee in banning a film that was "neither amusing nor educative nor anything else." Councillor T. Henderson felt that the whole banning episode was unnecessary and had given the film a lot of free publicity. He only wished the members of the Corporation would pay as much attention to the needs of the poor of the city. Alderman Nixon, who was one of the original group who had voted to ban the film, declared that as long as he was on the Police Committee anything that "purported to create life or to take the Divine out of God's hands" would be banned. The theme of a human being playing God and making life seemed to upset a number of councillors. Alderman Pierce disagreed, defending the film as "a sermon, well preached." Overall the discussions suggested that the Council was about evenly divided on the matter, but when the vote was taken the members decided by 24 to 20 to uphold the decision by the Police Committee to ban the film.

If "Frankenstein" was a test case, as the cinema managers suspected, they had lost the first round, and many felt uneasy about the future. In contrast there was general satisfaction in the ranks of the Belfast Film Committee, the Churches and their supporters. The Rev. Mr. W.Popham, the Episcopalian minister who had written to the Town Clerk on behalf of the Film Committee, explained that they took exception to "Frankenstein" in its entirety. There was nothing attractive or educational about it, he claimed. The total effect was unwholesome and "might have a criminal effect on abnormal minds." The banning was, in effect, a Pyrrhic victory because the ruling applied only to Belfast and, later in May, a short journey by train brought filmgoers to Lisburn where "Frankenstein" was showing without hindrance in the local Picture House. One year later, at the end of March 1939, Bangor's premier cinema, the Curran - owned Tonic, advertised a Triple Horror Show consisting of "Frankenstein," "Dracula," and the "sensational Ghost Organist" who was almost certainly Stendal Todd, the resident organist. The show was not recommended for "the very young or the squeamish... it's horrific... can you take it?" Special buses were put on by NIRTB from Belfast, Comber, Newtownards, Donaghadee and Millisle. Anyone who really wanted to see the film could easily do so regardless of the Belfast ban.

The arguments about the film were not confined to the Council Chamber, but continued in the newspapers. All the newspapers received a large mail on the subject, and feelings ran high. The majority of comments were critical of the actions of the Police Film Committee, and in defence of the film. A typical letter in the Irish News claimed that the people of Belfast were being treated like imbeciles who were unable to think for themselves, and the writer hoped that the letters of protest would be "many and vigorous." Another letter, in the News Letter, saw the banning as a "gross interference" by a small group of individuals in the liberty of conscience of the citizens. Another condemned the "rank hypocrisy" of "pandering to a few benighted, clerical and lay, who wanted everything according to their perverted view." That view, he contended, encompassed the public houses closed on Sundays, no music in the parks on Sunday, children's playgrounds closed on Sunday, no bookies..... a city ruled by people who had an "extreme abhorrence of all pleasures." Almost as an afterthought he added that "Frankenstein" contained nothing that was immoral, debasing or suggestive. A Mr Grahame of the Malone Road contemplated that depressing view of a joyless city and asked if things were to continue in a similar vein, what would the city be like in 1952? That question was probably most famously answered later in the comment of an American soldier based here during the war, who described Belfast on Sunday as "a cemetery with traffic lights."

One of the most balanced defences of the film appeared in the News Letter from an eminent cleric who signed himself Archdeacon. He claimed there were many films shown in Belfast which he regarded as "open to grave objections in that they were offensive to modesty, and treated sexual sins in a flippant manner." On occasion he had protested in writing to individual cinema managers about such films, but, he claimed, they had ignored his comments. He felt that "Frankenstein" was not in that category. It dealt with grave matters in a serious and impressive way. He had no objection to it being shown to adults, and felt that its banning was a mistake which sent out the wrong message. It undermined the efforts of those who supported a proper censorship.

The reference to the film being suited to adults was mentioned in many letters and there were complaints that children were seeing it despite the manager's clear warning. As if in response, the News Letter published a letter from a boy aged just under 16 years, who seemed to have wisdom beyond his years. He had seen the film, with his parent's permission, and claimed that he "experienced no symptoms of shock." He also found nothing objectionable about the film. He was of the opinion that the banning was the work of "interfering persons who are obviously unfitted to speak for the community." Others wrote that the banning only held the city up to ridicule. The News Letter also published a cynical comment by "Cato" who, tongue in cheek, chastised the Belfast public for their lack of consideration of the public spirit of the members of their Police Committee, who felt they had to attend every cinema performance suspected of even the slightest impropriety. "This voluntary martyrdom, which they suffer weekly, is sufficient to show their zeal for the moral welfare of our people." As future events were to reveal, the same caustic comments could still be effectively directed at the City Hall's official censors during the Sixties and Seventies.

Those who opposed censorship were a minority, and faced an uphill battle. Attacks on the cinema, and on films, continued, mostly clerical driven. Despite their divisions on theology and other differences it appeared that they could see eye-to-eye on certain things. On the Catholic side pulpit comments and official statements, especially in Lenten Pastorals, were directed at the faithful not to support films that condoned divorce, birth control or abortion. In January 1931 the Irish News published a statement from Pius XI in which the pope attacked films, novels and newspapers for not upholding the sanctity of marriage. Men like Will Hays in the USA were praised for their attempts to encourage wholesome films, and to put limits on what could be shown. When the League of Decency was established in Hollywood in 1934 Catholic parents here were encouraged to make themselves aware of the ratings the League gave to new films, and use those as a guide to decide what films they and their children should avoid.

On the Protestant side similar attitudes prevailed, and congregations were warned about the evils of certain films. In January 1933 the Whig published an account of a Sunday lecture given by the Rev. H.Atchinson in the Assembly Hall, on "Movies and Morals." An indication of the prevailing popularity of the topic was the fact that the meeting was packed. The speaker began by recalling the film shows that were once presented weekly in the CPA, the YMCA and the Grosvenor Halls, and he regretted the fact that they had to be discontinued because of a lack of suitable films. Too many films today gave a false and degrading view of life, he argued, presenting love as nothing more than sexual passion, while the vamp and the lounge lizard had become the new hero and heroine. People who tried to live ordinary decent lives were often depicted on screen as dull and foolish. The effect of such attitudes on young people was especially deplorable, and he agreed with the R.C. Bishop of Derry, Dr O'Kane, who had stated recently that "our children's morals are being sapped by the licentious picture house." Crime and gangster films, the lecturer claimed, were leading young men to crime. He directed particularly scathing comments at those cinema managers who showed such films just for financial gain, without reference to their impact or moral content. There was only one answer, and that was censorship. He felt that the Free State, with its firm censorship, had the right attitude. During the discussions of the Armagh Synod of the Church of Ireland in early October 1934 similar views were expressed. The Board of Temperance and Social Welfare of the church expressed concern in its report at the number of immoral and indecent films being shown, and suggested that a system of censorship similar to that in the Free State was needed in N.Ireland. They had consulted local councils on the matter but, while many agreed in principle, they argued that a complete and effective censorship was difficult to put into operation.

At the beginning of October 1934 a film was advertised for exhibition in the Ulster Hall which seemed, in the light of the comments above, a natural target for the local censors. Completed the year before, it was a sex hygiene film called "Damaged Lives," and it dealt with the forbidden topic of VD. It told the story of a pleasure loving young man, heir to a large shipping business, and engaged to be married to a beautiful girl called Joan. She postpones the wedding until he develops a more responsible attitude to life but during a visit to a night club he commits "an indiscretion" which results in him catching syphilis.

Official fears about socially transmitted diseases.

It was, the makers claimed, "the only picture of its kind since the advent of the talkies," a human drama which pointed out the dangers and results of contracting venereal disease. It had no BBFC certificate because the official censor felt that such topics were not suitable for places of general entertainment.

The Corporation had to decide on its fitness for local exhibition. According to the advertising blurb the film "shone a searchlight on the world's greatest social scourge," and the results were "Devastating.... Frank..... and Fearless." It was trade shown in the Picture House on Thursday 20th September to a specially invited audience which included members of the Police Film Committee, representatives of the Corporation's Public Health Committee, interested clergymen and reporters from local newspapers. It was one of an increasing number of "controversial" films being made in America by independent producers, which used sex and nudity to attract back audiences that had declined during the Depression. The films had been attacked in the USA by the clergy of all persuasions, by the Hays Office and later by the League of Decency for their perceived immorality, and by major Hollywood producers who saw scarce box office returns being siphoned off by crude and cheaply made products. According to one commentary

"Damaged Lives" was a mixture of sex education and titillation, which had been banned in New York, and cut in other states.

So how did what was obviously an exploitation film slip past the normally astute burghers of Belfast? The answer is simple. "Damaged Lives" purported to be a serious educational film, and as the manager of the Classic had pointed out during the Frankenstein furore, there were those in the City Hall who regarded the cinema as part of the educational system. The film claimed to have been made with the co-operation of the Canadian Health Council, and was shown throughout the UK with the blessing of the British Social Hygiene Council. To emphasise its educational intent the actual story was preceded by a short filmed address, delivered by a doctor, on the seriousness of the topic about to be illustrated. Belfast had experienced films and plays in the past dealing with contemporary "social problems", real and imagined, including white slavery, miscegenation, venereal disease and the need for sex education about matters like birth control. The contemporary worries over venereal disease had re-emerged in America in the mid - Thirties and, as usually happens, in time reached across the Atlantic Ocean, accompanied by verbal and visual arguments like "Damaged Lives." The type and pattern of discussion was very similar to the often strident deliberations that surrounded the more recent fears surrounding Aids, though, reflecting changed times, TV rather than the cinema was the major channel for discussion and the dissemination of information.

The response of the audience in the Picture House in late 1934 was quite positive, and the Police Committee readily gave permission for the film to be shown, though with the proviso that it would be for adults only. That, of course, gave the distributors more ammunition to fuel its "forbidden fruits" content. The Ulster Hall displayed large Adult Only notices for the two weeks' run, during which the film "aroused much controversy and wide public interest." (News Letter). The first show on Monday attracted "hundreds" of patrons, according to the News Letter. A special matinee was then arranged for the soldiers of the First Battalion King's Royal Rifles. As for the film itself, the News Letter found it "impressive and truthful," and praised the way in which the moral was intertwined with a story that contained romance and humour. The Belfast Telegraph commented under the heading: A film with a Message. Their critic thought it "a brilliantly enacted human drama....admirably produced and acted....most courageous and praiseworthy.... above all, highly entertaining." One wonders if he saw the film at all, and suspects that he was quoting liberally from the blurb that accompanied it. The Irish News made no comment, which indicated disapproval. The controversy that the News Letter mentioned revealed itself at the next monthly Council meeting when the film was discussed. Alderman Harry Midgley defended the showing as an event that would help to dispel the fog of ignorance on the topic that still enveloped some people. Councillor Maguire objected to the showing and argued that even if it was necessary to educate the public, there was no need to do it in the form of a drama. Alderman Pierce agreed, and held that there was no need to "make a dissecting room of the Ulster Hall" for educational purposes. He added, perceptively, that the film was a commercial venture, nothing else.

If anyone thought that the showing of "Damaged Lives" indicated a softening of the attitudes of the Police Committee and its supporters, they were to be proved very wrong.

An even larger censorship convulsion was waiting just around the corner. In 1935 Warner Brothers decided to produce a prestige film called "Green Pastures" (d. William Keighley), based on a much praised play of the same name by Marc Connolly. It was a biblical film, but with a difference. It had an all black cast, and it had no large set pieces like the parting of the Red Sea or such. An unusual feature was that God Almighty appeared as a black man, wearing a frock coat and a top hat. The play had been banned in Britain because the personization of God was not allowed on stage. From its release in 1936 the film had caused controversy, and details of its progress and the criticisms surrounding it were reported in papers and magazines, including the local newspapers. It was criticised by some black groups including the Universal Negro Improvement Association, who complained that it perpetuated the image of blacks as child-like people of simple faith. The story was set in the Deep South and concerned a Sunday schoolteacher describing characters and events of the Old Testament in terms that the local children would understand. The stories are told in a simple uncomplicated style using local language and local references. Thus God is presented in the person of the local pastor and His first appearance is preceded by a call: "Gangway for de Lawd God Jehovah," while heaven is a place where winged angels spend their time drifting around on cotton wool clouds, or attending fishfry picnics, and smoking ten cent cigars. The Almighty is played by Rex Ingram with impressive dignity and reverence. Humour is much in evidence, especially in the story of Noah, played again with suitable reverence, by Eddie Rochester Anderson. Negro spirituals were sung by the Hall Johnson Choir and proved to be one of the film's main attractions.

Lord Tyrrell, the British censor since 1935, admitted later in a lecture that "Green Pastures" caused him "much anxiety." After watching it and discussing it with leading churchmen he came to the conclusion that it was in no way blasphemous. After cuts of 211 feet it was given a "U" certificate. As more details about the film filtered into the local awareness, the ire of certain Protestant groups began to rise along with calls for the film to be banned in Belfast. In early August 1936 the Police Committee recorded the receipt of letters from the Belfast Film Committee of the Protestant Churches, the Belfast and District Baptist Council and the Belfast Council of Christian Churches detailing resolutions passed by their respective groups asking that appropriate steps be taken to prevent the exhibition locally of films which included the personification of God in human form. These were brought to the attention of the Council by Harry Midgley, who protested against what he called an "insidious attempt by medievally minded theological authorities to impose a mental dictatorship on the people." The problem, he claimed, involved the portrayal of the Deity in a manner that displeased the egos of certain small minded white men. Racism wasn't mentioned but the insinuation was certainly there. Lt. Com. Harcourt, the Chairman of the Police Film Committee, replied that he wasn't aware that the film had been booked into any local cinemas. If and when that happened the film would have to be passed by the local authority before being shown. Soon after that, it became known that the Classic cinema had booked "Green Pastures" for screening later that year.

The Protestant pressure groups continued to press the authorities to take action. At the beginning of December the powerful Belfast Presbytery of the Presbyterian Church wrote to the Police Committee requesting that the film be banned. A few days later the Film

Committee of the Protestant Churches decided to take the matter to higher authorities, and sent letters to the British Home Secretary in London, and the local Home Secretary, Sir Dawson Bates, calling for the banning of any film depicting the Almighty in human form. A few days later the Town Clerk received a protest letter from the Belfast and District Baptist Council concerning "Green Pastures." "We believe," the letter stated, that "the representation of God as depicted in this film to be both impious and blasphemous, and we are certain that as such it will have an evil effect on the community." That was followed by a plea that the film should not be shown in Belfast. At the same time the Police Committee recorded the receipt of a resolution forwarded by the Belfast Council of Christian Churches which called on the authorities to "take into consideration the question whether films such as "Green Pastures" which purport to represent the Invisible God in a fashion which perhaps legitimately and without irreverence appeal to people of another race and culture, are not entirely suitable for general exhibition to persons of our own community, who may be tempted to place a different construction on them, and whether such films ought not therefore to be prohibited in N.Ireland."

Green Pastures banned.
Source: N. Whig.

One of the problems was that very few people had actually seen the film but, as a letter from a minister pointed out, Belfast was "a great place for stirring up the righteous judgement of good folk on what their eye hath not seen nor their ear heard." To overcome that lack, a special showing was arranged for Friday morning, the 19th March, for members of the clergy, government officials, city councillors and aldermen, plus representatives of the Press. The Irish News reporter confessed that he had never seen so many clerical collars in a cinema before, adding that they were mainly Protestant. The absence of Catholic clergy didn't indicate a lack of interest, but most of them were involved in Lenten retreats and other Easter ceremonies. The showing was followed by an outpouring of comments in what the Whig described as "an animated controversy."

Newspapers claimed to have received hundreds of letters, pro and against. Clerical opinion was mixed and some eminent prelates expressed approval of the overall concept, emphasising its sincerity and reverence though noting its simplicity and lack of sophistication. The Church of Ireland Primate, Dr. d'Arcy, found it moving and impressive though marred in places by crudeness. Rev. Dr. Agnew, a Unitarian, felt it would be a scandal to ban such a reverent picture when so many other objectionable ones are shown. Dr. Breen from the Church of Ireland was deeply moved by its beauty and reverence. In contrast, Rabbi Shachter took a more intellectual approach and complained that historical facts were "distorted," while Biblical figures were shown in an "unpleasant" way. He felt its only interest would be to religious students. A Methodist, Rev. Stutt, the superintendent of the North Belfast Mission, agreed with the rabbi and dismissed the film as "pathetic." Evangelical groups attacked it for its "vulgarisation of the Sacred," and argued that it lessened the Scriptural conception of the Deity. One spokesman claimed that the film presented "naive, crude, and imperfect views of Biblical truth. "Another emphasised that "we take our conception of our Christian religion from Holy Scripture, not from Hollywood." Many commentators and letter writers described it with terms like simple, crude, childlike and naive, comments which carried overtones of racism. One writer felt that "the intelligent and religious citizens of Belfast had no wish to see their Maker caricatured and degraded on the screen by a "darkie" however gentlemanly he may appear.

The newspapers tended to be more tolerant in their comments. The Telegraph suggested that curiosity would probably influence many people to go and see it and that they would be persuaded to stay by the power of "its simplicity, its unimpeachable honesty, its grave humour and the beauty of its singing." The film was made with great sincerity which overcame the occasional crudity. The Whig was in general agreement though the writer admitted that some people would be offended by the presentation of God as a human figure. No-one could argue with the "moving dignity and reverence of spirit" with which Rex Ingram invests the part. The Irish News agreed and praised the film for showing a sense of respect for Christian ideals. There was nothing immoral or directly offensive about the film. The main objections revolved around the appearance of God as a person, and a black man at that. That offended some viewers who seem to have forgotten that God had appeared on stage since the days of the Medieval Morality plays. The main criticism of the film was, the writer insisted, that as a work of imagination it was poor. Even the simplest people, he concluded, rise far above top hats when they think of God.

On Saturday 20th March 1937, the day following the special showing, the Police Film Committee met in Room 42 in the City Hall, and after considering the various written resolutions referred to above, plus a verbal protest from the Ruling Elder's Union of the Presbyterian Church in Ireland, decided by a vote of 5 to 3 that "objection be not taken to the public exhibition in the City of the picture Green Pastures." That didn't settle the matter because the whole council still had to vote whether to approve, or to over-rule the decision of the Police Committee. The protests and letters continued. A woman wrote to the Whig to say she found it "unbelievable" that in a province of "God fearing and Bible reading people" that anyone could even contemplate the showing of such a film. Another equally appalled writer went on to ask: Will the Orangemen of Ulster stand idly by and allow the God of their fathers and His Divine Word, for which they fought and died, to be caricatured? In contrast the News Letter carried a letter calling on the clergy to develop a sense of humour. The film, claimed the writer, wasn't worth all the fuss that was being stirred up. If it was screened, those who objected to it could easily avoid it. Another letter in the same paper bemoaned the fact that Belfast already had a name for narrow bigotry, and if the film were banned "that ill opinion will be strengthened."

In the midst of the verbal storm the Council met on Thursday 25th March to discuss the matter. The chamber was crowded, both downstairs, and in the visitor's gallery. A protest deputation of about 100 members, both lay and clerical, from the Ruling Elder's Union of the Presbyterian Church in Ireland filled the ground floor. The atmosphere was tense and noisy. A reporter from the Irish Independent happened to be in the city, and she decided out of curiosity to attend the meeting. She was amazed at what she saw and heard. There was, she wrote, "a din" with members shouting each other down, while their supporters roared their approval. Tommy Henderson, in the midst of the fray, had a similar perception, describing the proceedings as "a bear-garden." Referring to the large deputation, the Independent reporter felt in size alone it "would have intimidated Mussolini or Stalin." The group consisted of both clerics and lay people, but their spokesmen were two laymen who delivered speeches that were more like sermons than arguments. There followed much shouting, but the only good speech, she maintained, was made by Alderman Midgley who showed "the clear reasoning of a highly intelligent mind."

Finally the vote was taken and the recommendation of the Police Committee was rejected by 31 to 12 votes. "Green Pastures" was banned. On leaving the chamber the confused Independent reporter noted "a look of grave approval" on the face of the portrait of Queen Victoria. That note of approval also surfaced in an editorial in next day's Whig. "We find it impossible to feel any pang of regret" the editor wrote, "that 'Green Pastures' has been banned in Belfast." The decision, he believed, only reflected the resentment of many of the citizens who felt that any representation of God in human form, "negro or otherwise," was repugnant. They also objected to the travesty in the presentation of certain Old Testament events. Finally they decried the "crude influence of Hollywood" that could be detected in the film.

The matter didn't end there because members of the Belfast Film Society decided that they would like to see the film, and instructed their Hon Sec. to make inquiries about the possibility of showing it. A minute of the Police Committee dated 04/11/ 37 refers to a letter from the Film Society about the matter and the willingness of the Police Committee to allow films not passed by the BBFC to be shown "on arrangement being made for the Police Committee to view them." The letter indicates some confusion (or maybe deliberate obfuscation) because the Film Society was well aware that according to the law it could only show films already passed by the BBFC. "Green Pastures" had been passed by the BBFC, before being banned by the Belfast Council. As such, special permission was needed from the Council to show the film even to the Police Committee, which had already seen it in March anyway. One can understand why the Film Society decided that such a viewing would be very difficult to arrange. Mr Mc Clelland, the Hon Sec of the Film Society, made a second approach to the Police Film Committee in a letter acknowledged by the latter on 14/ 07/ 38. He pointed out that the Film Society was a private organization whose 400 members were "representative of most walks of life in the city," and that it had "no political, religious, or other affiliations." The members were anxious to see the film "on the grounds of its artistic merit." His members felt that the objections already raised to its showing "do not seem to apply to it being shown by a private Society whose specific object is the study and advancement of the Art of the Cinema." After further futile exchanges the Film Society succumbed to the atmosphere of frustration, and decided that to pursue the matter wouldn't be worth all the "tiresome discussion and recrimination" it would cause. The request was dropped, and the showing was refused.

It had often been stated that while American film censorship was essentially moral, the British system was, in the main, political. A study of the events in Belfast Council during the early Thirties, as described above, wouldn't entirely support that thesis, but in fact the N.Ireland Government was quite adept at political censorship. Political censorship of films was a fact of life across Europe at the time, in Communist Russia, Nazi Germany, Fascist Italy and later in Spain. Film production and exhibition were strictly controlled in those countries, and what was shown was manipulated by the various governments. Individual voices were occasionally raised in the Belfast Chamber criticising what was happening on the Continent, but Unionist members seemed somewhat myopic about what was happening in their own city. While "Frankenstein" and "Green Pastures" were being banned in Belfast, and members were complaining about assaults on personal freedom, the Government at Stormont was at the same time keeping a firm hand on anyone or anything to do with Republicanism, or Nationalism. Magazines, pamphlets and newspapers from republican sources were forbidden, while all meetings and gatherings of a Republican nature were usually banned, especially over Easter. The Whig described the Falls Road on Easter Sunday in March 1937 as being overrun with police, and police vehicles. According to the reporter, nearly every street was patrolled, while whippet cars with machine guns, cage cars and tenders kept on the move. So it is no surprise that references to Republican matters in films came in for criticism, with demands that the films in question be banned. The Home Secretary, Sir Dawson Bates, stated the Unionist government position on one occasion when he claimed that "we are not dictators," but "the law must be obeyed." Among the laws at his disposal were the Special Powers Acts and he used them to impose restrictions on those public meetings and publications which he regarded as subversive. He was also quite ready to apply them to an entertainment medium like films, as he did in the case of "Ourselves Alone" (d. Brian Desmond Hurst, 1936).

The first local reference to "Ourselves Alone" appeared in the Whig on February 1936, detailing the plot of what was the first British film to be made at Elstree about the Irish War of Independence. Nine months later the film was booked for showing in the Hippodrome and, in keeping with the usual procedure, the cinema manager, George Dobler, arranged a trade showing on Wednesday morning for members of the trade, the Press, and invited friends. The Irish News critic attended and wrote that the film was one "to which not the slightest objection could be taken on political or any other grounds." The News Letter critic praised the film, and added that the makers had made an effort to keep a fair balance between the views of the Republicans and the RIC and Auxiliary forces. As a result he felt - quite rightly as it proved - the film would not appeal to those of extreme views. One such member of the audience, William Grant the Unionist MP for Duncairn felt that, as its name suggested, the film was "pure Sinn Féin propaganda," that would cause trouble in the city, and he suggested that the Home Secretary should see it. Sir Dawson Bates was sympathetic and stated that if the film was as Mr Grant described it, he would see that it was not shown. He pointed out, however, that the Belfast Council as the licensing authority had the last word on the matter.

In its defence it was pointed out that the film was entirely British in origin and concept, though its cast did contain Irish players, including Niall MacGinnis whose performance as the IRA leader was described by the News Letter as "excellent." The script was based on a play, "The Trouble," by two British officers who had served in Ireland. The main trade paper, The Kinematograph Weekly, had described it as "a vivid, exciting and thrilling portrait of life in Ireland during the rebellious days of 1921... without bias or provocation... intelligent and popular in its appeal... first rate entertainment." It had already had long runs, without incident, in many large cities in G.B., including Liverpool with its large Irish population. Despite being described by an Irish Press critic as "unhistoric history," and "a long lie," it drew large crowds in Dublin, running for five weeks in the Grafton cinema. The plot was in fact the familiar eternal triangle romance with a young Irish girl called Maureen being wooed by an RIC officer and an English intelligence officer. Her brother is the local IRA commander, and during a shoot - out he is killed by the RIC officer. The English officer nobly tells her that he was responsible, so that she could marry the man of her choice, the RIC officer. What was to happen in Belfast exhibited more of farce than romance.

George Dobler arranged a second showing on Thursday morning for the Home Secretary, who arrived with a high powered group which included George Hanna, the Parliamentary Secretary to the Ministry of Home Affairs, Lt Col Sir Charles Wickham the Inspector General of the RUC, and R.D.Harrison, the City Commissioner. An Irish News reporter described how they filed into the front row of the balcony, and "did not seem unduly perturbed by anything they saw." After the film they departed, without any comment, beyond what good manners decreed. During the day it became increasingly obvious that the Police Committee of the Corporation wanted to see the film for themselves, and so Mr Dobler, in a preview of groundhog day, arranged a third showing for Friday morning. Seven members of the Police Film Committee attended and decided, in the words of Lt Com. Harcourt, that "the film did not offend public morality" and that they would not prohibit its exhibition. The Irish News welcomed the decision and indicated that "Ourselves Alone" would be shown in the Hippodrome the following week, and later in the new Broadway.

That decision did not go down well with Sir Dawson Bates the Home Secretary, who announced on Saturday evening that he was banning the film under the Special Powers Act. The reason given was the fear of violence during the run -up to the imminent coronation of George VI. The management of the Hippodrome expressed amazement and anger, and George Dobler claimed that Wardour Film Co., the distributors, could lose up to £3,000 in the matter. In an editorial the Irish News criticised the ban and the way that it was done as "inconsiderate and stupid." The Home Secretary had seen the film on Thursday morning and yet had not acted until late Saturday. The editor pointed out that after the decision of the Police Committee on Friday Mr Dobbler had completed his preparations to show the film, including organising his publicity. All his preparations had to be undone at very short notice, and a replacement film found. There was also some discontent expressed by members of the Corporation and at the next Council meeting Cllr Hill suggested that the Council had been made a fool of. Ald. Pierce asked if the action of the Home Secretary was a censure of the Police Film Committee. Lt Com. Harcourt disagreed and argued that the powers of the Police Committee were confined to "the moral and spiritual aspects of the film." The Government took a different view, a political one, and on that basis had banned the film. One ironic aspect was ignored by all concerned. The film was directed by Brian Desmond Hurst who originally came from Belfast, from a family with a strong Unionist background.

While the arguments were raging about "Ourselves Alone," another film set in the same period was being prepared in America. In October 1936 Random Jottings (Irish News) referred to the recent success of the Abbey Players' tour of the USA and the fact that John Ford had invited a number of them (Barry Fitzgerald, Eileen Crowe, Denis O'Dea, Arthur Shields and Belfast's own Una O'Connor) to Hollywood to appear in a film based on Sean O'Casey's "Plough and the Stars." The Abbey Players were always welcomed in Belfast and their appearances at the Opera House drew packed houses. "The Plough and the Stars" was one of the plays they had presented there with great success, so local theatre and film goers looked forward to seeing Ford's version. The film was made for RKO Radio Studios whose executives interfered with Ford's concept, forcing him to make script changes, and to add the American actress, Barbara Stanwyck, to the cast. The result from Ford's point of view was that "they ruined the whole damned thing." Ford himself moved some of the action outdoors, adding scenes that were not in O'Casey's original vision, but which reflected his own personal admiration for the Irish rebels.

The film arrived in early 1937 but was not welcomed by the local authorities because of its theme and its political attitudes. The Police Film Committee saw it and voted 100% to ban it. Despite earlier claims that the Police Committee was concerned only about the moral and spiritual values of a film, everyone knew that the banning was political. Shortly after, in early May 1937, Harry Midgley, the bane of the local censors, highlighted the banning at a meeting of the Corporation. He condemned what he saw as the Police Committee's "own form of film censorship," and warned that it was leading to "an intellectual dictatorship." Councillor Agnew queried the decision, and the fact that no clear reason had been given for it. He had asked a number of members of the Committee the reason for the ban, and had been told that the film was "degrading and sordid." He pointed out that the original play had been performed in the Opera House, and that during its run it was almost impossible to get a seat. That hardly indicated that the contents were degrading. The Police Committee remained unmoved. The members of the White Cinema Club were especially angry at another attack on their commercial freedom, and decided to take action. At a special meeting they set up a committee of twelve members to liaise with the Police Committee on the matter of contentious films. They deplored the fact that the Police Committee seemed to listen to advice - usually hostile - from all quarters except from the cinema trade. In future their new committee would defend their position, and present the "reasoned views" of the trade. It was hoped, the out going President James Curran said, that such a move would assist the Corporation in reaching decisions that were "equitable and reasonable."

Films set during the Irish Troubles seemed, regardless of their quality, to have the potential to offend people of all persuasions. Part of the problem during the Thirties was that the events involved were so recent that many wounds were still open and festering. The fall out, by way of shootings and bombings, was still on going. Offence was taken by Unionists who regarded Republicans and Nationalists as trouble makers or worse, and expected their opinions and actions to be banned from the screen. Irish Nationalists, in turn, were angry with the British Government for not standing up to the Unionists, and giving Ireland the government promised by Home Rule. Then there were the pro - Treaty supporters who condemned those who had opposed the new government in Dublin, while the anti - Partitionists in the North felt that the Treaty supporters had abandoned them in a hostile sea of unionists. Finally Nationalists in general resented the implication in

British films that they were the legitimate rulers of Ireland whereas they (the Nationalists) regarded the actions of the British army and especially the hated Black and Tans as illegal, and often criminal.

In the Free State small groups took direct action against films which they objected to. Some film reels were stolen, or destroyed, to prevent the public seeing them. In April 1938 armed men intercepted goods being transported from Dundalk docks and stole two reels of the film "Beloved Enemy" (d. H.C.Potter, 1936), valued at £20, which were intended for a local cinema, the Magnet. The film, which was widely panned by critics, had been produced by Samuel Goldwyn, and was reputedly based on the life of Michael Collins. Due to pressures from the Motion Picture Producers and Distributors of America (better known as the Hay's Office), and the BBFC in London, the name of the main character was changed in the script as were details of the story, before filming began. What finally emerged was a love story involving an English girl and an Irish patriot played by Brian Aherne, which had no relation to specific historical fact, beyond being set against the background of the War of Independence. The group who stole the reels described it as "an insult to the men who fought for Irish freedom." The film was passed without cuts by the BBFC and shown, rather nervously, in N.Ireland, though as we have seen many such films were banned in Belfast to prevent them reaching a disapproving public.

The British Board of Film Censors tried to dissuade film producers from making such films at all. Universal's intention to make a film about Sir Roger Casement was killed off in that way. In 1922 T.P.O'Connor had appointed Col.J.C.Hanna as an assistant censor. Col. Hanna had been deputy head of British intelligence in Ireland during the Troubles and was particularly active in opposing the making of films about that period. Lord Tyrell, a Catholic, had been appointed censor in 1935 and was well aware of feelings in Ireland. In November 1937 the BBFC, presumably with his blessing, announced that some films with Irish themes had been passed "which might give offence in certain quarters." In future greater care would be taken in examining them, and, if necessary, the Censor's office would contact the Belfast Police Committee, and members of that group might be invited to view politically controversial films and give advice. There in no evidence that anything ever came of that suggestion, and Adolf Hitler's war plans soon put the idea on the back burner.

In the light of what was happening in Germany the government in London began, in 1935, to make preparations for a national censorship to cover the press, radio and cinema. A Ministry of Information (MOI) was established to organise the task, and in September 1939 the Police Committee received an official letter from that organization detailing the arrangements for a "security" censorship of films. The censorship was aimed at films "containing information which might be directly or indirectly useful to the enemy." The process would be carried out by the BBFC and would be on a voluntary basis, with producers submitting their films in the normal way. The censorship would however be extended to cover newsreels, topicals and other films not normally submitted. In certain circumstances the MOI had powers to "impose a compulsory censorship to such extent as may be necessary." Despite the reiteration of the voluntary nature of the censorship it was clear that the government was holding the very real threat of a compulsory system in reserve.

The new regulations did not remove the Police Film Committee's right to ban films that they did not approve of, and vestiges of the pre - war type of problem continued to appear in their discussions, notably with regard to "The Birth of a Baby," one of the most discussed and controversial films of the period. "The Birth of a Baby" (d. Al Christie, 1938) was made at Astoria Studios in Long Island New York at a reported cost of $43,000. That was much more than the average exploitation film of the time, which usually cost about $10,000, but less that a typical B movie, like those starring the popular hero Gene Autry, which could cost over $100,000. The extra money was reflected partly in the film's production values, which were often praised as being higher than one would expect from a film of that type. They, in turn, were due mainly to the influence of the producer Jack H. Skirball, who went on to produce, among other films, Alfred Hitchcock's "Saboteur"(1942) and "Shadow of a Doubt"(1943). The film was regarded by some as just another sex hygiene film aimed at the exploitation market, but, in fact, it was made as a serious health education film. Its aim was to explain, without sensationalism, the bodily changes that take place during pregnancy and birth. It's main concern, according to its distributors, was the health and welfare of mother and child, and in that it had the support of the American Committee on Maternal Welfare and other serious medical groups.

The film shows, in sequence, what happens to a young newly wed during her pregnancy, and the birth of a daughter. Her doctor, ever sympathetic, advises her during the whole process, and he and his nurse explain, often with the aid of animated diagrams, the physical and other changes that are occurring in her body. Scenes of an actual birth are then shown, and explained. There is no nudity or behaviour which could cause offence. The problems and criticisms arose when what was an educational film dealing with a sensitive and intimate subject, began to be presented in commercial cinemas as entertainment. People were divided in their opinions from the beginning. The powerful League of Decency praised its aims but withheld its approval on the grounds that it was not suitable material to be shown as entertainment in commercial cinemas. They also suggested that the cold, clinical approach adopted by the film makers made child bearing intimidating, and could put young women off the idea of getting married. Others saw it as subtle propaganda for hospital based pediatric care, that would entail increased expense for the couple concerned. It is interesting that the production was partly funded by a well known American company that manufactured medical materials of the type prominently displayed in the film. The wife in the film has her baby at home but a sequence is intercut extolling the advantages of a hospital delivery.

The main objections came from concerned groups who regarded the birth sequence as indecent or immoral, and who struggled to keep it off commercial screens. It even became the subject of legal argument, notably in New York State, where the courts upheld the state's censorship board's decision to withhold a licence on the grounds that the showing of an actual birth became indecent when shown in a place of entertainment. The film became a rallying cry for those who wanted a more liberal censorship, or none at all. Wherever it was shown there was controversy. And it made money.

In September 1941 the Police Film Committee received a request to allow the exhibition of the film, which had no BBFC license, in Belfast. Like the League of Decency, the BBFC believed that it contained material that was not suitable for showing in a place of entertainment. They preferred that such films should be shown in special halls. After viewing it, the Film Committee agreed, without exception, to forbid any showing anywhere, and hoped that the matter would end there. However they found themselves dealing with a Mrs Pleydell - Bouverie who, at the very least, could be described as a very persistent woman. Writing from an address in Salisbury, on paper with the heading Health Education Films Ltd., she queried the Committee's decision, and claimed that the film had already been seen by nearly 3 million people in Great Britain. It had been welcomed by eminent medical authorities, and she had received a large number of letters of thanks and praise from people of both sexes, of all ages and all creeds who had seen the film and found its message very beneficial. She asked to meet a member of the Committee to discuss the matter. The Committee replied that the decision not to show the film would not be reconsidered. On 3rd November she contacted the Committee again, and asked that they give permission for a special showing of the film. The Committee gave the necessary agreement, and the presentation took place in the Classic cinema on 10th December.

Mrs Bouverie arranged the screening, and invited members of the Ulster Medical Society, the local Nursing profession and recent medical graduates from Queen's University. The response from those professionals was, as she had hoped, generally favourable. The Film Committee remained adamant however, and the ban stayed in place. In response, Mrs Bouverie put pen to paper again. For anyone, she declared, to describe the natural function of birth as shocking indicates "an inhibited mind." There was nothing shocking in the film, she insisted, except for those who look at it "with the maladjusted mind." The attitude of the Film Committee, she wrote, suggests that they knew more about reducing the infant mortality rate in Belfast than the local medical authorities that had welcomed "The Birth of a Baby." If she thought that such comments would change attitudes, she completely misunderstood the Belfast character. The Film Committee were even more determined that local audiences would not see the film.

"Damaged Lives," with its theme of the dangers of venereal disease, surfaced again in late August 1939, when the Hippodrome requested and received permission to show it to audiences over the age of 16 years. The cinema advertisement was subdued, noting only that the film was shown under the auspices of the British Social Hygiene Council. The decision was a significant one because sex hygiene films had in the past been shown only in special halls, usually the Ulster Hall. The presentation in the Hippodrome was the first time that such a film had been advertised for showing in a local cinema given over to entertainment, and it opened the door for selected sex films to be shown, in the future, in normal entertainment surroundings.

For a time in the early Forties the Hippodrome departed from its usual policy of family entertainment and experimented with a series of "adult only" films. One of the most controversial of those was called "Marriage Forbidden," which dealt with the topic of VD. The request to show it produced a lively debate in the City Council at the beginning of 1940. The blurb that accompanied the film promised - modestly - a production "with all the impressiveness of an immortal drama... which paints the truth so frankly, and with such artistic force, that the mind is impressed as it could possibly be impressed in no other way." Not all the City Councillors swallowed that recommendation, and a number of them objected to the film on the grounds that it was immoral and offensive. Harry Midgley, as expected, defended it, and pointed out that the Council had already passed "Damaged Lives," which he described as "a film on the same lines." Councillor McKibben claimed that there wasn't one shot of an immoral nature in the film, and that it would "strike terror into the heart of anyone who had any thought of taking part in such conduct." The film was passed for viewing in the city by a vote of 15 for to 12 against. The production was American in origin, and was a filmed remake (in 1937) of Eugene Brieux's original play "Damaged Goods" which had been presented on the stage of the Grand Opera House in February 1918. It had already been filmed in 1914, but the new version had the advantages of sound, a script by Upton Sinclair, and a society that was more ready to accept such topics on the screen. The film was shown in early February 1940, advertised for "adults only."

The VD debate continued when "Damaged Lives" reappeared again in July 1942 and ran for two weeks in the Grosvenor Hall. Traditionalists were shocked to see the film advertised sensationally as "fearless, frank, devastating," and designated as suitable for adults only. It was not what one associated with the Methodist hall. Prices for seats were set at one shilling and two shillings, and during the first week it attracted - according to reports - over 33,000 patrons. The second week was equally successful. The News Letter critic was uncertain about

Sex hygiene for adults only.

its quality and content. He saw it as "an animated lecture presented in story form" but found it difficult to judge. It had, he commented, little relation to "the ordinary standards" used in evaluating a cinema entertainment. The fact that he described it as an entertainment was in itself significant of changing attitudes.

The topic of venereal disease, once taboo in polite conversation, was increasingly debated openly, especially after the beginning of the war in September 1939. Official wartime fears about the spread of socially transmitted disease reinforced the message of commercial films like "Marriage Forbidden' and made it easier for them to be shown. Ernest Brown, the Minister of Health in London, was widely quoted in the local papers whenever he spoke about the problem. He attacked the" heads -in-the-sand "attitude which characterised many people's response to the increasingly rapid spread of the disease. He believed the main cause was the collapse of traditional moral standards, and the growing disregard for sexual morality. Added to that were the "abnormal strains" of wartime living. He called on local authorities to educate the public on the problem. The government at Stormont undertook an advertising policy in the local press on the matter. It detailed VD as a growing menace and warned against contracting it. It explained that "abstention from free and easy sex relationships is the surest safeguard against infection" and directed the attention of those who feared they had already contracted the disease to special clinics where treatment was available. Many locals were shocked that such intimate matters were regarded as suitable for public debate.

The Minister of Health's call for education resulted in an Educational Film Season presented in the Grosvenor Hall during May - June 1943, dealing with the topic. The season began with a rerun of "Marriage Forbidden." More details were given in the adverts and newspapers than had accompanied its first showing in the Hippodrome. It promised to expose "the greatest evil the world has ever known... a menace as great as Hitler." It emphasised that the film was released under the auspices of the British Social Hygiene Council and warned that, in dealing with this matter, ignorance and secrecy were fatal. The "matter" wasn't mentioned in the adverts, but it was widely accepted that it was VD. A character in the film, a crusading doctor, was more outspoken, and claimed that syphilis was "a plague" that had to be eradicated. He called on young people to recognise the dangers, and to practise continence. Those sentiments reflected the warnings from local religious leaders, both Protestant and Catholic, who often deplored a perceived increasing laxity in sexual relationships.

"Marriage Forbidden" was followed on screen in the Grosvenor Hall by "Social Enemy No.1," which was advertised as the only new film on the dangers of VD. Do not be confused by other productions, the makers emphasised, in an obvious reference to "Damaged Lives." In a significant departure the term VD was used for the first time in a local film advert. The advert also included the Daily Mirror's comments about the film that "it pulls no punches... you must see it." The News Letter critic offered no personal criticism after viewing the film but quoted from the Minister of Health, thereby emphasising the political and educational implications of the production. The film, the Minister had written, was an interesting and helpful attempt to translate into human terms some of the consequences of a great social evil... the conditions and methods it portrays are American... but the film does bring out the essential points of the Government's campaign against venereal disease in this country. "To some viewers the films were useful educational aids, to others, more cynical, they were seen as exploitation films cashing in on a contemporary problem. Despite opposition from individual councillors the majority of members of the Police Committee and the City Council allowed themselves to be convinced, for the moment, that such films were playing a helpful role in educating the public about a serious social problem. They softened their opposition to them, at least during the period of the war. Reports suggested that large crowds attended all showings.

Taking advantage of the new "relaxed" approach to such matters, in late September 1942 the question of showing "The Birth of a Baby" was raised again with the Corporation. The Police Film Committee reluctantly advised that permission be given, allowing it to be shown, but only to women over 18 years of age. Mrs Pleydell - Bouverie tried to persuade the councillors to widen the potential audience base by allowing it to be shown to both women and men over 16 years, but the Council refused. It's screening was announced for a two week run in the Grosvenor Hall as part of the latter's Educational Film Season, beginning on 31 st May, with that proviso of women only. Despite the regulations restricting admittance, large crowds attended, and the producers - obviously skilled in manipulating the public - milked the situation by announcing that they had been granted permission to continue the showings for an extra six days, followed by a further three days. As a result the film actually ran for the most of June, becoming a lively talking point - and an obvious financial success.

The popularity of those films suggested that there was a substantial local audience for films with unabashed sexual themes. It was an indication of what the future held for film - going in the city.

CHAPTER TWENTY SIX
Good Feet and an Ability to Hold One's Tongue

In the late Thirties the cinema owners and managers had more to occupy their thoughts than censorship problems. To them films were a business and they had to take into account not only the requirements of the law, but the expectations of their paying patrons. The manager of one of the downtown cinemas (unnamed, but probably the Imperial) gave an interview in early 1940 about his job, which throws some light on the problems faced. Sitting at his desk in his office, he emphasised that running a cinema was a difficult, down - to - earth, full time occupation, quite different from the drama and romance shown on the screen. He had to keep his fingers on many strings, and he did that by making short term and long term decisions. The long term involved the renting of films, and he showed the reporter a file which he said covered his programmes for the following three months. When the films arrived he had to view them alone "from the point of view of copy and sound." Copy referred to the quality of the print, and if it was damaged or scored he had to immediately order a new copy from the renters. Sound quality was also very important, especially if the cinema was equipped with the latest type of projectors. Older projectors often distorted or even damaged the sound track. A good sound track was vital because of the precise timing involved. The film must run at a steady standard speed of eleven and one ninth minutes per thousand feet to ensure perfect sound. That regularity allowed him to work out exactly the time of a complete programme. In reply to a specific question, he admitted that he did not examine the films for "doubtful material," as the censor usually dealt with that. As far as he was concerned content had been passed as suitable for viewing, and he only took action when the film was restricted to "adults only." He made no mention of the Police Film Committee or other pressure groups in the city, though one suspects that he could have been quite voluble about their activities.

The next step was to organise the publicity to attract the customers. That task was, he admitted, greatly facilitated by the renters who sent him a packet of advertising materials to "sell" each film. The material could be very comprehensive and usually included posters, front-of-house stills, larger foyer stills, and press books. The latter contained hints for publicity campaigns, background on the stars, and on the making of the film. He had to decide what material to use, in the light of local attitudes and levels of co-operation from newspapers and such. The package included material that the local newspapers could readily use, even with prepared critiques for the critics who wrote about the films. Most cinemas had glass - fronted display cabinets attached to their front walls, in which the front - of - house stills from the film then showing were displayed. During the Forties the author, as a small boy, and some friends often did a tour of the downtown cinemas on a Sunday evening - there was little else to do - excitedly examining and commenting on the stills, while searching for their particular favourites like Maureen O'Hara, Randolph Scott, John Wayne, Jimmy Durante, Bing Crosby, Bob Hope and Dorothy Lamour among others. Of course, being Sunday, the cinemas were closed, as was the city centre, and one walked from cinema to cinema along quiet streets, meeting few people or vehicles. The stills just gave hints of the cinematic pleasures the future held, but looking at them today brings back many happy memories, not only of the films but also the whole social environment that regular film going involved. Many of those publicity items are now sought after by cineastes, and the rarest fetch high prices.

The day - to - day running of the cinema occupied much of the manager's time. Each day began early with meeting the cleaners who had already collected the usual piles of rubbish from the floor, consisting mainly of ice cream cartons, chocolate boxes, cigarette packets, sweet wrappings, newspapers and such. But there were also more personal objects found, which were listed and left for a month in a special room. The author recalls entering such a room in the Imperial and seeing piles of scarves, gloves, hats, raincoats, umbrellas, and even handbags. The reporter described the latest list covering the previous month which included five pipes, six bunches of keys, four pairs of stockings, ten umbrellas, two wallets plus assorted gloves, scarves and handbags. Some of the items were quite surprising, especially the numbers of handbags. Either the owners were extraordinarily absent - minded, or the films were so absorbing that they produced memory loss. The lost items were kept for one month before being disposed of.

Once the lost objects had been dealt with, the staff assembled and were inspected to see that their uniforms were neat, tidy and presentable. The better run cinemas were very conscious about their image. The doormen usually wore impressive peaked caps and long military style overcoats with brass buttons, which had to be polished and shining. The ushers and usherettes wore dark coloured uniforms and carried their indispensable aid, a flash - light. Usherettes were expected to do their job with tact and efficiency, and not to engage in conversations with the patrons. Some managers were stricter than others in such matters. The Regal on the Lisburn Road actually had a notice at the back, asking patrons not to speak to the usherettes. The usherettes were the members of staff that the public knew best so managers were careful whom they chose for the position. They had a wide spectrum to choose from because many girls were attracted to the job. The manager described how he had ten applicants for a recent vacancy, before he had even advertised it.

Conditions of work varied with the quality of the cinemas, but in 1940 in the best downtown cinemas the girls worked a 45 to 48 hour week with one day off, in return for a weekly wage of about 25 shillings, depending on seniority and length of service. There were also differences between continuous cinemas and non - continuous halls in the number of hours worked and the remuneration. In some of the less opulent halls non - continuous halls girls received only about one pound a week. The work in all cinemas was hard, in that the girls were on their feet most of the time. The manager, in his interview, said that, with regard to qualifications, he expected an elementary education, but he also looked for girls who had warm personalities, attractive appearance, carried themselves with authority, yet displayed tact in dealing with the public. An usherette summed the requirements up more tersely, saying that the job called for "good feet and an ability to hold one's tongue."

Besides attending to those human matters the manager had special duties demanded by the government. Firstly there was the contentious issue of entertainment tax. Every Saturday, without fail, after the last show, the tax for the past week had to be calculated and early the following week a cheque for the full amount was posted to the appropriate government department. After September 1939 there was also an added wartime requirement. The amplification system used in the projectors involved some special powerful valves that could also be used for radio transmission. Each one in Britain had been tabbed, and the manager had to check those lest they fell into the hands of an enemy agent. It suggested a MacGuffin worthy of Alfred Hitchcock. So, from litter to potential spies the manager's day was a full one. As he said, the picture on the screen was only a small part of running a successful cinema.

There were other matters the manager had to consider which weren't mentioned in the interview. The original Cinematograph Acts had come into force in the early days of "living pictures" mainly to ensure the safety of cinemagoers, especially from fire, and the regulations involved had since become ever more detailed, covering items like the level of lighting in the halls, and the question of sufficient and easy egress in case of an emergency. Fire remained a threat, and despite precautions, some cinemas suffered from a number of minor outbreaks. During a performance on July 1935, in the Windsor, the film burst into flames while it was being rewound. The brigade was called and quickly dealt with the outbreak. The damage was confined to the fire - proofed winding room, and consisted of scorching to the walls and ceiling. The performance was not interfered with, and most patrons, relaxing in their comfortable seats, were unaware of what was happening. Another small fire occurred in the roof space of the Willowfield on the Woodstock Road on a Saturday morning when the building was empty. Again the brigade dealt with it and the cinema opened as usual in the evening.

Another aspect of cinema safety, which was often monitored by the police, was the question of adequate facilities for rapid egress in case of emergency. In early 1938 the newly built Stadium on the Shankill Road was summoned in the persons of Norman Ellison the manager and Norman McLorinan the assistant manager. They were accused of being in breach of the Cinemagraph Act by having during a performance, according to police witnesses, 98 people standing in passageways, 46 along the back, 32 on the left hand side and 20 on the right side, thereby causing dangerous obstructions to movement if an emergency occurred. It was normal policy for cinemas to allow patrons, who were still queuing around 9:00pm, into the hall before the last film began, where they waited at the back and around the walls until seats became available. It was obviously a practice that the authorities frowned upon but the author recalls it as still being general practice during the Forties and Fifties.

Luckily any outbreaks of fire were minor and were quickly controlled by the fire brigade, until the conflagration which destroyed the Alhambra on Sunday morning 3rd Dec. 1939. Such a tragedy had been furthest from everyone's thoughts a few months before when, during August, under the guiding hand of the manager, the theatre had suitably celebrated its Diamond Jubilee (1879 - 1939), with a special programme called Alhambra Cavalcade. A distinctive Victorian style advert called upon its patrons to come and revive old memories of the great performers who had appeared on the Alhambra's stage in the past. They would hear once more the old familiar songs made famous by those who had occupied the stage, and they could join in the choruses. Performers would include the Alhambra's Discoveries of 1939, the best of local talent, plus favourites like the boxer Rinty Monaghan. The normal orchestra, directed by Hans Williams, was specially augmented for the occasion, The programme was a mixture of what the Alhambra did best, and what its patrons enjoyed most, namely nostalgia, popular music hall and sport. To complete the evening the advert announced in mock Victorian style that the management had arranged - at great expense, of course - for Mr Todd Slaughter to appear in his screen version of "Sexton Blake and the Hooded Terror."

According to the Irish News critic the programme was an outstanding success. Performers appeared in the dress of the Victorian and Edwardian periods, their impersonations were sympathetic and vigorous in interpretation, and the audience responded with loud appreciation. W.J.McNiece played W.J.Ashcroft, the Solid Man, and sang his most famous songs, while local discovery Ruby Campbell, in the guise of Florrie Ford, gave a rousing interpretation of "Down At the Old Bull and Bush." Rinty Monaghan, "the crooner - boxer," as the Irish News described him, always a welcome favourite, sang "The Man Who Broke the Bank at Monte Carlo." "Lily of Laguna," with its memories of Eugene Stratton, reduced the audience to appreciative silence. Another recent local discovery from the Alhambra's talent competition was Madge Magowan who sang "She Fought Like a Tiger for her Honour" in the style of Gracie Fields, followed by "Frankie and Johnny" as Mae West sang it. The evening, according to the Irish News critic, "gave old timers and sophists many moments of delight."

The menu was repeated the following week under the title The Alhambra Inn, advertised as "fully licensed for laughter and singing." That reminded patrons - if they needed reminding - of one of the theatre's main attractions, its lounge bar, located at the back on the first floor. One mature patron boasted that it was the only cinema in Belfast where one could stand at a bar with an elbow on the counter, a drink in the hand and watch a film. From the bar one could see the two wings of the balcony to right and left with, between them, on the ground floor, the stalls and the screen. Another drew attention to the large mirrors which adorned the walls of the balcony and pointed out that the film could be seen in one of them behind the lounge, though the images were reversed.

The Centenary raised the standing of the Alhambra and reminded people of its significance as a part of old Belfast, its place in the local history of live entertainment, and its involvement with the beginnings of projected films in the city. Someone estimated that since those pioneer days nearly 45,000 miles of film had passed through its machines. Over the years the Alhambra had generated a dedicated group of patrons who attended every week, often on the same evenings. There was the Monday crowd, the Tuesday crowd and so on, many of whom knew each other, meeting in the bar before retiring to see the film or live show. Frank Doherty the manager knew most of them and, like them, looked forward to the continuing success of the theatre/ cinema. When war was declared a few weeks later on 3rd September, the Alhambra published one of its distinctive adverts pointing out that it had survived three wars and "it will survive this one." Expect "Business as usual" it trumpeted, much to the delight of its patrons. But the gods do not take kindly to such hubris, as was sadly demonstrated exactly two months later.

And so, back to that early Sunday morning when a passing night watchman noticed a strange glow inside the building, and raised the alarm. When the firemen forced the doors open they faced a roaring furnace of flames. The stage area and screen were already devoured and the flames were moving into the ceiling. Sixty firemen fought to control the inferno, but when the roof collapsed there was little they could do to save the building. The interior was completely gutted, the seating reduced to rubble, most of the great mirrors cracked or smashed, though the frontage and some rooms were saved, including one where old historic posters and such were stored. The stage was a shambles, though the metal frame that had supported the screen still stood proudly upright. The firemen prevented the fire from spreading into the nearby premises including the branch of Woolworths next door. The historic Alhambra was reduced to a blackened cavity like a bad tooth which marred the smile on the face of a shocked North Street. Citizens who came to see were taken aback by the extent of the damage, which by then was estimated at £15,000. They realised that its destruction was a loss to local entertainment, an economic blow that would add to unemployment figures, and a social blow depriving those who met there regularly of conversation and companionship. The question most often asked was not if, but when, it would be rebuilt. "Let's hope," an Irish News reporter wrote, "it will arise once again from its ashes."

Besides fire the other element which posed a potential problem was water. The centre of Belfast is built on riverine and glacial muds which do not form strong foundations for heavy buildings. The water table in them is high so that, after heavy rain, flooding of buildings is always a possibility. As a result the owners of city centre cinemas have written into their plans an agreement that they will accept responsibility for dealing with any flood damage within their buildings. Central Belfast has a long and well documented history of flooding especially after heavy rain. During the week following 12th Oct. 1941 the whole Belfast area experienced prolonged and heavy rain which caused a rise in the water table accompanied by the overflow of local rivers like the Blackwater. The result was flooding across the city but especially around the lower Grosvenor Road, Great Victoria Street and nearby thoroughfares Among the buildings affected were the Ritz, the Coliseum, the Hippodrome and the Opera House. In some of the lowest parts of the buildings the water was nearly two meters deep. A patron in the Ritz described what happened. About ten o'clock the picture blurred and then disappeared from the screen. Almost immediately the power went off and the building was in complete darkness. The manager came on stage and announced that everyone would have to leave via Murray Street. Usherettes arrived with torches and guided the audience out through the air raid shelter into Murray Street. There they encountered some flooding. Men removed their shoes and socks and paddled to the drier pavements. The flooding extended down towards the Opera House where soldiers gallantly carried young ladies across the road to the pavements.

Other problems experienced were less dramatic. In some cinemas unruly patrons could be a problem. The Gaiety had its share of confrontations. On one occasion in May 1936 two men disrupted the performance by shouting and yelling. When an attendant told them to stop they assaulted him. They ended up in court where they were fined 20 shillings, and 10 shillings for disturbing the peace. On another occasion the manager of the Stadium was assaulted by fractious patrons. The Arcadian in Albert Street faced similar problems. In one famous incident in October 1938 trouble broke out among a group of youths, and the manager, John Irvine, with some of his staff ejected them. That evening after being warned about threats made by one of the youths, he and a few of his staff walked home in a group for safety. However, like a scene from a Western, they were ambushed in Lemon Street and a fight ensued. The leaders of the youths were reported by witnesses and ended up in court, where they were fined 20 shillings. The magistrate condemned their "outrageous hooliganism," and commented that people should be able to go to the cinema and home again in safety. On another evening fighting broke out among youths in the same cinema and spilled out on to Albert Street. The police were called and used batons to clear the road.

Another problem was vandalism and the manager of the Curzon, Harry Shepherd, complained that the slashing of seats had reached such a state that he had to employ a man for three hours a day, specially to deal with the damage. A boy, caught in the act, was fined £2 at the Juvenile Court, and ordered to pay fifteen shillings in compensation. There were also staff problems involving what today would be termed health and safety. In December 1936 a widow, who lived in Iveagh Street and had worked as a winder in the Diamond Cinema, earning £2 per week, took an action against the McKibben Estate over an accident she had suffered. In January 1934 she had cut her thumb while rewinding a film reel. Cuts were one of the hazards of rewinding because the edge of the moving celluloid film was as sharp as a knife blade. The wound didn't heal properly, and four months later the thumb had to be amputated. From January 1936 she had received compensation of £1-2-6 a week, reduced to 11/ 3d from the beginning of September. In response to her claim for general compensation she was awarded £350.

Preparations could be made to deal with the problems of fire or water but some managers were faced with situations that were completely beyond their control. Such was George Bradley, manager of the Popular on the lower Newtownards Road, who during a court appeal against the valuation on the cinema gave some interesting details about his problems. The Popular was located in what he called "borderline territory" or what would be called an interface today. The cinema drew its audience from the loyalist East Belfast streets and the nationalist Short Strand area. As such it was perculiarly susceptible to any sectarian disturbances, which usually resulted in reduced audience numbers. It had closed for two years during the Troubles of the Twenties, and in the Thirties interruptions to its working continued when street disturbances occurred. That happened regularly during the marching season, nearly every July, and especially during 1935. As a result, the manager claimed, the cinema operated at only 64% of total capacity. Over the period 1935 - 1938 the average annual takings before tax were £6949, while the takings for 1937 alone were only £6664. The loss of revenue was exasperated by increased competition from new cinemas which were, as the manager put it, "swamping the older ones."

Regardless of such problems it was the manager's task to produce a friendly environment in which patrons could enjoy the type of entertainment they expected. That meant a double bill, with a full supporting programme. The manager in turn depended on the renters to supply him with films that would attract the crowds. One body of films that proved very popular - despite the occasional censorship furore - was those that had an Irish dimension. There were serious films with Irish themes, notably john Ford's "The Informer" (1935), which ran for two weeks in the Lyric cinema in High Street, before moving on to the Clonard and the Alhambra. Another was "Parnell" which showed in the Hippodrome in January 1938, followed by a week in the Lyric. Most of the "Irish" films were from America, and the Whig critic claimed that only Hollywood could turn out such lively stories, full of attractive characters, bubbling over with family feuds and action interspersed with comedy, music and song. The Irish News agreed, praising them not only for their entertainment value, but also for being "good clean fun." They had names like "Laughing Irish Eyes," a "swift paced romantic comedy with an Irish background, Irish wit and fine singing" (Irish News), which starred Phil Regan, who sang among other songs the "Derry Air." Another was "The Pluck of the Irish" with James Cagney. The films were made mainly for the large Irish - American audience in the States, and usually starred James Cagney along with other members of the so-called Hollywood Irish mafia. That genial group included Pat O'Brien, who often played a priest, Spencer Tracy, Frank Mc Hugh, Allen Jenkins, and James Gleeson. James Cagney was immensely popular in Belfast, and the Strand ran a special Cagney Week, showing a

Deannese Nights. The popularity of Deanna Durbin.

different film of his every day. The only other star of the period who received a similar distinction was the charming singer Deanna Durbin whom the Mountpottinger Picturedrome in East Belfast presented in six different films for "six happy days" before they moved on to the Curran cinemas.

One of the best of Irish fare, according to the local papers, was "The Irish in Us" which arrived in the Picture House in April 1936, where it ran for two weeks. It then showed across the city, including the Alhambra, and was later revived more than once. The plotline was, according to the Whig, "familiar" and involved the prickly relationships between three brothers of the O'Hara family, a policeman, a fireman and a boxing promoter, with Cagney and O'Brien falling out over the affections of Olivia de Havilland. All problems are solved when Cagney stands in for boxer Allen Jenkins, faces the world champion in the ring, and, against the odds, defeats him.

The popularity of those films influenced British producers to enter the market, and a series of light hearted "Irish" films arrived in Belfast from British studios. "Fr. O'Flynn," starring Tom Burke, was a popular hit for the Picture House in June 1936, with the Whig describing it as "a sentimental but remarkably true picture of Irish life." It was entertaining, with lots of humour and "several rollicking Irish songs." The singer Tom Burke also starred in "Kathleen Mavoureen" with Sara Allgood, Arthur Lucan (Old Mother Riley) and Kitty McShane along with the Tara Irish Dancers and Frank Lee's Tara Ceilidhe Band to supply the music. "The Rose of Tralee" with Binkie Stuart was another success, as was "Macushla" which was described as "an exciting drama of the Irish border." Its cast included six Irish players one of whom was Jimmy Mageean, a leading member of Richard Hayward's Belfast Repertory Theatre Company. Like most of those films, it premiered in the Picture House, before showing across the city. Jimmy Mageean appeared in quite a few British films and became a familiar and recognisable figure on local screens. The Imperial showed the "Mountains of Mourne" in February 1939, a light - hearted piece that starred Niall Mac Ginnis in a story about a farmboy who became a radio personality. Outdoor scenes were filmed in Co, Down and Co. Wicklow, but interiors were completed in England. It was advertised as a "Picture with Charm and Irresistible Irish Appeal." Among the songs were Danny Boy, the Dear Little Shamrock, the Kerry Dance and With My Shillelagh Under My Arm. Many of those productions were quota quickies, cheaply made, with low production values. Despite their simple plots, their stage -Irish characters and their lack of pretensions they did well at the local box-offices with audiences enjoying the humour, the songs and the lively music. Observing their success, increasing number of voices were raised in Ireland asking why such films couldn't be made in this country.

During the Thirties there was a growing consensus that Ireland could, and should, produce its own films. It was an objective that found support in Belfast. In November 1936 the Irish News gave an editorial over to the matter, pointing out that films with Irish themes were very popular, though they were usually made in Hollywood or Elstree. The editor pointed out that the main requirement for a home industry was a studio where films could be finished and prepared for exhibition. He welcomed the suggestion that such a studio was planned be built on a former aerodrome 25 miles from Dublin, and expressed the hope that Ireland would soon be producing native films that would be "artistic, honest and sincere." It was taken for granted that such a development would take place in the Free State where commercial films had a history going back to the early silents made by Sidney Olcott near Killarney. Unfortunately the studio projected in 1936 came to nothing, and Ireland didn't get a modern film studio until 1958, when Ardmore Studios were opened by Sean Lemass a mile from Bray in Co. Wicklow. Before then films made in any part of Ireland, with a few exceptions like "The Dawn" (d. Tom Cooper, 1936), were processed and finished in Britain or Hollywood. The Irish News editor wasn't the only one in Belfast who hoped that that position could be changed.

In Belfast there was an increasing recognition of the importance of films for commercial, propaganda, and entertainment purposes. The Belfast Telegraph produced a short, "Going to Press," describing how the newspaper was put together for publication, and it was shown in local cinemas during 1936, causing great excitement. Another short film, about the work being done in the Royal Victoria Hospital, was also shown successfully the following year,

Star of Ulster. Richard Hayward, second from left.

THE "STAR OF ULSTER" FILM.—(Left to right) Major J. M. Henderson, Secretary of the Ulster Industries Development Association; Mr. Richard Hayward, who plays the principal role; Mr. J. Hanlon, Distributor of Films; and Mr. R. J. Frizzell, B.A., Assistant Secretary, photographed at the Royal Avenue Picture House, Belfast, after the private screening of the above picture yesterday.   ("Northern Whig" Photograph)

with a request at the end for financial support from the public to help fund an extension which was being built at the time. Samuel Goldwyn believed that a film shouldn't necessarily have a message, but the local approach was quite different, and the films produced were a combination of information, business and entertainment.

The Ulster Industries Development Association approached Richard Hayward, who devised and wrote the script for "The Star of Ulster" which, while only ten minutes long, put "Ulster industry on the screen," according to the Whig, when it was shown to the trade in the Picture House in January 1937. The Association had, over many years, advocated the need for local people to buy local goods, and thereby support local industries. That, in turn, would ensure local employment and help to overcome the industrial depression. The message of the film was "Ulster Goods for Ulster Folk, "and while it was actually photographed and processed by Fox British Pictures Ltd, in Wembley, the players were local, including Hayward himself (who sang its theme song), his wife Elma, and members of the public. The Whig thought that it put the message across successfully, "within a layer of amusement." In September 1938 it was screened in the museum, throughout a whole day, as part of Belfast Civic Week, with frequent showings between 11:30am and 9:00 pm. When it was shown in the Ritz, as part of the normal entertainment programme, it was advertised as an "Ulster film with Ulster players for Ulster's prosperity."

The recently revived Irish Linen Guild also recognised the influence of films for advertisement, or "propaganda" as one of their members referred to it. The Guild had £3,000 to spend on advertising their product and decided that they would get a wider coverage with a film rather than a more expensive newspaper campaign. Their plans were helped when the government gave them a further financial grant. It was decided to produce a special booklet, and film, to be released in tandem. Richard Hayward was engaged to write a script for the film, and the result was "The Wee Blue Blossom," which was unveiled to members of the trade and the trade unions in the Imperial Cinema in October 1936. The film contained many of Hayward's trademarks including local dialect, humour, beautiful countryside scenes and Irish music behind the commentary. The film opened with shots of the Mourne country during the flax harvest, and showed the pulling of the flax by hand, and its transport to the flax dams for retting. Then, taken from the dams, the fibres were transported to the mills and factories for scutching, weaving and the production of brown linen which, in turn, was laid out in long strips on the bleach greens. The finishing processes, with the making of tablecloths, bed linen, handkerchiefs and other products, was illustrated. Finally, the products were packed and sent down to the docks for export. Two versions were completed for exhibition, one of 500 feet which ran for five minutes, and a longer version of 2,000 feet. Cinemas could choose whichever length was more suitable for their programmes.

The main market for the linen was overseas, especially the United States, and when the film was shown in New York, Universal Pictures were so impressed that they requested that they be allowed to recut the film for a series they produced called "Going Places." The result was a ten minute version named "The Cloth of Kings," which was shown in Belfast in mid-October 1937. The Guild were happy with the result which, much to their relief, retained the essential Irish atmosphere of the original. The commentary was informative and well delivered by the eminent traveller and film maker Lowell Thomas, who had visited Belfast on a lecture tour some years before, though there was some complaints that he sometimes sounded "more Irish than the Irish themselves." Besides being impressed by Universal's cut, the Guild rejoiced when they learned the film would be shown in 4,500 cinemas in the USA, plus about another 3,500 worldwide. It was the type of coverage they had hoped for. Major Herdman, the chairman of the Guild, thanked everyone involved in the enterprise, including the Lord Mayor of Belfast, Sir Crawford McCullagh, who was always steady in his support of local industry, including the cinema. He also had special thanks for Mr McDowell the manager of the Imperial cinema who had allowed the use of the cinema by the Guild on four occasions.

The importance of those little films was not in their size, artistic impact, or originality. Advertising has a long history in the cinema, and audiences in the Thirties were quite familiar with short films, often musical and humorous in theme, advertising cars, cigarettes and such. The importance of the local films lay in the fact that they showed Ulster actors, workers, places and scenery on the big screen along with the stars of Hollywood and Elstree. It was, to use Neil Armstrong's moon-landing comment, a small step towards a local film industry. The next, bigger, and more important step, was taken by Richard Hayward.

Richard Hayward was one of a gifted trio of what could be called folk actor comedians, who wrote most of their own material. They entertained the population mainly from the stage by gently satirising the foibles of the Irish people. They did it with a warmhearted spirit based on observation and, above all, affection. The other two artistes were Cathal O'Byrne and Jimmy O'Dea. O'Byrne, like Hayward, was a local man and in the early decades of the century his plays, with their local characters, Irish themes, dances, music and song, were very popular on local stages, but also around Ireland, and among emigrants in England and America. Besides stage work he extended his interests into recordings, lectures and writing, but showed no desire to become involved in film making.

The third member of the group was Jimmy O'Dea. Jimmy was, of course, from Dublin but was a regular visitor to Belfast theatres, especially the Empire. He was, as the News Letter commented, "always welcome," and his appearances were usually accompanied by "House Full" notices. He was a skilled comedian and mime, but was also an impressive actor. His talents had attracted the attention of an Irish film maker, John Mac Donagh, for whom he made a number of silent films in the early Twenties. They included "The Casey Millions," "Wicklow Gold," and "Cruiskeen Lawn," all of which were shown in Belfast. The local critics didn't mention him then but, elsewhere, he was regarded as a matinee idol, which might surprise those who associate him only with the likes of Mrs Mulligan. He recognised films as a means of reaching a wider audience, and in the Thirties made a number of sound films. The first of them was "Jimmy Boy" (d. John Baxter, 1935), a British film comedy which had Jimmy trying to prevent a group of foreign spies from bombing London. It's first showing in N.Ireland was in the Imperial cinema in February 1936, and Jimmy and his stage partner, Harry Donovan, appeared personally in the hall for the evening performance. The plot called for him to do a number of impersonations which included Napoleon, a negro singer, a film actor, a waiter and a bootboy. The Belfast Telegraph thought that he "acquitted himself with credit,"while the Whig enjoyed the way that the film moved along "with a sparkle," and how Jimmy kept the comedy "at top pace." All the local critics praised the beautiful scenery of the early scenes filmed around Bantry, and their potential impact on the tourist trade was not lost on them. Though partly written by Harry O'Donovan, and having some Irish actors, notably Noel Purcell, in the cast, "Jimmy Boy" remained a British film, with a British director.

Jimmy wanted more control over the content, so he used his production company, O'D Productions, which he had set up in co-operation with Harry O'Donovan, to make another film. The result was "Blarney" written by both men, and directed by O'Donovan. It was filmed around Dundalk with some beautifully shot location scenes at Carlingford, Ravensdale and Greenore. He overcame the problem of the lack of an Irish studio by converting a concert hall in Dundalk into a makeshift film studio, for interiors. The completed film opened in the Savoy cinema in Dublin where it attracted large crowds during a three week run. It reached Belfast in September 1938 where it ran for two weeks in the Imperial. It was warmly received by the public and the critics, with the Whig describing it as "a delightful comedy of Irish life." While pleased with the outcome, Jimmy decided to sign with Basil Dean to make any future films in Britain. Belfast audiences didn't see him again on screen until the arrival of Walt Disney's "Darby O'Gill and the Little People" in which he starred with Belfastman, Albert Sharpe. It seemed that Irish films needed British or American finance and technical know-how to be made.

In the final scene of "Blarney" Jimmy attempts to kiss the heroine across a gate which was strategically located on the border. The gate collapsed, leaving no physical border between the hero and heroine. Some observers made much of that scene, and perceived it as a political statement about the unity of Ireland. In the North, Richard Hayward who, like Jimmy, recognised the cinema as the route to a larger audience, wouldn't have agreed with that conclusion. Hayward was a scholar, a Protestant and a member of the Orange Order. He saw himself first and foremost as an Ulsterman, but equally as an Irishman, though like that other talented Irishman Michael Mac Liammoir he was actually born in England. His main aim in his writings, recordings and films was to present - and preserve - what he saw as Ulster culture, with its distinctive dialects and characters. Hayward was born in 1892, lived for a time in Larne before moving with his parents to Belfast at an early age. He grew up with the silent cinema though his main interests were writing and acting. In time he developed into a man with a wide range of interests. When he died as a result of a car crash outside Ballymena on 13th October 1964 his passing was genuinely regretted. In the papers and at his memorial service in St Anne's Cathedral he was described as a "noted author and folklorist" (Irish News), an "author, musician, folklorist, archaeologist, film star, broadcaster, and raconteur" (Belfast Telegraph), "a wonderful Irishman" (News Letter) and "a great Irishman"(the Lord Mayor, Councillor W. Jenkins). Jeanne Cooper Foster summed him up with the words that "Ulster has lost one of her most colourful characters, and Ireland a little of its magic." Even allowing for the emotional nature of the occasion it is clear that Hayward was held in high regard because of his intellectual and cultural achievements.

Before he showed an interest in films Richard Hayward had pursued his enthusiasm for writing. He was attracted to radio and was writing for the fledgling BBC as early as 1924. Five years later, as already indicated, in conjunction with Jimmy Mageean, he established the Belfast Repertory Theatre based in the Empire Theatre. One of his aims was to encourage local writers, and at the same time establish a theatre group that would represent Ulster in the same way that the Abbey Theatre served the Free State. His successes in Dublin and elsewhere in the South, both on the stage and on Radio Eireann, made him well known and respected in cultural and entertainment circles both north and south of the border. During those travels he met Col Victor Haddick and joined with him in making an "experimental film" (as Hayward referred to it) called "The Voice of Ireland." The success of the latter convinced him that audiences wanted films with Irish themes, acted "in a natural manner." He hoped to meet that need, and the opportunity arose when he met the Irish journalist and script writer, Donovan Pedelty.

Pedelty had travelled to America and had worked in Hollywood, before returning to England in 1933. Pedelty, Hayward and Haddick joined forces to make a film, "Luck of the Irish" in 1935. It was a British film, a "quota quickie,"based on a novel by Victor Haddick, scripted and directed, very competently, by Pedelty, and produced by Hayward and Pedelty. The star was Richard Hayward supported by members of his Belfast Repertory Company, with popular English actress Kay Walsh supplying the glamour. The story concerned the nearly destitute Sir Brian O'Neill (Jimmy Mageean) who tried to escape from debt by entering his horse Knockavoe in the Grand National. The horse was ridden by his son (Niall McGinnis) who was in love with Eileen O'Donnell, played by Kay Walsh. To everyone's delight the horse wins the race but is then disqualified, leaving Sir Brian facing ruin. Sam Mulhern (Richard Hayward) joins with the local schoolmaster (R.H.McCandless) to save the situation, but makes things worse, until an American buys the horse and all is saved. When the film was completed, a special showing was arranged for the premiere in the Capitol Cinema in Dublin on 10th January 1936. In preparation Richard Hayward, a noted ballad singer, appeared on local radio singing the songs from the film, which included the Royal Blackbird, Nellie Bly, The Wee Shop, and the Bright Silvery Light of the Moon. Decca also recorded the songs on record, selling at 1/6 each. After the Dublin opening the film had its Belfast première, on 27th January, in the Picture House Royal Avenue, after which it was shown in Derry before going on general release. Richard Hayward appeared in person in the Empire Theatre during the week, singing the songs from the film.

The film caused great excitement and was soon the talk of the city. It was advertised as Ulster's first film, which was only partly true because, while the exteriors were photographed around Glynn and Templepatrick, the interiors had been shot in England and the film was completed there. Distribution was organised by Paramount Pictures who were impressed by the final product. Local critics and filmgoers were equally impressed and were soon referring to Richard Hayward as "our local film producer... or, local film star." The critics went out of their way to praise the film. The Belfast Telegraph welcomed it as "Ulster's first full - length talking picture" and rejoiced in the fact that it was performed by local actors, that it was filmed against local scenery and that it was full of Ulster humour. The News Letter was equally enthusiastic, praising the beauty of the landscape photography, and making special mention of the "charming ballads, homely humour and convincing characterisation." There were also kind words for Richard Hayward's acting, with an admiring reference to the "droll wit and dry philosophy" of his character, "subtly observed and cleverly portrayed." The film got a wonderful reception from Belfast filmgoers, resulting in long queues and crowded houses.

That "great local interest" (News Letter) wasn't confined to the city. Wherever it was screened audiences responded positively to the film. When Dan MacAllister booked it into his cinema, the Moyle, in Cushendall in July, the locals were especially excited to recognise some of John Bamber's horses that had appeared in the recent Cushendall Show. Besides the horses, the film included an interesting example of product emplacement in the form of White's Wafer Oats (porridge), which appeared

White's Wafer Oats.
Source: Irish News.

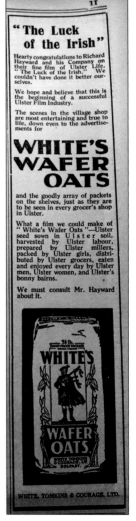

prominently in a scene in the village shop. When the film was showing in the centre of Belfast White's took out an advertisement in the newspapers congratulating Richard Hayward and his company on the "fine film of Ulster life." We believe, the advert continued, that this is the beginning of a successful Ulster Film Industry. They then suggested that, if Mr Hayward wanted another Ulster topic, he could make a great film about White's Wafer Oats, which was the product of Ulster seed planted in Ulster soil, harvested by Ulster labour, prepared by Ulster millers, packed by Ulster girls, distributed by Ulster grocers. That gives a flavour of the reaction to the film.

The obvious success of the venture and its appeal to Irish audiences was not lost on the distributors and Richard Hayward was dispatched in April 1936, with Paramount's blessing, to New York to sell the film. During his six weeks' tour Hayward was well received by the Americans. The film itself opened on 15th January 1937 in the 47th Street Cinema on Broadway, where it ran for two weeks, doing very good business. It's audience was mainly Irish emigrants and the distributors arranged for it to tap similar groups at showings in Boston, Philadelphia, Detroit, Los Angeles, San Francisco and Seattle. By the time of the American showings Hayward was back in Belfast and involved in other film making.

Before he left Belfast he announced that he had formed a Production Company, Richard Hayward Film Productions Ltd., with a group of fellow citizens including Wilson Boyd, Councellor Collier, Harold Goldblatt and Hugh McAlevey, with the aim of making Ulster films. They had plans for three films to be completed in 1936, and he hoped to begin the first of them when he returned from the USA in May. He had chosen "The Early Bird" based on a play by a new young writer, James Douglas of Coleraine, which the Belfast Repertory Players had presented in the Empire in January 1936. The script and direction would again be in the hands of Donovan Pedelty, while Hayward and the members of the Belfast Repertory Players would supply the cast. As with the "Luck of the Irish" the exteriors would be shot locally while the interiors and finishing touches would be added in England. He hoped that the choice of exteriors would encourage tourism. His ultimate aim was to build a studio in Belfast to support "a real Irish film industry." The response of the Irish News was to wish him "all success to his venture."

It was decided to shoot "The Early Bird" in the Glens of Antrim and, at the beginning of June, Richard Hayward and a crew of 15 actors and technicians arrived in Glenarm for a week's shooting. For that week Glenarm became "Ballytober," much to the amusement of the inhabitants. They watched the film makers at work and some of them played bit parts in the action. Scenes were shot around the village and on the Coast Road near Carnlough, all in excellent weather, to the relief of the cameramen. Their professional skills impressed the Irish News critic later when he commented on the beauty of those scenes, adding that "there seems to be something in the quality of the light in N.Ireland which lends itself to first class photography." Outdoor scenes were completed by 8th June and the crew left, allowing life in Glenarm to return to normal. Filming continued at Highbury Studios near London, and the finished film was previewed for the trade in the Imperial Cinema on 7th August 1937 in the presence of Donovan Pedelty, Richard Hayward and others. The speed with which the project was completed gives one indication why such films are described as "quickies." In early November "The Early Bird" was released to the public in the Picture House, and received a very positive welcome from the critics. The storyline was slight, and involved the attempts of the villagers to circumvent the strictures of the puritanical village matriarch. The Belfast Telegraph found it "an enjoyable comedy of life and love" in rural Ireland, with a good performance from Richard Hayward, who delighted the audience with his songs and comedy. The Irish News thought it was "out of the ordinary screen entertainment," characterised by diverting dialogue and clever direction. There was special mention of Hayward, who played the main role of Daniel Duff, a "philosophic countryman whose astuteness is only paralleled by his good nature." Equally, Jimmy Mageean was singled out for special praise.

"The Early Bird" was a success with local audiences and after a two week ruin in the Picture House it moved on to the Alhambra, the Clonard, and other halls across the city. It was chosen by Michael Curran as the inaugural film for the newly opened Broadway Cinema on 13th December. Richard Hayward was on stage that evening when he sang songs from the film and introduced members of the cast. By that time his next film, "Irish and Proud of It, "had been completed, and had already been given a special showing to the trade and press in the Picture House on 3rd November It premiered in the same cinema on the 7th of the following month. The plot had a familiar mix of comedy, song, Irish charm and eye catching scenery, but with a number of twists and changes that added freshness, The script was from the pen of Dorothea Donn Byrne, and presented Hayward as an unpopular businessman who is kidnapped by inhabitants of his Irish village and smuggled to London. There, he gets mixed up with Chicago - type gangsters, who are involved in illegal poteen making, but he manages to round them up for the police before returning, a hero, to Ireland. The Irish News critic thought that it was the best film made so far by Hayward's company, and praised him for what he had achieved in putting "Ulster and Ireland as a whole on the cinema map." The scenery, he maintained, photographed in Co Louth, was splendid, the direction was "brisk," and the acting excellent. Hayward, Jimmy Mageean and a young British actress called Dinah Sheridan were singled for special praise. He described Miss Sheridan as a delightful addition to the cast with her "looks, charm, a pleasant voice and acting ability." Dinah Sheridan, in due course, was to become much better known when she played the female lead opposite John Gregson in "Genevieve" (1953). The Whig critic referred to the story as "satisfactory," but was happy that it allowed Richard Hayward to show more versatility, and escape from the "kitchen courtship comedy formula." He also commended the acting of Hayward, Jimmy Mageean and Dinah Sheridan. The inclusion of English actors and London exteriors were obviously an attempt to increase the film's appeal to audiences other than Irish. In the main, English critics were not overly sympathetic to the Ulster stories. One commentator described the humour of "Irish and Proud Of It" as "boring," and the continual attempts to introduce local Ulster colour as "tiresome."

Another, more serious, criticism was directed at the films, namely that they were stage - Irish. The Irish News, which had long complained about stage Irishism on stage and screen, interviewed Richard Hayward about that problem. He was fully aware of the complaints, and had collected a scrapbook of cuttings on the subject from Irish, English and Canadian and American newspapers. The Irish News reporter quoted from a recent edition of the "Gaelic American" which deplored the fact that many films, including "Irish and Proud ot It," gave the impression that Ireland was "a land of poverty, dirt and drunks." Hayward pointed out that a similar criticism had been levelled at the plays of the Abbey Theatre. Certain Irish people, especially emigrants, refused to accept that the traditional "Land of Saints and Scholars" no longer existed. They took exception to the realist plays and films of modern Ireland presented by the Abbey and himself. He emphasised that he had spent his whole life "in the study of Irish folklore, literature, archaeology and music '" and that, like the Abbey Theatre, he wanted to "kill the old Irishman of Punch, and give the public a realistic Irishman." In defence of "Irish, and Proud of It" he quoted the conservative "Irish Catholic" which wrote that it was a film that offered "clean entertainment worthy of national respect, comedy without suggestiveness, and action without immodesty."

Richard Hayward decided to take fuller control of his next film by writing the script himself. He also acquired special sound equipment and lighting so that the film could be made entirely in N.Ireland. Donovan Pedelty and Victor Haddick were not involved, the production and direction being undertaken by Germain Burger, while Paramount were replaced by Columbia as distributors. The outcome was the 54 minutes long "Devil's Rock," which was filmed in the Glens of Antrim and in Co Down - around, and in, Bangor. Hayward arranged with Michael Curran to use the Tonic Cinema for interiors, and the music for the film was arranged and played by Stendal Todd, the Tonic's resident organist. Full use was also made of local talent and "local colour," and a concert sequence included St Gall's School Choir from the Falls Road, and the Lambeg Folk Dance Society. The cast were all from Ulster except Geraldine Mitchel (Gate Theatre, Dublin), and Michael Gleeson from Limerick. The film was shown to the trade in November 1937 and at a dinner afterwards in the Carlton Restaurant Hayward claimed that it was his first really "all - Ulster film." The star played a poacher and sheep drover who hopes to establish a restaurant in the local seaside village with the Widow Huggins. They put on a concert to collect money for the venture but the takings are stolen. A little girl falls into the sea and is swept away but our hero dives into the waves and saves her at the dangerous Devil's Rock. Meantime the thieves are caught and the money recovered. Just when everything seems to be working out satisfactorily, Hayward decides to give up the idea of the restaurant and return to the life he knows, sheep droving.

THE LATEST ULSTER FILM.—Mr. Richard Hayward (centre) interested in "stills " of his latest film " Devil's Rock " at a luncheon in the Carlton Restaurant, Belfast, yesterday. Also included are Mr. L. Morrison (left) and Mr. T. Hanlon, the " Renter " of the film (right). This new film was photographed in the Glens of Antrim and Bangor during the summer.

Devil's Rock; Richard Hayward (centre) disscusses its release. Source: N. Whig.

"Devil's Rock" didn't have the success of his former films and, with it, Hayward's Ulster cycle of fiction films came to an end. He realised that outside Irish audiences the films had restricted appeal, and it became increasingly difficult to get financing for them, especially with the outbreak of war. Some critics argued that the situations and characters depicted in the plots were more suited to the stage than the cinema, and that Hayward was a writer rather than a film maker. Richard Hayward himself maintained his popularity, but he decided to move from making fiction films, to documentary style films of Ireland, hoping to convey visually his feelings about the history and landscape of the Irish countryside. Most of them were made for the Tourist Boards both north and south of the border. The first of those "featurettes" (I.S.N.) was "In The Footsteps of St. Patrick" which was shown in the Alhambra in November 1939, followed by "Where the Shannon Flows," in the Royal Hippodrome at the beginning of the following March. The latter was part of a programme which ran for a week, and included Richard Hayward, in person on stage, in "Song and Story," plus his most popular film "Luck of the Irish." Later programmes included other Hayward films notably "Lough Corrib" and "In West Kerry." During November - December 1942 the Grosvenor Hall presented two Richard Hayward evenings with a personal appearance, followed by the "Luck of the Irish," a film that could still draw in the crowds.

Belfast had its own film stars like Richard Hayward, Jimmy Mageean, Una O'Connor, and Moyna Magill. On a visit home in early 1940 Miss Magill mentioned, with some satisfaction, that her daughter, Angela, had decided to study for a stage career. That daughter became known as Angela Lansbury and, between solving murders on TV, she visited Belfast many years later in search of her Irish roots. When an interviewer on TV suggested that she appeared quintessentially English in her manner, she replied that in her day to day activities she was English, but when she started acting her Irish half took over her personality. Indirect references to her mother have appeared in a number of her "Murder She Wrote" plots. The Belfast actors were distinguished by talent rather than glamour, and they didn't attract the media attention of other Irish born stars like Maureen O'Sullivan and Geraldine Fitzgerald.

In late 1938 the Random Jottings scribe mentioned that a new star had emerged in Dublin, a young girl with an acting background in radio and the Abbey Theatre, called Maureen Fitzsimmons. She used that name for a walk - on part in "Kicking The Moon Around" which came to the Imperial in early 1939, but, on Charles Laughton's insistence, she changed it to Maureen O'Hara. Mr Laughton, who regarded her as his special protégée, arranged for her first film, "My Irish Molly" (d. Alex Bryce, 1938) which was a gentle comedy of the type that Richard Hayward was making. In it she was co - starred with the "British Shirley Temple," Binkie Stuart. It arrived in the Ritz in August 1939 with Miss O'Hara getting top billing, and was well, if not overwhelmingly, received by critics and audiences. The Irish News critic described it as "a story with natural charm, simplicity, and glorious singing." The Whig found it pleasant entertainment, and recommended its Irish songs and music. The outspoken Miss O'Hara is on record as referring to it as "a stinker."

She was much more upbeat about her next film, "Jamaica Inn," directed by Alfred Hitchcock and starring Charles Laughton. The film is much better than some critics have suggested, with a strong performance from Laughton (an actor much admired in Belfast), and a splendid atmosphere evoked by Hitchcock. The local critics were impressed by the realism of the shipwrecking scenes, and Miss O'Hara has described how Hitchcock directed them with boyish enthusiasm. His attitude towards her was always that of a perfect gentleman, and far from ignoring her as some commentators have implied, he was always helpful. In the film she stood up to the buffeting of the wind and waves, faced a gang of violent ship - wreckers, and showed glimpses of that sturdy persona that was to emerge during the 40's and 50's. The film was scheduled for a première at a midnight Press gala in the Ritz, on 13 October, but Hitler upset those arrangements. With the outbreak of war a blackout was imposed on the city and the late night gala had to be abandoned. The film arrived quietly in the Ritz in mid - October and showed widely across the city. The Whig critic wrote that "Miss O'Hara more than justifies the praise lavished on her by the critics," while he praised the film for its realism and its "atmosphere of terror and dark doings." It is coincidental that during its run in the Ritz the nearby Hippodrome was showing John Ford's "Stagecoach" starring John Wayne, two men with whom Miss O'Hara's future career was to become entwined to the artistic benefit of cinema, and the enrichment of local audiences. Maureen O'Hara would become the epitome of Irish womanhood on the screen.

But all that lay in the future, and in the late Thirties the local fans continued to grumble when they saw top Hollywood personalities like Ramon Navarro visiting the Theatre Royal in Dublin, and ignoring Belfast. Thus it was that they enthusiastically embraced one whom they regarded as their own star, namely the dashing Errol Flynn. In early 1936 the News Letter published a comment from the Hollywood Reporter that Warners had "a million dollar property in the person of Errol Flynn." Errol Flynn was actually born in Hobart, Tasmania, but the local press referred to him as "the Belfast star" on the grounds that his father was Professor of Zoology in Queen's University, and that the family lived in Broomhill Park off the Malone Road. When Flynn's first major film, "Captain Blood,"

"CAPTAIN BLOOD."—Photograph taken yesterday morning in the Classic Cinema, Belfast, at a private screening of "Captain Blood," in which the leading part is taken by Mr. Errol Flynn, son of Professor T. T. Flynn, of Queen's University, Belfast. (Left to Right) Mr. T. H. MacDermott (manager), Professor Flynn, Miss Flynn, and Mrs. Flynn. The film is the chief feature next week. ("Northern Whig" Photograph.)

Proud father.
Source: N. Whig.

arrived in the Classic in early March 1937 Prof. Flynn, his wife and daughter, were invited by the manager to a special showing, before its general local release. The Professor addressed the invited audience from the cinema trade, the press and friends and described, with diplomatic omissions, his son's progress from his early days of "roughing it" as a "travelling soldier of fortune" to his screen success. He admitted his son lacked academic stage training, but made up for that by the impact of his natural talent and personality, "inherited from his very charming mother." His commentary was informed, not by Hollywood ballyhoo, but by family pride.

The film was well received, with the Whig critic praising its "pace, humour, character and life," through which the star moved "with ease." Errol Flynn himself flew quietly into Newtownards Airport nine months later for a short family visit, and a rest. A reporter from the Whig visited his home at 10:00 pm the next evening and found - to his surprise - the star already in his dressing gown, preparing for bed. He explained that he was tired, and needed a rest before he attended a number of local events that he had been invited to. He rode with the Co. Down Staghounds the next day, and he attended a Bridge Party in the Carleton Restaurant organized by Queen's Rag Committee to collect money for local hospitals. He presented the prizes and circulated among the crowd, chatting, and signing autographs. The Irish News reporter at the event was impressed by his "shy, quiet, almost deferential manner," that contrasted with the normal conception of a film star. During the following few days, before his departure for Hollywood, he moved about the city without encountering any displays of hysteria on the part of his fans. In the main people were polite and respected his privacy.

The next important visitor arrived in late January 1939, again quietly. He was Adolph

Zukor, one of the founders of Paramount Studios. who was on a good will tour of Europe, returning to America via Australia. He was one of the most powerful men in Hollywood, and the inclusion of Belfast in his itinerary reflected the importance of the local film industry. An impressive reception was arranged in the Grand Central Hotel in his honour, where the invited guests included Harry Wilton the President of the White Cinema Club, Sir Crawford McCullagh the Lord Mayor well known for his support of local cinemas, John Hicks the vice -president of Paramount, David Rose the managing director of Paramount in Great Britain, the publicity director of Paramount from Dublin (Mr Zukor's next stop), local cinema managers, members of the press and others associated with the film industry. Mr Zukor was presented with a shillelagh by the Lord Mayor, before making a speech and answering questions. He emphasised that as film makers they were there to entertain. "We are not propagandists," he stressed. The key to good films is good stories, and yes - in answer to a question - they were interested in good stories with Irish themes. He believed that films should tell their stories with action rather than words. He noted the recent increase in colour films, but colour was more expensive to use than black and white, so he couldn't see it replacing black and white entirely. Films would continue to develop technically and he saw a great future for 3D productions. Local managers must have shaken their heads at that statement, because they knew that audiences regarded 3D as a gimmick, and complained about having to wear special glasses.

A series of short 3D films called Audioscopics had been shown across the city during 1935 - 38. They consisted of familiar scenes of objects flying out from the screen into the audience. When they arrived in the Regal in December 1935 the adverts announced a "new novelty feature... uproarious success... more next week... glasses provided." Later they were screened in the Alhambra (March 1938) and the posters gave a flavour of their content: Have you ever been hit by a motor car? See Audioscopics and "see "what it "feels" like. Feature length 3D films were to return in the Fifties, but after a short period of audience interest they stalled, and disappeared. There are only so many spears and other missiles that intelligent people are willing to dodge for entertainment. Today (2014) Hollywood is trying again, using much improved technology, with digitally produced three dimensions. but it is too early to say if the films will be any more successful than in the past.. People still voice their reluctance at having to wear the special glasses, while complaints of eyestrain and headaches have surfaced again. The studios have responded by releasing both 2D and 3D versions of the films.

Visit of Gene Autry. Source: Irish News.

The greatest excitement was engendered by the visit of Gene Autry to the city in August 1939. Gene was the first of the singing cowboys, making films for Republic Studio, where John Wayne also worked. The Gene Autry films were a combination of action, humour (usually supplied by his sidekick, Smiley Burnett), and songs. The star had begun his career as a radio and recording act but had quickly taken to films. The latter were carefully tailored as family fare, and nothing offensive to children was allowed to be shown. That and his attractive voice had combined to build up a massive fan base across America and the English speaking world. During the summer of 1939 he brought his Western show to Britain and thrilled both adults and children. In August he came across from Wales to appear for a week in Dublin, where his show was a sellout with 62,000 tickets sold, and he was mobbed wherever he went, including at the Dublin Horse Show. He reared horses on his ranch in California, and readily praised the quality of Irish horses. At the end of the week, in response to requests from the film trade here, arrangements were made for him to travel back to Britain via Belfast. Notices in the papers alerted his fans and they looked forward to his arrival with rising excitement. The day of his visit saw the most extraordinary scenes of welcome.

He arrived at 10:30 am dressed in cowboy gear, and headed for the Grand Central Hotel, his headquarters for the day. He was met by a large crowd which had been gathering for over an hour, so that it nearly blocked Royal Avenue. All available police had to be rushed to the venue to control them. According to the Irish News reporter it took Gene three full minutes to cross 10 yards (9 metres) of pavement from his car to the hotel through a "crowd of shouting children and excited adults." From the Grand Central his car made its way with difficulty to the City Hall for an official welcome from the Lord Mayor. On emerging from the City Hall large crowds met him, many seeking autographs. After a time signing books, photographs and such he gave up and announced that he would sing a song for them all. He then sang "South of the Border" with many joining in the last chorus. Then it was back again to the hotel for a rest from hand shaking and signing autographs, followed by lunch. The latter was an impressive affair. Besides Gene and his wife the official party included Herbert J. Yates, the chairman of Republic Pictures, and the man who would later produce "The Quiet Man", R.J.Beaverstock the American Vice - Consul, Patrick McIlroy the N.I. representative of Republic Pictures and Louis Ellerman the Irish representative of the company. Special guests included the Lord Mayor, Richard Hayward, Harry Wilton, local film renters and cinema managers.

The Lord Mayor presented the actor, his wife, and employer with sets of Irish Linen. Gene replied at some length beginning with an appreciation of the warmth and friendliness of the crowds, here and in Dublin. They were much more demonstrative and warm hearted than anything he had experienced in London. He explained that he had made over 30 films since he began acting in 1934 and that his output was eight films a year. He emphasised that they made clean films for the youth of America and Europe and that parents greatly appreciated that. Replying to a question he explained that he had left his horse Champion with his company in South Wales where he was appearing. But such was the welcome he had received in Belfast he promised to bring his complete show here the following year. Unfortunately the outbreak of war in September put an end to those plans.

In the afternoon he made his way, again through welcoming crowds, to the Children's Hospital on the

Gene Autry in the Children's Hospital. Source: N. Whig.

AT THE BELFAST HOSPITAL FOR SICK CHILDREN, where his visit was greatly appreciated, especially when he sang "South of the Borde r" and "Boob and Saddle" played his own accompaniment on the guitar.

Falls Road. He caused some blushing among the nurses when he described them as "lovely Irish colleens," but his main goal was the children. They couldn't believe it when their hero, dressed in a powder blue sombrero, blue pants (not denims), and pointed leather cowboy boots sauntered through the wards chatting to them, and sitting on some of their beds. The nurses also listened in awe as he sang "Boots and Saddles" and "South of the Border," accompanying himself on the guitar. From the hospital he went to St Mary's Hall in Bank Street where 4,000 expectant children and adults were waiting. His appearance caused the hall to erupt and he had great difficulty distributing the prizes for the Irish Weekly Gene Autry competition. He then sang "Mexicali Rose" and "South of the Border" for them. As he waved goodbye the children responded with "Come Back to Erin."

Meantime Arthur Square was filling with enthusiastic fans awaiting his visit to the Royal Cinema and the Imperial. Even with the assistance of the police Gene had a difficult time negotiating the crowds in front of the Royal Cinema, but he made it into the cinema, where his films usually premiered in Belfast. The crowds milled around good-naturedly both outside and inside the foyer, and were silenced only when he sang for them. He inspected the Imperial, and then his party wended their way to the docks, and the Liverpool boat. As usual a big crowd had collected to say goodbye and after much waving and singing the boat left carrying the star and what one reporter called "a touch of the blue skies and hot sun of California" with it.

But it carried more than that. Gene Autry knew that his films had a large following especially among the young. He took the responsibilities that position implied seriously. His films, like most Westerns, were essentially about the victory of good over evil, of righting wrongs, of protecting the weak and vulnerable in society. They also projected positive personal values. On screen he never smoked or drank, he never used offensive language, he showed respect for women, he refused to hit anyone smaller than himself, and used his guns only as a last resort. His screen persona reflected decency and a clear morality. He may not have been seeking the Holy Grail, but he was still a knight whose values were worth emulating. His visit gave Belfast one of its most exciting days to remember. It brought warmth, colour and song to a dour city still struggling with the results of economic depression, its reputation marred by political bigotry and sectarian hatreds.

The next cinematic visitor arrived five months later, but without any of the excitement that had surrounded Gene Autry. Tod Slaughter, described in the I.S.N. as "the last of the barnstormers," was less well known to the new generation of filmgoers. He was a Victorian style actor who specialised in the thrills of old time melodrama. In interviews with local reporters he commented on his career. Originally from Newcastle-on-Tyne, he had entered the profession after the First World War, touring as a serious actor. In that guise he recalled playing the old Theatre Royal in Arthur Street, but, in time,

TOD SLAUGHTER, master villain of the screen, who is making a personal appearance before every screening of "The Face at the Window" in the Royal Cinema, Belfast. On the left is Mr. G. M. King, manager Royal Cinema, and on the right Mr. P. M'Ilroy, Northern Ireland Representative of the British Lion Film Corporation.

("Northern Whig" Photograph.)

Tod Slaughter.
Source: N. Whig.

experience told him that there was still an audience for melodramas like "Maria Martin," "Sweeney Todd," "The Ticket of Leave Man" and others. He toured the halls and built a reputation as a popular, over-the-top performer, usually playing, with obvious relish, very hissable villains. He later realised there was a cinema audience for those shockers, and his visit to Belfast was to advertise his latest film, "The Face at the Window," which was showing in the Royal Cinema for a week beginning on 15th January 1940, in a double bill with Gene Autry and Smiley Burnett in "Home on the Prairie." The advertising encouraged the public to come and see "the master villain of the screen," who would appear in person on stage before every showing. As for the film, it advised, "'Laugh at it, or with it... no matter... you will enjoy a hearty essay in calculating villainy. "The audiences obviously did enjoy both the stage appearances and the film, because, after a week of packed houses, the film moved on to the Coliseum, and then the Forum. Mr Slaughter stayed in the city for a few weeks greeting audiences before each showing, as promised. The News Letter critic described how the audiences responded enthusiastically to his "fund of good stories, told with the effectiveness of a born trouper." The combination of the old style experienced actor in the flesh followed by his film performance would have been perfect entertainment for the Alhambra, but regretfully the latter was still a burnt shell.

Despite the popularity of the projected image, the human presence on stage was still appreciated by Belfast audiences. One aspect of that was the success of the visits of film personalities as described above. Another was cinevariety. The latter was as old as the cinema itself though its make - up and presentation had changed with the passing years. In the early days films were a minor part of the mixed music hall programmes, but, by the Thirties, the tables were well and truly turned and the film was the dominant attraction, supported by live quality acts. The Ritz introduced modern cinevariety to Belfast in November 1936, with top class films and acts, a combination which was a big success with local audiences. Meantime the Hippodrome was passing through a period of uncertainty during which it couldn't decide if it was a cinema or a music hall. In July 1938 the lease on the hall, held by Associated British Cinemas, expired and the building was leased by David Forrester Theatres Ltd. Forrester was new to the entertainment business, but he had built up a group of theatres and cinemas in England, and saw the possibilities of promoting the Hippodrome. He persuaded George Dobler, the incumbent manager, to stay on, and announced that the hall would close for renovation. The stage would be modernised with new equipment which would allow entertainments other than films to be presented. Other improvements would include the latest electrical effects available, and the installation of a new projection system. Work began immediately and the hall reopened on 1st August with Cecil B.DeMille's "The Buccaneer" starring Frederick Marsh. That was followed by a series of quality productions which included John Ford's "The Hurricane," starring the exotic Dorothy Lamour and Jon Hall, battling some very strong winds. Another presentation was "Blockade," starring Henry Fonda, which was a story set during the recent civil war in Spain. "Blockade" (d. William Dieterle, 1938) arrived surrounded with controversy, notably the accusation that it was a one - sided piece of propaganda supporting the Communists. Despite the paucity of communists on the ground in Belfast it ran for two weeks, proving once again that controversy tends to increase box office takings.

Behind the scenes there must have been differences of opinion between the manager and the new owner about the future direction to be taken. At Christmas 1938 the Hippodrome presented the annual pantomime"Cinderella "which, according to the Irish News, "broke all records." While Cinders lost only her slipper, Mr Dobler the manager lost his job, and departed. David Forrester travelled over to Belfast in the New Year with his general manager, Harry Murray. At a highly organised press conference Forrester told local reporters that he was a firm believer in the superiority of "flesh and blood" for entertainment, and that Harry Murray would take over the running of the theatre. The latter, who had wide experience in cinemas and theatres, announced that in keeping with Mr Forrester's wishes the Hippodrome would revert to live entertainment, beginning with Hawaiian Paradise, followed by Alfredo and his Gypsy Band. However after only four live shows, a letter from Mr Murray appeared in the local press in mid - February announcing a change of policy. He thanked the Belfast audiences for their enthusiasm and their "marvellous support," though he also noted that they could be quite critical. He explained that he had found it impossible to book sufficient acts of the high calibre they demanded, so he had decided to revert to showing films alternating with "first class productions." That policy continued to May, but at the end of that month the Hippodrome reverted back entirely to showing films. Despite the talk about the shortage of quality shows it was obvious that films filled more seats than expensive live acts and shows from London and overseas. The problem was mainly about money, and Mr Murray even tried to increase receipts by showing the controversial sex hygiene film "Damaged Lives." Obviously the whole venture didn't turn out to David Forrester's liking and by the following year he had sold the lease to local businessman G. L. Birch, who took over the running of the hall until April 1951, when his interest was passed over to George Lodge, who by that time already controlled the Imperial, Royal Cinema and the Grand Opera House. G.L.Birch proved to be a very popular and efficient manager, who imposed his personality on the Hippodrome over the years. He had been involved in the cinema industry for over twenty years, and was a skilled cameraman, who actually made a number of small amateur films.

Other cinemas in the city, like the Arcadian, the Gaiety and the Sandro, also introduced variety into their programmes by incorporating live acts, mainly of a local and amateur nature. The cinema with the strongest amateur tradition was the Alhambra. In the late Thirties its new young manager, Frank Doherty, initiated a "do - as - you - please" amateur competition, which became an annual event. Entrants were encouraged to "sing, dance, croon, play an instrument... do as you please." The crowds and the critics enjoyed it immensely. Its appeal, according to a writer in the Irish News, was the approach adopted by Mr Doherty. He didn't hold rehearsals but accepted on faith that the entrants could perform. As a result the acts, good or bad, had a freshness and spontaneity which appealed to the listeners. In May 1939 he launched a special competition, the New Discoveries of 1939 (auditions required), with the slogan that today's amateurs are tomorrow's stars.

The success and appeal of the Alhambra lay in its closeness to its audiences, who enjoyed not only the films but also the local talent which it enthusiastically encouraged: the singers, the comedians, the boxers like Rinty Monaghan or Spider Kelly, and the all - rounders like Richard Hayward or Albert Sharpe. Thus, the burning of the hall in December 1939 was seen as a serious loss to the entertainment scene. Shortly afterwards, the Coliseum, which was owned by the same company, Irish Theatres Ltd, and which had been closed for renovations and redecoration, opened its doors again. Mr Doherty was installed as manager and immediately introduced the do - as - you - please competition. But the attempt to keep the Alhambra tradition alive was unsuccessful. There was only one Alhambra, and the experiment ended in February 1940 when Mr Doherty left the Coliseum and moved to a new position in Dublin.

After a time, the Alhambra reopened but it was only a shadow of its former self. The author remembers visiting it in the late Forties with some friends to see a Western, and being saddened by the general air of deterioration. The building was showing its age in wear and tear, while the wooden benches in the stalls reflected its general decline, and loss of comfort. It was bought by the Rank Organization in 1956 but even they couldn't revive its flagging fortunes. Rank put it up for sale but there were no takers. The final blow came at 8:20pm on Thursday 10th September 1959 when an audience of about 500 "men, women and children" were laughing at the antics of Terry -Thomas and George Cole in "Too Many Crooks."(d. Mario Zampi, 1958). A young man, Maurice McGuigan, noticed flames and called an attendant, Hugh O'Neill, who began dousing them using a fire extinguisher. He soon realised that the fire was becoming more intense. The fire brigade was summoned, and the manager, Mr Bronagh, a former manager of the Coliseum, had the hall cleared. The audience had barely left when the fire - later traced to an electrical fault - really took hold. Five brigades fought the flames for two hours, mainly to prevent the conflagration spreading to nearby premises, especially Woolworth's next door. The following day crowds flocked to North Street to view the smoking remains. The facade had survived, blackened but erect, but behind it were the charred remains of the auditorium, now open to the sky. "The remains of old decency," someone commented. A spokesman for Rank announced that the future of the hall was not yet decided, but most people felt there was little chance of it reopening. It never did. It was the end of an historic hall, and the end of an era in entertainment in Belfast.

The cinemagoing public paid little attention to changes in managers, or ownership. Their main concern was the entertainment presented for their enjoyment, and the basis of that was still the full supporting programme. Organists like Joseph Seal (Ritz), and Leslie Simpson (Classic), live acts both professional and amateur, international or local, and personal appearances, all helped to fill out programmes of two and a half to three hours, for admittance prices of between only one and three shillings. On screen two films were expected, plus cartoons and short documentaries on interesting topics. The cartoons were dominated by Walt Disney and included Mickey Mouse, Donald Duck (whose righteous and not so righteous anger could put even Charles Laughton in the shade), Goofy, and Pluto. Also available were the products of other studios, notably Popeye and Betty Boop, while Bugs Bunny made his screen debut in 1940.

Disney amazed everyone by producing a feature length colour cartoon, the unique "Snow White and the Seven Dwarfs," which was released in the U.S.A. just before Christmas, 1937. Disney's folly, as the cynics called it, proved to be an artistic and financial success. It reached Belfast in October 1938, showing in the Classic. The adverts modestly acclaimed it as "the greatest film of all time" which to many in the city was an understatement. The critics heaped praise on it, and the public responded with packed houses wherever it was shown. From the Classic it moved to the Curran Theatres, before showing across the city. The author still recalls watching it, with immense pleasure, as his first unforgettable experience of the cinema, when his parents took him to see it in the Broadway. There had been worries expressed about the frightening nature of some of the scenes involving the Wicked Queen, but the author remembers being more intrigued by the echo in the well, as Snow White sang the wistful "I'm Wishing." There was a rumour - sadly untrue - in Belfast at the time that the voice of Snow White was actually that of a local singer, Agatha Turley, whose father was the organist in St Mary's Church in Chapel Lane, a fact which, according to a report in the Irish News, gave the film "added interest."

Travel films, especially in colour, were very popular. Those were the days before cheap air fares and the majority of people spent their holidays in local resorts like Bangor, Newcastle, Ballycastle, Portrush and Portstewart. They enjoyed seeing exotic places and people on screen, and weren't bothered by the knowledge that it was most unlikely they would ever see or experience them in reality. One man who had, was the film maker James A.Fitzpatrick, an American of Irish parentage, who had filmed all over the world. His colour productions of romantic or unusual locales like Hawaii or Bali often appeared on local screens supporting the feature films. His films had a distinctive and recognisable style. He caused some excitement when he arrived in Belfast with two cameramen in June 1938, at the invitation of the Ulster Tourist Development Association. His intention was to make a colour film highlighting the natural scenery and other attractions of N. Ireland.

One of the most popular items on the programme was the newsreel. For a good newsreel a manager had to pay about £400 a year, but as one of them commented "it was money well spent." People expected to see a newsreel in the programme, and were annoyed if there was none. One writer in the Irish News mentioned that even if the films were uninteresting he would still go to the cinema to see the latest newsreel. Newsreels weren't subject to censorship like films, but the threat was always there, and the companies were expected to maintain certain standards in their presentation. Despite that apparent freedom of expression, newsreels have been criticised and accused of being more concerned with entertainment and propaganda than news, that they were highly selective and distorted reality, and that their approach to important events was superficial. That may have been true on some occasions but seen from today's perspective they form a comprehensive and fascinating social document of their period. Many modern documentaries shown on TV make maximum use of them. The audiences of the period took them seriously, and regarded them as the visual extension of what they read in the newspapers, and heard on the radio. Their overall importance was reflected in the prominence given to them in the daily cinema advertisements, and the respect with which the local critics treated them.

The newsreels were produced by five main companies: Pathé, British Movietone, Gaumont - British, British Paramount and Universal, the names and logos of which were well known to filmgoers. Cinemas went out of their way to ensure that patrons were aware of the particular brand they showed. Pathé News and its offshoots were the most widely shown, appearing in the Picture House, the Lyric, the Alhambra and the Curran Theatres. The Classic and Royal Cinema had British Movietone News and Gaumont British News, the Ritz projected Paramount News, while the Clonard also showed Movietone News. A number of Belfast cinemas had their official opening recorded by the newsreels and shown as a special attraction later. Newsreel cameras were present when the Ritz, the Strand and the Castle on the Castlereagh Road opened. The latter emphasised that Paramount News, including the local event, would be shown "all week."' To satisfy their patrons, and to save money, the cheaper halls often shared newsreels, which meant that the reels had to be moved on time quickly from one cinema to the other, either by car, or even by bicycle. Shades of a silent Keystone comedy!

The items in the newsreels are still with us on a daily basis on television, and the television programmes concerned still reflect the different types of newsreel events. Among the most popular were those dealing with sporting occasions. Sports fans were well served with major football and rugby matches, classic horse races including the Grand National and the Derby, cricket, and the Boat Race. They could also watch Henry Cotton's successes on the golf course, or see Fred Perry or Dorothy Round win Wimbledon titles. Local sporting events attracted the news cameramen, and their coverage was enthusiastically followed. In September 1934 the Ards Tourist Trophy took place on the first Saturday of the month with an entry of 40 cars, and on the following Tuesday, the normal day for the newspaper film comments, the News Letter carried the heading: "T.T. Thrills in Current Newsreels." The critic praised the "fine pictures" taken by the British Movietone cameramen, showing spills and thrills including a car somersaulting at Quarry Corner. Gaumont British also included exciting shots of the race plus another local item, the official opening of Ards Airport, when Lady Londonderry named the first training plane Finnian the White, called after a local Celtic saint. The opening was followed by a display of military and commercial planes, including an autogyro and about 20 privately owned machines. Also shown were the preparations for the coming America's Cup, with the British challenger, Endeavour, in full sail. Later newsreels showed the races, with the American yacht retaining the Trophy. The critic drew attention also to the fact that the same newsreel included shots of Prince George, the Duke of Kent, posing with his intended bride, Princess Marina.

Scenes of the British Royal family always went over well in Belfast, except in the Nationalist areas where they were usually omitted. One characteristic of newsreels was that individual unwanted items could be removed without damaging the continuity of the whole. When newsreels of the Royal wedding were shown in December 1934, the Belfast Telegraph reported that they "got a tremendous reception in packed houses." The Royal Hippodrome was showing De Mille's "Cleopatra" that week, but on Thursday the manager added a note to the adverts advising people that the newsreel of the wedding was being flown into Belfast and would be on the screen that evening. In Dublin, by contrast, the newsreel had to be withdrawn after strong objections from members of the audience. Audiences had become more familiar with King George the Fifth than any other of the royals due mainly to his frequent appearances in newsreels. His death in January 1936 resulted in a great outpouring of grief, and cinemas in the city closed as a mark of respect on 21st January. During the following weeks audiences packed the cinemas to see the scenes of his funeral. The critic of the Belfast Telegraph described being in the Classic and experiencing the "intensity of silence" in the cinema during the newsreel. The newsreel also included the official proclamation of the new king, Edward VIII. That was followed by the playing of the National Anthem, during which the whole audience stood in silence. In early March the Whig reported that a copy of the funeral film was presented by the film company to the

HOW BELFAST SAW THE LIGHT

Corporation. It probably lies, forgotten, in some store in the City Hall.

Life moved on and the newsreels later in the year were soon showing pictures of the events surrounding the abdication of Edward in December. The newsreel companies consulted with the government about the filming of the coronation of the new king, George VI, in March. There were fears expressed that the presence of cameras and lights would be at odds with the solemnity of what was not only a State, but also a religious occasion. The newsreel companies agreed not to release the finished film until it had been viewed and approved by the Archbishop of Canterbury and the Duke of Norfolk. When the film arrived in Belfast public interest was high. The Royal Cinema added a statement in heavy black print to its normal film advert, informing its patrons that it would be screening "special" pictures of the Coronation procession, which included scenes filmed inside Westminster Abbey.

Meantime international developments dominated the news. The writer of Random Jottings in the Irish News, a dedicated and knowledgeable filmgoer, congratulated the Classic on the "excellent" British Gaumont newsreels on the Italian invasion of Abyssinia. Apart from their content, he felt that they illustrated the advances that had taken place in the art of the cinema. In contrast with the newsreels from the Great War they showed a greater appreciation of the value of movement, while technically the pictures showed a decided improvement in clarity. He felt that the soundtrack added to their fluidity, as there were no printed titles to interrupt the flow of the images. The early scenes as the Italian army advanced over difficult terrain were "amazing." The pictures contrasted the highly mechanised nature of the Italians with the poorly equipped Ethiopians. There were lengthy scenes of the latter charging the Italian forces. The Ethiopians included female warriors, and one of them spoke "some broken English" to the camera, at which she was cheered by the audience. Scenes like that brought the campaign alive for local audiences. Another newsreel, showing in the Hippodrome, interviewed the former Prime Minister, Ramsey Mac Donald, about the attitude of the British Government to the invasion. After giving his opinion Mr Mac Donald ended with a rhetorical question: What will we do? which he repeated three times. There was complete silence in the cinema until a voice from the gallery shouted: "Send out the Specials, and they'll finish the war," causing the audience to dissolve into laughter.

Scenes of war or preparations for war became more frequent as the Thirties progressed, and, more ominously, came closer to home, in Europe. Scenes of Hitler and his well drilled army became familiar to every filmgoer, while shots of the new German autobahn shown in newsreels in January 1938 indicated the level of the country's development. A commentator from the Irish News expressed admiration for "the long dazzling stretches of road" and pointed out that there was nothing to compare with them here. Watching the cars moving along them at high speed, he felt he was watching scenes out of "Things to Come," a vision of the future. In contrast the Royal Cinema advertised its Gaumont - British News showing the first pictures of "the Mighty Maginot Line, the secret fortifications built by the French." Sadly, unlike the autobahn, the Maginot Line proved to belong to the past.

The world was shrinking and the newsreels played a part in making ordinary people aware of the fact. Speed and the conquest of distance were ever in the news. In 1933 cinemagoers watched pictures of Malcolm Scott as he pushed his car Bluebird to a world record speed of 272 miles per hour at Daytona, Florida. But it was mainly upwards that cameras and eyes were directed as intrepid airmen and women like Charles Lindburgh, Amy Johnson and Amelia Earhart strove to break old air records, and establish new ones. The aura of courage, adventure and glamour surrounding flight spilled over into fiction films. Cecil B deMille set his comedy, Madame Satan (1930), partly in a Zeppelin that crashes in flames, and the musical even took to the skies with "Flying Down to Rio" in which chorus girls performed feats of wing walking. That film landed in the Royal Hippodrome in October 1934, and introduced Belfast audiences to the first pairing of that magnificent dancing duo, Fred Astaire and Ginger Rogers.

One of the criticisms of newsreels was that they were superficial in content, so some news companies responded by making longer, more detailed studies of specific topics. The most famous and respected of those was the American series called "The March of Time," produced by Time Inc., which published Time and Life magazines. The declared aim of the series was to inform as well as entertain. With the resources of Time behind them they were well researched, intelligent and often thought provoking. Cinematically they introduced a new documentary format involving a stirring and distinctly American commentary, married to scenes of actuality, and reconstructions of relevant incidents using professional actors. This is an approach still widely used by television documentary makers today. The March of Time series of two reelers began in 1935 and remained in prominence through the Thirties and the Forties until its functions were taken over by the new medium of television. The films were very popular with Belfast audiences. They were shown in downtown cinemas, especially the Hippodrome, before moving on to the Curran cinemas. They dealt with a wide range of subjects like urban slums, the problems of India, the future of China, and even Ireland.

March of Time No. 5, titled "Ireland's New Deal" arrived in Belfast, at the Hippodrome, in early December 1936. It was included in a programme supporting the popular musical "Rose Marie," starring Nelson Eddy and the "fascinating" (Irish News) Jeanette Mac Donald. It was a study of Eamon deValera's Ireland. A few weeks before, a summary of the film had been sent to the major newspapers, which claimed that "not since O'Connell and Parnell has any man had so strong a hold over the hearts of the Irish people as this scholarly mathematics professor." The critic on the Irish News was impressed by the film which he described as "excellently constructed." He commented on its content, beginning with Mr deValera launching his plan for a new self - sufficient Ireland in 1932. The film then went in search of evidence of the implementation of that policy with interviews, shots of full theatres, new industries like sugar beet factories, modern turf cutting schemes, the Ford works in Cork where cars were assembled, and the Guinness complex in Dublin. Reference was also made to the economic war with Britain. As a climax the cameras were allowed to film a meeting of the Executive Council of the Free State, and to interview Mr deValera himself. After the interview a choir of schoolboys sang "The Soldier's Song" in Irish.

The critic thought the content was excellent, though he felt it was very biased in favour of Fianna Fail. The writer of Random Jottings also described seeing the film on its first run in the Hippodrome. The hall was well filled, and there was some unease about how it would be received. The Pathé newsreel which preceded it included an item on the Royal family, which was greeted, as usual, with applause. When the March of Time began it was watched intently and quietly, though when Mr deValera made his first appearance there was a spirited round of clapping. Throughout, the audience remained quiet, watching as the Tricolour flew, and the boy's choir sang in Irish. The writer optimistically interpreted the general reaction as an indication that tolerance was possible among local ordinary people

Another topic that the March of Time discussed in a later edition was "Adolph Hitler and Peace." But it was already too late. War was declared on 3rd September 1939. The editor of the Irish News summed up the general feeling in the city when he wrote: "The catastrophe that has been dreaded for years has come upon us, another European war."

CHAPTER TWENTY SEVEN
Why Worry?

As part of its Christmas programme in December 1939 the Ritz presented "Its A Wonderful World." (d. W. S.VanDyke, 1939). It was one of the last of the screwball comedies, and starred James Stewart, but is not to be confused with his more famous life - affirming post war production, "It's a Wonderful Life." (d. Frank Capra, 1946). It certainly made critics and audiences smile, but the title seemed at odds with the general atmosphere in the city. A great darkness had descended, and it wasn't only the blackout. People could gloomily and, with cause, ask just how wonderful the world really was. A few weeks earlier the Grand Opera House had presented Jimmy O'Dea in a variety show of comedy, music, dancing and speciality turns. It comprised in all of 21 scenes involving Jimmy as Mrs Mulligan, Maggie Murphy or, just as himself, in a series of sketches that had the hall shaking with laughter. Behind all the stage fun and frolic reality lurked, because, significantly, the name of the show was "WHY WORRY." The title itself must have brought a wry smile to many a local face because, since the beginning of September, the name of the game was worry.

Within a few weeks people found that their whole way of life was altered. Writing in early October, a correspondent in the Irish News contemplated those changes. The war, he wrote, dominated everything, and evidence of it could be seen and heard on all sides Shop windows were decorated with war posters and models of bombers, submarines and other war machines. Men's clothing shops were full of officers' uniforms. Some of the city's finest buildings were "defaced by sandbags." Food shortages were an increasing problem, with sugar already in short supply, and eggs becoming a luxury. The prices of some essential foods had risen, and even beer had gone up by one penny a pint. Bus services had been reduced, and taxi fares had increased. Conversations, wherever people collected, in restaurants, on buses and trams were mainly about war topics. Even sports seemed to have been forgotten. In the cinemas the newsreels were all about war. Street hawkers were selling copies of Hitler's last will and testament in the centre of the city. Even the children were affected, and had abandoned traditional and favourite street songs in favour of "The Siegfried Line."

After the official declaration of war the government immediately put into operation plans to protect the country, and its population, plans that impacted on every aspect of the lives of the people. Entertainment did not escape, and one of the first directives issued from London closed theatres, cinemas and other places of entertainment, where large crowds might assemble and form a target for bombing. In N.I. the Order in question stayed in place for only a few days. It was introduced on Friday but the following Monday the Amusement Caterers Association (the White Cinema Club) published a notice which stated that the Government of N.Ireland "did not consider it necessary at present to apply the Order closing cinemas and theatres." The public was assured that all halls would remain open, and operate as usual. The official reason given for relaxing the Order was that the government at Stormont believed that the danger of attack was not as great here as in England. Indeed there were many in local public life who felt that it was unlikely that the Germans would ever attack Belfast. During a debate in the City Council on 1st December 1939, Alderman Pierce criticised the amount of money being spent on the A.R.P., adding that "it was a million to one chance that there would ever be an air - raid on Belfast." The A.R.P. controller in the city disagreed, and stated - accurately, as it turned out - that Belfast was "not well prepared for heavy bombing." The Government felt that the very positive effect that cinemas and theatres had in boosting public morale had to be taken into account. The News Letter supported that view, adding that "the cinema did more than most" to distract and relieve the population from the worries and pressures of blackouts, shortages of food and petrol, and the dangers of air attack. The population were officially warned in future to differentiate between orders that applied to the whole U.K., to Britain, or just locally to N.Ireland.

In England the strictures against opening cinemas remained in place for nearly two weeks (until Sept. 16th) by which time the trade began to complain that they would soon have to lay off workers. In the interim, staff were given training in air raid precautions, and cinema managers made plans to deal with an emergency. When some English cinemas were allowed to reopen the manager of one addressed the audience before each show and told them that if a raid began during the performance they would be warned from the stage. Those who lived nearby could then go home, but those who lived further away would find it safer to stay in the cinema until the all-clear. The manager pointed out that modern cinemas were well built, and could withstand most bombs. The Stormont government, and many local managers, thought likewise, though the air-raids of Easter 1941, during which a number of cinemas were destroyed, would cause many to think again. The authorities in London also came round to accept the argument that cinemas could be a major boost to public morale.

The chief problem that citizens had to cope with was the blackout, which affected everyone. When darkness descends today the city becomes a blaze of electric light, but in early September 1939 when darkness descended a government Order meant that it stayed dark. No lights could be shown, and the police and air raid wardens patrolled the streets to see that the blackout, as it was called, was respected. A writer in the News Letter wrote that lights were only appreciated now when they were gone, while another in the Irish News described the eeriness of the city in complete darkness, with searchlight beams flashing across the sky. People no longer stayed out late, and the streets were deserted by 11:00pm. No street lights, no lighted shop windows, dimmed car lights, no theatre or cinema lights. The welcoming display of lighting outside each cinema was turned off, though one downtown manager commented that at least it reduced costs. For a time it also reduced patronage. It is difficult for a modern citizen to appreciate the intensity of the darkness, though it was ameliorated a little when people were allowed to carry small torches. On New Year's Eve a small crowd collected at the Albert clock and when midnight came they shone their torches on the clock so they could see its face, sang Auld Lang Sang, and departed wondering what 1940 would hold for them.

Some time later the writer of Random Jottings (Irish News) described leaving a brightly lit Dublin and travelling north by train. The carriages were well lit and passengers sat back contentedly. When the train reached Goraghwood on the border, the atmosphere changed. The customs men with their peaked caps entered the train and moved from carriage to carriage, asking "anything to declare?" searching baggage looking mainly for tea, tobacco and butter. The lights were lowered and the blinds drawn, as the train steamed through a darkened countryside to its destination at Great Victoria Street Station. When the passengers emerged into Great Victoria Street it was completely dark despite the presence of the Grand Opera House, the Royal Hippodrome and the Ritz cinema. The crowd dispersed quietly as their eyes adjusted to the conditions, but they moved with care.

The blackout was widely criticised not only for the inconvenience it caused but for the dangers it carried. When it was first introduced groups in some Nationalist areas lit small bonfires in the streets in political protest but the majority of people realised, as the Irish News editor wrote, that the black out was "in those days of danger an imperative obligation... an inconvenience that must be cheerfully suffered... for the protection of the community. "That didn't prevent editors and citizens complaining about its severity, how it was policed, its impact on shopkeepers, and the part it played in increasing levels of crime, and accidents. In January 1940 the Belfast coroner Dr Lowe expressed alarm at the increase in accidents, varying from falls to vehicle impacts. In the last two months he had dealt with 61 inquests, 20 of which were black-out related. Only small torches were allowed and the bulb or glass had to be covered with two layers of tissue paper. As a result elderly people were at risk of tripping or falling. The cars had special metal fixtures over their headlights, reducing visibility so that some pedestrians didn't see them coming, or the drivers didn't see the walkers. Dr Lowe suggested that for their own safety the elderly and those with poor eyesight should stay indoors during blackout hours. Certain supporters of Temperance in the city argued that alcohol played a part in many of the accidents, and called for the public houses to be closed during the periods of black-out.

Others saw the blackout as an opportunity, and the number of burglaries increased. In January 1940 a number of armed men walked into the foyer of the Royal Cinema, held up the staff of the Grand Opera booking office located there, and fled with £40. They ran out into Arthur Square and disappeared into the darkness before anyone could catch them. Even some children took advantage of the dark. Three children including a schoolgirl, all under 12 years of age, were caught breaking into cars, one of which was parked outside the Capitol Cinema. Their "loot" consisted of a bag, cigarettes, two containers of sweets, a Christmas pudding, a box of pastries and a box of chocolates. The R.M. gave them the benefit of the Probation Act, put them under probation for two years, and banned them from going out after the beginning of black-out. If they were caught out after dark he threatened to send them to an industrial school.

A widespread result of the blackout was that many people tended to stay indoors after dark and, as mentioned above, the streets were nearly deserted well before midnight. Even cars became a rare sight because of petrol rationing and fuel shortages. The only pedestrians in the city centre were policemen and air-raid wardens on the lookout for breaches of the blackout. The shops and department stores noted that trend and in the run-up to Christmas prominently advertised a range of indoor hobbies. Robinson and Cleaver suggested that for the Black Out evenings(sic) their customers turn to knitting, embroidery, tapestry work and bridge. More typical was Cecil Marcus of Donegall Street whose advert advised the public to "Black Out your Troubles with party games. We stock games, cards, jigsaws, and toys of all kinds." The decline in the number of people going out for the evening inevitably reduced the attendance at theatres, and especially cinemas. In early February 1940 the Troxy reflected the problem in an advert which read "Short of petrol? Well, just take a number 7 tram and see The Four Feathers." But humans are extremely adaptable and as the weeks passed without any sign of German bombers, people began to venture out again by the light of their torches. Musical groups in particular experienced increased attendances, while discussion groups, debating societies and such also began to report larger audiences, as did the theatres and cinemas. Full houses were experienced over the Christmas period and especially for the cinemas it was the beginning of a return to long queues and packed houses, a trend which lasted through the Forties and well into the Fifties. Paradoxically the cinemas, which depended for their existence on light, actually benefited from the darkness. For many people they became a refuge from the harsh realities of a wartime regime.

The cinemas had their own problems. The increase in patronage came at a time when the city had lost nearly 800 seats due to the destruction of the Alhambra. The Coliseum, owned by the same company Irish Theatres Ltd., carried on with the Alhambra tradition but the pressure on seating remained, but was partly relieved when the Grosvenor Hall began evening film shows. Beginning in November 1939 it presented a form of cine variety, usually involving Richard Hayward on stage, accompanied by one of his films on screen. They were evening presentations of one or two days duration which culminated in December with a show advertised attractively as "melody that charms and movies that satisfy" with Richard Hayward in person followed by the film "You're Out of Luck." The Belfast Film Society and the Belfast Film Institute Society also began to use the hall regularly for their specialist film meetings during the early Forties. Later the decision was taken to move from discrete programmes to continuous programming. That change of policy was associated, one suspects, with a change of exhibitor and resulted in the surprising presentation of "Damaged Lives," for adults only, in July 1942. That was followed by a series of first release programmes beginning with "Ladies in Retirement," (d. Charles Vidor, 1941), starring Ida Lupino and Louis Hayward, the proceeds from which were donated to the Red Cross, St John's Ambulance and the Cinematograph Benevolent Fund. The film, a Gothic style murder mystery, was welcomed by the local critics, and the News Letter commented that in view of the marked increase in cinema audiences "this addition to the city's cinemas should be welcomed, and supported." In May 1943 an Educational Film Season was announced which turned out to consist of the controversial sex hygiene films "Marriage Forbidden," "Social Enemy No.1," and "The Birth of a Baby," the details of which have already been discussed. Traditional supporters of the Grosvenor Hall entertainments were not happy with the direction that the hall seemed to be taking.

One of the more positive cinematic developments during the war was the purchase and updating of one of the city's oldest cinemas, the Kelvin. Over the years the Kelvin had lost its original gloss, and, being a small independent, struggled to get bookings for first run - films. As a result it had lost patronage and had come to depend mainly on small, less affluent, audiences who still enjoyed B movies. In April it was bought by Raymond Stross, a British film producer, and husband of Anne Heywood. His declared aim was to restore the Kelvin to its place "among the many fine cinemas in Belfast." Despite the shortages imposed by war time, the building was completely refurbished and its facilities upgraded. A new R.A.C. sound system was installed, with a new screen. The auditorium was reseated, and a new uniform was introduced for the staff, supplied by Goorwitch Ltd. of Castle Junction. The cinema, renamed the New Kelvin, opened in September 1942 with "China Fights," a war film which claimed to expose Japanese war crimes in Chima. It attracted packed houses, and Mr Stross announced that, in future, first - run films would be the rule. He backed that promise up with a series of large, illustrated adverts in the I.S.N. proclaiming "Who knows what tomorrow may bring... come what may, you are always sure of first rate entertainment at the New Kelvin." His next presentation - "direct from London" - was a French film with the English title "Judas Was a Woman," starring Jean Gabin and Simone Simon. The original French title was "La Bete Humaine," based on Zola's novel of the same name. The advert described it as "the story of a faithless wife goading a man to destruction." Later "The Mystery of Marie Roget," based on a story by Edgar Allen Poe, was presented with the challenge: we dare you to see it.

The success of the new policy coincided with a decision to introduce Cine - variety in mid - November. During Christmas week the programme consisted of "Girl's Town," starring Edith Fellows a former American child star, showing for the first time in N.Ireland, with a promise to disclose "the sensational, dramatic and revealing story of the heartaches, and headaches behind the glamour of the film racket." It was accompanied, on stage, with "Christmas Crackers," eighty minutes of non - stop variety with 14 star artists. The show ran for two weeks, to packed houses. That selection of shows summed up the cinema's approach of visceral thrills allied to the suggestion of naughtiness on screen, supported with good quality live entertainment. Audiences obviously enjoyed the mix, and the New Kelvin became the talk of the town. It also benefited from being one of the few cinemas in the city (along with the Imperial and the Picture House) given permission to show films on Sunday to the troops. Even after the war ended the hall, despite a change of name, continued to be called "the soldier's cinema." By 1942 the New Kelvin seemed to be on its feet again, its programmes vying successfully for audiences with the other downtown cinemas. Its economic future looked secure, and, after surviving the war, it underwent another change in 1946, emerging with a new name, the Mayfair.

During the devastating Easter blitz of 1941 a number of cinemas were hit by bombs. In the York Street area the Midland and the Queen's were destroyed, and never rebuilt. Their destruction undermined the belief that cinemas would stand up to aerial attack, but it also robbed a working class area of two of its most popular halls. The only downtown cinema to suffer was the Lyric in High Street. An official photograph taken after the raid - civilians were forbidden by law to take photographs - shows the sturdy frontage still standing, advertising a double bill of "Old Mother Riley in Business," and "The Door With Seven Locks," but the damage within was so great that it was decided not to rebuild. It's loss was greatly felt by regular cinemagoers because it had combined a reputation for showing good quality films, in comfortable surroundings, at reasonable prices. The building was in time demolished along with other badly damaged adjacent buildings, and the cleared area, on the Lagan side of Bridge Street, became known, during the war, as Blitz Square. It's space was utilised for many purposes, including car parking. As a child, the author remembers being taken there to see a display of warplanes and other military hardware. For a time, Barry's Amusements located there, erecting a large tent where musical shows were staged, as well as individual attractions like the Mexican film star Movita. The elimination of the Lyric ended the link with the old Panopticon hall, and its owner, the cinema pioneer Mr Stewart. In a later blitz the only cinema in East Belfast to suffer was the Popular, which was severely damaged by bombs, and forced to close. It remained boarded up for the duration of the war, much to the disappointment of its local audiences, though it was rebuilt and reopened to them once again in 1946.

The industry faced another threat of bombing, closer to home, from Republicans who objected to the cinemas being used for what they regarded as pro - British propaganda, especially in newsreels. The threats came to nothing in Belfast but resulted in violence in Derry where, in late February 1940, two cinemas, the Strand and the Midland were bombed. The attacks occurred after the halls were closed so no one was hurt, and only minor damage was inflicted on the buildings. The cinema managers of Derry took the matter seriously, and met to discuss the attacks. After the meeting the managers of issued a statement saying that they would continue to show newsreels because the majority of their patrons wanted to see them. They argued that the newsreels only showed "in pictorial form "what had already been printed in the newspapers, or broadcast on the radio. They felt that the cinema should have the same freedom of expression as those other media. The managers supporting that statement represented the City, Opera House, Rialto, Strand and Midland cinemas. As a precaution police guards were put on those buildings. Despite that, the Opera House, which had recently been completely refurbished, was destroyed by a fire which was widely regarded as the work of the I.R.A.

There is no doubt that the newsreels were heavily censored, despite statements to the contrary, so as to give as optimistic a view as possible of how the war was progressing. The Government regarded the cinema as an important channel, not only of propaganda, but also of information to the public, and the Ministry of Information (M.O.I.) produced a wide range of films dealing with topics encompassing advice on what to do in an air - raid, or how to use a gas mask in the event of a gas attack, to how to grow vegetables on an allotment, and many other subjects relevant to wartime survival. The members of the White Cinema Club, the managers and the renters all co - operated with the M.O.I. in showing those films. There were complaints of poor organization and lack of understanding, and the News Letter described how the M.O.I. tended to "dump" films on cinemas without warning. The managers then had to integrate them into programmes that had in many cases been carefully timed and prepared weeks before.

The disruption of transport caused by the war interfered with the distribution of entertainment films. As major new films became scarcer rental costs began to rise, and new hire agreements made matters financially difficult for many cinemas, especially independents. According to an article in the Whig a "war" had begun between the renters and the exhibitors in Britain over recent changes. The Cinematograph Exhibitors Association (CEA) of Great Britain told its members not to accept the new excessive demands. Some renters were asking for 40% to 50% return on the pound for the hire of their top films. The distributors of "Gone with the Wind" were asking for 70% of the take, along with a written guarantee that the lowest seat price at the matinee would be 3/ 6, and 4/ 6 in the evening. They also required a minimum booking period of 12 weeks. The new conditions worried the local exhibitors who, because of their smaller size and markets, hadn't the bargaining power of the larger cinema groups in Britain. A number of prominent people in the business were invited to N.Ireland to see how the problems facing exhibitors and renters here could be dealt with. One result was a meeting in the Grand Central Hotel in early December 1941 at which a N.I. section of the Cinematograph Exhibitors Association was established to take over the system of local film distribution. It replaced the White Cinema Club (the Amusement and Caterers Association of N.Ireland) which reverted to its original role as the organizer of social and charity work for the local entertainment industry. Members of the latter were appointed to prominent positions in the new organization, indicating their acceptance of it. J.D.Russell, the manager of the Ritz, was appointed president, John Curran of Curran Theatres was elected vice president, while the committee included George Lodge the owner of the Imperial, and Harry Wilton.

Lifting the gloom. Gone with the Wind in the Ritz.

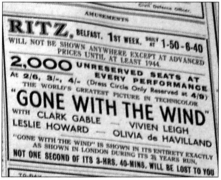

Beloved Enemy in the Broadway. Source: Irish News.

But the problem still remained of getting sufficient films to meet local needs. That was partly met by reissues, and past successes like the once controversial "From the Manger to the Cross," Cecil B. deMille's "The Sign of the Cross," Charlie Chaplin's "The Gold Rush," and Howard Hughes' "'Hell's Angels" all of which attracted new young audiences. The Irish News critic described the latter film as "still one of the most exciting films of its kind," which was not only highly entertaining, but also "allowed older cinemagoers to regret the loss to cinema that the death of Jean Harlow represented." She had died in June 1937. "The Gold Rush" proved its continuing appeal by running concurrently, and successfully, in both the Imperial and the Picture House, while "From the Manger to the Cross" attracted "large audiences"(News Letter) to the Broadway.

Despite such successes most people wanted to see new films, and a reduced but steady stream of those arrived from Hollywood and Britain. In February 1942 the Classic presented one of the greatest films to come out of America. It was "Citizen Kane," directed by Orson Welles, who among his other exploits had appeared on the stages of the Gate and the Abbey in Dublin in the early Thirties. The posters outside the Classic described the film as"..stark...realistic...emotional" which gave little indication of its real content. The News Letter critic was impressed, describing it as "a remarkable film" characterised by "stimulating technique and a wealth of inspired camerawork." Welles and his cast, he thought, gave "powerful" performances, but, above all, the film impressed with its "new uses of the screen's untapped potentialities." Seen today the film still towers in intelligence and style above most modern screen fare. Sadly it made little impact at the time on Belfast filmgoers, whose minds were focused on less serious entertainment.

The film which dominated the war years, and helped to lift the gloom temporarily, was "Gone With The Wind." The film magazines and newspapers had been full of details of its progress since the choice of Vivien Leigh to play Scarlett O'Hara to the filming of the burning of Atlanta. In the film Clarke Gable caused shock when he told Vivien Leigh that he "didn't give a damn," but everyone else seemed to care. Audiences in Belfast, their appetites suitably whetted by the advance publicity, waited to see it and their patience was rewarded when the Ritz announced that "the world's greatest picture in technicolor" would open on 17th August 1942. The Ritz promised that local audiences would see the full 3 hours 40 minutes that had been projected in London over its two and a half years run there. Because of its length there would be only two showings daily, at 1:50 pm and 6:40 pm. The prospect of such a long film was a novelty in itself. While seats could be booked in the Dress Circle (at four shillings and ninepence) the remaining 2,000 seats would be unreserved at prices of 2/ 6, 3 / -, and 4/ -. The result was long queues and packed houses over the following seven weeks, which must have brought smiles to the the face of Mr Russell, the manager. Audiences loved it, and it became a major topic of conversation in the city. Not to have seen GWTW was regarded as being very odd indeed. The critics praised it, but with some reservations. There was general admiration for the production values, the sets, the superb colour photography, the acting and the Civil War action sequences but a feeling that the later sections, dealing with the postwar problems of Scarlett O'Hara, were less interesting, despite the fine acting of Vivien Leigh. The News Letter critic agreed that for once the film lived up to its Hollywood hype, and was well worth seeing. He concluded that it was excellent entertainment with "undeniable greatness for two of its nearly four hours."

The other downtown cinemas struggled to compete with the Ritz. The Hippodrome decided to emphasise the length factor by promising patrons two hours of films, with one hour of stage variety. The main feature was called "Affectionately Yours," and starred Rita Hayworth. It was supported by Richard Hayward's much praised documentary "Loch Corrib." The variety consisted of The Irish Troubadours who included Richard Hayward and Anna Meakin singing Irish songs, plus an American act called the Mahoney Brothers., described as "comedy jugglers," who became quite popular in Belfast, appearing the following December in the Hippodrome Christmas circus. The News Letter thought that the combination of Hayworth on screen, and Hayward on stage, represented "a generous entertainment." Another Ritz special was the award winning war film, "Mrs Miniver" (d.William Wyler, 1942), which ran for four weeks beginning at the end of the year (1942). The News Letter critic opined that it was the best film made so far which accurately illustrated Britain at war, and he praised "its restrained sentiment and unemphasised drama." Besides its propaganda content it had special local appeal because it starred Greer Garson, who, though born in England had an Irish mother. She was very proud of her Irish roots and often described how she had spent her youthful summer holidays in Castlewellan, where her maternal grandparents lived. Her many Belfast fans were attracted by her beauty, and appreciated the serenity and quiet nobility in her acting, qualities that inspired Errol Flynn to describe her in a note, reputedly written on the wallpaper of his parent's home at Stranmillis, as "a cathedral on wheels." She won an Oscar for her performance in "Mrs Miniver" and at the Oscar presentation she replied with the longest reception speech ever recorded.

Another Irish actress who was very popular in Belfast during the war years(and later) was Maureen O'Hara. Sometimes two or three of her films were showing across the city at the same time. In February 1940, during the week that Paris fell to the Germans, the Classic presented her first Hollywood film, "The Hunchback of Notre Dame," in which she starred with her mentor, Charles Laughton. The film was welcomed by the local critics and the Irish News praised Mr Laughton for "his fine performance." The critic recalled the silent version starring Lon Chaney and commented that Laughton's make-up was "more repulsive" than Chaney's. He also added that Maureen O'Hara "added charm to the picture" and that her natural beauty came across as "the Irish antithesis to Hollywood syntheticism." Charles Laughton appeared again with his protegee in Jean Renoir's "This Land is Mine," a grim story of life in German occupied France. She also starred, as a proto-feminist, with Lucille Ball in "Dance, Girl, Dance," and later in John Ford's '' How Green was my Valley "with one of the top actors of the period, Walter Pidgeon. In a complete change of pace she also appeared in her first pirate film in colour," The Black Swan, "alongside Tyrone Power and George Sanders, who looked suitably villainous in a fierce red beard. Miss O'Hara, with her own mane of shining auburn hair and green eyes, came to be known as "The Queen of Technicolour." One New York critic wrote that the sunset itself faded into insignificance before Maureen O'Hara in Glorious Technicolor! Many in Belfast agreed.

The Irish Antithesis of Hollywood Syntheticism. Source: Irish News.

Musicals were always welcome and Fred Astaire, Bing Crosby, Betty Grable, Deanna Durbin, Alice Faye, the Andrews Sisters and the exotic Carmen Miranda all had their fans. One indication of the amazing popularity of Deanna Durbin was a series of Deannese Nights presented by Curran Theatres. Each ran for a week and consisted of six of her films: Three Smart Girls, 100 Men and a Girl, Mad About Music, That Certain Age, Three Smart Girls Grow Up, and First Love. A different film each evening, plus, on stage, a singing competition. The Deannese Nights travelled around the Curran cinemas with the finale of the competition held in the Tonic Cinema in Bangor. Comedies were also very popular and audiences laughed at the antics of Abbot and Costello, the ghostly adventures of Topper (Roland Young), and the frenetic exploits of Three Stooges. Bing Crosby, Bob Hope and their beautiful foil, Dorothy Lamour, made their first road picture, "The Road to Singapore," quickly followed by "The Road to Zanzibar," which showed in the Hippodrome in December 1941. Arguably one of the best films of the period was "The Great Dictator," Chaplin's serious comedy on the rise of Hitler. Before the war the censor did not permit any offence to be given to leaders of foreign governments, so popular films gave no real idea of what was happening politically on the Continent. Films dealt with the Depression, Prohibition, bootleggers, gangsters and juvenile delinquency, but, in general, avoided the rise of fascism.

With the outbreak of hostilities in 1939 official attitudes changed, and Belfast cinemas were soon showing films with titles like "Hitler, the Beast of Berlin," supported by the Three Stooges in "You Nazty Spy" (Royal Cinema), "Confessions of a Nazi Spy" with Ed.G.Robinson (Royal Cinema), "'Arf A Mo Hitler" (Imperial) which was advertised as "a topical feature of the mood of the moment," and "Professor Mamlock"(Royal Hippodrome). The News Letter critic was impressed by the effective style of the Edward G.Robinson film, which dealt with the exposure of a German spy ring in the U.S.A. He found it "semi documentary, but dramatic." He wasn't so enthusiastic about "Professor Mamlock" which was a Russian film, showing in conjunction with a reissue of "M," in an adults only programme. The News Letter critic described it as "a scathing Soviet exposure of Hitlerism, which was more interesting than entertaining." It was the first of a number of Russian films shown in the city during the war, with names like "One Day in Soviet Russia," and "Our Russian Allies. "As an ally Soviet Russia, its people and culture were officially much in favour, and the frontage of the Ritz was even decorated with three large, quite intimidating, posters of Churchill, Roosevelt and "Uncle Joe" Stalin.

Chaplin was still held in high regard in Belfast and his latest film "The Great Dictator" was awaited with impatience. It finally opened in both the Classic and the Picture House on 6th January 1941. In the neutral Free State the censor still applied the rule of not giving offence to heads of state, so the film was banned there. When Mr McDermott, the manager of the Classic, tried to put adverts in the Dublin papers for the film they were refused. Despite that, people were aware of the Belfast premiere, and some enthusiasts booked tickets and travelled even from Donegal to see it. The opening in two downtown cinemas was a rare recognition of the significance of Charles Chaplin as a film maker, and the importance of his film. Queues began forming on the first morning as early as 8:00 a.m. and during the day 7,500 people filed into the Classic to see it, breaking all previous records for a first day opening. Similar numbers filled the Picture House. The film engendered citywide excitement. The critics praised it as a "splendid comedy" though the News Letter felt - rightly one would have to agree - that it wasn't as good as "Shoulder Arms," or the "Gold Rush." Such comments, valid or otherwise, didn't prevent the crowds packing both cinemas all week.

Of equal appeal were the full length colour cartoons of Walt Disney, and Pinocchio, Bambi, Dumbo, Fantasia and others drew critical praise and popular support in equal measure from adults and children. Serious filmgoers also appreciated the output from Walt, and Disney shorts also appeared regularly in the programmes of the local Film Societies. The war years are not noted for their Westerns. A handful of entertaining Westerns did appear, notably Cecil B.deMille's "Union Pacific," (1939), "Dodge City"(d. Michael Curtiz, 1939) with Errol Flynn, and "The Return of the Cisco Kid" but most Westerns made were cheap B films, which were intended as supports for the main features. They were no less entertaining for that, and were widely approved of as suitable for young people. Bill Boyd righted wrongs as Hopalong Cassidy, while Charles Starrett could rein in behind a large rock and reappear, Superman like, as the masked Durango Kid, to deal with the villains. Gene Autry faded from the screens and was replaced by Roy Rogers who was, according to the posters for "Under Western Skies" outside the Royal Cinema in September 1939, "the screen's newest singing action star." Roy Rogers and his horse Trigger carried on where Gene Autry had left off, usually assisted by Smiley Burnett who supplied comedy, the Sons of the Pioneers with music and song and, later, by his wife, Dale Evans. Those and similar films became very popular with children at the Saturday morning film clubs in cinemas across the city.

One group who didn't benefit from the surge in cinema attendances was the minority societies for serious film goers and students. Both the Belfast Film Society and the Belfast Institute Film Society experienced increasing difficulties in securing venues, and suitable films for their shows. The increased demands on the city cinemas meant that halls, especially downtown venues, were no longer available for hire. The Institute Film Society, which announced a policy of showing films made in Allied countries, put on a number of such shows on Saturday afternoons in the Park Cinema on the Oldpark Road. Typical, in early January 1942, was "Janosik," part of a special Czech programme, shown at 2:45 pm. The main feature was supported by a Lotte Reiniger cartoon, and a George Pal short, "The Birth of a Robot." Besides the fee - paying members, the prices charged were visitors 2| 6, military officers 1| 10, other ranks 1|- The recurring question of a suitable location was finally answered by using the more centrally placed facilities of the Grosvenor Hall, and both societies held their meetings there throughout the remainder of the war years.

Another problem concerned the difficulties involved in getting suitable films of the quality demanded by the members of the societies. It became increasingly difficult to acquire Continental films, and more expensive to insure them for postage. The loss of a Continental film in the post was a serious matter because it was impossible to replace it. The Institute Society, with the resources of the British Film Institute behind it had an advantage over its rival and continued to source interesting quality films. Examples included Rene Clair's "Le Quatorze Juillet," ' Les Disparus de St Agil "which included Erich Von Stroheim in its cast," La Grande Illusion., ""Quai de Brume," with Jean Gabin, and a new Russian film called "The New Teacher." A fine documentary, Cavalcanti's "Film and Reality" dealt with the problem of depicting reality in films, and provoked much debate among the critics and the members. Those main features were supported by a mixture of shorts including Disney cartoons and nature documentaries (Disney was regarded as a true artist), Lotte Reiniger silhouette cartoons (always greatly appreciated) and such. To increase the size of audiences special reduced rates were offered to military personnel. The Belfast Film Society, in particular, experienced financial shortfalls. Their first show of the 1940-41 season registered a loss of £20, while the second lost £10, but after appeals in the local papers for more members, an improvement in attendances was recorded, and the Society was able to continue to produce its usual five or six programmes per season. As costs continued to rise it became obvious that the future lay in a merger between the two societies, which duly took place in 1945.

One of the reasons for the increase in cinema audiences during the war was the influx of military personnel into the region for training after September 1939. They were further augmented by the arrival of American G.I's or "doughboys" as they were called, beginning in early 1942. According to a local newspaper (News Letter) the new arrivals were warmly received, and quickly settled in though they complained about "the climate, the black-out, and the beds, which they found too hard." In turn the locals were intrigued by their "round hats" (helmets), and the fact that the army nurses wore trousers. The reporter noticed that one characteristic of the new arrivals was that they did enjoy having a good time. They were, he concluded, "party people." The need for entertainment was officially acknowledged from the beginning of the war when E.N.S.A. (Entertainments National Service Association) was established in Britain, with a local branch (N.I.E.N.S.A.) following here. Its aim was to organise and present stage shows, concerts and film shows for the military. Stage shows were put on in the Royal Hippodrome, the Grand Opera House, the

Ulster Hall, Wellington Hall, the Assembly Hall and elsewhere, in which local and outside professional and amateur talent performed. Jimmy O'Dea was a popular attraction in many N.I.E.N.S.A. shows in the early years of the war. George Formby, the most popular English performer of the time, came over in January 1942 to appear at the Royal Hippodrome in a show in aid of the Lord Mayor's Air Raid Distress Fund. He also toured the hospitals and military camps, and wherever he went was a great hit with his songs and skill on the ukulele. He also seemed to enjoy himself, and spoke warmly of Ireland, and its people. He recalled how he had trained as a jockey here and had ridden at the Curragh and the Maze. After the arrival of the Americans, E.N.S.A. co-operated with the American United Services and other organizations in bringing over big name American stars to entertain the troops.

A recurring complaint from local filmgoers over the years was the fact that so few Hollywood stars visited Belfast, despite coming to London. The war saw an end to that situation with an influx of screen stars, who came to entertain the soldiers. The first major Hollywood star to arrive was Robert Montgomery, though he didn't come as an entertainer. He was a naval attache in London and came on a visit to American technicians working in Derry. He took time to walk the historic walls and meet the press. He praised the Ulster scenery and insisted that he preferred his present job to working in Hollywood, though whether anyone believed that, is not recorded. In mid - September 1942 the first large group of stars arrived, and appeared in a show in the Royal Hippodrome for British and American servicemen. The group included Al Jolson, Merle Oberon, Frank McHugh and Allen Jenkins. Jolson, the main attraction, sang on stage for about three quarters of an hour. A large crowd collected outside the Hippodrome, but civilians were not admitted. That was the pattern that was followed over the next few years - the shows were for military personnel only. The stars then spent the next few days visiting hospitals and military camps across the province. In November a second group arrived which included Kay Francis, Martha Raye and Carol Landis. Martha Raye met the press and explained that her father had emigrated to the U.S.A. from Drogheda, while her mother's parents were both Irish. She regarded herself as Irish, and her real name was Margie Reed. It was, she claimed, "just swell" to be here. Other recorded visitors were the actresses Ann Dvorak and popular Bebe Daniels, plus the singer Stubby Kaye. Many others came quietly, without any mention in the press, notably Bing Crosby and Bob Hope, who entertained the troops at Langford Lodge. In August 1944 Glenn Miller and his Band flew in and played to large crowds in the American Red Cross Club (the Plaza Ballroom), and at Langford Lodge. The soldiers forgot their worries as they responded enthusiastically to the personal appearances, the glamour, the music and the humour.

As early as October 1939 the Home Office in London was considering the contentious issue of opening cinemas on Sundays as an added means of recreation for military personnel. There was opposition from the Lord's Day Observance Society in England, who argued that nothing should be done to undermine the sacredness of the Sabbath. Despite the war, cinemas and theatres should be kept closed, as the law demanded. They specifically complained about how the law was already being subverted increasingly by the number of so-called Sunday charity performances involving films and live acts, which they described as a "war-time racket." There were many in Belfast who agreed with that interpretation.

The Archbishop of Canterbury also expressed disapproval that such a move would take away from the special religious and family atmosphere of Sunday. The Home Office was in favour of opening cinemas (but not theatres) on Sunday, though it recognised that the final decision on such a matter lay with the local authorities. Many of the latter responded positively, and in a short time nearly every major city in Britain allowed the opening of at least one cinema on Sundays for military personnel. One local paper declared that Belfast was the only big city in the U.K. where the cinemas remained closed on Sundays, while the Irish News commented that any attempt to change that situation would come up against local "Sabbatarian rigidity."

The truth or otherwise of that prediction was tested seven months later, in May 1940, when Major-General Huddleston, the commander of troops in N.Ireland wrote to the Police Committee asking that one cinema be opened in Belfast on Sundays for troops in uniform. He pointed that there were few if any entertainments available in the city on Sundays for the soldiers, most of whom were far from home and friends. Cinemas were somewhere warm and comfortable where they could relax, unwind, and enjoy a film for a few hours. On the surface the problem seemed to be a simple one. The City Council was being asked to relax the legal ban in the light of the wartime emergency, as other cities had done. The response in Belfast was anything but simple, and the Sunday opening of cinemas became one of the "most controversial topics" (News Letter) that the city had experienced in many years. It became a conduit for the expression of deep - rooted religious, political and social prejudices. Everyone, the News Letter reporter wrote, seemed to have an opinion on the subject, and were determined to be heard. Not everyone, however...

The Nationalists, mainly Catholic, regarded the whole matter with a certain amount of cynicism, and detached humour. They regarded Sunday as a special holy day, but, after attending Mass, they could spend the rest of the day relaxing. In Nationalist areas in Belfast on Sundays, the parks were full and people enjoyed football and hurling and other pursuits. Only the swings and such in the children's areas were chained up, as they were across the city. While Catholics were often warned from the pulpits against "dangerous" company keeping, and the obligation to avoid certain "objectional" films, there was no general admonition against attending a dance or a cinema on Sunday. In Nationalist rural areas some halls, including cinemas, had special permission in the form of seven day licences to open on Sundays, but the cinemas along the Falls Road remained closed and locked like the rest of the city. In Belfast, Nationalists also knew that their opinions would count for little when the Council finally made its decision.

The Police Committee duly met under its chairman Councillor George Gray (who incidentally was also the Hon. Treasurer of the White Cinema Club) to consider the request for the Sunday opening of one cinema for the soldiers, but didn't come to any conclusion. The whole Council would have to be involved in the discussions. When it became known that the Council was going to discuss the matter at its monthly meeting on 2nd May, and make a decision, those opposed - mainly the Protestant Churches, the loyal Orders, the Evangelical groups and their associated societies - girded themselves for battle. They fell back on the traditional methods of protest used so successfully in past censorship disputes, a combination of public meetings, behind the scenes pressures, pulpit statements, and letters to the local press. The public meetings were to remind the people about the nature of the problem as they saw it. The main theme was to protect the sacredness and special social nature of the Sabbath, as required by Biblical teaching and tradition. They argued that there was no demand from the soldiers for Sunday films, and that rest and recreation were already available in the many Protestant halls in the city.

Some speakers perceived the problem in wider, more sinister, terms. The Rev. Dr. T.M.Johnstone, speaking in Newington Church, repeated the claim that there was no need to open cinemas on Sunday because there was no demand for it among the soldiers. From his experience many of the soldiers were devout young men, and it was wrong to suggest that all they wanted was cheap beer and secular entertainment. They needed the support of the Church, not the cinema. The arguments of the "Sunday cinema openers," he continued, were part of a plot by "traitor Quislings who would open the gates to the enemy. "The Independent Loyal Orange Institution also insisted that the agitation wasn't caused by the forces but emanated from those "who would seek to pervert our Protestant Faith and heritage." The Ulster Protestant League maintained that Sunday opening was part of "an insidious campaign of falsehood" spread by enemies of the Empire, including "the disloyal minority in N.Ireland." Rev. Dr. Little, Unionist M.P. for Down, saw Sunday opening as part of a general decline in morality which had gained momentum since the beginning of the war. He had raised the matter at Westminster, asking that something be done to curtail the increased nudity in London club acts, and the "bottle parties" which were so popular. His strictures, however, had amused rather than alarmed the other members in the Commons. He insisted that soldiers would prefer to have a cup of tea in a church hall on Sundays rather than attending a cinema.

Not every churchgoer accepted those extreme views. Individual voices were raised in opposition, notably that of the Dean of Belfast, the very Rev. W.S.Kerr. That eminent and respected Church of Ireland cleric explained that while he was against Sunday opening of cinemas in principle, he thought an exception should be made in the present circumstances. A supporter called his statement "a breath of fresh air in a foggy atmosphere," but the Dean was much criticised by the Orange Order, and Evangelical spokesmen. A representative of the Society of Religious Liberty League, writing from an address on the Ravenhill Road, called on the people to awaken to the fact that their personal liberty was being threatened. He claimed that the strictures against Sunday opening could be traced legally to the Sunday Observance Act of 1781, a "musty old law" that was completely out of date. Today, he claimed, people should be free to keep Sunday "as a holy day or a holiday," as they saw fit. In support another letter writer asserted that the local Sunday closures of theatres, cinemas, restaurants, public houses, bookies, and even the museum were acts "engineered by the same class of Puritanical tyrants." They should, he suggested, be "relegated to obscurity." It is interesting that arguments for and against extending Sunday trading still continue along similar lines today,

War conditions; to close or not to close.

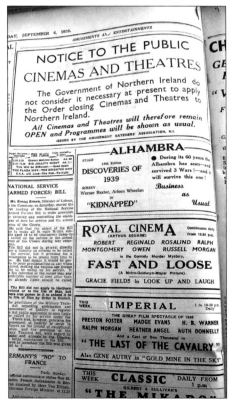

with the added spice of economic and social factors. Actually a social aspect did emerge obliquely in the Forties, when those opposed argued that it would be unfair to ask workers to work on Sundays when most others were off. A minority would be penalised for the entertainment of the majority.

The White Cinema Club discussed the matter and issued a statement saying that Sunday opening of cinemas was a matter for the military, and the Belfast Corporation. The cinema trade would accept whatever ruling was agreed upon. Later they added that if Sunday opening was allowed, no-one would be asked to work on that day who objected on religious or other grounds, nor would any worker lose their normal free days. A similar promise was made more recently with regard to the Sunday opening of shops and supermarkets, but there have been complaints that pressures can be applied to non co-operative workers to make them reconsider their positions.

A writer in Random Jottings (Irish News) complained in late 1939 that since the beginning of the war the debates in the City Council had lost a lot of their liveliness. That couldn't be said about the debate on the Sunday opening of cinemas which took place on Monday 3rd June 1940. The chamber was crowded, especially by a large, intimidating deputation of about 300 representatives from the Orange Order, the Independent Orange Order, the Presbyterian Church, the Church of Ireland,the Methodists, the Baptists, the Congregational Church, the Salvation Army, the Society of Friends, the Belfast City Mission, and the Belfast Sunday Observance Vigilance Committee. The deputation was formally introduced by Rev W.B.McMurray, the Moderator of the Belfast Presbytery, who described the proposal to open a cinema on Sundays as "deplorable." That set the tone for the spokesmen of the deputation, Sir Joseph Davidson, the Grand Master of the Orange Institution and Rev Dr James Little, MP for Down, who reiterated the arguments against opening mentioned above. The members of the deputation were unruly at times, interrupting the proceedings with cheers and shouts, much to the annoyance of many councillors and the Lord Mayor, who had to struggle to keep order. He reminded them that they were a deputation, and not a demonstration. When their submissions were completed they filed out, some of them singing "Rock of Ages." According to the Irish News reporter the din was so great that Council business was at a standstill for about ten minutes.

The discussion that followed in the Chamber was noisy and acrimonious, with caustic exchanges. Councillor Henderson growled, as he often did, that the churchmen didn't show the same enthusiastic support for the starving poor of the city as they did for closing the cinemas, while Mr Harry Midgley deplored, as he often did, the heated atmosphere that negated logical discussion. The views of the Sabbatarians carried the day and by 29 votes to 14 the corporation decided that the cinemas should stay closed on Sundays. In its editorial comment the Irish News regretted the decision. The editor argued that the request that one cinema should be opened to soldiers in uniform seemed quite "moderate." He emphasised that no-one wished to decry the observance of the Sabbath, but a Puritanical stance against entertainment could be carried too far. He felt that the opening of one cinema in the city would not put the holiness of the Sabbath at risk. It would give the young men a warm, comfortable place where they could rest, relax and have a smoke. It would give them an alternative to aimlessly wandering the wet streets. With regard to the argument that people would be working on what was traditionally a holiday, the editor claimed that only a minority of employees would be affected, and that the impact on them could be reduced by rotating which cinema should open. He summed up by saying that overall the City Council "had not acted sensibly."

That 1940 vote did not solve or settle the matter. Behind the scenes the Government in London still emphasised its support for Sunday opening. In the House of Commons Herbert Morrison, the Home Secretary, declared that he favoured keeping the cinemas open as long as possible. In today's jargon they were regarded as a national "resource" which boosted civilian and military morale. The local army commander in N.Ireland also favoured Sunday opening, and many ordinary citizens supported him. One letter writer who signed herself "a soldier's mother" praised the cinemas for their atmosphere of rest and recreation, but also because "they kept the troops out of mischief." She was referring, discreetly, to the worries being expressed officially about the increase in the incidence of V.D. since the outbreak of war. Such worries had played a part in persuading the Council to permit the showing of a number of sex-hygiene films on the subject in the Grosvenor Hall, as discussed earlier. Finally, a group of influential persons in the local film trade were sympathetic to the army commander's wishes, and were willing to co-operate with any scheme to open some cinemas on Sundays. They included G.L.Birch (owner of the Royal Hippodrome), G.Lodge (owner of the Imperial), Raymond Stross (owner of the New Kelvin), and the proprietors of the Ritz.

The problem emerged into the open again in 1942, with the arrival of the first American fighting troops, and battle positions were resumed for another round. The Protestant Churches and the Orange Order again united in opposition, and promised another large deputation at the Council meeting which would discuss the matter. The usual suspects were trotted out. There was no real demand among the soldiers for the opening of cinemas on Sunday. Over the last few years Protestant organizations like the Salvation Army, and the Churches had taken steps to supply, on Sunday evenings, musical shows with communal singing, and free non - alcoholic refreshments for those who wished to attend. The Wellington Hall, Assembly Hall, Y.M.C.A. and others presented more lavish family type productions. The traditional Sunday must be defended from spreading secularism, and the opening of the cinemas was a step too far in that direction. Rumours spread again that the opening of the cinemas was part of a plot by the enemies of N.Ireland, while it was even suggested that the White Cinema Club was behind it. Moderate voices, like those of the Dean of Belfast, who called for less legalism and more Christian understanding were criticised or ignored. In contrast large crowds attended the Grosvenor Hall to listen to the Rev. Alfred Binks who came over from London to warn about the dangers of opening cinemas on Sundays. He claimed that in London, where he had laboured for the last 20 years, he had seen two generations of young people growing up without experiencing the traditional Sunday. They knew little or nothing about religion. Most never entered a church on Sunday, but many of them could be found in the queues waiting outside the cinemas on Sunday evenings.

Those in favour of opening ridiculed the extremes of Sabbatarianism and emphasised the fact that cinemas were open in most British cities on Sundays for the soldiers, even in Scotland "the stronghold of the Presbyterian Sabbath." They highlighted the plight of the soldiers, tired from strenuous training, who came to Belfast on Sunday for recreation. What they found was "a grim place" (Councillor S.B.Thompson) with most recreational facilities closed to the general public. Councillor Henderson, the outspoken representative of the Shankill area, described seeing groups of British and American soldiers sheltering in doorways on wet evenings, with nowhere to go. He had been an opponent of Sunday opening, but scenes like that had caused him to change his mind. The efforts of the churches to supply entertainment was appreciated but it only coped with the surface of the problem. The army's position was clarified in February 1942 when members of the Cinematograph Exhibitor's Association of Gt. Britain and Ireland arrived in Belfast for a two day conference, during which the local branch of the Association, which had been formed two months before, would be officially inaugurated. The high powered delegation was led by the National President Col. Lewis, accompanied by influential figures in the film trade, and one suspects that the decision to come to Belfast at that time was more than just coincidence. The meeting gave undeclared but, nevertheless, strong support to the Sunday openers.

The conference was held in the opulent surroundings of the Ritz Cinema and involved an inaugural lunch in the cinema restaurant, combined with the discussion of official business, and various social activities. The latter included visits to the City Hall and Stormont, plus a pleasant evening at the annual Cinema Ball arranged by the White Cinema Club in the Floral Hall. At those events the members of the Association were made welcome, and the contribution of the cinema industry to the social and economic life of the area was duly praised. The meal was the highlight of the conference, and special guests included the Lord Mayor, the G.O.C. N. Ireland Lieut - General Franklyn, the chiefs of the three services and prominent members of the cinema trade. Col Lewis revealed that negotiations were ongoing for the earlier release of Hollywood films. At the moment there was a time - lag of up to eighteen months, but the Association wanted that reduced to facilitate the incoming American troops. One of their main objects in coming to Belfast, he explained, was to extend the arrangement made by the Association with the War Office to show training films to the Army, Home Guard and Civil Defence on Sundays. Sunday was chosen because it was the only day that the personnel involved were free from work. The government in London was anxious to make maximum use of the facilities available in the cinemas, and had asked the exhibitors to co-operate. The showings would include only official training films, and there would be no entertainment films. Civilians would not be admitted. The shows would be free of charge, so no special licence would be needed. He assured people that this "was not the thin edge of the wedge" where Sunday films were concerned.

The local G.O.C. continued with that theme. The shows would not include entertainment films, because as he put it, "Greta Garbo and tommy-guns do not go well together." He fully recognised the benefits of entertainment films. and he praised the vital role the cinema played in the war effort, how it boosted morale, and supplied rest and recreation. The soldier, he claimed, whose leisure time was filled with pleasant entertainment was "much more teachable next day." In that way, he explained to laughter, glamour girls played their part in maintaining army efficiency. Other speakers supported those views, and the wishes of the Home Secretary, Herbert Morrison, that maximum use be made of the cinemas was emphasised. While such comments were claimed not to be the thin edge of any wedge, they certainly encouraged and gave support to those who favoured showing films on Sunday. The scales were partly rebalanced by an editorial in the News Letter (9th March 1942) which declared that "we range ourselves unreservedly with the opponents of any proposal to open cinema theatres to the general public on Sundays. The moral sense of the community as a whole is against it." The editor didn't say that cinemas should stay closed regardless, but suggested that either the G.O.C. could use the special powers he had to requisition a cinema for Sunday films; or, if the general was reluctant to do so, the Council could produce some compromise that would allow one cinema to open, for uniformed personnel only.

The debate on the matter took place on 9th March, and both sides entered the Council Chamber feeling confident about the outcome. The arguments followed the lines laid down over the previous two years. The pros and cons of opening the cinemas were exchanged across the chamber, interspersed with bouts of sarcasm and insults. But there were signs of movement, with a small number of councillors declaring that they had changed their minds after seeing soldiers on Sundays sheltering from inclement weather in doorways and such, with nowhere to go for entertainment. There had been fears expressed among the anti - openers that the main danger to their cause was from a number of councillors who were threatening to change their vote. One of those was unionist Tommy Henderson who complained that pressures were being put on such councillors behind the scenes. His comments shine a light on the murky world of City Hall politics. He had been told - he asserted - that if he didn't vote against opening he would not be supported by the party machine in any future election. He loudly condemned that kind of coercion, and declared he would not accept such behaviour. In the end the Council voted by 22 to 17 to take no action on the matter, which meant that the cinemas stayed closed on Sundays, though they agreed that there would be no objection to the showing of training films to members of the Civil Defence. The Chairman of the Sabbath Observance Vigilance Committee publicly noted that they were "deeply grateful to the members of the Council who remained staunch and true to their convictions not to open cinemas on this sacred day." That stance was backed up with a series of city wide protests by the churches and their supporters on Sunday 15 March. Anti - openers packed six venues at the North Belfast Mission, St Enoch's Presbyterian Church, the Antrim Road Baptist Church, the Shankill Road Mission Hall, the Cooke Centenary Church on the Ormeau Road, and St Aidan's Parish Church on the Donegal Road. Clergy of all Protestant denominations sat with members of the Council on the various platforms and condemned any attempt to open cinemas on Sundays. Feelings and emotions ran high and were matched by strong words. One speaker avowed that "the opening of cinemas would only be achieved over our dead bodies."

The Council decision had reverberations outside Belfast. Questions were asked in the Commons about the continued closure of the cinemas on Sunday but the official reply was that it was a matter for the local authority. However it was pointed out that the G.O.C. had the right to use certain defence regulations at his discretion to have cinemas opened for troops on Sundays if he so decided. And that was what happened in Belfast, where it was well known that Lieu. Gen. Franklyn favoured Sunday opening, under strict conditions. When the Council refused to make a decision, the army moved to requisition a cinema.

In late March, G.L.Birch received a letter from the G.O.C. authorising him, at the order of the War Office, to open the Royal Hippodrome on Sundays for members of the Forces. Mr Birch was only too willing and arranged an ENSA stage show for Sunday evening, the 29th March. Military Police were on duty in the foyer, and in the auditorium, to ensure that only military personnel were admitted. The hall was crowded and large numbers had to be turned away. The G.O.C. regarded the evening as a great success, but those who opposed Sunday opening protested loudly. Dr Little M.P. asked, in the Commons, how the military could take such action when the Council had refused to allow the opening of cinemas on Sundays even for E.N.S.A. concerts. In reply Sir James Grigg explained that the decision of Belfast Council referred to the opening of cinemas to the general public, but that the G.O.C. had used a section of the Army Act to provide entertainment for members of the military only. He also added rather tartly that he didn't consider wholesome amusement inconsistent with the worship of God, or the defeat of the country's enemies.

Back in Belfast the Royal Hippodrome prepared for the second Sunday concert, but not everything went to plan. On the Saturday evening, after the audience had left, the hall and stage were being prepared before being handed over to the army. At about 10:35 there was a small explosion in a seat in the gallery followed by a puff of smoke, and flames. The chief operator, T. McAllister, acted quickly and extinguished the fire. Over the following few hours another three fire bombs ignited in the gallery and the stalls. In each case a seat had been slashed and a rather unsophisticated device inserted. A search by the police found another four before they ignited. Damage was very slight, and the Sunday concert went ahead as planned. The bombs were seen by many as the work of the "enemies of Ulster," but the police had suspicions that they might had been planted by extreme opponents of Sunday opening. The culprits were never found or named. The Sunday concerts continued, uninterrupted, through April and May, attracting large crowds. The final free concert took place on Sunday 31st May, presenting "three and a half hours of variety" which included music, song, dance (the Hippodrome Girls) and speciality acts. The main attraction was Jimmy Campbell with the Theatre Royal Orchestra from Dublin, which was on stage for 45 minutes. In the elaborate advert for the show, Mr Birch included the statement that over 25,000 members of the Forces had come to be entertained at the free concerts in the Royal Hippodrome over the preceding two months. He believed that that level of support proved "that there was room in Belfast for Sunday opening for troops." His final words were, "Now it is up to you..."

In June an influential and high profile group from the cinema trade arrived from Britain at the invitation of the local branch of the Cinematograph Exhibitors Association It included, among others, the presidents of the Kinematograph Renters Society, and the C E A, with the managing editor of the trade newspaper, the Daily Film Renter. At a special lunch in the Grand Central Hotel they announced that the details had been agreed for showing training films on Sundays to the Forces, and the Civil Defence, on the same terms as applied in England. The distribution of new films had also been speeded up, but only directly to American troops here. Discussions were under way to extend this availability to the commercial cinemas. The public were assured that there was no shortage of new films available. Finally, special mention was made of the work being done by George Lodge, the owner of the Imperial, as a member of the War Office Committee. Mr Lodge advised the N. Ireland government on all aspects of the local film industry, including the matter of showing films on Sundays, and his opinions were much valued. The contribution of the cinema to the war effort was widely recognised, and, in June 1945, at the end of the War, the Prime Minister, Sir Basil Brook, referred to the "splendid co-operation" which the Government had received from the local industry, especially from George Lodge.

The supporters of the traditional Sunday did not give up. When the manager of the Ritz requested permission from the Council to put on a film show in aid of the RAF Benevolent Fund on a Sunday afternoon, the request was refused, even though the event was for charity, and the timing was carefully chosen not to clash with religious services One councillor commented that the cinema owners could just as easily make a donation without desecrating the Sabbath. As pressure built up behind the scenes Sunday films soon did became available. By September, Sunday evening film shows, for military personnel only, were a weekly event in the Imperial and the New Kelvin. The cinemas were under army control during those shows, and patrons had to produce evidence that they were members of the Forces. Local youths joined the Cadets or similar organizations to acquire a uniform, and thereby, hopefully, the right of entry to a cinema on Sunday. Others were tempted to gain entrance by other means. One man from Conway Street accompanied his cousin, who was a soldier, to a Sunday cinema. The cousin went in, but slipped his paybook to his companion. When the latter presented it at the box-office, a Military Policeman noticed that the photograph wasn't an exact likeness, and questioned the man, who made a run for it. He was apprehended, and the whole story came out. A slide was projected on to the cinema screen asking the cousin to come to the foyer, where he was arrested by the MPs. The other man was handed over to the civilian police. When he appeared in court., the magistrate, wisely, commented that his offence was not a serious one, but "the law has to be upheld." He imposed a fine of 2/ 6.

The opening of a few cinemas on Sunday in 1942 was a wartime measure which was supposed to end with the return of peace and normal conditions. By 1945 a more relaxed attitude had grown up with regard to Sunday entertainment in general, and the Police Committee decided to flex its legal muscles. It warned hall owners that many Sunday stage entertainments were illegal, and that the Committee intended to put an end to them. As a result of that threat many Sunday entertainments in parochial halls were immediately cancelled. But the Committee was anxious to make an example of one, and soon had a golden opportunity. In mid January an appalling train crash took place in Belfast, as a result of which 18 people were killed and many others injured. The Mayor of Bangor set up the Bangor Relief Fund to aid the families of those involved. Mr G. Birch the owner of the Royal Hippodrome decided, at short notice, to put on a charity stage show for the fund. He chose Sunday evening, January 21st, and the event proved to be a great success. Despite the choice of Sunday, so large were the crowds that turned up that the police were needed to control them. Financially the event did well, and Mr Birch added a personal cheque of 100 guineas to the kitty. In his haste to arrange the event he neglected to inform the police, or give the necessary month's warning to the Police Committee. The Police Committee met to discuss his actions, and agreed that Mr Birch had broken the law with regard to Sunday entertainments, and breached the conditions of his licence. They recommended that the

Corporation should prosecute him.

The matter was, in time, discussed by the whole Council, and the responses of the members varied. Some sympathised with Mr Birch's aims and were willing to overlook his legal omissions. They were partly influenced by a letter of explanation and apology from Mr Birch, in which he explained that he hadn't the time to inform the Police Committee because many of the acts, all of whom gave their services free, were leaving Belfast the following morning. He claimed that, in principle, he was not in favour of Sunday entertainments but was so moved by the tragedy, that he wanted to do something to help. That did not placate some members who felt that the law should take its course. That group included Councillor E.Thompson, who insisted that the people he represented from the Shankill Road were opposed to the opening of places of entertainment on Sundays "especially on the hypocritical plea of charity." He was supported by Councillor Lavery who found Mr Birch's actions quite provocative. He also claimed, with bizarre logic, that the Royal Hippodrome had become "a rendezvous for the Communist Party." In the end it was decided to refer the matter back to the Police Committee for their further consideration. The latter discussed the matter again, and then repeated their recommendation in favour of prosecution. The Council decided to accept Mr Birch's explanation, and his letter of apology, so the matter was dropped.

While the matter of Mr Birch's licence was being debated the whole matter of Sunday entertainments took another turn, one with decided sectarian undertones. In the Catholic areas of Belfast local parochial halls usually presented Sunday evening entertainments, most prominently in St Mary's Hall in Bank Street, and the Holy Cross Hall at Ardoyne. St Mary's Hall had been putting such stage shows on over the previous 60 years, while Holy Cross had done likewise for 25 years, without giving offence or causing complaints from citizens, or the police. The recent pronouncement from the Police Committee suggested that those shows were illegal and must stop. St Mary's and Holy Cross therefore applied for seven day licences to safeguard their legality, and as a test case for other Catholic halls. The Catholics had kept out of the disputes over Sunday cinemas, but when the arguments used to keep the cinemas closed were extended to all Sunday stage entertainments, one began to detect a growing resentment over the behaviour and attitudes of certain Sabbatarian and Protestant groups. A letter to the Irish News (January 45) reflected that change. Ironically signed "Not An Inch," the writer claimed "it is time the Catholics of Belfast asserted themselves," and made it clear that those Protestant groups had "no right to dictate as to how Catholics should spend their Sunday evenings." Those groups claimed to represent the feelings of the Protestant population, but in the light of the large numbers who assembled to see Mr Birch's charity show, he doubted that. He called on the Catholics of Belfast to make their voices heard.

The Police Committee discussed the matter on the 29th March, and the Catholics sent a deputation of eminent laymen, women, and clerics to present their case. They found themselves facing a similar deputation from the Sunday Observance Vigilance Committee, various Protestant ministers, a number of Protestant organizations and the Orange Order. The Catholics argued that their shows took place in the evening after Evening Devotions, and did not interfere with religious services, and that they presented "clean and wholesome entertainment." They attracted large crowds, and played an important part in keeping young people off the streets at night. But, above all, they were not commercial enterprises. All profits went to charity, to parish organizations, and to the financial upkeep of Catholic schools. Fr. Mullally, the bishop's secretary, emphasised the positive social and economic aspects of the concerts and complained that "a handful of intolerant tyrants" whom he likened to the Pharisees, were attempting to deprive the people of those innocent pleasures. Their attempts to end the Catholic entertainments were an "insolent attack on our liberty of conscience,"he concluded.

Those in the opposing deputation rejected such accusations, and were notably riled by the comparison with the Pharisees. They argued that their main aim was the protection of the sacredness of the Sabbath. A spokesman for the Orange Order agreed, but went further, claiming that the crux of the matter was "the maintenance of their Christian civilisation," which, he believed, was menaced by secularisation. Mr Porter of the Protestant Action Society detected a more sinister political side to the Catholic request. He declared that "this is a Protestant country, governed by Protestant people... and they (the Catholics) are trying to sabotage the Protestant community so that they may ultimately have ruling power."

After listening to the arguments, the Police Committee retired to a room nearby, to consider their decision. Fifteen minutes later they emerged and announced that the application had been rejected by 9 votes to 3. The Sabbatarians and their supporters were pleased. The Irish News, in an editorial next day, summed up the Catholic reaction when it described the decision as "an impudent attack on Catholic rights and liberties." Unlike the topic of Sunday cinemas, the ban on Sunday entertainments was not just a question of protecting the sanctity of the Sabbath. It also had important social and economic implications in that it deprived Catholic charities and parishes of much needed, even vital, income. Catholics perceived it as an attack on their communities. The decision was therefore appealed, and the case was heard by the Belfast Recorder, Judge Fox, at the end of June. After considering the arguments, for and against, the judge gave permission for the Catholic halls to hold Sunday entertainments, excluding boxing, between 8:00 and 11:00 pm. He recognised the "deep and sincere convictions" of those opposed to Sunday entertainments but pointed out that there was nothing in the Local Government Act (NI), 1934 which prohibited the granting of a licence for public entertainment on Sunday. Also the entertainments in question were for charity, and gave no offence to non Catholics. The Sunday Observance Committee were unhappy with the decision, and with the law that permitted it. At a meeting organised by the Protestant Truth Society in the Wellington Hall the following day, Councillor Wilton, a well known opponent of Sunday entertainments, deplored the decision and insisted that "in a Protestant community like ours, the law should be amended so that we get what we want." There was nothing now, he continued, to prevent local cinemas and theatres from applying for 7 day licences. He felt that "Protestants must make a stand," or their Sabbath Day - horror of horrors - would soon become a Continental Sunday.

In the meantime momentous events had occurred that temporarily overwhelmed local affairs. The conflict in Europe ended on Tuesday 8th May with Germany's unconditional surrender, and the Irish News editor announced that "the long nightmare of war" was ended. As rumours spread on Monday evening, celebrating crowds began to converge on the city centre. Despite the fact that restrictions against the showing of lights were still in force, the City Hall was floodlit that night, some shop windows were lit up, and for the first time in nearly six years a number of downtown cinemas switched on their flashing neon lights. Bonfires glowed in many areas, and everywhere singing and dancing crowds collected to show their relief. Celebrations continued next day and large crowds collected around the City Hall to hear special victory radio broadcasts by King George, and Mr Churchill. The Churches, Protestant and Catholic, called on the people to attend specially arranged services, and masses of thanksgiving.

The cinemas, which had done so much to brighten the dark war years, were part of the general celebrations, and joined in the chorus of thanks to the fighting personnel. Over a combined advertisement for the Ritz, Majestic and Strand a statement from Associated British Cinemas congratulated the Allied forces on their great victory and those "who did the job so gallantly. "During that week the Royal Hippodrome was showing Korda's magical "The Thief of Baghdad" which had begun filming in England before the production was transferred to Hollywood for completion, because of the war. Now it had returned in the full glory of Technicolor. The Classic was, fittingly, screening "A Song to Remember"(d. Charles Vidor, 1945), with Cornel Wilde as Chopin, espousing Polish freedom while dying at the piano, his drops of red blood contrasting dramatically with the white keyboard, and reducing many a young girl to tears. Hollywood at its melodramatic best! Many years later a sensible and mature woman recalled that moment for the author, and described it as one of the most traumatic of her young life. In contrast the New Kelvin dispensed humour with "Old Mother Riley, Detective." The Imperial was showing "The Story of Dr Wassell" (d. Cecil B. deMille, 1944), a war film, which reminded local audiences that the struggle against Japan was still continuing in the Pacific.

A few months later, the CEA held a meeting in Belfast to discuss the future of the cinema trade. The national president (Mr Scarborough) presided, and at a luncheon in the Grand Central Hotel the guests included the Lord Mayor, the Governor of N.Ireland and the Premier, Sir Basil Brooke. The struggles over Sunday films were forgotten for the moment. The president emphasised that the CEA was not a political organization, but he admired the contribution of the local cinema industry to the war effort. There was praise for the amount of money raised for military charities, and for the fine entertainment presented week after week. The Premier took up that theme, expressing his thanks for the way the cinemas had boosted morale, and allowed the use of their halls and screens for education, and the disseminate of information to the public. The government, he said, had always received the full co-operation of the trade during the war. The representatives then settled down to discuss the future of the industry which, at that time, looked quite bright.

CHAPTER TWENTY EIGHT
Is This Belfast?

The return of peace brought widespread relief, and the hope of better times. When news of the ending of hostilities reached Stormont all business was suspended, and the Prime Minister, Sir Basil Brooke, expressed relief that "the horror, misery and death" were behind them, adding that he hoped that "a new era" lay ahead. The Irish News, in contrast, pointed out that large sections of Europe lay "bleeding and broken," and that many countries faced a titanic struggle to recover from the "wholesale devastation" that the war had visited upon them. Britain itself faced economic ruin. In such conditions, the paper warned, it was useless to portray a rosy future that may be nothing but a mirage, and fatal to confuse airy dreams with stark realities. Audiences in local cinemas watched, in shocked silence, newsreels of some of those "stark realities." They saw scenes of urban devastation, of vast areas covered with the remains of bombed - out buildings, of roads and streets fringed with piles of rubble, of shocked half - starving people scrabbling for whatever they could eat or use to survive. Worst of all were the terrible scenes filmed in the concentration camps.

While conditions at home were not as awful as the scenes presented on the cinema screens, the daily struggle for existence was depressing and bleak. Day to day living was still dominated by shortages of food, materials and power, while the rationing of essentials like foodstuffs, clothing, petrol, and even sweets, elevated ration books and coupons to the status of currency. In 1945 a Dubliner who had often enjoyed visiting Belfast before the war wrote in the Irish News about the changes he saw in the public face of the post-war city. The city, he wrote, bore the evidence of wartime shortages and pressures. The cityscape was pitted with ugly bomb sites, buildings showed signs of neglect. There was a lack of good houses and especially in working class areas the housing stock was inadequate, rundown and overcrowded. Shops were poorly stocked, with no evidence of luxuries of any kind. Their facades were worn, most needed painting, and their displays were equally dull and uninspiring. A greyness permeated everything. The people looked worried and seemed to have forgotten how to appear in their Sunday best. Even the young women had adopted the wartime dress code of shapeless slacks and headscarves, removing any signs of feminine colour from the pavements. There seemed to be no real sense of enjoyment. Sundays were especially dull with theatres, most cinemas, all public houses, the museum and art gallery, children's playcentres closed under the stern watchful eyes of the Sunday Observance Vigilance Committee. There was much talk about the future and what it would bring. Thinking people felt that a new era was coming, but the writer wondered if Belfast was prepared for it. He had a point, because ten years later the Telegraph, in an editorial calling for a planned future, could still describe Belfast as "an ugly city" dominated by shipyards, drab textile mills, areas of slums and blitzed spaces

A Whig reporter who was present at the New Year celebrations around the Albert Clock in January 1947, reflected the Dubliner's mood. He found the whole affair very low key, with a smaller crowd present than usual. A few bottles were, by tradition, thrown at the clock, accompanied by some singing, but the people obviously had no enthusiasm for merrymaking, and they soon headed off home. If the beginning of the year was cheerless, things went from bad to worse as the months passed. Even the weather turned unpleasant and, beginning in February, the Br. Isles experienced one of the worst winters on record. Blizzards and bitter temperatures cut off many rural areas for days, closed factories, and, above all, disrupted rail and road communications. Rail transport was especially badly hit

Odd Man Out: Children chosen to act in the film. Source: Irish News.

in England, and coal, a vital resource, piled up at the recently nationalised mines, as the railway system struggled to cope with the problems of distributing it. Even passenger trains were taken out of service and used to move the coal.

The main problem locally was the dwindling stocks of coal at the power stations and gasworks. In response the Stormont government introduced cuts in the use of domestic electricity from late February. Power could only be used in residential areas between 9:00 am and 11:00 am in the morning, and between 2:00pm and 5:00 pm in the afternoon. No power could be used in places of entertainment between midnight and 4:00 pm, and the general ban on exterior electrical displays remained in force. Official discussions took place with representatives of the cinema industry about the situation, and the cinema owners agreed not to open before 4:00pm, and to close before 11:00 pm, with the exception of Saturdays, when they would operate normally. Notices in the papers informed patrons of the closures, and apologised to parents because the Junior Cinema Clubs on Saturday mornings would be cancelled. The manager of the Classic announced that a special trade showing of "Odd Man Out" arranged for the following Friday morning had been cancelled. Another notice pointed out that many cinemas - especially those owned by Irish Theatres Ltd. - generated their own power and that those would function as normal. They included the Alhambra, the New Princess, the Stadium, the Forum, and the Windsor.

On the economic front the country was finding it difficult to pay for its imports. The government in London therefore, in August, introduced a super austerity plan which, according to the Irish News, represented the return of war-time conditions. Food rationing was tightened up, even with essentials. Citizens, for example, were allowed only two ounces of tea per week. Foreign holidays were forbidden in an attempt to save foreign currency, though that veto affected very few in Belfast. Businessmen, however, were permitted to travel abroad, but only on vital business, and on such excursions were limited to an allowance of £8 a day for their upkeep. Petrol rationing was strictly enforced, and all pleasure driving in cars was forbidden.

During those crises the cinema industry continued to flourish, and the two decades following 1945 were years of packed houses. A visit to the cinema was still a cheap, comfortable and satisfactory escape from the realities of post-war life. But cinema going wasn't just a form of social relaxation, it was also a habit. Most cinemagoers went regularly, once or twice a week, often regardless of what was showing, and many younger persons attended more often. In Belfast it was necessary to reach the cinema before 7:00 pm to be sure of a seat, otherwise one had to queue for admittance, often to 9:00 pm. A stroll around the quiet city centre on most evenings about 8:00 pm revealed long queues waiting patiently outside the Ritz, the Royal Hippodrome, the Mayfair, the Imperial, the Classic, the Royal Cinema, the Picture House and the Alhambra. Attendances at most suburban cinemas showed a similar pattern. The cinema owners and managers encouraged such support with good value double bills, cine-variety, late evening shows, special midnight matinees, amateur singing and musical competitions. They also tried to rent films that caught the attention of the local newspapers, which gave them good coverage, and publicity.

Writing in the Irish News in the mid - Fifties, a correspondent noted that matters cinematic were widely reported in the local newspapers, while films were a topic for discussion and argument wherever people met. They were, the writer argued, an excellent way to break the ice at parties and similar social gatherings. People who were reluctant to give an opinion on books, opera, ballet or even politics became quite voluble in response to the question: Have you seen such and such a film? Everyone had opinions on films and their stars. One way that the cinema managers and owners responded to that obvious interest was with gimmicks. During the Fifties and Sixties horror films became a major attraction, and the cinemas catered to those who enjoyed them, gleaning good publicity in the process. Typical was the case of Agnes Mc Kenzie, a young stenographer from Oswald Street, who, in February 1956, won a competition to watch "The Quatermass Xperiment," all alone, at midnight, in the palatial Ritz. Miss McKenzie, who thoroughly enjoyed the experience, explained to the press that while she enjoyed a good thrill, her favourite relaxation was actually embroidery. A few years later, Herbert Bell, manager of the Crumlin cinema, responded to a written plea from a regular filmgoer, a young girl who wanted to see the original film "Dracula" again. He arranged a special free showing, beginning at midnight, for her and 150 other Dracula fanatics. On the following day the papers carried a photo taken at the event of two local girls, Geraldine Downey and Margery Murphy, wide - eyed, watching the vampire, and looking suitably frightened.

Other cinemas held amateur talent contests which always engendered local interest, like the Deanna Durbin singing contest organized by Curran cinemas. In April 1956 the Society of Cinema Managers organized a Miss Cinema of Belfast contest, which was open to all cinema workers. It was won by Mrs Bridie Adams of Southport Street, who was crowned by the singer David Whitfield, at a special function in the Orpheus Ballroom. Mr Whitfield was appearing that week in the Opera House, and on his arrival at the Orpheus he was mobbed by waiting teenage fans, and experienced some difficulty reaching the door of the dancehall. Mrs Adams was presented with an engraved gold watch, and she and the runner-up, Margaret Mc Cann, a salesgirl in the Gaumont (the former Classic), won free holidays in Butlin's Holiday Camp at Mosney. Some events had special cinematic significance, as, for example, when the Forum cinema celebrated its 21st birthday in November 1958. The manager, N. McLorinan, introduced a special guest to the audience. He was "the man they never see," Michael Bunting, the chief projectionist, who had just completed 21 years working in the cinema.

Michael recalled how he had projected the first film ever shown in the Forum, "Men Are Not Gods," starring Miriam Hopkins. He had entered the cinema business during the silent era as a page boy in the Lyric Cinema in High Street in the late Twenties, earning only ten shillings (50p) per week but remembered those early years as being full of excitement. Silent films weren't really silent, he explained. Besides the musicians there was a group of men who were responsible for special effects. During the presentation of a First World film, "The Sinking of the Emden," a small container of gunpowder was placed below the screen and was exploded electrically by one man when a torpedo hit the ship. Another then began rubbing pieces of sandpaper together to suggest the sea pouring in. At the same time another man fired blanks while yet another produced machine gun effects using what Bunting called "a corncrake affair." His ambition had always been to become a projectionist and he later moved to the Alhambra to work for Irish Theatres Ltd. There he had to help out with other tasks, one of which was blacking up for a stage minstrel show to introduce the showing of "Uncle Tom's Cabin." After stints in projection booths in Larne and Lisburn he joined the team in Irish Theatre's new Forum in March 1937. When Mr Bunting returned to the projection room a ballot was held for a celebratory cake, presented by Stewart's Cash Stores, which was won by a local man, Mr H.Watson.

Lockwood and Mason: "codswallop".

Audiences enjoyed such diversions but what they really wanted were good entertaining films, and the cinemas tried to meet that demand. As an Irish News critic was to remind his readers later, in the cinema the film was the Thing (sic). Typical was "The Wicked Lady" (d. Leslie Arliss, 1945) in which the usually demure Margaret Lockwood donned a highwayman's attire, and engaged in robbery, murder and other dire deeds. The exotic storyline was, according to her co-star James Mason, "bloody codswallop." Before its release the film gained a certain notoriety because of its subject-matter, coupled with reports of Miss Lockwood's rather extensive decolletage. The news that American censors were demanding changes, including the re-shooting of more modest shots of the dresses worn by Miss Lockwood and Patricia Roc, before the film could be released in the USA, added to the anticipation. The local papers stoically ignored those more sensational aspects, but highlighted the fact that the script was based on a book by a local woman, Magdalen King - Hall who, in private life, was Mrs Patrick Perceval - Maxwell of Downpatrick. Members of her family were specially invited to the premiere in the Gaumont, London, though the main guest of honour was Queen Mary, who,after watching it in passive silence, told Margaret Lockwood, as she left the cinema: "I enjoyed it very much." The Royal approval went a long way in counteracting any negative comments. The film reached the Classic in Belfast in February 1946, accompanied by newspaper advertisements informing the populace that Miss Lockwood played a character who was "bad, bold and beautiful." The intrigued crowds duly arrived, but the critics weren't over - impressed. The Belfast Telegraph critic thought the plot was "eventful but hardly convincing." He praised the production values, the black and white photography and the acting of the principals. Margaret Lockwood, as Lady Skelton, brought "fascination" to her role, while James Mason swashbuckled competently. He added that he "doubted if those virtues compensated for uncertain narration, some awkward dialogue and a lack of morality." Seen today, the film is just an entertaining piece of fluff, which shows that James Mason's original view was correct.

In Hollywood, RKO Radio studios decided to make a film that would lift the spirits of audiences. The result was "The Spanish Main" (d. Frank Borzage, 1945), an exciting pirate adventure, with a contemporary theme of the struggle between personal freedom and oppression. It was decided to overlook wartime shortages. The film was to be made in Technicolor, and the studio was scoured for rich - looking fabrics for the costumes for the cast especially for the gowns of the heroine, the beautiful Maureen O'Hara. Production values were high, and audiences gaped at tables groaning under the weight of dishes of tropical fruits they hadn't seen - or tasted - for many years. Scenes of thundering broadsides and flashing sword blades were interspersed with humour, including a duel between Maureen O'Hara and Binnie Barnes involving bullets of soot. Seen today the film still glows with colour, and looks impressive, with great sailing ships manoeuvring on blue seas, past castles whose walls bristle with cannon. The hero was played by Paul Henreid, better known as Lazlo in "Casablanca," while the wily villain was the splendid Walter Slezak. Audiences responded enthusiastically, and the film made a fortune wherever it was shown. It arrived in Belfast in June 1946, and showed in the Classic to packed houses for two weeks, before moving on to the Curran circuit. The News Letter welcomed it as "a spirited adventure romance played with the necessary derring do and charm by Paul Henreid and Maureen O'Hara." The critic pointed out that it was accompanied by an interesting second feature, "Victory Day," a special documentary in colour showing the celebrations in Britain, official and unofficial, at the end of the war. Marching troops, official salutes, flags,and street parties filled the screen. The News Letter critic encouraged everyone to see it. "It has", he wrote, "a splendour of pageantry, and a story which for years will thrill the world."

The film, however, that had the greatest impact on Belfast, and on local audiences, was the J.Arthur Rank, Two Cities production of "Odd Man Out," (d.Carol Reed, 1946), which had nothing to do with the war. The source novel was published in 1945, and the filming rights were immediately bought up by film maker, Carol Reed. The project was first mentioned in the local papers in Jan.- Feb. 1946 with a report that a film script was being prepared based on the novel by "local author," F.L.Green. In fact Green was English by birth, but had lived in Belfast long enough (since 1932) to be regarded as "local.". Another report mentioned that the director, Carol Reed, had visited the city to study locations, and let it be known that he was anxious to engage local actors. He visited the Group Theatre and met its players, including Joe Tumelty whom he engaged for an acting part (as a cabbie), and as an advisor. Joe encouraged his mother-in-law, Mary (Min) Milligan, who lived in Dover Street, to attend an interview for a role, and she got the part of Fr Tom's housekeeper. She admitted later that, at first, she was apprehensive about working in Denham Studios, but she actually enjoyed the experience. She found the working conditions relaxed, while the staff were friendly and helpful. Min was later to become famous as Aunt Sarah in the Mc Cooeys on local radio, written by her son-in-law. Small parts also went to Min's niece Maura Milligan, who lived in Iris Drive, and Maureen Cusack. Those small parts helped give the film an

Still from Odd Man Out with thanks to Irish News.

authentic local atmosphere. News of those developments also kept interest in the film alive in the city, and people were already looking forward to seeing it.

Reed told the local press that he was impressed by the visual potential of Belfast which he felt would photograph well. With regard to the possibility of the city attracting other film makers, he pointed out that there was the problem of its unpredictable weather, so little would happen until a film studio was built. Richard Hayward had highlighted that same problem over a decade before, which had forced him to film interiors in English studios. It took another sixty years before Belfast could boast its own Paint Hall film studio. The interiors for "Odd Man Out" would be filmed at Denham Studios, strengthening that studio's connections with film making in Ireland. Denham Studios were the largest and best equipped studios in England. They had been built by Alexander Korda, but in 1939 were taken over by J.Arthur Rank. Over the years a number of films with Irish themes were filmed there, and they represented a welcome source of income for Ireland. During the filming of "Captain Boycott" there was a story that Irish soldiers hired as extras - as often happened after 1943 when Laurence Olivier, directing "Henry V," used them so successfully in recreating the Battle of Agincourt in the estate at Powerscourt south of Dublin - during a lull in filming caused by heavy rain, were heard singing: "Every time it rains, it rains, pennies from Denham." It is interesting that Olivier originally wanted Carol Reed to direct "Henry V," but he was not available because of other commitments Also, the finances for Olivier's film were supplied by Two Cities Films, the same company which backed "Odd Man Out."

This time however, the pennies fell on Belfast. By the end of February some outdoor shots filmed around Boomer Street and Hamilton Place were already in the can. According to the Irish News, extras included "two boys from the Falls, plus a stray dog." The Whig added that the boys' parts involved playing a game of "marleys." Children played important roles in catching the local atmosphere, and, according to the Irish News critic, everything they said and did in the film was "dead right." Many children were interviewed by Cecil Ford the Irish technical advisor to Two Cities Films for parts, and he finally chose 15 boys from St Patrick's Industrial School at Milltown on the Upper Falls Road. The boys were a familiar sight on the Falls Road, and every Saturday afternoon a group of them, accompanied by two Christian Brothers, marched in orderly fashion from the school down the road into the balcony of the Broadway cinema for a free film show After filming outdoor scenes in the city the excited new extras, suitably supervised, left on the Heysham steamer for Denham Studios, to film interiors. A special party was organized in Belfast for those other disappointed children who had failed the interviews.

The official U.K. release date for "Odd Man Out" was St Patrick's Day, 1947 but, in fact, the film opened in London at the beginning of February, winning, according to the Whig, "golden opinions" from leading critics. Belfast awaited its arrival with mounting excitement. One experienced picturegoer described how the atmosphere reminded him of the days before the coming of sound to the Picture House. Their patience was rewarded when the film opened in the Classic on Monday, 3rd March. From lunch time a large crowd began to collect and queue along the pavement in Castle Lane. The show couldn't begin until 4:00 p.m. because of the power restrictions in force. The doors were opened early, and patrons were guided to their seats by usherettes carrying carriage candles. In the audience were F.L.Green who had written the original novel, accompanied by his wife. Also, Sir Richard Pym, the Inspector General of the R.U.C., and Joe Tumelty. Notably there was a large body of uniformed police and plain clothes detectives, presumedly as a deterrent to trouble. Nothing untoward happened, but the presence of the extra police led to questions being asked at Stormont a few days later. Mr Hanna (Lab.) commented that those responsible for the presence of such a large body of police had obviously "lost their sense of humour." If someone thought that such a precaution was needed, then the cinema owners should pay for it, not the ratepayers. Others pointed out that such a decision would create a precedent. Would the idea, for example, be extended to political meetings, where there might be trouble? Mr Warnock, the Minister of Home Affairs, firmly rejected the suggestion.

The response to the film was generally favourable, both from the critics and the public. Most Belfast people probably went to see it because of the locations rather than the story. They recognised the Albert Clock, the streets still with their air raid shelters, the trams, the public houses and the distinctly uniformed police. But the geography, as often happens in films, was confused and inaccurate, while the scenes around the docks looked rather phoney. Great care was taken by the film makers to avoid absolute political positions or statements, but Belfast audiences knew what the Organization was, and what the R.U.C. represented. All those matters became the occasions for discussion and argument. One writer commented that everywhere you went the film was a topic of conversation. The newspaper critics for their part were very impressed. The Whig described it as a "screen triumph," and summed it up as a film of "authentic emotion, realistic scenes, characters that, with one exception, are credible, brilliantly drawn and acted." The News Letter critic described the film as "the story of a gunman on the run in Belfast," but agreed with the Whig that it was much more than a thriller. The theme he felt was elevated from the particular to the universal, producing a psychological drama of high quality. That duality of content was also recognised by the Irish News critic who, while impressed, added that the film was not a masterpiece, but came "within hailing distance of it," just missing greatness. The first half was superb, filmed with a "relentless objectivity," but the symbolism of the second half didn't succeed. He had praise for Carol Reed's direction, and for the photography of Robert Krasker, whose combined talents produced a portrait of a city that stayed long in the mind. The visuals caught superbly "the flavour of the city, the coarse tang of its life." He particularly liked the superb black and white images of "the back streets, the alley-ways, the shining pavements, the football bouncing into the air raid shelter, the little girl with one roller skate, the old women looking out from a lighted room before quickly pulling the curtains, the children gazing at the wonder of the snow....the black avenging forms of the police blocking every exit.... clocks striking, children playing, ship's sirens, the murmur of the city." They were images and sounds which were to reappear in various forms in Reed's later film about Vienna, "The Third Man." There was praise for the acting of James Mason (as the doomed hero Johnny), F.J. McCormick, Kathleen Ryan ("a lovely calm heroine," according to the Whig), Joseph Tumelty ("a real joy" said the Whig, though the Irish News found his cabbie "too Dickensian").

Despite the high praise, all the critics felt that the film suffered from minor flaws - a Fred Karno tram sequence (Irish News), jumbled topography(News Letter), and unauthentic accents. The most severe criticism came from an ordinary filmgoer who wrote to the Whig, signing himself "Bangor Picturegoer." He implied having a wide knowledge of films, claiming that he had seen, on average, five films per week over the previous ten years. He admitted being extremely disappointed with "Odd Man Out," especially with the performance of James Mason. He couldn't understand all the fuss over Kathleen Ryan, and thought that the best thing in the film was the acting of the children. Finally he condemned the scenery as "unreal", and having no connection with the actual city of Belfast. Those weren't just narrow local criticisms. Some years later, in February 1960, that most elegant and refined of film critics, Dilys Powell, who wrote in the Sunday Times, came to Belfast to give a lecture in the Whitla Hall, called "365 films a year." It was, as one would expect, a perceptive view of the development of the cinema, especially British cinema. During it she mentioned "Odd Man Out" and recalled that she found the James Mason character "rather negative" and that it was the people in the streets, often minor characters, who made a special impact on her. Belfast experienced at least one recorded "special impact" during the showing of the film when an ex-soldier from Boundary Street, who had a few drinks taken, voiced his feelings when the R.U.C. appeared on the screen, by shouting "Up the Rebels." He left quietly when asked to, was arrested in the foyer, and after a court appearance, was jailed for a month. The film ran for three weeks in the Classic.

There were other films with Irish themes, notably the Sam Goldwyn production of "Beloved Enemy," (d. H.C.Potter, 1936) which starred Brian Aherne and Merle Oberon. It was advertised as "a dramatic love story told against the turbulent background of Ireland, 1916 to 1921." It was in fact a thinly veiled fiction based on the life of Michael Collins (Brian Aherne) and his purported relationship with Lady Lavery (Miss Oberon). Because of its delicate political content involving pro and anti Treaty elements, the film was not immediately shown in Belfast, but was held back until the Broadway presented it in a Gala Premiere in February 1945, as part of a charity cine-variety entertainment which included Irish dancers, singers, musicians and local comedians, to collect funds for the Mater Hospital. The fact that it could be shown, even in a Nationalist area, was an indication of how attitudes seemed to have changed during the war. The cinema was crowded and there were no reports of objections from the audience, who obviously enjoyed the Irish flavour of the evening. The studio made alternative endings, one in which Collins is shot and another in which he is still alive at the end of the film. There is no indication, unfortunately, which ending was shown in the Broadway.

Other films shown were more light hearted, including the comedy "I See a Dark Stranger," starring Deborah Kerr and Trevor Howard. Belfast actress, Siobhan McKenna, from the Falls Road, had been offered the leading role but turned it down, preferring to remain on the stage. She did appear briefly in "Hungry Hill," (d. Brian Desmond Hurst, 1946) which was shot partly in Co. Cork. The little known and rarely shown "Crime on the Irish Border" featured Kieron Moore, while "Captain Boycott" starred Stewart Granger and Kathleen Ryan. All came in for their share of criticism. When "Jacqueline" (d. Roy Baker, 1956), which dealt with the problems of a shipyard worker played by John Gregson, arrived in the Imperial in October 1956 the Telegraph critic asked in mock horror: is this Belfast? Those and other films made in Ireland brought money into the country, gave employment to local actors and actresses, and experience to Irish technicians, but in general they were forgettable, and most are rarely mentioned today.

Not so "The Quiet Man" (d. John Ford,1951), which arrived in the Ritz in August 1952, to begin a run of five weeks to packed houses. The Belfast Telegraph critic described as one of the "most refreshing" films with an Irish background to reach Belfast in a long time. A preview was arranged in the Ritz on the 18th August for a specially invited audience, which consisted mainly of ordinary filmgoers. The Press and members of the trade attended a second showing and one of the local critics wrote that he had rarely heard such laughter at a Press preview. From the first public showing the Ritz was crowded and audiences poured in for the next five weeks. The Belfast Telegraph critic commented that the film may not depict the real Ireland, but it was still a "joyous entertainment." John Wayne, Victor Mac Laglan and the Irish cast were splendid. The critic was especially generous in his praise of Maureen O'Hara, maintaining that it was one of her best roles, and that "she has never done anything better." The film had everything - humour, drama, music, song, and colour which showed the scenery of the West of Ireland at its best, plus an unusual love story involving the two principals. The public took to the film from the beginning, and it went on to become one of the most enduring and popular films ever made. Over sixty years later it still returns to Belfast, showing to capacity audiences at venues like the Q.F.T. and the Waterfront Hall.

"Odd Man Out" paints a bleak, menacing environment dominated by dark film noir shadows, in which the increasingly helpless hero is buffeted by implacable forces and human indifference. Realism is the keynote, and his girlfriend, Kathleen Ryan, quietly acquiesces to the inevitable, and joins Johnny in death, in a sequence that the Irish News critic dismissed with some cynicism, as unbelievable. "The Quiet Man," in contrast, vibrates with colour and life, though the hero is again buffeted, not by the forces of the law, but by social pressures he doesn't fully understand. The driving force of the film is Mary Kate (Miss O'Hara) whose positive vitality contrasts with the quiet acceptance of Kathleen Ryan. Mary Kate's insistence on her rights finally results, not in death, but in family unity, with the prospect of future life. The films share heroes in conflict with the values and attitudes of their societies, and heroines whose aim is to "save"' them. A characteristic of "Odd Man Out" is its paucity of humour, and its dour urban realism contrasts with the warm rural images of "The Quiet Man." The latter work is set firmly in the imaginative vision of John Ford, and is essentially a personal, and, above all, affectionate picture of Ireland and its people. Within the story there are serious comments on pre-industrial Irish society, and how outsiders view it, but the overall approach annoyed some people who accused it of being too stage Irish. Together the films illustrate both sides of the Irish coin, and both make serious comments about the country, its people and its society.

Another popular film with an Irish theme was Disney's "Darby O'Gill and the Little People," (d. Robert Stevenson, 1958) which arrived in the Opera House in July 1959, a month after its world premiere in Dublin. It was hailed on the posters as "... it's different... it's delightful," and for once the publicity department was correct. The film had a special connection with Belfast because the main player was Albert Sharpe, who lived near the Broadway cinema, and was a familiar figure on the Falls Road. After a long career in music hall and variety, beginning in the Empire theatre, he had proved his worth with a splendid performance on Broadway in "Finian's Rainbow," which had led to the film role as Darby O'Gill. The film was an Irish fairy tale in which O'Gill outwits the King of the Fairies, played by Jimmy O'Dea. The Irish News critic praised both performances, noting how Albert Sharpe "frolicked his way through his part with a gleam in his eye." On the other hand he felt that Jimmy O'Dea was hampered by a script that ignored his true comic genius. Sean Connery, in an early part, lacked the experience to compete with the two old pros, but the Banshee held her own, and is still as frightening today as only the Disney special effects department could make her.

As the postwar demand for screen entertainment remained high, the local industry felt confident enough to undertake a policy of refurbishing their cinemas, and even building new venues. The Popular on the lower Newtownards Road was rebuilt and reopened in 1946, much to the delight of locals. Raymond Stross had the New Kelvin in College Square East refurbished and adorned with a new frontage, including the addition of a canopy to protect prospective queuers. The auditorium was modified to hold 506 seats, and among the new decorations was a special curtain of spun glass material. In those days the screen was always covered with a curtain, partly to protect it and partly to maintain a certain mystique and sense of anticipation about what was to come. Mr Stross, the general manager, promised that the cinema would continue to be highly selective, and show only first - rate films. His aim was to present about 20 films a year, each running for a few weeks. He hoped in time that such a policy would build up a discerning clientèle. It was a worthy ambition. To indicate a new beginning, the hall was renamed the Mayfair. The reopening, on the 19th March 1946, was an impressive affair graced by the singing and dancing star Jesse Matthews, who flew in especially for the occasion. The opening film was "Salty O'Rourke" starring the very popular Alan Ladd. The proceeds from the first day were donated, by tradition, to charity, to the Ulster Hospital for Children and Women on the Falls Road, and the Cine Trade Benevolent Fund.

The Mayfair soon established itself with the film - going public with a series of entertaining and popular films. Mr Stross also made the cinema available for meetings of the Institute Film Society, and the enthusiasm shown for their quality foreign films must have impressed him because he began to present more and more continental films, especially during the Fifties, a period when tastes in films were changing. Many of the films - mainly French - were adult only, X rated, and they brought the cinema into conflict with local clergy, prominent citizens, and the official Police Committee. The titles often promised more than they delivered, and included exotic gems like "Enticement," "Summer Manoeuvres,"(with Brigitte Bardot), "Intimate Relations," "Birth of a Baby"(again!), an updated reissue which showed for two weeks, "Lady Chatterly's Lover" ("much reduced in significance" in comparison with the novel, commented the News Letter), and "The Seven Deadly Sins." They were the type of films discussed in the magazine, Continental Film Review, an avant garde publication, liberally illustrated, which was available only in Marshall's excellent and comprehensive bookshop in Donegall Street. Some years later the Continental Film Review was one of a group of magazines seized by the R.U.C. from local shops as "indecent." The case against the Review was summarily dismissed, though many of the other titles taken were destroyed as "pornographic," on the order of a magistrate.

To some people the films shown in the Mayfair represented modern quality cinema, especially presentations like Roberto Rossellini's "Paisa" (1946), Vittorio de Sica's "Bicycle Thieves" (1948), and Akira Kurosawa's "Rashomond"(1950). But others regarded them as morally suspect, or worse, and as a result the Mayfair developed a reputation - quite undeserved - of being a purveyor of risqué and blue films. One put one's reputation for probity at risk being seen entering its foyer. The local critics had an ambivalent attitude to the films, recognising the cinematic qualities of some, while admitting that their relaxed moral attitudes to sex could cause local offence. The Irish News critics just ignored most of them, while the other critics laced their criticisms with sardonic humour. They never hesitated to praise films of quality, like Jean Cocteau's hauntingly beautiful "Beauty and the Beast," or the moving Spanish religious story of a young boy experiencing a miracle in "Marcelino, Pan y Vino." Martin Wallace, writing in the Telegraph, described the latter as a simple, warm hearted, restrained and reverent film, and added that it illustrated perfectly "how a religious theme should be translated to the screen." Church congregations were encouraged from the pulpits to go and see it. It proved to be a great success, and the Mayfair brought it back for a re-run later in the year.

Another film that came in for special mention of a different kind, was Jacques Becker's "Touchez Pas Au Grisbi," a much praised French gangster film starring Jean Gabin, whom the Telegraph critic described as an outstanding actor graced "with a face like a squashed hamburger." He thought the film itself was very well acted and directed, but was "wholly reprehensible" because it failed to criticise Gabin's celluloid misdeeds. Overall, the Mayfair management deserve to be congratulated, because for the first time since the silent era the cinema gave the general public the opportunity to see a wide selection of continental films, and to realise that there was cinematic life outside Hollywood.

Visits by film stars were always popular affairs, and during the following years many British stars came to the city. On the evening before Jesse Mathews opened the Mayfair, the Ritz presented a midnight matinee of cine variety. The main attractions on stage were Deborah Kerr and Michael Redgrave who flew over specially, landing at Nutt's Corner, from where they were taken to the Grand Central for a reception. There they were greeted by J.D.Russell, the manager of the Ritz, Louis Hyman the president of the local branch of the CEA, and a group of cinema owners and managers. The matinee was in aid of the Cinematograph Trade Benevolent Fund, and the hall was crowded. The two stars held an autographed photo auction, with Deborah Kerr's picture fetching £30, Michael Redgrave's going for £20, and other stars for £15 and £10 each. The chief attraction on stage was the David Curry's Belfast Light Orchestra, with songs by local favourite Lelia Webster, and dancing by the Barry Babes and the Glamourettes. The live acts were followed by the film, "Valley of Decision" (d. Tay Garnett, 1945) starring Greer Garson and Gregory Peck. The whole represented nearly three hours of top quality entertainment.

A few months later, in early July, Jean Kent arrived in a specially chartered plane at Nutt's Corner. From there she was driven to the Grand Central Hotel, and after a meal with representatives of the trade she travelled to the City Hall where she was welcomed by the deputy Lord Mayor. "Red haired and vivacious" (Irish News), she made a memorable impact wherever she went. The main reason for her visit was to attend a Charity midnight matinee in the Classic in aid of the Newspaper Press Fund. The event included the Irish premiere of her latest film "Caravan" - described on the posters as "Gainsborough's lovely gypsy romance" - which also starred Stewart Granger, at the height of his popularity then. When she appeared on the stage the packed hall gave her a rousing welcome. She entertained them with stories about her career and films, recalling that it was actually her second visit to Belfast, because she had appeared at the Empire in 1939, but as a lowly member of the chorus. The reporter commented on the contrast of her return, "glamorised," and looking as only a film star could.

At the end of February 1947 it was announced that Curran Theatres had purchased a large area of property from Barron Trust Ltd. and Northern Theatres Ltd for a six figure amount. The area included the Picture House and property extending along Garfield Street to Smithfield. The Curran organization had a much respected reputation in Belfast's cinema business and had played an important role in local cinema history. Its cinemas were modern, well managed, and popular with audiences. Geographically they were located in the suburbs, but, after the war, the company decided that it was time to move into the city centre, a move which reflected the generally optimistic mood of the local industry. The main aim of the purchase was to completely renovate and refurbish the historic but aging Picture House, and turn it into a first class modern cinema. The Picture House was duly closed in August, and reopened on 26th September 1947, renamed the Regent. With its acquisition Curran Theatres then controlled twelve cinemas, and could claim to be Belfast's own home grown circuit. Technically a circuit referred to a chain or group of more than ten cinemas. The new cinema was little changed on the outside, but, within, despite a difficulty in obtaining suitable building materials, the auditorium had been greatly modified. It had been redesigned in an unembellished, uncluttered style, with modern clean lines to improve sound reproduction. The latter was also augmented by the installation of new sound and projection equipment. The seating had been reduced from 830 units to 706, giving the audience more leg room. James Gribben was transferred from the Astoria at Knock, as manager. He announced that the hall would be run on modern lines with four separate shows per day, and that all seats would be bookable at no extra cost. The company expressed the hope that the easy booking system would do away with queueing. The experiment was not the success that James Curran had expected. The majority of Belfast filmgoers were slow to change their habits, the booking system lapsed over time, the cinema quickly reverted to continuous shows, and the nightly queues remained. The author remembers waiting patiently in Garfield Street for admittance on many an evening, sheltering under the decorated glass canopy. Despite the weather or other problems down-town queues remained quiet and orderly.

The opening was much anticipated, and the appetites of fans were heightened by a suitable fanfare of publicity. The film chosen to introduce the new cinema was the RKO production "So Well Remembered" (d. Edward Dmytryk, 1947), starring John Mills and Trevor Howard, and it was announced that its presentation would be a Grand Charity affair in aid of the Ulster Hospital for Children and Women building fund. On that first evening all seats would cost 10 shillings. John Mills and his wife Hayley Bell Mills, whose family came from near Greyabbey, flew into Nutt's Corner to perform the official ceremony. The couple were met by James Curran, the general manager of the circuit, James Gribben, the manager, and the publicity director for RKO studios. From the airfield the couple were driven the usual VIP route to the Grand Central Hotel where they were guests of honour at a special luncheon, presided over by Louis Hyman, the chairman of the local CEA. In the afternoon the couple made a number of local visits culminating in Robinson and Cleavers, where they purchased a few items before having tea in the cafe with the manager. Wherever they went there were crowds of fans and sightseers, with requests for autographs. At 8:00 pm they arrived through a large crowd at the Regent and John Mills performed the official opening. After the film he and his wife had supper with the manager in the new "spacious" (Irish News) cafe. Every detail of the visit was described in the local papers.

The post -war enthusiasm for more cinema seats wasn't confined to Belfast. In July 1947 the Mayor of Bangor opened a new cinema, the Astor, in that popular seaside resort. It wasn't a new building but had been converted from the former Flamingo Cafe and dance hall, to a hall that seated 400, with the aim of serving the Ballyholme area. The Mayor, in his speech, declared that "a progressive town like Bangor" needed a third cinema, reflecting the widely held belief that cinemas were indicators of development and social standing. In Enniskillen planning permission was also given for the conversion of a garage to a cinema, a move much welcomed by the local population.

But there were also those in the business who felt that what was needed were not conversions, but new buildings of modern design. They called upon the expertise of the eminent cinema architect J. McB Neill of Chichester Street, who designed two cinemas which incorporated the latest developments in building, design and equipment. The first was the Lido on the Shore Road which was opened on the 25th March 1955. It was an elegant, unfussy building with a welcoming ambience, which could seat 1150 persons. According to Sir James Norritt, a former Lord Mayor, who carried out the opening ceremony, it "brightened up a rather drab stretch of road." But its location had nothing to do with the scenic state of the area but everything to do with the fact that it was a growing suburban district. Besides comfort the cinema was up-to-date in its style, and presentation. The auditorium was designed to give the finest acoustics, and to accommodate the latest widescreen equipment. By the mid - Fifties audiences expected widescreen projection combined with stereophonic sound, and the Lido supplied both. Clarity of viewing was enhanced by a special air flow system which drew in filtered air at the screen end which was then drawn out at the rear stalls. In keeping the air clean and clear the system had to cope with the fact that most of the audience smoked. A smoky atmosphere was still accepted as part of the cinema going experience. In May of the following year the suggestion was made in the House of Commons that smoking should be forbidden in cinemas. In reply, the Home Secretary declared that the danger of serious fires resulting from smoking was not sufficient to justify the making of a regulation to prohibit it. There was no reference to the health hazard. The Lido included in the foyer a large cafe-shop to cater to the audiences' needs, though, on opening night, work was still continuing to complete it. The Lido was owned by the same company that owned the Troxy, and its managing director was Harry Wilton, a man experienced in the cinematic trade.

The opening night was organized by the local branch of the Variety Club, with the proceeds going to charity. The entertainment consisted of a stage show plus the film "Take the Stage," a comedy Western starring the lively Donald O'Connor. O'Connor, a fine dancer, made many enjoyable films but is probably best known for "Singing In The Rain" in which he starred with Gene Kelly and Debbie Reynolds. The Lido had much going for it in the form of good management, comfort, reasonable prices, entertaining films presented with modern equipment, but was unable to cope with the fact that times and tastes were changing. It had a relatively short life span of only fifteen years before closing in 1970. It didn't suffer the indignity of being bulldozed as others had, and is still operating, but as a Catholic Church. Maybe there is some truth in the suggestion that religion does involve some element of showmanship.

Three months later, in June 1955, another J.McBride Neill designed cinema was officially opened by the governor, Lord Wakehurst. It was the Tivoli, located in an expanding suburban area at Finaghy corner on the Lisburn Road. It was designed in a modern style, without a balcony, but with a wide auditorium that encompassed 1000 green moquette - covered seats, and which had been specially adapted to showing the latest Cinemascope films. The "miracle mirror" screen incorporated a special automatic masking device which could change the shape and dimensions of the screen to suit the ratio of the film. The manager, Jack Wright, who was a former assistant manager at the Ritz, claimed it was one of the largest screens in N. Ireland. The high quality projection - and the author can testify that it lived up to its reputation - was backed up by four track stereophonic sound with 13 strategically placed loudspeakers. Such details may seem commonplace today but in the mid - Fifties they represented the apogee of projection technology. In retrospect the building represented a halfway stage between the large and highly ornate picture palaces of the Thirties and the unadorned halls of today. Lord Wakehurst, who had a lively interest in film making, described the Tivoli as one of the largest and most attractive cinemas in the Six Counties, and congratulated its owners, Odeon (NI) Ltd, its managing director, George Lodge, and the new house manager, Jack Wright. The cinema had every facility including a cafe, shop and car parking space. It is interesting that, like the Lido, all the main work was carried out by local firms, an indicator of the continuing importance of the cinema industry to the local economy. The opening film was "The Night My Number Came Up," starring Michael Redgrave and Sheila Sim. It continued to present good quality films and was well supported until the outbreak of the Troubles in the late Sixties and early Seventies.

Two more cinemas were built outside the urban boundary, but within the city region. On the 1st September 1956 the Metro was officially opened, built at a cost of £50,000, at the corner of East Link, to serve the Dundonald area. On that first evening 200 specially invited guests, and a crowded house, watched James Stewart and Grace Kelly in Hitchcock's "Rear Window." The building itself was impressive, with an exterior style that was more reminiscent of the Thirties, than the Fifties. It is interesting historically in that it was the last cinema in which the electrics were completed by Curran Bros., who were soon to retire from the cinema scene. The most modern equipment was installed, including a 40 feet Cinemascope screen, while the auditorium had seating to hold nearly 1000 patrons. The Metro was the most recent addition to the expanding Supreme Cinemas Ltd group, and its owner was T.J.Furey, a director of that company. He admitted that it was "a calculated risk" to open a new cinema because of the competition from television, and the high level of entertainments tax on the cinema. Despite the commercial uncertainty he felt that a cinema was needed in Dundonald, and he intended to compete by showing the best films available, at the lowest possible prices. Despite the attraction of reasonably priced seating of one shilling for the stalls, and one and six for the balcony the Metro never really caught on with the local people, and after a struggle, closed its doors in 1961. Its cinematic life-span was only five years. Today a MacDonald's stands on the site.

On 1st April 1957 the last traditional style cinema was built, again for the Supreme Cinemas Ltd. group. It was the Alpha, intended to serve the Rathcoole estate, but, like the Metro, it was a financial failure. During the Fifties Supreme Cinemas continued to expand outside Belfast, and with the completion of the Metro and the Alpha they owned 15 cinemas across N.Ireland. They were never a major force within the city boundary where they owned only one cinema, the Park. Within the industry in general the outlook was still optimistic. The failure however of the Metro and the Alpha, in working class areas where they might be expected to do well, were warning signs that among the film going public, attitudes and habits were changing. Just how much began to make itself clear in the late Fifties.

Meantime the fascination with the cinema in Belfast was heightened and strengthened by the almost continuous flow of film personalities who visited the city, bringing a whiff of film glamour with them. The complaints that celebrities tended to bypass Belfast abated in the post war years as more and more film personalities visited the city. Some came for private or personal reasons, like Moyna Magill, the mother of Angela Lansbury, who arrived in November 1952 to visit her own mother at her home in Mount Charles. She spoke to reporters about her warm feelings for Belfast, and recalled how, as Chattie Mc Idowie, she had first come to public attention during the sad days of the First World War, with her poetry readings from the works of Moira O'Neill and others. She still gave those readings in California where she now lived, and they still proved very popular. She also continued to make films and the keen eyed aficionado can recognise her in "Frenchman's Creek," "The Unsinkable Molly Brown," and "My Fair Lady."

Another family visitor was locally born Beatrice Campbell, "Belfast's own film star," as the Irish News called her. In June 1952 Miss Campbell was preparing to film the "Master of Ballantrae" with Errol Flynn, when she flew into the city to open Robb's new Furniture department. The official opening was at 11:00 a.m. but long before that time Castle Street was crowded, and the police had to struggle to hold fans and sightseers back on both pavements. When her car arrived there was a great surge forward which overwhelmed the police lines. The actress remained unruffled, and after opening the department she mixed with the crowds, speaking to individuals, and signing autographs. The reporter described the obvious delight of the crowd and noted how her mother stood nearby watching her daughter with pride. She returned to England to complete the "Master of Ballantrae" which premiered at a midnight matinee in the Ritz in October of the following year, a grand affair attended by its other female star Yvonne Furneaux. The exotic Miss Furneaux was awaited and greeted with great excitement. After

Beatrice Campbell: Errol Flynn romances another Belfast girl.

seeing the film the local papers commented mainly on Beatrice Campbell's performance, describing it as "excellent." Another visitor was Frankie Laine, who though essentially a singer, had appeared in a number of films which showed locally. Douglas Fairbanks jr, his swashbuckling days behind him, was another visitor who arrived with his wife, quietly and privately, in the following month for a special Trafalgar Day event in the Empire Theatre.

Stephen Boyd was another local actor, working in Hollywood, who made personal visits to Belfast to see his family. In early December 1960 he flew in from London where he was making "Cleopatra" with Elizabeth Taylor. Miss Taylor had taken ill and the production had been stopped for a time. The actor took the opportunity to fly over with his personal secretary, for a 24 hour visit to see his mother, and view the new bungalow he had recently bought her. He spoke highly of Miss Taylor to the local reporters, and expressed the hope of resuming filming, when she had recovered. One wonders if he maintained his golden opinions of her when her amorous pursuits and ill health combined to delay the film, so that Boyd and others left the cast in professional disgust. That was a pity because he would have made a fine Mark Anthony.

Stephen Boyd was one of the few truly international stars that Belfast has produced. He probably would have taken issue with that statement because he regarded himself as an actor, rather than a star. Born in July 1931 and Christened Billy Millar, he grew up in the Glengormley area and got his first taste of the stage in the Carnmoney Amateur Dramatic Society. From there he graduated to the Group Theatre, a seedbed for Ulster acting talent. His abilities were soon noticed, and in September 1950 the Belfast Telegraph critic referred

Cast of McCooeys - Stephen Boyd's first publicity shot with thanks to News Letter. Boyd is third from the right.

to him in a new play "The Square Peg," commenting that "William Millar proves himself an able actor in the fairly difficult part of the elder son. He handles his final scene especially with a skilled touch." Joseph Tumelty also recognised his talents and gave him the part of the detective who made "one or two inquiries," in his popular radio serial "The McCooeys." It was that part that really introduced him to the Ulster public. In the News Letter of 21st April 1952 there is a photograph of the cast of the "McCooeys," celebrating the 100th programme of the serial. At the front is the writer Joseph Tumelty, with Min Milligan and J.G.Devlin nearby, but clearly recognisable at the back is William Millar, in what is probably the first publicity shot of Stephen Boyd.

Anxious to ascend the theatrical ladder he went to England, acting in repertoire, and, with the help of Michael Redgrave and Sir Alexander Korda, moved into television and films. He changed his name to Stephen Boyd, the latter being his mother's maiden name. After a number of short appearances in films like "An Alligator Named Daisy," he got his first important part in "The Man Who Never Was." (d. Ronald Neame, 1956). In March 1956 the Belfast Telegraph alerted the public with a report about a new local star, Stephen Boyd, who had travelled from the Group Theatre to a film contract with London Films, and who would soon be appearing in an important new film. The N.Ireland premiere of "The Man Who Never Was" was on Tuesday 24th March and was billed as a Royal Film

Première in aid of the National Playing Fields Association, whose patron was the Duke of Edinburgh. The Duke arrived and spent the day doing a rapid tour of the area around Belfast before attending the cinema, where he was photographed shaking hands with Stephen Boyd, who had flown over from London for the occasion. The film was very well received. it's plot was set in the early Forties, and was based on an actual event when British intelligence placed a dead body complete with "secret" documents in the sea off Spain in an attempt to fool the Germans into thinking the invasion of Europe would take place from the south. Boyd plays an IRA agent who is sent by the Germans to London to check up on the dead man's background. It was a relatively small part but he played it well, and came across very impressively on the big screen. He moved gracefully, and delivered his lines effectively, while at the same time giving depth to the character. In an interview with a Telegraph reporter, who questioned him about his acting technique, Boyd explained that he was studying the theoretical side of acting, and at that moment was investigating the psychology of movement. He obviously took his craft seriously.

Stephen Boyd at the Royal Hippodrome.

That was his only official visit to the city, though he did make many private, unrecorded visits to see his family, and especially his widowed mother, of whom he was very fond. He told local reporters that one of the rewards of film acting was that it gave him the money to see that she lived in comfort. He was a family man, and a private, reserved person. There are no recorded instances of him being mobbed by fans on the streets of Belfast. "My career," he admitted to another local reporter, "is the art of making a living. My life is another matter." After "The Man Who Never Was," his good looks attracted the attention of the film world. Brigitte Bardot requested him for her next film, in which he played a handsome villain, and he followed that experience, which he didn't seem to enjoy, with a number of average films which did little for his career, until "Ben Hur" gave him the strong part of Massala that brought him widespread praise. "Ben Hur"(d. William Wyler, 1959) opened in the Ritz in April 1961 and his local fans hoped - in vain as it proved - that he might come for the

Cartoon of Ben Hur, with thanks to Belfast Telegraph.

event. However he saw to it that his mother and family were present, and they joined other specially invited guests that included Lord Wakehurst, the Deputy Lord Mayor, and high powered M-G-M representatives. Also present were leaders of the local churches, including Dr Mageean, the Bishop of Down and Connor, the Bishop of Down and Dromore and the Rabbi, Dr Carlebach, along with the mayors of Newtownards, Lurgan and Portadown.

It was Stephen Boyd's finest hour but the rest of his career, varied as it was, didn't match it. It was with great sadness that the papers announced in early June 1977 news of his sudden death at Tarzana in the San Fernando Valley where he lived, after a game of golf with his wife. The local critics regretted his passing as did many of the general public. One of them reflected the general feeling when he wrote to the Telegraph expressing thanks for all the pleasure Boyd had given his fans. The letter ended with a heart felt "thank you, Stephen," and was signed, a Ben Hur fan. The actor never returned home, his ashes being buried in the USA where his friends in the film business set up a Stephen Boyd Heart Foundation to

STEPHEN BOYD WAS ULSTER'S MOST SUCCESSFUL FILM STAR. HIS GREATEST CINEMATIC ACHIEVEMENT WAS HIS DYNAMIC PERFORMANCE AS 'MESSALA' IN WILLIAM WYLER'S MIGHTY EPIC 'BEN HUR' FOR WHICH HE RECEIVED AN OSCAR NOMINATION.

HE WAS BORN, WILLIAM MILLAR, THE YOUNGEST OF NINE CHILDREN TO MARTHA AND JAMES MILLAR, AT CARNMONEY, BELFAST ON JULY 4th, 1931. HE LEARNED HIS ART AT THE GROUP THEATRE, BELFAST IN THE COMPANY OF SUCH DISTINGUISHED ACTORS AS J.G. DEVLIN, JOSEPH TOMELTY AND THE LATE HAROLD GOLDBLATT. HIS POTENTIAL WAS SPOTTED BY THE LATE SIR MICHAEL REDGRAVE AND HE SOON BEGAN APPEARING IN BRITISH FILMS OF THE EARLY FIFTIES. HIS PERFORMANCE IN ONE OF THESE FILMS, THE 1956 WAR DRAMA 'THE MAN WHO NEVER WAS' LED DIRECTLY TO A CONTRACT WITH 20th CENTURY FOX AND HIS HOLLYWOOD DEBUT OPPOSITE GREGORY PECK IN THE 1958 WESTERN 'THE BRAVADOS', THEN CAME 'BEN HUR'.

STEPHEN BOYD DIED PREMATURELY ON JUNE 2nd, 1977 NEAR HIS HOME AT TARZANA CALIFORNIA. HIS WIFE ELIZABETH BY HIS SIDE. HE MADE OVER 30 FEATURE FILMS IN A 21 YEAR CAREER, FILMS SUCH AS 'THE INSPECTOR', 'THE FALL OF THE ROMAN EMPIRE', 'GENGHIS KHAN', 'THE BIBLE', 'THE OSCAR', AND MANY OTHERS. HIS LEADING LADIES INCLUDED SUSAN HAYWARD, SOPHIA LOREN, BRIGITTE BARDOT, DORIS DAY, AND JOAN COLLINS.

HIS ROLES WERE MANY AND VARIED BUT IT WILL BE FOR MESSALA, IN 'BEN HUR', AND THAT LEGENDARY CHARIOT RACE, WITH CHARLTON HESTON THAT HE WILL BEST BE REMEMBERED.

DEDICATED TO STEPHEN BOYD

THE MAN WHO LOST THE CHARIOT RACE

Source: Belfast Telegraph.

Visit to Ritz projection room. Source: Belfast Telegraph.

commemorate his name. Disappointingly, there is no such gesture to preserve his memory in his birthplace. In December 1987 a plaque outlining his career was put up in the QFT but sadly during later refurbishment it disappeared.

Most stars came to Belfast for professional purposes, usually to attend charity midnight matinees in the Ritz. They flew into Nutt's Corner and were taken by car to the Grand Central Hotel for luncheon or dinner with local dignitaries, members of the cinema trade and, of course, the Press. Publicity for the films involved was an essential part of the visits, and the Press co-operated by publishing photographs and descriptions of the events. Among the list of personalities that visited were Richard Todd (March 1951) whose Irish origins were suitably emphasised, David Lean, John Houston, Ann Todd, John Mc Callum, Derek Bond, Deborah Kerr, Michael Redgrave, Janette Scott, June Thorburn, Jerry Colonna, Phyllis Calvert, Eunice Gayson and Cary Grant. Most of them appeared on the stage of the Ritz or the Royal Hippodrome. The Ritz, in particular, played host to major stars, emphasising its position as Belfast's elite cinema, a position it worked hard to maintain. In November 1949 the cinema celebrated its 13th birthday by opening its doors to the public for a series of guided tours "behind the scenes," a publicity stratagem which proved most successful. Large numbers of curious citizens took advantage of the offer. People were delighted to get up close to the great Compton organ whose sounds were so much a part of the Ritz going experience. But central to that experience were the films and inquisitive citizens, which the Belfast Telegraph noted "included many women," came to inspect the projection room which housed the latest type of projectors. Local members of staff were on duty to explain what they saw, and how the machines worked.

Besides major stars the Ritz also presented impressive premieres, often with special attractions (gimmicks, according to cynics) of local interest. In November 1952 "The Sound Barrier" (d.David Lean, 1952) was premiered as part of a midnight cine-variety show, with David Lean and Ann Todd making personal appearances. The film's Belfast connections were highlighted in the papers, with the presence of Joseph Tumelty and Nigel Patrick, the husband of Beatrice Campbell, in the cast. In September of the following year the cinema hosted an even more elaborate affair, the N.Ireland gala premiere of "Angels One Five" (d. George More O' Farrell,1954), a story of the Few, which starred Jack Hawkins, Michael Denison and Dulcie Gray. On the opening evening, in the presence of the Prime Minister, Lord Brookeborough, the audience were treated to a unique and memorable event. Members of Ulster's 502 Auxiliary Squadron set up an operations room on the stage of the Ritz. Their Squadron leader Matthews took off in a Vampire jet from Aldergrove and when he was exactly above the cinema at a height of 1500 feet he sent a radio signal down to the stage. The radio crackled and his voice was heard saying: "On target at angels one five."

At that the projector was started and the film appeared on the screen. The audience was delighted, including his wife, who according to the Belfast Telegraph, sat in the circle "in a shimmering blue gown. "Pathé News cameras were present that evening and members of the audience could see themselves in the newsreel which was shown the following week in the cinema. When the colour film "Conquest of Everest" was screened in January 1954 members of the Irish Mountaineering club, in full climbing gear, greeted patrons in the foyer. The premiere of "The Dam Busters," starring Richard Todd, was attended by Lord and Lady Wakehurst, and when they arrived the passage from their car to the foyer was lined by one hundred airmen in full uniform.

One of the biggest evenings in the cinema's social calendar occurred when "Helen of Troy" (d. Robert Wise, 1955) premiered in the Ritz on 26th January 1956. Warner Bros.,who produced the film, arranged a World Premiere in which the film was shown at the same time in 130 cinemas, scattered across 56 countries, in 23 different languages. Warners claimed it was the first time such an ambitious release had been attempted, and the Belfast Ritz was one of 8 cinemas in the British Isles chosen to participate. To add to the occasion two competitions, with cash prizes, were organized connected to the film. The first was to design a classical styled dress of the type that Helen may have worn. The local winner was Sandra Reid, a 15 year old schoolgirl from Finaghy, who produced a quite sophisticated sketch which greatly impressed the panel of local judges. The other competition was to select a local Helen of Troy. The Belfast winner was part time model, Miss Freida Campbell. She was in the foyer on the opening night, wearing an elegant classical styled dress, designed in London but made by Robinson and Cleaver's, greeting the special visitors. The distinguished guests included Lord and lady Wakehurst, Lord Brookeborough, members of the Stormont cabinet, top military personnel and members of the cinema trade. The cinema was packed, every seat having been booked by eight days before the event. In keeping with the elegance of the evening those seated in the circle wore evening wear, with a number of the ladies in classical type gowns. Before the film there was a gala stage show with music, local dancers and singers, and, of course, Stanley Wylie playing the Compton organ. Then the film began at the same time as elsewhere across the globe.

The film itself was fine entertainment, well directed, with plenty of action and colour, though there was some criticism of the acting of he inexperienced Rossana Podesta, an Italian actress, who played the main part. By the time the film had ended, around 11:00 pm, a large crowd had collected outside in Fisherwick Place, to see and admire the sight of the departing dignitaries, the dresses, and the style. The film itself ran for three weeks, and many schools used it as a source to encourage their students to take an interest in classical history. The whole affair was Hollywood at its most extravagant, and the people loved it. For most filmgoers going to the pictures was primarily fun and entertainment. All of those extras, the visiting stars, the competitions, the airmen, the mountain climbers and others added to the excitement of the occasions, stimulated audience interest, as well as generating good publicity for the films.

Orson Welles brings a whiff of cigar smoke and Hollywood to the Grand Opera House for Chimes at Midnight

Belfast experienced another world premiere in February 1956, a much quieter affair, but, to many, no less significant. It concerned a stage play, but one that had close cinematic links in the person of Orson Welles, and the fact that the play in question was "Chimes at Midnight." A report in the local papers in early February alerted the populace that a new Dublin Gate Theatre Production written by Orson Welles, and directed by Hilton Edwards would have its debut in the Grand Opera House on Tuesday 23rd February After five nights in Belfast it would then transfer to the Gate Theatre in Dublin. The cast, which consisted of 30 persons, including Orson Welles, 8 local and 2 Dublin actors, were already in rehearsal in London, but would be in Belfast on Monday the 22nd for a full dress rehearsal. As promised, Orson, complete with a large Hollywood type cigar, and accompanied by Hilton Edwards, arrived in the city on that day and gave a press conference. He recalled how he had begun his acting career in Dublin at the Gate Theatre, under the guidance of his "great friend," Hilton Edwards. He admitted that he (and Shakespeare) were responsible for writing the play, but that the direction was entirely Hilton's.

The play dealt with the career of Sir John Falstaff and his relationship with Prince Hal, played by Keith Baxter. Welles had adapted the appropriate sections from Shakespeare's Henry IV and Henry V, using Shakespeare's dialogue but linking the episodes with a commentary from Holinshed's Chronicles of England. It was a clever idea, but Welles was clearly anxious to see how audiences would respond. He didn't say so, but the production was partly a dry run to see if the play could be turned into a film. Hilton Edwards, in his comments, added that the emphasis was on the commoners and comedy rather than royalty and history. The World Premiere on Tuesday evening was graced by the presence of Lord and Lady Wakehurst who, from their box, looked over a packed theatre. It was an evening to savour with Welles giving a performance "on the grand scale" (Belfast Telegraph). The acting was fine and the critics were particularly moved by the denial scene when Prince Hal, now king with new responsibilities, rejected his old friend and all that he stood for. The stage settings were essentially simple but highly effective (Telegraph). The News Letter critic was equally impressed by what he called "this interesting if controversial theatrical experiment." The audience was in no doubt about its quality, and at the conclusion there was loud and prolonged applause, accompanied by many curtain calls.

Finally Orson Welles himself, bulky from the padding used to increase his size - one local critic unkindly compared him to the Michelin Man - came forward to speak to them, and to thank them for their enthusiastic response. He explained that he had appeared at first with some trepidation after a reporter warned him that he was to perform in what had been called "the deathtrap of the theatre." At that his voice rose and he "denounced this libel on your city." He found the Belfast audiences "attentive and warmly appreciative." Both the audience, and Welles, left the Opera House happy. Welles had already decided that he would turn "Chimes at Midnight" into a film. As was usual with him it took some time to get the necessary finances and set up the filming. The film was finally shot in Spain with an international cast, and first shown at the Cannes film festival in May 1966. Its release in Britain was not until March 1967. Welles still played the main part, and he had retained Keith Baxter to play Prince Hal, but the rest of the cast was changed. The narrator was Ralph Richardson, Jeanne Moreau played Doll Tearsheet, John Gielgud was Henry IV, and the unique Margaret Rutherford was Mistress Quickly. Wherever it was shown the film was praised as one of Welles's best, and it gave many local people satisfaction to think that it all began in the Opera House in Belfast.

During the Fifties a number of well known American stars visited the city. Bob Hope was the first, arriving by Enterprise from Dublin on Saturday 26th May 1951, for two shows in the Royal Hippodrome. He was accompanied by Marilyn Maxwell and Jerry Desmond.

He stayed in the Grand Central Hotel and it was there he met the Press. The News Letter reporter described him as "a small man, chewing gum, dressed conservatively in a sports jacket and dark flannels." His manager explained that they were at the end of a European tour and that Mr Hope was quite tired. The reporter commented that the tiredness didn't show. When he was presented with a shillelagh he swung it like a driver and wondered if it would help to improve his golf. He explained that it was only the second shillelagh he had been presented with, the first being in 1943 when he had come to entertain American troops stationed here during the war. After that he launched into a series of quips and one liners that had the room in fits of laughter. It was the same, later, in the Hippodrome, which was crowded for both houses. During the first show he was on stage for 72 minutes, and had the audience in the palm of his hand. Besides Marilyn Maxwell and Jerry Desmond, the audience was entertained by local acts including the singer Lelia Webster who later described the experience as one of the most treasured in her career. He left early the following morning, flying to France, and then on to the USA.

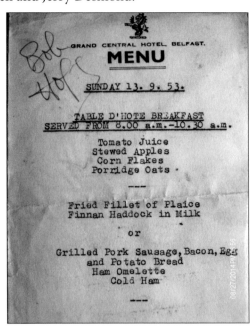

Memento of Bob Hope's visit to Belfast in 1953.

Two years later the Opera House announced that George Lodge had received a letter from Hope's manager recalling the "wonderful reception" they had received from the people during his last visit, and asked if another visit could be arranged, The result was that Bob Hope flew from London into Nutt's Corner along with Gloria de Haven and Jerry Desmond on Thursday 27th August 1953 for two shows in the Opera House. It was a bitterly cold day and the low temperatures took the performers by surprise, causing them to retreat into the plane before reappearing in overcoats, and in Hope's case, a five gallon stetson. The visit consisted of two shows in the Opera House on Wednesday, a trip to appear in Dublin, and back again for another two shows on Saturday evening. The prices were high, ranging from 30/`- in the circle down to 5/- in the gallery but the Telegraph critic thought it was worth every penny. Hope received a warm and rousing welcome. He was "in full vigour" from the beginning, and remained on stage for one hour and twenty minutes. He only stopped because of the large crowd collecting outside for the second show. The second show also overran and because of the lateness of the hour many of the audience missed the last buses and had to walk home. But no one complained, as they passed the time repeating Hope's one liners and jokes. He started with some local jokes, asking if those in the gallery got oxygen with their tickets, and was it true that the gallery had been used as a training ground for the assault on Everest. Bing Crosby came in for the usual "slegging" with Hope commenting that when Crosby squeezed an orange he got gold, while he was lucky to get juice. Dorothy Lamour and the Road films got due mention, and there were lots of golfing stories. It wasn't only the jokes, but the rapid fire delivery that delighted the crowd. It was widely accepted that the shows were a preparation for his coming appearance at the London Palladium, and the local critics noted that some old material from the appearance at the Hippodrome reappeared. Gloria de Haven added glamour, pleasing the women in the audience with her striking wardrobe, and the men with her singing and dancing.

The critics approved, and the happy faces of the audiences leaving the Opera House reflected their satisfaction. But a small minority were not entirely pleased. A letter to the Telegraph signed "a voice from the gods," with an address in Dundonald, was highly critical of the show. The writer had always enjoyed Hope's films but expressed "amazement" at what he regarded as "his lack of stagecraft." He complained that the performer forgot his lines on occasion, missed cues and even turned his back on the audience, so that some of his patter was inaudible in the gods. He wondered if he was watching a rehearsal instead of the real thing. He obviously was not in sympathy with the American style of humour, but his opinions were decidedly at odds with the majority view.

During the Fifties differences in styles of entertainment became more blurred, and performers who had made their reputations via records, or the variety stage, became better known to the public through their appearances in films or on television. American performers of that genre, who had also appeared in films, drew large crowds to the Opera House, the Royal Hippodrome and the King's Hall. Burl Ives, the folk singer, was a popular visitor. The News Letter reporter described his warm personality as "a refreshing breeze." He was completely relaxed and full of stories about his travels, his music and his film performances. He recalled that he had come to Europe in the Thirties as a hobo, travelling around with his guitar, singing and collecting folk songs. His travels had brought him to Belfast in 1933, but he was unknown then. Now, twenty years later,(September 1953), he was recognised wherever he went. He met local folk singers, and took lessons from Richard Hayward on playing the Irish harp. He also met fans and admirers in the Gramophone Shop in Donegal Street North, and signed autographs for them. His concerts in the Opera House where he performed for two weeks, were a sellout.

A short time after Burl Ives left Frankie Laine arrived at the Grand Central Hotel, to give two shows in the Royal Hippodrome, and caused great excitement. He had driven up from Dublin and was scheduled to appear later in the London Palladium. Crowds who had obviously bought his records, or seen him in his few appearances in films, collected outside the theatre and later in Royal Avenue, where traffic was blocked, and police struggled to keep the crowd under control. They shouted for him, and finally he appeared at a hotel window and sang to them. The Fifties are often described as dull and oppressive, but with moments like that the citizens of Belfast certainly didn't think so. Another outstanding performer, Jerry Colonna, arrived in the Opera House in August 1956 and made its walls vibrate with his amazing voice. He was combining his professional engagements with a tour of Europe, and an Irish News reporter described seeing him and his family attending mass every morning in St Mary's, Chapel Lane. Interviewers from all the local papers found him friendly, humorous and co-operative.

Another Hollywood actor who visited Belfast - in person as Dracula, the billboards promised - was Bela Lugosi, who came on 16th July 1951 for a week's run in the Grand Opera House. He had first chilled local audiences with his performance in the film "Dracula," which had shown in the Classic exactly twenty years before. By the Fifties, Lugosi, then approaching his seventies, was past his best and had decided to resurrect the original play of "Dracula" in an attempt to revitalise his career. The early performances in England proved disappointing to the actor and his cast. Audiences had refused to be frightened, and had laughed at some of the dialogue and stage situations. He was however, like Orson Welles, pleasantly impressed by Belfast audiences, who, according to the Whig critic, entered fully into the spirit of the play. They were "prepared to be thrilled and superbly horrified." Even before the curtain was raised he detected a pleasurable but tense aura of anticipation in the auditorium. During the play the audience responded to every climax, and the critic actually heard one or two screams.

Visit of Bela Lugosi in July 1951.

Sheila Wynn, who played the heroine Lucy in the play, recalled those screams in a later interview, and recalled how pleased Lugosi was to hear them. The production did have drawbacks, with off - stage music being played at the wrong times, and the special effects being rather disappointing. Lugosi rose above those problems and, according to the Whig critic, did produce moments of "authentic thrills of horror and menace," mainly by the use of his voice. He was well supported by Sheila Wynn and Arthur Hoskin, who played Van Helsing. At the end of the play Lugosi took a special curtain call, leaning forward to remind his watchers that there was no such thing as vampires, before disappearing in a sudden cloud of smoke, much to the approval of the audience.

The News Letter reporter was quite critical in his response to the play. He found Lugosi less horrifying at close quarters than in the "fantasy of film-land." He thought the mechanics of the presentation were disappointing, and was annoyed by the use of a badly scratched record off - stage for effects like the howling of werewolves. On the other hand he was impressed by the standard of the acting, and the effective use of lighting. The Irish News critic was more positive in his comments. He welcomed the opportunity of seeing Lugosi, "the great Hollywood master of thrills "in person, and was not disappointed. He found him a star performer who dominated the play. Overall, he thought, the play was skilfully presented, and he approved of the introduction of humour to relieve the horror. In all, he decided, it was well worth seeing, though he wondered why the Opera House had brought the play in July, when it obviously was more suited to "the dark days of winter." Sadly, Lugosi was struggling with his own "dark days." Unable to get serious parts he turned to drugs, and the local papers reported his death in August 1956. A year before, he had appealed for help to break his drug habit, and after rehabilitation, had announced that he was cured. Unfortunately his health continued to deteriorate. One sad report described him, before his death, as having a

Visit of Laurel and Hardy in June 1952.

tragic appearance, and being so weak that he couldn't stand without support. In contrast filmgoers preferred to remember him, bowing elegantly in a dress suit, while eyeing his intended victims with a sinister smile.

The following year the Opera House played host to two performers who were more than welcome whenever they arrived. They were Stan Laurel and Oliver Hardy, two of Hollywood's finest and most widely loved clowns, funnymen with a worldwide reputation. They opened on 9th June 1952 for a two - week appearance, playing to packed houses. Audiences, many of whom had enjoyed their adventures on screen from the days of the silent films, couldn't believe they were there on the Opera stage in front of them. Their reaction was a combination of affection and admiration as they laughed at what the Telegraph critic called "the hilarious technique so familiar on the screen." The sketches, in a railway waiting room, and in a burglary episode, were not original but they evoked roars of laughter. The Telegraph critic commended them for the fact that "their patter (was) spotlessly clean." Laurel and Hardy came across as gentlemen, both on stage and off. People who met them in Belfast commented on their lack of hauteur, and the fact that they seemed so "ordinary." There was no Grand Central for them, but they settled happily in the Midland Hotel on York Road. They enjoyed their stay in the city, and the sight seeing trips they took along the Antrim Coast Road and elsewhere. There was genuine regret when their engagement ended. Sadly, Ollie died five years later, but Stan had another ten years left during which he received an special Oscar for his contribution to screen comedy. He insisted that their only aim was to make people laugh. In that they succeeded.

Two months after their departure the Opera House presented a show that was very different in its attractions and content. It was headed by Gypsy Rose Lee, advertised as "the Queen of Glamour." Miss Lee, who was a sister of the film star June Havoc, was technically a stage performer who had made her reputation as a strip-tease dancer in burlesque. When the censors in New York forced the closure of the burlesque theatres, Gypsy Rose Lee went to Hollywood seeking work. She appeared in approximately a dozen mediocre films, but didn't have the success she had achieved on the stage. Many producers were reluctant to hire her because they believed that her name would keep family audiences away. Her arrival in Belfast was very low key, and little was written about her appearance on the Opera House stage. The Telegraph critic saw her show and admitted that she had little to learn about showmanship. She was, he wrote, supported by a group of "willowy lasses," and their lively display of dancing raised a few eyebrows in the audience. No serious objections were raised, and the show continued quietly for its week long run. If the same dances had featured in a film, the censor's scissors would have been busy. Of particular interest is the fact that one of the supporting acts in the Opera House was an unknown duo called Morcambe and Wise who, according to the local critic, got "a lot of fun from simple material." It was the same duo - who often expressed their admiration for Laurel and Hardy - that went on to dominate comedy on British television over the following decade.

Gypsy Rose Lee was later to write her biography, published in 1957, which became the basis of a successful stage musical, and, later, a film called "Gypsy, "(d. Mervyn LeRoy,

1962), starring Rosalind Russell, with Natalie Wood as Gypsy. The film arrived without any fanfare in Belfast in March 1963. It didn't open in a downtown cinema but had a combined premiere in the suburbs, in the Curzon, Majestic and Strand where it ran for one week only. Despite being described on the posters as being about "the girl who became the greatest show in show business" "Gypsy" didn't take off with the citizens of Belfast, either critics or public. It was an enjoyable musical with the more unattractive side of burlesque life toned down so as not to offend. Certainly it contained nothing that annoyed the censor.

In March 1958 another famous cinema glamour girl, Diana Dors, flew into the city to open a new hairdressing salon in Robb's city centre store. She was mobbed by a crowd estimated at about 3,000 who chanted "we want Diana." As the police struggled to control the largely female gathering, teenagers screamed and a number of women fainted. Miss Dors finally appeared at an upper window and showed her appreciation by throwing her bouquet of flowers down to her admirers. Later at a Press conference in the Grand Central Hotel she admitted that crowds frightened her, but they were one of the hazards of her profession. A few days later Mario Lanza arrived to give a concert in the Kings Hall, and into an even greater reception. He was greeted everywhere with wild enthusiasm, so much so that his concert had to be cut short short to prevent him being mobbed by his teenage fans. Like Miss Dors he found it all "very unsettling." Such visits were welcomed by fans, and caused much comment in the local papers, some of it unfavourable.

Roy Rogers and his wife, Dale Evans, arrived in Belfast yesterday. Among those who made sure of getting autographs were page boys Harry M'Guckian and Gabriel Fearon of the Grand Central Hotel.

Visit of Roy Rogers March 1954. Source: News Letter.

The children were not overlooked in those star visits. In March 1954 Roy Rogers arrived in Belfast, and appeared for two days in the Royal Hippodrome, giving six shows in all. He was accompanied by his wife Dale Evans and, of course, Trigger "the smartest horse in the movies." He came in via Nutt's Corner where he was greeted by a large crowd of admirers, and proceeded by car to the Grand Central where the crowds were so large that traffic in Royal Avenue was held up for a time. Trigger arrived that same morning in Larne on the ferry, and was met by a large group, mainly of children. There were cheers of delight when the horse turned towards them and curtseyed. He was taken to Belfast and stabled in Thompson's Yard in Chichester Street. Roy Rogers, like Gene Autry, took his responsibilities as a Western hero seriously. There was nothing offensive or upsetting to children in his films. He was known to children through his films and Saturday morning clubs, notably in the Curzon. Roy and his wife, Dale Evans, had a special interest in handicapped children, and made a point in Belfast of visiting local sick

Roy's companion, Trigger, coralled in a yard in Chichester Street. Source: Irish News.

children in hospital, and singing for them. Roy travelled around in a car, and stories of him riding Trigger in the streets are, sadly, untrue. The stage shows were crowded with family groups, and the audiences were treated to a programme of "homely and wholesome fun" (Belfast Telegraph) including clay pigeon shooting by Roy, roping and other Western pursuits, lots of singing, jokes, and demonstrations of Trigger's abilities. Children, many dressed in cowboy outfits, were amazed when Trigger demonstrated, among other skills, his ability to add, subtract, divide and multiply. One critic expressed surprise at the "evangelistic content" of some of the material, but children who were members of Saturday clubs would already have been familiar with that. After his Belfast appearance, Roy departed for Dublin, leaving the children with rich memories. Needless to say the sales of Roy Rogers cowboy costumes increased greatly in the months that followed.

The American West and its characters continued to fascinate children of all ages, and after Gene Autry and Roy Rogers their next hero to visit the city was Davy Crockett. The Disney film about his adventures, starring Fess Parker, showed in the Imperial in May 1956. The film was preceded by high level publicity, so that well before the film arrived, Davy Crockett and his coon - skin hat had entered into the local consciousness. The fact was illustrated when the man himself, in the shape of Fess Parker, who played him on the screen, reached Belfast a month before the arrival of the film. On the 16th April an advert in the local papers announced the personal appearance of Fess Parker at Robb's store in Castle Street. Parents were asked to bring their children to meet the "King of the Wild Frontier" at Robb's new Davy Crockett Trading Post. "They've all heard about him, sung about him," and they could now meet him. The visit was actually part of a three week tour of Britain, Ireland and Europe to boost the sales of Davy Crockett outfits.

The Belfast visit proved to be full of incident. Mr Parker and his party left Dublin and drove north, unaware that a group of five students from Queens dressed as Native American Indians waited in ambush near Portadown. Their plan was to fake a bicycle accident involving art student, Ethel Jenkins, and when Davy Crockett's car stopped they would emerge and kidnap him. He would then be held until a donation was made to a designated charity. Despite the careful planning it all came to nothing when the actor's car made a detour and avoided the trap. When Fess Parker was told about it later at a press conference in the Grand Central Hotel, he responded in his Southern drawl, "That would have been interesting." He told reporters that he had to declare his 120 year old flintlock rifle at the border, but that the officials let it pass. In the city he was received by the Lord Mayor in the City Hall, to whom he conveyed greetings from the Lord Mayor of Los Angeles. Meanwhile parents and children were collecting in Castle Street awaiting his appearance. The Irish News reporter calculated that about 4,000 people were soon pushing and shoving as the excitement rose. The children chanted, "We want Davy," but the crowd was so large that the star had to be smuggled in through a back door. When word spread that he was already in the building there was a surge forward, resulting in the breaking of panes of glass in the front door. Inside the shop the children climbed over furniture and pushed barriers aside to meet their hero. Attempts by staff, parents, police and Parker failed to restore order, so Davy made a strategic retreat back to the Grand Central. That evening he drove to Nutt's Corner and from there flew to Birmingham, and then on to Paris and other European cities.

One Davy may have gone but there were still others around, as was proved in December. A local Davy Crockett, complete with coon skin hat, arrived in the grounds of St Patrick's Training School by helicopter at the beginning of the month, to join Santa in a Christmas Parade along the Falls Road, which was awash with festive crowds. They sat side by side on a lorry decorated as a sleigh, which followed the school Brass Band to St Mary's Hall where a Christmas charity bazaar was officially opened. Davy Crockett had - temporarily at least - entered local culture in response to children's wishes. The enthusiasm of the children also meant bumper sales of coon hats and Davy Crockett outfits over Christmas. Many years later it emerged that there were direct descendents of Davy Crockett actually living in Belfast, and the Lord Mayor, Alderman William Geddis, was introduced to two of them, Olivia Crockett and her nephew Edgar Henderson.

Children had always formed a substantial segment of filmgoers, and since the Twenties cinemas had organized special matinees to cater for them. Those took place mainly on Saturday mornings when the schools were closed. In some of the neighbourhood cinemas they could be noisy and ill - disciplined affairs. As such they came in for criticism from those in charge of children's education and moral welfare. It wasn't only the general behaviour that was frowned upon, but also the contents of the films shown. Films were blamed at the time for all types of juvenile delinquency. Pressure brought by parents on cinema owners and managers convinced some of the latter that children's matinees needed to be better organized. One result was the formation of Children's Cinema Clubs with a clear set of rules, showing films carefully chosen to suit children. One of the best run local clubs was on the Ormeau Road, the Curzon Cinema Children's Club, which met on Saturday mornings. The poster advertising its films was adorned with an outline of Roy Rogers astride a rearing Trigger. Rogers was a special favourite in the Curzon.

The major circuits also had Saturday morning clubs. The Rank club was called the Gaumont and Odeon Boys and Girls Club, and it met every Saturday morning in the Gaumont cinema. It had been formed on 10th September 1946, after the war. It was well run, with well defined rules of behaviour. Children had to register to join, and in 1955 it had over 1000 registered Belfast children. The upper age of acceptance was 16 years, and the rules included no smoking, and no pets. The manager, John Mc Dougall, personally kept an eye on the club, applying the rules firmly but in a flexible manner. Dogs often followed their owners into the cinema, and he described spending Saturday morning at his desk, often with one or two dogs tethered to its legs. A typical show consisted of a cartoon, a serial (a western or space adventure), a Children's Film Foundation picture made especially for children with child actors, and an educational short on road safety or such. Lectures on topics appealing to children were also included. All the films shown were chosen and vetted by a panel of experts. Mr McDougal welcomed visits by parents, teachers, youth welfare workers and such to observe the proceedings.

The A.B.C. circuit also had a similar club called the ABC Minors which met on Saturday mornings in the Strand and the Majestic. The driving force behind it in Belfast was David Slane who established it in the Strand when he was manager there. When he was moved to the Majestic he set up a second branch there, which by the mid - Fifties had almost 1000 members. The pattern was similar to the Gaumont club. Only U certificate films were shown, mainly comedy and adventure films. Educational material included citizenship lectures, and films on topics like safety first. The meetings themselves were well ordered - the members could be as noisy as they liked but had to remain well behaved - and to ensure that, Mr Slane had the assistance of members of his staff, plus "monitors" specially chosen from the club members. Safety was a major concern, and the first four rows of the circle were not used in case of accidents. The monitors had special duties. They kept watch to ensure that the children themselves were safe, they led the community singing at the beginning of the show, and they introduced any visitors who came along. In return they were given special treats, like a visit behind the scenes to the projection room. The children were encouraged to bring any overseas visitors they knew, and Mr Slane told of one young Canadian visitor who came on a number of occasions wearing a cowboy outfit. Those visiting children were introduced from the stage by the monitors. When possible Mr Slane arranged visits from visiting celebrities, who in the Fifties included Edgar Bergen, Arthur Lucan (better known as Old Mother Riley) and Bob Monkhouse. Society's less fortunate children were not forgotten, and special visits to the cinema were arranged for orphan children and others.

The professed aims of the clubs were to supply suitable entertainment, and to encourage a sense of social responsibility in the children. Cynics and critics of films in general argued that the main aim was actually commercial: to encourage the cinema - going habit in its members and thereby ensure future audiences. In contrast, when the Magistrates Association of England submitted a memorandum to the Home Office in 1948 on the problems of children and the cinema, they highlighted and welcomed the growth of cinema clubs, which they believed could be "an influence for good." Speaking to mature persons who, in their youth, had attended local cinema clubs in Belfast one gets the feeling that the better run ones were not only fun, but, in the main, an enriching experience for young minds. Older cinemagoers look back on them with great affection.

Clever studio publicity which reached the public via the fan magazines and the local papers engendered an aura of glamour and excitement around films and their stars. With that atmosphere and the long nightly queues, one would have been forgiven for thinking that in the midst of national shortages, ration books and cutbacks the cinema was an exception, sailing along without problems. But appearances were deceptive, for behind the public facade the cinema trade faced serious problems during the post - war period. Mention has already been made of the power shortages in the Forties which curtailed the number of shows, and forbade outside displays of lights. Inside there was the continuing burden of entertainments tax which by then had reached 36% of the price of each seat. What had been introduced in 1916 to aid the war effort had become a sizeable source of income for the government, which was reluctant to give it up. Another serious problem after the war was a shortage of foreign currency, especially dollars.

The cash-strapped Labour government noted that Hollywood films earned about £17 million in Britain per year, and they decided to get a return for that. In August 1947 the government imposed a 75% tax on all American films entering Britain, thereby precipitating a major crisis in cinema circles. In response Hollywood announced that no more American films would be sent to Britain. According to the Irish News, Eric Johnson, a spokesman for the Hollywood producers stated that if Britain wanted American films, they would have to pay for them. "They shouldn't expect to get a dollar's worth of films for a quarter, which is what this tax will do." The government were taken aback because they hadn't expected such a sudden and dramatic response from Hollywood. Government ministers, including

Hugh Dalton, appeared in newsreel interviews and explained that while they would miss seeing the likes of Humphrey Bogart this was a matter of "Food before Flicks." Local audiences were not impressed. The cinema trade in Britain was appalled. A special meeting of the C.E.A. representing 4,500 cinemas, including those from N.Ireland, condemned the government tactic as "stupid" and repeated their belief that it would cause cinema closures. The local trade had no way of influencing the outcome of the problem, except by supporting the C.E.A., and hoping that some kind of compromise would be reached. After much posturing by both sides, an agreement was signed on 3rd May 1948 by which the tax would be lifted and the import of Hollywood films could begin again. In the meantime the renters drew on the pool of recent Hollywood films already in Britain which weren't liable for the new tax. There were also older films which could be revived, and an increasing number of those began to appear on local screens. British films also tried to fill the gap, and the Classic even showed a programme of snippets from Rank productions that were in the pipeline but, the problem, according to one local cinema manager, was that Belfast patrons preferred American films.

The threat to the film - going habit meant different things to different groups. To the government and the trade it was a matter of money and employment, to the general populace it represented a loss of their favourite relaxation, but to those interested in cultural matters it opened up the possibility of educating the general public on the delights of quality film - making. Writing in the Irish News, a commentator, using the cover name Gianni, discussed what he called the Anglo-American film war, and suggested that a period without American films might be culturally beneficial. He was obviously a person of mature years who was familiar with silent films as well as talkies, probably a member of a local Film Society, and, certainly, a regular film goer. He deplored the poor quality of many American films, which he blamed on those who go to the cinema two or three times a week regardless of what is showing. Their choice, he argued, was based on habit and was completely indiscriminate. As long as people acted like that, he argued, they would get the films they deserved. If American films were stopped people might think more about what they were watching, and become more selective in their choice. There were many possibilities for interesting films in the form of documentaries such as John Grierson and Robert Flaherty had made. Who wouldn't appreciate the delicate beauty of the silhouette films of Lotte Reneiger? Why don't film makers turn to the work of Irish writers like Maurice Walsh (what would he have made of "The Quiet Man"?), or Erskine Childers' "Riddle of the Sands" (filmed in 1979 with Simon MacCorkindale). Why not more continental films, or quality revivals? He pointed out that audiences had been surprised recently by revivals shown in the city, at their quality, and how well they had stood the test of time. There were endless opportunities to be explored with the careful choice of older films by Hitchcock, Lang, Korda and others. The main thrust of his argument was that cinema could be both entertaining and serious. Ironically many of the suggestions he made, especially with regard to older and foreign films, first reached the general public through the medium of the "great enemy," television.

A major film renter whose offices, Gresham Film Services, were located at 18, Gresham Street, was interviewed by the Telegraph on the problem of the lack of new films, and pointed out that the use of revivals had many advantages. They were free of the new tax,

Garbo returns.

they met the filmgoers' preferences for American films, and they were cheaper to rent. As a result revivals, or reissues as they were called, became an integral part of cinema programmes during the Forties and the Fifties, giving filmgoers an opportunity to see films they had missed, or to renew acquaintance with old favourites. The Opera House gave its patrons the opportunity to see Charlie Chaplin again in "The Gold Rush," and Greta Garbo in "Camille". Both films were warmly received and well supported. "The Gold Rush" had a soundtrack added in which Chaplin explained the silent narrative. The result, according to the Telegraph critic, was an excellent revival. He also welcomed the opportunity to see Garbo again. The film was advertised as having "the most fabulous personality of our time in her greatest screen romance," and he encouraged the younger generation to go along and see her. While much about the film had dated, he felt that that she still came across as fresh and modern. "Gone With the Wind" packed cinemas again in 1956 and 1962, as did the Charles Laughton version of "The Hunchback of Notre Dame" which ran in the Imperial for two weeks. The Imperial also successfully presented Laurence Olivier and Greer Garson in "Pride and Prejudice". Equally popular reissues were Alexander Korda's "The Thief of Baghdad," "Each Dawn I Die" with James Cagney and George Raft, and "Thanks For the Memory" with Bob Hope. "Rebecca", advertised with the slogan "to see again," drew large crowds to the Mayfair, as did Jane Russell in "The Outlaw" to the Royal Cinema. Charles Laughton in "The Private Life of Henry VIII", Cecil B. deMille's "The Plainsman" with Gary Cooper, and "The Black Swan" with Maureen O'Hara and Tyrone Power also drew the crowds. John Ford's "The Quiet Man" in which Miss O'Hara and Barry Fitzgerald starred starred with John Wayne, was reissued more than once. The Telegraph critic noted the fact and wrote approvingly that no film was more worthy of such treatment, because it was the one of the most enjoyable films he had ever watched. So, despite the shortage of new films, Belfast audiences were well catered for, and the local cinemas survived the crisis. But the trade knew that the main problem hadn't gone away. That problem was the growth of television.

Television began to take audiences away from the cinemas in the United States during the post - war years. The trend coincided with post - war social changes and population migration to the new urban suburbs. In Belfast the papers mentioned the numerical decline in American cinema audiences, but during the Forties and early Fifties it seemed to be an essentially American phenomenon, probably because Belfast didn't have a television service yet. Television pictures were already available in England and Scotland, and some lucky households in North East Antrim and along the east coast of Ireland could receive them, though Belfast remained outside the range of the English and Scottish transmitters. The occasion that spurred locals to demand a service was a Royal event. When King George VI died in early February 1952 Belfast citizens depended on the cinema newsreels to see the funeral and State ceremonies. When it was announced that the crowning of his successor was to be shown on television people began to ask: why can't we see it? One of the main topics of conversation among the Unionist population during early 1953 was the imminent coronation of the new queen, Elizabeth, on 2nd June. The BBC was pressurised to do something about allowing local people to see the historic proceedings on TV. A temporary station was set up at Glencairn and was officially opened on 1st May, in time for the ceremonies. The BBC covered the whole proceedings with an amazing - for the time - seven hours of almost continuous reporting. Interest was high both here, though the station only covered the Belfast area and parts of the east coast, and abroad. Outside the British Isles (including Dublin) pictures were beamed to France, Belgium, Holland, Denmark, and Germany. Special planes waited for tele film of the event and flew them directly to the U.S.A. Technicians on board processed the pictures so that when the planes landed they were ready for immediate transmission. It was the first great test of television as a popular medium and the BBC rightfully gleaned fulsome praise for its organisational skills. The whole exercise was a flash forward to what the future held.

The television reception in Belfast was, according to the Irish News "well nigh perfect." Observers were impressed by the immediacy of the images, an immediacy that film makers couldn't yet meet. Where possible family groups watched television sets in their homes, while other groups watched in halls. The Arts Theatre cancelled their play (The Colleen Bawn) that day, but erected a screen, 4 feet by 3 feet, on its stage which showed the television pictures from 10:15 a.m. Belfast Corporation arranged entertainment in the parks for those who celebrated in the fresh air, with band music, children's fancy dress parades, football and other games, cycle races and gymnastics. Many buildings, including some cinemas (notably the Crumlin), and streets were a blaze of colour, with flags and bunting, both downtown and in Unionist working class areas. Many streets off the Shankill and in East Belfast had organized street parties with outdoor dances later in the day. By mid - afternoon the city centre was nearly empty as the citizens enjoyed those diversions.

Most locals still had no access to television sets, (according to the BBC only about 600 households had TV licences) and followed events on the radio. One local firm rented radios at 20 pence a week. Many waited for the cinema newsreels to see images of the day's events The newsreel companies, which were well used to deadlines, rose to the occasion. Highlights of the ceremonies were quickly processed in London and flown to Nutt's Corner, arriving by 10:00 p.m. From there the reels were driven to the city and shown in the Royal Hippodrome, Royal Cinema and the Imperial at around 10:30 pm that same evening. Pathé, British Movietone and others produced longer newsreels with pictures that were large in size and rich in detail, on local screens the next day. In the days following the Coronation, normal programmes in the cinemas included "special" pictures of the historic occasion. The Regent offered a "special extra long" Coronation Newsreel; the Royal Cinema presented "Coronation News"; the Curzon had "Coronation Flashes"; the Astoria a "special newsreel," while the Troxy showed special scenes in a Coronation Day Pageant. The ABC group, the Ritz, Majestic and Strand, showed a "special" Pathé News coverage, and on Wednesday. evening switched their projectors off at 9 o'clock so that their patrons could hear the Queen's speech to the nation (sound only, of course). That was followed by yet another "special" film called Coronation Day. The newsreels were followed with intense interest, and in most of the cinemas there was cheering and clapping when the new Queen appeared. Despite the obvious success of the newsreels and documentaries astute cinema owners, like the Currans and the Gastons, realised that independent halls and small groups were facing a difficult and changing situation.

The Nationalist areas reacted like another world. The cinemas quietly ignored the whole proceedings, and carried on normally, as did most of their audiences. The roads and streets were bare of bunting or flags. The Nationalist response was cool, even bemused. On the Falls Road people were more interested in the imminent opening of Casement Park. In contrast the excitement remained high elsewhere in the city, especially when the Imperial and the Gaumont presented "A Queen is Crowned" the following week. It was advertised as "the only Coronation film in Technicolor." It ran for nearly 80 minutes, and had a commentary spoken by Sir Lawrence Olivier. It was the cinema's reply to TV, a vast panorama of the ceremonies which made the small black and white pictures look a little primitive. The critic from the Belfast Telegraph described it as "incomparable," and "equal to Hollywood's brightest and best." An overreaction, perhaps, but the film caused great excitement in the city, not only because of the richness and detail of its content, but because of its magnificent colour photography. The latter even impressed the discerning eyes of George Shanahan, the experienced chief projectionist in the Gaumont. Equal praise was lavished on another film version of the event, "Elizabeth Is Queen," an hour long colour (Warnercolor) documentary which showed in the ABC cinemas and the Regent. Mr G.W.Irvng, the manager of the Ritz, described how he had received lots of inquiries from Dublin about the Coronation films. After discussions with Mr Irving, and F. Murray, the manager of the Regent, the Great Northern Railway company agreed to charge special fares from Dublin to Belfast for those who wanted to see the Coronation films. How many availed of the offer is not recorded.

In certain quarters the Coronation films were not welcomed, and were regarded merely as English propaganda. Vague threats of violence were made against those cinemas which showed them. Nothing of note happened in Belfast but the Savoy in Newry, and the Picture House in Banbridge, both of which had booked "A Queen is Crowned" were bombed, and badly damaged. In Dublin the Minister of Justice admitted that he was not aware of any threats, specific or anonymous, made to cinema managers showing the film. Any objections reported were of a minor nature, like the man who entered a Dublin pub where a crowd were watching the ceremonies on TV, and smashed the set, before being arrested for disturbing the peace.

There were those in the cinema trade in Belfast who wished that all the television sets in the country could be broken, but they had to watch as sets and their ugly aerials spread across the city. On 31st Oct 1959 - that day of infamy, as John Gaston, the owner of the Curzon called it - the ITV transmitter was officially inaugurated by Sir Lawrence Olivier, and Ulster Television began its broadcasts. At the beginning the cinema trade had turned its face firmly against television but as the number of TV sets increased, and as cinemas began to experience what the Telegraph called "the lean days of audience attendance," the more progressive members of the trade began to reassess their position, and to consider that maybe the two could exist side by side. In June 1955 the deputy chairman of Associated British Pictures visited Belfast to attend the première of "The Dam Busters" in the Ritz, and at a press conference he declared that the cinema could meet the competition from television. Thus the policy of his company would continue to be one of expansion, and he inspected a site that ABC had bought on the Crumlin Road, where they hoped to build a new cinema comparable to the Majestic or Strand. The project never got off the ground, though the chairman of the company later said that the company had plans to rebuild some of their cinemas, and to modernise 20 others. Other visitors to Belfast had similar messages of optimism. There wasn't much that the Belfast owners could do. The main battle was being fought in America, and they could only wait for the fallout.

In the meantime the cinematic map was changing around them. The big boys, mainly in the person of J. Arthur Rank, were moving in. Major English circuits had long been part of the local cinema scene but not to the same extent as Rank. During and after the war the Rank Organization had expanded and brought under its umbrella the main arms of film production, distribution and exhibition in Britain. That policy of expansion included Ireland, which Rank perceived as a natural and worthwhile market for its films. In January 1946 J. Arthur Rank himself and his chief advisors visited Belfast to discuss matters relating to the cinema with local representatives, and then travelled on to Dublin where he acquired a "substantial interest" (Irish News) in cinemas in Cork, Limerick and Dublin, including the impressive but cavernous Theatre Royal. He announced that more British films would be shown in the Free State in future. But he also had an eye on Belfast and made a number of visits there during the late Forties and early Fifties. He was made welcome in quarters where cinema moguls were not usually encouraged.

J. Arthur Rank was unique in many ways. His family had made their money in the flour business but he had always had an interest in films. His family were devout Methodists and their generosity in supporting church matters had made them well known in Methodist circles in Belfast. During one of his visits in the early Fifties he and his wife were guests at a luncheon given by the clergy and lay members of Belfast District of the Methodist Church in Donegall Square Church Hall. In his address to the members he praised films as a vital tool of evangelisation, and recalled how he had started his career making religious films in 1933. He now had seven mobile cinemas which toured the rural areas showing religious films in church halls and other venues He found they were an excellent way of attracting young people. His comments went down well with the audience and speakers thanked and praised him for all he had done to spread the message of Methodism. As a mark of their appreciation he and his wife were presented with gifts of Irish linen.

But Rank was also a business man and the results of his visits to the city bore other fruits. His organization hoped to build a new cinema in downtown Belfast but, after an investigation of the situation, decided to acquire an established successful cinema instead. So it was that the Classic passed into Rank ownership, and as a sign of that change was renamed the Gaumont, in 1950. In February 1955 the Rank organization consolidated its position by purchasing the eleven cinemas owned by Irish Theatres Ltd. That gave them control of the Alhambra, the Coliseum, Stadium, Forum, Mountpottinger Picturedrome,and the New Princess within the city, plus the Regal in Larne, the Regal Enniskillen, the Palladium Portstewart, the Palladium Coleraine and the Picture House in Lisburn. Included in the deal was a new cinema, the Tivoli, being built at Finaghy and which opened in June 1955. The new acquisitions became part of a new company, Odeon (N.I.) Ltd with George Lodge as Director.

George Lodge was a key player in the transfer of the the downtown cinemas to the Rank Organization. He had arrived in Belfast from England in 1929 during the changeover to sound. He brought with him a new sound system called Majestone which, according to some reports, he had perfected himself, and which he hoped to sell to the local cinema owners. His greatest success was to convince the Imperial to install it, and during the negotiations he became friendly with the Managing Director, Ben McDowell, who, in turn, opened doors for him to the local cinema establishment. Lodge was an astute business man, and he understood how to advance his financial and business standing. When McDowell died he replaced him as general manager of the Imperial and the Gaiety. At the beginning of the war he had filmed a ploughing demonstration at Stormont, meeting the Prime Minister, Sir Basil Brooke, and other political heavyweights in the process. From that event he produced a five minute propaganda film called "Plough for Victory," which was shown in local cinemas. It was much praised, with the News Letter describing it as "compact, informative and persuasive". From then onwards his profile continued to rise. During the war he was vigorous in support of the war effort. He was quick to open the Imperial on Sundays for the entertainment of the Forces, and he worked as Liaison Officer with the film industry, supplying the local Home Guard and other groups with government information and training films. In 1944 he was awarded an MBE for that work, and in 1947 he also received an OBE for providing entertainment for the Forces.

In the years following the war he consolidated his position in the local cinema business. He became a director on the board of Warden Ltd. and through the accumulation of stock took a controlling interest in the company, with responsibility for the Royal Cinema and the Opera House. When G.L.Birch, who had managed the Royal Hippodrome with spectacular success since 1940, retired in 1951, Lodge took over his interests in April of that year. He then had direct control of the Imperial, the Gaiety (which he sold in 1956), the Royal Cinema, the Opera House and the Royal Hippodrome. He was also a member of the Board of Irish Theatres Ltd. with responsibility for its booking policy, and played a major role in the sale of that group to the Rank Organization. By 1958 he was chairman of the local branch of the CEA. Recognising Lodge's prominent position in, and experience of, the local trade, Rank appointed him Director of Odeon (N.I.) Ltd, the company which ran their local business. George Lodge was probably the most influential figure in the local cinema scene then, and many saw him as the main obstacle preventing Rank from completely dominating the local industry. As such his activities were watched warily by the A.B.C. chain which owned the Ritz, Majestic and Strand, by the few independents, like the Mayfair, still operating city centre cinemas, and the Curran circuit which owned the only other first class downtown cinema, the Regent, still outside the Rank-Lodge net.

There was general surprise when it became known in early 1956 that the Currans were discussing the sale of their circuit to Rank. According to the Irish News a figure around £600,000 had been offered. Negotiations continued quietly during the year, interrupted by the unexpected death of John Curran in August. John J. Curran was only 58 years old and was the eldest son of the late Michael Curran (died 1940) who had founded Curran Cinemas. He had always had a passion for films and as a young man had worked as a projectionist in the Alhambra and Popular cinemas, before joining his father in the latter's expanding electrical engineering company. When the Curran company built the Astoria cinema at Knock in 1934, John was appointed its manager. He had a wide working knowledge of the industry, and his death was a blow to the company at a crucial period in its development. The remaining brothers, Michael, James, Paul, Gerard and Frederick, continued the negotiations and before the end of the year the Rank organization had added the Regent, Lyceum, Regal, Broadway, Astoria, Apollo, and Capitol to his Belfast cinemas, plus, outside the city, the Tonic (Bangor), the Midland and Strand (Derry), the Majestic (Portrush), and the Frontier (Newry). Rank moved the administrative centre of their local organization to the Capitol Cinema where Roy Eveleigh was brought over from England and installed as managing director of Odeon (N.I.), replacing George Lodge. The last Curran adverts appeared in the Belfast newspapers during the last week in 1956.

The expansion of Rank seemed to augur well for the future, but at the same time the local papers carried statements from the company which suggested otherwise. It was claimed that 230 Rank cinemas in Britain were running at a loss, and that 79 of them would be closed by the end of 1956. Some would be sold, others converted to dance halls, and the remainder turned into bowling alleys. By then the Rank Organization owned the majority of the best cinemas in the city, with the exception of the Ritz, the Royal Hippodrome, the Royal Cinema and the Grand Opera House. While the latter was technically a venue mainly for live theatre, it qualifies also as a cinema. It had played an important, if largely unrecognised, role in the early history of local cinema, and George Lodge had reintroduced showings of specialist films during the Fifties. The Ritz, still the premier cinema in the city, was owned by Associated British Cinemas and was not on the market, but Rank had their eyes on those theatres under George Lodge's control. Lodge recognised the financial possibilities of the situation and made his first move in late 1959, with the sale of the Imperial to a development company. A local reporter noted that there was no explanation given for the sudden closure of the Imperial, nor was there any apparent good reason for it. However Lodge was, above all, a businessman and the sale was essentially a matter of making money. The extinguishing of the Imperial's lights on that last night, the 28th November 1959, may have saddened regular patrons, but the majority of the audience treated it more like a celebration than a funeral. When the projectors were turned off for the last time after the final showing of the French murder mystery, "The Foxiest Girl in Paris," starring Martine Carol, George Lodge came onstage and spoke to the audience. He recalled the fact that the cinema had been opened in 1914 by Sir Crawford McCullagh who was Lord Mayor then, and that he had been presented with a gold key to celebrate the occasion. Sir Crawford's son had now presented the same key to him, in a very generous gesture. Lodge spoke of his own long association with the Imperial. He indicated that about half of the present staff would find employment in his other halls, the Royal Cinema, the Royal Hippodrome and the Opera House, and expressed the hope that the rest would be taken on by other halls in the city. Patrons were given permission to take away small souvenirs, but, almost immediately after the last show, workmen began stripping the building in preparation for its new owners, Scott Bros., who intended to turn it into shops and offices. The site is occupied today (2014) by a booking office for the Titanic experience. The association is appropriate because the Belfast cinema industry itself was beginning to founder.

The author has particularly warm feelings for the Imperial, a cinema he often visited. He recalls settling down one Saturday evening to enjoy "All About Eve" starring Bette Davis (d. Joseph Mankiewicz, 1950). About ten minutes into the film he felt a light tap on the shoulder and a voice behind him whispered "Excuse me, but I think you are on fire. I can see smoke rising." Suddenly he was aware of excessive heat at the base of his spine and on standing up discovered that the bottom of his jacket was burnt and smouldering. The culprit was a cigarette butt that had been carelessly disposed off and had become jammed into the bottom of the tip-up seat. The author, who wasn't a smoker, realised dramatically that smoking wasn't just a social nuisance but could damage a person both internally and externally. Not to mention what it could do to one's Saturday gear!

Across Arthur Square the Royal Cinema continued to show films for another two years, but it was a shadow of its former glory. The cinema that had once called itself the home of Art was reduced to presenting X certificate horror bills. The foyer walls which in the past had been covered with tasteful posters illustrating the films of Chaplin, Griffith, Mary Pickford, Douglas Fairbanks, Buster Keaton, Fritz Lang and other masters of the screen, sported lurid invitations to see "Street Corner," and "Lost Women," or "The Fiend Without a Face" and "The Killer Shrews," or "The Incredible Petrified World" and "Teenage Zombies." A typical advert proclaimed in red lettering: "she was a tigress! exciting! dangerous! untamed! see Eleanora Rossi in "Enticement". In December 1960 the Royal showed Belfast's first "nudie" film with the highly original title "The Nudist Story," which proved a source of humour for those local critics who even mentioned it. Now and again there were flashes of the old Royal Cinema, as when it presented Gael Linn's splendid documentary "Mise Eire," and later John Ford's "The Rising of the Moon." As the overall quality of its films declined, the fabric of the building both outside and inside was allowed to deteriorate. The manager, Cecil King, retired in 1959 after 50 years in the business and was succeeded by Norman Crayton, who remained at the helm until George Lodge arranged its sale for Warden Ltd, for development as shops and offices. It closed quietly in early April 1961, after showing its last film, "A Man Alone", a fine Western starring Ray Milland. Some time later the papers carried photographs of the building with its frontage torn away and its interior exposed as a mass of rubble. Another link with the past was severed, but Belfast just shrugged its shoulders, and went about its business. That complacency was disturbed somewhat by other events which took place in late 1960 and during the following year.

In late 1960 rumours began to circulate in Belfast that the Grand Opera House, regarded by theatre goers as the gem among the city's entertainment establishments, would soon be sold and converted to an American style bowling alley. George Lodge was questioned about the matter by reporters, and dismissed the rumours as untrue. He did admit that the Opera House was run as a commercial enterprise and could be sold for the right price. He defended his record at the Opera House and claimed that he had given the Belfast public the type of entertainment they wanted. He argued that the more esoteric types of attraction, like ballet or opera, that "a vociferous minority" sought, were not box office, and would not support the theatre financially. Agreement with that view was expressed by some working actors like James Young, but others saw it as a good argument for the theatre to be supported from public funds.. What soon became clear was that the negotiations about the Opera House's future also included the Royal Hippodrome, and rumours abounded about their fate. One option was that both buildings might be demolished and replaced by a cinema and bowling alley under one roof. Another was that the Opera House would be refurbished, while the Royal Hippodrome became Belfast's premier theatre with a government subsidy supporting the high costs of ballet, opera and drama. Lodge dismissed those scenarios, and insisted that he had bookings for the Opera House until the end of 1961, and that there would be no change in its status.

Not everyone was convinced. A public letter signed by eleven prominent members of the arts, including Havelock Nelson, Richard Hayward, Jack Loudan, William Conor and Jeanne Cooper Foster condemned any change to the Opera House, such as a conversion to a bowling alley, that would damage "the fate of this charming building." Any such move they believed, would "represent a loss to the cultural, social and civic life of Ulster". The theatre must be maintained even as a public trust. Despite their efforts, by the 28th November, the Opera House and the Royal Hippodrome had become part of the Rank organization. Mr Eveleigh issued a statement that Rank had no plans to use the buildings for anything other than entertainment. There was no necessity to worry about changes to the Opera House, he assured interested parties soothingly, as they had no plans to change policy "at the present time". A short time later the News Letter carried a report that both

buildings would be refurbished, and that the Opera House would, in time, become a Top Rank Cinema. In the meantime the Opera House continued with a mixture of films and live entertainment until May 1961 when the staff were given notice, and the hall was closed for renovations. On 23rd September of the same year the Gaumont closed without any fuss, and it was announced that the staff would transfer to the refurbished Hippodrome when it opened in October, renamed the Odeon.

Other developments were taking place at the same time which were changing the commercial geography of the Corn Market - Arthur Square district. In November George Lodge applied for

Changing city centre—The Royal Cinema, Arthur Square, Belfast, which is being demolished to make room for shops.

End of the Royal Cinema.

planning permission to replace the Royal Cinema with shops and offices, and by early December permission had been granted. As described above, the building was then sold to developers. Its site is now occupied by Starbucks. Another bombshell followed when it was announced that the Empire Theatre, which had opened on 3rd December 1894, and which had played an important part in the early history of the cinema in Belfast, had been sold and would close soon. The manager, Frank Reynolds, announced that they would go out with a "cheerful" farewell, a week of special charity events, headed by singer Bridie Gallagher. The last night, 3rd June 1961 saw the theatre packed with a highly emotional crowd, but police were also there to ensure that souvenir hunters didn't become too exuberant. The fittings were duly auctioned and the empty building was handed over to Littlewoods at the end of the month for conversion to a store. Sam Thompson, whose play "Over The Bridge" had been presented with great success in the Empire when the Group rejected it, echoed W.B.Yeats' admonition to the citizens of Dublin when he declared that the people of Belfast should be ashamed of themselves for allowing their two main theatres to be closed, while they did nothing to prevent it.

Ritz: Ben Hur.

The local secretary of the National Association of Theatrical and Kine Employees took a more practical approach to the closures, describing them as "a blow to theatregoers and workers." He called upon the government to do something about reducing the Entertainments Tax which he claimed was a major factor in the closure of local theatres and cinemas, thereby causing even more unemployment. By the end of the Fifties it was clear that the entertainment industry, and especially the cinema industry, was undergoing dramatic change. That process of change would continue, and accelerate, through the Sixties and later. By the end of the century the seemingly impossible had happened. The familiar picture palaces and their associated patterns and habits of cinema going had all but been swept away.

CHAPTER TWENTY NINE
Big Men, Big Horses and Fine Big Girls

At the beginning of the Fifties the distribution pattern of cinemas across the city was basically the same as in the late Thirties, before the outbreak of war. Physical changes, due mainly to the wear and tear of buildings, had produced a hierarchy of quality that was familiar to regular filmgoers. The Ritz, or ABC, as the new owners, Associated British Cinemas, vainly tried to call it from 1963, sat at the apex of the cinematic pyramid, dominating the cinematic landscape. It was distinguished by its size, its gleaming cream exterior, the comfort of its interior, its decor, its reverberating Compton organ and the quality of its first - run films. During the Fifties an evening at the Ritz was still a memorable event. In its shadow were the other downtown halls, the Royal Hippodrome, the Royal Cinema, the Regent and the Imperial, less opulent maybe but otherwise delivering quality and good taste. On the fringes of that group were the historic Alhambra, showing its age, and the brash Mayfair, each with their own personality and clientele. Below those were the quality suburban cinemas of the Curran circuit, and ABC's Majestic and Strand which were mini Ritzs in their own right. All those were comfortable, well - run cinemas, showing quality films which already had completed their first runs downtown in the Regent or Imperial, or the Ritz. Then there were the independents like the Windsor, the Castle, the Ambassador and the Clonard, and the halls owned by Irish Theatres Ltd which included the Mount Pottinger Picturedrome, the New Princess, the Coliseum, the Alhambra, the Stadium, and the Forum. The Windsor was beginning to fray a little at the edges, but always attracted large audiences, mainly from the Donegal Road and Grosvenor Road areas, with its excellent double bills of highly entertaining films that had already done the rounds but were still able to draw the crowds. The Windsor programmes were usually three hours of first class entertainment. The elegant but increasingly battered Clonard served the same purpose for the audiences on the lower and middle Falls road area.

At the bottom of the pyramidal heap were halls like the Central, the Gaiety, the Diamond, the West End, the Arcadian and the Sandro. They were basic, well - worn halls, located in or adjacent to crowded working class streets. They have become the stuff of myth, involving wooden benches in the pits, eccentric characters on the staff and among the customers, jamjars for payment, urine running down the carpets, ushers reducing exuberant youths to silence with the threat, and occasionally use of, sticks and clubs. Some of the stories have been exaggerated for effect (especially after the cinemas were gone) but there is no denying that they were the fleapits and bughouses of the system, and one, metaphorically speaking, took one's life in one's hands entering them. To passersby each of them exhaled its own special eau de cinema, a heady mixture of stale tobacco smoke, sweat, urine, cleansing fluids and other indefinable ingredients. They struggled not only to keep order, but to survive, their meagre profits eroded by the entertainment tax. They were the first to feel the chill winds of change. Most of them didn't have the financial resources to install the new wide screens and sound technologies that the film companies began to introduce in the Fifties, to fight the spread of television. Most of them closed during the late Fifties and Sixties.

The first to go was the Gaiety in 1956 and the workmen were soon rebuilding its interior. Rumour had it that it was being turned into a dance hall, but in fact it became a supermarket. The Central in Smithfield closed its doors and pulled its metal gates across for the last time in 1958. It lay derelict until 1965 when it was bought by the Post Office and turned into a car park for post office vehicles. Today it is part of the Castlecourt Shopping complex. The Shankill Picturedrome also closed in 1958, and the McKibben group then went on to close its two other cinemas, the Diamond in 1959 and the West End in 1960. The Arcadian closed in February 1960, its last film being a comedy with Red Skelton called "Public Pigeon Number One." To locals in the Albert Street area its departure was nothing to laugh about.

The Rank organization meantime was studying its new acquisitions from its purchase of the Curran and Irish Theatres circuits. Their policy was to sell off those cinemas that were not showing a profit, and to refurbish and update those that were. The Coliseum was closed in June 1959 and interested parties suggested that it would be perfect for a civic theatre. The Stormont government was approached for a grant of £50,000 to purchase and refurbish the building, but the request was turned down. Talk of a civic theatre remained a hot topic and when the Sandro in Sandy Row closed in September 1961. Mike Emmerson announced that if he could raise £20,000 he would buy the old cinema, and convert it to a theatre. His intention was to acquire a hall that he could use during Queen's Festivals to present plays or foreign films. The money was not forthcoming, and the project fell through. Attention then focused on the Opera House as a more appropriate venue but, as described above, Rank purchased the building and restyled it as a commercial cinema. The Alhambra was put on the market, causing concern at the prospective loss of one of the city's most historic places of entertainment, which had attracted crowds for over eighty years as a music hall, theatre and cinema. The first films shown in Belfast had flickered on a screen in the Alhambra but that didn't seem to interest the Rank organization. The problem solved itself when the building burned down in September 1959, giving the owners the opportunity to sell it on for demolition, and later development as an office block.

In East Belfast the New Princess closed in April 1960 though the Mountpottinger Picturedrome held on until May 1970 before switching off its projectors. In the city centre the Gaumont was sold to a supermarket chain (British Home Stores) and that, combined with the closure of the Imperial, the Royal Cinema and the Empire ended the entertainment functions of the Arthur Square area, concluding a tradition that extended back to the opening of what became the Theatre Royal in February 1793. Today there is a rather tenuous connection to those lively venues in the shop White Stuff, which now occupies the corner site where Mooney's Public House stood. Upstairs, there is a small rest - room where customers can sit on ten genuine tip-up cinema seats, and watch a film (DVD) on a flat screen television attached to the wall. Sadly the seats are not remnants from a local cinema, but were brought in from England by the builders. For those who still remember the past with its long queues and buskers they conjure up pleasant ghosts.

Between 1950 and 1960 nine cinemas closed, all of them, with the exception of the Imperial, old rundown buildings at the lower end of the market. During the same decade the Mayfair also closed, but was quickly transformed into a News and Cartoon cinema, the first in the city, by its new owners. Between 1961 and 1969 there were 12 more closures which included the Classic/ Gaumont and Royal Cinema (both in 1961), plus the former Curran cinemas the Lyceum (April 1966) the Apollo(December 1962) and the Regal (January 1967). Also closed were the independent cinemas the Castle (March 1966), the Popular (February 1962) and the Clonard (March 1966). The departure of the Clonard meant that there was only one cinema - the Broadway - left on the Falls Road, while the Shankill Rd., which had seen the closure of McKibben's West End and Picturedrome halls had only

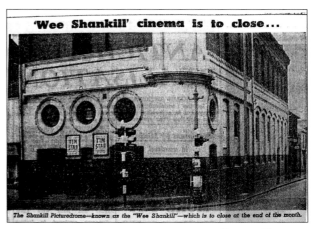

'Wee Shankill' cinema is to close...

The Shankill Picturedrome—known as the "Wee Shankill"—which is to close at the end of the month.

Closure of Joe McKibben's Shankill Picturedrome, 1959.

the Stadium remaining to turn to. Buildings that had played an important role in the social lives of so many people, with names that had enriched local conversations, disappeared, many with only the minimum of public comment, or with no comment at all. Their last days contrasted with the excitement and sense of occasion that had accompanied their inaugurations. There were some exceptions. The Arcadian's demise in February 1960 was well reported in the Irish News with nostalgic comments from the manager, T.Caffrey, and the chief projectionist, J.Reynolds. A former manager, Mike Kavanagh who had joined the staff in 1920, and stayed for 38 years, recalled its evolution from a dance hall built by John Donnelly to a cinema, and its survival despite being burned in the Twenties. As a silent cinema it had boasted a four - piece band with Henry McHenry as pianist. In those days cine variety was popular and among the artistes who had appeared on the Arcadian stage was Albert Sharpe. The last owner was the experienced Harry Wilton who made valiant efforts to keep it open, even going to the expense of installing a new wide screen in February 1955 to show cinemascope films, beginning with "The Robe."

PUBLIC NOTICES

ROYAL HIPPODROME   BELFAST 20971
IRISH GALA CHARITY PREMIERE
MONDAY, JANUARY 11, 1954, at 8 p.m.
PROCEEDS DEVOTED TO THE LORD MAYOR'S COAL RELIEF FUND

THE ROBE

COLOUR BY TECHNICOLOR   THE FIRST FILM IN

CINEMASCOPE

SEATS NOW BOOKABLE AT 2/-, 3/-, 5/-
From JAN. 12 onwards THE ROBE will be screened Daily at 12-25, 3-10, 5-50, 8-35, at Normal Admission Prices.

The Robe: counter attack against TV.

By the late Fifties the boom period was over. George Lodge addressed the local branch of the CEA in October 1958 and warned them that the following few years would probably be critical for the industry. Michael Mc Adam, a true cinema enthusiast who owned the Playhouse in Portrush, claimed that "all cinemas in the province are fighting for survival." To survive, he suggested, the industry needed to innovate and so he introduced (October 1958) the first credit card facility in N.Ireland for buying cinema seats. Mr McAdam went on to build up the Movie House group of cinemas. The local papers carried stories of the alarming and widespread decline in cinema attendance, especially in the U.S.A. There, it had been decided that the main cause was the impact of television, and the film industry came to the conclusion that the best way to combat television was with technology. Television in 1950 had two main drawbacks in that the pictures were in black and white, and, more importantly, they were small. When television came to Belfast, shops advertised "large" screens of 17 or 19 inches, which couldn't compare with the larger cinema screens, but which had a novelty factor which attracted family viewing. Something dramatic was needed to draw people away from their sitting rooms back into the cinemas.

The first round was fought with three dimensional (3-D) films. Belfast audiences were familiar with 3-D films like "Audioscopics", which had appeared periodically in local cinemas as part of the supporting programmes since the mid - Thirties, or the more recent Metroscopix, from M-G-M, which showed in the Ritz in June 1953. They were short films full of action, involving missiles of all kinds hurtling from the screen at the audience. The News Letter critic described Metroscopix as "a novelty of startling effects," and described how, during its twenty minutes run, the audience was bombarded with flying chairs, skulls, and burning wood; swamped by molten metal and crawled over by mice and crabs. Audiences regarded them as comedy gimmicks suitable only for passing the time while awaiting the main feature. Hollywood decided to change that perception by producing full length pictures with plotted storylines, filmed entirely in 3-D. During the early Fifties the local newspapers carried reports of that development, with comments about a bright future, and predictions that all films would soon be projected in 3-D.

The reaction in the city was one of interest, but hardly of overwhelming enthusiasm. Television hadn't really had any impact on Belfast at that time because the first TV station wasn't opened by the BBC until May 1953, while ITV didn't reach the city until October 1959. The cinema owners, for their part, were reluctant to accept the new technology because it involved extra expense in installing new equipment. The projectionists grumbled at the technical problems that could arise in showing the new films, the best of which required two reels to be running concurrently, accurately synchronised, on two projectors. Any imperfections in one of the reels destroyed the 3-D effect. However Hollywood producers were persuaded by the financial success of the first 3-D film, "Bwana Devil" which was completed in 1952 by an independent producer called Arch Oboler. Oboler used the Polaroid system of filming which produced two images, one for the left eye, and one for the right. The images were projected simultaneously from two projectors, and the distorted pictures that resulted were unscrambled by wearing special Polaroid glasses.

Bwana Devil advert: 3-D or not 3-D?

During the Fifties Hollywood studios, full of enthusiasm, produced over 40 films in 3-D, but only a handful were shown in Belfast, due mainly to the reluctance of the local owners to shoulder the cost of installing the extra equipment that was required. But there were exceptions, notably George Lodge. In early April 1953 the Belfast Telegraph carried a heading on its front page which announced that a 3-D film was coming to the Royal Hippodrome the following week. People assumed that it was one of the new full length films that were causing such excitement elsewhere. The heading was misleading because the film in question, "A Day in the Country", turned out to be a supporting short, made recently in Britain to cash in on the 3-D craze. The main feature that it accompanied was "Viva Zapata," starring Marlon Brando. The 3-D short was actually given top billing above the Brando film in the local advertisements.. A reviewer described how the audience were supplied with special cardboard glasses with green (left eye) and red (right eye) lenses. The best section of the film, he wrote, was a wild drive during which other vehicles, ladders, a clothes line of washing and even cattle seem to collide with the speeding car. All that was material that Belfast filmgoers were already familiar with, so the film made no great impact on audiences. The News Letter critic got his priorities right by discussing the Brando film at some length, and just dismissing "A Day in the Country" as "a three-dimensional novelty."

Mr Lodge, with an eye to new business, was just testing the waters to gauge local reaction before speculating in a full length film; and sure enough, a few weeks later, the Imperial announced it would show the first full length 3-D film to be presented in Belfast. Named "Bwana Devil," it was filmed in Ansco Color using an updated 3-D process called Naturalvision. Released in Hollywood in November 1952 the film had unexpectedly become a big hit with the public. The posters outside the Imperial promised viewers "a lion in your lap" and "a lover in your arms." The Imperial emphasised that a special screen, and extra speakers, had been installed to ensure realism. The audience would have to wear special glasses which would be supplied, but, as a consequence, prices had to be increased slightly. Even today 3-D versions of films are usually more expensive than the normal 2-D versions. Before 4:30 pm seats cost two shillings, and three shillings; after that the seat costs rose by five pence. Shows began every morning at 11:00 am which meant that one extra show could be put on each day.

"Bwana Devil" was an adventure film set about sixty years before, which involved an engineer, played by Robert Stack, building a railway in an isolated part of Africa. When the crew are attacked by man - eating lions they flee leaving him alone to protect his wife and himself against the animals. Hardly original, the plot, which was loosely based on an account of the building of the Uganda Railway, was used as an excuse to assail the audience with an assortment of missiles. Harris Deans, writing in the Telegraph, praised the acting, the colourful scenery and the direction but didn't seem to be much impressed by the story line. He complained that there was a limit to the number of times people could tolerate things flying at them from the screen. He didn't object, he wrote, to having a lady on his lap, as the advertising promised, but added that he preferred to be introduced first. Despite its inadequacies he felt the film would intrigue filmgoers, and give them much to talk about over the coming weeks. The News Letter critic admitted that the film treated the stereoscopic technique as more than a stunt, and that it was significant from an historic point of view. He agreed with Harris Deans that the plot was weak and lacking in any real distinction. In fact "Bwana Devil '" ran for only one week though whether that was due to poor audience reaction or booking limitations is not clear. Certainly people that the author spoke to at the time were not overwhelmed with the experience. Some complained of eyestrain, others about the extra cost of admission, while many found the glasses a nuisance to wear. A minority felt that the system still had technical flaws.

Curran Theatres with their tradition of innovation were among those intrigued, and a short time later the Regent screened Belfast's second 3-D film, "Man in the Dark." Audiences

Man in the Dark in the Regent.
Source: Irish News.

House of Wax in the Ritz, one of the better 3-D films.

were promised "ordinary prices for something extraordinary," which meant no seat price increases. Polaroid spectacles, carefully sterilised between each show, were loaned free of charge. The film, which starred Edmond O'Brien, was a thriller with an uninspired story line, according to the News Letter. Audience interest was maintained by the 3-D photography, and it ended with a thrilling climax in a runaway roller coaster. The film was in black and white and represented Columbia's first attempt at 3-D. It ran for two weeks. The inclusion of the roller coaster sequence indicated the maker's less than subtle approach to 3-D, taking the audience back to the fairground.

It was a different story with the next 3-D presentation. The Ritz announced the forth coming arrival of "House of Wax" (d. Andre de Toth, 1953) with the claim that "nothing that has gone before can compare with this 3-D." There was some truth in that statement, and many critics today agree that it was one of the best 3-D films, with impressive set-ups directed with an understanding of how 3-D should be used. The irony is that the director had only one eye and therefore was unable to "see" in three dimensions. When that drawback was mentioned to him he is reported to have replied that Beethoven couldn't hear music either. The film was a remake of the "Mystery of the Wax Museum" (d. Michael Curtiz, 1933) but with colour and stereophonic sound added. The Ritz, as one would expect, was well prepared, and eight extra effects speakers were fitted in the auditorium. The management regretted that seat prices would be increased slightly to cover the cost of the tax on the 3-D glasses, which technically were hired to the patrons. Reports from London about the film were positive and increased the level of anticipation among filmgoers, though the local critics weren't overly excited in the light of what they had already experienced of 3-D. Harris Deans expressed surprise when "a sophisticated audience shrieked at the preview."

The film had the distinction of having two certificates, a H for horror, and an X to exclude those under sixteen years of age. When it opened on Monday 20th July, it was advertised as suitable for "adults only" Audiences entered into the macabre spirit of the story, and watched as a cloaked Vincent Price chose his victims and turned them into wax figures. The colour and sound were well used to add to the underlying sense of horror. Even the cynical Deans admitted that both the sound and the 3-D were highly effective. During one dramatic sequence when the wax museum burned down, he almost felt the flames crackling under his seat. The author, just out of his teens then, remembers vividly the fire in question, and the eerie impact of the slowly melting wax figures. Deans found Vincent Price's special make-up quite "hideous" and felt that, despite its artistic brilliance, it was pushing at the boundaries of acceptability. One wonders what he would make of more recent blood stained special effects. He noted the novelty value of the film, the carefully engineered shocks, and the inevitable flying objects. His conclusion - "I had hoped for more from 3-D." - was ultimately one of disappointment. Belfast audiences disagreed with him, and the film ran for three weeks. During the third week long queues were still forming in the evenings.

Hollywood producers and the majority of filmgoers agreed with Harris Deans, because by the time "House of Wax" was shocking Belfast audiences, the 3-D mania was virtually over elsewhere. But Belfast audiences were noted for often acting against general trends, and while some managers felt that a market remained for 3-D films, most remained cautious. It was eight months later that the Ritz presented "The Charge at Feather River," (d.Gordon Douglas, 1953), advertised as the first film to be shown in the city that combined both 3-D and wide screen. It was a Warner production and everything about it proclaimed its origin. It was filmed in Warner Naturalvision (3-D), in Warnercolor, with WarnerPhonic sound. Each film company tended to have its own version of the new technology. The plot involved a trek by a group of ill - disciplined soldiers, led by Guy Madison, through dangerous country to rescue two white sisters who had been carried off by Cheyenne Indians. By Western standards the story was unoriginal, but was revitalised by careful use of 3-D. The scenery looked magnificent, and the audience was entertained by amusing shocks. In one a soldier, played by Frank Lovejoy, deters an advancing rattle snake by directing a spit of tobacco juice at it, and, with it, the audience. In another he fires his revolver directly into the audience recalling a famous scene in "The Great Train Robbery" (1906). Excitement was also kept high during clashes between the soldiers and bands of Indians. The film climaxed with a major battle between the two sides during which the audience was bombarded with arrows, spears, tomahawks and assorted missiles. Harris Deans thought the film "excellent," yet it ran for only four days. One reason may have been the charge of six pence for the special Polaroid glasses, a charge which most people resented. The cinema tried to soften the impact by selling the glasses to the patrons so that they could keep them and use them for future films. The problem was that there was no certainty of any more 3-D films. By 1954 the demand for them was over, even in Belfast.

The News Letter carried a report in which the President of the British Kinematograph Society described the reaction of the British public to the 3-D films as "lukewarm" due mainly "to the wearing of Polaroid glasses, and the eye fatigue and headaches that accompanied them." He believed that the problem didn't lie entirely with the glasses, but with the way in which the films were made. Most film makers, he stated, didn't understand the principles of stereoscopic photography, and viewers were forced to perform "unnatural and disconcerting optical gymnastics "while watching the films. Whatever the truth of that, locally the glasses continued to cause problems. There were reports from Belfast, and Dublin, of people objecting to paying extra for their use. Cinema managers in both cities complained that many patrons kept the glasses even though they were asked to return them, a habit that increased their running costs. By the middle of the decade it was obvious that 3-D had lost its appeal. In the issue of 7th November 1953 Picturegoer stated that "picturegoers hadn't taken to 3-D," and claimed that only 250 cinemas out of 4,500 in Britain had used the technology. Nor had it reduced the increasing popularity of TV.

The Telegraph reported a meeting in the Grand Central Hotel attended among others by the Lord Mayor and members of the Stormont cabinet to discuss the uses of documentary films. The meeting was chaired by a member of the Motion Picture Association of America who dismissed forecasts of the death of cinema. Films, he maintained, would continue to be made, and would exist parallel to TV, like live theatre, radio and gramophones. That kind of complementary existence was increasingly voiced by members of the cinema industry in

Belfast and elsewhere. The Irish News carried a report in December 1953 quoting Joseph Drew, a prominent member of the cinema industry in England, who argued that cinema should combine with TV rather than fight against it. He forecast - with commendable accuracy - that cinema, as people then knew it, would be greatly modified in the future by new technology, new systems of distribution, and increased co-operation with TV.

Meantime Hollywood found itself with a number of completed 3-D films that were no longer saleable. Managers wouldn't rent them when they weren't sure of an audience. "The Charge at Feather River" was the last major 3-D film to be shown in Belfast in its original format. The others arrived, without comment, on local screens in normal "flat" configuration. They included "The Creature from the Black Lagoon" which had been praised for its impressive underwater photography, the musical "Kiss Me Kate," the science fiction "It Came From Outer Space," the Western "Hondo" and Hitchcock's "Dial M For Murder." Tantalising glimpses of them appeared in a film history of three dimensional cinematography which was shown in the Imax cinemas in Dublin and Belfast during the Nineties.

In the main, 3-D films disappeared from local screens until developments in digital photography made them accessible again. They appear regularly in the multiplexes now, but, despite improvements in technique, they still reveal many of the problems associated with the products of the Fifties. The majority of them are unbearably noisy, full of visual gimmicks including, as ever, missiles hurling into the audience, and encumbered with the need to wear glasses. The latter are lighter and modern looking, and addicts can actually buy their own distinctive personal glasses, including a pair from Gucci costing £150. Thankfully, the Movie House on the Dublin Road sells them at a more economic £1. Whatever the cost, many people still find them a nuisance to wear, some people still complain of headaches, dizziness and feeling unwell. Despite that a Korean company is planning to build special cinemas which project what they call a 4-D experience, during which the 3-D images and multi - track stereophonic sound are accompanied by gimmicks like scratch-n-sniff cards, and moving tilting seats which have actually made people ill. All in the cause of entertainment. The first film advertised as being made in 4-D was shown in Belfast in September 2011. It's full title was "Spy Kids, All the Time in the World in 4-D."(d. Robert Rodriguez, 2011). To experience the full impact watching it required glasses and scratch-n-sniff cards (Aromascope), but in Belfast the latter were dispensed with, and the film was presented in versions in 3-D, 2-D and even in 35 mm. Regardless of what version people watched they couldn't avoid the conclusion that it was a silly and confused concoction. It added nothing of significance to the cinematic canon, and quickly disappeared from local screens.

George Lucas was quoted recently in the Irish News on 1st April 2011 (is there any significance in the date?) pointing out that digital technology was still in its infancy and that future developments would produce dramatic changes in how films are made and seen. One of those changes, he felt, would be the dominance of 3-D, which would take over film making in the same way that colour had replaced black and white. Observers were saying the same thing in the Fifties, but audiences remained unconvinced. George is now converting his Star Wars films to 3-D which may go some way to explaining his enthusiasm. Not many film makers in the Fifties had such a high regard for 3-D. In 1953 the

Belfast Telegraph carried details of a lecture by Anthony Asquith, the eminent director, in which he highlighted the nub of the matter. Speaking to the Association of Cinematograph and Allied Technicians, he warned his colleagues that they must not "substitute bad 3-D films for good two dimensional ones." He added that 3-D was not a revolution that would change films in the way that sound had. That admonition is as valid today as it was then. Writing in the "Observer" in April 2010 the critic Mark Kermode reflected Asquith's view, maintaining that 3-D was not a creative leap similar to the coming of sound. It was a technical gimmick that added nothing to narrative cinema, and did not represent the future of film making. It was, he claimed, just a form of carnival entertainment. Not everyone agrees with that conclusion but film producers today cover their bets by releasing both 3-D and 2-D versions so that patrons can choose which to see. The success of 3-D versions notably the Oscar winner "Gravity," (d.Alfonso Cuaron, 2013) suggests that 3-D, glasses and all, will be part of cinema programmes for some time to come. Only the future will tell if digital technology can overcome its perceived shortcomings.

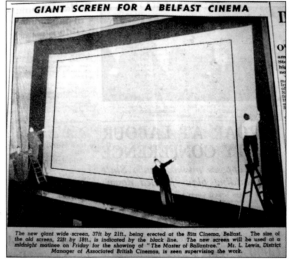

GIANT SCREEN FOR A BELFAST CINEMA

The new giant wide screen, 37ft by 21ft., being erected at the Ritz Cinema, Belfast. The size of the old screen, 22ft by 18ft., is indicated by the black line. The new screen will be used at a midnight matinee on Friday for the showing of " The Master of Ballantrae." Mr. L. Lewis, District Manager of Associated British Cinemas, is seen supervising the work.

Widescreen installed in the Ritz, Sept. 1953, with thanks to Belfast Telegraph. The Ritz always to the fore.

The Fifties did produce one major development that did become integrated successfully into the local cinema trade, and that was the widescreen. At the beginning of 1953 the Irish News carried a heading that announced that 3-D films would become the norm in most cinemas within a year. The statement had emanated from Spyros Skouras, the President of 20th Century Fox studios, and as such couldn't be ignored. A closer reading showed that Mr Skouras wasn't speaking about 3-D films of the "Bwana Devil" type, but of widescreen productions that gave the illusion of depth without the inconvenience of wearing glasses. He made his comments in Paris where he had gone to consult Prof.Henri Chretien about a process called Cinemascope which the professor had been experimenting with since the Twenties. The system used 70mm film and a special anamorphic lens that projected a wide image. He announced that the first film in Cinemascope, called "The Robe" would begin production in Hollywood on 16th Feb. The professor had promised that 5,000 special lenses would be available by the end of the year, and that the Fox company would then hire out the equipment to other studios and film producers.

The local cinema owners were interested, but waited to see how the public would respond. In its edition of 18th April 1953 Picturegoer magazine gave local film enthusiasts a first description of what was to come. The magazine's representative in Hollywood, Peter Day, wrote how he went to the old Fox studio on Western Avenue to see a preview of the new system. He noted the "giant" screen which was two and a half times the width of a normal screen, with a curvature that was five feet deep at the centre. He watched clips of racing cars, an orchestral musical piece, an unedited sequence from "The Robe" showing a sword fight between Richard Burton and Jeff Morrow, and shots from another film, "How to Marry a Millionaire," being photographed in the new system. He was impressed by the clarity of the images and the feeling of depth, enhanced by stereophonoic sound which followed characters and events across the screen. He celebrated the fact that all of that was achieved without the need to wear glasses. Cinemascope presented reality without shocks, or as he put it, "the story stays on its own side of the giant window." Dedicated filmgoers were intrigued and looked forward with keen anticipation to experience the new development.

When "The Robe" opened in the Roxy Theatre, New York its takings for the first day were £13,000, a world record at the time. The critics were impressed, and, most importantly, the people flocked in large numbers to see it, those numbers increasing as word of mouth spread. Wide screen had arrived in an impressive manner that couldn't be ignored. In fact the industry had already been experimenting with panoramic screens on which larger images could be shown. The first cinema to respond in Belfast was the Ritz which installed a new large screen at the end of September 1953, the first of its kind in Ireland. The screen, specially sprayed with silver to improve reflection, measured an impressive 37 feet by 21 feet, which compared with the 22 feet by 18 feet of the former screen. It was shown to the Press on the 30th Sept. by Mr G.W.Irving the manager who pointed out that the extension in width combined with a slight curvature resulted in an improved image, especially of outdoor scenes. The main problem was that films were not yet being filmed in widescreen, and when normal ratio films were enlarged on the new screen the image often lost its top or bottom. Patrons had the opportunity to experience the new screen for the first time when it was used for the local premiere of "The Master of Ballantrae" at a midnight matinee on 9th October. The film, in colour, starring Errol Flynn with Beatrice Campbell and Yvonne Furneaux, dealt with the aftermath of the rebellion of Bonnie Prince Charlie. It was an exciting, if undemanding, adventure story with lots of swordplay, thundering cannon and such. It was well received by the local critics but none of them mentioned the screen size. Their praises were reserved for Errol Flynn and local girl Beatrice Campbell.

Wide screen was not a new phenomenon. It had been used in the Twenties but had not caught on mainly for financial reasons. Cinema owners saw no reason to incur the costs of new large screens when their cinemas were packed with crowds quite satisfied with the normal sized screens. The Fifties differed in that audiences were decreasing, not increasing. Cinema owners wanted a system that was technically impressive yet financially reasonable. Cinemascope met those criteria, but it wasn't the only wide screen system available. When "The Robe" opened in 1953 there was another wide screen process, Cinerama, already causing a sensation in New York. Cinerama used a massive screen but it required three projectors working in unison to fill it. The three films projected concurrently produced an image similar to the width of normal vision, with the illusion of depth which could be experienced without having to wear glasses. Combined with stereophonic sound the result was amazing. The early films were documentaries like "The Seven Wonders of the World," with breath taking views of natural scenery and exotic places, including sequences like a dramatic flight into the Grand Canyon, or a memorable roller - coaster ride which was so realistic that it had even the sophisticated New York crowds shouting and screaming with excitement. It also proved once again that the carnival atmosphere was still alive in the cinema.

Cinerama was not only expensive to film but very costly to install and show, as it required a special screen and stereophonic sound as well as three projectors running in unison, plus the skilled technical expertise to project the images correctly. Its high costs meant that admission prices were high, of the roadshow levels, which, in turn, meant that it could only survive financially where there were large concentrations of population. Thus it tended to locate in large urban centres and capital cities. Cinerama was high order entertainment that people were willing to travel some distance to see. The author remembers going to London and, later, to Dublin to see it, and can vouch that visually it was an overwhelming experience. Dublin actually had two Cinerama cinemas. One was the Dublin Cinerama Theatre which was the renovated former New Electric cinema at the bottom of Talbot Street, across from Amiens Street railway station, as it was then called. It opened in 1964 and remained in operation for a decade despite the disadvantages of noise from passing trains, and high prices which ranged from 4|6 to 10|6. The Telegraph carried an advertisement in July 1964 inviting Belfast citizens who might be in Dublin "for the Twelfth holiday" to come and experience the new sensation. The second Cinerama cinema opened in 1967 in the cavernous Plaza cinema on Granby Row, using a more simplified projection system. It showed Cinerama and widescreen films which proved very popular with audiences. "The Sound of Music" ran there for a year to full houses. Sadly, the Plaza closed in 1981, and, after refurbishment, reopened as the National Wax Museum, until that attraction closed in 2005.

For reasons of cost and population size the original Cinerama never came to Belfast. Yet Belfast filmgoers did see films made in Cinerama, but with the image reduced to Cinemascope proportions. The first such production, "How The West Was Won," arrived in the Ritz in October 1964, advertised as the original three panel version presented for the first time on a single wide screen. It was well received by the local critics and audiences. The film, with a strong cast headed by James Stewart and Debbie Reynolds, dealt with the opening of the American West and while it excelled in its scenic and action sequences, its very size undermined its more intimate moments. It tended to dwarf the actors, and distance them somewhat from the audience. Cinerama never really overcame those problems in the way that the other widescreen system, Cinemascope, did.

George Lodge was the man responsible for introducing Cinemascope to the Belfast public, in the Royal Hippodrome. The new screen and associated sound equipment were installed, reportedly at a cost of £2000, and it was announced that a special Irish Gala Charity premiere of "The Robe" would take place on Monday 11th January 1954. It was a suitably grand occasion with all proceeds going to the Lord Mayor's Coal Fund, and the packed house included specially invited guests like the Deputy Lord Mayor Councillor Harcourt, members of the Stormont government, and senior members of all the churches.

"The Robe" was a landmark production with a mission, and great care was taken in its filming and presentation. The film was based on a novel by Lloyd C. Douglas and dealt with events during the early days of Christianity. The storyline described how the Centurion (Richard Burton) who was present at Christ's crucifixion, came into possession of the seamless robe that Christ wore, and how its influence led him to reject the standards of the degenerate Roman state and go to a martyr's death in the arena with his Christian wife (Jean Simmons). The film had a fine cast which included Victor Mature, Jay Robinson (Caligula), and Michael Rennie (St. Peter). It was directed by Henry Koster and photographed in colour by Leon Shamroy. The main aim of 20th Century Fox was to convince the public that Cinemascope was the way forward for films. In that they succeeded. The success of the new technology played a major role in halting the decline in audience numbers.

The local critics gave the film a mixed reception. The News Letter critic was impressed by the wide screen with its grand scale and "vast spectacle." He felt it was designed to be panoramic rather than stereoscopic in its impact. He was not overwhelmed by the film itself which he contended was filmed in glorious colour which couldn't disguise the black and white nature of the characters and plot. Harris Deans in the Telegraph was more liberal with his praise. He thought that Cinemascope was "a great technical achievement," and he congratulated the director Henry Koster for his handling of the new technology. He praised the general design, the expert use of colour and the beautiful settings. The only fault he highlighted was the fact that the technology tended to dominate the actors. A few days later the Telegraph published a second review by MW, presumedly Martin Wallace, which was quite scathing in its comments. He attacked the film on two levels, the commercial and the artistic. He dramatically described Cinemascope as the end of films as they had been known for the previous 25 years. It was, he felt, merely a novelty which the commercially minded hoped would bring people back into the cinemas, ignoring the fact that the answer to that problem was better films. He admitted that its panoramic effect was more impressive than "the spear-tossing 3-D system," but, by its nature, it undermined the accepted grammar of film making. It did not lend itself to intimate angled shots, close-ups or rapid editing. With regard to "The Robe" he noted that shots tended to be longer and often stage - like, which slowed the film up. Discussing the plot and its presentation he was extra critical, calling it "a pseudo-religious spectacle," vulgar, and presenting a religion of "emotionalism and mass hysteria."

The opposing, and provocative, views presented in the Telegraph led to a lively debate in the letter pages of that paper, and provoked George Lodge to write defending his decision to bring the film to the Royal Hippodrome. He pointed out that "The Robe" was a popular and financial success wherever it was shown. Contemporaneously with Belfast the film was showing in 300 cinemas around the world, and in each case attendance records were being broken. With reference to its content he emphasised that the film had never claimed to be a morality play, but was merely an attempt to use the latest technology to present a good story associated with "the origins of our Christian faith." He finished by saying that "the Royal Hippodrome will leave the verdict to the public." Another letter writer who signed himself "a cinema projectionist" suggested it was too soon to pass judgement on Cinemascope and wide screen. He noted that many had praised the film but he thought that MW's comments were "unjust, unfair and much too severe." Another writer agreed with MW. He felt that too much money had been spent on lavish and spectacular scenes and not enough on the actors. "The tragedy," he added, "is not that The Robe is a bad film, but that millions will think that it is exceptionally good". A "Housewife" found the film disappointing and too commercial, while a "Film Fan" expressed disappointment because there was an over emphasis on technology and novelty at the expense of the story opportunities presented in the book. A different approach was taken by "An Artist" who praised the use of colour and sound, but expressed extreme disappointment with the oblong shape of the screen which, he suggested, made framing and visual balance difficult.

One of the clergy invited by Mr Lodge was the Bishop of Down and Dromore who wrote in defence of the film. He made no comment about the Cinemascope technology, but thought that the film was made with reverence and good taste, and he was particularly impressed by "the restrained portrayal of the Crucifixion scenes." He also praised the atmosphere of the scenes showing the early spread of Christianity. Talk of pseudo - religion, vulgarity and mass hysteria were, he wrote, "not deserved." No-one could say that Belfast took its cinema or its religion lightly.

As the discussions and comments continued, the crowds also continued to pack the Royal Hippodrome, much to George Lodge's delight. In response to suggestions from patrons early shows, beginning at 10:00 am, were introduced on Saturday mornings "for the benefit of our country patrons." By the end of January the 100,000th ticket of admission had been sold, and the lucky patron was rewarded with two return air tickets to London to spend a free weekend during which he and his wife were guests at the premiere of the second Cinemascope film to be released, "King of the Khyber Rifles," (d. Henry King, 1953) after which they met the stars (Tyrone Power an Terry Moore) of the film. The author still vividly remembers going to see "The Robe", and waiting in a crowded auditorium for the house curtains to open. There was a decided atmosphere of anticipation as they slowly parted to reveal another red curtain projected on the screen. As it parted slowly, revealing a wider and wider screen surface, a gasp went up from the audience especially when the camera tracked into a vast arena, and then surveyed a large slave market, rich in colour and sound. The image was three times bigger than anything seen in the Hippodrome before, and the audience was definitely impressed by pictures that filled their normal field of vision. It soon became clear that the director and his cameraman were learning by experience. As the camera panned sideways some large objects, especially pillars, distorted slightly and actually seemed to move. Such minor technical problems didn't destroy the overall impact, and were soon eliminated in later Cinemascope productions. Audiences took to the new technology immediately. It was the beginning of a new chapter in the history of the cinema. and its impact wasn't lost on other managers and cinema owners across the city. "The Robe" ran for five weeks in the Royal Hippodrome, and the Troxy immediately announced it was installing the second Cinemascope screen in the city. The management announced proudly that the new screen was 35 feet wide, and silvered with aluminium for extra brightness. With it extra loudspeakers were installed to cope with the four soundtracks that Cinemascope films carried. "The Robe" opened there, at normal prices on 15th March and ran for two weeks, with three separate performances daily.

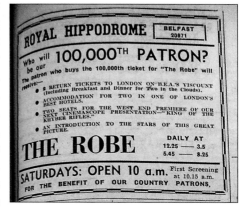

The Robe: 100,000th patron, a decided success.

Meantime in Hollywood the other big studios decided that Cinemascope was the answer to declining audiences, but each looked around for their own systems. Local audiences soon became familiar with Warnerscope (another French system bought by Warner Bros., and adapted for their use), Superscope (R.K.O), Naturama (Republic Studios), Vistavision (Paramount), and Todd-AO. Technicolor met the new demands by developing Technirama, a colour system which used 70 mm film. Many top directors complained about the practical drawbacks resulting from the "postbox" shape of the new wide screen systems, but the more creative of them soon began to overcome the technical and artistic problems involved. Wide screen, properly used, overwhelmed the spectator with landscape vistas and spectacle. Hollywood quickly realised that Cinemascope was ideally suited to the epic and during the late Fifties and Sixties Belfast's screens reflected that decision.

Actually the epic had already made its appearance in pre-widescreen days with the Italian made "Fabiola" (d.Allesandro Blasetti, 1949) which showed in the Royal Hippodrome just before Christmas in 1952. A local critic described it as "stupendous," and it attracted long queues. Hollywood had noted its popular success and decided to set up production in Europe where excellent studios like Cinecitta in Rome existed, where costs were lower than in America, and where producers had accumulated frozen financial assets. Most of the films produced in Europe had top stars and high production values, and they usually arrived in Belfast as road-shows with increased prices, and often bookable seats. They were presented as quality entertainment for general audiences. Some parents, and the British censor, found them too violent for their children. The exhibitors for their part were anxious to retain the young audience and emphasised to parents the literary origins and educational value of the films.

The first of the new epics was "Quo Vadis" (d. Mervyn Le Roy,1951) filmed before the advent of Cinemascope at the refurbished Cinecitta studios in Rome. Belfast audiences read the advanced publicity and waited expectantly for its arrival. During the Fifties it was normal for the distributor or the cinema manager to inform the Police Committee of forthcoming films, especially if there were any possible problems concerning censorship. George Lodge followed that procedure with "Quo Vadis," because the British censor had given it an "X" certificate which meant that no one under 16 years of age could be admitted. It was unusual for an expensive epic of that type to receive an adult only rating. The British censor felt that certain scenes, especially in the arena, were quite unsuited to children but M.G.M refused to trim them as he suggested. Mr Lodge's letter was headed re:Quo Vadis, after which someone in the City Hall had helpfully added, in longhand, Whither goest thou? In it he pointed out that a number of local authorities in England had given the film an "A" certificate, allowing children to be admitted, if accompanied by an adult. He felt that "the importance of the message, the faithfulness in production and the good taste in which it had been presented" were factors in the film's favour, and that parents should be allowed to decide if they wanted to bring their children to see it. He requested the Council to see the film in the hope that they would give a "sympathetic consideration" to allowing it to be shown with an "A" certificate. He enclosed copies of sermons and other comments in favour of the film. The Council viewed the film but made no change, so the "X" certificate remained.

"Quo Vadis", which Mr Lodge guaranteed was exactly the same as the version being shown in London, opened in the Imperial during the last week of March 1953, and ran for six weeks. The local critics praised the quality and scope of the production, its colour, its spectacle, its sets and large crowd scenes. That was before the days of CGI, and large crowds meant just that. Harris Deans, writing in the Telegraph, called it "an opulent melodrama of sex and religion" and predicted, correctly, that it would be a major box office attraction. It came across, he felt, as spectacle rather than serious drama. He praised the acting, especially Peter Ustinov as Nero. However he complained about the scenes in the arena which he described as "ghastly", with the added comment that they fully deserved an "X" certificate. Another complaint was that its running time of 2 hours 45 minutes was too long, but in the following years that was a problem he would have to get used to. One year later Mr Lodge brought the film back to Belfast with a modified "A" certificate, and presented it in the Royal Hippodrome "on the new magic miracle screen," with a reminder to parents that "now the children can see it."

"Fabiola," "Quo Vadis "and, above all, "The Robe" initiated a sequence of epics, or blockbusters as some local critics called them, which plundered Classical history for their plots. They were not noted for their historical accuracy, but, in the main, they delivered first class entertainment which local audiences appreciated in large numbers. The cinema owners rushed to install the latest wide screens and new sound systems, including even the larger Todd AO screens in the Regal and the ABC Ritz. The epics had everything, including large budgets which allowed vast sets and "casts of thousands." Producers and directors vied with each other to fill the big screens with action, colour, beautiful women and spectacle in films like "Helen of Troy," "Alexander the Great," '"Solomon and Sheba" (wherein there was local criticism of Gina Llobrigida's dancing), "The Greatest Story Ever Told," "Barabbas," Cecil B. deMille's "The Ten Commandments," the superior "Spartacus," and "Ben Hur". Charlton Heston dominated the widescreens in "Ben Hur" and "El Cid," and Belfast's own Stephen Boyd showed his acting mettle in "Ben Hur," and "The Fall of the Roman Empire." Anyone who saw the chariot race in "Ben Hur" will never forget it. The only regret expressed in Belfast, - in a Rowel Friers cartoon - was that Stephen Boyd didn't win it! All the major studios were involved, plus independent producers like Samuel Bronson who from his base in Spain produced, among others, "El Cid," (starring Charlton Heston, Mr Epic himself) and the controversial "King of Kings," in which Jeffrey Hunter played the role of Christ. Mike Todd (husband of Elizabeth Taylor) was another independent who produced "Around the World in 80 Days," starring David Niven. It was shown on the large Todd AO screen in the Regal cinema, preceded by George Méliès's silent "Voyage to the Moon" which had last been shown in Belfast at the beginning of the nineteenth century. Significantly its age and the relatively small size of its images didn't take away from its charm and impact. Its inclusion in the programme allowed a comparison between one of the earliest film systems and the latest. It must be admitted that Méliès successfully stood the test of time.

The Hollywood films had the advantage of being well financed, with money which translated into quality actors, massive sets and high production values. But parallel to their polished products was another series of Italian epics which the French critics called pepla, but which others referred to as the poor man's epic, the sword - and - sandals genre, or just plain rubbish. They were in widescreen, using systems like Totalscope or Dyaliscope, but made on a shoestring, and being cheaply made they employed actors who could barely act, with special effects which were often crude and amateuristic, along with dubbing into English that was often bizarre. What they lacked in polish they made up for in enthusiasm. They took their plots mainly from Mediterranean myths and history, with heroes named Hercules, Maciste, Ursus, Goliath, Samson or such. Those parts were played by musclemen,

Steeve Reeves arrives on the scene.

chosen for their physique rather than their acting ability. The most famous and successful of them was Steve Reeves, the Mr Universe of 1950, who became a fixture on Belfast screens during the Sixties. Others included Reg Park, Bob Mathias, Gordon Scott, Michael Lane, Ed Fury, Samson Burke and Kirk Morris, hardly household names. Opposite them were sensuous beauties like Sylvia Koscina, Sylvia Lopez, Sylvana Mangano, Gianna Maria Canale, Rosanna Schiaffino and Rossano Podesta.

Those films appealed mainly to the young and the less sophisticated who would collect outside the cinemas discussing the colourful and detailed posters with which the films were so well publicised. Typical was "Warlord of Crete," starring Bob Mathias, which showed in the suburban Rank (formerly Curran) cinemas. The action was set in Minoan Crete, and the associated well drawn colour poster promised visually a muscled hero, a beautiful endangered heroine, battles, and dancing girls against a background of impressive classical architecture. In fact, it displayed all the elements of the genre. Added to that was an invitation to see "the fabled palace of Minos, the dread labyrinth, captive maidens being sacrificed to the Minotaur monster, the goddess of the sea rising from its depths to claim her lover, and the raging revolt of the Cretans." Who, other than Sir Arthur Evans, could resist such attractions!

The Italian pepla inhabited a special world that was part pagan, part Christian, part Classical, part pre Classical, part realistic, and part mythical. Their heroes were uncomplicated supermen who spoke with booming dubbed voices, as they gently but firmly rejected the female wiles that would deflect them from their main function which was the defence of the weak and the victory of justice and right. That theme of personal freedom ran like a thread through all the films. But despite their inadequacies they were sometimes characterised by a distinctive visual style and striking colour images. Those were the contributions of the talents of a rising group of young directors and set designers like Mario Bava, Vittorio Cottafavi and Sergio Leone (who later directed the Dollar Westerns with Clint Eastwood). In Belfast the heyday of the Italian epics was short, covering mainly the first half of the Sixties though the first of them arrived much earlier, when George Lodge showed "Ulysses" in the Imperial during April 1956. "Ulysses" wasn't a true peplum because, though it was made in Italy, it starred a dubbed Kirk Douglas with Silvano Magnano. But it introduced audiences to the distinctive impoverished peplum style, and to the attractions of Italian cinema, especially in the person of Miss Magnano who enjoyed playing a double role as the temptress Circe, and the faithful wife Penelope.

The Italian invasion began in earnest in 1960 when, in February of that year, the Royal Cinema presented "Hercules" starring Steve Reeves, Sylvia Koscina and Sylvia Lopez. It was Reeves's first film, and proved a big success. The Telegraph described it as "a swift moving romp." Sometime later a sequel called "Hercules Unchained," with the same actors arrived in the Ritz, and again it attracted large crowds despite being dismissed by the critics. The Irish News scribe decried its low standard of acting, its "puerile" plot, and a script that was more suited to a comic book. The original success of the Hercules films was due mainly to the high powered advertising campaign carried out by Joseph E. Levine, an American producer who bought the films cheaply and then launched them with adverts in all the main newspapers plus, for the first time here, on television. Such was the intensity of the TV advertising in August 1960 that people were convinced that they simply had to see the films. The campaigns paid off handsomely, with Mr Levine raking in millions of pounds. Others realised that television could be used as a potent force to influence peoples' decisions, and that the success of Levine's campaigns suggested that film makers should co-operate with and use the new medium to increase their audience numbers.

Steve Reeves became a screen fixture over the next ten years, and earned enough money to retire to his ranch in California. His popularity is difficult to explain because he never played anyone but himself, while his performances were intense but wooden. The Irish News critic described how, in "Hercules Unchained," he moved from exploit to exploit "with all the finesse of a domesticated bull-dozer cum furniture-remover." "Despite such criticisms local audiences flocked to see him flex his muscles in "The Last Days of Pompeii," "Son of Spartacus," "The Wooden Horse of Troy," and "Goliath," the poster for which claimed that "a thousand women dream of his embrace." When the Regent showed "Goliath and the Barbarians" in July 1960 the Irish News critic described it in terms that could be applied to all of Steve Reeve's films. The plot had a stalwart Reeves contending with the barbarian invaders of N.Italy, and involved "much pillage, plunder, massacre, arson, torture, tests of strength, ritual dancing, intrigue, peeping from behind bushes, and "wait till I give the signal..." Interspersed between all the mayhem was some dubbed and tedious dialogue. His films, and other pepla, soon disappeared from the city centre cinemas, except the Regent (by then a Rank cinema), but continued to circulate in the suburbs. In January 1961 the Regent cinema presented "Carthage in Flames" starring Anne Heywood, and described as "blazing action with Super Spectacle." Later it showed "Sodom and Gomorrah," starring Stewart Granger, a more traditional epic. In October 1963 it was "Vengeance of the Gladiators," described as "a typical piece of Italian melodrama," and a few weeks later "The Mongols" starring Jack Palance and Anita Ekberg. The Telegraph dismissed the latter as a "swift moving spectacle about Genghis Khan's invasion of Europe." It was sad to see fading stars like Palance reduced to appearing in such material.

It was in the suburbs that the genre continued to flourish, attracting a mainly young following. The Stadium presented quite a few of them, claiming the first showing in N. Ireland of "Goliath and the Vampires," starring Gordon Scott, and the first run of "The Warrior and the Slave Girl" featuring George Marchal and Gianna Maria Canale. Meanwhile the Tivoli presented "Ulysses Against Hercules," while the Curzon, Strand and Majestic all showed "Giant of the Lost Tomb" with Kirk Morris, simultaneously, in January 1965. By the mid - Sixties even the suburban audiences had had a surfeit of exotic titles and strongmen, and their popularity was in decline. When the Regent had shown "Ulysses Against Hercules" in December 1964, Ulsterweek described it as "another slice of Italian beef-and-brawn mythology... which includes Birdmen and troglodytes among its attractions. "In July 1965 the Stadium trumpeted the arrival of "Perseus Against the Monsters," described as "containing thrills and monsters never before seen." Its highlight was the hero slaying the Medusa, but Ulsterweek dismissed it as "a jumpy, harshly coloured, dubbed Spanish-Italian romp of bronzed muscles and swords dripping with blood." The Castle gave its patrons a double bill of thrills with "Monster from the Unknown World" and "The Colossus of the Stone Age." In December 1965 the Lido presented what was probably the nadir of the genre with "Hercules Against the Moon Men." The scriptwriters were obviously running out of ideas, and the genre had degenerated into endless repetition. Above all, the audiences were bored, and what had once seemed exotic and fresh now looked ridiculous and silly.

At the same time the Hollywood epics were also showing evidence of decline. The Irish News critic, writing in December 1964, detected a move away from the spectacle of the epics towards more realism. The blockbusters he wrote, were still being made but "only the cost and the inanity of content (were) on a large scale." He had, like his local colleagues, always treated the Italian epics with humorous disdain but now they all began to be increasingly critical of the Hollywood productions. With regard to the latest epic, "Genghis Khan," which showed in Belfast in September 1964, the Ulsterweek critic complained that Stephen Boyd was forced to play second lead to Omar Sharif in what he summed up as "a big film with big horses, big men, fine big girls... but it's nobody's El Cid." More seriously there was criticism of "The Fall of the Roman Empire," which P.C.R, the Irish News critic, suggested "would make a Gibbon(sic) laugh." It wasn't really as bad as that. Stephen Boyd gave "a convincing performance," Alec Guinness was, as ever, impressive, and the film was visually superb, especially in the scenes of the winter fortress. Despite such praise the general feeling was that the final result was "a gallant failure" (Telegraph), with sections that were "deadly dull.... limp, and strangely pallid" (Irish News). Seen today, that seems to be rather harsh criticism, more applicable to 20th Century Fox's expensive "Cleopatra" (d. Joseph L. Mankiewicz, 1963), which emerged at the same time amid a plethora of publicity, and opened in Belfast, on Easter Monday 30th April 1964. It ran for four weeks in the Regal on the upper Lisburn Road. Rank chose a suburban release rather than the traditional city centre premiere because the Regal had a large Todd AO screen, which was the system "Cleopatra" was filmed in. Rank planned to make the Regal a super cinema and showed many top widescreen releases there, including "The Cardinal," and "Around The World in Eighty Days."

After all that had been said, reported, invented and written about the making of "Cleopatra," it was almost inevitable that the film itself would be an anti - climax. After its release in London at the end of July in 1963 reviews had been mixed but mainly lukewarm, with one English critic adding insult to injury by suggesting that it resembled an Italian Hercules spectacular, while lacking the latter's pace. Certainly its reception by Belfast audiences was subdued, despite arriving with suitable publicity flourishes as a road show, with special prices. The local critics welcomed it as less of an Easter egg, and more of a curate's egg. Martin Wallace in the Telegraph was unimpressed, describing it as "a bore," and was disappointed by Elizabeth Taylor's performance which presented the queen of the Nile as "a silky kitten...in gaudy wigs." The Irish News critic likewise described it as "three and a half hours of boredom and bathos... with gleams of stupidity rarely equalled even by de Mille." He found Elizabetth Taylor "superbly miscast," while Richard Burton came across as "the poor man's Olivier." The only acting to win his approbation was that of Rex Harrison in the role of Julius Caesar. He admitted that the production had its fair share of spectacle, sex, and exotic dancing, all of which he concluded, filled the eye, but touched nothing else. The News Letter gave a woman's view of the proceedings, written by Margaret Cavan. She found the film magnificent to look at, and praised the witty script and the acting. Rex Harrison was "perfect" in his role, Richard Burton was "dynamic" while Elizabeth Taylor showed she was "a great actress." Despite those positive qualities she admitted that the film was too slow moving, and its style set "the art of the film back about fifty years."

The author remembers seeing it later in the Avenue (the former Regent) during its general release at normal prices in late 1965, and was surprised to find the cinema only half filled, and that on a Friday evening. The dearth of enthusiasm soon became understandable because the film lacked vitality, especially during the second half. Camera movements were panoramic, and tended to be deliberate and painfully slow moving. The actors were too often dominated by the massive sets. Rex Harrison was splendid, and really carried the first half. Burton seemed to have wandered in from "The Robe," and Elizabeth Taylor proved too modern in the title role, and could have benefited from studying Claudette Colbert's interpretation of the part in De Mille's 1936 version of the story. No-one mentioned earlier screen versions of the Cleopatra story which had shown locally.

Many people in Belfast seemed to prefer the contemporary "Carry On Cleo" (d. Gerald Thomas, 1964) which was filmed on Cleopatra's abandoned sets at Pinewood, and arrived in the ABC during January 1965. It was the tenth Carry On, and took full advantage of the stir surrounding the exploits of Taylor and Burton. The audience were informed solemnly that the film they were about to see was based on historic characters, but that "certain liberties had been taken with Cleopatra." What followed was a lively and hilarious skit - a "nutty romp" or panto version according to the Belfast Telegraph - on the original, with Amanda Barrie obviously enjoying re-interpreting Elizabeth Taylor's performance. She was pursued by a suitably libidinous Sid James who played Mark Antony, wearing the same costume that Richard Burton had emoted in, though there the similarity of acting styles ended. Unlike the original, the film was fast moving, carrying the audience from one outrageous classical word play to the next. Kenneth Williams as Caesar, entered cinematic history with his famous pun, "Infamy, infamy... they all have it in for me," a comment that Joseph Mankiewicz could wryly have felt summed up most critical reaction to his film. The losses incurred by "Cleopatra" brought 20th Century Fox to its financial knees, but the studio was saved financially by the later success of "The Sound of Music." There is something ironic about the debris caused by the Siren of the Nile being swept up by a singing nun. When the critical, legal and financial dust had settled the only sensible reaction to "Cleopatra" could be "Oh Puer!" For non - classicists puer is the Latin for boy.

One topic that recurred frequently in films during the Forties, Fifties and Sixties was religion. Many of the American epics dealt with the life of Christ, and the early days of Christianity. The approach to the subject was always respectful though the local critics sometimes complained of the presence of what one of them called a vague emotionalism in the treatment. Films like Quo Vadis (May 1953), Ben Hur, The Robe, the Ten Commandments, King of Kings, Barabbas, and The Greatest Story Ever Told pleased or displeased local filmgoers in about equal numbers. The Irish News critic expressed surprise at the level of interest shown by Belfast audiences in religion onscreen. He mentioned especially films about nuns, referring to titles like "The Nun's Story"(which had a long run in the Ritz), "Conspiracy of Hearts," and "The Sound of Music.," all of which were very popular in Belfast. The latter, described by one local critic "as wholesome as home-made jam," was a hit with both critics and audiences, and ran for about seven months in the Odeon. According to one local critic it just went "on... and on... and on," as week followed week. All of those were family films, carefully tailored as essentially pieces of entertainment with positive values that would offend no-one. But, in Belfast, someone was always ready to be outraged. In December 1946 a clergyman at a luncheon of the Imperial Grand Chapter of the Orange Order complained that local cinemas were showing too many "Catholic" films like "Going My Way" and "The Bells of St Mary's "which, he claimed, offended many Protestants. The Irish News rejected that complaint, and pointed out that there was no Popish plot involved to subvert anyone's beliefs. In fact, the editor added, thousands of people both Catholic and Protestant, had seen and enjoyed the films. Thirty years later, in December 1977, a report in the Belfast Telegraph indicated that some individuals believed that "The Sound of Music" wasn't the innocuous entertainment it claimed to be. It had been shown in a local school in south Down, and the Kilkeel branch of the DUP, in what the paper called an "astonishing attack," condemned the event because they felt that the film exhibited "a distinctive Romanish trend," and that State schools shouldn't be used "to propagate something that would destroy their Protestant heritage." A letter in a later edition of the paper expressed amazement at the comments and suggested that the group in question must be the most narrow minded in the country.

Catholic themed films weren't shown only in Nationalist areas.

There is no doubt that "Catholic" films were good box office, and that was the main reason that Hollywood made them. Many of them were highly praised by the critics and won recognition within the industry. "Going My Way" (d. Leo McCarey, 1944) won five Academy awards for best picture, best director, best actor (Bing Crosby), best supporting actor (Barry Fitzgerald) and best song (Swinging on a Star), while Jennifer Jones received an Academy Award for best actress in "The Song of Bernadette," (d. Henry King, 1943) in which she played Bernadette Soubirous, the peasant girl who had visions of Our Lady at Lourdes. "The Song of Bernadette" drew large crowds in Belfast. It arrived in the Classic in August 1944 where it ran for three weeks. From there it went to the Clonard for a two week run, followed by week - long bookings in the Forum, the Troxy and the Curran theatres. The Irish News described it as "a rare experience" and praised newcomer Jennifer Jones for her "moving" performance. The author remembers, as a boy, seeing it in the Broadway, where the atmosphere, as it unreeled, was as reverential as in a church. In February 1958 the Imperial revived it again, specially for the Lourdes Centenary Celebrations. It ran for two weeks during which there were special morning performances arranged for school groups. While all those films dealt with Catholic attitudes and Catholic perceptions of events, no attempt was made in them to criticise or belittle other Faiths.

There were other, more serious, films on religious topics, often of Continental origin like "Marcelino Pan y Vino," which ran successfully for many weeks in the Mayfair, and in Curran theatres without complaints. The Currans were a leading Catholic family and showed such films in the Regent, and particularly in the Broadway on the Falls Road, where large audiences enjoyed the likes of "Mother Cabrini" (February 1947), "Miracle at Fatima,"(October 53), "Le Sorcier du Ciel" which dealt with the life of the Cure of Ars, "Bernadette of Lourdes" (February 62), or the grimmer "The Prisoner" (September 55) in which Alec Guinness had the role of a Cardinal - obviously Cardinal Mindsentzy - being interrogated by a Communist officer played by Jack Hawkins. The Broadway often showed films with religious themes during Holy Week though it always closed its doors respectfully on Good Friday. The main downtown cinemas also showed such films with great success.

Another source of religious films was Fr Patrick Peyton, the American preacher of Irish origin - he was born near Ballina - whose rallying call was that "the family that prays together, stays together." Catholics were slow to use films to spread their beliefs but Fr Peyton set about changing that during the Fifties. He had a special devotion to Our Lady and organized Rosary Crusades which attracted thousands of pilgrims He understood how to use the media to spread his message. He persuaded many stars in Hollywood to take part in a series of Christian themed radio plays and films, a selection of which were shown in Belfast during the late Forties, under the heading of Family Theatre. The stars who contributed their skills included Bing Crosby, Gregory Peck, Don Ameche, Jerry Colonna, Pat O'Brien, Loretta Young, Ethel Barrymore, Ruth Hussey, Gene Lockhardt, Rosalind Russell and Macdonald Carey. The films shown in Belfast included "Trial at Tara," "Triumphant Hour," and "A Star Shall Rise."

Later, colour documentary films were shot of the Rosary crusades held at Beechmount, Ballymena, Downpatrick and elsewhere. All the films were professionally produced on 16 mm stock for showing in parish halls and centres. They proved very popular, mainly with Belfast Catholics, when they were shown in St Mary's Hall and parish halls across the city. The documentaries in particular were very interactive in their impact, with bursts of clapping and much comment as people identified Fr Peyton and various Church dignitaries, but more so when they saw themselves, family members or friends. Entry was always free, but a collection for worthy causes was taken up after each presentation. The films were projected on equipment supplied by Erskine Mayne who was still in the business of selling or hiring projectors and films. From its art shop in Donegal Square West the company supplied 16mm films to boarding schools and other establishments, for entertainment and educational purposes. The commercial cinemas didn't regard Fr Peyton's films as competition, and to the people who went to see them the experience had little to do with "going to the pictures."

While the Irish Catholic authorities remained slow to use films as a means of spreading Christian beliefs, Protestant Evangelical groups had presented films in the Grosvenor Hall and other venues from the earliest days of the cinema, and continued that traditional on Saturday evenings. In the early Forties St Peter's Church on the Antrim road even introduced "films in church," an experiment where a religious film was shown during the service in place of the sermon. The rector, the Rev Breen, revived the practice in January 1951, showing "Dust or Destiny," a 40 minute religious film produced by the Moody Bible Institute (USA). He was unable to continue the practice because he found that there wasn't a sufficient supply of suitable films available. But, Protestant - themed films, mainly American in origin, were becoming more easily obtainable, and one of the most successful was "Martin Luther" starring Niall Mac Ginnis, produced by an American religious group called Lutheran Church Productions Ltd. The film was photographed at actual locations in Germany, overseen by Louis de Rochemont who had produced the popular March of Time series. The aim seemed to be more than just a riposte to the popular Catholic - themed films, because, before it was released in 1953, Paul Empie, Director of the National Lutheran Council, warned that the film pulled no punches, and that it would involve the Lutherans in controversy, "especially with members of the Roman Catholic Church." While admitting that it was a well - made film, and that there was nothing immoral or visually objectionable in it, many Catholics objected strongly to it because they felt that it misrepresented and distorted their beliefs. The American League of Decency put it in a Separate Classification which meant that they disapproved of some of its content.

"Martin Luther" was booked into the Grosvenor Hall, mainly through the efforts of George Lodge in mid - January 1955, and was warmly welcomed. A special preview was attended by, among others, 700 local Protestant clergymen, members of the Grand Orange Lodge of Ireland, and representatives of the Belfast Corporation Education Committee, who enthusiastically endorsed it. It then ran for five weeks, attracting large audiences. The News Letter gave it a write up which was more a eulogy on the life of Luther rather than a detached film review. The writer, in passing, did note that the film was a "work of outstanding merit" which presented "a deeply moving story... with impeccable dignity". The Whig critic found it "dramatic and moving," while the Telegraph, in an editorial, praised the achievements of Luther in regard to the Protestant Reformation. The Telegraph also noted that sectarian attitudes would ensure that many people would have their minds made up before actually seeing the film and pointedly welcomed the fact that those who wanted to see it could do so. That comment referred to local complaints that no major circuit had booked the film into its cinemas, because they regarded it as bad box office. The circuits maintained that view and the film showed in only one commercial cinema in the city, the Willowfield, which was owned by the Unionist Party.

George Lodge argued that it would do well financially in N.Ireland, and a number of letters, to the Whig especially, supported him in that view. But others ignored the financial arguments. Harry Midgely, the Minister of Education felt that the cinema industry didn't want to offend certain people, and insinuated that such a stance was akin to censorship. A letter from the Ulster Orange and Protestant Committee praised Midgely's attack on "the appeasement" that was spreading across Ulster. Another writer felt that the film would help "to further the interests of Loyalists and the Protestant religion," and praised those who supported it, with special reference to Norman Porter M.P. who took 800 of his supporters to see it on its second night in the Grosvenor Hall. Of course attitudes in N. Ireland are never straightforward, and it is noticeable that none of the letters published actually criticised the film as a visual artefact, but used it for political and religious comment. There was little adverse response in Belfast, as the Catholic population in general tended to ignore the film.

Another Protestant organization, called Youth for Christ, which had emerged in America during the war years to meet the spiritual needs of young people and fighting men often showed religious films as part of their services during the Fifties and Sixties. Youth for Christ was an evangelical movement with chapters located across the world, including Belfast. For a time in the mid - Forties Billy Graham was a member of their organization, and even after he left them and set up his own Billy Graham Evangelistic Association (BGEA) he continued to co-operate with them. Graham was a forceful and much admired evangelical preacher with fundamentalist views, and, like Fr Peyton, he recognised the power of the media in spreading his beliefs. In the early Fifties his organization acquired a small film company which became known as World Wide Pictures. Beginning with documentaries of Billy Graham rallies and Crusades, World Wide Pictures began making full length films for theatrical release. The plots usually dealt with someone who was experiencing difficulties in life but who finally finds peace in religion. Each film included scenes shot at one of Graham's rallies, including relevant parts of his sermons.

In March 1955 the Ireland Youth for Christ group hired the Opera House for two weeks and showed an early example of those full length films, called "Souls in Conflict." It was very successful, and its makers claimed that it attracted over 100,000 viewers across N.Ireland. The Opera House was hired again for two weeks in March 1957 for a showing of "Fire on the Heather" based on Graham's recent All Scotland Crusade. It dealt with the religious and industrial history of Scotland and was the usual mix of fundamentalist beliefs and facts, with appearances by Billy Graham, and the eminent Scottish actors Duncan Lamont and Duncan Macrae. It proved very popular with Protestant audiences in Belfast. The Youth for Christ Movement showed other Graham films in the Grosvenor Hall, notably "Oiltown U.S.A," which was preceded by a brief prayer service, and "The Heart is a Rebel" which transferred from its presentation at the London Coliseum, complete with a new 16mm projector using the latest Xenon bulb which gave a much clearer picture than normal. When the Midland Cinema in Derry was closed by Rank's Odeon circuit in 1959 the cinemascope screen and equipment were sold to the Grosvenor Hall, allowing it to show World Wide Pictures' s first Cinemascope production, "Mr Texas."

Grosvenor Hall.

The Youth For Christ movement continued to show films of a religious nature into the Sixties. In September 1965 they advertised a colour film of the life of Dr Albert Schweitzer, to be shown in the Wellington Hall, but, after internal complaints, withdrew it at short notice, on the grounds that many of their members didn't agree with Schweitzer's views. A film on the life of Billy Graham was substituted. Many who had gone in good faith, unaware of the change, were angered when an announcement of the change was made just before the beginning of the film. A number of people, including clerics, walked out. Some of them expressed their views later in letters to the Belfast Telegraph. One minister complained that "religious bigots get their own way too much in Belfast." Another writer felt that the action taken was "a slight on the memory of one of the world's greatest men," while another suggested that the Youth for Christ Movement should get its priorities right. It seemed that regardless of subject - matter, film had the unnerving facility of arousing controversy, though it must be admitted that the spat over the censoring of the Schweitzer film was of little consequence in comparison with the ongoing relations between the Corporation's Police Committee and the commercial cinema in the city.

Religious films of the type produced by Fr. Peyton and Billy Graham operated on the periphery of the commercial cinema and represented no real economic threat to mainline cinema. But in the years after the war another group of films, mainly of foreign origin, offered an alternative attraction to commercial cinema for a growing body of students and young sophisticated adults. Belfast had always had a small coterie of cineastes who sought out quality films, but they were a decided minority, numbered in the hundreds rather than the thousands. Like most people, the Belfast critics treated films essentially as entertainment, and recognised that the majority of people went to the cinema to relax and enjoy themselves. Belfast audiences certainly responded to quality entertainment, as the long running success of "The Sound of Music," "Mary Poppins," "The Nun's Story," "Jaws," and "Star Wars" attested. At the same time - to the frustration of managers - they could also be individualistic and ignore trends. Films that did well in London and throughout England sometimes flopped locally, as Brendan Keenan - a former Garron Tower student who had first experienced film making in the Film Society there - writing in the Telegraph in 1979, noted. But there were always those like the Irish News critic, who believed that films could be more than entertainment. They could be used to instruct, educate, enlighten, and even uplift their audiences. Such ideas were not over popular in Hollywood, an attitude summed up by Sam Goldwyn's oft quoted comment: if you want to send a message, use Western Union.

While Hollywood had produced fine, challenging films over the years, serious films, intelligent and artistic in content and form, were traditionally associated with Europe, where the seeds of cinema had originally germinated. During the Silent Era, as already noted, French, German, Italian, and Danish films were shown on Belfast screens and were accepted as normal. After the Great War foreign films struggled to penetrate the local market, and with the coming of sound they disappeared from local screens. As the majority of filmgoers indicated their approval and support for the English - speaking talkies, especially from Hollywood, a small sophisticated section of the population kept alive their ambition to see foreign films, despite the difficulties of language. Their wishes were met, as already described, by the British Film Institute which opened a local branch in Belfast, as well as by the enthusiastic Belfast Film Society. Unfortunately the Second World War cut off the supply of foreign films, and saw the demise of the worthy Belfast Film Society. The film industry became part of the war effort and Belfast's cinemas showed mainly British and American films that were either propaganda (notably "Mrs Miniver"), pure entertainment (comedies, musicals, Westerns) or a combination of both. The cinemas became refuges from the harsher realities of life in wartime.

After the war, attitudes underwent a change and during the Fifties and Sixties a greater appreciation of foreign language films permeated intellectual circles, especially in the universities. Film societies, and a knowledge of serious cinema became de rigueur for students. The new attitudes surfaced in the Sunday supplements, Film, Sight and Sound, Films and Filming, Movie and other film magazines, all of which were available in local bookshops and newsagents. Films and Filming was typical of the time. It was a monthly, left - wing magazine which took an intelligent approach to films. Its reviews covered the normal British and American releases as well as major foreign language films. It had representatives in major film making centres across the globe, including Hollywood, Rome, Paris and elsewhere. It ran comprehensive articles on the history of cinema, including the silent era, as well as commentaries on the careers of top directors like John Ford, Howard Hawkes, Orson Welles, and their European counterparts - from Jean Renoir to Ingmar Bergman. Of course London was the main centre of attention for foreign language films. Besides the many facilities of the British Film Institute, the city was able to offer a wide range of "specialist" cinemas to meet the growing demands of its large and culturally mixed population.

Despite its provincial outlook Belfast didn't remain entirely apart from those cultural developments. During the Fifties and Sixties, many local managers realised that there was a growing audience for foreign films. The Curran Theatres experimented by showing Rossellini's splendid "Open City" though the response of its regular patrons wasn't as enthusiastic as was expected. As already discussed, the first commercial cinema to show foreign language films on a regular basis was the Mayfair, a move that may have damaged its reputation somewhat but which did its box office no harm. When the Mayfair closed in 1958 it seemed that the last commercial outlet for foreign language films had closed with it. The main renter of foreign films in the city, Mr Sidney Durbridge, manager of the Gresham Film Service, decried the fact there was such a small local audience for foreign films in the city. He put that down mainly to the practice of using subtitles written across the bottom of the image. Students and film society members accepted them as normal, but general audiences found them a problem, though they were willing to accept them if they thought they would see something saucy or sexy. Local critics also complained about the poor quality of subtitles, and hoped for better from the new innovation of dubbing dialogue into English. Unfortunately their experience of the dubbed Italian spectaculars starring Steve Reeves and others left much to be desired. Even today dubbing can be unsatisfactory, and can put audiences off a film.

Sidney Durbridge and others in the trade may have thought that there was a very restricted commercial future for foreign films in Belfast, but their pessimism was to be confounded by later developments. The first developments looked decidedly gloomy. It was announced that an English company, Capital and Provincial News Theatres Ltd., had purchased the empty Mayfair and intended to convert it into a modern News and Cartoon cinema. The company already had similar cinemas in London, Liverpool, Manchester, Sheffield, Leeds, and Glasgow and claimed that they were all doing good business despite the competition of television. They catered for a special niche in the market with small, well - run cinemas where people could pass a short time resting from shopping, waiting for a train or a bus, or just enjoying a relaxing hour of light - hearted entertainment. Each programme consisted of an hour or more of cartoons, newsreels, travelogues in full colour, documentaries and, on occasion, shorts of the Three Stooges, Edgar Kennedy, Laurel and Hardy and even Charlie Chaplin and Buster Keaton. The cinema in Belfast would be the first of its kind in Ireland, and the citizens were promised modern and comfortable surroundings in which to enjoy the films. Douglas J.O'Brien, who had much experience of the local cinema trade, and was sensitive to local feelings, was appointed manager to organise the details, and seems to have been given considerable leeway in his task.

The company also hired a well known, progressive local architect, Henry Lynch-Robinson, who set about updating the building. The result indicated a clear break with the X certificate atmosphere of the past. He designed a new frontage, including a new canopy, and incorporated brighter outdoor lighting, including neon, to make the approach attractive and friendly. The foyer was redesigned and decorated with paintings and cutouts of favourite cartoon characters including Donald Duck, Pluto, Bugs Bunny, Sylvester the Cat with Tweetie Pie, and Tom and Jerry. Tom was shown nonchalantly leaning on a placard which informed patrons that seats cost 1/ 3 and 2 shillings. Among its facilities was a well stocked shop which sold everything from confectionery and cigarettes to cosmetics. In the auditorium the number of seats were reduced to under 500 to improve comfort by giving more leg room. The temperature of the filtered air was controlled by the most up to date oil fired heating and ventilation system. The main lighting was located in the ceiling giving an overall feeling of space. A small group of attractive girls toured the city handing out leaflets announcing that the new cinema was scheduled to open on Thursday 18th December 1959. at 11:00 am, and would stay open daily until 11 00pm. "Come and enjoy this new cinema - going experience," the adverts exhorted, adding that the cinema would present adult entertainment which children would also enjoy. A special preview for invited guests took place on the Wednesday evening which was attended by the Lord Mayor, Alderman Cecil McKee, members of the Corporation, representatives of the local cinema trade and the Press.

The reactions to the News and Cartoon cinema varied. Children and parents, not to mention grandfathers and grandmothers, welcomed and praised it. Retired people, tired businessmen, shoppers and such found it a marvellous place to relax for a short period. During the day there was a steady stream of people through the foyer. Regular filmgoers and serious film students tended to ignore it, except when a rare Chaplin film or such was shown, while the trade didn't regard it as a true cinema in the traditional meaning of the word. To them a cinema presented full length films. Its success showed that people were willing to support small modern halls, and added strength to the growing speculation that the days of the large picture palaces were over. The News and Cartoon became part of the entertainment scene, though it made no great impact until November 1964 when its manager was persuaded to contribute to Queen's Festival 64 by putting on a series of late night foreign films. A selection of ten notable films was presented at 11:00 pm during the Festival, including Ingmar Bergman's "Through A Glass Darkly," Polanski's "Knife in the Water," and Alain Resnais's inscrutable "Last Year in Marienbad." The management was completely surprised at the warmth and strength of the public reaction. The crowds were so large that a second showing of each film was arranged for 1:00 am.

The director of the Festival was a young man from Stratford-upon-Avon called Mike Emmerson. He had graduated from Queen's that year and had been given a small grant by the university to organise the festival, a task he set about with enthusiasm, assisted by his brother Charles. He felt that Queen's was too provincial in its outlook and reputation and that it needed to raise its profile by becoming integrated more prominently into contemporary cultural life. As part of that strategy he encouraged the incorporation of serious films, of films as art, into the festival. The successful experiment in the News and Cartoon cinema was the result. When the Festival ended he was able to announce that the News and Cartoon cinema would continue with its late night foreign film shows. Thus late night films became a regular feature of Belfast night life, and the News and Cartoon cinema entered Belfast cinema history as the first cinema to present rest and relaxation during the day, with art and cultural stimulation after 11:00pm. So it continued for two years until in November 1966 it was announced that the cinema was to have a £2,000 facelift, and would change its name to the Classic. For older filmgoers that brought back memories of the Classic cinema that had stood in Castle Lane, but there was no real comparison or connection. The name change indicated that the cinema had become part of the progressive Classic Circuit which already had similar cinemas in London and across Britain. The manager of each Classic was expected to cater to local tastes, and the success of the late night films had convinced the company that it was time to end the News and Cartoon era in Belfast, and to introduce a new policy more suited to local tastes.

Mr R.M.Morgan, the man in charge of booking films for the Classic circuit, gave a press conference in Belfast and explained that in future the cinema would show interesting full length feature films which had not originally been given the widespread release they deserved. The first of them was "War and Peace" (d. King Vidor, 1956) starring Audrey Hepburn and Henry Fonda. An important part of the new policy was that the presentation of late night films would continue. The revamped cinema opened on 7th November 1966 with a special showing which was attended by the deputy Lord Mayor, Councellor Lewis and his wife, the local French Consul Mon.P.Lunet, the manageress Miss Sally Feenan and R.J.Dowdeswell, the general manager of Classic cinemas.

The response in the city was positive. On the one hand filmgoers were given the opportunity to see good films, including reissues, that they had missed or wanted to see again. At the same time the late night film sessions went from strength to strength. The Irish News critic welcomed the new policy as one that every filmgoer "can only applaud sincerely." It was, he wrote, a bold experiment that recognised the increased maturity of Belfast filmgoers. The development was also warmly welcomed by the Queen's Film Society in its Film News, which praised the Classic circuit as "one of the most successful of the independent groups (which) fulfills a valuable function in providing an opportunity for films which have received a raw deal from the major circuits." It also mentioned that the Circuit had an enlightened approach to Continental and World cinema and often showed quality foreign films. The Classic management kept its word and over the following years presented many excellent Continental films by top directors. On his many visits the author always found the cinema full, or nearly so. The audience for stimulating quality films may have been small but it remained faithful, even in the early Seventies when bombings and shootings made it more and more dangerous to be about late. Sadly, at the end of December 1971 a large bomb aimed at the nearby Kensington Hotel also damaged the Classic beyond reasonable repair. It closed during the first week in January, and a rich vein of cinematic history in Belfast disappeared with it. There is no physical evidence that it ever existed, its site having been swallowed up by a combination of shops and offices.

By the Fifties an increasingly wide range of foreign films had become available for hire, and small groups of enthusiasts availed of them. One such group was the Lagan Film Society which showed specialist and esoteric films in the mid - fifties, in the Ulster Farmer's Union Hall in 18, Donegall Square East. The films included "The White Haired Girl" advertised as the first all - Chinese film shown in Ireland, "Childhood of Maxim Gorky," and "The Condemned Village"(X), the official U.N. film of Auschwitz's Women's Concentration Camp. There is little information about the society but the films give an indication of a move from purely entertaining fare. In the early Sixties a local business man, Trevor Jackson, founded an International Film Club at 36 College Sq. North, where members met every Monday and Tuesday at 8:00pm. The aim of the club was to offer members "the best discriminating films from the four corners of the globe." It was a noble and worthwhile aim, and the club attracted around 200 members. That number was insufficient to ensure financial viability, and like the Lagan Film Society it was didn't survive for long.

The demand for serious foreign films in the city was met mainly and successfully by Queen's University with its own Film Society, organised by the Dept. of Extra-Mural Studies, with a major input from the British Film Institute. The Film Society began operating, with a season of seven films, in October 1951. Its stated aim was to present a selection of the best available English speaking and foreign language films. The society was open to all, students and non students, who responded with their support so that within a short time its numbers had reached well over the thousand mark. The Society flourished throughout the Fifties and Sixties with a mix of silent and early sound classics, sophisticated French comedies, Italian neo-realist dramas, sombre East European and Scandinavian narratives, along with the best of British and American cinema. Its annual seasons of 16 films were able to fill the Whitla Hall on specified Wednesday and Saturday evenings with enthusiastic crowds. The author was a member, and still recalls the excitement and intellectual challenge of seeing the films of Antonioni, Fellini, Pasolini, Truffaut, Ray, Ingmar Bergman, Andrzej Wajda and many others in the company of other devoted cineastes. A special atmosphere permeated the hall, emanating from the bond of shared interests. A certain formality also prevailed and there were fewer beards and duffle coats than film societies in London usually attracted. Each showing was accompanied by a printed handout, Film News, which gave background information about the making of the films, plus critical reviews. The latter were often taken from Sight and Sound, and the BFI Monthly Film Bulletin.

The Society also had an interest in supporting amateur films. The making of amateur films was quite popular throughout Ireland, and many schools engaged in it. St Mac Nissi's College at Garron Point near Carnlough had a lively Film Society, organised by Fr. Gerard Mc Conville, where the emphasis was on both the theory and practice of film making. On the practical side the society produced a number of interesting prize winning films. Queen's Film Society showed two of them one Saturday evening (21st March 1964) and the large audience responded with a rousing standing ovation, much to the student film - makers' delight. The films, scripted and made entirely by the students, were treated in the Film News with the same seriousness as the professional films. Details of production, direction and actors were given along with a commentary on their merits. The first film, "A Question of Time," which dealt with the threat of nuclear attack, was a serious affair which won a number of major awards, while the other, "Fly Bonnie Prince," was a swashbuckler in the Hollywood style with lots of swordplay, spies, and narrow escapes involving the adventures of Bonnie Prince Charlie. The amateur films were a prelude to the main feature, the Greek tragedy "Antigone" (d. George Tzavellas, 1961).starring Irene Papas. After the fearful prospect of nuclear disaster implied in "A Question of Time," those of a more thoughtful demeanor must have trembled within when, ninety minutes later, the chorus in "Antigone" concluded the Greek film with the warning that "mortal men cannot escape from predestined disaster."

In the years that followed, the Queen's Society didn't exactly suffer a disaster, but unfortunately due to falling audience numbers and competition, especially from TV, which had taken to discussing and showing quality foreign language films, it found itself in financial difficulties in 1969. Despite selling their own 16mm camera the organizers were unable to accumulate sufficient funds to survive, and in 1973 the Society was wound up. The hope expressed at the time was that the financial situation would improve in the future and allow the society to be reactivated. Sadly, that didn't happen, though the spirit of the original society lived on, and continues to do so today, in its successor, the QFT. Unlike the Film Society the Queen's Film Theatre was an actual cinema, though quite unlike any other in Belfast, and its arrival was announced as "a new concept in cinema going." It was designed as a small (seating 252) specialised art house cinema that showed mainly quality English - speaking and foreign language films. It was owned by the university which, in association with the local Arts Council, supplied the initial funding of £4000. It was the brainchild of Michael Emmerson and Michael Barnes, two former directors of the Belfast Festival, and despite the university link, was expected to make its own way financially.

Its establishment was organised by its first administrator, an Englishman called Andrew Douglas-Jones. He had studied theatre management but worked for the British Film Institute, managing their art cinemas in Malvern and Tyneside. It was in the latter that he met Mike Emmerson, who persuaded him to come to Queen's to establish the Queen's Film Theatre as part of Festival 68. When interviewed in Belfast about the project he admitted that the facilities available were only a modified lecture theatre, but he pointed out, optimistically, it had the advantages of tiered seats, and a small size, which favoured the finances of an art cinema. His aim was to present local audiences with the best in world cinema. Programmes would begin in the evenings after lectures had finished and the cinema would be open on seven days. On Sundays a cinema club, similar to those already functioning in England, would cater for associates. Anyone over 16 years could become an Associate for a fee of ten shillings, though students and retired persons got a fifty percent concession. The club he explained, had the advantage that it could legally show films that hadn't been given a certificate, and other esoteric fare not available to the commercial circuits.

The official opening took place on the evening of 14th October 1968, and those present included the Vice - Chancellor of Queen's, Dr Vick, the director of the Arts Council, representatives of the BFI, and Mike Emmerson. After the introductory speeches the audience sat down to enjoy the exploits of Brigitte Bardot and Jeanne Moreau in "Viva Maria." The QFT was especially welcomed by the Queen's Film Society, though it was in the twilight of its own existence, and the programme secretary, T.E.Kennedy, exhorted all those interested in foreign films to support it. The problem for some filmgoers was finding it, because the entrance was located away from the bright lights, on University Square Mews. A mews it may have been called, but, in Belfast parlance, it was a back entry which in no way competed with the impressive approaches associated with most cinemas. In time the lack of decoration, the hard lecture seats and the unobtrusive entrance became part of the special ambiance of the place. Going to the QFT reflected a dedication to film rather than to place. Once inside, the atmosphere was always friendly and relaxed, with the intimacy of a small audience of like - minded aficionados.

The new QFT played its part in Festival 68 with two well - attended programmes of Great Westerns, and Scandinavian Films. No one mentioned that, strictly speaking, the cinema was illegal as it was functioning without planning permission. In fact the university didn't apply for planning permission until mid - January 1969, but the planners decided to postpone a decision on its future until the following month. The chief planning officer pointed out that there were problems regarding parking, plus the impact on what was a residential area. In mitigation was the fact that the site was within the university, so he suggested that its use as a cinema would be "reasonable" if admittance was confined to students and staff of Queen's. Such a restriction would have undermined the aim, and the financial viability of the project. However, with the strong support of the Arts Council the outstanding criticisms were dealt with and the necessary planning permission was granted.

Andrew Douglas-Jones nurtured the early days of the QFT with astuteness and skill. He distributed a questionnaire to ascertain what people wanted to see. He developed a successful sales policy backed by an aggressive advertising campaign which emphasised the uniqueness and attractions of the new venture. The cinema was described in newspaper adverts as "Belfast's new intimate picture house" where patrons could see the best of world films. Many of them, including Ingmar Bergman's "Persona," and Ichikawa's "An Actor's Revenge" were presented as Irish premières. He also developed the Sunday cinema club and promoted it in newspaper adverts with such success that by March 1968 the QFT had 3,500 Associate members. A large and prominent advert in January. encouraged people to join and see "Rocky Road to Dublin," "The Switchboard Operator," "Ulysses," and a variety of underground films "all in their original versions." It is interesting how Joseph Strick's much discussed "Ulysses," which had been refused a certificate by the BBFC in London, was slipped, without any special reference, in among the other coming attractions. It opened on Monday 27th January and showed to packed houses for a week. The News Letter described how it arrived "without a whisper of protest." The critic praised the acting, and overall found the film a "delight." The QFT notes described it as "a serious and unsensational attempt" to express Joyce's novel in cinematic terms. The response to the film was so enthusiastic that the QFT brought it back for another week at the end of June. After the January showing Andrew Douglas-Jones expressed his deep satisfaction, and now that the cinema was up and running, he departed back to England where he wanted to become more involved in live theatre administration again.

By February. his successor, another Englishman, had been appointed, and his name, Michael Open, became closely associated with the future development of the little cinema.

Michael Open was passionate about films and had worked for a time with the BFI in London. He little knew what he was letting himself in for, because the history of the QFT can best be described as a roller coaster, with ups and downs, and even a technical breakdown when it was forced to close for a few months in 1972. Despite financial problems, difficulties with distributors, the violence of the Troubles, and declining audiences the cinema has struggled on with financial help from Queen's, the N. Ireland Film Commission, the Arts Council of N.Ireland and other groups. It has managed to keep the flame of serious cinema lit, especially with its imaginative celebration of the Centenary of the birth of the Cinema in 1996. Over the years, alongside its modern films, it has often gone back to cinemas's roots by showing classic silent films usually accompanied by a piano and a pianist in the flesh. Young filmgoers were given the opportunity of seeing on the big screen films and personages they had only read about. Cinematic history became alive as Buster Keaton, Chaplin, the Gish sisters, Douglas Fairbanks, Valentino and many others appeared once again on a Belfast cinema screen. Parallel to those the QFT presented new prints of popular favourites like "Meet Me in St Louis" and "The Quiet Man," both of which attracted packed houses. The author remembers seeing the latter, with young people, mainly Queen's students, standing along the back of the hall, while others sat on the steps.

The whole complex was completely refurbished, within and without, in 2004, and reopened in October of that year with a new impressive entrance at 20, University Square. Today, as a result of that makeover it boasts two comfortable state of the art cinemas which seat 220 and 90 patrons respectively. Added to them is a 150 seat theatre performance space, plus a new bar serving tea, coffee and drinks. While the aim is still to screen quality films the overall atmosphere has subtly changed with a greater appreciation of commercial considerations. Since 2001 the QFT has had a marketing manager who has the almost impossible task of competing with the popular attractions of the multiplexes. Thus, added to the more sober and less commercial serious screenings, there have been Desert Island Movies, cult orientated films, Discussion Sundays when a film is screened and then followed by a discussion, and themed evenings. Typical of the latter was a Halloween Dracula Spectacula in October 2008 to celebrate the 50th Anniversary of Hammer Horror. The highlight was the screening of a new print of "Dracula," (1958) starring Peter Cushing and Christopher Lee. Then there are the club nights in which silent classics, accompanied by modern live soundtracks, are shown as a background to socialising. To some cineastes that is a step too far in the struggle for survival.

Despite such minor gripes the QFT continues in its own inimitable way to honour its dedication to serious cinema. Its high international standing is reflected in the type of guests it has attracted, including Daniel Day-Lewis, David Lynch, Mike Leigh, Ken Loach, Michael Palin, Jeremy Irons, Ciaran Hinds and others. Its future however depends on its ability to attract audiences, and it must be admitted that, in the main, Belfast audiences seem to prefer the noise and bluster of the fare shown in the multiplexes. The QFT still has a struggle on its hands to survive. In England many Art cinemas have been forced to close, while in Ireland only three still operate, in Dublin, Cork and Belfast.

Despite the addition of the QFT. in 1968 the cinema industry in Belfast continued to decline. Between 1950 and 1970 twenty five cinemas closed their doors as audience

The new Q.F.T.: the residence of good films. Photo: K. Hughes.

numbers continued to shrink, due mainly to the impact of television, combined with the changing pattern of film going. The number of family orientated films dropped after the introduction of the X certificate in 1951, persuading more parents to stay at home watching television. Sidney Durbridge, the film renter, who had his finger directly on the pulse of the local industry, warned cinema owners and managers that it wasn't the size or shape of their screens that would attract audiences back, but the quality of what was on those screens. The increasingly controversial content of the films being shown caused disquiet in some circles in Belfast, including the City Hall. The Police Committee was encouraged to act, and to stop what many members of the Corporation regarded as the moral rot of the permissive society. Those demands for more decisive action increased as the new X certificate allowed more graphic and challenging scenes of sex and violence to appear on local screens. Film censorship once again became a major topic of discussion in the city.

Food for thought: Even big John couldn't sort out the censorship problems.

CHAPTER THIRTY
Teddy Boys, Rock 'n' Roll and The Sash

No history of the cinema in Belfast would be complete without debating the topic of film censorship, and the actions of that august body of moral arbiters, the Police Film Committee. To some commentators the Police Committee was seen as a welcome and necessary expression of local democracy, but to others its actions implied a denial, or curtailment of free expression. During the Second World war years censorship matters had been concentrated in the hands of the Ministry of Information in London, and films shown in Belfast were vetted and passed there. Belfast Council had no say in their content, though it continued to involve itself controversially in cinematic matters, especially with regard to the question of Sunday performances, which it had vigorously opposed. At the end of the war the powers of local censorship were returned to the Councils, including Belfast. The return of its powers was welcomed by most members of the Council, and the Police Committee was quickly at work. If some members expected things to return to pre-war conditions, they were to be very disappointed. The members of the Committee and the Council found themselves making censorship decisions for a society that increasingly rejected the need for such restrictions.

The consequences of the impact of the war were already taxing minds in a wide range of fields, including film entertainment. Lord Tyrrell, the Film Censor, addressed the Cinematograph Exhibitors Association (the CEA) in June 1947, a short time before he died, on the problems that the film industry could expect to face in the coming years. He pointed out that social and moral conditions had changed as a result of wartime conditions. He drew special attention to the impact on society of the greater independence of women, which the war had engendered. Working women, separated from their menfolk, and with more money to spend, had experienced a greater freedom of behaviour, and had mixed socially with groups outside their normal class, which in turn, he felt, had put increased pressures on the bonds of marriage. Soldiers were returning home after the experience of army barrack life with its strong language and unadorned view of life in the raw. One result was that men and women were developing a more open view of sex. At the same time battlefield experiences had brought individuals face to face with the true nature of violence. All of that would, he felt, cause problems for future film censors and film censorship. Changes in social, moral and intellectual attitudes were certainly under way and would continue, though no-one, including Lord Tyrrell, realised just how far and how quickly they would proceed.

Post-war change accelerated through the late Forties and Fifties into the so-called Swinging Sixties. Historically, on the world stage, the decades after the war were an era

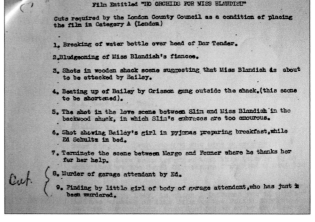

Discussion document with Police Committee's recommendations for cuts.

of political confrontation known as the Cold War, with its ever present threat of nuclear annihilation. The realities of the Cold War sent shock waves of mainly youthful protest through society. Demands for change, for justice and equality became more vociferous. Some protesters saw no future for society and released their frustrations in violence against it and its conventions. "Rebellion is the only thing that keeps you alive," explained the young heroine (Marianne Faithful) in the film "Girl on a Motorcycle."(1968). Others disagreed, and called on the youth to abandon violence and "make love not war." Some turned to "flower power," or a drug - fuelled hedonistic life style. Confusion spread as long held certainties, including moral certainties, came under intellectual scrutiny, causing concern especially among those responsible for young people.

With regard to censorship problems, it was a period that saw the introduction of X certificate films with less inhibited scenes of sex,violence and horror; the first nudist films; the Lady Chatterley test of the Obscene Publications Act in 1960 and the resulting legal decision in its favour; the antics of Teddy Boys, Mods, and Rock and Rollers; revulsion over horror comics; and, above all, worries about the impact of such changes on children. Addressing the jury at the opening of the Belfast City Commission in July 1947 Lord Justice Porter deplored the recent increase in juvenile crime which he put down to conditions in the aftermath of the war. He highlighted especially what he called the chaos, turmoil and unsettled state of moral and religious ideas, the lack of parental control, and poverty. There were, he complained, too many young people drifting aimlessly, open to crimes like burglary and theft from which they got money "to spend mainly on cigarettes and cinemas."

The connection between films and petty crime was taken seriously in legal circles. Films, in particular, were regarded by many prominent Protestant and Catholic spokesmen as purveyors of foreign and permissive society values, especially with regard to sexual mores, and violence. As early as 1947 Dr Mageean, the Catholic bishop of Down and Conor, addressing an Amateur Dramatic Feis in Lisburn, praised the value of local productions. "Home made cakes are better than all the canned food from Hollywood," he claimed, "better socially, morally, religiously and nationally." That same sentiment was reflected, thirteen years later, in the comments of Adrian Stanley when he addressed an audience at the Larne Drama Festival, and told them that it was important to introduce children to live theatre "to inoculate them against the type of film they would see as adults."

Among Belfast's ruling groups the majority view was that those outside changes should be resisted, or at least curtailed, because of their influence on youth. One youthful expression of change that caused concern was the appearance on Belfast's streets, during the Fifties, of Teddy Boys. They had a reputation for violence and when a group of them appeared on the pavement people gave them a wide berth. Certainly some of them caused trouble because, being Belfast, there was an added historical dimension with Shankill Teds and Falls Teds, who inevitably clashed. Teddy Boys featured prominently among those who appeared in court accused of disturbing the peace. A magistrate asked one such accused why he was dressed "in that ridiculous fashion," to which the young man replied, "I like it." Earlier in the year the Moderator of the General Assembly, attacked what he called the Vogue of the Gang, and especially the Teddy Boys with their distinctive Edwardian clothing. The Moderator received much support for his comments, with one letter writer referring to the Teddy Boys as "Devil's Boys" who went around with their "vamps of young women," causing trouble and "aping the stars of Hollywood, with their hair styles and clothes of 50 years ago." In response, another writer dismissed such attitudes as "silly," and called for positive action by way of youth clubs and other facilities to deal with the problems of the youth. In January 1957 the national secretary of the YMCAs, speaking in Belfast, took an equally sympathetic view. Draped jackets, drainpipe trousers and string ties, he insisted, were not signs of delinquency but "of youth seeking expression, and in need of counsel and understanding." Young people today were living in "a confused and confusing world" that they didn't understand. They were, he explained, easily swept along in the increasing tempo and excitement of modern day living. The city, and the Police Committee, were to experience some of that excitement with the arrival of rock and roll films.

In early January 1961 the Irish News published an editorial condemning the new Permissive Society that was emerging, and deplored the way that a section of the media, along with a handful of "cheap-jack prophets, pseudo theologians, and propagandists" were doing their best to undermine all traditional and accepted standards of decency. There had been, the editor wrote, a "frightening change" in public attitudes to pornography, abortion and euthanasia, which were becoming more and more socially acceptable. A short time later the Belfast Telegraph published an editorial on the increasingly serious problem of vandalism in Belfast, which it saw it as "one of the symptoms of social sickness." It suggested that the reasons for its upsurge included the lack of proper open play spaces for young people, antisocial films and, above all, a lack of parental control. The reference to antisocial films struck a responsive chord in certain local professional circles. In September 1964 the local papers quoted the evangelist Billy Graham, who, speaking at a rally in Boston, had condemned many commercial films for their use of "profanity, immorality, incest, and homosexuality" in their plots. Coverage was also given to the Pope and other senior religious figures when they took film makers to task for undermining family values by their depiction of divorce and immorality in their films. Bishop Farren of Derry told his flock that people had a right to protect the spiritual welfare of those they were responsible for. Many elected members in Stormont, and, more especially in Belfast Council, agreed with those sentiments. The Police Committee and the Council took what they saw as their responsibility to protect the morals of Belfast citizens very seriously - too seriously, some argued.

When, in 1955, the Council passed "The Wild One" as fit to be shown in a local cinema, Councillor Dixon castigated his fellow members and reminded them that they should be "in the vanguard of the campaign to maintain a high moral standard in the city." Such moral outrage was not approved of by some ratepayers who complained that Councillors were not elected for that purpose. A typical letter published in the Telegraph (August 1956) criticised "the arrogance of representatives of ratepayers acting as self - appointed custodians of the morals of the electors." Significantly, the writer questioned their qualifications to do so, a view that gained widespread acceptance during the Seventies. But public speakers and letter writers continued to express alarm at the changing state of society with its rising crime rate, sexual laxity and violence. Films, and increasingly TV, were seen as a major cause of many of those ills, which one writer insisted were fed by the "constant showing of crime and murder on films." In August 1953 the Telegraph gave details of a meeting of the T.U.C. at which a prominent member complained about the use of excessive violence in films. There was, he claimed, no artistic justification in most cases for it, and accused some film makers of using "base motives of profit through sensationalism." He called on the public to bring pressure on the authorities to put an end to the problem.

It was against that background that film censorship and the actions of the Police Committee took place. Many of the changes taking place in society were perceived as undermining moral stability, and many elected members of the Council believed it was their duty to protect the citizens in general from what they saw as a rising tide of sex and violence. That duty didn't just involve films, though they were the main target, but extended to other forms of entertainment, and means of communication like books, magazines, pop music and television. The majority of both Protestant and Catholic councillors disapproved of the New Morality, and felt threatened by it. They had widespread support in the city, especially from clerical groups, the teaching organizations, magistrates, certain trade unions and Womens' Leagues. Another high profile supporter was moral campaigner Mrs Mary Whitehouse who wrote from England to the local papers, and visited the city (in September 1977) to encourage the defence of traditional values. Mrs Whitehouse was mainly concerned with the topics of crude language, sex and violence on television, and had begun a Clean - Up TV campaign in 1964 to tackle those matters. Much criticised at the time, and often lampooned as an anachronistic figure of fun, it is now widely acknowledged that much of what she said, especially about screen violence, was quite valid. She had also recognised the need to protect children from early sexualisation and violence. The local newspaper editors often published letters from the public some of which supported the actions of Police Committee while others opposed them (making Belfast the laughing stock of Britain, some wrote). The editors themselves took a generally moderate and liberal tone, but occasionally expressed concerns about certain films, or the social trends that they reflected.

The local film critics tended to approach contentious films in a spirit of ridicule or humour, but only on rare occasions condemned any film as an outright menace to public morality. One exception was PRC in the Irish News who regarded a moral approach as an integral part of his critical duties. He complained that many of the films he viewed were "vulgar, witless, dull juvenile nonsense." He called for better quality films, and audiences that showed higher critical values. He wondered, as a critic, how he could contribute to bringing such a situation about. Any indication of improved quality was welcomed. When, in the early Sixties, the News and Cartoon cinema began showing quality Continental films at late night shows, he greeted the move as "a courageous and indeed almost recklessly daring experiment." The fact that it was being well supported by a discriminating public made it "one of the most hopeful portents of Belfast cinema-going" at the time. He also had special praise for the Troxy when it presented films by Ingmar Bergman, whom he regarded as "the most intense and most rewarding director of our time." When, in January 1964, the Troxy showed Bergman's "The Virgin Spring" he congratulated the management on giving the Belfast public the opportunity to see it. Unfortunately the Troxy closed shortly afterwards, and re-invented itself as the Grove Theatre, prompting the critic to regret the passing of "that most capricious cinema in which it was possible to see almost side by side, Bergman's "The Silence" and "How to throw off your clothes and be happy as nature intended on an island paradise set in the Humber Estuary." At the same time he believed that films should be categorised, and he contributed to the Irish News's own classification of films, which was mainly aimed at parents. The Irish News was the only local newspaper which published a critical and moral guide of that type.

Catholic parents - Catholics formed the majority of the Irish News readership - were encouraged to make themselves familiar with film classifications such as those of the American League of Decency, so that they could take steps to ensure that their children saw only films with positive moral values. They were encouraged to read magazines like "Focus," produced by the Catholic Film Institute in England. "Focus," which was available locally in Church bookstalls, reviewed major releases and classified them independently of the British Board of Censors, as being suitable for adults only, adults and adolescents, family audiences and especially for children. Also recommended was the National Film Quarterly produced by the National Film Institute of Ireland, which, besides reviews, published articles arguing the need for censorship, and a moral classification of films. The Irish News critic returned often to the problems of censorship, describing it as a struggle between the morally perfect and the practical, out of which, it was hoped, some sort of standard would emerge. He argued that ideally everyone should be their own censor, but accepted that in this imperfect world such a situation was unlikely. Thus, he argued, the State had to step in to protect those, especially children, who could be regarded as susceptible. Official censorship systems were not perfect, but he supported the efforts of the British Board of Film Censorship, which he described as "an imperfect attempt to combine protection and liberty in the optimum combination." He made no reference to the Police Committee, which didn't always share his opinion of the BBFC. One difficulty for the Committee and the City Council was that certain films arrived without a BBFC certificate, while others were regarded as having a rating that was unsuited to their content. The Belfast City Council through their control of cinema licences had, in law, the power to allow or ban

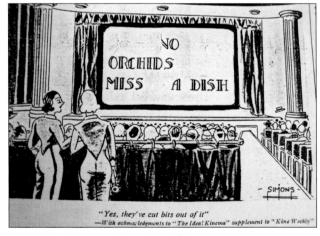

"Yes, they've cut bits out of it"
—With acknowledgments to "The Ideal Kinema" supplement to "Kine Weekly"

No Orchids For Miss Blandish - censored.

the showing of such films, a right that they applied enthusiastically. The result was that films shown in the city were censored at least twice, in London and in Belfast. The group appointed by the council to oversee that process locally was the 14 member Police Committee, few of whom, regrettably, ever showed any particular appreciation or understanding of film - making processes.

In City Hall politics the Police Committee was a very powerful cabal, and was treated as such by the cinema industry. As its records indicate, the Committee was part of a countrywide system involving the exchange of information on censorship. It was informed regularly by post of the decisions of the BBFC, but it also communicated with other English Councils, including the influential LCC, which, for one reason or another, sometimes took issue with the advice of the BBFC, and ignored its classification of certain films. When such a film with a "troublesome" reputation was booked into a local cinema the renter, sometimes the producer, or more often the cinema owner or manager wrote to the Police Committee informing them of the fact, and usually offered to put on a private preview so that they could form an opinion regarding its suitability or otherwise for local presentation. The application was usually accompanied by an outline of the film's plot and a publicity booklet on how best to "sell" the film. Members of the Committee (the whole committee rarely appeared), accompanied by interested members of the Council, the cinema industry and, initially, a scattering of journalists attended the preview. From the Fifties the details of such previews were kept secret, and journalists were not invited. After the showing those members of the Police Committee who were present consulted together, took a vote and then advised the Council either to allow the film to be screened, or not. The Council had the final decision which was announced after a public debate, and vote. Many films were banned, most were passed for exhibition, while some, like "The Birth of a Baby," were only permitted under strict conditions.

The Council were no strangers to "The Birth of a Baby" which, despite having no BBFC certificate, had been shown, with their reluctant permission, in the Grosvenor Hall in 1942, with entry restricted to females aged 18 years or over. In July 1947 the council received a letter from Health Education Films Ltd. requesting that the film - which still had no BBFC certificate - be shown to mixed audiences, with females under 16 years being allowed admittance. The Police Committee were not inclined to do that, but finally agreed to it being shown to adults, male and female, over 16 years. The company had to agree to keep to guidelines laid down by the National Baby Welfare Council which supported the showing of the film. All literature and publicity material would be approved by the NBWC, which would also have to approve any supporting films shown. A kiosk would be placed in the foyer with qualified persons who would answer any questions from patrons. The film opened in the Classic on 9th February 1948 where it ran for two weeks, drawing large audiences. Harris Deans writing in the Telegraph, gave it a very favourable review. He accepted that it dealt with a "delicate subject," but it was presented without offence in the unemotional style of a medical lecture. It told a simple story of a young married woman called Mary awaiting the birth of a baby, and through the advice given by her sympathetic doctor, learned what was happening to her, and what she needed to know. The critic praised the tone of the whole production but made no mention of the actual birth scene. Ten years later, in January 1957, the film popped up, cork-like, again in a revised and updated version distributed by Eros Films Ltd. The Police Committee gave permission again for it to be shown to adult audiences only.

A few years after the 1947 presentation another film in a similar vein arrived in the city. It was called "Street Corner," and the distributors arranged a special preview for the Police Committee in January 1951. The poster advertising it asked two questions: is forbidden fruit the sweetest? and, in an attempt to appeal to parents, where is your daughter tonight? It was an exploitation film posing as a sex educational treatise, about a young high school girl who becomes pregnant, and the problems,physical and mental, that she has to cope with. It also culminated with an explicit birth sequence. The Police Committee passed it for adults only, and it was shown in the Royal Cinema.

Sex education films didn't slip into Belfast via the suburbs, but usually began their runs in the city centre. Probably the most talked about and successful example of the genre was "Helga," a German film, with English subtitles, made for the German Ministry of Health, directed in colour by Erich Bender and starring Ruth Gassman. It followed the model established by "The Birth of a Baby" and told the story of a married woman going

The Snake Pit

through the experience of having a baby. The story line was punctuated by suitable comments from doctors, nurses and other experts. The distributors arranged a special preview in the ABC (the former Ritz) on 1st October 1968 for a selected audience of youth leaders, clergy, representatives of the local Marriage Guidance Council, birth control clinics and, most importantly, the Police Committee. Advertised as the first full length sex education film it proved to be a slow moving and rather ponderous eighty minutes which detailed the heroine's learning curve as she coped with the inquisitive stage of sex, courtship, sexual problems, the physiology of sex and - in glorious colour - childbirth. The producers emphasised its lofty motives and academic approach which had earned it an "A" certificate from the BBFC, meaning that children under sixteen could see it, if accompanied by an adult.

There were those in Belfast who thought that a detailed birth sequence in colour was quite unsuitable for presentation to anyone, not alone children, in a cinema which was, above all they argued, a venue for entertainment. During the preview at least one councillor, Brent Hughes, walked out in protest. He admitted that the film was well made but complained that he was "sickened by the birth scene" which he felt could "create panic among young expectant mothers." There was no public indication of such panic, though a small number of local people were later reported to have fainted during the birth sequence. After the preview the Police Committee and the Council passed the film as suitable for presentation with an "A" certificate, and it opened in the ABC in early Oct 1968, where It ran for two weeks. Its acceptance by the Police Committee indicated that between 1942 and 1968

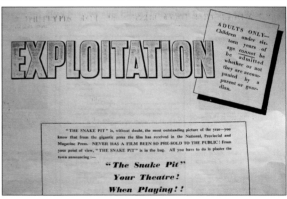

Was mental health a suitable subject for films? Publicity booklet (1948).

attitudes had changed to the extent that a birth scene which was deemed suitable only to women over 16 years was now passed as appropriate to mixed audiences including children in the company of adults. The poster, which was illustrated with a discreet image of a naked woman, carried a warning for parents stating that "this colour film contains scenes of an actual birth and may be unsuitable for some younger members of the public."

The News Letter critic noted that the film wasn't "the usual X certificate mush," but was a serious work which included no risqué material. It dealt "frankly and tastefully" with the delicate topic of conception and birth. On the negative side he felt it was too clinical in its approach, and "jerky" in its presentation. He also complained about the poor quality of the

dubbing. After its downtown run it moved to the Ambassador for two weeks, attracting large crowds. The Ambassador even arranged special children's matinees on Wednesday and Saturday, but made it clear that all children must be accompanied by adults. Later "Helga" showed in the Crumlin and the Grove cinemas, before disappearing from view.

Another controversial film with a clinical theme was "The Snake Pit"(d. Anatole Litvak, 1948), starring Olivia de Havilland. It dealt with the problem of mental breakdown, and many of its scenes showing conditions in a mental institution shocked audiences in the USA. It was the first serious attempt to deal with mental problems in the commercial cinema. The plot detailed the harrowing trials and tribulations of a writer called Virginia,(played by Miss de Havilland) who has a mental breakdown, losing all knowledge of her past including her marriage. Committed to an institution, she endures shock treatment and injections as her doctor (Leo Genn) tries to discover the underlying cause of her mental condition. The film arrived in Britain praised for its artistic integrity, and its sober approach to its delicate subject. Its theme caused the British censor much worry. It was seen by the BBFC five times, with and without the presence of medical personnel. The Minister of Health, Aneurin Bevan, saw it and approved. The censor finally gave it an "A" certificate but with a number of provisos. No child under 16 years could be admitted with or without an adult, and that prohibition had to be prominently displayed either outside or in the foyer of the cinema. A foreword was prefixed to the film emphasising that the conditions shown applied to an American hospital, and did not represent local conditions. On release the film was a great success in London, drawing large crowds over an eight week period, though there was little reference to it in the local press.

In a letter dated 28th September 1949 the district manager of Union Cinemas wrote to the Police Committee from the Ritz cinema informing them that the film had been booked into the Ritz for showing, beginning on the 7th November. He explained that the subject matter of the film was insanity, and though passed by the BBFC with an "A" certificate, he felt that "owing to its nature it should be viewed by members of the Police Committee in order to ascertain their reaction before presentation to the general public." A special showing took place on 12th October and two days later, members of the Police Committee met and decided by 4 votes to 2 to recommend that the film be passed for showing in Belfast. The full Council then discussed the matter but decided that the film's topic was unsuited for cinematic presentation, and banned it. Meantime, the Town Clerk (John Dunlop) received a letter about the film from the Dept of Affairs for Mental Patients (N.I.), saying that a number of doctors wished to see it. The producers, 20th Century Fox, arranged a private screening on November 24th in the Royal Cinema which over 150 people attended representing the Mental Health Services Committee, N.I. Hospital's Authority, the British Medical Association, the Royal College of Nursing and staff from Purdysburn Hospital. A letter from the N.I.Hospital's Authority a few days later informed the Council that there was nothing in the film that they could take exception to. They felt that it was an honest effort to deal with a very difficult problem, and "a considerable measure of success had been achieved." They suggested however that to be properly understood and appreciated the film should be seen from the beginning, and people should not enter during its presentation.

That was the type of response the producers welcomed, and they quickly wrote to the Council pointing out "the unanimously favourable expression of opinion" of the medical experts, and asked the Council to reconsider the possibility of showing the film. They referred to the suggestion that patrons should not be admitted after the film had begun but explained that would entail suspending continuous programming, which, they claimed, was not feasible for this film. Continuous programming was the norm at the time and it wasn't until 1960 that Alfred Hitchcock insisted on separate showings - a publicity gimmick, some complained - for his thriller "Psycho," which also touched upon the theme of mental derangement, though at a different level. A life sized cut - out of Hitchcock was displayed in the foyer with the warning that patrons were not allowed in after the film had begun. Fox's refusal to modify its continuous performance policy even for what was regarded as a serious topic didn't prevent the Council from discussing the film again at the end of January, when permission was given for its local presentation.

Hitchcock's Psycho - no admittance. Separate performances. Source: Irish News.

"The Snake Pit" opened in the Ritz on the 24th April. Reaction among the public was subdued, though critical opinion was very positive. Harris Deans, writing in the Telegraph was very impressed, describing it as "magnificent," and advised everyone to see it. However he warned that though it was made with sincerity it was also "a dreadful picture," because of the conditions it depicted in the mental hospitals. The images he claimed would live in the memory for a long time. It was a thought provoking film, but "it is not entertainment." He praised the acting, especially of Olivia de Havilland whose performance was an unexpected revelation to him. After a week the film moved to the Majestic and the Strand where it ran for another week. It then moved to the Adelphi in Bangor, but lasted only three days.

The involvement with delicate medical matters did not deflect the Council from its main targets of sex and violence, which unexpectedly revealed themselves in that normally stalwart morality tale, the Western. In 1941 in the USA, Howard Hughes had decided to make a Western to be called "The Outlaw," and he signed up Howard Hawkes to produce and direct it. The plot was a fiction built around the adventures of Billy the Kid. Hughes wanted a Western that was different in that there would be no moral condemnation of Billy, and that the story would include a strong dose of sex. Both those aims brought him into conflict with Joe Breen, the administrator of the Production Code Association, causing endless wrangling and script changes. Hawkes lost interest and withdrew from the project. Meanwhile Hughes organized a publicity stunt searching for new young actors to take the leading roles. He finally chose Jack Beutel to play Billy, and an unknown young woman called Jane Russell to play the main female lead. He then released a series of photos of her which emphasised her physical endowments. As expected they caused widespread complaints which gave the film the publicity Hughes sought. He personally directed the film but had to face rising criticism from the Production Code Association (PCA) over the plot's muddy morality, the visual presentation of the Jane Russell character which showed that she had more bosom than acting talent, and the poster adverts which also emphasised the actress's same physical characteristics.

The film engendered massive publicity and Jane Russell became a Forces pin-up despite the fact that no one had seen her on screen. Hughes held the film back until February 1943 when he released it in San Francisco without a seal of approval. As expected, the publicity had its effect and the film was a great commercial success, despite being artistically uninspiring. After that brief appearance Hughes withdrew it again in the face of continuing hostile reaction from local state censorship boards, the League of Decency, church groups and individuals, until 1946 when a much cut and censored version was released in the United States. The PCA reluctantly gave its approval but the League of Decency put it in a C for condemned category. When it crossed the Atlantic the British censor took a more lenient view of it and passed it with a "U" certificate, which meant that children could see it. It finally reached Belfast cinemas in 1947 but caused the Police Committee or the Council no problems. It showed in the Mayfair, opening on 18th August and running for six weeks, before moving on to the Majestic and the Strand. Harris Deans, writing in the Telegraph under the heading "a Western with Sex" described it as a "pretty good Western." He was confident that the crowds would go to see it because of its censorship history. He wasn't happy that it had been given a "U" certificate because he felt that it contained material that warranted an "A." He made no direct comment about the sexual content, but wasn't overimpressed by Jane Russell, whom he described as "a sulky looking girl." When the film was shown later that same year in the Royal Cinema he continued in a similar vein. Jane Russell, he wrote, showed her inexperience, but he admitted that she did appeal "to the masculine eye." Otherwise she was "an uninteresting young woman." Not everyone agreed, as the long queues outside the Mayfair and the Royal Cinema attested.

The lasting significance of "The Outlaw" is that it brought sex to the foreground in the Western. The first illustration of that new attitude reached Belfast a few months later in the form of "Duel in the Sun," (d.King Vidor, 1946) often referred to derogatorily as "Lust in the Dust." The film was based on a recent torrid best seller, but RKO, who had bought the rights, had censorship problems from the beginning with Joseph Breen of the PCA over the details of the script. The studio lost patience and sold the project to David O.Selznick, who had produced many fine films, including "Gone With the Wind." Selznick wanted to produce a film that would rival the latter, but, in the end, the script defeated him. He poured money into the project to ensure high production values. He persuaded King Vidor to direct, and he assembled a fine cast that included Lionel Barrymore, Charles Bickford, Joseph Cotton, Herbert Marshall and Lillian Gish. The progress of the film was surrounded by extensive publicity, and among the visitors reported on the set was D.W.Griffith himself.

The leading players were two young and promising actors, Jennifer Jones (whom Selznick was later to marry), and Gregory Peck. Both had screen personas associated with high morality. Jennifer Jones had recently played St Bernadette in "The Song of Bernadette," while Gregory Peck had played a missionary priest, Fr Chrisholm, in "The Keys of the Kingdom" The fiery, amoral and violent characters they played in "Duel in the Sun" were in complete contrast to those earlier roles. The film ended with a bizarre sequence in which they shot each other, before dying in each others arms. The final product was summed up by the writer Charles Brackett as "The Outlaw in bad taste." Most of the professional critical comment in the USA was equally negative. Belfast filmgoers waited to see if the film lived up - or down - to all the hype.

A letter dated 11th December 1947, and signed W. Cartlidge, supervisor for Union Cinemas, N.Ireland, reached the Police Committee from the Ritz Cinema informing them that the film was booked into the Ritz, beginning its run on 22nd December. With deadpan understatement Mr Cartlidge wrote that the film had been "the subject of comment" elsewhere but that he would be willing to arrange a private preview for the Committee on any morning, so that they could make up their own minds. He ignored the fuss the film had caused in the USA, but included newspaper clippings of the controversy it had caused recently in Derry, where, after a preview, the local Council had given permission for it to be shown, though to adults only. That decision had been greeted with outrage by the Derry Journal which described the film as "notorious" and "a thoroughly vile, salacious and damnable production unfit for exhibition in any Christian community." The editor referred to its condemnation by the League of Decency, and called on local public opinion to assert itself in defence of public decency by having films like it banned. The Londonderry Sentinel wasn't impressed by the story but argued, in contrast, that people should be allowed to make up their own minds about it. Banning it wasn't the answer. The duty of any council, the paper lectured, should be to implement the terms of the certificate awarded by the British Board of Film Censors, which in this case was an "A." Any individual who felt offended should stay away, or walk out.

A local MP, Eddie McAteer brought the matter up in Stormont, describing the film as "an exhibition of commercialised indecency," and asked the Minister of Home Affairs to have it banned throughout the Six Counties. The minister refused and pointed out that its banning or otherwise was a matter for the local authorities. In the light of such discussions the Derry Corporation decided to debate again their original decision at a special session. In general the Nationalist-Catholic members wanted the film banned while the Unionist -Protestant members supported its showing. One of the latter, Alderman Kennedy, claimed that the Roman Catholic Church didn't want the film shown, and for that reason alone he would vote for it. Another unionist complained that he wasn't going to accept that the Catholic Church could decide what he could see or not see. Alderman McCarroll asked the corporation to forget politics, and look after the morals of the people by "throwing out this piece of American filth." A division took place on the usual sectarian lines and it was decided by 9 votes to 8 to allow the film to be shown in Derry. Despite threats of disruption the initial programme went ahead without incident, and the large force of police on duty at the cinema was not needed.

In an editorial (Saturday 13th December) concerning the debate, headed "When the Screen is not Silver," the Irish News took issue with those unionists who would prevent Catholics making their views clear. Catholics, the writer claimed, had a right to speak out, especially on a subject like films which can exert such an "unparalleled influence for good or evil." Meantime in Belfast the Police Committee saw the film at a special preview in the Ritz, and recommended by 7 votes to 1 that it be shown in the city. The matter was then debated by the whole council in a meeting that lasted over one hour. Alderman Pierce, a

Unionist and outspoken Protestant, described the film as "loathsome" and nothing more than a "manifestation of filth, dirt and suggestive sexual conduct." He congratulated the Catholic Church on its opposition to it. Alderman McGlade (Nat) thought it advocated a view of life which was at complete variance with Christian standards. Others argued in favour of showing the film. One of them was Alderman Midgley (U) who thought that, overall, the film was "poor." It consisted, he claimed, of "two hours of long dreary nothings" relieved only by the inclusion of some beautiful scenery. Midgley had only recently joined the Unionist party so he probably felt it necessary to show his colours clearly. He hinted darkly at a plot or conspiracy backed by the Catholic Church to have it banned. His evidence for that involved the change in the roles played by the two leading stars from Catholic religious to illicit lovers. Nationalist councillors rightly dismissed his claims as ludicrous but some individual Catholics were quite shocked especially at Miss Jones's metamorphosis from saint to sinner. After a lively debate a vote was taken and the recommendation of the Police Committee to show the film was accepted by 28 votes to 9.

A special showing was arranged later for the press, in the late evening, followed by a party at 1:00 am where Marjorie Hearse, a representative from Selznick's company spoke about the film, and welcomed the decision to permit its presentation. The film opened in the Ritz in late December and, as expected, attracted large crowds. The critics had little to say about it. Harris Deans in the Telegraph thought it had little artistic value, though it was magnificently produced. His summing up was that sex appeared at the beginning and stayed to the end. The Newsletter critic was underimpressed. For him the main attraction was the splendid coloured outdoor shots. With regard to the content he wondered what all the fuss had been about, but did complain that "the finale plumbed a new depth of sadism." He agreed with his Telegraph colleague that the film was completely unsuited to children. It wasn't often that type of complaint was made about a Western, but it was an indicator of how even the Western was changing, with the introduction of more adult themes. It is interesting that the film version of "Duel in the Sun" with an "A" certificate ran for 138 minutes, while the latest video version (2008) runs for only 124 minutes, and has a PG certificate.

Hard on the heels of "Duel in the Sun" came "Forever Amber" (d. Otto Preminger, 1947), - like the former, based on a torrid best seller. It was set in the Restoration period and detailed the life of one Amber St. Clare (Linda Darnell) as she slept her way up the social scale to become the mistress of Charles the Second (George Sanders). From the beginning there were script problems. Joseph Breen rejected the first synopsis as "a saga of illicit sex ... without the slightest suggestion of compensating moral values." At a meeting of Hollywood producers it was decided that no major studio should attempt to film the book, but 20th Century Fox decided to go ahead, and handed the project to Daryll Zanuck who promised to produce a script that would be acceptable to the MPPA, the League of Decency and local censorship boards. His approach was to retain the spirit of the original without the objectionable detail. When the film was finally released in the USA the critical response was tepid, while the League of Decency was only appeased when a prologue was added which made it clear that Amber suffered for her immorality.

The BBFC viewed the film when it reached London and, after insisting on some small cuts, gave it an "A" rating. The Police Committee in turn watched it in mid - June and accepted the BBFC decision. The film was then presented in the Classic beginning on 6th August 1948. Despite its reputation and the furore that had surrounded it, the film caused no significant controversy in Belfast. Because of the publicity it attracted long queues, but the critics were unimpressed. They praised its lavish production values including the fashions, but found the acting and the script just passable. Harris Deans, writing in the Telegraph, commented that Linda Darnell as Amber, brought "no blushes to his cheeks," as her behaviour was always quite discreet. He wondered - tongue in blushless cheek - if the film, with its shots of the Great Plague and Fire of London, might not have some educational value for children. Certainly, he claimed, they "would suffer no moral harm." The League of Decency would not have approved of that conclusion. The author was too young to see or understand it, but he recalls one adult dismissing it as "forever boring."

Besides sex the other topic that occupied the film censors' minds was violence. In the years following the war the BBFC and the public became more aware of the increasingly violent nature of many films. Screen violence became the focus of outspoken criticism from magistrates, clerics, teachers, trade unionists and other concerned groups and citizens, who expressed worries about its impact on society, and especially on youth. Violence had usually been tolerated in epics and westerns where it was felt that its impact was lessened by cinematic environments that were exotic, and distanced from the observers in space and time. When it appeared in films set in more modern and familiar environments of streets and cities its impact was seen to be more immediate and dangerous.

One of the first post -war films that illustrated that trend was "No Orchids for Miss Blandish" (d.St John L.Clowes, 1948) based on a best selling book by James Hadley Chase. It was a British film, and like the American films mentioned above it had script problems from the beginning. The first script was rejected by the BBFC as unsuitable, and the president at the time (1944) Col Hanna dismissed it as "a story of pretty sordid crime and violence." The plot involved the kidnapping of a girl by gangsters, the murder of her fiancé, infighting between rival gangs which led to more violence, murder and robbery. The script was rewritten in the light of the censor's criticisms, and when the completed film was presented to the Board it was given a certificate as being suitable for adults only. The Board held that it was a typical gangster film that was no more brutal than most Hollywood examples of the genre. It was released in April 1948 and attracted large crowds in London, with over 100,000 passing the box office of the Plaza cinema in the first three weeks. However, the reception from the press, the critics and others was mainly hostile, and the film became the centre of controversy, with calls for it to be banned. Dilys Powell suggested that a special certificate of D for disgusting was needed. Even the LCC, which tended to be more liberal in its decisions than the BBFC, was appalled. They demanded and got 9 further cuts before they would allow it to be shown. The new President of the BBFC, Sir Sydney Harris, publicly apologised for having" failed to protect the public."

During the uproar, which was well reported in the English papers, the Belfast public could only watch and wait. Finally in June 1948 Renown Pictures, through their Belfast agent, Sydney Durbidge, wrote to Capt Nelson the chief executive of the Police Committee, informing him that they intended to show the film from 31st July. A wad of printed material was included to convince the Council that the film wasn't the crude affair that the public perception of it suggested. That material included a page detailing the cuts demanded by the LCC, a seven page (A4 size) defence of the film called The Other Side which consisted of quotes and newspaper clippings in favour of the film, and a two page Viewpoint detailing the views of the producer and distributor. The makers claimed that their primary aim was to produce an American - type gangster type film that would break into the American market, and earn much needed dollars. Mr Durbidge arranged a special showing in the Royal Hippodrome for the Police Committee and those members of the council who wanted to see it. Capt. Nelson asked to see both the LCC cut and the uncut versions, but Mr Durbidge persuaded him to watch the cut version, with, separately, clips of the scenes that had been removed.

Following the viewing, the Police Committee retired to Room 42 in the City Hall and after a discussion passed the film as suited for adults only. They demanded two further cuts, one showing the murder of a garage attendant, and another showing the discovery of his body by a little girl. The voting was 4 in favour, 2 against, with two abstentions. Councillor J.A.Mitchell, the vice chairman of the Police Committee, thought it was a "tough" gangster film but he could see no reason for it to be banned. One member, unnamed, criticised the censorship system rather than the film. He argued that the obligation to see and decide about the suitability of certain films "had the obvious danger of being misused for cheap publicity." That belief became more acceptable among members of the Council and was responsible for later special showings being kept secret from the press and the public. At their meeting, in July 1948, the Council accepted the Police Committee's recommendation, and passed the film for showing to adults only, with the cuts indicated. The producers agreed to those conditions, but it wasn't until the end of January 1949 that the film appeared in the Royal Hippodrome. The Council still felt some unease and, before it opened, the Police Committee sent a letter to Mr Durbidge reminding him, as the distributor, "it was incumbent" on him to keep the licensee of the theatre right in the matter of the Council's decision. Another letter to Mr G.Birch, at the Hippodrome, reminded him that only the cut version should be shown, and to adults only. The letter emphasised that he must ensure that the decision of the Council was adhered to "in every respect." The public response was subdued, while the critics wondered once again what all the fuss had been about. The News Letter dismissed it as just another gangster melodrama. The Telegraph admitted that the film was violent but, like the BBFC, felt that there was nothing in it to get worked up about. It was just "an average gangster film." That seemed to be the ordinary filmgoer's attitude also.

In the years following the war a number of British films were made which dealt with gangsters, crime and murder. A notable example was "Brighton Rock" (d. John Boulting, 1947) based on a novel by Graham Greene and starring a young Richard Attenborough. It concerned itself with the violent activities of a race course gang. The News Letter described it as a sordid tale, but admitted that its characters and their surroundings were filmed with impressive realism. Despite its violent scenes, which included the aggressive use of razors, it was passed without cuts by the censor in London, with an "A" certificate, which meant that a child could see it if accompanied by an adult. It also passed the eagle eyes of the Police Committee, and appeared on local screens.

Many parents and others were angry that children and young people could see such material. Some observers complained that there was a growing feeling that the censors were becoming too lax, and that the censorship system itself needed overhauling. A growing body of opinion in Britain called on the government to act, which it finally did in December 1949 by setting up a Committee to investigate and report on the relationship between children under 16 years and the cinema. Better known as the Wheare Committee after its chairman Prof K.C.Wheare, it carried out a detailed study of the behaviour and attitude of children with regard to the cinema. It reported its findings in May 1950, and from the point of view of censorship its main recommendation was the introduction of a new classification for adult films to be called the "X" certificate. That suggestion was accepted by the Censorship Board and put into operation from January 1951. It was to have a major impact on the content of films, the development of film censorship, and the future of the industry itself.

In February of the following year the Belfast Council received a letter from the BBFC signed by the then President S.W.Harris, which explained the aims of the new certificate. It would be awarded to films "which are wholly adult in theme and treatment" but which were "unsuitable for exhibition to children under sixteen." The hope of the Board was that the new category would produce "adult films of high quality, serious or light in character, which, though unsuitable for children, make a legitimate appeal to their parents." The Board did not wish to open the door to any undesirable type of film, but would ensure that films put in the new category would be free from matter likely to offend the majority of reasonable people. The tone was optimistic and suggested that, from its experience, the number of films involved would be small. That belief proved to be misplaced, and nearly everyone in the trade was surprised at how quickly film makers realised the opportunities that the new certificate opened up.

In 1955 the BBFC issued 35 of the new certificates, representing 14 % of the year's total, but by 1974 that number had increased to 212, representing 50% of the total. At the same time the Board's optimistic wish that the X certificate should not be used as a vehicle for films of "any undesirable type … designed to attract morbid curiosity" was subverted by unscrupulous operators who saw the new category as an open door allowing films to be made about the more lurid aspects of sex, violence and horror. As the Fifties progressed more and more of those films appeared on Belfast screens. The BBFC, major newspapers, and even a liberal magazine like "Films and Filming" protested at how the main aim of the X certificate to produce intelligent adult themed films was being undermined. In an editorial in October 1957 the magazine deplored "the tendency on the part of a group of film distributors and cinema owners to import only the sexually sensational, and to ignore many fine films." The editor saw that as "an unjustified exploitation of the X certificate," whereby it was being used to show films that were "moronic if not thoroughly distasteful."

Similar complaints circulated in Belfast where the Police Committee and the Council struggled with the problem of what they believed would be tolerated locally. Concerned citizens and pressure groups used their influence to get them to act. In February 1962 the Belfast Telegraph drew attention to an editorial in the Irish Christian Advocate which criticised the increase in the number of X certificate films being shown While accepting that there were some worthwhile X films, the paper insisted that there were too many which "pander to sensuality." Some time later, in 1964, the local Watch Committee of the Mother's Union of the C of I, which monitored social problems including that of children attending the cinema, expressed alarm at the increase in the number of X films showing in the city's cinemas, and called on the Police Committee to do something to curtail them. The Committee in turn wrote to cinema managers asking then to reduce the flow of X films voluntarily, or they, the Committee, would introduce measures to compel them to do so. Details of the steps they might take were kept vague, but the threat was there. In January 1965 the Telegraph called for higher standards of mass entertainment in an editorial which was praised by Mary Whitehouse, who wrote to the paper in support. She praised the stand taken by the local churches and others against sex films, and expressed thanks for the support of the 350,000 people in Northern Ireland who had signed her recent Clean - Up TV manifesto. The following month the Diocesan Synod of Down and Connor met in Belfast and among the topics discussed was the fact that too many X films dealt with the degradation of sex. In contrast to all the negative criticism very little was written or published locally in defence of the certificate.

Cinema managers were the butt of much criticism in the matter, but they had their own problems. John Mellor, manager of St Columbs Hall in Derry, summed up the main ones when, in early 1960, he announced that the hall would cease to operate as a cinema from 1st May. He explained that the closure was due to TV which was taking audiences away, but also because, on principle, he refused to show X rated sex films, despite the fact that they had become "the number one box office attraction." In Belfast managers had seen audience numbers drop over the preceding decade mainly because of TV, and as family films were replaced by X films that decline increased, especially among the older generation. The younger cinemagoers were more at ease with the less restrictive attitudes of the X certificates, and supported the increasing number of continental, sex, nudist and horror films that became available from the late Fifties onwards. It seemed for a time that the X certificate would attract audiences back, and financially reinvigorate the industry but, with hindsight it is clear that any improvement was only temporary and that in the final analysis it helped bring an end to a lucrative family orientated social habit that people had known and enjoyed over the former five decades.

The X certificate continued to test the conservative moral and social attitudes of the Police Committee, which found itself increasingly in conflict with distributors, producers and major film companies. Just before the new certificate was introduced, Mr Durbidge wrote, in July 1950, to Capt. Nelson, the executive officer of the Police Committee with information about a film called "Sins of the Fathers." It was a Canadian sex hygiene film which dealt with the scourge of V.D., and it replicated the pattern of similar films that had been shown in the city. A simple story showed how the disease was contracted, and its physical effects were illustrated by actual medical film clips. A sympathetic doctor and other experts interpolated comments on how it could be avoided, or treated and cured. The campaign book that accompanied the letter was clearly stamped "Adults Only" and contained advice to cinema managers on what advertisement strategy to follow. The educational aspects were to be emphasised above all. The film should be put across as "more than a film - a social service to your community," and a special appeal should be directed at parents with, "What

Dare you tell your sons and daughters? Sins of the Fathers does it for you." Cinema managers were further advised to contact the St John Ambulance Brigade because the medical scenes contained material that could cause "faints." They also represented good publicity. Mr Durbidge explained that he could get a booking in the Mayfair, subject to the Corporation agreeing to its exhibition. The Police Committee wrote back requesting more information, which the distributors duly supplied. The film did not have a BBFC certificate, but it had been passed by the LCC with an adult only classification. A few months later the Police Committee received a request to view "A Family Story," which resulted in a special showing in the Royal Hippodrome. It was another "educational" sex film which purported to relieve parents of the need to explain the facts of life to their children. The Police Committee were not impressed, and like "The Sins of the Father," it never reached Belfast screens.

Sins of the Father: The Police Committee said no.

Another topical social problem that some film makers felt they should enlighten the public about was the drug habit. In September 1948 the rumours about drug abuse in Hollywood were given credence when Robert Mitchum was arrested in the apartment of a young starlet called Lila Leeds, and accused of smoking marijuana. The resulting scandal didn't harm Mitchum's career (the charge against him was quashed later), but Miss Leeds went to prison. When she was released in 1949 she was ignored by the big studios, but was persuaded to make a cheap "quickie" which cashed in on her experiences. The film in question was bought by Kroger Babb, one of a group known in Hollywood as "the Forty Thieves," who made cheap exploitation films. Under his skilful guidance it crossed the Atlantic and arrived in Britain as "The Devil's Weed," an exploitation film dressed up as a serious educational and social study.

In May 1952 a request was received from International Film Distributors Ltd. with regard to the film. A letter signed by their Belfast representative, Mr S. Durbidge, asked the Police Committee to view the film. "We feel," he wrote "that as it concerns the marijuana menace the film may be of some use in a large seaport like Belfast." Those sentiments of concern however seem to be undermined by the accompanying campaign book which was illustrated by a reclining blonde under the headline "She has the curves but we have the box-office angles." Mr Durbidge arranged for the film to be shown to the Police Committee in the Mayfair on Monday 30th June at 10:00 am, but when the members arrived they were told that the film hadn't arrived from London. They were not amused. Capt. Nelson phoned, and then wrote to Mr Durbidge accusing him of lacking "elemental courtesy" in not informing the Committee of the delay. He, in turn, replied that he had written to explain what had happened, and it wasn't his fault if the letter hadn't been delivered. He complained about Capt. Nelson's "dictatorial tone" on the telephone. That was hardly good business practice, and obviously the London office thought that a damage limitation exercise was needed. Capt. Nelson got a letter from the company's Assistant Managing Director, a Mr Urry, who expressed his "sincere apologies" for Mr Durbidge's handling of the situation, and further apologised to the Police Committee. After more delays a new date of Monday 25th August was agreed. The Police Committee were somewhat irritated at how the situation had developed and in accepting the new date Capt. Nelson added, in his letter, that "it must be understood that neither the Press or the public should be permitted to attend this private viewing by members of the Corporation." After seeing the film the Police Committee

The Devil's Weed. Educational?

recommended that permission be granted for its presentation, but to adult audiences only. The film showed in the Mayfair during February 1953, when it ran for two weeks. The events surrounding the showing of "The Devil's Weed" are especially interesting in view of the light they throw on the relationship between the representatives of the film industry and the Police Committee. The reaction of International Film Distributors to Capt. Nelson's complaints reveal the company's desire to appease the Committee, because a ban on the film meant a loss of revenue. Thus Mr Durbidge was reprimanded like an errant schoolboy, while his complaint about Capt. Nelson's dictatorial attitude was ignored. Mr Durbidge's use of the term dictatorial, combined with the captain's demand for secrecy however, gives some indication of the power and influence that the Committee arrogantly felt it had. The Committee was also aware that their actions and comments presented strong publicity possibilities for film distributors, and tried to obviate that by insisting on secrecy. At the same time the decision to allow the film to be shown attests to the Committee's ignorance about the origins and production of the film. The film makers, and Kroger Babb, had the last laugh. The local critics showed their feelings by completely ignoring the film.

While those films were exercising the minds of the Police Committee, the new X certificate was beginning to make itself felt. The Police Committee continued to receive monthly reports from the BBFC which included the latest classifications. The Board drew attention to films that had in the past been refused certificates because they were not covered by the categories then available. Some of them were now being given X certificates, but before they could be shown they would have to be viewed and passed by local authorities. Examples of those, like the very French comedy "Clochemerle", were passed in Belfast and shown mainly in the Mayfair. The Police Committee continued to vet incoming films, and most X certificates were passed quietly and appeared on local screens. Typical was "M," which dealt with the unpleasant topic of a child murderer. It was a remake of Fritz Lang's classic German film of the same name, now directed by the much respected Joseph Losey. The original had caused much controversy at its release in 1931. In September 1951 George Lodge wrote to the Police Committee explaining that Columbia Pictures were "most anxious" that the Committee see the film before public exhibition in the city. Mr Lodge who was responsible for booking films for the Hippodrome, Imperial, Royal Cinema and Irish Theatres, vied with Mr Durbidge in the number of communications he had with the Police Commission. He offered to arrange a special showing for the Committee in the Imperial. He diplomatically emphasised that his offer was not "an exploitation stunt," and that no information would be given to the Press. The film was subsequently passed and shown in the Imperial, without comment. The News Letter critic wrote that it was "a horrific melodrama.... powerful in its suspense and thrills "but that it lacked "the imaginative quality which distinguished the original."

"Murder Incorporated," and "A Streetcar Named Desire" were among the earliest X films seen by the Police Committee, and were passed for presentation in the Ritz. In the past the former film would probably have been banned because of its violence, while "Streetcar..." would have suffered the same fate once the examiners realised that the exchanges between

Marlon Brando and Vivien Leigh had nothing to do with public transport. During the following years a growing number of X certificate films, mainly American and Continental in origin, were passed quietly by the Police Committee and the Council for presentation on local screens. Many had sex themes like "The Seven Deadly Sins" (1951), a French-Italian hodgepodge of short stories by different directors illustrating the aforementioned sins, which showed in the Royal Cinema during October 1953. Writing in the Telegraph, Harris Deans described it as "French, with an X certificate to prove it." He acknowledged it was a stylish exercise in Gallic sophistication, with sequences that showed how tolerant the censor had become. He found it, in turn, amusing, shocking and, on occasion, touching. Technically it couldn't be faulted, and he had special praise for the writer of the subtitles. Other films showed an increasing, and sometimes disturbing, social realism, like "Blackboard Jungle" which dealt with the frustrations of an idealistic teacher (Glenn Ford) as he struggled to make intellectual contact with uninterested young people in a tough district in New York. It painted a depressing educational environment where teachers' efforts were undermined by a disregard for discipline, an atmosphere of gang violence and a "who cares?" attitude among the students. The educational malaise had even spread to the staffroom. When asked for advice by a new and eager young female teacher, the cynical and experienced headmaster (the excellent Louis Calhern) replied with a succinct and telling comment, "Never turn your back on the class."

"Blackboard Jungle" arrived in Belfast minus six minutes of BBFC cuts, opening with a throbbing soundtrack that introduced Bill Haley and the Comet's version of "Rock Around the Clock." It was the first time that rock and roll music had been heard in any film, and its association with the juvenile violence shown in the film was to have repercussions for the Police Committee later in the decade. Another film concerned with the problems of youth, "Rebel Without A Cause" (d. Nicholas Ray, 1955) starring James Dean, had caused the BBFC some worries because it was felt it might have a "harmful influence... on young and impressionable members of the audience." The Mayfair showed "Cosh Boys" a controversial expose of youthful violence in Britain. It carried an X certificate and was advertised as "the film every parent should see." Some observers believed that films of youthful protest were an encouragement to violence and extreme behaviour within groups like the Teddy Boys. Normally such films would have received little sympathy from the Police Committee, but in the early Fifties, despite the doubts of a minority of members, the decisions of the BBFC were accepted, and "Rebel" was shown in the Ritz in March 1956 From its introduction Associated British Cinemas (ABC) who owned the Ritz, Majestic and Strand embraced the new certificate and presented quality X films. On the other hand the Rank organization, which was expanding its influence in Belfast, rarely if ever showed them at that time.

Just when the Police Committee seemed to have acquiesced completely to the decisions of the BBFC it suddenly showed its independence in a surprising manner, in its reaction to "The Wild One." (d. Laslo Benedek, 1954). The plot involved a motorbike gang of young thugs - a modern version of Quantrell's Raiders - led by Marlon Brando, who take over a small town and terrorise its inhabitants. In that sense it resembled a Western, but there was no John Wayne or Randolph Scott to restore order. Its modernity, the menacing roar of the engines and the inability of the police to control the situation produced an unsettling and threatening atmosphere which disturbed many viewers. The BBFC took strong exception to it, and after consideration, banned it as "a spectacle of unbridled hooliganism," a ban which remained in place until 1967. Most councils accepted the advice of the censorship board until Cambridge council allowed it to be shown with an X certificate. In March 1955 George Lodge, who, like Associated British Cinemas, was quite willing to show X films in the cinemas he controlled, wrote to the Police Committee with a view to showing the film in Belfast. He arranged a private showing in the Imperial cinema for members of the Council. In a letter of invitation from the Town Clerk, John Dunlop, members were told that the Police Committee were anxious "that the viewing will not attract publicity, and the exhibitors have agreed not to have representatives of the Press present."

Some time later the film was discussed in the Council chamber, in a debate which hardly sparkled intellectually. The Police Committee recommended its public showing. Councillor Dixon objected, pointing out that the BBFC had refused to grant the film a certificate, so a decision to pass it would be an implied criticism of the British censor. Also, he believed that such films only encouraged the "deplorable" conduct of gangs like teddy boys. Councillor Mrs Wilson, the only woman on the Police Committee, found the film "dull and stupid" but felt that was no reason why the public should not see it. She added that the Council had passed a number of certified films recently - unfortunately unnamed - that would better not to have been seen. Councillor Haig made it clear that he did not approve of censorship, but he found this film especially "disgusting" in the way that it showed contempt for the police. Councillor Jack Macgouran was in favour of passing it, though he thought it was "bad entertainment..... morbid and sordid...an indictment of a decadent culture." Councillor Tommy Henderson, always down-to-earth and never one to worry about logic, agreed that it should be shown. He compared it with incidents that had occurred during the recent university Rag Week. Things had happened then that were outrageous, he claimed, especially the white - washing of the statue of the Black Man. If Belfast people could cope with such behaviour they would have no problems with the film in question. The chairman of the Police Committee, Martin Wallace, took a more serious approach and advised against "a policy of restriction." He suggested that those who wanted real violence had only to go to the weekly boxing events held in the Ulster Hall. After a vote the film was passed as suitable for public viewing, to audiences over 16 years of age, and appeared on local screens in May 1955.

Not everyone was pleased with the decision. Councillor Dixon returned to the fray some time later and condemned the decision. He described how he had passed the Royal Hippodrome, where the film was showing, and was appalled to see long queues, mainly of Teddy Boys, waiting for admittance. The councillor obviously had strong feelings about Teddy Boys who he felt "were staining the fair name of the city." He called for a stricter censorship, claiming that over 50% of films presented in Belfast cinemas "appealed to the baser instincts of people." He must have been pleased with Harris Deans's criticism in the Telegraph. Deans admitted that the film was well made, and that Brando gave an "effective performance," but that overall it was "a noisy murderous film" that one wouldn't really want to see again. He complained about its "dubious morality," and the fact that the gang faced no retribution for their crimes. Because of its censorship history, and its banning by the

BBFC, he predicted - correctly - it would attract the crowds, regardless of its content.

While the discussions about "The Wild One" were in progress another uncertified film was waiting in the wings. It was "Wicked Woman" starring Beverly Michaels and Richard Egan which dealt with an amoral young woman's attempts to snare a rich man. United Artists wrote to the Police Committee from London with a request to examine the film and decide if it was suitable for presentation in Belfast. Their letter is dated 22nd March but it wasn't until 18th April that a private showing was arranged in the Royal Cinema. After viewing the film the Police Committee decided to recommend that it be shown to adults over 16 years.

To some observers it seemed that the Police Committee was becoming too lax, and foremost among its critics was the Presbyterian Church. On the 3rd May the Belfast Presbytery passed a resolution which emphasised the "deep concern" with which they viewed the decision of the Corporation to allow the showing of two uncertified films, "The Wild One," and "Wicked Woman." The Presbytery regarded such actions as an "encouragement of the production of films of a low moral standard." It reminded the Corporation that it had a responsibility to "maintain the good name of the city and the moral standards of the citizens." The sentiments weren't new but they were enunciated firmly, and accompanied by a request that the Council should meet a deputation of six persons appointed by the Presbytery to discuss the matter. The deputation met the Police Committee on the 12th May and soon afterwards it became clear that while the decision regarding "The Wild One" would remain, "Wicked Woman" would be banned. The Police Committee had been brought to heel, and their brief experiment with liberal censorship was deemed unacceptable.

The following year, 1956, saw the Committee wrestling with the question of whether or not to ban a film because of its musical soundtrack. The music in question was rock' n' roll. During the Forties Bill Haley made a name for himself on American radio, where he and his band, the Saddlemen, played hillbilly boogie. Advertised as "stars of stage, radio and records" their tours in America were very popular, and by the end of the decade the Saddlemen had evolved into the Comets (in 1952), playing a new brand of rhymic music called rock and roll. The generation who had listened and danced to the more formal Swing Bands found the new music rather frenetic, but it was taken up wholeheartedly by the youth, and Bill Haley became a national sensation. It was only natural that he and the Comets ended up in Hollywood making films, the first of which was "Rock Around the Clock" (1956), followed by "Don't Knock the Rock" (1956). They were not great films, but they exuded vitality and youthful spirits. The teenagers flocked to them, and some allowed themselves to be swept away by the rhythms. There were reports of dancing in the cinema aisles, and other excesses resulting in damage to seats and attacks on other people. Police were called on occasion to deal with over - excited teddy boys, young men and girls. During early 1956 the local papers carried reports of similar events in Britain and across Europe, associated mainly with screenings of "Rock Around the Clock."

The latter was booked into the Gaumont for 24th September 1956, and a routine request was made to the Council for permission to show it. The Police Committee were aware of its impact on some young people, and the vandalism that had occurred, and without waiting to see the film decided to recommend that it should be banned in Belfast. The newspapers continued to report events in London where 37 youths were arrested in a cinema; while in another, the Gaumont in Lewisham, 100 teenagers were ejected by police where they were joined outside by an estimated 1000, some of whom subsequently clashed with officers. There were reports in the local press and on TV of managers in London confronting noisy teenagers, of imposing dress codes for admittance (no cowboy boots, for example), of ejecting teddy boys and in some cases of completely banning teenagers. Similar events were reported from Oslo, Paris, Duisburg, and Groningen. Local managers discussed the problem. Mr John MacDougall, the manager of the Gaumont, thought that it was wrong to ban all teenagers, but admitted that his staff watched out for troublemakers who were either stopped at the box office, or, if they caused trouble in the auditorium were asked to leave. The manager of the ABC made it clear that disruptive behaviour would not be tolerated as he had to consider the feelings of most of his patrons, who only wanted an entertaining evening out. Another spokesman from the ABC circuit felt that, overall, local teenagers were better behaved than their counterparts across the water. However as a precaution his company was installing brighter lighting, known in the trade as "anti - hooligan lighting."

The Council were aware of those and similar reports when the matter was debated at the monthly meeting at the beginning of October. The unanimous recommendation of the Police Committee was accepted, and the ban on "Rock Around the Clock" was confirmed, without viewing the film. Some councillors disagreed with the decision. Councillor Macgouran was one of those. He argued that the ban was premature, and pointed out that the film had been shown in Dublin without incident, while Derry Corporation had approved its presentation, with the mayor describing it as "completely harmless." Another councillor agreed that there was nothing objectionable in the film, but there was the problem of what effect the music had on young people. Mr Macgouran commented that he had seen decent people here turned into "dancing dervishes" as a result of hearing The Sash, but he was not suggesting that it should be banned. Many councillors laughed, but made no moves to remove the ban.

"Rock Around the Clock" had its first public showing in N.Ireland, a few weeks later in Derry. After the first evening show there was what the Irish News called "wild scenes" as young people, emerging from the cinema, danced and clapped across the road, holding up traffic. Some attacked cars, shops and buildings, breaking windows, and causing damage estimated at about £30. The police were quickly on the scene and restored order. The cinema owners also acted rapidly. At their request representatives of Columbia Pictures, who distributed the film, rushed to the cinema and after discussions with the manager it was agreed to continue to show the rock film until 6:00pm after which time a substitute film, "Storm Centre" starring Bette Davis would be shown. That arrangement calmed the situation, and neither the police or the corporation interfered. Common sense prevailed.

The Rock phenomenon came to a head in Belfast at the beginning of March 1957 with two events, the arrival of Bill Haley in person to play two evenings in the Royal Hippodrome, and the showing of Haley's second film "Don't Knock the Rock" in the Gaumont Classic. Haley and his wife flew in from Dublin where his personal appearance had been followed by clashes between fans and the police. During an interview with the local press in the Grand Central Hotel he explained that he was a responsible father who had five children, and his aim was not to cause youthful disturbances. He felt that the "simplicity" of the music appealed to young people but that the troublemakers were not his true fans but those who gathered outside the venues where he was performing. Unfortunately on that Friday,1st March, the portents were not good. There was an unhealthy atmosphere of incipient violence in the city due mainly to the animosity between gangs of teddy boys and visiting Canadian sailors, from the crew of HMCS Bonaventure. As the evening progressed clashes took place in Donegall Place and Royal Avenue, including a major threeway punchup which recalled the old faction fights, between the sailors, youths and the Police. That spectacle was enjoyed by a large and appreciative crowd which collected on the pavement outside the G.P.O. (now part of Castlecourt) to watch. Shades of John Ford!

Inside the Royal Hippodrome the fans weren't disappointed. There were some empty seats, and the News Letter critic noted that the dearest seats were taken mainly by Canadian sailors. The crowd was well behaved, and one or two who stood to dance in the aisles were quickly directed back to their seats by the ushers. The audience were warmed up by Vic Lewis and his Orchestra, and local harmonica player Denis Forsythe. Bill Haley and the Comets were greeted with cheers and clapping. Their every move was applauded, while the music was accompanied by clapping and feet stamping. But people stayed in their seats and at the end showed every sign of having enjoyed themselves. As the evening progressed crowds began to collect outside the Hippodrome until there were about 800 young people blocking the pavements, and spilling over on to the road. There were shouts of "we want Bill Haley." The police struggled to contain the pushing crowd and at one point drew their batons. Passing cars and buses were thumped by the crowd, and during the melée three teenagers were arrested. When they appeared in court later they were given one month's prison for disorderly behaviour. While all the action was taking place at the front of the building, Bill Haley and his musicians were quickly smuggled out through a back door. The police then used a loud hailer to tell the crowd that they were gone, and after some persuasion they slowly dispersed. The uplifted voices calling "See you later, alligator, in a while crocodile," and their pithy Belfast equivalent of "See you later detonator, but not tonight gelignite" faded into the night sounds of the city. The overall excitement subsided rapidly and the Saturday show passed off without incident. By Sunday Haley's Comets had headed off to brighten another sky.

They were gone but not forgotten because on Monday the Gaumont presented a double bill consisting of "The Counterfeit Plan" starring Zachary Scott, supported by Bill Haley's second film "Don't Knock the Rock." The teenagers flocked to see it and as the music began to pound some took to dancing in the aisles, while others jumped on top of seats causing breakages to fittings. Total damage was later estimated at about £150. The management struggled to keep order, but finally had to summon police help. After discussions with the latter the manager, John Mc Dougall, withdrew the film on Wednesday and replaced it with "Ten Tall Men "starring Burt Lancaster and Jody Lawrence. The Police Committee decided that firm action was required and wrote to the City Commissioner asking for the reaction of the R.U.C to allowing the film to be shown elsewhere in the city. In his reply the City Commissioner gave his opinion that similar disturbances were very likely at other venues that would increase costs to the ratepayers, and put undue pressure on police resources, taking officers away from more important and useful duties. The letter ended with a clear statement that "the further showing of this film in Belfast should be banned." Armed with that information the Police Committee advised the Council to act accordingly. The Council agreed, and banned its future presentation in Belfast.

The Police Committee then went further and called for the banning of all rock' n' roll films within the city limits. A letter was sent to all city cinema licencees informing them of the ban plus the fact that, in future, one month's notice would be required if any cinema planned to show "any film of a similar nature." Cinema owners and managers were angry but had to co-operate, and the Police Committee soon received letters of future bookings from Odeon Cinemas, Associated British Cinemas and individual cinemas including the Imperial and the Castle. One of the films listed was "The Girl Can't Help It" which starred Jayne Mansfield and Tom Ewell, with a supporting cast that included rock 'n' roll performers like Fats Domino, Little Richard, Gene Vincent and Eddie Cochrane. The film was actually a satire on the pop industry, directed by Frank Tashlin. The distributors, Twentieth Century Fox, wrote from London explaining that the film had been shown widely across England without incident, and that they didn't expect any disturbances in Belfast. They added however that "we are of course desirous to co-operate with you to the full" in the matter. No one wanted to stand up to what many thought were the unreasonable demands the Police Committee. Principle was not involved. It was merely a matter of money. A ban meant loss of revenue.

The Royal Hippodrome had to cancel its booking of "The Girl Can't Help It" scheduled for 22nd April. But as councils in England, including Birmingham and Blackpool, lifted similar bans on rock' n' roll films, official attitudes in Belfast softened, and, by August, the Castle cinema had been given permission to show it. That relaxation didn't apply immediately to all rock films though. As the excitement around the music progressively subsided through late 1957 and 1958, the spotlight moved from rock films and they became an accepted part of weekly programmes. Most of them were cheaply made, harmless vehicles highlighting the talents of pop singers, aimed mainly at the teenage market. Controversial films continued to arrive, notably "Baby Doll" (d. Elia Kazan, 1956), which dealt with the tribulations of a child bride and her lecherous husband. In January 1957 the Police Committee received a request to show the film, in the Ritz. The film had had a rough ride in the USA where it had been widely criticised and attacked for what was described as its salacious content. In some cities opposition was so vehement that cinemas were forced to withdraw it. The League of Decency condemned it as immoral. When it reached Britain the BBFC made some minor cuts and released it with an X certificate.

In Belfast reactions were mixed. A small minority felt that the film dealt with a subject that was quite unsuited to a popular medium like cinema, and should not be shown locally Concerned citizens worried about its impact on young people, and many agreed with "Anxious Parent" who wrote to the papers reminding the Council of their duty to protect "the moral tone and health of our city." Other letters defended the film, and argued that "it was not in the same category as Rock Around the Clock," but was the work of distinguished artists Elia Kazan and Tennessee Williams. Among the letters of support was one from the secretary of the Stranmillis College Film Society who pointed out that the subject matter of "Baby Doll" was an adult one of the type that the X certificate had been introduced to allow the cinema to treat with the same freedom as theatre or the novel. The Police Committee attended a special viewing but were unable to reach a clear decision, being divided on whether to ban it or not. Councillor Marrinan wanted it banned because he felt that Hollywood standards of behaviour, as shown in X films, were lowering "standards of decency" in Belfast. Other members weren't so sure, and Alderman Mrs Wilson argued that the Council couldn't be arbiters of taste, but that they should only ban films that were clearly harmful. She had found "Baby Doll" "dull and dreary" rather than harmful.

The Council finally allowed the film to be shown, to adults only. When it opened in the Ritz on 11th February 1957 the Telegraph praised its direction and acting though it admitted that "it scraped the violent edge of Southern life." Martin Wallace, in a separate review, also praised its artistry and overall quality, adding that he found it "singularly moral, and less harmful" than many crime thrillers or sex comedies shown in the city recently. The News Letter critic joined the chorus of praise. It was "brilliant" though admittedly it dealt with a sordid theme. It was, above all, a controversial story made by adults for adult audiences." It ran for two weeks to full houses. Meanwhile the next major problem for the Police Committee was already looming on the horizon.

From its inception in 1912 the BBFC had one clear guideline, no nudity. That was still the situation at the beginning of the Fifties, but after the introduction of the X certificate that prohibition was increasingly tested by film makers. Of course there had always been nudity in films, especially in stag films which were cheaply made for showing in "gentlemen's" clubs and similar private gatherings. They never entered mainstream cinema, nor were they presented for certification. Any nudity that reached the commercial cinema in Belfast was dressed up in respectable educational or health clothing, and involved topics like venereal disease, birth control, giving birth, the dangers of drugs or such. Their studied social concern fooled no one but the very naive. Within the wider moral latitude allowed by the X certificate some film makers recognised another way to introduce acceptable nudity, and the route chosen was naturism. The gloves - and more - were off as far as the censors in London and Belfast were concerned.

There had been a number of financially successful American films on naturism made during the Thirties but they never reached Belfast, and their number declined during the world war. The Fifties saw a renewal of interest in them, beginning with "The Garden of Eden" in 1953. It was filmed in sunny Florida, and told a simple story of a quiet retiring girl who fell asleep under a tree and dreamed of casting off her clothes and wandering through the countryside. It had the distinction of being the first commercial naturist film shot in colour. It reached London the following year, but was firmly rejected by the BBFC. The distributor then submitted it to the LCC which gave permission for it to be shown with an "A" certificate. After that success it was submitted to 230 local authorities, and was passed for viewing by 180 of them with a "U," "A," or "X" certificate. It didn't reach Belfast until May 1957 when Mr Durbidge wrote to the Police Committee with a request to show it in the Royal Hippodrome. He arranged a private viewing in the cinema for the morning of 22nd May, and in his letter suggested that "it might be a good idea to keep this date very secret as the distributors are not desirous of having any Press at the viewing, at this stage of the proceedings." That element of secrecy from the Press also suited the Police Committee, and it became an increasingly important factor in the future relationships between the two parties.

Regardless of those precautions, the Police Committee advised that the film should be banned, and the council accepted that recommendation. Other similar films were treated in the same way. After a private showing in the Ambassador cinema, "The Naked World of Harrison Marks" was banned in June 1957. Marks was a photographer turned film maker who turned out pin-up type films rather than naturist sagas, though the latter continued to arrive from America. "Isle of Levant" and "Back to Nature "- which purported to be a documentary of life in a nudist camp - were rejected in 1958, though the latter had been given an" A "certificate by the BBFC. The Board gave a similar certificate to "Nudist Paradise," the first British nudist film which was filmed in Nudiscope, and starred Anita Love. In April 1959 the Police Committee received a request to see it with a view to allowing it to be screened locally. The Police Committee agreed, on condition that there was no publicity. A private screening took place in the Royal Cinema after which the Committee advised it be banned. The distributor, Orb International Ltd., protested and pointed out that the film already had an "A" certificate. They forwarded excerpts from a letter they had received from John Trevelyan (the influential secretary of the BBFC between 1958 and 1971) in which he suggested that the film was "entirely suitable for an A certificate, with a few minor cuts." The company were willing to make those cuts. The Police Committee were not impressed. The ban remained.

As more and more licensing authorities allowed nudist films to be shown the BBFC modified its rigid attitude and accepted that some nudity could be permitted depending on the type of film involved. By the late Fifties naturism, with its carefully posed nudes, had come to be regarded as inoffensive, and could be shown with an A certificate. "The Garden of Eden" was granted such a certificate in 1958. Documentary nudity was treated in the same way, but films of the pin-up variety, including those of Harrison Marks, were regarded as exploitative and were usually refused a certificate. Films showing stage shows which included nudity, striptease or such were usually cut before earning a certificate. Nudity in feature films was still a problem but its acceptability was judged in the overall context of each film. Those were guidelines which the BBFC found more and more difficult to apply as, during the Sixties and Seventies, producers and film makers pushed the limits of what they could show. In Belfast the Police Committee insisted that there be no screen nudity but in the face of changing attitudes they had to modify their position, and in mid - December 1960 the Royal Cinema presented Belfast's first commercial nudist film, called appropriately "The Nudist Story." The Irish News showed its disdain by ignoring it, while the News Letter critic mentioned it briefly and discreetly. It was, he noted, a film about the topic of the naturist's way of life, illustrated with a storyline involving the problems faced by a girl who inherits a nudist camp. The Telegraph critic, Martin Wallace, obviously a man of sterner stuff, decided to see for himself. He gave an amusing account of his visit to the Royal Cinema, beginning with a "bare outline" of the plot. He described how he joined the audience in the packed cinema. It consisted entirely of young males, a collection of "leering, cheering foot stampers." During the film the air was continually rent with "hoots and hollers" of appreciation. He doubted if the crowd were interested in, or learned anything about naturism, and he certainly saw no evidence that "minds were being improved." He made no reference to the quality of the film beyond the fact that the acting of the main players, Shelley Martin and Brian Cobby, was "immobile." The film ran for two weeks.

The flood gates were opening, and the Police Committee proved unable or unwilling to stem the flow. City cinemas were soon awash in a tidal wave of exploitation sex films. By January 1962 the Troxy could show a double X programme of "Nudes of the World" along "The Heat of Summer" featuring Patrecia "the Scorcher" Karen. The management claimed it was the first showing in Ireland of the films, which were "strictly adult only." The following year it screened a new naturist film from America, with Susan Baxter and Carol Mackenzie as "gorgeous Eves in search of Naked Freedom." Meantime the Royal Cinema in a desperate attempt to attract audiences showed the likes of "The Girl Rosemarie"(X) billed as "the film they tried to ban." The Royal Hippodrome presented "A Woman Like Satan," which starred Brigitte Bardot, which the Irish News critic dismissed as silly and tedious, but basically a "pernicious film... with salacious sequences." The Opera House presented the clever French film "La Ronde" which provoked some complaints, after which front -of - house stills were removed by the management. Critical comments from local clergy, parents, teachers, politicians and others increased. Dr Farren, the Catholic Bishop of Derry, speaking at Christmas 1960, regretted that the cinema "which used to be a means of pleasure and pastime had become a means of disseminating evil of the worst kind."

But while the sex and nudist films continued to march on, the Police Committee faced up to another problem, one with political overtones. There was one topic that sent shivers of fear into their hearts, and those of many Unionist councillors, and that was Irish Republicanism. Any film that included a Republican viewpoint involving violence was seen as a danger to the stability of the Northern state, and had to be banned.

Carol Reed's "Odd Man Out" was a rare post war exception. The Police Committee couldn't ignore its directorial qualities, its Belfast locations, and its use of local actors like Joe Tumelty and Albert Sharpe. The IRA was never mentioned in the film but everyone knew what the "organization" was that James Mason belonged to. The film was passed but there was a substantial police presence at the first showing in the Classic. The fact that they weren't needed suggested that the average cinemagoer was more mature than some observers believed. A few other British films with Irish themes, which pointed up the futility of violence were shown. They included "I Saw a Dark Stranger"(1946) a comedy starring Deborah Kerr and Trevor Howard, and "The Gentle Gunman" (1952) with John Mills and Dirk Bogarde. The unease with which the Police Committee viewed such films can be detected in the approach to the latter film. When a special showing was arranged in the Classic on Monday 20th Oct. 1952, a letter was sent by the Committee to the Commissioner of the RUC informing him of the fact and suggesting that "having regard to the nature of the film which deals with IRA wartime activities" it would be appreciated if a representative of the police could be present. Mr Mc Dougal, the manager of the Classic was then informed and asked to make certain that there was no publicity about the showing. The RUC raised no objections to the exhibition of the film. References, though minor, to the IRA in "The Quiet Man" (1952) didn't prevent it becoming a major success in Belfast.

It seemed to the general public, who were unaware of the involvement of the RUC, that the Police Committee was developing a sense of balance in its attitude to censorship, but that proved to be a myth when John Ford's "Rising of the Moon" arrived. Ford had joined Lord Killanin, Tyrone Power and Belfastman Brian Desmond Hurst to set up the Four Provinces Company to make films in Ireland. "The Rising of the Moon" (1957) was their first major production. It was filmed entirely in Ireland with an all Irish cast, with the exception of Tyrone Power who introduced it, and was based on three short literary works: Frank O'Connor's "The Majesty of the Law," Lady Gregory's play "The Rising of the Moon," and Martin McHugh's "A Minutes Wait." The result was an entertaining mix of comedy and drama filmed with Ford's characteristic flair. In due course, in October 1957, Odeon Ltd asked for clearance to show the film in Belfast. A private viewing was arranged for the Council and after it three members of the Police Committee met and recommended that the Council refuse permission to show it They objected especially to the section based on Lady Gregory's play which was set in the days of the Black and Tans. It was decided to discuss the matter at the next monthly meeting of the whole Council. Some council members argued that as only three members were present at the meeting of the Police Committee the minute calling for a ban was illegal. Most outsiders thought the whole episode was just ridiculous and agreed with Alderman S. McKearney who criticised those "thin - skinned members" who wanted to ban a film that most local picturegoers wanted to see. He could have added that the film was shown elsewhere in the North without incident, even in unionist strongholds like Bangor and Holywood. Before the matter was officially debated, however, Odeon Ltd, in exasperation, withdrew their application. The Police Committee, in response, withdrew the minute calling for the ban.

So the situation remained for three years until in, April 1960, Warner Bros. wrote to the Police Committee, and "respectfully requested" permission to show the film in the city. They pointed out that it had already been shown elsewhere in N.Ireland without "the slightest evidence of disturbance." The Police Committee were still unconvinced that the film should be exhibited, and when a special showing was arranged for them in the Royal Cinema on 11th May 1960 they informed every member of the Council, and encouraged them to see it. They also invited representatives of the RUC to be present. Three senior members did attend and in a written response voiced the opinion that "the public showing of this film is less likely to cause dissensun (sic) than that of Shake Hands With the Devil, which has been authorised by your committee," Permission was given, and, belatedly, those filmgoers who hadn't made the journey to Bangor were able to see and enjoy it in the Royal Cinema. The critics were favourable in their comments, with the unionist orientated News Letter declaring that it had "many deft touches" and reflected "a shrewd understanding of human nature." Most picturegoers wondered what all the fuss had been about. But there was more to come.

At the beginning of June 1959 the Police Committee had received a letter from the United Artist's office at 27, Garfield Street with a request to show a new film "Shake Hands With the Devil" (d. Michael Anderson, 1959) which had been given an "A" certificate by the BBFC. It was a British film made in the new Irish studio at Ardmore which had been opened the year before. It had a strong cast headed by James Cagney, Don Murray and Dana Wynter. The story highlighted the struggle between idealism and violence within the IRA in the early Twenties. It was a serious film and was much praised and discussed by critics at the time. The Police Committee decided that they needed advice on the matter, and on 5th June wrote to the City Commissioner asking him to see the film and let the committee have his observations about whether or not to show it. UA arranged a special showing on 11th June in the Gaumont cinema for the Committee at which the City Commissioner and one of his RUC officers attended. On 13th June the City Commissioner replied to the Police Committee informing them that he had discussed the film with his colleagues and "it is our view that it would not be in the interests of peace of the city that this film should be approved for public exhibition." The Police Committee discussed the matter and informed UA on 18th June that they had decided not to grant permission to show the film, subject to confirmation by the City Council at the monthly meeting on 1st July.

That meeting proved inconclusive. Councillor Lavery (Ind. Lab) was against the ban. He called on the Council to take a more balanced and commonsense approach to the question of censorship. He suggested that more attention be paid to films that might tend to lower moral standards, or corrupt the young. He pointed out that the Police Committee had passed controversial films such as "Room at the Top" and "Look Back in Anger." In contrast to those, "Shake Hands With the Devil" gave a balanced view of historical events which challenged the audience. Free speech meant that frank discussion and criticism of matters of public interest should be encouraged, not curtailed by unnecessary bans. The Unionists were divided in their attitudes. A small core wanted the film banned, but others demurred. At a private meeting of the party in the City Hall before the monthly meeting the argument was put forward that the proposed ban was attracting bad publicity, especially over the perceived matter of police censorship. It was therefore decided to support a motion of postponement until the September meeting, when a decision would be taken. In September the matter was debated again. Councillor Lavery returned to the attack and asked why the police were consulted, a step that had introduced another level of censorship into the discussion. Councillor Ross, chairman of the Police Committee argued with Machiavellian pedantry that the letter from the City Commissioner was not a letter of direction, but one of opinion. He still thought that the film should be banned. The Council members voted to allow it to be shown, and it duly appeared in the Imperial, opening on 7th Sept 1959. It ran for four weeks, attracting large crowds as filmgoers voted decidedly with their feet about what they wanted to see.

"A fine adventure story": News Letter. "Well worth seeing": Irish News.

The critics were generally favourable in their comments, praising the acting, especially of James Cagney, and Michael Anderson's direction. The Irish News critic noted that the story was set during the Black and Tan war in the Twenties, a period that could still arouse strong feelings both North and South of the border. He found it an "interesting film which was well worth seeing," providing one is prepared to be detached. There was violence, but there was no attempt to whitewash those involved, and the film finally came down on the side of peaceful negotiation. The Belfast Telegraph uncharacteristically dismissed it with a brief plot summary, and no critical comment. Their critic, Martin Wallace, might have been expected to comment, but, in the week that it opened he wrote instead about an inconsequential French comedy "Une Parisienne" starring Brigitte Bardot. The News Letter, by contrast, printed a detailed critique under the heading "Eire - made IRA film is fine adventure story." The writer recommended the film as one to see, but by mature audiences. He praised Michael Anderson's direction, and the "unmistakable richness" of the acting. He thought it was biased in places but gave no details, and warned that its violence could shock. His final conclusion was that "overall there was no denying its merit." The thorny problem of politics, and the rights and wrongs of the characters' actions were left to the audiences to decide.

"Shake Hands with the Devil" was soon followed by another British film called "A Terrible Beauty" (d. Tay Garnett, 1960), advertised in the local press as "the film you have been waiting for." There was nothing controversial in it and the Police Committee quickly passed it as suitable for showing. Despite its name it had nothing to do with the Easter Rising of 1916, but was set in a border area of N.Ireland. It starred Robt. Mitchum, Dan O'Herlihy, Cyril Cusack, Anne Heywood and Richard Harris. The plot involved the bombing of a police station and the refusal of a character to take part because the officer's wife and child also lived in the building. The Irish News critic thought it was a commendable but unsuccessful attempt to dramatise the moral issues involved. Overall he found the result unconvincing. The characters were unconvincing, the dialogue banal, and the plot "painfully" contrived. Richard Harris is on record describing it as one of the worst films he was ever in. The Belfast public didn't agree, and it ran for two weeks in the Royal Cinema. There was certainly nothing Yeatian about it, and later it was renamed "Night Fighters". Name change or not, it remains a typical example of the Irish fiction films made at the time mainly by British producers, They used the Irish political environment as a background for personal stories involving an eternal triangle of violence, peace and love. There was no detailed analysis of the Irish problem beyond a general view that peaceful accommodation was preferable to violence.

The next Irish film to test the Police Committee was quite different in its origin, aims, style and approach to its subject. It was "Mise Eire" an Irish made documentary using original materials to illustrate historical events in Ireland between 1896 and 1918. It was financed by Gael Linn, an organization set up in 1953 to further the Irish language and culture. "Mise Eire" (I Am Ireland) was the first part of a projected three part history of Ireland, and was directed by George Morrison who was born in Tramore, but spent part of his childhood living in Bangor with his grandparents. Morrison realised that most of the documentary and newsreel material filmed in Ireland in the early years of the 20th century had been mislaid or lost. He set himself the task of tracking down and collecting what he could find in Ireland, Britain, various European archives and in private ownership. In all he collected over 300,000 feet of celluloid and that unique material formed the raw material of the film. With the help of Louis Marcus, he expertly edited the newsreel clips, rare still photographs and newspaper cuttings

Mise Eire in the Royal Cinema: a critical success, Irish News.

into a visual history of the period. The effect of the images was increased by the moving and expressive music written by Sean O'Riada.

The impact was immediate wherever it was shown. It was premiered at the Cork Film Festival in September 1959 and caused a stir among the European critics present, which in time helped to raise the consciousness of Irish cinema across the continent. From the Festival it moved to Dublin and opened in the Regal Cinema to excellent reviews. In N.Ireland it was anticipated in Nationalist circles, though Unionists were less enthusiastic. That opinion was modified somewhat when Martin Wallace travelled to Dublin to see it, and wrote a glowing review in the Belfast Telegraph. It was, he claimed, one of the finest documentaries he had seen, and it breathed life into Irish history, better than any textbook. He felt it should be shown across Ireland, north and south. For Unionists there were many shots of Ulster Unionism in action with scenes showing Sir Edward Carson, James Craig and other leaders, while major Nationalist figures appeared including DeValera, Michael Collins and others. The Irish News critic journeyed to Newry to see it and found it "a truly historic film" made with "skill, love and pride". He drew special attention to the beautiful, evocative score by Sean O'Riada. On the Continent showings in major cities like Paris and Berlin were well received. In Ireland north and south Gael Linn showed the film in local cinemas and parish halls to large enthusiastic audiences. Belfast audiences waited to see what the Council would do.

In early September 1960 the film was shown privately in the Royal Cinema to the Police Committee and Council members. After the showing the Police Committee didn't disappoint, and revealed their usual narrow minded attitudes. They advised the Council that the film Mise Eire should be banned because the sound track was in a foreign language, Irish, that they didn't understand. Informed people were amazed at the perversity and illogicality of their decision. Some declared that the ban was a purely sectarian act. Surely, if the audience couldn't understand the commentary, that was censorship enough. Alderman Daley argued that the reason given was not a "valid" one, because many foreign language films were shown in the city without comment, and declared that he intended to bring the matter up for discussion again at the October monthly meeting. Liberal unionists were embarrassed by the decision, and a spokesman (unnamed) for them "clarified" the situation for an Irish News reporter. He explained, rarely lamely, that the proposed ban wasn't political because both sides of the story were presented with fairness, while the part played by Irishmen in the 1914 - 18 war was clearly shown. The issue was merely one of understanding. Whatever the stated reason the Police Committee was well aware that many Unionists just wanted the film banned. Finally good sense prevailed and in October the ban was rescinded without a debate. Permission was granted for its presentation in the Royal Cinema. On Saturday 12th November a special showing was arranged for an invited audience, including those members of the Council who hadn't seen it. George Morrison and representatives of Gael Linn came up from Dublin for the occasion. The film opened to the public on the following Monday.

The Irish News and Telegraph critics once again encouraged people to see it. The Whig was also positive in its comments. Their critic described it as "an absorbing historical document" and recommended it as a film that every Ulsterman should see "if only out of curiosity." He had some criticisms especially about the soundtrack being in "an alien tongue" without subtitles, which made it difficult to follow. He regretted that the film hadn't been given, what he called, the proper publicity it deserved. The News Letter was less effusive. The critic thought it was an "interesting account "of the historical events, but it was spoiled by the "ear distracting commentary in Gaelic." While the use of Gaelic seemed to annoy some of the critics it didn't deter the audiences. The author recalls seeing it in a packed Royal Cinema with the audience following the images intently. There was no noise, no clapping, shouting or other disruption. The film was essentially descriptive rather than critical but its originality, its richness of detail, its honesty and its evocative music inspired audiences across the country. The second part of the story called Saoirse (Freedom) covering the period from 1918 to 1922 hadn't the same level of critical success but was widely shown without comment in local parish halls and such in Nationalist areas. Part three was never made.

The Ambassador flirts with 'X' films.

Throughout the Sixties film makers continued to push the boundaries of what was acceptable by showing more and more (literally). In 1970 the BBFC responded by raising the minimum age for the X - certificate to 18 years. A steady stream of sex and horror films reached the city, and the Police Committee found itself overwhelmed with requests for viewings. Nearly every Thursday two special buses left the front of the City Hall at 10:00 a.m. carrying members of the committee, and interested members of the Council, to the Ambassador, the Troxy or the Castle to view the latest offerings that distributors wanted permission to show. Most of the films were destined for the three cinemas mentioned, but, increasingly, many were intended for downtown presentation. The ABC, once the home of the august Ritz, and a paragon of good taste, began putting on X rated double bills - including Virgin Witch (X), Female Animal (X), The Night She Rose From The Tomb (X) and Cold Blooded Beast (X) among others - which then moved to the Majestic and the Strand, but the main downtown centre for the films was the Avenue, formerly the Curran cinema, the Regent. The films shown would have appalled the former owners who had always been careful about the moral content of the films shown in the Curran theatres. Conditions had changed dramatically since the Regent had opened in the late Forties, and in October 1977 the Avenue could present "The Violation of Justine," starring Alice Arno, illustrated with a poster of a naked girl chained to a cellar wall. Other X gems that graced the Avenue during the Seventies were Erotic Pleasures, Eskimo Nell, Truck Stop Women, When Girls Undress (with, according to the adverts, "amazing sex scenes"), Erotic Inferno, and Hot Acts of Love.

The News Letter critic commented that the Avenue had done more for sex education over the years that any other institution in Belfast. Others failed to see the humour and complained, with good cause, that the Police Committee was letting too much "rubbish" through their net, while focusing their restrictions on more serious films. One of those was "Last Tango in Paris" (d. Bernardo Bertulicci, 1972) starring Marlon Brando and a new young actress called Maria Schneider. The film depicted a bleak view of human existence in parallel with an emotionless sexual relationship between the two principals. It gained notoriety because of its sexual frankness and, above all, a sex scene involving the use of butter. Miss Schneider complained bitterly about that scene in later life, blaming it for ruining her career. The film stirred up much controversy in the press, where it was dammed and praised in equal measure by both detractors and defenders. The BBFC weren't outraged when they saw it, and passed the film with a 10 seconds cut, giving it an X certificate. The Belfast Council had no hesitation in banning it, despite pleas from local serious cineastes and the efforts of Alexander Walker the prominent film critic (from Portadown) who came over from London to defend the film during a debate in the QFT. The effectiveness of the Belfast ban was undermined somewhat when it was shown in provincial centres outside the city, including Ballymena. It finally reached Belfast in late October 1980 and, like that other cause celebre, "Ulysses," it was presented, to club members only, in the QFT, where it ran for three weeks. Brendan Keenan, the perceptive film critic in the Telegraph, found it serious, challenging, sexually explicit, but "not especially erotic." On the other hand Sarah Denton, in the News Letter, wasn't all that impressed, and chastised the Police Committee for banning what she described as "ten minutes of sex out of two odd hours of boredom." Chacun a son gout!

During the Sixties and later, the volume of criticism over the actions of the Police Committee increased. James Kelly, the well respected commentator, wrote that their decisions branded Belfast as "a city of ancients ruled by ancients," while Sarah Denton described the city councillors as well - meaning but "completely ill -fitted" for the task. In a long critical letter a member of the public, who signed himself Ars Gratia Ars, took a similar line. He noted that the departments in the City Hall were run by people with suitable qualifications for the tasks involved. In contrast the members of the Police Committee had no special training or qualifications for their work. Ivor McNeely, film critic for the Belfast Telegraph, was more to the point when he wrote that "methinks the lads at the City Hall should stick to roads and sewage, and leave films to the BBFC, the local managers and the public."

The closest to a public defence of the Police Committee came from an editorial in the Irish News in March 1972. The writer admitted that the decisions of the Committee were often "confused and difficult to understand" but added that despite many blunders the members did acknowledge that a problem existed, especially with X certificate films. The editorial criticised the trend whereby some film makers used "the shock value of word and scene," while others exploited the increasing permissiveness in society by showing scenes of "sex, morbidity and violence." Those developments had to be coped with but, the editorial concluded, local film censorship was a problem that as yet "defied an adequate solution." The News Letter agreed, and commented editorially that the system whereby a film could be banned in Belfast while being allowed to be shown in a nearby venue like Bangor, only "highlighted the absurdity of local censorship." The Belfast Telegraph found the idea of the Council exercising its powers of film censorship "enough to send shivers down the spine," but at the same time deplored the surfeit of X certificate films showing in the local cinemas. The problem for the Council, the editorial felt, was to separate films of value from those aimed at "the sadistic or prurient minded."

All the papers agreed on the need for film censorship, but admitted that its application was problematical.

CHAPTER THIRTY ONE
Revival

During the late Sixties the Police Committee (PC) and the Council struggled, Canute like, to contain the increasing number of X films showing in the city. Clerical groups, youth representatives, and other concerned adults continued to pressurise the City Fathers to use their powers to impose some effective restraints. The PC blamed the cinema owners, and they in turn blamed the distributors. Relations between those various groups became quite tense at times. The cinema owners felt that they were being held responsible for a situation that was not of their making. William Dalton, the manager of the Crumlin cinema, spoke for many managers when he wrote an open letter complaining that the situation was more complex than the Council stated. He admitted that a few local managers were "cashing in" on the availability of sensational sex films

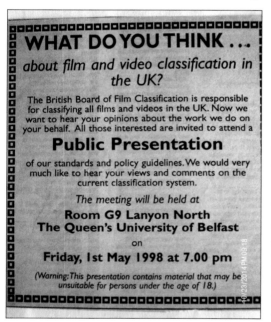

Censorship debate in QUB, May 1988, but few attended.

but insisted that they were unrepresentative. Managers, he claimed, were faced with the fact that there was an insufficient supply of family films and they were therefore forced to take X films to complete their schedules. He argued that the censorship system itself was at fault and that it might be better to abandon it entirely and allow people to follow their conscience in choosing what they saw.

That type of argument may have appealed to younger filmgoers but the Police Committee refused to accept it. In reply Alderman William Hinds, the chairman of the PC, admitted that there were "ambiguities" in the system but that the Police Committee tried to maintain "a reasonable balance" in their approach.. That was actually a quote from a letter from John Trevelyan the secretary of the BBFC to the Police Committee. The latter had written to him, in September 1968, complaining about the number of X certificates, and asking for clarification regarding the reasons for issuing certain certificates. In his reply Trevelyan, whose approach was essentially liberal, pointed out that films were throwing up more and more censorship problems, but at the same time audiences had become more permissive. In that situation, he argued, the BBFC tried to hold a reasonable balance. Many members of the PC and the Council had reservations about that approach and when it was announced that Trevelyan would soon be visiting Belfast it was decided to send a deputation to meet him.

The BBFC seemed a distant body to Belfast filmgoers but it became more personal and human in November 1968 when John Trevelyan, the secretary of the BBFC (1958 - 1971) came to the city to give the Gallagher lecture on Film Censorship, as part of Queen's Festival 68. Trevelyan had done much to raise the profile of the Board and its workings with the general public. He had the reputation of being a well - informed and entertaining speaker who was willing to discuss his decisions and the reasons for them. His lecture was keenly looked forward to and the crowd that turned up to hear it was so large that the venue had to be moved from the extra - mural conference room to the Whitla Hall He traced the history of film censorship up to the contemporary arguments over the X certificate. He understood peoples's concerns about the content of many films but emphasised that the Board couldn't stop the production of such films. He had to take into consideration the trend towards realism in films and the fact that most of the audience consisted of young people. In the final analysis the Board had to judge public taste, and what people would accept, rather than impose a politically dictated censorship. The lecture was well received and ended with a lively question and answer session.

Trevelyan believed in what would be termed transparency today, and answered honestly to a wide range of questions, many of which came from a large group of sixth-form students. One query was about the possibility of film censorship being ended, now that stage censorship had been abolished by the Theatres Act the month before (on 26th September). Surprisingly, he hazarded a guess that it would end but it would be a long, slow process. In the meantime he was in favour of some form of control especially with regard to violence, and the protection of children. He didn't object to local censorship though he thought it involved some absurdities. The PC noted his comments, and a deputation met him the following day to air their concerns. After their meeting it was announced that the Police Committee would in future receive written details of the BBFC's reasons for giving certain films X certificates. The information would, it was hoped, help the Committee in their decisions regarding which films could be shown locally. Despite the civilised exchange of views the meeting didn't really solve the problem of how the Police Committee should deal with X films.

As Mr Trevelyan had pointed out, X certificate films had become a fact of life, and despite their challenging moral, social and other cultural aspects, increasing numbers of film makers were producing them. At the same time audiences for them were also increasing, especially among the young. One of the most controversial examples to reach Belfast at the time was "The Exorcist" (d. William Friedkin, 1973). The film dealt with the demonic possession of a 12 year old girl but it was no coolly detached study of the subject. Its plot combined elements of the traditional horror film spiced up with pseudo - psychology, sex and religion. Parts of it were the stuff of nightmares. Jay Cocks in Time magazine described it as "vile and brutalising" with "cheap shocks and crude novelty," while other critics dismissed it as a dangerous mix of sex, violence and evil. Beneath the penny dreadful surface some critics detected hints of a struggle between good and evil, but admitted that it was its reputation for shock that attracted the audiences. When it was released in the US it caused a sensation, drawing large crowds, and causing hysteria, especially among young females. There were stories of people taking ill in cinemas, of faintings, of young girls unable to sleep after the experience. The film became a topic for discussion at all levels of society, but whatever else was said about it there was general agreement that it was completely unsuited to children. When the film reached London the BBFC agreed, and gave it an X certificate

The Belfast City Council accepted the Board's judgement and the film was allowed to be shown locally to those aged 18 or over. It opened in the A.B.C. in late October 1974. The hype in the London newspapers and on TV had done its work and the cinema was besieged by crowds on the opening day. House Full notices appeared in the foyer before the last show, and over 100 people were left standing on the pavement. A crowd of teenagers who had been refused entry because they were underage, pushed their way into the foyer and became noisy and unruly. The police had to be called to remove them. Brendan Keenan, the Telegraph critic, gained admittance with some difficulty, and described the film as a shocker which aimed to frighten, or even revolt, the audience. He dismissed the plot as silly, lacking in subtlety, and not to be taken seriously. He also suggested that anyone who was of a nervous, sensitive or superstitious disposition should avoid it. The Belfast Telegraph in its Viewpoint took a serious view of the whole furore surrounding the film. The film itself was "deeply disturbing" but no less so than the sight of so many local people rushing to see it. There were complaints that there were too many films available that were objectionable, and in many cases degrading. By supporting film makers who "exploit the baser aspects of human instinct" the public must accept some responsibility for that situation. If the editor was calling on audiences to be more judicious in their choice of films to support, the plea fell on deaf ears. Provocative films made money and so continued to arrive and attract audiences despite complaints from the City Fathers and others.

Some observers thought the matter was finally solved in 1973 when local government was reformed, and Belfast Corporation was replaced with the Belfast District Council. The new Council took office on 1st October 1973 and, as part of the reorganization involved, the former Police Committee was wound up. It didn't disappear as many people hoped, but just changed its spots. It became the 11 member Technical Services Committee, (referred to in future as the TSC) with the same powers and functions, and was soon at work again. Its first major test was the arrival in late 1975 of "Emmanuelle" starring Sylvia Kristel, passed by the BBFC with an X certificate. The film was a soft - porn catalogue of sex in exotic settings, characterised by high production values, lots of flesh (especially Miss Kristel's), the whole photographed in soft focus and glorious colour. In contrast to the bleakness of "Last Tango" the film coated its dubious morality with attractive locales, beautiful people and warm colours. After a special showing, the TSC recommended that it should be shown in the city, but at the monthly meeting on 1st September the Council voted by 12 votes to 10 (out of a total of 51 councillors) to ban it. During the council debate the film was described as "obscene," and "filthy from beginning to end." Councillor Murphy commented that "Last Tango was only a Bible story compared to this one," while Councillor Horan thought it would have a very bad effect on young people. Councillor John Carson agreed and deplored the film because he felt it promoted "adultery, rape, homosexuality, lesbianism and fornication". Councillor Spence, showing his grasp of cultural history, claimed that homosexuality and lesbianism had ruined many a nation and "they didn't want it ruining N.Ireland."

The low turnout for the debate indicated that the enthusiasm for vetting films was waning. One reason was that Council members had become aware of the growing criticisms among the citizens of their actions. Frank Millar, the deputy chairman of the TSC, let it be known that the committee had taken those criticisms into account in suggesting that the film be shown, and that an acceptance of their recommendation would have been in the Council's best interests. But some members felt that they had to object on moral and religious grounds, regardless of the aftermath. Councillor Michael Brown voiced the opinion that film censorship shouldn't be left in the hands of local authorities, a position that was gaining increasing support within the Council. Frank Millar (U) was known to favour implementing the BBFC classification, a position supported by John Cushnahan (Alliance), Oliver Napier (Alliance), Cormac Boomer (SDLP) and the Republican Clubs.

The distributors of "Emmanuelle" may have detected some signs of a shift in local attitudes because two years later they applied once more for permission to show the film. A special preview was arranged on 15th September 1977 in the Avenue for the Council. Only 25 out of the 51 members turned up, but a number of them walked out during the screening. John Cushnahan (Alliance) found the film "uninteresting" but didn't object to persons over 18 years seeing it. In contrast Cormac Boomer (SDLP) thought it was unsuited to teenagers and promised to vote against its presentation After the viewing the chairman of the TSC, Frank Millar, recommended once again that the ban be lifted, but after a short debate the council voted to retain it by 21 votes to 14. Millar defended his committee's decision but threatened to resign his position because of what he called "back sliding" by some members, who voted "yes '" at the private Committee meeting, and then "no" at the public council meeting. Hugh Smyth described the ban as silly, because it meant that people in Belfast were denied seeing a film that had already been shown "in wee country towns and places where they haven't even got running water." A number of councillors, including Olivier Napier(All), agreed that the practice of film previews should stop and the decisions of the BBFC implemented instead. Fred Proctor (DUP) added that the previews only gave producers free publicity. Most of the criticism directed at "Emmannuele" came from the male members of the council, but three female councillors, all married women, who had attended the preview were unfazed. Muriel Pritchard (All) found it "frightfully repetitive and boring." She was not shocked. "I am only shocked by violence," she explained. That of course went to the nub of the problem. Many people were shocked by screen violence; but equally, others objected to nudity, frank sex, coarse language and lack of respect for religion. The latter had always posed problems in Belfast and it was to prove so again when "Monty Python's Life of Brian" reached the city in July 1980.

When it was completed the producers and distributors of "Life of Brian" (d.Terry Jones, 1979) realised they had a potentially controversial hit on their hands. The film was released in London but, because of its religious content, which they knew would probably cause offence, it was held back until after Christmas for general release throughout the country. The BBFC had given it an AA certificate which meant it could be seen by anyone over 14 years, and most local councils in England accepted that. The film was viewed by the TSC at a special preview at which only 14 members of the Council attended. Afterwards, the committee recommended a ban. The Council discussed the matter at the next monthly meeting on 1st July, and rejected the advice of an outright ban. Instead they agreed, by 18 votes to 12, to allow it to be shown with an X certificate to adults over 18 years. When the distributors, CIC, were informed of the decision they, in turn, refused to accept it. They argued that the BBFC certification should be adhered to and they would not show the film with an X. Glasgow and the Irish Republic had also demanded X certificate conditions

Source: Irish News.

Belfast seems set to resist Temptation

By TONY CURRY

THE controversial Martin Scorsese film about the life of Christ will be vetted by Belfast City Council if attempts are made to screen it in the city.

The council yesterday decided that the film, "The Last Temptation of Christ," would insult the majority of citizens and distributors must arrange a private viewing for councillors without publicity.

It is not yet known if local cinemas intend showing the film.

The decision by the Technical Services Committee gives councillors the opportunity to ban the film.

It is thought unlikely that the majority unionist council will give permission for it to be screened.

An amendment proposed by the SDLP's Cormac Boomer that no action be taken on the film was rejected by the Technical Services Committee.

"People have to make up their own minds. My mandate does not require me to make moral judgements," he said.

Mr Boomer said the film had been passed by the British Board of film censors.

He added: "There's no point in keeping a dog if you are going to bark yourself."

Mr Boomer said the council's decision only gave the film advance publicity.

Sinn Féin councillor, Teresa Holland said the committee decision was, "a farcical attempt at censorship."

Councillor Holland said she did not know how the film could be viewed privately by councillors in Belfast without publicity.

"The Technical Services Committee of the Belfast City Council cannot be the moral conscience for the entire population in Belfast.

"Following today's decision the Com-mittee are in fact acting as publicity managers for the film," she said.

Earlier the film opened for the first time to the British public — amid low-key protests outside cinemas.

But an Anglican priest, who has now seen the film, said his previous attacks were wrong — it was a "profoundly moving, spiritual poem", he said and urged Christians to go and see it.

The film, which includes a scene where Jesus fantasises about having sex with prostitute Mary Magdalene has been bitterly attacked by religious groups in Britain who have accused director Martin Scorsese of blasphemy.

Posters advertising The Last Temptation have been banned from London Underground and there were prayer vigils outside the three cinemas in London's West End where it opened.

Mr Scorsese urged people in Britain not to see it if they thought they might be offended.

and the film would not be shown there either. No distributor had stood up so firmly to the Council before, and the members were not entirely prepared for their refusal. They responded by pointing out that the councillors were split on the matter. Some had described the film as "blasphemous, profane, and obscene," others complained it was highly offensive, while others thought it was unsuited to children. The X decision was a compromise to accommodate the variety of views. Alderman Hugh Smyth (PUP), whose record showed that he had never voted in favour of banning any film in the city, was convinced that the film was not suitable for 14 year olds, and explained that was why he voted for an X certificate. He criticised the distributors, and accused them of using the Council's decision to attract patrons to showings outside the city. In that he was probably correct. The film remained banned in Belfast.

"Life of Brian" had its NI premiere two weeks later in the Rialto cinema in Derry. The opening was picketed by a crowd of about 50 members of the DUP and the Free Presbyterian Church who sang hymns as filmgoers made their way into the foyer. A short time later North Down Borough Council accepted the AA certificate, and the film opened in Bangor where patrons had to pass a silent protest by members of the Free Presbyterian Church. Cinema owners and managers in Belfast were not too pleased to see prospective customers siphoned off to out - of - town venues. Those showings gave the Telegraph critic an opportunity to see and comment on the film. He accepted that it was a sharp - witted and funny parody but "tasteless at times (with) a schoolboy crudity about the story." The makers of the film appeared on TV and defended it, insisting that it was a satire on the Hollywood epics based on the life of Christ. Belfast Council remained unconvinced and the film remained banned from city cinemas. Data released by the BBFC at the time showed that among local councils Belfast's decision reflected a minority view. Councils across England and Wales reacted differently to criticisms of the film, especially the accusation of blasphemy. Over 50 councils allowed the film to be shown without vetting it; another 62 previewed it and accepted the BBFC certificate; after seeing it 28 councils insisted on changing the certificate to an X; only 11 authorities banned it entirely. Thus the majority of councils accepted the BBFC certification, a situation that strengthened the growing belief that local censorship powers should be reduced or revoked. That line of thought was gaining support even in Belfast.

The government in London was fully cognisant of the disquiet being expressed over the perceived spread of pornography throughout society. There were daily complaints about the content of books, magazines, advertising, stage shows, films and television. No-one could have been unaware of the well publicised Festival of Light (1971), of the Longford Report on Pornography (1972), of Mary Whitehouse's Clean-up TV campaign, and of the many pertinent discussions in the newspapers and on TV. The Telegraph carried out a local - rather unscientific - survey on the question after the publication of Lord Longford's Report, and recorded that most people interviewed on the streets of Belfast didn't think that the city had a serious pornography problem, though they agreed that children should be protected from the excessive sexual images seen on TV and in magazines. Films were omitted from their strictures. In June 1977 a local magistrate, Mr John Fox, dealt with a case involving girlie magazines which had been seized in recent police raids. He ruled that 12 of the magazines - which included Playboy and Continental Film Review - selling 1200 copies per month between them, were not obscene. He deemed that 92 others were obscene and ordered them destroyed. In his summing up he claimed that publications like them "diminished human dignity," adding that he was sure that every decent man and woman "wholeheartedly believed that pornography ought to be stamped out." Many members of the Council would not only have agreed with those sentiments, but would have included films among the offenders against public decency..

Sarah Denton (News Letter) recalled a discussion on UTV circa 1975 about film censorship, after which she asked herself why was a group of concerned intelligent people wasting their time discussing such things when the real obscenities - the bombings, shootings, murders, and maimings - were taking place daily on the streets. Even in the extreme political conditions of 70's Belfast censorship issues, especially involving films, could rouse passions, with people demanding that something be done. In late 1977 the Labour government decided to act, and set up a committee chaired by Prof. Bernard Williams to "review the laws concerning obscenity, indecency and violence in publications, displays and entertainments in England and Wales.... and to review the current arrangements for film censorship." The Committee consisted of 13 members who met between September 77 and October 79, after which the findings of the Williams Committee were published. In a detailed study Prof. Williams came to the conclusion that pornography had little influence on the development of society. That was at variance with the earlier Longford Report which had concluded that pornography was capable of causing serious damage to individuals, and, by inference, to society. Prof. Williams went further and suggested that terms like obscene, indecent, depraved and corrupt were legally of little use, and should be avoided. He opposed any censorship of literature but, in contrast, felt that films, because of their special potency, should be subject to a more effective system of censorship. The new Conservative government, and its Prime Minister Margaret Thatcher, found the report too liberal in its conclusions, so it was quietly ignored, with the exception of some of the recommendations on film censorship.

The reception of the Williams Report in Belfast was rather subdued, with only minimal reference in the local papers. Among Council members its conclusions were widely regarded as too radical but, despite that, it was to have a major impact on one aspect of council business, that of film censorship. One of its recommendations was that censorship decisions should be overseen by a new Film Examining Board in London, and that the censorship powers of local authorities be rescinded. The London Times criticised the proposed new system as "too severe," while a letter in the News Letter warned that it would impose "a greater degree of dictatorship than democracy." The BBFC was asked to test reaction from the local authorities, so it drew up a document putting forward the arguments for and against such a change. Copies were sent to local authorities, and members were asked to respond to it. The document reached the T.S.C and was considered by its members on 10th September 1980 and again on the 8th October, followed by a more detailed discussion on 22nd October.

In the document the BBFC emphasised that it favoured the expression of local opinion on film content but pointed out that, while the majority of filmgoers were young (77% under 35 yrs., with 88% under 45 yrs), councillors tended to be older, and went to the cinema only rarely. Many were out of touch with recent trends in films and film criticism, and, as such, weren't competent to censor films. During the debate Cllr Cormac Boomer (SDLP) supported that argument, and questioned the right and qualifications of members of the committee to censor films. He felt that moral standards in Belfast were high enough to withstand the impact of the removal of local censorship powers. The committee finally agreed to accept a motion proposed by Cllr Boomer and seconded by Cllr McGuinness (All) that "this Committee considers that the retention of local authority censorship powers with regard to films rated by the BBFC serves no useful purpose and recommends to the Council that the rescinding of the powers be supported, on the following conditions - that the categories U, A, AA, and X should remain unchanged: that films not granted a certificate should not be permitted to be shown under any circumstances: that the proposed new Film Examining Board - which actually never materialised - should be extended to 18 members, and that at least 6 of those members should be nominated by local authorities." The motion was forwarded to the Council for debate at their next monthly meeting on 1st December 1980.

When the details of the motion became known it engendered some scepticism because, going on past decisions of the Council, the motion seemed lost even before the debate began. Again, in the light of past censorship furores, one might have expected, at least, group protests and verbal fireworks. In fact the response was quite muted. The main opposition came, as expected, from members of the Ulster Unionists and the DUP. Before the actual debate Mrs Dorothy Dunlop (U) took issue with the perception that the councillors were out of touch with modern trends in society, and, in a letter to a local paper, defended her fellow councillors as "upright concerned people" who wanted to restore Belfast's night life, and who supported the local cinemas. She insisted that they weren't out of touch with the modern world. What she objected to was that many of those current tendencies, driven by TV, the pop music scene and commercial pressures, were sometimes "decadent, degrading and even evil." Many films reflected those standards, and she believed that local councillors should have the power to prevent them being shown in the city. Among the letters supporting her position was one from a Mr Clyde who argued that local censorship was "not only desirable but essential." Unfortunately he undermined his position by adding, that in his experience "the average Belfast man (was) absolutely incapable of deciding for himself whether a film (was) shocking or not."

During the Council debate on 1st December Mrs Dunlop developed her arguments, and added that "we have a right to look after the morals and rights of the community at large." She put forward a motion which called upon the Council to retain its powers of censorship.

It was seconded by Cllr Ted Ashby (DUP) who described any decision to abandon the right of censorship as "retrograde." Other councillors disagreed. Dan McGuinness (All) thought it was silly to ban a film in Belfast when it could easily be seen a short journey away in a nearby town. David Cook (All) argued that banning a film in Belfast made certain that it became a box office success in provincial centres. Cinema owners in Bangor, Lisburn, Comber and elsewhere would have agreed with that; it was noticeable that provincial cinemas made a point of advertising in the Belfast papers. Hugh Smyth said that if people could marry and vote at 18 years, then they were old enough to decide what they wanted to see. The exchanges continued along similar lines, but fundamentally they revolved around arguments about moral responsibilities and freedom of choice, about conservative values and more liberal attitudes, leavened by practical considerations. When the vote was taken the result was very close, but Mrs Dunlop's motion was defeated by 18 votes to 17. The Lord Mayor, John Carson, didn't vote.

The Telegraph announced, without comment, that the Council was in favour of "scrapping its film veto powers,"while the Irish News stated soberly that the City Council had rescinded its "right to censor films." The more liberal citizens greeted the news as a victory for good sense, but there were others who saw it as a charter for further screen licence. One letter writer described it as "a strange and delusory" decision, and argued strongly for the retention of both the BBFC and local censorship powers. The general belief that Belfast City Council had given up its powers of censoring films was not entirely true. Certainly the weekly censorship previews ended and, with them, the ludicrous sight of councillors leaving the front of the City Hall in hired buses to view controversial productions. In theory any film which carried a certificate granted by the BBFC could be shown legally in the city, but the council could still intervene in special cases by using its control of entertainment licences. The delicate question of the rights and duties of local authorities, which can be traced back to the Cinematographic Act 1909, were tidied up later in the Cinematographic Amendment Act 1985, and the Cinemas (N.Ireland) Order 1999. They made it clear that councils have the duty to license all cinemas including clubs, and to ensure that fire and safety regulations are adhered to. They can also prohibit the presence of children at films which are regarded as unsuitable. They can insist on a change to the BBFC certificate before allowing a film to be shown, though that step is rarely taken today. They can attach special conditions to a licence regarding the content or otherwise of films that can be shown. Thus, if they felt so inclined, they can still ban certain films from being shown locally. That decision is however open to legal challenge. In the final analysis the councils, including Belfast Council, still have the final say in what films can be shown in their jurisdiction.

Just as the Council was making its decision to curtail its censorship duties another contentious film was ear-marked for showing on Belfast screens. It was "Texas Chain Saw Massacre"(d. Tobe Hooper, 1974). It was an early "slasher" film, advertised as a true story though it was actually a work of fiction, which had become notorious for its violence and blood letting. The TSC was well aware of the censorship problems it had caused in the USA and elsewhere, involving bans and court cases. The BBFC had refused it a certificate, and that was sufficient for the committee to act. Without seeing the film they recommended that the council ban it, and asked members to ignore any offer of a preview, because that would only give the film free publicity. The council accepted the advice, and the film was banned at the meeting on 6th January 1981.

The following year another film with a dubious reputation was advertised to be shown in the ABC, but the Council took no action. The film in question was "Caligula," made by Bob Guccione, the owner of Penthouse magazine. The film was widely condemned as pornographic, without any redeeming features. Many of the well known personalities involved in it, including Gore Vidal, John Gielgud, Peter O'Toole and Malcolm McDowell, withdrew their names from the finished product. The BBFC viewed it and, after removing 12 minutes, gave it an X certificate. What remained was still a crude mixture of pseudo - classical sexual excess and frolicking Penthouse Pets. Hugh Finlay, the manager of the ABC, said he had no regrets about showing the film here. It was, he explained with mock innocence, "just another film our circuit has released. "The critics didn't see it exactly in that light. The Telegraph critic described it as "a cine - sex circus" which was badly acted, badly edited, and badly scripted. He dismissed it as "sheer tedium." The News Letter critic agreed, describing it as "one long orgy of shocking sex and violence" and "a corruption of celluloid," which, he stated, would have been banned here in the past. The fact that it wasn't indicated the shift in attitudes to film censorship that were taken place, even within Belfast Council. The film, which was also screened in the Tonic in Bangor, ran for two weeks in the ABC.

Some time later, in 1984, the British Board of Film Censors changed its name to the British Board of Film Classification, declaring that it was more concerned with classifying films rather than in censoring them. The Board realised that technical developments like video and, later the internet, made censorship not only more difficult, but less effective. The BBFC struggled to hold the line on sex and violence while parents fretted at what their children were watching. More people began to pay attention to Mrs Whitehouse's warnings about the impact of the permissive society on children. Belfast Council were guided by the BBFC's advice and classifications until a subject arose which always stirred heated discussion in Belfast. That topic was religion, and it surfaced in the form of a film called "The Last Temptation of Christ" (d. Martin Scorsese, 1988). When Martin Scorsese announced in 1983 that he would make a film based on the life of Christ it was hoped that he might produce something to rival Pasolini's impressive "Gospel According to St. Matthew"(1966). Alas, it wasn't to be. Instead of going to the original source material in the Gospels, Scorsese based the script (by Paul Schrader) on a contentious novel by a Greek writer called Nikos Kazantzakis. The work was described as a "fiction" which purported to study the human side of Christ's personality. The novel had caused a furious reaction when it was originally released in Greece, and resulted in Kazantzakis being excommunicated from the Greek Orthodox Church. The English translation, in turn, was highly criticised when it was published in the USA.

Scorsese and his producers knew how controversial it had been, and expected a similar response to the film. They weren't disappointed, and the film was attacked during the filming, and from its premiere. It was condemned as offensive to Christians mainly because of its depiction of a relationship between Christ and Mary Magdalene, and was regarded by many as blasphemous. Its showings in America were accompanied by threats, protests, legal actions and bans. It was fiercely attacked by Fundamentalists, and criticised by the main Churches. The Catholic Church gave it an "O" rating, denoting that it was regarded as morally offensive. Scorsese, himself a Catholic, defended the film as a study of Christ's human nature.

The film arrived in England in September and Mrs Whitehouse led a vociferous campaign to prevent it being shown, mainly on the basis that it was blasphemous. The DPP however concluded that the film did not contravene criminal law, and was not blasphemous. The BBFC quickly passed it uncut with an "18" certificate, and it opened in London during the second week in September. Mrs Whitehouse pointed out that only the local councils could prevent its future presentations. She wrote a letter calling on all Christians to put pressure on local representatives to have it banned in their areas. The letter was published, without comment, by the three main Belfast papers. In Belfast, passions were rising, especially after it was announced by the distributors that the film would be shown soon in the Strand cinema. Pressure groups and concerned individuals prepared for a good old - fashioned censorship row. The battle lines were drawn between freedom of choice for adults on the one hand - all sides were agreed that the film was unsuited to children - and the duty of public bodies to prevent the showing of something that many people would find highly offensive. In the ensuing struggle protesters north and south of the border shared common ground, in what the News Letter described as "a cross-border holy war." It is ironic that religion, which is usually so divisive in Ireland, engendered a bond of unity, even if it only reflected the essentially conservative nature of shared religious values.

On both sides of the argument the opinions about the film were based on outlines and other secondary information, because very few, if any, of those involved had seen the actual film. The DUP were loud and clear in their opposition to it being shown anywhere in N.Ireland. Rev. William McCrea repeated Mrs Whitehouse's call for "all Christians" to let their local council know how they felt. The DPP decision was "very sad and very wrong" he declared, and he promised to organize protests and petitions "to keep it off Ulster screens." Rev Mr Paisley, leader of the party, never a man for understatement, described the film - without seeing it - as "a monstrous piece of hellish blasphemy against the Son of Man," and called upon all "right thinking people in Ireland to unite against its showing." In Ballymena Council Tommy Nicholl (DUP) appealed to Mrs Thatcher to have the film banned. The council supported his stand unanimously, and called on Belfast council to support them. Similar calls for a ban came from councils in Craigavon, Magherafelt, Larne, Ards, North Down and Castlereagh. One exception was Derry council which voted to allow the film to be screened in the city.

The first round went to the protesters when the owner of the Strand, Ronnie Rutherford, issued a statement to the effect that the Strand would not be showing the film. "I have not seen it," he explained, "but I do not want to annoy people. It is more trouble than it is worth". Castlereagh council sent him a letter of congratulations on his decision. Meanwhile the TSC in Belfast began to receive letters of protest mainly from Protestant groups who were worried that attempts would be made to show the film locally. They all agreed that the film should be banned in the city. The Reformed Presbytery Church of Ireland Committee of Public Morals (Cregagh Road) claimed that the film was offensive to both Catholics and

Protestants. The Great Victoria Street Baptist Church made the same claim, adding that the film was inaccurate in its historical detail, and was "actually, if not legally, blasphemous." The Shalom Christian Fellowship (Church Road) supported those views. The Independent Orange Order urged the council to act, and ban the film.

There were also a number of letters published by the newspapers supporting the showing of the film. One, from the secretary of the Belfast Humanist Society, attacked "Ulster's moral godfathers" with "their philistine hostility to any work of culture which challenged their blinkered visions of Christianity." Another writer used less inflammatory language to regret the pressures to ban the film, and suggested that the QFT might come to the rescue and show it to club members. Fr Pat Buckley stirred his own particular religious pot by praising the film as "recommended viewing for all Christians." There was also some support from an unexpected source, the C of I Archbishop of Dublin, Dr Caird.

During September protests took place in the Republic to prevent the film being shown there. The first presentation in Ireland took place during the Cork Film Festival at a special late night showing. The Bishop of Cork spoke out against the showing, dismissing the film as "bad art and bad theology." By law a film shown during the Festival didn't need the censor's permission, so the première went ahead. A large crowd attended, though they had to pass through hymn - singing protesters to reach the cinema. The distributors then arranged a special private showing in Dublin for clergy and other interested parties. The Catholic Archbishop of Dublin was invited; he didn't attend, but he made it clear that he regarded the content of the film as highly offensive, and that the film should be banned. Dr Caird did attend. He did not approve of the film but he thought that a ban wouldn't solve anything because the film would appear on television in the future. In fact ITV put on a special discussion on the problems surrounding the film, during which clips from it were shown. Martin Scorsese appeared on the programme and defended his work. He also asked people who felt they would be offended by it not to go to see it. Dr Caird worried about the impact of the film on ordinary filmgoers, especially those who were not familiar with the Gospels. The picture of Christ presented in the film was not Biblical. It was, he felt, a combination of events selected from the Gospels interwoven with what was a total invention of a secular 20th century imagination. The result was a mixture of "fact and fancy, dream and hallucination," which could seriously mislead people. The Republic's censor Sheamus Smith (who was not a Catholic) wasn't overimpressed with the film and, like the BBFC, he tended towards classification rather than censorship. He passed it with an over 18 certificate, but cinemas had to display a notice in the foyer explaining that the film was not based on the Gospels. Also, to put the sex sequence in its proper context, no one could be admitted after the film had started.

In Belfast the Council was in favour of some sort of control over its presentation. The TSC had concluded that the film would be offensive to the feelings of the majority of the citizens, and recommended that cinemas should be warned not to show it without written permission. The Unionists and the DUP favoured an outright ban, but other voices were raised in opposition. Cormac Boomer (SDLP) argued that adults should be allowed to make up their own minds. His mandate, he insisted, did not require him to make moral judgements. Teresa Holland (SF) took a similar position, cautioning that the TCS couldn't be the moral conscience for the entire population of Belfast. The Council ignored those sentiments and accepted the Technical Services committee's recommendation. A letter, dated 14th September 1988, was sent to local cinemas warning them that they could not show the film under the terms of their entertainment licence without the written consent of the Council. If they did decide that they wanted to exhibit it the TSC would require at least six weeks prior notice, plus a private viewing - "without any attendant media publicity" - for the whole Council at least five weeks before the proposed showing. Copies were sent to the Cannon Film Centre (the former Ritz and ABC), the New Vic Theatre, the Curzon Cinema Centre, the Strand Variety Theatre, Queen's Film Theatre, Queen's University with reference to the Sir William Whitla Hall, and the Director of Leisure Services with reference to the Group Theatre. Within and beyond Belfast the arguments rumbled on, even reaching the House of Lords where the film was denounced as being "immensely offensive to the founder of the Christian faith."

The Council's proscriptions achieved their aim of keeping the film off Belfast screens. How effective that action was is debatable because anyone who really wanted to see it could travel to Derry. Also, within a short time it became available on DVD. The whole landscape of film censorship was changing in response to the impact of TV, videos, DVDs and, later, the internet, all of which made pornography available for home viewing. In the UK and Ireland the emphasis continued to shift from censorship of films to a system of classification which restricted films to certain age groups, extending from U (suitable for all) to Restricted 18. The classifications included guidance for parents. The spotlight of controversy moved to video nasties, slasher films, torture porn, and violence with or without sex. The harm that home viewing of such material on TV or video could do to young people, especially children, caused - and still causes - much soul searching. Those battles were fought mainly in London and though local voices of protest continued to be raised about some films, local councils were reluctant to intervene, or to modify BBFC certificates. An indication that the fire had gone out of local censorship could be detected a decade after the "Last Temptation" furore.

The BBFC decided to hold a number of meetings throughout the country to explain to the public the history of the Board and the problems it faced in classifying films and videos. One of the meetings was arranged to take place on Friday 1st May 1998 in Queen's University (see page 692). An impressive team, which included the President of the Board Andreas Whittam Smith, the Director James Ferman, and two young examiners were present. However, most of the seats in the lecture room remained empty, as only about a dozen people were sufficiently interested to come. The situation contrasted dramatically with a similar meeting that had taken place thirty years before when John Trevelyan had addressed an enthusiastic audience that filled the Whitla Hall. The President expressed disappointment that so few had turned up, and compared the situation with recent meetings in Liverpool and Glasgow which had been packed by enthusiastic crowds, who had expressed strong views on the subject. The aim of the exercise, he explained, was to explain the workings of the Board, but also, vitally, to get the reactions from the public He then introduced the Director, James Ferman, who had been involved in film censorship since 1975. Ferman, an American, emphasised that the members of the Board were no longer censors, but "classifiers" of films and video. He then gave a brief illustrated lecture on the development of films and the changing attitudes to what could or could not be shown. What was acceptable, he explained, changed with time, and varied across the country from region to region. The Board had to be aware of and sensitive to those changes. Today he found that what upset people were drugs, violence, bad language, sex, blasphemy, horror and nudity in that order.

The meeting lasted for nearly three hours and the last hour consisted of a discussion which was dominated by two young women who obviously had growing families. They insisted that the present system was too lax and that a stricter censorship was needed especially to protect children. Mr Ferman tried to argue that he had to respect the individual's right of free choice and he had to balance that against the need to remove offensive material. About 5% of films were cut, but where possible he tried not to cut. A young man with a pigtail and a ring in his nose asked why he couldn't obtain certain video nasties that were freely available in Holland but which were banned here. Mr Ferman said that the problem of violence was one that worried the Board. He then - after a suitable warning - showed some clips of sexual violence that had been cut. The clips varied from eyebrow raising to hair raising, while some of them were just unbelievable. He told the young man that one of the videos he mentioned included a scene in which a wooden peg was driven into a girl's eye, and he just wouldn't pass material like that. One of the women rounded on the young man and accused him of being "completely desensitised" watching material like that. The young man looked confused and replied that he was interested in special effects, which he hoped to study. Other voices were raised in criticism of the apparent laxity of the present system, though there was sympathy for the examiners who couldn't please everyone, whatever they did. At the end of the meeting the author spoke to Mr Ferman who told him that he was looking forward to his imminent retirement - he went in January 1999 - because he could then "watch the films he wanted to see, and not those he had to watch." He implied that a censor's life was not exactly a happy one.

The decline of the TSC, and of the public interest in local censorship during the last decade of the 20th century was paralleled by a welcome resurgence of cinema - going in Belfast. At the end of the war in 1945 Belfast had 30 full-time cinemas, all of them experiencing good business, but by 1977 that number had been reduced to five (the Avenue, New Vic, Strand, Curzon and the QFT). As the cinema - going public became aware of what was happening, voices of concern were raised. Typical was a letter to the Irish News in February 1967 which pointed out that over the preceding two years the Clonard, Willowfield, Savoy, Forum, and Regal had closed, while the Castle had abandoned films for bingo, and the Lido had become a social club. The writer had no doubts as to the reasons, and he listed badly run halls, where noisy patrons were allowed to disrupt the comfort of others, combined with poor quality projection. He also took owners and managers to task for what he described as their aim of making money at the expense of order and quality. Some time later the Irish News critic blamed TV for the loss of the cinema going habit, which he perceived as a social change that could kill the cinema business. He wondered if there would be any cinemas left by the 21st century.

The purchase of Irish Theatres Ltd. and the Curran Theatres by the Rank Organization meant that most Belfast cinemas were owned by large British companies who responded to "market trends" by selling off uneconomic units, or by adapting them for bingo or bowling. At the same time such developments were matched by a loss of business confidence so that local entrepreneurs hesitated to invest money in what they perceived as a dying industry that was struggling to remain viable by showing cheap horror and sex programmes. Thus closures continued and the fabric of many of the surviving buildings was allowed to deteriorate. Owners and managers complained about increased vandalism, especially the slashing of seats which were costly to repair.

By the early Seventies there were signs of recovery in the USA and soon there was talk of a tailback of films waiting for release. The problem was a shortage of suitable cinemas to show them in. Both the Telegraph and News Letter critics discussed recent changes in the industry in general, and complained about the lack of initiative in Belfast. The honeymoon period with TV was over and young people were looking for other forms of entertainment, and top of their lists were films. Changing social habits and changing requirements meant that the traditional large picture palaces were no longer, to quote a phrase beloved of politicians, "fit for purpose." The future lay with carefully designed small units with a few hundred seats - modern equivalents of the bijou cinemas of the early 20th century - using the latest high quality projection and sound systems. For the patrons they offered a more friendly and attractive environment, especially with their new more comfortable seating, greater leg - room and subdued decor. For the owners they were easier to fill, cheaper to heat and above all more economic to run. The great picture palaces, those icons of the Thirties, beautiful as they were, often occupied desirable city centre sites and were quickly sold for other commercial purposes. Many in Belfast had already gone that way, including the Imperial, Royal Cinema, Classic, and the Alhambra. Others were being converted into smaller multi - cinemas, but that particular concept hadn't reached Belfast yet, though newly converted multi - cinemas had already been built in London, Edinburgh and Dublin. In the latter city the Savoy in O'Connell Street was twinned as early as 1969, and in 1988 it was redesigned as a six screen multiplex. The trend was towards clusters of smaller units, and more screens. But entrepreneurs in Belfast had still one major problem to cope with: the Troubles.

The bombs drove people off the streets after dark, and cinema audience numbers suffered as a result. Some cinemas were damaged by bombs directed at nearby hotels and business establishments. The Classic (News and Cartoon cinema) closed after bomb damage, as did the Opera House, in 1972. Despite bomb scares and nearby attacks the remaining cinemas continued to function, though it was a stressful time for all involved. Then, on 22nd September 1977 a major attack was mounted against the cinemas themselves, as economic targets. Fire bombs were hidden in the ABC, the New Vic and the Curzon. The first fire broke out in the ABC after it had closed following the last show, and despite the best efforts of the fire fighters took hold fiercely. Then smoke was noticed pouring from the New Vic just across the Grosvenor Road. The fire there was quickly brought under control with mainly smoke and water damage confined to the circle. As both fires were being fought news arrived that the Curzon was also on fire.

The following morning the damage was inspected. The New Vic announced it would open the next day though only the stalls would be used until the circle was cleaned and repaired. The ABC was beyond immediate repair due to widespread damage to the auditorium, while the roof was in danger of collapse. People were angry that what in its day had been the city's most elegant and comfortable cinema had been reduced to a shell. The Belfast promoter, Jim Aitken, who had brought many major acts including the Beatles and the Rolling Stones, to its stage, regretted the loss of "a first class venue." The owners, EMI, who were well aware of the new trends in cinema architecture decided, after some hesitation, to rebuild its interior as a multiple cinema. It reopened on Thursday 19th June 1981, a significant date in the history of cinema in Belfast which introduced the cinema of the future. The outside of the building was still recognisably the Ritz, its impressive size, its straight lines and shining cream faience tiles indicating a picture palace of the Thirties, but the interior had been radically modified. The large auditorium that had resounded to the thunder of the Compton organ and the laughter of past generations no longer existed. In its place were four units called Studios, seating 551, 444, 281 and 215 patrons respectively. The former circle with its comfortable seating and excellent sight lines had been converted into Studios 1 and 2, while the stalls had been divided to become Studios 3 and 4. A minority of filmgoers who remembered the Ritz in its heyday regretted what they regarded as architectural vandalism, but accepted that it represented the way forward.

The opening of Belfast's and N.Ireland's first multiple screen cinema caused "a minor sensation" according to the Telegraph. That may be a slight exaggeration, but certainly most of the local filmgoers were delighted because, at a stroke, the number of cinema screens available in the city was increased from five (Curzon, Avenue, Strand, New Vic. and QFT) to nine, and six of those were located in the city centre area. In an editorial the Telegraph expressed the hope that the opening of the new cinema would encourage more citizens back to the city centre in the evenings. The writer noted that people were willing to come out at night to see films of quality, and he predicted, optimistically, that "a new era of film-going has arisen from the ashes." The new ABC promised much. It boasted the most up to date cinematic technology, with two automated projection rooms, using the latest push button projectors. One projectionist could control the projectors for the four separate cinemas. The manager, Hugh Finlay, explained that the four screens gave him more flexibility to show a wider range of films, including both X and U certificates. He would be showing the same films as those available in England, a policy that would restore parity of release with London, and reduce the backlog of films waiting to be shown here. In reply to questions he regretted the loss of the cinema restaurant which had been converted to a waiting area and he admitted there would be no more live shows because none of the units was extensive enough to cope with the large audiences involved.

The multiple screens certainly increased the variety of new films available. The first programmes set the pattern for quality, and entertainment with "Apocalypse Now" (d. Francis Ford Coppola, 1979), Blake Edward's "Ten," "The Electric Horseman" and "Mission Galactica." The response of audiences was positive, especially among younger age groups. The novelty of four cinemas in one building gradually wore off, though not before some patrons, unsure of the internal geography, found themselves in the wrong Studio watching a film they hadn't intended seeing. But the old atmosphere was gone and, with it, the former

Cannon took over the ABC in 1986.

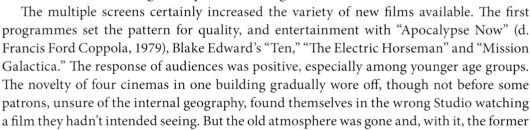

elegance, so that for more mature picturegoers a visit to the new ABC was always tinged with a certain melancholy at the memory of what had been lost. In 1986 the ABC became part of the expanding Cannon Group of film companies run by Menahem Golan and Yoram Globus, when they bought out Thorn EMI Screen Entertainment, and was renamed the Cannon Film Centre. Unfortunately the Cannon Group were financially overstretched and soon faced bankruptcy, but were bought out by Pathé, which, in 1990, merged with MGM and took control of MGM/ UA. Thus, though the name wasn't changed, the four screen Cannon was actually owned by MGM during its last years. When MGM decided to continue the process begun by the ABC, and to open Belfast's first ten screen multiplex on the Dublin Road, the days of the Cannon were numbered. It closed quietly on 1st July 1993 and was demolished the following year to make way for Jury's Hotel. The closure and destruction of the Cannon saddened many citizens especially those with long memories of the great days of the Ritz. A former usherette, quoted in the Irish News, spoke for many patrons when she claimed that she would "wallow in the red velvet-tinged nostalgia" of the old building. With the disappearance of the Cannon all the original downtown cinemas, those distinctive and welcoming centres of social activity that had enriched so many peoples lives during the Thirties, Forties and Fifties, were gone, with the exception of the New Vic (the former Royal Hippodrome), and it had ceased to function as a cinema since 1987.

A new chapter in cinema history. MGM opens a multiplex in July 1993 on Dublin Road.

From the late Fifties a characteristic of the cinema business had been the erosion of local control. The arrival of Rank and its absorption of Irish Theatres and Curran Theatres meant that decisions involving local cinemas and the films they showed were taken in London. The few independents like the Curzon, the Troxy, the Ambassador (closed 1972), the Castle (closed 1966) and the Windsor(closed 1970) found it more and more difficult to get the quality films they wanted to show. Rank and ABC, with their large circuits got first choice, and the independents took what was left, which often included cheap horror and sex films. Some sold out and the buildings became supermarkets or furniture and carpet stores, but still easily recognised today by their distinctive shapes. Others turned to bingo. By the late Seventies only the Curzon and the Strand had survived as cinemas, with of course the QFT, though it was always a special case with a distinctive audience.

By the early Seventies it was clear that Rank wanted to leave N.Ireland and began looking for a buyer for its halls. Reversing the trend of declining local cinema ownership, a group of local businessmen set up a company called Belfast Cinemas and bought out Rank Odeon (NI) in late 1974. They acquired 14 cinemas, 9 of which were in Belfast and included the Grand Opera House, Odeon, Avenue, Lyceum, Mountpottinger Picturedrome, Capitol, Stadium, Broadway, and Gaumont (Finaghy). Outside the city the group included the Odeon (Bangor), the Odeon and Midland (Derry), the Majestic (Portrush) and the Regal (Larne). They were a mixed bunch. The Lyceum was actually just an empty site as, after closing in 1966, the building had been destroyed in a fire, while the Grand Opera House,

Optimism in
June 1965.

Broadway, Picturedrome, Majestic and Midland had all closed.

There was much speculation about what the new owners would do. J.W McFetridge, the chairman of the group, refused to discuss their plans, and told a Belfast Telegraph reporter that "we are not prepared to say what we are doing with our business." There were rumours that some of the cinemas would be reopened, but that didn't happen. The empty buildings, and the Lyceum site, were sold off for development, and the Capitol was closed early in 1975. The Odeon in Bangor reverted to its original name, the Tonic, the Gaumont at Finaghy became the Tivoli again, the Odeon was given a new name, the New Vic, while the Avenue kept its present name, probably because it was always called that even when it was the Picture House. Alas, the attempts to highlight historical continuity, while well meaning, didn't pay off in audience numbers. The trend remained downwards. The Avenue struggled on regardless, wading through a flood of forgettable X epics like "Sexaphobia", "Emanuelle Queen Bitch," starring Laura Gemser who became as well known in Belfast as Sylvia Kristel, "Girls After Midnight," "Caligula's Hot Nights," and Mary Millington's "Star Sex." In October 1982 it turned to bingo, before closing in 1989. Today its site is part of the Castlecourt complex. The New Vic showed better films, but had a similar fate. Despite redecoration, the introduction of cinema variety, and bingo, the New Vic wasn't able to overcome the fact that it was too big and out of date. It showed its last film "Platoon "in June 1989 and became a bingo hall. It was finally closed and sold to Ewart Plc in August 1996 for redevelopment. By 1990, as the last decade of the 20th century began, the public realised that all the historic downtown cinemas were gone with the exception of the Ritz/ABC, in a much modified state, and the Opera House in a much dilapidated state.

No one seemed to know what to do with the Grand Opera House. It was no longer "grand," having lain derelict since it was bomb damaged in 1972. There was even talk of demolishing it but the Ulster Architectural Heritage Society and the Arts Council were determined to prevent that happening. Through their efforts it became a listed building which meant it couldn't be altered or demolished. The Arts Council bought it in 1978, and it was restored using a government grant before reopening in September 1980. In 1994 the Grand Opera Trust was formed which took over the running of the theatre. It functions today as Belfast's primary live theatre, but does not show films. It was never architecturally suited to being a cinema, and even Rank's modifications and subsequent attempts to turn it into a super Rank cinema were not a success. The angle of throw from the projection box was too steep, the seating was too cramped and the many pillars formed visual hazards between viewers and the screen.

During the September 1977 fire bomb attacks it was especially sad to see the Curzon being targeted. It was one of the few local independents which had continued to operate, and it still carried some of the original Thirties aura with it. Brothers Leslie and John Gaston, the cinema's directors and men of principle, had struggled on despite declining audiences. They believed in showing quality films, and declined to exhibit the cheap sex and horror stories that other suburban cinemas had turned to. They often praised family films like "Mary Poppins,'" "My Fair Lady," and "The Sound Of Music" which they felt were largely responsible for attracting audiences even during the darkest days of the Troubles. They later recalled with affection their two most successful attractions, "The Magnificent Seven," and - surprisingly - "Crocodile Dundee." They were genuinely surprised by the attack on their cinema, an event that inconvenienced no-one but their family patrons on the Ormeau Road. John Gaston often spoke of the "day of infamy" that marked the beginning of the decline of local cinemas but he wasn't referring to 22nd September 1977. The date in question was much earlier, on 31st October 1959 when UTV began broadcasting. He noted that audience numbers began to decline dramatically from then. He and his brother regarded the attack of 22nd September as a temporary setback, so they quickly and vigorously set about reconstruction. The Curzon reopened three months later, on 27th December 1977, with the N.Ireland premiere of "Star Wars," the same day the film opened in London and Dublin. At the end of that year Belfast had five cinemas still open for business, namely the Avenue and the New Vic in the city centre, with the Strand, the Curzon and the QFT in the suburbs.

The choice of "Star Wars" may have implied a faith in the future, but the Gaston brothers realised that change was needed to cope with that future. The days of the family audiences were over and the latter were being replaced with young vibrant groups who frequented clubs, restaurants and other entertainments besides films. The weekly habit of "going to the pictures" was out of date, and the large cinemas had lost their appeal. New smaller units were the in thing. The Gastons responded, and the Curzon was subdivided into three units by 1981, to which a fourth was added in 1989, with a fifth by 1992. The following year the first custom built multiplex was opened on the Dublin Road by M-G-M. It was new, trendy, and adjacent to the growing night life of the Golden Mile along the Dublin Road. It also had the latest sound and projection equipment and, above all, ten screens showing the latest releases. It was a new beginning.

The Curzon, despite its historic integration into the local community, just couldn't compete, and the decision was reluctantly taken to close, and sell the building for redevelopment. The Irish News reflected widespread reaction when it described the news as "extremely sad," and deplored the loss of a landmark which the paper insisted should have been a listed building. Mr Dennis Wright, the manager for the last 16 years, complained that the cinema couldn't compete with the multiplexes, and he deplored the fact that cinemas were now run by businessmen for profit, rather than by people who loved the cinema. Besides its special atmosphere Mr Wright confessed that he would miss the people, many of whom he had got to know personally over the years. John Gaston agreed that it was the support of the local people that had kept the cinema afloat but added that "its all a changed scene now." The adverts played the closure down with the simple statement that "patrons please note that the Curzon Film Centre will close on Sunday 11th April 1999." On that evening the staff wore fancy dress as the last audience watched "Shakespeare in Love." The Irish News described the occasion as "the end of an era for independent cinema in Belfast."

Actually it wasn't the last of the Independents because the QFT and the Strand still remained. The origin of the Strand dates back to March. 1935, when Harry Wilton, a local businessman with an address on the Antrim Road, presented to the Corporation for approval on behalf of the Strand Cinema Co. plans for a cinema to be built at Strandtown, designed by Thomas Guthrie of North Parade. The project was taken over by Union Cinemas, with Mr Wilton becoming a director of the Strand and Union Cinema Co. New plans were drawn up by McBride Neill and the completed building was opened on 7th December of the same year. From the beginning the building was highly praised for its style - a blend of Art Deco and International motifs - and became a popular resort for local East Belfast families. When Union Cinemas were taken over by ABC in 1938 the Strand joined the Ritz and the Majestic as part of the same company. The Strand, like the Majestic, flourished because it showed new, quality films a few weeks after they were screened downtown in the Ritz. By the Seventies the cinema was experiencing the effects of falling audiences due to the impact of TV, and the Troubles. In 1977 the Strand was fire - bombed a few weeks after the destruction of the ABC Ritz, but was quickly reopened. By then the early family film fare had been replaced with X rated attractions like "Untamed Sex," and "Daughter of Emmanuelle." Its days seemed to be numbered.

In 1981 the spectre of closure hovered ever closer over the building, and there were rumours of it being sold for redevelopment as a supermarket. Into the breach stepped local businessman, Ronnie Rutherford, and under his management it struggled on mainly with live variety, hosting musical shows with the likes of Dana, Jimmy Cricket and Philomena Begley, until the decision was taken to convert it to a four screen complex, a task completed in April 1988. It was always Mr Rutherford's ambition to restore it to its original function as a cinema. The new complex was widely welcomed, and the people of East Belfast and North Down were called upon to support it. Unfortunately the physical condition of the building continued to deteriorate and it was realised that something had to be done to protect a significant structure before it was too late. The DOE was persuaded to organise an urban development grant towards its refurbishment, and the architectural group, Robinson Patterson Partnership, were given the task of restoring the building, as far as possible, to its original Art Deco condition. The work was skillfully carried out during the first half of 1999 without interrupting the normal running of the cinema. The overall result was highly praised and the Strand once more came to dominate the lower Holywood Road, its outside proportions a delight to the eye, as befitted Belfast's sole surviving, still functioning representative of the Golden Age of cinemas of the Thirties.

The attractions of TV were no longer a problem, but the Strand still faced strong competition from the new multiplexes owned by the large cinema chains at the Odyssey, and in the city centre. In response the manager, Linda Smyth, reintroduced live entertainment in February 2013 to attract new audiences. Thus a month later Van Morrison, born and reared locally, entertained a crowded auditorium (250 patrons), while at the beginning of April the cinema hosted a special event in the form of the new film "Good Vibrations" (d. Lisa Barros D'Sa and Glenn Leyburn, 2012) at which local personality Terri Hooley, around whose life the film is based, appeared. A traditional talent contest called the Strand Star Search, similar to the very popular events that many former cinemas had presented in the past, also attracted the crowds. Variety nights and other activities are planned for the future. Linda Smyth believed that the Strand would survive if the local community could become more involved. "We just want people to realise that we're still here, and that we're still trying to operate." One hopes that she is right, but she faces a classic case of David versus Goliath; the big players, the cinema chains, operate in the world of money and business, not local sentiment. To cope with that reality the Strand has turned for advice to

Avec Solutions a non profit making company located on the Newtownards Road, and under their guidance has evolved into a "not -for -profit" cinema and arts centre, officially called the Strand Arts Centre. Its chief executive Mimi Turtle has high hopes that more people and organizations will make use of the building's facilities. In March 2014 the centre was given a loan of £40,000 by the Ulster Community Investment Trust to make improvements to its facilities. New modern projectors were needed, and the aim is to update three screens and to organise space for performing arts, drama and dance studios.

The closure of the Strand would be an architectural tragedy for Belfast which would deprive future generations of a window into what a true Picture Palace looked and felt like. Too much of the city's cinematic heritage has been lost already, and one could go so far as to say that the Strand must be preserved as a living and working venue, even though its interior has been modified. The surviving outlines of the Ambassador (now Wyse Buye) on the Cregagh Road, and the Majestic (now unoccupied) on the Lisburn Road at the corner of Derryvolgie Avenue give some idea of what a cinema of the Thirties and Forties looked like but the Strand shows the complete functioning building in 3-D and glorious technicolor. The key to its future lies in the response of audiences.

The Strand and the QFT are small independent islands in a sea of large multiplexes. The first multiplex in the Br. Isles opened in Milton Keynes in 1985 with ten screens. It took eight years for the concept to reach Belfast in the form of the M-G-M multiplex on the Dublin Road which opened on Friday 16th July 1993. "The greatest name in Hollywood brings to Belfast the ultimate cinema experience" claimed the advertisements. The new four storey brick building lacked the distinctive eye catching architecture associated with former cinemas, but within its factory - like walls it incorporated the latest developments in cinema presentation The complex was open seven days a week and had a fully computerised box office which included advanced booking by telephone. It was completely non - smoking, and had large seated waiting areas. There were 10 screens which catered for nearly 2,500 patrons (or customers, as the contemporary money based approach would have it) in small auditoria which seated 436 or less persons. The halls lacked any elaborate decoration, but had luxury seating with plenty of legroom. The equipment was top quality with the latest Kineton 35 mm projectors, and Dolby four channel stereo sound. The screens were uncovered and stared Balor like at the assembling audience, a situation that older cinemagoers found unsettling because in the former traditional cinemas the screen was always chastely covered with a curtain. One of the pleasures of the past was seeing the colour of the curtain changing as the lights dimmed, followed by a quiet opening, usually upwards, to reveal the first image. In over sixty years of cinema attendance the author never once saw a bare screen, until recently. The M-G-M was the first in Belfast of a new style of cinema going in units that were designed without frills, but with an eye to basics and profits. The architects envisaged buildings that were cheaper to build and maintain, and could be run with much fewer staff than the former cinemas. The cinemas displayed their products (films) for the customers to choose from, and it is no coincidence that many of them came to be located in large shopping centres.

The M-G-M multiplex was greeted warmly by local filmgoers, critics and newspapers. Under a byline "Cinema Scope" an editorial in the Belfast Telegraph proclaimed that "after

From York Street to Hollywood: Ken Branagh as Hamlet.

a long intermission the silver screen sparkles again." The article detailed the sad decline of local cinema since the high decades of the Forties and Fifties, comparing the situation to that of the extinction of the dinosaurs - the first major attraction at the M-G-M was Jurassic Park (d.Steven Spielberg 2003) - except that the cinema had made "a spectacular revival." The writer put the turnaround down to the attractive facilities of the new complexes, the great variety of exciting films available, and the fact that films were being released here at the same time as London. He could have added that the cinema was once again the "in" thing among the young and a night out at the cinema was an acceptable social experience for them. The studios and film makers responded to and manipulated those attitudes with action films, films based on comic book heroes, all with superb special effects, bigger and louder explosions, improved 3-D productions, and digital formats. A major attraction today are the "must see" blockbusters or event films which are released with maximum ballyhoo, their takings over their first weekend hailed as indicators of their importance. Much talent goes into those films, and many of them are quite entertaining, but critics have complained about their increasingly juvenile plots and characters. The old cliché that Hollywood made films mainly for 12 year olds has been heard recently again. One advantage claimed for the new multiplexes was that the multiplicity of screens would allow all tastes to be catered for. Films with narrower appeals to smaller audiences could be shown, but there is little evidence that that has happened so far in Belfast.

The geography of the cinema business in Belfast has changed in the early 21st century from a dispersed pattern of discrete cinemas to a clustered pattern of screens located in multiplexes. In the past major films showed firstly in the downtown cinemas and then moved to the suburbs, but today in each multiplex they open in the largest units and as audience numbers decline they move to the smaller units. The MGM multiplex bridged the gap into the present century, in the process changing hands from MGM to Virgin, then to UGC until it was purchased by Michael Mc Adam in December 2003, and became part of his Movie

Richard Attenborough at the opening of the Odyssey's 12 screen multiplex in May 2001 when he predicted a bright future for the industry in N. Ireland.

House group. Movie House now has 30 screens in the Greater Belfast area located at Dublin Road (10 screens), Yorkgate Cityside (14 screens) and Glengormley (6 screens), making it the dominant film exhibitor in the city. In East Belfast the Odyssey complex includes a multiplex with 12 screens. For a time the Odyssey included N. Ireland's one and only IMAX cinema owned by the Sheridan Group, which opened in November 2001. The Imax cinema had 380 seats and at the time boasted Ireland's largest screen, 62 feet (19 m) high and 82 feet (25m) wide. The Imax experience recalled the old Cinerama system but the technology and design were superior, producing a large clear image without any wobbles or joins. Also it could show excellent 3D pictures though still with the need for special glasses. It mainly presented specially made films of a documentary and educational nature. Sadly the company went into administration with large debts owed to the Anglo - Irish bank, and the cinema closed in 2009. The year before, Odeon Cinemas, the largest chain in Britain, opened a multiplex in Victoria Square with 8 screens. Another major player the Irish company Omniplex Holdings, the largest exhibitor in Ireland, has two large multiplexes in the Belfast area: in the Kennedy Centre on the Andersonstown Road with 8 screens, opened in 2010, and at the Dundonald Icebowl, with 8 screens, opened in January 2009. The new establishments were generally welcomed by the community but the Dundonald development was criticised as an unnecessary intrusion into the greenbelt. The Dundonald Greenbelt Association objected, and when the cinema received planning permission, described it as a "junk culture" proposal that would impair the local environment.

The QFT(2 screens) and the Strand (4 screens) remain as direct links to the past, but the cinema business is now dominated by the new multiplexes. In all, in the Belfast area, they offer 72 screens which is over twice the number available in 1945. The viewing areas may lack the elaborate decoration of the earlier cinemas but they compensate with their super comfortable tiered seating and up to date digital technology. The first cinema in N.Ireland to install a digital projector was the QFT in April 2007 thanks to financial help from the UK Film Council and the N.Ireland Film and Television Commission. The cinema welcomed its audience to "a new era" in film appreciation with digital prints of "Casablanca," "The Wizard of Oz," and "Dirty Dancing." Viewers were impressed by the improved quality of pictures and sound. Since then all the cinemas in Belfast have converted to digital projection. Contemporary film makers work only in digital, while studios are changing their old films to digital format. The age of celluloid is over though a few old - style projectors are retained in case they might be needed, but mainly because of their nostalgic value. Managers would agree with Mark Anderson when he stated at the opening of the Dundonald Omniplex in 2010 that "Digital is the future of cinema."

Jim Simpson, the Chief Digital Technician for the Movie House chain, agrees with that. He began his career as a trainee projectionist in the ABC/ Cannon, an experience he recalls with great pleasure, and has worked through the technical changes that have taken place since then. Celluloid has given way to digital and the former projectors with their whirring and clacking reels have been replaced by quiet digital computerised machines. The large circular reels, so redolent of historical continuity, along with their celluloid contents no longer arrive every week. Instead modern digitalised films come in portable enclosed box - like structures slightly bigger than the familiar videotapes that preceded DVD's. To prevent film piracy they cannot be projected until they are unencrypted over the telephone by the distributor, which in the case of major productions may not happen until the morning of the first showing. The older projection rooms could be rather noisy places but in contrast the modern equivalent is characterised by a low hum, barely audible. In the Dublin Road Movie House one projection room services the cinemas' ten screens. The computer systems are checked and prepared each morning usually by the assistant manager, and the computers switch on the various projectors as required during the day. There are no projectionists rushing in to check the times of reel changes or such. In fact projectionists as such no longer exist. They have been replaced by digital technicians. If any serious technical problem develops anywhere in the Movie House chain, Jim saddles up and rides to the rescue.

What skilled projectionists like George Shanahan, or progressive owners like Fred Stewart and Michael Curran would make of it all is difficult to know. Or the response of past audiences. They had always been willing to embrace technical change (excepting maybe 3-D) and they would have had no problems with the improved comfort, the superior picture clarity and sound and the emergence of the multiplexes. They would probably have complained about the reduced choice of films because the modern release policy combined with longer exhibition periods means that despite the increase in the number of screens the number of films to choose from has dropped. In 1945 patrons had over twenty five different films available in any one week to choose from but today that number has been halved.

The multiplexes reflect the attempted domination of the local industry by large outside organizations with an international view of the industry. Local needs are still met by the Omniplex group which is based in Dublin and emphasises that - like the former Curran Theatres - it has a family orientated approach, but more especially by the Movie House group which stands as a monument to one local entrepreneur, Michael McAdam. He once described himself, in an interview, as "a lucky wee fellah from Rathcoole." However it took more than luck to achieve what he did. It took ambition, hard work and, above all, a love of the cinema to put together his own chain of screens. He follows in the footsteps of the many local businessmen from John Y. Moore to Michael Curran who helped to found the industry and build the cinemas in Belfast. In those buildings over the years the light of film has glowed bright and clear especially from the Twenties to the Sixties; flickered and was nearly extinguished between the Seventies and the Nineties; then recovered its vigour in the 21st century. As long as enthusiasts like the Anderson family and Michael McAdam are around that local light will hopefully continue to brighten the city.

May the Force stay with them!

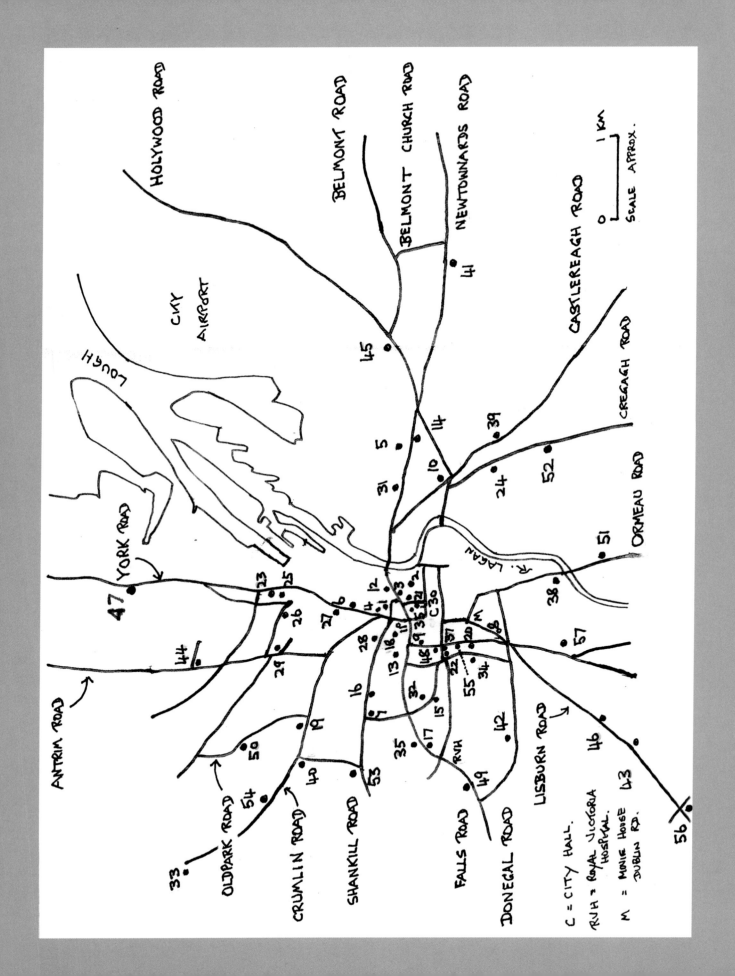

BELFAST CINEMAS : LOCATIONAL SUMMARY

(1) ALHAMBRA. 39 - 47 North Street. Original music hall opened 1872. Presented Belfast's first film show in July 1896. Regular film shows from 1903. Closed after a fire in 1959. Site now occupied by Human Rights Commission.

(2) EMPIRE THEATRE. Victoria Square at intersection with Telfair Street. Never a cinema, but presented the first Lumière Cinematographe in Belfast in November 1896. Closed in June 1961. Site now part of Victoria Square shopping complex.

(3) ST.GEORGE'S HALL 35 - now 39 - High Street, within St George's Building. Opened 1881. Silent cinema 1908 - 1914. Hall, much dilapidated, still exists.

(4) STAR MUSIC HALL. Church Street. Opened 1892. Renamed the Star Picture Palace and functioned as a silent cinema from 1908 to 1909. Closed 1919. Site now occupied by the headquarters of the ROAB.

(5) PRINCESS PICTURE PALACE. 308 Newtownards Road. Opened March 1910. Closed December 1926.

(6) ELECTRIC PICTURE PALACE 19 -21 York Street. Opened August 1910. Also known as the Palace and the Silver Cinema. Closed 1915.

(7) SHANKILL PICTUREDROME. 148, Shankill Road at the intersection with Northumberland Street. Opened December 1910, closed 1959. Now demolished.

(8) SHAFTESBURY PICTORIA 6,Shaftesbury Square. Opened December 1910. Closed 1917. New hotel being built on the site today.

(9) KELVIN. College Square East. Opened December 1910. Known also as the New Kelvin, the Mayfair, the News and Cartoon Cinema and the Classic (1967). Closed January 1972 after bomb damage. Site now occupied by retail units and offices. A Blue Plaque on the wall recalling Lord Kelvin indicates its location.

(10) MOUNTPOTTINGER PICTUREDROME. 112, Mountpottinger Road. Opened February 1911, rebuilt in 1934. Closed 1970. Demolished.

(11) PICTURE HOUSE. Royal Avenue at the intersection with Garfield Street. Opened June 1911. Also known as the Regent (from 1947), and the Avenue (from June 1965). Closed in October 1982 and later demolished. Site now part of the Castlecourt Shopping Complex.

(12) PANOPTICON. 42 -46, High Street. Opened February 1912. Renamed the Lyric from October 1924. Damaged by German bombing and closed May 1941. Now demolished.

(13) MELBOURNE ELECTRIC THEATRE. Melbourne Street. Opened 1st April 1912. Closed April 1914.

(14) NEW PRINCESS PICTURE PALACE. 307, Newtownards Road. Opened July, 1912. Closed April 1960. Site now has shops.

(15) WEST BELFAST PICTURE THEATRE. 74,Albert Street. Opened December 1912. Better known as the Arcadian from 1923. Closed February 1960. Demolished during housing redevelopment.

(16) WEST END PICTURE HOUSE. 108, Shankill Road. Opened October 1913. Closed 1960. In 1974 was remodelled as the Shankill Leisure Centre.

(17) CLONARD PICTURE HOUSE. 140, Falls Road. Opened December 1913. Closed March 1966. Later damaged during rioting and was demolished for housing redevelopment.

(18) CENTRAL PICTURE THEATRE. Smithfield. Known ironically as the Smithfield Ritz. Opened December 1913. Closed 1958. Lay derelict until it was demolished in 1965.

(19) CRUMLIN PICTURE HOUSE. 189, Crumlin Road. Opened March 1914. Closed after bombing in May 1972 Demolished.

(20) GREAT NORTHERN KINEMA. 17,Great Victoria Street. Opened April 1914. Closed March 1919. Site occupied by Avis car rental firm.

(21) IMPERIAL PICTURE HOUSE. 18-24 Cornmarket. Opened December 1914. Closed November 1959. Became a shoeshop, then a booking office for the Titanic Experience.

(22) COLISEUM. Grosvenor Road, at Barrack Street intersection. Originally the Alexandra Theatre (April 1911). Remodelled as the Coliseum cinema, opened in February 1915. Closed June 1959. Bought by Silver Cars and now mainly a parking area.

(23) QUEEN'S PICTURE HOUSE. 248,York Street. Opened December 1915. Sold to owners of the Gaiety the following year. Blitzed and closed in April 1941.

(24) WILLOWFIELD PICTURE HOUSE. Woodstock Road, near Cherryville Street. Opened 20th December 1915. Known locally as the Winkie, and officially as the Rex from 1968. Closed in 1973. Site now housing.

(25) MIDLAND PICTURE HOUSE. Canning Street, near York Street railway station. Opened March 1916. Closed April 1941, another victim of the blitz.

(26) DUNCAIRN PICTURE PALACE. 12, Duncairn Gardens. Known locally as the Donkey. Opened July 1916. Closed November 1969. Later demolished to make way for the North City Business Centre.

(27) NEW YORK PICTURE HOUSE. 68,York Street. Opened July 1916. Closed December 1922. Now demolished.

(28) GAIETY THEATRE 157 - 163, North Street just below Upp. Library Street. Opened November 1916. Closed 1956. Now demolished.

(29) LYCEUM PICTURE HOUSE. Antrim Road at intersection with New Lodge Road. The first Curran Cinema. Opened December 1916. Closed at end of April 1966. Demolished.

(30) ROYAL CINEMA. Arthur Square at junction with Castle Lane. A Warden cinema on the site of the historic Theatre Royal (opened 1793, closed March 1915). The Royal opened in December 1916. Closed April 1961. The site is now occupied by Starbucks.

(31) POPULAR PICTURE HOUSE. 49 - 55, Newtownards Road between Young's Row and Keenan's Street. Opened October 1917. Closed early 1962.

(32) TIVOLI. In Christian Place off Albert Street. Opened July 1918. Was fire bombed during the Troubles of the early Twenties, but was rebuilt. Closed in 1935 or 36. A venue fondly remembered in local myth.

(33) THE LIGONIEL. Opened in 1918. A short lived existence. Little information available about it beyond the fact that it was known locally as the Henhouse.

(34) THE SANDRO. 71 - 73, Sandy Row. Located in the Brewery Building. Opened 1919. Closed September 1961.

(35) DIAMOND PICTURE HOUSE. 35, Falls Road, at its intersection with Cupar Street. Opened February 1920. Closed 1959.

(36) CLASSIC. Castle Lane. Opened December 1923. Renamed the Gaumont in 1949. Closed by Rank in September 1961 when the staff moved to the Royal Hippodrome which was renamed the Odeon. The site is now occupied by British Home Stores.

(37) ROYAL HIPPODROME. Gtr. Victoria Street at intersection with Grosvenor Road. Originally a music hall, opened 1907 Leased by Union Cinemas in 1931, renamed Royal Hippodrome, a full time cinema from 1935. Bought by Rank, renamed the Odeon (1961), and later the New Vic (1974). Closed August 1996. Site now occupied by Grand Opera extension and the Fitzwilliam Hotel.

(38) APOLLO CINEMA. Ormeau Road at junction with Agincourt Avenue. Opened October 1933. Acquired by Curran Theatres 1939. Closed December 1962. Still standing, modified, now occupied by an Asian Supermarket.

(39) CASTLE CINEMA. 84,Castlereagh Road, at Clara Street. Opened October 1934. Closed March 1966. Modified, now a furniture store.

(40) SAVOY.294 - 296 Crumlin Road at Tennant Street. Opened November 1934. Closed 1967. Car showroom for a time. Demolished.

(41)ASTORIA CINEMA. Upp. Newtownards Road. A Curran theatre. Opened December 1934. Closed August 1974. Demolished. Telephone exchange now on the site.

(42) WINDSOR CINEMA. Donegal Road. Opened March 1935. Closed 1970.

(43) REGAL CINEMA. 366 - 372, Lisburn Road between Bawnmore Road and Lancefield Road. A Curran theatre. Opened October 1935. Closed at beginning of 1967.

(44) CAPITOL CINEMA. 407, Antrim Road at junction with Alexandra Park Avenue. A Curran theatre. Opened November 1935. Closed January 1972. Supermarket for a time, then demolished.

(45) STRAND CINEMA. Holywood Road at Gelson's Corner. Opened December 1935. Still operating as the Strand Arts Centre.

(46) MAJESTIC CINEMA. 208, Lisburn Road, at corner with Derryvolgie Avenue. Opened May 1936. Closed October 1975. Still standing,but now unoccupied.

(47) TROXY CINEMA. 194 - 196 Shore Road. Opened October 1936. Renamed the Grove Theatre in 1970. Closed in 1977.

(48) RITZ CINEMA. Fisherwick Place at junction with Grosvenor Road. A Union cinema. Opened November 1936. Renamed the ABC(1963), introduced the first multiple screen cinema to Belfast (1981),became the Cannon Film Centre (1986). Closed July 1993.

(49) BROADWAY CINEMA. 278, Falls Road, at Willowbank. A Curran theatre. Opened December 1936. Closed January 1972 after riot damage.

(50) PARK CINEMA. Oldpark Road at Torrens Avenue. Opened December 1936. Closed 1972. Bombed.

(51) CURZON CINEMA. 300, Ormeau Road. Owned by Gaston family. Opened December 1936. Closed April 1999. Site now occupied by the Curzon Apartments.

(52) AMBASSADOR CINEMA. 135, Cregagh Road. Opened December 1936. Closed March 1972. Still standing occupied by large store, Wyse Byse.

(53) STADIUM CINEMA. Shankill Road at junction with Tennant Street. Opened October 1937. Closed March 1976. Now the Spectrum Centre.

(54) FORUM CINEMA. 491 - 495, Crumlin Road opposite Twaddell Avenue. Opened November 1937. Closed January 1967. Front modified for offices. Auditorium still intact and used by the Star Social Club.

(55) GRAND OPERA HOUSE. Gt. Victoria Street and Glengall Street. A Warden Theatre. Opened 1895. Showed selected silent films. Functioned as a cinema on and off between October 1949 and April 1972. A Rank cinema from 1960 to 1972 when it closed because of bomb damage. Reopened as a live theatre in 1980.

(56) TIVOLI CINEMA. Lisburn Road above the Finaghy cross-roads. A modern style cinema built for Rank. Opened June 1955. Called the Gaumont between 1961 and 1974, when it reverted back to the Tivoli. Closed soon after. Modified as a car show room.

(57) QUEEN'S FILM THEATRE. 20, University Square. A specialist art cinema which began life as a lecture room. Opened October 1968. Renovated and extended in 2004. Still in operation.

(58) Group of cinemas connected to Belfast but outside the city boundary. LIDO. 812, Shore Road. Opened March 1955. Closed 1962. ALPHA, at Rathcoole. Opened 1957. Closed 1962. METRO at East Link to serve Dundonald. Opened September 1956. Closed 1961. Site now occupied by a Mac Donald's. TONIC, Bangor. Bangor's premier cinema. Opened July 1936, acquired by Curran Theatres in November 1936. Closed 1983. Demolished 1992.